SAT2000

Frontiers in Artificial Intelligence and Applications

Series Editors: J. Breuker, R. López de Mántaras, S. Ohsuga and W. Swartout

Volume 63

Previously published in this series:

Vol. 62, In production
Vol. 61, E. Kawaguchi et al. (Eds.), Information Modelling and Knowledge Bases XI
Vol. 60, P. Hoffman and D. Lemke (Eds.), Teaching and Learning in a Network World
Vol. 59, M. Mohammadian (Ed.), Advances in Intelligent Systems: Theory and Applications
Vol. 58, R. Dieng et al. (Eds.), Designing Cooperative Systems
Vol. 57, M. Mohammadian (Ed.), New Frontiers in Computational Intelligence and its Applications
Vol. 56, M.I. Torres and A. Sanfeliu (Eds.), Pattern Recognition and Applications
Vol. 55, G. Cumming et al. (Eds.), Advanced Research in Computers and Communications in Education
Vol. 54, In production
Vol. 53, E. Motta, Reusable Components for Knowledge Modelling
Vol. 52, In production
Vol. 51, H. Jaakkola et al. (Eds.), Information Modelling and Knowledge Bases X
Vol. 50, S.P. Lajoie and M. Vivet (Eds.), Artificial Intelligence in Education
Vol. 49, P. McNamara and H. Prakken (Eds.), Norms, Logics and Information Systems
Vol. 48, P. Návrat and H. Ueno (Eds.), Knowledge-Based Software Engineering
Vol. 47, M.T. Escrig and F. Toledo, Qualitative Spatial Reasoning: Theory and Practice
Vol. 46, N. Guarino (Ed.), Formal Ontology in Information Systems
Vol. 45, P.-J. Charrel et al. (Eds.), Information Modelling and Knowledge Bases IX
Vol. 44, K. de Koning, Model-Based Reasoning about Learner Behaviour
Vol. 43, M. Gams et al. (Eds.), Mind Versus Computer
Vol. 42, In production
Vol. 41, F.C. Morabito (Ed.), Advances in Intelligent Systems
Vol. 40, G. Grahne (Ed.), Sixth Scandinavian Conference on Artificial Intelligence
Vol. 39, B. du Boulay and R. Mizoguchi (Eds.), Artificial Intelligence in Education
Vol. 38, H. Kangassalo et al. (Eds.), Information Modelling and Knowledge Bases VIII
Vol. 37, F.L. Silva et al. (Eds.), Spatiotemporal Models in Biological and Artificial Systems
Vol. 36, S. Albayrak (Ed.), Intelligent Agents for Telecommunications Applications
Vol. 35, A.M. Ramsay (Ed.), Artificial Intelligence: Methodology, Systems, Applications
Vol. 34, Y. Tanaka et al. (Eds.), Information Modelling and Knowledge Bases VII
Vol. 33, P. Pylkkänen et al. (Eds.), Brain, Mind and Physics
Vol. 32, L. de Raedt (Ed.), Advances in Inductive Logic Programming
Vol. 31, M. Ghallab and A. Milani (Eds.), New Directions in AI Planning
Vol. 30, A. Valente, Legal Knowledge Engineering
Vol. 29, A. Albert (Ed.), Chaos and Society
Vol. 28, A. Aamodt and J. Komorowski (Eds.), Fifth Scandinavian Conference on Artificial

ISSN: 0922-6389

SAT2000

Highlights of Satisfiability Research in the Year 2000

Edited by

Ian Gent

School of Computer Science, University of St. Andrews, St. Andrews, United Kingdom

Hans van Maaren

Department of Mathematics, Computer Science and Electrical Engineering, Delft University of Technology, Delft, The Netherlands

and

Toby Walsh

Department of Computer Science, The University of York, York, United Kingdom

IOS Press

Ohmsha

Amsterdam • Berlin • Oxford • Tokyo • Washington, DC

ISBN 1 58603 061 2 (IOS Press)
ISBN 4 274 90363 X C3000 (Ohmsha)
Library of Congress Catalog Card Number: 00-102853

Publisher
IOS Press
Nieuwe Hemweg 6B
1013 BG Amsterdam
The Netherlands
fax: +31 20 620 3419
e-mail: order@iospress.nl

Distributor in the UK and Ireland
IOS Press/Lavis Marketing
73 Lime Walk
Headington
Oxford OX3 7AD
England
fax: +44 1865 75 0079

Distributor in the USA and Canada
IOS Press, Inc.
5795-G Burke Centre Parkway
Burke, VA 22015
USA
fax: +1 703 323 3668
e-mail: iosbooks@iospress.com

Distributor in Germany
IOS Press
Spandauer Strasse 2
D-10178 Berlin
Germany
fax: +49 30 242 3113

Distributor in Japan
Ohmsha, Ltd.
3-1 Kanda Nishiki-cho
Chiyoda-ku, Tokyo 101
Japan
fax: +81 3 3233 2426

PRINTED IN THE NETHERLANDS

Contents

SAT2000
I. Gent et al. (Eds.)
IOS Press, 2000

Preface

Scientific research is an ongoing human activity and its milestones are generally not achieved at particular dates or special years. However, our need to reflect on progress made or to anticipate discoveries to come is sensitive to such points in time. The transition from one millennium to another is such an event. Undoubtedly, this year will see the edition of many "State of the Arts", "Encyclopedia of ..." and "Recent Progress in...". The book you have just started to read is an example of such an effort.

In September 1998, Ian Gent and Toby Walsh sent out a call for papers to celebrate the start of a new age of Satisfiability research. They wanted to gather a representing sample of contributions and the editors of the Journal of Automated Reasoning were prepared to support this initiative with a special issue. Unfortunately, Ian and Toby were extremely successful in generating great enthusiasm for this project, and numerous high quality papers were submitted which together greatly exceeded the page constraints of the Journal. The original idea of a single special issue collecting all contributions was therefore not realizable.
Being a member of the organizing committee of an event which shared an identical heading, that is the "SAT2000: The Third International Workshop on Satisfiability", Ian and Toby asked me whether I was willing to cooperate in a second effort to collect all the papers together in one place, and what was a particular challenge, to have it appear in time for the conference. The result is now in your hands.

It is my pleasure to guide you through "SAT 2000" and to highlight some of the main contributions present. I have chosen to do this in an informal manner and to avoid an endless enumeration of facts and associated names: For the exact formulations of the results and statements, as well as the relevant references to earlier results, the reader must consult the quoted papers. If he or she doesn't, there is a danger of being inadequately informed about the roots of the issues under discussion. And he or she certainly would be mislead regarding credits to individual people and research groups associated with preceding achievements.

Before we start, let me express my gratitude to Ian and Toby for taking the initiative and for their confidence in letting me deal with this task. Also, without the approval of Kluwer Academic Publishers to re-edit the papers (they are still being published in the Journal of Automated Reasoning, but not all in identical form and spread out over several issues) it would not have been possible to put this volume together. We are very grateful that they were willing to cooperate with IOS Press in such a constructive manner.

This book is not an introductory textbook. The reader is supposed to be familiar with some elementary notions from Satisfiability Theory and Propositional Logic, although it must be said that all contributions contain an adequate introductory session and the unacquainted but persistent reader will find his or her way nevertheless.

We are glad to present a whole of contributions that cover a large part of Satisfiability research. A substantial part is dedicated to incomplete (local search) methods but

one can also find depth first-, breadth first- and restricted resolution based complete solvers and hybrid mixtures. Fascinating applications from Optimization Theory are there as well. Included we see examples of how to use SAT solvers (or SAT solving heuristics) for decision procedures in more expressive systems as modal- and quantified Boolean logics. We have contributions on the "implementational side" and on stochastic satisfiability. The performance of various existing methods is measured experimentally in some papers but is also provided with theoretical bounds in others. Algorithms to generate interesting test problems are discussed and new internet resources for the research community presented.
This book includes some intriguing new applications like quasigroups and product data management, and we see the first signs of SAT research contributing to the verification of cryptographic algorithms.
These contributions provide evidence that we are about to enter an exiting period of time, where real world problems will be tackled by SAT solvers with increasing frequency. And this not only by means of local search methods, since we are starting to encounter, as you will find documented here, more and more large structured problems which appear only to be solvable by complete algorithms.

Starting with our first contribution, imagine that you are trying to solve a SAT encoding of a logistic problem with a state of the art DPLL based solver. The branching variable heuristic used is a good one but you know that it frequently randomly tiebreaks between equally good variables. The procedure has solved similar problems in the past where it used 100.000 nodes on average, but some of them took only 2000 and others over 1.000.000. You notice that the run you just started has passed 2100 nodes. Do you abort the run and start all over again or will you patiently wait until the run is completed?
The paper of **Gomes**, **Selman**, **Crato** and **Kautz** deals with questions of this probabilistic nature. They use Pareto-Levy distributions to model the erratic runtime behavior of DPLL based techniques. These distributions are characterized by heavy tails. Such heavy tailed distributions have recently been seen in disciplines as varied as stock market analysis, Brownian motion and weather forecasting. The parameters of this distribution (which generally depend on both the problem and the solver) are estimated for a selected set of problems from timetabeling, planning, code optimization and circuit synthesis (using a SAT encoding) and from scheduling (using a CSP encoding). Backtrackings are used to measure runtime and slightly randomized variants of **SATZ** (Li and Anbulagan) and **RELSAT** (Bayardo and Schrag) are chosen as the state of the art solvers to deal with the SAT encoded problems. The latter solver uses intelligent backtracking while the first does not (in fact it is Chu Min Li's credo that the purpose of intelligent backtracking only is to correct for bad choices of branching variables). On the test example from logistic planning RELSAT has slightly less heavy tails but the influence of the randomization in the branching heuristics used, which Gomes et al necessarily had to put in, somewhat obscures this comparison, since SATZ had to be randomized substantially and RELSAT only a little.
To run the CSP encodings Gomes, Selman, Crato and Kautz used a solver based on the Ilog C++ constraint programming library (Puget and Leconte). It is important for the reader to realize that heavy tails have only been observed when applying DPLL methods to satisfiable instances. No heavy tails have been observed on unsatisfiable formulas yet and runtimes of local search methods, applied to satisfiable instances, seem to be modeled well by exponential distributions. The authors claim that very hard instances may not only exhibit heavy tail behavior on the right hand side of the distribution (an unfortunate property) but also one to the left (fortunate). Therefore they come up with a rapid restart backtracking device, which restarts when the search

exceeds a prescribed number of nodes (the cutoff value). The optimal cutoff values are estimated then for a 16-team round-robin scheduling problem (CSP) and for a logistics problem (SAT). For these choices, there is a very obvious optimal restart value. What is more, by applying this rapid restart strategy, the authors were able to solve some instances of problem types for the first time with a DPLL based algorithm and for other problems from their set it resulted in substantial savings. So far it looks that estimating optimal cutoff values for as yet unsolved problems must be done experimentally with good first guesses.
The very intriguing question whether we will be able to estimate optimal cutoff values for a variety of unsolved problem types remains open so far. However, some first results are given.

That the behavior of local search methods, when applied to hard satisfiable instances, does not show heavy tails, but seems to be modeled well by an exponential distribution is one of the outcomes of the study of **Hoos** and **Stützle**. This extensive contribution measures the performance of seven variants of local search methods on a variety of benchmarks. Their methodology consists of running a particular solver many times on the same problem to establish an empirical runtime distribution first. By aggregating the obtained RTD's over a specific problem class, the authors are able to give a functional description of the runtime behavior. The sensitivity of the methods on the benchmarks with respect to scaling (to size and to hardness), noise settings and cutoff values are questions which are addressed thoroughly. Over the benchmark set none of the seven variants dominated the others but **R-Novelty**, **Novelty**, **Walksat/Tabu** and **Gsat/Tabu** (all using a kind of search history) show superior performance many times. The hybrids **R-Novelty+** and **Novelty+**, developed by Hoos in earlier work, combine various aspects of the above methods. In fact, a random walk step is added to both and the authors claim that R-Novelty+ and Novelty+ might be the currently best performing stochastic local search algorithms for SAT.
The paper of Hoos and Stützle provides a standard approach to empirically investigate stochastic search methods. They clearly convince the reader that it is just not enough to measure performance of an algorithm by only collecting data of many runs. In addition, the introductory sections of their paper gives the reader a thorough survey of a large number of existing methods.

While the early papers on local search methods for Satisfiability showed a striking discrepancy between the simplicity of the method on the one side and its performance on the other, more elaborate "second generation" methods have been designed to solve problems with specific structure.
In the more general field of Constraint Satisfaction Problems (e.g. vehicle routing-, traveling salesman- and frequency assignment problems) there is a diversity of features which solutions might have, or are not allowed to possess. These features ask for additional notions and as most of the additional concepts guiding a local search, generally invoked either as "noise" or as penalties in an "overall" objective function, ask for new parameters to be tuned, the papers presented in this field show great ingenuity in dealing with this task.
The paper of **Mills** and **Tsang** is such an example. They discuss a form of Guided Local Search which has emerged out of neural networks and genetic algorithms. Not only do they give a nice overview of existing methods for escaping form local optima (which can be achieved for instance by weighting constraints dynamically, or by allowing sideway moves) they also contribute to Satisfiability research by specifying this Guided Local Search for Max-Sat problems. The method proposed is measured against **walkSAT**

(Selman, Kautz and Cohen) and Mills and Tsang provide experimental evidence for superior behavior of **GLS** applied to Weighted Max-Sat problems.
Applied to SAT problems it seems that differences are less pronounced for the moment: the larger Parity learning problems for instance, being solvable now using preprocessing techniques from Linear Programming, or by invoking equivalence reasoning into complete DPLL based solvers, still remain unsolved using their procedure.

As mentioned above, many researchers have wondered and still wonder about the occasional amazing efficiency of incomplete search methods in finding solutions to a variety of SAT problems. The question of how to extend these incomplete methods to complete ones is challenging, because some propositional reasoning must be added. But how much reasoning must be actually carried out and remembered during the execution of such a search algorithm?
The contribution of **Richards** and **Richards** consists of a procedure **learn-SAT** which records minimal partial assignments which cannot be extended to solutions (so called no-goods). These minimal assignments are constructed from the possible dead end situation after trying to extend a consistent partial assignment further. A forward checking procedure to reduce the domain of the variable selected to be set to a value, is carried out each time this consistent set is to be enlarged. In fact, their procedure is a generic Constraint Satisfaction solver where the typical Satisfiability features are captured by ordering the variables according to their appearance in (or their impact to create) 2-literal clauses. These type of counts are widely accepted as providing an important measure when selecting a branching variable, both in a full look-ahead situation, where the 2-literal clauses created are counted afterwards, or in the situation where a variable is to be selected without performing all the actual propagations and its potential to create 2-literal clauses is approximated by the number of times it appears in short clauses.
At first sight, the value of the learn-SAT procedure of Richards and Richards may not be apparent, simply because even its space-complexity is exponential! However, the authors show that their algorithm manages very well on a selected set of 3-SAT problems despite these worst-case storage constraints. They compare its performance with that of complete methods like (a somewhat extended versions of) **relsat** (Bayardo and Schrag) and **tableau** (Crawford and Auton), and incomplete ones like **weight** (Selman, Kautz and Morris). Their results encourage further investigations, not in the least because they pose some new intriguing questions about model density.

Despite the success of local search algorithms for Satisfiability, very little is known about the complexity of the current incomplete methods. Most papers on local search deal with the design of an algorithm by specifying its neighborhood structure, followed by an experimental evaluation of its performance which, it must be admitted once more, can be very impressive.
The paper of **Hirsch** however is of a different nature. It provides upper bounds (in a probabilistic sense) for the running times of **GSAT** (Selman, Levesque and Mitchell) and its non-greedy variant of Gent and Walsh referred to as **CSAT** (not to be confused with **C-SAT**, a branching algorithm of Dubois, Andre, Boufkhad and Carlier) when applied to CNF formulas of a specific type (called random k-CNF). Hirsch also establishes a lower bound on the running time performance (with respect to the whole class of CNF formulas) and a specific lower bound relative to the class of 3-SAT formulas. The formulas constructed in order to obtain these lower bounds (serving the purpose of "misleading" the search) may be the starting point for further attempts to analyse worst case behavior of local search methods.

In contrast to his first contribution, which is perhaps the first study of complexity issues regarding local search, Hirsch's second paper follows a well established tradition: investigating upper bounds for complete SAT branching algorithms.
Following on the well known results of Moniem and Speckenmeyer, with the subsequent work of Kullmann and Luckhardt, **Hirsch** presents a sharpening of the previous upper bounds by introducing a novelty: "the black and white literals principle". The exploitation of this principle (closely related to the autarky arguments used earlier by others) together with the use of the by now more or less standard concepts as the t-function and blocked clauses, leads to a further decrease in the exponent established in earlier bounds. The proofs are, as they generally are in this discipline, rather tedious and in some sense unnatural. Hirsch himself is concerned about this feature and expresses his hope (and mine) that some day more compact arguments might become available.

Incomplete methods are currently designed to locate solutions of Satisfiability problems. Comparable methods to find refutations are not yet present. But the paper of **de Klerk**, **van Maaren** and **Warners** can be considered as a first attempt to fill this gap. They define a certificate of Unsatisfiability as the outcome of a certain Semi-Definite Optimization problem, which can be associated to a CNF formula in a natural way. It is shown that, given a vector of the appropriate dimensions, it can be checked in polynomial time whether this vector is a certificate (by an eigenvalue computation) but what is more, that such a certificate can be constructed in polynomial time also. The class of formulas for which this method works contains the (unsatisfiable) 2-SAT formulas and (surprisingly) the **pigeon-hole-** and **mutulated chessboard** formulas. This is the more interesting if one realizes that the latter formulas can be shown to take resolution exponential time. Cutting plane proofs for the unsolvability of pigeon-hole formulas which are of polynomial size are already known but in those cases the underlying tree of clauses to combine is supposed to be given. In contrast, the method of de Klerk, van Maaren and Warners is a fully automated polynomial time procedure. The particular Semi-Definite Relaxation of a CNF formula they consider is still a weak one. In fact there are many ways to strengthen this relaxation. For that reason it is to be expected that the above class of "SDR infeasible" formulas will be enlarged considerably in the next future. Also, an international effort to improve interior point methods for Semi-Definite Optimization is still going on. This will undoubtably result in faster code. A promising fact is also that, following the initial success of Goemans and Williamson, who used SDR methods to construct approximation algorithms for Max 2-SAT, numerous applications of SDR to discrete problems have already been developed. However, whether SDR methods will be able to deal with large scale Satisfiability problems remains open.

The original work of Davis and Putnam lead to the DPLL algorithm which combines unit resolution with a branching device. But as **Rish** and **Dechter** point out, the early papers on resolution contain variants which nowadays seem to attract little attention. They reconsider what they call Directional Resolution **DR** which structures the resolution process by means of an ordering of the propositional variables. To be more precise, an ordering of variables induces an ordering on the clause set of a CNF formula, the equivalency classes of which are called buckets, and these classes are ordered in turn. Resolution then is performed within a bucket and resolvents are put into their corresponding classes. This procedure is then performed iteratively. The final output is a CNF which, if not shown infeasible, generates all models in time which is linear in its size. Of course, generally this size will be exponential in the size of the original formula.

To investigate the complexity of DR two variants are discussed, namely induced width and induced diversity. Starting with the interaction graph of a CNF, where nodes correspond to variables and edges between nodes represent the fact that the variables are together in at least one clause, an ordering under consideration induces additional structure on this graph, leading to an ordering dependent induced graph. The ordering dependent width then is the maximum of the widths of the nodes of this last graph. Finally, the induced width is the minimum over all possible orderings. Induced diversity is a similar minmax notion, but it is based on counting occurrences of literals within buckets. To find the optimal orderings involved is NP-complete. Rish and Dechter however use, when they come to experiments, surrogates for these optimal orderings, which can be determined by simple greedy algorithms.
But first they provide theoretical bounds for DR expressed in terms of the above two invariants and they show how 2-SAT and k-tree-formulas fit into these results, and in a separate chapter, they relate the knowledge-compilation aspects of DR to tree-clustering.
As is well known, the choice of an ordering of propositional variables influences the performance of backtracking algorithms (and similarly the sizes of Binary Decision Diagrams) drastically. It has a similar influence on the performance of DR. To the authors' knowledge (and mine) very little is known whether this is due to characteristics of the problems being solved or the methods being used or both. This fact, as the authors themselves point out, complicates any experimental comparison between DR with DPLL type algorithms.
DR can be restricted to resolution in which resolvents are only considered if their length is within a prescribed bound. This results in an incomplete algorithm, named **BDR(bound)**, which can be turned into a complete one by processing DPLL on the resulting formula. Another way is to resolve only with respect to a subset (selected dynamically in a branch tree) of variables, in order to obtain resolvents which lengths do not exceed the prescribed bound, and by invoking this restricted form of resolution into a DPLL algorithm, another hybrid solver **DCDR(bound)** is obtained. Rish and Dechter provide interesting data on the performance of these hybrids on both random and structured formulas. They especially focus on the sensitivity of these performances with respect to the bounds prescribed, showing that refinements are needed to explore more of the possible benefits.

The solver **Heerhugo** is named after a Dutch railway station since it emerged from a study concerning the validity of a procedure called Vital Processor Interlocking. This procedure is meant to prevent conflicting situations with regard to safety. The solver is in the spirit of Stallmarck's patented procedure, and can be characterized as a breadth-first backtracking algorithm. Its input is an arbitrary proposition which is (linearly) transformed into a 3-CNF formula. This transformation is even carried out when the input is already of this form, resulting in a larger 3-CNF. This may look odd, but it sometimes has dramatic consequences: by this feature the Dubois instances from the **DIMACS** collection for instance, are readily solved.
In phase 0 the solver applies some standard elements from propositional reasoning as unit resolution, elimination of cycles obtained from 2-literal clauses, restricted size resolution, monotone variable fixing, subsumption, etc. The key argument is carried out in phase 1. In this phase a variable is set to 0 and phase 0 is applied and when not solved the variable is set to 1 and phase 0 is entered again. Now the common clauses of the resulting two CNF formulas are added to the current formula (branch and merge) and another variable is then selected and the procedure is repeated. Having done this

for all variables (in an iterative manner) the current formula (now being invariant under phases 0 and 1) enters phase 2, when it is not resolved yet.
Phase 2 is a nested form of phase 1, where pairs of variables are successively set to their truth values, and so on. In principle the algorithm may reach any phase but **Groote** and **Warners** report that when a formula is not solved in phase 0, 1 or 2, the chances that it will be solved anyway by their algorithm are vanishing.
Heerhugo is hybrid in that sense that it also performs a local search method at some stages to enhance its performance on satisfiable instances. Groote and Warners performed numerous tests on various benchmarks (DIMACS and UCSC) and made comparisons with other methods as **SATO3.0** and **SATO2.2** (Zhang), **GRASP** (Marques Silva and Sakallah), **POSIT** (Freeman) and **modoc** (Van Gelder and Okushi) with varying results. We conclude with them that, apparently because of its breadth-first aspects, Heerhugo provides a powerful complementary approach to SAT solving. The solver is available to the research community: an appendix to the paper explains how to obtain and use it.

The impact of the internet on society is still growing. The scientific community has realized its importance now for some time. Nevertheless, the creation of a web site with valuable resources for research is the dedicated work of a minority of individuals. Its maintenance so that it remains of value over a longer period of time is something which is often too much of an effort for many of us. **Hoos** and **Stützle** present their Satisfiability Library **SATLIB** as a new resource for the SAT community. The site was started in 1998 and was frozen for some time but after its last update it now contains many new benchmarks (and older ones as the well known but somewhat outdated **DIMACS** problems), solvers, comparisons and a bibliography. Various links to researchers and events are there. Let us all hope that this initiative is a lasting one and that its announced frequent updates will continue to serve us all.

In order to evaluate the performance of SAT-solvers researchers use either a universally accepted and frequently consulted set of benchmark test problems, as provided for example by SATLIB, or they select a well defined class of problems, the instances of which are easily generated.
The paper of **Motoki** and **Uehara** provides new possibilities of generating hard 3-SAT instances with other probabilistic properties than those of the widely used "threshold" formulas. They discuss three algorithms to generate formulas admitting only one solution, or at least with high probability such. For two of these procedures they derive theoretical bounds on the number of clauses needed. Their experiments show that these bounds might be somewhat pessimistic and, moreover, that the algorithms involved are indeed capable of generating instances which are hard to solve by complete solvers (they selected **A-SAT** of Dubois) as well as incomplete ones (**Walksat** of Selman, Kautz and Cohen). And what is most important, these instances are of relative small size.

One of the striking achievements of Satisfiability research over the past years is the solution of some open problems in de theory of quasigroups. The award-winning IJCAI paper of Fujita, Slaney and Benett with the follow up of Slaney, Fujita and Stickel inspired other researchers to consider quasigroup problems as ideal benchmarks to evaluate the performance of their solvers. Even small quasigroups give rise to huge CNF formulas and a DPLL algorithm has to visit a unit propagation procedure millions of times. Therefore, efficiently dealing with data structures can make the difference between solving such a problem in realistic time and waiting for an answer in vain.

Zhang and **Stickel** push the boundaries somewhat further by going deeply into the implementational aspects of unit propagation.
They use a trie data structure to enhance the DPLL procedure and they consider seven variants, depending on how to explore this data structure, which are compared through their success on quasigroup problems. Three of their variants, of which **SATO** seems to perform the best, are measured against other state of the art solvers as **MACE** (McCune), **POSIT** (Freeman), **SATZ** (Li and Anbulagan) and **NTAB** (Crawford and Auton). Within the time limits set, SATO and MACE solve all quasigroup problems from the list and SATZ solves all but one. Zhang and Stickel believe, however, that these other solvers are also capable of comparably dealing with quasigroups after slight modifications. Finally, SATO was used to settle some new open quasigroup problems, which took several weeks of CPU time on a powerful workstation.

Another victory for SATO is recorded by **Küchlin** and **Sinz** in their application of propositional reasoning to product data management of Daimler Chrysler AG with respect to processing orders for Mercedes-Benz automobiles.
Since there is a vast variety of such cars, due to all possible models and supplementary equipment, an order from a customer is processed a number of times before it enters the production department as a so called parts list. During this processing, inconsistencies may be generated. For instance, a customers order which is constructible originally may become unconstructible by the order completion process, which consists of adding orders (properties of the car, like steering wheel left, no lighter, metallic, no airconditioning,) because of technical dependencies. The outcome of this process might depend on the arbitrary succession in propagating these dependencies.
The authors manage, after formalizing the whole process sketched above, to characterize confluentness of the associated term rewriting process as a propositional formula. Also they express other possible inconsistencies similarly. These formulas are not CNF formulas and after converting them, CNF formulas result with approximately 1000-2000 variables and 9000-22000 clauses. Küchlin and Sinz report, and this may be considered flattering to our research community, **SATO** outperformed other methods as resolution, term rewriting and Binary Decision Diagrams.

The US Data Encryption Standard DES was designed by IBM and NSA and, although it is currently under review, still plays an important role as a standard for international banking transaction services. It is an example of a cryptographic algorithm. Such algorithms play a key role in computer security and their formal verifications are of utmost relevance. **Massacci** and **Marraro** have encoded various desirable and undesirable properties for cryptographic algorithms as propositional formulas and they present their results for DES.
A logical formula E(P,K,C) is derived which evaluates to true if and only if DES transforms the plain text P into the cipher text C through the key K. Here, text is supposed to be represented as a 0,1 sequence. As they argue, such a formula might be obtained in a rather straightforward fashion, but to keep its size acceptable requires tricks and the authors even use CAD tools to reach this goal. They give a nice insight in the clause-variable structure of the formula which finally resulted.
A plain text attack is an attempt to break the code by comparing a cipher text C with a (perhaps obscurely obtained) plain text input, thus an attempt to obtain K from a given input P and C. If more such pairs are available conjunctions of the E(P,K,C) 's over the known (P,C) 's encode the fact that DES used K to transform the plain text samples at hand into the corresponding ciphers. A round is a procedure within DES

which may be repeated several times to make it harder to find the key. In fact, DES as such uses 16 rounds.
Massacci and Marraro report in their contribution that **RELSAT** so far was the only solver able to find the key for a 3-round DES under a two pairs plain text attack in reasonable time. **SATO** also succeeded in this but needed 8 such pairs, thus needing a much more constrained and easier problem. (By the time of writing this preface it is known however that a modification of **SATZ** has matched the RELSAT performance.) From a cryptographic viewpoint these are not impressive results, because existing methods can do much better, even up to 8 rounds. However, those methods need far more text pairs to do so and this is one of the reasons why the SAT approach is promising. Also, the work of Massacci and Marraro has an important spin-off, namely, it provides new possibilities to generate easily an abundance of "real world" problems of arbitrary size.

A Boolean formula can be compiled onto an FPGA (field-programmable gate array; sometimes called the poor man's chip) where after the corresponding feasibility problem can be attacked using the devices (e.g. PODEM and FAN) developed by the ATPG (automatic test generation problem) community. Such an attempt benefits from the fact that, on an FPGA, propagations are performed parallel.
This approach is subjected to a number of trade-off issues. First, the compilation time must be smaller than the hardware speed up. In their contribution, **Abramovici** and **De Sousa** argue, that by using ILAs (iterative logic arrays), compilation can be done in time which is linear in the size of the input CNF formula. These ILAs are building blocks, to be placed and routed on an FPGA, and can be used to represent any CNF, possibly at the cost of creating empty space on the FPGA under construction. Further, FPGAs may be to small (perhaps also due to the use of ILAs) for a given CNF formula. In the latter case the formula must be decomposed (by setting some variables to both their truth values) to a number (possibly exponential) of subproblems which do fit on an FPGA. After solving a subproblem an FPGA however may be reconfigured immediately to attack another subproblem, hence there are trade-off possibilities between FPGA-size, the number of available FPGAs and overall time.
The authors discuss all these trade-off issues and they present a clear view on what has been established so far with the reconfigurable hardware approach just sketched.
Typically new is the introduction of high- and low priority objectives, to be propagated on an LPGA. These objectives enable them to simulate, within the current possibilities of FPGAs, some typical SAT solving features as pure literal setting, don't care identification (the more don't cares the better in ATPG) and (some weak form of) splitting heuristics. The crucial aspect is that all these objectives are propagated simultaneously along all possible paths in the layout of the FPGA. Abramovici and De Sousa give us an insight in what might be gained (against **GRASP**) by this approach in solving a selection of DIMACS benchmarks. Times reported are calculated from a simulation of the actual process, but indicate that substantial speed up is to be expected.

From a pure logician 's point of view, propositional logic may have lost its attractions. But this is certainly not the case with modal logic, which variants are widely studied by the logicians community. The decision problems for these logics are, most of the time, hard combinatorial problems and it is a natural question whether SAT solvers can contribute to actually implement and perform the decision procedures involved.
Giunchiglia, **Giunchiglia** and **Tacchella** present a SAT based procedure, called ***SAT**, which they designed to deal with eight different existing modal logics. There approach is modular and differs essentially from more traditional methods as the tableau-

based- (Smullyan) or translation-to-first-order-logic-based procedures (van Benthem). Horrocks and Patel-Schneider also followed a similar approach but as they developed their own specifically suited SAT solver Giunchiglia, Giunchiglia and Tacchella argue that it might be better to built a procedure on top of (any) existing SAT solver, since then it can profit from the improvements resulting from ever ongoing work.
In their analysis they selected **SATO** as a state of the art solver. The approach they follow consists of two main parts. The first part is to generate a complete set of assignments satisfying a formula at hand. In this context an assignment is a conjunction of propositional literals and formulas starting with a modal operation (eventually preceded by a negation sign) without internal conflicts (no conjunct is the negation of another). Such an assignment satisfies a formula if it implies it by propositional reasoning. A set of satisfying assignments is complete if its disjunction is propositionally equivalent with the formula involved and to generate such a complete set efficiently requires a not straightforward approach. This first part is independent of the logic involved.
The logic dependent part consists of checking consistency with the axioms of the logic considered of all satisfying assignments from the complete set, a task performed again by propositinal reasoning. The authors show the soundness and completeness of the overall procedure for the eight modal logics considered. *SAT is measured against **KSATC** (Giunchiglia et al.), **DLP** (Patel-Schneider) and **TA** (Hustadt and Schmidt) for the logic K (=EMCN) and as tests they use randomly generated 3CNF-K formulas (a modal variant of 3CNF formulas) of modest size (up to 7 propositional variables) as well as the benchmarks from the Comparison of Theorem Provers for Modal Logics at Tableaux '98 (de Swart). For the logic E the authors come up with a generalization of the class of 3CNF-K formulas which is more suitable for testing procedures for non-normal modal logics. The results as presented certainly show superior or comparable performance of *SAT.

As it is generally hard, if not impossible, to compare performances of different SAT solvers, this is the more true for Modal Satisfiability checkers. One of the main reasons for this is the fact that it is considerably harder to generate meaningful random formulas in a modal logic language.
Horrocks and **Patel-Schneider** present a serious attempt to compare the procedures **DLP** and **KSATC** (with respect to the logic K) which are already commented above. They nicely describe the similarities and differences between the two methods in much detail and they convince the reader of the need of having an appropriate random formula generator first.
The original generator of Giunchiglia and Sebastiani allowed certain repetitions which could make a formula trivially false or tautological. As they argue, this fact obscured the earlier comparisons. Hustadt and Schmidt modified this generator to eliminate these problems where after Giunchiglia, Giunchiglia, Sebastiani and Tacchella again made some further improvements. Horrocks and Patel-Schneider in turn added some new parameters to the generation process to refine the possibility of comparisons even further.
And this is what they present here. A very extensive experimental study in the behavior of the two mentioned modal checkers, emphasizing on the sensitivities of both methods with respect to the parameter settings. Easy-hard-easy patterns are detected, but not as pronounced as in the propositional 3SAT cases we know. They also give a plausible explanation of the fact that (random) formulas with modal depth 2 appear to be easier solved than those of depth 1, a fact which was notified already in foregoing studies, but evidence is provided that it does not make sense to restrict one selves in testing on depth 1 for that reason only. In fact DLP outperforms KSATC on a range of problems

with depth 2. In the end, however, no clear winner shows itself and the authors conclude that both checkers should be considered as the best in the field.

Hustadt and **Schmidt** propose a translation based resolution decision procedure for the multi modal logic $\mathbf{K_{(m)}}$, a far reaching extension of **K**. $\mathbf{K_{(m)}}$ finds its motivation through its relations to description logics, which are used in the field of knowledge representation. The procedure, called **Rmod**, is not based on literal ordering refinements but on literal selection refinement and is shown to possess some nice properties.
First, models can be reconstructed from its output (resulting in a finite model property) and second, the relation to the original modal formula stays transparent during its execution. Because of this, proofs are easily transformed to obtain tableaux proofs.
Hustadt and Schmidt argue that tableaux (the single step prefixed tableaux of Massacci)- and sequent-style proof systems can be polynomially simulated by their procedure. They focus on various logics in between **K** and $\mathbf{K_{(m)}}$ with respect to the validity or generalizibility of their results.
Although the paper is mainly of theoretical nature, they include the outcome of some first modest experiments with an implementation of Rmod. To this end, the theorem prover **SPASS** (a first order logic resolution based theorem prover with equality by Weidenbach et al.) is modified to cope with randomized modal formulas (the original splitting heuristics is replaced by a Jeroslow-Wang heuristic) and extended by adding the literal selection functions. The authors conclude with expressing their hope to obtain a tableaux proof system for the guarded fragment by exploring refinements of literal selection, just as De Nivelle was able to give a resolution-type decision procedure based on ordering refinements.

In Quantified Boolean Logic propositional variables are put under the scope of an existential or universal quantifier. If a variable is under the scope of, for example, a universal quantifier it is meant that the formula following the quantifier should be true for both truth values of this variable. In principle, a formula from QBL can be expressed in propositional logic, but at the cost of an exponential growth: the decision procedure for QBL is PSPACE-complete.
Cadoli, **Schaerf**, **Giovanardi** and **Giovanardi** present **Evaluate**, a decision procedure for QBL. The underlying idea of Evaluate is straightforward in that sense that a branching tree is designed where both branches under a universally quantified splitting variable must result in a true formula and at most one in case the splitting variable is existentially quantified. Thus the backtracking laws are different than for SAT. This has considerable consequences for the value of known splitting heuristics, since the balancing aspects with respect to the growth of the search tree depend on the nature of the covering quantifier.
Much of the work of Cadoli, Schaerf, Giovanardi and Giovanardi consists of reducing a QBF to a certain form to eliminate trivially true or false formulas and to reduce the search space. Here, analogies of unit resolution and monotone variable fixing play a key role.
The data structures they use are redundant because the simplifying rules Evaluate performs need a lot of syntactic investigation.
The authors use randomly generated QBF's to get a first impression of the solvers abilities. It is understood that more parameters play a significant role in generating test formulas: the number of quantifier alterations and the numbers of variables under the scope of a given quantifier. They give a first insight into the threshold- and easy-hard-easy phenomena of QBF's, experimentally observed when shifting parameters. A remarkable feature they detected is that Evaluate solves a formula from their test

environment even before it is reduced to a plain SAT instance, most of the time. Therefore they conclude that typical DPLL splitting heuristics might be less valuable and that in the QBF case the key problem is to design quantifier-sensitive splitting heuristics.

If we extend QBF by adding a randomized quantifier we arrive at Extended Stochastic SAT, the subject of **Littman**, **Majercik** and **Pitassi**. If a variable is covered by such a quantifier it is meant that the formula in succession is to be valid for random choices of the variable in question. More precise, the value of an expression in Extended Stochastic SAT is defined recursively, where existential quantifiers are eliminated by a maximum value-, universal quantifiers by a minimum value- and randomized quantifiers by an averaging value-operation over the two truth values of the covered variable. An instance is called positive if its value exceeds a prescribed threshold. SSAT is PSPACE complete.
The main motivation to study this logic is that decision problems under uncertainty can be modeled in a quite natural fashion. The authors thus generalize an approach initiated by Papadimitriou ("game against nature").
A MAJSAT instance is a formula where all variables are under the scope of a randomized quantifier and a E-MAJSAT instance has two consecutive quantifier blocks, the first existential and the second randomized. These two specific subclasses of SSAT play an important role in the experiments provided by Littman, Majercik and Pitassi, but also in the complexity hierarchy between SAT and SSAT. The authors discuss this part of the hierarchy and also report of some known approximation results for computing values of SSAT formulas.
Next they propose the **Evalssat** procedure. This algorithm computes the value of a SSAT instance in a DPLL like fashion. As we know from our previous contribution, variables must be treated in fixed order, determined by the succession of quantifier blocks where they appear, with only some freedom with regard to the unit- or monotone literals and variables within a block. If one only wants to decide whether the value exceeds a given threshold, the authors add so called threshold pruning to Evalssat: keeping track of whether the threshold is already met or cannot possibly be met anymore downwards the decision tree.
The authors used random 3CNF formulas as the body of MAJSAT and E-MAJSAT instances to test the performance of the procedure and to investigate the threshold behavior with respect to clause-variable ratio and, for E-MAJSAT, the ratio of the lengths of the consecutive quantifier blocks. The formulas are rather small, but yet they reveal new interesting patterns, sometimes counterintuitive and not what one would expect on the basis of complexity theoretic arguments.
Also the sensitivity with regard to some widely used SAT splitting heuristic is experimentally studied: some influence is there if the quantifier blocks are not too small. It should be noted here that the investigated formulas are of a very specific nature.
Since the value of a SSAT formula can be computed in time linear with respect to the size of a canonical decision tree (a tree which takes into account the prescribed partial order of the variables), the authors address the question of finding small such trees. Based on earlier work of Clegg, Edmonds, Impagliazzo, Beame, Pitassi, Ben-Sasson and Wigderson they provide a method which generates decision trees of "almost" smallest size.
A third algorithmic device proposed by Littman, Majercik and Pitassi is a combination of sampling and local search. The variables under scope of a randomized quantifier are sampled to obtain a partial policy tree for the formula at hand while the local search part deals with the existentially quantified variables. The objective value directing the hill

climbing however is much more complex than in the SAT case, where only satisfied clauses are counted. In SSAT cases one also has to take into account the number of paths in the reduced policy tree satisfied by an assignment. The proposed device **Randevalssat**, which approximates expected values, is also experimentally tested, the results showing the expected trade-off between error and sample size. Formulas tested are small because the exact values had to be calculated first: the weakness of Randevalssat consists of the fact that the correctness (quality of approximation) of its output is not easily verified.

This concludes our preview of the presented material. We hope that the reader will enjoy SAT2000 as much as we enjoyed our editing tasks.
Finally, my personal thanks go to Peter van der Wijden for his great help in reformatting all files and managing all the type setting issues which arose and to all contributing authors for there support in establishing this volume.

Hans van Maaren

SAT2000
I. Gent et al. (Eds.)
IOS Press, 2000

Heavy-Tailed Phenomena in Satisfiability and Constraint Satisfaction Problems

Carla P. Gomes† and Bart Selman§
Dept. of Computer Science, Cornell University, Ithaca, NY 14853, USA

Nuno Crato||
Dept. of Mathematics, ISEG, Technical University of Lisbon, Portugal

Henry Kautz††
AT&T Shannon Laboratories, Florham Park, NJ 07932, USA

Abstract. We study the runtime distributions of backtrack procedures for propositional satisfiability and constraint satisfaction. Such procedures often exhibit a large variability in performance. Our study reveals some intriguing properties of such distributions: They are often characterized by very long tails or "heavy tails". We will show that these distributions are best characterized by a general class of distributions that can have infinite moments (*i.e.*, an infinite mean, variance, etc.). Such non-standard distributions have recently been observed in areas as diverse as economics, statistical physics, and geophysics. They are closely related to fractal phenomena, whose study was introduced by Mandelbrot. We also show how random restarts can effectively eliminate heavy-tailed behavior. Furthermore, for harder problem instances, we observe long tails on the left-hand side of the distribution, which is indicative of a non-negligible fraction of relatively short, successful runs. A rapid restart strategy eliminates heavy-tailed behavior and takes advantage of short runs, significantly reducing expected solution time. We demonstrate speedups of up to two orders of magnitude on SAT and CSP encodings of hard problems in planning, scheduling, and circuit synthesis.

Keywords: satisfiability, constraint satisfaction, heavy-tails, backtracking

1. Introduction

Procedures for solving propositional satisfiability (SAT) problems often exhibit a remarkable variability in the time required to solve any particular problem instance. For example, we see significant differences on runs of different heuristics, runs on different problem instances, and, for stochastic methods, runs with different random seeds. The inherent exponential nature of the search process appears to magnify the unpredictability of search procedures. In fact, it is not uncommon to observe a satisfiability procedure "hang" on a given instance, whereas a different heuristic, or even just another stochastic run, solves the instance quickly.

The fastest complete procedures for SAT are based on the Davis-Putnam-Logemann-Loveland method [12, 13]. These procedures essentially perform a backtrack search through the space of truth assignments. We study the runtime distributions of such backtrack search methods on a variety of problem instances. As we will see, these distributions have a number of intriguing properties. In particular, the distributions

† gomes@cs.cornell.edu
§ selman@cs.cornell.edu
|| crato@iseg.utl.pt
†† kautz@research.att.com

are often characterized by very long tails or "heavy tails". We will show that these distributions are best captured by a general class of distributions that can have infinite moments. Aside from our experiments on SAT, we also demonstrate the heavy-tailed phenomenon for backtrack search on general constraint satisfaction problems. In fact, we believe our results apply to backtrack search techniques in general.

Heavy-tailed distributions were first introduced by the Italian-born Swiss economist Vilfredo Pareto in the context of income distribution. They were extensively studied mathematically by Paul Lévy in the period between the world wars. Lévy worked on a class of probability distributions with heavy tails, which he called *stable* distributions. However, at the time, these distributions were largely considered probabilistic curiosities or pathological cases mainly used in counter-examples. This situation changed dramatically with Mandelbrot's work on fractals. In particular, two seminal papers by Mandelbrot [42, 43] were instrumental in establishing the use of stable distributions for modeling real-world phenomena.

Recently, heavy-tailed distributions have been used to model phenomena in areas as diverse as economics, statistical physics, and geophysics. More concretely, they have been applied in stock market analysis, Brownian motion, weather forecasts, earthquake prediction, and recently, for modeling time delays on the World Wide Web (*e.g.*, [1, 44, 56]).

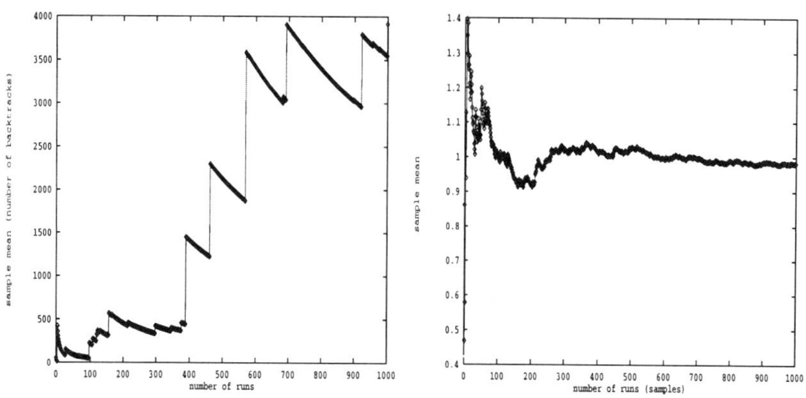

(a) (b)

Figure 1. Erratic behavior of the sample mean of backtrack search for completing a quasigroup (order 11, 30% pre-assignment) vs. stabilized behavior of the sample mean for a standard distribution (gamma).

Various researchers studying the computational nature of search methods on combinatorial problems have informally observed the erratic behavior of the mean and the variance of the search cost. In fact, this phenomenon has led researchers studying the nature of computationally hard problems to use the median cost, instead of the mean, to characterize search difficulty, because the median is generally much more stable [9, 20, 27, 35, 46, 64]. More recently, the study of runtime distributions of search methods — instead of just the moments and median — has been shown to provide a better characterization of search methods and much useful information in the design of algorithms [18, 23, 21, 29, 36, 55].

The work reported here provides a characterization of the tail behavior of backtrack-style SAT and CSP procedures, which often dominates their overall performance. We use the probabilistic model of heavy-tailed distributions. Such distributions provide a formal framework explaining the large variance and the erratic behavior of the mean of backtrack search. See Figure 1(a) for a preview of the erratic mean phenomenon. The figure shows the mean cost calculated over an increasing number of runs, on the same problem instance, of a randomized backtrack search procedure on a constraint satisfaction formulation of the quasigroup completion problem (described below). Contrast this behavior with that of the mean of a standard probability distribution (*e.g.*, a gamma distribution; no heavy tails), as given in Figure 1(b). In this case, we see that the sample mean converges rapidly to a constant value with increasing sample size. On the other hand, the heavy-tailed distribution in Figure 1(a) shows a highly erratic behavior of the mean that does not stabilize with increasing sample size.[1]

Previous authors have discovered the related — and quite surprising — phenomenon of so-called exceptionally hard SAT problems in fixed problem distributions [20, 62]. For these instances, we further observed that when a small amount of randomization was introduced into the heuristic used by the search algorithm, then, on some runs, the instances were solved quickly [58]. Thus, the "hardness" did not necessarily reside only in the instances, but rather in the combination of the instance with the details of the deterministic algorithm. When we plotted the solution times for many runs of the randomized complete algorithm (with different random seeds) on a *single* problem instance, we discovered the same heavy-tailed behavior as we had seen before on a collection of instances.

In our empirical work, we analyze cost distributions of collections of runs on single SAT instances, as well as on ensembles of instances. When running a search procedure on an ensemble of instances, we encounter two sources of variability: One is due to the variability between problem instances and the other one is due to the search algorithm itself. In order to isolate the latter source of variability — to better understand the nature of our search methods — we emphasize the study of distributions obtained from collections of runs (with different random seeds) on single problem instances. By considering instances from a range of problem domains, we also obtain insights into the variability across domains. See [29, 31] for a similar methodology.

As a direct practical consequence of the heavy-tailed behavior of backtrack search methods, we show how *rapid randomized restarts* (RRR) can dramatically reduce the variance in the search behavior. In fact, as we will see, a search strategy with restarts can eliminate heavy-tailed distributions.

For our experiments, we used SAT encodings of known hard problem instances from timetabling, planning, code optimization, and circuit synthesis. We also considered CSP encodings of scheduling problems. For our solvers, we used two state-of-the-art satisfiability engines: Satz by Li and Anbulagan [39] and Relsat by Bayardo and Schrag [5], and an efficient CSP solver built using the Ilog C++ constraint programming library [53]. It is important to note that the underlying deterministic complete search engines are among the fastest (and on many problems, *the* fastest) in their class. Thus, the techniques discussed in this paper extend the range of complete methods to problems that were often previously beyond their reach.

The paper is structured as follows. In the next section, we describe how we randomize Davis-Putnam style search methods and define our problem domains. In the following section, we introduce the notion of heavy-tailed distributions and analyze our empirical data. In the fourth section, we discuss how one can exploit the underlying heavy-tailed distributions to improve satisfiability and constraint satisfaction methods. The final section summarizes our results and gives directions for future research.

---

[1] The median, not shown here, stabilizes rather quickly at the value 1.

2. Search procedures and problem domains

2.1. Randomization

We consider a general technique for adding randomization to complete, systematic, backtrack search procedures, such as the Davis-Putnam procedure. These procedures construct a solution (or truth assignment) incrementally. At each step a heuristic is used to select an operation to be applied to a partial solution, such as assigning a value to an unassigned variable. Eventually either a complete solution is found, or the algorithm determines that the current partial solution is inconsistent. In the latter case, the algorithm backtracks to an earlier point in its search tree.

If several choices are heuristically determined to be equally good, then a deterministic algorithm applies some fixed rule to pick one of the operations, for example, by selecting the variables in lexicographic order. The most obvious place to apply randomization, therefore, is in this tie-breaking step: if several choices are ranked equally, choose among them at random. Even this simple modification can dramatically change the behavior of a search algorithm, as we will see below.

However, if the heuristic function is particular powerful, it may rarely assign more than one choice the highest score. To handle this, we can introduce a "heuristic equivalence" parameter to the algorithm. Setting the parameter to a value H greater than zero means all choices that receive scores within H-percent of the highest score are considered equally good. This expands the choice set for random tie-breaking.

With these changes, each run of the search algorithm on a particular instance will differ in the order in which choices are made and potentially in time to solution. We should note that introducing randomness in the branching variable selection does not affect the completeness of the backtrack search. Some basic bookkeeping ensures that the procedures do not revisit any previously explored part of the search space, which means that we can still determine inconsistencies, unlike local search methods. The bookkeeping mechanism involves some additional information, where for each variable on the stack, we keep track of which (truth) assignments have been tried so far.

We modified two state-of-the-art SAT solvers, Satz [39] and Relsat [6].[2] Both procedures are versions of the Davis-Putnam-Logemann-Loveland procedure [12, 13] with sophisticated heuristics for choosing which variable to branch on at each branching point. Relsat incorporates random tie-breaking and look-back strategies, such as conflict directed backjumping (CBJ, [52]) and relevance bounded learning [5]. These procedures are the fastest SAT methods we have found for the instances discussed in this paper. In both procedures the powerful heuristics often only yield a relatively small set of variables to branch on. We therefore added the heuristic equivalence parameter H to enlarge the choice set.

We also randomized the Ilog constraint solver for our experiments on constraint satisfaction formulations. Ilog provides a powerful C++ constraint programming library [53]. We randomized the first-fail heuristic and various variants of the Brelaz selection rule, which has been shown to be effective on graph coloring style problem domains [7].

2.2. Problem domains

In our study, we consider a series of problem domains.[3] Our first domain is the so-called Quasigroup Completion Problem. This domain was introduced in Gomes and Selman

[2] We thank Chu Min Li and Roberto Bayardo for making their source code available to us. See also SATLIB at www.informatik.tu-darmstadt.de/AI/SATLIB/.

[3] Problem instances and data are available from the first author (gomes@cs.cornell.edu). All experiments were performed on a 194 MHz SGI R10000 processor.

[22] to bridge the gap between purely random instances and highly structured problems, such as those from finite algebra [19, 37, 61].

A quasigroup is an ordered pair $(Q, \cdot)$, where Q is a set and $(\cdot)$ is a binary operation on Q such that the equations $a \cdot x = b$ and $y \cdot a = b$ are uniquely solvable for every pair of elements a, b in Q. The *order* N of the quasigroup is the cardinality of the set Q. The best way to understand the structure of a quasigroup is to consider the N by N multiplication table as defined by its binary operation. The constraints on a quasigroup are such that its multiplication table defines a *latin square.* This means that in each row of the table, each element of the set Q occurs exactly once; similarly, in each column, each element occurs exactly once [14].

An *incomplete* or *partial latin square* P is a partially filled N by N table such that no symbol occurs twice in a row or a column. The Quasigroup Completion Problem is the problem of determining whether the remaining entries of the table can be filled in such a way that we obtain a complete latin square, that is, a full multiplication table of a quasigroup. We view the pre-assigned values of the latin square as a *perturbation* to the original problem of finding an arbitrary latin square. Another way to look at these pre-assigned values is as a set of additional problem constraints on the basic structure of the quasigroup. (See www.cs.cornell.edu/gomes/ for a java applet demonstrating the quasigroup completion problem.)

The quasigroup completion problem is NP-complete [3, 8]. In previous work, we identified a phase transition phenomenon for the completion problem [22]. At the phase transition, problem instances switch from being almost all solvable ("under-constrained") to being almost all unsolvable ("over-constrained"). The computationally hardest instances lie at the phase transition boundary. This phase transition allows us to tune the difficulty of our problem class by varying the percentage of pre-assigned values. The location of the phase transition for quasigroups of order up to around 20 occurs around 42% of preassigned colors. For larger quasigroups, the exact location of the phase transition appears dependent on the order of the quasigroup, which is a topic for further study.

Figure 2 shows the median computational cost and phase transition as functions of the percentage of pre-assigned values for quasigroups up to order 15. Each data point is generated using 1,000 problem instances. The pre-assigned values were randomly generated in a incremental fashion with forward checking to eliminate obvious conflicts. For interesting related work using a somewhat different model of pre-assignment, see [59].

In our experiments, we used a constraint satisfaction formulation (CSP) formulation of the quasigroup completion problem. We did some preliminary experiments with a satisfiability (SAT) encoding but found that the formulas grow very large rather quickly, making it difficult to study quasigroup problems of interesting size. However, our preliminary SAT experiments agreed with our experiments using the CSP encoding.[4]

Our second problem domain is from the area of timetabling. In this domain, the problem is to determine whether there exists a feasible schedule that takes into consideration a set of pairing and distribution constraints. We consider two types of timetabling problem domains: school timetabling ([32]; we used a SAT encoding), and round-robin sports team scheduling ([45]; we used a CSP encoding). For some of the background literature in this fast growing area and to get a sense of the range and mathematical difficulty of the problems encountered, see, *e.g.*, [48].

---

[4] We thank Mark Stickel for randomizing his implementation of the Davis-Putnam procedure and for providing us with a SAT generator for the quasigroup problem.

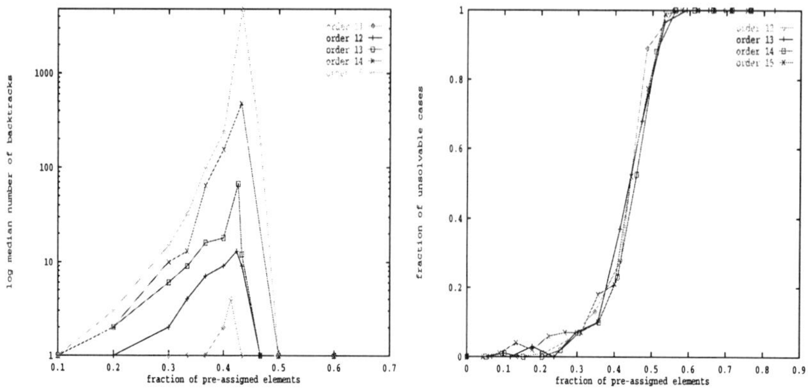

(a) (b)

Figure 2. (a) Cost profile, and (b) phase transition for the quasigroup completion problem (up to order 15).

Our third problem domain is planning. Kautz and Selman [34] showed that propositional SAT encodings of STRIPS-style planning problems could be efficiently solved by SAT engines. While both a complete backtrack-style engine and an incomplete local search engine worked well on moderate-sized problems, the largest problems from the domain of logistics scheduling could only be solved by local search. However, as it turns out, the deterministic version of Satz can solve all of the logistics instances from that paper in less than 2 minutes. Therefore we constructed a still-larger planning problem, labeled "logistics.d". This domain involves moving packages on trucks and airplanes between different locations in different cities. While the largest logistics problem from the Kautz and Selman [34] paper involved 1,141 variables and $10^{1}0$ states, "logistics.d" involves 2,160 variables and 10^{16} states. In the logistics domain, a state is a particular configuration of packages and vehicles. Satz takes over 100 minutes on logistics.d.

Our fourth and final domain involves several SAT encodings of problems from the Dimacs Challenge benchmark [32]. We consider a code optimization problem, involving register allocation ("mulsol" instance), and circuit synthesis problems ("adder" instances). For the circuit synthesis problems, Kamath *et al.* [33] developed a technique for expressing the problem of synthesizing a programmable logic array (PLA) as a propositional satisfiable problem. The statement of the problem includes a table specifying the function to be computed, and an upper-bound on the number of gates that may appear in the circuit. In general, these problems become more difficult to solve as the number of gates is reduced, until the limit is reached where the instance becomes unsatisfiable. These problems are quite hard to solve with complete SAT procedures, and have been used as part of the test-beds for numerous SAT competitions and research studies. The problems considered in this paper, "3bit-adder-32" and "3bit-adder-31" are (as one would guess) based on synthesizing a 3-bit adder using 32 and 31 gates respectively. Although Selman *et al.* [57] solve the instances using local search, they have not previously been solved using a backtrack procedure.

3. Cost distributions of backtrack search

As mentioned in the introduction, our first experiments demonstrate some of the puzzling features of backtrack search procedures, such as an extreme variability and a seemingly "wandering sample mean" of the search cost. See Figure 1(a). The data is based on runs of a randomized backtrack search procedure (Ilog) on an instance of the quasigroup problem of order 11 with 30% of pre-assignment. The figure shows the highly erratic behavior of the mean, which does not stabilize with increasing sample size. On the other hand, as we noted earlier, the median is 1 and stabilizes rather quickly.

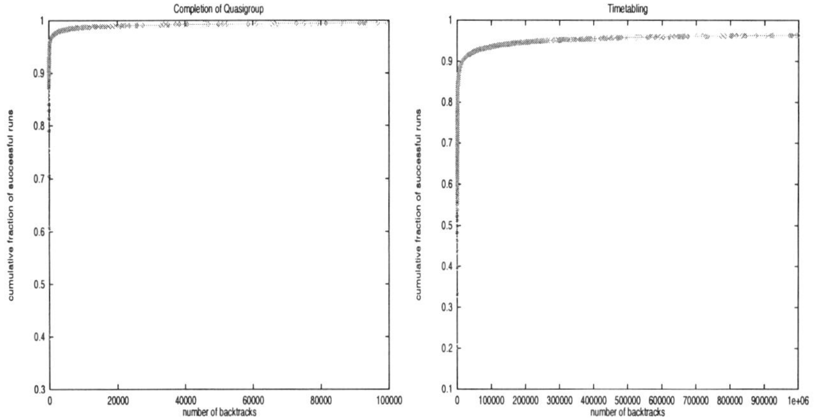

(a) (b)

Figure 3. Long tails for (a) quasigroup completion (CSP formulation), and (b) timetabling (SAT formulation).

Figure 3 provides some insights into the cause of the "wandering mean phenomenon." The figure shows surprisingly long "tails" in the distributions for two experimental domains. Each curve gives the cumulative fraction of successful runs as a function of the number of backtracks, and was produced by running the randomized backtrack search procedure 10,000 times on the same instance. Figure 3(a) shows the performance profile for the quasigroup completion problem; the data is from the same instance as shown in Figure 1. Figure 3(b) shows the cost profile of a randomized search procedure for a school timetabling problem ("school1_nsh" [32]).

The long tail phenomenon is apparent in both curves. In the case of the quasigroup completion problem, even though 50% of the runs solve the instance in 1 backtrack or less, after 100,000 backtracks 0.5% of the runs were still not completed. For the school timetabling problem, in 80% of the runs, a solution is found in 1,000 backtracks or less. However, 5% of the runs do not result in a solution even after 1,000,000 backtracks. (Note that, given that our procedure is complete, each of these runs would eventually find a solution.)

In order to model the long tail behavior of our distributions, we will consider non-standard probability distributions, referred to as "heavy-tailed" distributions. These distributions have recently received much attention because of their suitability to model stochastic phenomena subject to extreme fluctuations. In the next section, we provide a brief introduction to heavy-tailed distributions, and some of their mathematical properties. In the following section, we show how the long tails of the runtime distributions of backtrack search methods can be captured using the heavy-tailed model.

Table I. Comparison of tail probabilities, $P\{X > c\}$, for standard Normal, Cauchy and Lévy distributions. (Adapted from [51].)

c	Normal	Cauchy	Lévy
0	0.5000	0.5000	1.0000
1	0.1587	0.2500	0.6827
2	0.0228	0.1476	0.5205
3	0.001347	0.1024	0.4363
4	0.00003167	0.0780	0.3829
5	0.0000002866	0.0628	0.3453

3.1. Heavy-Tailed Distributions

Standard probability distributions, such as the normal distribution, have exponentially decreasing tails, which means that events that are several standard deviations from the mean of the distribution ("outliers") are very rare.[5] In this section, we consider distributions which have rather different properties, often leading to non-intuitive behavior. More specifically, we consider distributions which asymptotically have "heavy tails" — also called tails of the Pareto-Lévy form, *viz.*

$$P\{X > x\} \sim Cx^{-\alpha}, \quad x > 0 \tag{1}$$

where $0 < \alpha < 2$ and $C > 0$ are constants. These are distributions whose tails have a *power-law* decay.

An important source of heavy-tailed distributions is the class of so-called *stable* distributions. Stable distributions have been proposed in the study of several types of physical and economic systems. This class of distributions was extensively studied by Paul Lévy to model phenomena characterized by sums of independent identically distributed random variables. Informally, a random variable X is stable if the distribution of the sum of independent copies of it has the same shape as the distribution of X. The name of these distributions emphasizes the fact that the shape of a stable distribution is *stable* under addition.

Formally, a random variable X is *stable* if we have the following relation between X and two copies of X, X_1 and X_2, and any positive constants a and b:

$$aX_1 + bX_2 \stackrel{\mathcal{D}}{=} cX + d \tag{2}$$

for some positive c and $d \in R$. The symbol $\stackrel{\mathcal{D}}{=}$ means equality in distribution, *i.e.*, both expressions have the same probability law, possibly with different scale and location parameters [16]. In effect, (2) states that the distribution of the sum of two copies of X behaves essentially the same as X itself (up to a location and scaling factor).

Most standard probability distributions are not stable. For example, although the sum of two independently distributed gamma distribution is still a gamma, the shape of

[5] The tail of the standard normal distribution (mean 0 and standard deviation 1) decays as $P\{X > x\} \sim \frac{1}{x\sqrt{2\pi}} e^{-x^2/2}$ [16]. We write $h(x) \sim g(x)$ to mean $\lim_{x \to \infty} h(x)/g(x) = 1$.

the resulting gamma is generally not preserved. The normal or Gaussian distribution, however, is stable. There are two more cases of stable distributions for which one can write down explicit (closed form) expressions for their probability density functions. These are the Cauchy distribution and the Lévy distribution.[6] These distributions differ, however, in a fundamental way from the normal distribution in that the Cauchy and the Lévy distributions are heavy-tailed distributions: That is, the tails decay as in equation (1). Stable distributions are heavy-tailed, with the notable exception of the normal distribution [51]. The normal distribution is a stable distribution but not heavy-tailed. The other standard distributions, such as the exponential, Weibull, lognormal, gamma, etc., are neither stable nor heavy-tailed. Such standard distributions all have exponentially decaying tails and finite moments.

In Table I, we compare the tail probabilities for the three distributions. It is clear that the tail probability for the normal quickly becomes negligible, whereas the other two distributions have a significant probability mass in the tail.

The α in (1) is referred to as the *index of stability* of the distribution. The lower the index, the heavier the tail. For example, the Cauchy has $\alpha = 1.0$ and the Lévy distribution has $\alpha = 0.5$.

Heavy-tailed distributions have a number of surprising properties. For example, let's consider the moments (mean, variance, etc.) of these distributions. For standard distributions, these moments are well-defined. In the case of heavy-tailedness, due to the large probability mass in the tails, some of the integrals that define the moments do not converge. In particular, for $\alpha < 2$, moments of X of order less than α are finite while all higher order moments are infinite, *i.e.*, $\alpha = \sup\{b > 0 : \mathrm{E}|X|^b < \infty\}$. So, when $1 < \alpha < 2$, the distribution has a finite mean but no finite variance. With $\alpha \leq 1$, the distribution has neither a finite mean nor a finite variance.

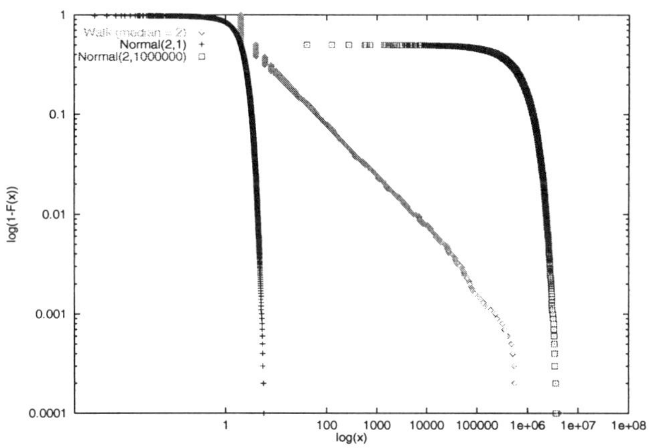

Figure 4. The heavy-tailed nature of a random walk with the exponential decay of the normal distribution for comparison.

Many aspects of random walks involve heavy-tailed distributions [16, 17]. Consider a one-dimensional random walk, where at each time step one takes a unit-step to the left or right with equal probability. One can show that after starting at the origin, with probability one, the walk will eventually return to the origin. However, the *expected*

[6] For the normal distribution, $X \sim N(\nu, \sigma^2)$, the probability density is given by $f(x) = \frac{1}{\sqrt{2\pi}\sigma} e^{-\frac{(x-\nu)^2}{2\sigma^2}}$. For the Cauchy, $X \sim \text{Cauchy}(\gamma, \delta)$, we have $f(x) = \frac{1}{\pi}\frac{\gamma}{\gamma^2 + (x-\delta)^2}$. And for $X \sim \text{Lévy}(\gamma, \delta)$, $f(x) = \sqrt{\frac{\gamma}{2\pi}} \frac{1}{(x-\delta)^{3/2}} e^{-\frac{\gamma}{2(x-\delta)}}$ [51].

time before return is infinite and, on average, the walk will reach all values on the x-axis before its return. Another intriguing phenomenon involves the expected number of returns to the origin ("zero-crossings") in a given number of steps. Intuition would dictate that if in k steps one has on average l crossings, then in a walk that is m times as long, one would expect on average $m \times l$ crossings. However, it can be shown that in $m \times l$ steps, one will only observe, on average, $\sqrt{m} \times l$ crossings. This means that there can be surprisingly long periods in a walk between two crossings. In fact, when doing a series of r random walks, each terminating at the first crossing, on average, some of the walks will be of the same order as the length of all other walks combined, *no matter what the value of* r *is.* Such events would normally be dismissed as outliers but when dealing with heavy-tailed distributions, they are far from rare and are an inherent aspect of the distribution. These distributions are therefore good models for dealing with phenomena that exhibit extreme fluctuations.

To provide a visual illustration of the heavy-tail effect in random walks, consider Figure 4. The figure shows simulation data for 10,000 runs of a symmetric random walk. For each walk we recorded the number of steps before the walk returned to the origin. In the figure, we plot the complement-to-one of the cumulative distribution, *i.e.*, $1 - F(x) = 1 - \mathrm{P}\{X \leq x\} = \mathrm{P}\{X > x\}$, with $F(x)$ being the cumulative distribution of $f(x)$. The probability function, $f(x)$, gives the probability of returning to the origin in exactly x steps. So, $1 - F(x)$ gives us the probability of returning in more than x steps. It can be seen that $f(1) = 0$ and $f(2) = 0.5$, so we have $F(x) = 0.5$, which means that with 50% chance the walk returns to the origin in at most two steps. In the figure, we give the log-log plot for $1 - F(x)$. (In the figure, the walk data is given by the diagonal straight line.) As we can see, we obtain a near straight line for the tail of the distribution. This suggests that the $1 - F(x)$ has power law decay, *i.e.*, we have $1 - F(x) = \mathrm{P}\{X > x\} \sim Cx^{-\alpha}$, and thus the distribution is heavy-tailed according to our definition (1) above. The slope of the line gives us an estimate of the index of stability, α, which in this case is equal to 0.5 (also known by rigorous analysis). The relatively high frequency of large outliers is clear from the figure. For example, although 50% of the walks return in just 2 steps or less, 1% of the walks take more than 5,000 steps to return to the origin, and about 0.1% take over 200,000 steps. In fact, several of the walks in our sample take almost $1,000,000$ steps.

To demonstrate how different such a heavy-tailed distribution is from a standard distribution, we included simulation data of the complement-to-one of the cumulative distribution for a normal distribution. We used a mean value of 2 and give the curves for two different standard deviations ($\sigma = 1$, left-most curve, and $\sigma = 10^6$, right-most curve). The key property to observe is the sharp, faster-than-linear, decay of the normal distribution in the log-log plot, which is consistent with the exponential decay in the tail of the distribution. We included a normal distribution with $\sigma = 10^6$ to show that the drop-off of the tail remains sharp even when the normal distribution has a large standard deviation. (The normal distribution is symmetrical; the figure only gives the right-hand side.)

There is a substantial literature on heavy-tailed distributions. Mandelbrot in [44] provides a good introduction to these distributions with a discussion of their inherently self-similar or fractal nature. For a complete treatment of stable distributions see either [66], or the more modern approach of [56].

3.2. Empirical Results

In order to check for the existence of heavy tails in our runtime distributions for backtrack search, we proceed in two steps. First, we graphically analyze the tail behavior of the sample distributions. Second, we formally estimate the index of stability.

From (1), we have $1 - F(x) = \mathrm{P}\{X > x\} \sim Cx^{-\alpha}$. As in the case of the random walk example, given the power-law decay of $1 - F(x)$, its log-log plot should show an approximate linear decrease in the tail. Moreover, the slope of the curve provides an estimate of the index α. In contrast, for a distribution with an exponentially decreasing tail, the log-log plot should show a faster-than-linear decrease.

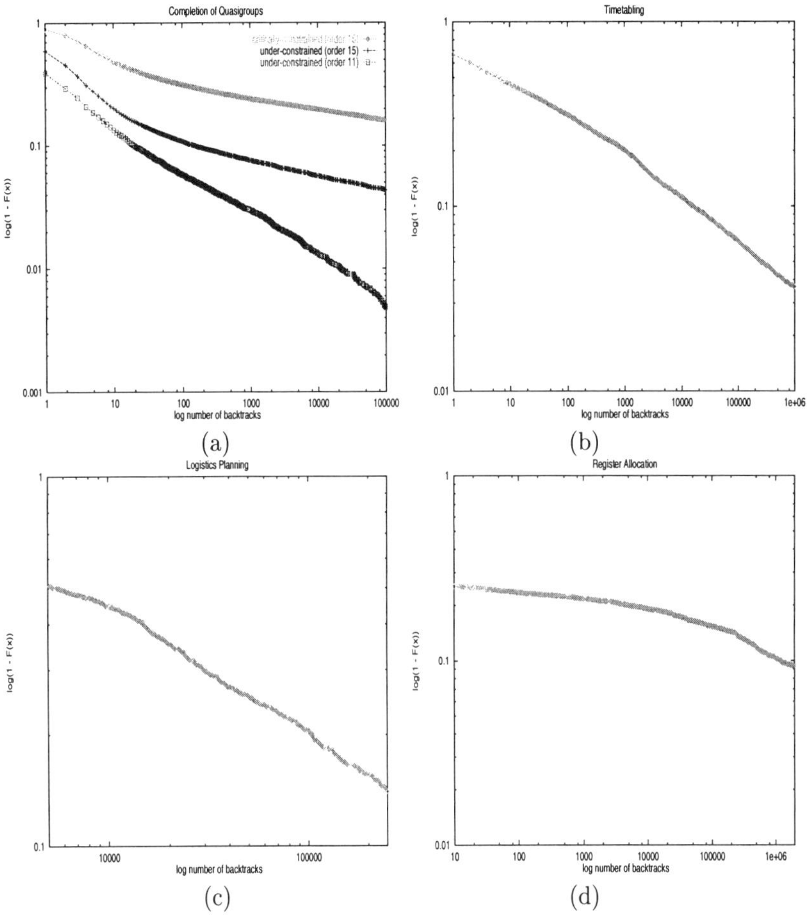

Figure 5. Log-log plot of heavy-tailed behavior for (a) quasigroup completion (CSP formulation), (b) timetabling (SAT formulation), (c) logistics planning (SAT formulation), and (d) register allocation (SAT formulation).

Figure 5 displays the log-log plots of the complement-to-one of the cumulative distributions for our experimental domains. In Figure 5(a), we give the data for a solvable critically-constrained instance of the quasigroup completion problem (order 15, 40% pre-assignment), and two solvable under-constrained instances of the quasigroup completion problem (one of order 15, 30% pre-assignment and the other of order 11, 30% pre-assignment, the same instance as used in Figure 1(a) and 3(a)). Figure 5(b) gives the data for the school timetabling problem; 5(c) for the logistics planning problem; and 5(d) for the register allocation problem. The linear nature of the tails in these log-log plots directly reveals the heavy-tailed behavior.

Note that our data is based on solvable problem instances. We considered additional distributions of over two dozen randomly picked quasigroup completion problems, from both the under-constrained and the critically constrained area, and other instances from the domains described above, as well as some ensembles of instances at various degrees of constrainedness. For sufficiently large instances (and therefore requiring substantial search), we found heavy-tailed distributions for most of our solvable instances. Some easy solvable instances did not exhibit heavy tails. We also have not encountered inconsistent instances with heavy-tailed behavior, which is consistent with the work on unsolvable instances by [18].

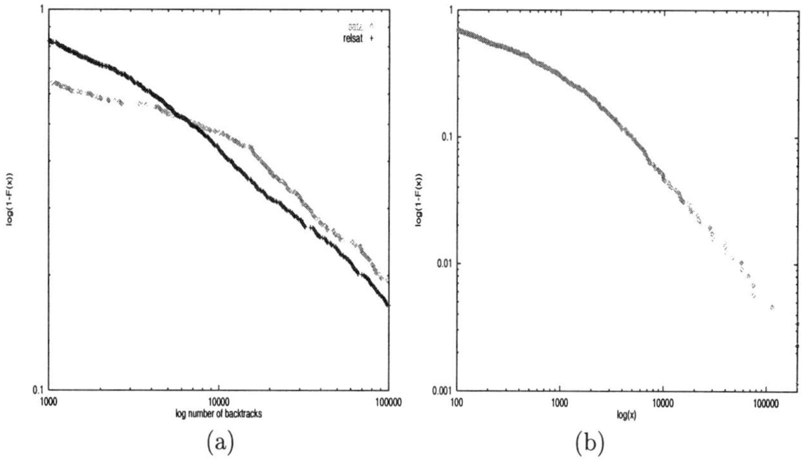

Figure 6. (a) Comparing Satz to Relsat on logistics planning (SAT formulations). (b) Heavy tail for quasigroup completion with extensive propagation (CSP formulation).

Figure 6(a) shows a comparison between two different SAT procedures on the logistics planning problem. We compare Satz [39] with Relsat [6]. As mentioned earlier, both procedures use sophisticated propagation rules and heuristics to guide their search. However, the Relsat backtracking strategy also includes look-back, based on conflict directed backjumping and relevance bounded learning [52, 5]. We present this comparison to consider the possible influence of such lookback strategies on the heavy-tailed behavior. From the figure, we see that Relsat still results in heavy-tailed behavior but the slope of the distribution in the log-log plot is steeper than for Satz. This means the index of stability for Relsat is higher, meaning a tail that is somewhat less heavy. This observation is consistent with related work where lookback strategies were shown to be effective for solving so-called exceptionally hard SAT instances [6]. In effect, the lookback approach reduces the variability in the search, even though it may not necessarily eliminate it.

We now consider the effect on heavy-tailed behavior of more compute-intensive propagation methods. For the quasigroup completion problem, when using so-called "all-different-constraints", one can solve substantially larger problems, as discovered by Shaw *et al.* [59]. In this approach, one maintains general arc consistency on the N-ary all different constraints using the algorithm of Regin [54]. This method uses a matching algorithm to ensure that at each point during the search, in each row, the set of remaining colors for the yet to be assigned cells is such that there is a different color available for each cell (similarly for the columns). Using an efficient Ilog-based implementation, we can solve instances of order 30 in under five minutes, which allows us to gather runtime information within a reasonable time frame.[7]

By using the all-different-constraint method, we observed that the heavy-tailed phenomenon disappears for quasigroups of low orders. The reason for this is that the instances are solved mostly by propagation, almost without any search. However, as we increase the order of the quasigroups, the heavy-tail phenomenon reappears. Figure 6(b) shows the heavy tail for an instance of order 30 with 55% preassigned when using the all-different-constraints (55% is close to the phase transition for order 30).

To complement our visual check of heavy-tailed behavior, we have calculated maximum likelihood estimates of the indices of stability (the values of α). There is a standard estimator for the index, called the Hill estimator [26, 24]. We adapted this estimator, since some of our data is not observable due to the fact that we ran our experiments with a certain high cutoff (usually 10^6) for the maximum number of backtracks, to avoid literally getting stuck in the most extreme outliers in the tail of the distribution during our data collection.

As shown in Appendix A, following an argument similar to the one in [26], we can derive the following maximum likelihood estimator for the index of stability α, which takes into account the data truncation:

$$\hat{\alpha}_{r,u} = \left(\frac{1}{r} \sum_{j=1}^{r-1} \ln X_{n,n-r+j} + \frac{u+1}{r} \ln X_{n,n} - \frac{u+r}{r} \ln X_{n,n-r} \right)^{-1} \tag{3}$$

$X_{n,1} \leq X_{n,2} \leq \ldots \leq X_{n,n}$ give the order statistics, *i.e.*, the ordered values of the sample $X_1, X_2 \ldots, X_n$ of the observed number of backtracks for different runs of our procedure. The highly extreme variable values $X_{n,n+1} \leq X_{n,n+2} \leq \ldots \leq X_{n,n+u}$ are not observable due to the limit that we imposed on the maximum number of backtracks allowed in the experiments. We used a limit of 10^6. The parameter r ($< n$) is a lower-bound cutoff on search cost, which enables us to focus only on the tail end of the distribution, *i.e.*, observations $X_{n,n-r} \leq X_{n,n-r+1} \leq \ldots \leq X_{n,n}$. Without a practical limit on extreme values ($u = 0$), the estimator reduces to the Hill estimator. In our analysis, we considered tails that correspond to roughly 30% of each sample (*i.e.*, $r = 0.3\ k$, with k the size of the sample).

Table II displays the maximum likelihood estimates of the indices of stability (the values of α) for the instances shown in the various figures. Note that for all the instances shown in the table, the estimates of α are consistent with the hypothesis of infinite mean and infinite variance, since $\alpha < 1$.[8]

For contrast with our heavy-tailed results, in Figure 7(a), we show the log-log plot for the same instance from the logistics planning domain used in Figure 5(c), but rather than using a randomized complete search method, we used Walksat [57], a randomized

[7] We thank Jean Charles Regin for his highly efficient Ilog implementation of this propagation strategy. A similar propagation, more efficient but somewhat less powerful, can be obtained by using so-called conjugate constraints [63].

[8] Of course, the computational cost of complete backtrack algorithms has a finite upper-bound. Technically speaking, we are dealing with "truncated heavy-tails". That is, when allowing for a very large number of backtracks such that one can explore most of the complete search tree, one will observe truncation effects in the heavy-tailed distribution. (Personal communication, Holger Hoos, Dec. 1999.) Nevertheless, the heavy-tailed model provides a good approximation for the tail-behavior of the search cost when dealing with realistic-size NP-complete problems. The heavy-tailed model emphasizes the power law decay over several orders of magnitude of the tail of the distribution. Also, since the upper-bound of the search space is exponential in the size of the problem, it is generally not reached in practice.

Table II. Estimates of the index of stability, α, with sample size k. The values within parentheses are the estimated asymptotic standard deviations. (Quasigroup instances encoded as CSP; other instances encoded as SAT).

Cases	k	α
Quasigroup (order 11, 30%)	9731	0.466 (0.009)
Quasigroup (order 15, 30%)	10000	0.319 (0.006)
Quasigroup (order 15, 40%)	10000	0.153 (0.003)
Quasigroup (order 30, 55%)	10000	0.392 (0.007)
School Timetabling	10000	0.219 (0.004)
Logistics Planning (Satz)	1442	0.360 (0.017)
Logistics Planning (Relsat)	1000	0.670 (0.009)
Register Allocation	10000	0.102 (0.002)

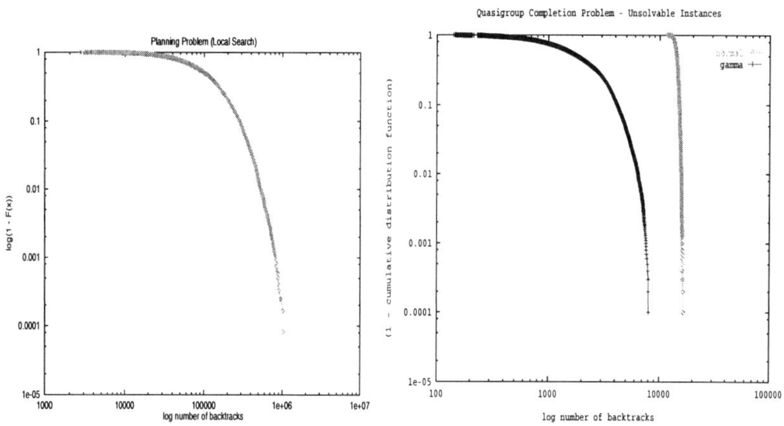

(a) (b)

Figure 7. No heavy-tails — (a) local search (SAT formulation) and (b) unsolvable instances (CSP formulation).

local search procedure. It is clear from that plot that the distribution does not exhibit heavy-tailed behavior, given the faster-than-linear decrease of the tail. This observation is consistent with the recent (independent) results by Hoos [29], showing that the exponential distribution generally provides a good model for the runtime profile of local search.

Another example of non heavy-tailed behavior is given in Figure 7(b), which shows the log-log plots of two unsolvable instances from the quasigroup completion domain. We see the sharp rounded drop-off of both curves — indicating the absence of heavy tails. One is a rare unsolvable instance in the under-constrained area (best fit: a gamma distribution), the other is an unsolvable instance in the critically constrained region (best fit: normal distribution). As noted above, we have not found unsolvable instances with heavy-tailed behavior, again consistent with Frost *et al.* [18].

3.3. Heavy-Tails on the Left-Hand Side of the Distribution

The heavy-tailed behavior we have seen so far shows that in backtrack search, extremely long runs can occur much more often than one would expect if the process were covered by a standard probability distribution. Similarly, in further experiments, we have found an indication that, when dealing with relatively hard problem instances, short runs may also occur much more frequently than expected. Figure 8 gives the log-log plot of the cumulative distribution ($F(x) = \mathrm{P}\{X \leq x\}$) for a 14 team round-robin scheduling problem (panel a) and for a logistics planning problem (panel b). The data from Figure 8(a) shows that even though 70% of the runs take more than 25,000 backtracks, roughly 1% of the runs take less than 650 backtracks. In the case of the 16 team scheduling instance, we observed that roughly 1% of the runs takes less than 10,000 backtracks, compared to a median value of the distribution which is over 2,000,000. For the logistics problem in Figure 8(b), we found that roughly 2% of the runs find a solution in at most 200 backtracks, while 70% of the runs take more than 100,000 backtracks. Figure 8 reveals a substantial fraction of very short runs. However, the left-hand side tails in Figure 8 are not heavy enough to qualify as "heavy". Nevertheless, our conjecture is that very hard instances may indeed exhibit heavy-tailed behavior on the left-hand side. We are currently investigating such a conjecture. The existence of a considerably mass of probability in the left-hand side of the distribution, as well as the heavy-tailed phenomena on the right-hand side, have significant consequences for algorithmic strategies.[9] In particular, we will show in the next section, how by rapid restarting a randomized backtrack procedure one can take advantage of the left-hand side probability mass and eliminate the heavy-tailed behavior on the right-hand side.

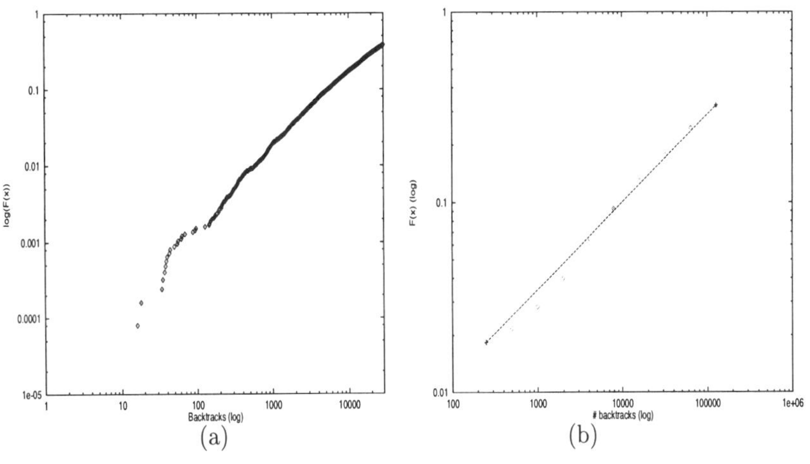

Figure 8. Log-log plot of left-hand side tail of the distribution for (a) 14 team round-robin scheduling (CSP formulation) and (b) logistics.d planning instance (SAT formulation).

---

[9] The long tails on the left also provide an explanation for the so-called "super-linear" speedup phenomenon, observed in practice when solving hard combinatorial problems using several parallel runs [15, 41, 28, 60]. Basically, a long tail on the left implies that some of the parallel runs have a non-negligible probability of finishing early.

3.4. Heavy-Tailedness and Structure of Search Space

Why do heavy-tailed distributions occur in backtrack search? An intuitive explanation involves the notion of *critically constrained* variables. In most combinatorial problems, it is much harder to find good values for some of the variables than for others. However, once these *critical* variables are set, the values for the other variables are largely determined. For example, in scheduling problems it is often the case that once a subset of critical tasks is scheduled, the other tasks immediately fall into place. The most efficient backtrack search strategy is to first concentrate on finding a consistent set of values for these critical variables. The variable choice heuristic employed in backtrack search tries to identify such critical variables, but is in practice inaccurate. The very short runs occur when the heuristic works well and critical variables are chosen at the beginning of the search. The very long runs occur when the algorithm makes some unfortunate choices early on and explores an exponential number of ways of setting non-critical variables, none of which allows a consistent assignment to the critical variables, *i.e.*, the search explores an exponentially large subtree containing no solutions. We are currently formalizing this intuitive explanation of critical variables by studying the close connection between phase transition phenomena and computationally hard problems, using models from statistical physics [25, 35, 47]. We show that the number of critical variables is linked to the nature of the phase transition underlying the computational task. Furthermore, heavy-tailed behavior suggests that the underlying search space for combinatorial problems is inherently self-similar in nature. We are exploring more direct measures to characterize such self-similarity geometrically. Intuitively speaking, self-similarity arises from repetitive patterns in the search tree, leading to a possible fractal dimension of the overall search tree.

Another step towards a further understanding of heavy-tailed behavior can be found in recent work by Walsh [65]. In searching graphs with so-called "small-world" properties, Walsh [65] identifies heavy-tailed behavior. He puts forward the conjecture that a small-world topology will induce heavy-tailed behavior. A small-world topology is characterized by a small number of global constraints combined with a large number of local connections. In such problems, the long range interactions may define the critical variables of the problem. Clearly, more work is needed to clarify these issues.

4. Consequences for Algorithm Design

We have shown the special heavy-tailed nature of the cost distributions of randomized SAT and CSP procedures, and we have seen how the distributions can be modeled with Pareto-Lévy type (heavy) tails. Our estimates for α are consistent with the hypothesis of infinite variance ($\alpha < 2$), and infinite mean ($\alpha < 1$), which is consistent with the empirically observed erratic behavior of the mean and extreme variance of the cost of backtrack search methods. We have also found long tails on the left-hand side of the cost distribution for certain classes of problem instances. Given the heavy-tailed phenomenon, a randomized backtrack procedure is, in a sense, most effective early on in the search, which suggests that a sequence of short runs instead of a single long run may be a more effective use of computational resources. In this section, we show how a *rapid randomized restart* strategy can take advantage of the heavy-tailed behavior.

4.1. *Cost Distributions With Restarts*

In Figure 9, we show the result of applying a strategy of fixed-length short runs ("restarts") of a randomized backtrack procedure. Figure 9(a) shows the results on a quasigroup completion instance of order 20 with 5% pre-assignment. Without restarts and given a total of 300 backtracks, we have a failure rate of around 70%. Using restarts (every 4 backtracks), this failure rate drops to around 0.01%. The figure also shows a clear downward curve for the log-log plot of the complement-to-one of the cumulative distribution of the restart strategy, which is an indication that the heavy-tailed nature of the original cost distribution has disappeared. In fact, we can show that the restart strategy follows a geometric distribution, and therefore, does not have heavy tails. For a derivation of this result and a formal characterization of restarts, see Appendix B.

Figure 9(b) shows the effect of restarts on the logistics.d planning problem. The figure gives the distributions resulting from running randomized Satz with a cutoff of 16 (near optimal) and a cutoff of 250. The sharp drop off in the log-log plot shows again the resulting geometric distribution. We see, for example, that with restarts using a cutoff value of 16, after a total of around 5,000 backtracks, we obtain a failure rate of around 5%. On the other hand, *without restarts*, even after 100,000 backtracks, the failure rate is still only around 70%.

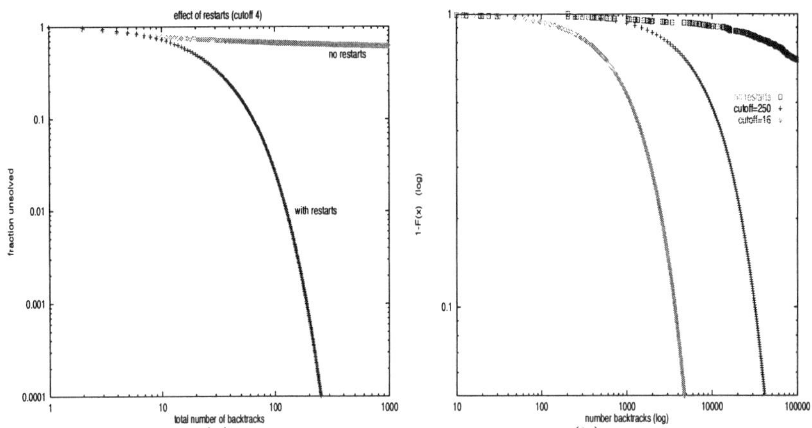

(a) (b)

Figure 9. A rapid restart strategy to speed up backtrack search. Failure rate $(1 - F(x))$ as a function of the total number of backtracks for a quasigroup instance (CSP formulation; panel a) and a logistics instance (SAT formulation; panel b). In panel b, the left-most curve is for a cutoff value of 16; the middle curve for a cutoff of 250; and, the right-most curve is without restarts.

4.2. *Rapid Randomized Restarts*

A restart strategy clearly eliminates the heavy-tails on the right of the cost distributions. Perhaps more surprisingly, such restarts can also take advantage of the long tails to the left of the median (section 3.3). In general, a restart strategy exploits *any significant probability mass early on in the distribution.*

Different cutoff values will result in a different overall mean solution time. Table 4.2 shows the mean solution time (based on 100 runs)[10] for a range of cutoff values on a

[10] Note that due to the geometric nature of the underlying restart strategy, the standard deviation in the runtime is of the order of the mean.

Table III. Solving (a) a 16-team round-robin scheduling problem (CSP formulation) and (b) the logistics.d instance (SAT formulation) for a range of cutoff values.

cutoff	success rate	mean cost ($\times 10^6$)
200	0.0001	2.2
5,000	0.003	1.5
10,000	0.009	1.1
50,000	0.07	0.7
100,000	0.06	1.6
250,000	0.21	1.2
1,000,000	0.39	2.5

(a)

cutoff	success rate	mean cost
2	0.0	>300,000
4	0.00003	147,816
8	0.0016	5,509
16	0.009	1,861
32	0.014	2,405
250	0.018	13,456
128000	0.32	307,550

(b)

timetabling problem (panel a, round-robin scheduling; 16 teams), and the logistics.d planning problem (panel b). Both tables show the same overall pattern, revealing a clear optimal range of cutoff values.[11] For the timetabling problem, the mean cost is minimized with a cutoff around 50,000, and for the planning problem the optimal cutoff value is near 16. (For both instances, these results exploit the long tail on the left.) With a higher than optimal cutoff value, the heavy-tailed behavior on the right of the median starts dominating the overall mean. Whereas, for cutoffs below the optimal range, the success rate is too low, requiring too many restarts to give a good overall mean cost value.[12]

Figure 10 gives the data from Table 4.2(b) in a graphical form. The logarithmic vertical scale indicates that one can shift the performance of the procedure over several orders of magnitude by tuning the cutoff parameter.

4.3. Restart Results on a Range of Problem Instances

In Table IV, we give the mean solution times of randomized backtrack procedures with rapid restarts, for a range of problem instances. The averages were computed over 100 runs each. For comparison, we included the runtime of the original deterministic

[11] It should be noted that random restarts involving a cutoff value are regularly used for local search methods. The novelty here is in the use of restarts in randomized backtrack search, to eliminate the heavy-tailed phenomena and to exploit short runs. Restarts are used in local search to avoid local minima, but the underlying runtime distributions do not appear to be heavy-tailed (Figure 7 [29]), resulting in less dramatic speedups.

[12] Note that the long tails in Figure 8 do not extend all the way to zero. This suggests that a pure "probing" strategy, *i.e.*, repeatedly going down a random branch of the search tree without any backtracking, is not effective on these instances. This also is apparent from Table 4.2. So, at least a small number of backtracks is required. This is in contrast with the scheduling problems considered by Crawford and Baker [11], who obtain good results with a pure probing strategy on SAT encodings in their scheduling domain.

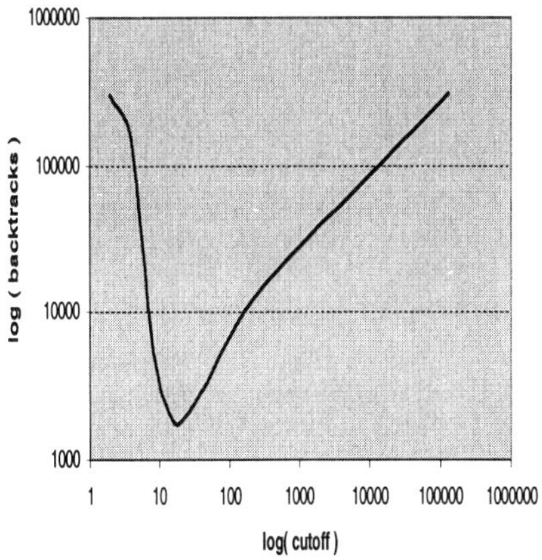

Figure 10. The effect of random restarts on solution cost for the logistics.d planning problem (SAT formulation).

Table IV. Randomized rapid restarts (RRR) versus deterministic versions of backtrack search procedures (Satz solver used on SAT encodings; Ilog solver on CSP encodings).

Problem	Solver	Deterministic soln. time	RRR mean soln. time
logistics.d	Satz	108 min	95 sec
3bit-adder-32	Satz	> 24 hrs	165 sec
3bit-adder-31	Satz	> 24 hrs	17 min
round-robin 14	Ilog	411 sec	250 sec
round-robin 16	Ilog	> 24 hrs	1.4 hrs
round-robin 18	Ilog	> 48 hrs	≈ 22 hrs
block-world.d	Satz	30 min	23 min

procedures (Satz for the logistics, adder, and blocks-world instances; Ilog for the round-robin problems).[13]

Our deterministic Ilog procedure on the round-robin scheduling problem gives us a solution for the 14 team problem in 411 seconds; randomization improves this to 250 seconds. We could not find a solution for the 16 and 18 team problem with the deterministic version. Apparently, the subtle interaction between global and local constraints makes the search for a globally consistent solution surprisingly difficult. These problem instances are too hard to obtain a full cost distribution, making it difficult to calculate an optimal cutoff value.[14] For example, in the 16 team case, running with a cutoff of 1,000,000 gives a success rate of less than 40%. So, we do not even reach the median point of the distribution. Each run takes about 2 hours to complete. (We

[13] The deterministic runs can also be viewed as single runs of the randomized procedure with an infinite cutoff value. Note that, of course, one might be "lucky" on any any given instance, and have the deterministic procedure branch in the right way. However, on the harder instances, we often need several hundred restarts to find a solution. On those instances, it becomes quite unlikely that a single deterministic run would succeed.

[14] For problems for which we can empirically determine the overall cost profile, we can calculate the *optimal* cutoff value that minimizes expected cost of finding a solution.

estimate that the median value is around 2,000,000.) In order to find a good cutoff value for very hard problem instances, one available strategy is a trial-and-error process, where one experiments with various cutoff values, starting at relatively low values, since the optimal cutoff for these problems tends to lie far below the median value of the distribution. Using such a strategy with RRR, we could solve the 16 team instance in 1.4 hours and the 18 team in approximately 22 hours.

For the SAT encodings of the 3bit-adder problems (examples of Boolean circuit synthesis problems from the Dimacs benchmark [32]) the RRR solution times are — to the best of our knowledge — the first successful runs of a backtrack search procedure (Davis-Putnam-Logemann-Loveland) on these instances. (These instances were previously solved with local search methods [57].)

On the blocks-world problem, the table shows that we obtain little improvement over our deterministic result. We ran the randomized version of Satz on this instance over a wide range of cutoff values and with different levels of randomization ("heuristic equivalence" settings). However, there was no evidence of a heavy-tailed distribution, and, therefore, randomization only slightly increases the effectiveness of Satz.

The results in Table IV show that introducing a stochastic element into a backtrack-style SAT or CSP procedure, combined with an appropriate restart strategy, can significantly enhance the procedure's performance. In fact, as we see here, it allows us to solve several previously unsolved problem instances.

Niemela [49, 50], in independent work, made randomization and restarts a standard feature of his procedure for finding stable models of propositional theories. Niemela did not study directly the cost profiles of his search procedures, but empirically found that randomization and restarts can greatly boost the performance of his solver. Although we have not studied the cost profiles of Niemela's solver directly, it seems likely that they will be heavy-tailed, which would explain the effectiveness of restarts.

Bayardo and Schrag [6], independently, included randomized tie-breaking and restarts in Relsat, but with only a fixed, high cutoff value. The focus of that work was on the effect of different backtrack techniques. The inclusion of random tie-breaking was based on the observation of the sensitivity of any fixed heuristics to individual problem instances [4].

Walsh [65] introduces a novel restart strategy in which the cutoff value increases geometrically. The advantage of such a strategy is that it is less sensitive to the details of the underlying heavy-tailed distribution. For further interesting related work, of a more purely theoretical nature, on minimizing the expected cost of randomized procedures and shortening the tails of randomized algorithms, see [2, 15, 40]. Luby *et al.* [40] provide a universal strategy for minimizing the expected cost of randomized procedures: one that is suitable for all distributions. For example, an efficient *universal* strategy consists of a sequence of runs whose lengths are powers of two, and each time a pair of runs of a given length has been completed, a run of twice that length is immediately executed. In our case, where we empirically determined the distribution of our search procedure, the optimal strategy is just a sequence of runs of a fixed length. Luby *et al.* [40] showed that such fixed restart strategy is optimal when the underlying runtime distribution of the randomized procedure is fully known. The work behind Luby's universal strategies was motivated by Ertel's observation of possible long runs of theorem proving methods and their effect on parallel strategies [15]. Although the universal strategy of Luby *et al.* is provable within a constant factor from optimal in the limit, we found that in practice the schedule often converges too slowly.

It should be noted that Luby *et al.*'s analysis for the universal strategy is based on two key assumptions: (1) no information about the prior distribution (2) unlimited time resources. One can show that when one has some prior knowledge about the problem instance (which is reasonable if you have some experience with solving previous instances of a problem class) or when one has some time constraints (*e.g.*, you need to solve this instance within, say, two days of cpu time) then more sophisticated strategies are needed. Further work on selecting the best restart strategy is needed.

Other related work is that of Huberman et al. [30] who show how one can reduce expected performance on hard combinatorial problems by running several different heuristic algorithm in parallel in a "portfolio" approach. In [21], we show that portfolios are quite effective when mixing heavy-tailed distributions arising from different heuristic strategies.

5. Conclusions

Heavy-tailed probability distributions have been used to model a variety of real-world phenomena, such as weather patterns and delays in communication networks. Our results show the suitability of such distributions in modeling the runtime behavior of Davis-Putnam style satisfiability procedures, which are the current fastest complete SAT procedures. Such procedures are based on a backtrack search through the space of possible truth assignments. Our results elucidate a series of puzzling characteristics of the computational cost of Davis-Putnam style methods. In particular, the heavy-tail model explains the informally observed highly erratic behavior of the mean and variance, as well as the long tails of the cost profiles. After observing such distributions in a variety of practical domains (including CSP formulations), it appears that the heavy-tailed behavior may be the rule rather than the exception for backtrack search methods.

The understanding of these characteristics explains why a "rapid restart" strategy is an effective remedy against heavy-tailed phenomena. In addition, restarts can exploit mass of probability on the left of the cost distributions. Restarts therefore reduce the variance in runtime and the probability of failure of the search procedure, resulting in a more robust overall search method.

An interesting question for future research is to determine what characteristics of SAT instances lead to heavy-tailed behavior and exactly how the heavy-tailedness depends on the backtrack search strategy itself. For dealing with unsolved problem instances, one would want to develop measures that are predictive of heavy-tailedness for a problem instance without having to obtain cost profiles of actual runs on the instance. If such measures can be found, one could develop apriori optimal or near-optimal restart schedules. However, even without such measures, we have found that one can often use restarts effectively because good schedules tend to be relatively uniform within a problem domain.

Finally, as we discussed, there are still many interesting research questions regarding the best restart policy. However, in practical terms [4, 38], we already see that randomization and restarts are being added to the state-of-the-art complete satisfiability procedures.

Acknowledgments We thank Karen Alguire, Roberto Bayardo, Nort Fowler, Ian Gent, Neal Glassman, Joseph Halpern, Holger Hoos, Richard Karp, Jean Charles Regin, Gennady Samorodnitsky, Mark Stickel, and Toby Walsh for useful suggestions and discussions.

The first author is supported by the Air Force Research Laboratory and the Air Force Office of Scientific Research, under the New World Vistas Initiative. The second author is supported by an NSF Faculty Early Career Development Award, an Alfred P.

Sloan fellowship, and by the Air Force Research Laboratory. The views and conclusions contained herein are those of the authors and should not be interpreted as necessarily representing the official policies or endorsements, either expressed or implied, of the Air Force Research Laboratory or the U.S. Government.

Appendix

A. Adaptation of Hill Estimator

Assume a sample of $k = n+u$ *iid* random variables is drawn. Let the order statistics for the smallest n $(n \leq k)$ values on the sample be $X_{n1} \leq X_{n2} \leq \ldots \leq X_{nn}$. Assume that, for $X_{n,n-r} \leq X \leq X_{nn}$, the tail distribution is of the Paul Lévy type. We will show that the conditional maximum likelihood estimator for the maximal moment exponent α is

$$\hat{\alpha}_{r,u} = \left(\frac{1}{r} \sum_{j=1}^{r-1} \ln X_{n,n-r+j} + \frac{u+1}{r} \ln X_{n,n} - \frac{u+r}{r} \ln X_{n,n-r} \right)^{-1} \quad (4)$$

and its variance is given by

$$\widehat{\mathrm{Var}}(\hat{\alpha}) = \frac{\hat{\alpha}^2 (r+1)^2}{r^2 (r-1)}.$$

In order to simplify the derivation, we will change momentarily the notation and derive the estimator in the context of a lower tail of the Pareto-Lévy form. The modification of the estimator for dealing with upper-tail values is straightforward. We will follow the approach of Hill (1975). For further details, see [10].

Let the order statistics be

$$Z^{(k)} \leq Z^{(k-1)} \leq \ldots \leq Z^{(l+s)} \leq \ldots \leq Z^{(l+1)} \leq Z^{(l)} \leq \ldots \leq Z^{(2)} \leq Z^{(1)}.$$

We have a total of k random variables. We assume that for $Z \leq Z^{(l)}$, at least, these are of the Pareto-Lévy type. However, we only observe the $l+s+1$ variables $Z^{(l+s)} \leq \ldots \leq Z^{(l+1)} \leq Z^{(l)}$, and not the $k-l-s$ variables $Z^{(k)} \leq \ldots \leq Z^{(l+s+1)}$. Thus, only the $s+1$ variables $Z^{(l+s)} \leq Z^{(l+s-1)} \leq \ldots \leq Z^{(l)}$ are included in the maximum likelihood estimator.

As in Hill (1975), the derivation is based on the Renyi (1953) representation theorem. Assume that the cumulative distribution function for Z, F, is continuous and strictly increasing. Then,

$$Z^{(i)} = F^{-1}\left(\exp\left\{ -\frac{e_1}{k} - \frac{e_2}{k-1} - \ldots - \frac{e_i}{k-i+1} \right\} \right),$$

where the e_i are independent exponential random variables with mean 1. Restricting our attention to the $s+1$ variables $Z^{(l+s)} \leq \ldots \leq Z^{(l+1)} \leq Z^{(l)}$, we have

$$\ln F(Z^{(l+i)}) = -\frac{e_1}{k} - \frac{e_2}{k-1} - \ldots - \frac{e_{l+i}}{k-l-i+1}$$

and so

$$(k-l-i+1)\left(\ln F(Z^{(l+i)}) - \ln F(Z^{(l+i+1)})\right) = e_i, \quad \text{for } i = 0, 1, \ldots, s.$$

Unlike Hill (1975) we assume directly that $F(z) = Cz^{\alpha}$ for the range above, which rewritten as $\ln F(z) = C + \alpha \ln z$ and introduced in the previous equation shows that the random variables T_j

$$T_{k-l-i+1} = (k-l-i+1)\left(\ln Z^{(l+i)} - \ln Z^{(l+i+1)}\right) = e_i/\alpha, \quad \text{for } i = 0, 1, \ldots, s,$$

are independent and exponentially distributed with parameter α. Therefore, conditioning on the boundary variables $Z^{(l)}$ and $Z^{(l+s)}$, the maximum likelihood estimator for α is $\hat{\alpha} = s/\sum T_i$. It is easy to verify that the sum $\sum T_i$ collapses to

$$(k-l)\ln Z^{(l)} - \sum_{i=1}^{s-1} \ln Z^{(l+i)} - (k-l-s+1)\ln Z^{(l+s)}.$$

Therefore, the estimator becomes

$$\hat{\alpha} = \left(\frac{k-l}{s} \ln Z^{(l)} - \frac{1}{s}\sum_{i=1}^{s-1} \ln Z^{(l+i)} - \frac{k-l-s+1}{s} \ln Z^{(l+s)} \right)^{-1}.$$

In order to modify this estimator for working with upper tails of the Pareto-Lévy type, we just note that letting $Z = X^{-1}$ we have $\mathrm{P}\{Z \le x\} = \mathrm{P}\{X \ge x^{-1}\} = Cx^{-\alpha}$. The changes lead directly to equation (4).

An estimator of the estimator's variance can be obtained by noticing that $\hat{\alpha} = s/\sum T_i$ has an inverted gamma distribution. Therefore

$$\widehat{\mathrm{Var}}(\hat{\alpha}) = \frac{\hat{\alpha}^2 (r+1)^2}{r^2 (r-1)}.$$

B. A Formal Characterization of Restarts

In this section, we formalize the restart strategy of a complete randomized backtrack search method. We show that the probability distribution associated with such a restart strategy does not exhibit heavy tails. Furthermore, the moments of the restart strategy are finite.

Given a randomized backtrack search procedure, let us consider the number of choice points (or backtracks) performed by such a procedure. We introduce random variable B, such that,

> B is the number of choice points that the backtrack search procedure takes to find a solution or prove that it does not exist. $B = \{1, 2, \cdots\}$

Now consider a Rapid Randomized Restarts (RRR) strategy for running our backtrack procedure: run the procedure up to a fixed number of choice points c (the cutoff); if the procedure finds a solution or proves that no solution exists, then RRR has also found a solution (or proven that no solution exists) and stops; otherwise restart the backtrack procedure from the beginning (using an independent random seed) for another c decision events, and so on. We associate with RRR the random variable S, such that,

> S is the number of choice points that RRR takes to find a solution or prove that no solution exists. $S = \{1, 2, \cdots\}$

Let's define a "run", as the execution of the randomized backtrack search method for up to c steps. We now define the random variable R, such that,

> R is the number of runs executed by RRR.

Figure 11 illustrates how the different random variables relate to each other.

The runs executed by RRR are independent (no information is carried over between runs, and each run uses a new random seed) and therefore can be seen as a sequence of Bernoulli trials, in which the success of a trial corresponds to finding a solution (or

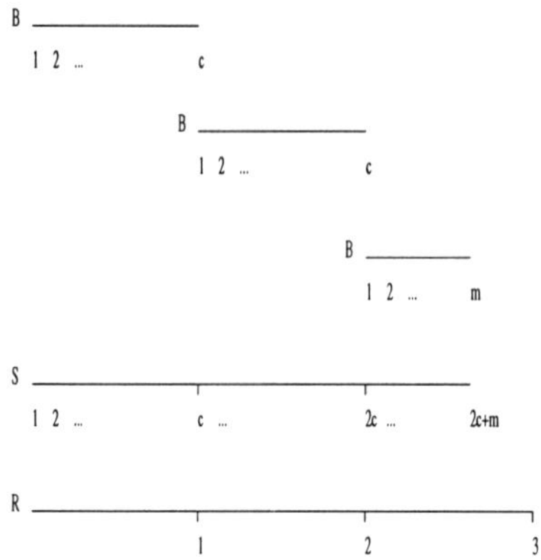

Figure 11. B — number of choice points searched by the randomized backtrack procedure (running with cutoff c); S — number of choice points searched by RRR; R — number of runs executed by RRR. In this case, a solution was found in the third run ($R = 3$), with a total of $2c + m$ choice points ($S = 2c + m$). The third run of the randomized backtrack search method took $m \leq c$ choice points.

proving that one does not exist) during a run; its probability is given by P[B$\leq$ c]. Therefore, R follows a *geometric distribution* with parameter $p = P[B \leq c]$.

The probability of the tail of S, $P[S > s]$, corresponds to the probability of not finding the solution in the first $\lfloor s/c \rfloor$ runs of RRR, and finding it with more than (s mod c) choice points in the next run. We obtain the following expression:

$$P[S > s] = P[B > c]^{\lfloor s/c \rfloor}\ P[B > s\ mod\ c] \tag{5}$$

The distribution of S is not heavy-tailed since its tail exhibits exponential decay:

$$P[S > s] \leq P[B > c]^{\lfloor s/c \rfloor} = P[R > \lfloor s/c \rfloor] \tag{6}$$

In words, the tail of S is limited from above by the tail of R. Since R follows a geometric distribution, it has finite moments, and therefore so does S. The full distribution of S is given by the following expression:

$$P[S = s] = \begin{cases} P[B > c]^{\lfloor s/c \rfloor}\ P[B = s \bmod c] & s \bmod c \neq 0 \\ \\ P[B > c]^{\lfloor s/c \rfloor - 1}\ P[s\ =\ c] & \text{otherwise} \end{cases} \tag{7}$$

Note that the second branch of (7) corresponds to the case in which the total number of choice points executed by strategy S is a multiple of c. This situation occurs when the solution is found when the cutoff c is reached.

Based on the distribution of B, we can determine a cutoff, c, that minimizes the expected runtime of S. Alternatively, one can determine a cutoff value that minimizes both the expected runtime and variance of the RRR strategy, using the tools from portfolio analysis (*e.g.*, [30, 21]). In our experiments, we determined the cutoff for the restart strategy (RRR) based on the empirical distribution of B, which was computed, when possible, by performing 10,000 runs of the backtrack search methods with a very high cutoff.

References

1. Adler, R., R. Feldman, and M. T. (Eds.): 1998, *A practical guide to heavy tails.* Birkhäuser.

2. Alt, H., L. Guibas, K. Mehlhorn, R. Karp, and A. Wigderson: 1996, 'A method for obtaining randomized algorithms with small tail probabilities'. *Algorithmica* **16**(4–5), 543–547.
3. Anderson, L.: 1985, 'Completing partial latin squares'. *Mathematisk Fysiske Meddelelser* **41**, 23–69.
4. Bayardo, R.: 1999. Personal communications.
5. Bayardo, R. and D. Miranker: 1996, 'A complexity analysis of space-bounded learning algorithms for the constraint satisfaction problem'. In: *Proceedings of the Thirteenth National Conference on Artificial Intelligence (AAAI-96)*. Portland, OR, pp. 558–562.
6. Bayardo, R. and R.Schrag: 1997, 'Using CSP look-back techniques to solve real-world SAT instances'. In: *Proceedings of the Fourteenth National Conference on Artificial Intelligence (AAAI-97)*. New Providence, RI, pp. 203–208.
7. Brelaz, D.: 1979, 'New methods to color the vertices of a graph'. *Communications of the ACM* **22**(4), 251–256.
8. Colbourn, C.: 1983, 'Embedding partial steiner triple systems is NP-complete'. *J. Combin. Theory* **A**(35), 100–105.
9. Cook, S. and D. Mitchell: 1998, 'Finding hard instances of the satisfiability problem: a survey'. In: Du, Gu, and Pardalos (eds.): *Satisfiability Problem: Theory and Applications. Dimacs Series in Discrete Mathematics and Theoretical Computer Science, Vol. 35.*
10. Crato, N., C. Gomes, and B. Selman, 'On estimating the index of stability with truncated data'. Manuscript in preparation.
11. Crawford, J. and A. Baker: 1994, 'Experimental Results on the Application of Satisfiability Algorithms to Scheduling Problems'. In: *Proceedings of The Tenth National Conference on Artificial Intelligence (AAAI-94)*. Austin, TX, pp. 1092–1098.
12. Davis, M., G. Logemann, and D. Loveland: 1979, 'A machine program for theorem proving'. *Communications of the ACM* **5**, 394–397.
13. Davis, M. and H. Putman: 1960, 'A computing procedure for quantification theory'. *Journal of the ACM* **7**, 201–215.
14. Denes, J. and A. Keedwell: 1974, *Latin squares and their applications.* London: Akademiai Kiado, Budapest, and English Universities Press.
15. Ertel, W. and M. Luby: 1994, 'Optimal Parallelization of Las Vegas Algorithms'. In: *Symp. on Theoretical Aspects of Computer Science, Lect. Notes in Computer Science 775*. pp. 463–475.
16. Feller, W.: 1968, *An introduction to probability theory and its applications Vol. I.* New York: John Wiley & Sons.
17. Feller, W.: 1971, *An introduction to probability theory and its applications Vol. II.* New York: John Wiley & Sons.
18. Frost, D., I. Rish, and L. Vila: 1997, 'Summarizing CSP hardness with continuous probability distributions'. In: *Proceedings of the Fourteenth National Conference on Artificial Intelligence (AAAI-97)*. New Providence, RI, pp. 327–334.
19. Fujita, M., J. Slaney, and F. Bennett: 1993, 'Automatic generation of some results in finite algebra'. In: *Proceedings of the International Joint Conference on Artificial Intelligence.* France, pp. 52–57.
20. Gent, I. and T. Walsh: 1993, 'Easy Problems are Sometimes Hard'. *Artificial Intelligence* **70**, 335–345.
21. Gomes, C. P. and B. Selman: 1997a, 'Algorithm Portfolio Design: Theory vs. Pratice'. In: *Proceedings of the Thirteenth Conference On Uncertainty in Artificial Intelligence (UAI-97)*. Providence, RI, pp. 190–197.
22. Gomes, C. P. and B. Selman: 1997b, 'Problem Structure in the Presence of Perturbations'. In: *Proceedings of the Fourteenth National Conference on Artificial Intelligence (AAAI-97)*. New Providence, RI, pp. 221–227.
23. Gomes, C. P., B. Selman, and N. Crato: 1997, 'Heavy-tailed Distributions in Combinatorial Search'. In: G. Smolka (ed.): *Principles and practice of Constraint Programming (CP97) Lecture Notes in Computer Science.* Linz, Austria., pp. 121–135.
24. Hall, P.: 1982, 'On some simple estimates of an exponent of regular variation'. *Journal of the Royal Statistical Society* **44**, 37–42.
25. Hayes, B.: 1996, 'Computer science: Can't get no satisfaction'. *American Scientist* **85**(2), 108–112.
26. Hill, B.: 1975, 'A simple general approach to inference about the tail of a distribution'. *Annals of Statistics* **3**, 1163–1174.
27. Hogg, T., B. Huberman, and C. W. (Eds.): 1996, 'Phase Transitions and Complexity (Special Issue)'. *Artificial Intelligence* **81**(1–2).

28. Hogg, T. and C. Williams: 1994, 'Expected gains from parallelizing constraint solving for hard problems'. In: *Proceedings of the Twelfth National Conference on Artificial Intelligence (AAAI-94)*. Seattle, WA, pp. 1310–1315.
29. Hoos, H.: 1998, 'Stochastic Local Search — Methods, Models, Applications'. PhD Thesis,TU Darmstadt.
30. Huberman, B., R. Lukose, and T. Hogg: 1993, 'An economics approach to hard computational problems'. *Science* **275**, 51–54.
31. Johnson, D.: 1996, 'A theoretician's guide to the experimental analysis of algorithms'. Preliminary manuscript. Invited talk presented at AAAI-96, Portland, OR.
32. Johnson, D. and M. Trick: 1996, 'Cliques, Coloring, and Satisfiability: Second DIMACS Implementation Challenge'. In: *Dimacs Series in Discrete Mathematics and Theoretical Computer Science, Vol. 36.*
33. Kamath, A., N. Karmarkar, K. Ramakrishnan, and M. Resende: 1990, 'Computational experience with an interior point algorithm on the satisfiability problem'. In: *Proceedings of Integer Programming and Combinatorial Optimization*. Waterloo, Canada, pp. 333–349.
34. Kautz, H. and B. Selman: 1996, 'Pushing the envelope: planning, propositional logic, and stochastic search'. In: *Proceedings of the Thirteenth National Conference on Artificial Intelligence (AAAI-96)*. Portland, OR, pp. 1188–1194.
35. Kirkpatrick, S. and B. Selman: 1994, 'Critical behavior in the satisfiability of random Boolean expressions'. *Science* **264**, 1297–1301.
36. Kwan, A.: 1995, 'Validity of normality assumption in CSP research'. In: *Proceedings of the Pacific Rim International Conference on Artificial Intelligence*. pp. 459–465.
37. Lam, C., L. Thiel, and S. Swiercz: 1994, 'The non-existence of finite projective planes of order 10'. *Can. J. Math.* **Vol. XLI**(6), 1117–1123.
38. Li, C. M.: 1999. Personal communications.
39. Li, C. M. and Anbulagan: 1997, 'Heuristics based on unit propagation for satisfiability problems'. In: *Proceedings of the International Joint Conference on Artificial Intelligence*. pp. 366–371.
40. Luby, M., A. Sinclair, and D. Zuckerman: 1993, 'Optimal speedup of Las Vegas algorithms'. *Information Process. Letters* pp. 173–180.
41. Macready, W., A. Siapas, and S. Kauffman: 1996, 'Criticality and parallelism in combinatorial optimization'. *Science* **271**, 56–59.
42. Mandelbrot, B.: 1960, 'The Pareto-Lévy law and the distribution of income'. *International Economic Review* **1**, 79–106.
43. Mandelbrot, B.: 1963, 'The variation of certain speculative prices'. *Journal of Business* **36**, 394–419.
44. Mandelbrot, B.: 1983, *The fractal geometry of nature*. Freeman: New York.
45. McAloon, K., C. Tretkoff, and G. Wetzel: 1997, 'Sports league scheduling'. In: *Proceedings of Third Ilog International Users Meeting*.
46. Mitchell, D. and H. Levesque: 1996, 'Some pitfalls for experimenters with random SAT'. *Artificial Intelligence* **81**(1–2), 111–125.
47. Monasson, R., R. Zecchina, S. Kirkpatrick, B. Selman, and L. Troyansky: 1999, 'Determining computational complexity from characteristic 'phase transitions''. *Nature* **400**(8), 133–137.
48. Nemhauser, G. and M. Trick: 1998, 'Scheduling a major college basketball conference'. *Operations Research* **46**(1), 1–8.
49. Niemela, I.: 1998. Logic programs with stable model semantics as a constraint programming paradigm. Ext. version of paper presented at the Workshop on Computational Aspects of Nonmonotonic Reasoning.
50. Niemela, I.: 1999. Personal communications.
51. Nolan, J.: 1999. Stable Distributions, Manuscript, in preparation.
52. Prosser, P.: 1993, 'Hybrid algorithms for the constraint satisfaction problem'. *Computational Intelligence* **9**(3), 268–299.
53. Puget, J. F. and M. Leconte: 1995, 'Beyond the black box: constraints as objects'. In: *Proceedings of ILPS'95*. Lisbon, Portugal., pp. 513–527.
54. Regin, J. C.: 1994, 'A filtering algorithm for constraints of difference in CSP'. In: *Proceedings of the Twelfth National Conference on Artificial Intelligence (AAAI-94)*. Seattle, WA, pp. 362–367.
55. Rish, I. and D. Frost: 1997, 'Statistical analysis of backtracking on inconsistent CSPs'. In: *Proceedings of Third International Conference on Principles and Practices of Constraint Programming*. pp. 150–162.

56. Samorodnitsky, G. and M. Taqqu: 1994, *Stable Non-Gaussian Random Processes: Stochastic Models with Infinite Variance.* Chapman and Hall.
57. Selman, B., H. Kautz, and B. Cohen: 1993, 'Local search strategies for satisfiability testing'. In: D. Johnson and M. Trick (eds.): *Dimacs Series in Discrete Mathematics and Theoretical Computer Science, Vol. 26.* pp. 521–532.
58. Selman, B. and S. Kirkpatrick: 1996, 'Finite-Size Scaling of the Computational Cost of Systematic Search'. *Artificial Intelligence* **81**(1–2), 273–295.
59. Shaw, P., K. Stergiou, and T. Walsh: 1998, 'Arc consistency and quasigroup completion'. In: *Proceedings of ECAI-98, workshop on binary constraints.*
60. Shonkwiler, R., E., and van Vleck: 1994, 'Parallel speedup of Monte Carlo methods for global optimization'. *Journal of Complexity* **10**, 64–95.
61. Slaney, J., M. Fujita, and M. Stickel: 1995, 'Automated reasoning and exhaustive search: Quasigroup existence problems'. *Computers and Math. with Applications* **29**, 115–132.
62. Smith, B. and S. Grant: 1995, 'Sparse constraint graphs and exceptionally hard problems'. In: *Proceedings of the International Joint Conference on Artificial Intelligence.* pp. 646–651.
63. Stickel, M.: 1998. Personal communications.
64. Vandengriend and Culberson: 1999, 'The G_{nm} Phase Transition is Not Hard for the Hamiltonian Cycle Problem'. *Journal of Artificial Intelligence Research* **9**, 219–245.
65. Walsh, T.: 1999, 'Search in a Small World'. In: *Proceedings of the International Joint Conference on Artificial Intelligence.* Stockholm, Sweden.
66. Zolotarev, V.: 1986, 'One-dimensional Stable Distributions'. Vol. 65 of "Translations of mathematical monographs", American Mathematical Society. Translation from the original 1983 Russian Ed.

SAT2000
I. Gent et al. (Eds.)
IOS Press, 2000

Local Search Algorithms for SAT: An Empirical Evaluation

Holger H. Hoos †
Department of Computer Science
University of British Columbia
Vancouver, Canada

Thomas Stützle §
FG Intellektik, FB Informatik, TU Darmstadt
Darmstadt, Germany

Abstract. Local search algorithms are among the standard methods for solving hard combinatorial problems from various areas of Artificial Intelligence and Operations Research. For SAT, some of the most successful and powerful algorithms are based on stochastic local search and in the past 10 years a large number of such algorithms have been proposed and investigated. In this article, we focus on two particularly well-known families of local search algorithms for SAT, the GSAT and WalkSAT architectures. We present a detailed comparative analysis of these algorithms' performance using a benchmark set which contains instances from randomised distributions as well as SAT-encoded problems from various domains. We also investigate the robustness of the observed performance characteristics as algorithm-dependent and problem-dependent parameters are changed. Our empirical analysis gives a very detailed picture of the algorithms' performance for various domains of SAT problems; it also reveals a fundamental weakness in some of the best-performing algorithms and shows how this can be overcome.

Keywords: SAT, Stochastic Local Search, Empirical Evaluation, Run-time Distributions, Robustness

1. Introduction

The satisfiability problem in propositional logic (SAT) is the task to decide for a given propositional formula whether it has a model. This problem plays a prominent role in various areas of computer science, as it is one of the conceptually simplest $\mathcal{NP}$-complete problems. Local search approaches for SAT became prominent in 1992, when independently Selman, Levesque, and Mitchell [60] as well as Gu [27] introduced algorithms based on stochastic local hill-climbing which could be shown to outperform state-of-the-art systematic SAT algorithms like ASAT [13] on a variety of hard subclasses of SAT [4, 59]. Since then, numerous other stochastic local search (SLS) schemes for SAT have been proposed. To date, state-of-the-art SLS algorithms can solve hard SAT problems with up to several thousand variables, including SAT-encoded problems from other domains. But because of their inherent randomness, the behaviour of SLS algorithms is generally difficult to analyse theoretically and even in the cases where theoretical results do exist, their practical applicability is often very limited. Given this situation, the performance of SLS algorithms is usually analysed using empirical methodology.

In this paper, we empirically analyse the behaviour of algorithms from the GSAT and WalkSAT architectures of SLS algorithms for SAT. These algorithm families were

† hoos@cs.ubc.ca
§ stuetzle@informatik.tu-darmstadt.de

chosen for two reasons: Firstly, they provided a major driving force in the development and application of SLS algorithms for SAT. Secondly, for most algorithms from these families, very efficient, thoroughly optimised implementations are available which could easily be modified and extended to cover some more variants and to yield a sufficiently coherent framework for practically conducting experiments. Although our empirical methodology allows us to abstract from machine- and implementation-specific details of algorithmic performance, some of our analyses are so computationally expensive that efficient implementations are indispensable.

Our empirical analysis addresses several important issues. Maybe the most straightforward question to ask is how the performance of different algorithms compares across a range of problem instances from different subclasses of SAT. But furthermore, as the behaviour of these algorithms (like for most other SLS algorithms) is controlled by a number of parameters which have to be chosen before running them, it is crucial to investigate the influence of these parameters on the algorithms' behaviour. In particular, optimal parameter settings are often not known exactly, but rather a range of reasonably good parameter settings is available. Therefore, one might be interested in the robustness of SLS performance *w.r.t.* these parameters. Similarly, the influence of problem dependent parameters, in particular problem size, on SLS behaviour is of considerable interest.

To adequately address these issues, a refined empirical methodology is needed. Therefore, different from many previous studies, our experimental methodology goes considerably beyond just measuring a small number of basic statistics, such as the mean run-time and its standard deviation. Instead, we use the methodology developed in [36] which is based on measuring and analysing run-time distributions (RTDs) on individual problem instances. This allows us to study the behaviour of SLS algorithms on single problem instances as well as on whole subclasses of SAT, while cleanly separating between different sources of randomness, such as the randomised generation of instances from a problem distribution and the inherent randomness of the SLS algorithm applied. Measuring RTDs does not incur any significant overhead in data acquisition, and from the RTD information, the commonly used basic descriptive statistics of the run-time, like its mean, standard deviation, and arbitrary percentiles can be easily derived. At the same time, RTDs provide important information on an algorithm's behaviour in a more precise and accessible way. For instance, the probability for finding a solution within any given time-limit or stagnation behaviour of the search process can easily be determined from a graphical representation of an RTD.

Using the RTD-based methodology, we analyse the behaviour of GSAT and WalkSAT algorithms for a carefully selected subset of problems from the SATLIB Benchmark Suite. Our selection covers a broad range of SAT instances which are well-known from the literature and which are hard for both systematic and local search algorithms. In particular, we study three fundamentally different types of problems: SAT instances from randomised distributions of native SAT problems (type 1), SAT-encoded instances from randomised distributions of other combinatorial problems (type 2), and SAT-encoded, hand-crafted individual instances from other domains (type 3). For type 1, we decided to focus on sets of uniform Random-3-SAT instances from the solubility phase transition, as these are known to be very hard for both systematic and SLS-based algorithms [10, 47, 64] and they have played a prominent role in the majority of the studies in literature [55, 60, 59, 22]. For type 2, we selected sets of graph colouring problems from randomised distributions of 3-colourable graphs [54, 35]. Finally, for type 3 we chose SAT-encoded planning instances which have been used in a number of previous studies, as well as a subset of the instances which have been originally collected for the DIMACS Satisfiability Benchmark Library. All benchmark problems, as well as the WalkSAT and GSAT implementations used in this work, are available from the SATLIB website at http://www.informatik.tu-darmstadt.de/AI/SATLIB (see also Chapter *SATLIB: An Online Resource*).

The results of our study can be summarised as follows. For optimal parameter settings the relative performance of the SLS algorithms studied here varies with the problem domain such that there is no single best algorithm over the full benchmark set. However, we can identify a subset of the algorithms studied (this subset comprises the WalkSAT variants R-Novelty, Novelty, WalkSAT/TABU) which show superior performance compared to the remaining algorithms. At the same time, these algorithms show premature stagnation of the search when applied to some instances. As a consequence these algorithms are very sensitive with respect to the setting of the cutoff parameter (which determines after how many steps the search is aborted and restarted from a new initial assignment). However, as we show later, this deficiency can be overcome by a relatively simple and generic modification of the algorithms, the so-called *random walk extension*. The accordingly modified algorithms show improved performance and a significantly increased robustness *w.r.t.* the cutoff parameter setting.

Our investigation of the robustness of SLS performance confirms and extends earlier observations that for relatively hard problem instances, all algorithms exhibit approximately exponential RTDs and are thus very robust *w.r.t.* the cutoff parameter setting. As a consequence of this characterisation result, by using the "multiple independent tries" parallelisation scheme, which is easy to implement and extremely scalable, optimal speedup and parallelisation efficiency can be obtained. At the same time, the exponential RTDs suggest a novel interpretation of SLS behaviour as independent random picking from a drastically reduced search space. However, as we show, the RTDs are only exponential if the noise parameter, which controls the greediness of the search process, is sufficiently high. If the noise setting is too low, i.e., the search is very greedy, the robustness of SLS performance *w.r.t.* the cutoff parameter deteriorates rapidly. Furthermore, there are considerable differences between the individual algorithms in the robustness *w.r.t.* the setting of the so-called noise parameter.

Another interesting result is the fact that across test-sets of randomly generated problem instances (such as Random-3-SAT at the solubility phase transition) the relative performance of the different algorithms tends to be tightly correlated, such that problem instances that are hard for one algorithm tend to be hard for all the other algorithms. This is somewhat surprising when considering that the algorithms studied here are different enough to yield absolute performance differences of more than one order of magnitude. At the same time, this result suggests that the same structural features are responsible for rendering a problem instance hard or easy for all the algorithms.

Finally, we investigate the scaling of SLS performance with problem size. We found no evidence of any substantial differences between different WalkSAT algorithms *w.r.t.* their scaling behaviour for growing problem size. But, somewhat surprisingly, our results indicate that the local search cost grows exponentially only for the hardest Random-3-SAT instances, while for easier instances the scaling of SLS performance appears to be polynomial. This phenomenon could not be observed for the graph colouring test-sets, where the scaling was generally exponential.

Knowledge on which algorithms perform best under various criteria, such as maximum performance or robustness, is useful for directing future efforts in designing even better SAT algorithms. Given the recent successes of solving combinatorial problems from other domains by encoding them into SAT, especially in various domains of AI planning [45, 46], using SAT algorithms for solving encoded real-world problems seems to become a serious alternative to using specialised algorithms under certain circumstances. In the context of this development it seems to be of crucial importance to make sure that the best-performing SAT algorithms are used and that when comparing their performance to the performance of domain-specific algorithms all important aspects of their behaviour are taken into account. Moreover, since most SLS algorithms for SAT can be easily generalised to more general problem classes, such as finite Constrained Satisfaction Problems or MAX-SAT, the potential impact of this knowledge would very likely reach beyond SAT. It is unfortunate that most of the empirical studies of SLS algorithms for SAT that can be found in the literature are incompatible with each other. Because of differences in either the methodology or the reference problem instances being used their results cannot be easily assembled to yield a comprehensive picture. Additionally, most of these previous studies are rather limited in their methodology and scope. The empirical methodology presented in this paper, the benchmark library used, and the results obtained, are intended to provide the starting point for a series of empirical studies which are compatible with each other and can thus be used to approach a comprehensive picture of the state-of-the-art in solving propositional satisfiability problems.

The remainder of the paper is structured as follows. Section 2 introduces a general framework for SLS algorithms, and in particular, the GSAT and WalkSAT families of SAT algorithms. In Section 3, we give an overview of the RTD-based methodology for empirically investigating SLS behaviour on individual problem instances as well as on problem distributions and introduce the benchmark suite which provides the basis for our empirical study. The results of a comparative analysis of SLS performance across these test-sets are reported in Section 4. In Section 5 we present our characterisation of parameter robustness and scaling of SLS behaviour, including an overview of some theoretical results concerning the asymptotic behaviour of prominent GSAT and WalkSAT algorithms. Furthermore, we show how these results can be exploited to improve some of the best known SLS algorithms for SAT. The concluding Section 6 summarises the main results presented in this paper and points out directions for future research.

2. Stochastic Local Search Algorithms for SAT

Local search is a widely used, general approach for solving hard combinatorial search problems. The general idea is to examine the search space induced by the given problem instance for solutions by initialising the search at some point and from there to iteratively move from one search space position to a neighbouring position where the decision on each step is based on information about the local neighbourhood only. Thus, the following components are required to define a local search procedure for problem class Π applied to a given problem instance $\pi \in \Pi$:

- the *search space* S_π of π which is a set of *positions* $s \in S_\pi$ (also called candidate solutions or states)

- a *set of solutions* $S' \subseteq S_\pi$

- a *neighbourhood relation* $\mathrm{N} \subseteq S_\pi \times S_\pi$ on S_π which specifies for each position the set of positions which can be visited in one local search step.

- an *initialisation function* $\mathrm{init} : \emptyset \mapsto (S_\pi \mapsto \mathbb{R})$ which specifies a probability distribution over initial search positions.

- a *step function* $\mathrm{step} : S_\pi \mapsto (S_\pi \mapsto \mathbb{R})$ mapping each position onto a probability distribution over its neighbouring states, for specifying the local search steps.

Typically, local search algorithms also make use of an *objective function* $f : S_\pi \mapsto \mathbb{R}$, mapping each search space position onto a real (or integer) number in such a way, that the global optima of the objective function correspond to the solutions. In SLS algorithms for SAT, generally the search space is defined as the set of all possible truth value assignments for the variables occurring in the given problem instance and the solutions are the satisfying assignments (models). Of course the search space thus defined is of exponential size in the number of propositional variables. Most SLS-based SAT algorithms use a 1-flip neighbourhood relation for which two truth value assignments are neighbours if they differ in the truth value of exactly one variable. Thus, the local search steps modify the truth value assigned to one propositional variable; such a move is called a *variable flip*. Almost all SLS algorithms for SAT work on propositional formulae in conjunctive normal form (CNF), i.e., on sentences of the form $\bigwedge_{i=1}^{k} c_k$ with $c_k = \bigvee_{j=1}^{l_k} L_{kj}$ where the L_{kj} are propositional variables or their negations. Typically, they use an objective function which is defined as the number of clauses which are unsatisfied under the given variable assignment. Hence, for satisfiable problem instances the models of the given formula correspond to global minima of this function. The general idea for finding these models is to perform a random walk in the search space which is biased towards minimising the number of unsatisfied clauses (obviously, this is equivalent to maximising the number of satisfied clauses). The main difference between different SLS algorithms for SAT is in the step function, that is, in the strategy used to select the variable to be flipped next.

SLS algorithms for SAT are typically incomplete, i.e., even for satisfiable problem instances they cannot be guaranteed to find a solution. The reason for this is the non-systematic nature of the search. Furthermore, SLS algorithms can get trapped in local minima and plateau regions of the search space [22, 15], leading to premature stagnation of the search. One of the simplest mechanisms for avoiding premature stagnation of the search is random restart, which reinitialises the search if after a fixed number of steps (cutoff time) no solution has been found. Random restart is used in almost every SLS algorithm for SAT.

A general outline of an SLS algorithm for SAT is given in Figure 1. The generic procedure initialises the search at some truth assignment and then iteratively flips some variable's truth value, where the selection of the variable depends on the formula Φ and the current assignment. If after a maximum of *maxSteps* flips no solution is found, the algorithm restarts from a new random initial assignment. If after a given number *maxTries* of such tries still no solution is found, the algorithm terminates unsuccessfully.

For many concrete algorithms, and in particular, for all algorithms investigated here, *initAssign* randomly chooses the initial assignment from the set of all possible assignments according to a uniform distribution. Hence, the main difference between SLS algorithms for SAT is typically the implementation of the step function as given by the procedure *chooseVariable*. In the following, we will focus on the GSAT and the WalkSAT families of algorithms, which have provided a major driving force in the development of SLS algorithms for SAT, and review some of the most widely used members of these families. Later, we will briefly discuss other algorithms and further GSAT and WalkSAT variants known from the literature.

2.1. The GSAT Architecture

The GSAT algorithm was introduced in 1992 by Selman, Levesque, and Mitchell [60]. It is based on a rather simple idea: GSAT tries to minimise the number of unsatisfied clauses by a greedy descent in the space of variable assignments. Variable selection in GSAT and most of its variants is based on the *score* of a variable x under the

procedure *StochasticLocalSearch for SAT*
  input *CNF formula* Φ, *maxTries*, *maxSteps*
  output *satisfying assignment of* Φ *or "no solution found"*
  for $i := 1$ **to** *maxTries* **do**
    $s :=$ *initAssign*(Φ);
    for $j := 1$ **to** *maxSteps* **do**
      if s satisfies Φ **then return** s;
      else
        $x :=$ *chooseVariable*(Φ, s);
        $s := s$ with truth value of x flipped;
      end if
    end for
  end for
  return "no solution found";
end *StochasticLocalSearch for SAT*

Figure 1. Outline of a general stochastic local search procedure for SAT.

current assignment s, which is defined as the difference between the number of clauses unsatisfied by s and the assignment obtained by flipping x in s.

2.1.1. *Basic GSAT*

The basic GSAT algorithm uses the following instantiation of the procedure *chooseVariable*(s, Φ). In each local search step, one of the variables with maximal score is flipped. If there are several variables with maximal score, one of them is randomly selected according to a uniform distribution. A straightforward implementation of GSAT may be rather inefficient, since in each step the score of all variables would have to be calculated from scratch. The key to efficiently implementing GSAT is to evaluate the complete set of scores only once at the beginning of each try, and then after each flip to update only the scores of those variable which were possibly affected by the flipped variable. Details on these implementation issues for GSAT and related algorithms can be found in [32]. One problem with basic GSAT is that it can easily get stuck in local minima of the objective functions. As these might contain a large number of search space positions between which GSAT can arbitrarily wander, local minima cannot be efficiently detected in general and the built-in random restart mechanism is the only way for escaping from these. This means that for GSAT there exist search space positions from which a solution cannot be reached without reinitialising the search. We call SLS algorithms which have this property *essentially incomplete.*

2.1.2. *GSAT with Random Walk (GWSAT)*

An important extension of the basic GSAT algorithm is GSAT with Random Walk (GWSAT) [59]. Here, besides the above defined greedy local search step, a second type of local search step, the so-called *random walk step*, is introduced. In a random walk step, first a currently unsatisfied clause c' is randomly selected. Then, one of the variables appearing in c' is flipped, thus effectively forcing c' to become satisfied. The basic idea of GWSAT is to decide at each local search step with a fixed probability wp (called *walk probability* or noise setting) whether to do a standard GSAT step or a random walk step. The random walk mechanism has been added to basic GSAT to avoid getting stuck in local minima of the objective function. Obviously, for arbitrary $wp > 0$ this algorithm allows arbitrarily long sequences of random walk steps; as detailed in [35], this implies that from any given assignments, a model (if existent) can be reached with a positive, bounded probability. This means that applied to a satisfiable formula, even without using random restart (that is, for *maxTries*=1), the probability that GWSAT finds a solution converges to 1 as the run-time approaches infinity (the so-called *PAC property*, or *probabilistic approximate completeness*).

2.1.3. *GSAT with Tabu Search (GSAT/TABU)*

Another well-known mechanism for preventing the search from getting stuck in local optima is Tabu Search [23, 28]. The general idea is to forbid reversing the effect of a particular move for a number tl of iterations; the parameter tl is called the *tabu tenure*. This mechanism can be easily added to basic GSAT [50, 61]; in the resulting algorithm, after a variable x has been flipped it cannot be flipped back within the next tl steps. GSAT/TABU can be efficiently implemented by storing for each variable x the iteration number i_x when it was last flipped. When initialising the search, all the i_x are set to $-tl$ and every time a variable x is flipped, i_x is set to the number j of the current iteration. Obviously, a variable x can only be flipped if $j > i_x + tl$.

Note that, unlike for GWSAT, it is not clear whether for arbitrary satisfiable formulae there exists a tl value such that GSAT/TABU has the PAC property for fixed *maxTries*. This means that adding Tabu Search does not necessarily guarantee that the algorithm will never get stuck in local minima. Intuitively, the problem is that for low tl values the local minima region might be big enough that the algorithm still cannot escape without using restart, while for high tl values all the routes to a solution might be cut off because too many variables cannot be flipped.

2.1.4. *HSAT and HWSAT*

HSAT [21] is another GSAT variant where the local search steps make use of history information. When in a search step there are several variables with identical score, HSAT selects the least recently flipped variable. Only shortly after search initialisation, when there are still variables which have not been flipped, a random selection like in GSAT is done. The intuition behind HSAT is that in GSAT some variables might never get flipped although they are frequently eligible to be chosen. This might cause stagnation of the search, as such a variable might be the one which has to be flipped for the search to make further progress. Although when compared to plain GSAT, HSAT was found to show superior performance [21], it is clear that it is even more likely to get stuck in local minima from which it cannot escape, as the additional history-based tie-breaking rule effectively restricts the search trajectories when compared to GSAT. Therefore, it appears to be attractive to extend HSAT with the same random walk mechanism used in GWSAT. The resulting variant is called HWSAT [20]; like GWSAT it has the PAC property.

2.2. *The WalkSAT Architecture*

The WalkSAT architecture is based on ideas first published by Selman, Kautz, and Cohen in 1994 [59] and it was later formally defined as an algorithmic framework by McAllester, Selman, and Kautz in 1997 [51]. It is based on a 2-stage variable selection process focused on the variables occurring in currently unsatisfied clauses. For each local search step, in a first stage a currently unsatisfied clause c' is randomly selected. In a second step, one of the variables appearing in c' is then flipped to obtain the new assignment. Thus, while the GSAT architecture is characterised by a static neighbourhood relation between assignments with Hamming distance one, WalkSAT algorithms are effectively based on a dynamically determined subset of the GSAT neighbourhood relation.

2.2.1. *WalkSAT*

WalkSAT, originally introduced in [59], differs in one important aspect from the other local search variants discussed here: The scoring function $score_b(x)$ used by WalkSAT counts only the number of clauses which are broken, i.e., currently satisfied, but will become unsatisfied by flipping variable x. Using this scoring function, the following variable selection scheme is applied: If there is a variable with $score_b(x) = 0$ in the clause c' selected in stage 1, i.e., if c' can be satisfied without breaking another clause, this variable is flipped (so-called *zero-damage flip*). If no such variable exists, then with a certain probability p (noise setting) the variable with minimal $score_b$ value is selected; in the remaining cases, one of the variables from c' is randomly selected (random walk flip).

Conceptually as well as historically, WalkSAT is closely related to GWSAT. However, there are a number of significant differences between both algorithms, which in combination account for the generally superior performance of WalkSAT. While both algorithms use the same kind of random walk steps, WalkSAT applies them only under the condition that there is no variable with $score_b(x) = 0$. In GWSAT, however, random walk steps are done in an unconditional probabilistic way. From this point of view, WalkSAT is greedier, since random walk steps, which usually increase the number of unsatisfied clauses, are only done when every variable occurring in the selected clause would break some clauses when flipped. Yet, in a greedy step, due to the two-stage variable selection scheme, WalkSAT chooses from a significantly reduced set of neighbours and can therefore be considered to be less greedy than GWSAT. Finally, because of the different scoring function, in some sense, GWSAT shows a greedier behaviour than WalkSAT: For a GSAT step, it would prefer a variable which breaks some clauses but compensates for this by fixing some other clauses, while in the same situation, WalkSAT would select a variable with a smaller total score, but breaking also a smaller number of clauses.

To our best knowledge it is unknown whether WalkSAT has the PAC property, i.e., whether it can theoretically escape from any local minima without using random restart. Unlike for GWSAT, it is not clear whether arbitrarily long sequences of random walk steps are always possible, because random walk steps can only be executed when no zero-damage flip is available. However, there is plenty of empirical evidence that in practice WalkSAT can effectively escape from any local minima [35, 37].

2.2.2. *WalkSAT/TABU*

Analogously to GSAT/TABU, there is also a WalkSAT variant which uses a Tabu Search mechanism; this algorithm is called WalkSAT/TABU [51]. It uses the same two stage selection mechanism and the same scoring function $score_b$ as WalkSAT and additionally enforces a tabu tenure of tl steps for each flipped variable. Here, if no zero-damage flip can be made, from all variables which are not tabu, the one with the highest $score_b$ value is picked; when there are several variables with the same maximal score, one of them is randomly selected according to a uniform distribution. As a result of the two-level variable selection scheme, it may happen that all variables appearing in the selected clause cannot be flipped because they are tabu. In this case, no variable is flipped (a so-called *null-flip*).

As has been shown in [35], WalkSAT/TABU is essentially incomplete for all tl settings, as it can get stuck in local minima regions of the search space. Although this is mainly caused by null-flips, it is not clear whether replacing null-flips by, e.g., random walk steps, would be sufficient for obtaining the PAC property.

2.2.3. *Novelty*

Novelty, introduced in [51], is one of the most recent SLS algorithms for SAT. Conceptually, it combines the algorithms based on the WalkSAT architecture with a history-based variable selection mechanism in the spirit of HSAT. Novelty, too, is based on the intuition, that repeatedly flipping back and forth the same variable should be avoided. Additionally, like for tabu search variants, the number of local search steps which have been performed since it was last flipped (also called the variable's *age*) is taken into consideration. Also, differently from WalkSAT or WalkSAT/TABU, Novelty uses the same scoring function as GSAT.

In Novelty, after an unsatisfied clause has been chosen, the variable to be flipped is selected as follows. If the variable with the highest score does not have minimal age among the variables within the same clause, it is always selected. Otherwise, it is only selected with a probability of *1-p*; in the remaining cases, the variable with the next lower score is selected. In Kautz's and Selman's implementation, if there are several variables with identical score, the one appearing first in the clause is always chosen.

Note that for $p > 0$, the age-based variable selection of Novelty probabilistically prevents flipping the same variable over and over again; at the same time, flips can be immediately reversed with a certain probability if a better choice is not available. Generally, the Novelty algorithm is significantly greedier than WalkSAT, since always one of the two most improving variables from a clause is selected, where WalkSAT may select any variable if no improvement without breaking other clauses can be achieved. Also, Novelty is more deterministic than WalkSAT and GWSAT, since its probabilistic decisions are more limited in their scope and take place under more restrictive conditions. For example, different from WalkSAT, the Novelty strategy for variable selection within a clause is deterministic for both $p = 0$ and $p = 1$.

On one hand side, this often leads to a significantly improved performance of Novelty when compared to WalkSAT. On the other hand, because of this property, it can be shown that Novelty is essentially incomplete [35], as selecting only among the best two variables in a given clause can lead to situations where the algorithm gets stuck in local minima of the objective function. As we will see later, this situation can be observed for some of our benchmark problems where it severely compromises Novelty's performance.

2.2.4. *R-Novelty*

R-Novelty, also introduced in [51], is a variant of Novelty which is based on the intuition that when deciding between the best and second best variable (using the same scoring function as for Novelty), the actual difference of the respective scores should be taken into account. The exact mechanism for choosing a variable from the selected clause can be seen from the decision tree representation given in Figure 2. Note that the R-Novelty heuristic is quite complex – as reported in [51], it was discovered by systematically testing a large number of WalkSAT variants.

R-Novelty's variable selection strategy is even more deterministic than Novelty's; in particular, it is completely deterministic for $p \in \{0, 0.5, 1\}$. Since the pure R-Novelty algorithm gets too easily stuck in local minima, a simple loop breaking strategy is used: every 100 steps, a variable is randomly chosen from the selected clause and flipped. However, it can be shown that this mechanism is insufficient for effectively escaping from local minima and consequently R-Novelty is essentially incomplete.

2.3. *Other SLS algorithms for SAT*

Apart from the presented GSAT and WalkSAT algorithms and their variants, numerous other SLS algorithms for SAT have been proposed. One particularly interesting tech-

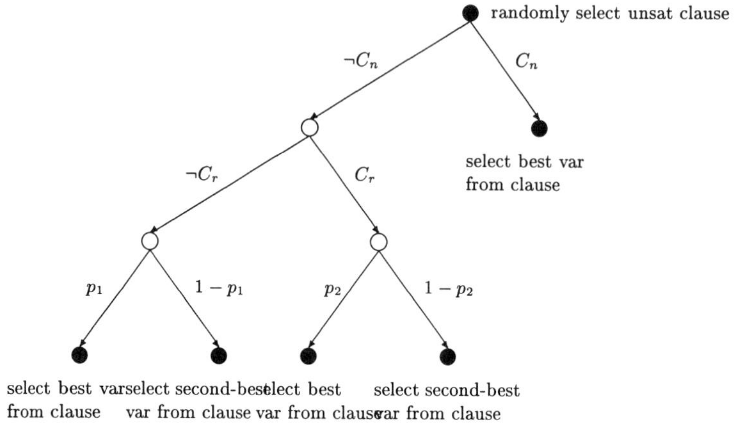

Figure 2. Decision tree representation for R-Novelty variable selection mechanism; condition $C_n \equiv$ "best var does not have minimal age"; condition $C_r \equiv$ "score diff between best and second best var ¿ 1"; "best" and "second-best" relate to the GSAT-score of variables; $p_1 = \max\{1 - 2p, 0\}$, $p_2 = \min\{2 - 2p, 1\}$.

nique which provides the basis for a number of SLS algorithms studied in literature is *clause weighting*. The underlying idea is to associate the clauses of the given CNF formula with weights which are modified during the local search process [7, 16, 17, 53, 58]. The objective function, on which the choice of the variable to be flipped is based, then reflects the weight of the satisfied clauses such that clauses with a high weight are more likely to become satisfied. Typically, the weights of the clauses which are unsatisfied at a local minimum are increased by some constant. One interpretation of clause weighting is that local minima are "filled in" by adapting the weights.

In [58], weights are only modified after each GSAT try by increasing the weight of unsatisfied clauses by one. A different approach, the breakout method [53], adjusts the clause weights during a single try. In particular, each time the algorithm encounters a local minimum, the weights of the currently violated clauses are increased. In [7, 16, 17] different strategies of how to change the weights during a single try are investigated. When evaluating the performance of a particular weighting scheme on a class of randomly generated instances which have only one single solution [2], it was observed that for the hardest of these instances the weighing scheme performed considerably better than GSAT and GWSAT [7]. Yet, the instances used in that comparison are not intrinsically hard because they can be solved by polynomial simplifications (unit propagation and unary / binary failed clauses). Experimental results presented in [16, 17] show that the weighting strategies significantly improve over GSAT and give somewhat better results than HSAT on Random-3-Sat instances. More concretely, using the weighting schemes proposed, the average number of flips needed to find a solution is reduced by ca. 50% when compared to HSAT. Yet it is not clear how efficiently the proposed schemes can be implemented since the weights have to be modified rather frequently and therefore the single search steps are more expensive — in terms of CPU time — than for GSAT. Considering our results reported in Section 4, it will become clear that even when arguing based on the most efficient implementations of GSAT, these variants will generally not be competitive with the best-performing WalkSAT algorithms. In this study we do not investigate local search algorithms with clause weighting schemes. There are two main reasons for this: On the one side, using clause weighting is a general mechanism which could be combined with almost any SLS algorithm; in particular it could be added to each of the GSAT and WalkSAT algorithms studied here. On the other side, except for GSAT with clause weighting, as proposed in [58], there are no efficient implementations of the weighting schemes available, which would render the type of empirical analysis performed in this study extremely expensive in terms of computation time. However, we feel that a systematic investigation of weighting schemes and their effect on the performance of various SLS algorithms, especially the best-performing WalkSAT variants, would be an important extension of the work presented here.

Another interesting SLS algorithm is the GSAT variant using cycle-cutsets (GSAT + CC) [43]. This algorithm additionally incorporates a number of other extensions to GSAT, including random walk and clause weighting. To our best knowledge, so far it has only been applied to binary constraint satisfaction problems (CSPs); the results reported in [43] suggest that GSAT+CC might show a performance roughly similar to WalkSAT for a very limited subclass of CSPs (those with small cutsets) while on other subclasses of CSPs it seems to be about a factor of 2 inferior to the GWSAT variant used for comparison.

Many other local search variants which are very popular in the Operations Research community have been applied to SAT. These include methods based on Simulated Annealing [3, 63, 59], Evolutionary Algorithms [26, 14], and Greedy Randomized Adaptive Search Procedures (GRASP) [56]. Some of these algorithms have been directly compared to the algorithms used in this study, but from the data published on the performance of these algorithms, there is no evidence that they might generally perform significantly better than the algorithms considered here.

3. Empirical Methodology

SLS algorithms like those presented in Section 2 strongly involve random decisions such as the choice of the initial assignment, random tie-breaking, or biased random moves. Due to this inherent randomness, given a specific soluble problem instance, the time needed by an SLS algorithm to find a solution is a random variable, as it varies from run to run. Consequently, the most detailed characterisation of such an algorithm's behaviour is given by its run-time distribution (RTD), which for a given instance maps the run-time t to the probability of finding a solution within time t [36, 37, 35].

3.1. RTD-based analysis of SLS algorithms

To measure RTDs, one has to take into account that most SLS algorithms have some cutoff parameter bounding their run-time, like the *maxSteps* parameter in the generic algorithm schema of Figure 1. Practically, we measure empirical RTDs by running the respective Las Vegas algorithm for a fixed number of times (without using restart, i.e., setting *maxTries* to one) on a given problem instance up to some (very high) cutoff value (optimal cutoff settings may then be determined a posteriori using the empirical run-time distribution) and by recording the time required to find a solution for each successful run (*cf.* Figure 3, *left*). The empirical run-time distribution is the cumulative distribution associated with these observations. More formally, let $rt(j)$ denote the run-time for the jth successful run, and n be the number of runs performed, then the cumulative empirical RTD is defined by $\widehat{P}(rt \leq t) = |\{j | rt(j) \leq t\}|/n$. Instead of actually measuring run-*time* distributions in terms of CPU-time, it is often preferable to use representative operation counts as a more machine (and implementation) independent measure of an algorithm's performance. An appropriate operation count for local search algorithms for SAT is the number of local search steps; the run-time distributions obtained by measuring the run-time in terms of local search steps (here: variable flips) instead of CPU time are also called run-*length* distributions (RLDs) (*cf.* Figure 3, *right*).

From the RTD information, the commonly used basic descriptive statistics of the run-time, like its mean, standard deviation, and arbitrary percentiles can be easily derived. At the same time, measuring RTDs does not incur any significant overhead in data acquisition, because the amount of experimentation required for obtaining stable estimates for basic statistics (like the mean run-time) is also sufficient for measuring RTDs with a reasonable accuracy. But compared to measuring standard descriptive statistics, an RTD-based empirical analysis has a number of advantages.

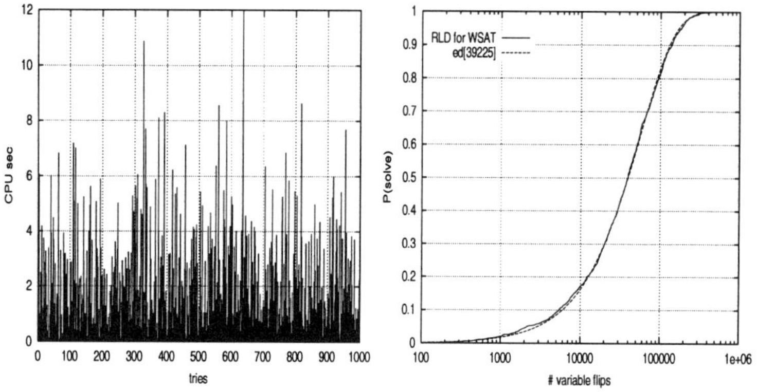

Figure 3. Run-time data of WalkSAT, applied to a hard Random-3-SAT instance for approx. optimal setting of *wp*, 1000 tries. *Left:* Bar diagramm of $rt(i)$ (vertical axis: run-time in CPU seconds). *Right:* Corresponding RLD with best-fit approximation by an exponential distribution (horizontal axis: run-time in local search steps; vertical axis: probability of solving the instance).

Firstly, it does not make any assumptions regarding the application scenario, i.e., the time constraints in finding a solution. To see why this is important, consider a SAT-based planner working in a real-time environment, where the run-time of the SAT solver is severely limited. When using an SLS algorithm in such an application context, the expected time for solving a particular problem instance is typically not relevant; the correct performance criterion is the probability of solving the problem within the given time-limit — which can be easily derived from an estimate of the RTD.

Secondly, RTDs give a graphic representation of the algorithm's behaviour which is well suited for analysing and describing the qualitative behavior of an algorithm. Especially when comparing the performance of different algorithms, a graphic representation of the RTDs is very useful. Let us consider two algorithms which, when applied to the same problem instance, show a cross-over in the corresponding RTDs. This immediately implies that for short runs one algorithm gives a higher solution probability than the other, while for longer run-times the situation is reversed. The location of the cross-over indicates the critical time at which both algorithms give the same solution probability. If on the other hand no such cross-over occurs, this provides evidence that for the given problem instance, one algorithm dominates the other in the sense that it gives consistently higher success probabilities, regardless of the run-time. Note that when only comparing the mean or median run-time, or even a number of percentiles, domination can typically not be tested but is often implicitely and misleadingly suggested by this data. The graphic representation of an RTD often also gives an indication whether an algorithm shows stagnation behaviour and thus gives hints on the possible incompleteness of an algorithm. Stagnation in an RTD is indicated by the fact that the RTD shows a horizontal section with a solution probability smaller than one over one or more orders of magnitude on the run-time axis. Moreover, as argued in [36], given the RTD data, optimal cutoff times (i.e., *maxSteps* settings) can be determined in a rather straight-forward way.

3.2. Analysing SLS performance for problem distributions

As specified above, RTDs are measured for individual problem instances rather than for sets of instances. While at the first glance this might seem like a disadvantage of the RTD-based approach, in fact it is one of its biggest advantages. To see why this is so, consider the prominent case of evaluating an SLS algorithm on a set of problem instances sampled from a random instance distribution, such as uniform Random-3-SAT (*cf.* Section 3.4) for a given number of variables and clauses. There is two sources of randomness which have to be taken into consideration: the variability in the run-time when applying the algorithm to an individual problem instance and the stochastic generation of the instances. For various reasons we feel that it is very desirable to investigate these two types of random influences seperately; one of these is the fact that the type of randomness captured in the RTD might strongly depend on the algorithm being used while the instance-related variation might be caused by properties of the instance which affect a large number of algorithms. Later, in Section 5, we will show that for Random-3-SAT this is actually the case.

Another important argument for analysing RTDs based on individual instances is the following (see [36] for details): Consider a situation where for a set of problem instances the RTDs on all individual instances are exponential distributions. As we will show in Section 5, this implies that this algorithm is very robust *w.r.t.* the *maxSteps* setting and cannot be improved by using restart. If, however, one looks at an "average RTD" obtained by summing up the RTDs over the instances of the test-set and dividing by the number of instances, this RTD is generally not an exponential distribution, as the family of exponential distributions is not closed under the operation of averaging [57]. As argued in [36], this RTD will generally suggest the existence of an optimal setting of the *maxSteps* parameter. Using this setting will indeed maximise the algorithm's performance — but only in the sense that within a given time period, the number of problem instances randomly drawn from the instance set (or distribution) which are solved within this time period will be maximal. However, as an RTD-based analysis shows, in this case the "optimal parameter setting" will not affect the performance on any individual instance from the set — it will only make sure that not too much is wasted trying to solve hard instances. Thus, using the optimal setting will effectively introduce a bias for solving easier problems — an effect which, except for very special application situations, will most likely be undesirable and can potentially give rise to erroneous interpretations of the observed behaviour. This problem becomes very relevant when the inter-instance difficulty within the test-set has a high variance, as is the case for Random-3-SAT and Graph Colouring test-sets (see also Section 4).

Using the RTD-based approach requires estimating the RTDs for each individual problem instance from a given test-set such as the Random-3-SAT and Graph Colouring instance sets used for this study. In all cases, when evaluating an algorithm's behaviour for a test-set of instances, we follow this approach. However, it is impractical to actually report the RTD data for 100 or 1,000 instances (the typical size of our test-sets). Instead, we usually report RTD data for a small number of instances (Section 4) or perform functional characterisations of the individual RTDs (Section 5). Additionally, we analyse and report distributions of the RTDs' means or percentiles (typically the median) across the given test-set. These *hardness distributions* reflect the variation in search cost arising from the random structure of the instances. Interestingly, using this approach one can easily see (cf. Section 4) that the RTDs are usually very different from the hardness distributions; in particular, the hardness distributions are typically heavy-tailed (cf. [24]), while we never observed a heavy-tailed RTD for any of the SLS algorithms studied here.

3.3. Functional characterisations of RTDs

In addition to the advantages discussed above, an RTD-based methodology provides the basis for more advanced types of empirical evaluations, such as the functional characterisation of the RTDs for a given algorithm. Here, one idea is that if a given algorithm displays the same type of RTDs for a range of problem instances and this type can be determined, then the RTD data can be represented in a much more compact and informative way. Practically, this can be done by approximating RTDs using parameterised families of distribution functions, where the parameters are estimated from the measured RTD data (*cf.* Figure 3, *right*). Once such characterisations are obtained, they provide a basis for studying the dependence of the RTD parameters on various factors such as problem size or constrainedness.

Note that this type of empirical analysis can be used to produce hypotheses, such as "when applying WalkSAT and using an optimal setting of *wp* to hard Random-3-SAT problem instances, the RTDs are well approximated by exponential distributions", which can be tested for statistical significance. Therefore, this type of RTD-based analysis follows suggestions made by Hooker [30, 31], that the empirical analysis of algorithms should not remain at the stage of simply collecting data. Rather, analogous to empirical methodologies used in other sciences, one should attempt to formulate hypotheses based on this data which, in turn, can be experimentally refuted or validated. As we will see in Section 5, this approach is extremely useful for investigating the robustness of SLS performance. Furthermore, functional characterisations of RTDs may also help in relating the empirical behaviour of algorithms to more general statistical phenomena and thus provide a basis for new interpretions of the observed behaviour [24, 18, 37, 35].

Finally, it should be noted that the same RTD-based methodology we are using here for analysing the run-time behaviour of SLS algorithms for SAT can generally be applied to empirical studies of a much broader class of algorithms, the so-called *Las Vegas algorithms.* These are algorithms which, if they find a solution, guarantee its correctness but generally have a run-time which is characterised by a random variable [49, 1, 35]. Also, this methodology can be generalised to optimisation problems, which is of interest as many SLS algorithms for decision problems can be analogously used for solving the corresponding optimisation problems (e.g., the SAT algorithms covered here can be equally well used for solving MAX-SAT problems) [35, 62].

3.4. The Benchmark Set

The benchmark selection we are using as a basis for the empirical evaluation of SLS algorithms for SAT is a subset of SATLIB (see also Chapter: *SATLIB: An Online Resource*) and comprises three different types of problems: test-sets sampled from Random-3-SAT, a well-known random problem distribution; test-sets obtained by encoding instances from a random distribution of hard Graph Colouring instances into SAT; and small sets of SAT-encoded instances from various other domains. All these benchmark instances are hard in general and difficult to solve for SLS algorithms. For the SAT-encoded problems, the hardness of the instances is inherent rather than just induced by the encoding scheme that was used for transforming them into SAT. The SAT-encodings used here are mostly very simple and well-known from the literature.

The selection of the benchmark problems was influenced by a number of criteria. First, we want to facilitate the combination of the results reported in this study with future evaluations of other SAT algorithms (not necessarily based on SLS) by using the same benchmark library, in order to obtain an overall picture of the performance of different SAT algorithms. Thus, the benchmark set should be as diverse as possible and avoid any bias towards the selection of algorithms studied here. A large and diverse benchmark set also allows us to investigate whether there are performance differences between these algorithms which are so fundamental that they can be consistently observed over a broad range of benchmark problems. Our choice of particular problem classes focuses on fairly well-known instances and instance distributions, which have been used widely in the literature. But secondly, as the goal here is to evaluate SLS algorithms which are typically incomplete, we have to restrict the benchmark suite to satisfiable instances. Finally, because of the detailed RTD-based analysis to be applied, each SLS algorithm has to solve each problem instance a large number of times (typically, at least 250) which limits the size and number of problem instances we could use in our experiments. Nevertheless, the benchmark set used in the context of this work contains ca. 4,500 problem instances.

Based on these consideration, we included various sets of satisfiable instances from SATLIB into our benchmark selection: a number of test-sets of satisfiable uniform Random-3-SAT (`uf*`) and SAT-encoded flat random Graph Colouring instances (`flat*`); individual SAT-encoded instances from the Blocks World and Logistics plannning domains (`bw_large*` and `logistics*`); several large SAT-encoded Graph Colouring instances and SAT-encoded instances from the problem of learning a parity function from given data, which were originally part of the Second DIMACS Challenge [41].

The details on almost all the instances applied in our experimental study are given in the chapter on SATLIB *SATLIB: An Online Resource*). An exception are the instances from the DIMACS benchmark set which are described in the following.

The large SAT-encoded Graph Colouring instances we used stem originally from a study performed by Johnson et.al. [40]. In our experimental analysis we used the three instances `g125.18`,(125 vertices, 18 colours), `g125.17` (125 vertices, 17 colours), and `g250.29` (250 instances, 29 colours). For a fourth instance (`g250.15`), we found that, despite its size, it is extremely easy for all algorithms considered here and consequently decided not to use it in our analysis. Instances `g125.18.cnf` and `g125.17.cnf` are based on the same graph, but use a different number of colours (17 is conjectured to be the chromatic number of this graph).

The parity learning instances `par*` are very hard for the SLS algorithms we used. We limited our RLD-based study to the smaller instances, which encode learning a parity function with eight variables based on a sample of (potentially noisy) input/output pairs. These formulae have been simplified using unit propagation and subsumption. The resulting formulae are rather small: each of the five instances contains approx. 70 variables and approx. 270 clauses. Some larger parity learning instances (the largest we tried encoded a parity function with sixteen variables and were simplified by polynomial preprocessing techniqies) can be solved by some of the best-performing SLS algorithms identified in this study, but the search cost is too high for a systematic empirical analysis of SLS behaviour.

Other classes of SATLIB instances stemming from the original DIMACS benchmark set have been deliberately excluded from our study. Among these are the instances obtained from the AIM instance generator [2] which are generated randomly for clauses/variable ratios of 1.6, 2.0, 3.4, and 6.0 in such a way that each formula has exactly one satisfiable assignment. However, different from all problem classes used in our benchmark collection, the resulting instances are polynomially solvable by simplification procedures (using binary failed clauses) and thus cannot be considered intrinsically hard. When practically solving SAT instances, such simplification procedures are typically applied as a preprocessing step.[1] Considering this, we regard instances which are solved by the preprocessing procedure alone to be of minor interest in the context of our study of SLS performance. Without simplification, when using reasonably optimised noise settings, the best WalkSAT variants typically solve the instances with high clauses per variable ratio with an average of less than 1000 flips. But for lower clause per variable ratios, such as 1.6 or 2.0, some of the instances are very difficult to solve using the algorithms considered here. In contrast, weighting schemes for GSAT solve this type of instances much more efficiently [7, 8]. It is not clear whether this is just an artifact of this problem class or a more general phenomenon which can be also observed for hard problem classes that cannot be efficiently solved by polynomial simplification methods. It would be interesting to further investigate this question; however, this would require additional methodology which is beyond the scope of this study.

Similary, also the instances from a test pattern generation program for VLSI circuits [48] can be solved, despite their relatively large size (they contain from 1,363 to 1,501 variables and 3,032 to 3,575 clauses), by preprocessing techniques alone. They are also relatively easily solved by the SLS algorithms applied here. Of the other instances there are some satisfiable ones (16 out of 50) among the randomly generated instances `jnh`x (where x is the instance identifier) with variable clause lenghts. Some initial experiments showed that these instances are easily solved and therefore we preferred to focus rather on our large-sets of hard Uniform Random-3-SAT instances. Finally, we also excluded the instances stemming originally from an integer programming formulation of an inductive inference problem [42]. These are easily solved by, for example, WalkSAT and therefore do not provide a challenging benchmark for the local search algorithms applied here.

4. Peak Performance Comparison

In this section, we present the results of our comprehensive performance analysis for the algorithms introduced in Section 2 applied to the suite of benchmark problems described in the previous section. As motivated and introduced in Section 3, we use an RLD-based methodology. In particular, two basic methods are applied: For individual instances, we compare the RLDs of the algorithms using approximately optimal settings of the noise parameters *wp*, *p*, or *tl*. As an optimality criterion we use the expected number of steps required for finding a solution. For test-sets sampled from random instance distributions, we additionally analyse the distribution of the mean search cost per instance for different algorithms, again using approximately optimal noise settings. More advanced aspects of our empirical investigation, in particular functional characterisations of the RLDs, as well as robustness and scaling issues, are deferred to Section 5, where we also study the influence of the noise parameters in more detail.

[1] Note that for SAT-encoded problems from other domains, this preprocessing is known to be crucial for finding solutions using SLS or systematic SAT algorithms.

Table I. Test-set uf100-430, basic descriptive statistics of hardness distributions for various algorithms with approx. optimal noise, based on 100 tries / instance; noise settings as for medium instance (*cf.* Table XXIV).

algorithm	mean	stddev	$\frac{\text{stddev}}{\text{mean}}$	med	Q_{75}	Q_{90}	$\frac{Q_{75}}{Q_{25}}$	$\frac{Q_{90}}{Q_{10}}$
GWSAT	6,532	10,639	1.63	3,398	7,040	13,880	3.82	12.62
GSAT/TABU	4,783	9,741	2.04	1,621	4,260	11,399	5.62	24.93
HWSAT	3,039	3,365	1.11	1,914	3,622	6,605	3.33	9.71
WalkSAT	3,672	5,698	1.55	1,995	4,142	7,296	3.62	10.40
WalkSAT/TABU	2,485	6,263	2.52	1,041	2,215	4,751	3.92	13.51
Novelty	28,257	191,668	6.78	851	1,845	4,390	3.85	14.50
R-Novelty	1,245	1,893	1.52	640	1,402	2,625	3.73	11.30

4.1. Random-3-SAT

For Random-3-SAT, we first empirically analysed SLS performance for test-set uf100-430 (1,000 instances) by measuring an RLD for each algorithm applied to each individual instance using approximately optimal noise settings (*wp*, *p*, or *tl*).[2] In this case, the RLDs are based on 100 tries per instance; using an extremely high cutoff parameter setting of *maxSteps* $= 10^7$ we made sure to obtain a maximal number of successful tries. To get an impression of the variability of the search cost within the test-set, we analysed the distribution of the mean search cost (number of local search steps) over the instances from the test-set. Figure 4 shows these cumulative hardness distributions, while Table I reports the corresponding basic statistics.

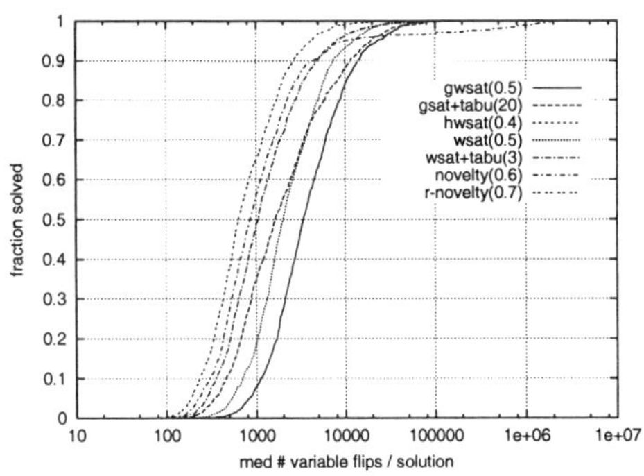

Figure 4. Hardness distributions across test-set uf100-430 for various algorithms; x-axis: median number of local search steps per solution.

For all algorithms, we observe a huge variability in search cost between the instances of each test-set. In particular, as can be seen from the long tails of these distributions, a substantial part of the problem instances is dramatically harder than the rest of the test-set. Furthermore, looking at the graphic representation of the hardness distributions in Figure 4, one might notice that the curves are roughly parallel in a semi-log plot. This indicates that the differences in search cost for these algorithms can be characterised by a uniform factor across the whole hardness distribution. However, examining the top 10% of the cumulative distribution curves, there are three notable exceptions from

[2] The noise settings have been optimised in preliminary runs. It was found that the approximately optimal noise settings did not considerably differ between different instances from the same test-set.

that rule: those for GSAT/TABU, WalkSAT/TABU, and — far more dramatically — Novelty have a significantly heavier tail than the curves for the other algorithms. That GSAT/TABU, WalkSAT/TABU, and Novelty cause considerably more inter-instance hardness variation can also be seen when comparing the normalised standard deviations and percentile ratios in Table I. This oberservation indicates that the variants using tabu search, as well as Novelty, have greater difficulties escaping from highly attractive areas in the search spaces of some instances than the other variants. For the tabu search variants this is most probably caused by the fixed length of the tabu list which limits the ability to escape from local minima regions. For Novelty, 33 of the 1,000 instances had a solution rate between 75% and 99%, whereas for identical *maxSteps* settings all other algorithms solved all instances in each try. This explains the huge standard deviation observed for the Novelty hardness distribution. It also indicates that due to its greedy bias, Novelty can get permanently stuck in local minima regions.

Table II. Problem instance `uf100-430/easy`, basic descriptive statistics of RLDs for various algorithms, approx. optimal noise (in parentheses after algorithms' names), based on 1,000 tries.

algorithm	mean	stddev	$\frac{\text{stddev}}{\text{mean}}$	median	Q_{75}	Q_{90}	$\frac{Q_{75}}{Q_{25}}$	$\frac{Q_{90}}{Q_{10}}$
GWSAT(0.5)	270.63	240.62	0.89	202	313	504	2.35	5.54
GSAT/TABU(20)	137.78	91.31	0.66	108	170	255	2.18	4.40
HWSAT(0.3)	190.58	154.25	0.81	145	223	365	2.40	5.21
WalkSAT(0.5)	177.86	135.78	0.76	139	206	336	2.22	4.87
WalkSAT/TABU(5)	97.79	49.04	0.50	86	119	164	1.92	3.28
Novelty(0.9)	77.36	37.29	0.48	68	92	124	1.77	3.02
R-Novelty(0.9)	76.63	34.79	0.45	68	90	121	1.70	2.81

Table III. Problem instance `uf100-430/med`, basic descriptive statistics of RLDs for various algorithms, approx. optimal noise, based on 1,000 tries.

algorithm	mean	stddev	$\frac{\text{stddev}}{\text{mean}}$	median	Q_{75}	Q_{90}	$\frac{Q_{75}}{Q_{25}}$	$\frac{Q_{90}}{Q_{10}}$
GWSAT(0.5)	2,432	2,159	0.89	1,785	3,345	5,434	3.78	11.51
GSAT/TABU(20)	1,368	1,297	0.95	995	1,804	2,903	3.83	12.62
HWSAT(0.4)	2,015	1,727	0.87	1,509	2,687	4,502	3.59	10.67
WalkSAT(0.5)	1,877	1,776	0.95	1,333	2,510	4,133	3.90	12.84
WalkSAT/TABU(3)	532	365	0.69	433	689	999	2.43	5.52
Novelty(0.6)	504	372	0.74	416	647	962	2.62	6.13
R-Novelty(0.7)	580	467	0.80	440	767	1,213	3.09	7.93

Next, we analysed the RLDs obtained by applying the algorithms to individual problem instances. For practical reasons, we restrict our presentation here to the instances corresponding to the minimum, median, and maximum of the hardness distribution for WalkSAT; these are referred to as the "easy", "medium" (med), and "hard" hardness instances from the underlying test-set. The RLDs shown in Figures 5 and 6 offer an easily accessible, yet comprehensive and precise picture of our results. As can be seen from the figures, the RLDs for the different algorithms have all roughly the same shape, and, with one exception (R-Novelty and WalkSAT/TABU on the medium instance), no cross-overs occur. Thus, generally there is a dominance relation between the algorithms when applied to the same instance, i.e., when comparing two algorithms' performance,

Table IV. Problem instance **uf100-430/hard**, basic descriptive statistics of RLDs for various algorithms, approx. optimal noise, based on 1,000 tries.

algorithm	mean	stddev	$\frac{\text{stddev}}{\text{mean}}$	median	Q_{75}	Q_{90}	$\frac{Q_{75}}{Q_{25}}$	$\frac{Q_{90}}{Q_{10}}$
GWSAT(0.6)	177,468	181,843	1.02	119,666	247,047	400,466	5.27	22.78
GSAT/TABU(20)	84,578	84,301	1.00	57,778	120,286	196,493	5.01	24.95
HWSAT(0.4)	37,822	37,717	1.00	26,481	52,008	89,132	4.96	22.98
WalkSAT(0.5)	86,773	90,538	1.04	56,666	120,583	198,109	5.41	27.07
WalkSAT/TABU(5)	87,031	86,692	1.00	60,019	119,246	206,822	5.14	26.23
Novelty(0.7)	26,995	27,165	1.01	19,434	36,972	58,661	4.43	18.06
R-Novelty(0.7)	19,118	19,827	1.04	12,819	26,707	43,911	4.71	23.36

one is uniformly better or worse than the other. Note that based on our earlier observation of stagnation behaviour for some of the algorithms, there are instances, for which this is not true, but it holds for the majority of the instances. This indicates that for Random-3-SAT problems, the relative effectivity of different search mechanisms, when compared to each other, does typically not change with increasing length of the search trajectory. Thus, search space features which affect the different search mechanisms non-uniformly are the exception rather than the norm.

Additionally, we give the descriptive statistics in numerical form in Tables II to IV. Because the different algorithm's RLDs typically do not cross-over, it is admissible to base performance comparisons mainly on descriptive statistics. One interesting observation which is even more obvious when looking at the numerical data rather than the graphical representation of the RLDs is the huge variability in the time required to find a solution (see standard deviation and percentile ratios in the tables) and the fact that this variability increases with instance hardness, as can be seen comparing the stddev/mean values or the percentile ratios between the easy, medium, and hard instance.

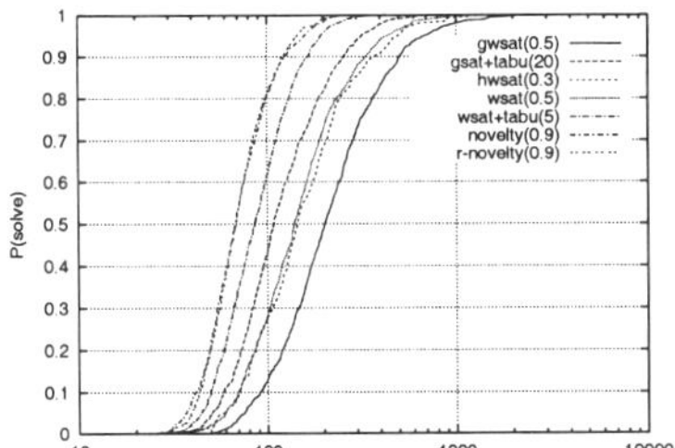

Figure 5. Problem instance **uf100-430/easy**, RLDs for various algorithms, approx. optimal noise, based on 1,000 tries.

From the RLDs and the numerical data, one can easily see that GWSAT is generally the worst performing algorithm, while R-Novelty performs best. Apart from this, however, the relative performance of the algorithms on Random-3-SAT generally depends on the instance hardness. Only for the hard instance, a significant difference between Novelty and R-Novelty can be observed, which suggests that the more complicated variable selection mechanism used in R-Novelty only pays off for extremely hard instances. At the same time, the performance differences observed between WalkSAT, WalkSAT/TABU, and GSAT/TABU for the easier instances are no longer observed for the hard instance. This suggests that the tabu mechanism might be considerably more

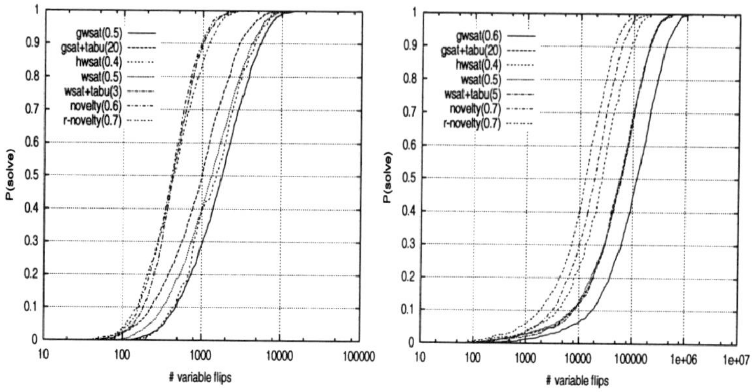

Figure 6. Problem instance `uf100-430/med` *(left)* and `uf100-430/hard` *(right)*, RLDs for various algorithms, approx. optimal noise, based on 1,000 tries / instance.

effective for easier instances. HWSAT ranks between GWSAT and GSAT/TABU for the easy and medium instance; for the hard instance however, this algorithm shows very competitive performance and ranks third after R-Novelty and Novelty. Thus, compared to rigid tabu lists the more flexible memory-based mechanism used in HWSAT, Novelty, and R-Novelty seems to be more effective for hard instances. It may be further noted that the differences in performance between the best and the worst performing algorithm (GWSAT and R-Novelty) is far more dramatic for the hard instance (a factor of approx. 10 in the median) than for the medium (factor ≈ 4 in the median) and the easy instance (factor ≈ 3 in the median). This suggests that especially for the features which make instances hard for the SLS algorithms considered here, R-Novelty's sophisticated search mechanism is particularly effective. As we will show in Section 5.3, by using advanced analysis techniques, additional evidence for this interpretation can be obtained.

4.2. Graph Colouring

Applying the same RLD analysis as used for Random-3-SAT to the `flat100-329` Graph Colouring test-set (100 instances), we observe some surprising differences (*cf.* Figures 7 and 8, and Tables V–VII). These concern mainly the performance of GSAT/TABU and R-Novelty. The latter algorithm, which dominated the scene for the Random-3-SAT test-set, shows a relatively weak performance on the Graph Colouring domain tested here, where it ranks third (on the easy and hard instance) or fourth (on the medium problem). Novelty is significantly better than R-Novelty on all three test instances; the performance difference is uniformly characterised by a factor of ca. 2 in the number of steps required to find a solution with a given probability. This suggests that R-Novelty's sophisticated variable selection mechanism might be too much tuned towards search space features which tend to occur only in Random-3-SAT problems. Alternately, R-Novelty might have difficulties with the more structured search spaces of SAT-encoded problems.

GSAT/TABU, on the other hand, is much stronger when applied to the Graph Colouring test-set than for Random-3-SAT. Here, for the easy and medium instance, GSAT/TABU is only second after Novelty, which is the best algorithm for these instances; for the hard instance, GSAT/TABU is slightly better than Novelty and thus leads the field. But analogously to what we observed for Random-3-SAT, WalkSAT/TABU's performance is relatively poor on the hard instance where, for `flat100-239`, it is inferior to WalkSAT. This is somewhat surprising given the huge

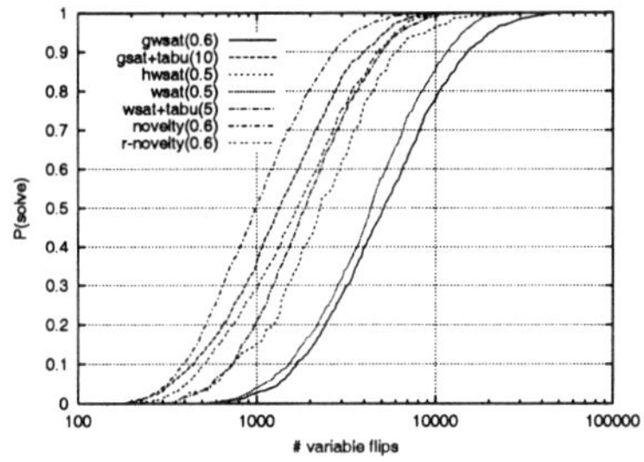

Figure 7. Problem `flat100-239/easy`, RLDs for various algorithms, approx. optimal noise, based on 1,000 tries.

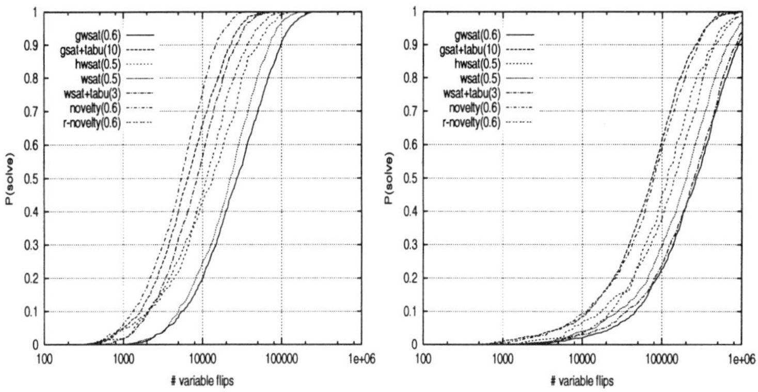

Figure 8. Problem `flat100-239/med` *(left)* and `flat100-239/hard` *(right)*, RLDs for various algorithms, approx. optimal noise, based on 1,000 tries / instance.

advantage GSAT/TABU realises over GWSAT (for the hard instance, we observe a factor of ca. 3 between the performance of these two algorithms). Obviously, the more global tabu mechanism in GSAT/TABU is particularly effective for the more structured search spaces of the Graph Colouring instances. HWSAT's performance is consistenly inferior to both, Novelty's and GSAT/TABU's.

Additionally to these RLD analyses, like in the case of Random-3-SAT, we performed an analysis of the instance hardness distribitions for the different algorithms. For practical reasons (computing time limitations and higher accuracy because of a larger number

Table V. Problem instance `flat100-239/easy`, basic descriptive statistics of RLDs for various algorithms, approx. optimal noise, based on 1,000 tries.

algorithm	mean	stddev	$\frac{\text{stddev}}{\text{mean}}$	med	Q_{75}	Q_{90}	$\frac{Q_{75}}{Q_{25}}$	$\frac{Q_{90}}{Q_{10}}$
GWSAT(0.6)	7,268	6,898	0.95	5,146	9,031	15,168	3.24	9.07
GSAT/TABU(20)	1,636	1,156	0.71	1,320	2,242	3,215	2.97	6.68
HWSAT(0.5)	3,142	3,080	0.98	2,271	3,878	5,946	2.84	8.11
WalkSAT(0.5)	5,602	4,358	0.78	4,341	7,398	11,577	2.93	7.61
WalkSAT/TABU(5)	2,453	1,924	0.78	1,863	3,155	4,978	2.82	6.78
Novelty(0.6)	1,333	1,097	0.82	980	1,733	2,704	2.96	6.97
R-Novelty(0.6)	2,253	1,912	0.85	1,687	2,958	4,721	3.44	9.15

Table VI. Problem instance `flat100-239/med`, basic descriptive statistics of RLDs for various algorithms, approx. optimal noise, based on 1,000 tries.

algorithm	mean	stddev	$\frac{\text{stddev}}{\text{mean}}$	med	Q_{10}	Q_{75}	Q_{90}	$\frac{Q_{75}}{Q_{25}}$	$\frac{Q_{90}}{Q_{10}}$
GWSAT(0.6)	41,784	41,629	1.00	27,288	5,426	58,159	97,410	4.83	17.95
GSAT/TABU(10)	9,811	9,765	1.00	6,539	1,656	13,041	22,443	4.07	13.55
HWSAT(0.5)	20,377	21021	1.03	13,469	2,023	28,089	49,004	5.08	24.22
WalkSAT(0.5)	31,260	28,586	0.91	22,595	4,995	42,567	70,267	4.23	14.07
WalkSAT/TABU(3)	11,881	11,094	0.93	8,548	2,091	16,086	26,590	3.87	12.72
Novelty(0.6)	7,070	5,928	0.84	5,455	1,297	9,951	14,826	3.77	11.43
R-Novelty(0.6)	16,183	16,333	1.01	11,291	1,997	20,790	36,645	4.36	18.35

Table VII. Problem instance `flat100-239/hard`, basic descriptive statistics of RLDs for various algorithms, approx. optimal noise, based on 1,000 tries.

algorithm	mean	stddev	$\frac{\text{stddev}}{\text{mean}}$	med	Q_{75}	Q_{90}	$\frac{Q_{75}}{Q_{25}}$	$\frac{Q_{90}}{Q_{10}}$
GWSAT(0.6)	306,886	249,012	0.81	240,302	451,475	700,129	4.35	15.96
GSAT/TABU(10)	107,872	111,690	1.04	73,594	142,838	251,477	4.51	21.35
HWSAT(0.5)	166,365	161,314	0.97	113,981	220,950	405,482	4.35	26.20
WalkSAT(0.5)	254,373	222,835	0.88	192,788	375,285	578,138	4.73	21.45
WalkSAT/TABU(3)	297,778	245,045	0.82	229,496	453,820	674,915	4.66	20.79
Novelty(0.6)	116,773	117,259	1.00	79,307	159,525	276,180	4.78	24.50
R-Novelty(0.6)	195,965	183,408	0.94	140,671	284,093	433,875	5.18	19.36

of instances), we used the `flat50-115` test-set for this analysis; however, our experimental experience indicates that these results translate directly to `flat100-239`. The hardness distributions shown in Figure 9 confirm and refine the observations from studying the three sample instances. Novelty, R-Novelty, and GSAT/TABU clearly dominate the other algorithms on the major part of the test-set; the hardness distributions of these algorithms appear to be almost identical. However, for Novelty and R-Novelty, as well as for WalkSAT/TABU, the distributions have heavy tails which indicate that the algorithms get stuck in local minima for a relatively small number of instances. Consequently, their worst-case performance on the given test-set is drastically worse

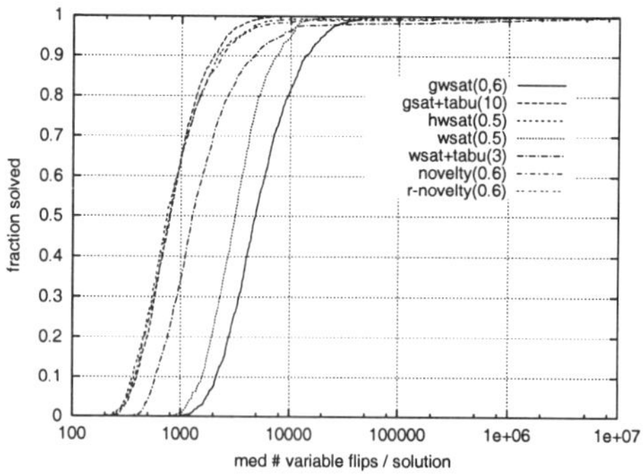

Figure 9. Hardness distributions across test-set `flat50-239` for various algorithms; x-axis: median number of local search steps / solution.

Table VIII. Test-set `flat50-115`, basic descriptive statistics of hardness distributions for various algorithms with approx. optimal noise, based on 100 tries / instance; noise settings as for medium instance (*cf.* Table XXVII).

algorithm	mean	stddev	$\frac{\text{stddev}}{\text{mean}}$	median	Q_{75}	Q_{90}	$\frac{Q_{75}}{Q_{25}}$	$\frac{Q_{90}}{Q_{10}}$
GWSAT	7,023	7,060	1.01	4,846	8,122	13,640	2.65	6.44
GSAT/TABU	1,040	855	0.82	787	1,220	1,963	2.26	4.99
HWSAT	2,641	2,056	0.78	2,042	3,139	4,926	2.30	4.95
WalkSAT	3,913	2,779	0.71	3,132	4,648	7,287	2.22	4.63
WalkSAT/TABU	61,393	720,406	11.73	1,265	2,252	4,675	2.70	8.00
Novelty	20,065	330,262	16.46	776	1,282	2,335	2.50	6.19
R-Novelty	7,109	97,543	13.72	739	1,282	2,142	2.62	6.01

than the other algorithms'. Note that for Novelty, a similar situation was observed in the case of Random-3-SAT — where, however, neither WalkSAT/TABU, nor R-Novelty showed any signs of essential incompleteness.

4.3. Blocks World and Logistics Planning

After evaluating the different algorithms on random distributions of hard problem instances, we now turn to single SAT-encoded instances from the Blocks World and Logistics Planning domains. Here, we compare the RLDs for individual instances, like it was done for the easy, medium, and hard instances from the distributions studied before. After preliminary experiments indicated that the GSAT variants are substantially outperformed by the more efficient WalkSAT variants on these problems (see also Section 4.5), we focused mainly on algorithms of the WalkSAT family.

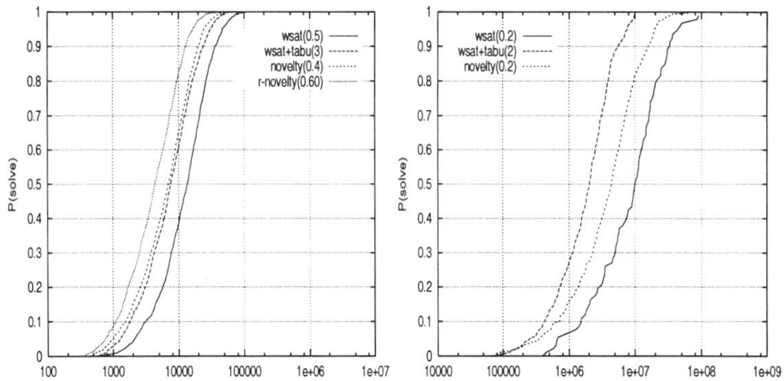

Figure 10. Problem instance `bw_large.a` *(left)* and instance `bw_large.c` *(right)* for various algorithms, approx. optimal noise, based on 1,000 and 250 tries, respectively.

For the smallest Blocks World instance (`bw_large.a`), as well as for similar small instances from the SATPLAN distribution, we observe a uniform performance pattern: R-Novelty is uniformly better than Novelty, which shows slightly improved performance over WalkSAT/TABU, which in turn is significantly better than WalkSAT (see Figure 10 on the left side and the numerical data given in Table IX). For the larger instances, however, the situation is considerably different: Applied to `bw_large.b`, R-Novelty ranks only third behind WalkSAT/TABU and Novelty, which show a very similar performance

Table IX. Problem instance `bw_large.a`, basic descriptive statistics of RLDs for various algorithms, approx. optimal noise, based on 1,000 tries.

algorithm	mean	stddev	$\frac{\text{stddev}}{\text{mean}}$	median	Q_{75}	Q_{90}	$\frac{Q_{75}}{Q_{25}}$	$\frac{Q_{90}}{Q_{10}}$
GWSAT(0.6)	26,994	24,784	0.92	18,653	38,041	58,679	4.09	11.61
GSAT/TABU(10)	10,635	10,515	0.99	6,977	14,917	25,291	4.72	20.02
WalkSAT(0.5)	17,490	15,320	0.88	13,505	23,446	35,981	3.44	11.77
WalkSAT/TABU(3)	10,603	9,665	0.91	7,563	14,169	23,870	3.84	13.41
Novelty(0.4)	9,315	8,587	0.92	6,932	12,877	20,202	4.02	13.17
R-Novelty(0.6)	6,053	5,583	0.92	4,317	8,413	12,875	4.01	11.87

Table X. Problem instance `bw_large.b`, basic descriptive statistics of RLDs for various algorithms, approx. optimal noise, based on 250 tries.

algorithm	mean	stddev	$\frac{\text{stddev}}{\text{mean}}$	median	Q_{25}	Q_{75}	$\frac{Q_{75}}{Q_{25}}$
WalkSAT(0.35)	582,384	570,626	0.98	414,744	166,326	782,842	4.71
WalkSAT/TABU(2)	152,104.03	137,108.76	0.90	107,586	54,611	215,564	3.95
Novelty(0.30)	191,715	195,045	1.02	131,494	53,629	254,779	4.75
R-Novelty(0.55)	234,304.18	215,100.55	0.92	166,922	73,673	341,827	4.64

(see Table X). For `bw_large.c`, WalkSAT/TABU is significantly better than Novelty (factor ≈ 2), while Novelty's performance is between WalkSAT's and WalkSAT/TABU's (see Figure 10 on the right side and Table XI). The big surprise, however, is that R-Novelty performs extremely poorly: for noise parameter settings up to 0.5, we observed stagnation behaviour with extremely low asymptotic solution probabilities ($< 10\%$). However, if a solution is found, this requires only a relatively small number of steps on average – thus by using restart and a small cutoff value, competitive performance can be achieved. Nevertheless, even using an optimal cutoff value, R-Novelty's performance is still inferior to WalkSAT/TABU's (the best estimated factor between the corresponding average local search steps / solution values is 1.75).

On the SAT-encoded instances from the Logistics Planning domain, similar to the blocks world instances, none of our algorithms dominates all the others. For example, on the smallest instance (`logistics.a`, see Table XII), Novelty and R-Novelty are the best performing algorithms, followed by WalkSAT and HWSAT which take roughly twice as many steps. WalkSAT/TABU is the worst algorithm of the WalkSAT-architecture and GWSAT is quite significantly outperformed by all the others, requiring – on average – roughly 15 times as many flips as the best performing algorithm. We were not able to solve this instance with GSAT/TABU trying various values for the tabu tenure. For instances `logistics.b` and `logistics.c` (not shown here), the performance ranking of the algorithms is the same as for `logistics.a`. Yet, for instance `logistics.d`, R-Novelty performs substantially worse than all other WalkSAT variants, while Novelty shows the best performance followed by WalkSAT/TABU and WalkSAT (see Table XIII).

4.4. Instances from the DIMACS Benchmark Set

Finally, we present the comparison of the SLS algorithms on instances of the DIMACS Benchmark set. We started with comparing the algorithms' performance on the large

Table XI. Problem instance `bw_large.c`, basic descriptive statistics of RLDs for various algorithms, approx. optimal noise, based on 250 tries.

algorithm	mean	stddev	$\frac{\text{stddev}}{\text{mean}}$	median	Q_{75}	$\frac{Q_{75}}{Q_{25}}$
WalkSAT(0.2)	$14.06 \cdot 10^6$	$15.60 \cdot 10^6$	1.11	$9.76 \cdot 10^6$	$17.0 \cdot 10^6$	4.85
WalkSAT/TABU(2)	$2.52 \cdot 10^6$	$2.12 \cdot 10^6$	0.84	$2.00 \cdot 10^6$	$3.53 \cdot 10^6$	3.89
Novelty(0.2)	$6.4 \cdot 10^6$	$7.13 \cdot 10^6$	1.12	$4.40 \cdot 10^6$	$8.16 \cdot 10^6$	4.70

Table XII. Problem instance `logistics.a`, basic descriptive statistics of RLDs for various algorithms, approx. optimal noise, based on 1,000 tries for algorithms of WalkSAT-architecture and 250 tries for algorithms of GSAT architecture.

algorithm	mean	stddev	$\frac{\text{stddev}}{\text{mean}}$	median	Q_{75}	Q_{90}	$\frac{Q_{75}}{Q_{25}}$	$\frac{Q_{90}}{Q_{10}}$
GWSAT(0.30)	711,033	682,080	0.96	500,970	904,361	1,464,615	3.79	9.95
HWSAT(0.15)	107,143	76,633	0.72	86.609	148,109	213,285	2.96	6.75
WalkSAT(0.3)	95,205	91070	0.96	65,566	120,207	200,325	3.33	9.92
WalkSAT/TABU(1)	177,169	139,661	0.79	139,647	246,933	365,434	3.49	10.55
Novelty(0.45)	55,748	41,323	0.74	46,366	72,153	108,518	2.81	6.53
R-Novelty(0.65)	45,220	36,219	0.80	33,713	62,321	93,278	3.18	8.32

SAT-encoded graph colouring instances. In Table XIV we give the computational results on instance `g125.18`. All the algorithms we applied solve this instance in relatively few steps; consistently with the results for the smaller, randomly generated graph colouring instances, GSAT/TABU and Novelty show the best performance. Novelty, however, as well as WalkSAT/TABU and R-Novelty show stagnation behaviour and hence do not find solutions in every run, even when using extremely high *maxSteps* settings (here: 10^6 steps). Of these, R-Novelty is affected worst which is reflected by the high standard deviation of the run length (see Table XIV). A similar situation can be found for instance `g125.17` (corresponding to the same graph but using only 17 instead of 18 colours), which is considerably harder to solve. On this instance, R-Novelty (not shown in the table) suffered from extreme stagnation behaviour.

Next, we did an analogous performance analysis for the DIMACS parity instances mentioned in Section 3.4. In Table XVI we give the basic descriptive statistics for instance `par8-5-c`, which we found to be the hardest for the SLS algorithms considered here. Here, R-Novelty and Novelty are the top performing algorithms, followed by the two other WalkSAT variants and the algorithms based on the GSAT-architecture. Of these latter, HWSAT shows the the best performance and GSAT/TABU the worst. On

Table XIII. Problem instance `logistics.d`, basic descriptive statistics of RLDs for various algorithms, approx. optimal noise, based on 1,000 tries.

algorithm	mean	stddev	$\frac{\text{stddev}}{\text{mean}}$	median	Q_{75}	Q_{90}	$\frac{Q_{75}}{Q_{25}}$	$\frac{Q_{90}}{Q_{10}}$
WalkSAT(0.4)	499,956	373,354	0.75	398,277	641,438	972,765	2.56	6.29
WalkSAT/TABU(2)	400,005	276,011	0.69	332,494	526,125	750,234	2.61	5.77
Novelty(0.35)	134,695	96,288	0.71	109,297	174,384	254,862	2.58	5.91
R-Novelty(0.6)	936,537	885,835	0.95	671,914	1,251,464	2,081,376	3.88	12.57

Table XIV. Problem instance `g125.18`, basic descriptive statistics of RLDs for various algorithms, approx. optimal noise, based on 1,000 tries.

algorithm	mean	stddev	$\frac{\text{stddev}}{\text{mean}}$	median	Q_{75}	Q_{90}	$\frac{Q_{75}}{Q_{25}}$	$\frac{Q_{90}}{Q_{10}}$
GSAT/TABU(20)	7,799	5,168	0.66	6,466	10,087	13,874	2.39	4.52
HWSAT(0.15)	12,442	9,591	0.77	9,566	16,281	24,510	2.89	6.76
WalkSAT(0.15)	44,923	34,731	0.77	34,712	59,574	87,705	2.89	6.75
WalkSAT/TABU(2)	21,215	71,263	3.36	13,856	20,653	29,786	2.30	4.78
Novelty(0.45)	9,304	31,989	3.43	7,125	10,124	14,873	2.17	4.36
R-Novelty(0.2)	27,501	138,038	5.02	6,933	10,220	15,353	2.18	4.32

Table XV. Problem instance `g125.17`, basic descriptive statistics of RLDs for various algorithms, approx. optimal noise, based on 100 tries.

algorithm	mean	stddev	$\frac{\text{stddev}}{\text{mean}}$	median	Q_{75}	Q_{90}	$\frac{Q_{75}}{Q_{25}}$	$\frac{Q_{90}}{Q_{10}}$
GSAT/TABU(20)	$1.21 \cdot 10^6$	$1.26 \cdot 10^6$	1.04	$0.76 \cdot 10^6$	$1.53 \cdot 10^6$	$3.06 \cdot 10^6$	5.03	29.27
WalkSAT(0.15)	$5.74 \cdot 10^6$	$5.52 \cdot 10^6$	0.77	$4.11 \cdot 10^6$	$8.29 \cdot 10^6$	$12.53 \cdot 10^6$	4.19	17.79
WalkSAT/TABU(1)	$2.94 \cdot 10^6$	$14.20 \cdot 10^6$	3.36	$0.64 \cdot 10^6$	$1.20 \cdot 10^6$	$2.01 \cdot 10^6$	2.73	7.87
Novelty(0.25)	$1.87 \cdot 10^6$	$10.10 \cdot 10^6$	5.38	$0.64 \cdot 10^6$	$1.14 \cdot 10^6$	$1.95 \cdot 10^6$	3.89	15.43

the other parity instances, the relative ranking of the algorithms has been found to be identical to the one on this instance.

4.5. Absolute CPU-times

In the comparative analysis above, we measured and reported the run-time in terms of variable flips, which implicitely suggests a uniform cost model for all algorithms. In practice, however, this assumption does not hold. For our experiments, we were using the highly optimised GSAT and WalkSAT implementations by Henry Kautz and Bart Selman, which we extended to implement HWSAT. Comparing the absolute CPU-time per local search step (i.e., variable flip) on a PC System with a single 400 MHz Pentium II CPU and 256 MB RAM running Redhat Linux 5.2, we found that for all benchmark instances the GSAT variants were consistently slower (in terms of variable flips per CPU second) than the WalkSAT variants by a factor of at least 3.

Table XVI. Problem instance `par8-5-c`, basic descriptive statistics of RLDs for various algorithms, approx. optimal noise, based on 1,000 tries.

algorithm	mean	stddev	$\frac{\text{stddev}}{\text{mean}}$	median	Q_{75}	Q_{90}	$\frac{Q_{75}}{Q_{25}}$	$\frac{Q_{90}}{Q_{10}}$
GWSAT(0.6)	27,143	44,044	1.62	18,634	37,812	63,169	4.65	21.45
GSAT/TABU(25)	62,687	80,268	1.28	45,027	88,950	146,843	5.42	25.58
HWSAT(0.45)	18,631	19,066	1.02	12,538	26,263	43,190	5.08	24.33
WalkSAT(0.2)	19,182	17,995	0.77	13,345	25,737	43,693	3.78	14.18
WalkSAT/TABU(7)	12,338	12,654	1.03	8,388	17,017	28,233	4.78	25.01
Novelty(0.80)	4,273	4,287	1.00	2,879	5,916	9,659	4.92	18.65
R-Novelty(0.85)	4,052	4,149	1.01	2,711	5,643	9,546	5.28	20.22

Table XVII. Absolute CPU timing for different algorithms and benchmark instances; all timings were measured on a 400 MHz Pentium II CPU.

instance	algorithm	flips per sec	instance	algorithm	flips per sec
uf100-430	GWSAT	38,400	uf250-1065	GWSAT	31,300
	GSAT/TABU	56,100		GSAT/TABU	60,100
	WalkSAT	248,000		WalkSAT	223,000
	R-Novelty	214,000		R-Novelty	191,000
flat100-239	GWSAT	48,300	flat200-479	GWSAT	42,900
	GSAT/TABU	44,100		GSAT/TABU	33,000
	WalkSAT	389,000		WalkSAT	378,000
	R-Novelty	320,000		R-Novelty	318,000
bw_large.a	GWSAT	21,500	bw_large.c	GWSAT	7,810
	GSAT/TABU	26,100		GSAT/TABU	16,100
	WalkSAT	170,000		WalkSAT	76,500
	R-Novelty	145,000		R-Novelty	74,000

Table XVII shows the typical numbers of flips for a selection of instances from our benchmark suite. Note that for structured problems, the observed differences are usually greater; also, the difference between GSAT and WalkSAT variants typically increases with problem size. Under the assumption that both implementations are optimised to approximately the same degree, this implies that for our benchmark suite the best WalkSAT variants would consistently outperform any GSAT variant considered here. In particular, this applies to the cases where the best GSAT variant (typically GSAT/TABU) was found to be competitive with the best WalkSAT variant (as for the Graph Colouring instances) when counting local search steps. This can be explained by the fact that different from GSAT, WalkSAT uses a two-stage variable selection scheme which means that in each search step, only the consequences of flipping a typically small number of variables occuring in one particular unsatisfied have to be considered.

It is also worth noting that for the Random-3-SAT and Graph Colouring instances, the number of flips per CPU second is almost unaffected by increasing the problem size. The reason for this is the fact that for these formulae, the connectivity of the constraint graph (in which variables correspond to nodes and edges connect variables which occur in a same clause) as well as the length (number of literals) of the clauses are independent of the problem size. In the most efficient implementations, these two factors dominate the CPU time per variable flip.

In summary, our comparative analysis of different SLS algorithms' performance across various problem domains shows that there is no single best algorithm for all domains. This is an interesting and new result because previously, a comprehensive study of the most recent and best performing GSAT and WalkSAT variants was not available. In particular, while the more limited results in [51] suggested that R-Novelty might be the overall best performing SLS algorithm for SAT, our results show clearly that this is not the case. We observed a tendency indicating that Novelty and R-Novelty are performing best for random, unstructured problems, but WalkSAT/TABU and GSAT/TABU are competive or better (when run-time is measured in terms of variable flips) on some of the relatively hard, large, structured problem instances like the large Blocks World Planning and Graph Colouring instances. However, all of these algorithms potentially suffer from stagnation behaviour which, in some cases, severely compromises their performance. Additionally, given the currently best known implementations for these algorithms, GSAT/TABU is never competitive with the best-performing WalkSAT variants in terms of absolute CPU time.

5. Robustness and Scaling

Up to this point, our analysis was mainly focused on peak performance; like most other studies in this field we analysed and reported results for optimal parameter settings (such as the cutoff time *maxSteps* or the noise parameters *wp*, *p*, or *tl*). But in practice, optimal parameter settings are often not known a priori, and as we have seen in the last section, for the same algorithm they may differ considerably between problem instances or domains. Therefore, robustness of an SLS algorithm *w.r.t.* suboptimal parameter settings is an important issue. At least of equal importance are the scaling aspects of SLS behaviour. These comprise scaling *w.r.t.* problem size, scaling *w.r.t.* constrainedness, and scaling *w.r.t.* the mean hardness of instances within test-sets sampled from problem distributions.

Of these, scaling with problem size is at least implicitly covered to some degree in many experimental studies in the sense that problem instances or test-sets for different problem sizes are used; but only a few studies, such as [19], investigate and model the scaling behaviour of SLS algorithms for SAT in more detail. The influence of constrainedness on SLS performance has been investigated in great detail in a number of studies, especially in the context of phase-transition phenomena (e.g., [19, 52]). Finally, as we will show in this section, the performance of the different SLS algorithms studied here is typically tightly correlated within test-sets, i.e., the same instances tend to be relatively hard for all algorithms. This suggests that the relative hardness of problem instances within the same test-set of, e.g., Random-3-SAT instances, is an intrinsic feature of the problem instance. Consequently, the distribution of the mean performance of an SLS algorithm over such a test-set can be viewed as a kind of scaling *w.r.t.* this intrinsic hardness.

Scaling dependencies and robustness are related in that the former can be interpreted as robustness of an algorithm's performance *w.r.t.* problem instance or domain specific properties. In this section we study the robustness and the scaling behaviour of SLS algorithms *w.r.t.* problem size and instance hardness, building on the methodology used in the previous section.

5.1. Robustness w.r.t. *the cutoff parameter*

As almost all SLS algorithms for SAT, and in particular all algorithms considered here, use a restart mechanism and therefore need the cutoff parameter *maxSteps* to be specified, robustness *w.r.t.* to this parameter is generally an important issue. Obviously, for a given algorithm and problem instance, the robustness *w.r.t.* the cutoff parameter is tightly related to the run-time distribution. Specifically, if the algorithm (without random restart) is essentially incomplete and stagnation occurs, the performance critically relies on reasonably small settings for the cutoff parameter. But good *maxSteps* settings are extremely difficult to find *a priori* and currently, to our best knowledge, there exist no theoretical results on how to effectively determine good settings. The only empirical results we are aware of, are for GSAT when applied to hard Random-3-SAT problem distributions [22]; but these results are limited to Random-3-SAT and rely on properties of the respective problem distributions rather than the individual instances. On the other hand, while using random restart with inappropriately chosen *maxSteps* settings theoretically eliminates essential incompleteness, in practice it leads to extremely poor performance. Thus, for obtaining a reasonable robustness *w.r.t.* the *maxSteps* parameter setting, an SLS algorithm should have the PAC property.

In [35, 34], the following results regarding the essential incompleteness or the PAC property of the algorithms considered here are established:

- plain GSAT (= GWSAT with *wp=0*) is essentially incomplete.
- GWSAT is PAC for arbitrary $wp > 0$;
- WalkSAT/TABU is essentially incomplete for arbitrary tl;
- Novelty is essentially incomplete for arbitrary p;
- R-Novelty is essentially incomplete for arbitrary p;

Furthermore, it is easy to see the following:

- HSAT is essentially incomplete;
- HWSAT is PAC for arbitrary $wp > 0$.

Unfortunately, it has not been proven whether or not WalkSAT is PAC; the same holds for GSAT/TABU. However, our experimental analysis suggests that WalkSAT might be PAC for $p > 0$, as in thousands of experiments, we never observer any indication of stagnation behaviour. Furthermore, our results indicate that GSAT/TABU is probably essentially incomplete at least for sufficiently low tabu tenure. It should be noted that the theoretical results mentioned above do not necessarily imply that the performance of the algorithms are affected in practice. In particular, the two following questions have to be answered:

1. For PAC algorithms, is the convergence of the success probability fast enough to be observable when applying these algorithms to hard problem instances?
2. For essentially incomplete algorithms, is the characteristic stagnation behaviour observable for any of the common benchmarks for SAT algorithms?

Considering the results reported in Section 4, both questions can be answered positively: PAC behaviour as well as essential incompleteness is reflected in the presence or absence of stagnation behaviour observed in the RTDs of the algorithms under considerations when applied to our benchmark problems.

Given this situation and the fact that with Novelty and R-Novelty, two of the overall best performing algorithms are affected by the adverse effects of essential incompleteness, it seems to be very desirable to modify these algorithms in such a way that their overall superior performance is retained while their essential incompleteness is removed in a way which makes them significantly more robust *w.r.t.* the *maxSteps* parameter setting.

Fortunately, as demonstrated in [35, 34], this can be done in a rather simple and uniform way by extending them with random walk as used in GWSAT in such a way that for each local search step, with a fixed probability a random walk step is performed. Note that for any algorithm using this mechanism, arbitrarily long sequences of random walk steps can occur, which directly implies the PAC property [35, 34]. Furthermore, the amount of perturbation introduced by a random walk sequence probabilistically depends on the length of the sequence such that small perturbations are much more likely to occur than large ones which, intuitively, should make the algorithms more robust than techniques like the deterministic loop-breaker in R-Novelty (see Section 2.2.4). Based on these considerations, we extended Novelty and R-Novelty with random walk such that in each search step, with probability *wp*, the variable to be flipped is randomly picked from the selected clause, while in the remaining cases, the variable is selected according to the heuristic for Novelty or R-Novelty, respectively. Obviously, WalkSAT/TABU can be analogously extended. For R-Novelty, we furthermore omit the deterministic loop breaking strategy which randomly flips a variable from the selected clause every 100 steps. The two algorithms thus obtained, Novelty$^+$ and R-Novelty$^+$, are obviously PAC as argued above. Furthermore, testing their performance against Novelty and R-Novelty on instances from our benchmark set shows that the stagnation behaviour observed for Novelty and R-Novelty is effectively eliminated even when using a fixed setting of 0.01 for the newly introduced parameter *wp*. Consequently, the new variants show a superior performance when applied to instances in which the original algorithms suffered from the effects of their essential incompleteness as can be seen from Tables XVIII and XIX.

Table XVIII. Performance comparison for Novelty and R-Novelty (approx. optimal noise) *vs.* Novelty$^+$ and R-Novelty$^+$ for Random-3-SAT and Graph Colouring test-sets. The reported basic descriptive statistics refer to the hardness distributions (mean number of steps / solution) over the test-sets.

test-set	algorithm	mean	stddev	$\frac{\text{stddev}}{\text{mean}}$	median	q_{25}	q_{75}	q_{10}	q_{90}
uf100-430	Novelty(0.6)	28,257	191,668	6.78	851	479	1,845	302	4,390
	Novelty+(0.6)	1,570	2,802	1.78	801	467	1,663	288	3,049
flat50-115	R-Novelty(0.6)	7,109	97,543	13.72	739	490	1,282	356	2,142
	R-Novelty+(0.6)	1,084	1,053	0.97	747	486	1,245	358	2,167

Table XIX. Performance comparison for Novelty and R-Novelty (approx. optimal noise) *vs.* Novelty$^+$ and R-Novelty$^+$ for Blocks World Planning and large Graph Colouring instances; $\widehat{p_s}^*$ indicates the asymptotic maximal success probability, $\widehat{E_s}$ denotes the expected number of steps for finding a solution (using random restart); the reported basic descriptive statistics refer to the corresponding conditional RLDs.

instance	algorithm	$\widehat{p_s}^*$	ms	$\widehat{E_s}$	mean_c	stddev_c	median_c
bw_large.c	R-Novelty(0.3)	0.028	10^8	$3.47 \cdot 10^9$	169,810	157,752	32,334
	R-Novelty+(0.3)	1.0	10^8	$8.09 \cdot 10^6$	8,086,468	8,414,928	5,292,830
g125.18	R-Novelty(0.2)	0.981	10^7	27,501	8133	5107	6,866
	R-Novelty+(0.2)	1.0	10^7	10,012	10,012	27,325	7,115
g250.29	R-Novelty(0.8)	0.904	$2.5 \cdot 10^8$	1,376,845	359,146	454,448	263,995
	R-Novelty+(0.8)	1.0	$2.5 \cdot 10^8$	501,464	501,464	1,313,066	280,333

Note, that in cases where the original algorithm did not show stagnation behaviour, the performance is not negatively affected by adding random walk, a fact which we verified in all the experiments we have run. When evaluating the performance of Novelty$^+$ and R-Novelty$^+$, we generally used a fixed setting of $wp = 0.01$. By optimising this additional parameter, further improvements in performance and robustness can be achieved.

While, as we have seen, the PAC property is of considerable theoretical interest and also affects the robustness of SLS algorithms in practice, a more detailed analysis has to focus on the overall shape of the RTDs, which is the factor which ultimately and uniquely determines the robustness of an algorithm *w.r.t.* the cutoff parameter. As pointed out in [36], the maximal robustness *w.r.t.* the cutoff parameter is encountered for exponential run-time distributions. To see this, consider an exponential RTD characterised by the cumulative distribution function $ed[m](x) = 1 - 2^{-x/m}$. Obviously, the probability for finding a solution within the first k steps is $ed[m](k) = 1 - 2^{-k/m}$. Now, if already j search steps have been done without success, using complementary probabilities and Bayes' Rule gives the probability for finding a solution within the next k steps as:

$$1 - \frac{1 - ed[m](j+k)}{1 - ed[m](j)} = 1 - \frac{2^{j+k}}{2^j} = ed[m](k)$$

Thus, an SLS algorithm characterised by an exponential RTD is memoryless in the sense that the probability of finding a solution within a fixed number of local search steps does not depend on the number of search steps done in the past. Consequently, as also argued in [36, 35, 39], in case of an exponential RTD, the probability to find a solution within a given time would not depend on the setting of the *maxSteps* parameter and thus, the number of random restarts.

It can be shown that for approximately optimal noise parameter settings, all GSAT and WalkSAT variants considered here show exponential RTDs when applied to hard problem instances [35, 36, 37, 39]. Here, "hard instance" refers to a problem instance which is relatively hard compared to instances of comparable size and structure, such as the 25% fraction of a Random-3-SAT test-set for which the mean of the RLD for a given algorithm is highest. Note that the claim is of such a nature that it can easily be tested, especially for the test-sets sampled from random instance distributions used in this study.

We systematically tested all algorithms considered here for the problem sets `uf100-430`, `flat100-239`, as well as for the individual planning and DIMACS instances. This analysis was based on the same RLDs used in Section 4. For each individual instance and algorithm, the RLD was approximated[3] using the cumulative form of an exponential distribution $ed[m](x) = 1 - 2^{-x/m}$ where m is the median of the distribution and x the number of steps required to find a solution.[4] For testing the goodness of this approximation we use a standard χ^2-test [57]. Basically, for a given empirical RLD this is done by estimating the parameter m and comparing the deviations to the predicted distribution $ed[m]$. The result of this comparison is the χ^2 value, where χ^2 values below a critical threshold indicate a close correspondence between empirical and predicted distribution. For the results reported here, we used the acceptance thresholds corresponding to a maximal probability of 0.05 or 0.01 of false negatives for the test (these values are commonly used in the statistical literature).

Figure 11 shows a scatter plot of the correlation between the median search cost per solution and the χ^2 values for WalkSAT applied to test-set `uf100-430`. Obviously, there

[3] All approximations were done using C. Gramme's "Gnufit" implementation of the Marquart-Levenberg algorithm.

[4] In the statistical literature, the exponential distribution $Exp(\lambda)$ is usually defined by $P(X \leq x) = 1 - e^{-\lambda x}$, which is equivalent to our representation $ed[m]$ using $m = \ln 2/\lambda$. A similar argument applies to the Weibull distribution mentioned later.

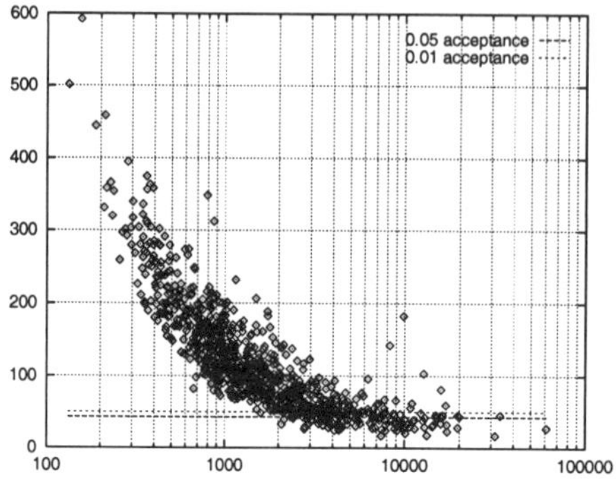

Figure 11. Correlation between hardness of problems (horizontal) and χ^2 values (vertical) from testing the RLDs of individual instances versus a best-fit exponential distribution for test-set `uf100-430`. The horizontal lines indicate the acceptance thresholds for the 0.01 and 0.05 acceptance level.

Table XX. Fraction of instances from the hardest 25% of the `uf100-430` Random-3-SAT test-set passing the χ^2 test for different algorithms with approximately optimal noise settings; the last column indicates the number of instances for which essentially incomplete behaviour was observed, these were removed from the test-set.

algorithm	acceptance level α	fraction passed	number removed
WalkSAT(0.55)	0.01	57.6%	0
WalkSAT/TABU(3)	0.01	49.6%	1
Novelty(0.7)	0.01	57.2%	35
R-Novelty(0.7)	0.01	49.6%	0

is a strong negative correlation, indicating that, indeed, for harder problem instances, WalkSAT's behaviour can be more and more accurately characterised by exponential distributions. As can be seen from the plot, for high median search cost, almost all instances pass the χ^2 test. Table XX shows the overall percentage of the instances from the hardest quarter of the test-set which passed the test for the different acceptance levels when performing this analysis for different WalkSAT variants. As indicated in Table XXI, analogous results were obtained for the `flat100-239` Graph Colouring test-set; the results for the GSAT variants (not reported here) are very similar. When

Table XXI. Fraction of instances from the hardest 25% of the `flat100-239` Graph Colouring test-set passing the χ^2 test for different algorithms with approximately optimal noise settings; the last column indicates the number of instances for which essentially incomplete behaviour was observed, these were removed from the test-set.

algorithm	acceptance level α	fraction passed	number removed
WalkSAT(0.5)	0.01	52%	0
WalkSAT/TABU(3)	0.01	64%	1
Novelty(0.6)	0.01	84%	1
R-Novelty(0.6)	0.01	100%	1

Table XXII. RLD approximations using exponential distributions *ed*[*m*] for Novelty (approximately optimal noise) applied to Blocks World Planning instances and an instance for learning the parity function; for the Graph Colouring instances we applied Novelty+ since Novelty shows stagnation behaviour on these instances. The last column indicates whether the approximation passed the χ^2 test.

instance	median #steps m	χ^2 for ed[m]	ν	passed (α)
bw_large.a	6,839	60.37	29	no
bw_large.b	119,680	11.40	16	yes (0.05)
bw_large.c	$4.27 \cdot 10^6$	8.71	16	yes (0.05)
bw_large.d	$8.51 \cdot 10^6$	10.14	10	yes (0.05)
par8-5-c	4,273	29.83	29	yes (0.05)
g125.18	8,558	579.24	29	no
g125.17	1,151,392	29.15	16	yes (0.01)

applying the same analysis for different problem sizes, it can furthermore be noted that a relatively higher number of instances pass the test, i.e., the deviations of the RLDs from ideal exponential distributions apparently become less prominent for larger problems (for details see [35]).

For the single instances from various SAT-encoded problems we performed the same analysis. The results are consistent with those for the Random-3-SAT and Graph Colouring test-sets: For the harder instances, the RLDs are well approximated by exponential distributions (see Table XXII). The only exception is instance `g125.18` which corresponds to finding a suboptimal colouring of a 125 nodes graph. For this relatively easy instance (considering its size) the test is clearly rejected. Yet, if for the same graph the conjectured optimal solution should be found (corresponding to instance `g125.17`) the χ^2 value is much smaller and, in fact, the test for an exponential distribution is passed at the 0.01 level.

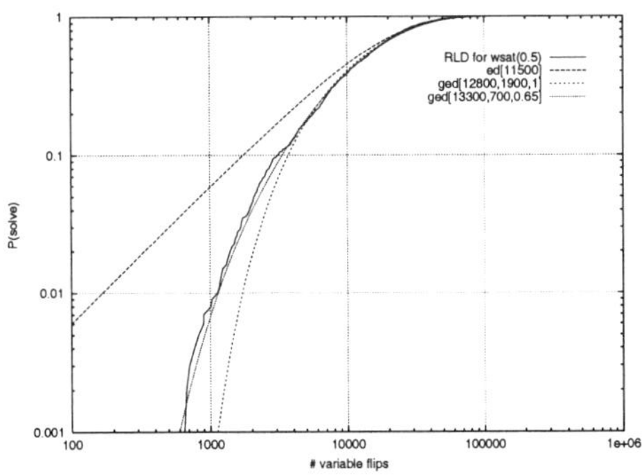

Figure 12. RLD for WalkSAT (approx. optimal noise) applied to Blocks World instance `bw_large.a` and three functional approximations.

Interestingly, exponential distributions are characteristic for the simplest randomised search technique: uniform random picking from a set of solution candidates. Thus, observing this type of behaviour for more sophisticated and much more efficient algorithms (such as the SLS algorithms studied here) suggests that their behaviour might be interpreted as random sampling from a much smaller space. Intuitively, this hypothetical "virtual searchspace" should be linked to features of the actual search space, such as the number, size, and topology of local optima. Unfortunately, the existing results on the topology of search spaces for SLS algorithms cannot be exploited to establish such a link [22, 64, 15, 35, 34]. While further investigating of this issue is beyond the scope of this paper, we are confident that it can be adequately addressed by combining the methodology for characterising SLS performance applied in this study with established methodology for analysing search space topology.

Note that for relatively easy instances the exponential approximations of the RLDs are rejected by the χ^2 test. Further analysis shows that in these cases typically the tail of the RLDs is still well approximated by an exponential distribution $ed[m]$, while for shorter run-times, the success probability is systematically lower than given by $ed[m]$. Figure 12 illustrates this situation for a typical example. Intuitively, this can be explained by the fact that SLS algorithms typically go through an initial search phase (cf. [22]), during which the probability of finding a solution is rather low. For hard instances, the successful runs are long enough that the impact of this initial search phase is only minimal, whereas for easy instances, it is clearly observable from the RLD.

Based on RLD data, the effect of this initial local search phase can be modeled using a slightly generalised family of distributions. Such a distribution has been introduced in [35]; it is based on the family of Weibull distributions[5] $wd[m,\beta](x) = 1 - 2^{-(x/m)^\beta}$, a well-known generalisation of the exponential distribution. The new model is defined by the following cumulative distribution function:

$$ged[m,\gamma,\delta](x) = wd[m, 1 + (\gamma/x)^\delta](x) = 1 - 2^{-(x/m)^{1+(\gamma/x)^\delta}}\quad .$$

Although the full defining term looks quite complicated, the definition simply reflects the idea of a Weibull distribution with a dynamically changing β parameter. More precisely, the new distribution is obtained from a Weibull distribution by introducing a hyperbolically decaying β parameter. Like for the exponential and Weibull distributions, m is the median of the distribution. The two remaining parameters intuitively correspond to the length of the initial search phase (γ) and to its impact on the overall behaviour (δ). High γ values indicate a long initial search phase, while high δ values are used to model a strong influence of the initial search phase.

Note that the exponential distribution is a special case of this new class of distributions, since $ed[m] = ged[m,0,\delta]$, while generally, Weibull distributions cannot be represented within this family. As can be easily seen from the definition, $ged[m,\gamma,\delta](x)$ asymptotically approaches an exponential distribution $ed[m](x)$ for large x. For decreasing x, however, the relative difference between $ged[m,\gamma,\delta](x)$ and $ed[m](x)$ increases monotonically, which is qualitatively exactly what we observed for the empirical RLDs of SLS algorithms (see also Figure 12).

Using this model, the RLDs measured for the SLS algorithms considered here can be modeled in great detail. Performing an analogous analysis as above, only now using *ged* approximations instead of *ed* approximations, the fraction of instances from test-sets like `uf100-430` or `flat100-239` which pass the χ^2 test increases to ca. 80% (for details, see [35]). At the same time, the correlation between instance hardness and goodness-of-fit cannot be observed any longer — which indicates that indeed the initial search phase is correctly modeled. In the relatively few remaining cases, where even these approximations are not sufficient, we generally found multi-modal RLDs which can be well approximated by weighted linear combinations of *ged*-type distributions.

[5] Weibull distributions are used in reliability theory to model failure rates in systems which are subject to aging phenomena [6].

Table XXIII. *ed*[*m*] approximations of RLDs for WalkSAT applied to Blocks World Planning instance `bw_large.a`, using optimal and larger-than-optimal noise parameter settings.

algorithm	median of RLD	m	χ^2 for ed[m]	passed (α)
WalkSAT(0.5)	13,505	13,094	98.41	no
WalkSAT(0.6)	15,339	16,605	76.17	no
WalkSAT(0.7)	27,488	27,485	42.13	yes (0.5)
WalkSAT(0.8)	72,571	74,289	20.78	yes (0.5)

Intuitively, these instances seem to contain "traps", i.e., singular, highly attractive regions of the search space which are hard to escape from. Clearly, further investigation is required for ultimately explaining this phenomenon, and the RLD-based approach, combined with advanced methods for search space analysis as proposed in [15, 35, 64] provides a good basis for such an endeavour.

5.2. *Robustness* w.r.t. *the noise parameter*

The noise parameter is more specific to the given algorithm than the cutoff parameter; e.g., the *wp* parameter used for the algorithms utilising random walk steps (such as GWSAT or HWSAT) is conceptually quite different from the tabu tenure parameter controlling the behaviour of SLS algorithms incorporating tabu search. Nevertheless, as emphasised in [51], the effect of high noise settings (high *wp*, *p*, *tl* parameter values) is generally similar: the algorithm's ability to escape from local minima increases. On the other hand it might be expected that this comes at a price, as high noise settings also decrease the probability for an algorithm to rapidly descend into local minima which are solutions.

Here, we investigate the robustness of SLS algorithms *w.r.t.* the setting of the noise parameter. It should be noted that according to a result by Selman, Kautz, and McAllester [51], the optimal noise setting seems to be closely related to a simple statistical property of the search trajectory. However, it is not clear whether this result is accurate enough to provide a basis for automatically and dynamically determining the approximately optimal noise parameter setting. To our best knowledge, as of this writing there exists no successful GSAT or WalkSAT variant with self-adjusting noise. Therefore, evaluating the sensitivity of the SLS algorithms considered here *w.r.t.* non-optimal noise settings seems to be a reasonable endeavour.

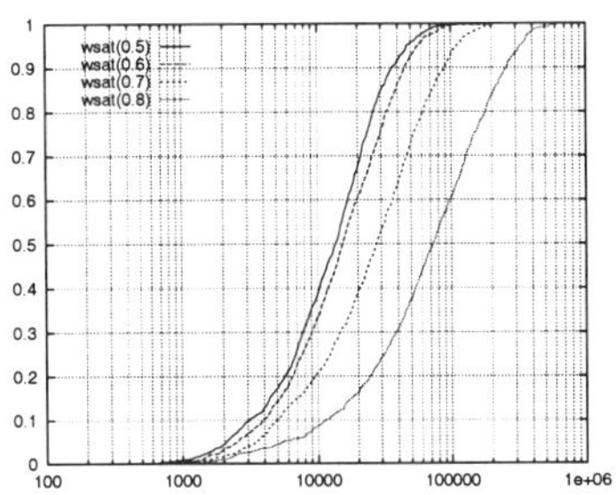

Figure 13. RLDs for WalkSAT applied to Blocks World Planning instance `bw_large.a`, using different noise parameter settings (0.5 is approximately optimal).

Table XXIV. Fraction of instances from the hardest 25% of the `flat50-115` Graph Colouring test-set passing the χ^2 test for Novelty with optimal and larger-than-optimal noise settings; instances, for which essentially incomplete behaviour was observed, were removed from the test-set.

algorithm	median hardness	acceptance level α	fraction passed
R-Novelty(0.6)	739	0.01	19.0%
R-Novelty(0.7)	832	0.01	23.8%
R-Novelty(0.8)	1043	0.01	40.7%

Based on our results on the functional characterisation of RLDs, it is an interesting question how these are affected by non-optimal noise settings. To investigate this question, we measured and analysed RLDs for the different algorithms when applied to the instances from our benchmark library. Here, we summarise the corresponding results and give a few representative examples. Generally, we find that if the noise setting is increased above the optimal value, the RLDs can still be well approximated using exponential (or, when the initial search phase is modeled, *ged*) distributions. Thus, for larger-than-optimal noise settings, SLS performance is very robust *w.r.t.* the cutoff parameter. At the same time the run-times compared to optimal noise are uniformly higher for all success probabilities. This is reflected in larger values of the m parameter when fitting the exponential distributions and can also be easily seen in the semi-log plots of the corresponding RLDs, where for larger-than-optimal noise, the RLD curves have the same shape while being shifted to the right (see Figure 13 for a typical example). Furthermore, when increasing the noise, the effects of the initial search phase become less prominent — consequently, the approximations using exponential distributions are usually better for higher noise (see Table XXIII). The same effects can be observed when using other GSAT or WalkSAT variants or different benchmark instances.

As a second example, we report the results of analysing the effects of increasing the noise parameter for R-Novelty, applied to the Graph Colouring test-set `flat50-115`. Table XXIV shows the fraction of instances from this test-set, for which a best-fit *ed* approximation passed the χ^2 test. As can be seen from this data, the fraction of the hardest 25% of the test-set which passed the test increases for larger-than-optimal noise, as the effects of the initial search phase become less prominent. At the same time the median hardness (mean number of steps per solution) increases considerably. Analogous results were obtained for different SLS algorithms and other problem domains from our benchmark suite.

While for larger-than-optimal noise, the SLS performance decreases but the algorithms still show approximately exponential RTDs, for lower-than-optimal noise parameter settings we find a completely different situation: For all algorithms the performance decreases non-uniformly for different solution probabilities and some of them show stagnation behaviour. We demonstrate this here by giving a small number of examples, which are nevertheless typical for our overall observations. As shown in Figure 14, GSAT and WalkSAT show a similar behaviour for smaller-than-optimal noise: While for short runs, the performance even improves slightly, for longer runs and the corresponding higher success probabilities, the performance deteriorates considerably. Consequently, the RLDs are less steep than exponential distributions and suffer from an increasingly long and heavy tail. Both GSAT/TABU and R-Novelty show a similar, but additionally essentially incomplete behaviour; as can be seen from Figure 15, the maximal success

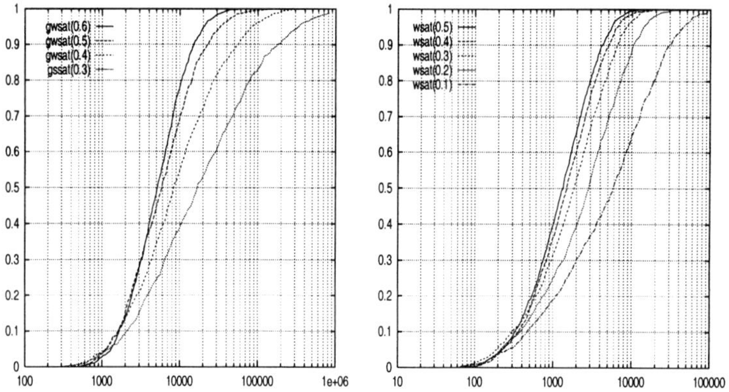

Figure 14. Left: RLDs for GWSAT applied to easy instance from Graph Colouring test-set `flat100-239`, using different noise parameter settings (0.6 is approx. optimal); *right:* same for WalkSAT applied to medium instance from Random-3-SAT test-set `uf100-430` (approx. optimal noise = 0.5).

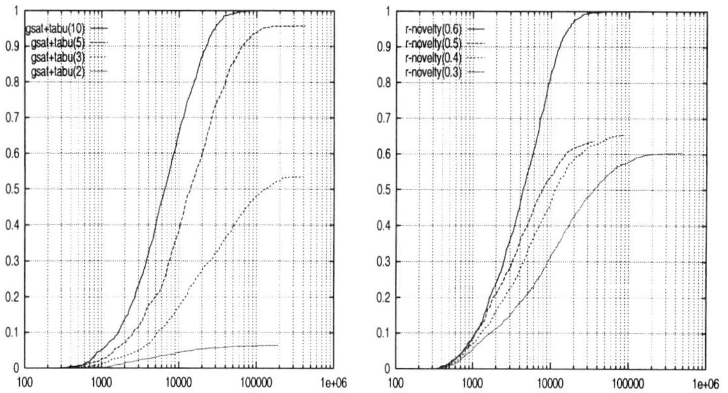

Figure 15. Left: RLDs for GSAT/TABU applied to medium instance from Graph Colouring test-set `flat100-239`, using different noise parameter settings (10 is approx. optimal); *right:* same for R-Novelty applied to Blocks World Planning instance `bw_large.a` (approx. optimal noise = 0.6).

probabilities for both algorithms are decreasing with the noise parameter. For Novelty, no increasingly essential incomplete behaviour is observed, but the performance also decays non-uniformly as for GSAT and WalkSAT. In comparison, WalkSAT/TABU seems to be relatively mildly affected; the main reason for this might be that typically, both the clause length and the optimal tabu-list-length are rather small.

Summarising these results, typically the detrimental effects of non-optimal noise parameter settings are much worse for lower-than-optimal noise settings than for larger-than-optimal noise. This is particularly the case for the higher percentiles of the corresponding RLDs; additionally, for essentially incomplete SLS algorithms, stagnation behaviour occurs more frequently with decreasing noise settings. However, the behaviour for very short runs is usually not affected by lower-than-optimal noise and sometimes, even performance improvements can be observed for the early phases of local search. This is consistent with the intuition that greedier local search behaviour should pay off during the initial search phase, where gradient descent dominates the search.

5.3. *Scaling with instance hardness*

After discussing robustness *w.r.t.* the parameter settings of the algorithms, we now turn towards the influence of problem-specific properties on SLS performance. In Section 4, when comparing the distributions of mean local search cost over the instances of our Random-3-SAT and Graph Colouring test-sets we observed that these hardness distributions are mostly similarly shaped. This suggests that the hardness of instances for different algorithms might be tightly correlated. To test this hypothesis, we performed a pairwise hardness correlation analysis of the different algorithms across test-sets `uf100-430` and `flat50-235`. Like before, as a measure for hardness we chose the expected number of steps required for finding a solution, based on 100 tries with a high cutoff value of 10^7 steps per try. In our analysis, we determined this hardness measure for each instance from the problem set and analysed the correlation between the hardness for different algorithms. To reduce the overall amount of computation, we chose GWSAT as a reference algorithm, i.e., for each other algorithm we analysed the correlation between its performance and GWSAT's on an instance per instance basis. The results of this analysis confirm the hypothesis that there is a tight correlation between the performance of any two algorithms over the test-sets, i.e., instances which are hard for one SLS algorithm tend to be hard for all the others. Figure 16 shows the correlation data for two pairs of algorithms applied to `uf100-430` as log-log scatter plots. These plots are typical for the correlation relations we observed.

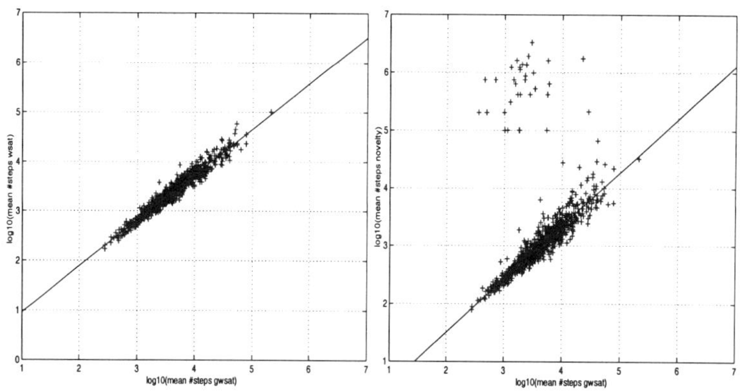

Figure 16. Left: Correlation between average local search cost for GWSAT (horizontal) and WalkSAT(vertical) for test-set `uf100-430`, using approx. optimal noise. *Right:* Same for GWSAT and Novelty. The outliers indicate instances on which Novelty showed stagnation behaviour.

To quantitatively characterise the strong correlations suggested by the scatter plots, we performed a correlation and least-mean-squares (*lms*) linear regression analysis of the logarithm of the hardness (mean search cost per solution); the regression lines shown in the log-log plots (Figures 16) correspond to power functions of the type $y = x^a \cdot exp(b)$. The results of this analysis are reported in Tables XXV and XXVI. This data confirms that the correlation between the hardness for different algorithms is very strong; this holds also for algorithms which show stagnation behaviour for some instances, after these outliers have been removed from the test-set. This indicates that the hardness for any of these algorithms (neglecting the outliers) is an intrinsic property of the instances. As a possible explanation for this observation we assume that the same structural features render a particular instance hard for all SLS algorithms. From the regression data we see that the a parameter is relatively close to one for all algorithms; this means that there is only minor variation in the performance differences between

Table XXV. Test-set `uf100-430`, pairwise hardness correlation for various algorithms with approx. optimal noise, based on 100 tries / instance; r is the correlation coefficient, a and b are the parameters of the *lms* regression analysis, and o the number of outliers which have been eliminated before the analysis (see text).

algorithms	r	a	b	o
GWSAT *vs.* GSAT/TABU	0.9171	1.1456	-0.8007	0
GWSAT *vs.* WalkSAT	0.9725	0.9229	0.0471	0
GWSAT *vs.* WalkSAT/TABU	0.9464	0.9962	-0.4814	0
GWSAT *vs.* Novelty	0.9431	0.9211	-0.3331	33
GWSAT *vs.* R-Novelty	0.9492	0.9044	-0.3628	0

Table XXVI. Test-set `flat50-115`, pairwise hardness correlation for various algorithms with approx. optimal noise, based on 100 tries / instance; r is the correlation coefficient, a and b are the parameters of the *lms* regression analysis, and o the number of outliers which have been eliminated before the analysis (see text).

algorithms	r	a	b	o
GWSAT *vs.* GSAT/TABU	0.9021	0.7673	0.0715	0
GWSAT *vs.* WalkSAT	0.9527	0.7738	0.6353	0
GWSAT *vs.* WalkSAT/TABU	0.8417	0.8885	-0.1149	27
GWSAT *vs.* Novelty	0.8398	0.8212	-0.1217	9
GWSAT *vs.* R-Novelty	0.8247	0.7848	-0.0205	6

the individual algorithms as the intrinsic hardness varies. Nevertheless, some systematic differences can be observed. In particular, for both test-sets, the tabu-variants show the lowest b value, indicating a superior performance on easy instances. However, except for GSAT/TABU on the Graph Colouring test-set,[6] they scale worse than the other variants as the intrinsic hardness increases. Also, we observe a consistent scaling advantage of R-Novelty over Novelty (comparing the a values), of Novelty over WalkSAT, and of WalkSAT over GWSAT.

Two more observations are worth noting. First, our data indicates that within a test-set, the hardness correlation gets noisier for harder problems. This holds especially for the more effective variants of WalkSAT, like WalkSAT/TABU or R-Novelty and suggests that for relatively hard instances, SLS procedures differ more in their effectiveness. Furthermore, the occurrence of stagnation behaviour, as can be seen from Figure 16, is not related to the intrinsic hardness of an instance, as outliers occur for instances which are relatively easy for another algorithm as well as for intrinsically hard instances.

5.4. Scaling with problem size

In a final analysis, we investigated the scaling of local search cost with problem size. First, we determined the hardness distributions for WalkSAT with approximately optimal noise parameter settings on the Random-3-SAT test-sets for $n = 50, 75, 100, ..., 250$

[6] Recall that for the instances considered here, GSAT/TABU is the best performing algorithm when counting variable flips; apparently it can exploit the specific structure induced by encoding Graph Colouring instances into SAT.

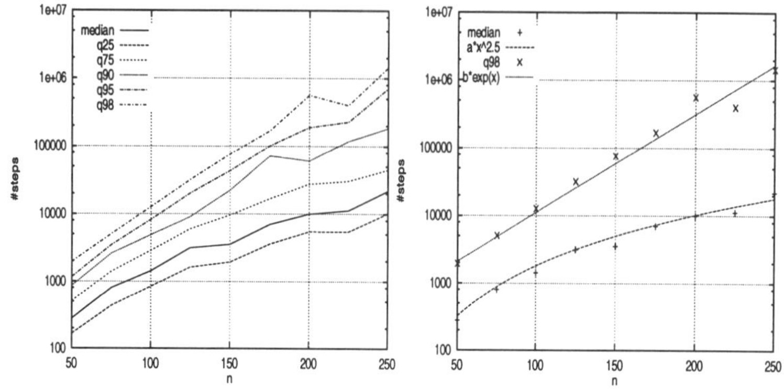

Figure 17. Left: Scaling of instance hardness with problem size for WalkSAT, approx. optimal noise, applied to Random-3-SAT test-sets. *Right:* Functional approximations of median and 0.98 percentile; the median seems to grow polynomially with n while the 0.98 percentile clearly shows exponential growth.

as described in Section 4. The scaling behaviour of the median and some higher percentiles thus determined is shown in Figure 17. The data clearly suggests, that the highest percentiles grow exponentially with the problem size; as shown on the left side of Figure 17, the 0.98 percentile can be well approximated with the exponential function $y = 400 \cdot exp(n/30)$. The lower percentiles, including the median, however, appear to be growing polynomially in n, the best approximation for the median was found as $y = 89.44 \cdot (n/30)^{2.5}$. Note however, that in both cases for small n, the actual value of the percentiles falls slightly off the approximations. This effect might explain why [19] observed a polynomial scaling behaviour of the 0.9 percentile in a similar analysis for GSAT when using smaller problems (up to $n = 100$); another potential explanation for the discrepancy between our result might be given by differences in the empirical methodology. However, considering the tight performance correlation established in Section 5.3, we assume that the difference in the algorithms being used is not responsible for the different results.

The qualitative difference in the scaling of the lower and higher percentiles is surprising and leaves at least two different interpretations. Either, there is a sharp transition between the polynomial and exponential behaviour as we study increasingly high percentiles of the hardness distributions. Or, all percentiles are exponential, but the lower ones show exponential behaviour only for much higher n. Either way, the higher percentiles grow much faster than the lower ones and, as a consequence, the variation of hardness within the test-sets (as measured by the percentile ratios Q_x/Q_{1-x}), increases strictly monotonically with problem size. An intuitive explanation of this phenomenon is the assumption that with growing problem size, as more variables and clauses are available, more complex "traps" (local minima or plateau regions which are hard to escape from) for SLS-based algorithms can occur in the search spaces of the randomly generated instances.

Performing the same analysis using R-Novelty$^+$, the best-performing algorithm for Random-3-SAT according to our earlier results, yields exactly analogous results: The median curve can be well approximated by $y = 26.83 \cdot (n/30)^{2.5}$, while the 0.98 percentile's scaling is ca. $y = 200 \cdot exp(n/30)$. Comparing these results with the one for WalkSAT given above, we note that the difference in the percentiles for the two algorithms is independent of n (ca. 3.5 for the median, and ca. 4 for the 0.98 percentile).

In other words, the performance difference between R-Novelty$^+$ and WalkSAT does not depend on the problem size, which is mildly disappointing as it means that for this problem class, R-Novelty$^+$ improves only by a small constant factor over WalkSAT.

Next, we applied an exactly analogous analysis for the Graph Colouring test-sets with $k = 50, ..., 200$ vertices in the original graph (this corresponds to 150–600 propositional variables in the SAT-encoded instances). Here, surprisingly, we obtain a different result: For WalkSAT (with approximately optimal noise for each n), the scaling of all the percentiles can be approximated by $y = a \cdot exp(k/b)$ with $(a, b) = (800, 33)$ for the median and $(800, 23)$ for the 0.98 percentile. When using Novelty$^+$ instead of WalkSAT, we get analogous results with $(a, b) = (220, 30)$ for the median and $(220, 20)$ for the 0.98 percentile. In general, for this problem class we have no evidence for a polynomial scaling of any percentile. At the same time, the phenomenon that for small k the percentile curves fall off the approximations is less obvious here. As a third difference, the variation in instance hardness is generally much smaller within our Graph Colouring test-sets than within the Random-3-SAT test-sets. As an example, consider the $Q_{0.95}/Q_{0.05}$ percentile ratio which is ca. 47 for test-set `uf150-645` and only ca. 5.1 for test-set `flat50-115` (all instances have 150 propositional variables). Hence, there seems to be a qualitative difference in the scaling behaviour for WalkSAT between Random-3-SAT and the Graph Colouring problem distribution considered here. One reason for this might be the fact that compared to Random-3-SAT, the Graph Colouring instances are structurally much more restricted because of the effects of the SAT-encoding used for transforming the original problems into CNF formulae. Also the fact that all instances are generated to be exactly 3-colourable might keep the variation of instance hardness within the test-sets somewhat smaller.

6. Conclusions

In this work, we have studied several of the most prominent and best-performing SLS algorithms for SAT. The published empirical results on the performance of these algorithms are mostly incompatible with each other because different methodologies and/or different sets of benchmark instances were used. Thus, in order to obtain a comprehensive picture of these algorithm's performance, we systematically evaluated them on a significant subset of the SATLIB Benchmark Suite including sets of randomly generated SAT instances as well as more structured SAT-encoded problems from various other domains. All problem classes used here are known from the literature and most of them have been used in the context of several studies of SLS performance. For our empirical study, we have used a novel empirical methodology which allowed us to characterise the behaviour of the various algorithms in great detail. This methodology has a number of advantages over traditional methods for the empirical evaluation of SLS-based SAT algorithms; in particular, it allows the functional characterisation of run-time distributions.

From our comparative analysis we obtained a number of new and interesting insights. First of all, of the algorithms considered here, no single one dominates all the others on all domains. However, we identified a subset of algorithms which show superior performance compared to the others across our benchmark set. These algorithms are: R-Novelty, Novelty, WalkSAT/TABU and GSAT/TABU; they all suffer from occasional stagnation behaviour, which for some instances severely compromises their performance. GWSAT, WalkSAT and HWSAT, on the other hand, are generally dominated by at least one of the aforementioned algorithms. Interestingly, all the best performing SLS variants for SAT make use of some aspects of the search history, such as a tabu list or the age of variables for guiding the local search process. This suggests that an adequate use of the search history may be generally crucial for obtaining superior SLS performance. This is very much in tune with recent results on local search algorithms for other combinatorial optimisation problems where, on a wide variety of problems, history-sensitive algorithms have been shown to perform better than local search methods which do not take into account the search history.

Additionally, when comparing the performance of the different SLS algorithms studied here, one has to take into account that when using the currently best-known implementations, the GSAT variants are by at least a factor of 3 slower than the WalkSAT variants, such that effectively, even GSAT/TABU is never competitive with the best-performing WalkSAT variants when absolute CPU-time is measured. Since the implementations of all GSAT and WalkSAT variants used in this study are highly optimised, we believe that this performance difference is inherent to the algorithms. There are several implementation related reasons which may be responsible for this fact. One is that WalkSAT algorithms are much simpler to implement efficiently and require less sophisticated data structures because they evaluate only the scores of a small number of variables in each search step. Furthermore, clauses are typically rather short — in many instances stemming from SAT-encodings of other problems, most of the clauses are actually binary clauses. Therefore WalkSAT algorithms actually often select only between two variables while GSAT algorithms select the variable to be flipped from a potentially much larger set.

As we have shown, the essential incompleteness which compromises the performance especially of the high-performing WalkSAT variants can be effectively overcome by adding an unconditional random walk mechanism as used in GWSAT. The Novelty$^+$ and R-Novelty$^+$ variants thus obtained show superior performance compared to the original algorithms and, to our best knowledge, might currently be the best-performing SLS algorithms for SAT. Compared to Novelty and R-Novelty they are particularly superior in terms of their robustness *w.r.t.* the setting of the cutoff parameter, which plays an important role in practice.

Regarding the functional characterisation of SLS behaviour, we empirically studied the run-time behaviour of WalkSAT, WalkSAT/TABU, Novelty, and R-Novelty. We showed that, using optimal noise parameter settings, the RLDs of these algorithms when applied to hard problem instances from various domains can be approximated by exponential distributions. The same phenomenon is observed for larger-than-optimal noise settings, while for smaller-than-optimal noise qualitatively different behaviour occurs. The insights gained by the functional characterisation of SLS behaviour also explain the observations made by other researchers that the use of random walk reduces the sensitivity of SLS algorithms to the particular value of the *maxSteps* parameter [20, 55]: for exponentially distributed RLDs, the solution probability does not depend on a particular *maxSteps* setting. However, due the effects of the initial hill-climbing phase, *maxSteps* should not be chosen too low.

We further introduced a refined mathematical model based on a new distribution type which is asymptotically exponential, but allows to model the effects of the initial search phase. As we have shown, this extended model allows a precise characterisation of SLS behaviour for a vast majority of the problem instances from our benchmark suite. Thus, for the first time, we can model the behaviour of some of the most powerful and prominent SLS algorithms for SAT in great detail. As a direct consequence of these results, when using optimal or larger-than-optimal noise settings, the algorithms are very robust *w.r.t.* the cutoff parameter setting.

Furthermore, we analysed the correlation between the different algorithm's performance across the Random-3-SAT and Graph Colouring test-sets. As a result, we found that there is a strong linear correlation between the logarithm of the average local search cost for each pair of algorithms. In other words, instances which are hard for one algorithm tend also to be hard for all other algorithms. Consequently it is justified to talk about the intrinsic hardness of problem instances for local search. The existence of the tight correlation in search cost we observed for various SLS algorithms is somewhat surprising, because the underlying concepts are sufficiently different to cause significant differences in performance. This suggests that the local search cost for these algorithms depends on the same structural features of the search space. Finally, we investigated the scaling of SLS performance with problem size. Surprisingly, our results indicate that while for the hardest fractions of problem instances from the randomly generated test sets, the local search cost grows exponentially, for fractions of easier instances the scaling of SLS performance might be polynomial. This phenomenon could not be observed for the Graph Colouring test-sets, where the scaling was generally exponential. When comparing different SLS algorithms *w.r.t.* their scaling behaviour for growing problem size, we found no evidence of any substantial differences.

Of course, this study has a number of limitations and leaves many issues for further investigation. In particular, we did not attempt to explain the observed performance behaviour in terms of structural features of the underlying search spaces [64, 15, 35]. Clearly, any advances in obtaining a deeper understanding of the factors which affect SLS performance, such as search space topology, the effects of various SAT-encodings, and polynomial simplification techniques (which can be applied as a preprocessing step), will improve the chances of designing better performing and more robust SAT algorithms. Search space analyses may also be helpful for understanding the rather poor performance of the SLS algorithms studied here compared to algorithms using clause weighting schemes on certain types of problems, such as the single solution instances with very low clause per variable ratio generated with the AIM generator [2]. We are currently investigating these issues, using the same methodology underlying this study (for first results, see [35, 33]).

Furthermore, the algorithms considered here can be extended in many directions, e.g., by considering clause weighting schemes, multiple variable flips per local search step, and learning schemes for certain parameters or the objective function. In particular, for the algorithms considered here it would be highly desirable to develop schemes for automatically tuning the noise parameter setting to a given problem instance. Given such a method, the effort for fine-tuning the algorithms would be significantly reduced. To achieve this goal, the local search invariants from [51] or a reaction mechanism as suggested in [5] could be very useful. Another interesting direction is the design and investigation of hybrid methods which combine different SLS strategies (or even SLS methods with systematic SAT algorithms) using a simple control mechanism [35]. In fact, the improved WalkSAT variants Novelty$^+$ and R-Novelty$^+$ are examples of such hybrid algorithms as they combine the Novelty and R-Novelty strategies with the random walk mechanism used in GWSAT.

We feel, based on the empirical results presented here, that as algorithms are further improved, robustness of performance will become a major issue, and hybrid combinations of different algorithms or heuristics might become the key to obtaining maximal performance over a broad range of problem classes. Finally, one of the big questions in SAT solving remains to be answered: how the best SLS algorithms and the best systematic methods compare in terms of peak performance and robustness. We started investigating this question [38], for which this study provides a good basis, as it is based on a carefully selected and widely available benchmark set, offers an advanced empirical methodology for empirically analysing the performance of stochastic algorithms, and identifies the candidates for the best-performing SLS algorithms. We are convinced that these contributions will also prove valuable for research on many of the issues mentioned above and thus bring us another step closer to a deep understanding and profound assessment of stochastic local search algorithms for SAT and other hard combinatorial problems.

Acknowledgements

A large part of this research was done at FG Intellektik, TU Darmstadt in Germany. We would like to thank Wolfgang Bibel and the Intellectics Group for their support, as well as Bart Selman, Henry Kautz, David McAllester, David Poole, Ian Gent, Toby Walsh, and Joe Culberson for interesting discussions in earlier stages of this work. Furthermore we extend our gratitude towards Henry Kautz and Bart Selman for providing the code for GSAT and WalkSAT. Finally, we thank the anonymous reviewers and Kevin O'Neill for their comments and suggestions which considerably helped to improve this article. This work was in part supported by a Postdoctoral Fellowship awarded by the University of British Columbia to Holger H. Hoos and by a Marie Curie Fellowship awarded to Thomas Stützle (CEC-TMR Contract No. ERB4001GT973400).

References

1. H. Alt, L. Guibas, K. Mehlhorn, R. Karp, and A. Wigderson. A Method for Obtaining Randomized Algorithms with Small Tail Probabilities. *Algorithmica*, 16:543–547, 1996.
2. Y. Asahiro, K. Iwama, and E. Miyano. Random Generation of Test Instanzes with Controlled Attributes. In [41], pages 377–394.
3. A. Beringer, G. Aschemann, H.H. Hoos, M. Metzger, and A. Weiß. GSAT versus Simulated Annealing. In A.G. Cohn, editor, *Proceedings of ECAI'94*, pages 130–134. John Wiley & Sons, 1994.
4. M. Buro and H. Kleine-Büning. Report on a SAT Competition. Technical Report 110, Dept. of Mathematics and Informatics, University of Paderborn, Germany, 1992.
5. R. Battiti and M. Protasi. Reactive Search, A History-Based Heuristic for MAX-SAT. *ACM Journal of Experimental Algorithmics*, 2, 1997.
6. R.E. Barlow and F. Proschan. *Statistical Theory of Reliability and Life Testing.* Holt, Reinhart and Winston, Inc., 1981 (reprint).
7. B. Cha and K. Iwama. Performance Tests of Local Search Algorithms Using New Types of Random CNF Formula. In *Proceedings of IJCAI'95*, pages 304–309. Morgan Kaufmann Publishers, 1995.
8. B. Cha and K. Iwama. Adding New Clauses for Faster Local Search. In *Proceedings of AAAI'96*, pages 332–337. MIT Press, 1996.
9. P. Cheeseman, B Kanefsky, and W.M. Taylor. Where the really hard problems are. In *Proceedings of IJCAI'91*, pages 331–337. Morgan Kaufmann Publishers, 1991.
10. J.M. Crawford and L.D. Auton. Experimental Results on the Crossover Point in Random 3SAT. *Artificial Intelligence*, 81(1–2):31–57, 1996.
11. M. Davis, G. Logemann, and D. Loveland. A Machine Program for Theorem Proofing. *Communications of the ACM*, 5:394–397, 1962.
12. J. de Kleer. A Comparison of ATMS and CSP Techniques. In *Proceedings of IJCAI'89*, pages 290–296. Morgan Kaufmann Publishers, 1989.
13. O. Dubois, P. Andre, Y. Boufkhad, and J. Carlier. SAT versus UNSAT. In [41], pages 415–436.
14. A.E. Eiben and J.K. van der Hauw. Solving 3-SAT with Adaptive Genetic Algorithms. In *Proceedings of the 4th IEEE Conference on Evolutionary Computation*, pages 81-86. IEEE Press, 1997.
15. J. Frank, P. Cheeseman, and J. Stutz. When Gravity Fails: Local Search Topology. *(Electronic) Journal of Artificial Intelligence Research*, 7:249–281, 1997.

16. J. Frank. Weighting for Godot: Learning Heuristics for GSAT. In *Proceedings of AAAI'96*, pages 338–343. MIT Press, 1996.
17. J. Frank. Learning Short-term Clause Weights for GSAT. In *Proceedings of IJCAI'97*, pages 384–389. Morgan Kaufmann Publishers, 1997.
18. D. Frost, I. Rish, and L. Vila. Summarizing CSP Hardness with Continuous Probability Distributions. In *Proceedings of AAAI'97*, pages 327–333. MIT Press, 1997.
19. I.P. Gent, E. MacIntyre, P. Prosser, and T. Walsh. The Scaling of Search Cost. In *Proceedings of AAAI'97*, pages 315-320. MIT Press, 1997.
20. I. Gent and T. Walsh. Unsatisfied Variables in Local Search. In J. Hallam, editor, *Hybrid Problems, Hybrid Solutions*, pages 73–85. IOS Press, 1995.
21. I.P. Gent and T. Walsh. Towards an Understanding of Hill–Climbing Procedures for SAT. In *Proceedings of AAAI'93*, pages 28–33. MIT Press, 1993.
22. I.P. Gent and T. Walsh. An Empirical Analysis of Search in GSAT. *Journal of Artificial Intelligence Research*, 1:47–59, 1993.
23. F. Glover. Tabu Search - Part I. *ORSA Journal on Computing*, 1(3):190–206, 1989.
24. C.P. Gomes and B. Selman. Problem Structure in the Presence of Perturbations. In *Proceedings of AAAI'97*, pages 221–226. MIT Press, 1997.
25. C.P. Gomes, B. Selman, and H. Kautz. Boosting Combinatorial Search Trough Randomization. In *Proceedings of AAAI'98*, pages 431–437. MIT Press, 1998.
26. J. Gottlieb and N. Voss. Improving the Performance of Evolutionary Algorithms for the Satisfiability Problem by Refining Functions. In A.E. Eiben, T. Bäck, M. Schoenauer, and H.-P. Schwefel, editors, *Proceedings of PPSN V*, volume 1498 of *LNCS*, pages 813–822. Springer Verlag, 1998.
27. J. Gu. Efficient Local Search for Very Large-Scale Satisfiability Problems. *SIGART Bulletin*, 3:8–12, 1992.
28. P. Hansen and B. Jaumard. Algorithms for the Maximum Satisfiability Problem. *Computing*, 44:279–303, 1990.
29. T. Hogg. Refining the Phase Transition in Combinatorial Search. *Artificial Intelligence*, 81:127–154, 1996.
30. J.N. Hooker. Needed: An Empirical Science of Algorithms. *Operations Research*, 42(2):201–212, 1994.
31. J.N. Hooker. Testing Heuristics: We Have It All Wrong. *Journal of Heuristics*, pages 33–42, 1996.
32. H.H. Hoos. Aussagenlogische SAT-Verfahren und ihre Anwendung bei der Lösung des HC-Problems in gerichteten Graphen. Master's thesis, Technische Universität Darmstadt, Darmstadt, Germany, 1996.
33. H.H. Hoos. SAT-Encodings, Search Space Structure, and Local Search Performance. In *Proceedings of IJCAI'99*, 1999.
34. H.H. Hoos. On the Run-time Behaviour of Stochastic Local Search Algorithms for SAT. In *Proceedings of AAAI'99*, pages 661–666. MIT Press, 1999.
35. H.H. Hoos. *Stochastic Local Search — Methods, Models, Applications.* PhD thesis, Department of Computer Science, Darmstadt University of Technology, 1998.
36. H.H. Hoos and T. Stützle. Evaluating Las Vegas Algorithms — Pitfalls and Remedies. *Proceedings of UAI-98*, pages 238–245. Morgan Kaufmann Publishers, 1998.
37. H.H. Hoos and T. Stützle. Characterizing the Run-time Behaviour of Stochastic Local Search. Technical Report AIDA–98–1, FG Intellektik, TU Darmstadt, January 1998.
38. H.H. Hoos and T. Stützle. Systematic vs. Local Search for SAT. To appear, *Proceedings of the 23rd National German Conference on Artificial Intelligence (KI-99)*, 1999.
39. H.H. Hoos and T. Stützle. Towards a Characterisation of the Behaviour of Stochastic Local Search Algorithms for SAT. To appear, Artificial Intelligence Journal.
40. D.S. Johnson, C.R. Aragon, L.A. McGeoch, and C. Schevon. Optimization by Simulated Annealing: An Experimental Evaluation: Part II, Graph Coloring and Number Partitioning. *Operations Research*, 39(3):378–406, 1991.
41. D.S. Johnson and M.A. Trick, editors. *Cliques, Coloring, and Satisfiability*, volume 26 of *DIMACS Series on Discrete Mathematics and Theoretical Computer Science.* American Mathematical Society, 1996.
42. A.P. Kamath, N.K. Karmarkar, K.G. Ramakrishnan, and M.G.C. Resende. A Continuous Approach to Inductive Inference. *Mathematical Programming*, 57:215–238, 1992.

43. K. Kask and R. Dechter. Graph-based Methods for Improving GSAT. In *Proceedings of AAAI'96*, pages 350–355. MIT Press, 1996.
44. H. Kautz, D. McAllester, and B. Selman. Encoding Plans in Propositional Logic. In *Proceedings of KR'96*, pages 374–384, 1996.
45. H. Kautz and B. Selman. Pushing the Envelope: Planning, Propositional Logic, and Stochastic Search. In *Proceedings of AAAI'96*, volume 2, pages 1194–1201. MIT Press, 1996.
46. H. Kautz and B. Selman. BLACKBOX: A New Approach to the Application of Theorem Proving to Problem Solving. In *Working notes of the Workshop on Planning as Combinatorial Search*, held in conjunction with AIPS-98, Pittsburgh, PA, 1998.
47. S. Kirkpatrick and B. Selman. Critical Behavior in the Satisfiability of Random Boolean Expressions. *Science*, 264:1297–1301, 1994.
48. T. Larrabee. Test Pattern Generation Using Boolean Satisfiability. *IEEE Transactions on Computer-Aided Design*, 11(1):6–22, 1992.
49. M. Luby, A. Sinclair, and D. Zuckerman. Optimal Speedup of Las Vegas Algorithms. *Information Processing Letters*, 47:173–180, 1993.
50. B. Mazure, L. Sais, and É. Grégoire. Tabu Search for SAT. In *Proceedings of AAAI'97*, pages 281–285, 1997.
51. D. McAllester, B. Selman, and H. Kautz. Evidence for Invariants in Local Search. In *Proceedings of AAAI'97*, pages 321–326. MIT Press, 1997.
52. D. Mitchell, B. Selman, and H. Levesque. Hard and Easy Distributions of SAT Problems. In *Proceedings of AAAI'92*, pages 459–465. MIT Press, 1992.
53. P. Morris. The Breakout Method for Escaping from Local Minima. In *Proceedings of AAAI'93*, pages 40–45. MIT Press, 1993.
54. S. Minton, M.D. Johnston, A.B. Philips, and P. Laird. Minimizing Conflicts: A Heuristic Repair Method for Constraint Satisfaction and Scheduling Problems. *Artificial Intelligence*, 52:161–205, 1992.
55. A.J. Parkes and J.P. Walser. Tuning Local Search for Satisfiability Testing. In *Proceedings of AAAI'96*, pages 356–362. MIT Press, 1996.
56. M.G.C. Resende, T.A. Feo. A GRASP for Satisfiability. In [41], pages 499–520.
57. V.K. Rohatgi. *An Introduction to Probability Theory and Mathematical Statistics.* John Wiley & Sons, 1976.
58. B. Selman, Henry A. Kautz. An Empirical Study of Greedy Local Search for Satisfiability Testing. In *Proceedings of AAAI'93*, pages 46–51. MIT Press, 1993.
59. B. Selman, Henry A. Kautz, and B. Cohen. Noise Strategies for Improving Local Search. In *Proceedings of AAAI'94*, pages 337–343. MIT Press, 1994.
60. B. Selman, H. Levesque, and D. Mitchell. A New Method for Solving Hard Satisfiability Problems. In *Proceedings of AAAI'92*, pages 440–446. MIT Press, 1992.
61. O. Steinmann, A. Strohmaier, and T. Stützle. Tabu Search vs. Random Walk. In *Advances in Artificial Intelligence (KI97)*, volume 1303 of *LNAI*, pages 337–348. Springer Verlag, 1997.
62. T. Stützle. *Local Search Algorithms for Combinatorial Problems — Analysis, Improvements, and New Applications.* PhD thesis, Department of Computer Science, Darmstadt University of Technology, 1998.
63. W.M. Spears. Simulated Annealing for Hard Satisfiability Problems. Technical Report, Naval Research Laboratory, Washington D.C., 1993.
64. T. Yokoo. Why Adding More Constraints Makes a Problem Easier for Hill-Climbing Algorithms: Analyzing Landscapes of CSPs. In *Proceedings of CP'97*, pages 357–370. Springer Verlag, 1997.

SAT2000
I. Gent et al. (Eds.)
IOS Press, 2000

Guided Local Search for solving SAT and weighted MAX-SAT Problems

Patrick Mills† and Edward Tsang§
Department of Computer Science, University of Essex, UK

Abstract. In this paper, we show how Guided Local Search (GLS) can be applied to the SAT problem and show how the resulting algorithm can be naturally extended to solve the weighted MAX-SAT problem. GLS is a general, penalty-based meta-heuristic, which sits on top of local search algorithms to help guide them out of local minima. GLS has been shown to be successful in solving a number of practical real life problems, such as the travelling salesman problem, BT's workforce scheduling problem, the radio link frequency assignment problem and the vehicle routing problem. We present empirical results of applying GLS to instances of the SAT problem from the DIMACS archive and also a small set of weighted MAX-SAT problem instances and compare them against the results of other local search algorithms for the SAT problem.

Keywords: SAT problem, Local Search, Meta-heuristics, Optimisation

1. Introduction

Guided Local Search [41] has been applied to a number of real life problems, including BT's workforce scheduling problem [40], the travelling salesman problem [43], the vehicle routing problem [20], function optimization [42] and the radio link frequency assignment problem [44].

GLS is a meta-heuristic, which sits on top of local search procedures for helping them escape from local minima. GLS is a generalisation of the GENET neural network [4], for solving constraint satisfaction and optimisation problems. Recently, Lau and Tsang [22, 23] have shown how GLS can be sat on top of a specialised Genetic Algorithm, resulting in the Guided Genetic Algorithm (GGA, [21]) for solving constraint satisfaction and optimisation problems. They apply GGA to a number of problems including the processor configuration problem [23] and the generalised assignment problem [22]. In this paper, we show how GLS can be successfully applied to the SAT problem and weighted MAX-SAT problem.

The SAT problem is an important problem in mathematical logic, inference, machine learning, VLSI engineering, and computing theory [14], and has been the focus of a lot of successful research into local search algorithms. The SAT problem is a special case of a constraint satisfaction problem (CSP) where the variables take boolean values and the constraints are disjunctions (logical OR) of literals (variables or their negations). The weighted MAX-SAT problem is an extension of the basic SAT problem, where each clause has a weight associated with it, and the goal is to minimise the sum of the weights of violated clauses.

In this paper, we show how GLS can be used to solve the SAT and weighted MAX-SAT problems, by sitting it on top of a local search algorithm, which is similar to GSAT [35] without restarts. We give an evaluation of GLS's performance on benchmarks from

† millph@essex.ac.uk
§ edward@essex.ac.uk

the DIMACS archive, and a set of weighted MAX-SAT problems, comparing the results against the results of similar local search algorithms.

2. The SAT and weighted MAX-SAT problem

The SAT problem is an important class of constraint satisfaction problem [39], where the domain of a variable is always { false, true }, and each constraint is a clause. The SAT problem is important in solving many practical problems in mathematical logic, constraint satisfaction, VLSI engineering and computing theory [14].

The SAT problem and it's extension, the weighted MAX-SAT problem are defined as follows:

- A set of m (boolean) variables, $Z = \{x_1, x_2, .., x_m\}$, each of which may take the values true or false.
- A set of n clauses, $C = C_1, C_2, .., C_n$, each of which is a disjunction of a set of literals (a variable or it's negation), e.g. $x_1 \vee \neg x_2 \vee x_3$. In the weighted MAX-SAT problem, a weight w_{C_i} is associated with each clause.
- The goal of the SAT problem is to find an assignment of values to variables, if one exists, where all the clauses are satisfied (evaluate to true) or prove it is unsatisfiable if no valid assignment exists (currently only complete algorithms can prove unsatisfiability). In the weighted MAX-SAT problem the goal is to minimise the sum of weights of violated clauses.

Both complete and incomplete algorithms have been used to solve the SAT problem. Of the complete algorithms, one of the best known is the Davis-Putnam procedure [6], which is based on resolution. Of the incomplete stochastic algorithms, the best known is probably GSAT (first reported in [35]), based on steepest gradient descent and the related WalkSAT [33] based on random walk with greedy variable selection heuristics.

Whilst a lot of work has been done on the basic SAT problem, only a small amount of work has been done on the weighted MAX-SAT problem by comparison. Examples include [18], where GSAT is extended to solve instances based network steiner trees, and their results compared against non-MAX-SAT techniques for the native network steiner tree problems. Resende et al. ([29]) show how GRASP can be applied to the instances of the weighted MAX-SAT problem based on soluble and insoluble instances of the jnh* problems from the DIMACS benchmarks archive with random weights associated with each clause. Borchers et al. ([1]) show how a branch and cut algorithm can be used to solve the MAX-SAT and weighted MAX-SAT problems. Recently, Wah and Shang ([45]) have shown how DLM how can be applied to the same set of instances of the weighted MAX-SAT problem as GRASP with excellent results. Later, in this paper we also give results compared with GRASP and DLM for these problems.

3. Other methods related to GLS

GENET ([46], [5], [4]), the direct ancestor of GLS, is a Min-Conflicts ([26]) based repair algorithm with a simple weight update scheme for solving constraint satisfaction problems (CSPs), inspired by neural networks and the earliest such scheme we know of which has been applied to solving CSPs, where the weights of all constraints are increased each time the algorithm converges to a local minimum. Morris ([27]) describes a very similar scheme called Breakout, which increases the weights of all violated constraints, every time there are no local moves available which will decrease the objective function. Selman and Kautz ([32]) modify GSAT to include clause weights, increasing the weights of all clauses which are unsatisfied at the end of each try (when the maximum number of flips of variable values has been exhausted and the algorithm is restarted from a new point in the search space) of GSAT. Hampson and Kibler ([16]) suggest a heuristic for deciding when to restart, based on the number of flips required to reach the current plateau, according to how many flips it took to reach the current plateau, from the initial solution. Later, Cha and Iwama ([2]) suggest a scheme called weight, which is the equivalent to breakout. Frank ([8]) increases the weights of violated clauses after each flip, and later ([9]) refines his scheme, with decaying weights, where after each flip, weights of all clauses are multiplied by a constant very close to 1.0. Recently, Shang and Wah ([38]) have applied DLM to the weighted MAX-SAT and SAT problem with excellent results. DLM could be seen to be quite similar to GLS, although it does not use selective penalisation (see Section 5.2), and originated from theoretical mathematical foundations, whereas GLS is the result of many years of research based on empirical results. The two methods are related by the use of some kind of augmented objective function, with extra terms to guide the search out of local minima (Lagrangian multipliers in DLM, and penalties in GLS). So far DLM has been applied to a number of problems (e.g. nonlinear integer programming problems, nonlinear mixed integer programming problems, and the design of multiplierless filter banks), as well as the SAT problem (see [36] and [49] for a full description), whilst the GLS framework is more general and has also been applied to a wide variety of other problems (and local search algorithms, for example in the travelling saleman problem with 2-opting, [43]) as well (see Section 1).

4. Local Search for the SAT problem

To cast the SAT problem as a local search problem, we simply want to minimise the number of unsatisfied clauses, which we will give as our basic objective function, g, given in (1), below.

$$g(\mathbf{s}) = \sharp\{c_i \mid c_i \text{ is violated by the truth assignment } \mathbf{s}\} \tag{1}$$

The local search algorithm we use is based on ideas reported by Gent and Walsh in [12], who conduct extensive experiments on lots of different variations of the basic GSAT algorithm ([35]), and find HSAT to be the best hill climbing algorithm to use with GSAT at that time (although other schemes have now been divised which may outperform HSAT). Following Gent and Walsh's HSAT, we use a history mechanism in our local search algorithm, to help diversify the search as much as possible. We sort the variables into buckets of downward (if the variable is flipped the objective function will decrease) and sideways moves (if the variable is flipped the objective function remains the same). We then select the least recently flipped variable, which will result in a decrease in the objective function if one is available and flip it. Otherwise we select a so-called sideways move and flip that variable. We allow the maximum number of consecutive sideways moves to be a parameter (*smax*) to the local search algorithm. Pseudo code for our local search algorithm is given in Figure 1. In this paper *smax* is always set to 20, unless otherwise stated.

In our implementation, we incrementally update the changes in the objective function, which would result when a variable is flipped, and also the buckets storing the

```
Function LocalSATSearch(s, g, smax)
{

    while(g(s) > 0)
    {
            Modify s, by flipping the least recently flipped
            variable, which will decrease the objective function
            g(s), if one exists.

            Otherwise, if no such variable exists, which will
            decrease the objective function g(s), modify s by,
            flipping the least recently flipped variable, which
            does not increase or decrease the objective function.

            If the last smax moves were sideways moves or no
            downwards or sideways move is available return s.
    }

    return s
}
```

Figure 1. Pseudo code for local search for the SAT problem

variables which if flipped result in downwards and sideways moves for the current search state, as this is more efficient than re-calculating every time.

5. Guided Local Search

Guided local search, (See [41] for more examples of applications of GLS) sits on top of a local search algorithm. Given a candidate solution **s** and a cost function g, a local search algorithm is expected to return a candidate solution **s'** according to its neighbourhood function. **s'** is hopefully better than **s** (i.e. hopefully $g(\mathbf{s'}) < g(\mathbf{s})$ in a minimisation problem).

5.1. Solution features

Solution features are used to distinguish between solutions with different characteristics, so that undesirable features can be penalised by GLS. The choice of solution features therefore depends on the type of problem, and also to a certain extent on the local search algorithm. Each feature, f_i defined must have the following components:

- An Indicator function, indicating whether the feature is present in the current solution **s** or not:

$$I_{f_i}(\mathbf{s}) = \begin{cases} 1 \text{ if feature present in solution } \mathbf{s} \\ 0 \text{ otherwise} \end{cases} \quad (2)$$

- A cost function $c_{f_i}(\mathbf{s})$, which gives the cost of having the feature present in the solution **s** (in the SAT and MAX-SAT problems, this is only used when the search is in a local minimum).

- A penalty p_{f_i}, initially set to 0, used to penalise occurrences of the feature, in local minima of the augmented objective function, h.

In the SAT problem, we define features as violated clauses (to be elaborated below). A more complex feature, might be an edge between cities in the travelling salesman problem, where the cost of the feature is the length of the edge, and the indicator function is whether a candidate solution contains the edge or not.

5.2. *Selective penalty modifications*

When the local search algorithm returns a local minimum, **s**, which does not satisfy the termination criteria (e.g. all clauses satisfied), GLS penalises all the features present in that solution which have maximum utility, $Util(\mathbf{s}, f_i)$ (as defined in Equation 3, below), by incrementing it's penalty.

$$Util(\mathbf{s}, f_i) = \frac{c_{f_i}(\mathbf{s})}{1 + p_{f_i}} \tag{3}$$

The idea is to penalise features with higher costs first, with the utility of doing so decreasing, the more times they are penalised. This is more beneficial for problems with lots of different features of different costs (e.g. the MAX-SAT problem), although even on problems with features with equal cost, this may still have some benefits in reducing the number of penalties imposed.

5.3. *Augmented cost function*

GLS uses an augmented cost function (see Equation 4, below), to allow it to guide the local search algorithm out of the local minimum, by penalising features present in that local minimum. The idea is to make the local minimum more costly than the surrounding search space, where these features are not present, thus guiding the local search algorithm out of the local minimum.

$$h(\mathbf{s}) = g(\mathbf{s}) + \lambda \sum_{i=0}^{n} I_{f_i}(\mathbf{s}) \cdot p_{f_i} \tag{4}$$

The parameter λ may be used to alter the intensification of the search for solutions. A higher value for λ will result in a more diverse search, where plateaus and basins in the search space are searched more coarsely; a low value will result in a more intensive search for the solution, where the plateaus and basins in the search landscape are searched with more care. In this paper λ is always set to 1, unless otherwise stated.

6. Guided Local Search for the SAT and MAX-SAT problems

To use Guided Local Search for a particular application, a set of features must be defined, and the local search algorithm must be called within the GLS procedure.

6.1. *Features in the SAT and MAX-SAT problem*

In the SAT problem unsatisfied clauses seem to make a good feature to penalise, as they are solution features, which we wish to eliminate from the final solution, and moves made by the local search algorithm (flipping a variable), will usually result in a different set of violated clauses.

$$I_{f_i}(\mathbf{s}) = \begin{cases} 1 & \text{if clause } C_i \text{ violated by solution } \mathbf{s} \\ 0 & \text{otherwise} \end{cases}$$

$$c_{f_i}(\mathbf{s}) = \begin{cases} 1 & \text{if standard SAT problem} \\ w_{C_i} & \text{if weighted MAX-SAT problem} \end{cases}$$

Figure 2. Clauses as features in the SAT and MAX-SAT problems

```
Function GLSSAT1(s, g, λ, smax)
{
        ∀f_i, p_{f_i} = 0
        s = random assignment
        do
        {
                h = g augmented as in equation 4
                s = LocalSATSearch(s,h, smax)
                For each feature, f_i, with maximum utility, Util(s, f_i)
                        p_{f_i} = p_{f_i} + 1
        }
        while (h(s) > 0 or termination condition)
        return s
}
```

Figure 3. Pseudo code for GLSSAT1

This is similar to using constraints as features as in the Radio Link Frequency Assignment Problem [44]. We define the indicator and cost functions associated with clause features in Figure 2. The feature is present if the clause is unsatisfied, and not present if it is satisfied. The cost of any unsatisfied clause is 1 for the standard SAT problem (since we have no preference for any particular unsatisfied clauses to be eliminated from the solutions, as we want to eliminate all of them) and w_{C_i} for the weighted MAX-SAT problem (as we want to eliminate the most costly violated clauses first). In a sense the standard SAT problem is a weighted MAX-SAT problem where the weight w_{C_i} of each clause is always 1 (note the weight w_{C_i} does not appear in the augmented objective function for the MAX-SAT problem (the same objective function is used as in the SAT problem); instead we leave GLS's selective penalisation to do the job of removing costly clauses from the solution).

6.2. Modifying the local search to use GLS

As GLS usually uses a simple augmented evaluation function, as defined in (4), we need to augment the objective function for the local search algorithm in Section 4, to take into account the penalty terms. This means passing the local search algorithm the augmented objective function h, instead of original objective function g, so that it searches for flips, which minimize h instead of minimising g. Pseudo code for the overall algorithm including GLS is given in Figure 3.

We shall call this new local search algorithm GLSSAT1. GLSSAT1 can solve most of the instances in the DIMACS archive with little difficulty. However, we have found that we are not able to solve the par8-*, par16-*-c, par16-*, par32-*-c, par32-*, f2000, g250-29, g125-17, hanoi4 or hanoi5 using GLSSAT1.

```
Function GLSSAT2(s, g, λ, smax)
{
        ∀f_i, p_{f_i} = 0
        s = random assignment
        do
        {
                h = g augmented as in equation 4
                s = LocalSATSearch(s,h,smax)
                For each feature, f_i, with maximum utility, Util(s, f_i)
                        p_{f_i} = p_{f_i} + 1
                If (number of calls to LocalSATSearch mod 200 = 0)
                        For each p_{f_i}
                                p_{f_i} = p_{f_i} * (4/5)
        }       while (h(s) > 0 or termination condition)
        return s
}
```

Figure 4. Pseudo code for GLSSAT2

We believe that GLSSAT1 has difficulty with these harder problems, as it learns incorrect information about the search space, penalising the wrong features, so that the search landscape becomes more and more rugged (the reader might like to refer to [7] for a study of the search landscape of the SAT problem) as time goes on, making it slower and slower to traverse, crippling the local search algorithm and forcing GLS to do all the work, and making it difficult to find a path to the solution. Frank ([9]) uses a weight decay scheme to try to counter this sort of problem, by multiplying all the clause weights by a small constant close to 1.0, after every flip with some success on random problems. Shang and Wah [38] address the same kind of problem with their DLM A3 algorithm, by using a scheme whereby the langrangian multipliers are scaled down every 10000 iterations. They report that this stops the langrangian multipliers becoming too large, too quickly. We tried a very similar method, whereby the penalties are multiplied by 4/5 every 200 iterations of GLS's outer loop (rather than every 10000 iterations), which seems to have a very similar effect on GLS as Shang and Wah's scheme does on DLM, allowing us to solve some of the harder problems in the DIMACS archive. We call this version of the GLSSAT algorithm, GLSSAT2 (see figure 4).

7. Empirical results

In this section, we give an empirical evaluation of GLSSAT1 and GLSSAT2 on instances of the SAT problem from the DIMACS archive, and a set of weighted MAX-SAT problems.

7.1. *The easier DIMACS benchmark problems*

We ran GLSSAT1 on the easier problems in the DIMACS benchmark archive with the λ parameter set to 1, and the *smax* (the maximum number of consecutive sideways moves) set to 20. GLSSAT1 was run 10 times (this is to show that it is not just chance that GLSSAT1 finds a solution, rather than to study the effect of restarts) on each problem, allowing a maximum of 3,000,000 flips to solve each problem, starting from random

Table I. Summary of results on the easier DIMACS SAT instances

Problem	Percent successful		Average CPU time		Average flips	
group	GLSSAT1	WalkSAT	GLSSAT1	WalkSAT	GLSSAT1	WalkSAT
ssa*	100.0	100.0	0.655	0.137	71025	51552
ii*	100.0	100.0	0.376	0.074	2331	2521
as*	100.0	100.0	0.295	0.127	1660	8818
tm*	100.0	100.0	0.244	0.024	724	602
aim*	99.8	51.5	0.259	0.144	20513	55263
jnh*	100.0	100.0	0.121	0.035	2989	5229
par8-*-c	100.0	100.0	0.609	0.085	55853	27080

starting points each time. We compared the results of GLSSAT1 against WalkSAT [33] (with Maxflips set to 3,000,000 and noise set to 0.5) to give the reader another local search algorithm to compare with. We give both the average number of flips to find a solution (for an implementation independent comparison) and also the average CPU time and success rate of each algorithm to find a solution. All experiments on the easier DIMACS problems, were performed on a Pentium II 300 Mhz PC running Windows NT 4.0, with 256MB of ram. GLSSAT1 was implemented in C++, and compiled using Microsoft Visual C++ 6.0.

Full results are listed in Appendix A.

7.2. The harder DIMACS problems

For the harder DIMACS problems, we used GLSSAT2 and allowed it 10,000,000 flips for the g*, f* and par8-* problems, and 150,000,000 for the par16-*-c problems to find a solution averaged over 10 runs from random starting points. The maximum number of consecutive sideways moves (*smax*) allowed was set to 20. For the graph coloring problems, we found that if we ran GLSSAT2 with *lambda* set to 1 we could not solve g125-17 and g250-29. By lowering *lambda* to 0.05 and thus making the search more intensive, so that the plateaus and basins in the search space are searched with more care, we found that we could find solutions to these problems. In a similar way to the graph coloring problems we found that we could not solve f1000 and f2000 using GLSSAT2 with the *lambda* parameter set to 1, so we tried lowering it to 0.05 and found again that we could find solutions for these problems. For the parity problems, we set lambda to 1.0. We also ran the standard WalkSAT on these problems to give the reader a reference point, with the maxflips paramter set to 10,000,000 on the g*, f* and par8-* problems and 150,000,000 flips for the par16-*-c problems. The noise parameter was tuned in 0.05 increments, between 0 and 1 (for the par8 problems, noise = 0.1, for the par16 we could not find a suitable noise setting which yielded solutions, for the g problems noise = 0.1 and for the f problems, noise = 0.55) for each problem group to maximise the number of successful runs. We allowed 10 tries to find a solution for each problem. All the experiments on the harder benchmark problems were run under Linux on identical Pentium III 450Mhz PCs with 128MB of ram, compiled using g++/gcc.

7.3. Weighted MAX-SAT benchmark problems

For these problems, we used smax = 2 and lambda = 1. We ran the algorithm 20 times with a maximum of 10000 flips allowed. We compare our results against the results

Table II. Results on harder DIMACS SAT instances

	Success rate / 10		Average CPU time		Average flips	
Problem	GLSSAT2	Walksat	GLSSAT2	Walksat	GLSSAT2	Walksat
par8-1	10	6	8.14	11.58	856626	4996298
par8-2	10	6	8.23	9.85	856772	4197080
par8-3	10	3	7.71	9.50	799245	4003199
par8-4	10	1	4.38	23.08	480596	9878630
par8-5	10	2	12.24	4.83	1219965	2030019
par16-1-c	10	0	281.81	-	25259873	-
par16-2-c	6	0	413.17	-	38414206	-
par16-3-c	10	0	522.28	-	48584078	-
par16-4-c	10	0	386.39	-	35490303	-
par16-5-c	9	0	441.03	-	41180575	-
g125-17	9	10	308.20	61.16	3500340	2511688
g125-18	10	10	1.23	1.07	9629	43033
g250-15	10	10	1.59	0.52	2524	4666
g250-29	10	10	905.24	119.81	3797486	1935538
f600	10	10	8.61	1.07	542008	217203
f1000	9	10	50.89	3.11	2877619	570843
f2000	6	10	113.97	8.53	4458712	1431990

of DLM, MaxWalkSAT [18] (with noise set to 0.3, which we found to give the best performance, out of 0.0,0.1,0.2,0.3,0.4,0.5,0.6,0.7,0.8,0.9 and 1.0) and GRASP over 20 runs, with a maximum of 10000 flips allowed for each, giving the best, worst and average deviation from the optimal solution for GLSSAT1 and the number of optimal solutions found for each problem. All the weighted MAX-SAT experiments were performed on a Pentium II 300 Mhz PC running Windows NT 4.0, with 256MB of ram. GLSSAT1 was implemented in C++, and compiled using Microsoft Visual C++ 6.0.

8. Analysis

Overall, GLSSAT performs robustly in solving the SAT problem and solves problems in a comparable number of steps to WalkSAT, whilst on the weighted MAX-SAT problem, GLSSAT performs extremely well (performing better than any of the other local search algorithms, including WalkSAT, in terms of both solution quality and robustness).

However, we could not find solutions to the following problems using GLSSAT1 or GLSSAT2 in the DIMACS archive within 30 minutes: Hanoi4, Hanoi5, par16-*, par32-*, par32-*-c, f2000. Warners and van Maaren [47], report on a new approach to solving the parity problems, whereby they use linear programming to extract conjunctions of equivalencies from the original SAT formulation, so that they can solve a reduced problem, with a modified Davis-Putnam solver in a reasonable time.

In terms of average CPU time, GLSSAT1 was generally outperformed by WalkSAT on most of the easier SAT problems in the DIMACS archive, although it outperformed WalkSAT on the aim problem instances in both terms of average number of flips and success rate at finding a solution. GLSSAT2 solves the parity learning problems, quite well, whereas WalkSAT has difficulty in solving the uncompressed par8-* instances and

Table III. Weighted MAX-SAT Results (continued on next page)

	Over 20 runs/tries with a maximum of 10,000 flips for each algorithm						
		GLSSAT1			DLM	MaxWalkSAT	GRASP
Problem		Deviation from optimal solution					
name	No. Optimal	Worst	Average	Best	Best	Best	Best
Jnh1	20	0.00	0.00	0.00	0.00	0.00	188.00
Jnh4	8	50.00	19.50	0.00	41.00	41.00	215.00
Jnh5	15	131.00	29.35	0.00	0.00	114.00	254.00
Jnh6	18	11.00	1.10	0.00	0.00	0.00	11.00
Jnh7	20	0.00	0.00	0.00	0.00	0.00	0.00
Jnh8	19	121.00	6.05	0.00	0.00	0.00	578.00
Jnh9	7	192.00	33.80	0.00	7.00	0.00	514.00
Jnh10	20	0.00	0.00	0.00	0.00	0.00	275.00
Jnh11	5	90.00	11.95	0.00	0.00	13.00	111.00
Jnh12	20	0.00	0.00	0.00	0.00	0.00	188.00
Jnh13	19	18.00	0.90	0.00	0.00	0.00	283.00
Jnh14	18	87.00	7.40	0.00	0.00	0.00	314.00
Jnh15	16	94.00	12.50	0.00	0.00	0.00	359.00
Jnh16	8	5.00	3.00	0.00	0.00	0.00	68.00
Jnh17	20	0.00	0.00	0.00	0.00	0.00	118.00
Jnh18	9	98.00	20.65	0.00	0.00	0.00	423.00
Jnh19	15	107.00	21.15	0.00	0.00	0.00	436.00
Jnh201	20	0.00	0.00	0.00	0.00	0.00	0.00
Jnh202	19	79.00	3.95	0.00	0.00	0.00	187.00
Jnh203	18	64.00	6.40	0.00	0.00	0.00	310.00
Jnh205	20	0.00	0.00	0.00	0.00	0.00	14.00
Jnh207	17	9.00	1.35	0.00	0.00	0.00	137.00
Jnh208	18	146.00	13.80	0.00	0.00	0.00	172.00
Jnh209	20	0.00	0.00	0.00	0.00	0.00	207.00
Jnh210	20	0.00	0.00	0.00	0.00	0.00	0.00
Jnh211	19	154.00	7.70	0.00	0.00	0.00	240.00
Jnh212	15	11.00	2.75	0.00	0.00	0.00	195.00
Jnh214	19	11.00	0.55	0.00	0.00	0.00	462.00
Jnh215	17	96.00	9.40	0.00	0.00	0.00	292.00
Jnh216	13	118.00	27.50	0.00	0.00	0.00	197.00
Jnh217	20	0.00	0.00	0.00	0.00	0.00	6.00
Jnh218	20	0.00	0.00	0.00	0.00	0.00	139.00
Jnh219	19	163.00	8.15	0.00	0.00	103.00	436.00
Jnh220	19	43.00	2.15	0.00	0.00	0.00	185.00
Jnh301	18	12.00	1.20	0.00	0.00	0.00	184.00
Jnh302	20	0.00	0.00	0.00	338.00	129.00	211.00

Table III. Weighted MAX-SAT Results (continued from previous page)

Over 20 runs/tries with a maximum of 10,000 flips for each algorithm							
	GLSSAT1				DLM	MaxWalkSAT	GRASP
Problem	Deviation from optimal solution						
name	No. Optimal	Worst	Average	Best	Best	Best	Best
Jnh303	16	152.00	28.60	0.00	143.00	80.00	259.00
Jnh304	19	273.00	13.65	0.00	0.00	31.00	319.00
Jnh305	9	258.00	91.90	0.00	194.00	196.00	609.00
Jnh306	20	0.00	0.00	0.00	0.00	0.00	180.00
Jnh307	12	63.00	15.70	0.00	0.00	0.00	155.00
Jnh308	13	156.00	34.40	0.00	0.00	156.00	502.00
Jnh309	19	49.00	2.45	0.00	0.00	0.00	229.00
Jnh310	16	38.00	7.60	0.00	0.00	0.00	109.00
Average	17	65.89	10.15	0.00	16.43	19.61	233.43

par16-*-c instances (in fact it didn't find any solutions to the par16-*-c instances). On the f and g problems, the tuned walksat performs much better than GLSSAT2, suggesting that walksat may be a more suitable algorithm for these problem instances.

On the weighted MAX-SAT problem, GLS's selective penalisation mechanism comes into it's own. Of the best of 20 runs of GLSSAT1 on the weighted MAX-SAT problem, GLSSAT1 finds the optimal solution for every problem, in fact in 85% (on average 17 out of 20) runs, GLSSAT1 finds the optimal solution. Furthermore, the average deviation, *averaged over 20* runs of GLSSAT1 is less than the average deviation of the *best of 20* runs for DLM and MaxWalkSAT. This shows that GLSSAT1 produces better quality solutions than both DLM and MaxWalkSAT. In the worst of 20 runs, GLSSAT1 outperforms GRASP for every problem. We believe that one of the reasons for GLSSAT1's superiority on these weighted MAX-SAT problems, is because we do not include the weights for each clause in the objective function (this is backed up by the fact that when we ran GLSSAT1 with clause weights in the objective function, it's performance was worse). Instead GLS uses selective penalisation based on the cost of features (i.e. weights of clauses) and the number of times they have already been penalised to select which features to try to remove. This means that clauses with large weights are penalised first, and thus discouraged earlier, so that GLS guides the search in a direction which favours unsatisfied clauses with low costs.

9. Conclusion

Guided Local Search gives good results on most of the SAT instances in the DIMACS archive, comparable with those of WalkSAT in terms of the number of flips to find a solution and on some problems more reliable in finding solutions than WalkSAT (an algorithm considered to be state of the art). However, where GLSSAT comes into it's own is on the weighted MAX-SAT problem instances, where it comfortably outperforms DLM, MaxWalkSAT and GRASP, in both solution quality and robustness. We believe this is due to GLS's selective penalisation mechanism which is specifically designed for optimisation problems, whereas DLM and WalkSAT are not really designed for this purpose. This means the GLS does not need to include the weights for clauses in the objective function and thus the local search algorithm has less difficulty exploring the search space than DLM does, whilst GLS's selective penalisation mechanism takes the responsibility for removing high cost clauses from the solution.

In conclusion, we believe GLS has a place in the SAT problem, and that it is particularly effective for solving weighted MAX-SAT problems. GLS is a general meta-heuristic, with very few parameters and has been shown to be successful in solving a number of real life problems, as mentioned earlier. In general, we speculate that GLS will add value to many more local search algorithms, particular those dealing with soft constraints with varying costs.

Acknowledgements

Our thanks to John Ford, Dick Williams, Nathan Barnes, James Borrett, Christos Voudouris, Ian Gent, Toby Walsh and the anonymous referees for their useful comments and suggestions. Also, we would like thank Henry Kautz and Bart Selman for making a version of MaxWalkSAT available to us.

Appendix A: Full results on DIMACS benchmark problems

Table IV. Results on Technology mapping problems

Problem	Success rate / 10		Mean CPU time		Mean flips	
name	GLSSAT	WalkSAT	GLSSAT	WalkSAT	GLSSAT	WalkSAT
tm1-yes	10	10	0.47	0.05	1287	1074
tm2-yes	10	10	0.02	0.00	161	129

Table V. Results on Circuit diagnosis problems

Problem	Success rate / 10		Mean CPU time		Mean flips	
name	GLSSAT	WalkSAT	GLSSAT	WalkSAT	GLSSAT	WalkSAT
ssa7552-038	10	10	0.73	0.32	70052	118122
ssa7552-158	10	10	0.88	0.09	102904	32339
ssa7552-159	10	10	0.65	0.06	74412	24185
ssa7552-160	10	10	0.36	0.08	36732	31563

Table VI. Results on the Asynchronous circuit synthesis problems

Problem	Success rate / 10		Mean CPU time		Mean flips	
name	GLSSAT	WalkSAT	GLSSAT	WalkSAT	GLSSAT	WalkSAT
as2-yes	10	10	0.01	0.00	147	250
as3-yes	10	10	0.01	0.00	190	240
as4-yes	10	10	0.12	0.03	1078	2271
as5-yes	10	10	2.75	1.46	13014	102867
as6-yes	10	10	0.06	0.02	660	1419
as7-yes	10	10	0.53	0.09	2061	3705
as8-yes	10	10	0.04	0.00	696	350
as10-yes	10	10	0.10	0.01	969	643
as11-yes	10	10	0.08	0.01	1268	625
as12-yes	10	10	0.01	0.00	164	232
as13-yes	10	10	0.04	0.01	488	798
as14-yes	10	10	0.01	0.00	142	82
as15-yes	10	10	0.09	0.02	706	1157

Table VII. Results on Circuit synthesis problems

Problem	Success rate / 10		Mean CPU time		Mean flips	
name	GLSSAT	WalkSAT	GLSSAT	WalkSAT	GLSSAT	WalkSAT
ii8a1	10	10	0.00	0.00	92	42
ii8a2	10	10	0.01	0.00	171	109
ii8a3	10	10	0.01	0.00	219	203
ii8a4	10	10	0.03	0.00	499	364
ii8b1	10	10	0.02	0.00	226	132
ii8b2	10	10	0.06	0.01	933	706
ii8b3	10	10	0.10	0.02	1197	1645
ii8b4	10	10	0.15	0.03	1634	2641
ii8c1	10	10	0.03	0.00	304	213
ii8e2	10	10	0.08	0.01	692	402
ii8c2	10	10	0.09	0.01	735	422
ii8d1	10	10	0.04	0.00	505	256
ii8d2	10	10	0.08	0.01	651	436
ii8e1	10	10	0.03	0.00	320	240
ii16c1	10	10	0.28	0.02	1403	781
ii16c2	10	10	0.34	0.61	3357	23108
ii16d1	10	10	0.28	0.03	1482	1452
ii16d2	10	10	0.24	0.52	1974	20238
ii16e1	10	10	0.29	0.02	1118	1005
ii16e2	10	10	0.16	0.03	871	1479
ii16a2	10	10	0.37	0.16	2358	6410
ii16b1	10	10	0.41	0.05	2053	1711
ii16b2	10	10	0.28	0.32	2217	11069
ii16a1	10	10	0.31	0.02	1777	897

Table VII. Results on Circuit synthesis problems (continued)

Problem	Success rate / 10		Mean CPU time		Mean flips	
name	GLSSAT	WalkSAT	GLSSAT	WalkSAT	GLSSAT	WalkSAT
ii32a1	10	10	1.05	0.03	5543	1246
ii32b1	10	10	0.15	0.00	3931	252
ii32b2	10	10	0.34	0.01	4865	627
ii32b3	10	10	0.48	0.02	2560	974
ii32b4	10	10	0.33	0.02	1582	952
ii32c1	10	10	0.05	0.00	904	136
ii32c2	10	10	0.11	0.00	1216	299
ii32c3	10	10	0.80	0.01	8385	394
ii32c4	10	10	2.23	0.78	4315	11021
ii32d1	10	10	0.22	0.00	4832	480
ii32d2	10	10	0.63	0.02	7039	1519
ii32d3	10	10	3.41	0.11	13187	3199
ii32e2	10	10	0.21	0.01	2319	389
ii32e3	10	10	0.23	0.01	1483	685
ii32e4	10	10	0.57	0.03	2590	1046
ii32e5	10	10	0.86	0.13	2901	4057
ii32e1	10	10	0.05	0.00	1124	104

References

1. Borchers, B., Mitchell, J.E. and Joy, S.: 1997, 'A Branch-And-Cut Algorithm for MAX-SAT and weighted MAX-SAT', In *Satisfiability Problem: Theory and Applications*, DIMACS Series in Discrete Mathematics and Theoretical Computer Science, volume 35, pages 519-536, American Mathematical Society, 1997.
2. Cha, B. and Iwama, K.: 1995, 'Performance Test of Local Search Algorithms Using New Types of Random CNF Formulas', In *Proceedings of IJCAI'95*, pages 304-310. Morgan Kaufmann Publishers, 1995.
3. Cha, B. and Iwama, K.: 1996, 'Adding New Clauses for Faster Local Search', In *Proceedings of AAAI'96*, pages 332-337. MIT Press, 1996.
4. Davenport, A.: 1997, 'Extensions and Evaluation of GENET in Constraint Satisfaction', *Ph.D. thesis*, Department of Computer Science, University of Essex, 1997.
5. Davenport A., Tsang E.P.K., Zhu K. and Wang, C.J.: 1994 'GENET: A connectionist architecture for solving constraint satisfaction problems by iterative improvement', *In Proceedings AAAI 1994, p.325-330.*
6. Davis, M. and Putnam, H.: 1960, 'A computing procedure for quantification theory', *Journal of the ACM* **Vol. no. 7**, pp. 201-215
7. Frank, J., Cheeseman, P. and Stutz, J.: 1997, 'When Gravity Fails: Local Search Topology', *Journal of Artificial Intelligence Research*, 7:249-281, 1997.
8. Frank, J.: 1996, 'Weighting for Godot: Learning Heuristics for GSAT', *Proceedings of AAAI'96*, pages 338-343, MIT Press, 1996.
9. Frank, J.: 1997, 'Learning Short-term Clause Weights for GSAT', *Proceedings of IJCAI'97*, pages 384-389, Morgan Kaufmann Publishers, 1997.
10. Garey, M.R. and Johnson, D.S.: 1979, 'Computers and intractibility', W.H.Freeman and Company.
11. Gent, I. and Walsh, T.: 1995, 'Unsatisfied Variables in Local Search', *In 'Hybrid Problems, Hybrid Solutions', ed. J. Hallam, IOS Press, Amsterdam, 1995, pp 73-85. (Proceedings of AISB-95)*
12. Gent, I. and Walsh, T.: 1993, 'Towards an Understanding of Hill-climbing Procedures for SAT', it In Proceedings of AAAI-93.

Table VIII. Results on Artificial 3-SAT problems

Problem name	Success rate / 10 GLSSAT	WalkSAT	Mean CPU time GLSSAT	WalkSAT	Mean flips GLSSAT	WalkSAT
aim-50-2_0-yes1-3	10	10	0.01	0.17	1181	81560
aim-50-1_6-yes1-1	10	1	0.02	0.03	1918	12359
aim-50-1_6-yes1-2	10	0	0.02	-	1636	-
aim-50-1_6-yes1-3	10	7	0.02	2.18	1709	1110424
aim-50-1_6-yes1-4	10	0	0.01	-	1444	-
aim-50-2_0-yes1-1	10	0	0.01	-	1268	-
aim-50-2_0-yes1-2	10	9	0.01	0.04	889	19688
aim-50-2_0-yes1-4	10	10	0.01	0.37	817	186927
aim-50-3_4-yes1-1	10	10	0.03	0.01	2146	3632
aim-50-3_4-yes1-2	10	10	0.01	0.00	517	1392
aim-50-3_4-yes1-3	10	10	0.01	0.00	342	882
aim-50-3_4-yes1-4	10	9	0.00	0.00	137	749
aim-50-6_0-yes1-1	10	10	0.01	0.00	86	778
aim-50-6_0-yes1-2	10	10	0.00	0.00	86	325
aim-50-6_0-yes1-3	10	10	0.01	0.00	162	543
aim-50-6_0-yes1-4	10	10	0.01	0.00	138	513
aim-100-1_6-yes1-2	10	0	0.08	-	8581	-
aim-100-1_6-yes1-3	10	0	0.10	-	11225	-
aim-100-1_6-yes1-4	10	0	0.09	-	10246	-
aim-100-2_0-yes1-1	10	0	0.09	-	8436	-
aim-100-2_0-yes1-2	10	0	0.10	-	9270	-
aim-100-2_0-yes1-4	10	0	0.08	-	7780	-
aim-100-3_4-yes1-1	10	10	0.13	0.04	9064	11587
aim-100-3_4-yes1-2	10	10	0.02	0.02	1459	6734
aim-100-3_4-yes1-3	10	0	0.03	-	1750	-
aim-100-3_4-yes1-4	10	10	0.02	0.01	1471	2624
aim-100-6_0-yes1-1	10	10	0.01	0.00	197	782
aim-100-6_0-yes1-2	10	10	0.01	0.01	330	1243
aim-100-6_0-yes1-3	10	10	0.01	0.01	294	1866
aim-100-2_0-yes1-3	10	0	0.09	-	7957	-
aim-100-6_0-yes1-4	10	6	0.01	0.01	309	824
aim-100-1_6-yes1-1	10	0	0.09	-	9206	-

13. Ginsberg, M. and McAllester, D.: 1994, 'GSAT and Dynamic Backtracking', *In Fourth Conference on Principles of Knowledge Representation and Reasoning (KR-94), May, 1994, pp 226-237*
14. Gu, J.: 1993 Local search for Satisfiability (SAT) Problem. *In IEEE Transactions on Systems, Man and Cybernetics, Vol. 23, No. 4, July/August 1993.*
15. Gu, J.: 1994 Global Optimization for Satisfiability (SAT) Problem. *In IEEE Transactions on Knowledge and Data Engineering, Vol. 6, No. 3, June 1994, pages 361-381.*
16. Hampson, S. and Kibler, D.: 1993 'Large plateaus and plateau search in Boolean Satisfiability problems: When to give up searching and start again', *In DIMACS Series, Cliques, Coloring and SAT, Vol. 26, pp437-456.*
17. Hoos, H.H. and Stutzle, T.: 1998 'Evaluating Las Vegas Algorithms - Pitfalls and Remedies', *In Proceedings of UAI-98*, pages 238-245, Morgan Kaufmann.

Table VIII. Results on Artificial 3-SAT problems (continued)

Problem name	Success rate / 10 GLSSAT	WalkSAT	Mean CPU time GLSSAT	WalkSAT	Mean flips GLSSAT	WalkSAT
aim-200-6_0-yes1-4	10	10	0.03	0.02	715	2747
aim-200-1_6-yes1-1	10	0	0.52	-	50884	-
aim-200-1_6-yes1-2	10	0	0.58	-	57444	-
aim-200-1_6-yes1-3	10	0	0.54	-	53104	-
aim-200-1_6-yes1-4	10	0	0.56	-	54488	-
aim-200-2_0-yes1-1	10	0	0.95	-	86069	-
aim-200-2_0-yes1-2	10	0	0.67	-	60978	-
aim-200-2_0-yes1-3	10	0	0.69	-	62791	-
aim-200-2_0-yes1-4	10	0	0.80	-	72276	-
aim-200-3_4-yes1-1	10	10	3.27	0.20	218214	55052
aim-200-3_4-yes1-2	10	10	0.13	0.13	7639	35660
aim-200-3_4-yes1-3	9	5	2.20	3.27	138974	1008856
aim-200-3_4-yes1-4	10	9	0.29	0.31	17014	91361
aim-200-6_0-yes1-1	10	5	0.03	0.02	786	2932
aim-200-6_0-yes1-2	10	10	0.04	0.04	768	6042
aim-200-6_0-yes1-3	10	6	0.02	0.03	458	4518

Table IX. Results on the Random SAT problems

Problem name	Success rate / 10 GLSSAT	WalkSAT	Mean CPU time GLSSAT	WalkSAT	Mean flips GLSSAT	WalkSAT
jnh1	10	10	0.04	0.01	741	1934
jnh7	10	10	0.02	0.00	403	438
jnh12	10	10	0.05	0.04	951	5097
jnh17	10	10	0.04	0.01	762	810
jnh201	10	10	0.02	0.00	233	390
jnh204	10	10	0.04	0.02	916	2180
jnh205	10	10	0.04	0.01	904	1076
jnh207	10	10	0.19	0.09	4954	13996
jnh209	10	10	0.06	0.04	1285	5919
jnh210	10	10	0.01	0.01	205	791
jnh212	10	10	0.82	0.10	21652	14763
jnh213	10	10	0.02	0.02	421	3104
jnh217	10	10	0.02	0.01	426	605
jnh218	10	10	0.02	0.01	407	903
jnh220	10	10	0.33	0.16	8625	24381
jnh301	10	10	0.22	0.05	4943	7276

Table X. Results on easier Parity learning problems

Problem	Success rate / 10		Mean CPU time		Mean flips	
name	GLSSAT	WalkSAT	GLSSAT	WalkSAT	GLSSAT	WalkSAT
par8-1-c	10	10	0.07	0.03	6390	10320
par8-2-c	10	10	0.05	0.03	4358	9049
par8-3-c	10	10	2.32	0.04	213274	12956
par8-4-c	10	10	0.18	0.21	15925	67803
par8-5-c	10	10	0.43	0.12	39316	35272

18. Jiang Y., Kautz H., and Selman B.: 1995 Solving Problems with Hard and Soft Constraints Using a Stochastic Algorithm for MAX-SAT. *1st International Joint Workshop on Artificial Intelligence and Operations Research.*
19. Kautz, H., McAllester, D. and Selman, B.: 1997 Exploiting Variable Dependency in Local Search. DRAFT. *Abstract appears in Abstracts of the Poster Sessions of IJCAI-97, Nagoya, Japan, 1997.*
20. Kilby, P., Prosser, P. and Shaw, P.: 1997 Guided Local Search for the Vehicle routing Problem, *In Proceedings of the 2nd International Conference on Metaheuristics, July 1997.*
21. Lau, T.L.: 1999 Guided Genetic Algorithm, PhD Thesis, Department of Computer Science, University of Essex 1999.
22. Lau, T.L. and Tsang, E. P. K.: 1998a Solving the generalized assignment problem with the guided genetic algorithm. *In Proceedings of 10th IEEE International Conference on Tools for Artificial Intelligence, 1998.*
23. Lau, T.L. and Tsang, E. P. K.: 1998b Guided Genetic algorithm and its application to the large processor configuration problem. *In Proceedings of 10th IEEE International Conference on Tools for Artificial Intelligence, 1998.*
24. Li, C.M. and Ambulagon: 1997 'Look-Ahead Versus Look-Back for Satisfiability Problems. *In Proceedings of CP'97,* pages 341-355. Spring Verlag, 1997.
25. McAllester, D., Selman, B. and Kautz, H.: 1997 Evidence for Invariants in Local Search. *In Proceedings AAAI-97, Providence, RI, 1997.*
26. Minton, S., Johnson M.D., Philips A.B. and Laird P.: 1992 Minimizing conflicts: a heuristic repair method for constraint satisfaction and scheduling problems. *In Artificial Intelligence 58 (1992), pp161-205.*
27. Morris, P.: 1993 The Breakout method for escaping from local minima. *In Proceedings of AAAI-93, pp40-45. AAAI Press/MIT Press.*
28. Resende, M.G.C. and Feo, T.A.: 1996 A GRASP for Satisfiability *In "Cliques, Coloring, and Satisfiability: Second DIMACS Implementation Challenge," David S. Johnson and Michael A. Trick, Eds., DIMACS Series on Discrete Mathematics and Theoretical Computer Science, vol. 26, pp. 499-520, American Mathematical Society, 1996.*
29. Resende, M.G.C., Pitsoulis, L.S. and Pardalos, P.M.: 1997 Approximate Solution of Weighted MAX-SAT Problems using GRASP. *In DIMACS Series on Discrete Mathematics and Theoretical Computer Science, vol. 35, pp. 393-405.*
30. Richards, T. and Richards, B.: 1998 Non-systematic search and learning: an empirical study. *In Lecture Notes in Computer Science 1520, Maher, M. and Puget J-F. (eds.). (Proceedings of 4th International Conference on Principles and Practice of Constraint Programming), Springer Verlag, pp370-384.*
31. Selman, B. and Kautz, H.: 1993 An Empirical Study of Greedy Local Search for Satisfiability Testing. *In Proceedings AAAI-93, 1993.*
32. Selman, B. and Kautz, H.: 1993 Domain-Independent Extensions to GSAT: Solving Large Structured Satisfiability Problems. *In Proceedings IJCAI-93, 1993.*
33. Selman, B., Kautz, H. and Cohen, B.: 1994 Noise Strategies for Improving Local Search. *In Proceedings AAAI-94, 1994.*
34. Selman, B., Kautz H. and McAllester, D.: 1997 Ten Challenges in Propositional Reasoning and Search. *In Proceedings of the Fifteenth International Conference on Artificial Intelligence (IJCAI-97), NAGOYA, Aichi, Japan, 1997.*

35. Selman, B., Levesque, H. and Mitchell, D.: 1992 A New Method for Solving Hard Satisfiability Problems. *In Proceedings AAAI-92, 1992.*
36. Shang, Y.: 1997 Global Search Methods for Solving Nonlinear Optimization Problems, *Ph.D. Thesis, Department of Computer Science, University of Illinois at Urbana-Champaign, August 1997.*
37. Shang, Y. and Wah, B. W.: 1998 Improving the Performance of Discrete Lagrange-Multiplier Search for Solving Hard SAT Problems. *In Proceedings 10th International Conference on Tools with Artificial Intelligence, IEEE, (accepted to appear) Nov. 1998.*
38. Shang, Y. and Wah, B.W.: 1998 A Discrete Lagrangian-Based Global-Search Method for Solving Satisfiability Problems. *In Journal of Global Optimization, Kluwer Academic Publishers, vol. 12, no. 1, Jan. 1998, pp. 61-99.*
39. Tsang, E.: 1993 Foundations of Constraint Satisfaction. *Academic Press, 1993.*
40. Tsang E. and Voudouris C.: 1997 Fast local search and guided local search and their application to British Telecom's workforce scheduling problem. *In Operations Research Letters 20 (1997), 119-127.*
41. Voudouris, C.: 1997 Guided Local Search for Combinatorial Optimisation Problems, *Ph.D. thesis. Department of Computer Science, University of Essex, 1997.*
42. Voudouris, C.: 1998 Guided Local Search - an illustrative example in function optimisation. *In BT Technology Journal, Vol. 16, No. 3, July 1998, pp46-50.*
43. Voudouris, C. and Tsang, E.P.K.: 1998a Guided local search and its application to the traveling salesman problem. *In European Journal of Operational Resaerch, Vol.113, Issue 2, November 1998, pp469-499.*
44. Voudouris, C. and Tsang, E.P.K.: 1998b Solving the Radio Link Frequency Assignment Problem using Guided Local Search. *In Proceedings, NATO Symposium on Radio Length Frequency Assignment, Sharing and Conservation Systems (Aerospace), Aalborg, Denmark, October 1998.*
45. Wah, B.W. and Shang, Y.: 1997 Discrete Lagrangian-Based Search for Solving MAX-SAT Problems. *In 15th International Joint Conference on Artificial Intelligence, 1997, pp378-383.*
46. Wang, C.J. and Tsang, E.P.K.:1991 Solving constraint satisfaction problems using neural-networks. *Proceedings, IEE Second International Conference on Artificial Neural Networks, 1991, p.295-299*
47. Warners, J.P. and van Maaren, H.: 1998 A Two Phase Algorithm for Solving a Class of Hard Satisfiability Problems. *Report SEN-R9802 (CWI). Operations Research Letters 23 (1999), pp. 81-88.*
48. Warners, J.P. and van Maaren, H.: 1997 Satisfiability problems with balanced polynomial representation. *Report of the Faculty of Technical Mathematics and Informatics 97-47, Deft University of Technology, 1997.*
49. Wu, Z.: 1998 The Discrete Lagrangian Theory and its Application to Solve Nonlinear Discrete Constrained Optimization Problems, *M.Sc. Thesis, Department of Computer Science, University of Illinois at Urbana-Champaign, May 1998.*

SAT2000
I. Gent et al. (Eds.)
IOS Press, 2000

Non-systematic Search and No-good Learning

E Thomas Richards[†] and Barry Richards[§]
IC-Parc, Imperial College, London SW7 2AZ, UK

Abstract. Non-systematic search algorithms seem, in general, to be well-suited to large-scale problems with many solutions. However, they tend to perform badly for problems with few solutions, and they cannot be used for insoluble problems, since they are incomplete.
Here we present a new algorithm *learn-SAT* which, although based on non-systematic search, is complete. Completeness is realised through a process of no-good learning, learning-by-merging. This requires exponential space in the worst case. We show, nevertheless, that *learn-SAT* performs very well on certain SAT problems that are tightly constrained or insoluble. Indeed, its performance generally approximates the best SAT algorithms, and does much better at lower clause densities. *Learn-SAT* also maintains much of the efficient performance of non-systematic search for large scale problems with many solutions, at least relative to backtrack search algorithms.
These results indicate that the burden on memory, imposed by no-good learning, is not generally a problem for *learn-SAT*. This is perhaps surprising in view of previous work. What is even more surprising is the scaleability of *learn-SAT*. For some types of problem it scales very much better than the nearest competitive algorithm. There are other types, however, for which this is not the case.
The performance profile of *learn-SAT* emerges from an experimental methodology related to the one outlined in [21]

Keywords: complete, non-systematic, search, 3-SAT, empirical studies

1. Introduction

No single algorithm is universally the best for solving constraint satisfaction problems (CSP's). Some algorithms are effective at solving tightly constrained problems with few solutions, or proving inconsistency for over-constrained problems. Among these are complete backtrack-search techniques [43, 41, 28]. Other algorithms are more effective for large-scale problems with many solutions, although they typically perform badly for problems with few solutions. Among these are incomplete, non-systematic techniques, which use local information to guide search [38, 36, 25, 9].

The basic question in this paper is the following.

- Is there a complete algorithm, based on non-systematic search, which is competitive with the best backtrack-search algorithms on 3-SAT problems, in particular those with few solutions or insoluble ones?

The answer, we think, is broadly yes. Here we describe a new algorithm *learn-SAT*, which incorporates a form of non-systematic search, *RestartRepair*, together with a procedure for no-good learning, learning-by-merging.

The basic search strategy of *learn-SAT* is to construct a solution to a CSP incrementally by extending a consistent labelling to a subset of the variables (a consistent

[†] etr@icparc.ic.ac.uk
[§] ebr@icparc.ic.ac.uk

partial labelling). If at some point in the search the current consistent partial labelling cannot be extended consistently, a new constraint, called a no-good, is added to the constraint set; this no-good removes the current dead-end labelling from the subsequent search. Search then restarts with the empty labelling. At each dead-end a new no-good is learned and stored.

Learning-by-merging generalises the no-goods learned at each dead-end. It uses a form of resolution to derive no-goods that prune more than just the associated dead-end labelling. The effectiveness of *learn-SAT* depends greatly upon the level of pruning achieved by the no-goods learned. Nevertheless, in the worst case *learn-SAT* will discover an exponential number of dead-ends, since it records a new no-good at each dead-end. This raises a fundamental question.

- Can *learn-SAT* manage the burden on memory?

We show that it can for 3-SAT problems with just one solution and for certain insoluble problems. Indeed, *learn-SAT* competes effectively on these problems with the best SAT-specific backtrack algorithms, whose complexity is at worst quadratic. This is perhaps puzzling, since one might expect these problems to be especially difficult for *learn-SAT*.

One of the underlying aims in this paper is to build an empirical profile of *learn-SAT*. This empirical profile is designed to support future study into why it behaves well when it does, and why it behaves less well when that happens.

1.1. Empirical study and methodology

We focus on four different sets of 3-SAT problems: (1) problems with exactly one solution, (2) structured insoluble problems, (3) large-scale problems with many solutions and (4) selected DIMACS benchmarks.

The first consists of randomly generated problems constructed using the method of [1]. [5] showed that for certain non-systematic search techniques, including *GSAT* [36], *walk-SAT* [38] and *weight* [37, 25], these problems, which have exactly one solution, are very difficult to solve. One might expect that an algorithm like *learn-SAT* will also find these problems very difficult.

The random generator designed by Asahiro et al. is essential to the methodology of this empirical study. The generator takes as inputs the number of variables of the problem and the clause density. And it always delivers a problem with exactly one solution. By systematically varying the number of variables and the clause density, we build up a profile of the relative performance of different algorithms. If we did not know how many solutions there were, there would be an uncontrolled parameter in the study. This parameter is fixed here.

Below we compare the performance of *learn-SAT* with one of the most effective algorithms for these problems. This is a systematic technique based on the *Tableau* algorithm of [8] which incorporates *conflict-directed backjumping* [28] and 3rd order learning [13]. We refer to this systematic algorithm as *Tableau*{CBJ+3rdLrn} [3].

The second set of problems consists of structured insoluble 3-SAT problems generated using the method of [3]. Here an insoluble sub-problem is embedded as part of a larger problem. The random generator takes four parameters as inputs: the number of variables and the clause density of the whole problem, and the number of variables and the clause density of the sub-problem. Obviously the number of solutions is fixed at zero and hence does not vary.

Again one might expect these problems to be particularly difficult for *learn-SAT*, since the burden of proving insolubility is carried wholly by the learning mechanism.

The no-good set must prune out the entire search space before the algorithm terminates and, therefore, the memory burden on *learn-SAT* should be prohibitive.

Here we compare the performance of *learn-SAT* with another effective SAT algorithm closely related to *Tableau*{CBJ+3rdLrn}, viz. *relsat* [4]. By systematically varying the parameters of the problem generator, we build a profile of the relative performance of *relsat* and *learn-SAT* with respect to both the sub-problem and the whole problem.

The third set of problems consists of large 3-SAT problems of a certain type, viz. literal-regular problems at low clause density. These have many solutions, and are thought to be well-suited to non-systematic techniques. We compare the performance of *learn-SAT* with another non-systematic algorithm *weight,* which is incomplete. We also compare their performance with *relsat.*

The final set of problems consists of selected insoluble problems from the DIMACS benchmarks. These serve to provide a different perspective on the relative performance of *learn-SAT* and *relsat.* Here the results are more anecdotal since the problem set has not been systematically varied. They are nevertheless interesting.

1.2. Summary of empirical results

On the single solution problems *learn*-SAT performs well compared to *Tableau*{CBJ+3rdLrn}. It does consistently better than *Tableau*{CBJ+3rdLrn} at low clause densities and only slightly worse elsewhere, although there is an anomalous case, as we shall see. In general, the burden of learning no-goods does not create much of a burden for *learn-SAT.*

On structured insoluble problems the performance profile of *learn-SAT* is in some respects similar. Relative to *relsat, learn-SAT* again performs competitively. The memory burden, imposed by learning no-goods, is never a problem. The two performance profiles, however, reveal something interesting. There is a clause density which separates the performance of *learn-SAT* from *relsat.* Below that point *learn-SAT* always does better, while above that point *relsat* is always better. We call this clause density the *performance cross-over.* The experiments show that this moves as the problem structure varies.

This shift is particularly significant in connection with scaleability. When the size of the sub-problem is fixed and that of the whole problem increases, the cross-over moves rightwards to ever higher clause densities. The right shift indicates that *learn-SAT* scales more effectively than *relsat* on the size of the whole problem. Conversely, when the size of the whole problem is fixed and that of the sub-problem increases, the cross-over moves leftwards to ever lower clause densities. The left shift indicates that *relsat* scales better than *learn-SAT* on sub-problem size. In effect, scaleability is not a uniform phenomenon.

As for literal-regular problems, *learn-SAT* preserves much of the good performance of non-systematic algorithms, but *weight* is definitely the better algorithm, regardless of clause density. Nevertheless, *learn-SAT* uniformly outperforms *relsat.* Together, these two phenomena are interesting, although it is premature to speculate about the explanation.

On the selected insoluble DIMACS benchmarks, *learn-SAT* outperforms *relsat* on all but one, viz. the SAT encodings of the pigeonhole problems. These involve clauses with up to ten literals. The other problems are all 3-SAT encodings. This raises an interesting question regarding the relationship between problem modelling and *learn-SAT.* Should *learn-SAT* be applied only to problem models which involve small clauses? We cannot pursue this question here.

1.3. Overview

In the next section we describe *learn-SAT* in some detail, specifying each of its key components. We then focus in Section 3 on the complexity of *learn-SAT*. In Section 4 we compare the performance of *learn-SAT* and *Tableau*{CBJ+3rdLrn} on the single solution 3-SAT problems of [1]. In Section 5 we compare *learn-SAT* and *relsat* on the structured insoluble problems of [3]. Lastly, we address the large-scale soluble literal-regular problems and the selected DIMACS benchmarks in Section 6. We conclude with a brief summary in Section 7.

2. *Learn-SAT*

Before we describe *learn-SAT*, we first define the concept of a constraint satisfaction problem (CSP) and a few other concepts which we use throughout.

Constraint satisfaction problem A *constraint satisfaction problem* consists of a set of variables V, where each $v \in V$ has an associated finite domain D of possible values and a set of constraints C. Each constraint $c \in C$, containing the variables $v_1, v_2, \ldots, v_k$ is represented as a subset of $D_1 \times D_2 \times \ldots \times D_k$ which specifies the set of prohibited n-tuples.

Labelling A *labelling* is an assignment of values to a subset of the variables V.

Complete labelling A *complete labelling* is an assignment of values to all the variables.

Consistent labelling A *consistent labelling* is an assignment where no constraint in C is violated.

Solution A *solution* is a complete and consistent labelling.

We now turn to *learn-SAT* which has four basic components: *RestartRepair*, learning-by-merging (LbM), forward checking and the SAT-specific heuristic binary ordering. Only the heuristic is specific; the other components are fully generic. We first describe *RestartRepair* and learning-by-merging separately, and then show how they are integrated to form the algorithm *RestartRepair*{LbM}, which is itself a component of *learn-SAT*. We next prove the soundness and completeness of *RestartRepair*{LbM}. These properties are maintained when we subsequently enhance *RestartRepair*{LbM} with forward checking and the binary ordering heuristic, thereby yielding *learn-SAT*.

2.1. RestartRepair

RestartRepair combines a simple non-systematic search procedure and a repair mechanism. Search begins with a complete labelling to the variables, referred to as *VarsLeft*; this is usually inconsistent. It then incrementally builds a consistent partial labelling, *VarsDone*, by randomly selecting a conflict variable from *VarsLeft*, i.e. a variable whose current assignment violates a constraint, and attempting to re-assign it a value consistent with *VarsDone*. If there is a consistent assignment, this is added to *VarsDone* and the previous assignment is deleted from *VarsLeft*. As long as *VarsDone* can be consistently extended, the repair process continues. This will either terminate in a complete consistent solution or encounter a dead-end, where a conflict variable cannot be assigned a value consistent with *VarsDone*. At a dead-end, search restarts from the empty partial solution; that is, *VarsDone* is reset to and *VarsLeft* is reset to the labelling consisting of the current assignments to all the variables. The domains of all variables are also reset.

Note that *RestartRepair* is incomplete; that is, it will not always find a solution if one exists, and if a problem is insoluble, it will never terminate. The algorithm becomes complete, however, when learning-by-merging is incorporated.

2.2. Learning-by-merging

When *RestartRepair* reaches a dead-end, the partial labelling *VarsDone*, which is under construction, cannot be extended to any value of the selected conflict variable. Therefore, *VarsDone* cannot participate in any solution to the problem. As it stands, *RestartRepair* might subsequently re-construct the same partial labelling to *VarsDone*, i.e. after restarting. We can prevent this happening by adding no-good learning to the process.

A simple learning mechanism would be sufficient. When *VarsDone* cannot be consistently extended, this can be treated as a no-good and added to the constraints of the problem. The concept of a no-good is defined as follows.

No-good Given a CSP, a *no-good* is a labelling to a set of variables that either violates a constraint or cannot be extended to a solution. For a labelling P and a no-good ng, P violates ng if $ng \subseteq P$. Any labelling that violates a no-good is also a no-good. All labellings violate the empty no-good denoted by $\emptyset$.

The simple approach to learning no-goods treats the partial labelling encountered at a dead-end as a whole; that is, it does not distinguish the particular assignments which render the labelling no-good. As a result, it adds the whole partial labelling to the set of constraints. This can lead to a considerable amount of unproductive search in the context of *RestartRepair*. To mitigate this we adopt a more sophisticated form of learning, viz. learning-by-merging. This is designed to focus on the particular assignments in *VarsDone* which cause the dead-end. The technique is defined below.

Learning-by-merging Given a CSP, let P be a consistent partial labelling which cannot be extended consistently to a variable v. Then for each value $x_i (1 \leq i \leq m)$ in the domain of v, there exists a no-good $ng_i \subseteq P \cup (v, x_i)$, that prohibits that assignment to v. *Learning-by-merging* generates a new no-good ng by merging the no-goods $ng_1, ng_2, \ldots, ng_m$ at v, where $ng = \bigcup(ng_i - (v, x_i))$. P violates this new no-good.

In learning-by-merging, each ng_i is identified during consistency checking with respect to the value x_i; ng_i is the first constraint found to prohibit the assignment of x_i to v. The best way to explain learning-by-merging is through an example.

Example Given a particular CSP, let P be the consistent partial labelling $\{(s,1), (t,2), (u,3)\}$, and suppose we attempt to extend this labelling to the variable v whose domain is $\{0,1\}$. Suppose further that there exist two constraints (no-goods) *ng1* $= \{(s,1), (v,0)\}$, and *ng2* $= \{(t,2), (v,1)\}$. Together these no-goods rule out the two possible assignments to v; there is no consistent extension of the labelling P to v. At this point learning-by-merging generates a new no-good ng which is derived as follows.

$$ng = \bigcup_{1 \leq i \leq 2} ng_i - (v, x_i) = \{(s,1)\} \cup \{(t,2)\} = \{(s,1),(t,2)\}$$

Note that here the no-good, which is subsequently added to the constraints of the CSP, consists of just two assignments, viz. $\{(s,1), (t,2)\}$. In contrast, the simple learning mechanism, described earlier, would add the whole of *VarsDone*, viz. $\{(s,1), (t,2), (u,3)\}$.

The implementation of learning-by-merging within *RestartRepair* is given in Figure 1. This algorithm, referred to as *RestartRepair*{LbM}, always terminates, either with a solution or with the empty no-good.

```
VarsDone ← a consistent partial labelling (initially)
VarsLeft ← a labelling to all variables not in VarsDone
Status ← Unknown
whileStatus ← Unknowndo
  if select variable/value pair (v, val) in conflict from VarsLeft
    then Consistent ← False
    ng ← ∅
    whileConsistent = False do
      val' ∈ D_v, the domain of variable v
      Consistent ← check( VarsDone ∪ {(v, val')})
      if Consistent = False then D_v ← D_v - {val'}
        ng ← ng ∪ VarsDone ↓_c, where c is
                   a violated constraint (no-good)
      else vl ← val'
      endif
    if D_v = ∅ then
      restart( VarsDone, VarsLeft)
      record(ng)
      if ng = ∅ thenStatus ← Insoluble
      endif
    else VarsDone ← VarsDone ∪{(v, vl)}
      VarsLeft ← VarsLeft - {(v,val)}
    endif
  else return VarsDone ∪ VarsLeft is a solution
    Status ← Solved
  endif
```

Figure 1. RestartRepair{**LbM**}

2.3. Soundness and completeness

We first show that *RestartRepair*{LbM} is sound; that is, it never leads to the elimination of any solutions. This could happen only through learning-by-merging, which generates new constraints. Second, we show that *RestartRepair*{LbM} will either terminate with a solution or derive the empty no-good in a finite time.

Proposition *RestartRepair*{LbM} is **sound**.

Proof Suppose that *RestartRepair*{LbM} has reached a dead-end at some point in the search. Let v be the dead-end variable, i.e. the variable that cannot be consistently assigned a value; and let $ng_1, ng_2, \ldots, ng_m$ be a set of no-goods that rule out the entire domain of v, say $\{x_1, x_2, \ldots, x_m\}$. Let ng be the no-good generated by learning-by-merging. Suppose now that ng is not a no-good. Then there exists a solution S of the CSP such that $ng \subseteq S$. Let x_i be the value of the variable v in S. Then $ng \cup \{(v, x_i)\}$ is not a no-good. However, $ng_i \subseteq ng \cup \{(v, x_i)\}$. This is contradictory and hence, ng must be a no-good.

Proposition *RestartRepair*{LbM} is **complete**.

Proof Having shown that the no-goods generated during search never eliminate any solutions, we need only prove that search will always terminate either with a solution or with the empty no-good after a finite number of steps. It is sufficient to show that the no-good set eliminates a strictly increasing amount of the search space.

After each dead-end is reached, a new no-good is added to the set of constraints. This no-good eliminates at least the dead-end labelling, which consists of the union of *VarsDone* and *VarsLeft* at the dead-end. Plainly, the new no-good will also eliminate any labelling which contains it. Since no-goods are never deleted, the set of labellings removed is strictly increasing.

2.4. Forward Checking

Since *RestartRepair*{LbM} progressively extends a consistent partial labelling, viz. *VarsDone*, it is possible to incorporate look-ahead techniques into the algorithm. One of the simplest and most successful of these is forward checking [17, 26, 41]. This has been widely used in backtrack search, and has also been implemented more recently in restart search [44]. Following this trend, we enhance *RestartRepair*{LbM} with forward checking. The implementation is slightly more complicated than that required for simple restart search; this is due to the role of learning-by-merging.

As we have seen, *RestartRepair*{LbM} builds a consistent partial labelling until a dead-end is encountered. At this point the dead-end variable cannot be assigned a value consistent with the current partial labelling *VarsDone*. A no-good is then generated from a set of existing no-goods (constraints), where each one eliminates a possible value from the domain of the dead-end variable. The strategy in forward checking is a little different. It uses propagation to eliminate values from the domains of variables. Here a dead-end is reached when every value of the dead-end variable eliminates all possible values from the domain of a variable which has not yet been assigned a value. This is known as domain wipe-out [26].

Since all variables are assigned in *RestartRepair*{LbM}, one might wonder how propagation works in this context. The answer is that it works with respect to the variables in *VarsLeft*. When a variable-value pair is added to *VarsDone*, the effect of this choice is propagated to the domains of the variables in *VarsLeft*. Recall that although these variables have assignments, they can be altered when the variables are selected for repair. At the time a variable in *VarsLeft* is selected for repair, the new assignment must be chosen to be consistent with *VarsDone*. The set of possible choices may have been reduced by propagation generated by previous extensions to *VarsDone*. The values eliminated for this variable, and for other variables in *VarsLeft*, are those which are inconsistent with *VarsDone*. Here there is no conflict between reducing the domains of these variables under propagation and their having a current "tentative" assignment.

In the context of forward checking, each time a variable from *VarsLeft* is repaired, i.e. moved with a possibly new assignment to *VarsDone*, propagation may update the domains of the remaining variables in *VarsLeft*. There is no need to maintain the domain of the repaired variable, since its assignment is now fixed until the algorithm restarts.

But for every variable still in *VarsLeft* it is necessary to maintain the state of the domain after propagation.

To integrate forward checking and learning-by-merging, when a value is eliminated under propagation from the domain of a variable in *VarsLeft*, it is essential to record the reason for the elimination. This will be some combination of assignments in *VarsDone*. For example, let v be a variable in *VarsLeft* whose domain has been reduced by propagation. Let the eliminated value be a. Then (v,a) belongs to a no-good whose other assignments are contained in *VarsDone*. These other assignments constitute the elimination reason for (v,a). The definition of an elimination reason is given below.

Elimination reason Given a partial labelling VarsDone, and a variable v in VarsLeft, if a value val is eliminated from the domain of v by propagation, an **elimination reason** is a set of variable-value pairs in VarsDone that cause the elimination of val from the domain of v, given the current constraints of the problem.

For each variable v in *VarsLeft* we maintain one elimination reason for each value eliminated from its domain. These are held in the form of a single set of assignments; the union of the elimination reasons for each eliminated value. In the algorithm this set is referred to as E_v. These E_v sets will be used to construct a no-good when a dead-end variable is encountered.

Figure 2 specifies the extension of *RestartRepair*{LbM} incorporating forward checking; this is referred to as *RestartRepair*{LbM+FC}. The algorithm proceeds as follows. Initially, the set of elimination reasons for each variable in *VarsLeft* is empty. A conflict variable is then selected for repair, and the algorithm seeks to choose a value for this variable from its current domain which is not only consistent with *VarsDone* but does not cause the domain of any other variable in *VarsLeft* to be wiped-out. If there is such a choice, the new assignment is added to *VarsDone*, and the effect of the new assignment is propagated to the domains of all the variables remaining in *VarsLeft*. If a value is removed from the domain of one of these variables, the elimination reason is added to the set of elimination reasons for that variable.

As long as the domains of all the variables in *VarsLeft* are non-empty, the process continues. If a dead-end variable v is encountered, each of its remaining values val_i leads to domain wipe-out of some other variable w_i in *VarsLeft*. At this point a no-good is constructed by the following equation:

$$ng = \bigcup_i E_{w_i} \cup E$$

Note that ng is the combination of the elimination reasons for the w_i's and the elimination reasons for v. It is important to emphasise here that no-goods are learned only at dead-ends; this is true for *RestartRepair*{LbM} and remains true for *RestartRepair*{LbM+FC}.

There is a special case of elimination reasons generated under forward checking. Let v be the variable selected for repair from *VarsLeft*. If the propagation of a choice of value for v reduces the domain of a variable w to a single value, this value is assumed to be assigned to w and that may initiate further propagation. Suppose a value is removed from another variable u in *VarsLeft*, where the no-good involves the assumed assignment to w. The elimination reason for this value will consist of those variable-value assignments of the no-good which are in *VarsDone*, together with the elimination reasons E_w for w.

Why must E_w be included in the elimination reason added to E_u? Note that the assumed assignment to w is not included in *VarsDone*. It is, however, part of the elimination reason for the eliminated value for u. Recall that only assignments in *VarsDone*

```
VarsDone a consistent partial labelling (initially)
VarsLeft a labelling to all variables not in VarsDone
foreach variable v, E_v, (reasons for eliminated values)
Status ← Unknown
while Status = Unknown do
  if Randomly select variable/value pair (v, val) in
                 conflict from VarsLeft
    then Consistent ← False
    ng ← E_v
    while Consistent = False do
      val' ∈ D_v, the uneliminated domain of variable v
      Consistent ← forward-check(VarsDone ∪ {(v,val')},
                VarsLeft-{(v,val)})
      if Consistent = False then D_v ← D_v-{val}
        ng ← ng ∪ VarsDone↓E_w, where w is the
              domain wipe-out variable
        undo-forward-check(VarsDone ∪ {(v,val')},
                   VarsLeft-{(v,val)})
      elsevl ← val'
      endif
    if D_v = ∅ then
      restart(VarsDone, VarsLeft)
      record(ng)
      if ng = then Status ← Insoluble
      endif
    else VarsDone ← VarsDone ∪ {(v,vl)}
      VarsLeft ← VarsLeft-{(v,val)}
    endif
  else return VarsDone ∪ VarsLeft is a solution
    Status ← Solved
  endif
```

Figure 2. RestartRepair{**LbM+FC**}

may be included in elimination reasons. This excludes the assumed assignment to w. This is circumvented through E_w, the elimination reasons for w. These include those assignments in *VarsDone* that eliminated all but one value, viz. the assumed assignment of w. Since E_w identifies this assignment uniquely, it is tantamount to the assignment of that value to w in *VarsDone.*

We now turn to the role of the **undo_forward_check** procedure. This undoes the propagation of the **forward_check** procedure, restoring the domains and the elimination reasons for each variable. This is involved when trying different values for a selected conflict variable. If a prospective value leads to domain wipe-out through propagation, the effects of that propagation must be undone.

In the presence of forward checking, or any consistency technique, the **restart** and **record** procedures must be extended. The **restart** procedure now restores not only the domains of variables, but also resets the elimination sets. The **record** procedure records a new no-good and propagates this new no-good.

2.5. Binary ordering and learn-SAT

Binary ordering is a heuristic designed specifically for SAT problems in conjunctive normal form. Moreover, it is constructed to work in the context of *RestartRepair* with no-good learning. This heuristic directs search towards discovering dead-ends as early as possible. The idea is to construct no-goods which remove parts of the search space that do not contain any solutions. This is done by selecting variables and values that cause the greatest amount of pruning.

In general, however, it is computationally too expensive to calculate the pruning achieved for every possible variable-value assignment. Hence, binary ordering approximates the pruning by first counting the number of binary clauses in which each of the variables in *VarsLeft* is involved. It then selects, from among the conflict variables, the variable that appears in the most binary clauses. The value chosen for this variable is a value consistent with *VarsDone* that leads to the greatest number of binary clauses. The use of binary clauses to approximate pruning originates from the Tableau heuristic of [8].

Binary ordering Given a SAT problem, let P be the current partial labelling. (1) Select a variable not in P with the maximum count C(v), where C(v) is the number of binary clauses involving either v or its negation. (2) Select the value for v that maximises the resulting number of binary clauses.

Figure 3 specifies the implementation of *learn-SAT*, which incorporates the binary ordering heuristic. Note that the heuristic is integrated in a modular form; that is, *RestartRepair*{LbM+FC} is augmented only slightly. This indicates that it would be easy to enhance the algorithm with other heuristics, which may themselves be domain specific. In effect, *RestartRepair*{LbM+FC} is fully generic and easily enhanceable.

One might wonder about the effect that each component of *learn-SAT* has on the performance of the algorithm. While this would require a very extensive study, we shall illustrate the situation in Section 4 with respect to one of the problems in the empirical study undertaken there.

2.6. Related work

The origins of *learn-SAT* lie in *ng-backmarking* [18, 30]. *Ng-backmarking* is based on a non-systematic search procedure and uses no-good learning to ensure the completeness. The search strategy is similar to that in *arbitrary choice dynamic backtracking* [15] although it was developed independently. The learning method is simple dead-end learning. That is, when a dead-end is discovered, the entire dead-end partial labelling is recorded as a no-good. [18] also explore several other forms of learning, among them learning-by-merging.

The basic search strategy of *learn-SAT* is related to the *weak-commitment* algorithm of [44], which combines a form of restart search with the minimising-conflicts heuristic for repair. Recall, however, that the minimising-conflicts heuristic is not used in *learn-SAT*. Moreover, the *weak-commitment* algorithm uses a very basic form of no-good learning, which generates a very heavy burden on memory. There is no strategy here for mitigating this.

Learning-by-merging originates from the work of [22] and [18], and is fully developed in [30]. [34] and [14] independently developed similar no-good learning mechanisms, although they are designed specifically for backtrack search. [13] introduce a related learning technique called jump-back learning. This is also designed for backtrack search.

```
VarsDone a consistent partial labelling (initially)
VarsLeft a labelling to all variables not in VarsDone
foreach variable v, E_v, (reasons for eliminated values)
Status ← Unknown
while Status = Unknown do
  if Randomly select variable/value pair (v,val) in conflict
    from VarsLeft such that v is involved in the
    greatest number of binary clauses
    then Consistent ← False
    ng ← E_v
    val ∈ D_v, the uneliminated domain of variable v
    Consistent ← forward – check(VarsDone∪ {(v,val')},
                    VarsLeft-{(v,val)})
    if Consistent = False then D_v ← D_v – {val'}
      ng ← ng ∪ VarsDone ↓E_w, where w is the
                    domain wipe-out variable
      undo-forward-check(VarsDone ∪ {(v,val')},
                    VarsLeft-{(v,val)})
    else nb ← no_of_bin_clauses((VarsDone ∪ {(v, val')})∪
                    (VarsLeft-{(v,val)}))
      ValList ← ValList ∪ {(nb, val')}
    endif
    if ValList = ∅ then
      restart(VarsDone, VarsLeft)
      record(ng)
      if ng = ∅ then Status ← Insoluble
      endif
    else select (nb,vl) ∈ ValList with smallest nb
      VarsDone ← VarsDone ∪ {(v,vl)}
      VarsLeft ← VarsLeft - {(v,val)}
    endif
  else return VarsDone ∪ VarsLeft is a solution
    Status ← Solved
  endif
```

Figure 3. Learn-SAT

The binary ordering heuristic of *learn-SAT* is original, although it is not without antecedents. Among these is the heuristic in the *Tableau* algorithm of [8]. This is designed for backtrack search where the most important choices are made at the top of the tree. The heuristic focuses on these choices. In *learn-SAT* there is no notion of important early choices, since there is no backtracking. But there is a common task, viz. to prune as much of the search space as possible, as quickly as possible. This is achieved in backtrack search by discovering dead-end labellings as close to the top of the tree as possible. In *learn-SAT* it is achieved by discovering no-goods with the greatest pruning factor.

3. Complexity

The aim of the section is to reveal the nature of the computational burden which must be managed by *learn-SAT*. This burden is widely believed to be unmanageable for hard problems, which require a considerable amount of search. The potential scale of the task is evident in the complexity of *learn-SAT*. Here it is sufficient to examine the complexity of its component algorithm *RestartRepair*{LbM}. For reference we compare this with the complexity of *conflict-directed backjumping* [28]. The comparison is on three dimensions: search nodes, constraint-checks, and space.

3.1. *RestartRepair{LbM}*

Search nodes The search-node complexity of *RestartRepair*{LbM} is measured by the number of nodes visited before termination. To illustrate the situation in the worst case, let us consider an insoluble CSP with three variables, each having a domain with two elements. Here *RestartRepair*{LbM} will terminate with the empty no-good only after discovering that every possible assignment is a dead-end, i.e. a no-good. In the worst case this will require the algorithm's progressing through all partial assignments.

To discover the first dead-end *RestartRepair*{LbM} labels two variables and then tries both possible values for the dead-end variable. At this point it has visited 4 nodes. Since neither value represents a consistent extension of the two-variable labelling, the algorithm restarts. As before it labels two variables, although not necessarily the same two, and again tries both possible values, in each case failing to find a consistent extension. It has now visited a further 4 nodes and again restarts. The algorithm proceeds to consider all two-variable labellings and their possible extensions to the third value. Each time it visits 4 nodes.

Given that there are three variables, there are 3 distinct pairs to consider in the labelling process. And for each pair there are 4 possible pairs of assignments; that is, there are 2^2 ways of mapping a given pair of variables into two possible values. Since there are 3 different pairs, there are 3×4 assignments which are addressed. This is, in effect, the number of times the algorithm restarts in this part of the search. Each time 4 nodes are visited in attempting to assign the third variable consistently. The total number nodes visited is then $3 \times 4 \times 4 = 48$.

At this point *RestartRepair*{LbM} has learned a set of no-goods which rule out all labellings to any pair of variables. It now restarts and labels one variable. It then attempts to extend this consistently to a second variable, but the no-goods rule out both choices. Here it has addressed a further 3 nodes. Again it restarts, labelling a variable and as before attempting to extend this consistently to another variable. Again it fails, addressing another 3 nodes in the process. The total number of nodes visited in this part of the search is calculated as follows. Since there are three variables and two values for each, *RestartRepair*{LbM} restarts 3×2 times, and each time it visits 3 nodes in attempting to find a consistent extension. Thus the total number nodes visited is $3 \times 2 \times 3 = 18$.

At this point *RestartRepair*{LbM} has generated no-goods which rule out all assignments to any variable. Now it restarts one last time. It selects any variable and tries to label it consistently. Clearly, it fails, generating the empty no-good, and terminates. Here it addresses just 2 additional nodes.

The total number of nodes visited in the process of proving the given CSP to be insoluble is $48 + 18 + 2 = 68$. This reflects the search complexity in the worst case. In general, the total number of nodes visited in the worst case by *RestartRepair*{LbM} is

$$O(n(d+1)^n)$$

The question is whether this is indicative of the performance of *learn-SAT* on hard problems.

Constraint checks As for the number of constraint checks performed in the worst case, this is clearly bounded by the product of the number of nodes visited in the worst case and the maximum number of constraints or no-goods that may be stored. To illustration situation in the worst case we again consider a three-variable insoluble CSP.

Since there are 8 possible assignments to the three variables and they are all inconsistent, there are at most 8 no-goods (constraints) necessary to rule out all the complete labellings. Let us assume that there are 8 such constraints in the original problem definition.

In the first phase of the search *RestartRepair*{LbM} checks all 8 constraints. Here each time the algorithm attempts to extend a labelling of a pair of variables to a consistent assignment to the third variable it fails. It then generates a new no-good and restarts. Recall that this occurs 12 times in the worst case, giving rise to 12 additional no-goods. The algorithm then attempts to extend each possible assignment to a single variable to a consistent assignment for another. Again it fails on each occasion, generating a new no-good, and restarts. This can happen at most 6 times, yielding another 6 no-goods. When the algorithm terminates, there are at most 26 no-goods (8 + 12 + 6) which could have been generated during search.

The total number of nodes visited in the worst case is 68. Therefore, the total number of constraint checks performed in the worst case can be no greater than 1768 (68×26). In general, the number of constraint check in the worst case is

$$O(n(d+1)^{2n})$$

Again there is a question as to whether this is a guide to the typical number of constraint checks performed in solving hard problems.

Space The real challenge, however, arises in connection with space complexity, i.e. from the burden of storing no-goods. To fix the limit of this burden in the worst case, we need only recall the limit on the number of constraints which could have been checked during search. This will include the original constraints of the problem plus all the no-goods generated at dead-ends. Every time the algorithm restarts, it generates a new no-good. In the worst case the algorithm addresses all complete assignments, which are ruled out by the original constraints, and it considers all partial assignments, which are ruled out by the no-goods. Thus the limit on the number of constraints is equal to the number of assignments, both complete and partial.

Since each no-good can be at most n variables in length, space consumed in the worst case is

$$O(n(d+1)^n)$$

The burden on memory grows exponentially with the size of the problem, measured in the number of variables. This is the key factor for *learn-SAT*.

3.2. Comparison

One search method which avoids an exponential growth in the demand for space is backtracking based on tree search [16]. *Conflict-directed backjumping* (*CBJ*) [28] is an enhanced version of this, designed to allow a certain flexibility in the construction of the search tree and to support an intelligent form of backtracking.

Table I. Complexity measures

	CBJ	*RestartRepair*{LbM}
Search	$O(nd^n)$	$O(n(d+1)^n)$
Constraint Checks	$O(nd^{2n})$	$O(n(d+1)^{2n})$
Space	$O(n^2)$	$O(n(d+1)^n)$

In *CBJ* the search proceeds by selecting a variable and attempting to assign it a value which is consistent with a current partial assignment. The order in which the variables in this partial assignment have been selected forms the basic structure of the tree. If a variable is selected which cannot be assigned a value consistent with the current assignments to the previously selected variables, the algorithm backjumps to the variable which has been most recently assigned and contributes to this dead-end. The set of variables implicated in this dead-end is established during search using a form of no-good learning similar to learning-by-merging. Each variable v which has been selected will have an associated conflict set; this will consist of all those previously selected variables whose current assignment has been discovered to be in conflict with a value for v.

CBJ is a complete algorithm, and visits no more nodes and performs no more consistency checks than chronological backtracking [19]. In general, it visits significantly fewer nodes and performs significantly less constraint checks on average.

The complexity of *CBJ* relative to *RestartRepair*{LbM} is summarised in Table I. In regard to search nodes and constraint checks, *CBJ* is slightly better than *RestartRepair*{LbM}; but in regard to space it is very much better. While the space requirement for *CBJ* is quadratic in the worst case, the requirement for *RestartRepair*{LbM} is exponential.

From these figures one might expect that *learn-SAT* could never compete with *CBJ*.

4. Single Solution 3-SAT Problems

In this section we begin the empirical study of *learn-SAT*. Here the focus is on single solution 3-SAT problems generated using the method of [1]. These, known as AIM problems, have been shown to be difficult for certain non-systematic search algorithms [5], in particular *GSAT* [36] *walk-SAT* [38] and *weight* [37, 25]. One might expect that *learn-SAT* will also find these difficult since it should explore an excessive number of dead-ends before finding the solution. This will progressively generate an excessive number of no-goods, thereby increasing the computational burden and decreasing the performance.

[3] develop a *CBJ* algorithm based on *Tableau* [8] and 3rd order jump-back learning [13]. We refer to this as *Tableau*{CBJ+3rdLrn}. Since this algorithm performs extremely well on AIM problems, it provides a searching benchmark for the study of *learn-SAT*.

To compare the two algorithms we use constraint checks as the measure of relative performance. Counting constraint checks accounts for the effort undertaken by all aspects of both algorithms, including search, no-good learning and heuristics. Counting constraint checks is also insensitive to the quality and eccentricities of implementation and environment, which affect CPU time.

4.1. Tableau{CBJ+3rdLrn}

The *Tableau* method of [8] enhances the Davis-Putnam algorithm [10] with a sophisticated variable selection strategy. The Davis-Putnam algorithm is based on simple backtrack search combined with the following simplification procedures.

- **Literal-tautology** reduces all clauses of the form $\neg x \vee x \vee x_2 \vee \ldots \vee x_n$ to $x_2 \vee \ldots \vee x_n$.

- **Pure-literal** removes all clauses involving a literal l if literal $\neg\ l$ does not appear in any clause in the formula.

- **Unit-propagation** reduces a SAT formula by removing all occurrences of unit clauses. This amounts to the following inference. Given a SAT formula involving the two clauses and x_1 and $\neg x_1 \vee x_2 \vee \ldots \vee x_n$, unit propagation replaces these with the single clause $x_2 \vee \ldots \vee x_n$. A single application of unit propagation removes all unit clauses.

The variable-selection method of *Tableau* search focuses on unit propagation; variables that cause significant unit propagation are preferred. Similarly, when selecting a variable to label, preference is given to a variable and a particular assignment which creates a significant number of unit clauses, thus increasing the amount of unit propagation. This strategy serves to minimise search by identifying assignments which lead to dead-ends early.

To compute the exact amount of unit propagation for each variable at each choice point is, in general, computationally very expensive. As an alternative, the *Tableau* algorithm seeks to approximate this by counting the number of binary clauses in the formula whose satisfiability is at issue.

[8] report the results of empirical studies which confirm that their variable-selection heuristic can significantly improve the performance of *Tableau* search. They could find no similarly effective heuristic for value selection.

As for the learning component of *Tableau*{CBJ+3rdLrn}, i.e. jump-back learning, this is not unrelated to learning-by-merging. In the context of *CBJ*, jump-back learning constructs a no-good from a dead-end using the conflict set. The procedure is as follows.

Jump-back learning Let P be a dead-end label reached by CBJ search. Let *conf_set* be the conflict set generated in *CBJ*. **Jump-back learning** derives a new no-good *ng* from the assignments to the *conf_set* variables in P. This is specified by the equation

$$ng = P \downarrow_{conf\_set}$$

[11] proposes that in certain cases it can be effective to record only no-goods of a limited size, e.g. those with m variables or less. In this case all other no-goods are discarded. Note that a no-good with m variables prunes more labellings than a no-good having more than m variables. In general, the shorter no-goods achieve the greater pruning.

Note, furthermore, that if unrestricted learning were added to *Tableau*{CBJ}, the resulting algorithm would cease to have polynomial space complexity. In *Tableau*{CBJ+3rdLrn} learning is restricted to three variables, and hence the space complexity remains polynomial.

```
P ← a consistent partial labelling (initially empty)
Status ← Unknown
Consistent ← True
while Status ← Unknown do
  while Consistent ← True do
    if P is a labelling to all variables then Status ← Solved
    else v ← tab_select(P), Consistent ← False
      while Consistent ← False do
        foreach val ∈ CD_v, the 'current' domain of variable v
          Consistent ← propagate(P∪ {(v,val)})
          if Consistent = False then
            conf_set_v ← conf_set_v ∪ conf_set_x,
            where x is the domain wipe-out variable,
            CD_v ← CD_v - {val},
            undo_propagate(P ∪ {(v,val)},{v})
          endif
      if Consistent = False (i.e. CD_v = ∅) then
        if conf_set_v = ∅thenStatus ← Insoluble
        else jump_back_learn(conf_set_v,P,3)
          let u ∈ conf_set_v be most recently assigned in P
          let Vars be all variables in P assigned after u,
          let val_u be the value of u in P, CD_u ← CD_u − {val_u}
          P ← P - Vars, undo_propagate(P, Vars ∪ {u})
          conf_set_u ← conf_set_u ∪ conf_set_v − {u}
          foreach variable w ∈ Vars do
            conf_set_w ← ∅, CD_w ← D_w, v ← u
        endif
      else Consistent = True, P ← P ∪ {(v,val)}
      endif
    endif
```

Figure 4. *Tableau*{CBJ+3rdLrn}

4.2. Empirical study

We now turn to the single solution AIM problems of [1]. To enhance the granularity of the study, we look at more clause densities than those addressed in the original problem set.

We study a range of problems of three different sizes, viz. with 50, 100, and 200 variables, at various clause densities ranging from 1.6 to 6.8. We consider four different problems at each clause density, and for each problem randomly generate 100 instances. At each data point we measure the performance in terms of the average number of constraint checks needed to solve all 400 instances.

One may feel that this is a relatively small data set, particularly in comparison with empirical studies which consider many thousands of problems. The present study, however, addresses problems of a very specific type, viz. those having just one solution, at a range of clause densities. As a result, the sample set represents a much more extensive sampling at each data point than would be achieved in a less focused study with many more problems.

Figure 5 presents the results of the first experiment. At clause densities between 1.6 and 2.6, *learn-SAT* always performs better than *Tableau*{CBJ+3rdLrn}. This becomes very pronounced on the 200-variable problems, which suggests that *learn-SAT* scales better than *Tableau*{CBJ+3rdLrn} at these clause densities. We explore this further when we look at insoluble problems in the next section.

Between clause densities 4.2 and 6.8 the situation is different. For the 50-variable problems, *learn-SAT* does considerably better than *Tableau*{CBJ+3rdLrn}, but as the problem size increases, the performance of *Tableau*{CBJ+3rdLrn} improves. It is only marginally worse on the 100-variable problems and slightly better on the 200-variable problems. This suggests that at these higher clause densities *Tableau*{CBJ+3rdLrn} may scale better than *learn-SAT*. We also address this later.

At clause density 3.4 there is an interesting anomaly. Although the two algorithms are equivalent on the 50-variable problems, *Tableau*{CBJ+3rdLrn} is approximately three times better than *learn-SAT* on the 100-variable problems and an order of magnitude better on the 200-variable problems.

One might wonder whether the results in Figure 5 are related to the phenomenon of phase transition [7, 24]. The phase transition for a set of randomly generated problems is the point at which the parameter settings generate problems that have only a 50% probability of being soluble. It is at this point that algorithms are expected to perform worst. The phase transition is the same for all algorithms. This seems to be unrelated to the results in Figure 5. First, all of the AIM problems are soluble and second, there are two transition points, one for *learn-SAT* at approximately 3.4 and another for *Tableau*{CBJ+3rdLrn} at approximately 2.6.

Let us summarise what has emerged so far. For the extended set of AIM problems, *learn-SAT* performs extremely well at every clause density tested in comparison to *Tableau*{CBJ+3rdLrn}, with the single exception of 3.4. Recall that the memory burden of *learn-SAT* in the worst case grows exponentially in the size of the problem. From previous studies of other non-systematic search techniques applied to AIM problems [5], one might expect these problems to approximate the worst case for *learn-SAT*. The algorithm should typically have to undertake a large amount of search to find the solution, thereby generating a very large number of no-goods and thus degrading the performance. But in most cases this does not happen. In fact, it happens in only one case in our tests. *Learn-SAT* manages its overheads either better than or broadly equivalently to those of *Tableau*{CBJ+3rdLrn}, except at clause density 3.4.

The results in Figure 5 suggest that *learn-SAT* scales better than *Tableau*{CBJ+3rdLrn} at lower clause densities. To explore this further we look at problems having 400 variables at clause density 2. As before, we address four different problems of this size and density, and consider 100 randomly generated initial assignments for each problem.

On these problems the gap in performance between *learn-SAT* and *Tableau*{CBJ+3rdLrn} is much wider than on the 200 variable problems. *Learn-SAT* solves all the problems and requires roughly 500,000 constraint checks on average to do so. *Tableau*{CBJ+3rdLrn} solves only 40% of the problems within a pre-set limit of 10,000,000 constraint checks. Here *learn-SAT* performs nearly 20 times better than *Tableau*{CBJ+3rdLrn}, while it is only 3 times better on the 200 variable problems.

Before moving to consider the space required to solve the problems addressed in Figure 5, let us first look at the average number of nodes visited by each of these algorithms. The results are shown in Figure 6. On the 200 variable problems we see that *Tableau*{CBJ+3rdLrn} visits on average roughly 17,500 at clause density 2.6. This is about 8 times more than *learn-SAT*, which is similar to the difference in the average number of constraint checks at 2.6. At 3.4 the situation is different. We see

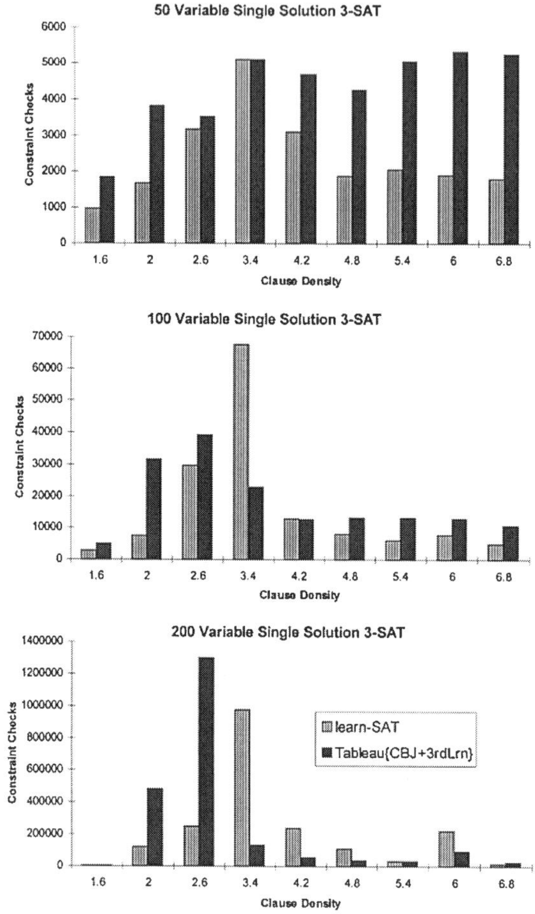

Figure 5. Average number of constraint checks

that *learn-SAT* visits on average about 4,500 nodes, which is about 5 times more than *Tableau*{CBJ+3rdLrn}. But *learn-SAT* requires about 10 times the number of constraint checks. This seems broadly as it should be, since *learn-SAT* checks most of the constraints at each node.

This suggests an interesting relation between the nodes visited and the average number of constraint checks. Comparing Figures 5 and 6, we see that when *Tableau*{CBJ+3rdLrn} visits more nodes than *learn-SAT*, the difference between the two is the same as that between them with respect to the average number of constraint checks. However, when *learn-SAT* visits more nodes than *Tableau*{CBJ+3rdLrn}, the difference here is only half that with respect to the number of constraint checks.

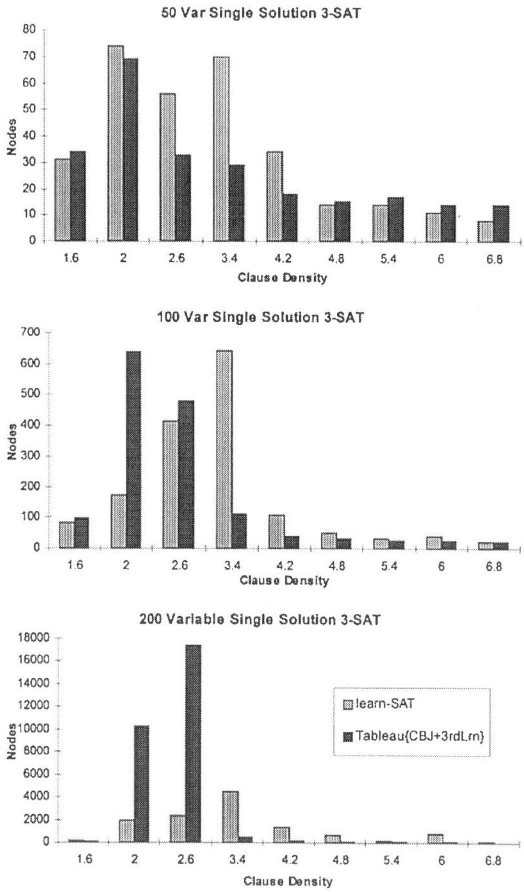

Figure 6. Average number of nodes visited

4.3. Memory requirement

We now turn to measure the memory required to solve the problems we have been considering. This is determined by the space required to store the problem and the space consumed by the no-goods generated during search. The former is measured by the sum of the sizes of all the clauses; the latter by the sum of the sizes of the no-goods generated.

In Figure 7 we compare at each clause density the space required to store the problem with the average total space required to solve its 400 instances. It is immediately evident that the additional space consumed during search is not a significant factor. Even in the worst case, i.e. at clause density 3.4 on the 200-variable problems, this is only just over twice the space required for the problem itself.

Nevertheless, the additional space consumed during search grows with problem size. Note that the growth is greatest at clause densities 2, 2.6 and 3.4. While the additional space consumed is negligible for 50-variable problems, it is greater for the 100-variable problems and even greater for the 200-variable problems. This suggests that for larger problems space will become an important factor.

In Figure 8 we show the average number of no-goods generated at each clause density. These results, together with those in Figure 6, point to an interesting question. On the 200-variable problems there is plainly a significant amount of learning at clause densities 2 and 2.6; many no-goods are discovered during search, consuming nearly as much space as that needed to store the problem itself. The situation does not change much at 3.4, although many more no-goods are discovered. Here the space consumed by the generated no-goods is only slightly more than that required by the problem. However, the average number of constraint checks is very different. There is nearly 5 times the number of constraint checks at 3.4 as compared to 2.6, and over 5 times at 2. Why is there such a difference here?

One explanation might be that the no-goods at 2 and 2.6 are pruning the search space more effectively than at 3.4. This would arise if the size of the no-goods learned at 2 and 2.6 were smaller than those learned at 3.4. Recall that smaller no-goods typically achieve more pruning than larger ones. This explanation, however, is eliminated by Figure 9, which measures the average size of the no-goods learned on the different problems. Note that on the 200-variable problems the average size is virtually the same at clause densities 2, 2.6 and 3.4.

Where there is a difference is in the average number of nodes visited. The results, which correspond to the graphs of Figure 6, are shown in Figure 10. On the 200 variable problems the average number of nodes visited at clause density 3.4 is significantly larger than at 2 and 2.6, roughly twice as many. This is the source of the difference in constraint checking. Visiting more than twice the number of nodes requires more than four times the amount of constraint checking. This is just what we see in Figure 5.

To explain the performance of *learn-SAT* we must explain why it visits so many more nodes at 3.4 than it does at 2 and 2.6. Note that this cannot be traced simply to the increase in clause density since the number of nodes visited at 4.2 drops sharply. The experiments here have revealed a deep question, which can only be resolved by further investigation. The aim in this section has been to fix the question to be pursued.

4.4. *Comparison to* **weight**

One might naturally ask how *learn-SAT* compares with incomplete non-systematic algorithms on the AIM problems. Here we examine the *weight* algorithm, which is an incomplete non-systematic technique introduced independently by [37], and [25].

Figure 11 describes *weight*. Each constraint has an associated weight, which is initialised to 1. The weighted number of conflicts of a labelling is the sum of the weights of the violated constraints. Two labellings are said to be neighbours if they differ in exactly one variable-value assignment. Suppose that the current labelling is inconsistent. Then search progresses by identifying the neighbour with the smallest weighted number of conflicts. Where there are several neighbours with the same weighted sum, one is selected at random. If the selected neighbour has a sum which is less than that of the current labelling, this neighbour becomes the new current labelling.

Otherwise, the conflict-count of each of violated constraint in the current labelling is incremented by 1, and the current labelling remains the same. The search then attempts to find a neighbour with a smallest weighted number of conflicts given these incremented weights. Note that the *weight* algorithm will only terminate if a solution is found.

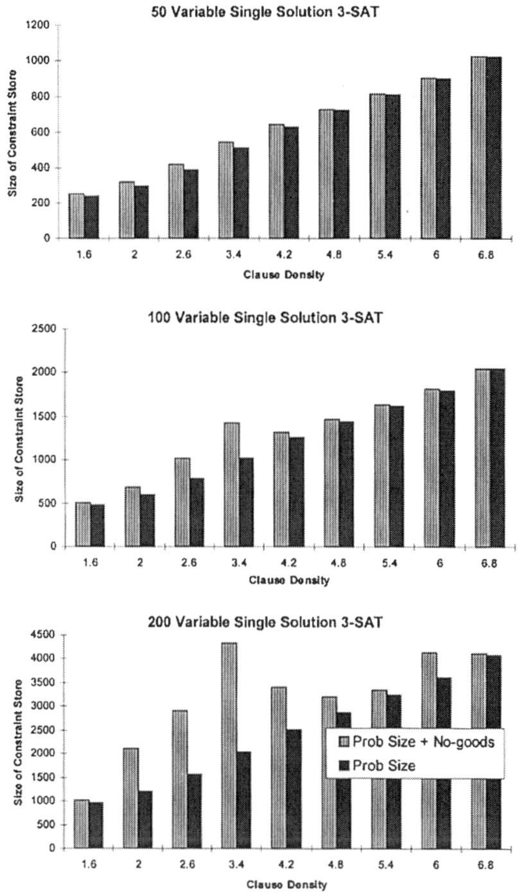

Figure 7. Space required by *learn-SAT*

[5] used the AIM problems to compare several non-systematic search techniques, including *GSAT*, *GSAT* with random walk, and *weight*. *Weight* was by far the best; at low clause density it outperformed the other algorithms by at least an order of magnitude.

Figure 12 compares the performance of *learn-SAT* and *weight* on the four AIM problems.As in previous experiments, each data point represents the average result for 100 different instances of each problem (400 cases in all). Clearly, *weight* performs very poorly relative to *learn-SAT*. The margin of difference is typically 1 to 2 orders of magnitude. It is interesting, moreover, that *weight* is at its worst at clause density 2.6. One might have thought that it would do better at the lower clause densities, but this is plainly not the case. In fact, the opposite holds; as clause density increases, *weight* begins to perform much better.

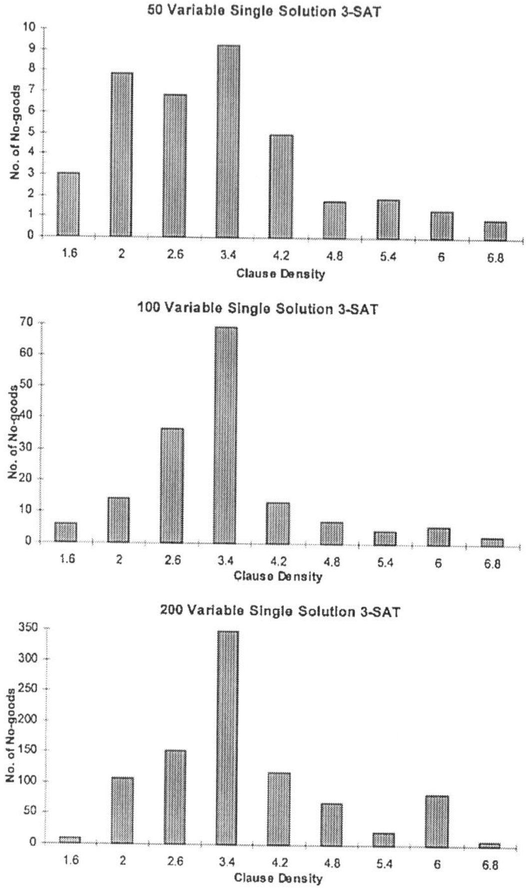

Figure 8. Average number of no-goods generated by *learn-SAT*

Figure 13 compares *weight* and *learn-SAT* with respect to the average number of nodes visited. Their relative behaviour here is very similar to that on the average number of constraint checks. Both measures show *weight* to be at its worst at low clause densities. [5] venture an explanation for this, and its better behaviour at higher clause densities. This is not immediately relevant.

4.5. Summary

The main result of this section concerns the relative performance of *learn-SAT* and *Tableau*{CBJ+3rdLrn} on the extended set of AIM problems. *Learn-SAT* outperforms *Tableau*{CBJ+3rdLrn} by a large margin at lower clause densities. At higher clause densities it often performs better than *Tableau*{CBJ+3rdLrn}, and when it

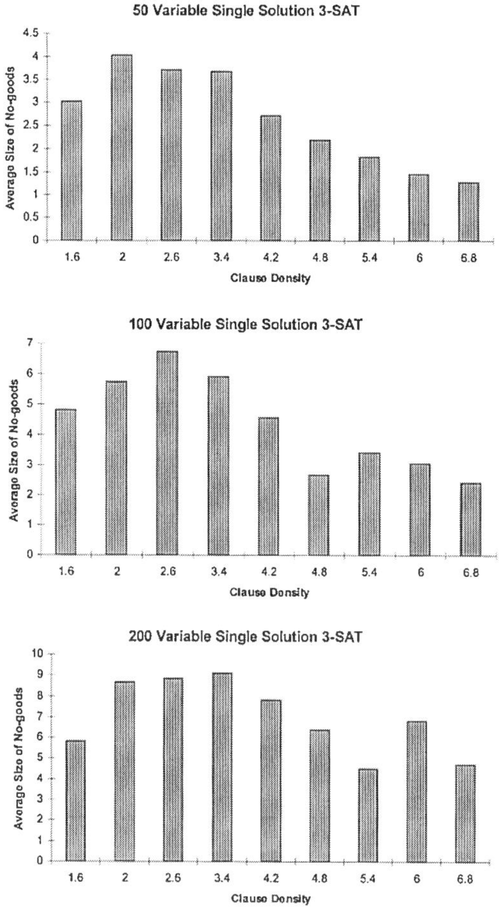

Figure 9. Average size of no-goods generated by *learn-SAT*

does not, the margin is quite small. The only exception is at clause density 3.4, where *Tableau*{CBJ+3rdLrn} performs very much better than*learn-SAT*.

On the matter of scaleability *learn-SAT* scales much better than *Tableau*{CBJ+3rdLrn} at lower clause densities. At the higher clause densities, however, there is some evidence that *Tableau*{CBJ+3rdLrn} scales better, although this is not pursued further. Scaleability will be addressed in the next section.

As for the anomalous performance of *learn-SAT* at 3.4, this is puzzling. We know that *learn-SAT* visits many more nodes here, but we do not know why. Explaining this, we conjecture, is critical to understanding the general performance of *learn-SAT*. We think we know at least one of the key questions. Resolving it is beyond the scope of this paper.

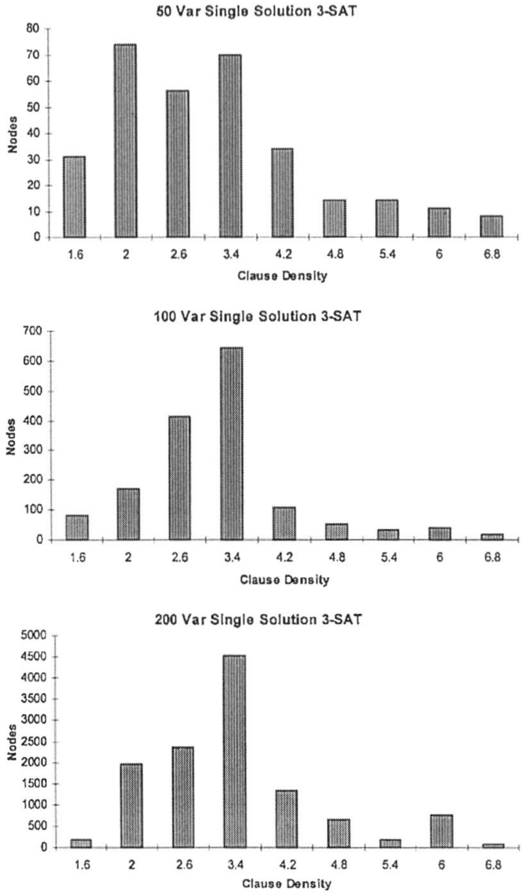

Figure 10. Average number of nodes visited by *learn-SAT*

One matter we have not addressed is the contribution which the individual components of *learn-SAT* make to its performance. This may be important to revealing an explanation for its performance profile. Although we cannot pursue this here, we show the contribution of the different components for 100 variable problems at clause density 2.6. The results are given in Table IV of Appendix B.

Despite the anomaly at 3.4, it is clear that the AIM problems we have studied do not impose much of a memory burden on *learn-SAT*. The leading question now regards the memory burden for insoluble problems. This is the focus of the next section.

```
A← a complete (possibly inconsistent) labelling to the variables
Initialise weight of each constraint to 1
Status ← Unknown
while Status = Unknown do
  let A' be a neighbouring labelling of A with the lowest
  weighted number of conflicts
  if (no. of conflicts in A') < (no. of conflicts in A)
    then A ← A'
  else increment the weight of each violated constraint in A
  endif
  if A is a solution
    then Status ← Solved
  endif
```

Figure 11. **Weight**

5. Insoluble 3-SAT Problems

Memory will definitely be a limitation on *learn-SAT* for some insoluble problems. We shall explore this limitation, particularly with respect to scaleability.

Here we focus on structured insoluble problems generated using the method of [3]. These problems are constructed by randomly generating an insoluble sub-problem and embedding this into a randomly generated larger problem. This structure allows the scaleability of algorithms to be investigated on two dimensions, i.e. the size of the sub-problem and the size of the whole problem.

[4] developed a new algorithm *relsat*, which they showed to be very effective for these structured insoluble problems. Below we compare the performance of *relsat* and *learn-SAT* on these problems. The results are striking and perhaps unexpected. Overall *learn-SAT* performs comparatively well, but the most interesting results arise when the two algorithms diverge.

5.1. Relsat

Relsat is similar to *Tableau*{CBJ+3rdLrn} in that it is based on conflict-directed back-jumping and jump-back learning. But unlike *Tableau*{CBJ+3rdLrn}, it incorporates a different variable selection heuristic and uses a different method for restricting the no-goods stored.

In *Tableau*{CBJ+3rdLrn} only those no-goods involving at most 3 variables are stored. In *relsat* all no-goods are stored but the set is reduced during search by "relevance bounding" [15, 2]. When a no-good differs in more than a fixed number of assignments from the current partial label, it is removed from the set. The idea here is that as the assignments in the current label diverge more and more from the no-good, the no-good becomes less and less relevant in pruning search.

Figure 14 describes *relsat.*

5.2. Empirical study

We now turn to the structured insoluble problems of [3]. These are generated by first constructing a literal-regular insoluble sub-problem and then extending this into a larger variable-regular problem. The sub-problem remains literal-regular, whereas the whole problem is variable-regular. The addition of regularity-inducing parameters into the

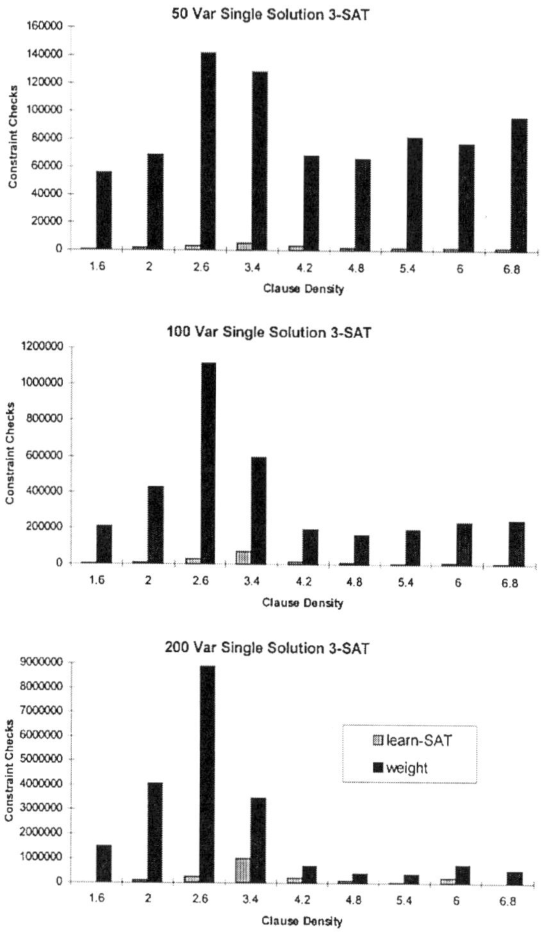

Figure 12. Average number of constraint checks

problem generator is designed to increase the difficulty by minimising the information available to heuristics when solving the problem.

The sub-problem and the whole problem can have different clause densities and will typically be of different size. We let n and d designate the size and clause density of the whole problem, and n and d the size and clause density of the insoluble sub-problem. In the experiments below we explore the relative performance of *learn-SAT* and *relsat* on two dimensions, viz. the size of the whole problem and the size of the sub-problem.

The first experiment explores the issue of scaleability with respect to the whole problem. We look at problems where the whole problem consists of 75, 100 or 150 variables (n); as above, we consider a range of clause densities d from 3 to 10. In all cases the size n and density d of the insoluble sub-problem is the same; $n = 15$ variables, and d is fixed by the formula $n \times d = (3.5 \times n) + 5$.

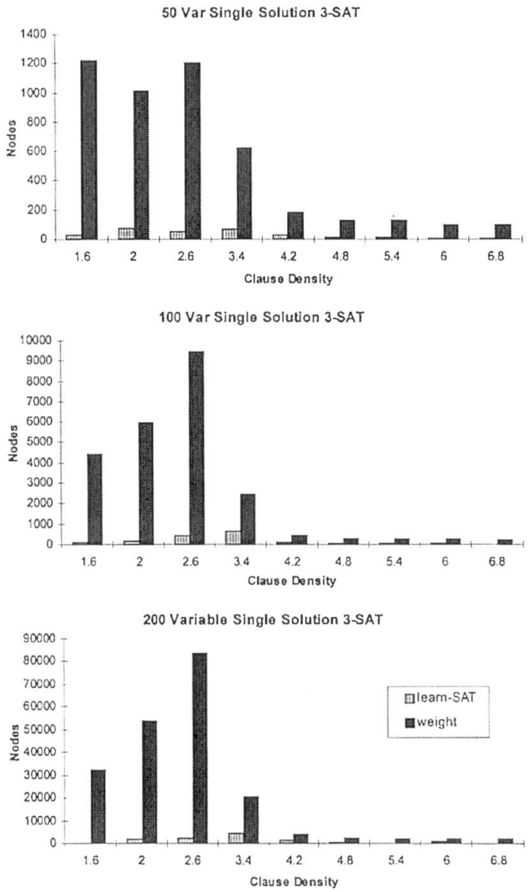

Figure 13. Average number of nodes visited

Figure 15 gives the average number of constraint checks for *learn-SAT* and *relsat* on 100 randomly generated problems at each data point.

Three things emerge from Figure 15. First, the overall performance of *learn-SAT* relative to *relsat* is far better than one might expect. When *learn-SAT* fails to reach the performance of *relsat*, which is only at the higher clause densities, it is by a modestly small margin. We saw something similar in the case of the AIM problems. Second, at the lower clause densities the performance of *learn-SAT* is very much better than that of *relsat*, again not unlike the results on the AIM problems.

But perhaps the most striking phenomenon concerns scaleability. As we move from the lower to the higher clause densities, we see a cross-over in the relative performance of the two algorithms on all three problem sizes. That is, *learn-SAT* performs uniformly better at lower clause densities than *relsat*, and then at a certain point *relsat* overtakes

```
P← a consistent partial labelling (initially empty)
Status ← Unknown
Consistent ← True
while Status ← Unknown do
  while Consistent = True do
    if P is a labelling to all variables then Status ← Solved
    else v ← relsat_select(P), Consistent ← False
      while Consistent ← False do
        foreach val ∈ CD_v, the 'current' domain of variable v
          Consistent ← propagate(P ∪ {(v, val)})
          if Consistent = False then
            conf_set_v ← conf_set_v ∪ conf_set_x
            where x is the domain wipe-out variable,
            CD_v ← CD_v - {val},
            undo_propagate(P ∪{(v, val)}, {v})
          endif
      if Consistent = False (i.e. CD_v = ∅)
        if conf_set_v = ∅thenStatus ← Insoluble
        else jump_back_learn(conf_set_v, P)
          let u ∈ conf_set_v be most recently assigned in P
          let Vars be all variables in P assigned after u,
          let val_u be the value of u in P, CD_u ← CD_u − {val_u}
          P ← P - Vars, undo_propagate(P, Vars ∪ {u})
          relevance_check_nogoods(O)
          conf_set_u ← conf_set_u ∪ conf_set_v - {u}
          foreach variable w ∈ Vars
            conf_set_w ← ∅, CD_w ← D_w, v ← u
        endif
      else Consistent = True, P ← P ∪ {(v, val)}
      endif
    endif
```

Figure 14. **Relsat**

learn-SAT and performs consistently better. We call this the *performance cross-over.* Note that the performance cross-over moves as the size of the whole problem increases. When it has 75 variables, the cross-over lies between densities 4 and 5; when it has 100 variables, the cross-over is between 5 and 6; and when it has 150 variables, it is between 6 and 7. This right shift is a clear manifestation of relative scaleability. *Learn-SAT* performs relatively better as the whole problem becomes larger and the sub-problem remains fixed in size.

Figure 15 also reveals an interesting phenomenon concerning the transition points, i.e. the clause density at which the performance of an algorithm is at its worst. Note that the transition point for *relsat* seems stable over all problem sizes at a clause density of roughly 4. In contrast, the transition point for *learn-SAT* moves with the three different problem sizes, from approximately 5 to 7 to 9. For one algorithm the transition point is stable; for the other it is not. It is interesting to note, moreover, that *relsat* performs very poorly at 4, rather like *learn-SAT* at 3.4 on the problems in the previous chapter.

But *learn-SAT* does not always scale better than *relsat.* Let us now vary the size of the sub-problem while fixing the size of the whole problem. In the next experiment the

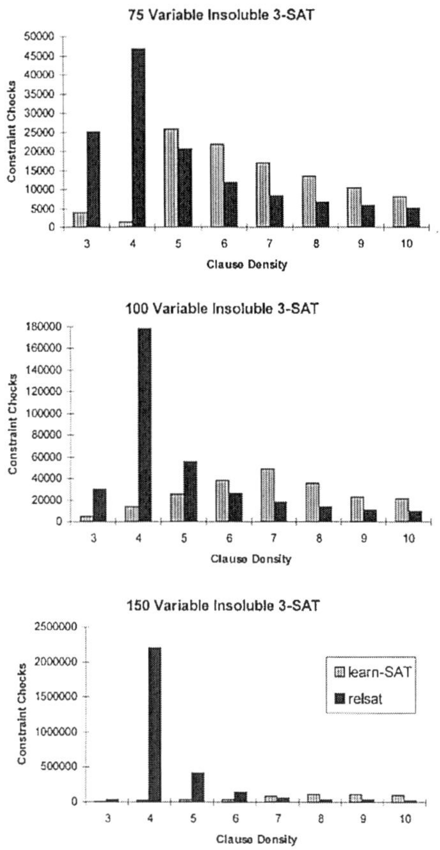

Figure 15. Varying the size of the whole problem

whole problem always has 100 variables. Again we explore different clause densities, ranging from 3 to 10. We consider sub-problems of four different sizes: 10, 15, 20 and 25 variables. For all sub-problems we again use $n \times d = (3.5 \times n) + 5$ to fix clause density. For each data point we randomly generate 100 problem instances and show the average constraint checks executed. The results are given in Figure 16; note that the clause densities on the x-axis are those of the whole problem.

The results in Figure 16 show that the performance cross-over moves to the left as the size of the sub-problem grows. For sub-problems consisting of 10 variables, *relsat* begins to outperform *learn-SAT* between clause densities 6 and 7; for 15-variable sub-problems the cross-over is between 5 and 6; and for 25-variable sub-problems it is between 4 and 5.

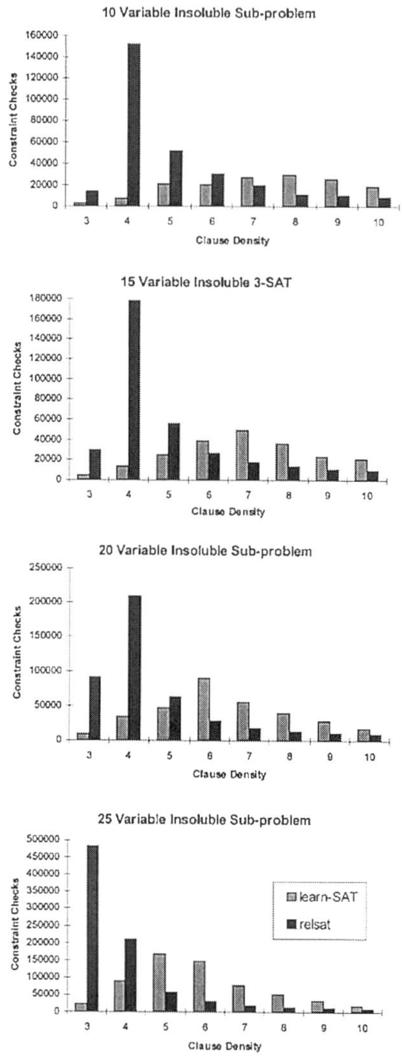

Figure 16. Varying sub-problem size

Again the conclusion is unmistakable. *Relsat* outperforms *learn-SAT* at ever lower clause densities as the size of the sub-problem grows. In effect, *relsat* scales better than *learn-SAT* on these problems. However, when *relsat* performs poorly relative to *learn-SAT*, it performs very poorly indeed. Between clause densities 3 and 4 its performance is far below that of *learn-SAT*. Note, moreover, that the transition point shifts slightly, from approximately 4 on 20-variable sub-problems to 3 on the 25-variable sub-problems;

Table II. Problems with large insoluble sub-problems

	$n = 40$	$n = 45$	$n = 50$
learn-SAT	423,433	1,133,353	1,940,050
relsat	1,052,013	1,116,188	878,623

it is otherwise stable at 4. In contrast, the transition point for *learn-SAT* moves from approximately 7 to 6 to 5.

Despite the relative stability and high peak of the *relsat* transition point, one would expect that *relsat* will eventually overtake the performance of *learn-SAT* at a clause density below 4. To explore this we consider three sets of 100 problems with 100 variables and clause density 3.5. In the first set each problem contains an insoluble sub-problem where the number n of variables is 40 and the clause density d is determined by the equation $n \times d = (3.5 \times n) + 5$. In the second set of problems n is 45, and in the third set n is 50; and again clause density d is determined by the same formula. The results of these experiments are shown in Table II.

When n is 40, *learn-SAT* requires approximately 400,000 constraint checks, less than half the count for *relsat* which is approximately 1,000,000 on average. When n is 45, the two algorithms require approximately the same number of constraint checks on average, roughly 1,100,000. But when n is 50, *relsat* requires 900,000 constraint checks on average, less than half that of *learn-SAT*.

While this result is as one might expect, it may be surprising that the sub-problem has to be so large before *relsat* outperforms *learn-SAT* at a lower clause density.

5.3. *Memory requirement*

We now measure the space required by *learn-SAT* to prove insolubility. Figure 17 relates to Figure 15, where the size of insoluble sub-problem is fixed and the whole problem varies in size. Figure 17 shows both the space required to store the problem and the average total space consumed in proving each of the problems insoluble at a given data point. Each data point represents the average over 100 problem instances. Recall that the clause densities here are those of the whole problem.

The most striking result is that on all problems the additional space required by the no-goods to prove insolubility is only a small fraction of the size of the problem itself. Note, moreover, that the additional space consumed grows slowly with problem size. In Appendix E we show the average number of no-goods generated for the largest problems, i.e. those having 150 variables in the whole problem. Clearly, space is not a significant factor here.

Figure 18corresponds to Figure 16 where the size of the whole problem is fixed and the sub-problem varies in size. Figure 18 shows the space required to store the problem and the average total space consumed in proving each of the problems insoluble. Once again, each data point represents the average over 100 problem instances, and the clause densities are those for the whole problem.

Here we see that as the insoluble sub-problem grows, the additional space requirement also grows. This is particularly evident at clause densities 4 and 5, where the proportional rate of growth is largest. But still the overall growth is low; in the worst case, viz. for problems with clause density 5 and sub-problems of 25 variables, the additional space consumed is less than 40% of the size of the problem itself. In Appendix E we show the average number of no-goods generated for these problems.

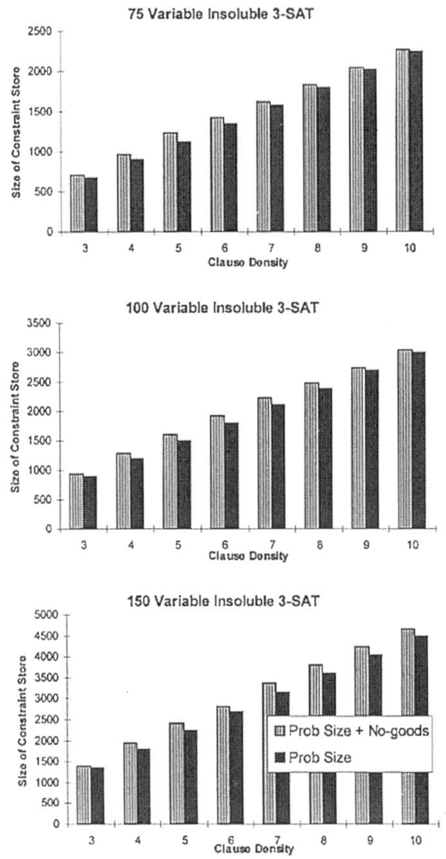

Figure 17. Space required by *learn-SAT* as the whole problem size increases

In general Figure 18 reveals that *learn-SAT* is well behaved for this problem set. There are no "outlying" results and the growth rate of the extra burden on memory is slow.

The behaviour at low clause densities is of particular interest. The burden on memory for *learn-SAT* grows as the sub-problem increases in size. One might wonder when the additional space requirements will become prohibitive, for surely they will at some point. We look at the space requirements for the insoluble problems considered in sub-section 5.2. Here the whole problem is fixed at 100-variables, and the sub-problems are of three different sizes, viz. 40, 45 and 50 variables.

When the insoluble sub-problem has 40 variables, the average space consumed in proving insolubility is approximately 2.5 times the problem size. At 45 variables the

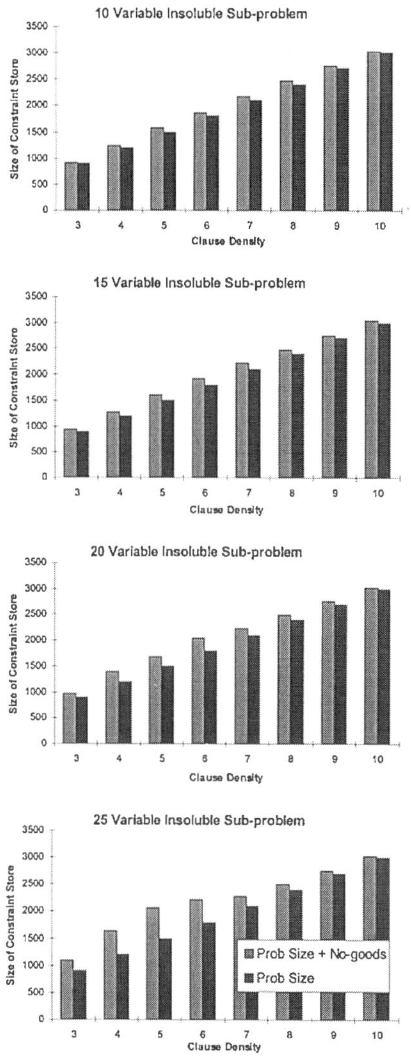

Figure 18. Space required by *learn-SAT* as the whole problem size increases

space required is approximately 4.5 times the problem size, and at 50 variables roughly 6 times the problem size. Clearly, the size of the sub-problem has a significant impact on the memory overhead. Nevertheless, it must be relatively large before this becomes an issue.

5.4. Search nodes

Finally, we look at the average number of nodes visited by *learn-SAT* and *relsat* when proving insolubility. These are given in Figures 19 and 20, which correspond respectively to Figure 15 and Figure 16.

The important correlation relates to the performance cross-over. Recall that the results reported in Figure 15, where the measure is the average number of constraint checks, show a right shift. As the whole problem increases in size, the cross-over is delayed to higher clause densities. When the whole problem has 50 variables, the cross-over occurs at clause density 5; when it has 100 variables, it occurs at 6; and when it has 150 variables, it does not occur until 7. Exactly the same holds for the results in Figure 19, where the measure is the average number of nodes visited. The cross-over is at the very same clause densities.

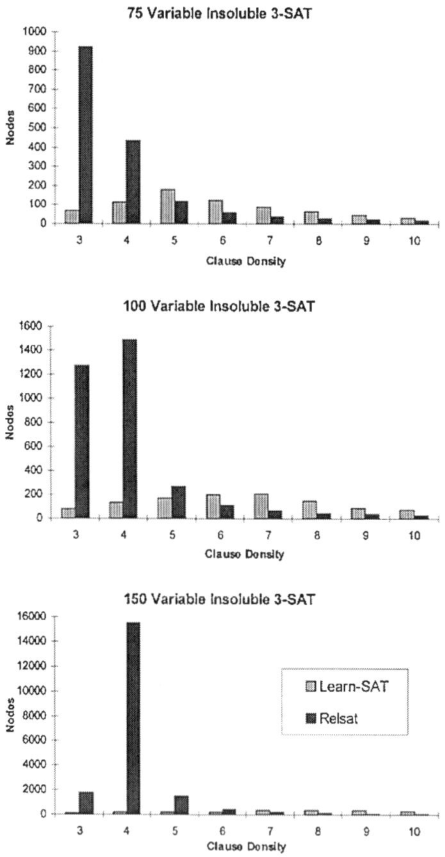

Figure 19. Average number of nodes visited

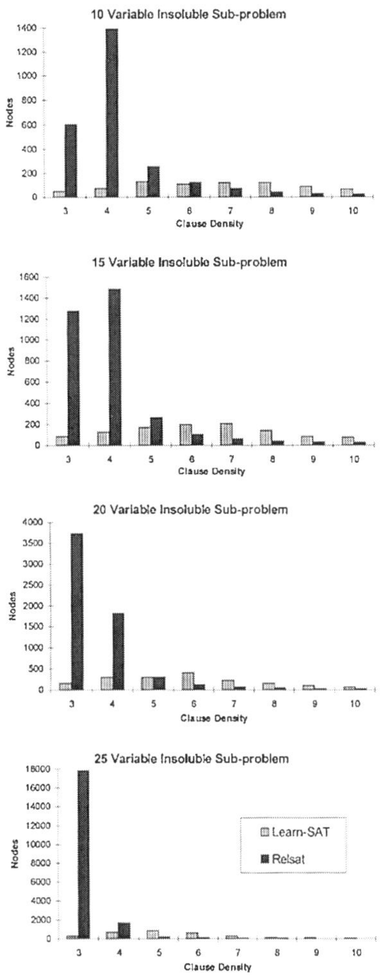

Figure 20. Average number of nodes visited

A similar situation holds for the results given in Figure 19. Here there is a left shift in the cross-over, which occurs at the same clause densities for the corresponding problems in Figure 16.

The correlation in regard to the performance cross-over confirms that this phenomenon is not an artefact of the way performance is measured. We see the same thing whether performance is measured in terms of average constraints checks or average nodes visited.

5.5. Summary and significance of results

Overall *learn-SAT* performs well on structured insoluble problems in comparison with *relsat*. It scales much better than *relsat* with respect to the size of the whole problem. It also performs very much better at all lower clause densities. But *relsat* scales better with respect to the size of the insoluble sub-problem; this is as one would expect. Nevertheless, the margin of difference is not very great, and *learn-SAT* continues to perform particularly well at lower clause densities.

Surprisingly, space is not a problem for *learn-SAT* in proving insolubility. This is perhaps unexpected since some of the problems tested are reasonably large; one might anticipate that a large volume of no-goods would be generated during search, thereby creating a heavy burden on memory. This does not happen. Moreover, *learn-SAT* performs in a roughly uniform way. The space requirements grow slowly, and there are no "outlying" results, unlike *relsat*.

At this point a picture is beginning to emerge, even if only tentatively. On insoluble problems there are two key factors affecting the relative performance of *learn-SAT* and *relsat*, viz. the size of the insoluble sub-problem and the size of the whole problem. The behaviour of *learn-SAT* is determined principally by the size of the insoluble sub-problem. As this becomes larger, *learn-SAT* performs less well. Its behaviour is less affected by the size of the whole problem. Indeed, provided the insoluble sub-problem is not too large, the size of the whole problem can be very large; *learn-SAT* scales well on this dimension. This suggests that the basic strategy of *learn-SAT* is to focus its search around the insoluble sub-problem; it tends not to investigate irrelevant parts of the search space.

The behaviour of *relsat* is more subtle. It is affected principally by the ratio of the size of the insoluble sub-problem to the size of the whole problem: the higher the ratio, the better the performance, at least relatively. *Relsat* is less affected than *learn-SAT* simply by the size of the insoluble problem. It more sensitive, however, to the size of the whole problem; this increases as the above ratio decreases. This suggests that *relsat* tends to undertake more and more irrelevant search as this ratio decreases. On the other hand, it deals efficiently with the insoluble sub-problem once it finds it.

To confirm these conjectures more empirical work is necessary. Our aim here has been to bring the conjectures into focus and provide some evidence that they are correct. In the next section we begin the task of placing them in a wider context.

6. Large-scale Problems & Benchmarks

At this point one may be tempted to think that *learn-SAT* will always be the best algorithm at lower clause densities. To explore this we study a set of literal-regular 3-SAT problems, all of which are soluble. Here we compare the performance of *learn-SAT* to both *weight* and *relsat*. We also consider a soluble type of problem from the DIMACS benchmarks, viz. par8-c, and again compare the three algorithms.

6.1. Literal-regular 3-SAT problems

The literal-regular problems studied below are constructed using a random generator such that each literal appears the same number of times. The motivation for having an even literal distribution is to minimise the impact heuristics might have in finding a solution. Heuristics tend to use irregularities in a problem to guide search. We focus here on low clause density problems where there are typically many solutions.

A literal-regular problem involving n variables has $2n$ different possible literals, consisting of the set of variables and their negations. To generate a literal-regular problem involving n variables with clause density d first collect a set containing $3d/2$ occurrences of each literal. A randomly selected set of unique literals is added to this set to ensure that there are exactly $3m$ literals, where m is the number of clauses in the problem, $m=nd$. Each clause is generated by removing three literals involving distinct variables

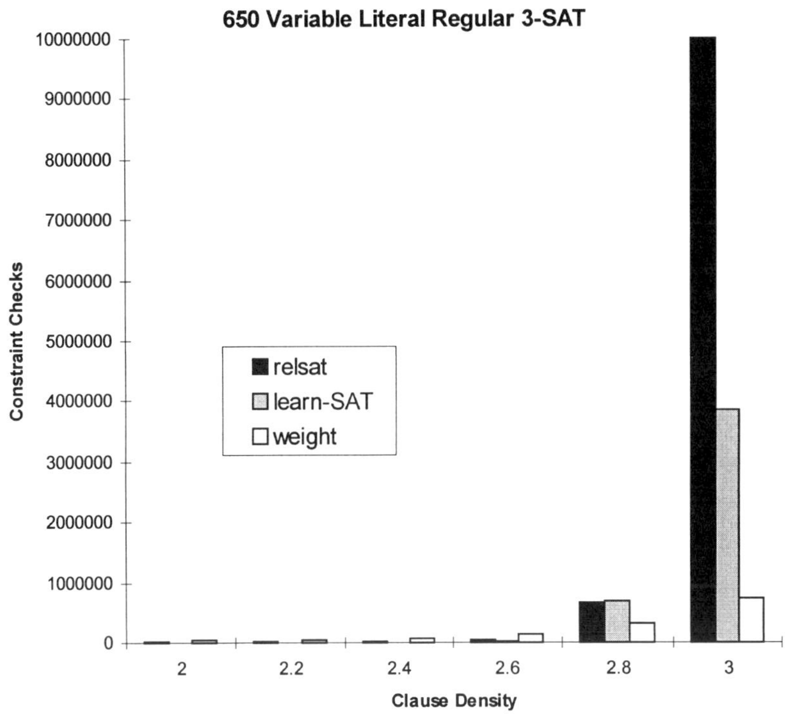

Figure 21. Average number of constraint checks

We study problems having 650 variables at 6 clause densities, ranging between 2 and 3 at increments of 0.2. These are all soluble. The results are given in Figure 21. Each data point represents the average number of constraint checks required by each of the algorithms over 100 different problem instances. There is a cut-off bound of 10,000,000 constraint checks.

There is not much difference in the performance of the three algorithms between 2 and 2.6. At 2.8, however, *weight* requires only half the number of constraint checks needed by the other two; these execute nearly a million constraint checks. At 3 the situation is more extreme. Although *learn-SAT* solves all the instances, it performs over 4 times the number of constraint checks on average 3.8 million. *Relsat* fails to solve any of the instances within the cut-off.

Figure 22 shows the average number of nodes visited during search for each of the algorithms. *Weight* visits far fewer nodes than the other two at 2.8 and 3. Curiously,

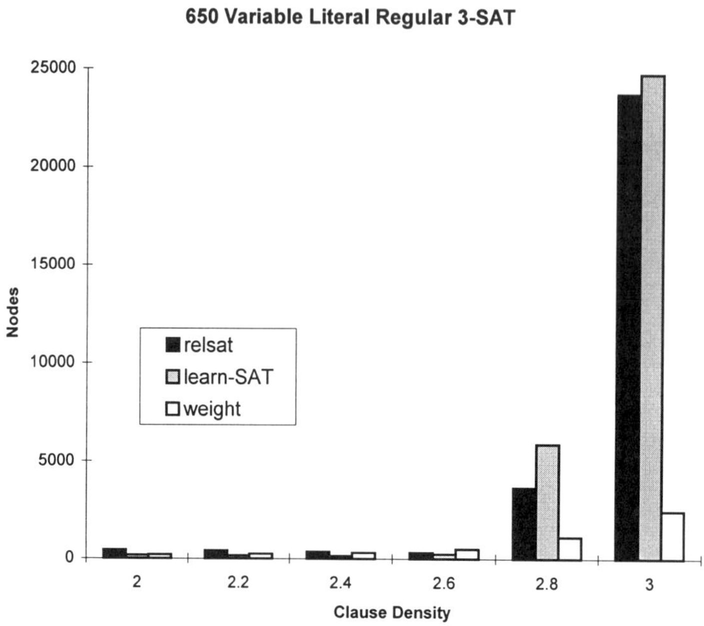

Figure 22. Average number of nodes visited

relsat visits fewer nodes on average than *learn-SAT* at these clause densities. Plainly *relsat* does much more work at each node than does *learn-SAT*. This is due to the heuristic in *relsat*.

Finally, we consider the par8-c problems from the DIMACS benchmarks. These are all soluble and are relevant to the earlier comparison of *weight*, *relsat* and *learn-SAT* on the AIM problems. Recall that on these problems *weight* never challenges the other two algorithms; they always perform better. It is interesting to see what their relative performance is on the par8-c problems, which have clause densities close to 4. Here there should not be many solutions.

We look at 5 problems of this type and as usual consider 100 different initial assignments for each problem. The number of constraint checks is averaged over 500 instances. *Learn-SAT* requires 3153 constraint checks and *relsat* 5996; in contrast, *weight* needs 1,433,700. What does this mean? Perhaps the par8-c problems are like the AIM problems in having very few solutions? If so, one would expect that *weight* would perform poorly, while *learn-SAT* and *relsat* should perform well.

6.2. Insoluble DIMACS benchmark

We have seen that *learn-SAT* performs well on structured insoluble 3-SAT problems. The question is whether this holds for other insoluble problems. Here we consider three insoluble problems drawn from the DIMACS benchmarks, viz. aim-no, dubois and hole, and compare *learn-SAT* and *relsat*.

We look at a number of different problems of each type, and for each problem we consider 100 different, randomly generated instances. The results, given in Table III, are the average number of constraint checks required to prove insolubility. Here there is

Table III. Benchmark Problems

	aim_no						dubois	hole
No. vars.	50		100		200			
Clause denity	1.6	2.0	1.6	2.0	1.6	2.0		
No.Probs.	4	4	4	4	4	4	11	5
learn-SAT	3,039	3,142	13,375	7,226	17,446	25,284	17,850,000 (97%)	(0%)
relsat	5,197	13,833	84,499	60,768	104,382	232,366	31,020,000 (54%)	11,340,000

a cut-off bound of 10,000,000 constraint checks for the aim-no problems, and 50,000,000 for the other problems. The percentages in brackets show the percentage of problems shown to be insoluble within the cut-off bound. Where this is not specified, all the instances were proved insoluble within the cut-off.

The results again reveal a curiosity. *Learn-SAT* outperforms *relsat* everywhere except on the hole instances, of which it proves none insoluble. On the aim-no instances it not only performs better than *relsat*, it scales better. On the dubois instances it proves insolubility in 97% of the cases, while *relsat* succeeds on only 54%. But on the hole instances *relsat* shows insolubility for all instances, while *learn-SAT* never does so.

Here there may be an important difference in the modelling of the problems. In the case of the aim-no and dubois problems, the maximum clause size is 3; that is, they are 3-SAT problems. The hole problem, however, is not. There are several clauses involving 10 literals. This invites one to wonder whether *learn-SAT* might be best deployed on 3-SAT models, not arbitrary SAT models.

7. Conclusions

The aim in this paper has been twofold: first, to show that *learn-SAT* can compete effectively with the best algorithms on selected hard problems; and second, to begin to build a profile of its performance which might be used to explain its behaviour.

7.1. Learn-SAT

The key issue has been the burden on memory arising from no-good learning. We have seen that this is managed well on both the AIM problems and structured insoluble problems.

On the AIM problems *learn-SAT* outperforms *Tableau*{CBJ+3rdLrn} by a large margin at lower clause densities. At higher clause densities it often performs better than *Tableau*{CBJ+3rdLrn}, and when it does not, the margin is usually quite small, with one interesting exception. Moreover, *learn-SAT* scales much better than *Tableau*{CBJ+3rdLrn} at lower clause densities. At higher clause densities *Tableau*{CBJ+3rdLrn} may scale better, although the results are less clear. Most important, the memory overhead on *learn-SAT* is not significant, except at clause density 3.4.

For structured insoluble problems *learn-SAT* performs well in comparison with *relsat.* At lower clause densities *learn-SAT* outperforms *relsat* by a large margin. Although the memory burden is handled efficiently on all the problems tested, the performance of *learn-SAT* deteriorates as the size of the insoluble sub-problem grows. This will eventually reach a size that *learn-SAT* cannot cope with.

The most striking results arise with respect the performance cross-over. When the size of the insoluble sub-problem is fixed, the cross-over shifts consistently to the right as the size of the whole problem increases. Here *learn-SAT* scales more effectively than *relsat*. When the size of the whole problem is fixed, the cross-over shifts consistently to the left as the size of the insoluble sub-problem increases. On this dimension *relsat* scales more effectively.

The results on large-scale literal-regular problems with many solutions show that *learn-SAT* is not always the best algorithm at low clause densities. Here *weight* is up to 5 times better. On the AIM problems, however, *learn-SAT* significantly outperforms *weight* everywhere.

In general, the experimental results indicate that *learn-SAT* is an effective scaleable algorithm for 3-SAT problems relative to the best backtrack search algorithms. But there remain many questions.

7.2. Two Questions

How does *learn-SAT* perform with respect to clause size? We have seen that it performs very poorly on the hole problems. Is this an anomaly or is the performance of *learn-SAT* dependent on clause size?

This points to a larger issue regarding modelling and *learn-SAT*. If the exceptional performance of *learn-SAT* is confined to 3-SAT models, one may seek to model SAT problems as 3-SAT problems to exploit the strengths of the algorithm. This may or may not be a good strategy. Only a detailed study will tell.

A second question relates to strategies for reducing the memory overheads of the no-good set. It is often the case that a no-good generated during search subsumes other no-goods already stored. For example the no-good $\{(x,\mathrm{r}),(y,\mathrm{s})\}$ subsumes the no-goods $\{(x,\mathrm{r}),(y,\mathrm{s}),(z,\mathrm{t})\}$ and $\{(u,\mathrm{q}),(x,\mathrm{r}),(y,\mathrm{s})\}$. The latter two achieve no additional pruning over the former $\{(x,\mathrm{r}),(y,\mathrm{s})\}$. Moreover, they consume more space. The question is, can subsumed no-goods be removed efficiently to save space and reduce constraint checking?

Appendix

A. Median contraint checks for *learn-SAT* and *Tableau*{CBJ+3rdLrn}

Figure 23 shows the median number of constraint checks for *learn-SAT* and *Tableau*{CBJ+3rdLrn} for 200 variable single solution 3-SAT problems.

B. Contribution of components in *learn-SAT*

Here we compare four stages in the development of *learn-SAT* on AIM problems with 100 variables at clause density 2.6. These are *RestartRepair*, *RestartRepair*{FC},*RestartRepair*{LbM+FC} and *learn-SAT*, and they represent the addition of one key component of the final algorithm.

Table IV gives the results on a problem set generated as in Section 5, i.e. on 100 instances of 4 different problems. There is a cut-off bound of 500,000 constraint checks on each run. In the table we show the percentage of problems solved within the cut-off and the average number of constraint checks required.

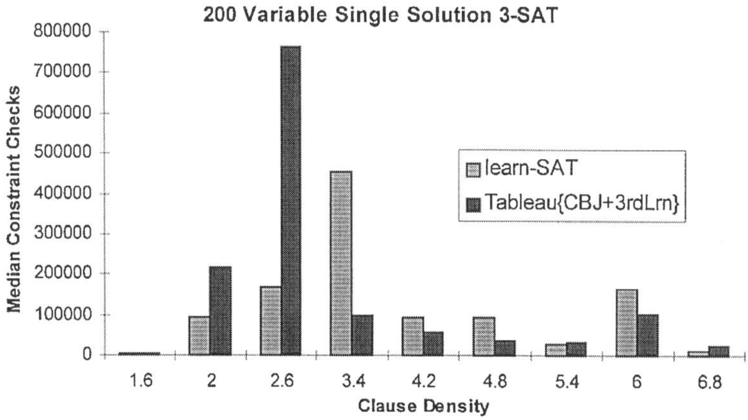

Figure 23. Median number of constraint checks for 200 variable single solution 3-SAT problems

Table IV. Contribution of components in *learn-SAT*

	Ave. constraint checks	% problems solved
RestartRepair	500000	0%
RestartRepair{FC}	457329	18.5%
RestartRepair{LbM+FC}	243277	85%
Learn-SAT	29655	100%

C. Median constraint checks for *learn-SAT* and *relsat* on 150-variable insoluble problems

Figure 24 shows the median number of constraint checks *learn-SAT* and *relsat* for insoluble problems where $n = 150$, $n' = 15$, and d is given by $n' \times d' = (3.5 \times n') + 5$.

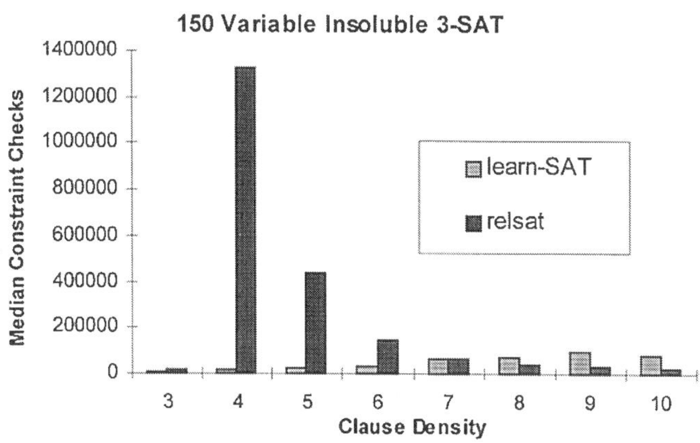

Figure 24. Median number of constraint checks for insoluble problems where $n = 150$, $n = 15$, and d' is given by $n' \times d' = (3.5 \times n') + 5$

D. Median constraint checks for *learn-SAT* and *relsat* on 100-variable insoluble problems

Figure 25 shows the median number of constraint checks for *learn-SAT* and *relsat* for insoluble problems where $n = 100$, $n = 25$, and d' is given by $n' \times d' = (3.5 \times n') + 5$.

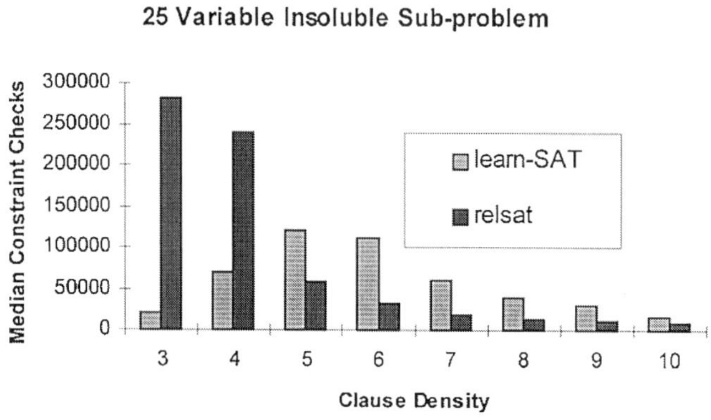

Figure 25. Median number of constraint checks for insoluble problems where $n = 100$, $n = 25$, and d' is given by $n' \times d' = (3.5 \times n') + 5$

E. Number of no-goods generated by *learn-SAT* to prove insolubility

For reference we record in Figure 26 the number of no-goods generated by *learn-SAT* to prove insolubility on two of the problem sets studied, one relating to the size of the whole problem (150 variables) and the other to the size of the insoluble sub-problem (25 variables).

Acknowledgements

We are particularly grateful to Jonathan Lever for many valuable suggestions, and to Yuichi Asahiro for extending the AIM problem set. We would also like to thank Roberto Bayardo, Hani El-Sakkout, Eugene Freuder, Robert Rodosek, Barbara Smith and Mark Wallace; and the two anonymous reviewers for detailed comments on an earlier draft of this paper. The early stages of this research were supported in part by BT Laboratories, Martlesham Heath, Ipswich.

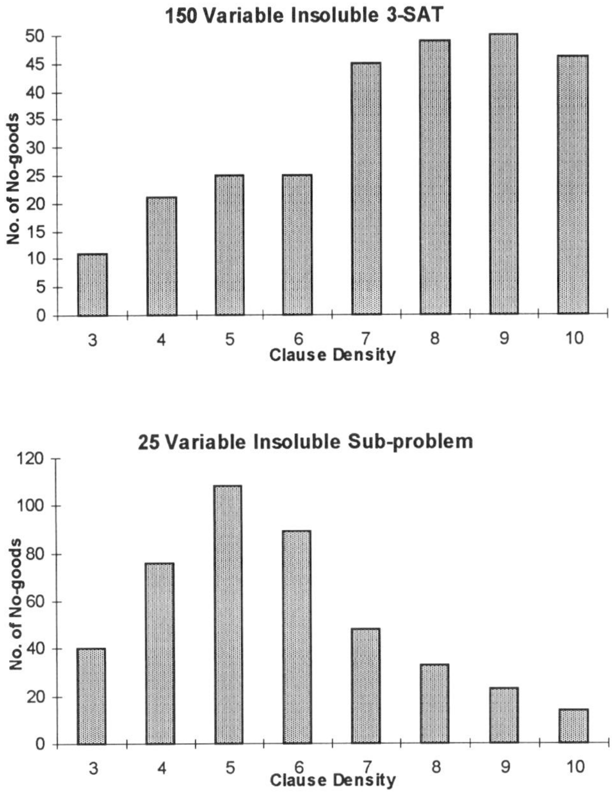

Figure 26. Average number of no-goods generated by *learn-SAT*

References

1. Y. Asahiro, K. Iwama and E. Miyano. Random generation of test instances with controlled attributes, Cliques, Colouring and Satisfiability. *DIMACS Series in Disc. Math. and Theory Comp. Sci.*, 1995.
2. R. J. Bayardo and D. Miranker. A complexity analysis of space bounded learning algorithms for the constraint satisfaction problem. *Proceedings AAAI-96*, 1996.
3. R. J. Bayardo and R. Schrag. Using look-back techniques to solve exceptionally hard SAT instances. *Proceedings CP-96*, Cambridge, MA, USA, August, 1996.
4. R. J. Bayardo and R. Schrag. Using CSP look-back techniques to solve real-world SAT instances. *Proceedings AAAI-97*, Providence, RI, USA, July, 1997.
5. B. Cha and K. Iwama. Performance test of local search algorithms using new types of random CNF formulas. *Proceedings IJCAI-95*, 1995.
6. B. Cha and K. Iwama. Adding new clauses for faster local search. *Proceedings AAAI-96*, 1996.
7. P. Cheeseman, B. Kanefsky and W. Taylor. Where the really hard problems are. *Proceedings IJCAI-91*, 1991.
8. J. M. Crawford and L. D. Auton. Experimental results on the crossover point in random 3SAT. *Artificial Intelligence 81*, 1996.
9. J. M. Crawford and A. B. Baker. Experimental results on the application of satisfiability algorithms to scheduling problems. *Proceedings AAAI-93*, 1993.

10. M. Davis and H. Putnam. A computing procedure for quantification theory. *Journal of the ACM*, 1960.
11. R. Dechter. Enhancement schemes for constraint processing: backjumping, learning and cutset decomposition. *Artificial Intelligence 41*, 1990.
12. O. Dubois and Y. Boufkhad. From very hard doubly balanced SAT formulae to easy unbalanced SAT forumlae, variations of the satisfiability threshold. *Proceedings of the DIMACS workshop on the satisfiability problem: Theory and Applications*, 1996.
13. D. Frost and R. Dechter. Dead-end driven learning. *Proceedings AAAI-94*, 1994.
14. M. Ginsberg. Dynamic Backtracking. *Journal of Artificial Intelligence Research*, 1993.
15. M. Ginsberg and D. McAllester. GSAT and Dynamic Backtracking. *Principles of Knowledge Representation and Reasoning 4th International Conference*, 1994.
16. S. Golomb and L. Baumert. Backtrack programming. *Journal of the ACM*, 1965.
17. R. Haralick and G. Elliott. Increasing tree search efficiency for constraint satisfaction problems. *Artificial Intelligence*, 1980.
18. Y. Jiang, E. T. Richards, and B. Richards. No-good backmarking with min-conflict repair in constraint satisfaction and optimisation. *Proceedings PPCP-94 2nd International Workshop*, Washington State USA, 1994.
19. G. Kondrak and P. van Beek. A Theoretical Evaluation of Selected Backtracking Algorithms. *Proceedings IJCAI-95*, 1995.
20. P. Langley. Systematic and non-systematic search strategies. *Artificial Intelligence and Planning Systems: Proceedings of 1st International Conference*, 1992.
21. D. L. Mammen and T. Hogg. A New Look at the Easy-Hard-Easy Pattern of Combinatorial Search Difficulty. *Journal of Artificial Intelligence Research*, 6:47-66, 1997.
22. F. Maruyama, Y. Minoda, S. Sawada, Y. Takizawa, and N, Kawato. Solving Combinatorial Constraint Satisfaction and Optimization Problems Using Sufficient Conditions for Constraint Violation. *Proceedings ISAI-91 4th International Symposium on AI*, 1991.
23. S. Minton, M. D. Johnston, A. B. Phillips and P. Laird. Minimising conflicts: a heuristic repair method for constraint satisfaction and scheduling problems. *Artificial Intelligence 58*, 1992.
24. D. Mitchell, B. Selman, and H. Levesque. Hard and easy distributions of SAT problems. *Proceedings AAAI-92*, 1992.
25. P. Morris. The breakout method for escaping local minima. *Proceedings AAAI-93*, 1993.
26. B. Nadel. Constraint Satisfaction Algorithms. *Computational Intelligence*, 1989.
27. C. Papadimitriou and K. Steiglitz. Combinatorial Optimisation: Algorithms and Complexity. *Englewood Cliffs, NJ: Prentice-Hall Inc.*, 1982.
28. P. Prosser. Hybrid algorithms for the constraint satisfaction problem. *Computational Intelligence 9*, 1993.
29. E. T. Richards. Non-systematic search and No-good Learning. *PhD Thesis*, IC Parc, Imperial College, 1998.
30. E. T. Richards, Y. Jiang and B. Richards. Ng-backmarking - an algorithm for constraint satisfaction. *AIP Techniques for Resource Scheduling and Planning, BT Technology Journal* Vol 13 No 1, January, 1995.
31. E. T. Richards and B. Richards. No-good Learning for Constraint Satisfaction. *Proceedings CP-96 Workshop on Constraint Programming Applications*, 1996.
32. E. T. Richards and B. Richards. Restart-repair and Learning: An empirical study of single solution 3-SAT problems. *Proceedings CP-97 Workshop on the Theory and Practice of Dynamic Constraint Satisfaction*, 1997.
33. E. T. Richards and B. Richards. Non-systematic search and learning: an empirical study. *Principles and Practice of Constraint Satisfaction CP-98*, 1998.
34. T. Schiex and G. Verfaillie. No-good Recording for Static and Dynamic Constraint Satisfaction Problems. *Proceedings IEEE 5th International Conference on Tools with Artificial Intelligence*, 1993.
35. T. Schiex and G. Verfaillie. Stubbornness: a possible enhancement for backjumping and no-good recording. *Proceedings ECAI-94*, 1994.
36. B. Selman, H. J. Levesque and D. G. Mitchell. A new method for solving hard satisfiability problems. *Proceedings AAAI-92*, 1992.
37. B. Selman, H. Kautz. An empirical study of greedy local search for satisfiability testing. *Proceedings AAAI-93*, 1993.
38. B. Selman, H. Kautz. Local search strategies for satisfiability testing. *Proceedings 2nd DIMACS Challenge Workshop*, 1993.

39. P. Siegel. Representation et utilisation des connaissances en calcul propositionnel. *These d'Etat*, Groupe d'Intelligence Artificielle, Universite d'Aix-Marseille II. 1987.
40. B. Smith. How to solve the Zebra problem, or path consistency the easy way. *Proceedings of ECAI-92*, Austria, 1992.
41. E. Tsang. Foundations of Constraint Satisfaction. Academic Press, 1993.
42. G. Verfaillie and T. Schiex. Dynamic Backtracking for Dynamic Constraint Satisfaction Problems. *Proceedings ECAI-94*, 1994.
43. P. van Hentenryck. Constraint Satisfaction in Logic Programming. MIT Press, London, England, 1989.
44. M. Yokoo. Weak-commitment search for solving constraint satisfaction problems. *Proceedings AAAI-94*, 1994.

SAT2000
I. Gent et al. (Eds.)
IOS Press, 2000

SAT Local Search Algorithms: Worst-Case Study *

Edward A. Hirsch‡
Steklov Institute of Mathematics at St.Petersburg,
27 Fontanka, 191011 St.Petersburg, Russia

Abstract. Recent experiments demonstrated that local search algorithms (e.g. GSAT) are able to find satisfying assignments for many "hard" Boolean formulas. A wide experimental study of these algorithms demonstrated their good performance on some important classes of formulas as well as poor performance on some other ones. In contrast, theoretical knowledge of their worst-case behaviour is very limited. However, many worst-case upper and lower bounds of the form $2^{\alpha n}$ ($\alpha < 1$ is a constant) are known for other SAT algorithms, e.g. resolution-like algorithms. In the present paper we prove both upper and lower bounds of this form for local search algorithms. The class of *linear-size* formulas we consider for the upper bound covers most of the DIMACS benchmarks, the satisfiability problem for this class of formulas is $\mathcal{NP}$-complete.

Keywords: SAT, greedy local search, worst-case time bounds.

1. Introduction

Recently there has been an increased interest to local search algorithms for the Boolean satisfiability problem. Though this problem is $\mathcal{NP}$-complete (see e.g. [19]), B. Selman, H. Levesque and D. Mitchell have shown in [27] that an algorithm that uses local search can easily handle some of "hard" instances of SAT. They proposed a randomized greedy local search procedure GSAT (see Fig. 1) for the Boolean satisfiability problem and presented reassuring experimental results for graph coloring and n-queens problem. Starting with a random assignment, GSAT changes at each step the value of one variable so that the number of satisfied clauses increases as much as possible (the increase can be non-positive). If the satisfying assignment is not found in a certain number of steps, GSAT starts with another random assignment. Later many experimental results concerning various modifications of GSAT were obtained [5, 23, 6, 26, 25, 7, 24, 15, 11]. In particular, B. Selman and H. Kautz demonstrated in [24] that GSAT variants can solve large circuit synthesis and planning problems. Also, some average-case upper bounds are known for local search algorithms [13, 8].

Starting from [17] (see also [18]) and [2], there are many theoretical results proving "less-than-2^N" upper bounds for SAT and its subproblems w.r.t. the number N of variables, the number K of clauses and the length L of a formula. However, most of them use splitting algorithms. For example, splitting algorithms give the upper bounds $O\left(2^{0.309K}\right)$ and $O\left(2^{0.103L}\right)$ [9] for SAT and the bounds near $O\left(2^{0.59N}\right)$ [14, 21] for the satisfiability problem for formulas in 3-CNF. On the other hand, a lot of exponential lower bounds for different proof systems (in particular, for regular resolution which is equivalent to splitting algorithms [1]) were proved ([28] is a good survey).

The only known worst-case bound for a local search algorithm is the upper bound $O\left(2^{(1-\frac{1}{kd})N}\right)$ for formulas in k–CNF–d (i.e. each of the variables occurs at most d times,

‡ `http://logic.pdmi.ras.ru/~hirsch`
* Research is supported by grants from INTAS and RFBR.

and each clause contains at most k literals) [10]. This bound was proved for a variant of GSAT that does not use greediness, namely, for algorithm CSAT ("cautious" SAT, see Fig. 2) suggested and studied by I. P. Gent and T. Walsh [5, 6, 7] who provided experimental evidence that greediness is not very important for GSAT efficiency. Given a formula F in CNF and a truth assignment I, we say that a variable v increases (decreases) the number of satisfied clauses, if the assignment that differs from I only by the value of v satisfies more (respectively, less) clauses of F than I does. CSAT chooses a variable at random from the set of variables increasing the number of satisfied clauses, if there are no such variables, it chooses one that does not decrease the number of satisfied clauses, if there are none of those, it chooses any variable.

In this paper we study local search algorithms CSAT and GSAT. We concentrate on worst-case upper and lower bounds of the form $2^{\alpha N}$ ($\alpha \leq 1$ is a positive constant). Namely, we

(1) improve the worst-case upper bound [10] for CSAT and extend this result to all *linear-size* formulas;

(2) prove the first worst-case lower bounds for CSAT and GSAT for formulas in CNF (the bound is $\Omega\left(2^N/p(N)\right)$, where p is a polynomial) and 3–CNF (the bound is $\Omega\left(2^{0.0817N}\right)$).

We consider CSAT and GSAT as Monte Carlo randomized algorithms that always output "no" if the input formula is unsatisfiable and output "yes" with probability greater than 50% if the input formula is satisfiable. In fact, in the latter case the algorithm finds a satisfying assignment.

Upper bounds. A Boolean formula is *linear-size* if the number of literal occurrences in it is linearly dependent on the number of variables, i.e., $L \leq \lambda N$ for a constant λ. For each $\lambda > 1$, the satisfiability problem is $\mathcal{NP}$-complete for formulas with $L \leq \lambda N$.

In addition, it is a common belief that there is a threshold $K/N \approx 4.25$ such that about 50% of formulas in 3–CNF located near it are satisfiable (see [4, 12, 3] for lower and upper bounds for this threshold). Computational experiments show that random formulas picked from this region are probably the most "hard" (see, e.g., [16]). Clearly, these formulas are linear-size.

We prove that CSAT can solve the satisfiability problem for linear-size formulas in the time

$$2^{\left(1-\frac{1}{4(k-1)(\lambda-1)+2}\right)N}p(N)$$

with error probability $1/e$ independent on the input formula (p is a polynomial, $e = 2.71828\ldots$ is the base of the natural logarithm). We also prove a better bound for a very similar algorithm which combines CSAT with pure literal elimination. As a by-product, we improve the upper bound for CSAT on formulas in k–CNF–d to $2^{\left(1-\frac{1}{(k-1)d+1}\right)N}$.

For simplicity, we reduce the power of CSAT by disabling downward moves (moves that decrease the number of satisfied clauses) and moves on plateaus (moves that do not change the number of satisfied clauses). We show that even in this form CSAT solves the satisfiability problem for linear-size formulas significantly better than a simple algorithm that just picks an assignment at random. Though the bound presented in this paper is worse than the recent bounds for k-CNF which are due to R. Paturi, P. Pudlak and M. E. Saks and F. Zane [20] (their algorithm uses neither splitting nor local search) and U. Schöning [22] (obtained by a random walk algorithm), the result is nevertheless of particular interest because together with our conference paper [10] we present the first theoretically proved upper bound for experimentally well-studied local search algorithms for SAT.

Lower bounds. Many researchers claimed that some formulas are "hard" for local search algorithms. For example, B. Selman, H. Levesque and D. Mitchell [27] *claimed* (but not *proved*) that it could take exponential time for GSAT to find a satisfying assignment for the formula

$$\begin{aligned}&(x_1 \lor \overline{x_2} \lor x_3) \land (x_1 \lor \overline{x_3} \lor x_4) \land (x_1 \lor \overline{x_4} \lor \overline{x_2}) \land \\ &(x_1 \lor x_5 \lor x_2) \land (x_1 \lor \overline{x_5} \lor x_2) \land \\ &(\overline{x_1} \lor \overline{x_6} \lor x_7) \land (\overline{x_1} \lor \overline{x_7} \lor x_8) \land \ldots \\ &\qquad \ldots \land (\overline{x_1} \lor \overline{x_{N-1}} \lor x_N) \land (\overline{x_1} \lor \overline{x_N} \lor x_6). \qquad (1.1)\end{aligned}$$

In this paper we concentrate on such "hard" examples and on *theoretical proofs* of their hardness for local search algorithms GSAT and CSAT.

All variables but x_1, x_2, x_5 occur in the formula (1.1) only twice. Our Theorem 3.1 gives the worst-case upper bound $2^{\frac{4}{5}N}p(L)$ for the running time of CSAT on such formulas[1] (p is a polynomial). On the other hand, in Sect. 4 we prove a lower bound of the order $2^{0.0817N}$ for formulas with at most three literals per clause. We use hard examples different from (1.1). These examples are very similar to hard examples presented in [19] (Exercise 11.5.6) for a random walk algorithm (and thus it is highly probable, but not proved here, that similar examples fail algorithms that combine local search with random walk, e.g., as those in [26, 25]). As to the general case (formulas in CNF without any additional restrictions), we prove a lower bound of the order 2^N, which mean that CSAT and GSAT perform on these formulas not much better than a trivial algorithm. This bound is based on a different set of hard examples. The number of clauses in these examples is linearly dependent on the number of variables. Thus, we obtain the lower bound $2^{K/4}$ w.r.t. the number K of clauses in the input formula. Our lower bounds hold both for CSAT and GSAT.

Structure of the paper. In Sect. 2 we give definitions and formulate precisely the algorithms we study. In Sect. 3 we prove various worst-case upper bounds for CSAT and its simple modification. Section 4 contains the proofs of the lower bounds. In Sect. 5 we discuss the current situation with upper and lower bounds for SAT and further directions of the work.

2. Preliminaries

Let Var $= \{x_1, x_2, \ldots\}$ be a set of Boolean variables (that take the values $True$ and $False$). Literals are variables $x_1, x_2, \ldots$ and their negations $\overline{x_1}, \overline{x_2} \ldots$ A clause is a finite set of literals. In this section F is a formula in CNF (i.e. a finite set of clauses), I and J are truth assignments for the variables of F (i.e. finite sets of literals corresponding to the variables occurring in F). We consider only complete assignments, i.e. assignments that contain one of the literals v or $\overline{v}$ for each variable v occurring in F.

If a variable $v \in I$, we say that the value of the variable v in the assignment I is $True$, and write $v[I] = True$; if $\overline{v} \in I$, we write $v[I] = False$. We denote by $\mathrm{dist}(I, J)$ the number of variables that have different values in I and J.

[1] In fact, by a similar argument an upper bound $2^{\frac{2}{3}N}p(L)$ can be proved.

The values of all variables in assignment $I^{(v)}$ coincide with their values in I except the variable v which has the opposite value. We say that we flip the value of v in I to obtain $I^{(v)}$.

We say that I satisfies a clause C if $I \cap C \neq \emptyset$. We denote by $\text{sat}(F, I)$ the number of clauses that I satisfies in F. If I satisfies all clauses of F, we say that it satisfies the formula F.

A formula is in k–CNF if each of its clauses contains at most k literals. A formula is in k–CNF–d if each of its clauses contains at most k literals and every variable occurs in it at most d times.

We now describe the algorithms we study. Their input is a formula F in CNF. Both algorithms start with a random assignment and at each step change the value of exactly one variable. If a satisfying assignment for the input formula is not found in a certain number of steps (parameter `MAXFLIPS`), the algorithm chooses at random another initial assignment. The maximal number of assignments the algorithm examines, is determined by parameter `MAXTRIES`.

The difference between algorithms CSAT and GSAT is in the choice of the variable whose value is changed. Algorithm GSAT (see Fig. 1) chooses the variable such that the number of clauses satisfied by the new assignment is the largest (however, this number can be less than the number of clauses satisfied by the current assignment). There can be several variables leading to the largest number of satisfied clauses. However, it is not important for us in this paper whether one of them is chosen in a random way or deterministically.

Algorithm CSAT (see Fig. 2) has greater freedom of choice. It constructs a set that contains every variable such that flipping its value increases the number of satisfied clauses. Then it chooses one of these variables at random. If there are no such variables, then it chooses one at random from the set of variables that do not lead to the decrease of the number of satisfied clauses. If all variables lead to such decrease, it chooses a variable at random from the set of all variables occurring in F.

To estimate the worst-case running time of CSAT, we reduce the power of CSAT by disabling downward moves (moves that decrease the number of satisfied clauses) and moves on plateaus (moves that do not change the number of satisfied clauses). However, our result holds for the original CSAT as well.
We first prove an upper bound for a “shortened” version called Algorithm SimpleCSAT (see Fig. 3) of this simplified algorithm. This version considers only one initial assignment (i.e., `MAXTRIES` $= 1$). Algorithm SimpleCSAT either outputs a satisfying assignment after having considered at most K assignments (K is the number of clauses in the input formula), or answers “No” (when it cannot choose a variable to change). Algorithm CSAT (with reduced power) then can be obtained by repeating Algorithm SimpleCSAT.

3. Worst-case upper bound for CSAT

In this section k and d are positive integers, e is the base of the natural logarithm, F is a satisfiable formula in k–CNF given as input to Algorithm SimpleCSAT, N is the number of variables in it, $D = (k-1)d + 1$. Let $\delta \cdot N$ be (some) lower bound for the number of variables occurring at most d times in the formula F.

Let I be a truth assignment for the variables of F. Let S be a satisfying assignment for F. We say that a variable v has the S-*correct* value in I, if $v[I] = v[S]$. Otherwise we say that v has the S-*incorrect* value in I (note that this value is uniquely defined since v is a Boolean variable). The variable v is *in a good position* w.r.t. formula F and assignment I, if it does not occur in any clause containing a variable which has the

Algorithm GSAT.
Input:
A formula F in CNF, integers `MAXFLIPS` and `MAXTRIES`.
Output:
A truth assignment for the variables of F, or "No".

Method.

Repeat `MAXTRIES` times:

— Pick an assignment I at random.

— Repeat `MAXFLIPS` times:

— If I satisfies F, then output I.
— Choose a variable v in F such that $I^{(v)}$ satisfies the maximal possible number of clauses of F.
— Flip the value of v in I.

Output "No".

Figure 1. Algorithm GSAT

Algorithm CSAT.
Input:
A formula F in CNF, integers `MAXFLIPS` and `MAXTRIES`.
Output:
A truth assignment for the variables of F, or "No".

Method.

Repeat `MAXTRIES` times:

— Pick an assignment I at random.

— Repeat `MAXFLIPS` times:

— If I satisfies F, then output I.
— Choose at random a variable v in F such that $\mathrm{sat}(F, I^{(v)}) > \mathrm{sat}(F, I)$.
If there are no such variables, choose at random a variable v such that $\mathrm{sat}(F, I^{(v)}) = \mathrm{sat}(F, I)$.
If there are none of those, choose a variable v at random from the set of all variables occurring in F.
— Flip the value of v in I.

Output "No".

Figure 2. Algorithm CSAT

Algorithm SimpleCSAT.
Input:
A formula F in CNF.
Output:
A truth assignment for the variables of F, or "No".

Method.
Pick an assignment I at random.
While I is not a satisfying assignment:

— Choose at random a variable v in F such that $\mathrm{sat}(F, I) < \mathrm{sat}(F, I^{(v)})$. If there are no such variables, output "No".

— Assume $I = I^{(v)}$.

Output I.

Figure 3. Algorithm SimpleCSAT

S-incorrect value in I (maybe except the variable v itself). Otherwise we say that v is *in a bad position.* We say that I is *changed locally* w.r.t. S if all variables that have the S-incorrect values in I, are in a good position and occur at most d times in the formula. We omit S in the above notation if its meaning is clear from the context.

Let i be an integer. We say that I satisfies the property $P_S(i)$ if $\mathrm{dist}(I, S) = i$ and I is changed locally w.r.t. S. Informally speaking, I satisfies the property $P_S(i)$ if it is obtained from S by changing the values of i variables such that

(1) each clause of F contains at most one of these variables;

(2) each of these variables occur at most d times in F.

We estimate the running time of Algorithm SimpleCSAT in two steps.

1. We prove that there are many assignments satisfying $P_S(i)$ and thus it is likely that Algorithm SimpleCSAT picks one.

2. We prove that it is likely that starting with an assignment satisfying $P_S(i)$, Algorithm SimpleCSAT stops in a polynomial time and outputs a satisfying assignment.

REMARK 3.1. *S is the only assignment satisfying $P_S(0)$.*

LEMMA 3.1. *Let S be a satisfying assignment for F. If an assignment I satisfies the property $P_S(i)$, then there are at most $(k-1)di$ variables v in a bad position that have the correct values in I.*

Proof. There are at most id clauses in F that contain variables having the incorrect values in I. These clauses contain at most $(k-1)di$ variables having the correct values in I. □

LEMMA 3.2. *Let S be a satisfying assignment for F. If an assignment I satisfies the property $P_S(i-1)$ for $1 \le i \le 1 + \frac{\delta N}{D}$, then there are at least $\delta N - (i-1)D$ variables v such that $I^{(v)}$ satisfies the property $P_S(i)$.*

Proof. There are at least $\delta N - (i-1)$ variables having the correct values in I and occurring at most d times in the formula. By Lemma 3.1 at most $(k-1)d(i-1)$ of them are in a bad position. The remaining $\delta N - (i-1) - (k-1)d(i-1)$ variables are exactly what we want. □

LEMMA 3.3. *Let S be a satisfying assignment for F. There are at least*

$$\frac{\delta N(\delta N - D)(\delta N - 2D)\ldots(\delta N - (i-1)D)}{i!}$$

assignments satisfying the property $P_S(i)$ for $1 \le i \le 1 + \frac{\delta N}{D}$.

Proof. We prove this statement by the induction on i.

Base ($i = 1$). Trivial.

Step. Suppose the statement holds for $i-1$. By Lemma 3.2 we can map each assignment I satisfying $P_S(i-1)$ to at least $\delta N - (i-1)D$ assignments $I^{(v)}$ satisfying $P_S(i)$. Thus we have mapped each of the

$$\frac{\delta N(\delta N - D)(\delta N - 2D)\ldots(\delta N - (i-2)D)}{(i-1)!}$$

assignments guaranteed by the induction hypothesis, to at least $\delta N - (i-1)D$ assignments. Since we have mapped at most i assignments into one assignment, the number of assignments satisfying $P_S(i)$ is at least

$$\frac{(\delta N - (i-1)D)}{i} \cdot \frac{\delta N(\delta N - D)\ldots(\delta N - (i-2)D)}{(i-1)!} =$$
$$= \frac{\delta N(\delta N - D)\ldots(\delta N - (i-1)D)}{i!}.$$

□

LEMMA 3.4. *Let S be a satisfying assignment for F. If an assignment I satisfies the property $P_S(i)$ and a variable v has the incorrect value in S, then $I^{(v)}$ satisfies the property $P_S(i-1)$.*

Proof. All variables having the correct values in I, have the correct values in $I^{(v)}$. □

LEMMA 3.5. *Let S be a satisfying assignment for F. If an assignment I is changed locally w.r.t. S, a variable v has the S-incorrect value in I, and $S^{(v)}$ is not a satisfying assignment for F, then* $\mathrm{sat}(F, I^{(v)}) > \mathrm{sat}(F, I)$.

Proof. W.l.o.g. we suppose $v[S] = \mathit{True}$. In the assignment I, the values of all variables in each of the clauses containing the literal $\overline{v}$, are correct. Thus, $I^{(v)}$ satisfies all these clauses, i.e. $\mathrm{sat}(F, I^{(v)}) \ge \mathrm{sat}(F, I)$.

Suppose $\mathrm{sat}(F, I^{(v)}) = \mathrm{sat}(F, I)$. Then I satisfies all clauses containing the literal v. Hence, the assignment $S^{(v)}$ satisfies the formula F, because I is changed locally w.r.t. S. □

LEMMA 3.6. *Let S be a satisfying assignment for F. If Algorithm SimpleCSAT starts with an assignment I that satisfies the property $P_S(i)$, then the algorithm stops in a polynomial time and outputs a satisfying assignment with probability at least D^{-i}.*

Proof. There are i variables v having the S-incorrect values in I. By Lemma 3.5 for each such variable v, either $S^{(v)}$ is a satisfying assignment for F (suppose there are j such variables) or $\mathrm{sat}(F, I^{(v)}) > \mathrm{sat}(F, I)$. Now consider an assignment J that differs from S exactly in the values of the above mentioned j variables. Since I is changed locally, J is a satisfying assignment. For all $(i-j)$ variables v having the J-incorrect values in I, $\mathrm{sat}(F, I^{(v)}) > \mathrm{sat}(F, I)$.

Since I satisfies $P_J(i-j)$, by Lemma 3.1 there are at most $(k-1)d(i-j)$ variables u having the J-correct values in I, such that $\mathrm{sat}(F, I^{(u)}) > \mathrm{sat}(F, I)$. Thus, the algorithm chooses a variable having the J-incorrect value in I with probability at least $\frac{i-j}{i-j+(k-1)d(i-j)} = \frac{1}{D}$. By Lemma 3.4 in this case the algorithm proceeds with processing an assignment having the property $P_J(i-j-1)$, etc. Thus, the algorithm stops after changing the values of at most i variables and outputs a satisfying assignment with probability at least D^{-i}. □

LEMMA 3.7. *If a satisfiable formula F in k–CNF is given as input to Algorithm SimpleCSAT, and δN is the number of variables occurring at most d times in F, then Algorithm SimpleCSAT stops in a polynomial time and outputs a satisfying assignment with probability at least $2^{-(1-\frac{\delta}{D})N}/p(N)$, where p is a polynomial.*

Proof. Let S be a satisfying assignment for F. By Lemmas 3.3 and 3.6, the probability of outputing S after i flips is at least

$$\frac{\delta N(\delta N - D)\dots(\delta N-(i-1)D)}{i!\cdot 2^N} D^{-i}$$
$$= \frac{1}{2^N}\cdot\frac{\frac{\delta N}{D}\cdot\frac{\delta N - D}{D}\cdot\ldots\cdot\frac{\delta N-(i-1)D}{D}}{i!}$$
$$\geq \frac{\left\lfloor\frac{\delta N}{D}\right\rfloor!}{2^N i! \left\lfloor\frac{\delta N}{D}-i\right\rfloor!}.$$

We assume $i = \frac{1}{2}\left\lfloor\frac{\delta N}{D}\right\rfloor$. Then, using the Stirling formula, the above probability is at least $2^{-(1-\frac{\delta}{D})N}/p(N)$ for some polynomial p. □

By Lemma 3.7, the algorithm obtained by repeating Algorithm SimpleCSAT $2^{(1-\frac{\delta}{D})N}p(N)$ times is a Monte Carlo algorithm for SAT with error probability

$$(1-2^{-(1-\frac{\delta}{D})N}/p(N))^{2^{(1-\frac{\delta}{D})N}p(N)} < 1/e.$$

Thus we have proved the following theorem.

THEOREM 3.1. *Given a formula in k–CNF, the Monte Carlo analog of Algorithm SimpleCSAT performs correctly with error probability at most $1/e$. Its worst-case running time is at most*

$$2^{\left(1-\frac{\delta}{(k-1)d+1}\right)N}q(N),$$

where N is the number of variables in the input formula, δN is the number of variables occurring at most d times in the input formula, q is a polynomial.

The result also holds for the original CSAT algorithm, since we may consider only the cases when it performs exactly as the Monte Carlo analog of Algorithm SimpleCSAT.

COROLLARY 3.1. *There exist polynomials p and q such that, given a formula in k–CNF with K clauses and N variables, δN of which occur at most d times, and values* $\mathtt{MAXFLIPS} = K$ *and* $\mathtt{MAXTRIES} = 2^{(1-\frac{\delta}{(k-1)d+1})N}p(N)$, *Algorithm CSAT returns a correct*

Table I. Approximate values of $1 - \frac{1}{(k-1)d+1}$.

$k \backslash d$	3	6	9	12	15
3	0.858	0.924	0.948	0.960	0.968
4	0.900	0.948	0.965	0.973	0.979
5	0.924	0.960	0.973	0.980	0.984

Table II. Approximate values of $1 - \frac{1}{4(\lambda-1)(k-1)+2}$.

$k \backslash \lambda$	3	6	9	12	15
3	0.945	0.977	0.985	0.989	0.992
4	0.962	0.984	0.990	0.993	0.995
5	0.971	0.988	0.993	0.995	0.996

answer with probability at least $1-1/e$ independent on the input formula. Its worst-case running time is at most

$$2^{\left(1-\frac{\delta}{(k-1)d+1}\right)N}q(N).$$

For formulas in k–CNF–d this gives us immediately the worst-case upper bound

$$2^{\left(1-\frac{1}{(k-1)d+1}\right)N}q(N).$$

(Approximate values of $1 - \frac{1}{(k-1)d+1}$ are given in Table I, for example, CSAT finds a satisfying assignment for a formula in 3–CNF–3 in time $O\left(2^{0.858N}\right)$.) We cannot directly apply our arguments to arbitrary formulas in k–CNF. However, if the length of a formula is upper bounded by a linear function λN of the number N of its variables, a certain number of variables must occur in it rarely. Thus, by appropriate choice of δ, we can get a more or less good upper bound.

Let $\delta = \frac{1}{2}$. Since $\lambda \geq \delta + (d+1)(1-\delta)$, we have that $d \leq \frac{\lambda-1}{1-\delta} = 2(\lambda-1)$. Therefore,

$$\frac{\delta}{(k-1)d+1} \geq \frac{1}{4(\lambda-1)(k-1)+2}$$

(approximate values of $1 - \frac{1}{4(\lambda-1)(k-1)+2}$ are given in Table II). Thus, we have proved[2]

COROLLARY 3.2. *There exist polynomials p and q such that, given a formula in k–CNF of length at most λN, with K clauses and N variables, and values* MAXFLIPS $= K$,

$$\texttt{MAXTRIES} = 2^{(1-\frac{1}{4(k-1)(\lambda-1)+2})N}p(N),$$

[2] A slightly better bound can be proved by more accurate choice of δ and d. However, this bound looks very complicated and we do not present it here since

(1) our purpose is only to prove a less-than-2^n bound for CSAT, and

(2) below we prove a better bound for a very similar algorithm.

Table III. Approximate values of $1 - \left(\frac{\sqrt{M+1}-\sqrt{M+1-k}}{k}\right)^2$.

$k \backslash \lambda$	3	6	9	12	15
3	0.925	0.974	0.984	0.989	0.991
4	0.948	0.983	0.990	0.993	0.994
5	0.961	0.987	0.992	0.995	0.996

Algorithm CSAT returns a correct answer with probability at least $1 - 1/e$ independent on the input formula. Its worst-case running time is at most

$$2^{\left(1-\frac{1}{4(k-1)(\lambda-1)+2}\right)N} q(N).$$

However, if we augment Algorithm CSAT with pure literal elimination prior to processing the formula (we call this modified algorithm CSAT+P), then we can suppose that each literal occurs at least twice in the formula. In this case d can be estimated via δ from $\lambda \geq 2\delta + (d+1)(1-\delta)$, i.e. $d \leq \frac{\lambda-\delta-1}{1-\delta}$ (we assume $\delta < 1$). Let $M = (k-1)(\lambda-1)$. Assuming $\delta = \frac{M+1-\sqrt{(M+1)(M+1-k)}}{k}$, we have $\frac{\delta}{(k-1)d+1} \geq \left(\frac{\sqrt{M+1}-\sqrt{M+1-k}}{k}\right)^2$. Approximate values of this bound for concrete values of k and λ are presented in Table III; for example, CSAT+P solves the satisfiability problem for a 3-CNF formula with $L \leq 3N$ in time $O(2^{0.925N})$. More precisely, we have proved

COROLLARY 3.3. *Let λ be a positive number, k be a positive integer, $M = (k-1)(\lambda-1)$. There exist polynomials p and q such that, given a formula in k-CNF of length at most λN, with K clauses and N variables, and values* `MAXFLIPS` $= K$,

$$\texttt{MAXTRIES} = 2^{\left(1-\left(\frac{\sqrt{M+1}-\sqrt{M+1-k}}{k}\right)^2\right)N} p(N),$$

Algorithm CSAT+P returns a correct answer with probability at least $1-1/e$ independent on the input formula. Its worst-case running time is at most

$$2^{\left(1-\left(\frac{\sqrt{M+1}-\sqrt{M+1-k}}{k}\right)^2\right)N} q(N).$$

4. Lower bounds for CSAT and GSAT

4.1. Formulas in general CNF

We now prove a lower bound for the running time of the algorithms CSAT and GSAT on formulas in CNF. We construct formulas F_N that are "hard" for the algorithms GSAT and CSAT. We then prove that it takes time of the order 2^N for CSAT or GSAT to find a satisfying assignment for F_N. For an integer $N \geq 6$, the formula F_N contains N Boolean variables and consists of $4N+1$ clauses of three types (see Fig. 4). Clauses of the first type express that in every satisfying assignment for F_N the values of all variables should be equal. The clause $\{x_1, x_2\}$ implies that all these values are equal to *True* (since together with $\{x_1, \overline{x_2}\}$ it implies that x_1 must have the value *True* in

Type 1:

$$\{x_1, \overline{x_2}\}$$
$$\{x_2, \overline{x_3}\}$$
$$\dots$$
$$\{x_n, \overline{x_1}\}$$

Type 2:

$$\{x_1, x_2\}$$

Type 3:

$$\{x_1, \quad \overline{x_2}, \dots, \overline{x_{N-3}}, \quad \overline{x_{N-2}}, \overline{x_{N-1}}\}$$
$$\{x_1, \quad \overline{x_2}, \dots, \overline{x_{N-3}}, \quad \overline{x_{N-1}}, \overline{x_N}\}$$
$$\{x_1, \quad \overline{x_2}, \dots, \overline{x_{N-3}}, \quad \overline{x_N}, \overline{x_{N-2}}\}$$

$$\{x_2, \quad \overline{x_3}, \dots, \overline{x_{N-2}}, \quad \overline{x_{N-1}}, \overline{x_N}\}$$
$$\{x_2, \quad \overline{x_3}, \dots, \overline{x_{N-2}}, \quad \overline{x_N}, \overline{x_1}\}$$
$$\{x_2, \quad \overline{x_3}, \dots, \overline{x_{N-2}}, \quad \overline{x_1}, \overline{x_{N-1}}\}$$

$$\dots$$

$$\{x_n, \quad \overline{x_1}, \dots, \overline{x_{N-4}}, \quad \overline{x_{N-3}}, \overline{x_{N-2}}\}$$
$$\{x_n, \quad \overline{x_1}, \dots, \overline{x_{N-4}}, \quad \overline{x_{N-2}}, \overline{x_{N-1}}\}$$
$$\{x_n, \quad \overline{x_1}, \dots, \overline{x_{N-4}}, \quad \overline{x_{N-1}}, \overline{x_{N-3}}\}$$

Figure 4. Formula F_N

every satisfying assignment). Hence, the formula F_N has only one satisfying assignment $S_N = \{x_1, x_2, \dots, x_N\}$ (it satisfies also all clauses of the third type).

Clauses of the third type are intended for "misleading" the algorithm. For each variable x_i, the formula F_N includes three clauses of the third type containing non-negated x_i. Each of these clauses also contains the negations of the next (modulo N) $N-4$ variables and the negations of two of the remaining three variables. Every assignment that differs from the satisfying assignment by the values of at least three variables, satisfies all clauses of the third type. However, assignments that differ from the satisfying assignment by the values of only one variable, satisfy only $3N-3$ of these clauses. In the following lemmas we prove that if GSAT or CSAT encounters an assignment that differs from the satisfying assignment by the values of exactly two variables, then it chooses a wrong variable for flipping. Thus, the assignments that differ from the satisfying assignment by the values of exactly two variables, form an "insurmountable ring" around the satisfying assignment. Hence, in this case the satisfying assignment cannot be found until the algorithm restarts from another initial assignment.

In the next two lemmas and in the theorem, S_N denotes the only satisfying assignment for the formula F_N.

LEMMA 4.1. *Let I be an assignment for F_N ($N \geq 6$), such that* $\text{dist}(I, S_N) = 2$. *Then for every variable v if* $\text{dist}(I^{(v)}, S_N) = 1$, *then* $\text{sat}(F_N, I^{(v)}) < \text{sat}(F_N, I)$.

Proof. Let I differ from S_N by the values of variables $v = x_i$ and x_j. Note that $I^{(v)}$ satisfies the clause $\{x_1, x_2\}$, $3N-3$ clauses of the third type and $N-1$ clauses of the first type, i.e. $4N-3$ clauses in total. We consider three cases.

CASE 1: $|(i-j) \bmod N| \neq 1$.

In this case I satisfies $N-2$ clauses of the first type, the clause $\{x_1, x_2\}$ and $3N-1$ or $3N$ clauses of the third type, i.e. $4N-1$ or $4N-2$ clauses in total.

CASE 2: $|(i-j) \bmod N| = 1$, but $\{i,j\} \neq \{1,2\}$.

In this case I satisfies $N-1$ clauses of the first type, $3N-1$ clauses of the third type and the clause $\{x_1, x_2\}$, i.e. $4N-1$ clauses in total.

CASE 3: $\{i,j\} = \{1,2\}$.

In this case I satisfies $N-1$ clauses of the first type and $3N-1$ clauses of the third type, i.e. $4N-2$ clauses in total. □

LEMMA 4.2. *Let I be an assignment for F_N ($N \geq 6$), such that* $\mathrm{dist}(I, S_N) = 2$. *Then there exists a variable v such that* $\mathrm{sat}(F_N, I) = \mathrm{sat}(F_N, I^{(v)})$ *and* $\mathrm{dist}(I^{(v)}, S_N) = 3$.

Proof. Let I differ from S_N by the values of variables x_i and x_j. We choose v such that

(1) $v \neq x_1, x_2$;

(2) exactly one of the conditions $v = x_{j+1}$, $v = x_{j-1}$, $v = x_{i-1}$ or $v = x_{i+1}$ holds.

(Such v exists since $N \geq 6$.) Then the assignment $I^{(v)}$ satisfies the same clauses of the second and the third types as I does. Also I and $I^{(v)}$ satisfy the same number of clauses of the first type. □

THEOREM 4.1. *Let $N \geq 6$. The algorithms CSAT and GSAT cannot find a satisfying assignment for F_N in expected time less than $\Omega(2^N/(N+1))$.*

Proof. Suppose that CSAT or GSAT starts its search from an initial assignment that differs from S_N by the values of *at least two* variables. We now prove that in this case the algorithm cannot find a satisfying assignment until it chooses another initial assignment.

Suppose that the algorithm outputs a satisfying assignment without choosing another initial assignment. Then the algorithm must encounter an assignment that differs from S_N by the values of *exactly two* variables. Let I be the last such assignment (i.e., after that the algorithm encounters only assignments that differ from S_N by the value of *exactly one* variable, and, finally, the satisfying assignment S_N).

By Lemma 4.2, at the next step the algorithm must flip the value of a variable v such that the number of satisfied clauses will *not decrease*, i.e. $\mathrm{sat}(F_N, I^{(v)}) \geq \mathrm{sat}(F_N, I)$. It follows that the assignment $I^{(v)}$ cannot differ from S_N by the value of *exactly one* variable since by Lemma 4.1 every such assignment satisfies strictly less clauses of F_N than I does.

Thus, the algorithm has a chance to succeed only if at some iteration it chooses S_N or one of its N neighbours as the initial assignment. The probability to choose one of these assignments is exactly $(N+1)/2^N$, i.e. the algorithm must perform $\Omega(2^N/(N+1))$ iterations to achieve a constant probability of error. □

4.2. Formulas in 3–CNF

We now prove a lower bound for the running time of the algorithms CSAT and GSAT on formulas in 3–CNF. The idea is the same as for formulas in general CNF, but the "insurmountable ring" around the satisfying assignment is not at the distance 2, but at the distance $\lceil \frac{N}{3} \rceil + 6$ from the satisfying assignment.

We now describe the "hard" formula G_N for an integer $N \geq 12$. It contains N variables and $\frac{N(N-1)(N-2)}{2}+N+1$ clauses of three different types. Clauses of the first two types are the same as in the formula F_N described in the previous section. These clauses imply that G_N has the only satisfying assignment $S_N = \{x_1, x_2, \ldots, x_N\}$. Similarly to the previous section, clauses of the third types are satisfied by S_N and are intended for "misleading" the algorithm. However, these clauses differ from the ones in the formula F_N since we are limited to clauses containing at most three literals. The clauses of the third type are all the $\frac{N(N-1)(N-2)}{2}$ possible clauses $\{x_i, \overline{x_j}, \overline{x_k}\}$ consisting of a variable x_i and the negations of two other variables x_j and x_k.

Let I be an assignment such that $\text{dist}(I, S_N) \geq \frac{N}{3}+6$. Let I and S_N assign different values to variable v and identical values to variable w. Easy calculation shows that flipping the value of the variable v leads to decrease in the number of satisfied clauses, and flipping the value of the variable w leads to increase in the number of satisfied clauses. Hence, CSAT or GSAT can output a satisfying assignment only if it chooses an initial assignment at the distance at most $\frac{N}{3}+5$ from the satisfying assignment S_N. There are at most $p(N)2^{H(\frac{1}{3})N}$ such assignments, where $H(\varepsilon) = -\varepsilon \log_2 \varepsilon - (1-\varepsilon) \log_2 (1-\varepsilon)$ is the binary entropy function and p is some polynomial. Since $H(\frac{1}{3}) < 0.9183$, the lower bound follows:

THEOREM 4.2. *Let $N \geq 12$. The algorithms CSAT and GSAT cannot find a satisfying assignment for G_N in expected time less than $\Omega(2^{0.0817N})$.*

5. Conclusion and further work

In this paper we studied the worst-case behaviour of the local search algorithms CSAT and GSAT. We proved a worst-case upper bound of the form $O\left(2^{\alpha N}\right)$ for the running time of CSAT on linear-size formulas in k–CNF (N is the number of variables, $0 < \alpha < 1$). On the other hand, we proved the lower bound of the order 2^N for formulas in CNF and the lower bound of the order $2^{0.0817N}$ for formulas in 3–CNF. In fact, the presented lower bound for formulas in 3–CNF holds also for GSAT and many other local search algorithms (e.g., for those that combine local search with random walk) and generalizes to k–CNF.

It would be interesting to obtain lower bounds for the running time of CSAT and GSAT on linear-size formulas, as well as to find more tight bounds for formulas in k–CNF of arbitrary size and for other interesting classes of formulas. Also, a wide variety of local search algorithms remains unstudied. It would be interesting to find classes of formulas on which these algorithms have better worst-case upper bounds than other (e.g., resolution-like) algorithms.

References

1. Cook S., Reckhow R. On the lengths of proofs in the propositional calculus (preliminary version). In: Conference Record of Sixth Annual ACM Symposium on Theory of Computing (1974) 135–148
2. Dantsin, E.: Two systems for proving tautologies, based on the split method. In: Journal of Soviet Mathematics **22** (1983) 1293–1305
3. Dubois, O., Boufkhad, Y., Mandler, J.: Typical Random 3-SAT Formulae and the Satisfiability Threshold, To appear in Proceedings of the 11th Annual ACM-SIAM Symposium on Discrete Algorithms (2000)

4. Frieze, A., Suen, S.: Analysis of two simple heuristics on a random instance of k–SAT Journal of Algorithms **20** (1996) 312–355
5. Gent, I., Walsh, T.: The Enigma of Hill-climbing Procedures for SAT. Research Paper **605**, Department of Artificial Intelligence, University of Edinburgh (1992)
6. Gent, I., Walsh, T.: Towards an Understanding of Hill-climbing Procedures for SAT. In: Proceedings of the 11th National Conference on Artificial Intelligence. Washington, DC, AAAI Press (1993) 28–33
7. Gent, I., Walsh, T.: Unsatisfied Variables in Local Search. In: Hallam, J. (ed.): Hybrid Problems, Hybrid Solutions (AISB-95). IOS Press, Amsterdam (1995)
8. Gu, J., Gu, Q.-P.: Average Time Complexity of The SAT1.2 Algorithm. In: Proceedings of the 5th Annual International Symposium on Algorithms and Computation (1994) 147–155
9. Hirsch, E. A.: Two new upper bounds for SAT. In: Proceedings of the 9th Annual ACM-SIAM Symposium on Discrete Algorithms (1998) 521–530. An improved journal version is to appear in Journal of Automated Reasoning and in the special issue "SAT-2000"
10. Hirsch, E. A.: Local Search Algorithms for SAT: Worst-Case Analysis. In: Proceedings of the 6th Scandinavian Workshop on Algorithm Theory, LNCS **1432** (1998) 246–254
11. Hoos, H. H., Stützle, T.: Local Search Algorithms for SAT: An Empirical Evaluation. To appear in Journal of Automated Reasoning and in the special issue "SAT-2000"
12. Kirousis, L. M., Kranakis, E., Krizanc, D., Stamatiou, Y. C.: Approximating the unsatisfiability threshold of random formulas, Random Structures and Algorithms **12(3)** (1998) 253–269
13. Koutsoupias, E., Papadimitriou, C. H.: On the greedy algorithm for satisfiability. Information Processing Letters **43(1)** (1992) 53–55
14. Kullmann, O.: New methods for 3–SAT decision and worst-case analysis. Theoretical Computer Science **223(1-2)** (1999) 1–72
15. McAllester, D., Selman, B., Kautz, H.: Evidence for invariants in local search. In: Proceedings of the 14th National Conference on Artificial Intelligence and 9th Innovative Applications of Artificial Intelligence Conference Providence, RI, AAAI Press (1997) 321–326
16. Mitchell, D. G., Selman, B., Levesque, H.: Hard and Easy Distributions of SAT Problems. In: Proceedings of the Tenth National Conference on Artificial Intelligence, San Jose, California, AAAI Press/MIT Press (1992) 459-465
17. Monien, B., Speckenmeyer, E.: 3-satisfiability is testable in $O(1.62^r)$ steps. Bericht Nr. **3/1979**, Reihe Theoretische Informatik, Universität-Gesamthochschule-Paderborn
18. Monien, B., Speckenmeyer, E.: Solving satisfiability in less than 2^n steps. Discrete Applied Mathematics **10** (1985) 287–295
19. Papadimitriou, Ch. H.: Computational Complexity. Addison-Wesley (1994)
20. Paturi, R., Pudlak, P., Saks, M. E., Zane, F.: An Improved Exponential-time Algorithm for k–SAT. In: Proceedings of the 39th Annual Symposium on Foundations of Computer Science (1998) 628–637
21. Schiermeyer, I.: Pure literal look ahead: An $O(1.497^n)$ 3-Satisfiability algorithm. In: Franco, J., Gallo, G., Kleine Büning, H., Speckenmeyer, E., Spera, C. (eds.): Workshop on the Satisfiability Problem, Technical Report. Siena, April, 29 – May, 3, 1996. University Köln, Report No. **96-230**
22. Schöning, U.: A probabilistic algorithm for k-SAT and constraint satisfaction problems. To appear in Proceedings of the 40th Annual Symposium on Foundations of Computer Science (2000)
23. Selman, B., Kautz, H.: An Empirical Study of Greedy Local Search for Satisfiability Testing. In: Proceedings of the 11th National Conference on Artificial Intelligence. Washington, DC, AAAI Press (1993)
24. Selman, B., Kautz, H.: Pushing the Envelope: Planning, Propositional Logic, and Stochastic Search. In: Proceedings of the 14th Conference on Artificial Intelligence (1996)
25. Selman, B., Kautz, H., Cohen, B.: Noise strategies for improving local search. In: Proceedings of the 12th National Conference on Artificial Intelligence. Seattle, Washington, AAAI Press (1994) **1**:337–343
26. Selman, B., Kautz, H., Cohen, B.: Local Search Strategies for Satisfiability Testing. In: Second DIMACS Challenge on Cliques, Coloring and Satisfiability (1993). A version of this paper is to appear in DIMACS Series in Discrete Mathematics
27. Selman, B., Levesque, H., Mitchell, D.: A new method for solving hard satisfiability problems. In: Swartout, W. (ed.): Proceedings of the 10th National Conference on Artificial Intelligence. San Jose, California, MIT Press (1992) 440–446
28. Urquhart, A.: The Complexity of Propositional Proofs. Bulletin of Symbolic Logic. Vol. **1** (N4) (1995) 425–467

SAT2000
I. Gent et al. (Eds.)
IOS Press, 2000

New Worst-Case Upper Bounds for SAT *

Edward A. Hirsch‡
Steklov Institute of Mathematics at St.Petersburg,
27 Fontanka, 191011 St.Petersburg, Russia

Abstract. In 1980 Monien and Speckenmeyer [23] proved that satisfiability of a propositional formula consisting of K clauses (of arbitrary length) can be checked in time of the order $2^{K/3}$. Recently Kullmann and Luckhardt [18] proved the worst-case upper bound $2^{L/9}$, where L is the length of the input formula. The algorithms leading to these bounds are based on the *splitting method* which goes back to the Davis–Putnam procedure. *Transformation rules* (pure literal elimination, unit propagation etc.) constitute a substantial part of this method. In this paper we present a new transformation rule and two algorithms using this rule. We prove that these algorithms have the worst-case upper bounds $2^{0.30897K}$ and $2^{0.10299L}$ respectively.

Keywords: SAT, worst-case upper bounds.

1. Introduction

SAT (the problem of satisfiability of a propositional formula in conjunctive normal form) can be easily solved in time of the order 2^N, where N is the number of variables in the input formula. In the early 1980s this trivial bound was reduced for formulas in 3-CNF by Monien and Speckenmeyer [22] (see also [24]) and independently by Dantsin [2] (see also [5] and [3]). After that, many upper bounds for SAT and its subproblems were obtained [23, 19, 27, 15, 16, 28, 18, 9, 25, 26, 29]. Most authors consider bounds w.r.t. three main parameters: the length L of the input formula, the number K of its clauses and the number N of the variables occurring in it. Before the conference proceedings version of this paper [10], the best known worst-case upper bounds for SAT were:

- $p(L)2^{L/9}$ [18],
- $p(L)2^{K/3}$ [23] (see also [18]),

where p is a polynomial. Also, the upper bound $p(L)2^{L/4}$ for satisfiability problem for general Boolean formulas (i.e., not necessarily in CNF) is known [31]. Recently Schöning [29] proved that 3-SAT is checkable in the randomized time $O\left(\left(\frac{4}{3}\right)^N\right)$, but it is still unknown whether the trivial upper bound 2^N for the general SAT problem can be improved. Kullmann and Luckhardt in [18] simplified the algorithm of Monien and Speckenmeyer from [23] and presented also an improved algorithm of the same complexity $p(L)2^{K/3}$ which works better when the ratio of the number of clauses to the number of variables is greater than 2.64557. In the conference proceedings version of this paper [10] we presented two algorithms which improve the bounds $p(L)2^{K/3} = p(L)2^{0.33333...K}$ and $p(L)2^{L/9} = p(L)2^{0.11111...L}$ to $p(L)2^{0.30897K}$ and $p(L)2^{0.10537L}$ respectively. In this journal version we improve the second algorithm and prove the worst-case upper bound $p(L)2^{0.10299L}$. Our new algorithm uses the $p(L)2^{0.30897K}$-time algorithm as a subroutine; the proof of the corresponding upper bound is much simpler than the proof in the conference proceedings version [10].

‡ `http://logic.pdmi.ras.ru/~hirsch`
* Research is supported by grants from INTAS and RFBR.

The most popular methods for solving SAT are the *local search method* and the *splitting method*. Many experimental and average-case results show the significant power of the local search method (for references, see the survey [8]). However, most best known worst-case upper bounds for SAT and its $\mathcal{NP}$-complete subproblems are obtained using the splitting method [23, 18, 9] (for worst-case upper bounds for the local search method see the papers [11, 12, 13]). The splitting method is also useful in proving worst-case upper bounds for exact and approximate MAXSAT solving [20, 4, 21, 1, 14].

The splitting method goes back to the Davis–Putnam procedure [7]. Let l be a literal occurring in a formula F. Let $F[l]$ be the formula obtained from F by assigning the value *True* to the literal l, i.e. by removing all clauses containing l and deleting all occurrences of $\bar{l}$ from the other clauses. In short, the main idea of the Davis–Putnam procedure is that F is satisfiable iff at least one of the formulas $F[l]$ and $F[\bar{l}]$ is satisfiable. In a wider sense [6], a splitting algorithm constructs a tree by reducing satisfiability of a formula F to satisfiability of several formulas $F[I_1], F[I_2], \ldots, F[I_s]$ obtained from F by assignments $I_1, I_2, \ldots, I_s$ respectively. Then, a splitting algorithm simplifies each of the formulas $F[I_1], F[I_2], \ldots, F[I_s]$ according to *transformation rules* which do not change their satisfiability. These transformations take a polynomial time. Their role is to reduce some of the parameters L, K or N of the formulas $F[I_1], F[I_2], \ldots, F[I_s]$ and to simplify these formulas by eliminating pure literals (a literal is *pure* if its negation does not occur in the formula), 1-clauses (1-*clause* is a clause consisting of one literal) and other "easy pieces".

Recurrent equations are often used in complexity analysis of algorithms. Kullmann and Luckhardt in [18] described a very similar, but simpler technique which is very useful in the estimation of the running time of splitting algorithms. One can consider an execution of a splitting algorithm as a *branching tree*, i.e. a tree such that formulas labelling children are simpler than formulas labelling parents (leaves are labelled with the simplest formulas). With each node of this tree we associate a *branching vector* of non-negative numbers and a polynomial constructed from this vector. One can estimate the number of leaves in the tree using the largest of the positive roots of these polynomials. Precise definitions and formulations are given in Sect. 3.

Transformation rules play an important role in splitting algorithms. Two simplest rules were proposed in the original paper of Davis and Putnam [7]: we can eliminate pure literals and 1-clauses. All transformation rules we use are described in Sect. 4. This paper introduces a new transformation rule which goes up to the following simple observation: if each clause of our formula contains at least one negative literal, then this formula is trivially satisfiable by the assignment in which all variables have the value *False*. Let $P(l, F)$ be a property of a literal and a formula, for example, "F contains exactly two occurrences of l and at least three occurrences of $\bar{l}$". In addition, we suppose that for each variable v in the formula F at most one of the literals v and $\bar{v}$ satisfies P. Given F, the literals that satisfy the property P will be referred as *P-literals*.

> *The black and white literals principle.* Let F be a formula in CNF. At least one of the following two alternatives holds.
>
> (1) There is a clause in F that contains a P-literal and does not contain the negations of any other P-literals.
>
> (2) Satisfiability of F is equivalent to satisfiability of the formula obtained from F by removing all clauses containing the negations of P-literals.

Figure 1. Two alternatives of the black and white literals principle.

A formal proof of the black and white literals principle is given in Lemma 4.3. Figure 1 illustrates this principle. White circles (○) denote P-literals, black circles (•) denote their negations, circles with dots (⊙) denote other literals (i.e., literals which are neither P-literals nor the negations of P-literals; note that the negation of such literal is again neither P-literal nor the negation of a P-literal). Columns correspond to clauses of the formula. The figure contains two formulas, the first one satisfies the condition (1), the second one satisfies the condition (2).

This principle is the key point of our algorithm corresponding to the upper bound $p(L)2^{0.30897K}$. In this algorithm we use the presence of clauses that contain a P-literal and do not contain the negations of other P-literals for a certain property P. The black and white literals principle is a kind of insurance: it guarantees that if we cannot find a required clause, then we can replace F by a simpler formula, or F does not contain any P-literals at all. This principle is one of re-formulations of the following simple property: for any partial assignment A (i.e., a set of literals which does not contain simultaneously x and $\overline{x}$ for any variable x) for a formula F in CNF, either there is a clause in F containing only literals from A, or setting the values of all these literals to *False* does not change the satisfiability of F.

Another known re-formulations of this property are the *generalized sign principle* [18] and the *autarkness principle* [22, 24, 19] (see also [18]). A comprehensive study of the autarkness principle can be found in [17].

The use of the black and white literals principle leads to two new bounds for SAT presented in this paper and also to several upper bounds for the satisfiability problem for formulas in CNF–(1,∞) [9] (a formula is in CNF–(1,∞) if each literal occurs in it positively at most once; the satisfiability problem for these formulas is $\mathcal{NP}$-complete).

In Sect. 2 we give basic definitions. Section 3 contains the technique that allows us to estimate the size of a branching tree. In Sect. 4 we explain transformation rules that we use in our algorithms. In Sect. 5 and Sect. 6 we describe the algorithms corresponding to the upper bounds $p(L)2^{0.30897K}$ and $p(L)2^{0.10299L}$ respectively, and give the proofs of this bounds.

2. Basic definitions

Let V be a set of Boolean variables. The negation of a variable v is denoted by $\overline{v}$. Given a set U, we denote $\overline{U} = \{\overline{u} \mid u \in U\}$. *Literals* are the members of the set $W = V \cup \overline{V}$. *Positive literals* are the members of the set V. *Negative literals* are their negations. If w denotes a negative literal $\overline{v}$, then $\overline{w}$ denotes the variable v. A *clause* is a finite set of literals that does not contain simultaneously any variable together with its negation. The empty clause is interpreted as *False*. A *formula in CNF* (*CNF-formula*) is a finite set of clauses. The empty formula is interpreted as *True*. The *length of a clause* is its cardinality, the *length of a formula* is the sum of the lengths of all its clauses. The length of a clause C is denoted by $|C|$. A *k-clause* is a clause of the length k. A *k^+-clause* is a clause of the length at least k. A *k^--clause* is a clause of the length at most k. If we say that *a literal v occurs* in a clause or in a formula, we mean that this clause or this formula contains the literal v. However, if we say that *a variable v occurs* in a clause or in a formula, we mean that this clause or this formula contains the literal v, or it contains the literal $\overline{v}$.

An *assignment* is a finite subset of W that does not contain any variable together with its negation. Informally speaking, if an assignment I contains a literal w, it means that w has the value $True$ in I. To obtain $F[I]$ from F and an assignment $I = \{w_1, \dots, w_s\}$, we

- remove from F all clauses containing the literals w_i,
- delete all occurrences of the literals $\overline{w}_i$ from the other clauses.

For short, we write $F[w_1, \dots, w_s]$ instead of $F[\{w_1, \dots, w_s\}]$.

An assignment I is *satisfying* for a formula F if $F[I]$ is the empty formula. A formula is *satisfiable* if there exists a satisfying assignment for it. We say that two formulas F and G are *equi-satisfiable* if both are satisfiable, or both are unsatisfiable.

Let w be a literal occurring in a formula F. This literal is a *i-literal* if F contains exactly i occurrences of w. It is a *(i,j)-literal* if F contains exactly i occurrences of w and exactly j occurrences of $\overline{w}$. It is a *(i,j^+)-literal* if F contains exactly i occurrences of w and at least j occurrences of $\overline{w}$. It is a *(i,j^-)-literal* if F contains exactly i occurrences of w and at most j occurrences of $\overline{w}$. Similarly, we define *(i^+,j^+)-literals, (i^+,j)-literals* etc.

We denote the number of occurrences of a literal w in a formula F by $\#_w(F)$. We denote the sum of the lengths of the clauses containing w by $\Diamond_w(F)$. When the meaning of F is clear from the context, we omit F.

3. Estimation of the size of a branching tree

Kullmann and Luckhardt introduced in [18] a notion of a branching tree. It is intended for estimating the time complexity of splitting algorithms, since a tree of formulas which such an algorithm splits, is a branching tree. One can consider an execution of a splitting algorithm as a tree whose nodes are labelled with CNF-formulas such that if some node is labelled with a CNF-formula F, then its sons are labelled with (simplified) formulas $F[I_1], F[I_2], \dots, F[I_s]$ for some assignments $I_1, I_2, \dots, I_s$.

Suppose we have a tree whose nodes are labelled with formulas in CNF. To each formula F we attach a non-negative integer $\mu(F)$ (*complexity of F*). The tree is a *branching tree* if, for each node, the complexity of the formula labelling this node is strictly greater than the complexity of each of the formulas labelling its sons. In this paper we use

(1) $\mu(F) = \mathcal{N}(F)$ is the number of variables in F;

(2) $\mu(F) = \mathcal{K}(F)$ is the number of clauses in F;

(3) $\mu(F) = \mathcal{L}(F)$ is the length of F.

We prove two upper bounds, w.r.t. $\mathcal{K}$ and w.r.t. $\mathcal{L}$. However, in this section we do not fix any concrete measure of complexity.

Let us consider a node in our tree labelled with a formula F_0. Suppose its sons are labelled with formulas F_1, F_2, ..., F_m. A *branching vector of a node* is an m-tuple $(t_1, \dots, t_m)$, where t_i are positive numbers not exceeding $\mu(F_0) - \mu(F_i)$. The *characteristic polynomial* of a branching vector $\vec{t}$ is defined by

$$\mathfrak{h}_{\vec{t}}(x) = 1 - \sum_{i=1}^{m} x^{-t_i}.$$

The characteristic polynomial $\mathfrak{h}_{\vec{t}}(x)$ is a monotone function of x on the interval $(0, +\infty)$, and $\mathfrak{h}_{\vec{t}}(0) = -\infty$, $\mathfrak{h}_{\vec{t}}(+\infty) = 1$. Hence, $\mathfrak{h}_{\vec{t}}(x) = 0$ has exactly one positive root. We denote this root by $\tau(\vec{t})$ and call it the *branching number*. We suppose $\tau(\emptyset) = 1$ for leaves. We omit one pair of parentheses and write $\tau(t_1, t_2, \dots, t_m)$ instead of $\tau((t_1, t_2, \dots, t_m))$.

EXAMPLE 3.1. For example,

$\tau(1, 1) = 2;$

$\tau(1, 2) = 1.61803... = 2^{0.69424...}$ is the golden ratio;

$\tau(6, 7, 6, 7) = 1.23881... = 2^{0.30896...};$

$\tau(10, 10) = 1.07177... = 2^{0.1}.$

The *branching number of a tree* T is the largest of the branching numbers $\tau(\vec{t})$ of its nodes. We denote it by $\tau_{max,T}$. The following lemma proved by Kullmann and Luckhardt allows us to estimate the number of leaves in a branching tree using its branching number.

LEMMA 3.1. (Kullmann, Luckhardt, [18]) *Let T be a branching tree, let its root be labelled with a formula F_0. Then the number of leaves in T does not exceed $(\tau_{max,T})^{\mu(F_0)}$.*

This lemma already allows us to estimate the running time of a splitting algorithm if we know the branching number of the splitting tree and the algorithm processes each its leaf in a polynomial time. However, our algorithm corresponding to the upper bound $p(L)\tau(6, 7, 6, 7)^{L/3}$ calls the algorithm corresponding to the upper bound $p(L)\tau(6, 7, 6, 7)^{K}$ as a subroutine and thus processes some of the leaves in an exponential time. To estimate the overall running time, we use the following simple generalization of Lemma 3.1.

LEMMA 3.2. [9] *Let T be a branching tree, let its root be labelled with a formula F_0. Let G_l denote the object labelling a leaf l of the tree T. Let $f(m) = \alpha\lambda^m$, where $\lambda > 1$, $\alpha \geq 0$. Then*

$$\sum_{l \text{ is a leaf of } T} f(\mu(G_l)) \leq \alpha(\max(\lambda, \tau_{max,T}))^{\mu(F_0)}.$$

Proof. Proof is the induction on the construction of the tree.

Base. The tree consisting of the unique node. In this case $\tau_{max} = 1$, $\alpha(\max(\lambda, \tau_{max}))^{\mu(F_0)} = \alpha\lambda^{\mu(F_0)} = f(\mu(F_0))$.

Step. Consider the tree T presented in Fig. 2. Let $\vec{t} = (t_1, t_2, \dots, t_s)$ be the branching

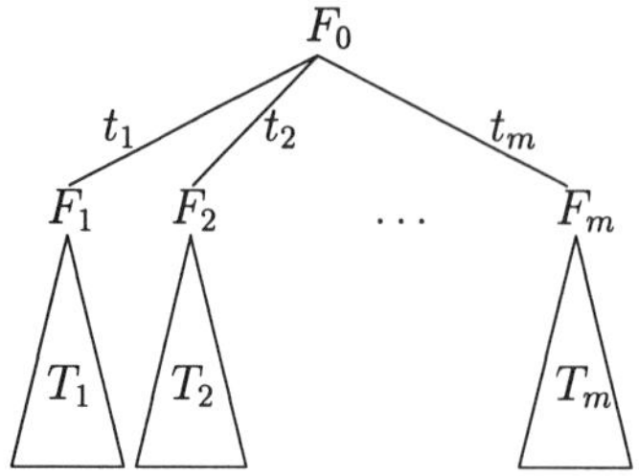

Figure 2. A splitting tree

tuple in its root.

$$\sum_{l \text{ is a leaf of } T} f(\mu(G_l)) =$$

$$= \sum_{j=1}^{s} \left(\sum_{l \text{ is a leaf of } T_j} f(\mu(G_l)) \right)$$

$$\leq \alpha \sum_{j=1}^{s} (\max(\lambda, \tau_{max,T_j}))^{\mu(F_j)} \qquad \text{(by induction hypothesis)}$$

$$\leq \alpha \sum_{j=1}^{s} (\max(\lambda, \tau_{max,T_j}))^{\mu(F_0)-t_j} \qquad \text{(by definition of the tuple } \vec{t}\text{)}$$

$$\leq \alpha \sum_{j=1}^{s} (\max(\lambda, \tau_{max,T}))^{\mu(F_0)-t_j} \qquad \text{(since } \tau_{max,T_j} \leq \tau_{max,T}\text{)}$$

$$= \alpha(\max(\lambda, \tau_{max,T}))^{\mu(F_0)} \cdot \sum_{j=1}^{s} (\max(\lambda, \tau_{max,T}))^{-t_j}$$

$$= \alpha(\max(\lambda, \tau_{max,T}))^{\mu(F_0)}(1 - \mathfrak{h}_{\vec{t}}(\max(\lambda, \tau_{max,T}))) \qquad \text{(by definition of } \mathfrak{h}_{\vec{t}}\text{)}$$

$$\leq \alpha(\max(\lambda, \tau_{max,T}))^{\mu(F_0)} \qquad \text{(by monotonicity of } \mathfrak{h}_{\vec{t}}\text{)}$$

□

Now if we know the branching number of the tree corresponding to a splitting algorithm, then we can estimate its running time. We explicitly require our algorithms to perform splittings with branching numbers not greater than we wish (and we only need to prove that there always exists a splitting satisfying this condition). For this purpose, the algorithm has to compare branching numbers corresponding to different vectors. Of course, this can be done just by the examination of a constant number of cases and the use of the monotonicity of τ. However, a more general statement holds.

LEMMA 3.3. (Kullmann, Luckhardt, [18]) *Let m, k be natural constants, $x_1, x_2, \ldots, x_m$, $y_1, y_2, \ldots, y_k$ be positive rational numbers. The problem whether $\tau(x_1, x_2, \ldots, x_m)$ is not greater than $\tau(y_1, y_2, \ldots, y_k)$ is solvable in time polynomial of* $\max(x_1, x_2, \ldots, x_m, y_1, y_2, \ldots, y_k)$.

In the following, when estimating the running time of our algorithms, we use frequently inequalities like $\tau(7,15) < \tau(5,17)$ or $\tau(5,17) < \tau(6,7,6,7)^{1/3}$ without proofs.

One can check these inequalities by approximate calculation of the branching numbers. However, there are several simple observations that may help to prove some of this inequalities easier.

LEMMA 3.4. (Kullmann, Luckhardt, [18])

(1) Permutations of the components of a branching vector do not affect the corresponding branching number.

(2) The branching number strictly decreases as one or more components of the branching vector increase.

(3) Let $0 < \alpha < t_1$. *Then* $\tau(t_1, t_2, t_3 \ldots, t_m) \gtreqless \tau(t_1 - \alpha, t_2 + \alpha, t_3 \ldots, t_m)$ *iff* $t_1 \gtreqless t_2 + \alpha$.

4. Transformation rules

In this section F denotes a formula in CNF.

Lemmas 3.1 and 3.2 allows us to take into consideration only the differences between the complexity of an input formula and the complexities of the formulas obtained from it by splitting. The higher these differences are, the smaller the number of leaves is. Thus, to obtain a good algorithm, we should reduce as much as possible the complexities of the formulas obtained by splitting. Here we explain transformation rules that allow us to do it. More precisely, we explain that in certain cases we can find a simpler formula equi-satisfiable with F. In the following we use these rules so that they never increase the parameter under consideration (the number of clauses in a formula or the length of a formula).

Elimination of 1-clauses. If F contains a 1-clause $\{a\}$, then the formulas F and $F[a]$ are equi-satisfiable since all assignments that contain $\overline{a}$ are unsatisfying.

Subsumption. If F contains two clauses C and D such that $C \subseteq D$, then F and $F \setminus \{D\}$ are equi-satisfiable since each assignment that satisfies the clause C, satisfies also the clause D.

Resolution with subsumption. Suppose we are given a literal a and clauses C and D such that a is the only literal satisfying both conditions $a \in C$ and $\overline{a} \in D$. In this case, the clause $(C \cup D) \setminus \{a, \overline{a}\}$ is called the *resolvent by the literal* a of the clauses C and D. We denote it by $\mathcal{R}(C, D)$.

Let now F contain such clauses C and D. It is clear that adding $\mathcal{R}(C, D)$ to the formula does not change its satisfiability. However, it increases its size. To avoid this effect, we use this rule only if $\mathcal{R}(C, D) \subseteq D$. In this case we reduce the satisfiability problem for the formula F to the satisfiability problem for $(F \setminus \{D\}) \cup \{\mathcal{R}(C, D)\}$.

Elimination of a variable by resolution. Given a literal a, we construct the formula $DP_a(F)$ by

- adding to F all resolvents by a;
- removing from F all clauses containing a or $\overline{a}$.

LEMMA 4.1. (Davis, Putnam, [7]) *The formulas F and $DP_a(F)$ are equi-satisfiable.*

This transformation can increase the size of a formula or/and the number of clauses in it, but we use this rule only if it does not increase the parameter under consideration (the number of clauses in a formula or the length of a formula). Note that in particular, this transformation does not increase any of the parameters of F if a is a pure literal, and thus it eliminates pure literals.

Elimination of blocked clauses. The clause C is *blocked* for a literal a w.r.t. F if C contains the literal a, and the literal $\overline{a}$ occurs only in the clauses of F that contain the negation of at least one of the literals occurring in $C \setminus \{a\}$. (Note that F may or may not contain C.) In other words, there are no resolvents by a of the clause C and any other clause of the formula F. For a CNF-formula F and a literal a occurring in it, we define the assignment $\mathcal{I}(a, F)$ as

$$\{a\} \cup \{x \in W \setminus \{a, \overline{a}\} \mid \text{the clause } \{\overline{a}, x\} \text{ is blocked for } \overline{a} \text{ w.r.t. } F\}.$$

When the meaning of F is clear from the context, we omit F and write $\mathcal{I}(a)$.

The notion of a blocked clause was introduced and investigated by Kullmann in [15, 16]. We use the following two facts about blocked clauses.

LEMMA 4.2. (Kullmann, [15, 16])

(1) If a clause C is blocked for a literal a w.r.t. F, then F, $F \setminus \{C\}$ and $F \cup \{C\}$ are equi-satisfiable.

(2) Given a literal a, the formula F is satisfiable iff at least one of the formulas $F[\overline{a}]$ and $F[\mathcal{I}(a)]$ is satisfiable.

Application of the black and white literals principle. Let P be a binary relation between literals and formulas in CNF, such that for a variable v and a formula F, at most one of $P(v, F)$ and $P(\overline{v}, F)$ holds.

LEMMA 4.3. *Suppose that each clause of F that contains a literal w satisfying $P(w, F)$ contains also at least one literal b satisfying $P(\overline{b}, F)$. Then F and $F[\{l \mid P(\overline{l}, F)\}]$ are equi-satisfiable.*

Proof. This is a particular case of the autarkness principle [22, 24, 19, 18]. We denote $G = F[\{l \mid P(\overline{l}, F)\}]$. Suppose G is satisfiable. Consider a satisfying assignment I for the formula G. It is clear that the assignment $I \cup \{l \mid P(\overline{l}, F)\}$ satisfies F. On the other hand, $G \setminus F = \emptyset$, hence, each assignment satisfying F satisfies also G. □

5. A bound w.r.t. the number of clauses

In this section we present Algorithm 5.1 which checks satisfiability of formula F in the time $p(\mathcal{L}(F))2^{0.30897\mathcal{K}(F)}$ (where p is a polynomial). This algorithm has two subroutines, Function $REDUCE_K$ and Function $SPLIT_K$. Function $REDUCE_K$ simplifies the input formula using the transformation rules (see Sect. 4). Function $SPLIT_K$ is intended for reducing the satisfiability problem for the input formula to the satisfiability problem for several simpler formulas. The execution of this algorithm can be viewed as follows: Function $REDUCE_K$ simplifies the input formula, then $SPLIT_K$ splits it into several formulas, $REDUCE_K$ simplifies each of these, and so on.

In the following, we denote by $REDUCE_K(F)$ the formula that Function $REDUCE_K$ outputs on input F. Similarly we define $SPLIT_K(F)$ etc.

Function $REDUCE_K$**.**

Input: A formula F in CNF.
Output: A (simplified) formula in CNF.

Method.

(KR1) **Elimination of 1-clauses.** If F contains a 1-clause $C = \{a\}$, then $F := F[a]$. Repeat this step while F contains 1-clauses.

(KR2) **Application of the black and white literals principle.** If each clause C in F that contains a (2,3$^+$)-literal, contains also a (3$^+$,2)-literal, then

$$F := F[\{a \mid a \text{ is a } (3^+,2)\text{-literal}\}].$$

(KR3) **Elimination of a variable by resolution.** Choose a literal a such that a or $\overline{a}$ occurs in F and $\Delta = \mathcal{K}(F) - \mathcal{K}(DP_a(F))$ is maximal. If there are several such literals, then choose a literal with $\#_a$ minimal. If $\Delta \geq 0$, then $F := DP_a(F)$. Repeat this step while F satisfies this condition.

(KR4) If F has been changed at steps (KR1)–(KR3), then go to step (KR1), otherwise return F.

□

Function $SPLIT_K$**.**

Input: A formula F in CNF.
Output: If F is satisfiable, then True, otherwise False.

Method.

(KS1) **The empty formula.** If $F = \emptyset$, then return $True$.

(KS2) **Formula containing the empty clause.** If $\emptyset \in F$, then return $False$.

(KS3) **Splitting into two subproblems.** For each literal a occurring in F, construct two formulas

$$F_1 = REDUCE_K(F[a]),$$
$$F_2 = REDUCE_K(F[\overline{a}]).$$

If there exists a literal a such that $\tau(\mathcal{K}(F) - \mathcal{K}(F_1), \mathcal{K}(F) - \mathcal{K}(F_2)) \leq \tau(6,7,6,7)$, then choose the formulas F_1 and F_2 corresponding to this literal. If $SPLIT_K$ returns $True$ for at least one of these, then return $True$, otherwise return $False$.

(KS4) **Splitting into four subproblems.** Choose a literal a occurring in F. For each two literals b and c occurring in $F[a]$ and $F[\overline{a}]$ respectively, construct four formulas

$$\begin{aligned}F_{11} &= REDUCE_K(F[a,b]),\\ F_{12} &= REDUCE_K(F[a,\overline{b}]),\\ F_{21} &= REDUCE_K(F[\overline{a},c]),\\ F_{22} &= REDUCE_K(F[\overline{a},\overline{c}]).\end{aligned}$$

If there exist literals b and c such that

$$\tau(\mathcal{K}(F)-\mathcal{K}(F_{11}),\mathcal{K}(F)-\mathcal{K}(F_{12}),\\ \mathcal{K}(F)-\mathcal{K}(F_{21}),\mathcal{K}(F)-\mathcal{K}(F_{22}))\le\tau(6,7,6,7),$$

then choose the formulas F_{11}, F_{12}, F_{21} and F_{22} corresponding to these literals. If $SPLIT_K$ returns $True$ for at least one of these, then return $True$, otherwise return $False$.

□

Algorithm 5.1.

Input: A formula F in CNF.
Output: If F is satisfiable, then True, otherwise False.

Method.

(KM1) Return $SPLIT_K(REDUCE_K(F))$.

□

In Sect. 4 we explained that none of the steps of $REDUCE_K$ changes the satisfiability of the formula. The steps (KR1)–(KR4) cannot be repeated more than $\mathcal{K}(F)+\mathcal{N}(F)$ times since none of them increases the number of clauses or the number of variables, and during each iteration (KR1)–(KR4)–(KR1) at least one of these quantities decreases. Each of these steps takes a polynomial time. Thus, $REDUCE_K$ does not change the satisfiability of the formula and returns the answer in a polynomial time.

We now construct a tree which reflects the behaviour of Algorithm 5.1 (together with Functions $REDUCE_K$ and $SPLIT_K$). Its internal nodes are labelled with formulas that Algorithm 5.1 splits at steps (KS3) and (KS4). Its leaves are labelled with formulas that satisfy the conditions of the steps (KS1) and (KS2). Each internal node labelled with F has two sons labelled with F_1 and F_2 or four sons labelled with F_{11}, F_{12}, F_{21} and F_{22}. Since the conditions of the steps (KS3) and (KS4) guarantee that the corresponding branching numbers do not exceed $\tau(6,7,6,7)$, by Lemma 3.1 the number of leaves in the tree is at most $\tau(6,7,6,7)^{\mathcal{K}(F)}$, where F is the input formula. Thus, the Algorithm 5.1 returns the answer in the time $p(\mathcal{L}(F))\tau(6,7,6,7)^{\mathcal{K}(F)}$, where p is some polynomial.

It remains to prove that Algorithm 5.1 performs correctly, i.e., each formula in CNF reduced by $REDUCE_K$ satisfies at least one of the conditions of the steps (KS1)–(KS4). To prove this statement, we need two simple lemmas concerning the output of $REDUCE_K$.

LEMMA 5.1. *Let F_1 be the value of F at step (KR1) of Function $REDUCE_K$ at some point of time (maybe after eliminating several 1-clauses), F_2 be the corresponding output formula of Function $REDUCE_K$, d and e be literals occurring in F_1.*

(1) If d is a $(1^-,1^+)$-literal, then $\mathcal{K}(F_2)\le\mathcal{K}(F_1)-1$.

(2) If d and e are $(1^-,1^+)$-literals, $\#_d+\#_e+\#_{\overline{d}}+\#_{\overline{e}}\ge 3$ and there are no clauses in F that contain d and e simultaneously, then $\mathcal{K}(F_2)\le\mathcal{K}(F_1)-2$.

Proof. (1). If $REDUCE_K$ modifies once more the formula at steps (KR1) or (KR2), then at least one clause will be deleted from it. Otherwise, at least one clause will be eliminated at step (KR3) since $\mathcal{K}(F_1) - \mathcal{K}(DP_d(F_1)) \geq 1$.
(2). W.l.o.g we suppose that F_1 contains at most one 1-clause, this clause (if any) contains a 1-literal and after eliminating this clause the formula F_1 does not contain 1-clauses at all. If F_1 contains exactly one 1-clause, then it will be eliminated at step (KR1), and one more clause will be eliminated by (1) since at least one of the literals d and e remains a $(1^-,1^+)$-literal.

Now let F_1 contain no 1-clauses. If $REDUCE_K$ modifies this formula at step (KR2), then at least one clause, i.e., at least two occurrences will be eliminated.

Now F has the value F_1 before the step (KR3). W.l.o.g. we suppose that $\Delta = 1$ in terms of the step (KR3). At step (KR3) a 1^--literal will be chosen. After the first application of DP, at least one of the literals d and e remains a 1^--literal and its negation or the literal itself remains in the formula. Hence, by (1) at least one more clause will be eliminated. □

LEMMA 5.2. *Let F be a formula in CNF. Then the formula $REDUCE_K(F)$ does not contain* 1*-clauses,* 1^-*-literals and* (2,2)*-literals.*

Proof. Function $REDUCE_K$ eliminates 1-clauses at step (KR1). If d is a 1^--literal or a (2,2)-literal, then $\mathcal{K}(DP_d(F)) \leq \mathcal{K}(F)$. Function $REDUCE_K$ eliminates such literals at step (KR3). □

THEOREM 5.1. *Algorithm 5.1 performs correctly and stops in the time* $p(L)\tau(6,7,6,7)^K < p(L)2^{0.30897K}$, *where L is the length of the input formula, K is the number of clauses in it, and p is a polynomial.*

Proof. We have shown above that it suffices to prove that each formula F in CNF reduced by $REDUCE_K$ satisfies at least one of the conditions of the steps (KS1)–(KS4). Suppose F does not satisfy the conditions of the steps (KS1)–(KS4). We now consider all possible cases. We prove that each of this cases is impossible. All symbols have the same meaning as they have at the corresponding steps of Function $SPLIT_K$. For $i, j = 1, 2$, we denote

$$\begin{array}{ll}
\Delta_i = \mathcal{K}(F) - \mathcal{K}(F_i), & \Delta_{ij} = \mathcal{K}(F) - \mathcal{K}(F_{ij}), \\
\mathrm{B}_1 = \mathcal{K}(F) - \mathcal{K}(F[a]), & \Gamma_1 = \mathcal{K}(F[a]) - \mathcal{K}(F_1), \\
\mathrm{B}_2 = \mathcal{K}(F) - \mathcal{K}(F[\overline{a}]), & \Gamma_2 = \mathcal{K}(F[\overline{a}]) - \mathcal{K}(F_2), \\
\Gamma_{1j} = \mathcal{K}(F[a]) - \mathcal{K}(F_{1j}), & \Gamma_{2j} = \mathcal{K}(F[\overline{a}]) - \mathcal{K}(F_{2j}).
\end{array}$$

The key observation is that if the formula F contains few "frequent" variables, then after the transformation of F into $F[a], F[\overline{a}]$ for some literal a we can apply Lemma 5.1. We now prove this more formally.

CASE 1: The formula F contains a $(3^+,4^+)$-literal a.

All clauses of the formula F containing the literal a disappear in $F[a]$, all its clauses containing the literal $\overline{a}$ disappear in $F[\overline{a}]$. Since a is a $(3^+,4^+)$-literal, $\mathrm{B}_1 \geq 3$, $\mathrm{B}_2 \geq 4$. Thus, in terms of the step (KS3), $\tau(\Delta_1, \Delta_2) \leq \tau(3,4) < \tau(6,7,6,7)$, i.e., the condition of the step (KS3) is satisfied.

CASE 2: The formula F contains a clause that contains a (3,3)-literal a and a $(2,3^+)$-literal b.

All three clauses of the formula F containing a disappear in $F[a]$, all three clauses containing $\overline{a}$ disappear in $F[\overline{a}]$. In addition, b becomes a $(1^-,1^+)$-literal in $F[a]$. Thus, in terms of the step (KS3) we have $\Gamma_1 \geq 1$ by Lemma 5.1. Hence, $\Delta_1 = \mathrm{B}_1 + \Gamma_1 \geq 4$, $\Delta_2 \geq 3$, i.e., the condition of the step (KS3) is satisfied.

CASE 3: The formula F contains a 2-clause $C = \{a, b\}$ consisting of 2-literals.

All clauses of the formula F containing a disappear in $F[a]$, all its clauses containing $\overline{a}$ disappear in $F[\overline{a}]$. By Lemma 5.2, a is a (2,3$^+$)-literal. Thus, $B_1 \geq 2$, $B_2 \geq 3$. Similarly to Case 2, in terms of the step (KS3) we have $\Gamma_1 \geq 1$. In addition, C becomes a 1-clause in $F[\overline{a}]$ and will be eliminated at step (KR1), i.e. $\Gamma_2 \geq 1$. We now have $\Delta_1 = B_1 + \Gamma_1 \geq 3$, $\Delta_2 = B_2 + \Gamma_2 \geq 4$, i.e., the condition of the step (KS3) is satisfied.

CASE 4: The formula F contains a 3$^+$-clause $C = \{a_1, a_2, \ldots, a_s\}$ consisting of 2-literals.

Let $i \in \{1, 2, \ldots, s\}$. All clauses of the formula F containing a_i disappear in $F[a_i]$, all its clauses containing $\overline{a_i}$ disappear in $F[\overline{a_i}]$. By Lemma 5.2, a_i is a (2,3$^+$)-literal. Thus, $\mathcal{K}(F) - \mathcal{K}(F[a_i]) \geq 2$, $\mathcal{K}(F) - \mathcal{K}(F[\overline{a_i}]) \geq 3$. In addition, a_2 and a_3 become (1$^-$,1$^+$)-literals in $F[a_1]$. If C is the only clause that contains a_2 and a_3 simultaneously, then by Lemma 5.1 we have

$$\mathcal{K}(F[a_1]) - \mathcal{K}(REDUCE_K(F[a_1]))) \geq 2.$$

Otherwise, a_3 becomes a (0,3$^+$)-literal in $F[a_2]$, i.e.

$$\mathcal{K}(F[a_2]) - \mathcal{K}(REDUCE_K(F[a_2])) \geq 2.$$

Depending on which of these two alternatives takes place, we choose a_1 or a_2 as a in terms of the step (KS3). We now have $\Delta_1 = B_1 + \Gamma_1 \geq 4$, $\Delta_2 \geq B_2 \geq 3$, i.e., the condition of the step (KS3) is satisfied.

CASE 5: The conditions of Cases 1–4 are not satisfied.

Since the step (KR2) does not change F, it contains only 3-literals. Since F does not satisfy the condition of the step (KS3), for each literal a,

$$\mathcal{K}(F) = \mathcal{K}(F[a]) + 3 = \mathcal{K}(REDUCE_K(F[a])) + 3. \tag{5.1}$$

Let a be a literal occurring in F. We now prove that there exist literals b and c such that the condition of the step (KS4) is satisfied. We consider three sub-cases (the first two of them are similar to Cases 2–4).

CASE 5.1: There exists a clause $C = \{a_1, a_2, \ldots, a_s\}$ in $F[a]$, such that a_1 is a (3,3)-literal and a_2 is a 2-literal.

We suppose $b = a_1$ in terms of the step (KS4). Similarly to Case 2, $\Gamma_{11} \geq 4$, $\Gamma_{12} \geq 3$.

CASE 5.2: There exists a clause $C = \{a_1, a_2, \ldots, a_s\}$ in $F[a]$, such that a_1 is a (2,3)-literal and $a_2, \ldots, a_s$ are 2-literals.

We suppose $b = a_1$ in terms of the step (KS4). Similarly to Cases 3–4, $\Gamma_{11} \geq 3$, $\Gamma_{12} \geq 4$, or $\Gamma_{11} \geq 4$, $\Gamma_{12} \geq 3$. (Note that by (5.1) the literals a_i and a_j cannot occur together in two clauses.)

CASE 5.3: The conditions of Cases 5.1–5.2 are not satisfied.

Since by (5.1) the steps (KR1)–(KR3) do not reduce the number of clauses in the formula $F[a]$ and the conditions of Cases 5.1–5.2 are not satisfied, this formula consists of clauses that contain only (2,2)-literals and clauses that contain only (3,3)-literals. Since exactly three clauses of the formula F disappear in $F[a]$, all occurrences of any (3,3)-literal cannot disappear in $F[a]$. Hence, it contains at least one (2,2)-literal b_1. Let b_1 be a 2-literal. The formula F does not contain 2-clauses by (5.1). Similarly, it cannot contain two clauses, each containing the literals $\overline{a}$ and b_1 simultaneously. Thus, $F[a]$ contains a 3$^+$-clause $C = \{b_1, b_2, \ldots, b_s\}$, where $b_1, b_2, \ldots, b_s$ are 2-literals.

We choose the literal b_1 as b. Both clauses of the formula $F[a]$ that contain $\overline{b_1}$ disappear in $F[a, \overline{b_1}]$. In addition, these clauses contain only (2,2)-literals which become $(1^-,1^+)$-literals. Thus, by Lemma 5.1

$$\mathcal{K}(F[a]) - \mathcal{K}(REDUCE_K(F[a, \overline{b_1}])) \geq 3.$$

On the other hand, two clauses of $F[a]$ containing b_1 disappear in $F[a, b_1]$, and two more clauses disappear by Lemma 5.1 since b_2 and b_3 become $(1^-,1^+)$-literals. We note that by (5.1) the formula F contains only one clause that contains b_2 and b_3 simultaneously. Thus,

$$\mathcal{K}(F[a]) - \mathcal{K}(REDUCE_K(F[a, b_1])) \geq 4.$$

We now have that in each of Cases 5.1–5.3 there exists a literal b in $F[a]$ such that $\Delta_{11} = \mathrm{B}_1 + \Gamma_{11} \geq 6$, $\Delta_{12} = \mathrm{B}_1 + \Gamma_{12} \geq 7$. A literal c can be chosen similarly. Hence, the condition of the step (KS4) is satisfied. □

6. A bound w.r.t. the length of a formula.

In this section we present Algorithm 6.1 which checks satisfiability of formula F in the time $p(\mathcal{L}(F))2^{0.10299\mathcal{L}(F)}$ (where p is a polynomial). As in the previous section, we define two subroutines, Function $REDUCE_L$ and Function $SPLIT_L$. We use them similarly to $REDUCE_K$ and $SPLIT_K$: Function $REDUCE_L$ simplifies the input formula, then $SPLIT_L$ splits it into several formulas, $REDUCE_L$ simplifies each of these, and so on.

Function $REDUCE_L$.

Input: A formula F in CNF.
Output: A (simplified) formula in CNF.

Method.

(LR1) **Elimination of 1-clauses.** If F contains a 1-clause $C = \{a\}$, then $F := F[a]$. Repeat this step while F contains such a clause.

(LR2) **Subsumption.** If F contains two clauses C and D such that $C \subseteq D$, then $F := F \setminus \{D\}$. Repeat this step while F contains such clauses.

(LR3) **Elimination of blocked clauses.** If F contains a blocked clause C, then $F := F \setminus \{C\}$. Repeat this step while F contains blocked clauses.

(LR4) **Resolution with subsumption.** If F contains two clauses C and D such that $\mathcal{R}(C,D) \subseteq D$, then $F := (F \setminus \{D\}) \cup \{\mathcal{R}(C,D)\}$. Repeat this step while F contains such clauses.

(LR5) **Elimination of a variable by resolution.** Choose a literal a such that a or $\overline{a}$ occurs in F and $\Delta = \mathcal{L}(F) - \mathcal{L}(DP_a(F))$ is maximal. If $\Delta \geq 0$, then $F := DP_a(F)$. Repeat this step while F satisfies this condition.

(LR6) If F has been changed at steps (LR1)–(LR5), then go to step (LR1), otherwise return F. □

Function *$SPLIT_L$*.

Input: A formula F in CNF.
Output: If F is satisfiable, then True, otherwise False.

Method.

(LS1) **The empty formula.** If $F = \emptyset$, then return $True$.

(LS2) **Formula containing the empty clause.** If $\emptyset \in F$, then return $False$.

(LS3) **Formula containing no 2-clauses.** If F does not contain 2-clauses, apply Algorithm 5.1 to F and return its answer.

(LS4) **Splitting into two subproblems.** For each literal a occurring in F, construct two formulas

$$F_1 = REDUCE_L(F[\mathcal{I}(a)]),$$
$$F_2 = REDUCE_L(F[\overline{a}]).$$

If there exists a literal a such that $\tau(\mathcal{L}(F)-\mathcal{L}(F_1), \mathcal{L}(F)-\mathcal{L}(F_2)) \leq \tau(5, 17)$, then choose the formulas F_1 and F_2 corresponding to this literal. If $SPLIT_L$ returns $True$ for at least one of these, then return $True$, otherwise return $False$.

□

Algorithm 6.1.

Input: A formula F in CNF.
Output: If F is satisfiable, then True, otherwise False.

Method.

(LM1) Return $SPLIT_L(REDUCE_L(F))$.

□

Similarly to $REDUCE_K$, Function $REDUCE_L$ does not change the satisfiability of the formula and returns the answer in a polynomial time.

We now construct a tree which reflects the behaviour of Algorithm 6.1 (together with Functions $REDUCE_L$ and $SPLIT_L$). Its leaves are labelled with formulas that satisfy the conditions of the steps (LS1)–(LS3). Algorithm 6.1 processes in a polynomial time formulas satisfying the conditions of the steps (LS1) and (LS2), and passes formulas satisfying the condition of the step (LS3) to Algorithm 5.1 which processes such a formula F in the time

$$p(\mathcal{L}(F))\tau(6,7,6,7)^{\mathcal{K}(F)} \leq p(\mathcal{L}(F))\tau(6,7,6,7)^{\mathcal{L}(F)/3},$$

where p is a polynomial (note that F contains no 2^--clauses since 1-clauses are eliminated at step (LR1)).

Internal nodes of our tree are labelled with formulas that Algorithm 6.1 splits at step (LS4). Each internal node labelled with F has two sons labelled with F_1 and F_2. Since the condition of the step (LS4) guarantees that the corresponding branching number does not exceed $\tau(5,17) < \tau(6,7,6,7)^{1/3}$, by Lemma 3.2 the running time of Algorithm 6.1 is upper bounded by $q(\mathcal{L}(G))\tau(6,7,6,7)^{\mathcal{L}(G)/3}$ for input formula G, where q is a polynomial.

It remains to prove that Algorithm 6.1 performs correctly, i.e., each formula in CNF reduced by $REDUCE_L$ satisfies at least one of the conditions of the steps (LS1)–(LS4). We need three simple lemmas concerning the output of $REDUCE_L$ to prove this statement.

LEMMA 6.1. *Let F be a formula in CNF, d be a literal occurring in it.*

(1) If d is a $(1,2^-)$-literal occurring in a 3^--clause, then $\mathcal{L}(DP_d(F)) \leq \mathcal{L}(F) - 1$.

(2) If d is a $(1,1^+)$-literal occurring in a 2^--clause, then $\mathcal{L}(DP_d(F)) \leq \mathcal{L}(F) - 2$.

(3) If d is a $(1,1)$-literal, then $\mathcal{L}(DP_d(F)) \leq \mathcal{L}(F) - 2$.

Proof. By straightforward calculations. □

LEMMA 6.2. *Let F_1 be the value of F at one of the steps (LR1)–(LR5) of Function $REDUCE_L$, F_2 be the corresponding output formula of Function $REDUCE_L$, d be a literal occurring in F_1.*

(1) If d is a $(1,2^-)$-literal occurring in a 3^--clause, then $\mathcal{L}(F_2) \leq \mathcal{L}(F_1) - 1$.

(2) If d is a $(1,1^+)$-literal occurring in a 2^--clause, then $\mathcal{L}(F_2) \leq \mathcal{L}(F_1) - 2$.

Proof. (1). Note that any change of the formula at steps (LR1)–(LR4) is a removal of some clauses and/or a change of other clauses by their subsets, and thus results in decreasing the length of the formula by at least one occurrence. If the formula does not change any more before the step (LR5), then at least one occurrence will be removed by Lemma 6.1(1).

(2). Suppose that after F gets the value F_1, Function $REDUCE_L$ modifies the formula before the step (LR4). This modifying cannot result in increasing the length of a clause or in increasing the number of occurrences of a literal. Moreover, if the formula changes at these steps, at least one occurrence is removed. If only one occurrence is removed, then at least one of the literals d, $\overline{d}$ remains in the formula. If this is the occurrence of d, then by Lemma 6.1(1) at least one more occurrence will be removed at step (LR5), and (2) holds. Otherwise, $\overline{d}$ becomes a pure literal and will be removed at step (LR5), thus (2) holds again.

Suppose now that $REDUCE_L$ does not modify the formula before the step (LR5). Then, (2) follows from Lemma 6.1(2). □

We use the following simple properties of the formula reduced by Function $REDUCE_L$ in the proof of 6.1 without explicit mentioning.

LEMMA 6.3. *Let* $F = REDUCE_L(G)$ *for some formula* G. *Then*

(1) F *does not satisfy any of the conditions of the steps (LR1)–(LR5);*

(2) there are no 1*-clauses in* F*;*

(3) there are no pure literals and (1,1)*-literals in* F*;*

(4) there are no 2*-clauses in* F *containing a* 1*-literal;*

(5) for any literal d *occurring in* F, $\Diamond_d(F) \geq max(3, 2\#_d)$*;*

(6) for any 1*-literal* d *occurring in* F, $\Diamond_d + \#_{\overline{d}} \geq 7$*;*

(7) for any literal d *occurring in* F, $\Diamond_d + \#_{\overline{d}} \geq 5$.

Proof. (1) is trivial; (2)–(7) since F does not satisfy the conditions of the step (LR1)and (LR5); see also Lemma 6.1. □

THEOREM 6.1. *Algorithm 6.1 performs correctly and stops in the time* $p(L)\tau(6,7,6,7)^{L/3} < p(L)2^{0.10299L}$, *where* L *is the length of the input formula and* p *is a polynomial.*

Proof. We have shown above that it is sufficient to prove that each formula F in CNF reduced by $REDUCE_L$ satisfies at least one of the conditions of the steps (LS1)–(LS4). Suppose F does not satisfy the conditions of the steps (LS1)–(LS3). We now consider the two possible cases: when F contains at least one 1-literal a, and when it contains no 1-literals. We prove that in each of these cases F satisfies the condition of the step (LS4).

Informally, this is done as follows. In the first case we show that the assignment $\mathcal{I}(a)$ contains many literals. The second case is handled by careful examination of sub-cases: we choose a 2-clause $\{c, d\}$ in F and examine the following sub-cases:

- there are many occurrences in the clauses containing the literal c (or d);

- F contains many occurrences of the literal $\overline{c}$ (or $\overline{d}$).

In these two sub-cases we show that many occurrences are eliminated during the transformation of F into $F[c], F[\overline{c}]$ (or $F[d], F[\overline{d}]$) and the subsequent elimination of 1-clauses obtained from the clauses containing the literals $\overline{c}, c$ (or $\overline{d}, d$). The third sub-case is:

- none of the previous sub-cases holds.

In this sub-case one of c and d is a (2,2)-literal occuring only in 2- and 3-clauses which allows us to use Lemma 6.1 after one occurrence of this literal is eliminated during the splitting by another literal.

In the following we denote $\Delta_1 = \mathcal{L}(F) - \mathcal{L}(F_1)$, $\Delta_2 = \mathcal{L}(F) - \mathcal{L}(F_2)$. Formulas F_1 and F_2 and a literal a have the same meaning as they have at step (LS4) of Algorithm 6.1.

CASE 1: The formula F contains a 1-literal a.

Let $D = \{a, a_2, \ldots, a_{|D|}\}$ be the only clause containing a. Let $r = \min\{5, |D|\}$. Since $\#_{\overline{a}} \geq 2$ and $\diamondsuit_a + \#_{\overline{a}} \geq 7$ by Lemma 6.3, we have $\#_{\overline{a}} \geq \max(7 - \diamondsuit_a, 2) \geq 7 - r$. Let γ be the number of 3^+-clauses among all clauses that contain $\overline{a}$.

During the transformation of the formula F into F_2, all occurrences of the literal a and all clauses containing $\overline{a}$ will be eliminated. Thus,

$$\Delta_2 \geq \diamondsuit_{\overline{a}} + \#_a \geq 2\#_{\overline{a}} + \gamma + \#_a \geq \\ 2(7-r) + \gamma + 1 = 15 - 2r + \gamma \geq 5.$$

During the transformation of the formula F into F_1, the clause D and all occurrences of the literal $\overline{a}$ will be eliminated; all 2-clauses containing $\overline{a}$ will be eliminated too (at step (LR1)). Since D is not blocked for any a_i w.r.t. F, for each $i \in 2, \ldots, r$ there exists clause D_i in F such that $D_i \cap \{\overline{a}, \overline{a}_2, \ldots, \overline{a}_r\} = \{\overline{a}_i\}$. All these clauses will be eliminated since all clauses $\{\overline{a}, \overline{a}_i\}$ are blocked for $\overline{a}$ w.r.t. F (i.e. $\{a, \overline{a}_2, \ldots, \overline{a}_r\} \subseteq \mathcal{I}(a)$). All clauses containing $\overline{a}$, all clauses D_i and the clause D are distinct. Thus, we have

$$\Delta_1 \geq |D| + \#_{\overline{a}} + (\#_{\overline{a}} - \gamma) + 2(r-1) \geq \\ r + (7-r) + (\#_{\overline{a}} - \gamma) + 2(r-1) = 5 + 2r + (\#_{\overline{a}} - \gamma) \geq 9.$$

We now have $\Delta_1 + \Delta_2 \geq 20 + \#_{\overline{a}} \geq 22$; $\Delta_1, \Delta_2 \geq 5$. Thus, $\tau(\Delta_1, \Delta_2) \leq \tau(5, 17)$, i.e., the condition of the step (LS4) is satisfied[1].

CASE 2: The formula F does not contain 1-literals.

Since F does not satisfy the condition of the step (LS3), it contains a 2-clause $D = \{c, d\}$. Let us note that

> The formula F does not contain other clauses that contain the literal d and the literal c, or the literal d and the literal $\overline{c}$, or the literal $\overline{d}$ and the literal c, simultaneously. (6.1)

This proposition is true since F does not satisfy the conditions of the steps (LR2) and (LR4). Also, in this case $\mathcal{I}(c) = \{c\}$ and $\mathcal{I}(d) = \{d\}$ by (6.1) and the definition of $\mathcal{I}(\ldots)$.

Let us denote one of the literals c, d by a (we shall choose later which one). We denote the remaining literal by b. Let α be the number of 3^+-clauses among all clauses that contain a (note that $\#_a - \alpha \geq 1$), let γ be the number of 3^+-clauses among all clauses that contain $\overline{a}$. We now count the occurrences that disappear during the transformation of the formula F into $F[\mathcal{I}(a)]$ $(= F[a])$ and $F[\overline{a}]$ and subsequent elimination of 1-clauses resulted from the 2-clauses containing the literals $\overline{a}$ and a.

During the transformation of the formula F into F_1, all occurrences of the literal $\overline{a}$ and all clauses containing a will be eliminated; all 2-clauses that contain $\overline{a}$ will be eliminated too (at step (LR1)), there are $(\#_{\overline{a}} - \gamma)$ such clauses.

The formula $F[\overline{a}]$ contains the 1-clause $\{b\}$ obtained from the 2-clause D. It will be eliminated at step (LR1). If F contains other 2-clauses containing a, the clauses obtained from them will be eliminated at step (LR1) too. The number of such clauses

[1] Kullmann and Luckhardt [18] prove for a very similar algorithm that in this case $\tau(\Delta_1, \Delta_2) \leq \tau(5, 21)$; thus, $\tau(5, 17)$ in the condition of the step (LS4) can be replaced by $\tau(8, 12)$. However, this would not improve our upper bound while would make the proof longer; thus, we present here this simpler proof.

is $(\#_a - 1 - \alpha)$. During the transformation of the formula F into F_2, all occurrences of the literal a and all clauses containing $\overline{a}$ or b will be eliminated. By (6.1), D is the only clause containing b in which the literals $a, \overline{a}$ can occur. Thus, even if we count only occurrences that disappear in clauses containing a or $\overline{a}$ before the first application of the step (LR2), we have

$$\Delta_1 \geq \Diamond_a + \#_{\overline{a}} + (\#_{\overline{a}} - \gamma), \tag{6.2}$$
$$\Delta_2 \geq \Diamond_{\overline{a}} + \#_a + (\Diamond_b - 1) + (\#_a - 1 - \alpha). \tag{6.3}$$

We consider several sub-cases.

CASE 2.1: $\Diamond_c \geq 6$ and $\Diamond_d \geq 6$.
From (6.2) and (6.3) we have

$$\begin{aligned} &\Delta_1 \geq 6 + 2 + (\#_{\overline{a}} - \gamma) \geq 8 + (\#_{\overline{a}} - \gamma) \geq 8, \\ &\Delta_2 \geq (2\#_{\overline{a}} + \gamma) + 2 + 5 = 11 + \gamma \geq 11, \\ &\Delta_1 + \Delta_2 \geq 19 + \#_{\overline{a}} \geq 21. \end{aligned}$$

Thus, $\tau(\Delta_1, \Delta_2) \leq \tau(8, 13) < \tau(5, 17)$, i.e., the condition of the step (LS4) is satisfied.

CASE 2.2: $\#_{\overline{c}} \geq 3$ or $\#_{\overline{d}} \geq 3$.
Let $a \in \{c, d\}$ be the literal for which $\#_{\overline{a}} \geq 3$ holds, let b be the remaining literal in $\{c, d\}$. Thus, we have

$$\begin{aligned} &\Delta_1 \geq (2\#_a + \alpha) + 3 + (\#_{\overline{a}} - \gamma) \geq 7 + \alpha + (\#_{\overline{a}} - \gamma) \geq 7, \\ &\Delta_2 \geq (2\#_{\overline{a}} + \gamma) + 2 + 2\#_b - 1 + (\#_a - 1 - \alpha) \geq \\ &\qquad\qquad 10 + \gamma + (\#_a - \alpha) \geq 11, \\ &\Delta_1 + \Delta_2 \geq 17 + \#_a + \#_{\overline{a}} \geq 22. \end{aligned}$$

Thus, $\tau(\Delta_1, \Delta_2) \leq \tau(7, 15) < \tau(5, 17)$, i.e., the condition of the step (LS4) is satisfied.

CASE 2.3: $\#_{\overline{c}} = \#_{\overline{d}} = 2$, and $\Diamond_c \leq 5$ or $\Diamond_d \leq 5$.
Let $a \in \{c, d\}$ be a literal such that $\Diamond_a = \max(\Diamond_c, \Diamond_d)$, let b be the remaining literal in $\{c, d\}$. Then $4 \leq \Diamond_b \leq 5$ and $\Diamond_a \geq \Diamond_b$. In this case b is a 2-literal, it occurs in D and in one other 2- or 3-clause. We denote this clause by C_b.

The literal b becomes a (1,2)-literal in $F[\mathcal{I}(a)]$ $(= F[a])$. We now complete the proof by showing that several literal occurrences will be eliminated in addition to the occurrences counted by (6.2). There are three sub-cases.

CASE 2.3.1: At least two occurrences are eliminated before the first application of step (LR2) in addition to the occurrences counted by (6.2).
In this case,

$$\begin{aligned} &\Delta_1 \geq \Diamond_a + \#_{\overline{a}} + (\#_{\overline{a}} - \gamma) + 2 \geq && (6.4) \\ &\quad (4 + \alpha) + 2 + (\#_{\overline{a}} - \gamma) + 2 \geq 8 + \alpha + (\#_{\overline{a}} - \gamma) \geq 8, \\ &\Delta_2 \geq (4 + \gamma) + 2 + 3 + (\#_a - 1 - \alpha) \geq 8 + \gamma + (\#_a - \alpha) \geq 9, && (6.5) \\ &\Delta_1 + \Delta_2 \geq 16 + \#_{\overline{a}} + \#_a \geq 20. && (6.6) \end{aligned}$$

CASE 2.3.2: Exactly one occurrence is eliminated before the first application of step (LR2) in addition to the occurrences counted by (6.2).

We remind that (6.2) counts only occurrences to the clauses containing one of the literals a,$\overline{a}$. By (6.1) the occurrence of the literal b to the clause C_b or any occurrence of the literal $\overline{b}$ cannot be eliminated during the transformation of the formula F into the formula $F[a]$. If we counted any of these occurrences in the $\#_{\overline{a}} - \gamma$ term of (6.2), then it was an elimination of a 1-clause $\{\overline{b}\}$ obtained from a 2-clause $\{\overline{a}, \overline{b}\}$. Since it is impossible to have two distinct identical clauses $\{\overline{a}, \overline{b}\}$ in the formula, the other two occurrences (another occurrence of the literal $\overline{b}$ and the occurrence of the literal b in C_b) eliminated at this moment are not counted by (6.2); this fact contradicts the assumption of Case 2.3.2.

Thus in this case b remains a (1,2)-literal before the first application of the step (LR2). By Lemma 6.2(1) at least one more occurrence will be eliminated after that and thus (6.4)–(6.6) hold.

CASE 2.3.3: No occurrences are eliminated before the first application of step (LR2) in addition to the occurrences counted by (6.2).

Similarly to Case 2.3.2, b remains a (1,2)-literal before the first application of the step (LR2) during transformations of the formula $F[a]$ by Function $REDUCE_L$. Thus, if $|C_b| = 2$, then two more occurrences are eliminated by Lemma 6.2(2), and (6.4)–(6.6) hold.

If, however, $|C_b| = 3$, then we can apply only Lemma 6.2(1), but in this case $\diamondsuit_a \geq \diamondsuit_b = 5$, and thus

$$\begin{aligned}
\Delta_1 &\geq \diamondsuit_a + \#_{\overline{a}} + (\#_{\overline{a}} - \gamma) + 1 \geq \\
&\qquad 5 + 2 + (\#_{\overline{a}} - \gamma) + 1 \geq 8 + (\#_{\overline{a}} - \gamma) \geq 8, \\
\Delta_2 &\geq (4 + \gamma) + 2 + 4 \geq 10 + \gamma \geq 10, \\
\Delta_1 + \Delta_2 &\geq 18 + \#_{\overline{a}} \geq 20,
\end{aligned}$$

Hence, in all three sub-cases 2.3.1–2.3.3, $\tau(\Delta_1, \Delta_2) \leq \tau(8, 12) < \tau(5, 17)$, i.e., the condition of the step (LS4) is satisfied. □

7. Conclusion and further work

In this paper we have improved the existing upper bounds for SAT with respect to K (the number of clauses) and L (the length of a formula). Although our bounds are theoretically the best known, we did not make any computational experiments, and thus it remains interesting to investigate how our algorithms behave in practice.

The key point in our algorithms and proofs is the *black and white literals principle*, a new transformation rule which can be viewed as a re-formulation of two previously known principles: the autarkness [22, 24, 19, 17] and the generalized sign principle [18]. However, our proofs (as well as the proofs of the previous upper bounds [23, 18]) are neither short nor elegant. It would be a kind of breakthrough to find a *compact way* to present proofs of upper bounds for splitting algorithms. It is believable that such a way could lead to even *better bounds*, since currently our possibilities to create new heuristics and prove the corresponding upper bounds are limited by the length of a comprehensible proof. On the other hand, it is a challenging problem to prove (more) *tight lower bounds* for (some class of) splitting algorithms: currently, the exponential lower bounds for resolution proofs (see, e.g., [30]) are far enough from the known upper bounds for splitting algorithms. (Most of splitting algorithms can be viewed as resolution proofs and vice versa.)

Another direction for work is to find *randomized* algorithms that give better upper bounds for SAT (or to find a way how to apply modern randomized algorithms that have already been invented for 3-SAT in recent breakthrough papers [25, 26, 29]). Also, it remains a challenging problem to find a *less-than-*2^N upper bound where N is the number of variables.

References

1. N. Bansal, V. Raman, *Upper Bounds for MaxSat: Further Improved,* Proceedings of ISAAC'99. To appear.
2. E. Dantsin, *Tautology proof systems based on the splitting method*, Leningrad Division of Steklov Institute of Mathematics (LOMI), PhD Dissertation, Leningrad, 1982 (in Russian).
3. E. Dantsin and L. O. Fuentes and V. Kreinovich, *Less than* 2^n *satisfiability algorithm extended to the case when almost all clauses are short*, Computer Science Department, University of Texas at El Paso, UTEP-CS-**91-5**, 1991.
4. E. Dantsin, M. Gavrilovich, E. A. Hirsch, B. Konev, *Approximation algorithms for Max Sat: a better performance ratio at the cost of a longer running time*, PDMI preprint 14/1998, available from ftp://ftp.pdmi.ras.ru/pub/publicat/preprint/1998/14-98.ps
5. E. Ya. Dantsin, V. Ya. Kreinovich, *Exponential upper bounds for the satisfiability problem*, Proc. of the IX USSR conf. on math. logic, Leningrad, 1988 (in Russian).
6. M. Davis, G. Logemann, D. Loveland, *A machine program for theorem-proving,* Comm. ACM, vol. **5**, 1962, pp. 394–397.
7. M. Davis, H. Putnam, *A computing procedure for quantification theory,* J. ACM, vol. **7**, 1960, pp. 201–215.
8. J. Gu, P. W. Purdom, J. Franco, B. W. Wah, *Algorithms for Satisfiability (SAT) Problem: A Survey*, Discrete Mathematics and Theoretical Computer Science: Satisfiability (SAT) Problem, American Mathematical Society, 1997.
9. E. A. Hirsch, *Separating the signs in the satisfiability problem*, Zap. nauchn. semin. POMI, vol. **241**, 1997, pp. 30-71 (in Russian). English translation of this collection is to appear in Journal of Mathematical Sciences in 1999.
10. E. A. Hirsch, *Two new upper bounds for SAT*, Proc. of the 9th Annual ACM-SIAM Symposium on Discrete Algorithms, 1998, pp. 521–530.
11. E. A. Hirsch, *Local Search Algorithms for SAT: Worst-Case Analysis*, Proc. of the 6th Scandinavian Workshop on Algorithm Theory, LNCS **1432**, 1998, pp. 246–254.
12. E. A. Hirsch, *Hard formulas for SAT local search algorithms*, PDMI preprint 19/1998, available from ftp://ftp.pdmi.ras.ru/pub/publicat/preprint/19-98.ps
13. E. A. Hirsch, *SAT Local Search Algorithms: Worst-Case Study*, To appear in Journal of Automated Reasoning and in the special issue "SAT-2000".
14. E. A. Hirsch, *A New Algorithm for MAX-2-SAT*, Technical Report TR99-036, Electronic Colloquium on Computational Complexity, 1999.
15. O. Kullmann, *Worst-case analysis,* 3*-SAT decision and lower bounds: approaches for improved SAT algorithms*, DIMACS Proc. SAT Workshop 1996, AMS, 1996, pp. 261–313.
16. O. Kullmann, *New methods for 3-SAT decision and worst-case analysis*, Theoretical Computer Science **223** (1-2), 1999, pp. 1–72.
17. O. Kullmann, *Investigations on autark assignments*, Submitted to Discrete Applied Mathematics, 1998, 19 pages.
18. O. Kullmann, H. Luckhardt, *Deciding propositional tautologies: Algorithms and their complexity*, Preprint, 1997, 82 pages; the ps-file can be obtained at http://mi.informatik.uni-frankfurt.de/people/kullmann/kullmann.html. A journal version, *Algorithms for SAT/TAUT decision based on various measures*, is to appear in Information and Computation, 1998.
19. H. Luckhardt, *Obere Komplexitätsschranken für TAUT-Entscheidungen,* Proc. Frege Conference 1984, Schwerine, Akademie-Verlag Berline, pp. 331–337.
20. M. Mahajan and V. Raman, *Parametrizing above guaranteed values: MaxSat and MaxCut*, Technical Report TR97-033, Electronic Colloquium on Computational Complexity, 1997. To appear in Journal of Algorithms.
21. R. Niedermeier and P. Rossmanith. *New upper bounds for MaxSat*, Technical Report KAM-DIMATIA Series 98-401, Charles University, Praha, Faculty of Mathematics and Physics, July

1998. Extended abstract appeared in Proceedings of the 26th International Colloquium on Automata, Languages, and Programming, LNCS **1644**, 1999, pp. 575–584. Submitted to Journal of Algorithms.
22. B. Monien, E. Speckenmeyer, *3-satisfiability is testable in* $O(1.62^r)$ *steps,* Bericht Nr. 3/1979, Reihe Theoretische Informatik, Universität-Gesamthochschule-Paderborn.
23. B. Monien, E. Speckenmeyer, *Upper bounds for covering problems,* Bericht Nr. 7/1980, Reihe Theoretische Informatik, Universität-Gesamthochschule-Paderborn.
24. B. Monien, E. Speckenmeyer, *Solving satisfiability in less then* 2^n *steps,* Discrete Applied Mathematics, vol. **10**, 1985, pp. 287–295.
25. R. Paturi, P. Pudlak, F. Zane, *Satisfiability Coding Lemma,* Proceedings of the 38th Annual Symposium on Foundations of Computer Science, 1997, pp. 566–574.
26. R. Paturi, P. Pudlak, M. E. Saks, F. Zane, *An Improved Exponential-time Algorithm for k-SAT,* Proceedings of the 39th Annual Symposium on Foundations of Computer Science, 1998, pp. 628–637.
27. I. Schiermeyer, *Solving 3-satisfiability in less than* 1.579^n *steps,* LNCS **702**, 1993, pp. 379–394.
28. I. Schiermeyer, *Pure literal look ahead: An* $O(1.497^n)$ *3-Satisfiability algorithm,* Workshop on the Satisfiability Problem, Technical Report, Siena, April, 29 – May, 3, 1996; University Köln, Report No. **96-230**.
29. U. Schöning, *A probabilistic algorithm for k-SAT and constraint satisfaction problems,* Proceedings of the 40th Annual Symposium on Foundations of Computer Science, 1999. To appear.
30. A. Urquhart, *The Complexity of Propositional Proofs,* Bulletin of Symbolic Logic **1**(4), 1995, pp. 425–467.
31. A. Van Gelder, *A satisfiability tester for non-clausal propositional calculus,* Information and Computation **79**, 1988, pp. 1–21.

SAT2000
I. Gent et al. (Eds.)
IOS Press, 2000

Relaxations of the Satisfiability Problem using Semidefinite Programming

Etienne de Klerk† and Hans van Maaren§
Department of Technical Mathematics and Informatics, Faculty of Information Technology and Systems, Delft University of Technology, P.O. Box 5031, 2600 GA Delft, The Netherlands

Joost P. Warners||**
Department of Technical Mathematics and Informatics, Faculty of Information Technology and Systems, Delft University of Technology, P.O. Box 5031, 2600 GA Delft, The Netherlands

SEN2, CWI, P.O. Box 94079, 1090 GB, Amsterdam, The Netherlands

Abstract. We derive a semidefinite relaxation of the satisfiability (SAT) problem and discuss its strength. We give both the primal and dual formulation of the relaxation. The primal formulation is an eigenvalue optimization problem, while the dual formulation is a semidefinite feasibility problem. We show that using the relaxation, a proof of the unsatisfiability of the notorious pigeon hole and mutilated chess board problems can be computed in polynomial time. As a byproduct we find a new 'sandwich' theorem that is similar to the sandwich theorem for Lovász' ϑ-function. Furthermore, the semidefinite relaxation gives a certificate of (un)satisfiability for 2SAT problems in polynomial time. By adding an objective function to the dual formulation, a specific class of polynomially solvable 3SAT instances can be identified. We conclude with discussing how the relaxation can be used to solve more general SAT problems and with some empirical observations.

1. Introduction

The satisfiability problem of propositional logic (SAT) is the original NP complete problem [5]. Many algorithms for SAT have been developed, both complete and incomplete; see for an overview [14]. Most of the incomplete algorithms are aimed at proving satisfiability; using some hill–climbing strategy a satisfying solution is sought, and if one is found the algorithm terminates; if no solutions are found, no definite answers about the (un)satisfiability of the formula can be given. In this paper we are primarily concerned with developing an (incomplete) algorithm for detecting *un*satisfiability. It is based on elliptic approximations of propositional formulas. Elliptic approximations of propositional formulas were first introduced by van Maaren [25, 24]. Since then they have been used to recognize polynomially solvable instances of satisfiability [35] and to derive effective branching rules and relative clause–weightings [26, 36]. In this paper we use elliptic approximations to derive sufficient conditions for unsatisfiability of a formula. These conditions can be expressed in terms of an *eigenvalue optimization* problem, which in turn can be cast as a *semidefinite program* (see e.g. [34, 8]). Semidefinite programming is a generalization of linear programming, and can be solved in polynomial time (to a given accuracy). Recently, much attention has been devoted

† `e.deklerk@its.tudelft.nl`
§ `h.vanmaaren@its.tudelft.nl`
|| `j.p.warners@its.tudelft.nl`
** Supported by the Dutch Organization for Scientific Research (NWO) under grant SION 612–33–001.

to this field. Using semidefinite programming, efficient approximation algorithms to various hard combinatorial optimization problems have been developed, including the *maximum–satisfiability* problem [13, 12, 32, 20]. Using duality theory, we show that the dual of our formulation is a semidefinite feasibility problem, which is related to the formulation used by Karloff and Zwick for 3SAT formulas [20]. However, it is our aim to use it for proving unsatisfiability rather than finding approximate MAX–SAT solutions. We show that using the relaxation, a proof of the unsatisfiability of the notorious pigeon hole problems can be obtained in polynomial time, in a truly automated way; i.e. without additional problem–specific information at all. As a byproduct, we obtain a new 'sandwich theorem' that is similar to Lovász' famous ϑ-function [22]. Furthermore, we show that it is complete for 2SAT formulas, and we indicate how it can be used to help solving 3SAT problems. In particular, a certain class of polynomially solvable 3SAT formulas can be recognized by adding an objective function to the dual formulation [28, 35].

This paper is organized as follows. In the next subsection we introduce some notation. In Section 1.2 we discuss some techniques for satisfiability solving based on a linear model, while the section thereafter is concerned with nonlinear approximations of satisfiability problems. In Section 3 we formulate a sufficient condition for unsatisfiability in terms of the eigenvalues of an appropriate matrix. Subsequently, we give a brief introduction to semidefinite programming and show that, using semidefinite programming, a certificate of unsatisfiability can be computed in polynomial time. The remainder of the paper is concerned with the investigation of the strength of the relaxation. Several subclasses of satisfiability problems are considered, namely 2SAT problems, a class of covering problems (to which the pigeon hole and mutilated chess board problems belong) and 3SAT problems. We conclude with some empirical observations and suggestions for further research. Where useful we provide geometrical interpretations of the notions introduced.

1.1. *The satisfiability problem (SAT)*

We consider the satisfiability problem in conjunctive normal form (CNF). A propositional formula Φ in CNF is a conjunction of clauses, where each clause $\mathbf{C}_k$ is a disjunction of *literals*. Each literal is an *atomic proposition* (or *variable*) or its negation ($\neg$). Let m be the number of clauses and n the number of atomic propositions. A clausal propositional formula is denoted as $\Phi = \mathbf{C}_1 \wedge \mathbf{C}_2 \wedge \ldots \wedge \mathbf{C}_m$, where each clause $\mathbf{C}_k$ is of the form

$$\mathbf{C}_k = \bigvee_{i \in I_k} p_i \vee \bigvee_{j \in J_k} \neg p_j,$$

with $I_k,\ J_k \subseteq \{1, \ldots, n\}$ disjoint. The satisfiability problem of propositional logic is to determine whether or not an assignment of truth values to the variables exists such that each clause evaluates to true (i.e. one of its literals is true) and thus the formula is true.

1.2. *SAT and linear programming*

1.2.1. *An integer linear programming formulation of SAT*

Associating a $\{-1, 1\}$–variable x_i with each proposition letter p_i, a clause $\mathbf{C}_k$ can be written as a linear inequality in the following way.

$$\sum_{i \in I_k} x_i - \sum_{j \in J_k} x_j \geq 2 - \ell(\mathbf{C}_k),$$

where $\ell(\mathbf{C}_k)$ denotes the length of clause k, i.e. $\ell(\mathbf{C}_k) = |I_k \cup J_k|$. Using matrix notation, the integer linear programming (ILP) formulation of the satisfiability problem can be stated as

$$(\text{IP}_{SAT}) \quad \text{find } x \in \{-1,1\}^n \text{ such that } Ax \geq b.$$

The matrix $A \in \mathbb{R}^{m \times n}$ is called the *clause–variable* matrix. By a_k^T the kth row of A is denoted. Obviously, $a_{ki} = 1$ if $i \in I_k$, $a_{ki} = -1$ if $i \in J_k$, while $a_{ki} = 0$ for any $i \notin I_k \cup J_k$. Furthermore, $b_k = 2 - \ell(\mathbf{C}_k)$.

For the reader unfamiliar with the concepts of mathematical programming, let us try to provide some geometrical insight. To this end, we introduce some additional notation:

$\mathcal{B}$: $\{-1,1\}$ hypercube of dimension n;
$\mathcal{B}_V$: the vertices of $\mathcal{B}$ — the *assignments*;
$\mathcal{P}$: the polyhedron $\{x \in \mathbb{R}^n \mid Ax \geq b\}$;
$\mathcal{P}_0$: $\mathcal{P} \cap \mathcal{B}$;
$\mathcal{P}_V$: $\mathcal{P} \cap \mathcal{B}_V$ — i.e. the *satisfying assignments.*

As a simple two–dimensional illustration, see Figure 1. It represents the above sets for a satisfiable and an unsatisfiable formula respectively. Note that these particular examples do not correspond to actual SAT instances as in two dimensions no meaningful examples can be constructed; as stated before, we merely aim to provide some geometrical insight. The box represents the unit hypercube $\mathcal{B}$; its vertices $\mathcal{B}_V$ are highlighted. Each of the lines (hyperplanes) corresponds to a linear constraint c.q. clause, expressing that any solution should lie either on, or on a specified side of the hyperplane. The polyhedron $\mathcal{P}$ is defined by the intersection of half–spaces defined by the hyperplanes. The shaded area is the intersection of the unit hypercube and the polyhedron $\mathcal{P}$, i.e. $\mathcal{P}_0$. This is called the *feasible* region. The intersection of $\mathcal{P}_0$ and $\mathcal{B}_V$ yields $\mathcal{P}_V$, which is the set of satisfying assignments; it is highlighted by the black circle. In the left hand example, $\mathcal{P}_V = \{(x = 1, y = -1)\}$, while in the right hand example $\mathcal{P}_V = \emptyset$. Thus, solving (IP_{SAT}) is equivalent to finding $x \in \mathcal{P}_V$, or showing that $\mathcal{P}_V$ is empty.

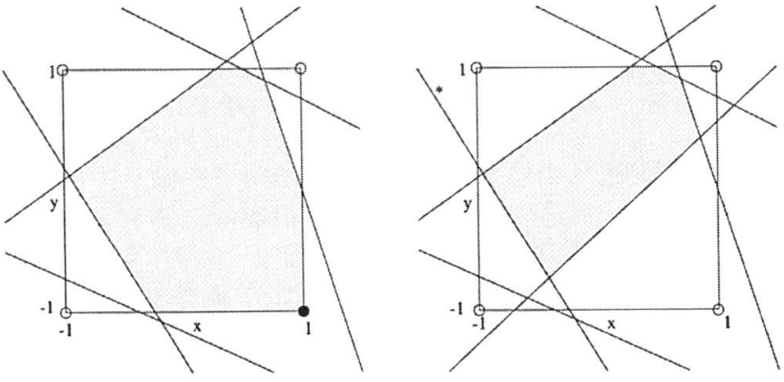

Figure 1. Illustration of LP approach to SAT solving.

1.2.2. *Remarks on solving* (IP_{SAT})

The most common approaches to solve integer linear programming problems include *branch and bound* and *branch and cut* algorithms. The integrality constraints are first relaxed to linear constraints (i.e. $x \in \{-1,1\}$ is relaxed to $-1 \leq x \leq 1$), and subsequently the resulting *LP relaxation* is solved using the simplex method or an interior point method (the latter of which runs in polynomial time). In other words, the problem of finding $x \in \mathcal{P}_0$ is solved. If the LP relaxation is infeasible (so $\mathcal{P}_0$ is empty), then the original ILP must also be infeasible and thus we are done. Unfortunately, the LP relaxation may be feasible, while the original ILP is infeasible (i.e. $\mathcal{P}_V$ is empty); this is illustrated by the right hand picture of Figure 1. If the LP relaxation is feasible, usually one or a combination of the following techniques is applied:

1. *Branch*: a variable is chosen to be fixed at -1 or $+1$. This value is substituted in the LP relaxation and subsequently the (lower dimensional) LP relaxation is solved. For example, if x is fixed at 1 in the right hand side example of Figure 1, the LP relaxation of lower dimension is infeasible, since the intersection of $\mathcal{P}_0$ and the hyperplane $x = 1$ is empty; if however y is fixed at 1, the resulting LP relaxation is still feasible.

2. *Cut*: the LP relaxation is tightened by adding *cuts* and again the LP relaxation is solved. A cut is a linear inequality that is redundant in the ILP formulation, but it cuts off a part of the feasible region of the LP relaxation (thus, denoting by $\mathcal{P}^*$ the tightened polytope, it holds that $\mathcal{P}^* \cap \mathcal{B} \subseteq \mathcal{P}_0$, while $\mathcal{P}^* \cap \mathcal{B}_V \equiv \mathcal{P}_V$; see also Section 6). As an example, consider the hyperplane marked with an asterisk in Figure 1; this is redundant for the ILP formulation since it does not cut off any vertices of the hypercube that are not already cut off by other hyperplanes. However, it does cut off a piece of the feasible region of the linear relaxation.

In general, procedures as sketched above will be effective only when the LP relaxations are *tight*; i.e. when $\mathcal{P}_0$ is a good approximation of the *convex hull* of $\mathcal{P}_V$. The convex hull of $\mathcal{P}_V$ is the polytope which only has the elements of $\mathcal{P}_V$ as its vertices. Since LP algorithms provide a solution that is a vertex of the feasible region, the solution to the LP will be a satisfying assignment, or the LP relaxation will be infeasible, when $\mathcal{P}_0$ and the convex hull of $\mathcal{P}_V$ coincide. Unfortunately, the LP relaxation of (IP_{SAT}) is weak; it is easily checked that the trivial all–zero solution is always feasible when no unit clauses are present. Thus it is virtually useless for deciding *un*satisfiability; for finding satisfying assignments the formulation can sometimes be of use since the solution to the LP relaxation could be either integer or rounded to a satisfying assignment. A specific kind of roundable solutions is the so–called *linear autarky*; see also Section 5[1].

As mentioned previously, to better suit the LP approach towards proving unsatisfiability, the LP relaxation can be tightened by adding cuts. Without going into too many details, we mention that Hooker [17] shows that *resolution* can in fact be interpreted as the addition of cuts. Thus, it follows that by adding sufficiently many cuts the feasible polytope becomes the convex hull of $\mathcal{P}_V$. Unfortunately, exponentially many cuts may be needed. Therefore, we are interested in deriving stronger relaxations of the satisfiability problem, using nonlinear rather than linear relaxations.

2. Elliptic approximations of SAT problems

2.1. *A weighted elliptic approximation*

In [24] elliptic approximations for satisfiability problems are introduced. For each individual clause we define its *elliptic representation* by

$$\mathcal{E}_k = \{x \in \mathbb{R}^n \mid (a_k^T x - 1)^2 \leq (\ell(\mathbf{C}_k) - 1)^2\}. \tag{1}$$

[1] Note that an alternative LP relaxation, namely the one based on polynomial representations of SAT problems, is capable of proving *un*satisfiability rather than satisfiability [37].

A geometric interpretation is given in the next section. It is easy to check that any assignment $x \in \{-1,1\}^m$ satisfying clause $\mathbf{C}_k$ lies in the interior or on the boundary of $\mathcal{E}_k$, since for such an assignment it holds that $b_k = 2 - \ell(\mathbf{C}_k) \leq a_k^T x \leq \ell(\mathbf{C}_k)$. On the other hand if x does not satisfy clause $\mathbf{C}_k$, it lies outside of $\mathcal{E}_k$ (since then $a_k^T x = -\ell(\mathbf{C}_k)$). Note that if $\ell(\mathbf{C}_k) \leq 2$, inequality in (1) may be replaced by equality.

Thus, basically the satisfiability problem can be expressed as finding a $\{-1,1\}$ vector x lying in the intersection of m ellipsoids, i.e.

$$x \in \bigcap_{k=1}^{m} \mathcal{E}_k \cap \{-1,1\}^n \equiv \bigcap_{k=1}^{m} \mathcal{E}_k \cap \mathcal{B}_V.$$

However, it is hard to characterize the intersection of two or more ellipsoids explicitly, therefore we need to find another way to aggregate the information contained in the m separate ellipsoids. It appears plausible to take the sum over all these ellipsoids; this again yields an ellipsoid. Unfortunately, during summation the discriminatory properties of the separate ellipsoids are partly lost, therefore we speak of an *approximation* of a propositional formula. Rather than weighting each clause equally in the summation, let us associate a nonnegative weight w_k with each individual clause. Then any satisfying assignment $x \in \{-1,1\}^n$ satisfies the following inequality:

$$\sum_{k=1}^{m} w_k (a_k^T x - 1)^2 \leq \sum_{k=1}^{m} w_k (\ell(\mathbf{C}_k) - 1)^2. \tag{2}$$

We define the *weighted elliptic approximation*:

$$\mathcal{E}(w) = \{x \in \mathbb{R}^n \mid x^T A^T W A x - 2w^T A x \leq r^T w\}, \tag{3}$$

where $w \in \mathbb{R}^m$, $W = \text{diag}(w)$ (i.e W is a diagonal matrix with the elements of the vector w on its diagonal) and $r_k = \ell(\mathbf{C}_k)(\ell(\mathbf{C}_k) - 2)$. We have the following theorem.

THEOREM 2.1. *Let Φ be a CNF formula with associated clause–variable matrix A and weighted elliptic approximation $\mathcal{E}(w)$. If $x \in \{-1,1\}^n$ is a satisfying assignment of Φ, then $x \in \mathcal{E}(w)$ for any $w \geq 0$.*
Proof. The proof follows by expanding (2) to

$$\sum_{k=1}^{m} w_k (a_k^T x)^2 - 2\sum_{k=1}^{m} w_k a_k^T x \leq \sum_{k=1}^{m} w_k \ell(\mathbf{C}_k)(\ell(\mathbf{C}_k) - 2),$$

which is equivalent to $x^T A^T W A x - 2w^T A x \leq r^T w$. Considering (3), we conclude that $x \in \mathcal{E}(w)$.

2.2. Ellipsoids and eigenvalues

For the reader who is uncomfortable with quadratic forms such as discussed in the previous section, let us now briefly consider some linear algebra to explain the name *elliptic* approximation and to provide some more insight in the structure of such quadratic forms. For a rigorous introduction to this field, see for example Strang [30].

Let Q be a real symmetric $n \times n$ matrix. Q has a so–called spectral decomposition $Q = S \Lambda S^T$, where Λ is a diagonal matrix containing the *eigenvalues* $\lambda_{\min} = \lambda_1 \leq \ldots \leq \lambda_n = \lambda_{\max}$ of Q, and the columns of S constitute an orthonormal base of corresponding eigenvectors. It holds that $S^TS = I$ (I denotes the identity matrix of appropriate dimension) and $Qs_i = \lambda_i s_i$, for any eigenvalue λ_i and corresponding eigenvector s_i. In case all eigenvalues are strictly positive, Q is called *positive definite.* If all eigenvalues are nonnegative Q is called positive *semi*definite. Equivalent definitions of positive semidefiniteness are that (i) $x^TQx \geq 0$ for any x, and (ii) there exists a matrix R such that $Q = R^TR$.

Now consider the quadratic form

$$\mathcal{Q}(x) = x^TQx - 2q^Tx,$$

where $q \in I\!R^n$ and let us assume that Q is positive definite. Letting $z = S^Tx$, we can rewrite x^TQx as follows:

$$x^TQx = x^TS\Lambda S^Tx = z^T\Lambda z = \sum_{i=1}^{n} \lambda_i z_i^2. \tag{4}$$

Considering (4), it is easy to see that the region $\{x \in I\!R^n \mid \mathcal{Q}(x) \leq \rho^2\}$ is a *bounded elliptic region* (i.e. it is an n–dimensional ellipsoid), which is nonempty if $\rho^2 \geq -q^TQ^{-1}q$. The family of ellipsoids associated with $\mathcal{Q}(x)$ is centered at $x = Q^{-1}q$ and its symmetry axes are parallel to the eigenvectors. The lengths of the axes are equal to $\rho/\sqrt{\lambda_i}$. This implies that the *longest* axis is the one parallel to the eigenvector corresponding to the *smallest* eigenvalue.

The elliptic approximation as introduced in the previous section is not necessarily bounded, since we can only guarantee that the matrix A^TWA is positive *semi*definite. This easily follows by noting that $A^TWA = R^TR$, where $R = W^{\frac{1}{2}}A$. Therefore, $x^TR^TRx = \|Rx\|^2 \geq 0$. In [36] a proof is given that a formula is either easily satisfiable or allows a bounded elliptic approximation.

Let us finish this section by deriving a well known and useful lower bound on the value of x^TQx over the vertices of the hypercube $\mathcal{B}_V$. Such a bound can easily be deduced from (4). Note that $x^Tx = n$ for any $x \in \{-1, 1\}^n$ and also that $z^Tz = x^Tx = n$. Thus,

$$x^TQx \geq \lambda_{\min} n, \text{ for any } x \in \{-1, 1\}^n. \tag{5}$$

2.3. Geometrical interpretation of elliptic approximations

Let us now consider the geometrical interpretation of the elliptic approximations. As indicated in Figure 1 the polytope $\mathcal{P}_0$ strictly separates between the satisfying and contradictory assignments; i.e. only satisfying assignments are contained in it. The elliptic approximation $\mathcal{E}(w)$ *circumscribes* $\mathcal{P}_0$. By adjusting the weights, its shape changes, but for any choice of weights $\mathcal{P}_0 \subset \mathcal{E}(w)$. Obviously, we are interested in finding a choice of weights such that $\mathcal{E}(w)$ is as tight as possible an approximation of $\mathcal{P}_0$. In particular, if $\mathcal{P}_V = \emptyset$ (so the formula under consideration is unsatisfiable), we want to find a set of weights such that $\mathcal{E}(w) \cap \mathcal{B}_V = \emptyset$ as well. See Figure 2. The elliptic approximation on the left hand side is not tight, since a (contradictory) assignment is contained in it. The approximation on the right hand side is tight.

In the next section we derive a condition on the weights for unsatisfiable formulas, under which the associated weighted elliptic approximation is tight.

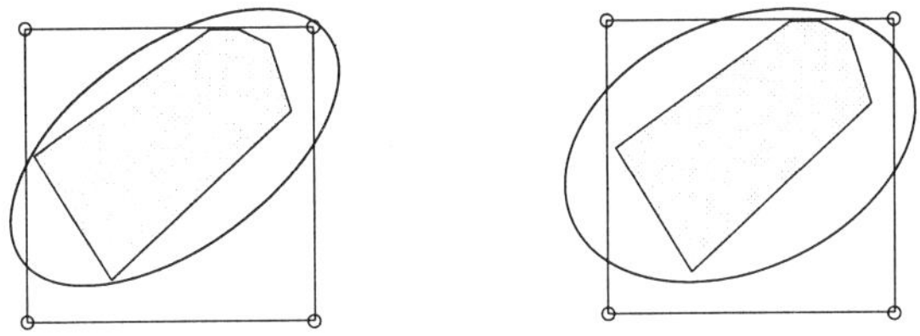

Figure 2. Elliptic approximations of the feasible polytope.

3. Relating unsatisfiability to eigenvalues

3.1. A sufficient condition for unsatisfiability

Let us again consider (3). By Theorem 2.1, for any satisfying assignment $x \in \{-1,1\}^n$ it must hold that

$$x^T A^T W A x - 2w^T A x - r^T w \leq 0, \qquad (6)$$

for all $w \geq 0$. Thus, we have a necessary condition for satisfiability. Reversing this argument gives a sufficient condition for unsatisfiability.

COROLLARY 3.1. *Let Φ be a CNF formula. If for some $w \geq 0$ it holds that $x \notin \mathcal{E}(w)$ for all $x \in \{-1,1\}^n$, then Φ is unsatisfiable.*

Relaxing the integrality constraint to a spherical constraint we obtain an alternative sufficient condition for unsatisfiability.

COROLLARY 3.2. *Let Φ be a CNF formula. If for some $w \geq 0$ it holds that $x \notin \mathcal{E}(w)$ for all x such that $x^T x = n$, then Φ is unsatisfiable.*

Observe that the condition of the second corollary is weaker than that of the first, since $x \in \{-1,1\}^n$ implies $x^T x = n$, but not the other way round.

Geometrically, we can interpret Corollary 3.2 as follows. Rather than trying to prove that a choice of weights exists such that no vertices of the unit hypercube are contained in the weighted elliptic approximation (this is still a difficult problem), it is our aim to find weights such that the intersection of the *unit sphere* and the weighted elliptic approximation is empty; see Figure 3.
Note that the condition stated in Corollary 3.2 appears to be closely related to the eigenvalues of the matrix $A^T W A$ involved in the weighted elliptic approximation. Assuming that the ellipsoid is centered at the origin, a choice of weights is required such that the minimal eigenvalue is as large as possible, since the minimal eigenvalue is related to the length of the longest axis of the ellipsoid. In the following, we will see that this is indeed a fruitful approach. We first illustrate its usefulness with an example.

Example. We consider the well known *pigeon hole* formulas, which can be stated as follows:

Given $h+1$ pigeons and h holes, decide whether it is possible to put each pigeon in at least one hole, while no two pigeons may be put in the same hole.

For more details on this problem and its SAT encoding see Section 6. The set of clauses

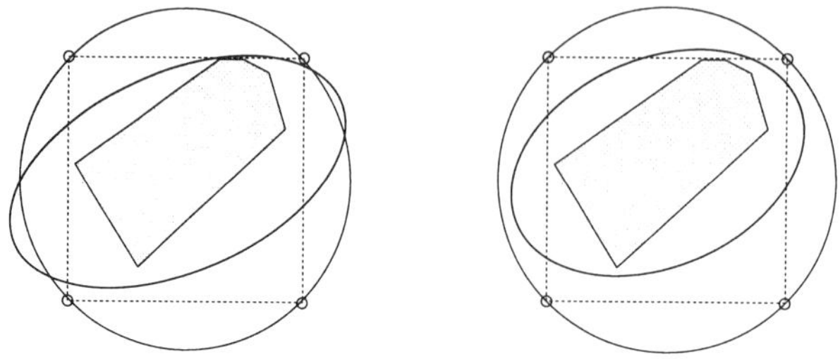

Figure 3. Illustration of the Corollaries 3.1 and 3.2. On the left unsatisfiability is proved by Corollary 3.1, on the right unsatisfiability is proved by both corollaries.

in such a formula can be divided into a set of *long* clauses and a set of *short* clauses. It can be shown that for the instance with h holes and $h+1$ pigeons, when all long clauses are given a weight of one, and all short clauses a weight of $h - 1 + \frac{2}{h+1}$, the minimal value of (6) over the sphere $x^T x = n$ is equal to $4(h - 1 + \frac{1}{h+1}) > 0$. These values can be explicitly computed by using the specific structure of the eigenspace of the matrix $A^T W A$ associated with the pigeon hole formulas. Thus by Corollary 3.2 it follows that the pigeon hole formulas are unsatisfiable. We conclude that, even by using only a low dimensional weight vector, pigeon hole formulas can be shown to be contradictory.□

3.2. A certificate of unsatisfiability based on eigenvalues

In this section we show how to reformulate Corollary 3.2 to obtain a condition for unsatisfiability in terms of eigenvalues. To this end we rewrite (6). Introducing an additional Boolean variable $x_{n+1} \in \{-1, 1\}$ we obtain the inequality

$$x^T A^T W A x - 2x_{n+1} w^T A x - r^T w \leq 0. \tag{7}$$

Once again, if Φ is satisfiable then inequality (7) is satisfied by some $\{x_1, \ldots, x_{n+1}\} \in \{-1, 1\}^{n+1}$ for all $w \geq 0$.

We can rewrite condition (7) as $\tilde{x}^T Q(w) \tilde{x} \leq 0$, where
$\tilde{x} := [x_1, \ldots, x_n, x_{n+1}]$ and $Q(w)$ is the $(n+1) \times (n+1)$ matrix:

$$Q(w) := \begin{bmatrix} A^T W A - \frac{r^T w}{n} I & -A^T w \\ -w^T A & 0 \end{bmatrix}.$$

This is valid, since $x \in \{-1, 1\}^n$ implies that $x^T(\frac{r^T w}{n} I)x = r^T w$. By this observation, it follows that we can further add a so-called *correcting vector* $u \in I\!R^n$ to $Q(w)$ to obtain

$$\tilde{Q}(u, w) := \begin{bmatrix} A^T W A - \frac{r^T w}{n} I - \operatorname{diag}(u) & -A^T w \\ -w^T A & e^T u \end{bmatrix}.$$

By e we denote the all–one vector; it is easy to verify that $\tilde{x}^T Q(w) \tilde{x} = \tilde{x}^T \tilde{Q}(u, w) \tilde{x}$.

Note that the family of ellipsoids defined by $\tilde{Q}(u, w)$ is in $n+1$–dimensional space which is a dimension higher than that of the feasible polytope $\mathcal{P}_0$. Due to the addition of the correcting vector, the ellipsoids in lower dimensional space no longer necessarily circumscribe $\mathcal{P}_0$. Thus, for appropriate choices of u and w, the elliptic approximation defined by $\tilde{Q}(u,w)$ can be a *tighter* approximation of $\mathcal{P}_V$ than $\mathcal{P}_0$ is.

By Corollary 3.1 we are interested in minimizing $\tilde{x}^T\tilde{Q}(u,w)\tilde{x}$ over the $n+1$–dimensional $\{-1,1\}$–vectors. Following Corollary 3.2 we relax the integrality constraint to a single spherical constraint $\tilde{x}^T\tilde{x} = n+1$. In particular, if the optimal value to this problem is positive for some $w \geq 0$ and u then Φ cannot be satisfiable. Thus we are facing the problem of finding choices of u and w such that the minimal value of $\tilde{x}^T\tilde{Q}(u,w)\tilde{x}$ over the unit sphere $\tilde{x}^T\tilde{x} = n+1$ is positive. By (eq. 5) this is equivalent to finding a pair $(w \geq 0, u)$ such that the minimal eigenvalue of $\tilde{Q}(u,w)$ is positive.

DEFINITION 3.1. *A pair $(w \geq 0, u)$ is called a* (u,w)–certificate of unsatisfiability *if the minimal eigenvalue of $\tilde{Q}(u,w)$ is positive.*

Note that given a (u,w)–certificate of unsatisfiability, its validity can be verified in polynomial time by computing the minimal eigenvalue of $\tilde{Q}(u,w)$.

In the next section, we show that an approach to find a (u,w)–certificate of unsatisfiability can be cast in terms of a *semidefinite programming* problem.

4. A semidefinite relaxation of the SAT problem

4.1. An introduction to semidefinite programming

Recently much attention has been devoted to the field of semidefinite programming. It was shown that efficient approximation algorithms for hard combinatorial optimization problems can be obtained using semidefinite relaxations [13, 1], while there are also applications in control theory [34]. Using interior point methods, semidefinite programs can be solved (to a given accuracy) in polynomial time. For the reader that is unfamiliar with semidefinite programming, we review some of the basic concepts.

The standard primal (SP) and dual (SD) semidefinite programming formulations can be denoted by (see e.g. [8]):[2]

$$\text{(SP)}\quad \begin{array}{rl} p^* = \inf & \mathbf{Tr}CX \\ \text{s.t.} & \mathbf{Tr}A_kX = b_k, \\ & X \succeq 0. \end{array} \qquad \text{(SD)}\quad \begin{array}{rl} d^* = \sup & b^Ty \\ \text{s.t.} & \sum_{k=1}^{m} y_kA_k + S = C, \\ & S \succeq 0. \end{array}$$

In the above programs, the A_k, C, X and S are symmetric real $(n \times n)$–matrices and b and y are m–vectors. The matrix X denotes the primal decision variables, while (S,y) are the dual decision variables; S is also called a *slack*–variable. The constraint $X \succeq 0$ (resp. $S \succeq 0$) indicates that X (resp. S) must be positive semidefinite. Positive semidefiniteness of a matrix can be characterized in several ways; see Section 2.2. **Tr** denotes the *trace*–operator. The trace of a matrix A is equal to the sum of its diagonal elements. For products of matrices, it holds that

$$\mathbf{Tr}AB = \sum_{i=1}^{n}\sum_{j=1}^{n} A_{ij}B_{ij},$$

[2] Note that the matrices in this section denote general matrices which are not necessarily related to the clause–variable matrix A introduced before.

where $A, B \in \mathbb{R}^{n \times n}$. A useful easy–to–check property of the trace operator is $\mathbf{Tr}AB = \mathbf{Tr}BA$. Also, the trace of a matrix is equal to the sum of its eigenvalues.

When all the data matrices involved in the pair (SP, SD) are diagonal matrices, the semidefinite programming problem reduces to a linear programming problem. Note that the (nonlinear) constraints $X \succeq 0$, $S \succeq 0$ then reduce to nonnegativity constraints.

The duality theory for semidefinite programming is similar to – but slightly weaker than – the duality theory of linear programming. For the pair (SP, SD) weak duality holds, i.e. $b^T y \leq \mathbf{Tr}CX$ if X is feasible for (SP) and y is feasible for (SD). As in linear programming, we call the nonnegative quantity $\mathbf{Tr}CX - b^T y$ the *duality gap*. It is easy to show that the duality gap equals $\mathbf{Tr}XS$ for feasible X, S.

We say that (SP, SD) are in perfect duality if $p^* = d^*$, where we use the convention that $p^* = \infty$ if (SP) is infeasible, $p^* = -\infty$ if (SP) is unbounded, etc. Perfect duality is guaranteed if one of (SP) and (SD) is *strictly feasible*; (SP) (resp. (SD)) is strictly feasible if a strictly interior solution $X \succ 0$ (resp. $S \succ 0$) exists. Infeasibility of one then implies unboundedness of the other. Note that perfect duality always holds in linear programming; in the semidefinite programming case pathological duality effects can occur where, for example, (SP) is infeasible but (SD) has a finite optimal value (i.e. $d^* < \infty$).

If *both* (SP) and (SD) are strictly feasible, then optimal solutions (X, S) exist for (SP, SD) with duality gap zero (i.e. $\mathbf{Tr}XS = 0$). Such solutions are called *complementary*, since $\mathbf{Tr}XS = 0$ is equivalent to $XS = 0$ for positive semidefinite matrices. In linear programming, all solutions to the primal and dual problems are complementary, but for semidefinite programming (SP) and (SD) may have optimal solutions with positive duality gap, if strict feasibility does not hold. We speak of *strict infeasibility* of (SP) if there exists an *improving direction* for (SD), and vice versa. An improving direction for (SD) is defined as a pair $(\Delta y, \Delta S)$ such that $\sum_{k=1}^{m} \Delta y_k A_k + \Delta S = 0$ and $b^T \Delta y \geq 1$. The objective function of (SD) can therefore be increased indefinitely along the direction $(\Delta y, \Delta S)$ which means that (SD) must be unbounded if it is feasible. Improving directions for (SP) are defined similarly. Once again, strict infeasibility is the only kind of infeasibility which can occur in linear programming, but in semidefinite programming *weak infeasibility* is also possible. The semidefinite programs we consider in this paper cannot give rise to these pathological duality effects, and the duality relations used here will be no more complicated than in the linear programming case. For more details on semidefinite programming duality issues we refer to [8].

4.2. An eigenvalue optimization problem

The problem of finding a (u, w)–certificate of unsatisfiability can be expressed in terms of an eigenvalue optimization problem. Note that, if μ is an eigenvalue of some matrix Q, then $\mu - \lambda$ is an eigenvalue of the matrix $Q - \lambda I$. This can be seen as follows: let s be the corresponding eigenvector, then $Qs = \mu s$ and $(Q - \lambda I)s = (\mu - \lambda)s$. Thus a valid approach for finding a (u, w)–certificate of unsatisfiability is to solve the following optimization problem.

$$
\text{(P)} \qquad \begin{array}{rl} \sup & (n+1)\lambda \\ \text{s.t.} & \tilde{Q}(u, w) \succeq \lambda I, \\ & w \geq 0. \end{array}
$$

If $\tilde{Q}(u,w) \succeq \lambda I$, then $\tilde{Q}(u,w) - \lambda I \succeq 0$. Thus it follows that $(w \geq 0, u)$ is a (u,w)–certificate of unsatisfiability, if (and only if) $\lambda > 0$. We call the optimal value of optimization problem (P) the *gap* of formula Φ (not to be confused with *duality gap*).

DEFINITION 4.1. *The gap of a formula Φ is defined as the optimal value of the optimization problem (P).*

$$gap(\Phi) := \sup_{w \geq 0, u} (n+1)\lambda_{\min}\left(\tilde{Q}(u,w)\right).$$

Thus, by Corollary 3.2, we have the following corollary.

COROLLARY 4.1. *If a formula Φ has a positive gap, it has a (u,w)–certificate of unsatisfiability and therefore Φ is a contradiction.*

We will show that the converse is also true if Φ is a *2–SAT* formula. Furthermore, the formulas corresponding to a specific type of covering problems, which include the notorious *pigeon hole problems* and *mutilated chess boards*, have a positive gap. Let us emphasize that having a (u,w)–certificate of unsatisfiability is still merely a sufficient condition for unsatisfiability.

4.3. The dual relaxation

Considering the eigenvalue optimization problem (P), we note that it fits the format (SD) (see Section 4.1). Thus, we can obtain the the dual of the optimization problem (P) via the primal–dual pair (SP, SD). It can be simplified to the following *semidefinite feasibility problem*:

$$\text{(D)} \qquad \begin{aligned} &\text{find } Y \in I\!R^{n\times n},\ y \in I\!R^n \\ &\text{s.t. } a_k^T Y a_k - 2a_k^T y \leq r_k,\ 1 \leq k \leq m, \\ &\qquad \text{diag}(Y) = e, \\ &\qquad Y \succeq yy^T. \end{aligned}$$

Since (D) does not have an objective function, we adopt the convention that its optimal objective value is zero if a feasible solution exists, while it is $+\infty$ if (D) is infeasible.

To see that (D) is indeed the dual of (P), note that the constraint on the diagonal of Y follows by dualizing the correcting vector, while the first set of constraints is obtained by rewriting the condition

$$\textbf{Tr}\begin{bmatrix} a_k a_k^T - \frac{r_k}{n} I & -a_k \\ -a_k^T & 0 \end{bmatrix}\begin{bmatrix} Y & y \\ y^T & 1 \end{bmatrix} \leq 0,$$

and using that $\text{diag}(Y) = e$. The last constraint of (P),

$$Y \succeq yy^T, \tag{8}$$

is called the *semidefinite constraint*. It follows using the well known *Schur complement* reformulation (see e.g. [18]):

$$\begin{bmatrix} Y & y \\ y^T & 1 \end{bmatrix} \succeq 0 \Leftrightarrow Y - yy^T \succeq 0.$$

When a formula Φ is satisfiable with an assignment x, the solution $Y = xx^T$, $y = x$ is feasible in its associated dual relaxation (D); note that then

$$a_k^T Y a_k - 2a_k^T y = (a_k^T x)^2 - 2a_k^T x \leq r_k,$$

which is exactly the elliptic representation of clause $\mathbf{C}_k$ (see (eq. 1)). Furthermore, $x \in \{-1, 1\}^n$, hence $\mathrm{diag}(Y) = e$, while (8) is satisfied as well.

Rather than via dualizing (P), (D) can be derived directly from the elliptic approximations of clauses in the following way. Expanding (1), it can be written as $a_k^T xx^T a_k - 2a_k^T x \leq r_k$. This equation can be linearized by replacing the variables x_i by *vectors* $v_i \in I\!R^{n+1}$ with the additional requirement that $\|v_i\| = 1$, adding a homogenizing vector v_0, and letting $Y = V^T V$ and $y = V^T v_0$ (here V is the matrix with the vectors v_i as columns). The constraint on the diagonal of Y follows immediately, and the semidefinite constraint follows using that $[V\ v_0]^T [V\ v_0] \succeq 0$ and the Schur complement. If Φ allows the satisfying assignment x, a feasible solution in terms of V is constructed by setting all entries of the vectors v_i to zero, except the first entries: the first entry of the vectors v_i $(1 \leq i \leq n)$ is set to x_i, while the first entry of v_0 is set to one.

Finally, note that (D) is closely related to the MAX3SAT relaxation proposed by Karloff and Zwick [20]. It appears to be slightly weaker, since in their formulation the constraints are further disaggregated; see also Section 8. In addition, we are only interested in proving unsatisfiability, rather than in MAX–SAT solutions.

4.4. Some properties of the gap

Let us now consider (P) and (D) to derive a number of properties of the gap. First note that (P) is strictly feasible, since there exist $w \geq 0$, u and λ such that the slack $\tilde{Q}(u, w) - \lambda I$ is positive definite. Thus, *perfect duality* holds, implying that unboundedness of (P) implies infeasibility of (D).

COROLLARY 4.2. *For any formula Φ, gap(Φ) is either zero or infinity. If gap(Φ) $= \infty$, then there exists a (u, w)–certificate of unsatisfiability, implying the unsatisfiability of Φ.*

We have an even stronger duality result.

LEMMA 4.1. *For the primal–dual pair (P, D) exactly one of the following two duality relations holds:*

1. *(D) is feasible and (P,D) have complementary optimal solutions;*

2. *(D) is strictly infeasible and (P) is unbounded.*

Proof.

1. Suppose (Y, y) is a feasible solution of (D). The all–zero solution $u = 0$, $w = 0$, $\lambda = 0$ is feasible for (P) and since the slack is then all–zero as well, this constitutes a complementary (and therefore optimal) solution. Thus, strong duality holds.

2. If (D) is infeasible, we conclude from the perfect duality of (P, D) that (P) is unbounded. Thus, it allows a solution $(w \geq 0, u)$ such that $\lambda > 0$. Using this solution, an improving direction for the objective function of (P) can be constructed, since $\lambda_{\min}\left(\tilde{Q}(\alpha u, \alpha w)\right) = \alpha \lambda_{\min}\left(\tilde{Q}(u, w)\right)$. This implies that (D) is *strictly* infeasible (see Section 4.1).

Since either complementary solutions exist for (P) and (D), or (D) is strictly infeasible, we have the following corollary (for a proof, see [8]).

COROLLARY 4.3. *Using semidefinite programming, it can be decided in polynomial time which of the two duality relations holds. Thus, the existence of a (u, w)-certificate of unsatisfiability can be established in polynomial time.*

Finally, we have a result on monotonicity of the gap.

LEMMA 4.2. *Let Φ be a CNF-formula and let $\Psi \subseteq \Phi$. Then it holds that $gap(\Psi) \leq gap(\Phi)$.*

Proof. Consider (P). Add to (P) the constraints that $w_k = 0$ for all clauses $\mathbf{C}_k$ which occur only in Φ. Solving this modified version of (P), gap(Ψ) is obtained. Obviously, it is a more restricted version of gap(Φ), so the lemma follows.

This leads immediately to the following corollary.

COROLLARY 4.4. *The gap is monotone under unit resolution.*

Proof. Unit resolution can be regarded as the addition of unit clauses to a formula. By the previous lemma, the gap cannot decrease.

In the next sections the gap for some specific SAT problems is considered.

5. The gap for 2SAT problems

In this section we prove that gap(Φ) $= \infty$ if Φ is an unsatisfiable 2SAT formula. It is well known that 2SAT problems are in fact solvable in linear time [2]. Furthermore, Goemans and Williamson [13] and Feige and Goemans [12] gave approximation algorithms with performance guarantee for the MAX2SAT problem, based on semidefinite programming. Hence it is not our aim to improve on any of the above algorithms; we merely want to show some properties of the gap approach. To this end we first characterize infeasibility of 2SAT formulas.

DEFINITION 5.1. (Autarky [27, 21]). *Let Φ be any CNF formula. A vector $z \neq 0$ is called a linear autarky of Φ if $Az \geq 0$.*

Two formulas Φ and Ψ are called *satisfiability-equivalent* if both are satisfiable or both are contradictory.

LEMMA 5.1. *A linear autarky z indicates a satisfiable subformula Ψ of Φ. The formula $\Phi \backslash \Psi$ is satisfiability-equivalent to Φ.*

Proof. For each linear inequality one of two possibilities is applicable:

1. All $z_i = 0$, $i \in I_k \cup J_k$ (so $a_k^T z = 0$).

2. At least one $z_i \neq 0$, $i \in I_k \cup J_k$ (so $a_k^T z \geq 0$).

In the second case, $a_k^T \mathrm{sgn}(z) \geq 2 - |I_k \cup J_k| = b_k$, implying that sgn($z$) restricted to its nonzero entries is a satisfying assignment of the subformula Ψ that is obtained by taking all clauses of Φ associated with linear inequalities with property 2. Note that each clause $\mathbf{C}_k$ is either satisfied by sgn(z) or remains invariant. Thus, $\Phi \backslash \Psi$ contains a subset of clauses of Φ. If it is satisfiable with some assignment x, then Φ is satisfied by

x extended with $\mathrm{sgn}(z)$. If it is unsatisfiable then this means that a subformula of Φ is unsatisfiable, implying that Φ is unsatisfiable.

We also make use of the notion of minimal unsatisfiability.

DEFINITION 5.2. (Minimal unsatisfiability). *An unsatisfiable CNF formula Φ is called minimally unsatisfiable if a satisfiable formula is obtained by omitting any given clause from Φ.*

By Lemma 4.2 we can restrict ourselves to the case that Φ is a minimally unsatisfiable formula.

LEMMA 5.2. *If a formula Φ is minimally unsatisfiable, then $Az \not\geq 0$ for all $0 \neq z \in \mathbb{R}^n$.*
Proof. If the condition in this lemma does not hold, the formula has a linear autarky, contradicting the fact that it is minimally unsatisfiable.

COROLLARY 5.1. *If Φ is minimally unsatisfiable, then A is of full rank.*

Now we can prove the key lemma of this section.

LEMMA 5.3. *Let Φ be a minimally unsatisfiable 2SAT formula. Then $gap(\Phi) = \infty$.*
Proof. ¿From the semidefinite constraint (see eq. (8)) we conclude that $a^TYa \geq (a^Ty)^2$ for any vector a. This implies that

$$(a_k^Ty)^2 - 2a_k^Ty \leq a_k^TYa_k - 2a_k^Ty \leq r_k \equiv 0$$

since $r_k = 0$ for 2SAT (for all $k = 1, \ldots, m$), from which it follows that $0 \leq a_k^Ty \leq 2$. The minimal unsatisfiability of Φ implies that $y = 0$. Hence, $a_k^TYa_k = 0$ for all $k = 1, \ldots, m$. Since $Y \succeq 0$ the a_k's must lie in the nullspace of Y[3], and since A is of full rank ($\mathrm{rank}(A) = n$) this implies $Y = 0$, contradicting the condition $\mathrm{diag}(Y) = e$ of (D). We conclude that (D) is infeasible, implying that $\mathrm{gap}(\Phi) = \infty$.

The main theorem of this section follows easily.

THEOREM 5.1. *Let Φ be any 2SAT formula. It holds*

$$gap(\Phi) = \begin{cases} \infty & \text{if } \Phi \text{ unsatisfiable;} \\ 0 & \text{if } \Phi \text{ satisfiable.} \end{cases}$$

Proof. Let Φ be a unsatisfiable 2SAT formula and let Ψ be a minimally satisfiable subformula of Φ. By Lemma 5.3, $\mathrm{gap}(\Psi) = \infty$, Lemma 4.2 implies that $\mathrm{gap}(\Phi) = \infty$. Conversely, assume now that Φ is a satisfiable 2SAT formula. Using any satisfying assignment x, a feasible solution $Y = xx^T$, $y = x$ to (D) can be constructed, implying that $\mathrm{gap}(\Phi) = 0$.

If $\mathrm{gap}(\Phi) = 0$ we can use the dual solution (Y, y) to construct a satisfying assignment x. First we set the entries of x corresponding to nonzero entries of y to $x = \mathrm{sgn}(y)$ as from the proof of Lemma 5.3 we know that y is an autarky. For all clauses that are not yet satisfied, a satisfying assignment can be constructed by considering Y^*, which denotes

[3] Let $Y = VV^T$, then $0 = a_k^TYa_k = \|V^Ta_k\|^2$, or $V^Ta_k = 0$ which implies $Ya_k = 0$.

the matrix Y restricted to the rows and columns corresponding to the zero entries of y. Note that $a_k^T y = 0$ implies that $a_k^T Y a_k = 0$, so $Y_{ij} = -a_{ki}a_{kj}$ where $I_k \cup J_k = \{i, j\}$. So we can assume that each of the rows and columns of Y^* contains an off-diagonal element that is equal to ± 1. Fixing all ± 1 elements, such a matrix Y^* can be completed to a rank one $\{-1, 1\}$ matrix that is feasible in (D). ¿From this matrix a $\{-1, 1\}$ solution x can easily be deduced. This construction is equivalent to the one given in [12].

6. The gap for a class of covering problems

In this section we consider SAT encodings of a particular class of covering problems, and show that these can be shown to be contradictory by our SDP approach.

6.1. A specific class of covering problems

Let V be a set of n propositional variables. Let $\mathcal{S} = \{S_1, \ldots, S_N\}$ and $\mathcal{T} = \{T_1, \ldots, T_M\}$ be sets of subsets of V. Both $\mathcal{S}$ and $\mathcal{T}$ form a partition of V. Furthermore, let us assume that $M < N$. Consider the following CNF formula Φ_{CP}.

$$\bigvee_{i \in S_k} p_i, \qquad 1 \leq k \leq N, \tag{9}$$

$$\neg p_i \vee \neg p_j, \ i, j \in T_k, i \neq j, \ 1 \leq k \leq M. \tag{10}$$

First, let us give two examples of problems that fit in this format.

Pigeon hole formulas. Let us state again the pigeon hole principle:

Given $h + 1$ pigeons and h holes, decide whether it is possible to put each pigeon in at least one hole, while no two pigeons may be put in the same hole.

We now argue that the standard encoding of the pigeon hole problem fits the format Φ_{CP}. For each pigeon–hole pair a proposition is introduced; thus, we obtain a total of $h(h + 1)$ variables in the set V. The long (positive) clauses (9) now express that each pigeon is put in at least one hole; thus there are exactly $N = h + 1$ of such clauses that all have length h. The short (negative) clauses (10) model that no two pigeons may be put in the same hole simultaneously; for each hole there is a set of short clauses, giving rise to $M = h$ separate sets T_k, each of size $h + 1$. It is easy to see that each proposition occurs both exactly once in the sets S_k and exactly once in the sets T_k, thus both $\mathcal{S}$ and $\mathcal{T}$ are a partition of V.

bf Mutilated chess boards. The problem of the mutilated chess board can be expressed as follows:

Given a chess board of size $2s \times 2s$ squares. Two of its diagonally opposite vertices are removed. Can the resulting 'mutilated' chess board be covered by rectangular dominoes of size 2×1 (i.e. a single domino covers exactly two adjacent squares), such that each square is covered exactly once?

The standard satisfiability coding for this problem is obtained by introducing a proposition for each pair of adjacent squares; thus we need $4(2s^2 - s - 1)$ variables. For each square there is a positive clause (of length 2, 3 or 4) expressing that it must be covered at least once, and a set of negative (2–)clauses expressing that it may be covered at most once. It is strongly conjectured that resolution requires exponential running time on this problem as well (despite the absence of 'long' clauses) [33]. Taking a subset of this set of clauses, a formula of the form Φ_{CP} is obtained. For all the *black* squares we keep the positive clauses, while for all the *white* squares we only use the negative clauses. The first set corresponds to (9) and the second set to (10). See also the graph in Figure 4; the nodes correspond to individual variables, the drawn edges indicate the *positive* clauses (all cliques with drawn edges constitute one positive clause) and the dotted edges the *negative* clauses (each pair of nodes connected by a dotted edge corresponds to a negative clause). Again, it is easy to see that each variable occurs in exactly one of the $N = 2s^2$ positive clauses, and in exactly one of the $M = 2s^2 - 2$ sets of negative clauses.

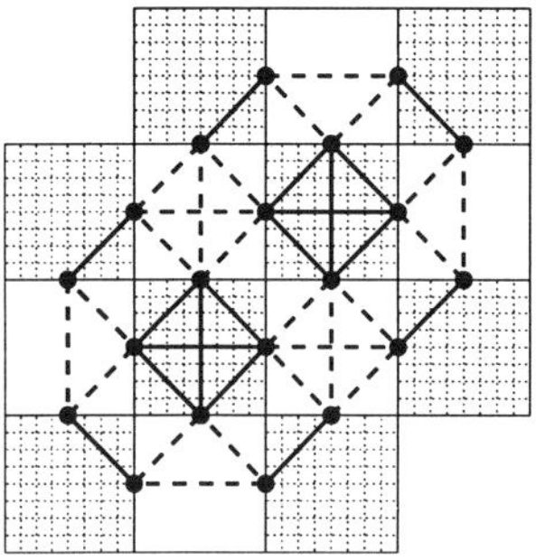

Figure 4. The mutilated chess board for $s = 2$.

Both of the above problems are easily concluded to be unsatisfiable. We verify that Φ_{CP} is unsatisfiable (when $M < N$), using *cutting planes* (this construction is well known, see e.g. [6]). To this end we introduce some more notation. By e_S (e_{ij}) we denote the vector with ones in the positions $i \in S$ (i and j) and zeros elsewhere. The integer linear feasibility formulation can be stated as

$$(\mathrm{IP}_{CP}) \qquad \begin{array}{ll} \text{find } x \in \{-1,1\}^n & \\ \text{s.t. } e_{S_k}^T x \geq 2 - |S_k|, & 1 \leq k \leq N, \\ \quad\;\; e_{ij}^T x \leq 0, & i,j \in T_k, i \neq j, \; 1 \leq k \leq M. \end{array}$$

Obviously, it is easy to find a solution of the linear relaxation of this problem (i.e. when the integrality constraints are relaxed to $-e \leq x \leq e$), by setting all variables to 0. However, using cutting planes one can show that for $\{-1,1\}$–variables, the set of inequalities for a set T_k implies that

$$e_{T_k}^T x \leq 2 - |T_k|, \; 1 \leq k \leq M. \tag{11}$$

(see [6]). A cutting plane is obtained by taking nonnegative combinations of the constraints, and subsequently adjusting the right hand side of the resulting equality, such that it is as sharp as possible. To determine this right hand side, we use the fact that the variables are binary [4].

For completeness, let us review the derivation (11). Taking a subset $U \subseteq T_k$, $|U| = 3$, and summing the (three) inequalities associated with this set, the inequality $2e_U^T x \leq 0$ is obtained. Since for any $\{-1,1\}$ vector x it holds that $e_U^T x$ is *odd*, the right hand side may be rounded down to the largest odd integer smaller than zero, thus we find that $e_U^T x \leq -1$. More generally, suppose we are given a set $U \subset T_k$ and an inequality $e_U^T x \leq 2 - |U|$. In addition let $j \in T_k \backslash U$, and denote $\overline{U} = U \cup \{j\}$. Summing for all $i \in U$ the inequalities $e_{ij}^T x \leq 0$ (with weight 1) and the initial inequality with weight $|U| - 1$, we obtain that $|U| e_{\overline{U}}^T x \leq (|U| - 1)(2 - |U|)$. Dividing both sides by $|U|$, and rounding the right hand side down to the nearest integer with same parity as $|\overline{U}|$ (thus the right hand side becomes $1 - |U|$, which is valid, since $((|U|-1)/|U|)(2-|U|) < 3 - |U|$) we obtain

$$e_{\overline{U}}^T x \leq 1 - |U| = 2 - |\overline{U}|.$$

We conclude that (11) is indeed implied by the inequalities in (IP_{CP}).

Summing all the inequalities (11), and using that $\mathcal{T}$ partitions V, we find that $-n \leq e^T x \leq 2M - n$. Similarly, taking the sum over the first set of inequalities in (IP_{CP}), we have $2N - n \leq e^T x \leq n$. Combining, we get

$$2N \leq e^T x + n \leq 2M, \tag{12}$$

from which it follows that $N \leq M$, implying the infeasibility of (IP_{CP}) and thus the unsatisfiability of Φ_{CP} when $M < N$. We conclude that using this cutting plane technique, a proof of unsatisfiability of Φ_{CP} can be constructed and verified in polynomial time.

Surprisingly, other techniques often require large running times to solve formulas of this type. Indeed, Haken [15] proves that no short resolution proof of the unsatisfiability of pigeon hole formulas exists. The length of any resolution proof is exponential in the size of the formula.

Note that to find the cutting plane proof sketched above efficiently, additional problem–specific information is used. In each step of the cutting plane proof, two linear inequalities are used to derive a new linear inequality. The cutting plane proof of the class (Φ_{CP}) is called a *tree–like* cutting plane proof, as each inequality is used only once [19]. To construct such a short tree–like cutting plane proof, additional searching is required, since the order in which linear inequalities are combined is crucial. For general CNF formulas, it is not clear how to efficiently find a (tree–like) cutting plane proof, even if it is known that one exists. It is our aim to show in this section that using our semidefinite programming approach formulas of the format Φ_{CP} are proven to be contradictory in polynomial time, while no additional problem–specific information whatsoever is required. This is due to the fact that (Φ_{CP}) allows a (u, w)–certificate of unsatisfiability whose existence can be computed in polynomial time (Corollary 4.3). Let us consider the semidefinite relaxation of Φ_{CP}. The SDP relaxation can be denoted as (see also (D))

$$(\mathrm{SD}_{CP}) \quad \begin{array}{ll} \text{find} & Y \in \mathbb{R}^{n \times n}, y \in \mathbb{R}^n \\ \text{s.t.} & e_{S_k}^T Y e_{S_k} - 2e_{S_k}^T y \leq |S_k|(|S_k| - 2),\ 1 \leq k \leq N \\ & e_{ij}^T Y e_{ij} + 2e_{ij}^T y \leq 0,\ i, j, i \neq j \in T_k,\ 1 \leq k \leq M \\ & \mathrm{diag}(Y) = e, \\ & Y \succeq yy^T. \end{array}$$

We prove the following theorem.

THEOREM 6.1. *The semidefinite relaxation (SD_{CP}) of Φ_{CP} is infeasible (if $M < N$). Equivalently, gap(Φ_{CP}) $= \infty$.*

Proof. Note that from the semidefinite constraint (see eq. (8)) it follows that $a^T Y a \geq (a^T y)^2$ for any n–vector a. Thus it follows that

$$(e_{S_k}^T y)^2 - 2e_{S_k}^T y \leq e_{S_k}^T Y e_{S_k} - 2e_{S_k}^T y \leq |S_k|(|S_k| - 2),$$

implying that

$$2 - |S_k| \leq e_{S_k}^T y \leq |S_k|, \ 1 \leq k \leq N. \tag{13}$$

Now we consider the inequalities corresponding to the sets T_k. Taking the sum over all the inequalities corresponding to set T_k, k fixed, we find that

$$e_{T_k}^T Y e_{T_k} + (|T_k| - 2) e_{T_k}^T \operatorname{diag}(Y) + 2(|T_k| - 1) e_{T_k}^T y \leq 0.$$

To verify this, note that each diagonal element Y_{ii}, $i \in T_k$, occurs in exactly $|T_k| - 1$ inequalities; similarly, each linear term y_i, $i \in T_k$, occurs in exactly $|T_k| - 1$ inequalities as well. Simplifying this expression using that $\operatorname{diag}(Y) = e$, we obtain

$$e_{T_k}^T Y e_{T_k} + 2(|T_k| - 1) e_{T_k}^T y \leq -|T_k|(|T_k| - 2).$$

Using the semidefinite constraint again, we conclude that

$$(e_{T_k}^T y)^2 + 2(|T_k| - 1) e_{T_k}^T y \leq e_{T_k}^T Y e_{T_k} + 2(|T_k| - 1) e_{T_k}^T y \leq -|T_k|(|T_k| - 2),$$

implying that

$$-|T_k| \leq e_{T_k}^T y \leq 2 - |T_k|, \ 1 \leq k \leq M.$$

Summing these inequalities we find that $-n \leq e^T y \leq 2M - n$ while from (13) we have that $2N - n \leq e^T y \leq n$, implying that $2N \leq e^T y + n \leq 2M$ (note that this is equivalent to what we obtained using cutting planes, see (12)). Thus we conclude that (SD$_{CP}$) is infeasible when $N > M$.

Thus by Corollaries 4.2 and 4.3 we have the following corollary

COROLLARY 6.1. *Using semidefinite programming, the unsatisfiability of Φ_{CP} can be decided in polynomial time.*

It may be noted that the proof of Theorem 6.1 and the cutting plane refutation of Φ_{CP} are essentially very similar. Indeed, the cutting planes (11) are automatically implied in (SD$_{CP}$).

6.2. Application to graph coloring

A famous result by Lovász is his 'sandwich' theorem [22], which states that for an undirected graph $G = (V, E)$ in polynomial time (using semidefinite programming), a number $\vartheta(G)$ can be computed which is bounded from above by the graph's coloring number $\gamma(G)$ (i.e. the minimal number of colors required to color the vertices of the graph such that no two adjacent vertices have the same color), and from below by its clique number $\omega(G)$ (i.e. the maximal complete subgraph of G). Applying our result from the previous section to the graph coloring problem (GCP) we obtain a similar result.

Suppose we are given a graph $G = (V, E)$ and a set of colors C. We introduce a proposition for each vertex–color combination. Then the GCP can be modeled as a formula Φ_{GCP} containing a set of $|V|$ long clauses, expressing that each vertex should be colored by at least one color, and a set of short clauses expressing that no two vertices may get the same color. We can construct the semidefinite relaxation of Φ_{GCP} in the usual way; we refer to it as (SD$_{GCP}$). Now let C^* be the smallest set of colors for which (SD$_{GCP}$) is feasible. Such a set must exist, since for $|C^*| \geq |V|$ the GCP and thus its relaxation (SD$_{GCP}$) are trivially feasible. We have the following theorem.

THEOREM 6.2. $\omega(G) \leq |C^*| \leq \gamma(G)$.
Proof. First note for any set of color C with $|C| < \omega(G)$, Φ_{GCP} has a subformula of the form Φ_{CP}, hence by Lemma 4.2 it has gap infinity. This subformula corresponds to the set of clauses corresponding to a clique of size $|C|+1$ or larger. Now consider set C^*. It holds that $|C^*| \geq \omega(G)$, since otherwise (SD_{GCP}) would be infeasible. Also, since removing one color from C^* implies infeasibility of (SD_{GCP}) (by assumption), it holds that $|C^*| \leq \gamma(G)$. This proves the theorem.

So by applying a binary search on the size of C, a number similar to Lovász ϑ–number can be computed.

In a forthcoming paper [9] the following theorem is proved.

THEOREM 6.3. $\omega(G) \leq |C^*| \leq \lceil \vartheta(G) \rceil \leq \gamma(G)$.

7. The gap for 3SAT problems

7.1. A modified formulation

So far we have seen that several classes of formulas can be solved efficiently by the gap approach. Let us now turn our attention to the most general class of CNF formulas, the 3SAT problems. First we have a negative result for pure 3SAT problems (the class of CNF formulas in which all clauses have length 3).

LEMMA 7.1. *Suppose Φ is a pure 3SAT problem. It holds that gap* $(\Phi) = 0$.
Proof. It is easy to verify that the solution $Y = I$, $y = 0$ is feasible in (D) since $a_k^T a_k = 3 = r_k$ for all clauses. By duality, gap$(\Phi) = 0$.

COROLLARY 7.1. *No pure 3CNF formula allows a (u, w)–certificate of unsatisfiability.*

Note that the proof of this lemma and the corollary easily extend to general CNF formulas in which no clauses of length one and/or two occur.

Of course the gap can be computed in nodes of a branching tree; during the branching process 2–clauses are created, thus making it possible for the SDP approach to be successful in specific cases. Note that (also) in this respect, the SDP approach is stronger than the LP approach (as mentioned in Section 2.1). However, computing the gap is computationally rather expensive, and especially in a DPLL–like branching algorithm (including unit resolution, although this can be simulated by the semidefinite relaxation as well) [7] the overhead will be substantial with the current state–of–the–art implementations. Several possibilities in this respect are discussed in the next section.

For now, let us slightly reformulate our gap relaxation to be able to say a little more about 3SAT formulas. Consider again the elliptic representation $\mathcal{E}_k$ associated with a clause k (1). By introducing a *parity*–variable, the inequality is turned into an equality constraint.

$$\mathcal{E}_k^p = \{x \in I\!R^n, 0 \leq s_k \leq 1 \mid (a_k^T x - 1)^2 + 4s_k = 4\},$$

where for all feasible $\{-1, 1\}$ assignments to x it holds that $s_k \in \{0, 1\}$. The ellipsoid $\mathcal{E}_k^p$ has the semidefinite relaxation

$$a_k^T Y a_k - 2a_k^T y + 4s_k = 3. \tag{14}$$

Obviously, the trivial solution (Lemma 7.1), is still feasible when simply setting all s_k to 0. However, if we are now going to maximize the sum of the s_k's, a solution other than the trivial one may be obtained. Thus we define the *parity* gap. Consider the semidefinite optimization problem (D').

$$
\text{(D')}\quad
\begin{aligned}
&\max \sum_{k=1}^{m} s_k \\
&\text{s.t. } a_k^T Y a_k - 2a_k^T y + 4s_k = 3, \quad 1 \le k \le m, \\
&\qquad \operatorname{diag}(Y) = e, \\
&\qquad Y \succeq yy^T, \\
&\qquad 0 \le s_k \le 1, \qquad\qquad 1 \le k \le m.
\end{aligned}
$$

DEFINITION 7.1. *The optimal value of optimization problem (D') is called the* parity *gap of a formula* Φ.

We then have the following lemma.

LEMMA 7.2. *If a pure 3CNF formula* Φ *has* parity *gap zero it is equivalent to an XOR–SAT formula, and as such efficiently solvable.*

Proof. If the parity gap is zero, $s_k = 0$ for all $1 \le k \le m$. Suppose that a satisfying solution x exists for which some clause $\mathbf{C}_k$ is satisfied in exactly two literals, so $a_k^T x = 1$. Using x, the solution $Y = xx^T$, $y = x$ is feasible in (D'), while $a_k^T Y a_k - 2a_k^T y = -1$, implying that $s_k = 1$. Thus the parity gap is not equal to zero. If (D') has objective value zero, no such solution exists, implying that if a satisfying assignment exists, then it must satisfy each clause in either exactly one or all three literals (i.e. $a_k^T x \in \{-1, 3\}$, $1 \le k \le m$). Thus the formula is equivalent to an XOR–SAT formula [35]. Checking whether such a solution exists can be done in polynomial time [28, 35].

If a formula has parity gap zero, its equivalent XOR SAT formula is obtained by simply replacing all occurrences of the 'or'–operator ('$\vee$') by the 'exclusive or'–operator ('$\oplus$').

A specific class of formulas that appear likely to have parity gap zero, is the class of *doubly balanced formulas* [24, 35]. By definition, for doubly balanced formulas it holds that $A^T A$ is a diagonal matrix and $A^T e \equiv 0$. Eliminating the s_k variables from (D') it can be rewritten to

$$
\text{(D'')}\quad
\begin{aligned}
&\min \mathbf{Tr} \begin{bmatrix} A^T A & -A^T e \\ -e^T A & 0 \end{bmatrix} \begin{bmatrix} Y & y \\ y^T & 1 \end{bmatrix} \\
&\text{s.t. } -1 \le a_k^T Y a_k - 2a_k^T y \le 3, \qquad 1 \le k \le m, \\
&\qquad \operatorname{diag}(Y) = e, \\
&\qquad Y \succeq yy^T.
\end{aligned}
$$

It holds that $\text{opt(D')} = \frac{3}{4}m - \frac{1}{4}\text{opt(D'')}$. Note that the objective function of (D") is essentially the same objective function as the one used by Goemans and Williamson in their MAX2SAT algorithm, only we are presently considering 3SAT formulas. Using formulation (D") it is straightforward to prove the next lemma.

LEMMA 7.3. *A doubly balanced formula has parity gap zero.*

Proof. By the definition of doubly balancedness and the constraint on the diagonal of Y the objective function of (D") reduces to the constant $3m$, implying that the parity gap is equal to zero.

We also have an autarky result.

LEMMA 7.4. *If all* $s_k > \frac{3}{4}$, $x = sgn(y)$ *is a satisfiable assignment of* Φ.
Proof. Note that

$$(a_k^T y)^2 - 2a_k^T y + (4s_k - 3) \leq 0.$$

This implies that

$$1 - 2\sqrt{1 - s_k} \leq a_k^T y \leq 1 + 2\sqrt{1 - s_k}.$$

If $s_k > \frac{3}{4}$, it holds that $a_k^T y > 0$. If all s_k have this property, then y is a linear autarky.

Note that y might be a linear autarky while not all s_k are larger than $\frac{3}{4}$. In this respect, a slightly stronger formulation is obtained by using *a single* slack variable t for all clauses, rather than a separate slack variable s_k for each of the clauses. The objective then becomes to maximize t; all s_k's must be replaced by t, and equality must be replaced by inequality. A drawback of this approach is that an optimum of zero only implies that a polynomially solvable *sub*formula is present. On the other hand, solving this subformula first, may speed up solving the full formula [37].

While it appears that the semidefinite relaxation as developed in this paper is not quite strong enough to completely solve 3SAT problems by itself, it can be used in various other ways. Apart from including it in a complete algorithm (see next section), both its primal and dual solution can be used for heuristic purposes. This is briefly discussed in Section 8.

7.2. Incorporating the gap approach in a complete algorithm

As mentioned in the previous section, the gap can be computed in each node of a branching tree to detect unsatisfiability early, so as to reduce the size of the search tree. Even though at present it appears that this might be computationally too expensive, there are several ways to reduce computational cost. We mention two possibilities.

1. Instead of using a primal–dual algorithm, it is possible to use a dual scaling algorithm to exploit sparsity of $\tilde{Q}$ to the full [3]. Computational experience with MAX2SAT problems indicates that for small sized problems this approach is competitive with other dedicated algorithms for the MAX2SAT problem [10].

2. For larger problems, spectral bundle methods can be used to solve the eigenvalue optimization problem (P) [16]. These have been shown to be able to handle problems with thousands of variables. Such methods solve only (P), so that the dual information is lost.

8. Remarks and further research

8.1. Some empirical observations

Both the primal and dual solutions obtained by solving a semidefinite relaxations can be used for heuristic purposes. The dual solution (Y, y) might be used to try to obtain good approximate MAX–SAT solutions. To illustrate the quality of the solutions thus obtainable, see Figure 5. We restricted ourselves to a set of random pure 3SAT formulas with 100 variables and a varying number of clauses, and used the dual formulation with a single slack variable. The SDPs were solved using the public–domain solver SeDuMi [31]. Approximate solutions are constructed by (i) taking the dual solution and rounding y (the drawn line), (ii) by applying a Goemans–Williamson–like randomized rounding procedure (the dotted line). For comparison we also included the solutions obtained by simply drawing random solutions; note that this in fact corresponds to the Karloff–Zwick algorithm for approximating (pure) MAX3SAT solutions. To obtain a good *ad hoc* lower bound on the optimal solution we applied a greedy weighted local search procedure. Considering the results, it is clear that the local search procedure gives the best results, but interestingly enough the drawn line is consistently above the dotted line, implying that the deterministic one–step procedure of rounding y gives better solutions than the randomized rounding procedure, which in turn is better than just drawing random solutions.

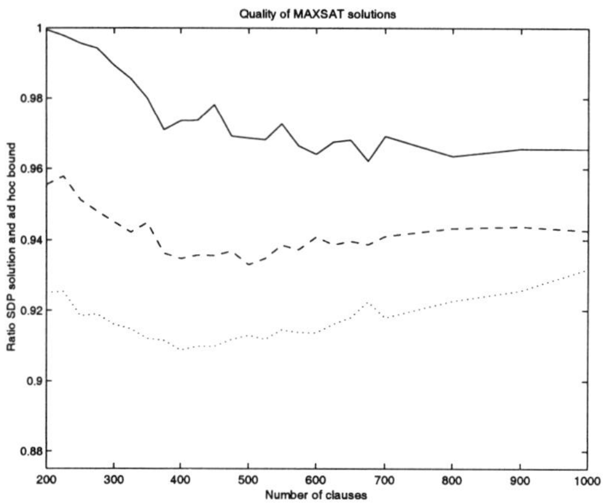

Figure 5. Comparison of MAXSAT solutions.

Let us finish this section by mentioning that using the primal optimal solution w, it is possible to identify hard subformulas. To this end, the sum of the weights is bounded (this corresponds to using a single slack variable in the dual formulation). Removing the clauses with 'small' weights, a subformula is obtained that appears to be the 'core' of the original formula. This yields a technique for finding approximately minimal unsatisfiable subformulas.

8.2. More general clause models

So far we have considered a fixed quadratic clause–model based on an elliptic approximation. Obviously there exist many other quadratic clause–models. Basically, all quadratic models $q(x)$ with the following property are valid.

PROPERTY 8.1. *If x is a satisfying assignment, then*

$$q(x) = \sum_{i=1}^{n}\sum_{j=1}^{n} q_{ij}x_ix_j + \sum_{k=1}^{n} q_kx_k + q_0 \leq 0.$$

As an example, let us consider the clause $\mathbf{C} = p_1 \vee p_2 \vee p_3$. Substituting the satisfying assignments of $\mathbf{C}$ in $q(x)$, a set of 7 inequalities is obtained. These inequalities, which are linear in the coefficients q_{ij} and q_k, define a cone. The extreme rays of this cone give rise to the following generic set of valid quadratic cuts (S).

$$\begin{aligned} x_1x_2 + x_1x_3 - x_2 - x_3 &\leq 0 \\ x_1x_2 + x_2x_3 - x_1 - x_3 &\leq 0 \\ x_1x_3 + x_2x_3 - x_1 - x_2 &\leq 0 \\ -x_1x_2 - x_1x_3 - x_2x_3 - 1 &\leq 0 \\ -x_1x_2 + x_1 + x_2 - 1 &\leq 0 \\ -x_1x_3 + x_1 + x_3 - 1 &\leq 0 \\ -x_2x_3 + x_2 + x_3 - 1 &\leq 0 \end{aligned}$$

An equivalent set is given by Karloff and Zwick [20]. So, each valid quadratic model of $\mathbf{C}$ is a linear combination of this set of inequalities. In particular, the elliptic approximation is obtained by taking the sum of the first three inequalities (see (1) and use that $x^2 = 1$ for $x \in \{-1, 1\}$). Karloff and Zwick show that using the first three inequalities a 7/8 approximation algorithm for MAX3SAT problems can be obtained. Thus, our relaxation is an aggregated version of the Karloff–Zwick relaxation.

Note that the SDP relaxations can be further strengthened by adding valid inequalities. An example of such cuts are the *triangle inequalities* [12]; note that many of these are in fact implied by (S) (namely those concerning variables that occur jointly in some clause). Another possibility is using (see also (1))

$$(a_k^T x - 1)(a_l^T x - 1) \leq (\ell(\mathbf{C}_k) - 1)(\ell(\mathbf{C}_l) - 1)$$

for any pair of clauses $\mathbf{C}_k$, $\mathbf{C}_l$ which share one or more variables. This is an example of a valid quadratic cut for *pairs* of clauses. Similar to (S), all valid quadratic cuts may be derived for pairs of clauses.

Generic procedures for deriving increasingly stronger relaxations of growing dimensions for binary programming problems in general, are given by Sherali and Adams [29] and Lovász and Schrijver [23]. These relaxations eventually describe the convex hull. While these results are of great theoretical interest, it is not entirely clear how to implement them in practice, due to the exponential size of the resulting relaxations. Using the elliptic approximations we obtain only one quadratic inequality per clause.

References

1. F. Alizadeh. *Combinatorial optimization with interior point methods and semi-definite matrices.* PhD thesis, University of Minnesota, Minneapolis, USA, 1991.
2. B. Aspvall, M.F. Plass, and R.E. Tarjan. A linear-time algorithm for testing the truth of certain quantified boolean formulas. *Information Processing Letters*, 8(3):121–123, 1979.
3. S.J. Benson, Y. Ye, and X. Zhang. Solving large-scale sparse semidefinite programs for combinatorial optimization. Technical report, Computational Optimization Lab, Department of Management Science, University of Iowa, Iowa City, USA, 1997.
4. V. Chvátal. Edmonds polytopes and a hierarchy of combinatorial problems. *Discrete Mathematics*, 4:305–337, 1973.
5. S.A. Cook. The complexity of theorem proving procedures. In *Proceedings of the 3rd annual ACM symposium on the Theory of Computing*, pages 151–158, 1971.
6. W. Cook, C.R. Coullard, and G. Turan. On the complexity of cutting plane proofs. *Discrete Applied Mathematics*, 18:25–38, 1987.
7. M. Davis, M. Logemann, and D. Loveland. A machine program for theorem proving. *Communications of the ACM*, 5:394–397, 1962.

8. E. de Klerk. *Interior point methods for semidefinite programming.* PhD thesis, Delft University of Technology, Delft, The Netherlands, 1997.
9. E. de Klerk, D.V. Pasechnik, and J.P. Warners. Approximate graph colouring algorithms based on the ϑ–function. Technical report, 1999. In preparation.
10. E. de Klerk and J.P. Warners. Semidefinite programming techniques for MAX–2–SAT and MAX–3–SAT: Computational perspectives. Technical Report 98–34, Department of Technical Mathematics and Informatics, Faculty of Information Technology and Systems, Delft University of Technology, Delft, The Netherlands, 1998.
11. D. Du, J. Gu, and P.M. Pardalos, editors. *Satisfiability problem: Theory and applications*, volume 35 of *DIMACS series in Discrete Mathematics and Computer Science.* American Mathematical Society, 1997.
12. U. Feige and M. Goemans. Approximating the value of two prover proof systems with applications to MAX 2SAT and MAX DICUT. In *Proc. Third Israel Symposium on Theory of Computing and Systems*, pages 182–189, 1995.
13. M.X. Goemans and D.P. Williamson. Improved approximation algorithms for maximum cut and satisfiability problems using semidefinite programming. *Journal of the ACM*, 42(6):1115–1145, 1995.
14. J. Gu, P.W. Purdom, J. Franco, and B.W. Wah. Algorithms for the satisfiability (SAT) problem: a survey. In Du et al. [11], pages 9–151.
15. A. Haken. The intractability of resolution. *Theoretical Computer Science*, 39:297–308, 1985.
16. C. Helmberg and F. Rendl. A spectral bundle method for SDP. Technical Report ZIB Preprint SC–97–37, Konrad–Zuse–Zentrum, Berlin, 1997.
17. J.N. Hooker. Resolution vs. cutting plane solution of inference problems: some computational experience. *Operations Research Letters*, 7(1):1–7, 1988.
18. R.A. Horn and C.R. Johnson. *Matrix analysis.* Cambridge University Press, 1985.
19. R. Impagliazzo, T. Pitassi, and A. Urquhart. Upper and lower bounds for tree–like cutting plane proofs. In *Proceedings of the 9th Annual IEEE Symposium on Logic in Computer Science*, pages 220–228, 1994.
20. H. Karloff and U. Zwick. A 7/8–approximation algorithm for MAX3SAT? In *Proceedings of the 38th Symposium on the Foundations of Computer Science*, pages 406–415, 1997.
21. O. Kullmann. Investigations on autark assignments. Technical report, Johann Wolfgang Goethe–Universität, Fachbereich Mathematik, 60054 Frankfurt, Germany, 1998. Submitted.
22. L. Lovász. On the Shannon capacity of a graph. *IEEE Transactions on Information Theory*, 25:1–7, 1979.
23. L. Lovász and A. Schrijver. Cones of matrices and set–functions and 0–1 optimization. *SIAM Journal on Optimization*, 1(2):166–190, 1991.
24. H. Van Maaren. Elliptic approximations of propositional formulae. Technical Report 96–65, Faculty of Technical Mathematics and Informatics, Delft University of Technology, Delft, The Netherlands, 1996. To appear in *Discrete Applied Mathematics.*
25. H. Van Maaren. On the use of second order derivatives for the satisfiability problem. In Du et al. [11], pages 677–687.
26. H. Van Maaren and J.P. Warners. Solving satisfiability problems using elliptic approximations - A note on volumes and weights. Technical Report 98-32, Department of Technical Mathematics and Informatics, Faculty of Information Technology and Systems, Delft University of Technology, Delft, The Netherlands, 1998.
27. B. Monien and E. Speckenmeyer. Solving satisfiability in less than 2^n steps. *Discrete Applied Mathematics*, 10:287–295, 1985.
28. T.J. Schaefer. The complexity of satisfiability problems. In *Proceedings of the Tenth Symposium on the Theory of Computing*, pages 216–226, 1978.
29. H.D. Sherali and W.P. Adams. A hierarchy of relaxations between the continuous and convex hull representations for 0–1 programming problems. *SIAM Journal on Discrete Mathematics*, 3(3):411–430, 1990.
30. G. Strang. *Linear algebra and its applications.* Harcourt Brace Jovanovich, third edition, 1988.
31. J.F. Sturm. Using SeDuMi 1.02, a MATLAB toolbox for optimization over symmetric cones. Technical report, Communications Research Laboratory, McMaster University, Hamilton, Canada, 1998.
32. L. Trevisan, G. Sorkin, M. Sudan, and D. Williamson. Gadgets, approximation and linear programming. In *Proceedings of the 37th Symposium on the Foundations of Computer Science*, pages 617–626, 1996.

33. A. Urquhart. Open problem posed at SAT'98, May 10–14, Paderborn, Germany. 1998.
34. L. Vandenberghe and S. Boyd. Semidefinite programming. *SIAM review*, 38:49–95, 1996.
35. J.P. Warners and H. Van Maaren. Recognition of tractable satisfiability problems through balanced polynomial representations. *Discrete Applied Mathematics*, ?, 199. To appear.
36. J.P. Warners and H. Van Maaren. Solving satisfiability problems using elliptic approximations - Effective branching rules. Technical Report 98–18, Department of Technical Mathematics and Informatics, Faculty of Information Technology and Systems, Delft University of Technology, Delft, The Netherlands, 1998. Accepted for publication in *Discrete Applied Mathematics.*
37. J.P. Warners and H. Van Maaren. A two-phase algorithm for solving a class of hard satisfiability problems. *Operations Research Letters*, 23(3–5):81–88, 1999.

SAT2000
I. Gent et al. (Eds.)
IOS Press, 2000

Resolution versus Search: Two Strategies for SAT *

Irina Rish‡ and Rina Dechter¶
Information and Computer Science, University of California, Irvine, USA

Abstract. The paper compares two popular strategies for solving propositional satisfiability, *backtracking search* and *resolution*, and analyzes the complexity of a directional resolution algorithm (DR) as a function of the "width" (w^*) of the problem's graph. Our empirical evaluation confirms theoretical prediction, showing that on low-w^* problems DR is very efficient, greatly outperforming the backtracking-based Davis-Putnam-Logemann-Loveland procedure (DP). We also emphasize the knowledge-compilation properties of DR and extend it to a tree-clustering algorithm that facilitates query answering. Finally, we propose two hybrid algorithms that combine the advantages of both DR and DP. These algorithms use control parameters that bound the complexity of resolution and allow time/space trade-offs that can be adjusted to the problem structure and to the user's computational resources. Empirical studies demonstrate the advantages of such hybrid schemes.

Keywords: propositional satisfiability, backtracking search, resolution, computational complexity, knowledge compilation, empirical studies.

1. Introduction

Propositional satisfiability (SAT) is a prototypical example of an NP-complete problem; any NP-complete problem is reducible to SAT in polynomial time [10]. Since many practical applications such as planning, scheduling, and diagnosis can be formulated as propositional satisfiability, finding algorithms with good average performance has been a focus of extensive research for many years [65, 12, 34, 50, 51, 4]. In this paper, we consider *complete* SAT algorithms that can always determine satisfiability as opposed to incomplete *local search* techniques [65, 64]. The two most widely used complete techniques are backtracking search (e.g., the Davis-Putnam Procedure [13]) and resolution (e.g., Directional Resolution [14, 25]). We compare both approaches theoretically and empirically, suggesting several ways of combining them into more effective hybrid algorithms.

In 1960, Davis and Putnam presented a resolution algorithm for deciding propositional satisfiability (the Davis-Putnam algorithm [14]). They proved that a restricted amount of resolution performed along some ordering of the propositions in a propositional theory is sufficient for deciding satisfiability. However, this algorithm has received limited attention and analyses of its performance have emphasized its worst-case exponential behavior [37, 43], while overlooking its virtues. It was quickly overshadowed by the Davis-Putnam Procedure, introduced in 1962 by Davis, Logemann, and Love-

‡ irinar@ics.uci.edu
¶ dechter@ics.uci.edu
* This work was partially supported by NSF grant IRI-9157636.

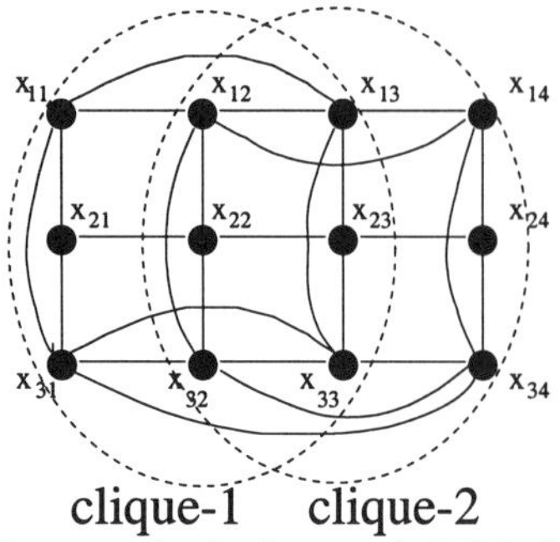

Unit #	Min Up Time	Min Down Time
1	3	2
2	2	1
3	4	1

Figure 1. An example of a "temporal chain": the unit commitment problem for 3 units over 4 hours.

land [13]. They proposed a minor syntactic modification of the original algorithm: the resolution rule was replaced by a splitting rule in order to avoid an exponential memory explosion. However, this modification changed the nature of the algorithm and transformed it into a backtracking scheme. Most of the work on propositional satisfiability quotes the backtracking version [44, 55]. We will refer to the original Davis-Putnam algorithm as *DP-resolution*, or *directional resolution (DR)* [1], and to its later modification as *DP-backtracking*, or *DP* (also called DPLL in the SAT community).

Our evaluation has a substantial empirical component. A common approach used in the empirical SAT community is to test algorithms on randomly generated problems, such as uniform random k-SAT [55]. However, these benchmarks often fail to simulate realistic problems. On the other hand, "real-life" benchmarks are often available only on an instance-by-instance basis without any knowledge of underlying distributions which makes the empirical results hard to generalize. An alternative approach is to use *structured* random problem generators inspired by the properties of some realistic domains. For example, Figure 1 illustrates the *unit commitment* problem of scheduling a set of n power generating units over T hours (here $n = 3$ and $T = 4$). The state of unit i at time t ("up" or "down") is specified by the value of boolean variable x_{it} (0 or 1), while the minimum up- and down-time constraints specify how long a unit must stay in a particular state before it can be switched. The corresponding constraint graph can be embedded in a chain of cliques where each clique includes the variables within the given number of time slices determined by the up- and down-time constraints. These clique-chain structures are common in many temporal domains that possess the *Markov property* (the future is independent of the past given the present). Another example of structured domain is circuit diagnosis. In [29] it was shown that circuit-diagnosis benchmarks can be embedded in a tree of cliques, where the clique sizes are substantially smaller than the overall number of variables. In general, one can imagine a variety of real-life domains having such structure that is captured by *k-tree-embeddings* [1] used in our random problem generators.

Our empirical studies of SAT algorithms confirm previous results: DR is very inefficient when dealing with unstructured uniform random problems. However, on structured problems such as k-tree embeddings having bounded *induced width*, directional resolu-

[1] Directional resolution can be viewed as a particular case of the first-order technique known as A-ordered resolution [52], or simply ordered resolution [8, 38, 2, 27], applied to propositional theories (see section 9 for more details).

	Backtracking	Resolution
Worst-case time	O(exp(n))	O(n exp(w*)) w*⩽ n
Average time	better than worst-case	same as worst-case
Space	O(n)	O(n exp(w*)) w*⩽ n
Output	one solution	knowledge compilation

Figure 2. Comparison between backtracking and resolution.

tion outperforms DP-backtracking by several orders of magnitude. The induced width (denoted w^*) is a graph parameter that describes the size of the largest clique created in the problem's interaction graph during inference. We show that the worst-case time and space complexity of DR is $O(n \cdot exp(w^*))$, where n is the number of variables. We also identify tractable problem classes based on a more refined syntactic parameter, called *diversity*.

Since the induced width is often smaller than the number of propositional variables, n, DR's worst-case bound is generally better than $O(exp(n))$, the worst-case time bound for DP. In practice, however, DP-backtracking – one of the best complete SAT algorithms available – is often much more efficient than its worst-case bound. It demonstrates "great discrepancies in execution time" (D.E. Knuth), encountering rare but exceptionally hard problems [67]. Recent studies suggest that the empirical performance of backtracking algorithms can be modeled by long-tail exponential-family distributions, such as lognormal and Weibull [35, 60]. The average complexity of algorithm DR, on the other hand, is close to its worst-case [20]. It is important to note that the space complexity of DP is $O(n)$, while DR is space-exponential in w^*. Another difference is that in addition to deciding satisfiability and finding a solution (a model), directional resolution also generates an equivalent theory that allows finding each model in linear time (and finding all models in time linear in the number of models), and thus can be viewed as a knowledge-compilation algorithm.

The complementary characteristics of backtracking and resolution (Figure 2) call for hybrid algorithms. We present two hybrid schemes, both using control parameters that restrict the amount of resolution by bounding the resolvent size, either in a preprocessing phase or dynamically during search. These parameters allow time/space trade-offs that can be adjusted to the given problem structure and to the computational resources. Empirical studies demonstrate the advantages of these flexible hybrid schemes over both extremes, backtracking and resolution.

This paper is an extension of the work presented in [25] and includes several new results. A tree-clustering algorithm for query processing that extends DR is presented and analyzed. The bounded directional resolution (BDR) approach proposed in [25] is subjected to a much more extensive empirical tests that include both randomly generated problems and DIMACS benchmarks. Finally, a new hybrid algorithm, *DCDR*, is introduced and evaluated empirically on a variety of problems.

The rest of this paper is organized as follows. Section 2 provides necessary definitions. Section 3 describes directional resolution (DR), our version of the original Davis-Putnam algorithm expressed within the *bucket-elimination* framework. Section 4 discusses the complexity of DR and identifies tractable classes. An extension of DR to tree-clustering scheme is presented in Section 5, while Section 6 focuses on DP-backtracking. Empirical comparison of DR and DP is presented in Section 7. Section 8 introduces the two hybrid schemes, BDR-DP and DCDR, and empirically evaluates their effectiveness. Related work and conclusions are discussed in Sections 9 and 10. Proofs of theorems are given in the Appendix A.

2. Definition and Preliminaries

We denote propositional variables, or propositions, by uppercase letters, e.g. P, Q, R, propositional literals (propositions or their negations, such as P and $\neg P$) by lowercase letters, e.g., p, q, r, and disjunctions of literals, or *clauses*, by the letters of the Greek alphabet, e.g., α, β, γ. For instance, $\alpha = (P \vee Q \vee R)$ is a clause. We will sometimes denote the clause $(P \vee Q \vee R)$ by $\{P, Q, R\}$. A *unit clause* is a clause with only one literal. A clause is *positive* if it contains only positive literals and is *negative* if it contains only negative literals. The notation $(\alpha \vee T)$ is used as shorthand for $(P \vee Q \vee R \vee T)$, while $\alpha \vee \beta$ refers to the clause whose literals appear in either α or β. A clause β is *subsumed* by a clause α if β's literals include all α's literals. A clause is a *tautology*, if for some proposition Q the clause includes both Q and $\neg Q$. A *propositional theory* φ in conjunctive normal form (*cnf*) is represented as a set $\{\alpha_1, ..., \alpha_t\}$ denoting the conjunction of clauses $\alpha_1, ..., \alpha_t$. A *k-cnf theory* contains only clauses of length k or less. A propositional cnf theory φ defined on a set of n variables Q_1,...,Q_n is often called simply "a theory φ".

The set of *models* of a theory φ is the set of all truth assignments to its variables that satisfy φ. A clause α is *entailed* by φ (denoted $\varphi \models \alpha$), if and only if α is true in all models of φ. A propositional satisfiability problem (SAT) is to decide whether a given cnf theory has a model. A SAT problem defined on k-cnfs is called a *k-SAT* problem.

The structure of a propositional theory can be described by an *interaction graph*. The interaction graph of a propositional theory φ, denoted $G(\varphi)$, is an undirected graph that contains a node for each propositional variable and an edge for each pair of nodes that correspond to variables appearing in the same clause. For example, the interaction graph of theory $\varphi_1 = \{(\neg C), (A \vee B \vee C), (\neg A \vee B \vee E), (\neg B \vee C \vee D)\}$ is shown in Figure 3a.

One commonly used approach to satisfiability testing is based on the *resolution* operation. Resolution over two clauses $(\alpha \vee Q)$ and $(\beta \vee \neg Q)$ results in a clause $(\alpha \vee \beta)$ (called *resolvent*) eliminating variable Q. The interaction graph of a theory processed by resolution should be augmented with new edges reflecting the added resolvents. For example, resolution over variable A in φ_1 generates a new clause $(B \vee C \vee E)$, so the graph of the resulting theory has an edge between nodes E and C as shown in Figure 3b.

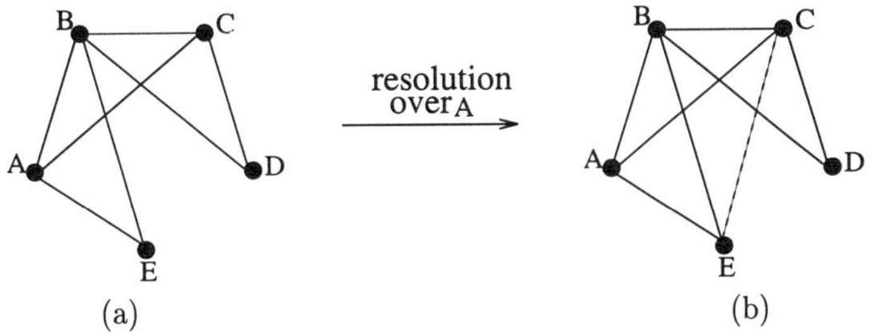

Figure 3. (a) The interaction graph of theory $\varphi_1 = \{(\neg C), (A \vee B \vee C), (\neg A \vee B \vee E), (\neg B \vee C \vee D)\}$, and (b) the effect of resolution over A on that graph.

Directional Resolution: DR
Input: A *cnf* theory φ, $o = Q_1, ..., Q_n$.
Output: The decision of whether φ is satisfiable.
If it is, the *directional extension* $E_o(\varphi)$ equivalent to φ.
1. **Initialize:** generate a partition of clauses, $bucket_1, ..., bucket_n$, where $bucket_i$ contains all the clauses whose highest literal is Q_i.
2. **For** $i = n$ to 1 do:
    If there is a unit clause in $bucket_i$,
    do unit resolution in $bucket_i$
    else resolve each pair $\{(\alpha \vee Q_i), (\beta \vee \neg Q_i)\} \subseteq bucket_i$.
    If $\gamma = \alpha \vee \beta$ is empty, return "φ is unsatisfiable"
    else add γ to the bucket of its highest variable.
3. Return "φ is satisfiable" and $E_o(\varphi) = \bigcup_i bucket_i$.

Figure 4. Algorithm Directional Resolution (DR).

Resolution with a unit clause is called *unit resolution. Unit propagation* is an algorithm that applies unit resolution to a given cnf theory until no new clauses can be deduced.

Propositional satisfiability is a special case of *constraint satisfaction problem (CSP)*. CSP is defined on a *constraint network* $< X, D, C >$, where $X = \{X_1, ..., X_n\}$ is the set of *variables*, associated with a set of finite *domains*, $D = \{D_i, ..., D_n\}$, and a set of *constraints*, $C = \{C_1, ..., C_m\}$. Each constraint C_i is a relation $R_i \subseteq D_{i_1} \times ... \times D_{i_k}$ defined on a subset of variables $S_i = \{X_{i_1}, ..., X_{i_k}\}$. A constraint network can be associated with an undirected *constraint graph* where nodes correspond to variables and two nodes are connected if and only if they participate in the same constraint. The *constraint satisfaction problem (CSP)* is to find a value assignment to all the variables (called a *solution*) that is consistent with all the constraints. If no such assignment exists, the network is *inconsistent*. A constraint network is *binary* if each constraint is defined on at most two variables.

3. Directional Resolution (DR)

DP-resolution [14] is an ordering-based resolution algorithm that can be described as follows. Given an arbitrary ordering of the propositional variables, we assign to each clause the index of its highest literal in the ordering. Then resolution is applied only to

find-model $(E_o(\varphi), o)$
Input: A *directional extension* $E_o(\varphi)$, $o = Q_1, ..., Q_n$.
Output: A model of φ.
1. **For** $i = 1$ to N
   $Q_i \leftarrow$ a value q_i consistent with the assignment to $Q_1, ..., Q_{i-1}$ and with all the clauses in $bucket_i$.
2. Return $Q_1 = q_1, ..., Q_n = q_n$.

Figure 5. Algorithm *find-model.*

clauses having the same index and only on their highest literal. The result of this restriction is a systematic elimination of literals from the set of clauses that are candidates for future resolution. The original DP-resolution also includes two additional steps, one forcing unit resolution whenever possible, and one assigning values to *all-positive* and *all-negative* variables. An all-positive (all-negative) variable is a variable that appears only positively (negatively) in a given theory, so that assigning such a variable the value "true" ("false") is equivalent to deleting all relevant clauses from the theory. There are other intermediate steps that can be introduced between the basic steps of eliminating the highest indexed variable, such as deleting subsumed clauses. Albeit, we will focus on the ordered elimination step and refer to auxiliary steps only when necessary. We are interested not only in deciding satisfiability but in the set of clauses accumulated by this process constituting an equivalent theory with useful computational features. Algorithm *directional resolution* (DR), the core of DP-resolution, is presented in Figure 4. This algorithm can be described using the notion of *buckets*, which define an ordered partitioning of clauses in φ, as follows. Given an ordering $o = (Q_1, ..., Q_n)$ of the variables in φ, all the clauses containing Q_i that do not contain any symbol higher in the ordering are placed in $bucket_i$. The algorithm processes the buckets in a reverse order of o, from Q_n to Q_1. Processing $bucket_i$ involves resolving over Q_i all possible pairs of clauses in that bucket. Each resolvent is added to the bucket of its highest variable Q_j (clearly, $j < i$). Note that if the bucket contains a unit clause (Q_i or $\neg Q_i$), only unit resolutions are performed. Clearly, a useful dynamic-order heuristic (not included in our current implementation) is to processes next a bucket with a unit clause. The output theory, $E_o(\varphi)$, is called the *directional extension* of φ along o. As shown by Davis and Putnam [14], the algorithm finds a satisfying assignment to a given theory if and only if there exists one. Namely,

THEOREM 1. : *[14] Algorithm DR is sound and complete.* □

A model of a theory φ can be easily found by consulting $E_o(\varphi)$ using a simple model-generating procedure *find-model* in Figure 5. Formally,

THEOREM 2. : (model generation)
Given $E_o(\varphi)$ of a satisfiable theory φ, the procedure find-model *generates a model of φ backtrack-free, in time $O(|E_o(\varphi)|)$.* □

EXAMPLE 1. : Given the input theory $\varphi_1 = \{(\neg C), (A \vee B \vee C), (\neg A \vee B \vee E), (\neg B \vee C \vee D)\}$, and an ordering $o = (E, D, C, B, A)$, the theory is partitioned into

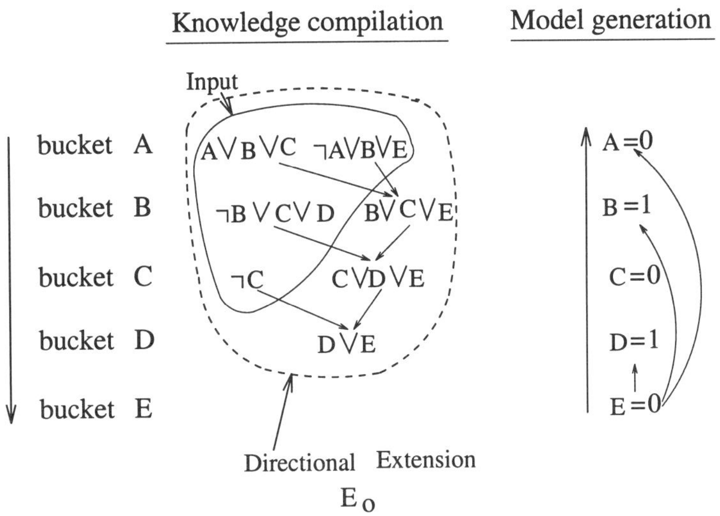

Figure 6. A trace of algorithm DR on the theory $\varphi_1 = \{(\neg C), (A \vee B \vee C), (\neg A \vee B \vee E), (\neg B \vee C \vee D)\}$ along the ordering $o = (E, D, C, B, A)$.

buckets and processed by directional resolution in reverse order[2]. Resolving over variable A produces a new clause $(B \vee C \vee E)$, which is placed in $bucket_B$. Resolving over B then produces clause $(C \vee D \vee E)$ which is placed in $bucket_C$. Finally, resolving over C produces clause $(D \vee E)$ which is placed in $bucket_D$. Directional resolution now terminates, since no resolution can be performed in $bucket_D$ and $bucket_E$. The output is a non-empty directional extension $E_o(\varphi_1)$. Once the directional extension is available, model generation begins. There are no clauses in the bucket of E, the first variable in the ordering, and therefore E can be assigned any value (e.g., $E = 0$). Given $E = 0$, the clause $(D \vee E)$ in $bucket_D$ implies $D = 1$, clause $\neg C$ in $bucket_C$ implies $C = 0$, and clause $(B \vee C \vee E)$ in $bucket_B$, together with the current assignments to C and E, implies $B = 1$. Finally, A can be assigned any value since both clauses in its bucket are satisfied by previous assignments.

As stated in Theorem 2, given a directional extension, a model can be generated in linear time. Once $E_o(\varphi)$ is compiled, determining the entailment of a single literal requires checking the bucket of that literal first. If the literal appears there as a unit clause, it is entailed; if not, its negation is added to the appropriate bucket and the algorithm resumes from that bucket. If the empty clause is generated, the literal is entailed. Entailment queries will also be discussed in Section 5.

4. Complexity and Tractability

Clearly, the effectiveness of algorithm DR depends on the the size of its output theory $E_o(\varphi)$.

---

[2] For illustration, we selected an arbitrary ordering which is not the most efficient one. Variable ordering heuristics will be discussed in Section 4.3.

THEOREM 3.: (complexity)
Given a theory φ and an ordering o, the time complexity of algorithm DR is $O(n \cdot |E_o(\varphi)|^2)$ where n is the number of variables. □

The size of the directional extension and therefore the complexity of directional resolution is worst-case exponential in the number of variables. However, there are identifiable cases when the size of $E_o(\varphi)$ is bounded, yielding tractable problem classes. The order of variable processing has a particularly significant effect on the size of the directional extension. Consider the following two examples:

EXAMPLE 2.: Let $\varphi_2 = \{(B \vee A), (C \vee \neg A), (D \vee A), (E \vee \neg A)\}$. Given the ordering $o_1 = (E, B, C, D, A)$, all clauses are initially placed in *bucket*(A). Applying DR along the (reverse) ordering, we get: *bucket*$(D) = \{(C \vee D), (D \vee E)\}$, *bucket*$(C) = \{(B \vee C)\}$, *bucket*$(B) = \{(B \vee E)\}$. In contrast, the directional extension along ordering $o_2 = (A, B, C, D, E)$ is identical to the input theory φ_2 since each bucket contains at most one clause.

EXAMPLE 3.: Consider the theory $\varphi_3 = \{(\neg A \vee B), (A \vee \neg C), (\neg B \vee D), (C \vee D \vee E)\}$. The directional extensions of φ_3 along ordering $o_1 = (A, B, C, D, E)$ and $o_2 = (D, E, C, B, A)$ are $E_{o_1}(\varphi_3) = \varphi_3$ and $E_{o_2}(\varphi_3) = \varphi_3 \cup \{(B \vee \neg C), (\neg C \vee D), (E \vee D)\}$, respectively.

In example 2, variable A appears in all clauses. Therefore, it can potentially generate new clauses when resolved upon, unless it is processed last (i.e., it appears first in the ordering), as in o_2. This shows that the interactions among variables can affect the performance of the algorithm and should be consulted for producing preferred orderings. In example 3, on the other hand, all the symbols have the same type of interaction, each (except E) appearing in two clauses. Nevertheless, D appears positive in both clauses in its bucket, therefore, it will not be resolved upon and can be processed first. Subsequently, B and C appear only negatively in the remaining theory and will not add new clauses. Inspired by these two examples, we will now provide a connection between the algorithm's complexity and two parameters: a topological parameter, called *induced width*, and a syntactic parameter, called *diversity.*

4.1. Induced width

In this section we show that the size of the directional extension and therefore the complexity of directional resolution can be estimated using a graph parameter called *induced width.*

As noted before, DR creates new clauses which correspond to new edges in the resulting interaction graph (we say that DR "induces" new edges). Figure 7 illustrates again the performance of directional resolution on theory φ_1 along ordering $o = (E, D, C, B, A)$, showing the interaction graph of $E_o(\varphi_1)$ (dashed lines correspond to induced edges). Resolving over A creates clause $(B \vee C \vee E)$ which corresponds to a new edge between nodes B and E, while resolving over B creates clause $(C \vee D \vee E)$ which induces a new edge between C and E. In general, processing a bucket of a variable Q produces resolvents that connect all the variables mentioned in that bucket. The concepts of induced graph and induced width are defined to reflect those changes.

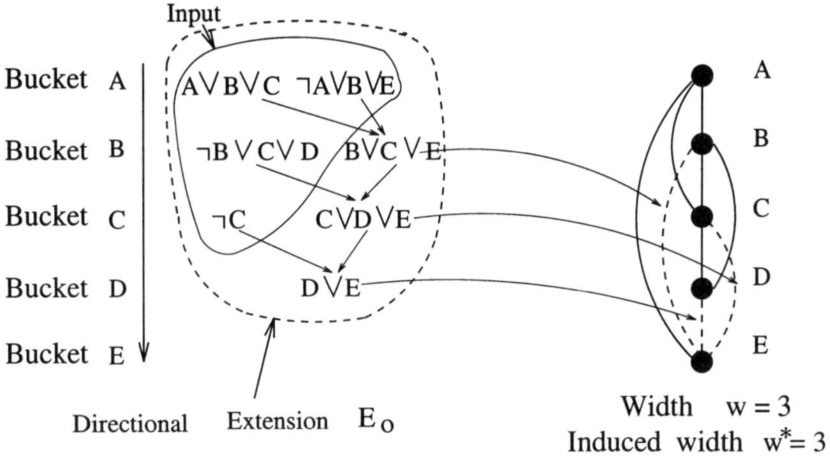

Figure 7. The effect of algorithm DR on the interaction graph of theory $\varphi_1 = \{(\neg C), (A \vee B \vee C), (\neg A \vee B \vee E), (\neg B \vee C \vee D)\}$ along the ordering $o = (E, D, C, B, A)$.

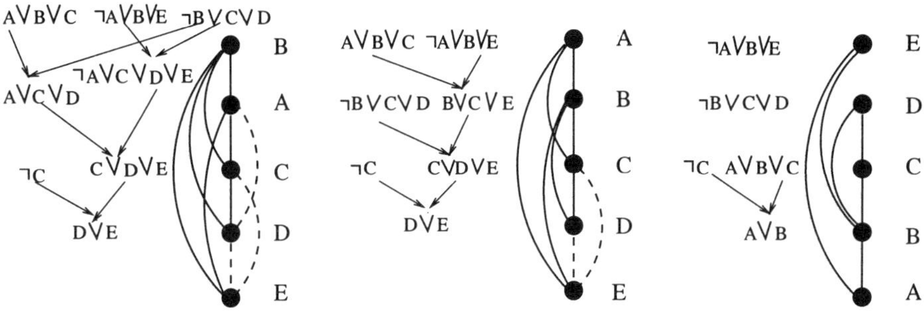

(a) $w^* = 4$ (b) $w^* = 3$ (c) $w^* = 2$

Figure 8. The effect of the ordering on the induced width: interaction graph of theory $\varphi_1 = \{(\neg C), (A \vee B \vee C), (\neg A \vee B \vee E), (\neg B \vee C \vee D)\}$ along the orderings (a) $o_1 = (E, D, C, A, B)$, (b) $o_2 = (E, D, C, B, A)$, and (c) $o_3 = (A, B, C, D, E)$.

DEFINITION 1.: Given a graph G, and an ordering of its nodes o, the *parent set* of a node X_i is the set of nodes connected to X_i that precede X_i in o. The size of this parent set is called the *width* of X_i relative to o. The *width of the graph* along o, denoted w_o, is the maximum width over all variables. The *induced graph* of G along o, denoted $I_o(G)$, is obtained as follows: going from $i = n$ to $i = 1$, we connect all the neighbors of X_i preceding it in the ordering. The induced width of G along o, denoted w_o^*, is the width of $I_o(G)$ along o, while the induced width w^* of G is the minimum induced width along any ordering.

For example, in Figure 7 the induced graph $I_o(G)$ contains the original (bold) and the induced (dashed) edges. The width of B is 2, while its induced width is 3; the width of C is 1, while its induced width is 2. The maximum width along o is 3 (the width of A), and the maximum induced width is also 3 (the induced width of A and B). Therefore, in this case, the width and the induced width of the graph coincide. In general, however, the induced width of a graph can be significantly larger than its width. Note that in this

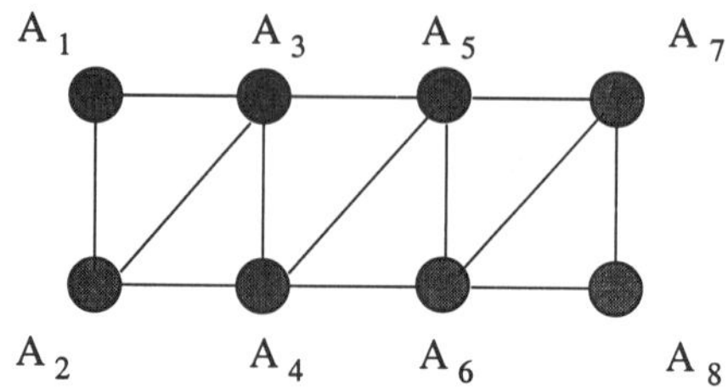

Figure 9. The interaction graph of φ_4 in example 4: $\varphi_4 = \{(A_1 \vee A_2 \vee \neg A_3), (\neg A_2 \vee A_4), (\neg A_2 \vee A_3 \vee \neg A_4), (A_3 \vee A_4 \vee \neg A_5), (\neg A_4 \vee A_6), (\neg A_4 \vee A_5 \vee \neg A_6), (A_5 \vee A_6 \vee \neg A_7), (\neg A_6 \vee A_8), (\neg A_6 \vee A_7 \vee \neg A_8)\}$.

example the graph of the directional extension, $G(E_o(\varphi))$, coincides with the induced ordered graph of the input theory's graph, $I_o(G(\varphi))$. Generally,

LEMMA 1.: *Given a theory φ and an ordering o, $G(E_o(\varphi))$ is a subgraph of $I_o(G(\varphi))$.* □

The parents of node X_i in the induced graph correspond to the variables mentioned in *bucket$_i$*. Therefore, the induced width of a node can be used to estimate the size of its bucket, as follows:

LEMMA 2.: *Given a theory φ and an ordering $o = (Q_1, ..., Q_n)$, if Q_i has at most k parents in the induced graph along o, then the bucket of a variable Q_i in $E_o(\varphi)$ contains no more than 3^{k+1} clauses.* □

We can now derive a bound on the complexity of directional resolution using properties of the problem's interaction graph.

THEOREM 4.: *(complexity of DR)*
Given a theory φ and an ordering of its variables o, the time complexity of algorithm DR along o is $O(n \cdot 9^{w_o^*})$, and $E_o(\varphi)$ contains at most $n \cdot 3^{w_o^*+1}$ clauses, where w_o^* is the induced width of φ's interaction graph along o. □

COROLLARY 1.: *Theories having bounded w_o^* for some ordering o are tractable.* □.

Figure 8 demonstrates the effect of variable ordering on the induced width, and consequently, on the complexity of DR when applied to theory φ_1. While DR generates 3 new clauses of length 3 along ordering (a), only one binary clause is generated along ordering (c). Although finding an ordering that yields the smallest induced width is NP-hard [1], good heuristic orderings are currently available [7, 16, 61] and continue to be explored [5]. Furthermore, there is a class of graphs, known as *k-trees*, that have $w^* < k$ and can be recognized in $O(n \cdot exp(k))$ time [1].

DEFINITION 2.: (k-trees)
1. A clique of size k (complete graph with k nodes) is a k-tree.
2. Given a k-tree defined on $X_1, ..., X_{i-1}$, a k-tree on $X_1, ..., X_i$ can be generated by selecting a clique of size k and connecting X_i to every node in that clique.

COROLLARY 2.: *If the interaction graph of a theory φ having n variables is a subgraph of a k-tree, then there is an ordering o such that the space complexity of algorithm DR along o (the size of $E_o(\varphi)$) is $O(n \cdot 3^k)$, and its time complexity is $O(n \cdot 9^k)$.* □

Important tractable classes are *trees* ($w^* = 1$) and *series-parallel networks* ($w^* = 2$). These classes can be recognized in polynomial (linear or quadratic) time.

EXAMPLE 4.: Consider a theory φ_n defined on the variables $\{A_1, A_2, ..., A_n\}$. A clause $(A_i \vee A_{i+1} \vee \neg A_{i+2})$ is defined for each odd i, and two clauses $(\neg A_i \vee A_{i+2})$ and $(\neg A_i \vee A_{i+1} \vee \neg A_{i+2})$ are defined for each even i, where $1 \leq i \leq n$. The interaction graph of φ_n for $n = 5$ is shown in Figure 9. The reader can verify that the graph is a 3-tree ($w^* = 2$) and that its induced width along the original ordering is 2. Therefore, by theorem 4, the size of the directional extension will not exceed $27n$.

4.1.1. *2-SAT*

Note that algorithm DR is tractable for 2-cnf theories, because 2-cnfs are closed under resolution (the resolvents are of size 2 or less) and because the overall number of clauses of size 2 is bounded by $O(n^2)$ (in this case, unordered resolution is also tractable), yielding $O(n \cdot n^2) = O(n^3)$ complexity. Therefore,

THEOREM 5. : *Given a 2-cnf theory φ, its directional extension $E_o(\varphi)$ along any ordering o is of size $O(n^2)$, and can be generated in $O(n^3)$ time.*

Obviously, DR is not the best algorithm for solving 2-SAT, since 2-SAT can be solved in linear time [28]. Note, however, that DR also compiles the theory into one that can produces each model in linear time. As shown in [19], in this case all models can be generated in output linear time.

4.1.2. *The graphical effect of unit resolution*

Resolution with a unit clause Q or $\neg Q$ deletes the opposite literal over Q from all relevant clauses. It is equivalent to assigning a value to variable Q. Therefore, unit resolution generates clauses on variables that are already connected in the graph, and therefore will not add new edges.

4.2. Diversity

The concept of induced width sometimes leads to a loose upper bound on the number of clauses recorded by DR. In Example 4, only six clauses were generated by DR, even without eliminating subsumption and tautologies in each bucket, while the computed bound is $27n = 27 \cdot 8 = 216$. Consider the two clauses $(\neg A \vee B)$ and $(\neg C \vee B)$ and the order $o = A, C, B$. When bucket B is processed, no clause is added because B is positive in both clauses, yet nodes A and C are connected in the induced graph. In this subsection, we introduce a new parameter called *diversity*, that provides a tighter bound on the number of resolution operations in the bucket. Diversity is based on the fact that a proposition can be resolved upon only when it appears both positively and negatively in different clauses.

DEFINITION 3.: (diversity)
Given a theory φ and an ordering o, let Q_i^+ (Q_i^-) denote the number of times Q_i appears positively (negatively) in $bucket_i$. The *diversity of* Q_i relative to o, $div(Q_i)$, is defined as $Q_i^+ \times Q_i^-$. The *diversity of an ordering* o, $div(o)$, is the largest diversity of its variables relative to o, and the *diversity of a theory*, div, is the minimal diversity among all orderings.

The concept of diversity yields new tractable classes. For example, if o is an ordering having a zero diversity, algorithm DR adds no clauses to φ, regardless of its induced width.

EXAMPLE 5.: Let $\varphi = \{(G \vee E \vee \neg F), (G \vee \neg E \vee D), (\neg A \vee F), (A \vee \neg E), (\neg B \vee C \vee \neg E), (B \vee C \vee D)\}$. It is easy to see that the ordering $o = (A, B, C, D, E, F, G)$ has diversity 0 and induced width 4.

THEOREM 6. : *Zero-diversity theories are tractable for DR: given a zero-diversity theory φ having n variables and c clauses, 1. its zero-diversity ordering o can be found in $O(n^2 \cdot c)$ time and 2. DR along o takes linear time.* □

The proof follows immediately from Theorem 8 (see subsection 4.3).

Zero-diversity theories generalize the notion of causal theories defined for general constraint networks of multivalued relations [24]. According to this definition, theories are *causal* if there is an ordering of the propositional variables such that each bucket contains a single clause. Consequently, the ordering has zero diversity. Clearly, when a theory has a non-zero diversity, it is still better to place zero-diversity variables last in the ordering, so that they will be processed first. Indeed, the *pure literal rule* of the original Davis-Putnam resolution algorithm requires processing first all-positive and all-negative (namely, zero-diversity) clauses.

However, the parameter of real interest is the diversity of the directional extension $E_o(\varphi)$, rather than the diversity of φ.

DEFINITION 4.: (induced diversity)
The *induced diversity of an ordering* o, $div^*(o)$, is the diversity of $E_o(\varphi)$ along o, and the *induced diversity of a theory*, div^*, is the minimal induced diversity over all its orderings.

Since $div^*(o)$ bounds the number of clauses generated in each bucket, the size of $E_o(\varphi)$ for every o can be bounded by $|\varphi| + n \cdot div^*(o)$. The problem is that computing $div^*(o)$ is generally not polynomial (for a given o), except for some restricted cases. One such case is the class of zero-diversity theories mentioned above, where $div^*(o) = div(o) = 0$. Another case, presented below, is a class of theories having $div^* = 1$. Note that we can easily create examples with high w^* having $div^* \leq 1$.

THEOREM 7.: *Given a theory φ defined on variables $Q_1, \ldots, Q_n$, such that each symbol Q_i either (a) appears only negatively (only positively), or (b) it appears in exactly two clauses, then $div^*(\varphi) \leq 1$ and φ is tractable.* □

min-diversity (φ)
1. **For** $i = n$ to 1 do:
   Choose symbol Q having the smallest diversity
   in $\varphi - \bigcup_{j=i+1}^{n} bucket_j$ and put it in the ith position.

Figure 10. Algorithm *min-diversity.*

4.3. Ordering heuristics

min-width (φ)
1. **Initialize:** $G \leftarrow G(\varphi)$
2. **For** $i = n$ to 1 do
   1.1. Choose symbol Q having the smallest degree in G and put it in the ith position.
   1.2. $G \leftarrow G - \{Q\}$.

Figure 11. Algorithm *min-width.*

min-degree (φ)
1. **Initialize:** $G \leftarrow G(\varphi)$
2. **For** $i = n$ to 1 do
   1.1. Choose symbol Q having the smallest degree in G and put it in the ith position.
   1.2. Connect the neighbors of Q in G.
   1.3. $G \leftarrow G - \{Q\}$.

Figure 12. Algorithm *min-degree.*

As previously noted, finding a minimum-induced-width ordering is known to be NP-hard [1]. A similar result can be demonstrated for minimum-induced-diversity orderings. However, the corresponding suboptimal (non-induced) min-width and min-diversity heuristic orderings often provide relatively low induced width and induced diversity. Min-width and min-diversity orderings can be computed in polynomial time by a simple greedy algorithm, as shown in Figures 10 and 11.

THEOREM 8. : *Algorithm* min-diversity *generates a minimal diversity ordering of a theory in time* $O(n^2 \cdot c)$*, where* n *is the number of variables and* c *is the number of clauses in the input theory.* □

The *min-width* algorithm [16] (Figure 11) is similar to the min-diversity, except that at each step we select a variable with the smallest *degree* in the current interaction graph. The selected variable is then placed i-th in the ordering and deleted from the graph.

max-cardinality (φ)
1. **For** $i = 1$ to n do
   Choose symbol Q connected to maximum number of previously ordered nodes in G and put it in the ith position.

Figure 13. Algorithm *max-cardinality.*

A modification of min-width ordering, called *min-degree* [30] (Figure 12), connects all the neighbors of the selected variable in the current interaction graph before the variable is deleted. Empirical studies demonstrate that the min-degree heuristic usually yields lower-w^* orderings than the induced-width heuristic. In all these heuristics ties are broken randomly.

There are several other commonly used ordering heuristics, such as *max-cardinality* heuristic presented in Figure 13. For more details, see [7, 16, 61].

5. Directional Resolution and Tree-Clustering

In this section we further discuss the knowledge-compilation aspects of directional resolution, and relate it to *tree-clustering* [23], a general preprocessing technique commonly used in constraint and belief networks.

As stated in Theorem 2, given an input theory and a variable ordering, algorithm DR produces a directional extension that allows model generation in linear time. Also, when entailment queries are restricted to a small fixed subset of the variables C, orderings initiated by the queried variables are preferred, since in such cases only a subset of the directional extension needs to be processed. The complexity of entailment in this case is $O(exp(min(|C|, w_o^*)))$, when w_o^* is computed over the induced graph truncated above variables in C [3].

However, when queries are expected to be uniformly distributed over all the variables it may be worthwhile to generate a compiled theory symmetrical with regard to all variables. This can be accomplished by tree-clustering [23], a compilation scheme used for constraint networks. Since cnf theories are special types of constraint networks, tree-clustering is immediately applicable. The algorithm compiles the propositional theory into a *join-tree* of relations (i.e., partial models) defined over *cliques* of variables that interact in a tree-like manner. The join-tree allows query processing in linear time. A tree-clustering algorithm for propositional theories presented in [6], is described in Figure 14 while a variant of tree-clustering that generates a join-tree of clauses rather than a tree of models is presented later.

The first three steps of tree-clustering (TC) are applied only to the interaction graph of the theory, transforming it into a *chordal* graph (a graph is chordal if every cycle of length at least four has a chord, i.e. an edge between two non-sequential nodes in that cycle). This procedure, called *triangulation* [69], processes the nodes along some order

[3] Moreover, since querying variables in C implies the addition of unit clauses, all the edges incident to the queried variables can be deleted, further reducing the induced width.

Tree-clustering (φ)
Input: A *cnf* theory φ and its interaction graph $G(\varphi)$, an ordering o.
Output: A join-tree representation of all models of φ, $TCM(\varphi)$.
Graph operations:
1. Apply triangulation to $G_o(\varphi)$ yielding a chordal graph $G_h = I_o(G)$.
2. Let C_1,...,C_t be all the maximal cliques in G_h indexed by their highest nodes.
3. **For each** C_i, $i = t$ to 1,
   connect C_i to C_j ($j < i$), where C_j shares the largest set of variables with C_i.
The resulting graph is called a *join tree* T.
4. Assign each clause to every clique that contains all its atoms, yielding φ_i for each C_i.
Model generation:
5. For each clique C_i, compute M_i, the set of models over φ_i.
6. Apply *arc-consistency* on the join tree T of models:
   for each C_i, and for each C_j adjacent to C_i in T, delete from M_i every model M that does not agree with any model in M_j on the set of their common variables.
6. Return $TCM_o(\varphi) = \{M_1, ..., M_t\}$ and the tree structure.

Figure 14. Model-based tree-clustering (TC).

of the variables o, going from the last node to the first, connecting edges between the earlier neighbors of each node. The result is the induced graph along o, which is chordal, and whose maximal cliques serve as the nodes in the resulting structure called a join-tree. The size of the largest clique in the triangulated (induced) graph equals $w_o^* + 1$. Steps 2 and 3 of the algorithm complete the *join-tree* construction by connecting the various cliques into a tree structure. Once the tree of cliques is identified, each clause in φ is placed in *every* clique that contains its variables (step 4), yielding subtheories φ_i for each clique C_i. In step 5, the models M_i of each φ_i are computed and replace φ_i. Finally (step 6), arc-consistency is enforced on the tree of models (for more details see [23, 6]). Given a theory φ, the algorithm generates a tree of partial models denoted $TCM(\varphi)$.

It was shown that a join-tree yields a tractable representation. Namely, satisfiability, model generation, and a variety of entailment queries can all be done in linear or polynomial time:

THEOREM 9. : *[6]*

1. *A theory φ and a $TCM(\varphi)$ generated by algorithm TC are satisfiable if and only if none of $M_i \in TCM(\varphi)$ is empty. This can be verified in linear time in the resulting join-tree.*

2. *Deciding whether a literal $P \in C_i$ is consistent with φ can be done in linear time in $|M_i|$, by scanning the columns of a relation M_i defined over P.*

3. *Entailment of a clause α can be determined in $O(|\alpha| \cdot n \cdot m \cdot log(m))$ time, where m bounds the number of models in each clique. This is done by temporary elimination of all submodels that disagree with α from all relevant cliques, and reapplying arc-consistency.* □

We now present a variant of the tree-clustering algorithm where each clique in the final output join-tree is associated with a subtheory of clauses rather than with a set of models, while all the desirable properties of the compiled representation are maintained. We show that the compiled subtheories are generated by two successive applications of DR along an ordering dictated by the join-tree's structure. The resulting algorithm *Clause-based Tree-Clustering (CTC)* (Figure 15) outputs a clause-based join-tree, denoted $TCC(\varphi)$.

CTC(φ)
Input: A *cnf* theory φ and its interaction graph $G(\varphi)$, an ordering o.
Output: A clause-based join-tree representation of φ
1. Compute the skeleton join-tree (steps 1-3 in Figure 14.
2. Place every clause in very clique that contains it literals.
Let C_1,...,C_t be a breadth first search ordering of the clique-tree that starts with C_1 as its root. Let φ_1,...,φ_t be theories in C_1,...,C_t, respectively.
3. For $i = t$ to 1, $\varphi_i \leftarrow res(\varphi_i)$ (namely, close φ_i under resolution)
put a copy of resolvents defined only on variables shared between C_i and C_j where C_j is an earlier clique, into C_j.
4. For $i = 1$ to t do $C_i \leftarrow res(C_i)$;
put a copy of resolvents defined only on variables that C_i shares with a later clique C_j, into C_j.
5. Return $TCC(\varphi) = \{\varphi_1^*, ..., \varphi_t^*\}$, the set of all clauses defined on each clique and the tree structure.

Figure 15. Algorithm clause-based tree-clustering (CTC).

The first three steps of structuring the join-tree and associating each clique with cnf subtheories (step 4) remain unchanged. Directional resolution is then applied to the resulting tree of cliques *twice*, from leaves to the root and vice-versa. However, DR is modified; each bucket is associated with a clique rather than with a single variable. Thus, each clique is processed by *full (unordered)* resolution relative to *all* the variables in the cliques. Some of the generated clauses are then copied into the next neighboring clique. Let $o = C_1 ... C_t$ be a *tree-ordering* of cliques generated by either breadth-first or depth-first traversal of the clique-tree rooted at C_1. For each clique, the rooted tree defines a parent and a set of child cliques. Cliques are then processed in a reverse order of o. When processing clique C_i and its subtheory φ_i, all possible resolvents over the variables in C_i are added to φ_i. The resolvents defined only on variables shared by C_i and its parent C_l are copied and placed into C_l. The second phase works similarly in the opposite direction, from the root C_1 towards the leaves. In this case, the resolvents generated in clique C_i that are defined on variables shared with a child clique C_j are copied into C_j [4]. Since applying full resolution to theories having $|C|$ variables is time and space exponential in $|C|$ we get:

THEOREM 10. : *The complexity of CTC is time and space $O(n \cdot exp(w^*))$, where w^* is the induced width of the ordered graph used for generating the join-tree structure.* □

[4] Note that duplication of resolvents can be avoided using a simple indexing scheme.

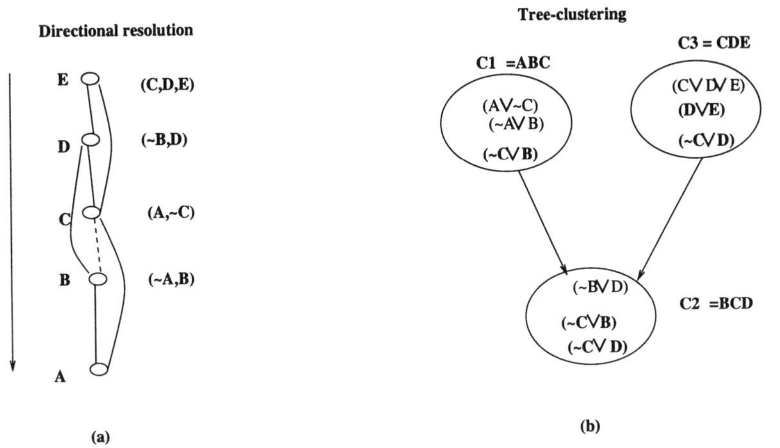

Figure 16. Theory and its two tree-clusterings.

EXAMPLE 6. : Consider theory $\varphi_2 = \{(\neg B \vee A)(A \vee \neg C), (\neg B \vee D), (C \vee D \vee E)\}$. Using the order $o = (A, B, C, D, E)$, directional-resolution along o adds no clauses. The join-tree structure relative to this ordering is obtained by selecting the maximal cliques in the ordered induced graph (see Figure 16a). We get $C_3 = EDC$, $C_2 = BCD$, and $C_1 = ABC$. Step 4 places clause $(C \vee D \vee E)$ in clique C_3, clause$(\neg B \vee D)$ in C_2 and clauses $(A \vee \neg C)$ and $(\neg B \vee A)$ in C_1. The resulting set of clauses in each clique after processing by tree-clustering using $o = C_1, C_2, C_3$ is given in Figure 16b. The boldface clauses in each clique are those added during processing. No clause is generated in its backward phase. In the root clique C_1, resolution over A generates clause $(\neg C \vee B)$ which is then added to clique C_2. Processing C_2 generates clause $(\neg C \vee D)$ added to C_3. Finally, processing C_3 generates clause $(D \vee E)$.

The most significant property of the compiled sub-theories of each clique C_i, denoted φ_i^*, is that each contains all the prime implicates of φ defined over variables in C_i. This implies that entailment queries involving only variables contained in a single clique, C_i, can be answered in linear time, scanning the clauses of φ_i^*. Clauses that are *not* contained in one clique can be processed in $O(exp(w^* + 1))$ time.

To prove this claim, we first show that the clause-based join-tree of φ contains the directional extensions of φ along all the orderings that are consistent with the tree-structure. The ability to generate a model backtrack-free facilitated by the directional extensions therefore guarantees the existence of all clique-restricted prime implicates. We provide a formal account of these claims below.

DEFINITION 5. : A *prime implicate* of a theory φ is a clause α such that $\varphi \models \alpha$, and there is no $\alpha_1 \subset \alpha$ s.t. $\varphi \models \alpha_1$.

DEFINITION 6. : Let φ be a cnf theory, and let C be a subset of the variables of φ. We denote by $prime_\varphi$ the set of all prime implicates of φ, and by $prime_\varphi(C)$ the set of all prime implicates of φ that are defined only on variables in C.

We will show that any compiled clausal tree, $TCC(\varphi)$, contains the directional extension of φ along a variety of variable orderings.

LEMMA 3.: *Given a theory φ, let $T = TCC(\varphi)$, be a clause-based join-tree of φ and let C be a clique in T. Then, there exist an ordering o that can start with any internal ordering of the variables in C, such that $E_o(\varphi) \subseteq TCC(\varphi)$.* □

Based on Lemma 3 we can prove the following theorem:

THEOREM 11.: *Let φ be a theory and let $T = TCC(\varphi)$ be a clause-based join-tree of φ, then for every clique $C \in T$, $prime_\varphi(C) \subseteq TCC(\varphi)$.* □

Consider again theory φ_3 and Figure 16. Focusing on clique C_3 we see that it has only two prime implicates, $(D \vee E)$ and$(\neg C \vee D)$.

Having all the prime implicates of a clique has a semantic and a syntactic value. Semantically, it means that all the information related to variables C_i is available inside the compiled theory φ_i^*. The rest of the information is irrelevant. On the syntactic level we also know that φ_i^* is the most explicit representation of this information. From Theorem 11 we conclude:

COROLLARY 3.: *Given a theory φ and its join-tree $TCC_o(\varphi)$, the following properties hold:*

1. *The theory φ is satisfiable if and only if $TCC(\varphi)$ does not contain an empty clause.*
2. *If $T = TCC(\varphi)$ for some φ, then entailment of any clause whose variables are contained in a single clique can be decided in linear time in T.*
3. *Entailment of an arbitrary clause α from φ can be decided in $O(exp(w^* + 1))$ time and space.*
4. *Checking if a new clause is consistent with φ can be done in linear time in T.* □

In the example shown in Figure 16, the compiled sub-theory associated with clique C_2 is $\varphi_2^* = \{(\neg B \vee D), (\neg C \vee B), (\neg C \vee D)\}$. To determine if φ entails $\alpha = (C \vee B \vee D)$, we must assess whether or not α is contained in φ_2^*. Since it is not contained, we conclude that it is not entailed. To determine if α is consistent with φ, we must see if φ entails the negation of each literal. If it does, the clause is inconsistent. Since φ_2^* does not include $\neg B$, $\neg C$, or $\neg D$, neither of those literals is entailed by φ, and therefore, α is consistent with φ.

6. Backtracking Search (DP)

Backtracking search processes the variables in some order, instantiating the next variable if it has a value consistent with previous assignments. If there is no such value (a situation called a *dead-end*), the algorithm *backtracks* to the previous variable and selects an alternative assignment. Should no consistent assignment be found, the algorithm backtracks again. The algorithm explores the *search tree*, in a depth-first manner, until it either finds a solution or concludes that no solution exists. An example of a search tree is shown in Figure 17a. This tree is traversed when deciding satisfiability of a

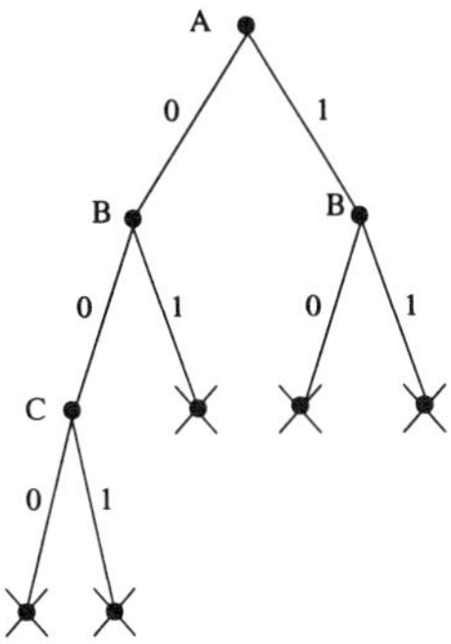

(a)

```
DP(φ):
Input: A cnf theory φ.
Output: A decision of whether φ is satisfiable.
Unit_propagate(φ);
If the empty clause generated return(false);
else if all variables are assigned return(true);
else
      Q = some unassigned variable;
      return(DP(φ ∧ ¬Q) ∨
              DP(φ ∧ Q) )
```

(b)

Figure 17. (a) A backtracking search tree along the ordering A, B, C for a cnf theory $\varphi_5 = \{(\neg A \vee B), (\neg C \vee A), \neg B \vee C\}$ and (b) the Davis-Putnam Procedure.

propositional theory $\varphi_5 = \{(\neg A \vee B), (\neg C \vee A), \neg B, C\}$. The tree nodes correspond to the variables, while the tree branches correspond to different assignments (0 and 1). Dead-end nodes are crossed out. Theory φ_5 is obviously inconsistent.

There are various advanced backtracking algorithms for solving CSPs that improve the basic scheme using "smart" variable- and value-ordering heuristics ([11], [36]). More efficient backtracking mechanisms, such as *backjumping* [39, 15, 57], constraint propagation (e.g., *arc-consistency, forward checking* [45]), or learning (recording constraints) [15, 33, 3] are available. The Davis-Putnam Procedure (DP) [13] shown in Figure 17b is a backtracking search algorithm for deciding propositional satisfiability combined with unit propagation. Various branching heuristics augmenting this basic version of DP have been proposed since 1962 [49, 11, 46, 41].

The worst-case time complexity of all backtracking algorithms is exponential in the number of variables while their space complexity is linear. Yet, the average time complexity of DP depends on the distribution of instances [31] and is often much lower then its worst-case bound. Usually, its average performance is affected by rare, but exceptionally hard instances. Exponential-family empirical distributions (e.g., lognormal, Weibull) proposed in recent studies [35, 60] summarize such observations in a concise way. A typical distribution of the number of explored search-tree nodes is shown in Figure 18. The distribution is shown for inconsistent problems. As it turns out, consistent and inconsistent CSPs produce different types of distributions (for more details see [35, 36]).

7. DP versus DR: Empirical Evaluation

In this section we present an empirical comparison of DP and DR on different types of cnf theories, including uniform random problems, random chains and (k,m)-trees, and benchmark problems from the Second DIMACS Challenge [5]. The algorithms were implemented in C and tested on Sun SPARCstations. We used several machines having different performance, such as Sun SPARCstation SLC 4/20 (20MHz CPU), SPARCsta-

[5] Available at *ftp://dimacs.rutgers.edu/pub/challenge/sat/benchmarks/volume/cnf.*

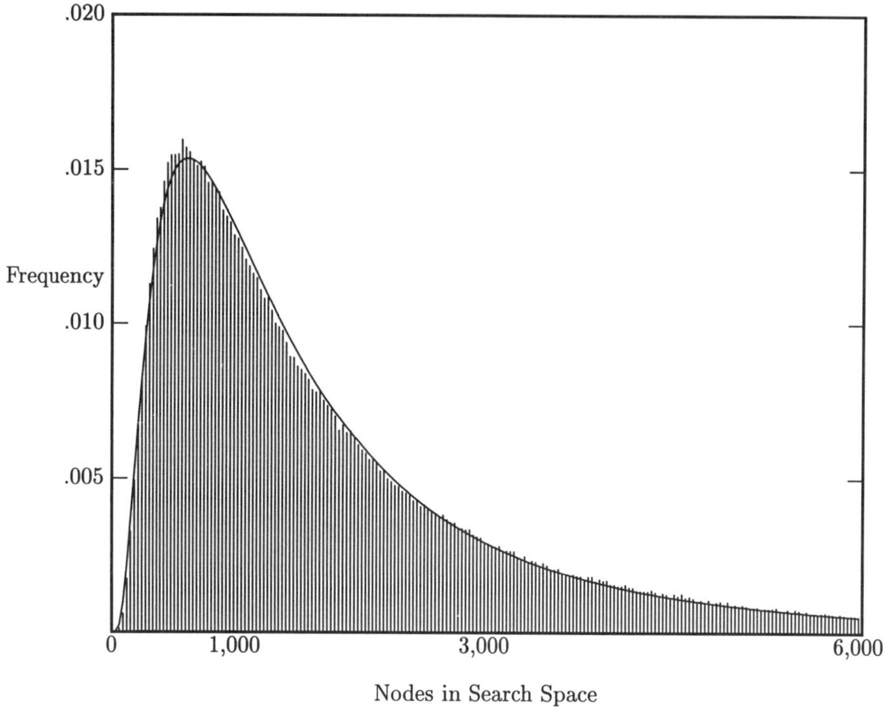

Figure 18. An empirical distribution of the number of nodes explored by algorithm BJ-DVO (backjumping+dynamic variable ordering) on 10^6 instances of inconsistent random binary CSPs having N=50 variables, domain size D=6, constraint density C=.1576 (probability of a constraint between two variables), and tightness T=0.333 (the fraction of prohibited value pairs in a constraint).

Figure 19. An example of a theory with (a) a chain structure (3 subtheories, 5 variables in each) and (b) a (k,m)-tree structure (k=2, m=2).

tion 4 Model 110 (110 MHz microSPARC II CPU), Sun SPARCstation 5 Model 170 (170 MHz FMI,MB86907 CPU), and Ultra 2 Model 2170 (168 MHz UltraSPARC CPU). We specify explicitly which machine was used for each set of experiments. Reported runtime is measured in seconds.

Algorithm DR is implemented as discussed in Section 3, using heuristic orderings described in Section 4.3. If it is followed by DP using the same variable ordering, no dead-ends will occur (see Theorem 2). Algorithm DP was implemented using the dynamic variable ordering heuristic of *Tableau* [11], a state-of-the-art backtracking algorithm for SAT. This heuristic, called the *2-literal-clause* heuristic, suggests instantiating next a variable that would cause the largest number of unit propagations approximated by the number of 2-literal clauses in which the variable appears. The augmented algorithm significantly outperforms DP without this heuristic [11]. Note that DP and DR use different ordering heuristics, each suited for particular algorithm's properties: namely, min-width, min-diversity, and similar DR's heuristics aim at decreasing the induced width, while DP's 2-literal-clause heuristic attempts to decrease the number of branches in the search tree by allowing more unit resolutions. One may raise a question about fairness of the comparison between DR and DP since the orderings are different. However, due to the different nature of backtracking- and resolution-based algorithms, a good DR ordering may not help DP and vice versa.

7.1. Random problem generators

To test the algorithms on problems with different structures, several random problem generators were used. The *uniform k-cnfs* generator [55] uses as input the number of variables N, the number of clauses C, and the number of literals per clause k. Each clause is generated by randomly choosing k out of N variables and by determining the sign of each literal (positive or negative) with probability p. In the majority of our experiments $p = 0.5$. Although we did not check for clause uniqueness, for large N it is unlikely that identical clauses will be generated.

Our second generator, *chains*, creates a sequence of independent uniform k-cnf theories (called *subtheories*) and connects each pair of successive cliques by a 2-cnf clause containing variables from two consecutive subtheories in the chain (see Figure 19a). The parameters of the generator are the number of cliques, $Ncliq$, the number of variables per clique, N, and the number of clauses per clique, C. A chain of cliques, each having N variables, is a subgraph of a k-tree [1] where $k = 2N-1$ and therefore, has $w^* \leq 2N-1$.

We also used a *(k,m)-tree* generator which generates a tree of cliques each having $(k+m)$ nodes where k is the size of the intersection between two neighboring cliques (see Figure 19b, where $k = 2$ and $m = 2$). Given k, m, the number of cliques $Ncliq$, and the number of clauses per clique $Ncls$, the *(k,m)-tree* generator produces a clique of size $k+m$ with $Ncls$ clauses and then generates each of the other $Ncliq - 1$ cliques by selecting randomly an existing clique and its k variables, adding m new variables, and generating $Ncls$ clauses on that new clique. Since a k-m-tree can be embedded into a $(k+m-1)$-tree, its induced width is bounded by $k+m-1$ (note that $(k,1)$-trees are conventional k-trees).

7.2. Results

As expected, on uniform random 3-cnfs having large w^*, the complexity of DR grew exponentially with the problem density while the performance of DP was much better. Even small problems having 20 variables already demonstrate the exponential behavior of DR (see Figure 20a). On larger problems DR often ran out of memory. We did not proceed with more extensive experiments in this case, since the exponential behavior of DR on uniform 3-cnfs is already well-known [37, 43].

However, the behavior of the algorithms on chain problems was completely different. DR was by far more efficient than DP, as can be seen from Table I and from Figure 20b, summarizing the results on 3-cnf chain problems that contain 25 subtheories,

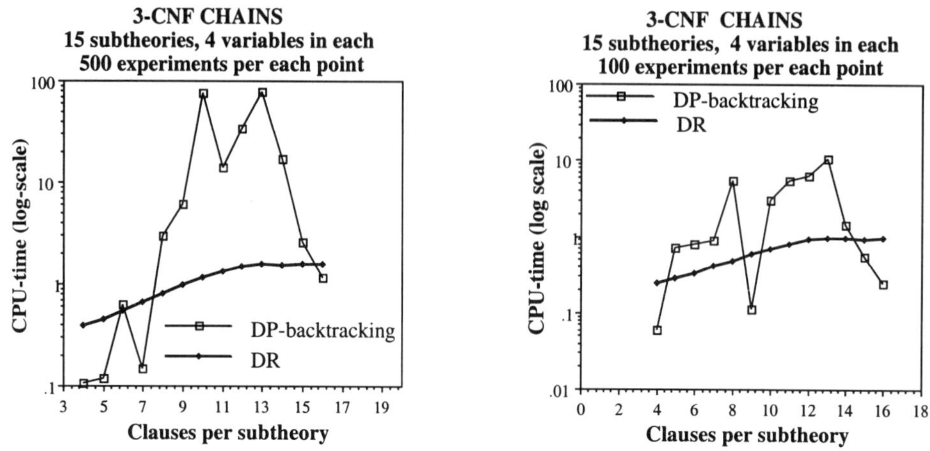

(a) input ordering (b) min-width ordering

Figure 20. (a) DP versus DR on uniform random 3-cnfs; (b) DP, DR, BDR-DP(3) and backjumping on 3-cnf chains (Sun 4/20).

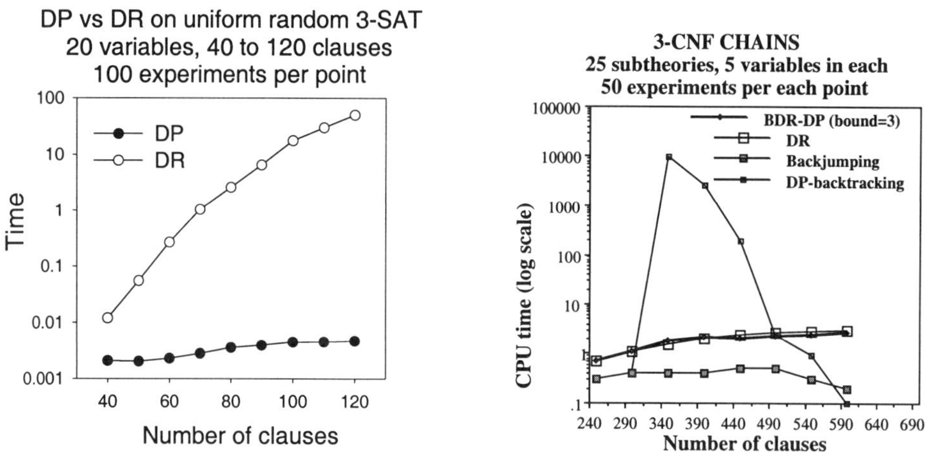

(a) uniform random 3-cnfs, $w^* = 10$ to 18 (b) chain 3-cnfs, $w^* = 4$ to 7

Figure 21. DR and DP on 3-cnf chains with different orderings (Sun 4/20).

each having 5 variables and 9 to 23 clauses (24 additional 2-cnf clauses connect the subtheories in the chain) [6]. A min-diversity ordering was used for each instance. Since the induced width of these problems was small (less than 6, on average), directional resolution solved these problems quite easily. However, DP-backtracking encountered rare but extremely hard problems that contributed to its average complexity. Table II lists the results on selected hard instances from Table I (where the number of dead-ends exceeds 5,000).

[6] Figure 20b also shows the results for algorithms BDR-DP and backjumping discussed later.

Table I. DR versus DP on 3-cnf chains having 25 subtheories, 5 variables in each, and from 11 to 21 clauses per subtheory (total 125 variables and 299 to 549 clauses). 20 instances per row. The columns show the percentage of satisfiable instances, time and deadends for DP, time and the number of new clauses for DR, the size of largest clause, and the induced width w^*_{md} along the min-diversity ordering. The experiments were performed on Sun 4/20 workstation.

Num of cls	% sat	DP		DR			
		Time	Dead ends	Time	Number of new clauses	Size of max clause	w^*
299	100	0.4	1	1.4	105	4.1	5.3
349	70	9945.7	908861	2.2	131	4.0	5.3
399	25	2551.1	207896	2.8	131	4.0	5.3
449	15	185.2	13248	3.7	135	4.0	5.5
499	0	2.4	160	3.8	116	3.9	5.4
549	0	0.9	9	4.0	99	3.9	5.2

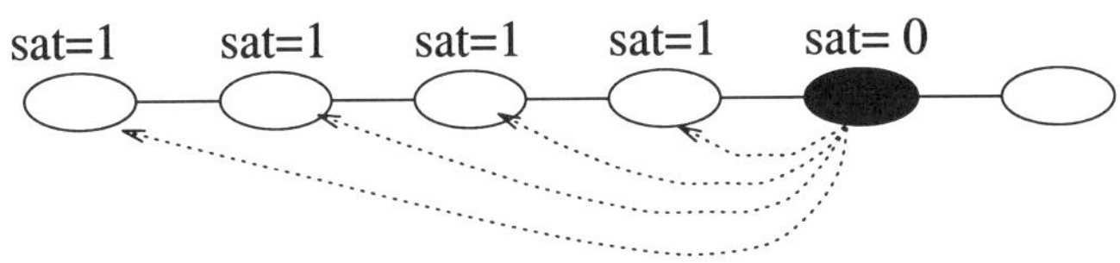

Figure 22. An inconsistent chain problem: a naive backtracking is very inefficient when encountering an inconsistent subproblem at the end of the variable ordering.

Similar results were obtained for other chain problems and with different variable orderings. For example, Figure 21 graphs the experiments with min-width and input orderings. We observe that min-width ordering may significantly improve the performance of DP relative to the input ordering (compare Figure 21a and Figure 21b). Still, it did not prevent backtracking from encountering rare, but extremely hard instances.

Table III presents the histograms demonstrating the performance of DP on chains in more details. The histograms show that in most cases the frequency of easy problems (e.g., less than 10 deadends) decreased and the frequency of hard problems (e.g., more than 10^4 deadends) increased with increasing number of cliques and with increasing number of clauses per clique. Further empirical studies are necessary to investigate phase transition in chains[7].

In our experiments nearly all of the 3-cnf chain problems that were difficult for DP were unsatisfiable. One plausible explanation is that inconsistent chain theories may have an unsatisfiable subtheory only at the end of the ordering. If all other subtheories are satisfiable then DP will try to re-instantiate variables from the satisfiable subtheories whenever it encounters a dead-end. Figure 22 shows an example of a chain of satisfiable

[7] The phase transition phenomenon observed in uniform random 3cnf and in CSPs corresponds to a sharp transition from mostly satisfiable to mostly unsatisfiable problems around a particular value of a critical parameter, such as clauses/variables ratio, and is usually associated with a sharp peak in the algorithm's complexity [9, 55, 42, 68, 47].

Table II. DR and DP on hard chains when the number of dead-ends is larger than 5,000. Each chain has 25 subtheories, with 5 variables in each (total of 125 variables). The experiments were performed on Sun 4/20 workstation.

Num of cls	Sat: 0 or 1	**DP** Time	**DP** Dead ends	**DR** Time
349	0	41163.8	3779913	1.5
349	0	102615.3	9285160	2.4
349	0	55058.5	5105541	1.9
399	0	74.8	6053	3.6
399	0	87.7	7433	3.1
399	0	149.3	12301	3.1
399	0	37903.3	3079997	3.0
399	0	11877.6	975170	2.2
399	0	841.8	70057	2.9
449	1	655.5	47113	5.2
449	0	2549.2	181504	3.0
449	0	289.7	21246	3.5

Table III. Histograms of the number of deadends (log-scale) for DP on chains having 20, 25 and 30 subtheories, each defined on 5 variables and 12 to 16 clauses. Each column presents results for 200 instances; each row defines a range of deadednds; each entry is the frequency of instances (out of total 200) that yield the range of deadends. The experiments were performed on Sun UltraSPARC.

Deadends	C=12			C=14			C=16		
	Ncliq			Ncliq			Ncliq		
	20	25	30	20	25	30	20	25	30
$[0, 1)$	103	90	75	75	23	8	7	2	2
$[1, 10)$	81	85	102	102	107	93	73	68	59
$[10, 10^2)$	3	4	7	7	21	24	40	37	43
$[10^2, 10^3)$	2	1	4	4	8	12	20	26	22
$[10^3, 10^4)$	1	3	2	2	10	8	21	10	21
$[10^4, \infty)$	10	17	10	10	31	55	39	57	53

theories with an unsatisfiable theory close to the end of the ordering. Min-diversity and min-width orderings do not preclude such a situation. There are enhanced backtracking schemes, such as *backjumping* [39, 40, 15, 56], that are capable of exploiting the structure and preventing useless re-instantiations. Experiments with backjumping confirm that it substantially outperforms DP on the same chain instances (see Figure 20b).

The behavior of DP and DR on *(k-m)*-trees is similar to that on chains and will be discussed later in the context of hybrid algorithms.

Table IV. DP versus Tableau on 150- and 200-variable uniform random 3-cnfs using the min-degree ordering. 100 instances per row. Experiments ran on Sun UltraSPARC.

Cls	% sat	Tableau time	DP time	DP de
150 variables				
550	1.00	0.3	0.4	81
600	0.93	2.0	3.9	992
650	0.28	4.1	10.1	2439
700	0.04	2.7	7.1	1631
200 variables				
780	0.99	11.6	10.0	1836
820	0.95	48.5	43.7	7742
860	0.40	81.7	125.8	22729
900	0.07	26.6	92.4	17111

7.2.1. *Comparing different DP implementations*

One may raise the question whether our (not highly optimized) DP implementation is efficient enough to be representative of backtracking-based SAT algorithms. We attempt to answer this question by comparing our DP with the executable code of Tableau [11].

The results for 150- and 200-variable uniform random 3-cnf problems are presented in Table IV. In order to make a quick comparison within a limited time frame, we ran experiments in the under- and over-constrained regions rather than at the phase-transition point. We used min-degree as an initial ordering consulted by both (dynamic-ordering) algorithms Tableau and DP in tie-breaking situations. In most cases, Tableau was 2-4 times faster than DP, while in some DP was faster or comparable to Tableau.

On chains, the behavior pattern of Tableau was similar to that of DP. Table V compares the runtime histograms for DP and Tableau on chain problems showing that both algorithms were encountering rare hard problems, although Tableau usually encountered hard problems less frequently than DP. Some problem instances that were hard for DP were easy for Tableau, and vice versa.

Due to the time limitations, we were unable to compare our implementation with various other state-of-the-art versions of the Davis-Putnam procedure available in the literature. However, although more sophisticated recent versions of DP (including Tableau) can be more efficient than our implementation, this difference does not change the key distinctions made between backtracking- and resolution-based approaches. Namely, good heuristics may reduce, but are unlikely to eliminate all rare extremely hard instances for backtracking-based algorithms; on the other hand, the complexity of directional resolution is always bounded by the induced width. Most of experiments in this paper use our implementation of DP. Having the source code for DP allowed us more control over the experiments (e.g., bounding the number of deadends) than having only the executable code for Tableau.

Table V. Histograms of DP and Tableau runtimes (log-scale) on chains having $Ncliq = 15$, $N = 8$, and C from 21 to 27, 200 instances per column. Each row defines a runtime range, and each entry is the frequency of instances within the range. The experiments were performed on Sun UltraSPARC.

Time	C=21	C=23	C=25
Tableau runtime histogram			
$[0,1)$	195	189	166
$[1,10)$	0	2	12
$[10,10^2)$	0	3	14
$[10^2,\infty)$	5	6	8
DP runtime histogram			
$[0,1)$	193	180	150
$[1,10)$	2	3	8
$[10,10^2)$	2	2	11
$[10^2,\infty)$	3	15	31

8. Combining search and resolution

The complementary properties of DP and DR suggest combining both into a hybrid scheme (note that algorithm DP already includes a limited amount of resolution in the form of unit propagation). We will present two general parameterized schemes integrating bounded resolution with search. The hybrid scheme BDR-DP(i) performs bounded resolution prior to search, while the other scheme called DCDR(b) uses it dynamically during search.

8.1. Algorithm BDR-DP(i)

The resolution operation helps detecting inconsistent subproblems and thus can prevent DP from unnecessary backtracking. Yet, resolution can be costly. One way of limiting the complexity of resolution is to bound the size of the recorded resolvents. This yields the incomplete algorithm *bounded directional resolution*, or $BDR(i)$, presented in Figure 23, where i bounds the number of variables in a resolvent. The algorithm coincides with DR except that resolvents with more than i variables are not recorded. This bounds the size of the directional extension $E_o^i(\varphi)$ and, therefore, the complexity of the algorithm. The time and space complexity of BDR(i) is $O(n \cdot exp(i))$. The algorithm is sound but incomplete. Algorithm $BDR(i)$ followed by DP is named *BDR-DP(i)* [8]. Clearly, BDR-DP(0) coincides with DP while for $i > w_o^*$ BDR-DP(i) coincides with DR (each resolvent is recorded).

[8] Note that DP always uses the 2-literal-clauses dynamic variable ordering heuristic.

Bounded Directional Resolution: BDR(i)
Input: A *cnf* theory φ, $o = Q_1, ..., Q_n$, and bound i.
Output: The decision of whether φ is satisfiable.
If it is, a *bounded directional extension* $E_o^i(\varphi)$.
1. **Initialize:** generate a partition of clauses, $bucket_1, ..., bucket_n$, where $bucket_i$ contains all the clauses whose highest literal is Q_i.
2. **For** $i = n$ to 1 do:
    resolve each pair $\{(\alpha \vee Q_i), (\beta \vee \neg Q_i)\} \subseteq bucket_i$.
    If $\gamma = \alpha \vee \beta$ is empty, return "φ is unsatisfiable"
    else if γ contains no more than i propositions,
    add γ to the bucket of its highest variable.
3.Return $E_o^i(\varphi) = \bigcup_i bucket_i$.

Figure 23. Algorithm Bounded Directional Resolution (BDR).

Table VI. DP versus BDR-DP(i) for $2 \leq i \leq 4$ on uniform random 3-cnfs with 150 variables, 600 to 725 clauses, and positive literal probability $p = 0.5$. The induced width w_o^* along the min-width ordering varies from 107 to 122. Each row presents average values on 100 instances (Sun Sparc 4).

Num of cls	DP		BDR-DP(2)				BDR-DP(3)				BDR-DP(4)				w_o^*
	Time	Dead ends	BDR time	DP time	Dead ends	New cls	BDR time	DP time	Dead ends	New cls	BDR time	DP time	Dead ends	New cls	
600	4.6	784	0	4.6	786	0	0.1	4.1	692	16	1.7	8.5	638	731	113
625	8.9	1487	0	8.9	1503	0	0.1	8.2	1346	18	1.9	16.8	1188	805	114
650	11.2	1822	0.1	11.2	1821	0	0.1	10.3	1646	19	2.3	21.4	1421	889	115
675	10.2	1609	0.1	9.9	1570	0	0.1	9.1	1405	21	2.6	19.7	1232	975	116
700	7.9	1214	0.1	7.9	1210	0	0.1	7.5	1116	23	3	16.6	969	1071	117
725	6.1	910	0.1	6.1	904	0	0.1	5.7	820	25	3.5	13.3	728	1169	118

8.2. *Empirical evaluation of BDR-DP(i)*

We tested BDR-DP(i) for different values of i on uniform 3-cnfs, chains, (k,m)-trees, and on DIMACS benchmarks. In most cases, BDR-DP(i) achieved its optimal performance for intermediate values of i.

8.2.1. *Performance on uniform 3-cnfs*

These results for BDR-DP(i) ($0 \leq i \leq 4$) on a class of uniform random 3-cnfs are presented in Table VI. It shows the average time and number of deadends for DP, the average BDR(i) time, DP time and the number of deadends after preprocessing, as well as the average number of new clauses added by BDR(i). An alternative summary of the same data is given in Figure 24, comparing DP and BDR-DP(i) time. It also demonstrates the increase in the number of clauses and the corresponding reduction in the number of deadends. For $i = 2$, almost no new clauses are generated (Figure 24c). Indeed, the graphs for DP and BDR-DP(2) practically coincide. Incrementing i by 1 results in a two orders of magnitude increase in the number of generated clauses, while the number of deadends decreases by 100-200, as shown in Figure 24c.

The results suggest that BDR-DP(3) is the most cost-effective on these problem clases (see Figure 24a). It is slightly faster than DP and BDR-DP(2) (BDR-DP(2) coincides with DP on this problem set) and significantly faster than BDR-DP(4). Table VI shows that BDR(3) takes only 0.1 second on average, while BDR(4) takes up to

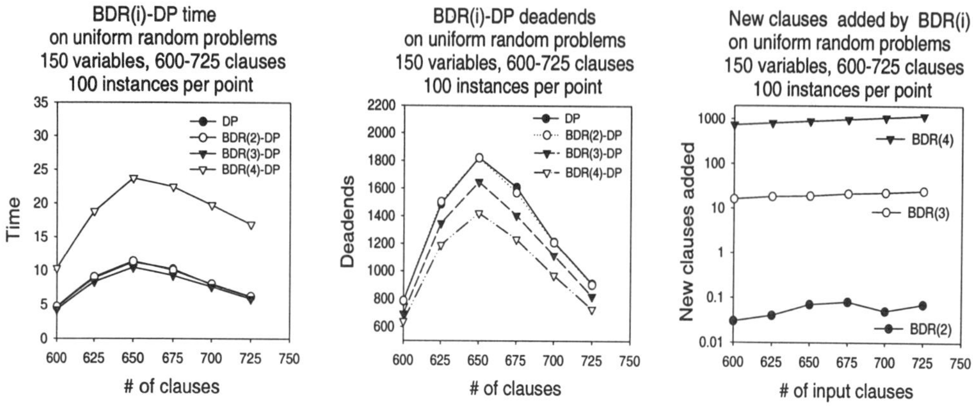

(a) time (b) deadends (c) new clauses

Figure 24. BDR-DP(i) on a class of uniform random 3-cnf problems. (150 variables, 600 to 725 clauses). The induced width along the min-width ordering varies from 107 to 122. Each data point corresponds to 100 instances. Note that the plots for DP and BDR(2)-DP in (a) and (b) almost coincide (the white-circle plot for BDR(2)-DP overlaps with the black-circle plot for DP).

Table VII. DP versus BDR-DP(i) for $i = 3$ and $i = 4$ on uniform 3-cnfs with 200 variables, 900 to 1400 clauses, and with positive literal probability $p = 0.7$. Each row presents mean values on 20 experiments.

Num of cls	DP		BDR-DP(3)				BDR-DP(4)			
	Time	Dead ends	BDR time	DP time	Dead ends	New cls	BDR time	DP time	Dead ends	New cls
900	1.1	0	0.3	1.1	0	11	8.4	1.7	1	657
1000	2.7	48	0.4	1.6	14	12	13.1	2.7	21	888
1100	8.8	199	0.6	27.7	685	18	20.0	50.4	729	1184
1200	160.2	3688	0.8	141.5	3271	23	28.6	225.7	2711	1512
1300	235.3	5027	1.0	219.1	4682	28	39.7	374.4	4000	1895
1400	155.0	3040	1.2	142.9	2783	34	54.4	259.0	2330	2332

Table VIII. DP versus BDR-DP(3) on uniform random 3-cnfs with $p = 0.5$ at the phase-transition point (C/N=4.3): 150 variables and 645 clauses, 200 variables and 860 clauses, 250 variables and 1075 clauses. The induced width w_o^* was computed for the min-width ordering. The results in the first two rows summarize 100 experiments, while the last row represents 40 experiments.

$< vars, cls >$	DP		BDR-DP(3)				w_o^*
	Time	Dead ends	BDR time	DP time	Dead ends	New cls	
$< 150, 650 >$	11.2	1822	0.1	10.3	1646	19	115
$< 200, 860 >$	81.3	15784	0.1	72.9	14225	18	190
$< 250, 1075 >$	750	115181	0.1	668.8	102445	19	1094

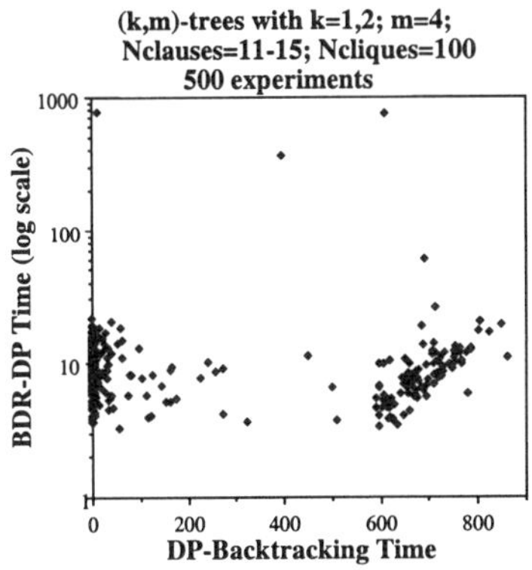

Figure 25. DP and BDR-DP(3) on (k-m)-trees, k=1,2, m=4, Ncliq=100, and Ncls=11 to 15. 50 instances per each set of parameters (total of 500 instances), an instance per point.

3.5 seconds and indeed generates many more clauses. Observe also that DP is slightly faster when applied after BDR(3). Interestingly, for $i = 4$ the time of DP almost doubles although fewer deadends are encountered. For example, in Table VI, for the problem set with 650 clauses, DP takes on average 11.2 seconds but after preprocessing by BDR(4) it takes 21.4 seconds. This can be explained by the significant increase in the number of clauses that need to be consulted by DP. Thus, as i increases beyond 3, DP's performance is likely to worsen while at the same time the complexity of preprocessing grows exponentially in i. Table VII presents additional results for problems having 200 variables where $p = 0.7$ [9].

Finally, we observe that the effect of BDR(3) is proportional to the theory size. In Table VIII we compare the results for three classes of uniform 3-cnf problems in the phase transition region. While this improvement was marginal for 150-variable problems (from 11.2 seconds for DP to 10.3 seconds for BDR-DP(3)), it was more pronounced on 200-variable problems (from 81.3 to 72.9 seconds), and on 250-variable problems (from 929.9 to 830.5 seconds). In all those cases the average speed-up is about 10%.

Our tentative empirical conclusion is that $i = 3$ is the optimal parameter for BDR-DP(i) on uniform random 3-cnfs.

8.2.2. *Performance on chains and (k,m)-trees*

The experiments with chains showed that BDR-DP(3) easily solved almost all instances that were hard for DP. In fact, the performance of BDR-DP(3) on chains was comparable to that of DR and backjumping (see Figure 20b).

Experimenting with (k, m)-trees, while varying the number of clauses per clique, we discovered again exceptionally hard problems for DP. The results on (1,4)-trees and on (2,4)-trees are presented in Table IX. In these experiments we terminated DP once it exceeded 20,000 dead-ends (around 700 seconds). This happened in 40% of (1,4)-trees with $Ncls = 13$, and in 20% of (2,4)-trees with $Ncls = 12$. Figure 25 shows a scatter diagram comparing DP and BDR-DP(3) time on the same data set together with an additional 100 experiments on (k,m)-trees having 15 cliques (total of 500 instances).

[9] Note that the average decrease in the number of deadends is not always monotonic: for problems having 1000 clauses, DP has an average of 48 deadends, BDR-DP(3) yields 14 deadends, but BDR-DP(4) yields 21 deadends. This may occur because DP uses dynamic variable ordering.

Table IX. BDR-DP(3) and DP (termination at 20,000 dead ends) on (k, m)-trees, k=1,2, m=4, Ncliq=100, and Ncls=11 to 14. 50 experiments per each row.

Number of	% sat	DP		BDR-DP(3)			
		Time	Dead ends	BDR(3) time	DP after BDR(3) time	DP after BDR(3) dead ends	Number of new clauses
(1,4)-tree, *Ncls* = 11 to 14, *Ncliq* = 100 (total: 401 vars, 1100-1400 cls)							
1100	60	233.2	7475	5.4	17.7	2	298
1200	18	352.5	10547	7.5	1.2	7	316
1300	2	328.8	9182	9.8	0.25	3	339
1400	0	174.2	4551	11.9	0.0	0	329
(2,4)-tree, *Ncls* = 11 to 14, *Ncliq* = 100 (total: 402 vars, 1100-1400 cls)							
1100	36	193.7	6111	4.1	23.8	568	290
1200	12	160.0	4633	6.0	1.6	25	341
1300	2	95.1	2589	8.4	0.1	0	390
1400	0	20.1	505	10.3	0.0	0	403

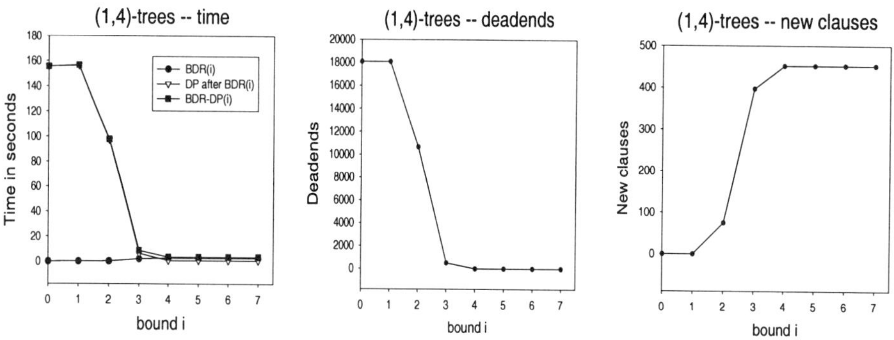

(a) time (b) deadends (c) new clauses

Figure 26. BDR-DP(i) on 100 instances of (1,4)-trees, $Ncliq = 100$, $Ncls = 11$, $w^*_{md} = 4$ (termination at 50,000 deadends). (a) Average time, (b) the number of dead-ends, and (c) the number of new clauses are plotted as functions of the parameter i. Note that the plot for BDR-DP(i) practically coincides with the plot for DP when $i \leq 3$, and with DP when $i > 3$.

As in the case of 3-cnf chains we observed that the majority of the exceptionally hard problems were unsatisfiable. For fixed m, when k is small and the number of cliques is large, hard instances for DP appeared more frequently.

The behavior of BDR-DP(i) as a function of i on structured bounded-w^* theories is demonstrated in Figures 26 and 27. In these experiments we used min-degree ordering that yielded smaller average w^* (denoted w^*_{md}) than input ordering, min-width ordering, and min-cardinality ordering (see [58] for details). Figure 26 shows results for (1,4)-trees, while Figure 27a presents the results for (4,8)-trees, (5,12)-trees, and (8,12)-trees. Each point represents an average over 100 instances. We observed that for relatively low-

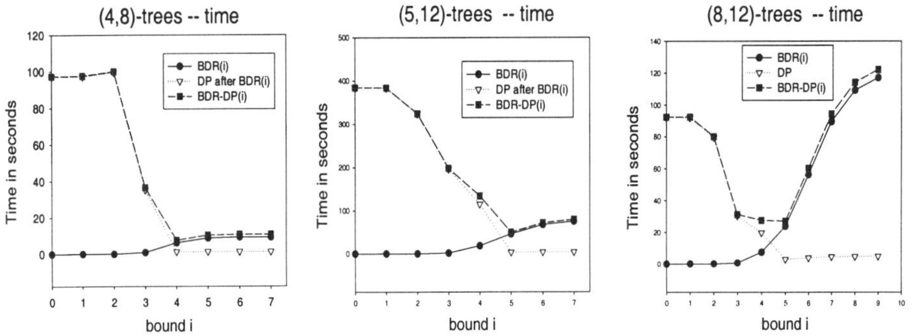

(a) (4,8)-trees, $w^*_{md} = 9$ (b) (5,12)-trees, $w^*_{md} = 12$ (c) (8,12)-trees, $w^*_{md} = 14$

Figure 27. BDR-DP(i) on 3 classes of (k,m)-tree problems: (a) (4,8)-trees, $Ncliq = 60$, $Ncls = 23$, $w^*_{md} = 9$, (b) (5,12)-trees, $Ncliq = 60$, $Ncls = 36$, $w^* = 12$, and (c) (8,12)-trees, $Ncliq = 50$, $Ncls = 34$, $w^* = 14$ (termination at 50,000 deadends). 100 instances per each problem class. Average time, the number of dead-ends, and the number of new clauses are plotted as functions of the parameter i.

Table X. Tableau, DP, DR, and BDR-DP(i) for i=3 and 4 on the Second DIMACS Challenge benchmarks. The experiments were performed on Sun Sparc 5 workstation.

Problem	**Tableau**	**DP**	Dead	**DR**	**BDR-DP(3)**			**BDR-DP(4)**			w^*
	time	time	ends	time	time	Dead ends	New cls	time	Dead ends	New cls	
aim-100-2_0-no-1	2148	>8988	$> 10^8$	*	0.9	5	26	0.60	0	721	54
dubois20	270	3589	3145727	0.2	349	262143	30	0.2	0	360	4
dubois21	559	7531	6291455	0.2	1379	1048575	20	0.2	0	390	4
ssa0432-003	12	45	4787	4	132	8749	950	40	1902	1551	19
bf0432-007	489	8688	454365	*	46370	677083	10084	*	*	*	131

w^* (1,4)-trees preprocessing time is not increasing when $i > 3$ since BDR(4) coincides with DR (Figure 26a), while for high-w^* (8,12)-trees the preprocessing time grows quickly with increasing i (Figure 26c). Since DP time after BDR(i) usually decreases monotonically with i, the total time of BDR-DP(i) is optimal for some intermediate values of i. We observe that for (1,4)-trees, BDR-DP(3) is most efficient, while for (4,8)-trees and for (5,12)-trees the optimal parameters are $i = 4$ and $i = 5$, respectively. For (8,12)-trees, the values $i = 3, 4$, and 5 provide the best performance.

8.2.3. *BDR-DP(i), DP, DR, and Tableau on DIMACS benchmarks*

We tested DP, Tableau, DR and BDR-DP(i) for i=3 and i=4 on the benchmark problems from the Second DIMACS Challenge. The results presented in Table X are quite interesting: while all benchmark problems were relatively hard for both DP and Tableau, some of them had very low w^* and were solved by DR in less than a second (e.g., *dubois20* and *dubois21*). On the other hand, problems having high induced width, such as *aim-100-2_0-no-1* ($w^* = 54$) and *bf0432-007* ($w^* = 131$) were intractable for DR, as expected. Algorithm BDR-DP(i) was often better than both "pure" DP and DR. For example, solving the benchmark *aim-100-2_0-no-1* took more than 2000 seconds for Tableau, more than 8000 seconds for DP, and DR ran out of memory, while BDR-DP(3) took only 0.9 seconds and reduced the number of DP deadends from more than 10^8 to 5. Moreover, preprocessing by BDR(4), which took only 0.6 seconds, made the problem backtrack-free. Note that the induced width of this problem is relatively high ($w^* = 54$). Interestingly, for some DIMACS problems (e.g., *ssa0432-003* and *bf0432-007*) preprocessing by BDR(3) actually worsened the performance of DP. Similar phenomenon was observed in some rare cases for (k,m)-trees (Figure 25).

In summary, *BDR-DP(i)* with intermediate values of i is overall more cost-effective than both DP and DR. On unstructured random uniform 3-cnfs BDR-DP(3) is comparable to DP, on low-w^* chains it is comparable to DR, and on intermediate-w^* (k,m)-trees, BDR-DP(i) for $i = 3, 4, 5$ outperforms both DR and DP. We believe that the transition from i=3 to i=4 on uniform problems is too sharp, and that intermediate levels of preprocessing may provide a more refined trade-off.

8.3. Algorithm DCDR(b)

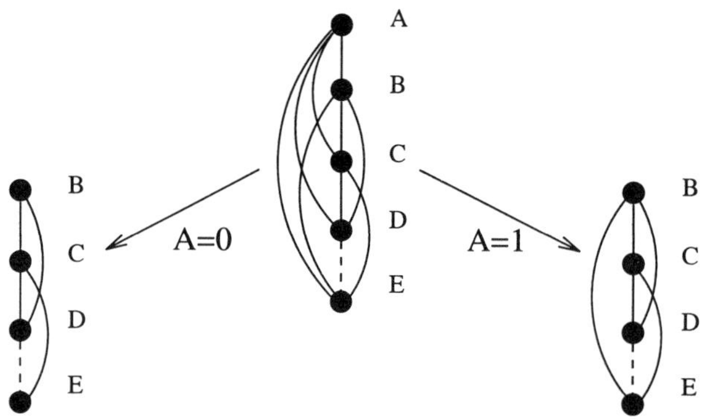

Figure 28. The effect of conditioning on A on the interaction graph of theory $\varphi = \{(\neg C \vee E), (A \vee B \vee C), (\neg A \vee B \vee E), (\neg B \vee C \vee D)\}$.

The second method of combining DP and DR that we consider uses resolution dynamically during search. We propose a class of hybrid algorithms that select a set of *conditioning* variables (also called a *cutset*), such that instantiating those variables results in a low-width theory tractable for DR [10]. The hybrids run DP on the cutset variables and DR on the remaining ones, thus combining the virtues of both approaches. Like DR, they exploit low-w^* structure and produce an output theory that facilitates model generation, while using less space and allowing less average time, like DP.

The description of the hybrid algorithms uses a new notation introduced below. An instantiation of a set of variables $C \subseteq X$ is denoted $I(C)$. The theory φ conditioned on the assignment $I(C)$ is called a *conditional theory* of φ relative to $I(C)$, and is denoted as $\varphi_{I(C)}$. The effect of conditioning on C is deletion of variables in C from the interaction

[10] This is a generalization of the cycle-cutset algorithm proposed in [22] which transforms the interaction graph of a theory into a tree.

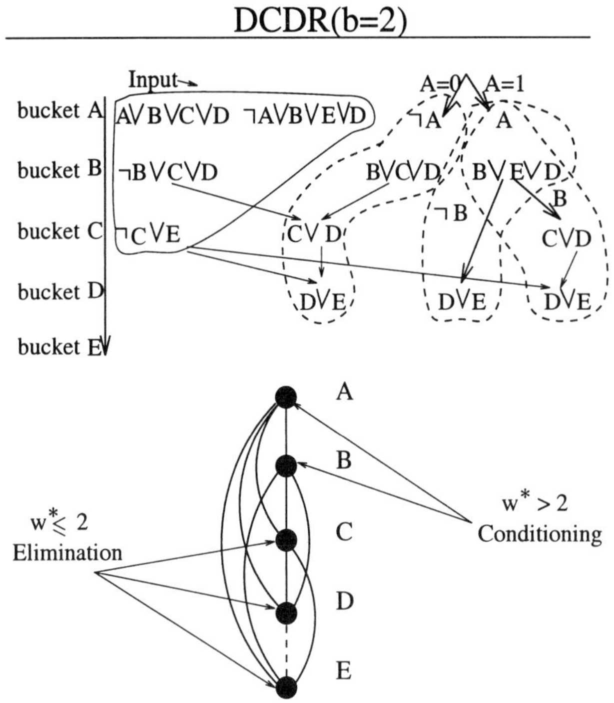

Figure 29. A trace of DCDR(2) on the theory $\varphi = \{(\neg C \vee E), (A \vee B \vee C), (\neg A \vee B \vee E), (\neg B \vee C \vee D)\}$.

graph. Therefore the *conditional interaction graph* of φ with respect to $I(C)$, denoted $G(\varphi_{I(C)})$, is obtained from the interaction graph of φ by deleting the nodes in C (and all their incident edges). The *conditional width* and *conditional induced width* of a theory φ relative to $I(C)$, denoted $w_{I(C)}$ and $w^*_{I(C)}$, respectively, are the width and induced width of the interaction graph $G(\varphi_{I(C)})$.

For example, Figure 28 shows the interaction graph of theory $\varphi = \{(\neg C \vee E), (A \vee B \vee C), (\neg A \vee B \vee E), (\neg B \vee C \vee D)\}$ along the ordering $o = (E, D, C, B, A)$ having width and induced width 4. Conditioning on A yields two conditional theories: $\varphi_{A=0} = \{(\neg C \vee E), (B \vee C), (\neg B \vee C \vee D)\}$, and $\varphi_{A=1} = \{(\neg C \vee E), (B \vee E), (\neg B \vee C \vee D)\}$. The ordered interaction graphs of $\varphi_{A=0}$ and $\varphi_{A=1}$ are also shown in Figure 28. Clearly, $w_o(B) = w^*_o(B) = 2$ for theory $\varphi_{A=0}$, and $w_o(B) = w^*_o(B) = 3$ for theory $\varphi_{A=1}$. Note that, besides deleting A and its incident edges from the interaction graph, an assignment may also delete some other edges (e.g., $A = 0$ removes the edge between B and E because the clause $(\neg A \vee B \vee E)$ becomes satisfied).

The conditioning variables can be selected in advance ("statically"), or during the algorithm's execution ("dynamically"). In our experiments, we focused on the dynamic version *Dynamic Conditioning + DR (DCDR)* that was superior to the static one.

Algorithm DCDR(b) guarantees that the induced width of variables that are resolved upon is bounded by b. Given a consistent partial assignment $I(C)$ to a set of variables C, the algorithm performs resolution over the remaining variables having $w^*_{I(C)} < b$. If there are no such variables, the algorithm selects a variable and attempts to assign it a value consistent with $I(C)$. The idea of DCDR(b) is demonstrated in Figure 29 for the theory $\varphi = \{(\neg C \vee E), (A \vee B \vee C \vee D), (\neg A \vee B \vee E \vee D), (\neg B \vee C \vee D)\}$. Assume that we run DCDR(2) on φ. Every variable is initially connected to at least 3 other variables in $G(\varphi)$. As a result, no resolution can be done and a conditioning variable is selected. Assume that A is selected. Assignment $A = 0$ adds the unit clause $\neg A$ which causes unit resolution in $bucket_A$, and produces a new clause $(B \vee C \vee D)$ from $(A \vee B \vee C \vee D)$. The assignment $A = 1$ produces clause $(B \vee E \vee D)$. In Figure 29, the original clauses are shown on the left as a partitioning into buckets. The new clauses are shown on the right, within the corresponding search-tree branches.

Following the branch for $A = 0$ we get a conditional theory $\{(\neg B \vee C \vee D), (B \vee C \vee D), (\neg C \vee E)\}$. Since the degrees of all the variables in the corresponding (conditional) interaction graph are now 2 or less, we can proceed with resolution. We select B, perform resolution in its bucket, and record the resolvent $(C \vee D)$ in $bucket_C$. The resolution in $bucket_C$ creates clause $(D \vee E)$. At this point, the algorithm terminates, returning the assignment $A = 0$, and the conditional directional extension $\varphi \wedge (B \vee C \vee D) \wedge (C \vee D) \wedge (D \vee E)$.

The alternative branch of $A = 1$ results in the conditional theory $\{(B \vee E \vee D), (\neg B \vee C \vee D), (\neg C \vee E)\}$. Since each variable is connected to three other variables, no resolution is possible. Conditioning on B yields the conditional theory $\{(E \vee D), (\neg C \vee E)\}$ when $B = 0$, and the conditional theory $\{(C \vee D), (\neg C \vee E)\}$ when $B = 1$. In both cases, the algorithm terminates, returning $A = 1$, the assignment to B, and the corresponding conditional directional extension.

Algorithm DCDR(b) (Figure 30) takes as an input a propositional theory φ and a parameter b bounding the size of resolvents. Unit propagation is performed first (lines 1-2). If no inconsistency is discovered, DCDR proceeds to its primary activity: choosing between resolution and conditioning. While there is a variable Q connected to at most b other variables in the current interaction graph conditioned on the current assignment, DCDR resolves upon Q (steps 4-9). Otherwise, it selects an unassigned variable (step 10), adds it to the cutset (step 11), and continues recursively with the conditional theory $\varphi \wedge \neg Q$. An unassigned variable is selected using the same dynamic variable ordering heuristic that is used by DP. Should the theory prove inconsistent the algorithm switches to the conditional theory $\varphi \wedge Q$. If both positive and negative assignments to Q are inconsistent the algorithm backtracks to the previously assigned variable. It returns to the previous level of recursion and the corresponding state of φ, discarding all resolvents added to φ after the previous assignment was made. If the algorithm does not find any consistent partial assignment it decides that the theory is inconsistent and returns an empty cutset and an empty directional extension. Otherwise, it returns an assignment $I(C)$ to the cutset C, and the conditional directional extension $E_o(\varphi_{I(C)})$ where o is the variable ordering dynamically constructed by the algorithm. Clearly, the conditional induced width $w^*_{I(C)}$ of φ's interaction graph with respect to o and to the assignment $I(C)$ is bounded by b.

THEOREM 12.: (DCDR(b) soundness and completeness) *Algorithm DCDR(b) is sound and complete for satisfiability. If a theory φ is satisfiable, any model of φ consistent with the output assignment $I(C)$ can be generated backtrack-free in $O(|E_o(\varphi_{I(C)})|)$ time where o is the ordering computed dynamically by DCDR(b).* □

DCDR(φ, X, b)
Input: A cnf theory φ over variables X; a bound b.
Output: A decision of whether φ is satisfiable. If it is, an assignment $I(C)$ to its conditioning variables, and the conditional directional extension $E_o(\varphi_{I(C)})$.
1. **if** unit_propagate(φ) = *false*, return(*false*);
2. **else** $X \leftarrow X -$ { variables in unit clauses }
3. **if** no more variables to process, return *true*;
4. **else while** $\exists Q \in X$ s.t. $degree(Q) \leq b$ in the current graph
5. resolve over Q
6. **if** no empty clause is generated,
7. add all resolvents to the theory
8. **else** return *false*
9. $X \leftarrow X - \{Q\}$
10. Select a variable $Q \in X$; $X \leftarrow X - \{Q\}$
11. $C \leftarrow C \cup \{Q\}$;
12. return(DCDR($\varphi \wedge \neg Q$, X, b) $\vee$
DCDR($\varphi \wedge Q$, X, b)).

Figure 30. Algorithm DCDR(b).

THEOREM 13. : (DCDR(b) complexity) *The time complexity of algorithm DCDR(b) is* $O(n2^{\alpha \cdot b+|C|})$, *where* C *is the largest cutset ever conditioned upon by the algorithm, and* $\alpha \leq log_2 9$. *The space complexity is* $O(n \cdot 2^{\alpha \cdot b})$. □

The parameter b can be used to control the trade-off between search and resolution. If $b \geq w^*_o(\varphi)$, where o is the ordering used by DCDR(b), the algorithm coincides with DR having time and space complexity exponential in $w^*(\varphi)$. It is easy to show that the ordering generated by DCDR(b) in case of no conditioning yields a min-degree ordering. Thus, given b and a min-degree ordering o, we are guaranteed that DCDR(b) coincides with DR if $w^*_o \leq b$. If $b < 0$, the algorithm coincides with DP. Intermediate values of b allow trading space for time. As b increases, the algorithm requires more space and less time (see also [18]). However, there is no guaranteed worst-case time improvement over DR. It was shown [7] that the size of the smallest *cycle-cutset* C (a set of nodes that breaks all cycles in the interaction graph, leaving a tree, or a forest), and the smallest induced width, w^*, obey the relation $|C| \geq w^* - 1$. Therefore, for $b = 1$, and for a corresponding cutset C_b, $\alpha \cdot b + |C_b| \geq w^* + \alpha - 1 \geq w^*$, where the left side of this inequality is the exponent that determines complexity of DCDR(b) (Theorem 13). In practice, however, backtracking search rarely demonstrates its worst-case performance and thus the average complexity of DCDR(b) is superior to its worst-case bound as will be confirmed by our experiments.

Algorithm DCDR(b) uses the 2-literal-clause ordering heuristic for selecting conditioning variables as used by DP. Random tie-breaking is used for selecting the resolution variables.

8.4. Empirical evaluation of DCDR(b)

We evaluated the performance of DCDR(b) as a function of b. We tested problem instances in the 50%-satisfiable region (the phase transition region). The results for

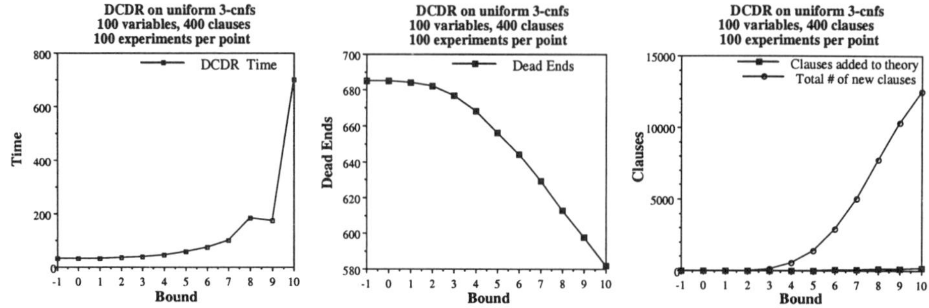

(a) uniform 3-cnfs

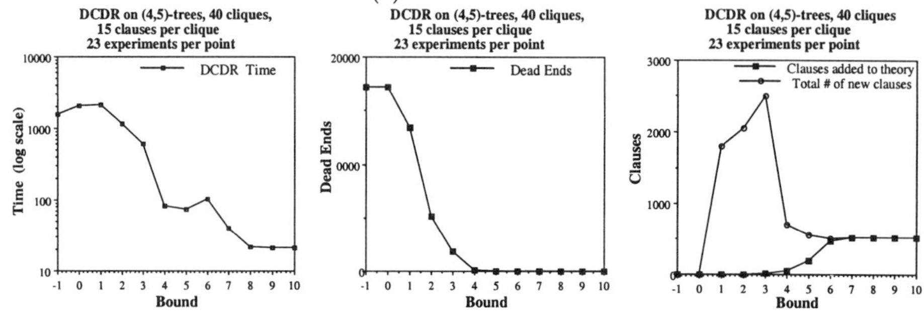

(b) (4,5)-trees

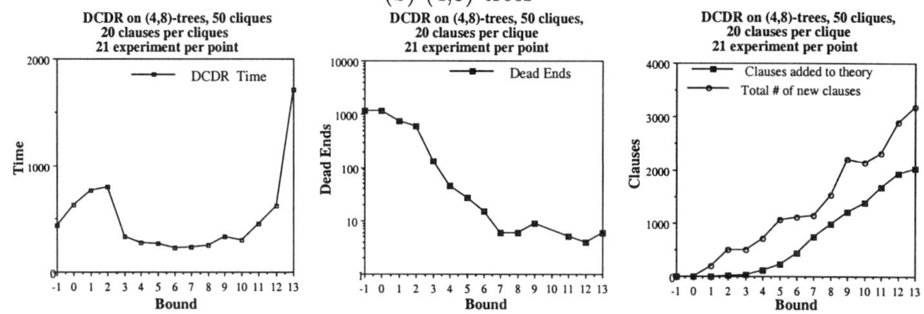

(c) (4,8)-trees

Figure 31. DCDR(b) on three different classes of 3-cnf problems. Average time, the number of dead-ends, and the number of new clauses are plotted as functions of the parameter b.

different b and three different problem structures are summarized in Figures 31-33. Figure 31(a) presents the results for uniform 3-cnfs having 100 variables and 400 clauses. Figures 31(b) and 31(c) focus on $(4,5)$-trees and on $(4,8)$-trees, respectively. We plotted the average time, the number of dead-ends, and the number of new clauses generated as functions of the bound b (we plot both the total number of generated clauses and the number of clauses actually added to the output theory excluding tautologies and subsumed clauses).

As expected, the performance of DCDR(b) depends on the induced width of the theories. We observed three different patterns:

– On problems having large w^*, such as uniform 3-cnfs in the phase-transition region (see Figure 31), the time complexity of DCDR(b) is similar to DP when b is small. However, when b increases, the CPU time grows exponentially. Apparently, the decline in the number of dead ends is too slow relative to the exponential (in b) growth in the total number of generated clauses. However, the number of new clauses actually *added* to the theory grows slowly. Consequently, the final conditional directional extensions have manageable sizes. We obtained similar results when experimenting with uniform theories having 150 variables and 640 clauses.

– Since DR is equivalent to DCDR(b) whenever b is equal or greater then w^*, for theories having small induced width, DCDR(b) indeed coincides with DR even for small values of b. Figure 31(b) demonstrates this behavior on (4,5)-trees with 40 cliques, 15 clauses per clique, and induced width 6. For $b \geq 8$, the time, the total number of clauses generated, as well as the number of new clauses added to the theory, do not change. With small values of b ($b = 0, 1, 2, 3$), the efficiency of DCDR(b) was sometimes worse than that of DCDR(-1), which is equivalent to DP, due to the overhead incurred by extra clause generation (a more accurate explanation is still required).

– On (k, m)-trees having larger size of cliques (Figure 31(c)), intermediate values of b yielded a better performance than both extremes. DCDR(-1) is still inefficient on structured problems while large induced width made pure DR too costly time- and space-wise. For (4,8)-trees, the optimal values of b appear between 5 and 8.

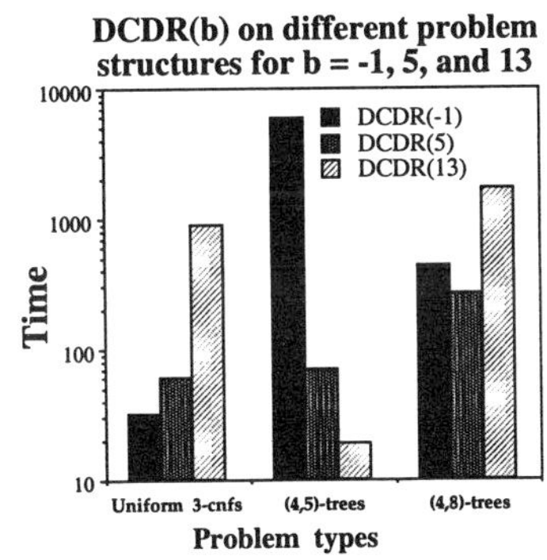

Figure 32. Relative performance of DCDR(b) for $b = -1, 5, 13$ on different types of problems.

Figure 32 summarizes the results for DCDR(-1), DCDR(5), and DCDR(13) on the three classes of problems. The intermediate bound b=5 seems to be overall more cost-effective than both extremes, b= -1 and b=13.

Figure 33 describes the average number of resolved variables which indicates the algorithm's potential for knowledge compilation. When many variables are resolved upon, the resulting conditional directional extension encodes a larger portion of the models, all sharing the assignment to the cutset variables.

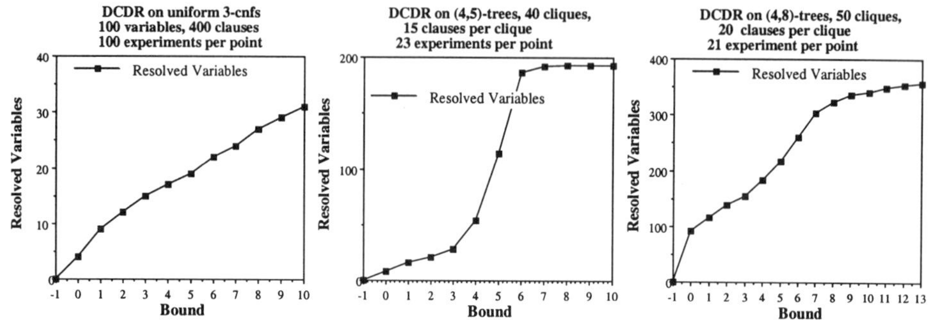

Figure 33. DCDR: the number of resolved variables on different problems.

9. Related Work

As mentioned before, directional resolution can be viewed as a particular case of a more general first-order method known as A-ordered resolution, or simply ordered resolution. Given a set of first-order clauses S, Kowalski and Hayes [52] defined an A-ordering as a total ordering on some subset of the set of literals appearing in S (subject to certain restrictions)[11] and proved the completeness of the resolution procedure that uses an A-ordering. Ordered resolution approach is widely used in the first-order literature [8, 38, 2, 27].

A propositional variant of ordered resolution, called here directional resolution, belongs to a family of elimination algorithms first analyzed for optimization tasks in dynamic programming [7] and later used in constraint satisfaction [63, 22] and in belief networks [53]. In fact, DR can be viewed as an adaptation of the constraint-satisfaction algorithm *adaptive consistency* to propositional satisfiability where the project-join operation over relational constraints is replaced by resolution over clauses [22, 26]. Using the same analogy, bounded resolution can be related to bounded consistency-enforcing algorithms, such as arc- path- and i-consistency [54, 32, 16], while bounded directional resolution, BDR(i), parallels directional i-consistency [22, 26]. Indeed, one of this paper's contributions is transferring constraint satisfaction techniques to the propositional framework.

The recent success of constraint processing which can be attributed to techniques combining search with limited forms of constraint propagation (e.g., forward-checking, MAC, constraint logic programming [45, 39, 62, 48]) that motivated our hybrid algorithms. In the SAT community, a popular form of combining constraint propagation with search is unit-propagation in DP. Our work extends this idea.

The hybrid algorithm BDR-DP(i), initially proposed in [25], corresponds to applying directional i-consistency prior to backtracking search for constraint processing. This approach was empirically evaluated for some constraint problems in [21]. However, those experiments were restricted to small and relatively easy problems, for which only a very limited amount of preprocessing was cost-effective. The presented experiments with BDR-DP(i) suggest that the results in [21] were too preliminary and that the idea of preprocessing before search is viable and should be further investigated.

[11] This definition of A-ordering is similar to Slagle's [66] but allows a finer discrimination between literals.

Our second hybrid algorithm, DCDR(b), proposed first in [59], generalizes the cycle-cutset approach that was presented for constraint satisfaction [15] using static variable ordering. This idea of alternating search with bounded resolution was also suggested and evaluated independently by van Gelder in [41], where a generalization of unit resolution known as *k-limited resolution* was proposed. This operation requires that the operands and the resolvent have at most k literals each. The hybrid algorithm proposed in [41] computes *k-closure* (namely, it applies k-limited resolution iteratively and eliminates subsumed clauses) between branching steps in DP-backtracking. This algorithm, augmented with several branching heuristics, was tested for k=2 (the combination called *2cl* algorithm), and demonstrated its superiority to DP, especially on larger problems. Algorithm DCDR(b) computes a *subset* of b-closure between its branching steps [12]. In this paper, we study the impact of b on the effectiveness of hybrid algorithms over different problem structures, rather than focus on a fixed b.

The relationship between clausal tree-clustering and directional resolutions extends the known relationship between variable elimination and the tree-clustering compilation scheme that was presented for constraint satisfaction in [23] and was extended to probabilistic frameworks in [17].

10. Summary and Conclusions

The paper compares two popular approaches to solving propositional satisfiability, backtracking search and resolution, and proposes two parameterized hybrid algorithms. We analyze the complexity of the original resolution-based Davis-Putnam algorithm, called here directional resolution (DR)), as a function of the induced width of the theory's interaction graph. Another parameter called diversity provides an additional refinement for tractable classes. Our empirical studies confirm previous results showing that on uniform random problems DR is indeed very inefficient. However, on structured problems such as k-tree embeddings, having bounded induced width, directional resolution outperforms the popular backtracking-based Davis-Putnam-Logemann-Loveland Procedure (DP). We also emphasize the knowledge-compilation aspects of directional resolution as a procedure for generating a join-tree. We show that it generates all prime implicates restricted to cliques in the clique-tree.

The two parameterized hybrid schemes, BDR-DP(i) and DCDR(b), allow a flexible combination of backtracking search with directional resolution. Both schemes use a parameter that bounds the size of the resolvents recorded. The first scheme, BDR-DP(i), uses bounded directional resolution BDR(i) as a preprocessing step, recording only new clauses of size i or less. The effect of the bound was studied empirically over both uniform and structured problems, observing that BDR-DP(i) frequently achieves its optimal performance for intermediate levels of i, outperforming both DR and DP. We also believe that the transition from i=3 to i=4 is too sharp and that intermediate levels of preprocessing are likely to provide even better trade-off. Encouraging results

[12] DCDR(b) performs resolution on variables that are connected to at most b other variables; therefore, the size of resolvents is bounded b. It does not, however, resolve over the variables having degree higher than b in the conditional interaction graph, although such resolutions can sometimes produce clauses of size not larger than b.

are obtained for BDR-DP(i) on DIMACS benchmark, where the hybrid algorithm easily solves some of the problems that were hard both for DR and DP.

The second hybrid scheme uses bounded resolution *during* search. Given a bound b, algorithm DCDR(b) instantiates a dynamically selected subset of conditioning variables such that the induced width of the resulting (conditional) theory and therefore the size of the resolvents recorded does not exceed b. When $b \leq 0$, $DCDR(b)$ coincides with DP, while for $b \geq w_o^*$ (on the resulting ordering o) it coincides with directional resolution. For intermediate b, DCDR(b) was shown to outperform both extremes on intermediate-w^* problem classes.

For both schemes selecting the bound on the resolvent size allows a flexible scheme that can be adapted to the problem structure and to computational resources. Our current "rule of thumb" for DCDR(b) is to use small b when w^* is large, relying on search, large b when w^* is small, exploiting resolution, and some intermediate bound for intermediate w^*. Additional experiments are necessary to further demonstrate the spectrum of optimal hybrids relative to problem structures.

Appendix A: Proofs

Theorem 2: (model generation)
Given $E_o(\varphi)$ of a satisfiable theory φ, the procedure find-model *generates a model of φ backtrack-free, in time $O(|E_o(\varphi)|)$.*
Proof: Suppose the model-generation process is not backtrack-free. Namely, suppose there exists a truth assignment $q_1, ..., q_{i-1}$ for the first $i-1$ variables in the ordering $o = (Q_1, ..., Q_n)$ that satisfies all the clauses in the buckets of Q_1,..., Q_{i-1}, but cannot be extended by any value of Q_i without falsifying some clauses in $bucket_i$. Let α and β be two clauses in the bucket of Q_i that cannot be satisfied simultaneously, given the assignment $q_1, ..., q_{i-1}$. Clearly, Q_i appears negatively in one clause and positively in the other. Consequently, while being processed by DR, α and β should be resolved, resulting in a clause γ that must reside now in a $bucket_j$, $j < i$. That clause can not allow the partial model $q_1, ..., q_i$, which contradicts our assumption. Since the model-generation is backtrack-free, it takes $O(|E_o(\varphi)|)$ time consulting all the buckets. □

Theorem 3: (complexity)
Given a theory φ and an ordering o, the complexity of algorithm DR is $O(n|E_o(\varphi)|^2)$ where n is the number of variables.
Proof: There are at most n buckets, each containing no more clauses than the output directional extension. The number of resolution operations in a bucket does not exceed the number of all possible pairs of clauses, which is quadratic in the size of the bucket. This yields the complexity $O(n \cdot |E_o(\varphi)|^2)$. □

Lemma 1: *Given a theory φ and an ordering o, $G(E_o(\varphi))$ is a subgraph of $I_o(G(\varphi))$.*
Proof: The proof is by induction on the variables along ordering $o = (Q_1, ..., Q_n)$. The induction hypothesis is that all the edges incident to $Q_n, ..., Q_i$ in $G(E_o(\varphi))$ appear also in $I_o(G(\varphi))$. The claim is clearly true for Q_n. Assume that the claim is true for $Q_n, ..., Q_i$; as we show, this assumption implies that if (Q_{i-1}, Q_j), $j < i-1$, is an

edge in $G(E_o(\varphi))$, then it also belongs to $I_o(G(\varphi))$. There are two cases: either Q_{i-1} and Q_j initially appeared in the same clause of φ and so are connected in $G(\varphi)$ and, therefore, also in $I_o(G(\varphi))$, or a clause containing both variables was added during directional resolution. In the second case, that clause was obtained while processing some bucket Q_t, where $t > i-1$. Since Q_{i-1} and Q_j appeared in the bucket of Q_t, each must be connected to Q_t in $G(E_o(\varphi))$ and, by the induction hypothesis, each will also be connected to Q_t in $I_o(G(\varphi))$. Since Q_{i-1} and Q_j are parents of Q_t, they must be connected in $I_o(G(\varphi))$. □

Lemma 2: *Given a theory φ and an ordering $o = (Q_1, ..., Q_n)$, if Q_i has at most k parents in the induced graph along o, then the bucket of a variable Q_i in $E_o(\varphi)$ contains no more than 3^{k+1} clauses.*

Proof: Given a clause α in the bucket of Q_i, there are three possibilities for each parent P: either P appears in α, or $\neg P$ appears in α, or neither of them appears in α. Since Q_i also appears in α, either positively or negatively, there are no more than $2 \cdot 3^k < 3^{k+1}$ different clauses in the bucket. □

Theorem 4: *(complexity of DR)*
Given a theory φ and an ordering of its variables o, the time complexity of algorithm DR along o is $O(n \cdot 9^{w_o^*})$, and $E_o(\varphi)$ contains at most $n \cdot 3^{w_o^*+1}$ clauses, where w_o^* is the induced width of φ's interaction graph along o.

Proof: The result follows from lemmas 1 and 2. The interaction graph of $E_o(\varphi)$ is a subgraph of $I_o(G)$ (lemma 1), and the size of theories having $I_o(G)$ as their interaction graph is bounded by $n \cdot 3^{w^*(o)+1}$ (lemma 2). The time complexity of algorithm DR is bounded by $O(n \cdot |bucket_i|^2)$, where $|bucket_i|$ is the size of the largest bucket. By lemma 2, $|bucket_i| = O(3^{w^*(o)})$. Therefore, the time complexity is $O(n \cdot 9^{w^*(o)})$. □

Theorem 7: *Given a theory φ defined on variables $Q_1, ..., Q_n$, such that each symbol Q_i either (a) appears only negatively (only positively), or (b) it appears in exactly two clauses, then $div^*(\varphi) \leq 1$ and φ is tractable.*

Proof: The proof is by induction on the number of variables. If φ satisfies either (a) or (b), we can select a variable Q with the diversity of at most 1 and put it last in the ordering. Should Q have zero diversity (case a), no clause is added. If it has diversity 1 (case b), then at most one clause is added when processing its bucket. Assume the clause is added to the bucket of Q_j. If Q_j is a single-sign symbol, it will remain so. The diversity of its bucket will be zero. Otherwise, since there are at most two clauses containing Q_j, and one of these was in the bucket of Q_n, the current bucket of Q_j (after processing Q_n) cannot contain more than two clauses. The diversity of Q_j is therefore 1. We can now assume that after processing $Q_n, ..., Q_i$ the induced diversity is at most 1, and can also show that processing Q_{i-1} will leave the diversity at most 1. □

Theorem 8: *Algorithm* min-diversity *generates a minimal diversity ordering of a theory in time $O(n^2 \cdot c)$, where n is the number of variables and c is the number of clauses in the input theory.*

Proof: Let o be an ordering generated by the algorithm and let Q_i be a variable whose diversity equals the diversity of the ordering. If Q_i is pushed up, its diversity can only increase. When it is pushed down, it must be replaced by a variable whose diversity is equal to or higher than the diversity of Q_i. Computing the diversity of a variable takes $O(c)$ time, and the algorithm checks at most n variables in order to select the one with the smallest diversity at each of n steps. This yields the total $O(n^2 \cdot c)$ complexity. □

Theorem 9: (DCDR(b) soundness and completeness)
Algorithm DCDR(b) is sound and complete for satisfiability. If a theory φ *is satisfiable, any model of* φ *consistent with the output assignment* $I(C)$ *can be generated backtrack-free in* $O(|E_o(\varphi_{I(C)})|)$ *time, where o is the ordering computed dynamically by DCDR(b).*
Proof: Given an assignment $I(C)$, DCDR(b) is equivalent to applying DR to the theory $\varphi_{I(C)}$ along ordering o. From Theorem 2 it follows that any model of $\varphi_{I(C)}$ can be found in a backtrack-free manner in time $O(|E_o(\varphi_{I(C)})|)$. □

Theorem 10: (DCDR(b) complexity) *The time complexity of algorithm DCDR(b) is* $O(n2^{\alpha \cdot b+|C|})$, *where C is the largest cutset ever instantiated by the algorithm, and* $\alpha \leq log_2 9$. *The space complexity is* $O(n \cdot 2^{\alpha \cdot b})$.
Proof: Given a cutset assignment, the time and space complexity of resolution steps within DCDR(b) is bounded by $O(n \cdot 9^b)$ (see theorem 4). Since in the worst-case backtracking involves enumerating all possible instantiations of the cutset variables C in $O(2^{|C|})$ time and $O(|C|)$ space, the total time complexity is $O(n \cdot 9^b \cdot 2^{|C|}) = O(n \cdot 2^{\alpha \cdot b+|C|})$, where C is the largest cutset ever instantiated by the algorithm, and $\alpha \leq log_2 9$. The total space complexity is $O(|C| + n \cdot 9^b) = O(n \cdot 9^b)$. □

References

1. S. Arnborg, D.G. Corneil, and A. Proskurowski. Complexity of finding embedding in a k-tree. *Journal of SIAM, Algebraic Discrete Methods*, 8(2):177–184, 1987.
2. D. Basin and H. Ganzinger. Complexity analysis based on ordered resolution. In *Proc. 11th IEEE Symposium on Logic in Computer Science*, pages 456–465. IEEE Computer Society Press, 1996.
3. R. Bayardo and D. Miranker. A complexity analysis of space-bound learning algorithms for the constraint satisfaction problem. In *Proceedings of the Thirteenth National Conference on Artificial Intelligence (AAAI-96)*, pages 298–304, 1996.
4. R.J. Bayardo and R.C. Schrag. Using CSP look-back techniques to solve real-world SAT instances. In *Proceedings of AAAI-97*, pages 203 –208, 1997.
5. A. Becker and D. Geiger. A sufficiently fast algorithm for finding close to optimal jnmction trees. In *Uncertainty in AI (UAI-96)*, pages 81–89, 1996.
6. R. Ben-Eliyahu and R. Dechter. Default reasoning using classical logic. *Artificial Intelligence*, 84:113–150, 1996.
7. U. Bertele and F. Brioschi. *Nonserial Dynamic Programming.* Academic Press, New York, 1972.
8. Chin-Liang Chang and Richard Char-Tung Lee. *Symbolic Logic and Mechanical Theorem Proving.* Academic Press, Inc., 1973.
9. P. Cheeseman, B. Kanefsky, and W.M. Taylor. Where the *Really* Hard Problems Are. In *Proceedings of the International Joint Conference on Artificial Intelligence*, pages 331–337, 1991.
10. S.A. Cook. The complexity of theorem-proving procedures. In *Proceedings of the 3rd Annual ACM Symposium on the Theory of Computing*, pages 151–158, 1971.
11. J.M. Crawford and L.D. Auton. Experimental results on the crossover point in satisfiability problems. In *Proceedings of the Eleventh National Conference on Artificial Intelligence*, pages 21–27, 1993.

12. J.M. Crawford and A.B. Baker. Experimental results on the application of satisfiability algorithms to scheduling problems. In *Proceedings of AAAI-94, Seattle, WA*, pages 1092 – 1097, 1994.
13. M. Davis, G. Logemann, and D. Loveland. A Machine Program for Theorem Proving. *Communications of the ACM*, 5:394–397, 1962.
14. M. Davis and H. Putnam. A computing procedure for quantification theory. *Journal of the Association of Computing Machinery*, 7(3), 1960.
15. R. Dechter. Enhancement Schemes for Constraint Processing: Backjumping, Learning, and Cutset Decomposition. *Artificial Intelligence*, 41:273–312, 1990.
16. R. Dechter. Constraint networks. In *Encyclopedia of Artificial Intelligence*, pages 276–285. John Wiley & Sons, 2nd edition, 1992.
17. R. Dechter. Bucket elimination: A unifying framework for probabilistic inference algorithms. In *Uncertainty in Artificial Intelligence (UAI-96)*, pages 211–219, 1996.
18. R. Dechter. Topological parameters for time-space tradeoffs. In *Uncertainty in Artificial Intelligence (UAI-96)*, pages 220–227, 1996.
19. R. Dechter and A. Itai. Finding all solutions if you can find one. In *UCI Technical report R23, 1992. Also in the Proceedings of the Workshop on tractable reasoning, AAAI-92*, 1992.
20. R. Dechter and I. Meiri. Experimental evaluation of preprocessing techniques in constraint satisfaction problems. In *International Joint Conference on Artificial Intelligence*, pages 271–277, 1989.
21. R. Dechter and I. Meiri. Experimental evaluation of preprocessing algorithms for constraint satisfaction problems. *Artificial Intelligence*, 68:211–241, 1994.
22. R. Dechter and J. Pearl. Network-based heuristics for constraint satisfaction problems. *Artificial Intelligence*, 34:1–38, 1987.
23. R. Dechter and J. Pearl. Tree clustering for constraint networks. *Artificial Intelligence*, pages 353–366, 1989.
24. R. Dechter and J. Pearl. Directed constraint networks: A relational framework for causal models. In *Proceedings of the Twelfth International Joint Conference on Artificial Intelligence (IJCAI-91), Sidney, Australia*, pages 1164–1170, 1991.
25. R. Dechter and I. Rish. Directional resolution: the Davis-Putnam procedure, revisited. In *Proceedings of KR-94*, 1994.
26. R. Dechter and P. van Beek. Local and global relational consistency. *Theoretical Computer Science*, pages 283–308, 1997.
27. A. del Val. A new method for consequence finding and compilation in restricted languages. In *Proceedings of AAAI-99*, 1999.
28. S. Even, A. Itai, and A. Shamir. On the complexity of timetable and multi-commodity flow. *SIAM Journal on Computing*, 5:691–703, 1976.
29. Y. El Fattah and R. Dechter. Diagnosing tree-decomposable circuits. In *International Joint Conference of Artificial Intelligence (IJCAI-95)*, pages 1742–1748, Montreal, Canada, August 1995.
30. Y. El Fattah and R. Dechter. An evaluation of structural parameters for probabilistic reasoning: results on benchmark circuits. In *UAI96*, pages 244–251, Portland, Oregon, August 1996.
31. J. Franco and M. Paul. Probabilistic analysis of the Davis-Putnam procedure for solving the satisfiability problem. *Discrete Appl. Math.*, 5:77 – 87, 1983.
32. E. C. Freuder. Synthesizing constraint expressions. *Communication of the ACM*, 21(11):958–965, 1978.
33. D. Frost and R. Dechter. Dead-end driven learning. In *AAAI-94: Proceedings of the Twelfth National Conference on Artificial Intelligence*, pages 294–300, 1994.
34. D. Frost and R. Dechter. In search of the best constraint satisfaction search. In *Proceedings of the Twelfth National Conference on Artificial Intelligence*, 1994.
35. D. Frost, I. Rish, and L. Vila. Summarizing CSP hardness with continuous probability distributions. In *Proc. of National Conference on Artificial Intelligence (AAAI97)*, pages 327–333, 1997.
36. D. H. Frost. Algorithms and heuristics for constraint satisfaction problems. Technical report, Phd thesis, Information and Computer Science, University of California, Irvine, California, 1997.

37. Z. Galil. On the complexity of regular resolution and the Davis-Putnam procedure. *Theoretical Computer Science*, 4:23–46, 1977.
38. H. Ganzinger, Chr. Meyer, and Chr. Weidenbach. Soft typing for ordered resolution. In *Automated Deduction — CADE'14*, volume 1249 of *Lecture Notes in Computer Science*, pages 321–335, Berlin, 1997. Springer-Verlag.
39. J. Gaschnig. A General Backtrack Algorithm That Eliminates Most Redundant Tests. In *Proceedings of the International Joint Conference on Artificial Intelligence*, page 247, 1977.
40. J. Gaschnig. Performance measurement and analysis of certain search algorithms. Technical Report CMU-CS-79-124, Carnegie Mellon University, 1979.
41. A. Van Gelder and Y. K. Tsuji. Satisfiability testing with more reasoning and less guessing. In *David, Johnson and Michael A. Trick, editors, Cliques, Coloring and Satisfiability*, 1996.
42. I. P. Gent and T. Walsh. The satisfiability constraint gap. *Artificial Intelligence*, 81:59–80, 1996.
43. A. Goerdt. Davis-Putnam resolution versus unrestricted resolution. *Annals of Mathematics and Artificial Intelligence*, 6:169–184, 1992.
44. A. Goldberg, P. Purdom, and C. Brown. Average time analysis of simplified Davis-Putnam procedures. *Information Processing Letters*, 15:72–75, 1982.
45. R. M. Haralick and G. L. Elliott. Increasing Tree Search Efficiency for Constraint Satisfaction Problems. *Artificial Intelligence*, 14:263–313, 1980.
46. J.N. Hooker and V. Vinay. Branching rules for satisfiability. In *Third International Symposium on Artificial Intelligence and Mathematics, Fort Lauderdale, Florida*, 1994.
47. B. A. Huberman and T. Hogg. Phase transitions in artificial intelligence systems. *Artificial Intelligence*, 33:155–171, 1987.
48. J. Jaffar and J. Lassez. Constraint logic programming: A survey. *Journal of Logic Programming*, 19(20):503–581, 1994.
49. R. Jeroslow and J. Wang. Solving propositional satisfiability problems. *Annals of Mathematics and Artificial Intelligence*, 1:167 -187, 1990.
50. K. Kask and R. Dechter. Gsat and local consistency. In *Proceedings of IJCAI-95*, pages 616–622, 1995.
51. H. Kautz and B. Selman. Pushing the envelope: planning, propositional logic, and stochastic search. In *Proceedings of AAAI-96*, 1996.
52. R. Kowalski and P. Hayes. Semantic trees in automatic theorem proving. *Machine Intelligence*, 4:87–101, 1969.
53. S.L. Lauritzen and D.J. Spiegelhalter. Local computation with probabilities on graphical structures and their application to expert systems. *Journal of the Royal Statistical Society, Series B*, 50(2):157–224, 1988.
54. A. K. Mackworth. Consistency in networks of relations. *Artificial Intelligence*, 8(1):99–118, 1977.
55. David Mitchell, Bart Selman, and Hector Levesque. Hard and Easy Distributions of SAT Problems. In *Proceedings of the Tenth National Conference on Artificial Intelligence*, pages 459–465, 1992.
56. P. Prosser. BM + BJ = BMJ. In *Proceedings of the Ninth Conference on Artificial Intelligence for Applications*, pages 257–262, 1983.
57. P. Prosser. Hybrid algorithms for constraint satisfaction problems. *Computational Intelligence*, 9(3):268–299, 1993.
58. I. Rish. *Efficient reasoning in graphical models.* PhD thesis, 1999.
59. I. Rish and R. Dechter. To guess or to think? hybrid algorithms for SAT (extended abstract). In *Proceedings of the International Conference on Principles and Practice of Constraint Programming (CP96)*, 1996.
60. I. Rish and D. Frost. Statistical analysis of backtracking on inconsistent CSPs. In *Proceedings of the International Conference on Principles and Practice of Constraint Programming (CP97)*, 1997.
61. N. Robertson and P. Seymour. Graph minor. xiii. the disjoint paths problem. *Combinatorial Theory, Series B*, 63:65–110, 1995.
62. D. Sabin and E. C. Freuder. Contradicting conventional wisdom in constraint satisfaction. In *ECAI-94*, pages 125–129, Amsterdam, 1994.

63. R. Seidel. A new method for solving constraint satisfaction problems. In *Proceedings of the Seventh International Joint Conference on Artificial Intelligence (IJCAI-81), Vancouver, Canada*, pages 338–342, 1981.
64. B. Selman, H. Kautz, and B. Cohen. Noise strategies for improving local search. In *Proceedings of AAAI94*, pages 337–343, 1994.
65. B. Selman, H. Levesque, and D. Mitchell. A New Method for Solving Hard Satisfiability Problems. In *Proceedings of the Tenth National Conference on Artificial Intelligence*, pages 440–446, 1992.
66. J.R. Slagle. Automatic theorem-proving with renamable and semantic resolution. *J. Ass. Comput. Mach.*, 14:687–697, 1967.
67. Barbara M. Smith and M. E. Dyer. Locating the phase transition in binary constraint satisfaction problems. *Artificial Intelligence*, 81:155–181, 1996.
68. B. M. Smyth and M. E. Dyer. Locating the phase transition in binary constraint satisfaction problems. *Artificial Intelligence*, 81:155–181, 1996.
69. R. E. Tarjan and M. Yannakakis. Simple linear-time algorithms to test chordality of graphs, test acyclicity of hypergraphs and selectively reduce acyclic hypergraphs. *SIAM Journal of Computation.*, 13(3):566–579, 1984.

SAT2000
I. Gent et al. (Eds.)
IOS Press, 2000

The Propositional Formula Checker HeerHugo

Jan Friso Groote[†]
SEN2, CWI, P.O. Box 94079, 1090 GB, Amsterdam, The Netherlands
Computing Science Department, Eindhoven University of Technology

Joost P. Warners[§¶]
SEN2, CWI, P.O. Box 94079, 1090 GB, Amsterdam, The Netherlands
Department of Technical Mathematics and Informatics, Faculty of Information Technology and Systems Delft University of Technology, P.O. Box 5031, 2600 GA Delft, The Netherlands

Abstract. HeerHugo is a propositional formula checker that determines whether a given formula is satisfiable or not. The underlying algorithm is based on a specific breadth–first search procedure, with several enhancements including unit resolution and 2–satisfiability tests. Its main ingredient is the branch/merge rule, that is inspired by an algorithm proposed by Stållmarck, which is protected by a software patent. In this paper, the main elements of the algorithm are discussed, and its remarkable effectiveness is illustrated with some examples and computational results.

Keywords: Satisfiability, Propositional logic, Theorem proving.
AMS subject classification: 03B05, 68Q20, 68T15.

1. Introduction

The satisfiability problem of propositional logic (SAT) is considered important in many disciplines, such as mathematical logic, electrical engineering, computer science, operations research etc. It was the first problem shown to be NP–complete [4], which means that it is considered unlikely that an algorithm exists that can solve any instance of SAT in polynomial time. It may be noted though that several subclasses of SAT exist, which allow a polynomial time algorithm, such as 2SAT and HornSAT [2, 8]. Over the years, many algorithms for solving satisfiability problems have been developed; for a comprehensive overview the reader is referred to [19]. The algorithms can basically be subdivided into two categories. Firstly, there are the *complete* algorithms; such algorithms find one or all satisfying solutions or prove that the formula under consideration is a contradiction. Examples of such algorithms are (variants of) the Davis–Putnam procedure (which we refer to as DPLL algorithms) [7, 6] and binary decision diagrams (BDDs) [3]. Secondly, there are *incomplete* algorithms. These search for a satisfying assignment; if one is found, the formula is solved. Unfortunately, such methods are not able to prove a formula contradictory. These methods include various kinds of local search [29, 18, 17].

In this paper, an implementation of a complete algorithm, called HeerHugo, is described. The initial purpose of this implementation was to validate correct operation of the Vital Processor Interlocking unit guarding the safety of all operations at the Dutch railway stations in Hoorn–Kersenboogerd and Heerhugowaard (see also [10, 16, 26]); hence the

† janfriso.groote@cwi.nl
§ j.p.warners@its.tudelft.nl
¶ Supported by the Dutch Organization for Scientific Research (NWO) under grant SION 612–33–001.

name of the solver. For this practical application HeerHugo turned out to be very effective and therefore it was decided to test HeerHugo's strength on other kinds of SAT problems as well.

HeerHugo is inspired by an algorithm proposed by Stållmarck[1], which can be interpreted as a *breadth first* search algorithm, with several enhancements (see also [31, 20, 37]). The actual algorithms implemented in HeerHugo differ substantially from Stållmarck's algorithm, as it operates on formulas in conjunctive normal form (CNF) and incorporates many logical rules that are more or less common in theorem proving. It seems to us that the breadth first search type algorithm is largely overlooked in the literature on practical satisfiability solving. The DPLL method [6], which seems to be the most widely used, is in fact a *depth first* search algorithm. It appears that for many classes of formulas breadth first search is substantially more effective than depth first search, especially for instances stemming from real–life applications; on the popular (at least for research purposes) difficult random 3SAT instances [27] depth–first search seems more effective. The effectiveness of HeerHugo is mainly due to its reasoning strength. Based on (nested) assumptions conclusions are drawn that are subsequently added to the formula; such conclusions include not only truth values of propositions, but also the equivalence of sets of variables. Note that implementations of DPLL algorithms that are enhanced with 'intelligent backjumping' techniques (such as GRASP [30] and SATO [40]), appear to have a comparable reasoning strength. Other (essentially depth first search) solvers that employ additional reasoning techniques are discussed in [14, 13].

Besides being a complete algorithm for determining satisfiability,
breadth first search can be applied as *preprocessing* technique to substantially reduce the size of the formula under consideration by restricting the number of nested assumptions. If during this process the empty clause is not derived, one could decide to switch to a DPLL or other algorithm.

This paper is organized as follows. In the next section we deal with the preliminaries and notation. HeerHugo is able to handle propositional formulas with all the well known connectives. It first translates a formula to a formula in conjunctive normal form, maintaining satisfiability, by introducing auxiliary variables. This transformation is briefly described in Section 3.1. Subsequently various simple inference rules are applied to simplify the formula under consideration as much as possible; these are specified in Section 3.2. The way the breadth–first search is carried out is discussed in Section 3.3. In the subsequent subsections some complexity issues and possible enhancements are mentioned. Section 4 and 5 are concerned with the description of HeerHugo's actual performance. Some specific effects of the simple inference rules are discussed, and a number of computational results are given. We conclude with a discussion in Section 6. In Appendix A it is explained how HeerHugo 2.0 can be obtained and used.

1.0.0.1. *Acknowledgements* Thanks go to Marc Bezem for helping to track some references, and to Bert Lisser and John Tromp for their comments on an earlier version of this manuscript. Also thanks are due to the referees whose suggestions contributed to the completeness and clarity of this paper.

[1] Stållmarck's prover is protected by a software patent [32].

2. Preliminaries and Notation

Let us start with introducing some notation. Let $\mathcal{P} = \{p, p_0, p_1, p_2, \ldots, q, r, \ldots\}$ be the set of *atomic propositions* or *variables*. Each proposition can be either *true* or *false*. We have a number of *connectives*: $\neg$ ('not' or 'negation'), $\vee$ ('or' or 'disjunction'), $\wedge$ ('and' or 'conjunction'), $\rightarrow$ ('implication') and $\leftrightarrow$ ('equivalence' or 'bi-implication'). Furthermore, a literal is an atomic proposition or its negation. Let $\mathcal{L} = \{l, l_0, l_1, l_2, \ldots\}$ be the set of *literals*. Propositional (sub)formulas are denoted by Φ and ψ. An example of a propositional formula Φ is

$$\Phi = (p_0 \leftrightarrow \neg p_1) \vee ((\neg p_0 \rightarrow p_2) \wedge (p_1)).$$

The satisfiability problem of propositional logic is to assign truth values to the propositions, such that the formula Φ evaluates to *true*, or to prove that no such assignment exists. If the formula is *true* for each assignment to the variables, it is called a *tautology*, while if it is *false* for each assignment it is said to be a *contradiction*. Otherwise it is said to be *satisfiable*.

In this paper, the satisfiability problem is studied in conjunctive normal form (CNF). A CNF formula consists of a conjunction of disjunctions, where each of the disjunctions is called a *clause*, in notation:

$$\Phi = \bigwedge_{k=1}^{n} C_k,$$

where each clause C_k is of the form

$$\bigvee_{i \in I_k} l_i,$$

with l_i a literal. The length $\ell(C_k)$ of a clause is defined as the number of distinct literals occurring in its minimal representation, i.e. tautological clauses have length zero, and doubled occurrences of identical literals in the same clause are reduced to a single occurrence. A CNF formula in which the maximum clause length is equal to ℓ is referred to as an $\leq \ell$CNF formula. In particular, $\leq$2CNF formulas are solvable in linear time [2], while $\leq$3CNF formulas are in general NP-complete [4].

Note that the $\leftrightarrow$ and $\rightarrow$ operators can be eliminated using the well known De Morgan's laws [5] to obtain a CNF formula. In general, this cannot be done efficiently; i.e. transforming an arbitrary formula to CNF using these laws requires a number of operations that is exponential in the length of the formula. However, using auxiliary variables, any formula can be put into the ($\leq$3)CNF format in linear time, maintaining satisfiability. This transformation is used by HeerHugo. It is described in the next section.

3. Algorithms and rules

We describe how HeerHugo is working in four parts. The first part describes how an arbitrary formula can efficiently be transformed to a conjunctive normal form, where clauses contain at most 3 literals. In the second section we describe efficient (mainly linear) operations that can be carried out on the conjunctive normal form to reduce the number of distinct propositions that occur in it. In the third section we describe Stållmarck's branch/merge rule, which is required to make the system complete. Subsequently, the way new clauses are derived is discussed, some complexity issues are addressed and finally the inclusion of additional satisfiability tests is mentioned.

3.1. *Transformation to ≤3CNF*

We describe a linear transformation of any formula Φ to $\leq$3CNF form, i.e. formulas in conjunctive normal form with at most 3 literals per clause. This transformation is believed to be first described by Tseitin [34] and therefore we refer to it as the Tseitin translation. The original formula allows a satisfiable assignment if and only if its transformed $\leq$3CNF counterpart allows a satisfiable assignment. More precisely, any satisfying assignment of the original formula can be extended to a satisfying assignment of the associated $\leq$3CNF formula. Note that if the original formula is a tautology, the resulting CNF formula is merely satisfiable; it is easy to see that (unless P=NP) no polynomial time transformation to CNF preserving tautology exists, since the tautology problem on CNFs is easy. Note that proving a formula to be a tautology is equivalent to proving the negation of its transformed counterpart to be a contradiction.

Take an arbitrary formula Φ. Introduce for any subformula ψ of Φ a new proposition p_ψ, except if ψ is itself an atomic proposition. First construct the following formula:

$$p_\Phi \wedge \bigwedge_{\substack{\psi \in Sub(\Phi) \\ \psi \equiv \psi_1 \oplus \psi_2}} (p_\psi \leftrightarrow (p_{\psi_1} \oplus p_{\psi_2})) \wedge \bigwedge_{\substack{\psi \in Sub(\Phi) \\ \psi \equiv \neg\psi_1}} (p_\psi \leftrightarrow \neg p_{\psi_1}).$$

Here $Sub(\Phi)$ is the set of subformulas of Φ, and $\oplus$ denotes one of the binary connectives. Obviously, the number of subformulas is linear in $|\Phi|$, and since each of the logical expressions involved can be expressed in at most 4 clauses the transformation is linear in the size of the formula.

Note that to obtain a slightly more concise formulation, the equivalence operators may be replaced by implications [38]. Thus satisfiability is maintained, but in case the original formula is satisfiable, the resulting formula allows more satisfiable solutions.

For completeness, we give an example of the result of transforming a 'triple' $(p_\psi \leftrightarrow (p_{\psi_1} \wedge p_{\psi_2}))$ and a formula $(p_\psi \leftrightarrow \neg p_{\psi_1})$ to $\leq$3CNF form. We obtain $(\neg p_\psi \vee p_{\psi_1}) \wedge (\neg p_\psi \vee p_{\psi_2}) \wedge (p_\psi \vee \neg p_{\psi_1} \vee \neg p_{\psi_2})$ and $(p_\psi \vee p_{\psi_1}) \wedge (\neg p_\psi \vee \neg p_{\psi_1})$, respectively. One of the differences between HeerHugo and Stållmarck's satisfiability checker is that the latter works with so-called 'triples', formulas of the form $p \leftrightarrow q \oplus r$, whereas HeerHugo operates on the larger $\leq$3CNF formulas, which allows for more logical rules to be applied.

Let us finish this section by emphasizing that all logical rules discussed in the remainder of this section are not restricted to $\leq$3CNF formulas, but can be used for unrestricted CNFs as well. The decision that HeerHugo operates on $\leq$3CNF formulas is mainly motivated by implementational issues. It is not clear whether not restricting the clause length would lead to better or worse results.

3.2. *Simple rules*

From now it is tacitly assumed that we consider $\leq$3CNF formulas. In order to simplify a formula, a number of transformations is simultaneously applied. By simplification of a formula we mean in general the removal of propositions and clauses, or the addition of short clauses (i.e. clauses that are likely to contain useful information). The transformations are described in the following paragraphs.

Unit resolution
Unit resolution is motivated by the occurrence of clauses of length one in the formula. Such clauses are called *unit clauses*. It relies on the obvious observation that a literal

occurring in a unit clause must be *true* in any satisfying assignment (if any). In the unit resolution phase, all unit clauses are found, and the corresponding literals are set to *true*. Subsequently, the truth values are propagated through the formula. During this process new unit clauses can emerge, or a contradiction can be found. The procedure is repeated until either a contradiction is found or no unit clauses remain. All unit resolution steps can be applied in linear time [8]. It is interesting to note that unit resolution is complete for Horn formulas, or propositional Prolog programs. These are formulas in conjunctive normal form (without a restriction on the clause length) where each clause contains at most one positive literal.

Removal of implication cycles
The second simplification procedure is motivated by the occurrence of clauses of length two. If the maximum clause length is equal to two the formula under consideration can be solved in linear time [2]. Moreover, by considering a 2CNF *sub*formula of a larger formula, it is possible to reduce the problem size, using this algorithm. Clauses of length two can be viewed as implications, i.e. $p \vee q$ is equivalent to $\neg p \rightarrow q$ and $\neg q \rightarrow p$. Such implications can form a cycle, for example $p \rightarrow q$, $q \rightarrow \neg r$ and $\neg r \rightarrow p$. Clearly, all literals in such a cycle are equivalent, and henceforth can be given the same name. This observation yields a complete linear time algorithm for 2CNF formulas [2]. Obviously, if the 2CNF subformula is found to be contradictory, the full formula is a contradiction as well.

Classical Davis–Putnam rule
One of the earliest rules in propositional reasoning is proposed in [7]. We refer to this rule as the *classical Davis–Putnam rule*. It can be formulated for a proposition p as follows. Given a CNF of the form

$$\Phi = (p \vee \psi) \wedge \psi',$$

where p does not occur positively in ψ' and it does not occur at all in ψ). (Note that ψ and ψ' both denote $\leq$3CNF formulas.) Basically, for every occurrence of $\neg p$ in ψ' we can substitute ψ, maintaining all satisfying assignments. When carrying out this substitution it is easy to obtain a CNF again, but auxiliary propositions must be introduced to maintain $\leq$3CNF. Moreover, if both p and $\neg p$ occur several times, the resulting $\leq$3CNF is likely to become considerably larger than the original. This is basically the motivation for Davis, Logemann and Loveland's modification of the original Davis–Putnam algorithm [6]. Their (depth–first search) algorithm is currently one of the most widely used algorithms for solving SAT problems.

In HeerHugo the classical Davis–Putnam rule is carried out only when the formula reduces in size, or when there is a limited growth. Just before applying the branch/merge rule (see below) to a proposition p, it is investigated whether it can be fruitfully applied. In this respect we mention two special cases:

- When $\neg p$ does not occur in ψ', then the Davis–Putnam rule implies that $(p \vee \psi)$ can be discarded. This is called *monotonic variable fixing* (also known as the *pure literal rule*).

- Another interesting case is when p occurs exactly once, in a clause of length 2, while $\neg p$ occurs arbitrarily often. For example, this clause has the form $p \vee q$. According to the classical Davis–Putnam rule all occurrences of $\neg p$ may be substituted by q, reducing the number of propositions and thus the size of the formula.

HeerHugo is facilitated to immediately (i.e. while applying unit resolution) detect whether one of these special cases of the classical Davis–Putnam rule can be applied. For general CNF formulas, the number of successful applications of this rule may be expected to be low. Due to the Tseitin translation however, a substantial number of variables has limited occurrence, thus often allowing the rule to substantially reduce problem size (see also Section 4).

Subsumption and ad hoc resolution

HeerHugo constantly changes its set of clauses by removing and adding clauses (see also the next section). Whenever a clause is added, it is checked whether a similar clause exists. For example, if a clause $C_1 \equiv p \vee q \vee r$ is added, then the set of clauses is checked for the occurrence of a clause C_2 of any of the forms listed in Table I, and the corresponding action is taken. The actions are motivated by *subsumption*, i.e. $C_2 \rightarrow C_1$, or *resolution*, i.e. $(C_1 \wedge C_2) \rightarrow C_3$ for some clause C_3 which is subsequently added. If no such clause C_2 is present, C_1 is simply added. Obviously, if p, q and/or r appear with negations, the obvious dual actions are taken. Similarly, in case a clause of the form

Table I. Actions following the derivation of a 'new' clause $C_1 \equiv p \vee q \vee r$.

C_2	Action
$p \vee q \vee r$	do not add C_1
$p \vee q \vee \neg r$	do not add C_1, remove C_2 and add $p \vee q$
$p \vee \neg q \vee r$	do not add C_1, remove C_2 and add $p \vee r$
$\neg p \vee q \vee r$	do not add C_1, remove C_2 and add $q \vee r$
$p \vee q$	do not add C_1
$p \vee \neg q$	do not add C_1, add $p \vee r$
$\neg p \vee q$	do not add C_1, add $q \vee r$
$p \vee r$	do not add C_1
$p \vee \neg r$	do not add C_1, add $p \vee q$
$\neg p \vee r$	do not add C_1, add $q \vee r$
$q \vee r$	do not add C_1
$q \vee \neg r$	do not add C_1, add $p \vee q$
$\neg q \vee r$	do not add C_1, add $p \vee r$

$C_1 \equiv p \vee q$ is added and a clause C_2 of any of the forms listed in Table II is present, the corresponding actions are taken. Again, if no such C_2 is present, C_1 is simply added. The dual cases, where p and/or q are negated, are left to the reader.

3.3. A branching scheme: The branch/merge rule

After applying all rules from the previous section, it might be that no contradiction has been derived. In this case a branch/merge rule is adopted. This rule stems from [31] where it is called the dilemma rule, and appears to be surprisingly effective in proving formulas. We actually believe that the success of the Stållmarck prover should be solely attributed to this rule, since its other aspect (namely the handling of triples), is a slightly enhanced variant of unit resolution, which is completely subsumed by all rules mentioned previously. The branch/merge rule is depicted in Figure 1. It must be interpreted as follows. Starting with a $\leq$3CNF formula Φ, the proof is split in two parts. In the first part, the assumption $\neg p$ is added to Φ. Exhaustively applying the simple

Table II. Actions following the derivation of a 'new' clause $C_1 \equiv p \vee q$.

C_2	Actions
$p \vee q$	do not add C_1
$p \vee \neg q$	do not add C_1, remove C_2 and add p
$\neg p \vee q$	do not add C_1, remove C_2 and add q
$\neg p \vee \neg q$	do not add C_1, remove C_2 and set $p \equiv q$
$p \vee q \vee r$	remove C_2
$p \vee q \vee \neg r$	remove C_2
$p \vee \neg q \vee r$	remove C_2, add $p \vee r$
$p \vee \neg q \vee \neg r$	remove C_2, add $p \vee \neg r$
$\neg p \vee q \vee r$	remove C_2, add $q \vee r$
$\neg p \vee q \vee \neg r$	remove C_2, add $q \vee \neg r$

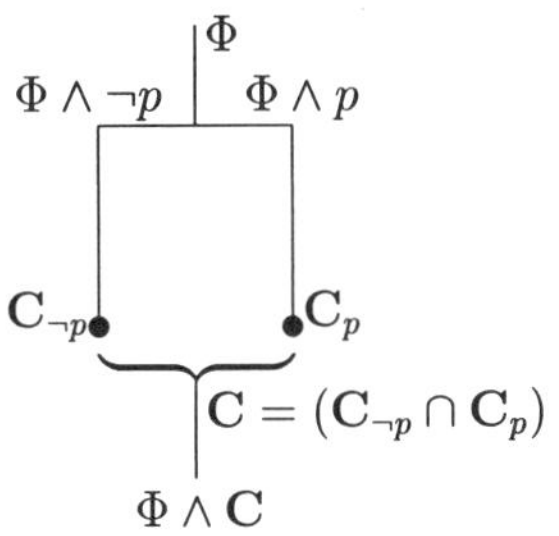

Figure 1. Illustration of the branch/merge rule.

rules, a set of *conclusions* $\mathbf{C}_{\neg p}$ is drawn. Similarly, assuming p a set of conclusions $\mathbf{C}_p$ is drawn. Subsequently, the intersection $\mathbf{C}$ of the conclusion sets $\mathbf{C}_{\neg p}$ and $\mathbf{C}_p$ is determined and each fact in $\mathbf{C}$ is added to Φ. Any *conclusion* is of the following forms:

- *Literal conclusion*: A certain proposition does or does not hold; q or $\neg q$.
- *Equivalency conclusion*: Two propositions are equivalent: $q \leftrightarrow r$, or two propositions are not equivalent: $q \leftrightarrow \neg r$.

The conclusion sets $\mathbf{C}_p$ and $\mathbf{C}_{\neg p}$ are made *closed* in the following way. It is checked whether $\mathbf{C}_{\neg p}$ (resp. $\mathbf{C}_p$) contains the conclusion that both q and $\neg q$ must hold, for some proposition q. If this is the case an inconsistency has been derived; then $\mathbf{C}_{\neg p}$ (resp. $\mathbf{C}_p$) is made to contain the set of all literals, as well as all (in)equivalences between literals (since out of a contradiction anything can be concluded); we refer to this conclusion as $\mathbf{C}_{unsat}$. Otherwise, for all conclusions of the form q, an equivalence $\neg p \leftrightarrow q$ is added to $\mathbf{C}_{\neg p}$ (resp. $p \leftrightarrow q$ is added to $\mathbf{C}_p$). Thus, sets of equivalent literals evolve. All literals that belong to a single equivalency class can be determined in almost linear time (using a path compression algorithm, see [1]). For example, if $\neg p \leftrightarrow q$ and $q \leftrightarrow r$ are in $\mathbf{C}_{\neg p}$, then using this algorithm $\neg p \leftrightarrow r$ is concluded. Calculating the intersection $\mathbf{C}$ of $\mathbf{C}_{\neg p}$ and $\mathbf{C}_p$ can be done in time linear in the number of conclusions. When $\mathbf{C}$ is not empty, the simple rules are applied to simplify $\Phi \wedge \mathbf{C}$. Note that if one of the branches lead to a contradiction, the conclusions of the other branch are all in the intersection.

HeerHugo applies the branch/merge rule for every proposition in turn, leading to a diagram of shape (*b*), shown in Figure 2. The branch/merge is repeatedly applied

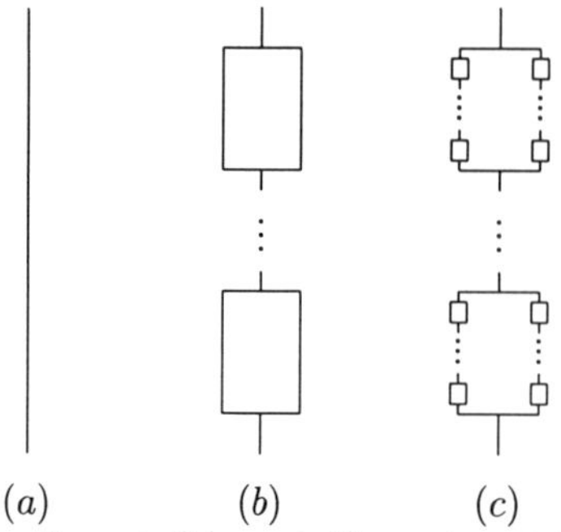

Figure 2. Schematic illustration of the application of simple rules (a), the branch/merge rule (b) and the nested branch/merge rule (c).

to all propositions in sequence until the stage is reached where for all propositions the intersection of $\mathbf{C}_{\neg p}$ and $\mathbf{C}_p$ is empty. This means that applying the rule to any proposition does not lead to any new facts. In this case the branch/merge rule is applied in a nested way (see (c), Figure 2). First, at level one, a single proposition is set to *true* and *false*, and under this assumption, the branch/merge rule is applied to all other propositions, until no new facts can be derived. Then a next proposition at level one is chosen, and so on. For a more precise outline, see the Figures 3 and 4.

Some additional explanation is in order. Figure 3 gives HeerHugo's main loop. First, a formula Φ is read into memory and translated to $\leq$3CNF. The procedure `UNSAT` checks whether the current representation of Φ can be declared a contradiction, i.e. it checks whether the empty clause is present. If not, the formula is simplified by applying the branch/merge rule with an increasing number of nestings, which is specified by the variable `level`. After all conclusions have been derived at a given level, they are added to the formula and subsequently the formula is simplified. If no conclusions have been drawn at the current level, it is increased. Figure 4 specifies the branch/merge procedure. If `level` equals zero, facts are derived using the simple rules and they are saved in the set of conclusions $\mathbf{C}$. HeerHugo verifies whether the current formula is empty (then `SAT`(Φ) evaluates to true and thus HeerHugo terminates with a satisfying (possibly partial) assignment, taking into account the equivalencies that have been derived so far) or contains the empty clause. In the second case HeerHugo returns the set of conclusions $\mathbf{C}_{unsat}$. As indicated before, it holds that $\mathbf{C}_{unsat} \cap \mathbf{C} = \mathbf{C}$ for any $\mathbf{C}$. Otherwise, if `level` is greater than zero, the procedure `branch/merge` is recursively called with the value of level decreased by one. If `level` equals zero, the set of conclusions is returned. Thus, the algorithm terminates when a satisfying assignment is discovered, or when it is proved that no such assignment exists. Note that at level n HeerHugo enumerates all solutions and therefore is guaranteed to terminate.

It may be noted that a less powerful variant of the branch/merge rule is employed in various depth first DPLL based solvers, such as C–SAT [9]. There it is used to detect possible variable fixings (if assuming $\neg p$ a contradiction is derived, it decides that p holds) and early closing of branches (if the assumptions p and $\neg p$ both lead to a contradiction); it does not take into account equivalencies of variables.

A note on adding 'expensive' clauses

It can happen that after assuming a literal p to be *true* , assuming the validity of a literal q leads to a contradiction. In this case we have derived $p \wedge q \rightarrow \mathit{false}$, which is equivalent to the clause $\neg p \vee \neg q$. We consider such a clause expensive, because we may have searched for quite a while before finding it. Furthermore, it is considered useful,

```
Φ = read_formula;
Φ = 3CNF(Φ);
level = −1;
while (¬UNSAT(Φ)) do
   level = level + 1;
   repeat
      C = branch/merge(Φ, level);
      (Φ, C) = simple_rules(Φ ∧ C);
   until C ≠ ∅
endwhile
```

Figure 3. HeerHugo's main loop.

```
procedure branch/merge(Φ, level)
(Φ, C) = simple_rules(Φ);
if SAT(Φ) then terminate;
if UNSAT(Φ) then return(C_unsat);
if level ≥ 1
   for all p ∈ Φ do
      C_p = branch/merge(Φ ∧ C ∧ p, level − 1);
      C_¬p = branch/merge(Φ∧C∧¬p, level−1);
      C = C ∪ (C_p ∩ C_¬p);
   endfor
endif
return(C)
```

Figure 4. The branch/merge procedure.

since it is a concise fact. Therefore, such a clause is added to the formula. This is also done when the nested assumption of three propositions leads to a contradiction. We have also experimented with adding a clause $\neg p \vee q$ ($\neg p_0 \vee \neg p_1 \vee q$) if we derive q under the assumption p (assumptions p_0 and p_1). We found a degradation of performance, due to the fact that many redundant clauses were generated in this way.

3.4. Including satisfiability tests

As may be clear from the description of the algorithm so far, it is basically a form of applying resolution [28] (enhanced with the capability to recognize equivalency of variables), and thus it is particularly suited for proving contradictory formulas. In order to make it effective for satisfiable formulas as well, it is necessary to include satisfiability tests. These look, guided by some heuristic, for a satisfying assignment of the formula. If such an assignment is found, the formula is proven satisfiable and the search can be cut short. Typically, a satisfiability test should be applied at each level of the search. We have experimented with two types of satisfiability tests:

- The first is based on the gradient of polynomial transforms of CNF formulas [25]. Essentially, a proposition is chosen and set to *true* if its number of unnegated occurrences is higher than its number of negated occurrences, otherwise it is set to *false*. Subsequently the simple rules are applied, and a next proposition is chosen, until either a contradiction is found, or a satisfiable assignment is constructed.

- The other is a weighted variant of a greedy local search algorithm [29]. Starting from a random assignment, variables are 'flipped' (set from *true* to *false* or vice versa), such that the weight of satisfied clauses increases. If no improving 'flip' is identified, the weights of the unsatisfied clauses are increased until an improving flip comes into existence. In this way, 'difficult' clauses are getting large weights and thus are more likely to be satisfied in the end. This process is repeated until either a satisfiable assignment is constructed, or the maximum number of flips is exceeded.

It may be noted that for many satisfiable formulas the local search algorithm is sufficient for finding a model quickly. Thus it tends to obscure HeerHugo's performance; therefore we did not make use of it in the computations in Section 5.

3.5. Some complexity issues

If a formula can be proven to be a contradiction using simple rules only (as in (a)), it is said to be in *hardness class* 0. If a formula is proven contradictory using the application of the branch/merge rule on level 1 (as in (b)), it is said to be in hardness class 1. Similarly, a formula that can be proven using i nested applications of the branch/merge rule, but cannot be proven using $i-1$ nested applications, is said to be in hardness class i [31]. If application of simple rules is linear (which is the case in Stållmarck's prover, and almost in HeerHugo) bounds on the lengths of proof size and search for a contradictory formula Φ in hardness class h can be derived [31].

$O((3\|\Phi\|)^{h+1})$	length of a proof to refute Φ
$O((3\|\Phi\|)^{2h+1})$	length of the proof search to refute Φ
2^h	lower bound on the proof length of Φ

Here $|\Phi|$ denotes the size of the formula Φ. It should be noted that the number of propositions occurring in Φ is a better measure than its size, except in constructed cases where large formulas contain an extremely low number of propositions.

The hardness class of a formula gives a very good intuition for the provability of a formula. A formula in hardness class 0 can without problem contain 10^6 propositions, whereas the refutability of a formula with 100 propositions in hardness class 3 is doubtful. Moreover, it appears that formulas belonging to a certain kind of application, have a typical hardness class associated with them. However, there also formulas of which the hardness class increases with size. E.g. prime number tests and the pigeon hole formulas appear to range over all classes.

It is worthwhile to note that the hardness class very much depends on the nature of the simple rules. We have observed that by increasing the strength of the simple rules, formulas shifted down from higher to lower hardness classes. As far as we know the relation between hardness classes and the nature of the simple rules has never been investigated.

Finally, the hardness classes appear to be related to the notion of hierarchies of polynomially solvable SAT problems as first introduced by Gallo and Scutellá [12]. It is however a different notion, since the hardness class is not a static property of a formula (as it depends on the simple rules that are applied). Moreover, it is not defined for satisfiable instances.

4. Detecting structure in formulas

In this section we show how HeerHugo detects and employs certain kinds of structure in a formula.

4.1. Identification and removal of identical subterms

Suppose we start with a formula (not yet in CNF) and this formula contains identical subterms, i.e. the subformula $q \oplus r$ occurs twice. Assume that the identical subformulas are assigned auxiliary propositions p_0 and p_1. It is easy to verify that for any operator, using simple rules and the single level branch/merge rule, it is concluded that $p_0 \leftrightarrow p_1$. In this way the equivalence between all pairs of equal subterms is detected. For example, if $\oplus \equiv \wedge$, we find in the $\leq$3CNF formula 6 clauses that are equivalent to $p_0 \leftrightarrow (q \wedge r)$ and $p_1 \leftrightarrow (q \wedge r)$. Now if for example q is considered in a branch/merge step, it is derived assuming $\neg q$ that $\neg p_0$ and $\neg p_1$. Assuming q, it is derived that $p_0 \leftrightarrow r$ and $p_1 \leftrightarrow r$. Taking the intersection of these results, we find that $p_0 \leftrightarrow p_1$.

In case the translation to $\leq$3CNF is applied where implications are used, rather than bi–implications, a similar effect occurs, but only if the simple Classical Davis Putnam rules are being applied.

4.2. Identification and removal of similar propositions

Suppose the propositions p and q occur in a similar way; more precisely, Φ can be expressed as

$$\begin{aligned}\Phi &\equiv (p \vee \psi) \wedge (\neg p \vee \psi') \wedge \psi'' \\ &\equiv (q \vee \psi) \wedge (\neg q \vee \psi') \wedge \psi'''.\end{aligned}$$

Using the branch/merge rule, monotonic variable fixing and subsumption and ad hoc resolution, the system detects that p and q can be made equivalent without violating satisfiability. Assume using the branch/merge rule that p holds; then ψ' is derived. This means that using ad hoc resolution the subformula $(\neg q \vee \psi')$ is proven superfluous. This implies that q only occurs positively. Therefore, using monotonic variable fixing q is set to *true*. In particular $p \leftrightarrow q$. Similarly, assuming $\neg p$, leads to the conclusion $p \leftrightarrow q$ as well. Thus HeerHugo concludes that p and q may be assumed to be equivalent in this case.

4.3. Recognition of 3CNFs

HeerHugo is not capable of recognizing whether a formula is in $\leq$3CNF already. Therefore, given a $\leq$3CNF formula, it will translate it into a satisfiability–equivalent $\leq$3CNF formula of larger size. However, already at level 0 the formula will be reduced to its original form, or better. Given a 3CNF formula consisting of n clauses and m variables, after the Tseitin translation and unit resolution, the associated $\leq$3CNF contains $m+n$ variables and $4n$ clauses (if bi–implications are used; otherwise it contains $2n$ clauses). Each clause of the form $p \vee q \vee r$ will be translated to $(a \leftrightarrow (p \vee q)) \wedge (a \vee r)$. It is easy to see that applying the classical Davis–Putnam rule, a is eliminated and the clause $p \vee q \vee r$ is obtained again. Thus, it can be argued that even though HeerHugo does not check explicitly whether a formula is in $\leq$3CNF format, it recognizes such formulas in 'almost' linear time.

5. Computational experience

The most common way to compare the efficiency of implementations of propositional checkers is by applying the tool to a set of benchmarks. In this section we provide computational results on various classes of benchmarks. All results are obtained on a Silicon Graphics PowerChallenge R10000 (250 Mhz R10000 CPU, 4MB secondary cache, Irix6.4) with sufficient main memory. Times reported are the wall clock times (in seconds) reported by HeerHugo to solve the formulas.

5.1. Safety at railway stations

The initial purpose of HeerHugo was to solve a collection of formulas expressing the safety of operations at the Dutch railway stations in Heerhugowaard (see also [26]). A method of expressing safety criteria for railway stations as a propositional formulas is developed and discussed in [10]. Here we only give a brief outline. Given the layout of a railway station (i.e. the infrastructure of the railroads, the position of the signals and level crossings etc.), a number of requirements is formulated (in terms of propositional formulas) to protect trains from colliding or derailing. Furthermore, a set of assignments is given that models the program of the *Programmable Logic Controller* (PLC), which guards that all operations are safe. For Heerhugowaard , we estimate that this system has 10^{1000} states. For each of these assignments all safety criteria must be satisfied *at any time* and for all situations that can occur at the yard. Thus, denoting by $\Phi_0, \ldots, \Phi_n$ the assignments at $n+1$ sequential moments in time, and by R a particular safety criterion, it must hold that $(\Phi_0 \wedge \ldots \wedge \Phi_n) \rightarrow R$ is a tautology, or equivalently, its negation is a contradiction. Even for small stations such formulas can grow quite large. Initially, it was attempted to solve the resulting formulas using BDDs [15], but unfortunately it appeared that these could not handle the instances `heerhugo*` associated with Heerhugowaard railway station. However, HeerHugo can solve them with ease. In Table III the results of HeerHugo on a number of benchmarks[2] are given. Given are the size of formula after transformation to $\leq$3CNF and after the application of exhaustive search at various levels; m gives the number of propositions and n gives the number of clauses. It is indicated at which level the formulas was decided to be contradictory or satisfiable.

5.2. DIMACS and UCSC benchmarks

The best known set of SAT benchmarks is the DIMACS suite [33]. It contains instances stemming from practical applications, as well as constructed hard instances. We used HeerHugo to solve a subset of these instances. Most of these instances are fairly hard for DPLL algorithms (see the various results in [22]). Many of the DIMACS benchmarks are satisfiable, and thus rather easily solved by local search methods[3]; therefore the main interest lies in the unsatisfiable formulas. Note that all the DIMACS instances are already in CNF; yet, HeerHugo applies the transformation to $\leq$3CNF anyway (even if the problem is already in $\leq$3CNF format; see also the previous section).

To give the reader an indication of the effectiveness of HeerHugo when compared to other solvers, we make use of results reported in [30, 40, 13]. Solvers that we compare against are:

[2] These formulas can be obtained by contacting one of the authors.
[3] This observation does not hold for the notorious `par32*` instances. These have only been solved making use of their special structure [36].

Table III. HeerHugo results railway station instances. 'brnch' refers to *branches*; one application of the branch/merge rule constitutes two branches.

name	≤3CNF		level 0		level 1		time	brnch
	m	n	m	n	m	n		
h-k1	660	1197	361	788	SAT		.12	229
h-k2	624	1140	FALSE				.01	0
h-k3	645	1190	FALSE				.01	0
h-k4	593	1074	FALSE				.01	0
heerhugo2	8353	18175	5225	13942	SAT		10.45	5097
heerhugo3	8351	18173	5223	13937	FALSE		3.77	1634
heerhugo4	8574	18669	5339	14284	FALSE		3.80	1301
heerhugo5	6286	13496	3922	10210	SAT		12.29	6925

- SATO3.0 [40], GRASP [30]; implementations of the DPLL algorithm, enhanced with intelligent backjumping techniques;
- POSIT [11], SATO2.2 [40]; two of the most efficient implementations of the DPLL algorithm (employing the usual branch and backtracking scheme);
- `modoc` [13]; a *model-elimination* algorithm.

Since HeerHugo provides a fundamentally different approach to SAT solving than these solvers, it is difficult to give a clear comparison of the relative effectiveness. In this section we report and compare the number of successes and solution times of HeerHugo on various classes of benchmarks; in the next section we provide some more details to try and give the reader a better intuition of HeerHugo's performance.

In the Tables IV and V the number of successes of the mentioned algorithms on various classes of benchmarks are reported. The DIMACS benchmarks stem from various sources [33]; the UCSC benchmarks are derived from the hardware application *Automated Test Pattern Generation* [24]. The maximum run time allowed for each benchmark was 10,000 seconds on the hardware used in [30]; when this threshold was exceeded the run was noted as a failure to solve the instance under consideration. For HeerHugo, we report the number of instances solved at each level separately, where the maximum level is set to 2, followed by the cumulated number of successes; if the solution time exceeded one hour, the execution of HeerHugo was aborted.

In the Tables VII and VIII the total run times for solving all benchmarks in each class are reported. All times are scaled to the times of the hardware we used, using Table VI to scale the times (these standard benchmarks were provided by Trick [22]). Following [30], if an instance was not solved, its 'solution' time was recorded as 10,000 (Zhang [40] also refers to these results); we subsequently scale these times (by a factor of 1/2.4). Considering the above results we conclude that HeerHugo is very effective in solving certain types of instances. We observe the following.

- HeerHugo seems to be especially effective on structured instances. It outperforms, or is as effective as the state–of–the–art implementations of the (un–enhanced) DPLL algorithm (POSIT, SATO2.2) on most classes of benchmarks, except the `ii`,

Table IV. Number of successes on UCSC benchmarks.

class	#	lev 0	lev 1	lev 2	HeerHugo	GRASP	modoc	POSIT	SATO2.2
bf0432	21		12	9	21	21	21	21	21
bf1355	149		149		149	149	149	64	22
bf2670	53	2	47	4	53	53	53	53	17
ssa0432	7		7		7	7	7	7	7
ssa2670	12		7	5	12	12	12	12	0
ssa6288	3	3			3	3	3	3	3
ssa7552	80		80		80	80	80	80	57

Table V. Number of successes on various DIMACS benchmarks. A * indicates that for these classes the search at level 2 was not always completed within the hour.

class	#	level 0	level 1	level 2	HeerHugo	SATO3.0	POSIT	SATO2.2
aim-50	24	1	23		24	24	24	24
aim-100	24		21	3	24	24	24	20
aim-200	24		17	7	24	24	13	9
dubois	13		13		13	13	7	7
ii8	14		14		14	14	14	14
ii16*	10			2	2	9	9	7
ii32*	17		8	6	14	17	17	16
jnh	50	2	31	17	50	50	50	50
par8	10		10		10	10	10	10
par16	10				0	10	10	10
pret	8			8	8	8	4	4

jnh and par instances. HeerHugo manages to solve all of the UCSC benchmarks in short times, where POSIT and SATO2.2 often struggle.

– HeerHugo's effectiveness on the dubois instances is particularly notable. On these instances it outperforms all other solvers. These instances are very hard for resolution based algorithms. HeerHugo's capability of identifying equivalencies of variables is of great importance in solving these formulas; see also the next section.

Table VI. Execution times for machine comparisons.

	r100.5	r200.5	r300.5	r400.5	r500.5
[30, 40]	0.03	0.68	6.12	39.05	149.92
[14, 13]	0.04	0.93	8.05	49.06	189.29
Present	0.01	0.31	2.62	16.08	61.35

Table VII. Solution times on various UCSC benchmarks.

class	#	HeerHugo	GRASP	modoc	POSIT	SATO2.2
bf0432	21	47.4	19.8	12.5	23.3	11739
bf1355	149	144	52.4	120	39422	563082
bf2670	53	23.9	28.5	151	1238	150000
ssa0432	7	.54	.46	.42	.08	271
ssa2670	12	9.5	21.4	74.5	1178	50000
ssa6288	3	5.2	.08	.30	0	.29
ssa7552	80	21.6	8.25	12.3	25.0	100940

Table VIII. Solution times on various DIMACS benchmarks.

class	#	HeerHugo	SATO3.0	POSIT	SATO2.2
aim-50	24	.27	.01	.17	5.29
aim-100	24	.95	.17	538	25162
aim-200	24	4.56	.46	49163	62540
dubois	13	.41	.63	32162	29803
ii8	14	17.8	.46	.96	.17
ii16	10	28804	2.21	4217	35634
ii32	17	11640	4.92	271	4168
jnh	50	1274	.88	.33	4.58
par8	10	.70	.09	.04	.08
par16	10	–	253	30.0	4353
pret	8	23.2	1.25	16955	16846

- On the other hand, the classes of benchmarks that HeerHugo has difficulty with are relatively easy for the other algorithms. HeerHugo cannot solve the par16 instances at level 2, while its solution times on the jnh instances are considerably larger than those of the other solvers. Also, the classes ii16 and ii32 appear very hard for HeerHugo. Interestingly, HeerHugo solves instances in these classes in either quite short times (within one minute on average) or extremely long times. It may be noted that most of these benchmarks are satisfiable (except a subset of the jnh instances); including stronger satisfiability tests in HeerHugo could vastly improve the solution times.

- Comparing HeerHugo to modoc, we note that HeerHugo is at least as effective on the instances considered. Overall their solution times and success rate are (more or less) comparable, while on the ssa2670 and bf2670 HeerHugo is considerably faster. The large difference on the ssa6288 instances can be attributed to the fact that HeerHugo first transforms these (quite large) formulas to $\leq$3CNF.

- The enhanced implementations of the DPLL algorithm GRASP and SATO3.0 in turn are as effective as, or outperform HeerHugo on all classes. Thus it appears that employing intelligent backtracking endows DPLL algorithms with a reasoning strength comparable to that of HeerHugo, while the solution finding power of the DPLL algorithm is preserved.

In addition, we observed that HeerHugo is in general not successful in solving random 3SAT formulas on the threshold with 200 variables and more (especially unsatisfiable ones), when the number of nested assumptions is restricted to 2. Obviously, increasing the number of nested assumptions will eventually lead to a correct answer, but this requires substantial computation times.

Concluding, HeerHugo is well capable of solving many classes of benchmarks. Its successes indicate that unsatisfiable formulas can efficiently be solved by rather general reasoning techniques; to solve satisfiable formulas however, some guessing is inevitable. HeerHugo appears to be successful on formulas where standard depth–first branch and backtracking algorithms struggle and the other way round. Thus HeerHugo provides a useful complementary approach to SAT solving. Let us emphasize that the current implementation does not contain any heuristics on variable orderings and such; to get a clearer picture of the extent to which the variable ordering influences the solution times requires further research.

5.3. More details on HeerHugo's performance

For the interested reader, we provide some more details of HeerHugo's performance. First, we compare the number of branches required by HeerHugo to the number of branches required by the depth–first solver `2cl` [14]. This implementation does not include intelligent backtracking, but it does include a similar recognition of implication cycles by resolving on clauses of length two (this is called *2–closure* in [14]). Of course, it also includes unit resolution. Therefore, the number of branches required by these solvers provide an interesting comparison of a depth–first and breadth–first solver. In [14], detailed results are provided on the classes `bf`, `ssa` and `ii`. In the Tables IX and X the results of HeerHugo and `2cl` on the `bf` and `ssa` instances are reported. In Table XI the results on the `ii8` and `ii32` instances are given. Both `2cl` and HeerHugo only solved two of the ten `ii16` instances; these results are left out. Note that the averages of HeerHugo on the `ii32` instances are taken over 14 solved instances, whereas `2cl` managed to solve 16 instances. As before, the solution times are scaled to match machines.
Overall, it appears that HeerHugo requires substantially fewer branches than `2cl` on the UCSC formulas; on the larger `ii32` formulas however, it is the other way round. Generally, HeerHugo appears more robust and it outperforms `2cl`; note however that more efficient depth–first solvers than `2cl` exist (see also previous section). For completeness, we mention that in [14] successes of `2cl` on hard random 3CNF formulas with up to 283 variables are reported; the current version of HeerHugo is in general not successful in solving such formulas, once again indicating that HeerHugo can be considered as a complementary approach to depth–first solvers.

To finish off this section, Table XII gives an indication of the importance of including equivalency conclusions. For a restricted set of benchmarks the average solution times and number of branches with and without inclusion of such conclusions are given. It is obvious that in almost all cases, the inclusion of equivalency conclusions has a great influence on the efficiency with which the instances are solved. Note that the `pret` instances are not solved at all when excluding equivalency conclusions and restricting the number of nested assumptions to 2. This illustrates the fact that in a number of cases, the number of nested assumptions required to solve particular formulas increases.

Table IX. Execution times of HeerHugo and 2cl on UCSC formulas. For each class of instances, HeerHugo's results are reported in the top row.

class	#	vars	mean	std	min	med	max
bf0432	21	421–1057	2.26	2.78	.06	.53	7.36
			1.90	2.10	.24	.99	7.23
bf1355	149	1450–298	.97	.21	.40	.98	1.71
			13.6	6.76	.95	12.2	28.0
bf2670	53	694–1784	.45	.42	.08	.35	2.27
			142	790	.26	4.60	5745
ssa0432	7	427–435	.08	.02	.07	.08	.12
			.25	.04	.20	.25	.29
ssa2670	12	986–1359	.80	.21	.48	.68	1.03
			499	207	57.4	481	786
ssa6288	3	10404–10410	1.85	.01	1.85	1.85	1.86
			12.8	1.98	10.5	13.9	13.9
ssa7552	80	1391–2013	.27	.10	.18	.23	.65
			.63	.09	.48	.62	.90

Table X. Branchings of HeerHugo and 2cl on UCSC formulas. An application of the branch/merge rule constitutes two branches. For each class of instances, HeerHugo's results are reported in the top row.

class	#	vars	mean	std	min	med	max
bf0432	21	421–1057	4052	5820	12	307	15624
			1407	2430	6	240	8412
bf1355	149	1450–298	158	94	2	147	346
			13254	9038	2	12472	31194
bf2670	53	694–1784	533	797	0	212	3912
			109347	576585	2	2428	4174892
ssa0432	7	427–435	80	50	54	55	191
			268	137	80	320	400
ssa2670	12	986–1359	1452	439	784	1163	1936
			520449	260399	99642	507782	866328
ssa6288	3	10404–10410	0	0	0	0	0
			0	0	0	0	0
ssa7552	80	1391–2013	118	186	1	1	702
			23	6	7	22	34

Table XI. Performance of HeerHugo and `2cl` on `ii` formulas. For each class of instances, HeerHugo's results are reported in the top row.

Solution times					
class	mean	std	min	med	max
`ii8`	1.27	1.70	.01	.51	5.82
	66.0	91.6	.02	35.0	252
`ii32`	59.5	96.8	.15	6.69	285
	81.5	185	.12	.58	642
Branches					
class	mean	std	min	med	max
`ii8`	723	903	1	1	2263
	31354	45902	8	22185	132210
`ii32`	52452	77200	1	11683	238047
	2753	6634	67	142	26125

Table XII. Performance of HeerHugo with and without including equivalency conclusions.

class	#	with		without	
		time	brnch	time	brnch
`bf0432`	21	2.26	4052	29.0	33675
`bf1355`	149	.97	158	1.50	318
`bf2670`	53	.45	533	2.80	5825
`dubois`	13	.03	63	50.9	326590
`pret`	8	3.21	18172	failed	
`ssa0432`	7	.08	80	.23	526
`ssa2670`	12	.80	1452	4.40	11197
`ssa6288`	3	1.85	0	1.85	0
`ssa7552`	80	.27	118	.28	123

6. Concluding remarks

The construction of HeerHugo, and its predecessors (a tool based on normal forms of proofs and a tool using binary decision diagrams (see also [15])) as well as experience with the first order theorem prover otter [39] led to the observation that there is hardly any fundamental understanding of proof search in propositional logic. Attempts at obtaining a deeper understanding that we are aware of can be found in [21] where it is tried to clarify the effects of different branching rules, while there also exists a wealth of probabilistic results (see for an overview [19]); unfortunately, these rely on assumptions on the distribution of the formulas. This makes these results, which are very interesting from a theoretical viewpoint, difficult to apply and interpret when it comes to understanding practical satisfiability solving. The same holds for the results on proof lengths [23, 35]; the existence of a short proof in some proof system, does not at all guarantee that a reasonably short proof will be found in an automated way.

Our experiences with HeerHugo and other solvers, clearly show that the current level of understanding how proofs can be found efficiently in practice is low; it is based mainly on computational experience, rather than on any theoretical foundations. Without truly understanding why, it appeared to be possible to achieve considerable improvements in performance for formulas in higher hardness classes. Rather typically the performance doubled with almost every round of improving HeerHugo. We expect that it is possible to double performance of HeerHugo in a similar way a few more times. The reason for this is that the logical rules and search algorithms that we use are quite standard; all can be found somewhere in the literature, and other existing efficiently implementable rules are not applied yet. We did not (yet) compare the rules with each other in order to remove redundancies in search; nor do we use any heuristics for finding the best propositions to branch on.

By applying HeerHugo to a number of well known benchmarks, we have concluded that it is a powerful complementary approach to solve SAT problems, that seems to be particularly effective on structured formulas, especially those stemming from real–life applications; see also [16]. Such formulas appear to be almost always in hardness class 2 or less, and thus efficiently solvable by HeerHugo. The efficiency with which HeerHugo solves structured instances should be attributed to its reasoning strength. Rather than just doing much guessing, HeerHugo derives as many facts as possible from increasingly complex assumptions. Thus inherent structure is recognized and subsequently exploited. As opposed to HeerHugo, standard implementations of DPLL (depth–first search) algorithms are less suited to exploit structure. When such implementations are enhanced with intelligent backjumping techniques, their reasoning strength increases [30, 40]. It appears that for efficiently solving many classes of formulas exploiting structure is of the utmost importance.

Even when HeerHugo does not manage to solve a formula at level 2 or lower, it is able to substantially reduce the size of the formula during the search. Subsequently, the reduced formula could be solved by another solver that might be better suited for that particular type of formulas. In this sense HeerHugo can be used as a *preprocessing* tool, which is especially useful for contradictory formulas.

On the other hand, many formulas that are difficult for HeerHugo, for example random 3SAT instances and large satisfiable formulas, are often rather easily solved by a depth–first DPLL approach or even by a greedy local search algorithm. Thus it appears that satisfiability solving has become an art of choosing the right algorithm for the right instance.

A. Using HeerHugo

Version 0.2 of HeerHugo is designed to have an extremely simple input/output behaviour, in order to guarantee that it can be used on any computer platform. An input formula must be in `Ain` and output will appear in a file called `Aout`. HeerHugo will also write progress information in `Aout`, which can be used for monitoring purposes. HeerHugo can be obtained by anonymous ftp from `ftp://ftp.cwi.nl/pub/jfg` for experimental purposes. Note that HeerHugo 0.2 is experimental software, and, although it appears to work correctly, may contain flaws. HeerHugo comes with a README file explaining the use of several flags, options and constants. In the file `Ain` a formula can be written using the operators `->` (implication), `&` (and), `|` (or) `~` (negation) and `<->` (bi-implication). Elementary propositions can be denoted by a sequence of letters and digits. Brackets can be used. A line starting with an `%` is taken to be a comment. The following expression is a correct input:

```
% This is an example input file for HeerHugo 2.0
% containing sufficient facts to derive that Jan and Gijs
% do not have the same birthday
( 13April <-> JanBirthday ) & ( 27September <-> GijsBirthday ) &
( ~13April | ~27September )
```

References

1. A.V. Aho, J.E. Hopcroft, and J.D. Ullman. *Data structures and algorithms.* Addison-Wesley, 1987.
2. B. Aspvall, M.F. Plass, and R.E. Tarjan. A linear-time algorithm for testing the truth of certain quantified boolean formulas. *Information Processing Letters*, 8(3):121–123, 1979.
3. R.E. Bryant. Graph-based algorithms for boolean function manipulation. *IEEE Transactions on Computers*, C-35(8), 1986.
4. S.A. Cook. The complexity of theorem proving procedures. In *Proceedings of the 3rd annual ACM symposium on the Theory of Computing*, pages 151–158, 1971.
5. D. Van Dalen. *Logic and structure.* Springer-Verlag, Berlin, 3rd edition, 1994.
6. M. Davis, M. Logemann, and D. Loveland. A machine program for theorem proving. *Communications of the ACM*, 5:394–397, 1962.
7. M. Davis and H. Putnam. A computing procedure for quantification theory. *Journal of the ACM*, 7:210–215, 1960.
8. W.F. Dowling and J.H. Gallier. Linear-time algorithms for testing the satisfiability of propositional Horn formulae. *Journal of Logic Programming*, 1(3):267–284, 1984.
9. O. Dubois, P. Andre, Y. Boufkhad, and J. Carlier. SAT versus UNSAT. In Johnson and Trick [22], pages 415–436.
10. W.J. Fokkink. Safety criteria for the vital processor interlocking at Hoorn-Kersenboogerd. In *Proceedings of the 5th Conference on Computers in Railways - COMPRAIL'96, Volume I: Railway Systems and Management*, pages 101–110. Computational Mechanics Publications, 1996.
11. J.W. Freeman. *Improvements to propositional satisfiability search algorithms.* PhD thesis, Department of Computer Science, University of Pennsylvania, USA, 1995.
12. G. Gallo and M.G. Scutellá. Polynomially solvable satisfiability problems. *Information Processing Letters*, 29:221–227, 1988.
13. A. Van Gelder and F. Okushi. A propositional theorem prover to solve planning and other problems. Technical report, Computer Science Department, University of California, Santa Cruz, CA, 1998.
14. A. Van Gelder and Y.K. Tsuji. Satisfiability testing with more reasoning and less guessing. In Johnson and Trick [22], pages 559–586.
15. J.F. Groote. Hiding propositional constants in BDDs. *Formal Methods in System Design*, 8:91–96, 1996.
16. J.F. Groote, J.W.C. Koorn, and S.F.M. van Vlijmen. The safety guaranteeing system at station Hoorn-Kersenboogerd (extended abstract). In *Proceedings 10th IEEE Conference on Computer Assurance (COMPASS'95)*, pages 57–68, Maryland, 1995.
17. J. Gu. Local search for the satisfiability (SAT) problem. *IEEE Transactions on Systems, Man and Cybernetics*, 23(4):1108–1129, 1993.
18. J. Gu. Global optimization for satisfiability (SAT) problem. *IEEE Transactions on Knowledge and Data Engineering*, 6(3):361–381, 1994.
19. J. Gu, P.W. Purdom, J. Franco, and B.W. Wah. Algorithms for the satisfiability (SAT) problem: a survey. In D. Du, J. Gu, and P.M. Pardalos, editors, *Satisfiability problem: Theory and applications*, volume 35 of *DIMACS series in Discrete Mathematics and Computer Science*, pages 9–151. American Mathematical Society, 1997.

20. J. Harrison. Stållmarck's algorithm as a HOL derived rule. In J. von Wright, J. Grundy, and J. Harrison, editors, *Proceedings of TPHOLs'96*, volume 1125 of *LNCS*, pages 221–234, 1996.
21. J.N. Hooker and V. Vinay. Branching rules for satisfiability. *Journal of Automated Reasoning*, 15(3):359–383, 1995.
22. D.S. Johnson and M.A. Trick, editors. *Cliques, Coloring and Satisfiability: Second DIMACS implementation challenge*, volume 26 of *DIMACS series in Discrete Mathematics and Computer Science*. American Mathematical Society, 1996.
23. J. Krajícek. *Bounded arithmetic, propositional logic, and complexity theory*, volume 60 of *Encycplodia of Mathematics and its Applications*. Cambridge University Press, 1996.
24. T. Larrabee. Efficient generation of test patterns using Boolean satisfiability. *IEEE Transactions on Computer-Aided Design*, 11(1):4–15, 1992.
25. H. Van Maaren, J.F. Groote, and M. Rozema. Verification of propositional formulae by means of convex and concave transforms. Technical Report 95–74, Faculty of Technical Mathematics and Informatics, Delft University of Technology, Delft, The Netherlands, 1995.
26. J. Mertens. Verifying the safety guaranteeing system at railway station Heerhugowaard. Master's thesis, University of Utrecht, Utrecht, The Netherlands, 1996.
27. D. Mitchell, B. Selman, and H. Levesque. Hard and easy distributions of SAT problems. In *Proceedings of the 10th National Conference on Artificial Intelligence (AAAI-92)*, pages 459–465, San Jose, CA, 1992.
28. J.A. Robinson. A machine–oriented logic based on the resolution principle. *Journal of the ACM*, 12:23–41, 1965.
29. B. Selman, H. Levesque, and D. Mitchell. A new method for solving hard satisfiability problems. In *Proceedings of the 10th National Conference on Artificial Intelligence (AAAI-92)*, pages 440–446, San Jose, CA, 1992.
30. J.P. Marques Silva and K.A. Sakallah. Conflict analysis in search algorithms for propositional satisfiability. Technical Report RT/4/96, Cadence European Laboratories, ALGOS, INESC, Lisbon, Portugal, 1996.
31. G. Stållmarck. A proof theoretic concept of tautological hardness. Incomplete manuscript, 1994.
32. G. Stållmarck. System for determining propositional logic theorems by applying values and rules to triplets that are generated from boolean formula. United States Patent number 5,276,897; Swedish Patent 467 076; European Patent 0 403 454; Canadian Patent 2,018,828, 1994.
33. M.A. Trick. Second DIMACS challenge test problems. In Johnson and Trick [22], pages 653–657.
34. G.S. Tseitin. On the complexity of derivation in propositional calculus. *Studies in Constructive Mathematics and Mathematical Logic*, part 2:115–125, 1968. Reprinted in J. Siekmann and G. Wrightson (editors), *Automation of reasoning* vol. 2, Springer–Verlag Berlin, 1983.
35. A. Urquhart. The complexity of propositional proofs. *The Bulletin of Symbolic Logic*, 1(4):425–467, 1995.
36. J.P. Warners and H. Van Maaren. A two-phase algorithm for solving a class of hard satisfiability problems. *Operations Research Letters*, 23(3–5):81–88, 1999.
37. F. Widebäck. Stållmarck's notion of n-saturation. Technical Report NP–K–FW–200, Logikkonsult NP AB, Sweden, 1996.
38. J.M. Wilson. Compact normal forms in propositional logic and integer programming formulations. *Computers and Operations Research*, 17(3):309–314, 1990.
39. L. Wos, R. Overbeek, E. Lusk, and J. Boyle. *Automated Reasoning.* McGraw–Hill, 1992.
40. H. Zhang. SATO: An efficient propositional solver. In W. McCune, editor, *Automated Deduction — CADE-14*, LNAI 1249, pages 272–275. Springer, 1997.

SAT2000
I. Gent et al. (Eds.)
IOS Press, 2000

SATLIB: An Online Resource for Research on SAT

Holger H. Hoos †
Department of Computer Science, University of British Columbia, Vancouver, Canada

Thomas Stützle §
FG Intellektik, FB Informatik, TU Darmstadt, Darmstadt, Germany

Abstract. SATLIB is an online resource for SAT-related research established in June 1998. Its core components, a benchmark suite of SAT instances and a collection of SAT solvers, aim to facilitate empirical research on SAT by providing a uniform test-bed for SAT solvers along with freely available implementations of high-performing SAT algorithms. In this article, we give an overview of SATLIB; in particular, we describe its current set of benchmark problems. Currently, the main SATLIB web site (http://www.informatik.tu-darmstadt.de/AI/SATLIB) and its North American mirror site (http://www.cs.ubc.ca/~hoos/SATLIB) are being accessed frequently by a growing number of researchers, resulting in access rates of about 250 hits per month. To further increase the usefulness of SATLIB as a resource, we encourage all members of the community to utilise it for their SAT-related research and to improve it by submitting new benchmark problems, SAT solvers, and bibliography entries.

Keywords: SAT, Benchmark Problems, SAT Algorithms

1. Introduction

The satisfiability problem in propositional logic (SAT) is one of the most prominent problems in artificial intelligence, logic, theoretical computer science, and various application areas. In the past, a large body of research has focussed on SAT and recently, the interest in SAT seems to be increasing as witnessed by a growing number of SAT-related papers published in journals and presented at major conferences. At the same time, in particular in AI, empirical studies of SAT problems and algorithms have become increasingly popular and lead to important insights into the nature of the problem as well as to dramatic improvements in SAT algorithms which, to date, can solve hard instances with thousands of variables.

Considering the increasing interest in SAT, in 1998 we created SATLIB as an online repository of benchmark problems and solvers for SAT. The original motivation behind SATLIB was to facilitate and encourage empirical studies of SAT algorithms that make use of a common set of benchmark instances and SAT solver implementations in order to improve the assessment of new algorithmic ideas or classes of SAT instances and to enhance the comparability of published empirical results. The advantages of widely used collections of benchmark problems and reference implementations of algorithms have been recognised in many areas of computer science and related fields; consequently, various such collections have been established and made available online. Some well known examples are TSPLIB (containing a variety of TSP and TSP-related instances), ORLIB (providing test instances for a variety of problems from Operations Research),

† `hoos@cs.ubc.ca`
§ `stuetzle@informatik.tu-darmstadt.de`

TPTP (a collection of problem instances for theorem provers), and, more recently, CSPLIB (a benchmark library for constraints). For SAT, two collections of benchmark instances have been existing prior to SATLIB: the benchmark collection from the Second DIMACS Challenge [16], and the collection from the Beijing SAT Competition (see http://www.cirl.uoregon.edu/crawford/beijing/). These benchmark sets are available online, but they are static in the sense that no new problems were added after the initial realse, and hence, when SATLIB was created, they were partly out-dated.

From the beginning, the concept of SATLIB was to provide not just a benchmark library for SAT, but rather an increasingly comprehensive resource for SAT-related research including implementations, results from the evaluation of SAT algorithms, a list of people involved in research on SAT, pointers to SAT-related web sites, events, and an annotated bibliography. SATLIB is meant to be an open resource and will be continuously extended in the future.

In the following sections we give an overview of the current release of SATLIB. In particular, we motivate and describe our selection of benchmark instances, outline the SATLIB solver collection, and state the submission guidelines for benchmark instances, solvers, and bibliography entries. We also discuss other currently available components of SATLIB, such as the annotated bibliography, and finish with some concluding remarks and future plans.

2. The SATLIB Benchmark Suite

The most obvious but also the most important function of a benchmark library is to facilitate the use of the same set of problem instances across different studies and thus to enhance the comparability of the respective results. Therefore, these problem instances have to be easily accessible and usable for experimental studies. Different from the situation for CSP, there exists a widely used format for SAT instances: the cnf format from the Second DIMACS Benchmark Challenge. This format is currently accepted by almost all of the best-performing SAT solvers and tools, it is simple to parse and generate, reasonably concise and flexible, portable across different platforms, and human-readable. Therefore, all SATLIB benchmark instances are currently offered in cnf format.

Generally, benchmark sets should contain a large variety of different types of problem instances, such that they can be used as a basis for evaluating different types of algorithms in as unbiased as possible a way. Furthermore, different types of studies will focus on problem instances with different properties, and a benchmark set becomes more useful if it can support a broader range of studies. SATLIB offers four different types of problems: randomly generated native SAT instances, SAT-encoded, randomly generated problem instances from other domains, instances from direct applications of SAT, and SAT-encoded instances from other application domains. For most of these problem types, there are instances of different sizes. For randomly generated instances, such as Random-3-SAT, SATLIB provides standardised test-sets sampled from the underlying distributions. Since it is known that for these distributions, instance hardness may often vary strongly between the sampled instances [12, 15], making standardised test-sets available rather than only providing the generators offers considerable advantages for the comparability and reproducibility of empirical results. For encoded instances, we avoid encodings which increase the difficulty of solving the instances significantly.

Generally, we focus on problem instances which are intrinsically hard or difficult to solve for a broad range of algorithms and avoid instances which are known to be trivially solvable. While easy instances can be sometimes useful for illustrating or investigating properties of specific algorithms (for example polynomially solvable instances which are hard for certain, otherwise high-performing algorithms), we believe that they should not be used as general benchmark problems, as this can easily lead to heavily biased evaluations and assessments of the usefulness of specific algorithms. Hence, SATLIB's benchmark collection comprises mostly instances which are known to be hard for a wide range of SAT algorithms.

To avoid some well-known pitfalls of benchmarking [10, 11], benchmark libraries should generally not be static, but allow to be updated with new challenging problems. As elaborated in Section 4, SATLIB therefore encourages the submission (and retraction) of benchmark problems and thus lives of the contribution of people involved in SAT research. In the following, we give a brief overview of the benchmark suite currently available through SATLIB.

2.1. Uniform Random-3-SAT

Uniform Random-3-SAT is a family of SAT instance distributions obtained by randomly generating 3-CNF formulae in the following way: For an instance with n variables and k clauses, each of the k clauses is constructed from 3 literals which are randomly drawn from the $2n$ possible literals (the n variables and their negations) such that each possible literal is selected with the same probability of $1/2n$. Clauses are not accepted for the construction of the problem instance if they contain multiple copies of the same literal or if they are tautological (i.e., they contain a variable and its negation). Each choice of n and k thus induces a distribution of Random-3-SAT instances. Uniform Random-3-SAT is the union of these distributions over all n and k.

One particularly interesting property of uniform Random-3-SAT is the occurrence of a phase transition phenomenon, i.e., a rapid change in solubility which can be observed when systematically increasing (or decreasing) the number k of clauses for fixed problem size n [19, 25]. More precisely, for small k, almost all formulae are underconstrained and therefore satisfiable; when reaching some critical $k = k^*$, the probability of generating a satisfiable instance drops sharply to almost zero. Beyond k^*, almost all instances are overconstrained and thus unsatisfiable. For Random-3-SAT, this phase transition occurs approximately at $k^* = 4.26n$ for large n; for smaller n, the critical clauses/variable ratio k^*/n is slightly higher [2, 25]. Furthermore, for growing n the transition becomes increasingly sharp.

Empirical analyses show that problem instances from the phase transition region of uniform Random-3-SAT tend to be particularly hard for both systematic SAT solvers [2] and stochastic local search algorithms [28]. Striving to test their algorithms on hard problem instances, many researchers used test-sets sampled from the phase transition region of uniform Random-3-SAT (see [7, 23, 24] for some examples). Although similar phase transition phenomena have been observed for other subclasses of SAT, including uniform Random-k-SAT with $k \geq 4$, these have never gained the popularity of uniform Random-3-SAT. Maybe one of the reasons for this is the prominent role of 3-SAT as a prototypical and syntactically particularly simple $\mathcal{NP}$-complete problem.

In SATLIB we included test-sets of satisfiable and unsatisfiable instances sampled from Uniform Random-3-SAT distributions from the solubility phase transition region at ca. 4.26 clauses per variable [19, 25], where the average instance hardness for both, systematic and stochastic local search algorithms is maximal [2, 28]. Satisfiable and unsatisfiable instances were separated using fast complete SAT algorithms. This separation is particularly advantageous when using the test-sets for evaluating incomplete SAT algorithms which cannot determine unsatisfiability. Table I shows the characteristics of the test-sets currently included in SATLIB; these range from $n = 50$ to $n = 250$

variables with 100 instances per test-set, except for $n = 50$ and $n = 100$, for which test-sets with 1,000 instances each are provided.

2.2. Graph Colouring

The Graph Colouring problem (GCP) is a well-known combinatorial problem from graph theory: Given a graph $G = (V, E)$, where $V = \{v_1, v_2, ..., v_n\}$ is the set of vertices and $E \subseteq V \times V$ is the set of edges connecting the vertices, find a colouring $C : V \mapsto \mathbb{N}$, such that neighbouring vertices have different colours. When transforming GCP into SAT, a decision variant is encoded for which the objective is to find a colouring for a given number of colours. (The optimisation variant, which searches for a colouring with a minimal number of colours, can be solved by solving a series of such decision problems.)

SATLIB contains seven test-sets based on 3-colourable flat random graphs with 50 to 200 vertices which were created using Joe Culberson's random graph generator (available from http://web.cs.ualberta.ca/~joe/Coloring, Joe Culbersons's Graph Coloring Page.). The connectivity (edges per vertex) of these graphs was adjusted in such a way that the instances have maximal hardness (on average) for graph colouring algorithms like the Brelaz heuristic [9]. Each test-set contains 100 instances except for the 50 vertex test-set, which comprises 1,000 instances. The GCP instances were transformed into SAT by using a straightforward, yet efficient encoding known from the literature [4]. The characteristic of the SATLIB test-sets thus obtained are shown in Table II.

Another interesting class of Graph Colouring Problems is obtained by morphing regular ring lattices with random graphs [6]: A (type B) p-morph of two graphs $A = (V, E_1)$ and $B = (V, E_2)$ is a graph $C = (V, E)$ where E contains all the edges common to A and B, a fraction p of the edges from $E_1 \setminus E_2$ (the remaining edges of A), and a fraction $1 - p$ of the edges from $E_2 \setminus E_1$. The problems considered here are obtained by morphing regular ring lattices, where the vertices are ordered cyclically and each vertex is connected to its k closest vertices in this ordering, and random graphs from the well-known class G_{nm}. The morphing ratio p controls the amount of structure in the problem instances, and by varying p, the behaviour of various algorithms depending on the degree of structure and randomness can be studied [6].

SATLIB contains 9 test-sets `sw100-8-lp`x`-c5`, where $x \in \{0, 1, \ldots\}$ indicates a morphing ratio of 2^{-x}. Each of these test-sets contains 100 instances which were generated using a generator program provided by Toby Walsh and then encoded into SAT using

Table I. Uniform Random-3-SAT test-sets; the `uf*` test-sets contain only satisfiable, the `uuf*` test-sets only unsatisfiable instances.

test-set	instances	clause-len	vars	clauses
uf50-218 / uuf50-218	2 × 1,000	3	50	218
uf75-325 / uuf75-325	2 × 100	3	75	325
uf100-430 / uuf100-430	2 × 1,000	3	100	430
uf125-538 / uuf125-538	2 × 100	3	125	538
uf150-645 / uuf150-645	2 × 100	3	150	645
uf175-753 / uuf175-753	2 × 100	3	175	753
uf200-860 / uuf200-860	2 × 100	3	200	860
uf225-960 / uuf225-960	2 × 100	3	225	960
uf250-1065 / uuf250-1065	2 × 100	3	250	1,065

Table II. SAT-encoded Graph Colouring test-sets (flat random graphs).

test-set	instances	vertices	edges	colours	vars	clauses
flat50-115	1,000	50	115	3	150	545
flat75-180	100	75	180	3	225	840
flat100-239	100	100	239	3	300	1,117
flat125-301	100	125	301	3	375	1,403
flat150-360	100	150	360	3	450	1,680
flat175-417	100	175	417	3	525	1,951
flat200-479	100	200	479	3	600	2,237

the same encoding as the graph colouring instances described above [4]. The underlying graphs have 100 vertices and 400 edges, the regular ring lattice used for morphing connects each vertex to its 8 nearest neighbours in the cyclic ordering. For $0 < p < 1$, the chromatic number of the graphs thus obtained varies. Using a special graph colouring program provided by Joe Culberson, we filtered out all instances with $c \neq 5$ colours (the regular ring lattice, i.e., the morphed graph for $p = 0$, has chromatic number 5). One additional test-set, `sw100-8-p0-c5` contains the unique problem instance corresponding to the ring lattice graph (morphing ratio $p = 0$). All instances in these test-sets are satisfiable and contain 500 variable and 3,100 clauses each. [6] show that for small p (around 0.01), these instances are hardest for local search algorithms, such as WalkSAT [26], while for higher p (around 0.2), some of the instances are extremely hard for systematic search algorithms, such as SATZ [20].

2.3. Planning instances

Recently it has been shown that some AI Planning problems can be efficiently solved by encoding them into SAT and then finding models of the SAT formulae using standard SAT algorithms. This approach has shown to be competitive with or even to outperform state-of-the-art general-purpose planning algorithms [18]. In SATLIB we included SAT encodings from two well-known planning domains, the Blocks World domain and the Logistics domain. In Blocks World Planning, starting from some initial configuration, a number of blocks has to be moved to reach some given goal situation; in Logistics Planning, packages have to be moved between locations in different cities using trucks and airplanes with limited capacity.

Our benchmark set contains the four largest Blocks World Planning instances and four Logistics Planning instances from Henry Kautz's and Bart Selman's SATPLAN distribution. These instances are described in Table III; despite the reductions mentioned above, they are still very large when compared to other instances of our benchmark suite.

The SAT encoding used for generating the benchmark instances relies critically on techniques for reducing the size of the CNF formulae. These concern the particular way of defining the propositional variables as well as the application of well-known propositional reduction strategies, like unit propagation and subsumption, which are used to simplify the formulae before applying stochastic local search. These reductions can be computed in polynomial time and eliminate a number of propositional variables whereby the search space is efficiently reduced. Details on the SAT encoding used to generate the benchmark instances can be found in [18, 17].

Table III. SAT-encoded Blocks World Planning and Logistics Planning instances.

instance	packages / blocks	plan steps	vars	clauses
logistics.a	8	11	828	6,718
logistics.b	5	13	843	7,301
logistics.c	7	13	1,141	10,719
logistics.d	9	14	4,713	21,991
bw_large.a	9	6	459	4,675
bw_large.b	11	9	1,087	13,772
bw_large.c	15	14	3,016	50,457
bw_large.d	19	18	6,325	131,973

2.4. Instances from older benchmark sets

Finally, SATLIB also contains the instances from the benchmark set established during the Second DIMACS Challenge [16] and those of the Beijing SAT Competition. These benchmark sets contain satisfiable as well as unsatisfiable instances of widely different size and hardness. Most of them are SAT-encoded instances from other problem domains, including graph colouring, boolean function learning, test pattern generation for VLSI circuits, and inductive inference; furthermore, there is also a number of instances which have been generated using various random techniques. Because of space restrictions, we cannot give detailed descriptions of all these instances here; however, such descriptions can be found in SATLIB.

It should be noted that some of the larger DIMACS and Beijing instances contain several thousands of variables and tenthousands of clauses. Yet, their size is not always indicative of their hardness. In the course of extensive evaluations of different SAT algorithms (see also Chapter *Local Search Algorithms for SAT*) we found that some of these benchmark instances could be solved using polynomial preprocessing techniques. Furthermore, there are instances of SAT-encoded problems which can be efficiently solved in the original problem domain, but seem to be very hard to current techniques for solving SAT problems. These aspects of instance hardness, as far as we are aware of them, are noted in the problem descriptions included in SATLIB.

3. The SATLIB Solver Collection

The SATLIB Solvers Collection contains the original distributions of some of the most powerful SAT algorithms we are currently aware of. It comprises solvers based on stochastic local search as well as systematic search algorithms, all of which are coded in C or C++ and are relatively easy to compile and run in any Unix-like environment. The solvers included in SATLIB generally accept the DIMACS cnf-format used for all the SATLIB benchmark instances. Hence, they can be easily used for the comparative analysis of newly developed SAT algorithms, for solving SAT problems of interest, or for analysing the relative advantages and disadvantages of the different implementations.

The solvers based on stochastic local search comprise the two probably best known families of local search algorithms for SAT: GSAT [27] and the more recent WalkSAT [26]. The implementations available from SATLIB cover the basic algorithms as well as numerous variants, such as GWSAT [26], GSAT/TABU, HSAT [7], WalkSAT/TABU,

Novelty, R-Novelty [24], Novelty$^+$ and R-Novelty$^+$ [13]. We refer to Chapter *Local Search Algorithms for SAT* for a detailed investigation into the performance of stochastic local search algorithms for SAT.

The systematic solvers, all of which are variants of the well known Davis-Logemann-Loveland procedure [3], fall into different categories. Some of the underlying algorithms, such as POSIT [5], NTAB [2], and SATZ [20], rely mainly on powerful branching rules to direct the search. Others, including GRASP [22], REL_SAT [1], and SATO [29], use various mechanisms, such as dynamic-backtracking techniques, to avoid the disadvantages of chronological backtracking. Recently, some high-performing systematic solvers have been randomised to further improve their performance [8]; SATZ-rand and REL_SAT-rand, which are variants of the basic implementations of these algorithms, fall into this category.

Note that many of the techniques these algorithms are based on, can be combined in various ways. Some of the solvers currently available realise such combinations while others are currently being extended to incorporate techniques initially used only by certain other solvers. Generally, over the past few years, the development of SAT algorithms has progressed rapidly, and we expect that new developments will lead to even more powerful solvers in the near future.

4. Submission Guidelines

To increase the usefulness and scope of SATLIB, we depend on contributions from the members of the research community. These submissions will help to further extend the SATLIB benchmark suite with challenging new instances (in particular, SAT-encoded instances from other application) and the solvers collection by new high-performing algorithms. To facilitate the use of SATLIB for testing and evaluating SAT algorithms and to ensure a uniform format and appearance, we ask contributors to follow some simple guidelines:

Benchmark Problems

All problem instances should be encoded in DIMACS cnf format. The description of this format and examples are available from the SATLIB Benchmark Section. The cnf files should be packaged into `*.tar.gz` or `*.zip` files. If you think it makes sense to divide the set of instances you are submitting into several packages which should be distributed separately, you may bundle them as you see fit.

You should provide information on the instances, at least number of variables, clauses, some background on the problem class, and give evidence for the potential interest of the instance for the SAT community (such as: they are hard for a specific class of solvers, they stem from interesting applications of SAT, ...). For examples, see the descriptions in the Benchmarks Section of SATLIB. The description you send should ideally be in the form of a HTML document, but can also be a Postscript or PDF file. Please do not send research papers instead of the problem description, unless the description of the problem class the benchmark problems are taken from is the main topic of the paper.

Solvers

All solvers should accept DIMACS cnf format (see above) or be bundled with a wrapper script (preferably perl) which translates cnf into the input format accepted by the solver. All sources and a makefile for at least Unix/Linux environments should be bundled into a `*.tar.gz` (or `*.zip`) file.

You should provide information on the solver (complete/incomplete, algorithm sketch, ...), possibly a short description in form of an HTML document. You may also send a research paper (or references to papers) if the solver is the main topic of the paper. Ideally, you should also submit evaluation data for your solver applied to SATLIB benchmark problems.

References for the Annotated Bibliography
Please send us the entries either as plain text or in BibTeX format. Submitted entries should contain all bibliographically relevant information. Additionally, you should include a URL if the paper is available online, as well as a short list of keywords and/or concise notes on its contents.

General Instructions
Please send your submissions as email attachments to `hoos@cs.ubc.ca`. When your submission is included in SATLIB, you will be automatically added to the "People Involved in SAT Research" section of SATLIB. If you want to have a link to your home page added, please send us the URL, otherwise, we will link to your email address.

Please be patient. We will try to include your submission into SATLIB as soon as possible, however, we usually will collect a number of update requests and submissions before releasing a new version of SATLIB.

5. Other SATLIB Components

While the Benchmark Suite and the Solver Collection are SATLIB's core components, SATLIB also provides a number of additional features which intend to support and stimulate SAT-related research. A list of people involved in research on SAT gives easy access to the homepages (or, if not available, to the email addresses) of active members of the SAT community. A list of SAT-related events and activities provides an overview over conferences, workshops, or journal special issues. Finally, SATLIB contains a collection of links to related sites, such as webpages on specific SAT or SAT-related topics or other benchmark libraries.

Only recently, with support from Toby Walsh and Ian Gent, a first version of an annotated bibliography on SAT has been added to SATLIB. The individual entries contain bibliographic data as well as URLs for electronic versions, some keywords and/or notes on the contents for most papers. Currently, this bibliography is still very incomplete. But we hope that with the support of the community, this will become a very useful resource, which will facilitate the access to an extensive collection of publications on SAT and may thus help in finding and locating relevant research papers as well as in providing a first orientation to new members of the SAT community.

6. Conclusions and Future Developments

We described SATLIB, an online resource for SAT-related research first established in 1998. SATLIB comprises a benchmark library as well as source code distributions for a number of the most popular and best-performing SAT algorithms known to date. These core components are aimed at facilitating empirical studies of SAT algorithms, which in the past have been instrumental in improving the performance of SAT solvers as well as in enhancing our understanding of their behaviour. SATLIB also contains various other components, including an annotated bibliography of publications on SAT, which are provided to support and stimulate SAT-related research activities.

Future releases of SATLIB will hopefully provide an extended benchmark collection and new SAT solvers, as well as a considerably extended version of the annotated SAT bibliography. In this context, we have to rely on the support from the SAT community — the continuing usefulness of SATLIB as a resource crucially depends on submissions and feedback from fellow researchers. Furthermore, we plan to extend SATLIB in various ways. Firstly, we intend to provide more tools, such as implementations of converters between different formats of SAT problems, implementations of polynomial simplification strategies for SAT instances, or tools for the empirical evaluation of the performance of SAT solvers. Secondly, we want to provide results on the performance of various SAT solvers, in particular the ones available through SATLIB, on the SATLIB Benchmark Suite. Finally, we consider to extend SATLIB to problems tightly related to SAT, such as MAX-SAT, QSAT, or the recently introduced stochastic SAT and dynamic SAT problems [21, 14].

Generally, we hope that SATLIB will continue to be a useful resource which, utilised and supported by the SAT community, may contribute to support and advance SAT-related research.

Acknowledgements

We thank all members of the community who contributed to SATLIB. In particular we would like to thank the following people for submitting benchmark problems, solvers, references, or providing some help in any other way: Roberto Bayardo, Wolfgang Bibel, James Crawford, Joe Culberson, Jon W. Freeman, Ian Gent, Carla Gomes, Jens Gottlieb, Henry Kautz, Chu-Min Li, Hans van Maaren, João P. Marques da Silva, Jussi Rintanen, Bart Selman, Geoff Sutcliff, Michael Trick, Toby Walsh, Joost Warners, and Hantao Zhang. Furthermore, we gratefully acknowledge the support of the Intellectics Group at the Computer Science Department of Darmstadt University of Technology (Germany), and the Laboratory for Computational Intelligence at the Computer Science Department of the University of British Columbia (Canada), who currently host the SATLIB web site. This work was in part supported by a Postdoctoral Fellowship awarded by the University of British Columbia to Holger H. Hoos and by a Marie Curie Fellowship awarded to Thomas Stützle (CEC-TMR Contract No. ERB4001GT973400).

References

1. R.J. Bayardo Jr. and R.C. Schrag. Using CSP Look-back Techniques to Solve Real World SAT Instances. In *Proceedings of AAAI'97*, pages 203–208. MIT Press, 1997.
2. J.M. Crawford and L.D. Auton. Experimental Results on the Crossover Point in Random 3SAT. *Artificial Intelligence*, 81(1–2):31–57, 1996.
3. M. Davis, G. Logemann, and D. Loveland. A Machine Program for Theorem Proofing. *Communications of the ACM*, 5:394–397, 1962.
4. J. de Kleer. A Comparison of ATMS and CSP Techniques. In *Proceedings of IJCAI'89*, pages 290–296. Morgan Kaufmann Publishers, 1989.
5. J.W. Freeman. *Improvements to Propositional Satisfiability Search Algorithms.* PhD thesis, Department of Computer and Information Science, University of Pennsylvania, Philadelphia, 1995.
6. I.P. Gent, H.H. Hoos, P. Prosser, and T. Walsh. Morphing: Combining structure and randomness. In *Proceedings of AAAI'99*, pages 654–660. MIT Press, 1999.

7. I.P. Gent and T. Walsh. Towards an Understanding of Hill–Climbing Procedures for SAT. In *Proceedings of AAAI'93*, pages 28–33. MIT Press, 1993.
8. C.P. Gomes, B. Selman, and H. Kautz. Boosting Combinatorial Search Trough Randomization. In *Proceedings of AAAI'98*, pages 431–437. MIT Press, 1998.
9. T. Hogg. Refining the Phase Transition in Combinatorial Search. *Artificial Intelligence*, 81:127–154, 1996.
10. J.N. Hooker. Needed: An Empirical Science of Algorithms. *Operations Research*, 42(2):201–212, 1994.
11. J.N. Hooker. Testing Heuristics: We Have It All Wrong. *Journal of Heuristics*, pages 33–42, 1996.
12. H.H. Hoos. *Stochastic Local Search — Methods, Models, Applications.* infix-Verlag, Sankt Augustin, Germany, 1999.
13. H.H. Hoos. *On the Run-time Behaviour of Stochastic Local Search Algorithms for SAT.* In *Proceedings of AAAI'99*, pages 661–666. MIT Press, 1999.
14. H.H. Hoos and K. O'Neill. Stochastic Local Search Methods for Dynamic SAT — an Initial Investigation. Technical Report TR-00-01, Computer Science Department, University of British Columbia, 2000.
15. H.H. Hoos and T. Stützle. Towards a Characterisation of the Behaviour of Stochastic Local Search Algorithms for SAT. *Artificial Intelligence*, 112(1–2):213–232, 1999.
16. D.S. Johnson and M.A. Trick, editors. *Cliques, Coloring, and Satisfiability*, volume 26 of *DIMACS Series on Discrete Mathematics and Theoretical Computer Science.* American Mathematical Society, 1996.
17. H. Kautz, D. McAllester, and B. Selman. Encoding Plans in Propositional Logic. In *Proceedings of KR'96*, pages 374–384, 1996.
18. H. Kautz and B. Selman. Pushing the Envelope: Planning, Propositional Logic, and Stochastic Search. In *Proceedings of AAAI'96*, volume 2, pages 1194–1201. MIT Press, 1996.
19. S. Kirkpatrick and B. Selman. Critical Behavior in the Satisfiability of Random Boolean Expressions. *Science*, 264:1297–1301, 1994.
20. C.M. Li and Anbulagan. Look-Ahead Versus Lock-Back for Satisfiability Problems. In *Proceedings of CP'97*, pages 341–355. Springer Verlag, 1997.
21. M. Littman Initial Experiments in Stochastic Satisfiablility. In *Proceedings of AAAI'99*, pages 667–672. MIT Press, 1999.
22. J.P. Marques-Silva and K.A. Sakallah. GRASP: A Search Algorithm for Propositional Satisfiability. *IEEE Transactions on Computers*, 48(5):506–521, 1999.
23. B. Mazure, L. Sais, and É. Grégoire. Tabu Search for SAT. In *Proceedings of AAAI'97*, pages 281–285, 1997.
24. D. McAllester, B. Selman, and H. Kautz. Evidence for Invariants in Local Search. In *Proceedings of AAAI'97*, pages 321–326. MIT Press, 1997.
25. D. Mitchell, B. Selman, and H. Levesque. Hard and Easy Distributions of SAT Problems. In *Proceedings of AAAI'92*, pages 459–465. MIT Press, 1992.
26. B. Selman, Henry A. Kautz, and B. Cohen. Noise Strategies for Improving Local Search. In *Proceedings of AAAI'94*, pages 337–343. MIT Press, 1994.
27. B. Selman, H. Levesque, and D. Mitchell. A New Method for Solving Hard Satisfiability Problems. In *Proceedings of AAAI'92*, pages 440–446. MIT Press, 1992.
28. T. Yokoo. Why Adding More Constraints Makes a Problem Easier for Hill-Climbing Algorithms: Analyzing Landscapes of CSPs. In *Proceedings of CP'97*, pages 357–370. Springer Verlag, 1997.
29. H. Zhang. SATO: An Efficient Propositional Prover. In *Proceedings of CADE-97*, pages 308–312. Vol 1104 in LNAI, Springer Verlag, 1997.

SAT2000
I. Gent et al. (Eds.)
IOS Press, 2000

Unique solution instance generation for the 3-Satisfiability (3SAT) problem

Mitsuo Motoki[†]
Tokyo Institute of Technology, Tokyo, Japan

Ryuhei Uehara[§]
Komazawa University, Japan

Abstract. For the 3-Satisfiability Problem (3SAT), we propose algorithms for generating its positive instance (and its solution) randomly. We design these algorithms so that each of them produces, with high probability, a *unique solution 3SAT instance* i.e., a 3SAT instance with only one satisfying assignment. First we investigate a naive algorithm. We proved theoretically that the algorithm yields a unique solution 3SAT instance with high probability if the number of clauses is $(7/3)n \ln n + O(n)$, where n is the number of variables. Then by modifying this algorithm, we propose two algorithms that need only $O(n)$ clauses to yield a unique solution 3SAT instance with high probability. Hardness of generated instances against standard heuristics is also investigated experimentally.

Keywords: SAT, instance generation

1. Introduction

The Satisfiability Problem (SAT Problem), the problem of deciding whether a given Boolean formula is satisfiable, is one of the well-known NP-complete problems. It appears in many basic applications such as automatic deductive reasoning, logic programming, machine learning, etc. Thus, while the problem is believed unsolvable in polynomial time in the worst case, many heuristic algorithms have proposed and some of them seem to be quite good "on average".

For testing the performance of these SAT solvers, it would be useful if we have efficient algorithms generating SAT instances. Such test instance generation algorithms have been proposed in the literature [2, 11, 1]. Those proposed algorithms are designed mainly to generate relatively "hard" instances; for example, Horie and Watanabe [8] gave an algorithm that generates hard SAT instances based on the factorization problem.

We propose algorithms for generating random instances of the 3SAT problem and investigate statistical features and hardness of generated instances.

We aim to generate instances "randomly" under some reasonable distribution whose domain covers almost all *positive SAT instances*, i.e., satisfiable Boolean formulae. We consider the problem of randomly generating a positive 3SAT instance together with its satisfying assignment. (A *positive 3SAT instance* is a satisfiable conjunctive normal form Boolean formula with three literals in each clause.) We consider one more requirement; our algorithm generates, with high probability, a positive 3SAT instance having exactly one satisfying assignment, which we call a *unique solution 3SAT instance.* Unique solution 3SAT instances are useful for investigating behavior of many heuristics such as the local search method. Furthermore, one can generate a negative 3SAT instance from

[†] mmotoki@is.titech.ac.jp
[§] uehara@komazawa-u.ac.jp

a unique solution 3SAT instance, just by adding one more clause that suppresses the unique solution. This provides us with a natural way to randomly generate large variety of negative 3SAT instances. (Note that unless NP = co-NP, it is impossible to generate each negative 3SAT instance in polynomial time with nonzero probability.)

In this paper we first consider one naive positive 3SAT instance generation algorithm and study the probability that it generates unique 3SAT instances. Then based on this analysis, we modify it to obtain two algorithms. Our algorithms, given parameters n and m, generate a positive 3CNF formula with n variables and m clauses. The naive algorithm, which we call $G1$, chooses a desired satisfying assignment uniformly at random and then selects m clauses satisfied by the unique assignment uniformly at random. Clearly, a formula obtained in this way is satisfiable. Furthermore, one can easily expect that if m increases, it becomes more likely that a formula obtained has no other satisfying assignment, i.e., it is a unique solution 3SAT instance. But this algorithm is so naive that needs many clauses to generate a unique solution 3SAT instance with high probability. This motivates us to modify the algorithm. By modifying $G1$, we propose two algorithms that yield unique solution 3SAT instances with smaller m.

We prove theoretically that algorithm $G1$ generates a unique solution 3SAT instance with high probability (say, with 90%) if $m = \frac{7}{3}n \ln n + O(n)$.

Based on this analysis, we propose two modifications and obtain algorithms $G2$ and $G3$. We prove theoretically that $G2$ generates a unique solution 3SAT instance with high probability if $m \geq c_2 n + o(n)$, where $c_2 = 40$. We also show experimentally that $G2$ generates a unique solution 3SAT instance with about probability 50% if m is $4.3n$, which is close to the crossover point in random 3SAT, estimated at $4.258n+58.26n^{1/3}$ [3]. Though we have not been able to get better theoretical bound, we show experimentally that the third algorithm $G3$ needs less number of clauses for generating a unique solution 3SAT instance with high probability.

We also examine experimentally the hardness of instances generated by our algorithms when they are solved by standard backtrack and local search algorithms [4, 10]. We show that for these two standard heuristics, instances generated by $G2$ are much harder than those generated by $G1$.

Preliminaries We recall some notions on the 3SAT problem and define some notations.

Throughout this paper, our SAT instance is a *3-conjunctive normal form* (3CNF) formula f over n *variables*, $x_1, x_2, \ldots, x_n$. That is, f is a sequence $c_1, c_2, \ldots, c_m$ of *clauses*, where each clause is a set of exactly 3 *literals*, i.e., variable x_i or its complement $\overline{x_i}$. Here we assume that any variable appears at most once in each clause. Let C denote the set of all such clauses; then $\|C\| = 8\binom{n}{3}$. Throughout this paper, we use n and m to denote the number of variables and clauses respectively.

For any truth assignment t of n variables, we denote by C_t the set of clauses in C satisfied by t, and let N denote $\|C_t\|$. For each k with $0 \leq k \leq n$, we use T_k to denote the set of assignments whose Hamming distance from $t_0 = 1^n$ is equal to k, and let N_k denote $\|C_{t_0} \cap C_t\|$ where $t \in T_k$.

PROPOSITION 1.1. *$N = 7\binom{n}{3}$ and $N_k = 6\binom{n}{3} + \binom{n-k}{3}$.*

Proof. If clause c includes at least one variable whose value is distinct on t_0 and t_k, there are 6 combinations of positive and negative literals. If clause c includes no variables whose value is distinct on t_0 and t_k, there are 7 combinations of positive and negative literals and there are $\binom{n-k}{3}$ combinations of variables.

We say that c *suppresses* t if an assignment t does not satisfy a clause c.

2. A Naive Instance Generation Algorithm

A naive way to generate positive 3SAT instances is to first choose a desired satisfying assignment and then select clauses satisfied by the assignment. We give theoretical analysis to this naive algorithm $G1$ stated as follows:

Algorithm $G1$
input n : the number of variables, m : the number of clauses;
begin
  choose truth assignment $\hat{t} \in \{0,1\}^n$ randomly;
  for $i = 1$ **to** m **do**
    choose a clause from $C_{\hat{t}}$ randomly as the ith clause c_i of f ;
  output $(f_{G1(n,m)}, \hat{t})$;
end.

Remark. One clause may be selected more than once.

Clearly $G1$ can output all positive instances with n variables and m clauses. Intuitively, $f_{G1(n,m)}$, an output formula of $G1(n,m)$, has fewer number of solutions if m is large. Hence, our interest is a condition of m that $f_{G1(n,m)}$ has only one solution with high probability. Hereafter, we assume that $t_0 = 1^n$ is chosen as $\hat{t}$, solution of $f_{G1(n,m)}$, without loss of generality.

We first prove an upper bound of the number of clauses that is sufficient to generate a unique solution instance with a given probability.

THEOREM 2.1. *For any positive constant $\delta < 1$ and any n with $n \geq 43$, if $m \geq \frac{7}{3}n\ln n - \frac{7}{3}n\ln\frac{\delta}{2}$, then $f_{G1(n,m)}$ has only one solution with probability at least $1-\delta$.*

Proof. We suppose that $f_{G1(n,m)}$ has another solution $t_k \in T_k$. Then, $f_{G1(n,m)}$ consists of only elements in $C_{t_0} \cap C_{t_k}$. Thus, the probability that $f_{G1(n,m)}$ has another solution $t \in T_k$ is $\left\{\frac{N_k}{N}\right\}^m$.

Then, the probability that $f_{G1(n,m)}$ has at least two solutions is bounded above as follows.

$$\Pr\left[\ f_{G1(n,m)} \text{ has at least two solutions}\right] \leq \sum_{k=1}^{n} \binom{n}{k} \left\{\frac{N_k}{N}\right\}^m .$$

The probability that $f_{G1(n,m)}$ has only one solution is greater than $1-\delta$, if this value is less than δ. Let $p(k)$ be $\binom{n}{k}\left\{\frac{N_k}{N}\right\}^m$.

Then since $m \geq \frac{7}{3}n\ln\frac{2n}{\delta}$, we get $p(1) = n\left\{1 - \frac{3}{7n}\right\}^m \leq ne^{-\frac{3}{7n}m} \leq \delta/2$. Thus it is sufficient to show that $p(k+1)/p(k) \leq 1/2$ for $0 < k < n$ and $m \geq \frac{7}{3}n\ln\frac{2n}{\delta}$.

When $k \geq \frac{2n-1}{3}$, $p(k+1)/p(k) \leq 1/2$ irrespectively of m. Thus our goal is to show that $p(k+1)/p(k) \leq 1/2$ for $k < \frac{2n-1}{3}$. Since $m \geq \frac{7}{3}n\ln\frac{2n}{\delta} \geq \frac{7}{3}n\ln 2n$, $n \geq 43$ and letting $k = \alpha n$, we have

$$\begin{aligned}
\frac{p(k+1)}{p(k)} &= \frac{(1-\alpha)n}{\alpha n+1}\left\{1-\frac{3}{\frac{6n(n-1)(n-2)}{(1-\alpha)^2(n-\frac{1}{1-\alpha})(n-\frac{2}{1-\alpha})}+(1-\alpha)n}\right\}^m \\
&\le \frac{(1-\alpha)n}{\alpha n+1}\left\{1-\frac{3(1-\alpha)^2}{7n}\right\}^m \\
&\le \frac{(1-\alpha)n}{\alpha n+1}\exp\left(\frac{-3(1-\alpha)^2 m}{7n}\right) \\
&\le \frac{(1-\alpha)n}{\alpha n+1}\exp\left(-(1-\alpha)^2\ln 2n\right) \\
&= \frac{(1-\alpha)n}{\alpha n+1}(2n)^{-(1-\alpha)^2}.
\end{aligned}$$

It is easy to see that $\frac{(1-\alpha)n}{\alpha n+1}(2n)^{-(1-\alpha)^2}$ is monotone decreasing function of n when $n \ge \frac{2-\alpha}{(1-\alpha)^2}$. Moreover, since $0 < \alpha \le \frac{2-\frac{1}{n}}{3}$, $\frac{2-\alpha}{(1-\alpha)^2} = \frac{1}{(1-\alpha)^2} + \frac{1}{1-\alpha} < 12$. Combining this together, $\frac{(1-\alpha)n}{\alpha n+1}(2n)^{-(1-\alpha)^2}$ is monotone decreasing when $n \ge 12$. We can check that $\frac{(1-\alpha)n}{\alpha n+1}(2n)^{-(1-\alpha)^2} \le 1/2$ when $n = 43$ by brute force. Thus $p(k+1)/p(k) \le 1/2$ for $n \ge 43$, which completes the proof of the theorem.

Next we prove a lower bound of the number of clauses that is required to generate a unique solution instance with a given probability. Intuitively, $f_{G1(n,m)}$ shall have some solutions near by $\hat{t}$, if m is too small. This observation leads us to the lower bound.

THEOREM 2.2. *For any positive constant $\varepsilon < 1$, when $m < \frac{7}{3}n\ln n + \left(\frac{7}{3}\gamma - \alpha - 1\right)n$, $f_{G1(n,m)}$ has at least two solutions with probability at least $1-\varepsilon$, where γ is the Euler's constant (≈ 0.57722) and $\alpha > \frac{7\pi}{3\sqrt{6\varepsilon}}$.*

Proof. For any 3CNF f, if a clause c is the first clause in f that suppresses an assignment t, then we say *c hits t*. It is easy to see that $f_{G1(n,m)}$ has unique solution if and only if all assignments except $\hat{t}$ are hit.

Let $t_1^i \in T_1$ be an assignment whose ith bit x_i is 0. We remark that when $f_{G1(n,m)}$ has unique solution, all possible t_1^is should be hit. We consider a clause c_i hitting t_1^i.

Then, since c_i suppresses t_1^i and does not suppress t_0, $c_i = (x_i \vee \overline{x_{a_i}} \vee \overline{x_{b_i}})$ for some a_i and b_i. Thus, c_i does not suppress t_1^j for each $j \ne i$, and the number of possible c_i is $\binom{n-1}{2}$.

Let X be a random variable defined to be the number of randomly chosen clauses from C_{t_0} required to hit all assignments in T_1. We first determine the expected value of X. Let $c_1, c_2, \ldots, c_X$ be the clauses, where $c_i \in C_{t_0}$ is the ith clause of $f_{G1(n,m)}$. We divide the sequence into *epochs*, where the epoch i begins with the clause following clause which hits a remaining assignment in T_1 and ends with the clause which hits another remaining assignment in T_1. Define the random variable X_i, for $0 \le i \le n-1$, to be the number of clauses in the ith epoch, so that $X = \sum_{i=0}^{n-1} X_i$. (See [9] for the notion "epoch" used in "Coupon Collector's Problem".)

Further, let p_i denote the probability that one of remaining assignments in T_1 is hit on any clause of the ith epoch. This is the probability of drawing a clause hitting one of the $n-i$ remaining assignments and so, $p_i = 3(n-i)/7n$. The random variable X_i is geometric distribution with parameter p_i. Thus, the expected value of X_i is $1/p_i$ and its variance is $(1-p_i)/p_i^2$.

By the linearity of expectation,

$$E[X] = \sum_{i=0}^{n-1} E[X_i] = \frac{7n}{3} \sum_{i=0}^{n-1} \frac{1}{n-i} = \frac{7n}{3} \sum_{i=1}^{n} \frac{1}{i} = \frac{7n}{3} H_n,$$

where H_n is the nth Harmonic number and $H_n \geq \ln n + \gamma + \frac{1}{2n} - \frac{1}{12n^2}$ (see [6] 6.4 (6.66)).
Since the X_is are independent, we have

$$\sigma_X^2 = \sum_{i=0}^{n-1} \sigma_{X_i}^2 = \frac{49n^2}{9} \sum_{i=0}^{n-1} \frac{1}{(n-i)^2} - \frac{7n}{3} \sum_{i=0}^{n-1} \frac{1}{n-i} < \frac{49\pi^2}{54} n^2.$$

Hence $\sigma_X < \frac{7\pi}{3\sqrt{6}} n$. Now, we have

$$\begin{aligned} \Pr[f_{G(n,m)} \text{ has unique solution}] &\leq \Pr[\forall t_1^i \in T_1 \text{ are hit}] \\ &= \Pr[X \leq m] \leq \Pr\left[|X - E[X]| \geq E[X] - m\right]. \end{aligned}$$

Since $m < \frac{7}{3} n \ln n + \left(\frac{7}{3}\gamma - \alpha - 1\right) n$, $E[X] - m \geq \alpha n \geq \frac{1}{\sqrt{\varepsilon}} \sigma_X$. Thus, using the Chebyshev's inequality, we have

$$\Pr\left[|X - E[X]| \geq E[X] - m\right] \leq \Pr\left[|X - E[X]| \geq \frac{1}{\sqrt{\varepsilon}} \sigma_X\right] \leq \varepsilon.$$

This completes the proof of the theorem.

In theoretical analysis of the algorithm $G1$, the upper and lower bounds have the same main term $\frac{7}{3} n \ln n$. Through some experiments, we located the average value between upper and lower bounds. We also estimated constant values. We assumed that the relation of the ratio of the number of clauses and the number of variables with the ratio of not unique solution formulae forms $m/n = \frac{7}{3} \ln n - x \ln \delta - \frac{y}{\sqrt{1-\delta}} + z$, and get $m/n = \frac{7}{3} \ln n - 2.58 \ln \delta - \frac{2.53}{\sqrt{1-\delta}} - 0.788$.

3. Improved Algorithms

In the previous section, we show that $G1$ generates a unique solution instance with high probability when $m = \Theta(n \ln n)$. On the other hand, it has been believed that hard 3SAT instances are more likely when m is close to the crossover point, i.e., $m \approx 4.258n + 58.26n^{1/3}$ [3], and researchers are interested in solving instances with approximately this number of clauses. Compared to this number, $\Theta(n \ln n)$ seems to be too large. In fact, Gent showed that instances generated by $G1(n, m)$ are very easy to solve on average, when m is $O(n \ln n)$ [5]. Thus, we modify the naive algorithm to generate a unique solution instance with less number of clauses.

3.1. Modification of the Naive Algorithm: Algorithm G2

In the proof of Theorem 2.2, we use the idea that the assignments in T_1 are likely to be other solutions. The idea also gives us an obvious lower bound n of the number of clauses for unique solution instances to suppress all assignments in T_1.

To improve $G1$, we first add clauses that suppress all assignments in T_1, which is the key idea of algorithm $G2$.

More formally, $G2$ is stated as follows.

Algorithm $G2$
input n : the number of variables, m : the number of clauses;
begin
choose a truth assignment $\hat{t} \in \{0,1\}^n$ randomly;
let $\hat{t}_1^i$ $(1 \le i \le n)$ be an assignment different from $\hat{t}$ on only the ith bit;
for $i = 1$ **to** n **do**
choose a clause which suppresses $\hat{t}_1^i$ from $C_{\hat{t}}$ randomly as the ith clause c_i of f;
for $i = n+1$ **to** m **do**
choose a clause from $C_{\hat{t}}$ randomly as the ith clause c_i of f;
output $(f_{G2(n,m)}, \hat{t})$;
end.

Note that $G2$ can generate all unique solution instances. We show that $\Theta(n)$ clauses are sufficient to generate a unique solution instance with high probability. This is a big advantage of $G2$ over $G1$.

THEOREM 3.1. *For any given fixed δ with $0 < \delta < 1$ and any n with $n \ge 163$, when $m \ge \max\left(\frac{7}{6}(n+3)\ln\frac{6}{\delta},\ 39n\right)$, $f_{G2(n,m+n)}$ has only one solution with probability at least $1-\delta$.*

Proof of Theorem 3.1 is similar to that of Theorem 2.1. Remind that we can assume that $\hat{t} = t_0 = 1^n$ without loss of generality.

Proof. We first consider the probability that any fixed t in T_k is not suppressed by the first n clauses. For each $c_1, c_2, \cdots, c_n$, we assume that c_i is the form $(x_i \vee \overline{x_{a_i}} \vee \overline{x_{b_i}})$. We denote by $t(x_i)$ the ith value of the assignment t. Then two cases arise. In the case $t(x_i) = 1$, c_i does not suppress t. On the other hand, when $t(x_i) = 0$, c_i suppresses t with probability $\frac{n-k}{n-1}\frac{n-k-1}{n-2}$ since t has $(n-k)$ 1s. Hence c_i does not suppress t with probability $1 - \frac{n-k}{n-1}\frac{n-k-1}{n-2} = \frac{(k-1)(2n-k-2)}{(n-1)(n-2)}$. The first case occurs $(n-k)$ times, and the second case occurs k times. Thus, t is not suppressed by $c_1, c_2, \cdots, c_n$ with probability $\left\{\frac{(k-1)(2n-k-2)}{(n-1)(n-2)}\right\}^k$.

Then, the probability that $f_{G2(n,n+m)}$ has at least two solutions is bounded above as follows.

$$\begin{aligned}
&\Pr\left[f_{G2(n,n+m)} \text{ has at least two solutions}\right] \\
&\qquad \le \sum_{k=2}^{n} \binom{n}{k} \left\{\frac{(k-1)(2n-k-2)}{(n-1)(n-2)}\right\}^k \left\{\frac{N_k}{N}\right\}^m \\
&\qquad \le \sum_{k=2}^{n} \frac{k}{2}\binom{n}{k} \left\{\frac{(k-1)(2n-k-2)}{(n-1)(n-2)}\right\}^k \left\{\frac{N_k}{N}\right\}^m.
\end{aligned}$$

We let $q(k) = \frac{k}{2}\binom{n}{k}\left\{\frac{(k-1)(2n-k-2)}{(n-1)(n-2)}\right\}^k \left\{\frac{N_k}{N}\right\}^m$ for short.
Then since $m \ge \frac{7}{6}(n+3)\ln\frac{6}{\delta} \ge \frac{7n(n-1)}{6(n-2)}\ln\frac{4n}{(n-1)\delta}$, we get

$$q(2) = \frac{2n}{(n-1)}\left\{\frac{N_2}{N}\right\}^m \le \frac{2ne^{-\frac{6(n-2)}{7n(n-1)}m}}{(n-1)} \le \frac{\delta}{2}.$$

Thus it is sufficient to show that $q(k+1)/q(k) \le \frac{1}{2}$. We have

$$\begin{aligned}\frac{q(k+1)}{q(k)} &= \frac{(n-k)(2n-k-3)}{(n-1)(n-2)}\left\{\frac{k(2n-k-3)}{(k-1)(2n-k-2)}\right\}^k\left\{\frac{N_{k+1}}{N_k}\right\}^m\\ &\le \frac{4(n-k)(2n-k-3)}{(n-1)(n-2)}\left\{\frac{N_{k+1}}{N_k}\right\}^m.\end{aligned}$$

Hence, $q(k+1)/q(k) \le \frac{4(n-k)(2n-k-3)}{(n-1)(n-2)} \le 1/2$ irrespectively m when $k \ge \frac{6n-6-\sqrt{6n^2-30n+40}}{4}$. Thus our goal is to show $q(k+1)/q(k) \le 1/2$ for $2/n \le \alpha \le \frac{6n-6-\sqrt{6n^2-30n+40}}{4n} \le \frac{486-\sqrt{38641}}{326}$.

By letting $k = \alpha n$ (where $2/n \le \alpha \le \frac{6n-6-\sqrt{6n^2-30n+40}}{4n}$) , $m \ge 39n \ge \frac{7n}{3(1-\alpha)^2}\ln\frac{8(1-\alpha)163((2-\alpha)163-3)}{162\cdot 161} \ge \frac{7n}{3(1-\alpha)^2}\ln\frac{8(1-\alpha)n((2-\alpha)n-3)}{(n-1)(n-2)}$ and $n \ge 163$, we have

$$\begin{aligned}\frac{q(k+1)}{q(k)} &\le \frac{4(1-\alpha)n((2-\alpha)n-3)}{(n-1)(n-2)}\left\{1-\frac{3(1-\alpha)^2}{7n}\right\}^m\\ &\le \frac{4(1-\alpha)n((2-\alpha)n-3)}{(n-1)(n-2)}\exp\left(\frac{-3(1-\alpha)^2m}{7n}\right) \le \frac{1}{2}.\end{aligned}$$

This completes the proof of the theorem.

3.2. Further Improvement: Algorithm G3

We here propose yet another improvement. The next algorithm $G3$ is obtained experimentally.

Algorithm $G3$
input n : the number of variables, m : the number of clauses;
begin
  choose a truth assignment $\hat{t} \in \{0,1\}^n$ randomly;
  let $\hat{t}_1^i$ $(1 \le i \le n)$ be an assignment different from $\hat{t}$ on only the ith bit;
  let $\hat{t}_{n-1}^i$ $(1 \le i \le n)$ be an assignment different from $\hat{t}$ on all bits but the ith bit;
  for $i = 1$ **to** n **do**
    choose a clause which suppresses $\hat{t}_1^i$ from $C_{\hat{t}}$ randomly as the ith clause c_i of f;
  for $i = 1$ **to** n **do**
    choose a clause which suppresses $\hat{t}_1^i$ from $C_{\hat{t}}$ randomly as the $n+i$th clause c_{n+i} of f;
  for $i = 1$ **to** n **do**
    choose a clause which suppresses $\hat{t}_{n-1}^i$ and is satisfied by $\hat{t}_n$ from $C_{\hat{t}}$ randomly as the $2n+i$th clause c_{2n+i} of f;
  for $i = 3n+1$ **to** m **do**
    choose a clause from $C_{\hat{t}}$ randomly as the ith clause c_i of f;
  output $(f_{G3(n,m)}, \hat{t})$;
end.

In this algorithm, we add clauses that suppress all assignments in T_1 two times, and clauses that suppress all assignments in T_{n-1} (but not suppress $t_n = 0^n$). Thus,

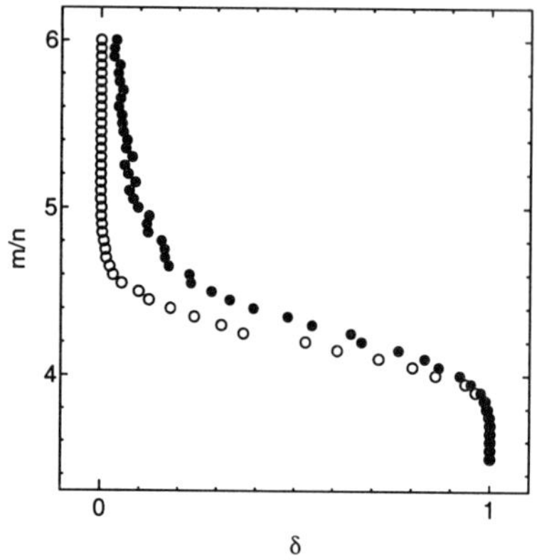

Figure 1. the ratio m/n to the ratio δ

$G3$ cannot generate all of unique solution formulae. But $G3$ has the advantage of the number of clauses over $G2$.

$G3(n, 3n + m)$ adds $2n$ clause to an instance generated by $G2(n, n + m)$. Thus, obviously, we can also apply the upper bound for $G2(n, n + m)$ to $G3(n, 3n + m)$.

COROLLARY 3.2. *For any given fixed δ with $0 < \delta < 1$, when $m \geq \max\left(\frac{7}{6}(n+3)\ln\frac{6}{\delta}, 39n\right)$, $f_{G3(n,3n+m)}$ has only one solution with probability at least $1 - \delta$.*

3.3. Experiments

In theoretical analysis of the algorithms $G2$ and $G3$, we show the linear upper bounds. We compare the theoretical upper bounds with the number of clauses that we obtained through experiments.

First, we describe the setup used in the experiments. The algorithm to check the unique solution formulae is based on a backtrack algorithm "A-SAT" [4]. To detect another solution, we add a size n clause that is not satisfied by only $\hat{t}$.

We fixed the number of variables to 100, and we selected the numbers of clauses being from 350 to 600 at intervals of 5. For each point, we checked the ratio of unique solution formulae to 1000 formulae chosen uniformly at random.

In Figure 1, along the horizontal axis we give the ratio of not unique solution formula δ, and along the vertical axis we give the ratio m/n. Black dot is the experimental result of $G2(n, m)$, and white dot is that of $G3(n, m)$.

With this graph, we can see that $G3$ can output unique solution formulae with less number of clauses than $G2$. Furthermore, the ratio of unique solution formula of $G3$ converges to 1 faster. This is the advantage of $G3$ over $G2$.

Both $G2$ and $G3$ can output unique solution formulae with high probability when the number of clauses is larger than the crossover point ($\approx 4.3n$). Furthermore, behavior of $G3$ is similar to crossover region of random 3SAT.

4. Hardness of Instances

In the previous sections, for generating a unique solution instance with high probability, we show that $G2$ and $G3$ need less number of clauses than $G1$. But if instances generated by $G2$ and $G3$ are solvable more easily than that of $G1$, they are not useful as test instance generators. In this section, we show experimentally that instances of $G2$ and $G3$ are much harder than that of $G1$ against two basic SAT solvers, a backtrack algorithm and a local search algorithm.

4.1. Backtrack Algorithm

Backtracking is one of the well-known strategy for solving NP problems, and many variations of backtrack algorithm have been proposed for SAT. Here we choose "A-SAT" [4]. We measure the number of branches to estimate hardness of instances.

In our experiment, we fixed the number of variables to 100, and we selected the numbers of clauses from 400 to 600 at intervals of 10. For each point, we checked the number of branches to solve by A-SAT for 1000 formulae generated by our generators. (For comparison, we used the same set of m for all three generators, though $G1$ needs much more clauses than $G2$ and $G3$ in order to generate unique solution SAT instances. But through our experiment, we have verified that the result does not change (even worse to $G1$) for larger m.)

Table II, III and IV show the number of branches to solve instances generated by $G1$, $G2$ and $G3$ respectively. From these tables, we see that (i) most of instances of $G1$ need between 1 and 2000 branches, and on the other hand, (ii) when $m \leq 500$, most of instances of $G2$ and $G3$ need between 500 and 10000 branches, (iii) when $m \geq 500$, there are quite difference between $G1$ and $G2$ (resp. $G3$). That is, the ratios of hard instances against A-SAT in instances generated by $G2$ (resp., $G3$) are quite higher than that of $G1$. Both $G2$ and $G3$ generate harder instances than $G1$ against a standard backtrack solver.

4.2. Local Search Algorithm

Local search is another standard strategy to solve NP problems, and again, many variations of local search algorithms have been proposed for SAT. For example, Gu and Gu proposed a local search algorithm that can solve 3SAT in polynomial time on average [7]. As a basic local search algorithm, we use "walksat" [10].

The outline of walksat is as follows. For a given formula, it starts with a randomly chosen initial assignment. Then it improves an assignment by flipping one bit of assignment so that either, with probability p, the number of satisfied clauses increases, or, with probability $1-p$, flip one bit to satisfying randomly chosen unsatisfied clause, until either it finds an satisfying assignment for the formula, or the number of flips is over MAXFLIPS. For the latter case, the algorithm restarts with a new initial assignment. For estimating the hardness of a instance, we measure the number of initial assignments used to find a solution.

Throughout this experiment, we fixed the number of variables to 50, and we selected the numbers of clauses from 200 to 300 at intervals of 5. For each point, we checked the number of initial assignments used to find a solution by walksat for 1000 (100, for $G3$) formulae generated by our generators. We set MAXFLIPS, the maximum number of flips, to 5000, and p to 0.5. Again we used, for comparison, the same set of m for all three generators, but we also have verified in our preliminary experiment that the result does not change (even worse to $G1$) for lager m.

Table V, VI and VII show the number of initial assignments to find a solution of instances of $G1$, $G2$ and $G3$ respectively. From these tables, we see that the ratio of hard instances against walksat in instances generated by $G2$ (resp., $G3$) is much higher than that of $G1$. In particular, $G3$ sometimes generates some extremely hard instances that needs more than 200 initial assignments.

To explain this result, we investigate the structure of search space of generated instances. For an instance f with a satisfying assignment $\hat{t}$, suppose that the number of satisfiable clauses tends to increase as an assignment gets closer to the correct assignment $\hat{t}$. Then we may expect that f is easy for the local search. That is, the structure of a search space of f is favorable to the local search. For checking whether generated instances have a favorable search space structure, we investigated the distribution of assignments that satisfy many, i.e., $m-2$, $m-1$, and m, clauses for generated instance.

In this experiment, we fixed the number of variables to 20, and the number of clauses to 100. (Since we need to count all assignments exhaustively, we had to use relatively small number.) Then for each generator, we generated 50 instances and computed the average number of assignments in each T_k that satisfy $m-2$, $m-1$, and m clauses respectively.

Table VIII shows the result. It is easy to see that compared to instances of $G1$, instances of $G2$ and $G3$ have few assignments near $\hat{t}$ that satisfy $m-1$ clauses. Furthermore, instances of $G3$ still have few assignments near $\hat{t}$ that satisfy $m-2$ clauses. This structure is somewhat clear from our generation algorithms. Recall that in $G2$ (resp., in $G3$) one clause is (resp., two clauses are) added to suppress each assignment with distance 1 from the designated solution $\hat{t}$. Thus, there must be only few assignments close to the solution that satisfy many, e.g., $m-2$ and $m-1$, clauses. On the other hand, this structure seems a reason why instances generated by $G2$ and $G3$ are hard for the local search.

On the other hand, when m is large enough and $G1$ generates a unique solution instance with high probability, the search space structure of a generated instance becomes quite favorable to the local search. For example, we found through another experiment that the maximum number of satisfied clause in T_k is monotonically decreasing with k.

5. Concluding Remarks

If there exists imbalance between the number of positive and negative occurrence of each variable in a generated formula, some solver may be able to find a solution using this imbalance.

We can theoretically estimate the expected number of positive and negative occurrence of each variable. (See Table I: the first three are for the general case and the last three are for the case that the total number of clauses is $6n$.)

From Table I, we can find that instances generated by $G1$ have large imbalance. On the other hand, instances generated by $G2$ and $G3$ have fewer difference between the expected number of positive and negative literals, and we believe that this type of imbalance does not cause serious problems for instances generated by $G2$ nor $G3$. However, a more clear explanation (based on theoretical analysis) is left for future topics.

This research is a part of the SAT instance generation project conducted at Watanabe group, Department of Mathematical and Computing Sciences, Tokyo Institute of Technology. Our algorithms and examples of instances are available through the SAT Instance Generation Page at http:// www.is.titech.ac.jp/~watanabe/gensat/.

Table I. The expectation number of literals

instance	The expected number of literals positive literals	negative literals	difference
$G1(n, m)$	$12m/7n$	$9m/7n$	$3m/7n$
$G2(n, n+m)$	$1 + 12m/7n$	$2 + 9m/7n$	$-1 + 3m/7n$
$G3(n, 3n+m)$	$4 + 12m/7n$	$5 + 9m/7n$	$-1 + 3m/7n$
$G1(n, 6n)$	$10 + 2/7$	$7 + 5/7$	$2 + 4/7$
$G2(n, 6n)$	$9 + 4/7$	$8 + 3/7$	$1 + 1/7$
$G3(n, 6n)$	$9 + 1/7$	$8 + 6/7$	$2/7$

Acknowledgements

The authors thank to the referees for their helpful comments. Especially, one referee kindly pointed us the problem for the imbalance between the number of positive and negative occurrences discussed in Concluding Remarks. We also thank to Prof. Osamu Watanabe and the members of Watanabe group.

Appendix

A. Tables

Table II. The number of branches to solve by A-SAT for $G1(100, m)$ instances

m	the number of branches 1 to 100	101 to 200	201 to 500	501 to 1000	1001 to 2000	2001 to 5000	5001 to 10000	10001 to 20000
400	345	257	214	119	46	16	3	0
410	296	240	225	120	82	32	5	0
420	263	211	222	130	98	68	8	0
430	180	201	251	169	121	64	14	0
440	156	217	218	171	137	84	16	1
450	139	187	201	181	155	122	15	0
460	120	141	194	188	196	143	17	1
470	87	135	208	176	193	188	13	0
480	106	98	201	213	185	177	19	1
490	70	116	189	220	214	177	14	0
500	61	115	176	220	231	190	7	0
510	58	114	208	219	244	151	6	0
520	66	102	200	214	259	157	2	0
530	45	104	208	248	260	134	1	0
540	63	108	212	259	263	95	0	0
550	47	95	235	284	259	79	1	0
560	67	99	235	279	256	64	0	0
570	50	102	247	318	232	51	0	0
580	56	111	275	315	208	35	0	0
590	57	115	291	317	195	25	0	0
600	82	115	292	331	170	10	0	0

Table III. The number of branches to solve by A-SAT for $G2(100, m)$ instances

m	the number of branches 1 to 100	101 to 200	201 to 500	501 to 1000	1001 to 2000	2001 to 5000	5001 to 10000	10001 to 20000	20001 to 50000
400	52	98	154	155	171	228	115	26	1
410	35	68	139	142	178	248	152	38	0
420	18	42	90	109	186	299	225	31	0
430	9	35	73	114	142	354	246	27	0
440	10	28	62	106	161	398	229	6	0
450	8	26	43	104	194	458	163	4	0
460	2	26	55	105	183	494	132	3	0
470	4	26	76	127	237	473	56	1	0
480	4	30	94	121	229	486	36	0	0
490	13	35	83	131	324	390	24	0	0
500	9	34	92	186	334	338	7	0	0
510	11	47	122	195	377	245	3	0	0
520	14	51	108	215	391	219	2	0	0
530	12	48	147	247	407	139	0	0	0
540	14	46	165	258	426	91	0	0	0
550	12	56	159	284	422	67	0	0	0
560	23	68	197	300	371	41	0	0	0
570	26	81	228	326	312	27	0	0	0
580	21	73	243	376	280	7	0	0	0
590	37	77	249	368	261	8	0	0	0
600	23	98	274	382	220	3	0	0	0

Table IV. The number of branches to solve by A-SAT for $G3(100, m)$ instances

m	the number of branches 1 to 100	101 to 200	201 to 500	501 to 1000	1001 to 2000	2001 to 5000	5001 to 10000	10001 to 20000	20001 to 50000
400	44	78	141	133	170	238	148	48	0
410	26	45	87	120	162	249	237	73	1
420	9	39	77	71	124	288	305	85	2
430	8	23	52	79	133	335	332	38	0
440	5	20	49	78	111	406	302	29	0
450	3	13	46	73	132	477	249	7	0
460	7	21	52	61	156	540	160	3	0
470	6	26	53	92	179	570	74	0	0
480	7	23	69	100	244	533	24	0	0
490	7	27	78	108	293	478	9	0	0
500	8	27	95	145	338	384	3	0	0
510	11	37	89	165	386	310	2	0	0
520	12	42	103	176	435	230	2	0	0
530	5	50	110	221	464	150	0	0	0
540	13	42	143	223	468	111	0	0	0
550	14	53	149	286	438	60	0	0	0
560	16	57	175	266	451	35	0	0	0
570	25	70	166	349	371	19	0	0	0
580	15	74	192	369	341	9	0	0	0
590	21	94	220	394	265	6	0	0	0
600	23	82	238	432	223	2	0	0	0

Table V. The number of initial assignments needed by walksat for $G1(50, m)$ instance

	# of initial assignments			
m	1	2	3 to 5	6 to 10
200	999	1	0	0
205	999	1	0	0
210	998	2	0	0
215	998	1	1	0
220	999	1	0	0
225	994	4	2	0
230	999	1	0	0
235	995	4	1	0
240	995	5	0	0
245	997	3	0	0
250	994	5	1	0
255	992	7	1	0
260	998	0	2	0
265	995	4	1	0
270	996	3	0	1
275	996	3	1	0
280	996	4	0	0
285	997	1	2	0
290	997	3	0	0
295	996	3	1	0
300	996	4	0	0

Table VI. The number of initial assignments needed by walksat for $G2(50, m)$ instances

	the number of initial assignments							
m	1	2	3 to 5	6 to 10	11 to 20	21 to 50	51 to 100	101 to 200
200	877	36	43	19	13	10	1	1
205	824	64	52	29	19	11	1	0
210	726	81	108	45	22	18	0	0
215	710	85	101	51	34	15	4	0
220	641	117	135	49	42	13	2	1
225	648	124	135	47	30	16	0	0
230	635	155	119	53	25	12	1	0
235	629	137	141	51	27	12	3	0
240	637	132	137	54	28	9	3	0
245	665	144	115	48	24	4	0	0
250	671	154	113	45	14	3	0	0
255	706	135	100	44	10	4	1	0
260	746	115	93	30	9	7	0	0
265	730	128	90	28	18	6	0	0
270	770	137	62	20	9	1	1	0
275	793	112	71	16	8	0	0	0
280	815	107	56	15	7	0	0	0
285	856	94	34	12	4	0	0	0
290	866	73	52	6	2	1	0	0
295	875	81	35	6	2	1	0	0
300	889	59	36	12	2	2	0	0

Table VII. The number of initial assignments needed by walksat for $G3(50, m)$ instances

m	1	2	3 to 5	6 to 10	11 to 20	21 to 50	51 to 100	101 to 200	201 to 500	501 to 1000	1001 to 2000	2001 to 5000
	the number of initial assignments											
200	100	0	0	0	0	0	0	0	0	0	0	0
205	100	0	0	0	0	0	0	0	0	0	0	0
210	99	0	0	0	0	0	0	0	0	0	1	0
215	99	0	0	0	0	0	0	0	1	0	0	0
220	92	1	0	0	0	0	1	1	2	0	3	0
225	92	2	0	1	0	0	1	3	0	0	1	0
230	81	0	0	0	0	1	2	3	4	8	1	0
235	74	3	1	1	0	2	1	5	10	3	0	0
240	65	0	0	0	0	4	4	8	11	7	0	1
245	61	3	1	0	4	2	3	8	11	5	2	0
250	51	1	0	0	2	4	7	13	14	6	2	0
255	43	1	0	1	2	4	12	12	21	4	0	0
260	24	1	1	4	7	7	13	16	21	5	1	0
265	17	0	1	2	3	16	17	15	24	3	2	0
270	8	0	2	3	4	16	20	30	12	4	1	0
275	5	2	4	2	6	18	14	26	19	4	0	0
280	3	2	4	3	14	18	23	21	10	2	0	0
285	7	0	4	5	4	16	23	25	13	3	0	0
290	5	1	3	5	9	22	22	20	12	1	0	0
295	2	1	3	8	8	23	18	22	14	1	0	0
300	3	1	2	11	9	25	27	16	5	1	0	0

Table VIII. The search space

Hamming distance from $\hat{t}$	the number of satisfied clauses								
	$G1$			$G2$			$G3$		
	100	99	98	100	99	98	100	99	98
1	2.02	5.46	5.18	0	3.86	5.84	0	0	8.42
2	2.56	12.38	26.84	0.06	1.58	11.16	0	0.14	1.56
3	2.28	16.22	55.34	0.04	1.38	9.58	0	0.08	1.28
4	1.46	16.18	71.88	0.02	1.48	9.50	0	0.08	1.52
5	0.90	13.14	72.56	0.04	1.36	10.36	0	0.20	1.98
6	0.68	9.92	63.44	0.04	1.42	11.64	0.02	0.30	2.80
7	0.70	7.38	51.92	0.12	1.72	12.24	0.02	0.52	4.38
8	0.64	6.00	40.24	0.18	1.86	14.00	0.04	0.74	6.58
9	0.50	4.38	29.54	0.12	2.04	15.90	0.02	0.96	9.04
10	0.30	2.88	19.36	0.16	2.02	17.64	0.02	1.52	11.04
11	0.10	1.66	11.58	0.22	2.40	16.54	0.18	1.74	12.88
12	0	0.96	6.38	0.24	2.12	13.96	0.22	1.88	14.38
13	0	0.46	3.34	0.22	1.36	9.66	0.16	2.14	13.00
14	0	0.12	1.44	0.12	0.90	5.28	0.18	1.52	11.06
15	0	0	0.36	0.02	0.46	2.66	0.10	1.04	7.52
16	0	0	0.06	0	0.10	1.16	0.04	0.62	4.40
17	0	0	0	0	0.06	0.16	0	0.38	1.94
18	0	0	0	0	0.02	0	0	0.12	0.76
19	0	0	0	0	0	0	0	0.02	0.36
20	0	0	0	0	0	0	0	0.02	0.04

References

1. Yuichi Asahiro, Kazuo Iwama, and Eiji Miyano. Random generation of test instance with controlled attributes. In David S. Johnson and Michael A. Trick, editors, *Cliques, Coloring, and Satisfiability*, volume 26, pages 377–393. DIMACS Series in Discrete Mathematics and Theoretical Computer Science, 1996.
2. Vašek Chvátal and Endre Szemerédi. Many hard examples for resolution. *Journal of the ACM*, 35(4):759–768, October 1988.
3. James M. Crawford and Larry D. Auton. Experimental results on the crossover point in random 3-SAT. *Artificial Intelligence*, 81(1-2):31–57, 1996.
4. O. Dubois, P. Andre, Y. Boufkhad, and J. Carlier. SAT versus UNSAT. In David S. Johnson and Michael A. Trick, editors, *Cliques, Coloring, and Satisfiability*, volume 26, pages 415–436. DIMACS Series in Discrete Mathematics and Theoretical Computer Science, 1996.
5. Ian P. Gent. On the stupid algorithm for satisfiability. http://www.cs.strath.ac.uk/~apes/reports/apes-03-1998.ps.gz, April 1998. Report APES-03-1998.
6. R. L. Graham, D. E. Knuth, and O. Patashnik. *Concrete Mathematics*. Addison-Wesley, 1989.
7. J. Gu and Q.-P. Gu. Average time complexity of the SAT 1.2 algorithm. *Lecture Notes in Computer Science*, 834:146–154, 1994.
8. Akira Horie and Osamu Watanabe. Hard instance generation for SAT. In *Proc. 8th International Symposium on Algorithms and Computation*, Lecture Notes in Computer Science 1350, pages 22–31, 1997.
9. R. Motowani and P. Raghavan. *Randomized Algorithms*, chapter 3.6. Cambridge, 1995.
10. Bart Selman, Henry A. Kautz, and Bram Cohen. Local search strategies for satisfiability testing. In David S. Johnson and Michael A. Trick, editors, *Cliques, Coloring, and Satisfiability*, volume 26, pages 521–531. DIMACS Series in Discrete Mathematics and Theoretical Computer Science, 1996.
11. Alasdair Urquhart. Hard examples for resolution. *Journal of the ACM*, 34(1):209–219, 1987.

SAT2000
I. Gent et al. (Eds.)
IOS Press, 2000

Implementing the Davis–Putnam Method

Hantao Zhang[†‡]
Dept. of Computer Science, The University of Iowa, Iowa City, IA 52242, U.S.A.

Mark E. Stickel [¶ ||]
Artificial Intelligence Center, SRI International, Menlo Park, CA 94025, U.S.A.

Abstract. The method proposed by Davis, Putnam, Logemann, and Loveland for propositional reasoning, often referred to as the Davis–Putnam method, is one of the major practical methods for the satisfiability (SAT) problem of propositional logic. We show how to implement the Davis–Putnam method efficiently using the trie data structure for propositional clauses. A new technique of indexing only the first and last literals of clauses yields a unit propagation procedure whose complexity is sublinear to the number of occurrences of the variable in the input. We also show that the Davis–Putnam method can work better when unit subsumption is not used. We illustrate the performance of our programs on some quasigroup problems. The efficiency of our programs has enabled us to solve some open quasigroup problems.

Keywords: propositional satisfiability, Davis–Putnam method, trie data structure.

1. Introduction

In recent years, there has been considerable renewed interest in the satisfiability (SAT) problem of propositional logic. The SAT problem is known to be difficult to solve — it is the first known NP-complete problem. Because the SAT problem is fundamental to many practical problems in mathematics, computer science, and electrical engineering, efficient methods that can solve a large subset of SAT problems are eagerly sought. Empirical research has been very fruitful for the development of efficient methods for SAT problems.

The method proposed by Davis, Putnam, Logemann, and Loveland for propositional reasoning [3, 4], often referred as the Davis–Putnam method, has long been a major practical method for solving SAT problems. It is based on unit propagation (i.e., unit resolution and unit subsumption) and case splitting. It is known that many factors affect the performance of the method: the data structure for clauses, the choice of variable for splitting, and so forth. In this paper, we will concentrate on the use of tries (discrimination trees) and related refinements for the Davis–Putnam method. In [5], de Kleer used tries to represent propositional clauses for efficient subsumption.

In the past, both of us have used tries to represent first-order terms and to implement efficient rewriting-based theorem provers. In autumn 1992, we independently started using tries in the Davis–Putnam method. By using the trie data structure, our programs gain something in efficiency, and much in elegance. Some preliminary results of our experiments are presented in [15, 16, 18]. In this paper, we present in detail the data structures used in our programs.

---

‡ `hzhang@cs.uiowa.edu`
|| `stickel@ai.sri.com`
† Research supported by NSF under Grants CCR-9202838 and CCR-9357851.
¶ Research supported by NSF under Grant CCR-8922330.

One of the major motivations for developing our programs was to solve open problems in algebra concerning the existence of quasigroups satisfying certain constraints [1]. The usefulness of computer programs to attack these quasigroup problems has been demonstrated in [19, 8, 15]. We prefer these quasigroup problems as benchmarks over randomly generated SAT problems for testing constraint solving methods: The problems have fixed solutions; descriptions of the problems are simple and easy to communicate; most important, some cases of the problems remain open, offering challenge and opportunities for friendly competition as well as contributions to mathematical knowledge. Besides having large search spaces, quasigroup problems are demanding examples for the Davis–Putnam method because their propositional representations contain n^3 variables and (depending on the constraint) from $O(n^4)$ to $O(n^6)$ clauses, so large sets of clauses with hundreds of thousands of literals must be handled.

Recently, some incomplete methods based on local search have been proposed that can solve very large size SAT problems [10, 14]. The usefulness of these methods for solving quasigroup problems remains to be seen. However, these methods cannot entirely replace the Davis–Putnam method because many quasigroup problems have no solutions, and incomplete methods cannot prove that no solution exists or count the number of solutions. Quasigroup completion problems (completion of partially filled in Latin squares, but without the constraints) are now a subject of research [9].

2. The Davis–Putnam Method

The Davis–Putnam method is based on three simple facts about truth table logic. First, where A and B are any formulae, the conjunction $A \wedge (\overline{A} \vee B)$ is equivalent to $A \wedge B$ and the conjunction $A \wedge (A \vee B)$ is equivalent to A. It follows that the application of unit resolution and subsumption to any set of propositional clauses results in an equivalent set. Second, where X is any set of formulae and A any propositional formula, X has a model iff either $X \cup \{A\}$ has a model or $X \cup \{\overline{A}\}$ has a model. Third, where X is any set of propositional clauses and A any propositional atomic formula, if A does not occur at least once positively in [some clause in] X and at least once negatively, then the result of deleting from X all clauses in which A occurs is a set which has a model iff X has a model.

A simple algorithm based on the first two of these facts[1] is shown in Figure 1. That it is sound and complete for propositional clause problems is well known.

Naturally, one important place at which heuristics may be inserted is in the choice of a literal for splitting. In this paper, to eliminate as much as possible other factors of the implementations, unless specified otherwise, all of our programs will use identical input and simply choose the minimally indexed variable not yet assigned a value for splitting. This literal selection strategy results in a substantial increase in the size of the search space (evident in Tables I and V), but ensures comparability of results; the focus of this paper is the effect of the trie data structure and other refinements on the speed of unit propagation, not the effect of splitting heuristics on search space size.

We have tested some other advanced SAT techniques, such as intelligent backjumping and lemma generation, with the trie data structure with good preliminary results [18].

[1] Eliminating "pure" variables that occur only positively or only negatively is not necessary for completeness. Moreover, in many types of problems, such as the quasigroup problems that we are especially interested in, the condition never occurs.

```
function Satisfiable ( clause set S ) return boolean
    /* unit propagation */
    repeat
        for each unit clause L in S do
            /* unit subsumption */
            delete from S every clause containing L
            /* unit resolution */
            delete L̄ from every clause of S in which it occurs
        od
        if S is empty then
            return true
        else if a clause becomes null in S then
            return false
        fi
    until no further changes result
    /* splitting */
    choose a literal L occurring in S
    if Satisfiable ( S ∪ {L} ) then
        return true
    else if Satisfiable ( S ∪ {L̄} ) then
        return true
    else
        return false
    fi
end function
```

Figure 1. A simple Davis–Putnam algorithm.

However, for quasigroup problems, these techniques seem not to have much positive impact on performance. A thorough discussion is outside the scope of this paper.

3. Trie Data Structure for Propositional Clauses

Our programs gain something in efficiency, and much in elegance, from using the *trie* data structure, first used to represent sets of propositional clauses in [5].

We assume that each propositional variable has a unique index, which is a positive integer. The index of the negation of a variable is the negation of the index of that variable. A clause is represented by the list of indices of the literals in the clause.

Conceptually, the trie data structure for propositional clauses is very simple. It is a tree all of whose edges are marked by indices of literals and whose leaves are marked by a clause mark. A clause is represented in a trie as a path from the root to a leaf such that the edges of the path are marked by the literal indices of the clause. If two clauses (represented as lists of integers in ascending order by absolute value) have the same prefix of length n, then they share a path of length n in the trie.

If all the nodes that have an edge of the same mark to the same parent node in a trie are made into a linear list, we may use a 3-ary tree to represent a trie as follows: Each node of the tree is empty (*nil*), or a clause end-mark ($\Box$), or a 4-tuple $\langle var, pos, neg, rest \rangle$, where *var* is a variable index, *pos* is its positive child node, *neg* is

```
function trie-merge (trie t1, trie t2) return trie
        if t1 = □ or t2 = □ then
                return □
        else if t1 = nil then
                return t2
        else if t2 = nil then
                return t1
        fi
        let t1 = ⟨v1, p1, n1, r1⟩
        let t2 = ⟨v2, p2, n2, r2⟩
        if v1 = v2 then
                let n = trie-merge(n1, n2)
                let r = trie-merge(r1, r2)
                return ⟨v1, trie-merge(p1, p2), n, r⟩
        else if v1 < v2 then
                return ⟨v1, p1, n1, trie-merge(r1, t2)⟩
        else
                return ⟨v2, p2, n2, trie-merge(r2, t1)⟩
        fi
end function
```

Figure 2. The *trie-merge* procedure.

its negative child node, and *rest* is its brother node. The interpretation is that the edge from this node to *pos* is implicitly marked by *var*; the edge from this node to *neg* is implicitly marked by $(-var)$; *rest* is the next node in the linear list of nodes that have the same parent node in the trie; *rest* does not contain any *var* or $(-var)$ edges.

A set S of (nontautologous) propositional clauses is represented by a trie T_S as follows: If S is empty, then $T_S = nil$; if S contains a null clause, then $T_S = \square$; otherwise, choose any variable index v and divide S into three groups:

$P = \{v \vee P_1, \ \ldots, \ v \vee P_n\}$ — the clauses that contain v positively.
$Q = \{\overline{v} \vee Q_1, \ \ldots, \ \overline{v} \vee Q_m\}$ — the clauses that contain v negatively.
$R = \{R_1, \ \ldots, \ R_l\}$ — the clauses that do not contain v.

Let

$P' = \{P_1, \ldots, P_n\}$ — P with occurrences of v removed.
$Q' = \{Q_1, \ldots, Q_m\}$ — Q with occurrences of $\overline{v}$ removed.

Let $T_{P'}$, $T_{Q'}$, and T_R be the trie nodes recursively representing P', Q', and R, respectively. Then S can be represented by $T_S = \langle v, T_{P'}, T_{Q'}, T_R\rangle$. For example, if $S = \{x_1 \vee x_2, \overline{x}_1 \vee \overline{x}_2\}$, then

$$T_S = \langle 1, \langle 2, \square, nil, nil\rangle, \langle 2, nil, \square, nil\rangle, nil\rangle.$$

A trie is said to be *ordered* if for any node $\langle var, pos, neg, rest\rangle$, var is smaller than any variable index appearing in *pos*, *neg*, or *rest*. The *trie-merge* operation, an extension of the merge-sort algorithm that merges two ordered tries into a single one, is shown in Figure 2. The insertion of one clause c into a trie T can be done using *trie-merge*, if we first create a trie T_c for c and then merge T_c and T.

If the value of *var* is true, $\langle var, pos, neg, rest\rangle$ is equivalent to $trie\text{-}merge(neg, rest)$. Similarly, $\langle var, pos, neg, rest\rangle$ is equivalent to $trie\text{-}merge(pos, rest)$ when the value of *var* is false. The nodes $\langle var, pos, neg, \Box\rangle$ and $\langle var, \Box, \Box, rest\rangle$ are equivalent to $\Box$. The node $\langle var, nil, nil, rest\rangle$ is equivalent to *rest*. We replace nodes by their simpler equivalents whenever possible in the *trie-merge* operation.

The *unit propagation* operation of the Satisfiable procedure can be easily implemented on tries: when a variable *var* is set to true, we simply replace each node $\langle var, pos, neg, rest\rangle$ in the trie by *trie-merge*$(neg, rest)$. The case when *var* is set to false is handled similarly.

The trie representation of a set of propositional clauses has several advantages for the Davis–Putnam method:

- Duplicate clauses are automatically eliminated when the trie is constructed.
- Memory usage is reduced because of shared clause prefixes.
- Unit clauses can be found quickly.
- Tail-subsumed clauses are automatically eliminated when the trie is constructed. A clause is said to be *tail-subsumed* by another clause if its first portion of the literals is also a clause. For example, $x_1 \vee x_2 \vee x_3$ is tail-subsumed by $x_1 \vee x_2$.
- Tail-resolutions are automatically performed when the trie is constructed. If $c_1 \vee L$ and $c_1 \vee \overline{L} \vee c_2$ are two clauses, the *tail-resolution* is the resolution on the last literal of the first clause and the result is $c_1 \vee c_2$ which subsumes the second clause. So the second clause will be replaced by $c_1 \vee c_2$. In our implementation, such resolutions will be performed no matter which clauses enters the trie first.
- The *unit propagation* operation can be performed relatively efficiently. Because the subtrie $\langle var, pos, neg, rest\rangle$ does not contain any variable $var' < var$, it does not need to be searched or altered when assigning a value to var'. Multiple variable assignments can be done in a single traversal of the trie.

4. Quasigroup Problems

The quasigroup problems are given by Fujita, Slaney, and Bennett in their award-winning IJCAI paper [8]. Roughly speaking, the problems concern the existence of $v \times v$ Latin squares — each row and each column of a Latin square is a permutation of $0, 1, \ldots, (v-1)$ — with certain constraints. Given $0 \leq i, j < v$, let $i * j$ denote the entry at the ith row and jth column of a square. The following clauses specify a $v \times v$ Latin square: for all elements $x, y, u, w \in S = \{0, \ldots, (v-1)\}$,

$$x * u = y, x * w = y \Rightarrow u = w \quad \text{: left-cancellation law,} \tag{1}$$
$$u * x = y, w * x = y \Rightarrow u = w \quad \text{: right-cancellation law,} \tag{2}$$
$$x * y = u, x * y = w \Rightarrow u = w \quad \text{: unique-image property,} \tag{3}$$
$$(x * y = 0) \vee \cdots \vee (x * y = (v-1)) \quad \text{: (right) closure property.} \tag{4}$$

It was shown in [15] that the following two clauses are valid consequences of the clauses above and adding them reduces the search space.

$$(x * 0 = y) \vee \cdots \vee (x * (v-1) = y) \quad \text{: middle closure property,} \tag{5}$$
$$(0 * x = y) \vee \cdots \vee ((v-1) * x = y) \quad \text{: left closure property.} \tag{6}$$

For any x, y, z in $\{0, \ldots, (v-1)\}$, the following constraints are given:[2]

[2] The QG7 constraint is the one used in [15], not [8].

Name	*Constraint*
QG1	$x * y = u, z * w = u, v * y = x, v * w = z \Rightarrow x = z, y = w$
QG2	$x * y = u, z * w = u, y * v = x, w * v = z \Rightarrow x = z, y = w$
QG3	$(x * y) * (y * x) = x$
QG4	$(x * y) * (y * x) = y$
QG5	$((x * y) * x) * x = y$
QG6	$(x * y) * y = x * (x * y)$
QG7	$((x * y) * x) * y = x$

In the following, problem QG$i.v$ denotes the problem represented by clauses (1)–(6) plus QGi for $S = \{0, ..., (v-1)\}$. In addition, clauses for the idempotency law, $x*x = x$, and a constraint such as $x * (v - 1) \geq x - 1$ to eliminate some isomorphic models are used for each problem here.

Propositional clauses are obtained by simply instantiating the variables in clauses (1)–(6) by values in S and replacing each equality $x * y = z$ by a propositional variable $p_{x,y,z}$. The number of the propositional clauses is determined by the order of the quasigroup (i.e., v) and the number of distinct variables in a clause. Constraints QG1 and QG2 can be handled directly, but constraints QG3–QG7, must be transformed into "flat" form. For example, the flat form of QG5 is

$$(x * y = z), (z * x = w) \Rightarrow (w * x = y).$$

It can be shown that the two "transposes" of the above clause are also valid consequences of QG5:

$$(w * x = y), (x * y = z) \Rightarrow (z * x = w),$$
$$(z * x = w), (w * x = y) \Rightarrow (x * y = z).$$

Experiments have shown that adding these "transposes" to the input can reduce the search space; this is also true of QG3, QG4, QG6, and QG7. More information on quasigroup problems can be found in [1], [8], [15], and [17].

5. DDPP: A Nondestructive Trie-based Implementation

DDPP (Discrimination-tree-based Davis–Putnam Prover) is a straightforward implementation of the Davis–Putnam method based on the *trie-merge* operation. It performs the operation nondestructively, and the result shares (nearly) maximal structure with the original trie to minimize the memory allocation. DDPP is written in Common Lisp. A detailed description can be found in [13].

Performance of DDPP (and LDPP) on some quasigroup problems is shown in Table I. Search was continued until the search space was exhausted and all models had been found. The number of branches is one plus the number of splittings in the Davis–Putnam method. The data was collected using CMU Common Lisp on a 200 MHz Pentium Pro processor with 128 MB memory. The same sets of clauses were used for all results in this paper.

Several open problems about quasigroups were first solved by DDPP [15]: QG5.13, QG5.14, and QG5.15 (negatively), and QG4.12 (positively), but DDPP was still hindered by the speed of the crucial *unit propagation* operation. Although the trie representation eliminated searching subtries $\langle var, pos, neg, rest \rangle$ for variables $var' < var$, extensive searching was still necessary. Moreover, the nondestructive *trie-merge* still required

Table I. DDPP (nondestructive trie representation) vs. LDPP (destructive list representation); LDPP′ omits unit subsumption.

Problem	Clauses	Models	Branches	DDPP Search (sec)	LDPP Search (sec)	LDPP′ Search (sec)
QG1.7	68083	8	958	5.8	13	6.1
.8	148957	16	590624	4011	11489	5101
QG2.7	68083	14	672	4.8	11	4.3
.8	148957	2	579624	4029	12282	5629
QG3.8	10469	18	1016	7.4	1.9	0.8
.9	16732	–	82405	717	122	71
QG4.8	9685	–	910	7.4	1.6	0.6
.9	15580	194	59514	610	98	61
QG5.9	28540	–	188	4.2	0.7	0.4
.10	43636	–	1454	63	10	4.2
.11	64054	5	12581	962	116	54
.12	90919	–	139582	18062	1807	853
.13	125464	–	1798177	370626	32704	15255
QG6.9	21844	4	52	1.7	0.3	0.1
.10	33466	–	314	14	2.0	0.7
.11	49204	–	2523	185	20	9.6
.12	69931	–	26848	3400	315	142
QG7.9	22060	4	42	1.1	0.3	0.1
.10	33736	–	817	28	4.5	1.8
.11	49534	–	11617	802	90	42
.12	70327	–	159908	20609	1942	913
.13	97072	64	2351662	552988	45573	19684

some storage allocation. Nevertheless, the approach remains appealing, particularly when destructive operations are undesirable or impractical as in logic programming.

6. LDPP: A Destructive Non-Trie-Based Implementation

LDPP (Linear-list-based Davis–Putnam prover) was written to avoid the cost of the nondestructive *trie-merge* operation in unit propagation. It uses reversible destructive operations on lists instead. Like DDPP, LDPP is written in Common Lisp.

LDPP is generally much faster than DDPP. It performs unit resolution and unit subsumption operations quickly by decrementing and setting fields. Resolvable or subsumable clauses need not be searched for because each variable contains pointers to all the clauses that contain the variable.

In LDPP, a set of clauses is represented by a list of clauses and a list of variables. Each clause contains the following fields:

- `positive-literals`, `negative-literals`: List of pointers to variables occurring positively (resp. negatively) in this clause.
- `subsumed`: If the clause has been subsumed, this field contains a pointer to the variable whose assignment subsumed this clause; otherwise it is `nil`.
- `number-of-active-positive-literals`,
  `number-of-active-negative-literals`: When `subsumed` is `nil`, this is the number of variables in `positive-literals` (resp. `negative-literals`) that have not been assigned a value.

Each variable contains the fields:

- `value`: This is `true` if the variable has been assigned the value true, `false` if it has been assigned false, and `nil` otherwise.
- `contained-positively-clauses`, `contained-negatively-clauses`: List of pointers to clauses that contain this variable positively (resp. negatively).

To assign true to a variable:

- Its `value` field is set to `true`.
- Unit subsumption: Every clause in `contained-positively-clauses` has its `subsumed` field set to the variable, unless `subsumed` was already non-`nil`.
- Unit resolution: Every clause in `contained-negatively-clauses` has its `number-of-active-negative-literals` field decremented by one, unless `subsumed` was already non-`nil`. Note that we *don't* modify `negative-literals` itself. If the sum of `number-of-active-negative-literals` and `number-of-active-positive-literals` reaches zero, the current truth assignment yields the unsatisfiable empty clause. If the sum reaches one, a new unit clause has been produced. The newly derived unit clause can be identified by finding the only atom in `positive-literals` or `negative-literals` whose value is `nil`. These are queued and assigned values before *unit propagation* finishes.

Assignment of false to a variable is done analogously. The set of clauses after a sequence of assignments is represented by those clauses in the list whose `subsumed` field is `nil`; the literals still present in these clauses are those in `positive-literals` and `negative-literals` whose `value` is `nil`. An assignment can be undone during backtracking before trying an alternative assignment. Many other implementations of the Davis–Putnam method employ a similar approach, including Crawford and Auton's NTAB [2], Letz's SEMPROP, and McCune's MACE [12].

LDPP′ is a faster variant of LDPP that explores exactly the same search space as LDPP but does not perform the subsumption operation (see Section 7.2.2).

7. SATO: A New Algorithm for Unit Propagation

The high cost of the *trie-merge* operation in DDPP, which motivated the abandonment of the trie representation in LDPP, does not imply that the trie data structure is ineffective for the Davis–Putnam method. Actually, the implementations of the Davis–Putnam method in the SATO program (SAtisfiability Testing Optimized) [16] did not use the *trie-merge* operation. In this section, we describe some ideas used in SATO to improve the performance of the Davis–Putnam method based on the trie data structure.

SATO was used to settle several open cases of quasigroup problems, including QG5.14 (without the idempotency law), QG6.15, QG7.15 (negatively), QG2.14, QG2.15, and QG7.16 (positively). Some of these problems required several weeks of CPU-time on a powerful workstation. The efficiency of SATO was indispensable for our success.

SATO possesses features of DDPP (trie representation) and LDPP (destructive operations and lists of pointers to atom occurrences to eliminate search).

The major idea used in SATO is to keep two lists of literals: The *head list* is a collection of the occurrences of the first literal of each clause, and the *tail list* is a collection of the occurrences of the last literal of each clause. If the first literal of a clause becomes true, that literal is simply removed from the head list. If that literal becomes false, it is removed from the head list, and we search for the next unassigned literal in the clause and add it to the head list, unless one of the following occurs: (a) if a literal with value true is found during the search process, no literal will be added to the head list since the clause was subsumed by a previous assignment; (b) if every literal in the clause has value false, then a null clause has been found and that information is returned; (c) if the next unassigned literal of the clause is also in the tail list, then a unit clause has been found and that literal is collected in a list of "unit clauses". The handling of literals in the tail list is analogous.

The idea implies that a clause should be represented as a double-linked list. When the trie data structure is used, a literal is represented by a trie node together with an edge from a node to its parent. That is, instead of the data structure $\langle var, pos, neg, rest\rangle$, we use $\langle var, pos, neg, rest, parent\rangle$, where *parent* is the parent of the current node.

For efficiency, both the head list and tail list are grouped according to the variable index of each node. That is, we use a variable table in which we not only record the value of each variable (true, false, or unknown), but also a head list and a tail list of nodes whose label is that variable. Initially, each head list contains at most one node. Whenever a variable's value goes from unknown to true (resp. false), we remove each node in the head list of this variable and try to add the negative (resp. positive) child node — together with its brothers — into the head list. We also remove each node in the tail list of this variable; if its negative (resp. positive) child is equivalent to $\square$, we try to add its parent node into the tail list.

The first version of SATO does not use the tail list and thus does not need the parent link in the trie data structure. While this implementation does not need dynamic memory allocation, our experiments indicate that more than half of the total search time is spent on deciding whether a trie is equivalent to $\square$ — this operation is necessary to locate unit clauses and to select literals for splitting. This is because not every node with an interpreted variable is removed from the trie. For example, the clause $x \vee y$ is represented by $T_c = \langle x, \langle y, \square, nil, nil\rangle, nil\rangle$, which is initially stored in the head list of variable x. Now suppose y has value false; then in our implementation, $\langle y, \square, nil, nil\rangle$ will not be replaced by $\square$. To decide that x is in a unit clause, we have to search the whole T_c.

Table II. SATO1 (atoms point to clauses whose first literal contains it) vs. SATO2 (atoms point to clauses whose first or last literal contains it).

Problem	Branches	SATO1 (sec)	SATO2 (sec)
QG1.7	958	1.20	0.53
.8	590624	4328.93	283.10
QG2.7	672	1.05	0.49
.8	579624	3698.32	228.32
QG3.8	1016	1.46	0.28
.9	82405	121.39	12.02
QG4.8	910	0.97	0.20
.9	59514	93.31	12.08
QG5.9	188	0.81	0.24
.11	12581	211.03	18.32
.12	139582	6923.66	377.14
.13	1798177	137902.56	10099.64
QG6.9	52	0.77	0.15
.10	314	2.61	0.34
.11	2523	47.10	3.70
.12	26848	953.59	63.23
QG7.9	42	0.68	0.14
.10	817	2.44	0.47
.11	11617	32.57	10.25
.12	159908	2580.45	412.21
.13	2351662	160396.05	13908.68

In Table II, results for two versions of SATO are given — SATO1 uses only the head list and SATO2 uses both the head and tail lists. The experimental results indicate that SATO2 is substantially faster than SATO1 on quasigroup problems. The times in Tables II and III were collected on an SGI Onyx R10000 processor (196 MHz) with 256 MB memory. SATO is written in C.

7.1. Complexity Analysis

In the following, we show that the technique implemented in SATO2 for unit propagation is better, both theoretically and practically, than the method of LDPP.

The Davis–Putnam method as given in Figure 1 consists of two major operations: *unit propagation* and *splitting*. The *unit propagation* consists of a sequence of *unit propagation* operations. For any moderate satisfiability problem, thousands of the *splitting* operations will be performed, and each *splitting* will invoke *unit propagation*. Other things being equal, the complexity of the *Satisfiable* procedure depends on that of *unit propagation*. In the following, we concentrate on the complexity of *unit propagation*.

Given a set S of input clauses and any variable v, let P_v be the number of clauses of S in which v appears positively, and let N_v be the number of clauses in which v appears negatively. It is easy to see that for LDPP, the complexity of the *unit propagation* operation is $O(P_v + N_v)$ when v receives a value, either true or false.

We show below that the *unit propagation* operation in SATO takes an amortized time of $O(N_v)$ when v is assigned to true and $O(P_v)$ when v is assigned to false. To facilitate understanding, we may assume that each clause is represented by a double-linked list, even though the trie data structure gives better results. We also assume that a literal cannot be in both the head list and the tail list: if this is the case, we remove it from both lists and add it to the unit-clause list.

Suppose x is assigned true and the number of $\overline{x}$ literals in the head list is $H_{\overline{x}}$. We need to perform $H_{\overline{x}}$ operations to add those literals that follow $\overline{x}$ in each of $H_{\overline{x}}$ clauses to the head list. Recall that in our implementation, not every node with an interpreted variable is removed from the trie. Because of this, when the first literal (i.e., $\overline{x}$) of a clause becomes false, adding the next (unassigned) literal of the clause to the head list does not always take constant time: If the next literal has value false, we have to pass by this literal and so on, until we find a literal whose value is true or unassigned, or until no literal is left in the current clause.

That is, if k literals are passed by in the adding process, the complexity of adding the next literal to the head list will be $O(k)$ and the worst complexity would be $O(k * H_{\overline{x}})$. However, if $\overline{y}$ is passed by because y was assigned true earlier, then this $\overline{y}$ is not in the head list at the time when y was assigned true. Hence, we can distribute the cost of passing $\overline{y}$ to that of assigning y to true (i.e., $O(N_y)$). After this kind of distribution, the cost of adding the next literal following each $\overline{x}$ in the head list is constant.

The case when $\overline{x}$ appears in the tail list is handled similarly. In short, the cost of assigning x to true, $O(N_x)$, consists of two parts: the cost of visiting each $\overline{x}$ literal in the head and tail lists and the cost prepaid for passing $\overline{x}$ literals neither in the head list nor in the tail list. Note that not every $\overline{x}$ in the clause set has to be visited when assigning x to true, i.e., $O(N_x)$ is a generous upper bound.

The above complexity analysis also applies when x is assigned false. When the set of clauses is represented by a trie, the number of $\overline{x}$ literals in the head list, $H_{\overline{x}}$, in the above analysis can be replaced by the number of the corresponding trie nodes (which is usually smaller than HN_v). However, we cannot say that the amortized complexity of assigning x to true is bounded by the number of the trie nodes representing $\overline{x}$ because, when assigning x to true, a trie node representing $\overline{x}$ may be visited more than once while an occurrence of $\overline{x}$ is visited at most once when clauses are represented by double-linked lists.

7.2. Experimental Comparison of Two Algorithms

While the theoretical analysis shows that SATO's method has an advantage over LDPP's, it also appears to perform better in practice (see Tables I and II). Because it is difficult to make accurate comparisons across different implementations in different languages, for purposes of comparison, we also carefully implemented LDPP's algorithm, which is similar to Crawford and Auton's method, in SATO. We discuss below the two key ideas that can be borrowed from SATO to improve on LDPP: (a) using a trie for clauses and (b) eliminating using unit subsumption.

Table III. SATO1.2 (list representation) vs. SATO1.3 (trie representation).

Problem	Branches	SATO1.2 Create (sec)	SATO1.2 Total (sec)	SATO1.3 Create (sec)	SATO1.3 Total (sec)
QG1.7	958	0.38	1.29	0.38	0.68
.8	590624	0.85	2084.10	0.86	408.93
QG2.7	672	0.39	1.05	0.39	0.64
.8	579624	0.85	2293.32	0.91	328.45
QG3.8	1016	0.05	0.46	0.05	0.32
.9	82405	0.08	36.26	0.08	24.29
QG4.8	910	0.05	0.39	0.05	0.28
.9	59514	0.08	27.70	0.08	18.26
QG5.9	188	0.14	0.31	0.14	0.26
.10	1454	0.22	2.51	0.23	1.57
.11	12581	0.32	50.03	0.35	23.45
.12	139582	0.46	1317.66	0.54	490.96
.13	1798177	0.64	29901.56	0.79	11167.84
QG6.9	52	0.11	0.17	0.11	0.17
.10	314	0.17	0.61	0.17	0.51
.11	2523	0.25	6.59	0.27	5.05
.12	26848	0.35	163.88	0.41	113.37
QG7.9	42	0.11	0.15	0.11	0.17
.10	817	0.17	1.09	0.17	0.77
.11	11617	0.25	31.48	0.27	19.30
.12	159908	0.35	1241.95	0.42	571.83
.13	2351662	0.49	57294.93	0.63	18495.21

7.2.1. *Using Trie for Clauses*

Using tries can automatically remove some subsumed clauses (including duplicates). LDPP and Crawford and Auton's method can take advantage of this. To test this idea, we implemented two versions of LDPP's algorithm in SATO: in SATO1.2, each clause is represented by a single linked list of integers; in SATO1.3, the trie data structure is used and each clause is represented by a path from a leaf to the root of a trie. Table III lists the results for SATO1.2 and SATO1.3. SATO1.3 always takes less time than SATO1.2 to finish the job. This is in part because the trie data structure eliminates duplicate clauses. Actually, it automatically deletes a class of subsumed clauses, that is, those clauses one of whose prefixes (regarding a clause as a list) is also a clause in the system.

It might appear that creating a trie for a set of clauses would be appreciably more expensive than creating lists of lists of literals. In fact, both operations have the same theoretical complexity. In practice, creating a list is slightly faster than creating a trie, as indicated by the creation times in Table III. The creation times for SATO1 and SATO2 are the same as those of SATO1.3.

Table IV. Summary of program characteristics (R: representation; US: unit subsumption).

Program	R	How Resolvable Literals Are Found	US
DDPP	trie	search trie; uses *trie-merge* operation instead of destructive operations like the other programs	yes
SATO1.3	trie	atom points to clauses that contain it	yes
SATO1.2 & LDPP	list	atom points to clauses that contain it	yes
LDPP′	list	atom points to clauses that contain it	no
SATO1	trie	atom points to clauses whose first active literal contains it	no
SATO2	trie	atom points to clauses whose first or last active literal contains it	no

7.2.2. *Eliminating Unit Subsumption*

The Davis–Putnam method performs unit resolution and unit subsumption operations. These are done in LDPP by decrementing literal counts for unit resolutions and setting a `subsumed` flag for unit subsumptions. Every assignment to a variable requires examining and possibly modifying every clause that contain the variable. A key issue in SATO is that only unit resolutions are performed, so only occurrences with one polarity or the other are examined.

This idea can be applied to LDPP by eliminating the use of the `subsumed` field. There are some extra costs: counts for resolved literals are decremented for subsumed clauses as well as unsubsumed ones, derived units might already be assigned a (subsuming) value and must be ignored, and subsumed clauses must be ignored by the process for selecting literals to split on. Despite these extra costs, there is substantial benefit to omitting the subsumption operation. LDPP′ is LDPP modified to eliminate the subsumption operations. As can be seen from Table I, it is appreciably faster than LDPP on quasigroup problems.

8. Conclusions

In this paper, we have concentrated on the use of the trie data structure and other refinements for implementing the Davis–Putnam method. Seven implementations of the Davis–Putnam method with their performance results on some quasigroup problems are presented: DDPP, LDPP, LDPP′, SATO1, SATO2, SATO1.2, SATO1.3. Table 7.2.2 summarizes the characteristics of the different programs described here.

We conclude the following:

- The trie representation for clause sets is more efficient than the list representation (e.g., SATO1.3 vs. SATO1.2).

Table V. DDPP and LDPP′ with standard literal selection strategy: a literal of a shortest positive clause is chosen for splitting; search is halted after finding a model in satisfiable cases (marked by *).

Problem	DDPP			LDPP′		
	Branches	Search (sec)	Total (sec)	Branches	Search (sec)	Total (sec)
QG1.7*	11	0.2	7.5	11	0.1	7.0
.8*	57421	640	658	39349	309	327
QG2.7*	5	0.2	8.3	45	0.4	10
.8*	50721	541	560	4405	48	69
QG3.8*	379	2.8	3.8	403	0.3	0.9
.9	26847	280	281	24673	25	26
QG4.8	564	4.3	5.2	602	0.4	1.6
.9*	450	6.0	7.5	904	0.9	1.8
QG5.9	15	0.6	3.7	15	0.1	2.2
.10	50	3.1	9.1	38	0.2	4.1
.11*	94	12	21	80	0.5	6.5
.12	443	70	84	369	2.9	11
.13	16438	2802	2826	12686	123	139
QG6.9*	4	0.5	2.7	12	0.0	1.5
.10	65	2.5	7.0	59	0.1	3.2
.11	451	27	35	539	2.1	7.1
.12	5938	564	576	7288	38	43
QG7.9*	1	0.2	2.5	1	0.0	1.9
.10	40	1.6	5.7	40	0.1	4.2
.11	321	24	31	294	1.2	5.5
.12	2083	219	231	1592	7.6	13
.13*	30	7.2	26	205	1.5	11

- Using lists of pointers to occurrences of atoms in clauses and reversible destructive updating is faster than using the DDPP's nondestructive *trie-merge* operation (e.g., SATO1.3 vs. DDPP).
- Eliminating the unit subsumption operation can improve performance (e.g., LDPP′ vs. LDPP).
- Restricting the unit resolution operation to operate only on clauses whose first or last literal contains the atom can improve performance (no single factor comparison was made, but see SATO2 vs. LDPP′ and SATO1.3; SATO2 vs. SATO1 shows the benefit of considering first and last literals instead of just first literals).

We have proposed a new method for efficiently implementing *unit propagation* in the Davis–Putnam method. We showed that this new method, used in SATO2, is better, both theoretically and practically, than the approach used in LDPP and many other systems. That approach appeared earlier in Dowling and Gallier's linear algorithm for satisfiability of Horn clauses [6]. We think our ideas can be used to design a new sublinear algorithm for the satisfiability of Horn clauses.

Table VI. SATO and MACE with standard literal selection strategy: a literal of a shortest positive clause is chosen for splitting; search is halted after finding a model in satisfiable cases (marked by *).

Problem	SATO Branches	SATO Search (sec)	SATO Total (sec)	MACE [12] Branches	MACE [12] Search (sec)	MACE [12] Total (sec)
QG1.7*	85	0.1	0.6	16	0.2	2.0
.8*	40755	29	30	39357	63	67
QG2.7*	33	0.0	0.7	53	0.2	2.1
.8*	28155	29	30	4410	11	15
QG3.8*	239	0.1	0.2	408	0.2	0.4
.9	20340	10	10	24763	14	14
QG4.8	924	0.3	0.4	602	0.2	0.4
.9*	54	0.0	0.2	913	0.5	0.8
QG5.9	15	0.1	0.3	15	0.1	0.7
.10	38	0.1	0.5	38	0.1	1.1
.11*	41	0.2	0.7	82	0.4	1.8
.12	354	1.6	2.4	369	1.7	3.7
.13	12781	65	66	12686	79	82
QG6.9*	9	0.0	0.2	13	0.0	0.5
.10	65	0.1	0.4	59	0.1	0.8
.11	625	1.2	1.7	539	1.0	2.1
.12	7270	18	19	7288	20	22
QG7.9*	6	0.0	0.2	3	0.0	0.5
.10	42	0.1	0.4	40	0.1	0.8
.11	324	0.7	1.1	294	0.6	1.6
.12	1642	4.4	5	1592	3.7	5.2
.13*	22801	81	81	210	1.0	3.0

Many aspects of the Davis–Putnam method are not addressed in this paper. To facilitate comparison, all of our programs use the same input and simply choose the minimally indexed variable not yet assigned a value for splitting in the Davis–Putnam method. Many selection heuristics can be efficiently implemented using the trie data structure; we ignore this because it is outside the scope of this paper. Our programs do not perform general subsumption checking; it would be interesting to see how de Kleer's subsumption algorithm on tries could be integrated into the Davis–Putnam method. We did little or no checking for pure literals and did not check for symmetries. Further research is needed to see how such operations can be done efficiently using the trie data structure.

Table VII. POSIT, SATZ, NTAB: default settings; search is halted after finding a model in satisfiable cases (marked by *).

Problem	POSIT [7] Branches	POSIT [7] Search (sec)	POSIT [7] Total (sec)	SATZ [11] Branches	SATZ [11] Total (sec)	NTAB [2] Branches	NTAB [2] Total (sec)
QG1.7*	6	0.0	3.0	7	33	75	3.4
.8*	5151	34	40	7770	218	2346	106
QG2.7*	21	0.1	3.0	10	53	12	2.5
.8*	5761	41	47	6975	270	4009	207
QG3.8*	49	0.2	0.6	221	1.2	6	0.3
.9	4803	19	19	8083	33	4585	59
QG4.8	113	0.3	0.7	255	1.5	104	1.0
.9*	63	0.2	0.9	585	3.6	134	2.0
QG5.9	1	0.1	1.2	3	6.2	4	0.9
.10	?	?	fault	29	12	19	2.8
.11*	?	?	fault	12	18	15	4.3
.12	?	?	fault	199	47	?	>13000
.13	6361	310	315	?	>18000	?	>2700
QG6.9*	?	?	fault	6	3.0	12	0.8
.10	55	0.7	2.1	60	6.0	77	3.3
.11	?	?	fault	462	22	1714	117
.12	?	?	fault	6623	318	?	>2700
QG7.9*	?	?	>2700	1	3.9	3	0.7
.10	15	0.2	1.6	3	6.6	16	1.4
.11	205	2.3	4.4	119	15	258	18
.12	?	?	fault	1116	70	1745	156
.13*	?	?	fault	2969	244	?	>2700

Finally, we conclude the paper with statistics comparing DDPP, LDPP′, and SATO with four other powerful SAT solvers: MACE [12], POSIT [7], SATZ [11], and NTAB [2] (Tables V, VI, and VII).[3] DDPP and LDPP are written in Common Lisp; all the others are written in C. We succeeded in solving all the problems only with our solvers and MACE. McCune's MACE uses data structures similar to those of LDPP, the same "choose an atom of a shortest positive clause" literal selection strategy as our solvers and has also been used to solve open quasigroup existence problems. We believe the other systems are competent to solve these problems with some adjustment, but the tables illustrate the nontriviality of the problems and that superior performance is not automatically and immediately transferrable between problem domains.[4] We welcome

[3] The data for these tables were collected on a 200 MHz Pentium Pro processor with 128 MB memory.

[4] Likewise, our solvers have not been adapted to random 3-SAT problems that benefit from features such as pure literal detection and different literal selection strategies.

readers to try these quasigroup problems — and harder ones, many still open — using their systems.

Appendix

The CSPLib problem library (`http://csplib.cs.strath.ac.uk`) contains the Common Lisp quasigroup problem generator used for this paper and an ILOG Solver generator. The code for SATO is available from `http://cs.uiowa.edu/~hzhang/sato/`. SATO (full version) can be used to generate clauses for the quasigroup problems presented in this paper. For instance, the command `sato -Q5 -G9 -o` will generate QG5.9 in Lisp format, while `sato -Q3 -G10 -o2` will generate QG3.10 in DIMACS format.

References

1. Bennett, F. E. and Zhu, L.: Conjugate-orthogonal Latin squares and related structures, in J. H. Dinitz and D. R. Stinson (eds.), *Contemporary Design Theory: A Collection of Surveys.* Wiley, New York, 1992.
2. Crawford, J. M. and Auton, L. D.: Experimental results on the crossover point in satisfiability problems, *Proceedings of the Eleventh National Conference on Artificial Intelligence (AAAI-93),* 1993, pp. 21–27.
3. Davis, M. and Putnam, H.: A computing procedure for quantification theory, *Journal of the Association for Computing Machinery* 7(3) (July 1960), 201–215.
4. Davis, M., Logemann, G., and Loveland, D.: A machine program for theorem-proving, *Communications of the Association for Computing Machinery* 5(7) (July 1962), 394–397.
5. de Kleer, J.: An improved incremental algorithm for generating prime implicates, in *Proceedings of the Tenth National Conference on Artificial Intelligence (AAAI-92),* San Jose, California, July 1992, pp. 780–785.
6. Dowling, W. F. and Gallier, J.H.: Linear-time algorithms for testing the satisfiability of propositional Horn formulae, *Journal of Logic Programming 3* (1984), 267–284.
7. J. W. Freeman, Improvements to propositional satisfiability search algorithms, Ph.D. Dissertation, Department of Computer and Information Science, University of Pennsylvania, May 1995.
8. Fujita, M., Slaney, J., and Bennett, F.: Automatic generation of some results in finite algebra, in *Proceedings of the Thirteenth International Joint Conference on Artificial Intelligence,* Chambery, France, 1993.
9. Gomes, C., Selman, B., and Crato, N.: Heavy-tailed distributions in combinatorial search, *Proceedings of the Third International Conference on Principles and Practice of Constraint Programming (CP97),* Linz, Austria, 1997.
10. Gu, J.: Local search for satisfiability (SAT) problem, *IEEE Transactions on Systems, Man, and Cybernetics* 23(4) (1993) 1108–1129.
11. Li, C.M., Anbulagan, M.: look-ahead versus look-back for satisfiability problems, in *Proceedings of International Conference on Principles and Practice of Constraint Programming,* 1997.
12. McCune, W.: A Davis–Putnam program and its application to finite first-order model search: quasigroup existence problems, draft manuscript, Mathematics and Computer Science Division, Argonne National Laboratory, Argonne, Illinois, May 1994.
13. Meglicki, G.: Stickel's Davis–Putnam engineered reversely, available by anonymous FTP from arp.anu.edu.au, Automated Reasoning Project, Australian National University, Canberra, Australia, 1993.
14. Selman, B., Levesque, H., and Mitchell, D.: A new method for solving hard satisfiability problems, in *Proceedings of the Tenth National Conference on Artificial Intelligence (AAAI-92),* San Jose, California, July 1992, pp. 440–446.
15. Slaney, J., Fujita, M., and Stickel, M.: Automated reasoning and exhaustive search: quasigroup existence problems, *Computers and Mathematics with Applications 29,* 2 (May 1995), 115–132.
16. Zhang, H.: SATO: a decision procedure for propositional logic, *Association for Automated Reasoning Newsletter,* No. 22 (March 1993), pp. 1–3.
17. Zhang, H.: Specifying Latin squares in propositional logic, in R. Veroff (ed.): *Automated Reasoning and Its Applications, Essays in Honor of Larry Wos,* Chapter 6, MIT Press, 1997.

18. Zhang, H.: SATO: An efficient propositional prover, in *Proc. of International Conference on Automated Deduction* (CADE-97), Lecture Notes in Artificial Intelligence 1104, Springer-Verlag, 1997, pp. 308–312.
19. Zhang, J.: Search for idempotent models of quasigroup identities, typescript, Institute of Software, Academia Sinica, Beijing, 1991.

SAT2000
I. Gent et al. (Eds.)
IOS Press, 2000

Proving Consistency Assertions for Automotive Product Data Management

Wolfgang Küchlin and Carsten Sinz
Symbolic Computation Group, WSI for Computer Science, University of Tübingen and Steinbeis Technology Transfer Center OIT, Sand 13, D-72076 Tübingen, Germany
`http://www-sr.informatik.uni-tuebingen.de`

Abstract. We present a formal specification and verification approach for industrial product data bases containing Boolean logic formulae to express constraints. Within this framework, global consistency assertions about the product data are converted into propositional satisfiability problems. Today's state-of-the-art provers turn out to be surprisingly efficient in solving the SAT-instances generated by this process. Moreover, we introduce a method for encoding special non-monotonic constructs in traditional Boolean logic. We have successfully applied our method to industrial automotive product data management and could establish a set of commercially used interactive tools that facilitate the management of change and help raise quality standards.

Keywords: formal specification, verification, product data management, product configuration, industrial application

1. Introduction

The use of formal methods is still uncommon in industrial practice [17]. Analysis of safety-critical systems and verification of both processors and protocols seem to be among the rare exceptions [10, 13, 15, 19]. The reason for this is manifold: First, there are intrinsic preconditions imposed on the process to be formalized. One is the requirement of precise, symbolic input data; this contrasts with the imprecise data delivered by physical measurement. Another is the algorithmic complexity of symbolic techniques which is usually much higher than that of numerical or heuristic procedures. Second, the industrial process to be formalized has to be understood very precisely in every aspect, and modeling has to start on a well-founded basis. The language in which the process is to be described must have sufficient expressive power, but should exclude intractable logics—incomplete, undecidable, or merely too time- or space-consuming for the intended purpose.

Besides these intrinsic reasons there are more practical ones: On the one hand, one is faced with industrial prejudice against the power of formal verification [4]; on the other hand, research in the ATP community is often not directly concerned with real-world application aspects. Further obstacles arise when communication between researchers and practitioners is hindered by different worlds of thought, or when incorporation of formal methods requires major changes in the actual production process. However, successful verification projects conducted in the realm of industry may further the acceptance of formal methods [3, 12].

In this article we describe a method to reveal inconsistencies in a data base used by DaimlerChrysler AG to check the constructibility of motor-vehicles of the Mercedes-Benz lines. This project was greatly helped by the fact that Boolean logic was already used to express constraints in the product data base. Difficulties were imposed by the mere complexity, as the data that had to be considered for some tests consisted of more than 18,000 rules (elementary Boolean formulae) and 1,700 propositional variables. In addition we had to formalize significant portions of the industrial process involved in order to prove assertions that could not be checked so far.

Although the general problem of product configuration has gained interest over the last years, we have not yet seen the formalization and verification of an existing large-scale industrial system.

The paper is organized as follows: First, we briefly describe the automobile constructibility data base, its integration into the order processing and production process, and show some potential inconsistencies that might occur in the data base. Then a formalization of the process to check individual car orders is presented, followed by a variety of global data base consistency criteria formulated as propositional satisfiability problems. Finally, we present experimental results achieved using a state-of-the-art propositional satisfiability checker.

2. Product Documentation and Order Processing

The Mercedes-Benz passenger car and commercial vehicle production encompasses a wide variety of different models customers can order. Apart from different model classes, design lines and engine variants, an extraordinary number of supplementary equipment may be selected. Not all theoretically possible combinations of variants can actually be produced, however. Geometrical, electrical or other engineering limitations are as common as legal or sales restrictions. Moreover, the availability of certain models can differ from country to country and undergo substantial temporal change. To automate administration and production tasks, exact knowledge about valid models is needed in electronic form. Thus, a data base (called product documentation) is employed to draw the distinction between models that can be manufactured and those that cannot.

A second, but equally important purpose of the product documentation is to transform a customer's model description into a parts list for the requested vehicle, which can then be fed into the production planning process.

2.1. Processing a Customer's Order

A customer's order consists of a basic model class selection together with a set of further equipment codes describing additional features. As model classes can be decoded into a few special equipment codes, all rules in the product documentation are formulated on the basis of these codes, which are just propositional variables.

Ascertaining the constructibility of an individual order as well as parts list generation and other intermediate steps are performed by evaluating Boolean formulae stored in the product documentation data base.

Within our application constructibility may only be checked with respect to the rules of the product documentation, not with respect to physical reality. Therefore, we call an order *constructible* (or *valid*) if the corresponding vehicle model can be manufactured according to the product documentation; otherwise an order is called *invalid.*

The most important of the aforementioned intermediate steps—and the only one considered here—allows the completion of orders by appending additional codes. This supplementing process is mainly used to add codes that are implied by technical dependencies or that make up equipment packages.

The whole order processing procedure (slightly simplified) consists of the following steps:

1. *Order completion:* Extend the customer's order by additional codes.

2. *Constructibility check:* Are all constraints on constructible models fulfilled by this order?

3. *Parts list generation:* Transform the (possibly supplemented) order into a parts list.

These three steps are illustrated in Figure 1, schematically on the left hand side and by a concrete example on the right.

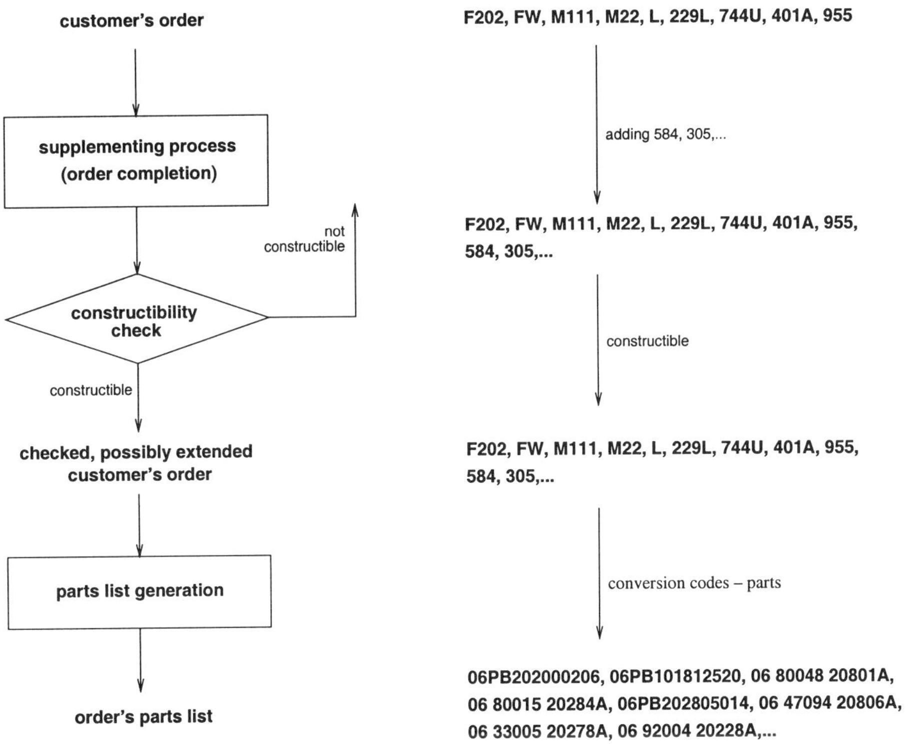

Figure 1. Processing customers' orders

2.2. Consistency of the Product Documentation

The mere complexity of the product documentation sometimes induces erroneous data base entries that are usually hard to find. Global usage and varying knowledge of the operating personnel aggravate this trend. In one of the evaluated settings, consisting of that part of the product documentation that specifies the limousines of the Mercedes-Benz C-class, 1,151 codes and formulae containing a total of more than 170,000 logical symbols had to be considered.

The formal specification of the complete process enables posterior verification of important aspects and thus offers new possibilities to reduce inconsistencies.

A priori, that is, without explicit knowledge of intended constraints on constructible models, the following data base consistency criteria may be checked:

Necessary codes: Are there codes that must appear in each constructible order?

Inadmissible codes: Are there any codes that cannot possibly appear in any constructible order?

Consistency of the order completion process: Are there any constructible orders that are invalidated by the supplementing process? Does the outcome of the supplementing process depend on the (probably accidental) ordering in which codes are added?

Superfluous parts: Are there any parts that cannot occur in any constructible order?

Ambiguities in the parts list: Are there any orders for which mutually exclusive parts are simultaneously selected?

By using additional information further checks may be performed. Most of them require only minor changes with respect to the above criteria. The existence of valid orders with certain constraints falls under this class of checks. They are an easy generalization of the search for necessary or inadmissible codes.

We see our main contribution in showing how to formalize these consistency checks and how to apply theorem proving methods to improve the data quality within an existing industrial process.

3. A Formal View of Product Documentation

We will now describe the data base and its functionality more thoroughly. Starting with constructibility, and continuing with the order completion process, we are finally led to parts list generation.

Thus, we achieve a formal description of the complete actual order processing procedure for Mercedes-Benz cars and trucks. This formalization will afterwards serve as the basis on which product documentation consistency criteria can be formulated.

3.1. Preliminaries

Let $\mathcal{C}$ be the set of all equipment codes used in the product documentation. Then a customer's order O is the subset of $\mathcal{C}$ corresponding to the equipment selected in the order. Obviously each order O may be interpreted as a truth assignment by using the characteristic function $\chi_O : \mathcal{C} \to \{0, 1\}$ of O relative to $\mathcal{C}$, where we interpret 1 as truth and 0 as falsity.

All checks and modifications performed on a customer's order O depend on the evaluation of formulae (rules of the product documentation) under the truth assignment χ_O. For a formula F this evaluation is denoted by $\chi_O^*(F)$. We will also use the notation $\chi_O \models F$, or even shorter $O \models F$, instead of $\chi_O^*(F) = 1$.

Furthermore, we assume that each order contains a specification (exactly one of the codes L and R) of whether left or right hand side steering is demanded.

3.2. Constructibility

In general, constructibility[1] of a customer's order O is checked according to the following scheme: For each code, there may be several rules indicating restrictions under which this code may be used. A code is called constructible within O if all constraining rules associated with this code are fulfilled, that is, all of these rules evaluate to *true* under χ_O. For an order to be constructible, each code of the order must be constructible.

The constructibility check consists of two independent parts: The first one is independent of the car model class considered, while the second one takes into account

[1] German: *Baubarkeit*

additional features of each car model class. The latter also depends on the kind of steering[2] (left or right hand side) under consideration.

The model class independent part of the constructibility check consists of a rule for each code indicating a constraint under which it may (or may not) be used. For a code c we use the notation $\mathrm{C}^{\mathrm{I}}(c)$ for the model class independent rule corresponding to c. To pass the model class independent constructibility check, an order O must fulfill the following condition:

$$O \models \mathrm{C}^{\mathrm{I}}(c) \quad \text{for each } c \in O \ . \tag{1}$$

The second part of the constructibility check is more complex, and the relevant rules are hierarchically organized, as shown in Figure 2.

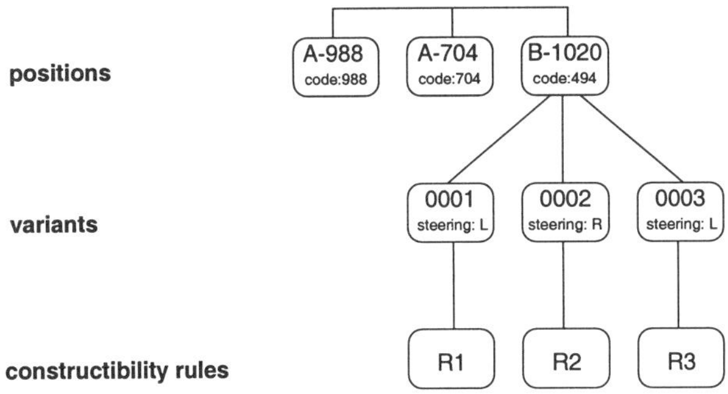

Figure 2. Structure of model class dependent constructibility

There is a set $\mathcal{P}$ of geometric positions and a set $\mathcal{V}$ of variants. Positions are grouped reflecting common functionality or usage. With each position $p \in \mathcal{P}$ a unique code c is associated; however, the converse need not hold: hence, a code may occur at different positions. We use the function $\mathrm{Pos} : \mathcal{C} \to 2^{\mathcal{P}}$ to denote all positions associated with a code. Positions are unique within the whole product documentation, and for each position a (possibly empty) set of variants $V \subseteq \mathcal{V}$ exists. Each variant possesses an additional steering attribute (left or right, L or R). The function $\mathrm{Var} : \mathcal{P} \times \{L, R\} \to 2^{\mathcal{V}}$ selects all variants at a position with matching steering type. The model class dependent constructibility rules[3] $\mathrm{C}^{\mathrm{D}}(p, v)$ are indexed by a pair $(p, v) \in \mathcal{P} \times \mathcal{V}$.

For a code c to be constructible, at least one variant v of matching steering type must exist for every position p associated with c, such that $\mathrm{C}^{\mathrm{D}}(p, v)$ is fulfilled. In a valid order O every code $c \in O$ must be constructible.

Thus we obtain the following condition for an order O of steering type s to pass the model class dependent constructibility check:

$$O \models \mathcal{B}(c, s) \quad \text{for each } c \in O, \tag{2}$$

where $\mathcal{B}(c, s)$ is defined as

$$\mathcal{B}(c, s) = \bigwedge_{p \in \mathrm{Pos}(c)} \bigvee_{v \in \mathrm{Var}(p,s)} \mathrm{C}^{\mathrm{D}}(p, v) \ . \tag{3}$$

The cardinalities of $\mathrm{Pos}(c)$ and $\mathrm{Var}(p, s)$ are usually less than a dozen, the individual rules $\mathrm{C}^{\mathrm{D}}(p, v)$ normally consist of much fewer than a hundred symbols.

[2] German: *Lenkungsvariante*

[3] German: *Baubarkeitsregeln*

For an order to be valid, it must pass both the model dependent and the independent check.

3.3. Order Completion Process

The order completion process adds implied codes to an order. The process is guided by special formulae, called supplementing rules[4], associated with each code. These rules are structurally organized in the same way as those of the model dependent constructibility check, that is, in positions and variants. Each rule application extends the order by exactly one code, so the whole completion process is iterated until no further changes result.

Ideally, the relationship between original and augmented order should be functional. However, the result of the order completion process may depend critically on the order of rule application, whereas the exact sequence in which individual codes are added is sometimes obscure. Therefore, the functional relationship cannot be assumed to hold in general. We will show below how to identify potential instances of this problem.

As is the case with the model class dependent constructibility check, supplementing rules $\mathrm{S}(p, v)$ are hierarchically organized in positions $p \in \mathcal{P}$ and variants $v \in \mathcal{V}$.[5] The semantics of positions is different, though. In order to activate a supplementing step for code c, it is sufficient that any rule for code c is fulfilled, independent of the position or variant of the rule. To avoid invalidation of correct orders, constructibility is also considered during such a step. This works as follows: Besides the supplementing rule $\mathrm{S}(p, v)$ for code c, the corresponding formulae $\mathrm{C}^{\mathrm{D}}(p, v)$ and $\mathrm{C}^{\mathrm{I}}(c)$ must evaluate to *true* under order O.

Thus, code c is added to order O of steering type s, if

$$O \models \mathcal{Z}(c, s), \tag{4}$$

where $\mathcal{Z}(c, s)$ is defined as

$$\mathcal{Z}(c, s) = \Bigg(\bigvee_{\substack{p \in \mathrm{Pos}(c) \\ v \in \mathrm{Var}(p,s)}} \left(\mathrm{S}(p, v) \wedge \mathrm{C}^{\mathrm{D}}(p, v)\right) \Bigg) \wedge \mathrm{C}^{\mathrm{I}}(c) \ . \tag{5}$$

Symbolically, we can express the admissible steps of the supplementing process as a rewrite relation $\longrightarrow_S \subseteq 2^{\mathcal{C}} \times 2^{\mathcal{C}}$. Thus $O \longrightarrow_S O'$ iff there is a code c such that $O \models \mathcal{Z}(c, s)$, where s is the unique steering code occurring in O, $c \notin O$ and $O' = O \,\dot{\cup}\, \{c\}$. We also use the notation $O \xrightarrow{c}_S O'$ if O' is obtained by adding code c to order O. Hence we have

$$\longrightarrow_S \;=\; \bigcup_{c \in \mathcal{C}} \xrightarrow{c}_S \ .$$

Note that relation $\longrightarrow_S$ is a terminating reduction-relation. The reflexive-transitive closure of $\longrightarrow_S$ is denoted by $\longrightarrow_S^*$, and the n-fold product of $\longrightarrow_S$ by $\longrightarrow_S^n$. Furthermore, we write $\longrightarrow_S^{\leq n}$ for $\bigcup_{0 \leq i \leq n} \longrightarrow_S^i$. Definitions of basic notions regarding rewrite systems can be found in [8].

---

[4] German: *Zusteuerungsregeln*

[5] $\mathrm{C}^{\mathrm{D}}(p, v)$ corresponds to $\mathrm{S}(p, v)$

3.4. Parts List Generation

The parts list[6] is subdivided into modules, positions and variants, with decreasing generality from modules to variants. Parts are grouped in modules depending on functional and geometrical aspects. Each position contains all those parts which may be used alternatively in one place. The mutually exclusive parts of a position are specified using variants. Admissible variants depend, as is the case with model class dependent constructibility, on the steering type under consideration. Each variant is assigned a formula called a code rule[7], and a part number. The structure of the parts list is depicted in Figure 3.

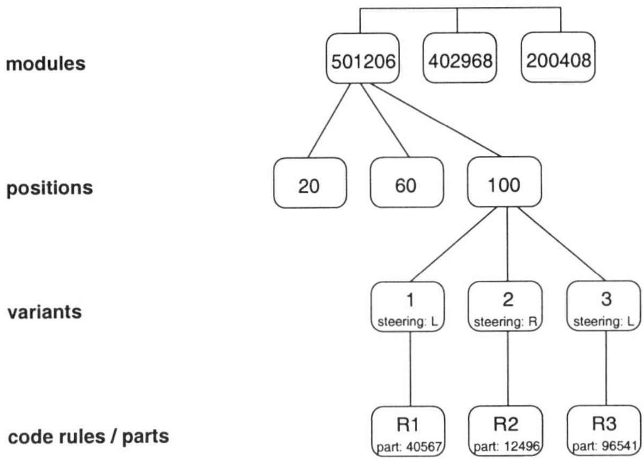

Figure 3. Structure of the parts list

The sets of part numbers, modules, positions, and variants of the parts list are denoted by $\mathcal{N}$, $\mathcal{M}$, $\mathcal{I}$, and $\mathcal{W}$, respectively. All variants of module $m \in \mathcal{M}$ at position $p \in \mathcal{I}$ with steering type s are delivered by function $\mathrm{PV} : \mathcal{M} \times \mathcal{I} \times \{L, R\} \to 2^{\mathcal{W}}$, the steering type of a variant v of module m and position p is determined by $\lambda(m, p, v)$. The code rule of variant v at position p in module m is accessible through $\mathrm{R}(m, p, v)$, the corresponding part is $\tau(m, p, v)$. The mapping $\tau : (m, p, v) \mapsto \tau(m, p, v)$ need not be injective: for each position there is a part, but a part may be used at many positions. Moreover, let the function $\Omega : \mathcal{N} \to 2^{\mathcal{M} \times \mathcal{I} \times \mathcal{W}}$ select all occurrences of a certain part in the parts list.

Variant v at position p of module m is selected for an order O of steering type s, if

$$\lambda(m, p, v) = s \quad \text{and} \quad O \models \mathrm{R}(m, p, v) \ . \tag{6}$$

In order to construct the parts list for a completed and checked customer's order O, one thus scans through all modules, positions, and variants, and selects those parts which possess a matching steering attribute and a code rule that evaluates to *true* under O.

Usually, exactly one variant has to be selected for each module position.

Let us end this section with two notes:

1. The product data base as described above is in use for the Mercedes-Benz passenger cars only. Commercial vehicles are documented in a slightly different fashion.

---

[6] German: *Teileliste, Stückliste*

[7] German: *Coderegel*

2. In the actual process some minor refinements and exceptional cases occur which we did not consider here.

4. Formalization of Consistency Assertions

In this section we want to develop criteria expressing various consistency aspects of the product documentation data base as a whole. These aspects were already briefly mentioned in Section 2.2.

Most of these consistency assertions require a characterization of the set of orders having passed the order completion process and the constructibility check, just before parts list generation.

Starting with a formula representing all constructible models, and extending it by a partial formula concerning the supplementing process, we finally reach the required characterization. Having this formula at hand, we can formulate the aforementioned consistency assertions as propositional satisfiability problems.

Throughout this section we assume the set of Boolean variables to be fixed to $\mathcal{C}$. The set of propositional formulae over $\mathcal{C}$ is denoted by $\mathcal{F}(\mathcal{C})$ or simply $\mathcal{F}$. Formula variables are implicitly assumed to range over $\mathcal{F}$, sets of orders are subsets of $2^{\mathcal{C}}$.

Furthermore, we assume $\wedge, \vee, \neg$ and $\perp$ as basic logical constants, whose semantics are defined, as usual, by

$$\begin{aligned}
\chi_O^*(F \wedge G) &= \min(\chi_O^*(F), \chi_O^*(G)) \\
\chi_O^*(F \vee G) &= \max(\chi_O^*(F), \chi_O^*(G)) \\
\chi_O^*(\neg F) &= 1 - \chi_O^*(F) \\
\chi_O^*(\perp) &= 0
\end{aligned}$$

Other symbols ($\Rightarrow$, $\top$) and their semantics are derived from the logical constants as usual.

Moreover, we restrict our attention to only one model class. This is no limitation in practice, because model classes are mutually independent.

DEFINITION 4.1. *A propositional formula F describes a set S of orders if S is the set of models of F (i.e., $O \models F$ iff $O \in S$).*

PROPOSITION 4.2. *The set of model class independent constructible orders is described by formula $\mathcal{B}^{\mathrm{I}}$, where*

$$\mathcal{B}^{\mathrm{I}} := \bigwedge_{c \in \mathcal{C}} (c \Rightarrow \mathrm{C}^{\mathrm{I}}(c)) \ . \tag{7}$$

Proof. Let S be the set of model class independent constructible orders. By (1) we know that $O \in S$ iff $O \models \mathrm{C}^{\mathrm{I}}(c)$ for each $c \in O$. So we have to show that

$$O \models \mathcal{B}^{\mathrm{I}} \quad \text{iff} \quad O \models \mathrm{C}^{\mathrm{I}}(c) \ \text{ for each } \ c \in O \ . \tag{$*$}$$

At first, note that evaluation of $\mathcal{B}^{\mathrm{I}}$ under any χ_O yields

$$\chi_O^*(\mathcal{B}^{\mathrm{I}}) = \min_{c \in \mathcal{C}} \{\max(1 - \chi_O(c), \chi_O^*(\mathrm{C}^{\mathrm{I}}(c)))\} \ .$$

We now prove both implications of $(*)$.

"⇒": Let $O \models \mathcal{B}^{\mathrm{I}}$ and $c' \in O$ arbitrary. Then $\chi^*_O(\mathcal{B}^{\mathrm{I}}) = 1$ and, in particular, $\max(1 - \chi_O(c'), \chi^*_O(\mathrm{C}^{\mathrm{I}}(c'))) = 1$. As $c' \in O$ implies $\chi_O(c') = 1$, we have $\chi^*_O(\mathrm{C}^{\mathrm{I}}(c')) = 1$ and thus $O \models \mathrm{C}^{\mathrm{I}}(c')$.

"⇐": Let $O \subseteq \mathcal{C}$ with $O \models \mathrm{C}^{\mathrm{I}}(c)$ for each $c \in O$. Choose any $c' \in \mathcal{C}$. If $c' \notin O$ then $\chi_O(c') = 0$. Otherwise we have $\chi^*_O(\mathrm{C}^{\mathrm{I}}(c')) = 1$. In both cases $\max(1 - \chi_O(c'), \chi^*_O(\mathrm{C}^{\mathrm{I}}(c))) = 1$ holds. As c' was chosen arbitrarily we have $\chi^*_O(\mathcal{B}^{\mathrm{I}}) = 1$.

PROPOSITION 4.3. *The set of model class dependent constructible orders is described by formula* $\mathcal{B}^{\mathrm{D}}$, *where*

$$\mathcal{B}^{\mathrm{D}} := \bigwedge_{c \in \mathcal{C}} \left(c \Rightarrow \bigwedge_{\substack{p \in \mathrm{Pos}(c) \\ s \in \{L,R\}}} \left(s \Rightarrow \bigvee_{v \in \mathrm{Var}(p,s)} \mathrm{C}^{\mathrm{D}}(p,v) \right) \right) \tag{8}$$

$$= \bigwedge_{\substack{c \in \mathcal{C} \\ s \in \{L,R\}}} \left(c \wedge s \Rightarrow \mathcal{B}(c,s) \right), \tag{9}$$

and $\mathcal{B}(c,s)$ *is defined by Equation* (3).

Proof. The equivalence of (8) and (9) is easily shown. The rest of the proof is similar to that of Proposition 4.2. Let s_O be the uniquely determined steering type of order O. Using Definition (2) we have to show that

$$O \models \mathcal{B}^{\mathrm{D}} \quad \text{iff} \quad O \models \mathcal{B}(c, s_O) \text{ for each } c \in O \ . \tag{$**$}$$

Formula (9) yields for arbitrary O

$$\chi^*_O(\mathcal{B}^{\mathrm{D}}) = \min_{c \in \mathcal{C}, s \in \{L,R\}} \{\max(1 - \chi_O(c), 1 - \chi_O(s), \chi^*_O(\mathcal{B}(c,s)))\} \ .$$

We again show the two implications of (**) independently:

"⇒": Let $O \models \mathcal{B}^{\mathrm{D}}$ and $c' \in O$ arbitrary. Furthermore, let s_O be the uniquely determined steering type of O. Then $\chi^*_O(\mathcal{B}^{\mathrm{D}}) = 1$ and $\max(1 - \chi_O(c'), 1 - \chi_O(s_O), \chi^*_O(\mathcal{B}(c', s_O))) = 1$. As $\chi_O(c') = \chi_O(s_O) = 1$ we have $\chi^*_O(\mathcal{B}(c', s_O))) = 1$ and thus $O \models \mathcal{B}(c', s_O)$.

"⇐": Let $O \subseteq \mathcal{C}$ with $O \models \mathcal{B}(c, s_O)$ for each $c \in O$ and uniquely determined $s_O \in O \cap \{L, R\}$. Choose any $c' \in \mathcal{C}, s' \in \{L, R\}$. For $s' \neq s_O$ we obtain $\chi_O(s') = 0$. If $c' \notin O$ then $\chi_O(c') = 0$. Otherwise $(s' = s_O, c' \in O)$ we have $\chi^*_O(\mathcal{B}(c', s')) = 1$. In each case $\max(1 - \chi_O(c'), 1 - \chi_O(s'), \chi^*_O(\mathcal{B}(c', s'))))\} = 1$ holds. As c' and s' were chosen arbitrarily we have $\chi^*_O(\mathcal{B}^{\mathrm{D}}) = 1$.

Formula $\mathcal{B}^{\mathrm{D}}$ allows orders with either no or multiple steering codes. To enforce exactly one $s \in \{L, R\}$ in each order, we use the following formula:

PROPOSITION 4.4. *The set of all orders containing exactly one steering code* $s \in \{L, R\}$ *is described by formula* $\mathcal{B}^{\mathrm{S}}$, *where*

$$\mathcal{B}^{\mathrm{S}} := (L \vee R) \wedge \neg(L \wedge R) \ . \tag{10}$$

Proof. By case distinction whether or not $L, R \in O$.

COROLLARY 4.5. *The set of (effectively) constructible orders is described by formula* $\mathcal{B}^{\mathrm{C}}$, *where*

$$\mathcal{B}^{\mathrm{C}} := \mathcal{B}^{\mathrm{I}} \wedge \mathcal{B}^{\mathrm{D}} \wedge \mathcal{B}^{\mathrm{S}} \ . \tag{11}$$

Proof. By Propositions 4.2, 4.3 and 4.4, and the fact that $\wedge$ corresponds to set intersection.

What we have achieved so far is the formalization of the constructibility check; the order completion process, however, is not yet integrated. At first glance, it may seem that the supplementing process requires modeling some kind of state transition. Describing each step in this way inevitably necessitates the use of non-monotonic or modal logic. Neither way seems to be desirable due to complexity considerations.

4.1. Avoiding State Transitions

The major part of the criteria to be checked requires no knowledge of the dynamic development caused by the supplementing process. This holds, e.g., for the (static) description of all possible states appearing after completion of the supplementing process. Moreover, formalization of changes caused by a fixed number of supplementing steps is also possible within propositional logic, as is shown later.

Before resuming with further criteria, we want to comment on some simple properties of relation $\longrightarrow_S$.

At first, note that an order is left unchanged by the supplementing process iff it is in $\longrightarrow_S$-normal form. Furthermore, an $\longrightarrow_S$-normal form of an order O of steering type s is characterized by the following property (compare with Equation (4)):

$$O \not\models \mathcal{Z}(c, s) \ \text{ for all } c \in \mathcal{C} \setminus O \ . \tag{12}$$

We therefore obtain

PROPOSITION 4.6. *The set of orders left unchanged by the supplementing process is described by formula* $\mathcal{Z}^{\mathrm{U}}$, *where*

$$\mathcal{Z}^{\mathrm{U}} := \bigwedge_{\substack{c \in \mathcal{C} \\ s \in \{L,R\}}} \left(s \wedge \Big(\bigvee_{\substack{p \in \mathrm{Pos}(c) \\ v \in \mathrm{Var}(p,s)}} \big(\mathrm{S}(p,v) \wedge \mathrm{C}^{\mathrm{D}}(p,v)\big) \Big) \wedge \mathrm{C}^{\mathrm{I}}(c) \ \Rightarrow \ c \right) \tag{13}$$

$$= \bigwedge_{\substack{c \in \mathcal{C} \\ s \in \{L,R\}}} \Big(s \wedge \mathcal{Z}(c,s) \Rightarrow c \Big), \tag{14}$$

and $\mathcal{Z}(c, s)$ *is defined by Equation* (5).

Proof. Formula (13) is just the version of (14) with the definition of $\mathcal{Z}(c, s)$ expanded, so equivalence is obvious. Furthermore, let s_O be the unique steering type of order O. Using (12) we now have to show that

$$O \models \mathcal{Z}^{\mathrm{U}} \quad \text{iff} \quad O \not\models \mathcal{Z}(c, s_O) \ \text{ for all } \ c \in \mathcal{C} \setminus O \ . \tag{***}$$

Evaluation yields for arbitrary O

$$\chi_O^*(\mathcal{Z}^{\mathrm{U}}) = \min_{c \in \mathcal{C}, s \in \{L,R\}} \{\max(1 - \chi_O(s), 1 - \chi_O^*(\mathcal{Z}(c,s)), \chi_O(c))\} \ .$$

As in similar proofs before, equivalence (***) is shown by proving the two implications directly, which we feel free to omit here.

We are now able to describe the set of orders that appear just before parts list generation:

COROLLARY 4.7. *The set of orders which have passed the supplementing process and the constructibility check are described by formula $\mathcal{B}^{\mathrm{Z}}$, where*

$$\mathcal{B}^{\mathrm{Z}} := \mathcal{B}^{\mathrm{C}} \wedge \mathcal{Z}^{\mathrm{U}} . \tag{15}$$

Proof. Corollary 4.5, Proposition 4.6.

Four of the five initially posed problems can now be solved:

Necessary codes: Code c is necessary iff the formula

$$\mathcal{B}^{\mathrm{Z}} \Rightarrow c$$

is a tautology, which is equivalent to $\mathcal{B}^{\mathrm{Z}} \wedge \neg c$ being unsatisfiable.

Inadmissible codes: Code c is inadmissible iff the formula

$$c \Rightarrow \neg \mathcal{B}^{\mathrm{Z}}$$

is a tautology. This holds iff $\mathcal{B}^{\mathrm{Z}} \wedge c$ is not satisfiable.

Superfluous parts: Part t is superfluous iff

$$\mathcal{B}^{\mathrm{Z}} \wedge \bigvee_{(m,p,v)\in\Omega(t)} \Big(\lambda(m,p,v) \wedge \mathrm{R}(m,p,v)\Big)$$

is unsatisfiable.

Ambiguities in the parts list generation process: There is an ambiguity between variants v_1 and v_2 at position p of module m iff the formula

$$\mathcal{B}^{\mathrm{Z}} \wedge \lambda(m,p,v_1) \wedge \mathrm{R}(m,p,v_1) \wedge \lambda(m,p,v_2) \wedge \mathrm{R}(m,p,v_2)$$

is satisfiable.

The interpretation of these formulae is straightforward using the set-of-orders view suggested by Definition 4.1.

Note that $\mathcal{B}^{\mathrm{Z}}$ occurs exclusively positive in all these cases, when formulated as satisfiability problems. We can greatly profit from this fact as follows. Most propositional provers require the input to be in conjunctive normal form. As $\mathcal{B}^{\mathrm{Z}}$ is a conjunction of smaller formulae, it can be converted relatively easily to conjunctive normal form (CNF), at least much more easily than its negation $N = \neg\mathcal{B}^{\mathrm{Z}}$. The CNF of N, which is structurally equivalent to the disjunctive normal form of $\mathcal{B}^{\mathrm{Z}}$, can be understood as an implicit enumeration of all valid orders. It seems hardly surprising that the enumeration-of-orders view is less efficient than the constraint view using $\mathcal{B}^{\mathrm{Z}}$.

We now concentrate on the remaining open question concerning the consistency of the supplementing process.

4.2. Ordering Dependencies in the Supplementing Process

At first, we investigate dependencies on the ordering in which the supplementing steps are performed. As the relation $\longrightarrow_S$ is terminating, it suffices to show that $\longrightarrow_S$ is locally confluent to assure (global) confluence and thus ordering independence.

LEMMA 4.8. *If $\longrightarrow_S$ is locally confluent, every order O has a unique $\longrightarrow_S$-normal form.*

Proof. This is just a variation of Newman's Diamond Lemma [14] applied to the terminating reduction relation $\longrightarrow_S$.

As we want to avoid the encoding of different states during the supplementing process in a modal or non-monotonic logic, we have to resort to constructs available in propositional logic. But a purely propositional formalization of the local confluence property of relation $\longrightarrow_S$ is hard to give, as the number of supplementing steps and thus supplementing possibilities can be quite large.

Therefore, we consider a stronger precondition by limiting the number of reduction steps:

DEFINITION 4.9. *The relation $\longrightarrow_S$ is n-step locally confluent if for all $O, O_1, O_2 \subseteq \mathcal{C}$ there is an $O_{12} \subseteq \mathcal{C}$ with*

$$O_1 \longleftarrow_S O \longrightarrow_S O_2 \quad \Rightarrow \quad O_1 \longrightarrow_S^{\leq n} O_{12} \longleftarrow_S^{\leq n} O_2 \ .$$

NOTE 4.10. *Obviously n-step local confluence implies local confluence.*

Let us now concentrate on developing a criterion describing 1-step local confluence. Before we can give this criterion, we need the following

DEFINITION 4.11. *Let $F \in \mathcal{F}(\mathcal{C})$, $x, y \in \mathcal{C}$ and $k \in \{\top, \bot\}$.*[8] *The restriction $F|_{x=k}$ is defined as the homomorphic extension of*

$$y|_{x=k} = \begin{cases} k & \textit{if } y = x \\ y & \textit{otherwise} \end{cases}$$

to the set $\mathcal{F}(\mathcal{C})$ of formulae.

Using this definition we can formalize properties about successor states in the supplementing process.

LEMMA 4.12. *Let $O \xrightarrow{c}_S O'$ and $F \in \mathcal{F}$. Then*

$$O \models F|_{c=\top} \quad \textit{iff} \quad O' \models F \ .$$

Proof. At first, note that $O' = O\dot{\cup}\{c\}$. We proceed by structural induction. The lemma is obvious for $F = \top$ and $F = \bot$. If $F = x \neq c$ is a propositional variable, then $x|_{c=\top} = x$ and $\chi_O(x) = \chi_{O'}(x)$. If $F = c$, we have $c|_{c=\top} = \top$ and $\chi_{O'}(c) = 1 = \chi_O(\top)$. Now, assume $F = \neg G$. Since $(\neg G)|_{c=\top} \equiv \neg(G|_{c=\top})$, the induction hypothesis already proves the lemma. The cases $F = G \vee H$ and $F = G \wedge H$ are handled accordingly using the fact that the restriction is a homomorphism.

Using Lemma 4.12 we can represent the effect of individual supplementing steps in propositional logic. The validity of a property F after adding code c is thus expressed by the validity of $F|_{c=\top}$ before supplementing c.

We therefore obtain

[8] $\top$ denotes truth, $\bot$ falsity.

PROPOSITION 4.13. *The supplementing process (i.e., $\longrightarrow_S$) is 1-step locally confluent iff*

$$\bigwedge_{\substack{c_1,c_2\in C\\ c_1\neq c_2}} \left(\neg c_1 \wedge \neg c_2 \;\Rightarrow\; \bigwedge_{s\in\{L,R\}} \left(s \;\Rightarrow\; \left(\mathcal{Z}(c_1,s) \wedge \mathcal{Z}(c_2,s) \;\Rightarrow\; \mathcal{Z}(c_2,s)|_{c_1=\top} \wedge \mathcal{Z}(c_1,s)|_{c_2=\top}\right)\right)\right) \tag{16}$$

is a tautology.

Proof. First we want to show that 1-step local confluence implies (16). We assume, for a contradiction, that (16) is not a tautology. Then there is a counterexample model O of steering type s_O, and codes c_1, c_2 with $c_1 \neq c_2$, such that $c_1, c_2 \notin O$, $O \models \mathcal{Z}(c_1, s_O)$, $O \models \mathcal{Z}(c_2, s_O)$ and $O \not\models \mathcal{Z}(c_2, s_O)|_{c_1=\top} \wedge \mathcal{Z}(c_1, s_O)|_{c_2=\top}$. Therefore, we also have $O \xrightarrow{c_1}_S O_1$ and $O \xrightarrow{c_2}_S O_2$ for appropriate O_1 and O_2. Moreover we get by using Lemma 4.12: $O_1 \not\xrightarrow{c_2}_S O_{12}$ or $O_2 \not\xrightarrow{c_1}_S O_{12}$. As $O_1, O_2 \neq O_{12}$ we have shown that $\longrightarrow_S$ is not 1-step locally confluent, a contradiction. The converse, namely that (16) implies 1-step local confluence is shown using a similar argumentation in reverse order.

Combining Lemma 4.8 and Note 4.10 with Proposition 4.13 we have a criterion at hand that captures the largest part of ordering dependencies occurring in our application.[9]

COROLLARY 4.14. *Assume (16) holds. Then the relation $\longrightarrow_S$ generates unique normal forms.*

4.3. Consistency of the Supplementing Process

The supplementing process adds codes to orders, thereby possibly converting non-constructible to constructible ones. The opposite, however, namely the conversion of constructible to non-constructible orders, may indicate a flaw in the process, especially since the supplementing formula (5) takes constructibility information ($\mathrm{C^D}, \mathrm{C^I}$) into consideration. We now want to elaborate on this.

Supplementing code $c \in \mathcal{C}$ while retaining constructibility is expressed by the validity of

$$\left(\mathcal{B}^{\mathrm{C}} \wedge \neg c \wedge \bigwedge_{s\in\{L,R\}} \left(s \Rightarrow \mathcal{Z}(c,s)\right)\right) \;\Rightarrow\; \mathcal{B}^{\mathrm{C}}|_{c=\top} \tag{17}$$

The subformula $\mathcal{B}^{\mathrm{C}}|_{c=\top}$ can be further simplified in this context by omitting certain subformulae as follows. For arbitrary formulae F we have $F \Rightarrow F|_{c=\top}$ as long as c does not occur negatively in F (this is easily proved by induction on F). As $\mathcal{B}^{\mathrm{C}}$ is a big conjunction $B_1 \wedge \cdots \wedge B_n$ we can drop those subformulae B_i not containing c negatively from the restriction $\mathcal{B}^{\mathrm{C}}|_{c=\top} = (B_1 \wedge \cdots \wedge B_n)|_{c=\top}$, without changing the validity of (17).

[9] Multiple supplementing steps can be simulated accordingly, although at the cost of increased complexity.

PROPOSITION 4.15. *The supplementing process preserves constructibility (in the above-mentioned sense) iff*

$$\bigwedge_{c\in C}\left(\left(\mathcal{B}^{\mathrm{C}} \wedge \neg c \wedge \bigwedge_{s\in\{L,R\}} \left(s \Rightarrow \mathcal{Z}(c,s)\right)\right) \Rightarrow \mathcal{B}^{\mathrm{C}}|_{c=\top}\right) \tag{18}$$

is a tautology.

Proof. Following the same idea as in the proof of Lemma 4.13.

5. Experimental Results

In order to solve the decision problems developed in the last section, we made experiments with different proving techniques, including resolution [16], term rewriting (using Stone polynomials to represent formulae [11]), BDDs [1, 5], and variations of the Davis-Putnam (DP) algorithm [7, 6]. Some of these techniques (e.g., BDDs) did not even permit a representation of the generated formulae (like $\mathcal{B}^{\mathrm{Z}}$). In general, run-times and memory requirements differed by orders of magnitude between these procedures. The DP algorithm turned out to be by far best-suited to solve the generated problems. This corroborates conclusions from [22].

Results of the experiments with a state-of-the-art implementation of the DP algorithm (SATO [20, 21]) are shown in Table I.

We used the test set

$$\mathcal{T} \quad = \quad \{\mathcal{B}^{\mathrm{Z}} \wedge c \mid c \in \mathcal{C}\} \cup \{\mathcal{B}^{\mathrm{Z}} \wedge \neg c \mid c \in \mathcal{C}\}$$

(representing the computation of necessary and inadmissible codes) as input for the propositional prover and split $\mathcal{T}$ into two disjoint subsets SAT and UNSAT containing satisfiable and unsatisfiable instances, respectively.

Table I. SATO average and maximal run-times for consistency proofs, in seconds.

data set	#vars	#clauses	$\bar{t}_{\mathrm{SAT}}$	$\bar{t}_{\mathrm{UNSAT}}$	$t_{\max}$
C-Class	1151	22036	0.49	0.38	0.68
Actros	1734	14264	0.19	0.13	0.21
Atego	1684	8973	0.12	0.09	0.15

The input data comprise the complete product documentation of the limousines of the Mercedes-Benz C-class, and parts of the product documentation of the Mercedes-Benz heavy and light trucks Actros and Atego, respectively (each restricted to one model line). To give an idea of the problem sizes, we have also included the number of propositional variables and the number of clauses in Table I.

Average run times for the elements of the two test sets SAT and UNSAT as well as the maximal run times are reported in seconds. All tests were performed on a SUN Ultra 1 running at 140 MHz under Solaris 2.5.1. Experiments using encodings of other consistency criteria resulted in similar prover run-times.

Most Davis-Putnam-style implementations require the input data to be in conjunctive normal form. We experimented with different transformation procedures including

BDD-based techniques (as they are used, e.g., for two-level hardware minimization) and the traditional satisfiability-conserving transformation method due to Tseitin [18]. Neither method showed clear advantages, be it in conversion times or in the impact on prover behaviour. We nevertheless believe that the relationship between CNF transformation technique and proof complexity could be an interesting field of research.

The statistical information about the data sets shown in Table I refers to a BDD-based CNF transformation (which results in fewer variables, but more and longer clauses).

Further experiments with the DP algorithm using different data structures (lists vs. tries), different variable selection heuristics, and different types of search-space pruning, indicated that most improvements on the DP algorithm (e.g., backjumping [2] or sophisticated literal selection heuristics [9]) were vital to achieve reasonable run-times for the complete set of generated SAT-instances.

6. Conclusions

In this paper we developed the formalization of an existing industrial process in automotive product data management. The formalization allows us to automatically check consistency criteria that could not be handled so far. We were thus able to increase the quality of the product documentation. Moreover, by establishing interactive tools for product data management, we could provide a push-button technology that helps the professionals cope with the continuous change of data.

Of course, practical acceptance of such tools crucially depends on reasonable run times, even more when used interactively. The state of development of current satisfiability checkers proved to be sufficiently advanced for our project.

But the integration into the users' workflow plays an equally important role. Users interact with our information system through a graphical interface in terms of their every-day work. The product documentation is imported through a standard interface to the data base. So, only little additional knowledge is demanded from the operating personnel.

As the product documentation's constraints and rules were already presented in Boolean logic, we could restrict our work to formalizing the process-inherent logic. A further encoding of the data was not necessary in order to apply propositional provers. While it would be comparatively easy to switch from one encoding to another, the critical issue is, however, how precise the industrial data and process are laid down initially.

Although the experiments were tailored to automotive product documentation, the underlying concepts should be applicable to neighboring fields of product data management (aviation, avionics, electronics, etc.), and especially to automotive supply industries.

Acknowledgements

The authors would like to thank Alfons Geser for fruitful discussions and suggestions during the early phase of the project. Special thanks are due to Dirk Bendrich from debis Systemhaus Industry GmbH (now with DaimlerChrysler AG), who was instrumental in initiating the project. Throughout the project, Alexander Krewitz (debis Systemhaus Industry GmbH) has been an extremely supportive industrial project leader. We are grateful to Ralph Wüsthofen (DaimlerChrysler AG) for patiently checking our processes and terminology from an industrial point of view.

References

1. S. B. Akers. Binary decision diagrams. In *IEEE Transactions on Computers*, volume C-27(6), pages 509–516, June 1978.
2. R. J. Bayardo Jr. and R. C. Schrag. Using CSP look-back techniques to solve real-world SAT instances. In *Proceedings of the 14th National Conference on Artificial Intelligence (AAAI'97)*, pages 203–208. AAAI Press, 1997.
3. A. Borälv. The industrial success of verification tools based on Stålmarck's method. In O. Grumberg, editor, *Computer Aided Verification*, volume 1254 of *Lecture Notes in Computer Science*, pages 7–10. Springer-Verlag, 1997.
4. J. P. Bowen and M. G. Hinchey. Seven more myths of formal methods: Dispelling industrial prejudices. In M. Naftalin, T. Denvir, and M. Bertran, editors, *FME'94: Industrial Benefit of Formal Methods*, volume 873 of *Lecture Notes in Computer Science*, pages 105–117. Springer-Verlag, 1994.
5. R. E. Bryant. Graph-based algorithms for boolean function manipulation. In *IEEE Transactions on Computers*, volume C-35(8), pages 677–691, Aug. 1986.
6. M. Davis, G. Logemann, and D. Loveland. A machine program for theorem-proving. In *Communications of the ACM*, volume 5, pages 394–397, July 1962.
7. M. Davis and H. Putnam. A computing procedure for quantification theory. In *Journal of the ACM*, volume 7, pages 201–215, 1960.
8. N. Dershowitz and J.-P. Jouannaud. Rewrite systems. In *Formal Models and Semantics*, volume 2 of *Handbook of Theoretical Computer Science*, chapter 6. Elsevier, 1990.
9. J. W. Freeman. *Improvements to Propositional Satisfiability Search Algorithms.* PhD thesis, University of Pennsylvania, Philadelphia, Pennsylvania, May 1995.
10. A. Geser and W. Küchlin. Structured formal verification of a fragment of the IBM 390 Clock Chip. Technical Report 97-50, RISC-Linz Report Series, Schloß Hagenberg bei Linz, Austria, Oct. 1997.
11. J. Hsiang. *Topics in Automated Theorem Proving and Program Generation.* PhD thesis, University of Illinois, Urbana, Illinois, Dec. 1982.
12. F. E. Marschner. Practical challenges for industrial formal verification tools. In O. Grumberg, editor, *Computer Aided Verification*, volume 1254 of *Lecture Notes in Computer Science*, pages 1–2. Springer-Verlag, 1997.
13. K. L. McMillan. *Symbolic Model Checking.* Kluwer Academic Publishers, Boston, 1993.
14. M. H. A. Newman. On theories with a combinatorial definition of "equivalence". In *Annals of Mathematics*, volume 43, pages 223–243. Princeton University Press, 1942.
15. R. Pugliese and E. Tronci. Automatic verification of a hydroelectric power plant. In M.-C. Gaudel and J. Woodcock, editors, *FME'96: Industrial Benefit and Advances in Formal Methods*, volume 1051 of *Lecture Notes in Computer Science*, pages 425–444. Springer-Verlag, 1996.
16. J. A. Robinson. A machine-oriented logic based on the resolution principle. In *Journal of the ACM*, volume 12, pages 23–41, 1965.
17. H. Saiedian. An invitation to formal methods. In E. A. Parrish, editor, *Computer*, volume 29, pages 16–30. IEEE Computer Society, Apr. 1996.
18. G. S. Tseitin. On the complexity of derivation in propositional calculus. In A. O. Silenko, editor, *Studies in Constructive Mathematics and Mathematical Logic*, pages 115–125, 1970.
19. A. L. Turk, S. T. Probst, and G. J. Powers. Verification of a chemical process leak test procedure. In O. Grumberg, editor, *Computer Aided Verification*, volume 1254 of *Lecture Notes in Computer Science*, pages 84–94. Springer-Verlag, 1997.
20. H. Zhang. SATO: A decision procedure for propositional logic. In *Association for Automated Reasoning Newsletter*, volume 22, pages 1–3, Mar. 1993.
21. H. Zhang. SATO: An efficient propositional prover. In *CADE'97: 14th International Conference on Automated Deduction*, volume 1249 of *Lecture Notes in Computer Science.* Springer Verlag, 1997.
22. H. Zhang and M. Stickel. Implementing the Davis-Putnam algorithm by tries. Technical report, Department of Computer Science, The University of Iowa, Iowa City, IA, Aug. 1994.

SAT2000
I. Gent et al. (Eds.)
IOS Press, 2000

Logical Cryptanalysis as a SAT Problem

*Encoding and Analysis of the U.S. Data Encryption Standard**

Fabio Massacci[‡]
Dipart. di Informatica e Sistemistica, Università di Roma I "La Sapienza", Italy & Dipart. di Ingegneria dell'Informazione, Università di Siena, Italy

Laura Marraro
Dipart. di Informatica e Sistemistica, Università di Roma I "La Sapienza", Italy

Abstract. Cryptographic algorithms play a key role in computer security and the formal analysis of their robustness is of utmost importance. Yet, logic and automated reasoning tools are seldom used in the analysis of a cipher, and thus one cannot often get the desired formal assurance that the cipher is free from unwanted properties that may weaken its strength.
In this paper, we claim that one can feasibly encode the low-level properties of state-of-the-art cryptographic algorithms as SAT problems and then use efficient automated theorem proving (ATP) systems and SAT-solvers for reasoning about them. We call this approach *logical cryptanalysis.*
In this framework, for instance, finding a model for a formula encoding an algorithm, is equivalent to finding a key with a cryptanalytic attack. Other important properties, such as cipher integrity or algebraic closure, can also be captured as SAT problems or as quantified boolean formulae. SAT benchmarks based on the encoding of cryptographic algorithms can be used to effectively combine features of "real world" problems and randomly generated problems.
Here we present a case study on the U.S. Data Encryption Standard (DES) and show how to obtain a manageable encoding of its properties.
We have also tested three SAT provers, TABLEAU by Crawford and Auton, SATO by Zhang, and rel-SAT by Bayardo and Schrag, on the encoding of DES, and we discuss the reasons behind their different performance.
A discussion of open problems and future research concludes the paper.

Keywords: Cipher verification, Data Encryption Standard, Logical Cryptanalysis, Propositional Satisfiability, Quantified Boolean Formulae, SAT Benchmarks

1. Introduction

Providing computer security in large open networks such as the Internet is one of the frontiers of computer science today [2, 38, 35]. Yet, providing security is not so simple and many technical challenges need to be solved to provide the high assurance that such an enterprise requests. These challenges are sketched in the excellent introduction by Anderson and Needham [2] and requires the use of particular security protocols for communication [1, 19, 45] and advanced cryptographic techniques [45]. Notwithstanding the amount of research and development work, the literature is full of "how to break a secure..." examples [10, 28, 43]. A protocol can be proven formally secure [39] and still be broken because the cipher used for its implementation has unwanted algebraic properties [43].

So, the use of logical encodings and automated reasoning tools for the analysis of cryptographic algorithms seems to be the next step towards greater assurance of secu-

‡ `massacci@dii.unisi.it`
* This is a longer and revised version of [30]. It contains also some of the experimental data reported in [31] for rel-SAT. Further details, problem instances and the encoder program can be found at the url: `http://www.dis.uniroma1.it/~massacci/cryptoSAT`

rity. Yet, in contrast with the large literature on formal verification of cryptographic protocols (see e.g. [10, 39, 28, 34]), we find little or no use of logics and automated reasoning tools in the proper cryptographic literature. Sophisticated and successful techniques such as linear cryptanalysis [33, 32] or differential cryptanalysis [7] use only statistical tools for solving cryptanalysis problems. The presence or absence of algebraic properties which may substantially weaken a cipher, such as algebraic closure, are often determined by ad-hoc methods or huge experiments [12, 26, 45].

In the absence of formal verification, the properties of many cryptographic algorithms are subject to intense debates and speculations[1]. Cryptographic key search has become THE search problem for many governments and large corporations, and the (lack of) resistance to key search is often the main concern behind the licensing of a cipher [23].

Thus, a new field of potential applications comes to one's mind:

- Can we encode low-level properties of ciphers into logic?
- Can we do it in such a way that finding a model of the encoded formula is equivalent to finding a key so that AI search techniques can be used to validate the strength of an algorithm?
- Can we do it in such a way that other problems, such as cipher integrity, existence of trapdoors, etc. can also be formally verified by complete automatic reasoning tools?
- Last, but not least, can we do it by using a *feasible encoding*, which might give hard-to-analyze formulae but not overwhelming?

In this paper we claim that propositional logic and automatic reasoning tools can be efficiently used to model and verify state-of-the-art cryptographic algorithms such as the (U.S.) Data Encryption Standard.

Among the various possibilities, we have chosen to encode cryptographic properties as SAT problems for a number of factors that are well summarized by Selman, Kautz, and McAllester [47]:

> First new algorithms were discovered, including ones based on stochastic local search as well as systematic search, that have better scaling properties than the basic Davis-Putnam algorithm. Second, improvement in machine speed, memory size and implementations extended the range of the algorithms. Third, researchers began to develop and solve propositional encodings of interesting, real-world problems such as planning and diagnoses, with others on the horizon [...]
>
> Between 1991 and 1996 the size of hard satisfiability problems grew from ones involving less than 100 variables to ones involving over 10,000 variables.

As we shall see, a number of interesting and challenging cryptographic problems are now at the border of tractability for SAT-based approach.

1.1. *Contributions of this paper*

In a nutshell, we show how to encode the abstract, functional, properties of a cryptographic algorithm[2] in a suitable logic so that, for instance, finding a model of the

[1] See e.g. [45][Chapter 12] for a survey of the long lived debate on whether the Data Encryption Standard has hidden trapdoors which would allow the US National Security Agency to decrypt all traffic.

[2] We only refer to the analysis of the algorithm itself and not to the verification of the program, software code or hardware circuit that implements it. Thus, we are not interested in software verification

corresponding formulae is equivalent to recovering a key in a cryptanalytic attack. Once the properties of the algorithm are represented as (propositional) formulae, then we can use efficient and effective automatic (SAT) reasoning tools for the analysis and the verification of the algorithm. We call this approach *logical cryptanalysis.*

To make our claims concrete, we show that by combining clever reverse engineering, advanced CAD minimization, and propositional simplification, it is possible to encode in propositional logic the properties of the U.S. Data Encryption Standard, DES for short, [36, 45].

The Data Encryption Standard, designed by IBM and NSA in the 70s, is the current U.S. Government standard, has been adopted for many financial and banking institutions, and is the recommended standard of the international banking transaction services. Although DES is currently under review [37], its widespread use and the fact that its security has been the subject of an intense scrutiny since its inception [7, 12, 33, 32] makes the case study significant. For many years DES has been (and still is) the algorithm on which cryptanalyst tested the final success of their techniques (see [45][Chapter 12] or Section 2 for a discussion and further references). Even partial successes with AI techniques, might be of substantial industrial relevance.

The encoding of the properties of DES that we have been able to generate is at the border of tractability for current search techniques: it is hard but not impossible. For examples, the encoding of a cryptographic attack with a known plaintext (where finding a model is equivalent to finding a key) for the commercial version of DES requires slightly more than 60,000 clauses and 10,000 variables (out of this only 56 are independent control variables, the key bits).

To check the effectiveness of AI techniques on this problem, we have used state-of-the-art SAT provers for cryptographic key search with our encoding. Here we focus on complete algorithms[3] based on the Davis-Putnam (DPLL) procedure [18, 17] and in particular on

- TABLEAU, by Crawford and Auton [15], a reference implementation of the DPLL procedure,

- SATO, by Zhang [51], which uses a sophisticated trie data structure for speeding up unit propagation,

- rel-SAT, by Bayardo and Schrag [5], a combination of the traditional DPLL procedure with back-jumping and learning.

In the experiments on the Data Encryption Standard, we didn't expect to be immediately competitive with twenty years of advanced cryptanalysis techniques, especially because AI Labs are not equally well funded to afford a specialized hardware machine of 250.000 USD, or the exclusive use of a network of 12 workstations for 50 days which have been used to break DES in the last few years [16, 32]. Still, we were pleasantly surprised by the result: a general purpose search algorithm such as rel-SAT using off-the-shelf hardware (Sparcs and Pentium II) can solve limited versions of DES without being told any information on the structure of the problem. Yet, there is a lot of research work that needs to be done since the commercial version is still out of reach for SAT-based

and in showing that an implementation matches a specification. We are interested in showing that the specification itself does not imply hidden, unwanted properties.

[3] Local search algorithms such as GSAT and Walk-SAT do not seem to perform well on this problem. See Massacci [31] for further details.

systems and on intermediate versions we cannot fully compete[4] with the performance of advanced cryptographic techniques based on statistical analysis [3, 7, 32].

Still, we believe that this approach might be beneficial for both the automated reasoning and the computer security communities.

For the *automated reasoning community*, it provides a set of challenging problems of industrial relevance ranging from satisfiability and validity in propositional logic to validity in quantified boolean logic. Thus we claim that this problem could be one of the reference benchmarks for propositional reasoning and search. We should not see such applications as tools for "electronic criminals". Verification and cryptanalysis of ciphers is the common practice of institutions responsible for international standards and of cryptographic research[5]. After all, before recommending an algorithm for encoding bank transactions, one may want to thoroughly test and verify it.

Moreover, the encoding of Feistel-type ciphers like DES has the same characteristics of challenging hard problems such as the hidden parity bit problem mentioned in [47]: defined and independent variables, a hierarchical and regular structure, and large affine subproblems (i.e. formulae with exclusive or). As we shall see, such encodings give the possibility of generating as many random instances as one wants and still each instance is as "real-world" as any instance that can be met in commercial cryptographic applications[6].

Thus, we believe that it can be a first step towards an answer to the last SAT challenge proposed by Selman, Kautz, and McAllester [47]. It is also an answer to the problem of generating hard solved instance discussed by Cook and Mitchell in their DIMACS survey [14]. As our experiments shows, our encoding can be used to generate solved instances which are hard to solve, in contrast with the standard generation methods for solved instances. We exploit the fact that cryptographic algorithms are *designed* to be hard to crack. Our proposal follows the spirit of Cook and Mitchell [14] where it was proposed to use RSA for generating hard solved instances.

For the *security community*, the formalization of the property of a cipher using logic might offer a simple solution to many issues regarding the strength of a cryptographic algorithm. Consider the hot debate about the existence of trapdoors or key escrow schemes. The formal proof that there is no universal key to escrow a cipher might be provided together with the algorithm. The proof might then be quickly machine checked for correctness by suspicious users. Even if finding the proof takes a long time, this can be done off-line once and for all. Also, to verify the strength of a cipher one may test it for resistance against SAT solvers and thus possibly avoid the risk of becoming the subject of a "how to break a secure..." paper at the next crypto conference.

1.2. Plan of the paper

In the rest of the paper we recall at first some basic things about cryptography, how the Data Encryption Standard works, and some of the main approaches used for the cryptanalysis of DES (§2).

Then we present the general idea behind logical cryptanalysis, and how different properties can be captured by this approach once we have encoded the functional description of a cipher into propositional logic (§3). The details of the encoding of

[4] Note however that these cryptographic methods require large amount of data to be effective. See further in Section 2.

[5] Most security firms offer cash prizes for those who are able to break their ciphers.

[6] This contrast with the most common benchmarks for propositional reasoning and search which are either totally random such as the Random 3-SAT CNF [48] or are fixed but have industrial relevance such as the IFIP benchmark for hardware verification [13]. Our proposal follows the line of the work by Gomes, Selman, et al. on generating structured CSP problems using quasi-group problems [21, 22].

the Data Encryption Standard are presented in Section 4, where we also presents some experimental data on the size and structure of the corresponding SAT-problem.

Third we present some preliminary experiments on the performance of the automated reasoning tools TABLEAU, SATO, and rel-SAT, for the simplest cryptographic problem that we can encode as a SAT problem (cryptographic key search on a limited version of DES) and discuss the reason behind their different performances (§5) .

We conclude the paper with some topics for future research (§6).

2. Basics of Cryptography

At high level (for a comprehensive introduction to the subject see [45]), a cryptographic algorithm transforms a sequence of bits into another sequence of bits with certain (desirable) properties. So, if we denote three vectors of bits by **P** (the plaintext), **C** (the ciphertext), and **K** (the secret key) we have

$$\mathbf{C} = \mathrm{E}_{\mathbf{K}}(\mathbf{P})$$

The important property of this transformation, called *encryption*, is that it must be difficult to recover **P** from **C** if one does not know **K**.

In most cases we have another transformation (*decryption*) that maps back **C** into **P** using **K** or another sequence of bits $\mathbf{K}^{-1}$ which is related to **K**.

$$\mathbf{C} = \mathrm{D}_{\mathbf{K}^{-1}}(\mathbf{P})$$

If **K** can also be used for decryption, we have a *symmetric cipher.*

The first thing a cryptanalyst may wish to do is to *search for a key* which produced a given ciphertext. This can be done by using only the ciphertext, or a number of known pairs of plaintext and ciphertext (known plaintext attack). This latter attack is not so impossible as one might expect: there are lot of standard parts in encrypted messages and files. In some cases it makes sense to assume that the cryptanalyst could choose such pairs (chosen plaintext attack). The cryptographic techniques we sketch in Section 2.2 can be classified along these lines.

There are other, more sophisticated properties which are more interesting though harder to analyze. The basic one regards the *existence of trapdoors* in a cipher. For instance, we may wonder if there is an *universal key* to decrypt any message encrypted with DES. As we already noted, this has been the subject of an intense debate till recent past [45][Section 12.3].

Almost all algebraic properties of a cipher that distinguish it from a pseudo-random permutation affect (weaken) its strength. A fairly simple property is the existence of *weak keys* i.e. of keys **K** such that $\mathbf{P} = \mathrm{E}_{\mathbf{K}}(\mathrm{E}_{\mathbf{K}}(\mathbf{P}))$. There is little sense in encrypting things twice with a weak key. For instance DES has an handful of weak keys [45][p. 280].

Even if no weak key exists, we may wish to know whether *a cipher is closed* [26, 45, 12] i.e. for any plaintext **P** and for any two key $\mathbf{K}^1$ and $\mathbf{K}^2$ we can always find a third key $\mathbf{K}^3$ such that encrypting a plaintext with the first key and then with the second key is perfectly equivalent to encrypting it is just once with the third key. In other words we want to know whether $\mathrm{E}_{\mathbf{K}^2}(\mathrm{E}_{\mathbf{K}^1}(\mathbf{P})) = \mathrm{E}_{\mathbf{K}}(\mathbf{P})$ for a suitable key **K**. In general we may wish to find a key **K** that is independent from the plaintext and just dependent on the other two keys.

If a cipher is closed this means that we cannot improve its security by encrypting things twice with the different keys. Even worse, the cipher is vulnerable to particular attacks that make it possible to reduce the search space of brute force attacks to half of the key bits [26]. Proving that a cipher is closed is equivalent to proving that the encryption transformations form a group. For instance, it has been proved with a huge amount of cyclic experiments that DES is not a group [12].

Another interesting combination of encryption with different keys is Tuchman's *triple encryption scheme*, which is an encryption of the plaintext with one key, its decryption with a different key and its final re-encryption with a third key. Again, we wish to known whether we are better off than by using a simple encryption, i.e. whether

$$\mathrm{E}_{\mathbf{K}^3}(\mathrm{D}_{\mathbf{K}^2}(\mathrm{E}_{\mathbf{K}^1}(\mathbf{P}))) \neq \mathrm{E}_{\mathbf{K}}(\mathbf{P})$$

for all plaintexts $\mathbf{P}$ and all keys $\mathbf{K}$.

As a final example, we may wish to know whether a cipher is *faithful* [26], i.e. if different keys can be used to generate the same plaintext-ciphertext pair. In symbols we may ask whether $\mathrm{E}_{\mathbf{K}}(\mathbf{P}) = \mathrm{E}_{\mathbf{K}'}(\mathbf{P})$ implies that $\mathbf{K} = \mathbf{K}'$. This is important if we want to use the data as court evidence.

2.1. The Data Encryption Standard

As the reader might now want to know how DES works, we start by saying that DES is a *block cipher*, which enciphers blocks of 64 bits (the plaintext) into blocks of 64 bits (the ciphertext) using a key of 56 bits[7]. We give here only a simple presentation to make the paper self-contained and the interested reader is referred to [36] or [45][Chap. 12] for more details.

DES and many other popular symmetric ciphers such as RC5 are built following a common architecture which is due to Feistel and his group [20]. After some initial preprocessing, the following operations are executed:

1. break the plaintext in two halves,
2. combine one half with the key using a clever function f,
3. XOR the combination with the other half
4. swap the two parts.

The combination of these operations is called a *round*. Figure 1 exemplifies the construction.

In the case of DES there are 16 rounds (i.e. the above operations are "repeated" 16 times) which are almost identical except for the keys: for each round a different subset of the 56 key bits is selected and combined with the input of the previous round. The strength of the cipher depends on the way this combination function is designed and on the number of rounds. This design is, to quote Ron Rivest, "part art, part science".

Following the notation introduced at the beginning of the section, we use superscripts to distinguish two different vectors of bits and subscripts to represents the single element within a vector. So, in $\mathbf{L}^1$, $\mathbf{L}^2$ etc. $\mathbf{L}^i$ is the i-th vector and not the i-th component. The j-th component of the i-th vector $\mathbf{L}^i$ is represented as $\mathbf{L}^i_j$.

After an initial permutation, whose purpose is to mix the input bits, the plaintext is divided in two halves, a left one and a right one. The 16 rounds in which the right part of the data is combined with the key can be described as follows:

$$\mathbf{L}^i = \mathbf{R}^{i-1} \tag{1}$$

$$\mathbf{R}^i = \mathbf{L}^{i-1} \bigoplus \mathbf{f}(\mathbf{R}^{i-1}, \mathbf{K}^i) \tag{2}$$

[7] The key is usually expressed as a 64 bits number, in which every eighth bit is used for parity checks and is ignored by the algorithm.

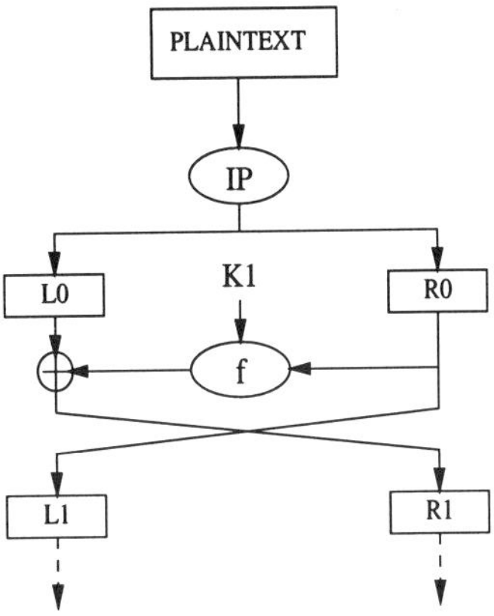

Figure 1. A Round of DES

where we indicate by $\mathbf{A} \bigoplus \mathbf{B}$ the xor of the j-th component of the vector $\mathbf{A}$ with the j-th component of the vector $\mathbf{B}$. After the 16th round, the right and left halves are joined and a final permutation (the inverse of the initial permutation) finishes the algorithm.

For each of the 16 rounds of DES a 48 bits subkey is generated. These subkeys, $\mathbf{K^i}$, are generated according a particular scheduling algorithm. Initially we divide the 56 bits key in two 28 bits blocks, $\mathbf{C^0}$ and $\mathbf{D^0}$, and, during the generic iteration, $\mathbf{C^{i-1}}$ and $\mathbf{D^{i-1}}$ are circularly shifted left of one or two bits based on the round i. This produces two blocks, $\mathbf{C^i}$ and $\mathbf{D^i}$, that are joined and permuted to produce the 48 bits subkey $\mathbf{K^i}$.

The round function f, which DES uses to mix up the key bits with the output of the previous round, takes as arguments the right half $\mathbf{R^i}$ from the previous round and the subkey from the actual round. Then the 32 bits which compose $\mathbf{R^i}$ are permuted and expanded to 48 bits and the xored together with the key bits:

$$\mathbf{X^i} = E(\mathbf{R^{i-1}}) \bigoplus \mathbf{K^i}$$

The 48 bits block $\mathbf{X^i}$ is then divided in eight sub-blocks of 6-bits each. Each sub-block specifies an entry in a *substitution matrix* called *S-box*. Every matrix has six input bits and four output bits, therefore it has four rows and sixteen columns. The six input bits specify in which row and column to see to find the four output bits. From the S-boxes we obtain eight 4-bits numbers that form a 32 bits block.

The pictorial representation in Fig. 2 should make it a bit clearer.

Substitution and permutation operations realize the properties that Shannon [49] named confusion[8] and diffusion[9], and that give a cipher its strength. So the S-boxes represent the most critical step that gives DES its strength [45][pp. 284 and 294].

2.2. Existing cryptanalytic approaches

The simplest approach is *exhaustive search*: try different keys until the right one is found. Testing 2^{55} keys on average is not easy unless one has specialized hardware or a large network of machines. This has proved to be finally successful in 1998: a specialized machine costing 250.000 US$ broke the DES challenge posted by RSA Security in 56 hours [16]. Although the search strategy exploited some of the algebraic properties of

[8] Confusion is created using operations that make an output sequence non-linearly dependent on an input bits sequence.

[9] With diffusion an output bit is made dependent on a great number of input bits.

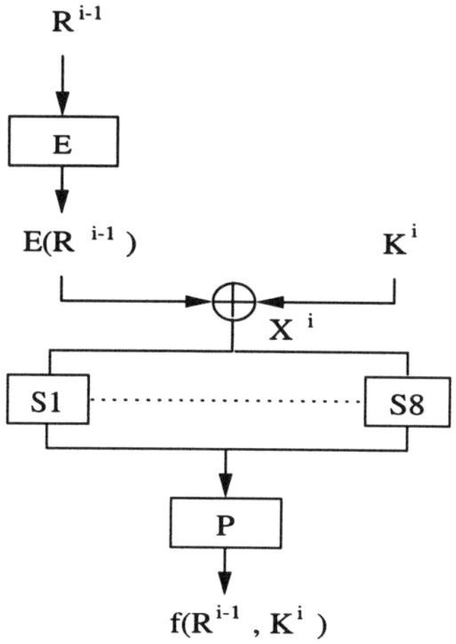

Figure 2. The Round Function f of DES

DES to cut the size of the search space, we can substantially classify it as exhaustive search.

Differential cryptanalysis was introduced in the early 90s by Biham and Shamir [7]. It considers ciphertext and plaintext pairs presenting particular fixed differences. Then, it analyzes the evolution of these differences as the plaintexts pass through the rounds of DES. Using the differences appearing in the actual ciphertexts, different probabilities can be assigned to different keys. Considering an increasing number of ciphertext and plaintext pairs, a key will emerge as the most probable.

Using this approach Biham and Shamir found a chosen plaintext attack that is more efficient than exhaustive search. For few rounds this approach is still feasible, although it requires larger and larger amount of data as the number of rounds increase. For instance, DES up to 8 rounds can be broken within few minutes on a PC if a sufficiently large pool of chosen plaintexts (50,000) is available [7][p. 6]. However, for the full DES with 16 rounds, this attack is only theoretical since it requires too many resources. To get the key, it uses 2^{47} chosen plaintext. The time complexity of the data analysis is about 2^{37} DES equivalent operations. If this approach is converted in a known plaintext attack, its efficiency is worse than exhaustive search.

Matsui's *linear cryptanalysis* [32, 33] works better. This method uses linear approximations (xor) to describe the behavior of a block cipher. By xoring together some plaintext bits with some ciphertext bits, one can get a bit that is the xor of some key bits. This is a linear approximation of a round that is correct with a certain probability. Using an increasing number of plaintext and related ciphertexts, it is possible to guess the value of some key bits. If more data is analyzed, the guess is more reliable.

To identify a good linear approximation for DES, it is necessary to find good linear approximations for each round, and then join them together. The base attack uses the best linear approximations for 16-rounds DES, and 2^{27} known plaintexts, returning two key bits. A refinement of this method uses the linear approximations of 14 rounds and then guesses the input and output values of the first and last rounds of DES. It can find 26 key bits and for the remaining bits uses exhaustive search. An experimental analysis by Matsui [32] showed that is possible to get the key of the full version of DES in 50 days using a network of workstations.

Davie (unpublished) proposed a potential attack on DES based on the non-uniformity of the distribution of the output of pairs of adjacent S-boxes. This attack is theoretical and requires $2^{56.6}$ known plaintexts to discover two key bits. The improved Davie's attack [6] finds 24 key bits by applying the analysis twice, one considering the odd rounds and the other considering the even rounds. The remaining 32 bits can be found by exhaustive search. The improved version is able to break DES faster than exhaustive search.

3. Logical Cryptanalysis

The main intuition behind logical cryptanalysis is that we should view each bit sequence **P**, **C**, **K** as a sequence of *propositional variables* P, C, K, in which every variable is true when the corresponding bit is 1 and false when it is 0.

Then we simply need to *encode the properties of the cryptographic algorithm with a logical formula* $\mathcal{E}(P, K, C)$, which is true if and only if for the corresponding sequences of bits we have that $\mathbf{C} = \mathrm{E}_{\mathbf{K}}(\mathbf{P})$ holds. Propositional logic is the straightforward choice but other logics (such as temporal logic) might give a more compact encoding.

The intuition behind logical cryptanalysis is as simple as that. Once we have the formula describing the cipher, the cryptanalysis problems we have described can be easily formalized.

However, before going forward to the examples, we need to notice that if $\mathcal{E}(P, K, C)$ holds there is no guarantee that $\mathcal{E}(C, K, P)$ holds too. $\mathcal{E}(C, K, P)$ does *not* model the fact that we can obtain **P** by decrypting **C** using **K**. Even for symmetric ciphers, where the same key is used for encryption and decryption, the algorithm used for decryption is slightly different from the algorithm used for encryption (e.g. in DES we need to change the key scheduling). This slight difference is sufficient to make the formula $\mathcal{D}(C, K, P)$ slightly different from $\mathcal{E}(C, K, P)$.

To model *key search*, let v_C be the truth values (true/false) of the available ciphertext. To find a key with a ciphertext only-attack, it is enough to find a model of $\mathcal{E}(P, K, v_C)$. In a known plaintext attack, we also know the values v_P of the propositional variables P. So, we only need to search for a model of $\mathcal{E}(v_P, K, v_C)$.

For reason of space efficiency we may need to introduce more variables in $\mathcal{E}(P, K, C)$ besides C, P and K to make use of abbreviations and definitions. Indeed, this is what we have done in the encoding of DES in Section 4. Still, if the encoding is well made, then K, C and P should be the only *control variables* of the problem, i.e. fixing their values should determine the values of all other variables. Thus, in $\mathcal{E}(v_P, K, v_C)$ the interesting variables are only K. For instance, in the case of the DES encoding we have only 56 control variables.

If we have n plaintext and ciphertext pairs we can constraint the search further by conjoining the corresponding formulae

$$\bigwedge_{i=1}^{n} \mathcal{E}(v_P^i, K, v_C^i).$$

We can thus encode cryptographic key search as a satisfiability problem.

In this way we can generate easily *solved instances* which might be very hard to solve: we generate randomly a key **K** and a plaintext **P**. Then we use the cryptographic algorithm itself to generate $\mathbf{C} = \mathrm{E}_{\mathbf{K}}(\mathbf{P})$. Finally we substitute in $\mathcal{E}(P, K, C)$ the corresponding boolean values v_P and v_C that we have so far generated. Then the pair $\langle v_K, \mathcal{E}(v_P, K, v_C)\rangle$ gives a solved instance of the satisfiability problem. If the encoding is well designed, one could also use $\mathcal{E}(v_P, v_K, C)$ and unit propagation to obtain v_C. Our encoding satisfied this property but using the original encryption algorithm is much faster.

Finding a model (v_K or another assignment) is then equivalent to break the cipher with a known plaintext attack which uses only one or few plaintext/ciphertext pair. Since the ciphers are designed to be hard to break, this will provide us with the hard solved instances asked for by Cook and Mitchell [14].

For the analysis of the strength of a cipher, we are often interested in other important properties that can be encoded as SAT problems or at worst as quantified boolean formulae (QBF) [9, 11]. For instance if we use QBF, finding a key would correspond to a constructive proof of

$$\exists K. \left(\bigwedge_{i=1}^{n} \mathcal{E}(v_C^i, K, v_P^i) \right)$$

The simplest property (but for importance) that can be encoded as a SAT problem is the property that a cipher is *faithful* [26]: for any pair of plaintext and ciphertext there is only one key that could have produced them. This property is captured by the following formula,

$$\mathcal{E}(P, K, C) \wedge \mathcal{E}(P, K', C) \Rightarrow \left(\bigwedge_{i} K_i \Leftrightarrow K_i' \right)$$

In the case of DES, by analyzing the algorithm it is possible to detect some (six) key pairs K and K' that do not satisfy this property. They are called *semi-weak keys*[10]. It is not known whether they are the only ones (see e.g. [45][p. 281]).

In some cases (e.g. when discussing the value of encrypted evidence in a court case), we may be interested in knowing whether a semi-weak key exists for given plaintexts and ciphertexts. This problem is just a slightly harder variant of the key search problem: we want to know whether $\mathcal{E}(v_P, K, v_C)$ has a unique solution.

Another problem that can be expressed as a SAT-problem is the *(non) existence of weak keys*: we want to prove that $\mathrm{E}_K(\mathrm{E}_K(\mathbf{P})) \neq \mathbf{P}$ for all values of $\mathbf{P}$. If we denote the result of the first encryption by C, this property can be captured by the propositional formula below:

$$\mathcal{E}(P, K, C) \Rightarrow \neg\mathcal{E}(C, K, P)$$

If the formula above is propositionally valid then no weak key exists for all values of the plaintext. We can restrict it further by looking at particular instances of v_P or v_K, if we suspect v_K to be a weak key. Since DES has few weak keys, this problem has a known answer. It might be interesting to see whether SAT-based approaches can find other weak keys automatically.

If the strong property above is not valid, we can weaken it by using a 2-QBF formula. Now we just require that for every key there is at least a plaintext that is not mapped into itself.

$$\neg\exists K.\forall P. \left(\mathcal{E}(P, K, C) \Rightarrow \mathcal{E}(C, K, P)\right)$$

Notice that we do not need to quantify over C: it should be uniquely determined by the values of K and P if the encoding is well designed.

If we want to prove that *a cipher is not closed* the formula we have to prove is slightly more complicated. Recall that we have to prove that for any pair of keys $\mathbf{K^1}$ and $\mathbf{K^2}$ we can never find a third key $\mathbf{K}$ such that $\mathrm{E}_{\mathbf{K^2}}(\mathrm{E}_{\mathbf{K^1}}(\mathbf{P})) = \mathrm{E}_{\mathbf{K}}(\mathbf{P})$. If we denote by C^1 the result of the first encryption and by C the result of the final encryption we get the following formula:

$$\left(\mathcal{E}(P, K^1, C^1) \wedge \mathcal{E}(C^1, K^2, C)\right) \Rightarrow \neg\mathcal{E}(P, K, C)$$

[10] For instance, including the parity bits (every eighth bit), the keys 01FE 01FE 01FE 01FE and FE01 FE01 FE01 FE01 are a pair of semi-weak keys.

If this formula is valid then the cipher is not closed: encrypting twice (with different keys) is better than encrypting once.

Notice that this property has never been formally proven for DES. There is only an indirect proof based on cyclic experiments [12] of the weaker property that the encryption with DES does not form a group, which is equivalent to the following one:

$$\exists K^1 \exists K^2 . \forall K \exists P . \left(\mathcal{E}(P, K^1, C^1) \wedge \mathcal{E}(C^1, K^2, C)\right) \wedge \neg\mathcal{E}(P, K, C)$$

Proving that Tuchman's *triple encryption is stronger than single encryption* can also be done by proving the following formula:

$$\left(\mathcal{E}(P, K^1, C^1) \wedge \mathcal{D}(C^1, K^2, C^2) \wedge \mathcal{E}(C^2, K^3, C)\right) \Rightarrow \neg\mathcal{E}(P, K, C)$$

This property can also be weakened using QBF.

The *existence of universal keys* which can decrypt all traffic can be characterized by a QBF formula. If we denote by C the result of the encryption we have

$$\exists K^u . \forall K . \forall P . \left(\mathcal{E}(P, K, C) \Rightarrow \mathcal{D}(C, K^u, P)\right)$$

Of course, we might be more interested in the negation of this formula, i.e. in proving that no universal key exists. It is easy to check that if a cipher is faithful then no universal key exists.

Among these problems, we believe that the encoding of key search as a SAT problem deserve particular attention as a SAT-benchmark. The main advantage behind our proposal is the combination of the seemingly contrasting needs of using "real-world" problems (possibly with lot of structures) and of generating a huge number of instances which can only be (pseudo)randomly generated.

Real problems are important because solving them is what one expects from SAT solvers. Yet, dealing with them is not simple [5]:

> Care must be taken when experimenting with real world instances because the number of instances available for experimentation is often limited.

Crawford and Auton [15] noted that working with random instances might be preferable because

> [...] random problems are readily available in any given size and virtually inexhaustible numbers. For example, ... [their experiments] required several million problems and it is hard to imagine collecting that many problems any other way.

Our main point is that by changing the plaintext and the key we can generate as many *solved instances* as we want. If we encode the full-fledged version of the cryptographic algorithm (such as the Data Encryption Standard) each instance would be identical to an actual plaintext and ciphertext used by a bank, financial institution or government department. In the case of the Data Encryption Standard we can generate $2^{56} \times 2^{64}$ instances which are fairly enough. Indeed, if we consider the encryption of binary or compressed data, we can substantially span the whole message space. If we restrict ourselves to ASCII plaintexts, the number of different plaintexts shifts from 2^{64} to 2^{56}, since every 8th bit of the 64 message bits will be fixed.

To generate *unsatisfiable instances*, it is sufficient to generate a plaintext and ciphertext pair and then give it to the encoder together with a wrong ciphertext (by randomly flipping few bits). Our experimental analysis (Section 5) on the Data Encryption Standard shows that few rounds or few plaintext and ciphertext pairs are sufficient to constraint the search to only one model. Changing one bit of the ciphertext would make the problem unsatisfiable.

Of course, the hard part is getting a manageable translation. We have done this for the Data Encryption Standard.

4. Encoding the Data Encryption Standard

The generation of the formula $\mathcal{E}(C, K, P)$ which describes the logical characteristics of DES has been a substantial operation of reverse "logical" engineering.

The straightforward approach would be describing the VLSI circuit implementing DES and transform the circuit into a logical formula. Unfortunately, the resulting formula is too big to be of any use.

Our basic idea is to walk through the DES algorithm, generating along the way the formulae corresponding to each operation that DES performs, with a clever trick. The trick to obtain manageable formulae is that not all stages of DES should be explicitly represented by a circuit and then encoded as formulae. Whenever possible, operations should be executed directly on the propositional variables representing the input bits. For instance a permutation is not encoded, rather we execute the permutation of the input bits and provide as output the permuted propositional variables.

Intuitively, to generate the encoding our programs must

- transform into boolean formulae the fixed matrix operations corresponding to the round function f (Fig. 2) and minimize them off-line using state-of-the-art CAD tools;
- encode each bit of the ciphertext, the plaintext and the key as a propositional variable;
- simulate the DES algorithm, and generate formulae corresponding to each DES operation on the way by
  - encoding complex transformations (previously minimized off-line);
  - encoding exclusive or and equivalences;
  - calculating simple operations and permutations;
- if requested, read from files the known values of the plaintext and ciphertext and substitute the corresponding boolean values in the formula;
- finally simplify the formula, propagate and eliminate boolean values, equivalences, duplicate variables, tautological or inessential clauses etc.

This process can be logically divided in three parts, one dealing with the general structure of Feistel-like ciphers, one dealing with the permutations and the key scheduling, one treating the S-boxes.

4.1. Encoding the general Feistel architecture

The encoding of the general Feistel-like structure of DES is straightforward. For every round i of the algorithm we generate the formulae

$$
\begin{array}{lll}
L_j^i & \Leftrightarrow R_j^{i-1} & j = 1 \dots 32 \\
R_j^i & \Leftrightarrow L_j^{i-1} \oplus F_j^i & j = 1 \dots 32 \\
X_j^i & \Leftrightarrow E(R^{i-1})_j \oplus K_j^i & j = 1 \dots 48 \\
F_j^i & \Leftrightarrow P(S^i)_j & j = 1 \dots 32
\end{array}
$$

In the previous formulae, the expression $E(R^{i-1})$ represents a permutation and an extension from 32 to 48 bits of the initial vector of 32 propositional variables represented by R^{i-1}. In practice this means that some variables in R^i are duplicated. The expression $P(S^i)$ represents the permutation of the S-boxes outputs. The vector of variables F^i is the output of the f function. The vector of propositional variables K^i represents the i-th subset of the initial key that is chosen by the algorithm for each round.

In the future we plan to study some possibility of off-line minimization for these formulae, using the CAD minimization tool we have used for the generation of the S-boxes in Sec. 4.3, since they are common to many other ciphers and are repeated for many rounds.

4.2. Encoding permutations and the key scheduling

The "encoding" of the permutations and the generation of the subkeys K^i have been the subject of the trick we mentioned at the beginning of the section.

So, let M be a permutation matrix and A the vector of propositional variables to be permuted. If m_j is the element j in the matrix M, then the variable M_j representing the element j of the matrix M, will be equal to the variable A_{m_j} representing the element m_j of the vector A. Then we can simply consider the permuted variables as the input of the next stage of the algorithm.

To generate the subkey K^i we consider a 64 elements vector in which every element is an integer representing the index of the variable that locates a particular key bit. The DES algorithm applies a permutation (the one that eliminates eight parity bits) and reduces these elements to 56. These 56 elements are divided in two halves and the shift operation is performed for each round. The two shifted parts are then joined and permuted again to give the subkey. To encode the shift operation, suppose that the number of shifts that have to take place at round i is denoted by s_i. Then, for each element in the vector to be shifted we calculate the position p_j with $(j = 1 \dots 28)$ that each element occupies in the shifted vector.

The new positions can be obtained using the following algorithm:

1. $p'_j = (j - s_i)$.
2. If $p'_j \leq 0$
   then $p_j = 28 - |p'_j|$
   else $p_j = p'_j$

With the new positions, the shift can be encoded as a permutation.

For instance, suppose that the processed round is the first round. Then $shift_i$ is equal to 1, and one of the two vectors containing half of the key bits to be shifted is C_0 : [57 49 41 33 ... 52 44 36].

Using the previous criteria is possible to see that:

$$\begin{array}{lll} j = 1 & \Rightarrow p'_1 = 1 - 1 = 0 & \Rightarrow p_1 = 28 \\ j = 2 & \Rightarrow p'_2 = 2 - 1 = 1 & \Rightarrow p_2 = 1 \\ \vdots & & \\ j = 28 & \Rightarrow p'_{28} = 28 - 1 = 27 & \Rightarrow p_{28} = 27 \end{array}$$

In this way we have obtained a permutation vector that have to be applied to C_0. Performing this permutation we obtain the shifted vector C_1 : [49 41 33 ... 52 44 36 57]. In the final formula, rather than adding a formula corresponding to the permutation relating the input variables $K_1, K_2, \dots K_{64}$ and the output variables of the permutation

Table I. Number of minterms per output

S-box	Multiple Outputs				Single Outputs			
	o_1	o_2	o_3	o_4	o_1	o_2	o_3	o_4
S1	20	20	21	22	17	16	19	20
S2	25	23	22	22	19	18	18	14
S3	25	24	25	23	22	17	18	18
S4	23	23	22	23	18	17	17	18
S5	22	24	23	21	17	23	17	17
S6	23	24	25	22	17	22	22	16
S7	23	22	24	26	19	16	18	23
S8	22	22	20	21	19	17	15	18

circuit K_1^2, K_2^2, ..., K_{64}^2 and then using the output variables K_1^2, K_2^i, ... in the rest of the circuit we use the corresponding permuted variables K_{49}, K_{41} etc. This is the twist that makes the encoding feasible.

4.3. Encoding the S-boxes

The fundamental problem in processing the S-boxes is to determine a representation that is adequate to translate these matrices into formulae. The simplest approach is to use Programmable Logic Arrays (PLAs) since these matrices are addressed by bits and their entries are bits too. Once every S-box is represented as a PLA, we get formulae of this kind:

$$M_{kh}^i \Leftrightarrow \bigwedge_{j=1}^{48} \pm X_{jkh}^i \qquad k = 1 \dots maxM_{ih}$$

$$S_h^i \Leftrightarrow \bigvee_{j=k_1}^{maxM_{ih}} M_{k_j h}^i \quad h = 1 \dots 32$$

where M^i are the minterms generated in the round i, the vector of propositional variables S^i represents the 32 output bits of the S-boxes for the round i, and $maxM_{ih}$ is the number of minterms generated in the round i for the h-th output bit of the S-boxes.

If we do this translation without using minimization techniques we introduce a lot of redundant minterms which make the search harder.

To minimize the PLAs representing the S-boxes we used a CAD program for PLA minimization [42, 41] named Espresso, a minimization tool for two level binary functions and multiple valued logic functions. Espresso accepts as input a two level description of a Boolean function. This function is represented as a character matrix with keywords embedded in the input to specify the size of the matrix and the logical format of the input function. In our case we automatically generate the inputs for Espresso from the standard S-box descriptions.

We tried two different approaches to minimization. In the first one every S-box was considered as a single PLA with multiple valued outputs. In the second one we modeled each output bit of each S-box as a separate PLA and minimized each PLA independently. The rationale behind the first choice is that we expected to have minterms common to different outputs.

In the first case we have 8 PLAs with six input variables and four output variables. After the minimization, the entries of the matrixes are reduced from 64 to 52 (51 for the eighth S-box). The distribution is presented in the first four columns of Table I. The column represents each S-box outputs.

$$\begin{aligned} L^i &= R^{i-1} \\ R^i &= L^{i-1} \oplus F^i \\ F^i &= P(S^i) \\ S^i &= \bigvee M^i \\ M^i &= \bigwedge \pm X^i \\ X^i &= E(R^{i-1}) \oplus K^i \end{aligned}$$

Figure 3. Formulae encoding DES

Considering each output bit of an S-box as a single output we got 32 PLAs with six input variables and one output variable. With this kind of minimization we obtain a further improvement in terms of the number of minterms associated with each output and the average number of variables associated with each minterm. The distribution of the number of minterms is presented in the last four columns of Table I.

As for the number of variables, we note that in the first case we have on average 5.4-5.6 variables per minterm and in the second case 4.8-5.0 variables per minterm.

Clearly, we have chosen the second approach for the final generation.

4.4. Building the final formula

After every step of DES has been encoded, we obtain a set of formulae whose conjunction is exactly the formula $\mathcal{E}(C, K, P)$ that characterizes DES. To give an intuitive feeling of how it looks like we present a sketch in Fig. 3. For sake of readability, we have dropped the subscript corresponding to single bits and use only the superscript i to indicate the i-th round of DES.

At this point, if we are interested in a known plaintext attack, it is necessary to introduce the values of particular (plaintext, ciphertext) pairs. This is done by setting each variable in L^0, R^0, L^r, and R^r to true or false, where r represents the total number of rounds considered.

Then a simplification phase composed by two operations starts:

1. a substitution of the variables defined by atomic equivalences[11] with the corresponding values to reduce the number of variables in other formulae, and to introduce the truth values.

2. a propositional simplification of the formulae using the rules listed in Table II

Propositional simplification may introduce other atomic equivalences and therefore the overall process is iterated while there are changes.

The formulae in Fig. 4 are the result of the elimination of equivalences and we have given some emphasis to the plaintext and the ciphertext, represented respectively by the values of the first and last rounds of the algorithm.

In a known plaintext-attack this formula can be simplified further, since L^0, R^0, L^r, and R^r are known, and we obtain the results in Fig. 5.

The final outcome of the encoder is a formula which represents the logical relations between the key bits, the known plaintext and the known ciphertext. Its structure is shown in Fig. 6.

[11] We define an atomic equivalence as a formula of the form $V \Leftrightarrow F$ where V is a variable and F is either another variable or a truth value.

Table II. Propositional simplification rules

Initial fml	Simplified
$A \Leftrightarrow X \wedge X$	$A \Leftrightarrow X$
$A \Leftrightarrow X \wedge 0$	$A \Leftrightarrow 0$
$A \Leftrightarrow X \wedge 1$	$A \Leftrightarrow X$
$A \Leftrightarrow X \wedge \overline{X}$	$A \Leftrightarrow 0$
$A \Leftrightarrow X \vee X$	$A \Leftrightarrow X$
$A \Leftrightarrow X \vee 0$	$A \Leftrightarrow X$
$A \Leftrightarrow X \vee 1$	$A \Leftrightarrow 1$
$A \Leftrightarrow X \vee \overline{X}$	$A \Leftrightarrow 1$
$A \Leftrightarrow X \oplus X$	$A \Leftrightarrow 0$
$A \Leftrightarrow X \oplus \overline{X}$	$A \Leftrightarrow 1$
$A \Leftrightarrow X \oplus 0$	$A \Leftrightarrow X$
$A \Leftrightarrow X \oplus 1$	$A \Leftrightarrow \overline{X}$

Initial Fml	Generated Fml
$1 \Leftrightarrow A \wedge B$	$A \Leftrightarrow 1$; $B \Leftrightarrow 1$
$0 \Leftrightarrow A \vee B$	$A \Leftrightarrow 0$; $B \Leftrightarrow 0$
$0 \Leftrightarrow A \oplus B$	$A \Leftrightarrow B$
$1 \Leftrightarrow A \oplus B$	$A \Leftrightarrow \overline{B}$
$A \Leftrightarrow A \oplus B$	$B \Leftrightarrow 0$
$\overline{A} \Leftrightarrow A \oplus B$	$B \Leftrightarrow 1$

$$
\begin{aligned}
R^1 &= L^0 \oplus S^1 & \\
R^2 &= R^0 \oplus S^2 & \\
R^i &= R^{i-2} \oplus S^i & j = 3 \ldots r-2 \\
R^{r-1} &= R^{r-3} \oplus S^{r-1} & \\
R^r &= R^{r-2} \oplus S^r & \\
S^i &= \bigvee M^i & i = 1 \ldots r \\
M^i &= \bigwedge \pm X^i & i = 1 \ldots r \\
X^1 &= R^0 \oplus K^1 & \\
X^i &= R^{i-1} \oplus K^i & i = 2 \ldots r-1 \\
X^r &= R^{r-1} \oplus K^r &
\end{aligned}
$$

Figure 4. DES Formulae for r rounds

$$
\begin{aligned}
R^3 &= \pm S^1 \oplus S^3 & \\
R^4 &= \pm S^2 \oplus S^4 & \\
R^i &= R^{i-2} \oplus S^i & i = 5 \ldots r-4 \\
S^i &= \bigvee M^i & i = 1 \ldots r \\
\pm S^{r-1} &= R^{r-5} \oplus S^{r-3} & \\
\pm S^r &= R^{r-4} \oplus S^{r-2} & \\
M^1 &= \bigwedge \pm K^1 & \\
M^i &= \bigwedge \pm X^i & i = 2 \ldots r-1 \\
M^r &= \bigwedge \pm K^r & \\
X^2 &= \pm S^1 \oplus K^2 & \\
X^3 &= \pm S^2 \oplus K^3 & \\
X^i &= R^{i-1} \oplus K^i & i = 4 \ldots r-3 \\
X^{r-2} &= \pm S^{r-1} \oplus K^{r-1} & \\
X^{r-1} &= \pm S^r \oplus K^r &
\end{aligned}
$$

Figure 5. DES formulae for r rounds with known plaintext and ciphertext

$$\begin{array}{lrcll} \text{Definitions} & & & & \\ & M^i & \Leftrightarrow & \bigwedge \pm X^i & 2 \leq i \leq r-1 \\ & S^i & \Leftrightarrow & \bigvee M^i & 2 \leq i \leq r \\ & X^{i+1} & \Leftrightarrow & S^i \oplus K^i & 1 \leq r-1 \\ & & & & \\ \text{Constraints} & & & & \\ & M^1 & \Leftrightarrow & \bigwedge \pm K & \\ & M^r & \Leftrightarrow & \bigwedge \pm K^r & \\ & \pm S^{r-1} & \Leftrightarrow & \bigoplus_i S^i & i \text{ even} \\ & \pm S^r & \Leftrightarrow & \bigoplus_i S^i & i \text{ odd} \end{array}$$

Figure 6. The final encoding of the Data Encryption Standard

4.5. Experimental data

Since it makes no sense to make this encoding by hand, a program[12] has been designed and implemented to generate formulae encoding DES in an entirely modular and automatic way.

We can easily generate the formulae describing DES-like crypto-systems for any number of rounds up to 16, for any key and any pair of plaintext and ciphertext. All the permutation and substitution matrices (S-boxes) are read from external files so that one can change them according one's wishes. In this manner one can evaluate the strength of DES when the number of rounds and the values of the matrices varies.

The use of Espresso [42] to generate minimal covers for the S-boxes is the only part in our approach were human intervention is necessary: due to interface problems, Espresso must be run on the input files using shell commands. Once Espresso files are generated (and this happen only once for each S-box) our encoder program reads directly from Espresso output files.

As output we can produce a textual representation using AND, OR, etc, to be used by BDD-like algorithms, a set of clauses to be used by CNF-based provers [25], and the TPTP non-clausal format [50].

We have made some tests to get information about execution times and use of memory. These tests were made on a Workstation UltraSparc using Solaris, and on a Pentium II 300Mhz using Windows 98 and Linux. Here we report only the data on Solaris and Windows 98, the data using Linux being somehow intermediate between the other two.

Execution times were better on the Pentium. In particular for the full 16 rounds version of DES,

1. to generate the generic circuit are needed almost 25.96 seconds;

2. to generate the simplified circuit are needed almost 71 seconds;

It is also possible to use the algorithm to verify that we are indeed encoding a solved instance i.e. we generate the simplified circuit, read plaintext, key and ciphertext and verify that everything simplifies to true. This took approximately 197 seconds. Proportionately smaller timings and memory requirements were found for reduced variant of DES. For instance one or two rounds can be done within one second.

Memory usage for the three previous cases is fairly substantial and is substantially smaller for the Unix machines:

[12] More details on the encoder can be found in [29] and at the cited web site.

1. to generate the generic formulae are needed 130 MB (167 MB for Windows 98)

2. to generate the simplified formulae are needed 136 MB (175 MB for Windows 98)

3. to verify the formulae are needed 137 MB (175 MB for Win 98)

This memory requirements are likely due to a poor (say inexistent) memory management of our algorithm. With better memory management it could also probably take much less time since it would not have to use the swap space.

Beside memory and time we have collected a substantial amount of quantitative data for what regard the size and nature of the final encoded formula. To this extents we have concentrated on the generation of solved instances of the SAT problem, according the methodology that we have presented in Section 3. Thus our algorithm for the generation of the benchmark suite worked as follows:

1. fix the number of rounds of DES we are interested with;

2. generate randomly a key $\mathbf{K}$ (the solution v_K of the SAT problem);

3. generate randomly 400 blocks of plaintext $\mathbf{P}$ (a block is 64 bits);

4. encrypt the plaintext with the key using DES limited to the requested number of rounds and generate the ciphertext $\mathbf{C} = \mathrm{E}_{\mathbf{K}}(\mathbf{P})$;

5. encode the limited version of DES as a formula $\mathcal{E}(P, K, C)$ and substitute the values of the plaintext v_P and ciphertext v_C.

Each block of plaintext and ciphertext gives a (satisfiable) formula $\mathcal{E}(v_P, K, v_C)$. We repeated the process for 5 randomly generated keys.

Table III reports the arithmetic mean of the number of equivalences, exclusive or, conjunctions, and disjunctions present in a formula $\mathcal{E}(v_P, K, v_C)$ for the various rounds of DES. For instance the fourth row shows that if we limit DES to 4 rounds (1st column) then $\mathcal{E}(v_P, K, v_C)$ is made (on average) by the conjunction of 2,432 equivalences out of which 96 contain exclusive or, 2,208 contain (multiple) conjunctions and 128 contain disjunctions. See again Fig. 5 or Fig. 6 for an intuitive idea of their shape.

The last two columns of Table III show the number of variables occurring in the formula which are different from the variables representing the key bits and the number of clauses that is generated when $\mathcal{E}(v_P, K, v_C)$ is translated into clausal normal form.

Note that the data in Table III are given per single pair of plaintext and ciphertext and therefore the total number of the formulae, clauses etc is obtained by multiplying those numbers by the number of plaintext and ciphertext pairs. For instance the clauses corresponding to 4 blocks of plain/ciphertext for DES limited to 2 rounds are over 13,000 (3,304 $\times$ 4) and the variables over 1,900 (489 $\times$ 4).

The variance of these numbers is not shown here since it is fairly small as we move beyond the fourth round. A simple explanation is that the known values of the plaintext and the ciphertext do not propagate through the rounds as soon as exclusive or starts to appear.

The clause length varies quite widely and therefore the mean clause length is not a good indicator. However, looking at the way in which clauses are generated more information can be obtained:

– for every equivalence containing an *exclusive or* we obtain 8 clauses of length 3;

Table III. Occurrences of formulae per single plaintext/ciphertext pair

Round	Equiv	Xor	And	Or	Clauses	Vars
1	520	0	504	16	1,645	243
2	1,042	0	1,010	32	3,304	489
3	1,738	48	1,609	80	9,064	1,430
4	2,432	96	2,208	128	14,811	2,368
5	3,096	176	2,760	160	18,738	3,032
6	3,760	256	3,312	192	22,665	3,696
7	4,424	336	3,864	224	26,592	4,360
8	5,088	416	4,416	256	30,519	5,024
9	5,752	496	4,968	288	34,446	5,688
10	6,416	576	5,520	320	38,373	6,352
11	7,080	656	6,072	352	42,300	7,016
12	7,744	736	6,624	384	46,227	7,680
13	8,408	816	7,176	416	50,154	8,344
14	9,072	896	7,728	448	54,081	9,008
15	9,736	976	8,280	480	58,008	9,672
16	10,400	1,056	8,832	512	61,935	10,336

- for every equivalence containing a *conjunction* we obtain a number of binary clauses (usually less than 5-6) and a large clause with 5-6 literals;
- for every equivalence containing a *disjunction* we obtain a number of binary clauses (as for conjunctions) and one large clause.

So, there is an overwhelming component of binary clauses with ternary clauses starting to appear as soon as exclusive or starts to appear.

For these formulae, the clause over variable ratio (the standard indicator of the hardness of random 3-SAT formulae [48]) does not explain well the hardness of the problem. Indeed, consider the case of the commercial version of DES, whose ratio clauses over variables can be identified by the following formula (where b is the number of blocks, i.e. plaintext/ciphertext pairs, and k the number of key bits):

$$c/v = \frac{61,935 \times b}{k + 10,336 \times b}$$

The number of key bits is less and less relevant as the number of blocks increases. With an infinite number of blocks, it converges to a fixed value. However, even if we add an infinite number of blocks, after 3 rounds the shift in the clause/variable ration would be less than 1-2%. This seems to imply that adding more blocks should not make the problem neither much easier nor much harder. As we shall see in Section 5, the experimental data contradict this hypothesis.

Table IV contains the average number of variables representing the key bits occurring in the formulae generated for each round.

Not shown here, is the fact that there are between 40 (1 round) and 90 (16 rounds) occurrences of each key bit. Moreover, key bits occur in approximately 17% of the total number of clauses and are the most frequently occurring variables, since other variables occur always in less than 100 formulae.

Table IV. Occurrences of key bits per single plaintext/ciphertext pair

Round	Avg	Max	Round	Avg	Max
1	40.99	57	9	89.03	115
2	82.01	113	10	90.79	115
3	84.79	112	11	91.64	119
4	85.64	111	12	92.5	118
5	86.50	115	13	93.36	119
6	87.36	112	14	94.21	118
7	88.21	113	15	95.07	118
8	89.07	116	16	95.93	126

This means that almost all SAT heuristics, which are usually variants of "choose the literal with most occurrences such that X" will select almost only key bits in the search process.

5. Experimental Cryptanalysis with Theorem Provers

To test the ability of a *generic* ATP to cope with cryptographic problems, we have chosen 3 state-of-the-art provers for propositional logic:

- TABLEAU by Crawford and Auton [15], because it is a reference implementation of the Davis-Putnam procedure and because it has been extensively tested on the random 3-SAT benchmark;
- SATO by Zhang [51, 53], because it uses the trie data structure to boost the speed of the unit propagation phase and because it has been successfully used on the encoding of semi-groups problems;
- rel-SAT by Bayardo and Schrag [5], because it combines the Davis-Putnam algorithm with back-jumping and learning of CSP algorithms and because it has been successfully used on "real-world" problems in scheduling.

The backbone algorithm used by all three provers is the Davis-Putnam-Longemann-Loveland (DPLL) algorithm [18, 17] which we only sketch for reference in Fig. 7. For the particular implementation details of each prover we refer to corresponding paper. We recall that a literal is either a propositional variable or a negated propositional variable and that a clause is a set of literals. A unit clause is a clause with only one literal.

Among the various possibilities described in Section 3 we have focused on key search assuming a known plaintext attack because it is the simplest problem available among the SAT-problems we can generate, and because it generates solved instances. To generate the benchmark suite we have followed the same methodology that we have presented in Section 4. The only difference here is that we have also grouped together the formulae corresponding to different plaintext using the same key. In other words we have tested the provers on the formulae

$$\mathcal{E}(v_C, K, v_P) \qquad \bigwedge_{i=1}^{2} \mathcal{E}(v_C^i, K, v_P^i) \qquad \ldots \qquad \bigwedge_{i=1}^{n} \mathcal{E}(v_C^i, K, v_P^i)$$

Let Σ be a set of clauses using variables in V.

- if Σ is empty return SAT;
- if Σ contains an empty clause return UNSAT;
- (Unit Propagation) if Σ contains a unit clause $\{l\}$ then assign l the value true and call recursively DPLL on the simplified set of clauses;
- (Splitting Rule) Select a variable v in V, assign v a truth value and call recursively DPLL on the simplified set of clauses. If DPLL returns SAT then return SAT, otherwise assign v the opposite truth value and return the result of DPLL on the simplified set of clauses.

Figure 7. Davis-Putnam-Longemann-Loveland Algorithm

for $n = 1, 2, 4, 8$ to test whether increasing the number of constraints can lead to an increase of performance (i.e. decrease of running time) in the same fashion of what happens in random 3-CNF problems [15]. Indeed, having large quantities of plaintext is necessary for all standard cryptanalytic approaches that do not rely on exhaustive search.

All tested ATP systems admit different settings and we have tried to stick to the recommended standards, eventually experimenting with heuristics. This was one of the main aim of the experiment: we wanted to see how a generic ATP system performed without being told any information on the problem i.e. whether SAT-solvers were able to automatically detect and exploit the underlying hidden properties of DES which have been the subject of intense cryptographic research. Indeed the SAT-based approach make sense only if we just need to specialize our SAT-algorithm at the level of heuristics or just add features (such as reasoning with affine subproblems) that are of general interest.

In this framework, the only reasonable re-engineering of the heuristics is the limitation of the branching search variables to the known independent control variables i.e. to the 56 bits of the key. We have explored this possibility with the various provers but without great successes. This contrast with other application of SAT-based encodings, such as planning, where branching on a restricted set of variables, the others being implied, considerably improves the performance [47]. We discuss this issue later in this section.

The tests have been run on SUN UltraSparcs running Solaris with 64M RAM and on a Pentium-II with the same memory and we obtained qualitatively the same results (to avoid normalization problems we only report here the CPU running time on the SUN machines).

For each prover, we report the results as follows: for each class of instances, characterized by the number of rounds of DES and by the number of blocks (i.e. number of $\mathcal{E}(v_C^i, K, v_P^i)$ formulae that are conjoined together) we report the *percentage of success* in finding a solution and the *mean time in seconds* necessary to find a solution. For mean time we intend the arithmetic mean[13] over the total number of instances of the class (see

[13] We have used the mean time rather than the median time because the running times do not show the big outliers exhibited by random 3-SAT [15, 48].

Table V. Performance of TABLEAU

Rounds	Blocks	% Success	Keybits	Branches	Mean Time (sec)
1	1	100%	33.7	1,8,325	12.96
1	2	100%	48.2	189,170	204.05
1	4	100%	50.7	64,813	117.95
2	1	100%	54.0	61,979	99.14
2	2	100%	55.8	80,133	222.07
2	4	100%	56.0	8,033	36.43

Section 4). We also report the mean number of branches explored during the search, with the caveat that each algorithm has a slightly different notion of what constitute a branch. So comparison of number of branches across different provers should only be made w.r.t. scaling rather than w.r.t. absolute values.

Since we didn't know whether the encoding of a plaintext and ciphertext pair would have admitted different models, i.e. keys[14], whenever a model was found it was compared with the "original key" used to generate the instance. The average number of matching key bits (arithmetic mean over all instances) is then reported in the tables for each benchmark class.

To be fully complete, our experiments should have also explored another source of randomness: varying the keys, i.e. the solutions of the SAT instances, while keeping the plaintexts fixed (recall that in the bulk of the experiments the key is randomly generated but stay fixed for all the 400 plaintexts we have generated). We have investigated this possibility only for one of the algorithm (i.e. rel-SAT) and we have not found any significant pattern (although our experiments were limited to 50 different keys). Since cryptography research has also investigated key patterns without much results, whereas plaintexts and ciphertexts analysis has led to substantial attacks we have postponed the analysis of key randomness to future works.

A further general observation concerning the organization of the experiments is the use of normalization: since all chosen ATP systems require clausal normal form we have used the CNF generation facilities provided by the encoder. Before using the clause file as input for the search algorithms, a preprocessing step was necessary to "compact" the integer values used for representing variables[15] since the encoding was so sparse that we exceeded the maximum number of atoms readable by the ATP systems. The running time of this auxiliary algorithm is not included in the running time of the provers.

The results are reported in separate subsections for each prover and a final part with general observations concludes this section.

5.1. TABLEAU *on DES*

Table V contains the running time of TABLEAU for the limited version of DES for which it could solve some problems. TABLEAU has been run with the standard setting, and eventually with purity disabled.

Note that the problem becomes easier as we add more ciphertext and plaintext pairs. We stopped at 8 blocks because the formulae could not be read by TABLEAU: there

[14] Recall that if we have more than one key for the same pair the cipher is not faithful and we have semi-weak keys. See again Section 2 for details.

[15] Our encoder used a redundant and sparse encoding so that one could detect from which round and which pair of ciphertext and plaintext a variable came from.

Table VIa. Performance of SATO searching for at least 2 models

Rounds	Blocks	% Success	Models	Keybits	Branches	Time
1	1	22%	2	32.8	71	0.04
1	2	2%	2	40.5	75	0.07
1	4	48%	1(75%)	50.8	63	0.12
1	8	100%	1 (100%)	52.0	19	0.10
2	1	72%	1 (30%)	53.9	641	0.54
2	2	88%	1 (84%)	56.0	150	0.25
2	4	98%	1 (98%)	56.0	29	0.16
2	8	100%	1 (100%)	56.0	6	0.15

Table VIb. Performance of SATO searching for 1 model

Rounds	Blocks	% Success	Keybits	Branches	Time
2	1	76%	53.3	458	0.36
2	2	96%	55.6	118	0.19
2	4	100%	56	18	0.10
2	8	100%	56	9	0.14
3	8	50%	56	269,804	2,192.73

were too many variables (see again Section 4 for the size of the problem). The running times had very limited variance which is not shown for readability.

Yet, it is not all so easy: TABLEAU could not solve 3 rounds of DES in two hours, no matter the number of blocks. Increasing the time limit before timeout has been also tried (up to one day) but to no avail. Increasing the number of rounds did not lead to any solution either.

Re-engineering TABLEAU to branch only on key bits was too hard a task (due to the poor documentation of the program), so we have relied on an alternative implementation using the same heuristics which have been used for finding minimal models [27]. This further experimental analysis was again not conclusive: by restricting to independent variables we do not seem to gain much. In particular we are still not able to crack DES with three rounds.

5.2. SATO *on DES*

The timings of SATO are shown in Table VIb and Table VIa. At the beginning we have tried SATO with the standard setting and then with different options (such as searching for more than one model) and search heuristics. Table VIa to the standard settings, but we stopped the search after the second model has been found (or the search space exhausted). Table VIb generated by stopping the search after the first model has been found.

Since we have not limited the search to the first model, this explains the greater running time and number of branches in comparison with TABLEAU. In the column "Models" we show between brackets the number of instances on which only one model was found. Also in this case the variance of the running time was limited, and it suggests that the running time distribution of the problem does not exhibit a heavy tail behavior.

Most of SATO's failures are due to virtual memory failure rather than the 2 hours timeout. Thus, we have decided to run SATO on a Pentium II with 64M but with a swap space of over 628M. It turned out that if we let SATO run on 3 rounds of DES without time limit we could solve all instances within few minutes of actual CPU time. Yet, if we looked at "real" time, it took over 12 hours for a single instance to be solved. In practice, the time is spent by swapping the trie data structure in and out main memory and then performing very few quick operations on each part of the trie. Then, we have decided not to include these latest running times into the table: they may give a wrong idea of the computational resources needed by SATO.

For the case of one round and eight blocks, the strange results that we get only one model and yet only 52 out of 56 bits can be explained by the fact that not all key bits occur in the corresponding formulae and SATO has been used with purity on (that is setting to false any bit that does not occur).

With SATO we have also experimented with different heuristics and a new feature of the algorithm that make it possible to generate lemmata corresponding to closed branches. We have also experimented with a simple list structure rather than the trie data structure. The worst heuristics for this problem seemed to be that proposed by Jeroslow and Wang. Without the trie data structure SATO offered the same qualitative performance of TABLEAU.

In this case we also tried to restrict the selection of the branching literals to the 56 independent control variables. The re-engineering of the algorithm was done by Zhang and again [52] it led to worse results and was abandoned.

5.3. rel-SAT *on DES*

rel-SATis a variant of the Davis-Putnam algorithm, enhanced with conflict directed back-jumping and learning [5] and is indeed the only algorithm which solves 3 rounds of DES within few minutes.

The basic working of the enhanced algorithm is worth repeating:

- unit propagation is applied to the clause set;
- if no contradiction is found, a new literal is selected and added either positively or negatively to the clause set;
- if a contradiction is found, then the algorithm backtracks to the literal that has caused the contradiction;
- the clause responsible for the contradiction is resolved with a clause representing the temporary assignment; the resolvent is learned as a reason to avoid the corresponding assignment;
- the procedure is iterated until all literals have been assigned (SAT) or no backtrack is possible (UNSAT).

More details and references can be found in [5]. The important parameter is the learning factor i.e. the size of the clauses that can be learned during the backtrack plus resolution stage.

Also in this case, the testing started with the recommend standard: a small learning factor (4), using relevance-based learning (see Table VIIa). Up to 2 rounds of DES rel-SAT is slightly faster but still comparable with the results of Davis-Putnam-like algorithms such as SATO and TABLEAU or local search algorithm like Walk-SAT [31].

Table VIIa. Performance of rel-SAT with learning factor 4

Rounds	Blocks	Keybits (Mean)	Branches (Mean)	Time (Mean)	Time (Variance)
1	1	31.0	28	0.02	0.009
1	2	48.9	105	0.11	0.047
1	4	50.9	104	0.22	0.083
1	8	52.0	83	0.45	0.103
2	1	54.0	231	0.20	0.105
2	2	56.0	111	0.23	0.106
2	4	56.0	68	0.36	0.123
2	8	56.0	57	0.81	0.252
3	1	-	-	$\geq$1h	-
3	2	56.0	174,612	983.22	1,034.598
3	4	56.0	19,312	159.13	66.894
3	8	56.0	3,596	75.03	32.783

Table VIIb. Performance of rel-SAT with no learning

Rounds	Blocks	Keybits (Mean)	Branches (Mean)	Time (Mean)	Time (Variance)
1	4	53.6	172	2.38	1.165
1	8	53.0	185	6.18	1.866
2	4	56.0	157	4.98	3.006
2	8	56.0	103	8.00	6.449
3	4	-	-	$\geq$1h	
3	8	56.0	8,154	822.35	164.792

Again, the performance of the algorithm increases with the number of blocks (plaintext-ciphertext pairs). Adding more constraints makes the search for the only (?) existing solution easier. The success rate (100%) is omitted. The variance of the running times is fairly limited but for the case of 3 round of DES and 2 blocks.

Other settings were tried, in particular we tried both without any learning at all and with larger learning factors. The analysis shows that with no learning we have a decrease in performance (see Table VIIb). With too large learning factors (order of 20) there is not a big gain in performance. With slightly larger learning factors (order of 5-6) we get a slight but not substantial increase in performance.

Since rel-SAT has the best readable code of the three ATP systems, we experimented with a small re-engineering in the attempt to exploit the knowledge of the domain. In the original algorithm, a first selection of potential branching variables is done and then all variables with a value of the heuristic function lower than a threshold were discarded. The modified algorithm didn't check the threshold if the selected variable was a keybit. In this way the algorithm gives preferences to dependent variables with very good properties or independent variables with medium properties. However, the running time of the algorithm didn't improved substantially.

Since this was also the best performing algorithm we have tried, including BDDs [4] and Walk-SAT [31], we have performed more experiments (on a SUN with 256MB) to determine whether the search space of the problem using rel-SAT was actually

Table VIII. Further experiments with rel-SAT with learning factor 5

Rnds	Blcks	Keybits (Mean)	Branches (Mean)	Time (Mean)	Time (Var)	Max Stack Depth (Mean)	Max Stack Depth (Abs)
1	1	31.6	25	0.02	0.010	22	37
1	2	46.1	83	0.09	0.048	17	26
1	4	51.9	97	0.21	0.059	17	20
1	8	52.0	98	0.50	0.068	17	20
2	1	54.7	238	0.22	0.129	16	20
2	2	55.9	108	0.22	0.091	15	18
2	4	56.0	66	0.34	0.116	14	17
2	8	56.0	45	0.66	0.170	14	19
3	2	56.0	99,908	1,314.94	3,078.913	31	34
3	4	56.0	8,883	105.40	37.255	30	33
3	8	56.0	5,491	142.57	23.067	29	31

Table IX. Changing the keys for rel-SAT with learning factor 5

Rnds	Blcks	Keybits (Mean)	Branches (Mean)	Time (Mean)	Time (Var)	Max Stack Depth (Mean)	Max Stack Depth (Abs)
3	4	56.0	8,892	285.37	160.922	29	35
3	8	56.0	3,641	260.14	108.360	28	32

smaller than the search space generated by brute force search[16]. This experiment can shown the potential of the CSP/SAT approach to the problem if constraint propagation substantially reduces the search space, even in absence of specific, problem-dependent information.

The results of this new set of experiments, with a slightly larger learning factor (5) are reported in Table VIII. Beside mean, variance and number of key bits found, we also report the absolute maximum depth of the stack during the search over all instances and the average maximum depth of the stack over all instances (i.e. for each instance we compute the maximum stack depth and then take the arithmetic mean over all instances). As we can see we are substantially below the 55 choice points that would have been necessary with brute force search. A caveat is that the table also suggests a trend of increasing search depth as the number of rounds increases. This may explain why four rounds cannot be solved by current SAT tools.

In Table IX we have described the results of the experiments when we keep the plaintext fixed and change the keys i.e. the solution of the SAT-problem. Even if the significance of the data is limited (50 different keys on 10 different plaintexts), we can observe that there is not a big difference between these data and those reported in Table VIII.

Given these promising results, the algorithm has been further engineered to accept larger formulae with more variables and tried on 4, 8 and full 16-rounds DES, also using 1, 2, and 4 blocks. The algorithm didn't return within one day.

[16] This experiment was suggested by an anonymous reviewer and the editors.

5.4. General observations

From a cryptanalyst viewpoint these results are not very impressive: three rounds of DES were cryptanalyzed long ago [3] and linear cryptanalysis [32] or differential cryptanalysis [7] can do much better for up to 8 round, although they need far larger amount of plaintexts than just 8 blocks.

What make these results interesting is the fact that the ATP systems do not know at all that the 56 variables of the key are the only "variables that count", the only variables that must be set to find a model. They do not known which of the thousands of clauses are just definitions in disguise and which are really constraints. With 4 block of plaintext and 2 rounds of DES they search in a space of almost $2^{2,000}$ solutions, and still they find the only one that exists. The constraints present in the encoding are sufficient to drastically reduce the search space. This is fairly close to what happens for the DIMACS parity problems where SAT procedures do manage to find the independent variables from the much larger set of all variables.

What makes these results puzzling is that knowing which are the "variables that count" does not seem to help. Moreover the hardness of the problem exhibits an abrupt jump: reasonably easy up to two rounds, then moderately hard at three, and then simply unsolvable.

We can explain the good performance by observing that there are many defined variables. Thus, few wrong assignments to control variables are enough to provoke a cascade of assignments to defined variables and then inconsistencies are quickly found. However, this would imply that formulae encoding more rounds should be easier and not harder. Indeed, ciphers are designed to exhibit an "avalanche" effect when the number of rounds is increased: the number of output bits influenced by the key bits increases in a non-linear fashion. With more rounds the propagation of inconsistencies should also be boosted. Since this is not the case, it seems the propagation of assignments is hindered.

We conjecture that the source of the complexity is the particular structure of the Feistel-ciphers, i.e. the xors which are added at each round. What really hinders state-of-art SAT-solvers is the inability of handling affine subproblems in an efficient way. Although these problems are themselves polynomially solvable [44] their presence, such as in the hidden parity bit mentioned in [47], makes the difference between hard and unsolvable problems.

This would also explain the abrupt jump in complexity: DES at 4 four rounds is the first problem where exclusive or starts to appear. If we remove those formulae the resulting formula can be shown to be satisfiable by all ATP systems without much effort.

The fact that there is no heavy tail phenomenon as in random 3-SAT can also be explained: the structure of the problem is fairly regular, and its hardness is well controlled by the number of blocks of known plaintext, whose increase makes the problem easier, and the number of rounds of DES, whose increase makes the problem harder.

What remains to be explained is why "knowing the control variables" does not help. We have already noted at the end of Section 4 that the key bits are the variables that occur most often and therefore it may simply be that knowing the control variables does not help because *in this problem the independent variables are already among the variables preferred by the standard heuristics.* An informal analysis of the stack of choice points of rel-SAT revealed that almost all variables that are selected by the standard heuristics are key variables. Thus, by giving the algorithm the full choice on the branching variables we do not give away our bias towards control variables (because the problem is such that the heuristics will likely choose them) and still gives the algorithm the possibility of exploiting shortcuts with defined variables.

A second observation is that branching on control variables alone is what brute force approaches do. In this respect, looking at linear and differential cryptanalysis might be instructive. If we set aside the problem of gathering the massive amount of data they need, we may observe that they can solve the problem better than we do because

1. they exploit the probability distribution of intermediate results to guess their value (this corresponds to splitting on defined variables in the SAT-based approach) without concentrating on key bits only;

2. they make use of the affine subproblems to determine the value of some independent variables out of the dependent variables they have set (whereas we are swamped by them because we perform search on them);

3. only after the first two steps have given an indication of a plausible solution they start searching on control variables alone.

So, we may conclude this point by observing that our ATP systems have been able to do the first step almost correctly by using their sophisticated heuristics, without human intervention, but they have not been able to do the second.

Another interesting point regards the integrity of DES, i.e. the number of keys which are consistent with the same pair of plaintext and ciphertext. If more than one key would be consistent with a plaintext and ciphertext pair (even worse that there was a key consistent with different plaintexts and ciphertexts), we would have discovered a trapdoor. Since only one key exists (at least for three rounds) this offers an independent evidence that DES was not designed to have hidden trapdoors (beside semi-weak keys). Since the number of models actually decreases quickly to one as the number of rounds or the number of plaintexts increase, this is a strong evidence that DES is almost faithful. Note that the outcome of the experiment with SATO can be easily converted into a *proof* that for each tested pair there is only one key which could have generated it.

It is worth noting that a number of extensive tests with BDDs has been also carried at our Department by Ascione [4], since BDDs are known to perform well on non-clausal problems [8]. Even on our optimized encoding, BDDs could not solve key search problems any better than SAT-based approaches [4]: the tests showed that the BDDs representing the encoded formula reached quickly a million and over nodes and then crashed the systems for virtual memory failure.

The tests with BDDs were however useful for confirming the experimental data regarding the integrity of DES: when the number of known plaintexts or the number of rounds increases the final BDD representing $\mathcal{E}(v_P, K, v_C)$ turns out to be a chain (i.e. there is only one model).

6. Open Problems and Conclusions

In this paper we have presented an application of propositional reasoning and search to a key security problem of industrial relevance.

We have shown that the translation of properties of ciphers in logic is doable (although not simple) and that a number of key properties can be modeled.

The effectiveness of general ATP systems in this framework has also been preliminary tested and looks promising, although ATP search strategies need to be improved to meet the full challenge provided by this benchmark. They seem promising because only one or few blocks of plaintext and ciphertext are necessary to identify a unique solution to the cryptographic problem (rather than the few hundreds or millions required by traditional methods).

Thus, we believe that the whole approach on encoding cryptographic problems as SAT-problems can be a step forward towards the development of generators "for problem instances that have computational properties that are more similar to real world instances" [47]. Even if cryptography is a limited application area (although an important one), the structure of the corresponding SAT-problems is such that a generic ATP system able to cope with them (e.g. able to handle affine subproblem) will be able to apply its techniques effectively to hard problems from other application areas.

This approach also offers a solution to the problem discussed by Cook and Mitchell [14]: how to randomly generate solved instances that are hard to solve.

Still, there is a lot of work to be done and a good conclusion of paper may just be the indication of open problems.

PROBLEM 1. *Find a key for the commercial 16 round Data Encryption Standard in less than 56 hours using off-the-shelf h/w and s/w but enhanced ATP systems.*

This is the subject of current investigation and, as we have already mentioned, our focus is the enhancement of ATP system with rules and techniques to cope with affine subproblems.

Further experiments are needed to better understand the structure of the problem, and which heuristics may be better suited to solve it.

PROBLEM 2. *Prove formally that the commercial 16 round Data Encryption Standard DES is not a group and is not pure using the encoding and an automated theorem prover.*

This might be an independent way to formally guarantee the experimental evidence obtained in [12] with cycling experiments.

PROBLEM 3. *Prove formally that the commercial 16 round Data Encryption Standard DES is* faithful *according to the definition in [26] i.e. for any pair of plaintext and ciphertext there is only one key that can generate that pair (setting semi-weak keys aside).*

Notice that this, in contrast with the previous two results, is an open problem for cryptography. If a solution of this problem could be found, this would have extreme relevance for the use of a cipher in applications such as electronic commerce where the impossibility of forging data is essential. This could become an established method to guarantee that a cipher has such properties.

Other problems involve QBF theorem proving and this field is still not mature enough to tackle such hard problems. A preliminary test has been done using the algorithm in [11] but it didn't returned in one hour even for reduced version of the algorithm limited to 1 or 2 rounds. New tests with an enhanced version of the algorithm that exploits defined variables are in preparation.

PROBLEM 4. *Develop heuristic techniques for propositional reasoning and search that work with every Feistel-type cipher with data independent permutations like DES.*

The highly regular structure of these ciphers should be exploited by search algorithms in two directions: the identification of no-goods which prune a substantial amount of the search space and the variable selection heuristics. Since the operations are data independent, a certain amount of preprocessing for the internal rounds could be done off-line. This is a case where knowledge compilation [46] may entirely pay off. Another algorithm that may work is Stålmark algorithm since it uses a data structure which well fits with those of a Feistel-cipher [24].

PROBLEM 5. *Find efficient encodings of Feistel-type ciphers with data-dependent permutations like RC5 [40, 45].*

Of course a straightforward encoding is always possible: just translate the cipher into a circuit and this into propositional logic. Unfortunately, we have noted this is already unworkable for DES.

PROBLEM 6. *Find efficient encoding into propositional (or any) logic of public-key cryptographic algorithms for digital signatures based on number theory such as RSA [45].*

This problem has been suggested by Cook and Mitchell [14] and might be the hardest since the way in which the algorithm is expressed (number theory) is fairly remote from propositional logic. Again, one can just encode multipliers and adders into propositional logic but this might be overwhelming. Moreover, factoring is known to be hard (see e.g. [45][p. 256] for related references) and it may be that SAT-based techniques will be inferior to factoring algorithms.

The coming adoption of an U.S. Advanced Encryption Standard [37] may open new directions of research.

As for all "real-world" problems, there might be a dark side: the measure of success might be the "privilege" (!?) of successful automated reasoning tools being denied export licenses as dangerous weapons.

Acknowledgements

We would like to thank L. Carlucci Aiello for her encouragement and support, M. Ascione for discussing with us his results on the logical cryptanalysis of DES using BDDs, and P. Baumgarten, P. Liberatore, I. Niemela, and H. Zhang for testing our problem using their provers, and for many useful discussions. We would also like to thank all members of the AI group at the Dipartimento of Informatica e Sistemistica in Rome for bearing with us and our machine swamping experiments. The comments and suggestions from the anonymous reviewers greatly improved the quality of this paper.

F. Massacci acknowledges the support of the CNR fellowship 201-15-9 at the Dipartimento of Informatica and Sistemistica at the Univ. di Roma I "La Sapienza". This work has been partly supported by CNR, MURST and ASI grants of the Dipartimento di Informatica e Sistemistica at the Univ. di Roma I "La Sapienza" and by the AMTEC research grant of the Dipartimento di Ingegneria dell'Informazione at the Univ. di Siena.

References

1. M. Abadi and R. Needham. Prudent engineering practice for cryptographic protocols. *IEEE Trans. on Software Engineering*, 22(1):6–15, 1996.

2. R. Anderson and R. Needham. Programming satan's computer. In *Computer Science Today - Recent Trends and Developments*, volume 1,000 of *LNCS*, pages 426–440. Springer-Verlag, 1996.
3. D. Andleman and J. Reeds. On the cryptanalysis of rotor machines and substitution-permutations networks. *IEEE Trans. on Information Theory*, 28(4):578–584, 1982.
4. M. Ascione. Validazione e benchmarking dei BDD per la criptanalisi del data encryption standard. Master's thesis, Facoltà di Ingegneria, Univ. di Roma I "La Sapienza", March 1999. In Italian.
5. R. Bayardo and R. Schrag. Using CSP look-back techniques to solve real-world SAT instances. In *Proc. of the 14th Nat. (US) Conf. on Artificial Intelligence (AAAI-97)*, pages 203–208. AAAI Press/The MIT Press, 1997.
6. E. Biham and A. Biryukov. An improvement of Davies' attack on DES. In *Advances in Cryptology - Eurocrypt 94*, *LNCS*, Springer Verlag, 1994.
7. E. Biham and A. Shamir. Differential cryptanalisis of DES-like cryptosystems. *J. of Cryptology*, 4(1):3–72, 1991.
8. R. Bryant. Graph-based algorithms for boolean function manipulation. *IEEE Trans. on Computers*, 35(8):677–691, 1986.
9. H. Büning, M. Karpinski, and A. Flögel. Resolution for quantified boolean formulas. *Information and Computation*, 117(1):12–18, 1995.
10. M. Burrows, M. Abadi, and R. Needham. A logic for authentication. *ACM Trans. Computer Systems*, 8(1):18–36, 1990.
11. Marco Cadoli, Andrea Giovanardi, and Marco Schaerf. An algorithm to evaluate quantified boolean formulae. In *Proc. of the 15th (US) Nat. Conf. on Artificial Intelligence (AAAI-98)*, pages 262–267. AAAI Press/The MIT Press, 1998.
12. K. Campbell and M. Weiner. DES is not a group. In *Proc. of Advances in Cryptography (CRYPTO-92)*, *LNCS*, pages 512–520. Springer-Verlag, 1992.
13. L. Claesen, editor. *Formal VLSI Correctness Verification: VLSI Design Methods*, volume II. Elsevier Science Publishers (North-Holland), 1990.
14. S. Cook and D. Mitchel. Finding hard instances of the satisfiability problem: A survey. In *Satisfiability Problem: Theory and Applications*, volume 35 of *DIMACS Series in Discrete Mathamatics and Theoretical Computer Science*, pages 1–17. American Mathematical Society, 1997.
15. J. Crawford and L. Auton. Experimental results on the crossover point in random 3SAT. *Artificial Intelligence*, 81(1-2):31–57, 1996.
16. Cryptography Research Inc. DES key search project information. Technical report, Cryptography Research Inc., 1998. Available on the web at `http://www.cryptography.com/des/`.
17. M. Davis, G. Longemann, and D. Loveland. A machine program for theorem-proving. *Communications of the ACM*, 5(7):394–397, 1962.
18. M. Davis and H. Putnam. A computing procedure for quantificational theory. *Journal of the ACM*, 7(3):201–215, 1960.
19. R. De Millo, L. Lynch, and M. Merrit. Cryptographic protocols. In *Proc. of the 14th ACM SIGACT Symposium on Theory of Computing (STOC-82)*, pages 383–400, 1982.
20. H. Feistel, W. Notz, and L. Smith. Some cryptographic techniques for machine-to-machine data communication. *Proc. of the IEEE*, 63(11):1,545–1,554, 1975.
21. C. Gomes and B. Selman. Problem structure in the presence of perturbation. In *Proc. of the 14th Nat. (US) Conf. on Artificial Intelligence (AAAI-97)*. AAAI Press/The MIT Press, 1997.
22. C. Gomes, B. Selman, and N. Crato. Heavy-tailed distributions in combinatorial search. In *Third Internat. Conf. on Principles and Practice of Constraint Programming (CP-97)*, volume 1330 of *LNCS*, pages 121–135. Springer-Verlag, 1997.
23. Group of Experts on Information Security and Privacy. Inventory of controls on cryptography technologies. OLIS DSTI/ICCP/REG(98)4/REV3, Organization for Economic Co-operation and Development, Paris, Sep 1998.
24. J. Harrison. Stalmarck's algorithm as a HOL derived rule. In *Proc. of the 9th Internat. Conf. on Theorem Proving in Higher Order Logics (TPHOLs'96)*, volume 1125 of *LNCS*, pages 221–234. Springer-Verlag, 1996.
25. D. Johnson and M. Trick, editors. *Cliques, Coloring, satisfiability: the second DIMACS implementation challenge*, volume 26 of *AMS Series in Discrete Mathematics and Theoretical Computer Science*. American Mathematical Society, 1996.
26. B. Kaliski, R. Rivest, and A. Sherman. Is the Data Encryption Standard a group? (preliminary abstract). In *Advances in Cryptology - Eurocrypt 85*, volume 219 of *LNCS*, pages 81–95. Springer-Verlag, 1985.

27. Paolo Liberatore. Algorithms and experiments on finding minimal models. Technical Report 09–99, Dipartimento di Informatica e Sistemistica, Università di Roma "La Sapienza", 1999.
28. Gavin Lowe. Breaking and fixing the needham-schroeder public-key protocol using CSP and FDR. In *Tools and Algorithms for the Construction and Analysis of Systems*, volume 1055 of *LNCS*, pages 147–166. Springer-Verlag, 1996.
29. Laura Marraro. Analisi crittografica del DES mediante logica booleana. Master's thesis, Facoltà di Ingegneria, Univ. di Roma I "La Sapienza", December 1998. In Italian.
30. Laura Marraro and Fabio Massacci. A new challenge for automated reasoning: Verification and cryptanalysis of cryptographic algorithms. Technical Report 05-99, Dipartimento di Informatica e Sistemistica, Università di Roma "La Sapienza", 1999.
31. Fabio Massacci. Using walk-SAT and rel-SAT for cryptographic key search. In *Proc. of the 16th Internat. Joint Conf. on Artificial Intelligence (IJCAI-99)*, page 290–295. Morgan Kaufmann, 1999.
32. M. Matsui. The first experimental cryptanalysis of the Data Encryption Standard. In *Proc. of Advances in Cryptography (CRYPTO-94)*, volume 839 of *LNCS*, pages 1–11. Springer-Verlag, 1994.
33. M. Matsui. Linear cryptanalysis method for DES cipher. In *Advances in Cryptology - Eurocrypt 93*, volume 765 of *LNCS*, pages 368–397. Springer-Verlag, 1994.
34. J. Mitchell, M. Mitchell, and U. Stern. Automated analysis of cryptographic protocols using Murphi. In *Proc. of the 16th IEEE Symposium on Security and Privacy*, pages 141–151. IEEE Computer Society Press, 1997.
35. Organization for Economic Co-operation and Development OECD emerging market economy forum (EMEF): Report of the ministerial workshop on cryptography policy. OLIS SG/EMEF/ICCP(98)1, Organization for Economic Co-operation and Development, Paris, Feb 1998.
36. National Institute of Standards and Technology. Data encryption standard. Federal Information Processing Standards Publications FIPS PUB 46-2, National (U.S.) Bureau of Standards, Dec 1997. Supersedes FIPS PUB 46-1 of Jan. 1988.
37. National Institute of Standards and Technology. Request for comments on candidate algorithms for the advanced encryption standard (AES). *(U.S.) Federal Register*, 63(177), September 1998.
38. Committee on Payment, Settelment Systems, and the Group of Computer Experts of the central banks of the Group of Ten countries. *Security of Electronic Money.* Banks for International Settlements, Basle, August 1996.
39. L. Paulson. The inductive approach to verifying cryptographic protocols. *Journal of Computer Security*, 1998.
40. R. Rivest. The RC5 encryption algorithm. In *Proc. of the Fast Software Encryption Workshop (FSE-95)*, volume 1,008 of *LNCS*, pages 86–96. Springer-Verlag, 1995.
41. R. Rudell. Espresso 1OCTTOOLS, January 1988.
42. R. Rudell and A. Sangiovanni-Vincentelli. Multiple valued minimization for pla optimization. *IEEE Trans. on Computer Aided Design*, 6(5):727–750, 1987.
43. P. Ryan and S. Schneider. An attack on a recurive authentication protocol. a cautionary tale. *Information Processing Letters*, 65(15):7–16, 1998.
44. T. Schaefer. The complexity of satisfiability problems. In *Proc. of the 10th ACM Symposium on Theory of Computing (STOC-78)*, pages 216–226. ACM Press and Addison Wesley, 1978.
45. B. Schneier. *Applied Cryptography: Protocols, Algorithms, and Source Code in C.* John Wiley & Sons, 1994.
46. B. Selman and H. Kautz. Knowlege compilation and theory approximation. *J. of the ACM*, 43(2):193–224, 1996.
47. B. Selman, H. Kautz, and D. McAllester. Ten challenges in propositional resoning and search. In *Proc. of the 15th Internat. Joint Conf. on Artificial Intelligence (IJCAI-97).* Morgan Kaufmann, Los Altos, 1997.
48. B. Selman, D. Mitchell, and H. Levesque. Generating hard satisfiability problems. *Artificial Intelligence*, 81(1-2):17–29, 1996.
49. C. Shannon. Communication theory of secrecy systems. *Bell System Technical J. n.28*, pages 656–715, 1949.
50. C. Suttner and G. Sutcliffe. The CADE-14 ATP system competition. *J. of Automated Reasoning*, 21(1):99–134, 1998.
51. H. Zhang. SATO: an efficient propositional prover. In *Proc. of the 14th Internat. Conf. on Automated Deduction (CADE-97)*, *LNCS*, 1997.

52. H. Zhang. Personal Communication, Nov 1998.
53. H. Zhang and M. Stickel. An efficient algorithm for unit-propagation. In *Proc. of the 4th Internat. Symposium on AI and Mathematics*, 1996.

SAT2000
I. Gent et al. (Eds.)
IOS Press, 2000

A SAT Solver Using Reconfigurable Hardware and Virtual Logic

Miron Abramovici[†] and Jose T. De Sousa[§]
Bell Labs - Lucent Technologies, Murray Hill, NJ 07974, USA

Abstract. In this paper, we present the architecture of a new SAT solver using reconfigurable logic and a virtual logic scheme. Our main contributions include new forms of massive fine-grain parallelism, structured design techniques based on iterative logic arrays that reduce compilation times from hours to minutes, and a decomposition technique that creates independent subproblems that may be concurrently solved by unconnected FPGAs. The decomposition technique is the basis of the virtual logic scheme, since it allows solving problems that exceed the hardware capacity. Our architecture is easily scalable. Our results show several orders of magnitude speedup compared with a state-of-the-art software implementation, and also with respect to prior SAT solvers using reconfigurable hardware.

Keywords: satisfiability, reconfigurable logic, virtual logic, massive parallelism.

1. Reconfigurable Computing

Reconfigurable computing is an emerging computing paradigm using reconfigurable hardware based on Field-Programmable Gate Arrays (FPGAs) to implement computationally intensive applications by tailoring the architecture to the needs of each application. An FPGA is a universal logic device structured as an array of programmable logic cells, interconnected by a programmable routing network, and programmable I/O cells. There are several methods of programming FPGAs to implement a specific function. For SRAM-based FPGAs (the most popular type of FPGAs), programming is simply done by writing the contents of a configuration memory contained in the device. The set of all programming bits establishes the *configuration* that determines the function of the device. A SRAM-based FPGA may be reconfigured an arbitrarily large number of times. A reconfigurable processor combines hardware speed with the flexibility of software and is usually attached as a coprocessor to a general-purpose host computer. The host prepares and downloads the data needed to configure the hardware as an application-specific processor. The reconfigurable logic benefits from eliminating or reducing the overhead of a general-purpose computer (instruction interpretation, fixed-width data-paths, limited register set, fixed functional units, etc.) and can be optimally designed for the target application by exploiting fine-grain parallelism. Unlike special-purpose accelerators (such as those used for simulation), reconfigurable processors support many different applications. To pick only one example, the same DEC reconfigurable processor [34] has been used to implement (1) long-integer arithmetic, (2) RSA cryptography, (3) DNA sequencing, (4) neural networks, (5) multistandard video compression, (6) solutions of Laplace equations, (7) image acquisition, analysis, and classification, (8) stereo vision, (9) sound synthesis, and (10) Viterbi decoding. In most applications, the reconfigurable processor achieved supercomputer-level performance, while its cost is only a small fraction of a supercomputer cost.

[†] miron@research.bell-labs.com
[§] sousa@research.bell-labs.com

Emulation is an application of reconfigurable computing increasingly used in design verification of complex systems (for example, see [16]). With emulation, one builds an FPGA-based hardware model of a new VLSI chip; typically, such a model is only about 10 times slower than the real hardware (hence many orders of magnitude faster than software simulation), which makes possible in-system verification and hardware-software co-design.

2. Motivation

SAT is a central problem in computer science, with many applications in many different domains [19]. Our main motivation in developing a reconfigurable hardware SAT solver was to obtain a low-cost tool for solving difficult SAT instances that occur in the area of Computer Aided Design (CAD) and test of electronic circuits. CAD and test problems that require solving large systems of Boolean equations include logic verification, timing verification [13, 22], layout and routability analysis [12, 35], and fault diagnosis [36]. The Automatic Test Generation (ATPG) problem may be formulated as a SAT problem [21, 30]. Computing the maximum circuit delay in the presence of false paths can also be solved by SAT [29]. Many problems in logic synthesis [8] – such as state assignment, state minimization, I/O encoding and asynchronous circuit design [20] – have SAT-based solutions. Many other computationally difficult problems, such as graph coloring, scheduling, theorem proving, and constraint satisfaction problems, have also been mapped into SAT. Because of the NP-completeness of SAT [10], even with the most advanced SAT algorithms, such as GRASP [28], difficult problems may require many hours of computation. In the DIMACS set of SAT benchmarks [14], there are still several problems so difficult that, to the best of our knowledge, no SAT algorithm has ever been able to solve them. Applied to complex VLSI circuits, SAT-based algorithms have long run-times. Thus speeding up SAT will result in improving the efficiency of many CAD and test algorithms relying on SAT. Note that in this area we cannot use approximate SAT algorithms, since unsatisfiable formulas occur often, and only an exact algorithm is guaranteed to recognize unsatisfiability.

3. Previous Work

Recently, several research groups have explored different approaches to implementing SAT on reconfigurable hardware [31, 2, 38, 25, 39, 24]. Figure 1 illustrates the general

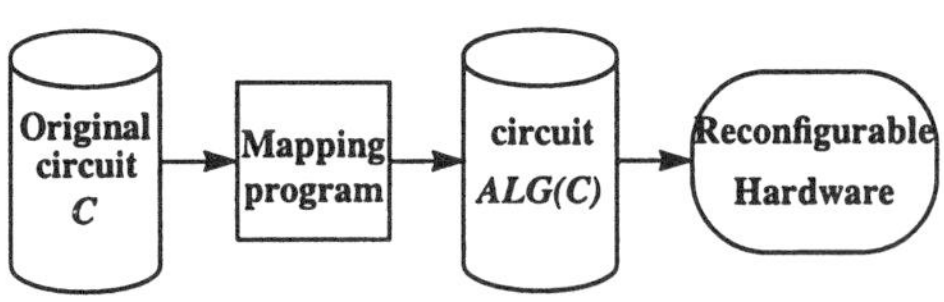

Figure 1. Speeding up algorithm ALG for circuit C.

data flow of such an approach, whose goal is to speed up an algorithm ALG working on a given circuit C. A mapping program generates the model of a new circuit $ALG(C)$, which executes ALG for C. Since $ALG(C)$ will be used only once, it would not be economically feasible to implement it in a conventional way. Using reconfigurable hardware allows one to "virtually" create the $ALG(C)$ circuit; then the algorithm is executed by emulating this circuit. In contrast to a hardware accelerator for ALG (for example, a simulation accelerator), where the same special-purpose hardware processes different circuits, in this approach the $ALG(C)$ hardware is designed specifically for a single circuit. The advantage is that *ALG will run at emulation speed, without incurring the cost of building special-purpose hardware.* Similar paradigms based on reconfigurable computing techniques have also been used or proposed to accelerate other computationally difficult problems, such as finding independent sets [5] and transitive closure [9] in graphs.

In the following, we will refer to a $SAT(C)$ circuit as a *hardware SAT solver*, or a *satisfier*. Suyama et al. [31] were the first to create a satisfier, which is downloaded into an emulator for execution. Although this method has been reported to be more efficient than a software SAT solver, its applicability to CAD is limited because the generated vectors are always fully specified. For example, for a problem with 200 variables, all of them will be assigned binary values, even if the function may be satisfied, say, with only 20 assignments. This overspecification is detrimental in most CAD and test applications, where typically we would like to minimize the number of specified variables. For example, in ATPG, full specification would preclude test set compaction [1] and may also preclude the generation of the obtained vector by a different circuit.

The satisfier of Zhong et al. [38, 39] implements a version of the classical Davis–Putnam SAT algorithm [11]. For every variable x_i, they construct an implication circuit and a state machine to manage the decision process for x_i. The implication circuit detects the conditions when values of other variables imply a value for x_i, and detects a conflict when both 0 and 1 are implied for x_i. The decision state machine keeps track of the current value of x_i (0, 1, or x for unassigned/unknown) and of the way the value has been obtained (assigned or implied). The decision state machines of all variables are connected as cells in a serial chain, where only one cell at a time may be enabled. The leftmost enabled cell whose variable x_i has an unknown value first assigns x_i to 1. All the implications of this assignment are determined (in several clock cycles), and if no conflicts are detected, the next cell to the right is enabled. If $x_i = 1$ leads to conflicts, the assignment $x_i = 0$ is tried next. When both 0 and 1 lead to conflicts, x_i is set to x and control is passed to the left (backtracking). A cell whose value has been implied simply passes control to the right for normal processing or to the left for backtracking. The architecture has been implemented using an IKOS emulator. A proposed extension [39] implements a sophisticated nonchronological backtracking mechanism. The published results show a median speedup of 64 on a subset (about 60%) of the DIMACS SAT benchmarks [14].

An important problem in any SAT solver is the method used to select the next decision variable and its value to be tried. In software, the most efficient techniques rely on dynamic (run-time) ordering of variables based on heuristic measures that allow selecting the best one [27, 28]. Dynamic selection, however, has been considered too expensive to directly implement in hardware. What all hardware SAT solvers do is order the variables statically (as a preprocessing step) based on some heuristic functions. This predetermines the basic order in which the search space will be explored at run-time. The only way this ordering may be altered is by skipping certain variables based on run-time conditions.

The static order used in [39] ranks variables based on their literal count and is used to arrange the variables in the serial chain. The only variables skipped at runtime are those already having a binary value, and for every decision variable the 1 value is tried before 0. This mechanism leads to unnecessary or detrimental decisions. For example, when variable A becomes enabled and A still has value x, $A = 1$ will be tried, even if no assignment to A is really needed in the current state (if A feeds only already satisfied clauses) or even if 1 is the wrong choice for A (when only $\bar{A}$ literals appear in the currently unsatisfied clauses); this results in a lot of unnecessary backtracking.

A satisfier architecture similar to [39] has been recently described by Platzner and De Micheli [24]. A proposed extension allows overcoming the problem of unnecessary decisions in [39] by introducing additional clauses to identify the conditions that make a variable become a *don't care* and logic that avoids decisions on these variables.

The satisfier proposed by Abramovici and Saab [2] executes a *justification* algorithm patterned after PODEM [17]. Here, we have a combinational logic circuit that represents the Boolean function to be satisfied, and the goal is to set the primary output (PO) to 1 by a suitable assignment of the primary inputs (PIs). Central to this algorithm is the concept of *objective*, which is a desired assignment $l = v$ of value v to signal l, which currently has an unknown value x. Initially all signals are set to x. An objective may be achieved only by PI assignments. A *backtrace* procedure propagates an objective $l = v$ along a single path from l to a PI i, where all the signals along the path have value x, and determines a PI assignment $i = v_i$ that is likely to contribute to achieving $l = v$. A major innovation introduced in [2] is logic for backtracing of objectives, thus realizing a backward circuit traversal in hardware. The search process is performed in a central control unit, using a hardware stack to support the backtracking process. Backtracing inherently avoids both decisions on *don't care*'s and assigning wrong values as done in [39]. However, the central control unit appears difficult to scale up with the size of the target CNF. Rashid et al. [25] discuss an implementation of this architecture using Xilinx 6200 series FPGAs [37]. No significant results are reported in either [2] or [25].

An important issue affecting not only SAT but also any algorithm implemented on reconfigurable hardware is the *compilation time* spent in preparing the FPGA-based circuit to be emulated. This process involves multi-FPGA partitioning taking into account the existing board interconnect, and then, for every FPGA, technology mapping, placement, and routing. If these tasks require more time than solving the original problem in software, then no overall speedup can be achieved. To realize a proper balance between the runtime of the FPGA physical design tools and the computational savings resulting from accelerating SAT, Zhong et al. [39] suggest that one should use a satisfier only for really difficult problems for which it is worth spending even a couple of hours in compilation if this saves many more hours (or days) of computation or if it allows solving problems that are impossible for a software SAT solver. Nevertheless, it would be a great advantage to have a more efficient design flow, less dependent on conventional FPGA design tools.

Another problem in accelerating SAT with reconfigurable logic is the capacity and the cost of the hardware platform used for emulation. All previous SAT solvers using reconfigurable hardware are limited in the size of the problems they can handle by the available hardware capacity; hence any problem that does not fit is automatically "out-of-bounds." Current logic emulators have large capacity (up to several million gates), but they are quite expensive (about $0.50 per emulated gate) and hence not easily affordable; however, most other platforms that are reasonably priced do not provide sufficient capacity. The ideal solution would be a *virtual logic* mechanism that allows a reconfigurable logic platform to process circuits much larger than its available capacity at the cost of some additional processing time. Note the analogy with *virtual memory,* where the logical address space is much larger than the physical address space.

4. Main Contributions

In this paper we survey our work in creating a new satisfier architecture [3, 4]. We first describe a *new massively parallel fine-grain satisfier architecture.* Like [2], our satisfier selects the next variable to assign based on backtracing objectives. But while in [2] only one objective is propagated along a single path and results in a unique variable assignment, the new architecture provides *new forms of massive parallelism – parallel backtracing of all objectives along all possible paths and concurrent assignments of several variables.* Conceptually, the parallel backtrace is similar (to a certain extent) to the multiple backtrace of the FAN algorithm [15]; but, unlike in software, where objectives must be processed serially, in hardware we backtrace all objectives concurrently. An important difference is that in places where FAN selects only one path to backtrace one objective, in hardware we allow *simultaneous exploration of all possible paths.* To make possible this massive parallel processing, we introduced the new concept of *objective propagation with several different priorities.*

Another significant contribution in our approach is the *identification of dynamically unate variables.* A *unate variable* has all its literals either complemented or not, and hence it can never cause a conflict. The literals of a unate variable are known in the SAT literature as *pure literals* [11]. After a variable is assigned, certain clauses become satisfied. All the unassigned literals of an already satisfied clause are said to be *dead*, because in the current state, their values can no longer influence the satisfied clause. When our satisfier detects that all inverting literals of a variable A have died, it immediately assigns $A = 1$, because this will satisfy all the clauses containing A without causing any conflicts. Similarly, detecting that all noninverting literals of A have died shows that A may be safely set to 0. In other words, although A is not unate, we can treat A as a variable that becomes unate in the current state (*dynamically unate*). Identifying and assigning dynamically unate variables represents an *opportunistic assignment* that is treated like a *new type of implication.* Increasing the number of implications reduces the search space and results in significant speedup. This new technique can be viewed as the hardware embodiment of the Pure Literal Rule [11].

When all the literals of an unassigned variable A have died (because all the clauses containing A are satisfied), A is said to be a *dead variable.* Our satisfier identifies dead variables and never assigns them, thus avoiding the unnecessary decisions taken in [39]. Our dead variables are equivalent to the *don't care*'s of [24] but are identified by a different mechanism.

We have implemented our satisfier using the ACE6264 reconfigurable processor board produced by TSI-TelSys Inc. This board employs the XC6200 series FPGAs [37], witch have been designed to support reconfigurable computing applications. To overcome the high computational costs of conventional FPGA physical design tools, we have developed *modular design techniques using iterative logic array (ILA) structures* that trade off some chip area and performance to obtain easy-to-construct circuits (a carry-ripple adder is a typical example of ILA). As in [25], we predesign several types of basic building blocks (including their placement and routing) and create a library of modules to be used by any satisfier. The novel aspects of our approach are the design of the library modules as ILA cells and the placement of these blocks using specific ILA structures parametrized for a target CNF. After the library modules have been created, *the complexity of the place-and-route algorithms grows only linearly with the size of the ILAs. The ILA-based approach is inherently scalable*, since adding more cells to an ILA does not change its regular structure. While an unstructured chip design ends up with many unrouted nets after 10–12 hours of CPU time, the same *circuit using ILA-based design techniques takes only a few minutes to successfully compile.* These techniques are applicable to any type of FPGA, and the reduction in compilation time they provide becomes even more significant when we need to compile a large number of FPGAs.

Multi-FPGA partitioning is necessary when the circuit to be emulated (in our case, the satisfier) does not fit into one FPGA. An additional complication is that such an FPGA partitioning algorithm must also deal with the constraints imposed by existing inter-FPGA board interconnect. Another significant contribution of this paper is *a method of decomposing a given SAT problem into several nondisjoint but nevertheless independent subproblems that may be solved in any order by unconnected FPGAs,* where every subproblem is assigned to one FPGA. Our decomposition technique combines partitioning into disjoint subproblems used in software SAT algorithms [27] with the simple variable decomposition previously used for running SAT on parallel processors [7]. Unlike circuit partitioning into multiple FPGAs, the unusual feature of our decomposition is that *inter-FPGA signals are not required.* This provides a *simple solution to the limited hardware capacity problem*: if we have more subproblems (n) than available FPGAs (k), we simply take turns in reusing every FPGA by reconfiguring it for n/k subproblems. This feature represents a *virtual logic mechanism*, which allows a reconfigurable logic platform to process circuits much larger than its available capacity. Additional advantages of our decomposition are discussed in Section 6.

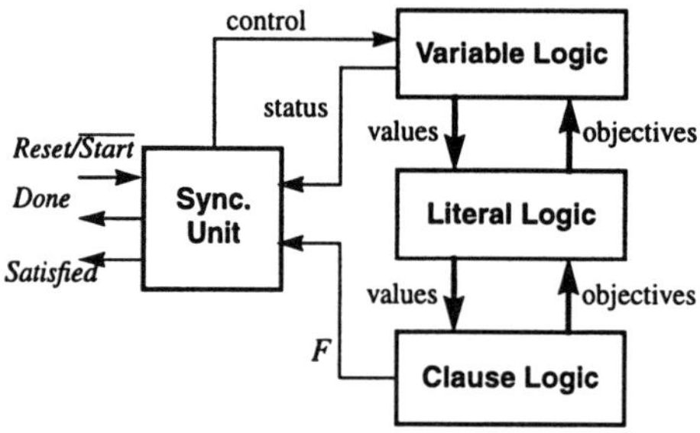

Figure 2. High-level view of the architecture.

The remainder of the paper is organized as follows. Section 5 presents the architecture of our satisfier. Section 6 describes our decomposition technique and the virtual logic scheme. Section 7 presents our experimental results. Section 8 discusses future research directions, and Section 9 concludes the paper.

5. The Satisfier Architecture

Figure 2 shows the high-level view of our satisfier. (More details will be given in the following subsections.) Variable Logic maintains the current values (0, 1, or x) of all variables. Their values are sent to Literal Logic, which distributes them as literal values to Clause Logic. Clause Logic computes the value of every clause and of the output function F, and also determines objectives for all the literals. These objectives are sent back to Literal Logic, which merges objectives arriving from different literals of the same variable into one objective for that variable. Both Clause Logic and Literal Logic are combinational blocks. Variable Logic maps the objectives arriving from Literal Logic into assignments (implications or decisions). The Synchronization Unit initiates backtracking when the function F becomes 0, performs some timing and control functions, and provides the interface with the outside world: *Reset/$\overline{Start}$* initiates the execution, *Done* is the completion signal, and *Satisfied* indicates whether the SAT problem has been successfully solved.

5.1. Concurrent Objectives

We model a CNF as a two-level circuit, as illustrated in Figure 3. Each PI represents a variable, each OR input represents a literal, and each OR gate represents a clause.

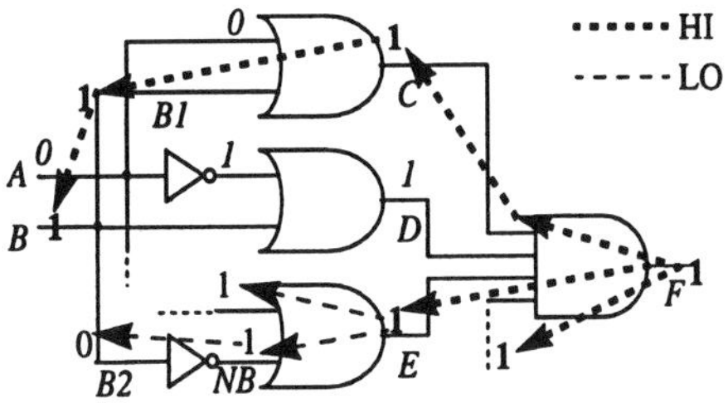

Figure 3. HI- and LO-objectives.

Structurally, a variable is also referred to as a fanout stem. We treat satisfiability as a justification problem to set $F = 1$.

To justify $F = 1$, all the inputs of the AND gate must be 1. While in software justification algorithms [17, 15] (and also in the hardware scheme of [2]) these simultaneous requirements are processed one objective at a time, in our massively parallel approach all the objectives are concurrently processed. Allowing concurrent objective propagation along several paths means that several objectives may reach the same variable, each one arriving from a different literal. Since these objectives may be conflicting, a first question should be: are all objectives equally important? The answer can be easily inferred by analyzing the objectives shown in Figure 3, where we assume that A has already been assigned value 0, which in turn satisfied clause D (logic values are italicized). Note that only signals with value x may have objectives. All the objectives shown in bold are necessary to set $F = 1$, while the 1 objectives at the inputs of E are not (since there are two alternative ways of setting $E = 1$). Thus we say that an objective has *high priority* if it *must be achieved* (in the current state) to set the function F to 1; the other objectives are said to have *low priority*. We will abbreviate "high- and low-priority objective" as "HI- and LO-objectives", respectively. Note that HI-objectives always form *continuous implication chains* (represented by bold arrows) starting with the PO objective. Clearly, a HI-objective on a fanout branch of a stem should override any LO-objectives on other branches of the same variable. In Figure 3, the HI-1 objective on $B1$ overrides LO-0 on $B2$, and it is transmitted to the stem B. HI-objectives reaching PIs denote *implications* and are mapped into value assignments for the corresponding variables in the next clock cycle. (Since every clause has always a HI-1 objective, these objectives are fixed in the logic and not propagated from the PO; but for the sake of clarity, we will show them as being propagated.) While in [2], processing of the HI-1 objective of E would result in only one input with value x being assigned a LO-1 objective, in our approach LO-1 objectives are simultaneously sent to every input of E with x value. The importance of this difference will be explained shortly.

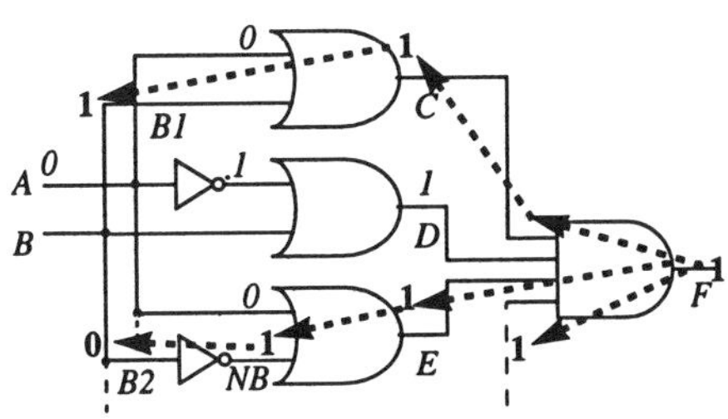

Figure 4. Conflicting HI-objectives.

Conflicts. Conflicting HI-objectives arriving at the same variable indicate an inconsistent state, because any binary value assigned to that PI in the current state would set the function F to 0 by reversing at least one of the implication chains arriving at the stem from the PO. Figure 4 illustrates such a case where the objectives at *B1* and *B2* are, respectively, HI-1 and HI-0. In such a situation we would like to backtrack immediately to cut useless wandering in a no-solution area of the search space. This is achieved by the same technique described above that maps any HI-objective reaching a PI into its corresponding variable assignment, because no matter which binary value is assigned to that PI, one of the implication chains will be reversed, and the result will be $F = 0$. This value of F is used in the Sync. Unit to initiate backtracking.

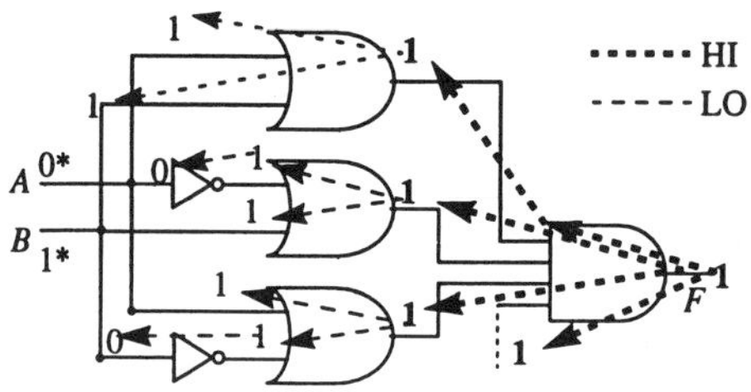

Figure 5. Potentially conflicting LO-objectives.

Potential Conflicts. An additional priority level is useful to differentiate among LO-objectives. A LO-objective means that this objective is useful to achieve an upstream HI-objective, but in the current state there are alternative ways of achieving the same HI-objective. In Figure 5, all the OR inputs have LO-1 objectives, and both A and B receive two LO-1 and one LO-0 from their fanout branches. Clearly, this indicates potential for conflicts in the future. Here the choice of the objective value to propagate to the variable is arbitrary (A gets 0 and B gets 1), but we flag the variable objective as a *potential conflict* using a *. Variable Logic will select the next decision variable among the PIs with a potential conflict flag. Propagating LO-1 objectives from all inputs of the OR gates guarantees that *all potential conflicts are identified.*

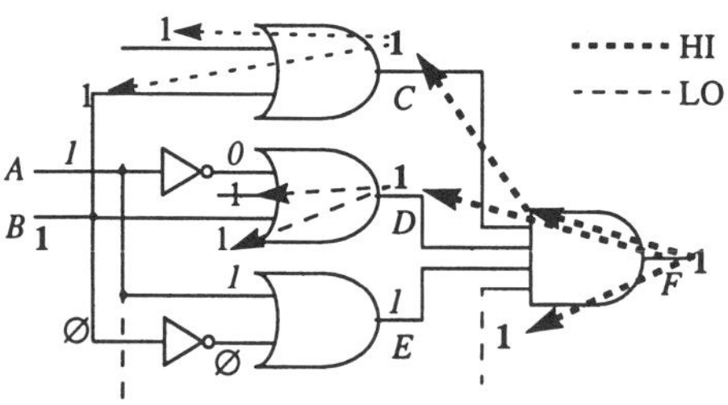

Figure 6. Dynamically unate variable.

Dead Literals and Dynamically Unate Variables. As a result of assigning $A = 1$ in Figure 6, clause E becomes satisfied. Then the value of its other input becomes a "don't care", and this input will be referred to as a *dead literal.* Although B is a binate variable, it may no longer cause a conflict in the current state; we say that B has become a *dynamically unate variable.* To transmit the information about dead literals from the satisfied clauses back to the variables generating the dead literals, we introduce a *dead objective*, denoted by $\oslash$ in Figure 6. Clearly, the priority of $\oslash$ should be the lowest. Then B is recognized as a dynamically unate variable because its fanout branches

Table I. OR2 objective priority computation.

O_r	V_l	V_{in}	O_l	O_{in}
∅	—	—	∅	∅
	1	—		
—	—	1	∅	∅
	0	0		
	x	x	LO	LO
H/L	x	0	H/L	∅
	0	x	∅	H/L

propagate only nonconflicting objectives (LO-1 and ∅). Although the value of B is not implied by the current state, we will *opportunistically assign* $B = 1$ to satisfy clauses C an D without causing any conflicts. To effectively treat $B = 1$ as an implication, Literal Logic converts the nonconflicting LO-1 objective into a HI-1, which will generate the implication $B = 1$ in the next clock cycle. This process will continue, since the newly satisfied clauses will create new dead literals, which in turn may cause other variables to become dynamically unate, and so on.

In summary, our satisfier recognizes four priorities for objectives: HI, $*$ (potential conflict), LO, and ∅ (dead). These are coded with two bits.

5.2. Clause Logic

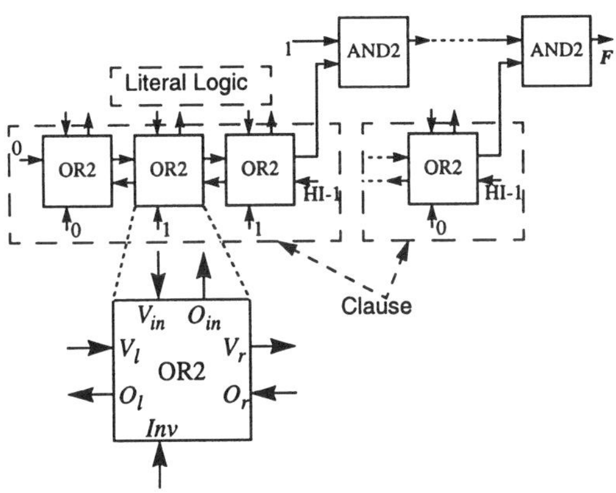

Figure 7. Clause logic.

As illustrated in Figure 7, every clause with m literals is implemented by a bidirectional ILA of m OR2 cells. Every cell receives the value of one variable (V_{in}), a flag (Inv) indicating whether V_{in} should be inverted, and the partial OR result from the cells on its left (V_l), and computes $V_r = (V_{in} \oplus Inv) + V_l$ for the next cell on its right (using 3-valued logic). The V_r value obtained at the right-most OR2 cell is the clause output value, which is sent to an AND ILA to iteratively compute the value of the function F.

While values propagate left to right through the ILA, the computation of input objectives advances in the opposite direction. Every OR2 cell receives its output objective O_r

from the cell on its right (O_r is initialized to HI-1 at the rightmost cell) and determines the objective for its input O_{in} and the output objective O_l for the cell to its left. In fact, the binary value of any (nondead) objective is known a priori (1 for O_l and $\overline{Inv}$ for O_{in}) and it is hard-coded in the logic. Thus only the computation of priorities is relevant, as given in Table I, where H/L denotes a HI or LO priority and "-" denotes a don't care entry.

5.3. Literal Logic

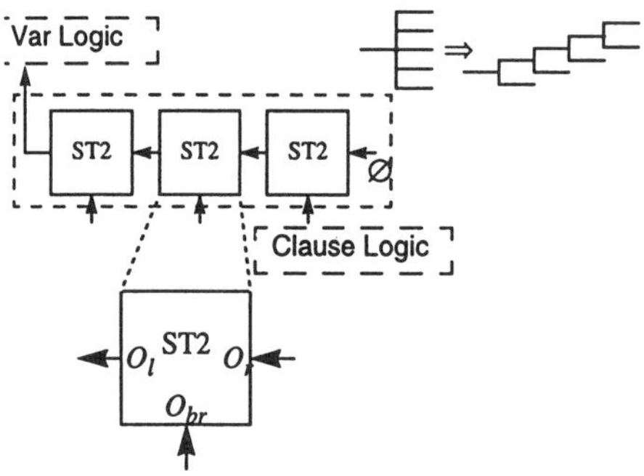

Figure 8. Literal logic.

Since the propagation of the variable values to literals is straightforward, we will discuss only the process of computing an objective for a variable from the objectives of its literals. As illustrated in Figure 8, we model a stem as a sequence of stems with two fanout branches. The stem objective is computed by an ILA composed of ST2 cells which iteratively merge the objectives arriving on fanout branches from Clause Logic. Every ST2 cell receives the partial result O_r from the cell on its right and the objective of one fanout branch O_{br}, and computes the objective for its stem O_l, which is sent to the next cell on its left. The O_l output from the left-most cell is the PI objective sent to Variable Logic. The rules for computing objectives are given in Table II, where v and a are arbitrary objective values, and H/L/* $\in$ {HI, LO, *}. Note that O_{br} cannot be a potential conflict (which may be generated only by Literal Logic) and that O_{br} is given priority over O_r in the case both have HI-priority. A conflict between HI-objectives will be detected because any value assigned to the stem will cause Clause Logic to output $F = 0$.

5.4. Variable Logic

As illustrated in Figure 9, Variable Logic is constructed as a bidirectional ILA of VL cells, where each cell corresponds to a variable. Every cell maintains its current value V in a 2-bit register, and receives the objective O from Literal Logic as a 3-bit field (2 bits for priority and 1 for value). A HI-objective indicates that the objective value must be assigned to this variable as an implication in the next clock cycle. All cells with HI-objectives are concurrently assigned. A LO-objective shows that this variable has become dynamically unate; its priority is immediately converted to HI so that it will be treated as an implication. A *-objective denotes a potential conflict; if no variable must be implied, one of the variables with a *-objective will be selected as the next decision variable. Finally, a dead objective denotes a variable that should do nothing.

Since all implications must be done before any decision is tried, the ILA iteratively determines whether HI-objectives are present anywhere in the array. For this, every cell

Table II. Variable objectives.

O_r	V_{br}	O_l	Notes
⊘	⊘	⊘	same
H/L-ν	H/L-ν	H/L-ν	objective
—	HI-ν	HI-ν	HI overrides
HI-ν	LO-a		any objective
⊘	H/L-ν	H/L-ν	any objective
H/L/*-ν	⊘	H/L/*-ν	overrides ⊘
LO-$\overline{\nu}$	LO-ν	*-ν	pot. conflict
*-ν	LO-a		* overrides LO

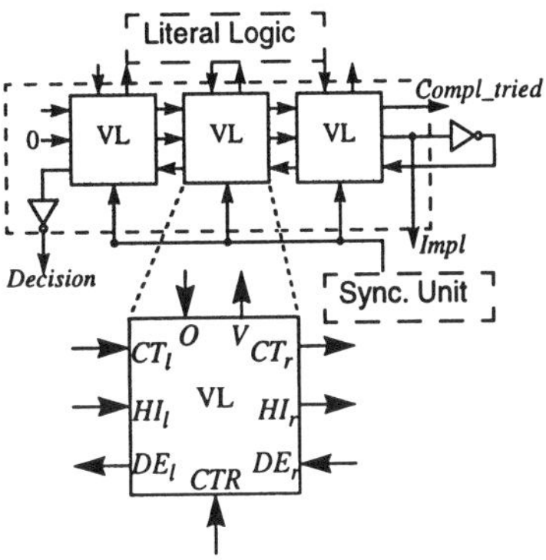

Figure 9. Variable logic.

computes a HI_r flag signaling whether its objective O or any of the objectives of the cells to its left has HI-priority; the result from the preceding cells is brought in by the input HI_l. The signal *Impl* obtained at the HI_r output from the right-most cell reports whether at least one variable is being implied. Since no decisions should be made while implications are in progress, *Impl* is complemented and fed back to the right-most cell as a decision-enable input (DE_r). A cell receiving a dead objective ($O = \oslash$), because either its value is binary or its variable is dead, just passes the decision enable signal through, that is, $DE_l = DE_r$. If the objective O of a cell denotes a potential conflict and the cell is enabled to take a decision (has $DE_r = 1$), then its variable will be the next decision variable, so it disables decisions for the cells to its left by setting its DE_l output to 0. The complement of the DE_l output from the left-most cell is the signal *Decision* which indicates whether any cell is taking a decision. Both *Decision* and *Impl* being 0 means that all arriving objectives are ⊘, since any nondead objective would produce either an implication or a decision; this may occur only when the function F has a binary value.

Each VL cell is a state machine with four states: (1) Unset (initial state with $V = x$), (2) Implied (V implied from a HI-objective), (3) Assigned (V assigned from a *-objective by a decision), and (4) Complemented (V is the result of reversing the last decision of this cell). Being in the Complemented state results in asserting the output CT_r if the variable is the current decision variable. Thus one can OR the left input CT_l with a flag indicating that the cell is the current decision variable and is in the Complemented state, to obtain the output CT_r. The signal *Compl_tried,* obtained at the CT_r output from the right-most cell, reports whether the decision variable has been complemented. *Compl_tried*, *Decision,* and *Impl* are sent to Sync. Unit to report the status of Variable Logic. State transitions in a VL cell are controlled by its arriving objective O, its decision-enable input DE_r, and the 2-bit control bus CTR, which is generated by Sync. Unit and shared among all cells.

Unlike the central stack used in [2], in our architecture each VL cell has an up/down counter DL to keep track of the current decision level, and a register AL to store the level at the time when its variable has been assigned (by a decision or an implication). The state of a cell is encoded in a two-bit state register, which can only be updated if the cell is at the current decision level ($AL = DL$). All DL counters are concurrently incremented or decremented as specified by the CTR inputs. (The DL counters are identical, but their replication simplifies routing.) Such a distributed control mechanism is easily scalable.

5.5. Synchronization Unit

Sync. Unit determines the state of the satisfier using the signal F from the Clause Logic, the signals *Impl, Decision*, and *Compl_tried* from Variable Logic, and another replica of the DL counter. From these signals it can tell if the problem has been satisfied ($F = 1$), if the problem is unsatisfiable ($DL = 0$ and there is still need to backtrack), or if execution should continue. In the latter case, different actions are issued to the VL cells via CTR. $F = 0$ indicates the need to complement the current decision or backtrack to the previous one, if *Compl_tried* is asserted. If $F = x$, we can (1) have a new decision, (2) have implications resulting from the previous decision, or (3) be in between consecutive backtracks. In the first two cases new variable assignments will be caused, and in the third case we have to decrement DL again.

Another function of Sync. Unit is to provide clocking signals to the rest of the circuit. After new variables are set, the longest delay until *Decision* becomes stable involves two traversals through the VL ILA. This delay T can be determined from post-layout timing analysis, and is programmed into Sync. Unit. We call $f_1 = 1/T$ the main clock frequency. We also have a secondary, faster frequency f_2, which we use for consecutive decrement operations of DL. Note that no variable assignments are made between consecutive DL decrement operations; we just need to wait for the *Compl_tried* signal to propagate through the VL array. Usually $f_2 \cong 2 \times f_1$. If $N1$ and $N2$ are the respective numbers of clock pulses of frequencies f_1 and f_2 used during a run, we will report the result by the number of equivalent main clocks $CK = N1 + N2/2$. Because of the ILA nature of our satisfier, f_1 is quite low (below 5 MHz), compared with more conventional designs.

6. SAT Decomposition

6.1. Simple Decomposition

In [7], an original SAT problem is decomposed into n subproblems, which are then distributed to n conventional processors, and interprocessor communications are used for load balancing. We reuse this technique for the case of reconfigurable hardware satisfiers. The principle underlying this decomposition is well known: we split the problem $F(x_1, x_2, \ldots, x_n) = 1$ into two subproblems obtained by setting one variable to 0 and 1, respectively. If we split on x_1, the two subproblems will be $F(0, x_2, \ldots, x_n) = 1$ and $F(1, x_2, \ldots, x_n) = 1$. Clearly, any solution to the first (second) subproblem is also a solution to the original problem if we add $x_1 = 0(1)$. To conclude that the original problem is unsatisfiable, every subproblem must be proven unsatisfiable. The CNF for a subproblem is a subset of the original CNF; the simplification process based on assigning one variable will be described in the next section. Thus any subproblem is smaller than the original problem. We can recursively repeat this splitting process for k variables. If we represent this decomposition process by a binary OR tree with k levels, the subproblems to be solved are obtained at the terminal nodes of the tree. The OR relation between the two branches of a node means that solving one of the two subproblems is sufficient to solve the original problem. The more variables we assign, the smaller the subproblems become. Of course, k should be limited since the number of subproblems is 2^k. *The subproblems share all the variables not assigned, so they are not disjoint. Nevertheless, they are independent*, since the values of the shared variables do not have to be correlated, as different subproblems may obtain different satisfying vectors for the original problem.

Let us assume that we continue to assign variables until each subproblem fits into one FPGA. Unlike circuit partitioning into multiple FPGAs, the unusual feature of this decomposition is that *inter-FPGA signals are never required.* The advantages of not having any inter-FPGA interconnect are very significant. First, the conventional *multi-FPGA partitioning step is no longer needed,* and hence the design flow becomes simpler and faster. Second, the *large delays* associated with signals propagating off-chip, on the board, and back on-chip *are avoided,* which allows a faster clock speed. Third, *we can use a reconfigurable hardware platform much simpler, smaller, and cheaper than an emulator*, where inter-FPGA communication is a complex problem requiring expensive solutions, such as hierarchical crossbar structures [33], or dedicated field-programmable interconnect chips [23], or time-multiplexing hardware [6]. Unlike multi-FPGA partitioning techniques, which have to deal with a specific board interconnect scheme, *our decomposition is independent of the architecture of the target hardware platform.*

The lack of any inter-FPGA interconnect also provides the basis for the virtual hardware mechanism: if we have more subproblems (n) than available FPGAs (g), we simply *take turns in reusing every FPGA by dynamically reconfiguring it for different subproblems.* An FPGA that has finished a subproblem may be immediately reconfigured for the next one. The reconfiguration time is in most cases negligible compared with the computation time. In the worst case where all n subproblems must be solved, every FPGA will process, on the average, n/g problems. Thus the worst-case loss of efficiency caused by the time-multiplexing of FPGAs is proportional to n/g, which also represents the *overflow ratio* between the "size" of the problem and the available hardware capacity. Note that, in extreme, this scheme works even with a single FPGA, which must be reconfigured at most n times. For example, assume that we decompose a large SAT problem into 1,000 subproblems so that each one fits into one FPGA, but our reconfigurable hardware platform is limited to 50 FPGAs. So the problem size is significantly larger (20 times) than the available capacity. Nevertheless, we can still solve it by simply reconfiguring every FPGA for at most 20 subproblems. Since we may stop as soon as one FPGA finds a solution, it is likely that only an unsatisfiable original problem will require all 20 runs to complete.

Another benefit of the decomposition is the additional speedup obtained by the g FPGAs working concurrently on different subproblems. Since each subproblem is simpler than the original and is restricted to a smaller search space, and also because we can stop all computations as soon as one solution is found, the average speedup is usually greater than g (this observation is also supported by the results in [7]).

The drawback of this simple decomposition method is that in some CNFs the reductions in the problem size are relatively small, and we need to assign too many variables until we can make every subproblem fit into one FPGA, which in turn results in too many subproblems. This occurs in CNFs characterized by a small ratio between literals and variables, because setting one variable in such a formula results in a small reduction in the size of the problem. The next section provides a more general solution applicable to any CNF.

6.2. *Decomposition for Disjoint Partitioning*

One type of partitioning used in software SAT solvers [27] is finding subsets of clauses that depend on disjoint subsets of variables. The resulting subproblems are independent and may be separately solved. If one subproblem is unsatisfiable, then so is the original problem. The solution to the original problem is obtained by concatenating the individual solutions of all subproblems. A disjoint partition provides an exponential reduction of the worst-case search space of a SAT solver, but it is seldom found in practical problems. However, such partitions may be created dynamically, as a consequence of the formula simplifications caused by assignments to variables.

The simple decomposition method described in the preceding section is inefficient when variable assignments result only in small reductions in the size of subproblems. In this section, we introduce a *new decomposition technique, whose goal is to assign variables so that the resulting subproblems are disjoint* [4]. This is motivated by the fact that disjoint partitioning significantly reduces the size of the resulting subproblems. The process of simplifying a formula based on an assignment $Var = val$ consists of removing those parts of the formula (variables, literals, and clauses) that become inactive, or *dead*, as a result of implying $Var = val$. The pseudocode of *Simplify* in Figure 10 outlines the simplification procedure. *To_imply* schedules assignments to be processed. If *val* conflicts with the current value of *Var*, the formula is recognized as unsatisfiable. All clauses satisfied by setting $Var = val$ are removed from the formula, along with all their literals. All remaining literals of *Var* and the variable itself are also removed. After this set of simplifications, we analyze all variables that lost some literals. A variable all of whose literals have died is also removed. If the remaining literals of a variable are all inverting or all noninverting, this dynamically unate variable may be safely assigned to the value that will satisfy all its clauses. Next we analyze all clauses that lost some literals (these are unsatisfied). If all the literals of a clause have been removed, this clause can no longer be satisfied, so the formula is recognized as unsatisfiable. If a clause is left with only one literal, its variable is assigned the value that satisfies the clause. We repeat this process until no more variables are assigned. If at this point all clauses are satisfied, the formula is recognized as satisfied.

Our decomposition relies on a simple clause bipartitioning algorithm, which starts by creating from each clause a one-component cluster, then repeatedly merges clusters (based on a "closeness" measure reflecting the number of common variables), until two final clusters are obtained such that their number of common variables is minimized. To separate these two clusters, we assign their common variables. Note, however, that we may not need to assign all the common variables; as some of them may be implied or become dead after other common variables are assigned. Figure 11 outlines the algorithm to select the best variable to assign. It tries tentative formula simplifications for both 0 and 1 assignments to each common variable, and evaluates them based on the reduction obtained in the set of common variables (as a tie-breaker, we use the reduction in the number of literals). These simplifications are tentative since the changes they introduce may be erased by the procedure *Restore*. This analysis also does some learning; namely, when one assignment $Var = val$ falsifies the formula, then *Var* is set to $\overline{val}$ on a permanent basis (without *Restore*). The analysis is restarted after each instance of learning-induced simplification.

```
Simplify (Var = val) {
To_imply (Var = val)
for every assignment Var = val to be implied {
  if value of Var is val̄ then return "UNSAT"
  if value of Var is val then continue
  assign Var = val
  for every clause cls satisfied by Var = val
    for every literal lit of cls Remove_literal (lit)
    Remove_clause (cls)
  for every literal lit of Var Remove_literal (lit)
  Remove_variable (Var)
  for every variable Var who lost literals {
    if Var has no literals then Remove_variable (Var)
    if Var has only non-inverting literals then To_imply (Var = 1)
    if Var has only inverting literals then To_imply (Var = 0) }
  for every clause cls who lost literals {
    if no literals left then return "UNSAT"
    if cls has only one literal lit of variable Var then
      if lit is inverting then To_imply (Var = 0)
      else To_imply (Var = 1) }
  } // no more assignments to imply
  if no clause left then return "SAT"
  return "SIMPLIFIED"
}
```

Figure 10. Formula simplification.

Figure 12 outlines the process of recursive decomposition trying to achieve a disjoint partitioning of the formula. MAX_SIZE is the capacity of the target FPGA and *Size*() provides the size of the current formula, both expressed as number of literals (after the library modules are defined, we can estimate how many literals will fit in the target FPGA [3]). The recursion terminates when the current formula fits into one FPGA. If the formula is too large, *Bipartition* clusters the clauses in two subformulas as disjoint as possible, and also computes the set *Common_vars*. If there are no common variables, the process continues recursively with the two disjoint subformulas. Note that here we need to satisfy both subformulas in order to satisfy the original one, so when one subformula is identified as unsatisfiable, the original one is also unsatisfiable.

When there are common variables, we select the best variable to assign using the procedure given in Figure 11, then recursively continue the decomposition with the two simplified formulas obtained by assigning the best variable. Here it is sufficient to satisfy one of the two subproblems, so when one subformula is satisfied, the original one is also satisfied.

Figure 13 shows the decomposition tree for *dubois*26 – one of the SAT benchmarks in the DIMACS set [14]; this formula has 78 variables, 208 clauses, and 624 literals. The number inside a node is the number of variables for the corresponding subproblem. Setting MAX_SIZE = 300 literals, and assigning 2 variables, we obtain 8 subproblems, each one having 38 variables, 100 clauses, and 296 literals. (In general, the subproblems have different sizes, and the OR/AND graph is not symmetric.) The dotted arcs denote OR decomposition, where it is sufficient to solve only one subproblem, while the heavy arcs denote AND decomposition obtained by disjoint partitioning, where both subproblems must be solved and their solutions concatenated. Thus *dubois*26 can be solved with 8 unconnected FPGAs. An additional advantage of the decomposition is the speedup resulting from the 8 FPGAs working concurrently solving subproblems much simpler than the original one (only 38 variables instead 78), and from the fact that we

```
Select_best_var () {
RESTART: for every variable Var to be analyzed {
   lowest_penalty = 0
   status = Simplify (Var = 0)
   if (status = "SAT") then return "SAT"
   if (status = "UNSAT") then {// Var must be 1
      Restore()
      status = Simplify (Var = 1)
      if (status = "SAT") then return "SAT"
      if (status = "UNSAT") then return "UNSAT"
      go to RESTART }
   penalty = number of unassigned common variables
   Restore()
   if (penalty < lowest_penalty) then {
      lowest_penalty = penalty
      best_var = Var }
   status = Simplify (Var = 1)
   if (status = "SAT") then return "SAT"
   if (status = "UNSAT") then {// Var must be 0
      Restore()
      status = Simplify (Var = 0)
      if (status = "SAT") then return "SAT"
      if (status = "UNSAT") then return "UNSAT"
      go to RESTART}
   penalty = number of unassigned common variables
   Restore()
   if (penalty ≥ lowest_penalty) then continue
   lowest_penalty = penalty
   best_var = Var
} // all variables analyzed
return "DONE"
}
```

Figure 11. Variable selection.

Table III. Execution times for two subproblems.

A	B	OR	AND
SAT	SAT	$\min(a, b)$	$\max(a, b)$
SAT	UNSAT	a	b
UNSAT	SAT	b	a
UNSAT	UNSAT	$\max(a, b)$	$\min(a, b)$

can stop execution as soon as the first pair of ANDed subproblems found a solution (or as soon as one FPGA from each pair identifies an unsatisfiable subproblem). If we have only 2 available FPGAs, we can solve the problem in at most four rounds of computation.

Table III summarizes the execution time for a pair of subproblems, A and B, obtained by decomposing a common parent problem. The execution time depends on the decomposition type (AND or OR), their results (SAT or UNSAT), and their execution times (denoted by a and b).

Although this is a more powerful decomposition technique, just like simple decomposition, when the target subproblem size is much smaller than the original problem

```
Decompose_to_Partition (formula) {
if (Size() ≤ MAX_SIZE) then { // it fits
   ++nparts
   return "DONE"}
Bipartition (first_subformula, 2nd_subformula)
if (Common_vars = ∅) then { // disjoint subformulas
   status1 = Decompose_to_Partition (first_subformula)
   if (status 1 = "UNSAT") then return "UNSAT"
   status2 = Decompose_to_Partition (2nd_subformula)
   if (status2 = "UNSAT") then return "UNSAT"
   if (status1 = "SAT" and status2 = "SAT") then return "SAT"
   return "DONE"}
// we have common variables
status = Select_best_var()
if (status ≠ "DONE") then return status
Simplify (best_var = 0)
status0 = Decompose_to_Partition (formula)
if (status0 = "SAT") then return "SAT"
Restore()
Simplify (best_var = 1)
status1 = Decompose_to_Partition (formula)
if (status1 = "SAT") then return "SAT"
if (status0 = "UNSAT" and status1 = "UNSAT") then
      return "UNSAT"
return "DONE"
}
```

Figure 12. Decomposition for partitioning.

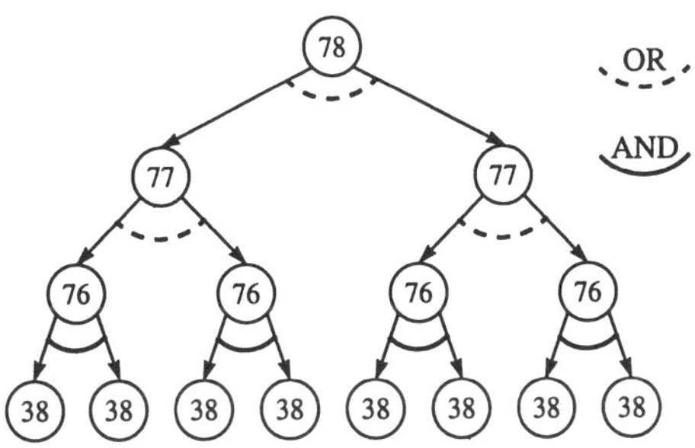

Figure 13. OR/AND decomposition tree for *dubois*26.

size, the procedure may take an excessive time and/or produce too many subproblems. Decomposition for disjoint partitioning attempts to find the leaves in the decomposition tree that contain subproblems with the required size or smaller; in the worst case, we may need to explore an exponential number of branches before finding such leaves. However, increasing the subproblem size significantly speeds up the decomposition and reduces the number of subproblems to solve.

6.3. Hardware Implementation

The block diagram shown in Figure 14 illustrates a possible architecture for a PCI board to implement a satisfier using our virtual logic mechanism. The board is attached to a general-purpose host processor via a PCI bus. The host will use this board to solve computationally expensive SAT problems. The board features a microprocessor (μP), several FPGAs, and RAM for storing configurations.

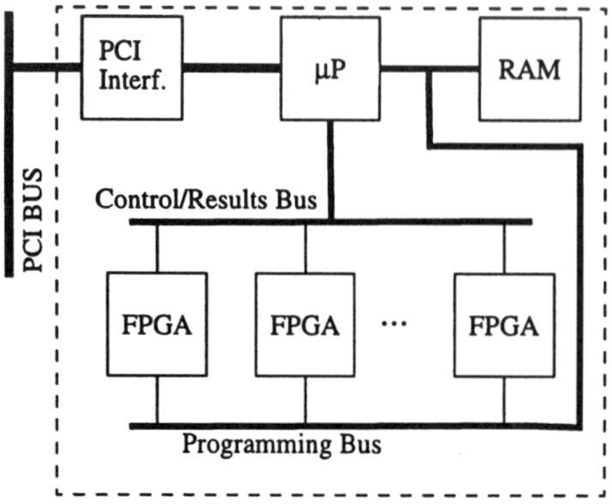

Figure 14. Satisfier board architecture.

The μP controls the virtual logic system, based on the OR/AND decomposition tree. It assigns subproblems to available FPGAs, starts their reconfiguration process, initiates the FPGA operation, and monitors the FPGA completion signals. Every FPGA communicates with the μP using four control signals: (1) *Start*; (2) *Done*; (3) *Satisfied*; and (4) *Stop*. When *Done* is asserted, *Satisfied* indicates whether the subformula assigned to that FPGA has been satisfied or it was proven to be unsatisfiable. *Stop* is used to abort a computation in progress in one FPGA when the μP has already determined that the result of that FPGA is no longer needed in computing the overall result. The four control signals of all FPGAs are bussed. Each FPGA has an address used by the μP to select that FPGA as the destination for *Start* or *Stop*, or to recognize the source of *Done* and *Satisfied*. The same *Control/ Results Bus* is used to retrieve the satisfying vectors computed by different FPGAs. The shared *Programming Bus* carries the configuration data from RAM to the selected FPGA. Since the computation does not require data path connections among FPGAs, this architecture is much simpler than an emulator.

7. Experimental Results

Figure 15 shows the layout of a satisfier for a formula having 13 variables, 29 clauses, and 69 literals, using an XC6264 FPGA. The layout is organized in alternating columns of clause logic and variable/literal logic. The space between these columns is reserved for the complex routing between the ST2 blocks of each variable and the OR2 blocks of each clause. It is this routing between variables and clauses that takes most of the compilation time, since the routing of the ILAs themselves is trivial. Nevertheless, the empty space reserved between columns guarantees efficient routing. No automatic place and route tool would achieve the compilation speed and compactness of this layout. These new features are very important in reconfigurable computing applications. The block in the lower left corner is the Sync. Unit. As can be seen, it represents a small fraction of the whole area, and it does not vary with the SAT instance being solved. The layout took about 3 minutes to be compiled from its original CNF file. In contrast, the unstructured version of the same satisfier (that is, without using ILA-based design) could never be successfully compiled (after 10 hours of CPU time, there were still more than 200 unrouted nets). We determined that a satisfier that occupies the whole chip area can be clocked with a main clock frequency f of about 3.5 MHz. From the small size of this SAT instance we conclude that larger devices, virtual logic schemes, or multiple device architectures are in demand. All these are current

Figure 15. Satisfier layout on XC6264.

Table IV. Comparison with GRASP.

Benchmark	#I	#C	#L	Sat	Time[T]	Time_G[T]	SU
aim100-6_0-yes1-1	100	600	1800	Y	12,388	129,500	10.4
aim200-6_0-yes1-1	200	1200	3600	Y	942,830	2,033,500	2.2
dubois20	60	160	480	N	10,486K	199,500	0.02
hole8	72	297	648	N	259,519	302,834K	1166.9
hole9	90	415	900	N	2,336K	12.3G	5,270.0
hole10	110	561	1210	N	23,357K	>12.6G	>539.3
ii8a2	180	800	2052	Y	60,587	168,000	2.8
ii32c1	225	1280	6081	Y	38	150,500	3960.5
ii32d2	404	5153	17940	Y	31,701	5,586K	176.2
jnh1	100	850	4392	Y	3,879	304,500	78.5
par16-1-c	317	1264	3670	Y	1,133K	748,160K	660.0
par16-2-c	349	1392	4054	Y	703,007	4.93G	7,000.0
par16-5	1015	3358	8980	Y	1,750K	814,415K	465.4
pret60_25	60	160	480	N	28,512K	210,000	0.01
ssa432-003	435	1027	2364	N	86,496	126,000	1.5

research topics; the virtual logic scheme presented in this paper is a step toward these directions.

We ran satisfier circuits for instances that fit in the XC6264 in order to validate a software simulator of our architecture developed in the C language. With this program we were able to obtain the exact times that our satisfier circuits would take to solve larger instances. The simulation time is orders of magnitude slower, which limits the number of examples that can be analyzed in this way. Nevertheless, we managed to simulate enough examples to make the strong points that follow.

We use 25 examples extracted from the DIMACS set of SAT benchmarks [14]. In Table IV we compare the results of our satisfier with GRASP [28], one of the most

Table V. Comparison with [38].

Benchmark	#I	#C	#L	Sat	H	HO	Time[T]	SU
aim-50-1_6-no-3	50	80	240	N	12,854	—	51,900	80
aim-50-1_6-no-2	50	80	240	N	12,854	—	75,415	38
aim-100-1_6-yes1-3	100	160	480	Y	25,554	—	1,711K	>58
aim-100-1_6-no-2	100	160	480	N	25,554	—	6,570K	>15
aim-200-6_0-yes1-1	200	1200	3600	Y	165,354	1.6	942,830	1
hole8	72	297	648	N	32,113	—	259,519	9
hole9	90	415	900	N	44,099	—	2,336K	12
hole10	110	561	1210	N	58,751	2.6	23,357K	>4
ii8a2	180	800	2052	Y	98,166	2.5	60,587	71
ii32d2	404	5153	17940	Y	790,349	—	31,701	27
par16-1-c	317	1264	3670	Y	174,054	2.1	1,134K	1
ssa432-003	435	1027	2364	N	124,277	1.1	86,496	1

efficient software SAT solvers available. We emphasize that these results are obtained without decomposition. The first 5 columns in Table IV show the benchmark data: name, number of inputs #I, number of clauses #C, number of literals #L, and a Yes/No indication of satisfiability. The following columns show the time taken by our satisfier in number of main clock cycles T, the time taken by GRASP using the same time unit, and the speedup SU gained with our approach. (For a meaningful comparison, we ignored instances for which runtimes were very short.) The main clock frequency is 3.5 MHz. GRASP was run on a Sun Ultra SPARC workstation with 1026 Mb RAM using a 248 MHz clock. Thus GRASP is running with a clock about 83 times faster than the emulation clock. Unlike in [39], where GRASP was run in a restricted mode, so that it matched the features implemented in hardware, we allowed GRASP to run "full speed," using all its sophisticated techniques. These include clause addition based on conflict analysis, nonchronological backtracking, heuristics for decision making, etc. Our experience has shown that for many instances, the restrictive mode slows down GRASP by several orders of magnitude. GRASP was allowed to run each example for up to one hour (equivalent to 12.6G clock cycles on our satisfier), before aborting the execution (only *hole*10 was aborted by GRASP). For 10 examples out of the 15 included in Table IV, our satisfier achieved significant speedups between 78 and 7,000, and for 3 instances the speedup was in the 1.5 to 2.8 range. For 2 examples GRASP was faster than our satisfier. This is due to its sophisticated search features that do not have a match in our satisfier. However, if we also use decomposition, our satisfier will be faster in most cases. Nevertheless we envision our satisfier not as a replacement of, but as complement to, software SAT solvers.

Table V shows a comparison with the reconfigurable hardware satisfier described in [38]. To reproduce their results, we simply switched off our capabilities for identifying dead variables and implying dynamically unate variables, which are not implemented in [38]. As the variable order is the same, this would produce a fair comparison but for the mechanism for implication undoing. It is unclear in [38] how implications are undone. It seems *all* implications are cleared, not only the ones resulting from the last decision, and all the previous decisions are re-implied when the last decision is modified. If this is the case, the comparison presented here is favorable to [38], since we undo only the implications of the last decision, and we do it in a single clock cycle. Column H

Table VI. Results with decomposition.

Example	#I	#C	#L	Sat	$\#P_d$	$\#P_{dp}$
dubois50	150	400	1200	N	>1024	46
dubois100	300	800	2400	N	>1024	320
hole7	56	204	448	N	12	13
hole8	72	297	648	N	99	128
ii8a1	66	186	450	Y	2	3
par8-2-c	68	270	780	Y	1	10
par8-5-c	75	298	864	Y	0	1
pret60_25	60	160	480	N	>1024	64
pret60_40	60	160	480	N	>1024	64

represents the "hardware cost" of our satisfier, defined as in [38] as the total number gates and flip-flops. *HO* is the ratio of *H* to the corresponding cost in [38], given only for the examples that are common in the two papers. Our hardware cost is between 1.1 and 2.6 times greater than [38]. However, this buys us 1 to 2 orders of magnitude speedup, as illustrated by the last two columns in Table V. Again, these results did not take advantage of decomposition. Also, we are not including the speedup that results from our faster compilation time: according to [38], their compilation time for one FPGA is about 40 minutes, one order of magnitude greater than our 3 minutes.

Finally, we address one of the difficult problems in reconfigurable computing - size. In fact, none of the instances we analyzed can completely fit in a XC6264 device. In [38] an IKOS emulator was used, so that an instance can be mapped to multiple FPGA devices. This is an expensive solution given the price of emulators and the time required to partition the problem into multiple devices. In [38] it was reported that this step requires an additional compilation time in the order of tens of minutes. This severely restricts the range of instances where the approach can be useful compared to software SAT solvers.

In this work our goal was to find a cheaper and therefore more useful solution to this problem. The result was the decomposition techniques explained in Section 6. The maximum FPGA size MAX_SIZE was set to 300 literals, and we looked at examples that could be quickly (10 minutes at maximum) decomposed in at most 1024 parts. The decomposition results are summarized in Table VI, where $\#P_d$ is the number of parts (subproblems) obtained with the simple decomposition technique, and $\#P_{dp}$ is the number of parts obtained with decomposition for disjoint partitioning, As we can see, in four examples the simple decomposition was aborted when the number of FPGAs passed the 1,024 limit, while decomposition for disjoint partitioning completed in all cases with a reasonably small number of parts. The problems where the simple decomposition obtained few parts are characterized by the presence of variables whose assignment contributes to significantly simplifying the formula without contributing toward achieving disjoint subproblems. In the future, we plan to combine the two methods to create an adaptive procedure that will dynamically switch between the two types of decomposition to take advantage of the benefits of each.

Another benefit of decomposition for disjoint partitioning is the fact that the resulting subproblems are much simpler and can run much faster than the original problem. Note that the number of variables in each disjoint part is significantly lower than the number of variables in the original problem. We observed that a subproblem can run 3 orders of magnitude faster than the original problem. Since there is a cost associated with decomposition, this acceleration can help compensate the cost incurred in decomposition. When the original problem is hard to solve, the speedup due to decomposition may decrease the overall computation time, even when the decomposition time is accounted for. However, further investigations are needed to determine which type of instance will benefit from this potential speedup.

8. New Directions

The satisfier architecture and the virtual logic scheme contributed by this research are just one of the few achievements in a promising and exciting new area: algorithms on reconfigurable hardware. In particular for SAT, many interesting aspects are still to be explored. It is the objective of this section to discuss some of these new directions.

8.1. Nondisjoint Partitioning

Both simple decomposition and decomposition for disjoint partitioning aim at producing independent subproblems that can be run by independent devices, concurrently or serially. However, the ability to do so depends on the *personality* of the instance. Some instances lend themselves better to these decomposition techniques than others. Not being able to handle instances whose personality is averse to these techniques represents a limitation in the usefulness of our approach.

To handle instances that resist decomposition by our techniques, we consider nondisjoint partition, that is, the decomposition in dependent subproblems. Suppose in decomposition for disjoint partition we obtain a residual set of common variables but, because we have exhausted our decomposition resources, we cannot proceed any further. One possible solution is to put these two parts in separate devices, and connect the devices with the necessary wires to carry the assignments to the common variables. Because we assumed a small number of common variables, we know only a few connections will be needed. This is not as general as full multi-FPGA partitioning, but is cheaper and enables handling more examples than with just our decomposition techniques. However, we would still have the disadvantages of communication across chips, longer delays, more complex hardware, and so on.

We are also looking into solving the dependent problems using the same platform. This would be accomplished in the following way: we would run one of the subproblems until we need to assign some of the common variables. Then we would swap the subproblems, while leaving on the platform the data concerning the common variables. The second subproblem would start running using these data, and generating its own, until more common variables are hit again. The first subproblem would be swapped in again and so on until the problem is solved. However, the overhead of swapping contexts may be excessive if the whole device need be reconfigured (current devices take tens of milliseconds for complete reconfiguration). One technology advance that can make this solution extremely attractive is the emergence of context switching FPGAs [32, 26]. Such devices can store different configurations or contexts in RAM, and switch between them in one clock cycle. In our case, switching between different SAT subproblems would become a trivial matter.

8.2. *Algorithmic Improvements*

The algorithm implemented by our architecture executes a basic SAT search, incorporating only the minimal features of trying variable assignments in a fixed order, computing implications (Boolean constraint propagations), avoiding branching on dead (irrelevant) variables and implying unate variables (pure literal rule). The architecture exploits the sheer speed of hardware and massive parallelism, rather than algorithmic sophistication. Nonetheless, if more algorithmic refinements can be introduced, while still maintaining the advantages of simplicity and massive parallelism, even more speed can be attained.

Whenever several subproblems must be concurrently solved, a general principle is to first solve the most difficult one, since solving easier problems first may be wasted effort. Of course, applying this principle depends on having good heuristic measures of "difficulty". In SAT, we can regard satisfying each clause as a subproblem, and consider the number of unassigned variables of a clause as an inverse measure of difficulty. One algorithmic improvement that we have been working on is a heuristic that favors decisions on variables feeding clauses having a small number of nondead literals. The objective mechanism is used to implement yet another priority level that signals these short clauses. In the simplest case we can signal only clauses containing two (nondead) literals. The clause would send, say, an objective LO+ instead of LO. This LO+ objective is accordingly merged with other objectives at the stem circuits, finally reaching the variables that will be given priority over the potential conflicts in the selection of the next decision variable. Such a heuristic is a variation of the well-known Jeroslaw–Wang heuristic [19], which is known to produce good results. This heuristic will require more hardware resources, of course, but will enhance the characteristics of massive parallelism.

A powerful algorithmic improvement introduced with GRASP [28] is the diagnosis of conflicting variable assignments. This analysis permits determining the variables that are responsible for the conflict, and enables (1) backtracking on the last assigned of these variables rather than on the last variable assigned (nonchronological backtracking), and (2) creating additional clauses from these variables, which will prevent the conflict from happening again (clause addition). In [38] a weak version of nonchronological backtracking in reconfigurable hardware is discussed. A considerable hardware overhead is needed for this scheme. A more plausible implementation of a complete conflict diagnosis procedure leading to both nonchronological backtracking and clause addition is put forward in [40]. Nonetheless, that scheme sacrifices massive parallelism and ignores dynamic variable selection. To be able to match the algorithmic sophistication of GRASP and add hardware acceleration and massive parallelism, we also need clever heuristics for dynamic variable selection.

8.3. *Multidevice Architectures*

The basic problem of SAT on reconfigurable hardware is a space problem. Solving large SAT problems requires more hardware resources than can be found in any single FPGA device. Thus a multiple device architecture for SAT appears necessary. This is not a substitute for the virtual logic schemes we have studied; it is rather a complement. The virtual logic mechanism can use a multidevice structure instead of one chip to solve one subproblem. This means that it would be able to handle larger parts, exponentially increasing the usefulness of our decomposition techniques.

The size problem also motivated the architecture described in [40]. This architecture uses multiple FPGA devices assembled in a pipelined ring. Each FPGA in this ring constitutes a processing element (PE) that implements a set of clauses. The variables circulate around the ring and get updated as they go along. One of the elements in the ring is a main control unit responsible for monitoring the global state of execution and selecting the next decision variable. This architecture has several advantages. Each PE is a shallow stage of logic, which can be clocked much faster (a frequency of 20 MHz is estimated). The need to route variables to clauses disappears, as variables become abstract entities. This contributes to structuring the layout, greatly improving the compilation time. Finally, and most important, the architecture is suitable for implementing dynamic addition of clauses derived by conflict diagnosis, using dynamic configurations. Despite these advantages, this architecture sacrifices the massive parallelism available in reconfigurable logic, and thus its scalability is questionable.

Our approach is to keep the massive parallelism of our architecture and to solve the size problem by extending the applicability of our decomposition technique. Instead of assigning a subproblem to one FPGA, we will assign it to a group of connected FPGAs. The virtual logic feature will result from the lack of connections among these groups. This will keep the cost lower compared with an emulation architecture. Our goal is a low-cost FPGA board that users can simply plug into their personal computers.

9. Conclusions

In this paper we have introduced a *new satisfier architecture*, using *new forms of fine-grain massive parallelism* to accelerate a SAT solver implemented on reconfigurable hardware: *parallel backtracing of multiple objectives along all possible paths and concurrent assignments of several variables.* This massive parallel processing is facilitated by *objective propagation with several different priorities.* One result of objective propagation is the identification of all the "dead parts" of a CNF formula, which in turn allows the satisfier to recognize *dynamically unate variables* and *dead variables*. These techniques generate more implications, avoid wrong and unnecessary decisions, and reduce the amount of back-tracking, thus providing significant speedups. Our results show several orders of magnitude speedup compared with both a state-of-the-art software SAT solver and a previous satisfier.

We have developed *modular design techniques using ILA structures.* These techniques result in *compilation time that grows only linearly with the size of the problem,* hence overcoming the high computational costs of conventional FPGA physical design tools. While an unstructured chip design ends up with many unrouted nets after 10–12 hours of CPU time, the same *circuit using ILA-based design techniques takes only a few minutes to successfully compile.* These techniques are applicable to any type of FPGA, and the reduction in compilation time they provide becomes even more significant when we need to compile a large number of FPGAs. Another advantage of the ILA-based approach is its *inherent scalability.*

We have introduced a *new virtual logic system for solving satisfiability problems using reconfigurable hardware.* We combine a simple decomposition method with a formula partition technique to create a *decomposition for disjoint partition.* This novel technique can effectively divide a formula into independent subproblems that can be concurrently run by multiple FPGAs.The unusual feature of our decomposition is that *inter-FPGA signals are never required.* Unlike the multi-FPGA partitioning used in a conventional design flow, our decomposition is a much faster algorithm, since it does not need to know how the FPGAs are interconnected in our platform. In fact, it is independent of the reconfigurable hardware platform, so it may be easily used on any emulator without using its inter-FPGA communication structures. But since it does not require any inter-FPGA routing, it can work on a platform much simpler and cheaper than an emulator. Also the clock frequency may be higher, because we avoid the delays involved in propagating signals off-chip, on the board, and back on-chip.

The decomposition algorithm is such that often the resulting subproblems can be serially run much faster than the original problem. This is a consequence of the sophisticated dynamic variable selection used by the algorithm. It is also the key to our *virtual logic mechanism*, which allows a reconfigurable logic platform to process circuits much larger than its available capacity. Although the sum of the size of the subproblems is greater than the size of the original problem, the summation of the execution times is often smaller than the execution of the original problem. The FPGAs can be run concurrently, introducing a new level of coarse-grain parallelism, and resulting in up to three orders of magnitude additional speedup. This comes from the disjoint partitioning of the search space. Our architecture is easily scalable, since all we need to handle larger problems is additional or larger FPGAs. Combined with our fine-grain massively parallel satisfier architecture, the virtual logic for SAT has the potential to offer a low-cost solution for solving computationally difficult problems in a wide variety of fields.

Acknowledgment

We acknowledge useful discussions with Prof. D. Saab on early versions of these ideas.

References

1. Abramovici, M., Breuer, M. A. and Friedman, A. D.: *Digital Systems Testing and Testable Design*, IEEE Press, 1995.
2. Abramovici, M. and Saab, D.: Satisfiability on reconfigurable hardware, in *Proc. Intn'l. Workshop on Field-Programmable Logic and Applications*, Sept. 1997.
3. Abramovici, M., Sousa, J. and Saab, D.: A massively-parallel easily-scalable satisfiability solver using reconfigurable hardware, in *Proc. Design Automation Conf.*, June 1999.
4. Abramovici, M. and de Sousa, J. T.: A virtual logic system for solving satisfiability problems using reconfigurable hardware, in *Proc. Symp. on Field-Programmable Custom Computing Machines*, April 1999.
5. Babb, J., Frank, M. and Agarwal, A.: Solving graph problems with dynamic computation structures, in *SPIE Photonics East: Reconfigurable Technology for Rapid Product Development & Computing*, November 1996, pp. 225–236.
6. Babb, J., Tessier, R. and Agarwal, A.: Virtual wires: Overcoming pin limitations in FPGA-based logic emulators, in *Proc. Symp. on Field-Programmable Custom Computing Machines*, April 1993, pp. 142–151.
7. Bohm, M. and Speckenmeyer, E.: A fast parallel SAT solver: Efficient workload balancing, *Ann. Math. Artificial Intelligence* **17**(3–4) (1996), 381–400.
8. Brayton, R., Hachtel, G., McMullen, C. and Sangiovanni-Vincentelli, A.: *Logic Minimization Algorithms for VLSI Synthesis*, Kluwer Academic Publishers, 1984.
9. Chakradhar, S. T. and Agrawal, V. D.: A novel VLSI solution to a difficult graph problem, in *Proc. Intn.l. Symp. on VLSI Design*, January 1990, pp. 124–129.
10. Cook, S. A.: The complexity of theorem-proving procedures, in *Proc. 3rd Annual ACM Symp. on Theory of Computation*, 1971, pp. 151–158.
11. Davis, M. and Putnam, H.: A computing procedure for quantification theory, *J. ACM* **7** (1960), 167–187.
12. Devadas, S.: Optimal layout via boolean satisfiability, in *Proc. Intn'l. Conf. on CAD*, November 1989, pp. 294–297.
13. Devadas, S., Keutzer, K., Malik, S. and Wang, A.: Certified timing verification and the transition delay of a logic circuit, in *Proc. Design Automation Conf.*, June 1992, pp. 549–555.
14. DIMACS Challenge Benchmarks, *ftp://dimacs.rutgers.edu/pub/challenge/sat/benchmarks/cnf/*.

15. Fujiwara, H. and Shimono, T.: On the acceleration of test generation algorithms, *IEEE Trans. Comput.* **C-32**(12), December 1983, pp. 1137–1144.
16. Gately, J. et al.: UltraSPARC-I emulation, in *Proc. Design Automation Conf.* June 1995, pp. 13–18.
17. Goel, P.: An implicit enumeration algorithm to generate tests for combinational logic circuits, *IEEE Trans. Comput.* **C-30**(3), March 1981, pp. 215–222.
18. Gu, J.: Satisfiability problems in VLSI engineering, in *DIMACS Workshop on Satisfiability Problem: Theory and Applications*, March 1996.
19. Gu, J., Purdom, P. W., Franco, J. and Wah, B. W.: Algorithms for the satisfiability (SAT) problem: A survey, in *DIMACS Workshop on Satisfiability Problem: Theory and Applications*, March 1996, pp. 19–51.
20. Gu, J. and Puri, R.: Asynchronous circuit synthesis with boolean satisfiability, *IEEE Trans. on CAD* **14**(8) (1995), pp. 961–973.
21. Larrabee, T.: Test pattern generation using boolean satisfiability, *IEEE Trans. on CAD* **11**(1) (1992), pp. 4–15.
22. McGeer, P. C. et al.: Timing analysis and delay-fault test generation using path recursive functions, in *Proc. Intn'l. Conf. on CAD*, November 1991, pp. 180–183.
23. *http://www.icube.com/prodpage/ProdPage.html*, I-Cube Co.
24. Platzner, M. and De Micheli, G.: Acceleration of satisfiability algorithms by reconfigurable hardware, in *Proc. Intn'l. Workshop on Field-Programmable Logic and Applications*, Sept. 1998.
25. Rashid, A., Leonard, J. and Mangione-Smith, W. H.: Dynamic circuit generation for solving specific problem instances of boolean satisfiability, in *Proc. Symp. on Field-Programmable Custom Computing Machines*, April 1998, pp. 196–204.
26. Scalera, S. M. and Vazquez, J. R.: The design and implementation of a context switching FPGA, in *Proc. Symp. on Field-Programmable Custom Computing Machines*, April 1998, pp. 78–85.
27. Silva, J. M.: An overview of backtrack search satisfiability algorithms, in *Proc. 5th Intn'l. Symp. on Artificial Intelligence and Mathematics,* January 1998.
28. Silva, J. M. and Sakallah, K. A.: GRASP – A new search algorithm for satisfiability, in *Proc. Intn'l. Conf. on CAD*, November 1996, pp. 220–227.
29. L. G. Silva et al.: Realistic delay modeling in satisfiability-based timing analysis, in *Proc. Intn'l. Symp. on Circuits and Systems (ISCAS)*, May 1998.
30. Stephan, P. R., Brayton, R. K. and Sangiovanni-Vincentelli, A.: Combinational test generation using satisfiability, *IEEE Trans. on CAD* **15**(9) (1996), 1167–1176.
31. Suyama, T., Yokoo, M. and Sawada, H.: Solving satisfiability problems on FPGAs, in *Proc. Intn'l. Workshop on Field-Programmable Logic and Applications,* 1996.
32. Trimberger, S., Carberry, D., Johnson, A. and Wong, J.: A time-multiplexed FPGA, in *Proc. Symp. on Field-Programmable Custom Computing Machines*, April 1997.
33. Varghese, J., Butts, M. and Batchller, J.: An efficient logic emulation system, *IEEE Trans. on VLSI* **1**(2) (1993), 171–174.
34. Vuillemin, J. et al.: Programmable active memories: reconfigurable systems come of age, *IEEE Trans. on VLSI Systems*, March 1996.
35. Wood, R. G. and Rutenbar, R. A.: FPGA routing and routability estimation via Boolean satisfiability, in *Proc. Intn'l. Symp. on FPGAs*, February 1997.
36. Wu, Y. and Adham, S.: BIST fault diagnosis in scan-based VLSI environments, in *Proc. Intn'l. Test Conf.*, October 1996, pp. 48–57.
37. *XC6200 Field-Programmable Gate Arrays*, Xilinx, June 1996.
38. Zhong, P., Martonosi, M., Ashar, P. and Malik, S.: Accelerating Boolean satisfiability with configurable hardware, in *Proc. Symp. on Field-Programmable Custom Computing Machines*, April 1998.
39. Zhong, P., Martonosi, M., Ashar, P. and Malik, S.: Using reconfigurable computing techniques to accelerate problems in the CAD domain: A case study with Boolean satisfiability, in *Proc. Design Automation Conf.*, June 1998.
40. Zhong, P., Martonosi, M., Ashar, P. and Malik, S.: Solving Boolean satisfiability with dynamic hardware configurations, in *Proc. Intn'l. Workshop on Field-Programmable Logic and Applications*, Sept. 1998.

SAT2000
I. Gent et al. (Eds.)
IOS Press, 2000

SAT-Based Decision Procedures for Classical Modal Logics

Enrico Giunchiglia
DIST, V.le Causa 13, 16145 Genova, Italy

Fausto Giunchiglia
DISA, Università di Trento., IRST, 38050 Povo, Trento, Italy

Armando Tacchella
DIST, V.le Causa 13, 16145 Genova, Italy

Abstract. We present a set of SAT-based decision procedures for various classical modal logics. By SAT-based, we mean built on top of a SAT solver. We show how the SAT-based approach allows for a modular implementation for these logics. For some of the logics we deal with, we are not aware of any other implementation. For the others, we define a testing methodology which generalizes the $3CNF_K$ methodology by Giunchiglia and Sebastiani. The experimental evaluation shows that our decision procedures perform better than or as well as other state-of-the-art decision procedures.

1. Introduction

Propositional reasoning is a fundamental problem in many areas of Computer Science. Many researchers have put, and still put, years of effort in the design and implementation of new and more powerful SAT solvers. Most importantly, the source code of many of these implementations is freely available and can be used as a basis for the development of decision procedures for more expressive logics (see, e.g., [14, 3]).

In this paper, we present a set of SAT-based decision procedures for various classical modal logics [26, 32]. By SAT-based, we mean built on top of a SAT solver. We show how the SAT-based approach allows for a modular implementation for these logics. For some of the logics we deal with, we are not aware of any other implementation. For the others, we define a testing methodology which generalizes the $3CNF_K$ methodology by Giunchiglia and Sebastiani [14]. The experimental evaluation shows that our decision procedures perform better than or as well as other state-of-the-art decision procedures.

Our approach, first suggested by Giunchiglia and Sebastiani [16], consists of two steps:

1. take off the shelf one of the fastest SAT procedures available, and

2. use it as the basis for your modal decider.

Our approach differs from most of the previous works in decision procedures for modal logics, which are either tableau-based, (i.e., based on Smullyan's tableau for propositional logic [34]: see, e.g., [9, 25, 1]), or translation-based (i.e., based on a reduction to first order logic: see, e.g., [37, 27, 22]). Some of the differences and advantages of the SAT-based approach with respect to the tableau based and translation based approaches have been already pointed out in [15, 16]. Here we show how the SAT-based approach provides for a simple and natural schema for the development of decision procedures for modal logics.

Our approach differs also from the approaches by Horrocks [21] and Patel-Schneider [28]. These authors developed their own SAT checker and used it as a basis for their modal decider. This approach allows for a better integration among the different modules of the system and for a finer tuning of the reasoning strategies. On the other hand, it does not exploit the great amount of ongoing work on SAT deciders. Each year, new and faster SAT engines are proposed. With some standard modifications of the source code we can inherit in the modal setting all the benefits of state-of-the-art propositional checkers.[1]

Finally, our system, called *SAT, improves also on previous works by Sebastiani and ourselves [14, 15, 16]. In particular,

- *SAT is built on top of the SAT decider SATO [40]. *SAT inherits many of the SATO configurable options, and allows for some more options (including early pruning, caching, two forms of backjumping, and the choice of various splitting heuristics); and

- *SAT is able to deal with 8 modal logics, namely E, EM (=M), EN, EMN, EC, EMC (=R), ECN, EMCN (=K) (see [4]). For EN, EMN, EC and ECN, we do not know of any other implemented decision procedure, nor of any reduction to a formalism for which a decision procedure is available.

The paper is structured as follows. In Section 2 we review some basic definitions about classical modal logics. Then, in Section 3, we present the idea of the SAT-based approach to modal reasoning, and discuss in detail the algorithms for the 8 logics we consider. Section 4 is devoted to *SAT: it discusses some of the motivations underlying its construction, and some of its features. The experimental analysis comparing *SAT with other state-of-the-art decision procedures is done in Section 5. Our analysis is restricted to K (for which there are several systems available) and E (for which there exists a reduction to bimodal K). We end in Section 6 with the conclusions and the future work.

2. Classical modal logics

Following [4], a *modal logic* is a set of formulas (called *theorems*) closed under tautological consequence. Most modal logics are closed under the rule

$$\frac{(\varphi_1 \wedge \ldots \wedge \varphi_n) \supset \psi}{(\Box\varphi_1 \wedge \ldots \wedge \Box\varphi_n) \supset \Box\psi}$$

for certain values of n. If $n = 1$ then the logic is said to be *monotone*. If $n = 2$ then the logic is said to be *regular*. If $n \geq 0$ then the logic is said to be *normal*. The smallest monotone, regular and normal modal logics are called M, R and K respectively (see, e.g., [4]).

Classical modal logics [26, 32] are weaker than normal modal logics. In fact, the only requirement is that the set of theorems is closed under the rule

$$\frac{\varphi \equiv \psi}{\Box\varphi \equiv \Box\psi}.$$

As a consequence, the schemas

[1] A similar point is made by Kautz and Selman [24] as an explanation for the better performances of SATPLAN with respect to specialized engines for planning problems.

N: $\Box\top$,[2]

M: $\Box(\varphi \wedge \psi) \supset \Box\varphi$,

C: $(\Box\varphi \wedge \Box\psi) \supset \Box(\varphi \wedge \psi)$,

which are theorems in K do not necessarily hold in classical modal logics. The three principles N, M, and C enforce closure conditions on the set of provable formulas which are not always desirable, especially if the $\Box$ operator has an epistemic (such as knowledge or belief) reading. If we interpret $\Box\varphi$ as "a certain agent a believes φ", then N enforces that a believes all the logical truths, M that a's beliefs are closed under logical consequence, and C that a's beliefs are closed under conjunction. These three closure properties are different forms of omniscience, and —as such— they are not appropriate for modeling the beliefs of a real agent (see, e.g., [13] and [8] Chapter 9). We can easily imagine situations involving a's beliefs, where only an arbitrary subset of the above properties holds.

There are eight possible ways to add the three schemas M, C, and N to the smallest classical modal logic E. The resulting modal logics are called E, EM (equivalent to the logic M), EN, EMN, EC, EMC (equivalent to R), ECN, EMCN (equivalent to K), where EX denotes the logic obtained adding the schemas in X to E.

3. SAT-based procedures for classical modal logics

We say that a conjunction μ of propositional literals and formulas of the form $\Box\varphi$ or $\neg\Box\varphi$ is an *assignment* if, for any pair ψ, ψ' of conjuncts in μ, it is not the case that $\psi = \neg\psi'$. An assignment μ *satisfies* a formula φ if μ entails φ by propositional reasoning. A formula φ is *consistent* in a logic L (or L-*consistent*) if $\neg\varphi$ is not a theorem of L, i.e., if $\neg\varphi \notin$ L.

Consider a formula φ. Let S be a set of assignments satisfying φ, and let L be a modal logic. As noticed by Sebastiani and Giunchiglia [31], the following two facts hold:

- If at least one assignment in S is L-consistent then φ is L-consistent.

- If no assignment in S is L-consistent then φ is not L-consistent as long as the set S is *complete for* φ, i.e., as long as the disjunction of the assignments in S is propositionally equivalent to φ.

From these facts, it follows that the problem of determining whether φ is L-consistent can be decomposed in two steps:

- *generate* an assignment μ satisfying φ, and

- *test* whether μ is L-consistent.

In all the logics we consider, testing the consistency of an assignment μ amounts to determining the consistency of other formulas whose depth (i.e., the maximum number of nested $\Box$ operators) is strictly minor than the depth of μ. This implies that we can check the consistency of these other formulas by recursively applying the above methodology, at the same time ensuring the termination of the overall process. The above methodology can be implemented by two mutually recursive procedures:

[2] The symbols $\top$ and $\bot$ are 0-ary connectives representing truth and falsity respectively.

- $\text{LSAT}(\varphi)$ for the generation of assignments satisfying φ, and
- $\text{LCONSIST}(\mu)$ for testing the L-consistency of each generated assignment μ.

In order to simplify the presentation, we first present $\text{LCONSIST}(\mu)$, and then $\text{LSAT}(\varphi)$.

3.1. $\text{LCONSIST}(\mu)$

Whether an assignment is consistent, depends on the particular logic L being considered. Furthermore, depending on the logic L considered, the consistency problem for L (i.e., determining whether a formula is consistent in L) belongs to different complexity classes. In particular, the consistency problem for E, EM, EN, EMN is NP-complete, while for EC, ECN, EMC, EMCN it is PSPACE-complete (see [38, 8]). Here, to save space, we divide these eight logics in two groups. We present the algorithms for checking the L-consistency of an assignment first in the case in which L is one of E, EM, EN, EMN, and then in the case in which L is one of the others.

3.1.1. *Logics E, EM, EN, EMN*

The following Proposition is an easy consequence of the results presented in [38].

PROPOSITION 1. *Let $\mu = \bigwedge_i \Box\alpha_i \wedge \bigwedge_j \neg\Box\beta_j \wedge \gamma$ be an assignment in which γ is a propositional formula. Let L be one of the logics E, EM, EN, EMN. μ is consistent in L if for each conjunct $\neg\Box\beta_j$ in μ one of the following conditions is satisfied:*

- *$(\alpha_i \equiv \neg\beta_j)$ is L-consistent for each conjunct $\Box\alpha_i$ in μ, and L=E;*
- *$(\alpha_i \wedge \neg\beta_j)$ is L-consistent for each conjunct $\Box\alpha_i$ in μ, and L=EM;*
- *$\neg\beta_j$ and $(\alpha_i \equiv \neg\beta_j)$ are L-consistent for each conjunct $\Box\alpha_i$ in μ, and L=EN;*
- *$\neg\beta_j$ and $(\alpha_i \wedge \neg\beta_j)$ are L-consistent for each conjunct $\Box\alpha_i$ in μ, and L=EMN.*

When implementing the above conditions, care must be taken in order to avoid repetitions of consistency checks. In fact, while an exponential number of assignments satisfying the input formula can be generated by LSAT, at most n^2 checks are possible in L, where n is the number of "$\Box$" in the input formula. Given this upper bound, for each new consistency check, we can cache the result for a future possible re-utilization in a $n \times n$ matrix M. This ensures that at most n^2 consistency checks will be performed. In more detail, given an enumeration $\varphi_1, \varphi_2, \ldots, \varphi_n$ of the boxed subformulas of the input formula, M[i,j], with $i \neq j$, stores the result of the consistency check for $(\varphi_i \wedge \neg\varphi_j)$. M[i,i] stores the result of the consistency check for $\neg\varphi_i$. Initially, each element of the matrix M has value *Undef* (meaning that the corresponding test has not been done yet). The result is the procedure LCONSIST in Figure 1.

Consider Figure 1 and assume that L=E or L=EN. Given a pair of conjuncts $\Box\alpha_i$ and $\neg\Box\beta_j$, we split the consistency test for $(\alpha_i \equiv \neg\beta_j)$ in two simpler sub-tests:

- first, we test whether $(\alpha_i \wedge \neg\beta_j)$ is consistent, and
- only if this test gives *False*, we test whether $(\neg\alpha_i \wedge \beta_j)$ is consistent.

Notice also that, in case L=EN or L=EMN, if we know that, e.g., $(\alpha_i \wedge \neg\beta_j)$ is consistent, then also $\neg\beta_j$ is consistent and we store this result in M[j,j].

```
function LCONSIST(⋀_i □α_i ∧ ⋀_j ¬□β_j ∧ γ)
  foreach conjunct □β_j do
    foreach conjunct □α_i do
      if M[i,j] = Undef then M[i,j] := LSAT(α_i ∧ ¬β_j);
      if L ∈ {EN,EMN} and M[i,j] = True then M[j,j] := True;
      if L ∈ {E,EN} and M[i,j] = False then
        if M[j,i] = Undef then M[j,i] := LSAT(¬α_i ∧ β_j);
        if L = EN and M[j,i] = True then M[i,i] := True;
        if M[j,i] = False then return False
    end
    if L ∈ {EN,EMN} then
      if M[j,j] = Undef then M[j,j] := LSAT(¬β_j);
      if M[j,j] = False then return False
  end;
  return True.
```

Figure 1. LCONSIST for E, EM, EN, EMN

PROPOSITION 2. *Let* $\mu = \bigwedge_i \Box\alpha_i \wedge \bigwedge_j \neg\Box\beta_j \wedge \gamma$ *be an assignment in which* γ *is a propositional formula. Let L be one of the logics E, EM, EN, EMN. Assume that, for any formula* φ *whose depth is less than the depth of* μ, LSAT(φ)

- *returns True if* φ *is L-consistent, and*

- *False otherwise.*

LCONSIST(μ) *returns True if* μ *is L-consistent, and False otherwise.*

Proof: The Proposition is an easy consequence of the hypotheses and Proposition 1. ♠

3.1.2. *Logics EC, ECN, EMC, EMCN*

The following Proposition is an easy consequence of the results presented in [38].

PROPOSITION 3. *Let* $\mu = \bigwedge_i \Box\alpha_i \wedge \bigwedge_j \neg\Box\beta_j \wedge \gamma$ *be an assignment in which* γ *is a propositional formula. Let* Δ *be the set of formulas* α_i *such that* $\Box\alpha_i$ *is a conjunct of* μ. *Let L be one of logics EC, ECN, EMC, EMCN.* μ *is consistent in L if for each conjunct* $\neg\Box\beta_j$ *in* μ *one of the following conditions is satisfied:*

- $((\bigwedge_{\alpha_i \in \Delta'} \alpha_i) \equiv \neg\beta_j)$ *is L-consistent for each non empty subset* Δ' *of* Δ, *and L=EC;*

- $((\bigwedge_{\alpha_i \in \Delta'} \alpha_i) \equiv \neg\beta_j)$ *is L-consistent for each subset* Δ' *of* Δ, *and L=ECN;*

- Δ *is empty or* $((\bigwedge_{\alpha_i \in \Delta} \alpha_i) \wedge \neg\beta_j)$ *is L-consistent, and L=EMC;*

- $((\bigwedge_{\alpha_i \in \Delta} \alpha_i) \wedge \neg\beta_j)$ *is L-consistent, and L=EMCN.*

```
function LCONSIST(⋀_i □α_i ∧ ⋀_j ¬□β_j ∧ γ)
  Δ := {α_i | □α_i is a conjunct of μ};
  foreach conjunct □β_j do
    Δ' := Δ;
    if L ∈ {EC, ECN} then
      foreach conjunct □α_i do
        if M[j,i] = Undef then M[j,i] := LSAT(¬α_i ∧ β_j);
        if M[j,i] = True then Δ' = Δ' \ {α_i}
      end;
    if L ∈ {ECN, EMCN} or Δ' ≠ ∅ then
      if not LSAT(⋀_{α_i∈Δ'} α_i ∧ ¬β_j) then return False
  end;
  return True.
```

Figure 2. LCONSIST for EC, ECN, EMC (R), EMCN (K)

Assume that L=EC or L=ECN. The straightforward implementation of the corresponding condition may lead to an exponential number of checks in the cardinality $|\Delta|$ of Δ. More carefully, for each conjunct $\neg\Box\beta_j$ in μ, we can perform at most $|\Delta| + 1$ checks if

1. for each formula α_i in Δ, we first check whether $(\neg\alpha_i \wedge \beta_j)$ is consistent in L. Let Δ' be the set of formulas for which the above test fails. Then,

2. in case L=ECN or $\Delta' \neq \emptyset$, we perform the last test, checking whether $((\bigwedge_{\alpha_i \in \Delta'} \alpha_i) \wedge \neg\beta_j)$ is consistent in L.

Furthermore, the result of the consistency checks performed in the first step can be cached in a matrix M analogous to the one used in the previous subsection.

If L=EC or L=ECN, the procedure LCONSIST in Figure 2 implements the above ideas. Otherwise, it is a straightforward implementation of the conditions in Proposition 3.

PROPOSITION 4. *Let* $\mu = \bigwedge_i \Box\alpha_i \wedge \bigwedge_j \neg\Box\beta_j \wedge \gamma$ *be an assignment in which* γ *is a propositional formula. Let L be one of logics EC, ECN, EMC, EMCN. Assume that, for any formula* φ *whose depth is less than the depth of* μ, LSAT(φ)

- *returns True if* φ *is L-consistent, and*

- *False otherwise.*

LCONSIST(μ) *returns True if* μ *is L-consistent, and False otherwise.*

Proof: The Proposition is an easy consequence of the hypotheses and Proposition 3. ♠

```
function LSAT(φ)
   return LSAT_DP(cnf(φ), ⊤).

function LSAT_DP(φ, μ)
   if φ = ⊤ then return LCONSIST(μ);                    /* base */
   if φ = ⊥ then return False;                          /* backtrack */
   if { a unit clause (l) occurs in φ }                 /* unit */
      then return LSAT_DP(assign(l, φ),μ ∧ l);
   l := choose-literal(φ, μ);
   return LSAT_DP(assign(l, φ),μ ∧ l) or                /* split */
          LSAT_DP(assign(l̄, φ),μ ∧ l̄).
```

Figure 3. LSAT and LSAT_{DP}

3.2. LSAT(φ)

Consider a formula φ. Let L be a modal logic. The generation of assignments satisfying φ is independent of the particular logic L being considered. Furthermore, it can be based on any procedure for SAT:

- if the SAT decider is complete, then we can generate a finite and complete set of assignments for φ as follows:

  - at step 0, ask for an assignment satisfying φ, and
  - at step $i + 1$, ask for an assignment satisfying φ and the negation of the assignments generated in the previous steps.

  By checking the L-consistency of each assignment, we obtain a correct and complete decider for L.

- if the SAT decider is correct but incomplete, then we cannot generate a complete set of assignments for φ, but we can still build a correct but incomplete decider for L by checking each generated assignment. Of course, whether an incomplete effective procedure for SAT can be turned into an effective incomplete procedure for a modal logic L, is still an open point.

The above method for generating a complete set of assignments for φ has the advantage that the SAT decider is used as a blackbox. The obvious disadvantage is that the size of the input formula checked by the SAT solver may become exponentially bigger than the original one. A better solution is to invoke the test for L-consistency *inside* the SAT procedure whenever an assignment satisfying the input formula is found. In the case of the Davis-Putnam (DP) procedure [5], we get the procedure LSAT represented in Figure 3. In the figure,

- *cnf*(φ) is a set of clauses —possibly with newly introduced propositional variables— such that, for any assignment μ in the extended language, the following two properties are satisfied:[3]

    1. if μ satisfies *cnf*(φ) then the restriction of μ to the language of φ satisfies φ, and
    2. if μ satisfies φ then there exists an assignment in the language of *cnf*(φ) which (i) extends μ and (ii) satisfies *cnf*(φ).

    Examples of such conversions are the "classical conversion" (which given a formula in negative normal form recursively distribute conjunctions over disjunctions), and the conversions based on "renaming", such as those described in [36, 30, 6].

- *choose-literal*(φ, μ) returns a literal occurring in φ and chosen according to some heuristic criterion.

- if l is a literal, $\bar{l}$ stands for A if $l = \neg A$, and for A if $l = \neg A$;

- for any literal l and formula φ, $assign(l, \varphi)$ is the formula obtained from φ by (i) deleting the clauses in which l occurs as a disjunct, and (ii) eliminating $\bar{l}$ from the others.

As can be observed, the procedure LSAT_{DP} in Figure 3 is the DP-procedure modulo the call to LCONSIST(μ) when it finds an assignment μ satisfying the input formula. Notice that in this procedure the pure literal rule, used by some DP implementations, is not implemented. In fact, our main interest is in correct and complete modal deciders. With the pure literal rule, the set of assignments checked by LCONSIST —assuming that each of such call returns *False*— is not ensured to be complete.[4]

In the following, for any formula φ and for any assignment μ in the (possibly extended) language of *cnf*(φ), μ_φ is the restriction of μ to the language of φ. Analogously, for any set of assignments Γ, $\Gamma_\varphi = \{\mu_\varphi \mid \mu \in \Gamma\}$.

PROPOSITION 5. *Let φ be any modal formula. Assume that, for any assignment μ,* LCONSIST(μ) *prints μ and returns False. Let Γ be the set of assignments printed as the result of invoking* LSAT(φ). *The disjunction of the assignments in Γ_φ is propositionally equivalent to φ.*

Proof: In the hypotheses of the Proposition, what we need to prove is that

$$\varphi \equiv \bigvee_{\mu \in \Gamma_\varphi} \mu.$$

First, it is clear that *cnf*(φ) $\equiv \bigvee_{\mu \in \Gamma} \mu$. For the thesis, the right-to-left implication is an easy consequence of the first of the two properties of *cnf*(φ). Assume that the left-to-right implication is false. This means that there exists an assignment μ in the language of φ such that

[3] Let μ be an assignment in a language L. Let $L' \subseteq L$ be a language. The *restriction of μ to L'* is the assignment obtained from μ by deleting the conjuncts not in L'. Let μ' an assignment. μ' *extends* μ if each conjunct of μ is also a conjunct of μ'.

[4] According to some authors (see, e.g., Freeman [11]) the pure literal rule only helps for a few classes of SAT problems. Furthermore, when this rule does help, it does not result in a substantial reduction in search tree size.

(1) for any propositional atom A, either A or $\neg A$ is a conjunct of μ,

(2) for any formula $\Box\psi$ in the language of φ, either $\Box\psi$ or $\neg\Box\psi$ is a conjunct of μ,

(3) μ satisfies φ, and

(4) μ does not satisfy $\bigvee_{\mu \in \Gamma_\varphi} \mu$.

Given (3) and the second of the properties of *cnf*(φ), there must exist an assignment μ' in the language of *cnf*(φ) which

(5) extends μ,

(6) satisfies *cnf*(φ), and thus also $\bigvee_{\mu \in \Gamma} \mu$.

(6) means that μ' entails $\bigvee_{\mu \in \Gamma} \mu$ by propositional reasoning. Thus, there must exist an assignment μ'' in Γ such that —given (1), (2), (5)— each conjunct of μ''_φ is also a conjunct of μ'_φ and thus of μ. This implies that μ entails μ''_φ. Since $\mu''_\varphi \in \Gamma_\varphi$, μ entails $\bigvee_{\mu \in \Gamma_\varphi} \mu$, contradicting (4). ♠

We can now state and prove soundness and completeness results for our procedures.

Theorem [Soundness and Completeness] *Let L be one of the logics E, EM, EN, EMN, EC, ECN, EMC, EMCN.* LSAT *is sound and complete for L, i.e., for any modal formula φ,* LSAT(φ) *returns True if φ is L-consistent, and False otherwise.*

Proof: First observe that LSAT(φ) returns

- *True* if there exists a call to LCONSIST(μ) which returns *True*, and
- *False* if each call to LCONSIST(μ) returns *False*.

The proof is by induction on the depth d of φ. If $d = 0$ the Theorem is trivial. Assume that $d = m + 1$. By induction hypothesis, for any formula ψ whose depth is less than d, LSAT(ψ) returns *True* if ψ is L-consistent, and *False* otherwise. In the following, we use the following two facts:

(1) For any two assignments μ and μ' differing only for propositional conjuncts, μ is L-consistent iff μ' is L-consistent.
This is a trivial consequence of Proposition 1 and Proposition 3.

(2) Let μ be an assignment such that LCONSIST(μ) is invoked during the execution of LSAT(φ). LCONSIST(μ) returns *True* if μ is L-consistent and *False* otherwise.
Given that the depth of μ is less than or equal to d, this is a consequence of the the induction hypothesis, Proposition 2 and Proposition 4.

There are two cases:

1. φ is L-consistent. From Proposition 5, it follows that there exists a call to LCONSIST(μ) in which the assignment μ (i) satisfies *cnf*(φ), and (ii) is such that μ_φ is L-consistent. Since μ possibly extends μ_φ in that it may assign some newly introduced propositional variables, from (1) it follows that μ is L-consistent, and from (2) it follows that LCONSIST(μ) —and thus also LSAT(φ)— returns *True*.

2. φ is not L-consistent. From Proposition 5, it follows that for each call LCONSIST(μ), the assignment μ_φ is not L-consistent. As above, from (1) it follows that μ is not L-consistent, and from (2) it follows that LCONSIST(μ) returns *False*. ♠

4. *SAT

*SAT is built on top of SATO ver. 3.2 [40]. The choice of adopting SATO as the basis for our system has been driven by the following motivations:

- SATO is fast. We have not performed and are not aware of any up-to-date extensive comparison among the different SAT solvers publicly available.[5] However, according to some experiments we have done and to the results presented in [40], SATO seems to behave better than most of the currently available SAT solvers.
- SATO has many options, including various splitting heuristics and backjumping. We have inherited some of these options, and they are available for experimentation.
- SATO has been written using some Software Engineering conventions which have made and will make much easier to tune it for our goals.

Besides the options inherited from SATO, our system allows for other possibilities that we have developed while implementing the system. It is out of the goals of this paper to describe *SAT structure, optimizations and configurable options. For a more detailed presentation, see [35] and the manual distributed with *SAT. For our goals, it suffices to say that the core of *SAT is a C implementation of the procedures LSAT and LCONSIST in Figures 1, 2, 3. In particular, with reference to Figure 3, in *SAT

- *cnf*(φ) is the set of clauses obtained from φ by applying a conversion based on renaming, such as those described in [36, 30].
- *choose-literal*(φ, μ) returns a literal according to a MOMS heuristic (Maximum Occurrences in clauses of Minimum Size) [11].
- *assign*(l, φ) is a highly optimized procedure which takes time linear in the number of occurrences of l in φ.

*SAT also implements two important optimizations which have been used in the tests presented in the next Section:

Early-pruning. Before each splitting step in LSAT, the L-consistency of the assignment generated so far is checked by a call to LCONSIST. As in KSATC, care is taken to avoid the repetition of L-consistency checks on the same branch of the propositional search tree.[6] Early pruning has proved to be very effective at least on some of the tests presented in the next Section (see [16]).

Caching for K. In the case of the logic K, *SAT uses an additional data structure which allows to associate to any formula φ the result of LSAT(φ). Before invoking LSAT

[5] See `http://aida.intellektik.informatik.th-darmstadt.de/~hoos/SATLIB/` for a list of publicly available SAT solvers and more.

[6] This is obtained through a pointer in the assignment stack which keeps track of the portion of the current assignment which has been already verified to be L-consistent.

on a formula ψ, LCONSIST checks whether the K-consistency of ψ has already been determined. As in DLP, caching introduces some additional costs, but it may produce dramatic speedups (see [20]).

We have not yet conducted an exhaustive experimental analysis to see, for each class of formulas, which combination of *SAT options leads to the best results (see [20] for a similar study of DLP options). In all the tests in the next Section, we used *SAT options which seemed more reasonable to us. In particular, we have set *SAT as to use

- early pruning on all tests, and
- caching (for K) when the depth of the input formula is greater than 1.

5. A comparative analysis

The availability of decision procedures for the logics we consider varies significantly. For EMCN, that we recall is equivalent to K, there are many implemented decision procedures available, see, e.g., [10, 7]. For E, EM and EMC, Gasquet and Herzig [12] provide a reduction to normal modal logics: by implementing this reduction we indirectly obtain decision procedures for these logics. Fitting [9] calls U the logic EM, and defines a tableau system for it. More recently, Governatori and Luppi [17] define a tableau-like proof system for classical, monotonic and regular modal logics. We are not aware of any implementation of these tableau systems. For EN, EC, EMN and ECN we are not aware of any other implemented decision procedure, nor of any reduction into a formalism for which a decision procedure is available.

Our comparative analysis is restricted to K and E. In fact, both our decision procedures for E and EM, and Gasquet and Herzig's reductions for E and EM, are similar. We expect that the experimental analysis for EM would lead to results similar to the ones we have for E. For EMC, Gasquet and Herzig's reduction is to a normal modal logic for which we do not have a system available.[7]

5.1. Modal K

As we said, there are several systems able to solve the consistency problem for K. In our comparative experimental analysis, we consider the four systems *SAT, KSATC [16], DLP [28] and TA [22], i.e., some among the fastest solvers for K. We remember that TA, given a modal formula φ, first determines a corresponding first order formula φ^* and then it performs conventional first-order theorem proving. In our tests, as in [22], TA uses FLOTTER to convert φ^* in a set of clauses $Cl(\varphi^*)$, and then the theorem prover SPASS to solve $Cl(\varphi^*)$. For a brief description of FLOTTER and SPASS, see [39].[8]

[7] The reduction maps the consistency problem for a formula φ in EMC, into the consistency problem for a formula φ' in the smallest normal modal logic with two modal operators $\Box_1$, $\Box_2$ and augmented with the schema

$$\psi \supset \Box_1\psi.$$

See [12] for more details.

[8] The experimental results have been obtained with DLP ver. 3.1, TA ver. 1.4 (SPASS/FLOTTER ver. 0.55), KSATC ver. 1.0, and *SAT ver. 1.2. To compile the systems we have used `sml-nj 110.0.3`, `sicstus prolog 3`, `ACL 5.0`, and `gcc 2.7.2.3`. The tests have been run on several Intel PCs, whose configuration varies from `P200MHz` with `64MbRAM`, up to a `PII350MHz` with `256 MbRAM`. All platforms are running `Linux 5.x`

We test these systems on three problem sets of randomly generated $3CNF_K$ formulas. A $3CNF_K$ formula is a conjunction of $3CNF_K$ clauses, each with three disjuncts. Each disjunct in a $3CNF_K$ clause is either a propositional literal or a formula having the form $\Box C$ or $\neg\Box C$, where C is a $3CNF_K$ clause. See [14] for a more detailed presentation. We only remark that for any formula φ there exist a $3CNF_K$ formula which is K-consistent iff φ is K-consistent.

Sets of $3CNF_K$ formulas can be randomly generated according to the following parameters:

(i) the modal depth d;

(ii) the number L of clauses at depth $d = 0$;

(iii) the number N of propositional variables;

(iv) the probability p with which a disjunct occurring in a clause at depth $< d$ is purely propositional.

Care is taken in order to avoid multiple occurrences of a formula in a clause, at the same time ensuring that the modal vs. the propositional structure of each generated formula only depends on p. In more detail, a clause is generated by randomly generating its disjuncts. When generating a disjunct, we first decide whether it has to be a propositional literal or not. Then a disjunct of the proper type is repeatedly generated as long as it does not occur in the clause generated so far.

In the tests we consider, a problem set is characterized by N and p: d is fixed to 1, while L is varied in such a way to empirically cover the "100% satisfiable – 100% unsatisfiable" transition. For each L in a problem set, 100 $3CNF_K$ formulas are randomly generated, and the resulting formulas are given in input to the procedure under test. Then, for each run, we consider the time the systems take for the main processing of the formula, thus excluding the negligible time the systems take to read and somehow normalize the input formula. (In particular, for TA this means that we take into account only the time needed by SPASS to solve the formula generated at the end of the translation process.) For practical reasons, a timeout mechanism stops the execution of the system on a formula after 1000 seconds of CPU time. Even more, for any pair N, p, the execution of *SAT, KSATC and TA is stopped after the system exceeds the timeout on 51 of the 100 samples corresponding to the fixed N, p. DLP instead, stops its execution on the 100 samples corresponding to a pair N, p if a super-majority of the first n tests timeout.[9] When this happens, it is assumed that DLP exceeds the timeout for more than 50% of the tests with that N, p.

The first three problem sets we consider have $N = 4, 5, 6$ while p is fixed to 0%: according to Hustadt and Schmidt [23], fixing $p = 0\%$ corresponds to particularly difficult tests. We call these problem sets PKN4p0, PKN5p0, and PKN6p0 respectively. PKN4p0 and PKN6p0 are called PS12 and PS13 respectively in [23]. In order to better highlight the behavior of *SAT and KSATC, we also run these systems on a problem set (called PKN7p0) having $N = 7$ and $p = 0\%$. In Figure 4, satisfiability percentages

RedHat. DLP is available at `http://www-db.research.bell-labs.com/user/pfps`. TA is available at `http://www.doc.mmu.ac.uk/STAFF/U.Hustadt/mdp`. KSATC is available at `ftp://ftp.mrg.dist.unige.it/` in `pub/mrg-systems`. *SAT is available at the WEB page `http://www.mrg.dist.unige.it/~tac/StarSAT.html`.

[9] In more detail, DLP stops its execution if there are at least 5 tests so far and more than 90% of them timeout, or if there are at least 10 tests so far and more than 75% of them timeout, or if there are at least 20 tests so far and more than 55% of them timeout [29].

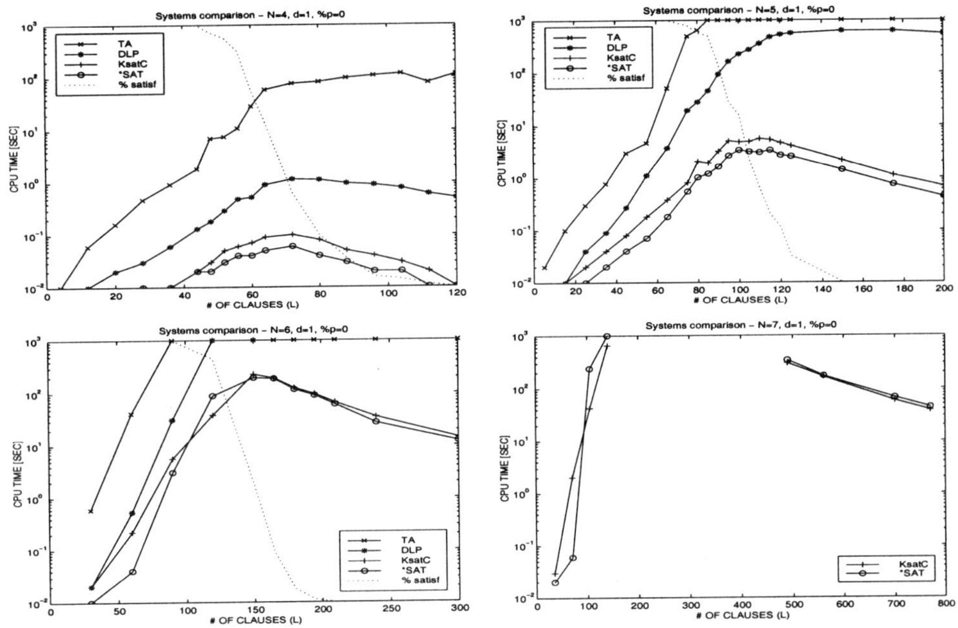

Figure 4. Logic K. *SAT, KSATC, DLP, and TA median CPU time. $N = 4, 5, 6, 7$. $p = 0\%$. 100 samples/point. Background: satisfiability percentage.

and the median of the CPU times for the four systems are plotted against the number of clauses L. Notice the logarithmic scale on the vertical axis, which causes that values equal to 0.00 do not get plotted.

Consider Figure 4. The first observation is that *SAT and KSATC are the fastest. The two systems perform roughly in the same way, with *SAT performing better when $L = 4, 5$. For $L = 6, 7$, the two systems have similar performances, one system performing better than the other for some values of L, but worse for other values of L. This comes at no surprise: the two systems have the same underlying structure, both use early pruning and a MOMS heuristic to select the splitting literal. The two systems do not have an identical behavior because they use different data-structures and implement slightly different MOMS strategies.

Considering the other systems, for PKN4p0 the gap between *SAT/KSATC and DLP [resp. TA] is of more than one order of magnitude at the cross-over point of 50% of satisfiable formulas, and goes up to almost 2 [resp. 4] orders of magnitude at the right end side of the horizontal axis. For PKN5p0 and PKN6p0, TA median values exceed the timeout for $L = 85$ and $L = 90$ respectively, while the corresponding values of *SAT [resp. KSATC] are 1.22 [resp. 1.83] and 3.32 [resp. 5.64] seconds. TA keeps exceeding the timeout for all the successive values. The gap between *SAT/KSATC and DLP on PKN5p0 is of more than one order of magnitude at the cross-over points of 50% satisfiable formula, and goes up to almost 3 orders at the very right of the plot. When $N = 6$, DLP median values exceed the timeout for $L = 120$ and $L = 150$. For $L > 150$, DLP does not terminate gracefully.[10] Comparing *SAT and DLP on PKN4p0 and PKN5p0, we see that

[10] DLP ver. 3.2 is able to successfully handle formulas with $N = 6$, $p = 0\%$ and $L > 150$.

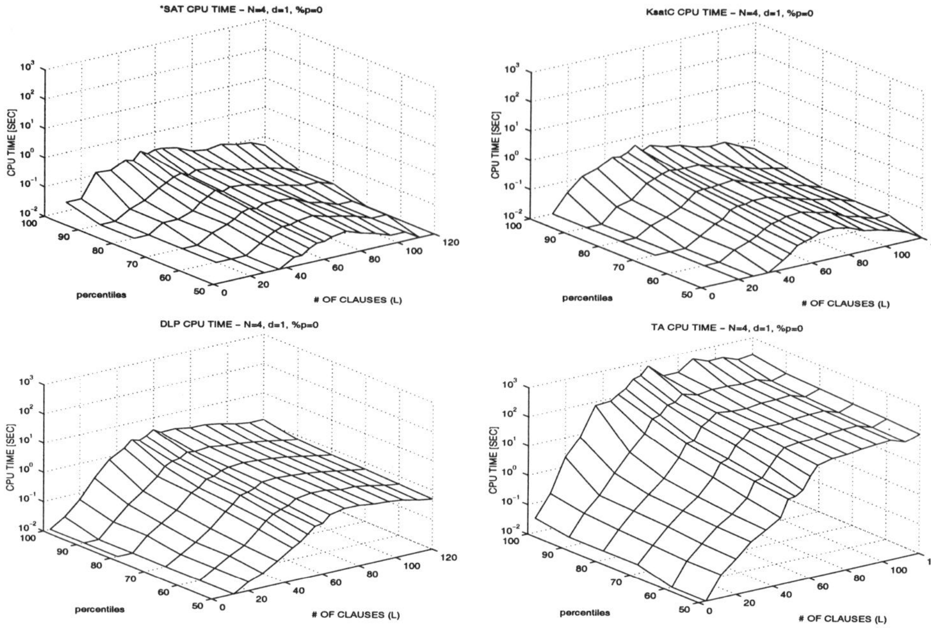

Figure 5. Logic K. 50%–100% percentile CPU times of *SAT, KSATC, DLP, and TA. $N = 4$. $p = 0\%$. 100 samples/point.

- the gap between *SAT and DLP seems to increase with L. Both for PKN4p0 and PKN5p0, the difference in logarithmic scale between *SAT and DLP is (almost always) monotonically increasing.

- At the crossover point of 50% satisfiable formulas, the gap between *SAT and DLP [resp. TA] is roughly 1s [resp. 60s] for PKN4p0; and ≥220s [resp. ≥1000s] for PKN5p0.

Such good performances by *SAT and KSATC are due to early pruning, which has revealed to be very effective on these problem sets. For example, if we disable early pruning in *SAT and rerun it on PKN5p0, the system keeps exceeding the time limit for $65 \leq L \leq 200$.

When $p = 0\%$, the better behavior of *SAT and KSATC than DLP and TA, is confirmed by the $Q\%$-percentile graphs in Figure 5, corresponding to $N = 4$. Formally, the *$Q\%$-percentile* of a set S of values is the value V such that $Q\%$ of the values in S are smaller or equal to V. The median value of a set thus corresponds to the 50% percentile of the set. Figure 5 reports the 50%, 60%, 70%, 80%, 90% and 100% percentile values of the CPU-times when *SAT (top left), KSATC (top right), DLP (bottom left) and TA (bottom right) are run on PKN4p0. The percentile plots for PKN5p0 and PKN6p0 look similar to the plots in Figure 5. This means that all the systems perform in roughly the same way on the 50 most difficult samples of the 100 tests corresponding to a fixed N and L.

We also run the four systems on problems with $N = 4, 5, 6, 7$ while p is fixed to 50%. We call these problem sets PKN4p50, PKN5p50, PKN6p50, and PKN7p50. In Figure 6 the satisfiability percentages and the median of the CPU times for the four systems are plotted against the number of clauses L. As for $p = 0\%$, *SAT and KSATC perform roughly in the same way and are the fastest. Differently from the tests in which $p = 0\%$,

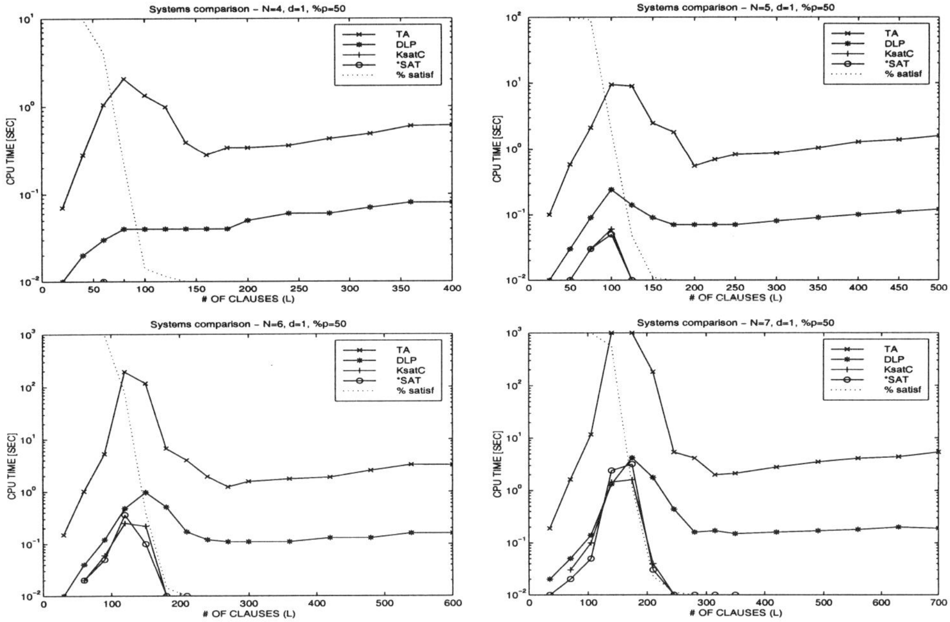

Figure 6. Logic K. *SAT, KSATC, DLP, and TA median CPU time. $N = 4, 5, 6, 7$. $p = 50\%$. 100 samples/point. Background: satisfiability percentage.

at the transition point of 50% of satisfiable formulas, the gap between *SAT/KSATC and DLP seems to diminish when the number of variables increases. Horrocks and Patel-Schneider [19] show that for values of L bigger than 7, DLP performances are superior to those of KSATC when $d = 1$ and $p = 50\%$. They also conclude that DLP performs better than KSATC when p is high and worse when p is low. We have not yet done such a broad comparison using *SAT instead of KSATC. However, we believe that Horrocks and Patel-Schneider's conclusions should extend also to *SAT, if *SAT is used with the parameter settings we have currently used, i.e., those which make *SAT most similar to KSATC. Of course, a big role can be played by *SAT already available configurable options, and this will be the issue of future research. In any case, both *SAT and KSATC perform better than the other systems for large values of L, when the formulas are trivially unsatisfiable. This is due to the fact that for large values of L, formulas become propositionally unsatisfiable, and thus both *SAT and KSATC mostly take advantage of their SAT-based nature, e.g., of their optimized data structures for handling large formulas.

As for $p = 0\%$, the percentile plots of the timings of the systems on PKN7p50, do not show big differences with respect to the plots of the medians. Considering DLP and *SAT 100% percentile plots, it is interesting to observe that DLP has a lower maximum than *SAT; on the other hand, *SAT values decrease more rapidly than those of DLP.

Finally, we see that for most of the problem sets we consider, all the systems seem to have an easy-hard-easy pattern, whose peak roughly correspond to the 50% of satisfiable formulas. When $p = 0\%$, this phenomenon is best evident for *SAT and KSATC.

We also consider the benchmarks formulas for K used at the Comparison of Theorem Provers for Modal Logics at Tableaux'98 (see [7]). These consist of nine provable parameterized formulas (ending with "_p") and nine unprovable parameterized formulas (end-

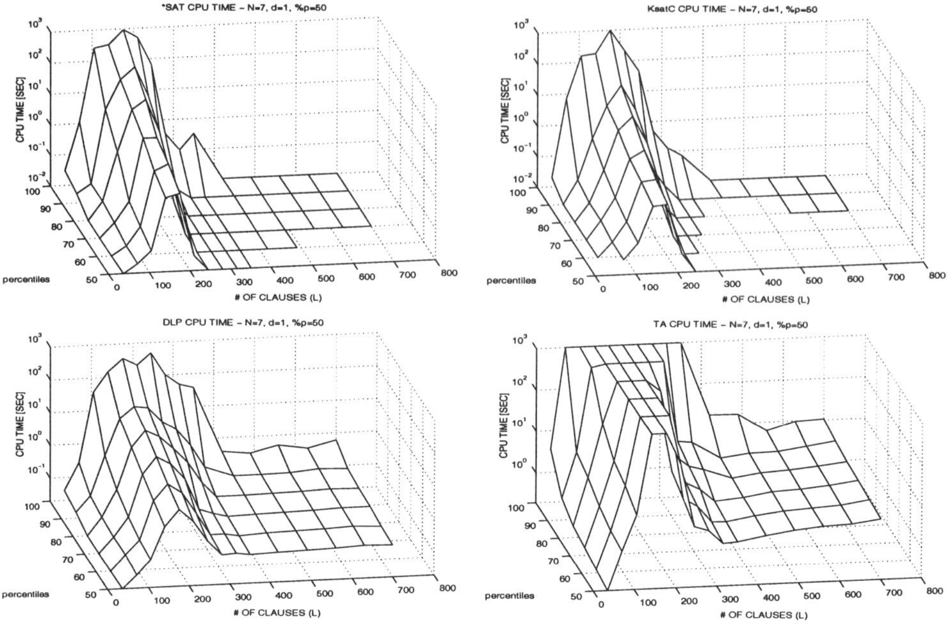

Figure 7. Logic K. 50%–100% percentile CPU times of *SAT, KSATC, DLP, and TA. $N = 7$. $p = 50\%$. 100 samples/point.

Table I. Logic K. *SAT, DLP and TA performances on Tableaux'98 benchmarks

	*SAT		DLP		TA		
Test	Size	Time	Size	Time	Size	SPASS	FLOTTER
k_branch_n	12	94.49	12	52.29	6	84.21	12.23
k_branch_p	21	0.21	18	44.56	6	51.95	13.81
k_d4_n	21	2.87	21	3.43	14	1.14	42.92
k_d4_p	21	0.06	21	0.17	15	0.64	70.47
k_dum_n	21	0.12	21	0.13	16	1.75	64.07
k_dum_p	21	0.04	21	0.07	17	3.32	61.67
k_grz_n	21	0.01	21	0.20	21	0.16	0.17
k_grz_p	21	0.04	21	0.11	21	0.35	0.16
k_lin_n	21	47.80	21	0.70	21	16.07	63.94
k_lin_p	21	0.01	21	0.08	21	1.03	8.21
k_path_n	21	0.96	21	1.29	4	58.70	2.14
k_path_p	21	0.72	21	1.19	5	22.85	2.18
k_ph_n	12	0.60	9	40.16	9	45.21	9.92
k_ph_p	8	48.54	6	11.34	6	42.19	0.97
k_poly_n	21	2.25	21	0.65	4	1.23	7.86
k_poly_p	21	1.73	21	0.34	5	2.48	51.00
k_t4p_n	21	1.28	21	0.45	9	3.37	84.35
k_t4p_p	21	0.29	21	0.21	16	3.91	84.75

ing with "_n"). For each parameterized formula $A(n)$, the test consists in determining the greatest natural number $n \leq 21$ satisfying the following two conditions:

1. the prover returns the correct result for the formulas $A(1), A(2), \ldots, A(n)$ in less than 100 seconds, and

2. the prover cannot do the formula $A(n+1)$ in less than 100 seconds or $n = 21$.

Even though it has been proved that most of these tests can be easily solved by current solvers, these are still interesting because

- they are not 3CNF$_K$ formulas, and

- some of these tests have not been solved yet.

The results for *SAT, TA and DLP are reported in Table I. KSATC has not been tested since KSATC is able to deal with 3CNF$_K$ formulas only. We also show the CPU time requested by the system to solve the last instance $A(n)$. Notice that *SAT has been run with caching enabled, since the depth of all the formulas in the Table is greater than 1. For TA, we do not take into account the time needed to compute the first order formula $A^*(n)$ corresponding to $A(n)$ (which is negligible), but we do take into account the time requested by FLOTTER to convert $A^*(n)$ into a set $Cl(A^*(n))$ of clauses (reported in the FLOTTER column), and the time requested by SPASS to determine the consistency or inconsistency of $Cl(A^*(n))$ (reported in the SPASS column). Furthermore, we stopped TA on $A(n)$ with $n < 21$, either because FLOTTER does not terminate gracefully when computing $Cl(A^*(n+1))$, or because SPASS or FLOTTER exceed the 100 seconds time limit. In the table, these three cases correspond to the rows in which the value for n/SPASS/FLOTTER respectively is underlined.

As can be observed from Table I, the three systems are able to solve all the instances of a formula in four cases. *SAT and DLP are able to solve all the instances except for k_branch_n, k_branch_p, k_ph_n, k_ph_p. Except for the first of these four parameterized formulas, *SAT is able to solve more instances than DLP. For k_branch_n, both *SAT and DLP are able to solve the 12th instance, with DLP taking less time than *SAT to solve it.

5.2. Modal E

Gasquet and Herzig [12] provide a translation which maps any formula φ into a formula φ_{GH} in K$_2$, i.e., the smallest normal modal logic with two modal operators $\Box_1$ and $\Box_2$. The translation is such that φ is satisfiable in E iff φ_{GH} is satisfiable in K$_2$. This translation is defined in the following way:

- $\varphi_{GH} = \varphi$, if φ is a propositional variable,

- $\varphi_{GH} = \neg\Box_1\neg(\Box_2\psi_{GH} \wedge \Box_1\neg\psi_{GH})$, if $\varphi = \Box\psi$,

and homomorphic for the cases of the propositional connectives.

Consider a formula φ. We compare *SAT performances on φ with respect to *SAT, DLP and TA performances on φ_{GH}. We could not run KSATC on φ_{GH}, since KSATC accepts only 3CNF$_K$ formulas with at most one modality. To make evident when a system is run using Gasquet and Herzig's translation, we append the string "+GH" to the name of the system. Therefore, in the following, we will have the systems *SAT, *SAT+GH, DLP+GH, and TA+GH.

In E, the 3CNF_K test methodology is not suited. Indeed, it is no longer the case that for any modal formula φ there exists a 3CNF_K formula which is E-satisfiable iff φ is E-satisfiable. Furthermore, checking the consistency of an assignment μ in E amounts to determine the consistency of $(\alpha \equiv \neg\beta)$ for each pair of conjuncts $\Box\alpha$ and $\neg\Box\beta$ in μ: most of these tests, in case α and β are 3CNF_K clauses, can be trivially satisfied.

We therefore consider sets of 3CNF_E formulas. A 3CNF_E formula is a conjunction of 3CNF_E clauses, each with three disjuncts. Each disjunct in a 3CNF_E clause is either a propositional literal or a formula having the form $\Box C$ or $\neg\Box C$, where C is a 3CNF_E formula. For example,

$$\Box((\Box(l_1 \vee l_2 \vee l_3) \vee l_4 \vee l_5) \wedge (l_6 \vee l_7 \vee l_8))$$

where each l_i $(1 \leq i \leq 8)$ is a propositional literal, is a 3CNF_E formula. For any formula φ, there exist a 3CNF_E formula logically equivalent to φ in E.

Sets of 3CNF_E formulas can be randomly generated according to the parameters used to generate 3CNF_K formulas, and a new parameter C representing the number of clauses at depth $d > 0$. A 3CNF_K is thus a 3CNF_E formula in which $C = 1$. As in the previous subsection, a problem set is characterized by N and p: d and C are fixed to 1 and L respectively; L is given increasing values in such a way to empirically cover the "100% satisfiable – 100% unsatisfiable" transition. We also check that in each sample there are no multiple occurrences of a formula in a clause, at the same ensuring that the propositional vs. the modal structure of the formula only depends on p. Notice that while increasing L also C is increased. As a consequence, for each pair of formulas $\Box\alpha_i$ and $\neg\Box\beta_j$ in an assignment satisfying a 3CNF_E formula, the recursive E-consistency check for $(\alpha_i \equiv \neg\beta_j)$ has itself a phase transition from 100% satisfiable to 100% unsatisfiable when increasing L. Overall, for low [resp. high] values of L we expect that each satisfying assignment should be trivially determined to be E-consistent [resp. not E-consistent].

As before, for each value of L in a problem set, 100 3CNF_E formulas are randomly generated, and the resulting formulas are given in input to the procedure under test. A timeout stops the execution of the system on a formula after 1000 seconds of CPU time. We consider the following problems sets:

- PEN4p0, PEN5p0, PEN6p0, PEN7p0 in which $p = 0\%$ while $L = 4, 5, 6, 7$ respectively, and

- PEN4p50, PEN5p50, PEN6p50, PEN7p50 in which $p = 50\%$ while $L = 4, 5, 6, 7$ respectively.

Given the huge amount of time that FLOTTER takes to prepare the formula for SPASS, we run TA+GH only on the problems sets PEN4p0 and PEN4p50. For PEN7p0 and PEN7p50, we run TA+GH only on the initial points. As in the preceding subsection, we only take into account the time the systems take for the main processing of the formula. In particular, for each system, we do not take into account the time needed to perform the Gasquet and Herzig's conversion; and for TA+GH we take into account only the time taken by SPASS. The median and the percentile plots of the systems on PEN4p0, PEN5p0, PEN6p0, PEN7p0 are shown in Figure 8 and Figure 9 respectively.

Consider Figure 8. As can be observed, *SAT is the fastest: the gap with the other systems is of more than one order of magnitude for certain values of L. However, both *SAT+GH and DLP+GH perform quite well, better than one could have imagined given that the consistency problem for E and K_2 belongs to two different complexity classes. However, a closer look to Gasquet and Herzig's reduction reveals that, considering a

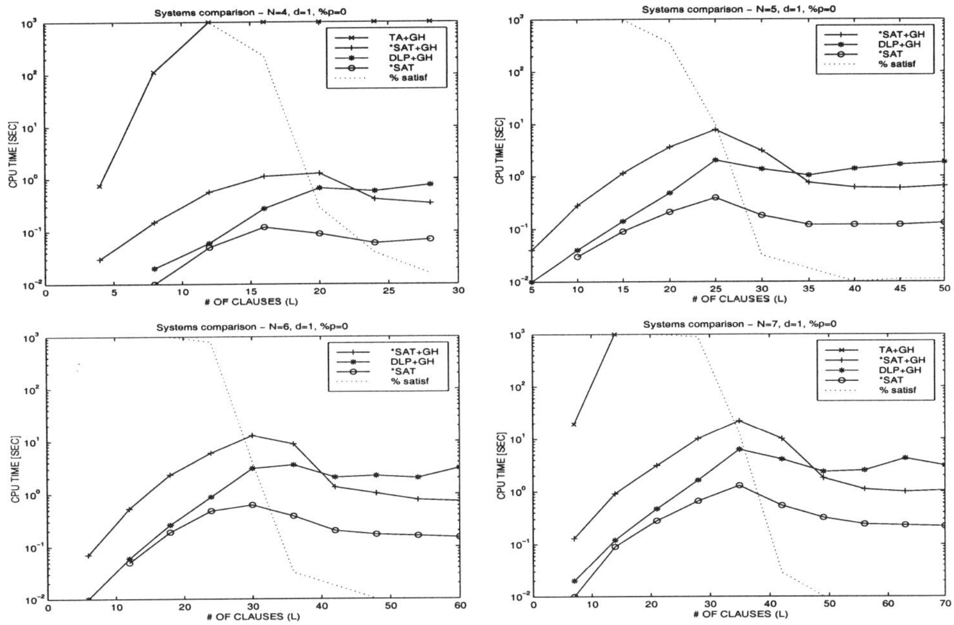

Figure 8. Logic E. *SAT, *SAT+GH, DLP+GH, and TA+GH median CPU time. $N = 4, 5, 6, 7$. $p = 0\%$. 100 samples/point. Background: satisfiability percentage.

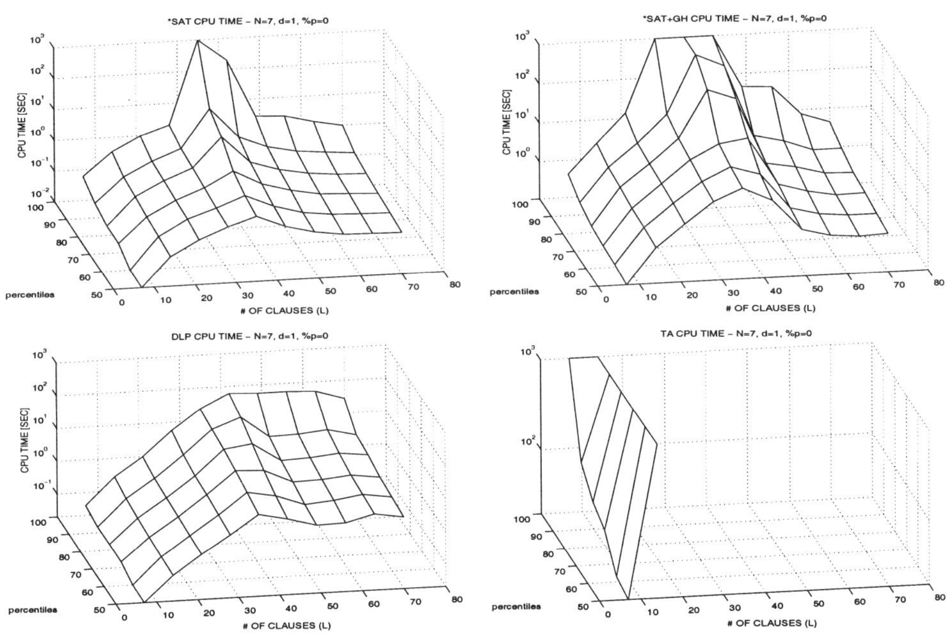

Figure 9. Logic E. 50%–100% percentile CPU times of *SAT, *SAT+GH, DLP+GH, and TA+GH. $N = 7$. $p = 0\%$. 100 samples/point.

3CNF_E formula φ, and an assignment $\mu = \bigwedge_{i=1}^{m} \Box\alpha_i \ \wedge\ \bigwedge_{j=1}^{n} \neg\Box\beta_j \ \wedge\ \gamma$ (as usual we assume that γ is a propositional formula) in the language of φ,

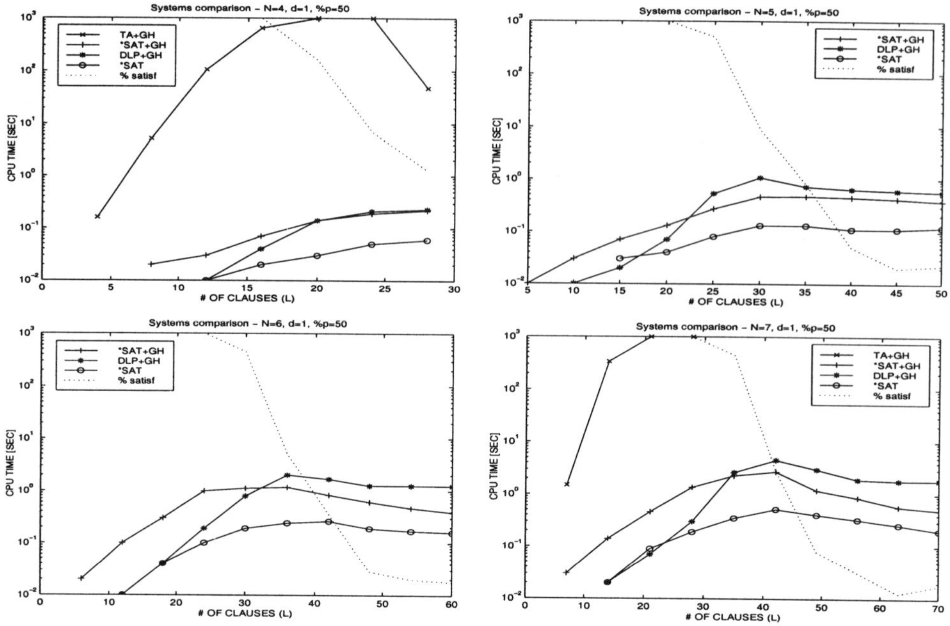

Figure 10. Logic E. *SAT, *SAT+GH, DLP+GH, and TA+GH median CPU time. $N = 4, 5, 6, 7$. $p = 50\%$. 100 samples/point. Background: satisfiability percentage.

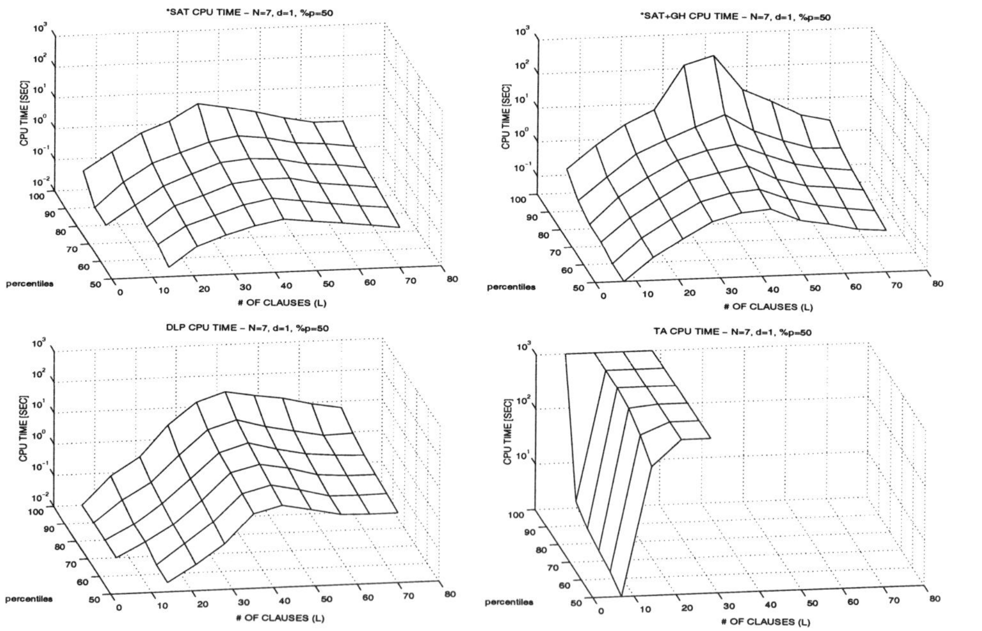

Figure 11. Logic E. 50%–100% percentile CPU times of *SAT, *SAT+GH, DLP+GH, and TA+GH. $N = 7$. $p = 50\%$. 100 samples/point.

1. μ satisfies φ iff μ_{GH} satisfies φ_{GH}.
2. for checking the E-consistency of μ, *SAT performs at most $2mn$ consistency checks involving the formulas $\alpha_1, \ldots, \alpha_m, \beta_1, \ldots, \beta_m$.
3. for checking the K_2-consistency of μ_{GH}, both *SAT+GH and DLP+GH perform at most $2mn$ consistency checks involving the formulas $\alpha_{1GH}, \ldots, \alpha_{mGH}, \beta_{1GH}, \ldots, \beta_{mGH}$.

The first two points are obvious. To understand the last, it suffices to notice that μ_{GH} is propositionally equivalent to

$$\bigwedge_{i=1}^{m} \neg\Box_1\neg(\Box_2\alpha_{iGH} \wedge \Box_1\neg\alpha_{iGH}) \ \wedge \ \bigwedge_{j=1}^{n} \Box_1(\neg\Box_2\beta_{jGH} \vee \neg\Box_1\neg\beta_{jGH}) \ \wedge \ \gamma.$$

Given that both *SAT+GH and DLP+GH use caching, these procedures will perform at most a quadratic number of checks in the number of subformulas of φ_{GH}. This is not the case for TA+GH, since SPASS does not have any caching mechanism. This explains the good behavior of *SAT+GH and DLP+GH, and the bad behavior of TA+GH.

It is interesting to compare *SAT+GH and DLP+GH performances. As can be observed, DLP+GH performs better than *SAT+GH for low values of L, but worse for high values of L. This behavior reflects the different mechanisms used by *SAT+GH and DLP+GH to prune the search space when checking the K-consistency of an assignment. As we said in Section 4, in all the tests we have set *SAT+GH as to use the early pruning strategy. DLP+GH instead implements a backjumping schema in the spirit of [2]: when an assignment is discovered to be not K-consistent, backtracking to a point which does not lead to the same contradiction is enforced. While implementing early pruning does not introduce overheads, this is not the case for backjumping, where a dependency set of each derived clause has to be maintained (see [28] for more details). Despite the additional costs introduced, backjumping clearly wins if compared to early pruning in logic K, for low values of L. In this case, almost each assignment is K-consistent and early pruning may cause additional (i.e., not performed by a backjumping strategy) checks. On the other hand, for high values of L, when the formula under test is not K-consistent but there are still assignments satisfying it, *SAT+GH is able to greatly cut off the search by checking the inconsistency of the assignment generated so far. DLP+GH instead checks the consistency of an assignment only when it satisfies the current formula. DLP+GH may therefore generate many assignments which, even though they satisfy the input formula, are not K-consistent. When L is so high that the input formulas become propositionally unsatisfiable, *SAT+GH may still perform additional K-consistency checks, but these get compensated by (*i*) *SAT+GH SAT-based nature and (*ii*) the costs DLP+GH has because of backjumping. Considering Figure 9, we see that DLP+GH has a better behavior than the other systems on some of the hardest instances. Evidently, on these tests, backjumping leads to a more uniform behavior than early pruning. Horrocks and Patel-Schneider [19] show that for some randomly generate 3CNF_K formulas, early pruning leads to a more uniform behavior than backjumping.

For $N = 4, 5, 6, 7$ and $p = 50\%$, *SAT, *SAT+GH, DLP+GH and TA+GH median and percentile times are plotted in Figure 10 and Figure 11 respectively. As it can be observed, the situation is very similar to the case in which $p = 0\%$. The only difference is that now *SAT+GH performs better than DLP+GH for a lower value of L. This is reasonable, since for each L, the number of consistency checks performed by *SAT+GH because of early pruning, diminishes when p increases.

Finally, notice the easy-hard-easy pattern of *SAT. To better appreciate it, Figure 12 shows the number of calls to LSAT done by LCONSIST on PEN4p0-PEN7p0 (left),

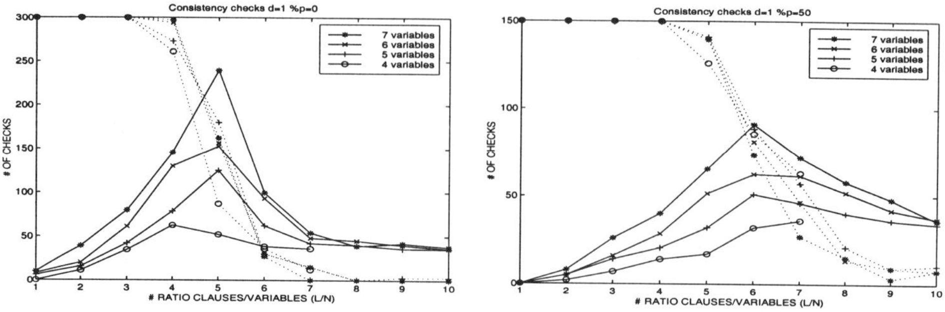

Figure 12. Logic E. *SAT median number of calls to LSAT. $N = 4, 5, 6, 7$. $p = 0\%$ (left) and $p = 50\%$ (right). 100 samples/point. Background: satisfiability percentages.

PEN4p50-PEN7p50 (right) against the ratio $\frac{L}{N}$ between L and N. As can be observed, *SAT performs a number of LSAT calls whose maximum roughly correspond to the 50% of satisfiable formulas. This transition happens when $\frac{L}{N}$ is close to 5 for $p = 0\%$ and to 6 for $p = 50\%$. This behavior reflects the above stated intuition according to which for low [resp. high] values of L all the formulas should be easily determined to be E-consistent [resp. not E-consistent].

6. Conclusions and future work

We have presented a set of SAT-based decision procedures for eight classical modal logics. We have shown how the SAT-based approach allows for efficient and modular implementations for these logics. We have presented *SAT. *SAT is the only system that is able to deal with EN, EC, ECN and EMN. In the case of the logic E, we have defined a testing methodology which generalizes the 3CNF_K methodology by Giunchiglia and Sebastiani [14], and which is suitable for testing systems for non-normal modal logics. The experimental evaluation shows that *SAT performances are superior to or comparable to the performances of other state-of-the-art systems.

In the future, we plan to conduct an extensive experimental analysis (similar to that presented in [18, 20]) to understand, for each class of formulas, which combination of *SAT options leads to the best results. We also plan to extend *SAT in order to handle more expressive decidable logics. We will also consider logics, like S4, for which more sophisticated methods than that described in Section 4 have to be employed in order to ensure the termination of the decision procedure.

Acknowledgments

We are grateful to Ullrich Hustadt, Peter F. Patel-Schneider, and Hantao Zhang for the assistance they provided on their systems. Special thanks to Roberto Sebastiani for the many useful discussions related to the subject of this paper. Thanks also to the anonymous reviewers for their helpful comments and suggestions. The first and last authors are partially supported by the Italian Spatial Agency.

References

1. F. Baader, E. Franconi, B. Hollunder, B. Nebel, and H.J. Profitlich. An Empirical Analysis of Optimization Techniques for Terminological Representation Systems or: Making KRIS get a move on. *Applied Artificial Intelligence. Special Issue on Knowledge Base Management*, 4:109–132, 1994.
2. A. Baker. Intelligent backtracking on the hardest constraint problems. *Journal of Artificial Intelligence Research*, 1995.
3. M. Cadoli, A. Giovanardi, and M. Schaerf. An algorithm to evaluate quantified boolean formulae. In *Proc. AAAI*, 1998.
4. B. F. Chellas. *Modal Logic – an Introduction.* Cambridge University Press, 1980.
5. M. Davis and H. Putnam. A computing procedure for quantification theory. *Journal of the ACM*, 7:201–215, 1960.
6. T. Boy de la Tour. Minimizing the Number of Clauses by Renaming. In *Proc. of the 10th Conference on Automated Deduction*, pages 558–572. Springer-Verlag, 1990.
7. H. de Swart, editor. *Automated Reasoning with Analytic Tableaux and Related Methods: International Conference Tableaux'98*, number 1397 in Lecture Notes in Artificial Intelligence. Springer-Verlag, May 1998.
8. R. Fagin, J.Y. Halpern, Y. Moses, and M. Y. Vardi. *Reasoning about knowledge.* MIT Press, 1995.
9. M. Fitting. *Proof Methods for Modal and Intuitionistic Logics.* D. Reidel Publishing, 1983.
10. E. Franconi, G. De Giacomo, R. M. MacGregor, W. Nutt, C. A. Welty, and F. Sebastiani, editors. *Collected Papers from the International Description Logics Workshop (DL'98).* CEUR, May 1998.
11. Jon W. Freeman. *Improvements to propositional satisfiability search algorithms.* PhD thesis, University of Pennsylvania, 1995.
12. O. Gasquet and A. Herzig. From classical to normal modal logics. In Heinrich Wansing, editor, *Proof Theory of Modal Logics*, volume 2 of *Applied Logic Series*, pages 293–311. Kluwer Academic Publishers, 1996.
13. E. Giunchiglia and F. Giunchiglia. Ideal and Real Belief about Belief. Technical Report 96-0138, DIST, University of Genoa, Italy, September 1997. Also IRST-Technical Report 9605-04. Submitted for the publication to JLC, Journal of Logic and Computation. A short version of the paper appeared in the Proc. International Conference on Formal and Applied Practical Reasoning, (FAPR'96).
14. F. Giunchiglia and R. Sebastiani. Building decision procedures for modal logics from propositional decision procedures - the case study of modal K. In *Proc. CADE-96*, Lecture Notes in Artificial Intelligence, New Brunswick, NJ, USA, August 1996. Springer Verlag.
15. F. Giunchiglia and R. Sebastiani. A SAT-based decision procedure for ALC. In *Proc. of the 5th International Conference on Principles of Knowledge Representation and Reasoning - KR'96*, Cambridge, MA, USA, November 1996. Also DIST-Technical Report 9607-08 and IRST-Technical Report 9601-02.
16. E. Giunchiglia, F. Giunchiglia, R. Sebastiani, and A. Tacchella. More evaluation of decision procedures for modal logics. In *Sixth International Conference on Principles of Knowledge Representation and Reasoning (KR'98)*, 1998.
17. G. Governatori and A. Luppi. Labelled tableaux for non-normal modal logics. In *Sixth Conference of the Italian Association for Artificial Intelligence, AI*IA '99, Bologna, Italy, September 14–17, 1999: proceedings*, 1999.
18. I. Horrocks and P. F. Patel-Schneider. Comparing subsumption optimizations. In E. Franconi, G. De Giacomo, R. M. MacGregor, W. Nutt, C. A. Welty, and F. Sebastiani, editors, *Collected Papers from the International Description Logics Workshop (DL'98)*, pages 90–94. CEUR, May 1998.
19. I. Horrocks and P. F. Patel-Schneider. Advances in propositional modal satisfiability, 1999. Manuscript.
20. I. Horrocks and P. F. Patel-Schneider. Optimising description logic subsumption. *Journal of Logic and Computation*, 1999. To appear.
21. I. Horrocks. Using an expressive description logic: FaCT or fiction? In *Sixth International Conference on Principles of Knowledge Representation and Reasoning (KR'98)*, pages 636–647, 1998.
22. U. Hustadt and R.A. Schmidt. On evaluating decision procedures for modal logic. In *Proc. of the 15th International Joint Conference on Artificial Intelligence*, 1997.

23. U. Hustadt and R.A. Schmidt. On evaluating decision procedures for modal logic. Research report MPI-I-97-2-003, Max-Planck-Institut für Informatik, Saarbrücken, Germany, February 1997.
24. Henry Kautz and Bart Selman. BLACKBOX: A new approach to the application of theorem proving to problem solving. In *Working notes of the Workshop on Planning as Combinatorial Search, held in conjunction with AIPS-98*, 1998.
25. F. Massacci. Strongly analytic tableaux for normal modal logics. In *Proc. CADE*, 1994.
26. Richard Montague. Pragmatics. In R. Klibansky, editor, *Contemporary Philosophy: A Survey. I*, pages 102–122. La Nuova Italia Editrice, Florence, 1968. Reprinted in *Formal Philosophy*, by Richard Montague, Yale University Press, New Haven, CT, 1974, pp. 95–118.
27. H. J. Ohlbach. Translation methods for non-classical logics - an overview. *Bulletin of the Interest Group in Pure and Applied Logic - IGPL*, 1(1), 1988.
28. P. F. Patel-Schneider. DLP system description. In E. Franconi, G. De Giacomo, R. M. MacGregor, W. Nutt, C. A. Welty, and F. Sebastiani, editors, *Collected Papers from the International Description Logics Workshop (DL'98)*, pages 87–89. CEUR, May 1998.
29. P. F. Patel-Schneider. Personal communication, June 1999.
30. D.A. Plaisted and S. Greenbaum. A Structure-preserving Clause Form Translation. *Journal of Symbolic Computation*, 2:293–304, 1986.
31. R. Sebastiani and F. Giunchiglia. From Tableau-based to SAT-based procedures - preliminary report. Technical Report 9711-14, IRST, Trento, Italy, November 1997.
32. Krister Segerberg. *An Essay in Classical Modal Logic.* Philosophical Studies, Uppsala, 1 edition, 1971.
33. Jörg Siekmann and Graham Wrightson, editors. *Automation of Reasoning: Classical Papers in Computational Logic 1967–1970*, volume 2. Springer-Verlag, 1983.
34. R. M. Smullyan. *First-Order Logic.* Springer-Verlag, NY, 1968.
35. Armando Tacchella. *SAT system description. In *Collected Papers from the International Description Logics Workshop (DL'99).* CEUR, July 1999.
36. G. Tseitin. On the complexity of proofs in propositional logics. *Seminars in Mathematics*, 8, 1970. Reprinted in [33].
37. Johan van Benthem. Correspondence theory. In D. Gabbay and F. Guenthner, editors, *Handbook of Philosophical Logic, Volume II: Extensions of Classical Logic*, volume 165 of *Synthese Library*, chapter II.4, pages 167–247. D. Reidel Publ. Co., Dordrecht, 1984.
38. Moshe Y. Vardi. On the complexity of epistemic reasoning. In *Proceedings, Fourth Annual Symposium on Logic in Computer Science*, pages 243–252, Asilomar Conference Center, Pacific Grove, California, 5–8 June 1989. IEEE Computer Society Press.
39. C. Weidenbach, B. Gaede, and G. Rock. SPASS & FLOTTER version 0.42. In M.A. McRobbie and J.K. Slaney, editors, *Proceedings of the 13th Conference on Automated Deduction (CADE-13)*, volume 1104 of *Lecture Notes in Artificial Intelligence*, pages 141–145, New Brunswick, New Jersey, USA, July/August 1996. Springer.
40. H. Zhang. SATO: An efficient propositional prover. In William McCune, editor, *Proceedings of the 14th International Conference on Automated deduction*, volume 1249 of *LNAI*, pages 272–275, Berlin, July13–17 1997. Springer.

SAT2000
I. Gent et al. (Eds.)
IOS Press, 2000

Evaluating Optimised Decision Procedures for Propositional Modal $\mathbf{K}_{(\mathbf{m})}$ Satisfiability

Ian Horrocks[†]
Department of Computer Science, University of Manchester, UK

Peter F. Patel-Schneider[§]
Bell Labs Research, Murray Hill, NJ, U.S.A.

Abstract. Heavily-optimised decision procedures for propositional modal satisfiability are now becoming available. Two systems incorporating such procedures for modal **K**, DLP and KSATC, are tested on randomly-generated CNF formulae with several sets of parameters, varying the maximum modal depth and ratio of propositional variable to modal subformulae. The results show some easy-hard-easy behaviour, but there is as yet no sharp peak as in propositional satisfiability.

1. Introduction

Propositional modal satisfiability has lagged behind standard propositional satisfiability in that until recently there have been no heavily-optimised propositional modal systems. This has changed in the last few years with the appearance of several heavily-optimised systems that can be used to determine the satisfiability of formulae in propositional modal logics.

One factor driving the development of such propositional modal systems is the relationship between propositional modal logics and description logics. A system that correctly reasons with information in an expressive description logic includes a decision procedure for an expressive propositional modal logic. This decision procedure must be heavily optimised if it is to be able to usefully reason with knowledge bases of any complexity. Description logic systems that incorporate a heavily-optimised propositional modal logic decision procedure include FACT [27], DLP [39], and HAM-ALC [24].

Another factor that has lead to the development of heavily-optimised propositional modal systems is the availability of heavily-optimised decision procedures for non-modal propositional logic. It is possible to use such a procedure as the core of a decision procedure for a propositional modal logic. Modal decision procedures built in this fashion include KSAT and its successor, KSATC [22, 23, 21].

These systems perform well on hand-generated problems. In the comparison at Tableaux'98 [7, 30], DLP solved many of the supposedly-difficult problems without even performing any search. Even when search was required, the optimisations in DLP resulted in very short execution times for many of the problems. A KSAT system also did well on the Tableaux'98 problems, although it did not perform as well as DLP.

There has also been some testing of decision procedures for propositional modal logics on random formulae. Giunchiglia *et al* [22, 23, 21] designed a random generator for formulae in the modal logic K and tested their systems, KSAT and KSATC, on formulae produced by the generator. Unfortunately, some versions of their generator

† horrocks@cs.man.ac.uk
§ pfps@research.bell-labs.com

suffered from problems which made the results of their testing suspect. The generator was modified by Hustadt and Schmidt[34, 35] to remove some of its problems and used to test the performance of their system, TA, a decision procedure for various propositional modal logics.

We have created a new generator that extends the previous generators, and tested both DLP and KSATC on the formulae produced by this new generator. The results show that it is easy to produce modal formulae that are difficult for both DLP and KSATC, even when there are only six propositional variables and the modal depth is limited to one or two. Nevertheless, both systems performed much better than previous decision procedures for propositional modal logic. The two systems have quite different behaviour on the generated formulae, with neither dominating the other, showing that their optimisations are effective for different kinds of formulae.

We also used the new generator to test the two systems on modal formulae with a maximum modal depth of 100. To our knowledge, this is the first time that propositional modal satisfiability procedures have been tested with such highly modal formulae. Although such problems are mostly very easy, the test did highlight an important difference between the two systems: KSATC finds a small number of these formulae very hard to solve, whereas DLP found them uniformly easy.

2. DLP and KSATC

The two systems we compare are similar in that they both systematically search for a model of a formula. Thus they are complete, non-stochastic procedures. They are quite different from stochastic systems like GSAT [42], or from the TA system, which translates propositional modal formulae into a fragment of first-order logic (basic path logic) and tests the satisfiability of the resulting formulae using a first-order prover (FLOTTER/SPASS [44]) that always terminates on this fragment.

Although DLP and KSATC both use search techniques, they are otherwise quite different. DLP was developed as the core of a description logic reasoner. It includes a complete decision procedure for a very expressive description logic; one that includes propositional dynamic logic as a subset. Because DLP can reason in a superset of propositional dynamic logic, it can be used as a decision procedure for many (multi) modal logics, including $\mathbf{K}_{(\mathbf{m})}$ and $\mathbf{K4}_{(\mathbf{m})}$, and, through simple embeddings, $\mathbf{KT}_{(\mathbf{m})}$ and $\mathbf{S4}_{(\mathbf{m})}$. DLP is similar in capabilities and design to other description logic systems, including FACT and HAM-ALC.

The system KSATC was designed as a reasoner for the propositional modal logic $\mathbf{K}_{(\mathbf{m})}$. Through the standard embedding it can be used to reason in the propositional modal logic $\mathbf{KT}_{(\mathbf{m})}$. However, KSATC cannot handle transitive modalities, so it is unable to reason in $\mathbf{K4}_{(\mathbf{m})}$, $\mathbf{S4}_{(\mathbf{m})}$, or propositional dynamic logic, except by using a complex encoding that produces very difficult to solve formulae.

2.1. DLP

DLP [39] is based on a modal tableaux procedure. Given an input formula, it attempts to create a modal structure that is a witness to the satisfiability of the input formula. This modal structure consists of a collection of nodes and binary relations between the nodes. Each relation corresponds to a particular modality, and if a node x is related to a note y by a relation r, then y is said to be an r-successor of x. Each node x is annotated with a set of subformulae called its label (denoted $\mathcal{L}(x)$), and a structure is said to be contradictory (or contain a *clash*) if some label contains both a formula and its negation. DLP incorporates and extends the implementation philosophy of FACT [27], a description logic system written in LISP. Disjunctions and other choice points are handled via a backtracking mechanism. If the procedure terminates with a suitable (non-contradictory) structure, the formula is satisfiable; if the procedure cannot find such a structure, the formula is unsatisfiable.

Because DLP allows transitive roles and the transitive closure of roles, it has to be able to handle loops in the modal structure. It does this by looking for nodes with the same label (annotated with the same collection of subformulae) and checking for satisfiability or unsatisfiability of the loop. As the testing analysed in this paper does not have transitive features we will not detail this mechanism of DLP, nor will we detail the other mechanisms that support transitive features.

Each diamond formula ($\Diamond_r \phi$) that is true at a node gives rise to an r-successor node labelled with $\{\phi\}$. Each box formula ($\Box_r \phi$) that is true at a node adds the formula ϕ to the label of each r-successor node. (Transitivity modifies this somewhat.) DLP delays the generation of successor nodes until there is no more propositional processing to be performed at a node. This delay is important for some of the optimisations and enhancements that DLP incorporates.

The details of the algorithm, including details of the processing of the various formulae constructors and the precise termination conditions, are fairly standard, and can be found in [41]. DLP is implemented in Standard ML of New Jersey, using a mostly-functional implementation style.

The basic algorithm sketched above is much too slow to form the basis of a useful decision procedure. DLP thus includes a variety of optimisations to improve its performance. These optimisations were initially chosen in an attempt to improve the processing of description logic knowledge bases but have since been revised based on several experiments with DLP. The optimisations include lexical normalisation, semantic branching search, unit resolution, dependency directed backtracking, caching, and heuristic guided search.

Theoretical descriptions of tableaux algorithms often assume that the formula to be tested is in negation normal form, with negations applying only to propositional variables [26, 4, 8]. Assuming that formulae are in negation normal form simplifies the (description of the) algorithm, but then clashes will only be detected when a propositional variable and its negation appear in the same node label, as in negation normal form negation only applies to propositional variables. If there are complex subformulae that occur both positively and negatively in the input formula, there are opportunities to detect clashes earlier.

Clashes can be detected early by transforming formulae into a lexically normalised form that does not move negation inward. Then a clash can be detected whenever any formula, not just propositional variables, and its negation occur in the same node label.

In the lexically normalised form used in DLP, formulae consist only of propositional variables, conjunctions, and diamond formulae, plus their negations. All other formulae are transformed into one of these forms using the obvious equivalences. The normalisation process used in DLP also removes repeated conjuncts and replaces conjunctions that directly contain a formulae and its negation with the negation of the empty conjunction. Further, conjunction is treated as working on a set of conjuncts, and nested conjunctions are flattened. Tableau expansion of formulae in this form is no more complex than if they are in negation normal form [28].

Unrestricted branching on disjunctions can be another source of inefficiency in tableaux procedures. If disjunctions are expanded by searching the different models obtained by adding each of the disjuncts, the alternative branches of the search tree are not disjoint, so there is nothing to prevent the recurrence of an unsatisfiable disjunct in different branches, as noted in [22]. The resulting wasted expansion could be costly if discovering the unsatisfiability requires the solution of a complex sub-problem.

This source of inefficiency is dealt with in DLP by using a semantic branching technique adapted from the Davis-Putnam-Logemann-Loveland procedure (DPLL) commonly used to solve propositional satisfiability (SAT) problems [11, 17]. Instead of choosing an unexpanded disjunction in $\mathcal{L}(x)$, a single disjunct ϕ is chosen from one of the unexpanded disjunctions in $\mathcal{L}(x)$. The two possible sub-trees obtained by adding either ϕ or $\neg\phi$ to $\mathcal{L}(x)$ are then searched. Because the two sub-trees are strictly disjoint, there is no possibility of wasted search as in syntactic branching. There are other methods for reducing repeated work in tableaux procedures, including improved analytic tableaux [43].

An additional advantage of using a DPLL based search technique is that a great deal is known about the implementation and optimisation of this algorithm. In particular, both *unit resolution* and *heuristic guided search* can be used to try to minimise the size of the search tree.

Unit resolution (UR) is a technique used to maximise deterministic expansion, and thus pruning of the search tree via clash detection, before performing non-deterministic expansion (branching) [17]. Before semantic branching is applied to the label of a node x, UR deterministically expands disjunctions in $\mathcal{L}(x)$ which present only one expansion possibility and detects a clash when a disjunction in $\mathcal{L}(x)$ has no expansion possibilities. In effect, UR is using the inference rule

$$\frac{\neg\phi, \phi \vee \psi}{\psi}$$

to simplify the expression represented by $\mathcal{L}(x)$.

Inherent unsatisfiability concealed in sub-problems can easily lead to large amounts of unproductive backtracking search known as thrashing. The problem is exacerbated when all propositional reasoning is performed at a node before any successors are examined.

This problem is addressed in DLP by adapting a form of dependency directed backtracking called *backjumping*, which has been used in solving constraint satisfiability problems [6] (a similar technique was also used in the HARP theorem prover [38]). Backjumping works by labeling formulae with a dependency set indicating the branching points on which they depend. A formula $\phi \in \mathcal{L}(x)$ depends on a branching point when ϕ was added to $\mathcal{L}(x)$ at the branching point or when $\phi \in \mathcal{L}(x)$ depends an another formula $\psi \in \mathcal{L}(y)$, and $\psi \in \mathcal{L}(y)$ depends on the branching point. A formula $\phi \in \mathcal{L}(x)$ depends on a formula $\psi \in \mathcal{L}(y)$ when ϕ was added to $\mathcal{L}(x)$ by a deterministic expansion which used $\psi \in \mathcal{L}(y)$, e.g., if $p \in \mathcal{L}(x)$ was derived from the expansion of $(p \wedge q) \in \mathcal{L}(x)$, then $p \in \mathcal{L}(x)$ depends on $(p \wedge q) \in \mathcal{L}(x)$.

When a clash is discovered, the dependency sets of the clashing formulae can be used to identify the most recent branching point where exploring the other branch might alleviate the cause of the clash. The algorithm can then jump back over intervening branching points *without* exploring alternative branches, which can result in considerable savings. It is possible for this backjumping to jump out of nodes into their ancestors.

During a satisfiability check there may be many successor nodes created. These nodes tend to look considerably alike, particularly as the labels of the r-successors for a node x each contain the same formulae derived from the box formulae $(\Box_r\phi)$ in $\mathcal{L}(x)$. Considerable time can thus be spent performing computations on nodes that have the same label, and as the satisfiability algorithm only cares whether a node is satisfiable or not, this time is wasted.

If the modal successors of a node are only created when all purely propositional processing at that node is exhausted, then all the formulae that would be added to a successor node because of modal formulae in the parent node can be determined when the successor node is first created. The satisfiability status of the successor node is then completely determined by this set of formulae. Under this condition, if there exists another node with the same set of "initial" formulae, then the two nodes will have the same satisfiability status [13].

If the satisfiability status of these sets of formulae are suitably stored, or *cached*, they can then be later retrieved and used to determine the satisfiability status of any new node whose set of initial formulae has already been encountered. Each time this cache is used to successfully determine the satisfiability status of a new node, a considerable amount of processing can be saved, as not only is the work at the new node saved, but also the work at any successors it may have had.

One downside of caching is that the dependency information required for backjumping cannot be effectively calculated for nodes whose processing is eliminated. This happens because the dependency set of any clash detected depends on the dependency sets of the incoming formulae, which will differ between the two nodes. Backjumping can still be performed, however, by combining the dependency sets of all incoming formulae and using that as the dependency set for the unsatisfiable node. This combination may underestimate the amount of backjumping possible, but is generally better than not performing backjumping. Another problem with caching is that it requires that nodes, or at least sets of formulae, be retained until the end of a satisfiability test, changing the storage requirements of the algorithm from polynomial to exponential in the worst case.

Heuristic techniques can be used to guide the search in a way which tries to minimise the size of the search tree. A method which is widely used in DPLL SAT algorithms is to branch on the disjunct which has the Maximum number of Occurrences in disjunctions of Minimum Size—the well known MOMS heuristic [16] and its variants, including the heuristic from Jeroslow and Wang [36]. By choosing a disjunct which occurs frequently in small disjunctions, this heuristic tries to maximise the effect of UR. For example, if the label of a node x contains the unexpanded disjunctions $\phi \vee \psi_1, \ldots, \phi \vee \psi_n$, then branching on ϕ leads to their deterministic expansion in a single step: when ϕ is added to $\mathcal{L}(x)$, all of the disjunctions are fully expanded and when $\neg\phi$ is added to $\mathcal{L}(x)$, UR will expand all of the disjunctions. Branching first on any of $\psi_1, \ldots, \psi_n$, on the other hand, would only cause a single disjunction to be expanded.

Unfortunately this heuristic interacts adversely with the backjumping optimisation by overriding any "oldest first" order for choosing disjuncts: older disjuncts are those that resulted from earlier branching points and will thus lead to more effective pruning if a clash is discovered [27]. Moreover, the heuristic itself is of little value in many interesting modal formulae because it relies for its effectiveness on finding the same disjuncts recurring in multiple unexpanded disjunctions: this is likely in SAT problems, where the disjuncts are propositional variables, and where the number of different variables is usually small compared to the number of disjunctive clauses (otherwise problems would, in general, be easily satisfiable); it is unlikely in modal satisfiability problems, where the disjuncts can be modal formulae, and where the number of different modal formulae is usually large compared to the number of disjunctive clauses. As a result, the heuristic will often discover that all disjuncts have similar or equal priorities, and the guidance it then provides is not particularly useful.

An alternative strategy is to employ a heuristic that tries to maximise the effectiveness of backjumping by using dependency sets to guide the expansion. Whenever a choice is presented, the heuristic chooses the formula whose dependency set includes the earliest branching points. This technique can be used both when selecting disjuncts on which to branch and when selecting the order in which r-successors are expanded.

The current version of DLP allows for various heuristics. The heuristics used in the tests are to use the oldest-first heuristic to select some disjunctions, and then use MOMS along with some weighting based on the size and kind of a formula to select the best-looking disjunct from amongst these disjunctions.

2.2. KSATC

KSATC is based on Böhm's C implementation of the DPLL algorithm. It implements a decision procedure for $\mathbf{K}_{(\mathbf{m})}$ (multi-modal $\mathbf{K}$). KSATC requires its input formulae to be in extended conjunctive normal form, where each formula is a conjunction of disjunctions of (possibly negated) propositional variables and box formulae. The subformula of these box formulae are disjunctions as above.

Böhm's DPLL algorithm was the winner of a 1992 SAT competition [9]. The algorithm is a standard DPLL algorithm that takes a propositional formula in conjunctive normal form and determines whether the formula is satisfiable by giving assignments to the propositional variables in the formula. It uses a very efficient set of data structures to minimise overhead in determining which variable to assign next and to modify the assignments of other variables. It also implements a collection of smart heuristics to determine the order of variable assignments, including the MOMS heuristic.

In KSATC this DPLL algorithm is modified by allowing modal formulae to masquerade as propositional variables as far as the DPLL algorithm is concerned. Thus the DPLL algorithm assigns values to both propositional variables and modal formulae. Further, the pure literal rule is removed, as it is not valid if the literal is a modal formula. Finally, the DPLL algorithm is modified to allow for the possibility of many instances of the algorithm being active at once.

KSATC uses this DPLL algorithm to determine the propositional satisfiability of a node. When a propositional assignment is found, successor nodes are generated as necessary, and their satisfiability is determined by a recursive call. If these successors are all satisfiable, then the node itself is satisfiable; if not, then the DPLL algorithm resumes control and continues to look for other propositional assignments.

KSATC includes one other important optimisation. Successor nodes are not only investigated when a complete propositional assignment is found, they are also investigated just before a new propositional variable is chosen as a branching variable. Only those successors that have new information are actually investigated, however. If some successor is unsatisfiable at this point, then both branches will be unsatisfiable and do not need to be explored, potentially saving a considerable amount of processing.

KSATC incorporates lexical normalisation, much as DLP does, although, of course, only for formulae in conjunctive normal form. This amounts mostly to sorting disjuncts and then checking for syntactic identity.

2.3. Differences between DLP *and* KSATC

DLP is tableaux-based, in that it allows assignment to any subformula, even though it performs semantic branching instead of syntactic branching. Because DLP is tableaux-based, it does not need formulae to be in conjunctive normal form—its normalisation steps do not increase the size of input formulae. KSATC is DPLL-based, in that it assigns only to propositional variables and modal formulae. KSATC requires its input formulae to be in a conjunctive normal form.

DLP includes a large collection of optimisations, including input formulae normalisation, semantic branching, unit resolution, backjumping between modal nodes, caching of modal node status, and heuristic optimisations. KSATC employs a fast DPLL procedure, and thus incorporates most of its optimisations inside each modal node, augmenting these with a modal lookahead optimisation.

DLP is implemented in a functional programming style. Its data structures and low-level algorithms are only moderately optimised. For example, DLP uses a binary tree with functional updates to store the collection of assignments for a node, resulting in changes to the assignments taking time logarithmic in the number of assignments and updates to the status of formulae taking time linear in the number of formulae in the node label. On the other hand, KSATC is written in an imperative programming style, with heavily optimised data structures and low-level algorithms. In KSATC updates to assignments take constant time and updates to the status of formulae take time linear in the number of occurrences of the assigned propositional variable.

We expected that these differences between DLP and KSATC would result in considerable differences between their performance on various test suites.

3. Previous Testing Methodology

Variants and precursors of DLP and KSATC have been tested on various test suites, including the test suite for the Tableaux'98 propositional modal logic comparison [25] and various collections of random formulae.

Randomly generated modal formulae were were first used by Giunchiglia and Sebastiani [22, 23] to test KSAT_0 and KSAT, two predecessors of KSATC that use the same DPLL-based methodology, but not the same optimised implementation of DPLL. Giunchiglia and Sebastiani took their cue from the testing of non-modal propositional satisfiability decision procedures on randomly-generated 3CNF formulae [14, 42]. Their generator generates formulae in $3\text{CNF}_{\mathbf{K_{(m)}}}$.

A $3\text{CNF}_{\mathbf{K_{(m)}}}$ formula is a conjunction of $3\text{CNF}_{\mathbf{K_{(m)}}}$ clauses. A $3\text{CNF}_{\mathbf{K_{(m)}}}$ clause is a disjunction of three $3\text{CNF}_{\mathbf{K_{(m)}}}$ literals, i.e., $3\text{CNF}_{\mathbf{K_{(m)}}}$ atoms or their negations. A $3\text{CNF}_{\mathbf{K_{(m)}}}$ atom is either a propositional variable or a formula of the form $\Box_r\phi$, where ϕ is a $3\text{CNF}_{\mathbf{K_{(m)}}}$ clause. $3\text{CNF}_{\mathbf{K_{(m)}}}$ formulae capture all $\mathbf{K_{(m)}}$ formulae, as there is a satisfiability preserving transformation from $\mathbf{K_{(m)}}$ into $3\text{CNF}_{\mathbf{K_{(m)}}}$.

The generator of Giunchiglia and Sebastiani has several parameters:

- the number of clauses in the main formula, L.
- the number of propositional variables, N.
- the number of modalities, m.
- the probability that an atom is propositional, p.
- the maximum modal depth, d.

A propositional variable is said to have modal depth 0, the modal depth of a propositional formula is the maximum modal depth of its components, and the modal depth of a modal atom $\Box_r\phi$ is one more than the modal depth of ϕ. Regardless of the value of p, the generator will not choose a modal atom if so choosing would result in an overall formula with depth greater than d.

The generator is similar to the one widely used for 3CNF formulae [42]: the first two parameters (L and N) correspond to two of the 3CNF parameters, and in both generators propositional variables (and modal subformulae in the $3\mathrm{CNF}_{\mathbf{K}_{(\mathbf{m})}}$ generator) are negated with probability 0.5.

Giunchiglia and Sebastiani proceeded by fixing N, m, p, and d. They then generated random formulae for various values of L, and used the resulting formulae to test both their own systems and older decision procedures. Their results showed that their systems, KSAT$_0$ and KSAT, were much more effective than previous decision procedures for $\mathbf{K}_{(\mathbf{m})}$. They also showed that multiple modalities, i.e., $m \neq 1$, were easier than single modalities. Subsequent testing has generally been restricted to a single modality.

Unfortunately, the generator of Giunchiglia and Sebastiani suffers from a serious flaw. Instead of selecting different atoms when generating a $3\mathrm{CNF}_{\mathbf{K}_{(\mathbf{m})}}$ clause, their generator allows for repeated $3\mathrm{CNF}_{\mathbf{K}_{(\mathbf{m})}}$ atoms to occur in a $3\mathrm{CNF}_{\mathbf{K}_{(\mathbf{m})}}$ clause. If the atoms are given the same negation status, then the size of the clause is effectively reduced, changing the character of the generated formula. If the atoms are given different negation status the situation can be even worse: tautological or contradictory clauses can be generated, such as $\neg\Box_1(p \vee \neg p \vee q)$. A contradictory clause, even nested deep in a modal subformula, can result in the entire formula being contradictory from just a single one of its clauses. When such formulae are used as input to a decision procedure that includes lexical normalisation, such as DLP, many of the formulae are determined to be satisfiable or unsatisfiable just by lexical normalisation.

Hustadt and Schmidt [34, 35] modified the generator of Giunchiglia and Sebastiani to eliminate some of these problems. The generator of Hustadt and Schmidt ensures that propositional variables only occur once in a $3\mathrm{CNF}_{\mathbf{K}_{(\mathbf{m})}}$ clause. In this way they eliminated many of the problematic formulae generated by Giunchiglia and Sebastiani. With this new generator, and turning off the normalisations of KSAT, they determined that KSAT is much less dominant over previous decision procedures and that their system, TA, is faster than KSAT. This result is somewhat controversial in that it can be claimed on the one hand that normalisation is an integral part of the KSAT system, while on the other hand it can be seen as extraneous to the underlying decision procedure.

We used the improved generator of Hustadt and Schmidt to test the performance of several systems [31, 29, 32], including a previous version of DLP as well as KSAT, as part of a larger series of tests of various modal decision procedures. We concluded that DLP was faster than KSAT, although the speed difference was least on the random formulae.

Giunchiglia, Giunchiglia, Sebastiani, and Tacchella [21] took the improved generator of Hustadt and Schmidt and further improved it. The generator of Hustadt and Schmidt only removes repetitions of propositional variables from clauses. Even if the depth parameter d is 1, this will not remove all repetitions from within clauses, as modal atoms can reoccur. This happens because the number of propositional variables is very small in current tests, and the number of different modal atoms of depth 1 is thus quite small: with 4 propositional variables there are only 32 different depth-1 modal atoms [27]. As the testing often involves top-level formulae with hundreds of clauses there is a significant chance that a top-level formula includes clauses that have repetitions or are tautologies or contradictions. The presence of such clauses can significantly change the expected difficulty of a formula. In our previous testing we found that with formulae from the Hustadt and Schmidt generator, as well as from the earlier Giunchiglia and Sebastiani generator, lexical normalisation was the most important optimisation in DLP.

Giunchiglia *et al* modified the Hustadt and Schmidt generator so that it does not generate repeated modal formulae and tested their improved system, KSATC, on generated formulae. They found that their improved system (with normalisation turned on) was much faster than TA, often by orders of magnitude.

This later testing suffers from flaws of a methodological nature. Hustadt and Schmidt observed that some of the formulae become unsatisfiable simply from top-level propositional interaction[1], and can be determined to be unsatisfiable without investigating any modal successors. They proposed that this factor be eliminated by ensuring that propositional letters only occur at the maximum modal depth, and that this be achieved by setting the parameter p to 0. Their own testing was of this form, as has been most subsequent testing.

Although it is true that formulae that are propositionally unsatisfiable are not very hard, it is not true that test suites that contain significant numbers of propositionally unsatisfiable formulae are uninteresting. First, even formulae with propositional variables only occurring within modal formulae can be determined to be unsatisfiable by DLP without examining any modal successors, because the modal subformulae may repeat in different clauses. Second, restricting propositional variables to only occur at the deepest level eliminates many kinds of formulae. As different systems may perform well (or badly) on different sorts of formulae, it is not a good idea to so severely restrict the sorts of formulae considered.

On the basis of Giunchiglia and Sebastiani's results for formulae of varying modal depth, Hustadt and Schmidt concluded that, relative to the size of formulae, the hardest problems were generated when the modal depth was 1, and they thus fixed d at 1 in all their subsequent experiments. Unfortunately, this result is partly an artifact of Giunchiglia and Sebastiani's generator in that the probability of generating formulae amenable to the normalisation optimisation increases with increasing modal depth.

4. Our Testing Methodology

To show the importance of testing with different sorts of formulae, and also to evaluate the performance of DLP and KSATC, the best-performing modal decision procedures, we have developed a new random formula generator and performed several experiments employing it. These experiments extend the range of hard problems for propositional modal logics and show the effects of the differing optimisations.

Our generator is similar to the twice-improved generator of Giunchiglia *et al* [21], but modified so that it is able to generate less uniform formulae, e.g., by employing different probabilities for negating propositional variables and modal formulae. The modified generator generates $\mathrm{CNF}_{\mathbf{K}_{(\mathbf{m})}}$ formulae employing the following parameters:

- the number of clauses in the main formula, L.
- the number of propositional variables, N.
- the number of modalities, m.
- the maximum modal depth, d.
- the minimum and maximum number of clauses in a disjunct, c_{min}, c_{max}, with equal probability for each number in the range.
- the probability that an atom is propositional, p (except at depth d where all atoms are propositional).

[1] They call these formulae ***trivially unsatisfiable***, although they are different from the problems called trivially unsatisfiable in random constraint satisfaction problems and random QSAT problems [18].

- the probability that a modal formula is negated, n_m.
- the probability that a propositional variable is negated, n_p.

When generating the atoms in a clause, our generator employs a scheme that is equivalent to picking formulae from a population, without repetition, so that the modal structure of a formula is defined by p. The generator does *not* ensure that the $3CNF_{\mathbf{K_{(m)}}}$ clauses in the main conjunctive formula are distinct, effectively picking clauses from a population, but in this case with the possibility of repetition. Because the generator is often employed for small N but large L, there is the distinct possibility that there would be too few clauses of a certain form, such as purely propositional clauses, to allow for distinct clauses while retaining the correct probabilities for modal structures.

We restricted the testing as follows. We used only 1 modality ($m = 1$) because, as discovered earlier, multiple modalities generally cause the problems to become easier. We used only $3CNF_{\mathbf{K_{(m)}}}$ formulae ($c_{min} = c_{max} = 3$). We set the probability of negated propositional variables to 0.5 ($n_p = 0.5$).

However, we varied all the other parameters, not just L and N as in recent testing. We varied the propositional probability (p), using 0.5 and 0.4, as well as 0.0. We varied the maximum modal depth (d), using 2 as well as 1. We varied the probability of negated modal formulae (n_m), using 0.1, as well as 0.5. We varied the number of propositional variables (N) from 3 to 9, ranging the number of clauses from N to $150N$ in increments of N, and generating 100 formulae at each data point. We also performed a separate series of tests with $d = 100$ and p between 0.9 and 0.7. The parameters used in the various tests are summarised in Figure 1.

Both DLP and KSATC were tested using the same seed for the random number generator in the formula generator. We did not see any disagreements between DLP and KSATC on any of the formulae although we did not make a systematic search for disagreements.

We would have liked to try all combinations of the parameters above. However, this would have taken much too long, so we had to pick various combinations of the parameters and various ranges of N. Moreover, we used a timeout of 1,000 seconds of CPU time, and terminated processing on a data point as soon as it became evident that the median time would exceed the timeout. All times reported are CPU times, provided from DLP and KSATC, exclusive of any time required to read, translate, or preprocess the formulae: the extra time just confuses the results, and would include different sorts of processing for the two systems.

4.1. Testing Details

The February 1999 version (version 3.2) of DLP was used for the tests. This version is very close to previous versions of DLP; the only differences are some optimisations to make processing of large formulae more efficient. This version of DLP is available at `http://www.bell-labs.com/user/pfps/dlp`. DLP was run under Standard ML of New Jersey, version 110.0.3.

A single setting of the options for DLP was used throughout the tests. All the optimisations mentioned above were turned on, and the heuristics were set to select a formulae from among the backjumping-oldest clauses using a MOMS-style heuristic. The code to handle the transitive closure of modalities was turned off.

For the tests KSATC was compiled under g++, version 2.7.2.3, with optimisation -O2, as in the supplied makefile. The version of KSATC used for previous testing was used in these tests. It is available at `ftp://ftp.mrg.dist.unige.it/pub/mrg-systems/KR98-sources/KSat-source/KSatC`.

Our testing was performed on two classes of machines. Most testing was performed on upgraded SPARCstation 20s with two 150 MHz Ross RT626 CPUs, roughly equivalent to a 140M SPARC Ultra-1, and 128M of main memory. Testing for propositional probability 0.0 was performed on a SPARC Ultra-2 with two 296 MHz UltraSPARC-II CPUs and 256M of main memory. The testing machines were otherwise very lightly loaded. Tests that were rerun showed almost exactly the same timing; in all examined cases the difference was less than the maximum of 0.02 seconds or 1 percent of the run time. Using a different seed for the random number generator *did* result in different timing results, but the qualitative and comparative results were unchanged in all examined cases.

The formula generator was coded in Standard ML of New Jersey. Each test started with a known random seed, which was not reset during the run. The random number generator was used only to generate formulae, so that the tests would be reproducible. If a test was terminated prematurely, it was restarted by reading the results of the previous run of the test, generating random formulae without testing them for each test performed by the previous run, and then continuing in the normal fashion.

For the DLP tests, the formulae were generated and tested in the same process. Each test was terminated as soon as the time limit of 1,000 CPU seconds was exceeded, as calculated by the built-in timing facilities of Standard ML of New Jersey. The times reported include any garbage collection that happened during the test. For the KSATC tests, the formulae were written in a format acceptable to KSATC and then read in and tested by a different process. This separate process was limited to 1200 seconds of real time; if this time limit was exceeded, the test was deemed to have take at least 1000 seconds of CPU time. This extra limit was needed, as KSATC sometimes did not terminate gracefully. As the testing systems were very lightly loaded, it is extremely unlikely that any results would have been different without this real time limit.

Tests	N	m	d	c_{min}	c_{max}	p	n_m	n_p
1	3–9	1	2	3	3	0.5	0.5	0.5
2	3–9	1	1	3	3	0.5	0.5	0.5
3	3–7	1	1	3	3	0.0	0.5	0.5
4	3–8	1	1	3	3	0.4	0.5	0.5
5	3–7	1	2	3	3	0.5	0.1	0.5
6	3–8	1	2	3	3	0.4	0.5	0.5
7	3–6	1	100	3	3	0.9–0.7	0.5	0.5

Figure 1. Test parameter settings

The results of our testing are presented in two kinds of graph. The first and most common kind of graph plots run time against the ratio of clauses to number of propositional variables (L/N) for a single test, i.e., various values of N, and fixed values of maximum modal depth (d), propositional probability (p), and modal negation probability (n_m). Each graph shows, on a log scale, either the median, the 90th percentile, or the worst case run time for either DLP or KSATC. The Pth percentile is the maximum time taken by the fastest $P\%$ of the tests, so the 50th percentile would be equivalent to the median.

The second kind of graph is three-dimensional and plots, again on a log scale, the fiftieth through one hundredth percentile run times against L/N for a single test and a single value of N. Overlaid on these plots are dotted surfaces that show the ratio of satisfiable to total solvable formulae, as determined by DLP or KSATC, provided that the program could solve at least half of the formulae at that point.

5. Test Results

The first series of tests that we performed was for maximum modal depth 2, propositional probability 0.5, and modal negation probability 0.5. We ran tests with 3 through 9 propositional variables. The tests with 3, 4, and 5 variables correspond to some of the original tests performed by Giunchiglia and Sebastiani [23], while those with 3, 4, 5, and 8 variables correspond to some of the tests performed by Hustadt and Schmidt, although in both cases the improved formulae generator now eliminates local redundancies, tautologies, and contradictions. The results for DLP and KSATC are given in Figure 2. These formulae are not all easy, and there is a general easy-hard-easy behaviour for both DLP and KSATC. However, the shape of the curves is very different from the narrow, pronounced peak in propositional satisfiability. Instead, there is a general "half-dome" shape to the curves. This shape is caused by two factors. First, there are many modal successors and if the formula is satisfiable they all have to be investigated. If the successors are all or almost all easily determined to be satisfiable then they contribute a polynomial growth in difficulty as the formula grows in size, resulting in the left-hand-side of the half-dome. Second, at some point enough formulae become trivially unsatisfiable, and thus easy for both DLP and KSATC, resulting in the steep "cliff". This point varies somewhat with the number of variables and there may be some "ringing", particularly at the higher percentiles.

The only major exception to this smooth half-dome shape occurs with small numbers of propositional variables, most prominently at $N = 3$. Here for L/N in the range 50–70 there are some formulae that are harder than would be indicated by half-dome-shaped successor evaluation. This behaviour shows up most clearly at the higher percentiles. The hard formulae are those where there are a significant number of modal successors whose satisfiability status is hard to determine, resulting in backtracking and a peak in the difficulty. These extra-hard formulae are highlighted in Figure 3.

The results for DLP and KSATC are given in Figure 2. These formulae are not all easy, and there is a general easy-hard-easy behaviour for both DLP and KSATC. However, the shape of the curves is very different from the narrow, pronounced peak in propositional satisfiability. Instead, there is a general "half-dome" shape to the curves. This shape is caused by two factors. First, there are many modal successors and if the formula is satisfiable they all have to be investigated. If the successors are all or almost all easily determined to be satisfiable then they contribute a polynomial growth in difficulty as the formula grows in size, resulting in the left-hand-side of the half-dome. Second, at some point enough formulae become trivially unsatisfiable, and thus easy for both DLP and KSATC, resulting in the steep "cliff". This point varies somewhat with the number of variables and there may be some "ringing", particularly at the higher percentiles.

The only major exception to this smooth half-dome shape occurs with small numbers of propositional variables, most prominently at $N = 3$. Here for L/N in the range 50–70 there are some formulae that are harder than would be indicated by half-dome-shaped successor evaluation. This behaviour shows up most clearly at the higher percentiles. The hard formulae are those where there are a significant number of modal successors whose satisfiability status is hard to determine, resulting in backtracking and a peak in the difficulty. These extra-hard formulae are highlighted in Figure 3.

DLP generally performs better than KSATC for these tests, being often two orders of magnitude faster than KSATC. However, DLP is not always faster than KSATC.

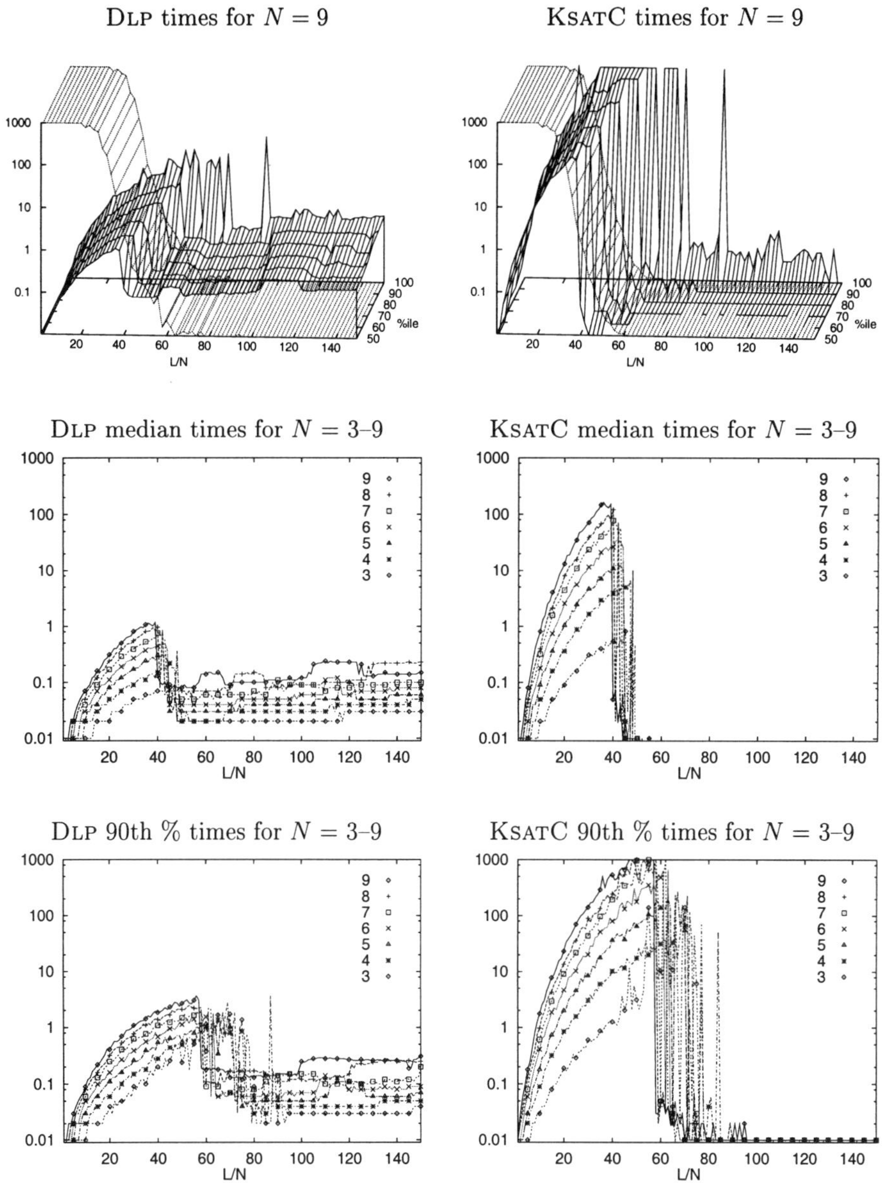

Figure 2. Results for test 1 ($d = 2$, $p = 0.5$, and $n_m = 0.5$)

In the trivially-unsatisfiable region KSATC is faster than DLP (less than 0.01 seconds compared with about 0.1 seconds). This is because DLP's data structures and low-level algorithms are not heavily optimised, and it takes several hundredths of a second just to go through these large formulae. The DPLL algorithm in KSAT can perform single passes over a large set of clauses in a very short time, and KSAT can thus process large trivially unsatisfiable formulae very quickly.

For data points in the L/N range from about 20–50, where all or most of the successors are satisfiable, DLP is uniformly faster than KSATC. Much of this difference is due to KSATC investigating modal successors every time a new branching variable is chosen. Modal successors do not produce much, if any, unsatisfiability in these tests, so the investigation of modal successors does not cut off search. Worse, KSATC has to investigate some modal successors very often, as each time a new box formula is assigned true, every modal successor has to be re-examined.

Even outside the above ranges (of L/N values), DLP consistently performs better than KSATC for *satisfiable* formulae. Although there may be some benefit in examining modal successors early for these formulae, this benefit would occur only when a large number of box formulae have been assigned true. Because of the repeated work performed by KSATC on such successors, it does not appear that the benefits are realised.

This series of tests shows that it is not a good idea to restrict testing to depth 1 and propositional probability 0, as this would ignore at least one area where DLP significantly outperforms KSATC.

The second series of tests that we performed was for maximum modal depth 1, propositional probability 0.5, and modal negation probability 0.5. We again ran tests with 3 through 9 propositional variables. These tests do not correspond to any previous tests, as all previous testing with propositional probability different from 0.0 was performed with maximum modal depth greater than 1.

The results of the tests for DLP and KSATC are given in Figure 4. In these tests there is a more distinct easy-hard-easy behaviour with a pronounced peak from both DLP and KSATC although the peak is quite wide by propositional satisfiability standards.

Again, DLP generally performs better than KSATC, but the difference is less: only slightly more than one order of magnitude. Also, there is a new area where KSATC outperforms DLP.

In these tests, when the formulae are mostly unsatisfiable but not trivially unsatisfiable, the modal successors do provide an important source of the unsatisfiability. KSATC's early investigation of the modal successors can thus be used to cut off search. This shows up in the results for values of L/N around about 40, where KSATC is considerably faster than DLP.

As pointed out by Hustadt and Schmidt, the tests with maximum modal depth 1 are in some sense *harder* than the tests with maximum modal depth 2. This is true almost uniformly for DLP for larger numbers of propositional variables, except where the low-level overhead is most prominent. It is also true in some sense for KSATC, as with a given number of propositional variables the hardest median depth-1 problems are harder for KSATC than the hardest depth-2 problems. If the difference in average formula size between the two sets of formulae is taken into consideration, the depth-1 formulae are decidedly harder.

This being the case, why should the depth-2 formulae be investigated at all? First, it is not appropriate to limit investigations to just some small group of formula unless the excluded formulae can be transformed into the investigated ones. This is certainly not the case here, as a limitation to a modal depth of 1 removes from consideration the vast majority of modal formulae. Second, the hardest formulae may change with different systems. Although this is not the case here, at least for DLP, there are significant differences in the results for the groups of formulae. If attention had been paid to only one group, these differences would not have been seen.

But why is modal depth 1 "harder" than modal depth 2? Well, both DLP and KSATC include the MOMS heuristic. Because there are more modal atoms than propositional variables, and because modal atoms and propositional variables are picked with the same probability (except at the deepest depth), the atom that has the highest MOMS score will almost certainly be a propositional atom. Therefore both DLP and KSATC will end up with assignments at the root node that are heavily weighted to giving values to propositional variables. The only modal atoms that will be given assignments are those that are required to make all the clauses evaluate to true.

So how many modal atoms will be given assignments? Clauses with three propositional literals will generate no assignments to modal atoms. Clauses with two propositional literals will, on average, have one of their propositional literals assigned to true in three out of four cases, and thus will produce an assignment to a modal atom in only one out of four cases. Clauses with one propositional literal will, on average, have it assigned to true in one out of two cases, and thus will produce an assignment to a modal atom in only one out of two cases. Clauses with no propositional literals will give rise to an assignment to a modal atom in every case.

If we make the assumption that modal atoms occur only once[2], then for propositional probability 0.5 about

$$\frac{3}{8}\frac{1}{4} + \frac{3}{8}\frac{1}{2} + \frac{1}{8}1$$

or 13/32 of the clauses will give rise to an assignment to a modal atom. About half of these assignments will result in a box formula and about half in a diamond formula. Therefore at the next depth there will only be about 13/64 or 1/5 as many clauses as at the current depth.

For maximum modal depth of 1, this means that a top-level formula with about $30N$ clauses will give rise to modal successors with about $6N$ clauses. Such clauses will be propositional, and because clauses can occur multiple times at the top level, this is just about at the hardest L/N point for propositional formulae. This is also near the point where the strictly propositional clauses in the formula as a whole (1/8 of the total clauses) are providing a non-trivial problem at that level. The compounding of the two sources of hardness results in very hard problems.

As the number of clauses increases, the sub-problems generated become more unsatisfiable, so early detection of this unsatisfiability becomes more beneficial. This is precisely where KSATC outperforms DLP.

For maximum modal depth of 2, a top-level formula with about $40N$ clauses will give rise to modal successors with about $8N$ clauses. Such clauses will have maximum modal depth 1, and give rise to problems similar to (but not exactly the same as) the maximum modal depth 1 problems generated by the formula generator. With only $8N$ clauses, the chance of such problems being satisfiable is almost exactly 1.0, and both DLP and KSATC are able to find a satisfying assignment in very little time and with very little search. Therefore, the time taken here is due to the very large number of modal successors investigated rather than to their individual hardness. As KSATC goes through this search multiple times for each top-level assignment, it takes longer on some depth 2 problems. As DLP does this investigation only once for each top-level assignment, and thus often only once in total, it is much faster on these sorts of problems.

Top-level formulae with more clauses are usually trivially unsatisfiable, and thus do not give rise to any modal processing. Those top-level formulae that are not trivially unsatisifiable, however, can be difficult, as their modal successors may have enough clauses to be moderately difficult in their own right. This is the cause of the occasional difficult problems for $L/N > 80$.

[2] This is not a valid assumption for small numbers of propositional variables and large numbers of clauses, but it is not too far off for the analysis here, except for very small numbers of propositional variables where the analysis breaks down somewhat.

Our third series of tests has maximum modal depth 1, propositional probability 0.0, and modal negation probability 0.5. We ran tests with 3 through 7 propositional variables. These are similar to some of the tests performed by Hustadt and Schmidt and by Giunchiglia *et al* [21].

The results of the tests for DLP and KSATC are given in Figure 5. The qualitative behaviour of both DLP and KSATC is yet again different. There is an easy-hard-easy pattern, but the hard section is spread over most of the L/N values and the formulae only gradually become easier.

In these tests KSATC performs much better than DLP. This is to be expected, as almost all of the unsatisfiability comes from the modal successors, which are all easy to investigate, because there are a small number of propositional variables and the maximum modal depth is 1. Because KSATC aggressively investigates the modal successors it can significantly reduce search in the root node, and for these formulae the advantage of this reduction outweighs the disadvantage of potentially repeated investigations of each successor. DLP, on the other hand, does not investigate modal successors until it has discovered a complete top-level assignment. It will therefore generate many more top-level assignments and have to examine the modal successors, although in many cases these will be nearly the same. DLP's caching of modal results does not help very much as there are so many different modal successors that can be generated.

We next ran a series of tests with an "intermediate" value for the propositional probability to see where the cross-over between DLP and KSATC lies. These tests have maximum modal depth 1, propositional probability 0.4, and modal negation probability 0.5.

The results of the tests for DLP and KSATC are given in Figure 6. Here the two systems are very close in performance, with KSATC being slightly faster and having a smaller range of L/N in which it finds hard problems. With a propositional probability of 0.4, the benefits of KSATC's aggressive modal investigation are starting to outweigh its detriments, especially in the slightly overconstrained area.

The qualitative behaviour of both systems is intermediate between the two previous tests, with a pronounced peak in difficulty but one quite a bit wider than the peak for $p = 0.5$.

So with a maximum modal depth of 1, DLP performs better than KSATC when the propositional probability is high and worse when the propositional probability is low. When the propositional probability is low the modal successors have a high chance of being overconstrained and KSATC's early investigation of the incomplete successors will find unsatisfiability early, thus cutting off considerable amounts of search. When the propositional probability is high the modal successors have a high chance of being satisfiable, or only being unsatisfiable when all information is known about them. Here, most or all of KSATC's early investigation of incomplete successors will be wasted effort.

Our fifth set of tests further investigated formulae with a maximum modal depth of 2. There are two ways to make the tests with maximum modal depth of 2 harder. The first approach is to reduce the propositional probability. The second approach to make the tests harder is to have fewer but larger modal successors by reducing the probability of negating a modal atom, which, in this generator, are always box formulae. This approach has the advantage that the change does not affect the size of the resulting formulae, whereas reducing the propositional probability considerably increases formula size.

We performed a series of tests with maximum modal depth 2, propositional probability 0.5, and modal negation probability 0.1. The results for DLP and KSATC are given in Figure 7. In these tests DLP has by far the better median performance, by a couple of orders of magnitude. However, DLP is slower on the harder formulae in this series. This is because the harder formulae provide places for KSATC's early investigation of modal successors to cut off search, whereas DLP has to investigate many more choice points before determining that the modal successors block any solution.

We also performed testing with maximum modal depth 2 and propositional probability 0.4. These results of these tests are given in Figure 8. Again DLP is generally faster than KSATC, often by several orders of magnitude. The only place where DLP is slower than KSATC is in the trivially unsatisfiable region.

KSATC's early investigation of modal successors performs very poorly in these tests, as indicated by the relative height of the half-dome section of the tests. Even where there are hard modal successors, and early investigation might provide some early cutoffs, KSATC performs worse than DLP. This is probably due to the backjumping optimisation in DLP.

These tests have some of the half-dome behaviour indicative of many but easy modal successors. However, there is even more indication of backtracking behaviour, most prominent for small numbers of propositional variables, but still evident with 8 propositional variables. Plots detailing this behaviour are given in Figure 9.

The plots show that, for DLP, the tests with smaller numbers of propositional variables are harder than the test with 8 propositional variables. This unusual behaviour occurs because of conditions in the modal successors for very small numbers of propositional variables having to do with the few modal formulae of depth 1 and the presence of conjunctions supplied by the top-level diamond formula. These conditions give rise to modal subproblems that are more difficult than they would otherwise be. KSATC experiences similar hardness effects but they are masked by its repeated examination of the modal successors.

For our last set of tests we investigated a very different kind of formulae. We wanted to see what would happen if there were no "hard stop" to the modal structure, and thus create formulae where the modal subformulae looked just like the main formula, except smaller. One way of creating such formulae would be to have no maximum modal depth. We approximated formulae with no maximum modal depth by setting the maximum modal depth parameter, d, to 100. We ran tests with the propositional probability, p, ranging from 0.9 to 0.7 and the number of propositional variables, N ranging from 3 to 6.

In these tests the propositional probability cannot be lowered much beyond 0.7 or else the generated formulae become too large to store. Even with a propositional probability of 0.7 the formulae generated are very large, as at each level the expected number of clauses shrinks by only about 5 percent. (However, the number of clauses in the modal successors shrinks by about 50 percent, because only half of the modal clauses are box formulae.)

The results for DLP and KSATC for propositional probabilities of 0.75 and 0.7 are given in Figures 10 and 11. It is obvious that these formulae are not nearly as difficult as some of the earlier formulae. DLP found all the formulae extremely easy—the processing required for the formulae that required the most search (for L/N from around 30 to 50) was less than the processing required for the largest formulae, which are trivially unsatisfiable and require almost no search.

KSATC found most of the formulae easy, although there is a small harder section for L/N around 10–30, resulting in behaviour qualitatively different from that of DLP. In this section there were even a few formulae that KSATC found very hard, as shown in the top graphs of Figures 10 and 11. To better illustrate this effect, the results for the hardest formulae at each data point for propositional probabilities of 0.8, 0.75, and 0.7

are given in Figure 12. As these results show, for propositional probability 0.7 KSATC usually took between 0.5 and 10 seconds to solve the hardest formulae at data points with L/N between 15 and 50. However, in some cases it took around 100 seconds, and in a very few cases it took longer than 1,000 seconds. The results for propositional probability 0.75 are similar, except that the usual worst-case was slightly under 0.1 seconds, and only a couple of formulae took a very long time.

These harder formulae are those where KSATC is investigating many modal successors multiple times. On the other hand, DLP found all these formula very easy, with the hardest of the hardest taking only around 0.1 seconds, except for the very large formulae where DLP's processing overhead pushed the processing time up to 0.5 seconds.

If the size of the formulae are taken into consideration, these formulae are much easier than the previous ones, even though KSATC finds some of them very hard. However, they do provide another useful data point indicating that concentration on one kind of formula does not present a complete performance picture.

6. Conclusion

Our experiments with DLP and KSATC show that they are both effective decision procedures. Both systems are vastly better than previous approaches. Neither system dominates the other: DLP is better when there are complex modal subproblems, or these modal subproblems are mostly satisfiable; KSATC is better for big, simple problems, and where the modal subproblems provide early cutoffs.

Both systems still have weaknesses. DLP suffers from a mostly-functional implementation style; KSATC suffers from the divorce between its propositional and modal components. While it would be relatively easy to reimplement DLP with better data structures and low-level algorithms, we believe that the problem with the KSATC approach is more fundamental as its use of a pre-existing propositional reasoner makes it extremely hard to employ any optimisation techniques, such as backjumping, that cut across the separate modal and propositional reasoning steps. This is because adding such optimisations to KSATC would involve significant modifications of its propositional reasoner which is not created by the authors of KSATC.

Further, the early investigation of modal successors, which is a major optimisation in KSATC, is also a source of inconsistent performance. This early investigation can be very effective if the modal successors can quickly shown to be unsatisfiable before all the propositional reasoning is performed. However, it can also result in much extra work if the modal successors are mostly satisfiable or only unsatisfiable when all information is known about them. In the experiment with maximum modal depth 100, the extra work caused by this optimisation produces a "false" peak in difficulty, which is completely absent in DLP.

Moreover, extending KSATC to deal with more expressive logics may be problematical as the loop-checking required to guarantee termination, and other processing required for the more-expressive logics, may be difficult to interface with the propositional reasoner. Tableaux systems on the other hand can easily be extended to deal with a wide range of expressive logics [2, 3, 5, 19, 33]: DLP, for example, already deals with a superset of propositional dynamic logic. However, in KSATC's favour is the fact that it can take advantage of most advances in propositional satisfiability testing simply by substituting Böhm's DPLL implementation with a more efficient SAT procedure and making the few changes required to eliminate optimisations that are not valid in a modal setting;[3] this would be more difficult in DLP where the propositional and modal components are tightly integrated.

Our experiments also show that concentrating on one set of tests is not appropriate, and can give misleading results if used as a methodology for comparing satisfiability testers. The two systems tested here behaved differently on the different sets of tests, and concentrating on one set of tests would have masked the benefits of certain optimisations and the drawbacks of others. Moreover, the increased complexity of propositional modal formulae, and the interaction between propositional and modal reasoning, gives rise to results that would have been difficult to predict without detailed analysis of both formulae and algorithms.

Our experiments generally show an easy-hard-easy distribution, as in propositional satisfiability. However, there is no hard peak evidenced in many of the experiments, and the different experiments produce qualitatively different results. The differences are partly due to the greater numbers of parameters in the modal case; with more ways of setting the parameters there are more kinds of behaviour possible. The lack of a hard peak may also be partly due to the inadequacies of the provers being tested, and there may be optimisations yet undiscovered that would restrict the hard problems to a small range of parameter values. The lack of a hard peak may also be partly due to the hardness of the problem: current provers cannot reach beyond small numbers of propositional variables, so asymptotic behaviour may not yet be evidenced.

There are other parameter settings that should be investigated. We have only reported results for modal depths 1 and 2 with a clause length of 3, and results for modal depth 100. We have mostly used a modal negation probability of 0.5. Changing any of these would result in different kinds of tests.

We are experimenting with new approaches for building modal decision procedures as part of a continuing effort to build effective systems for expressive description logics. Our newest system, in its early stages of development, employs an advanced form of backtracking, called dynamic backtracking [20]. It also performs early analysis of modal successors but does not throw away the successful successor nodes, retaining them instead for the duration of the proof. In this way we hope to further improve the performance of propositional modal satisfiability testing procedures.

[3] Some propositional reasoners may, of course, be implemented in a fashion that makes the changes required for the KSATC approach difficult or impossible. However, the changes are not extensive and should be possible for most propositional reasoners. They are certainly much less involved than the modifications required to augment the control structure of a propositional reasoner to incorporate an optimisation like backjumping across modal nodes.

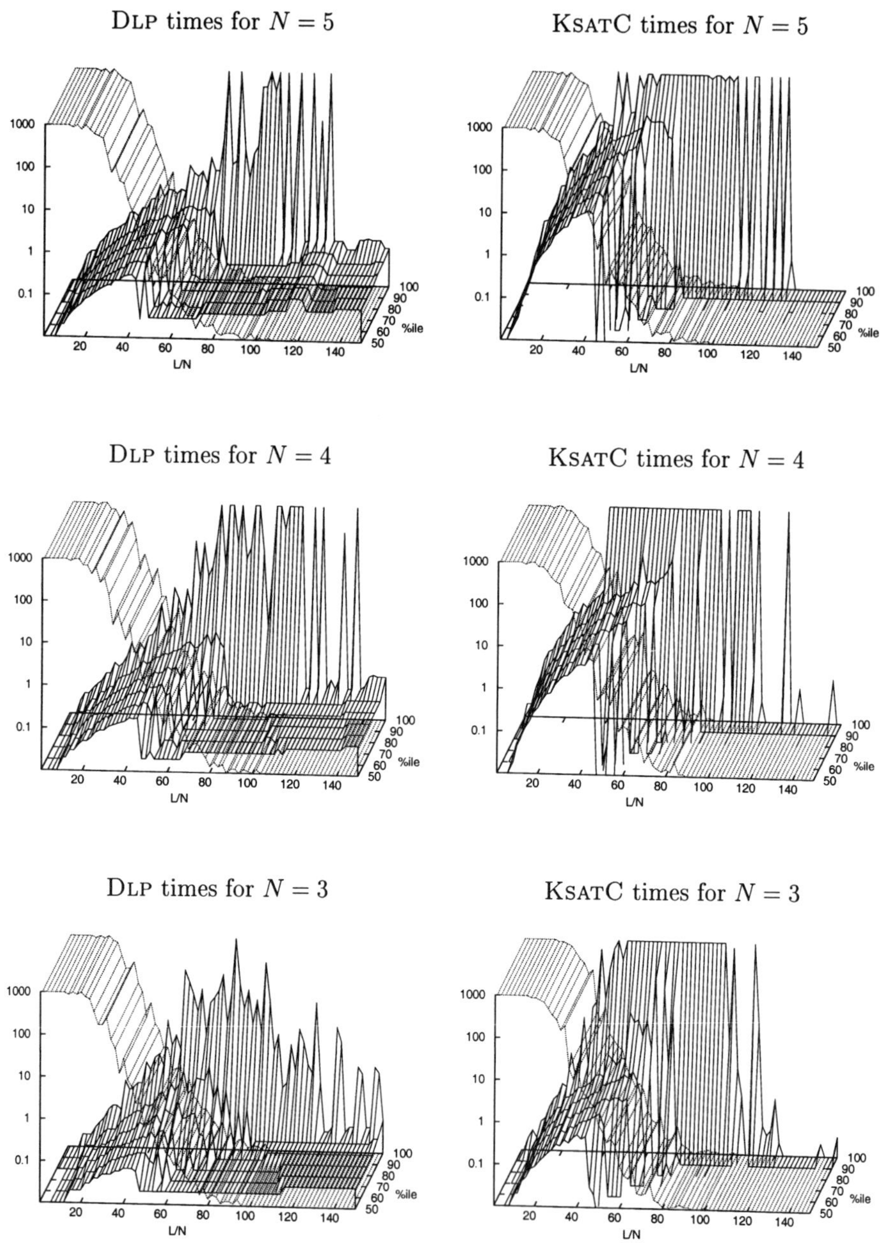

Figure 3. Detailed results for test 1 ($d = 2$, $p = 0.5$, and $n_m = 0.5$)

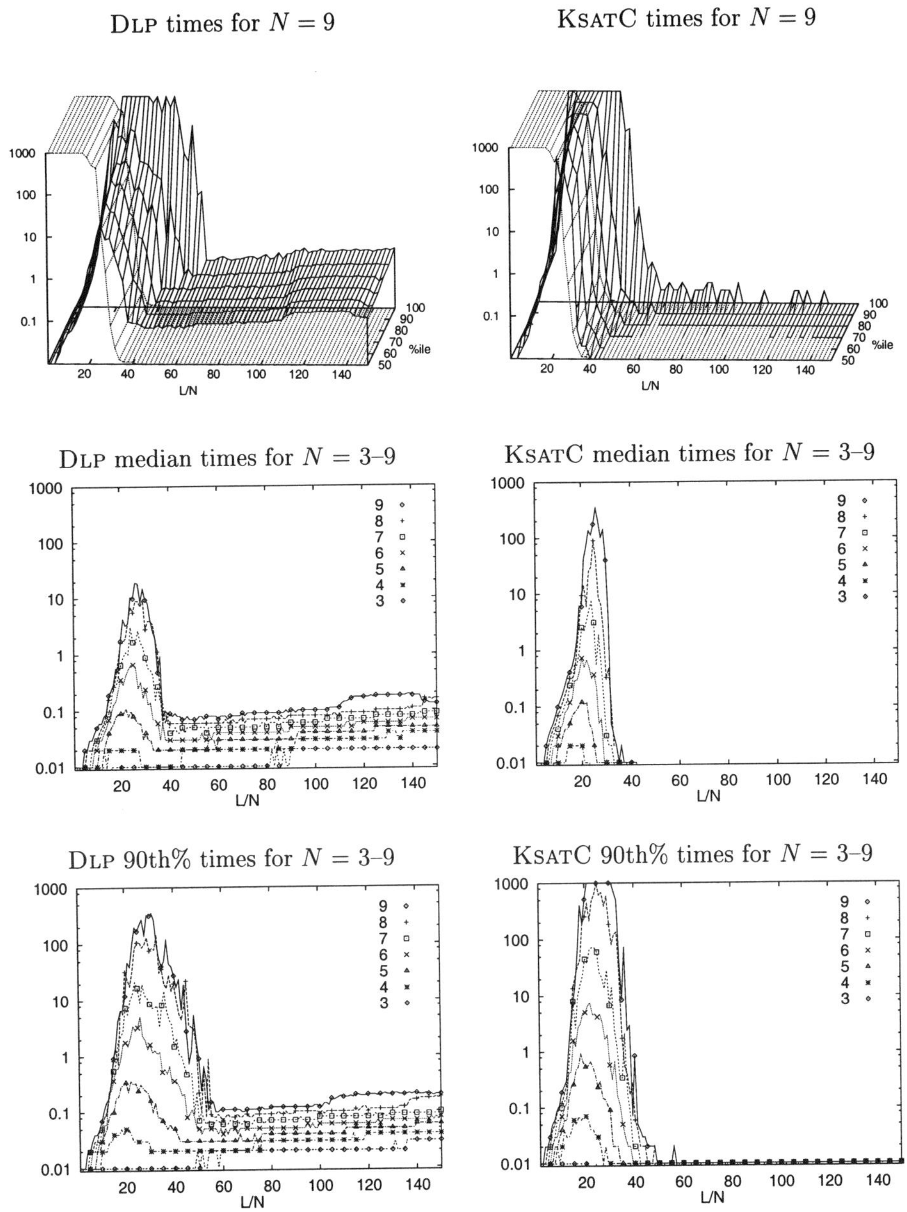

Figure 4. Results for test 2 ($d = 1$, $p = 0.5$, and $n_m = 0.5$)

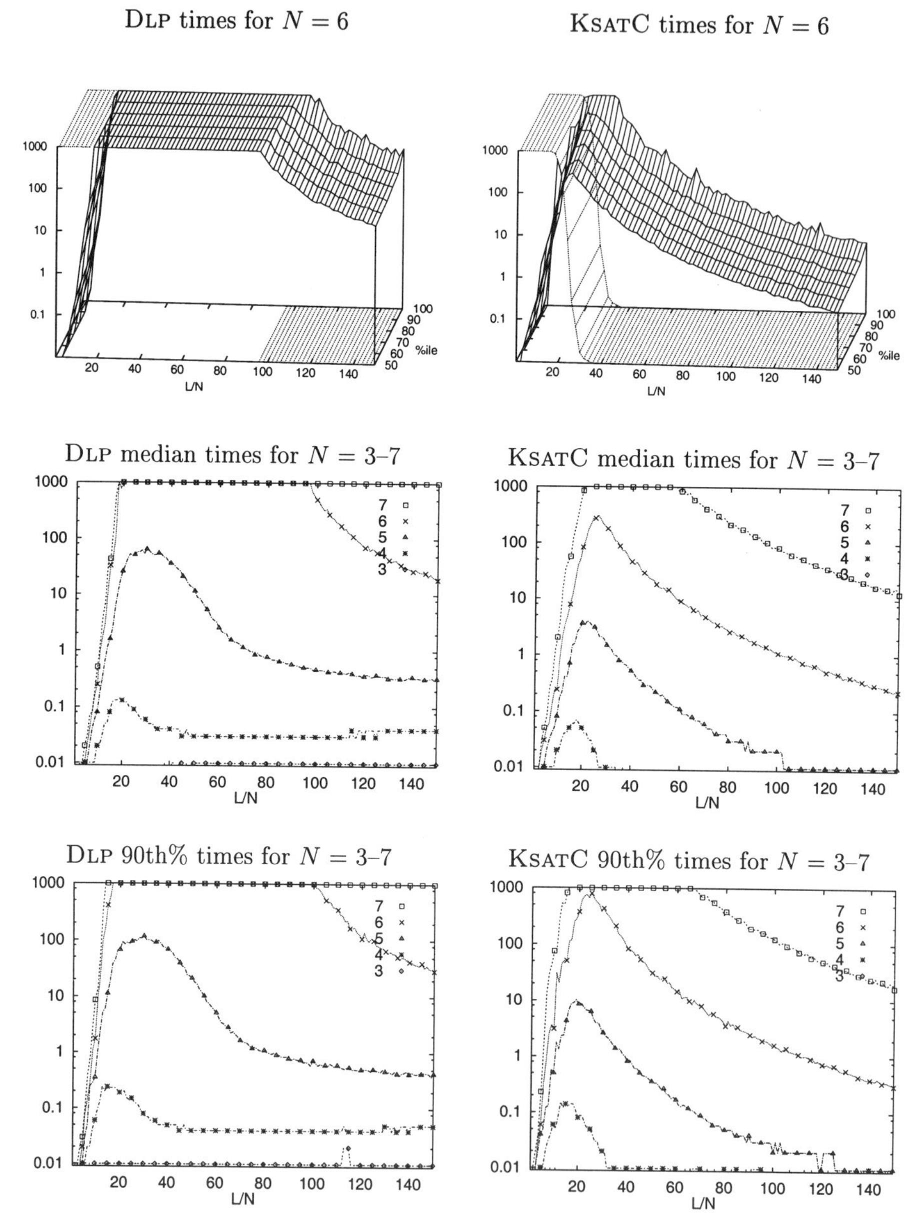

Figure 5. Results for test 3 ($d = 1$, $p = 0.0$, and $n_m = 0.5$)

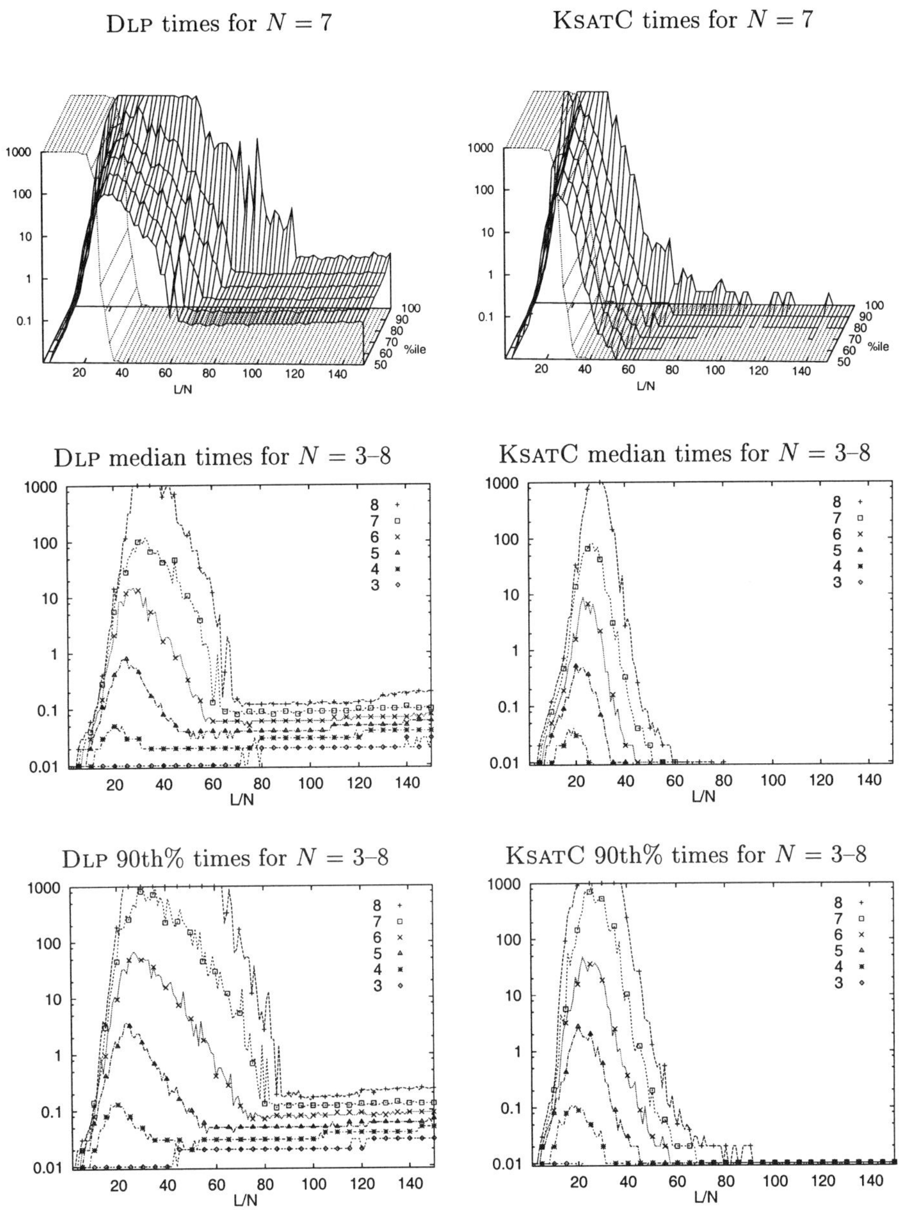

Figure 6. Results for test 4 ($d = 1$, $p = 0.4$, and $n_m = 0.5$)

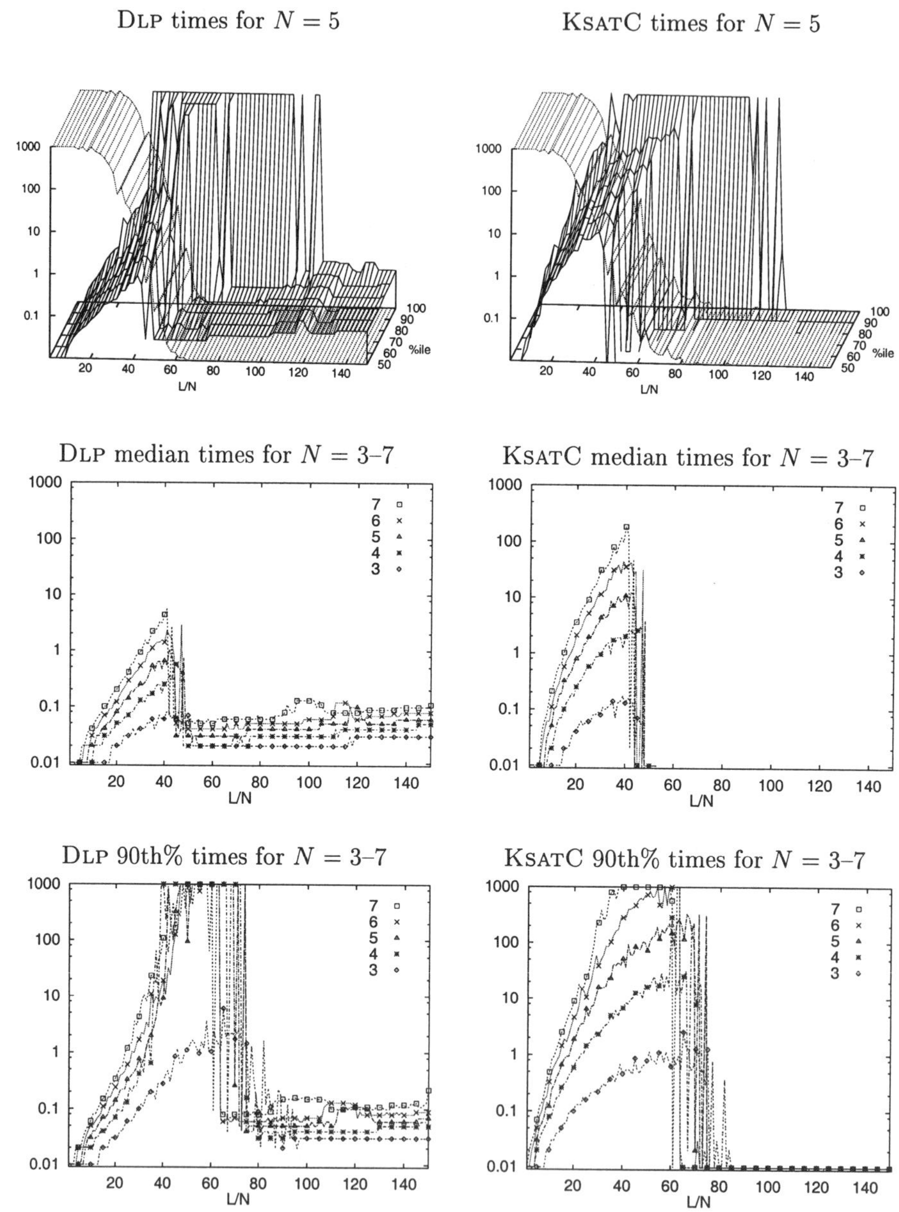

Figure 7. Results for test 5 ($d = 2$, $p = 0.5$, and $n_m = 0.1$)

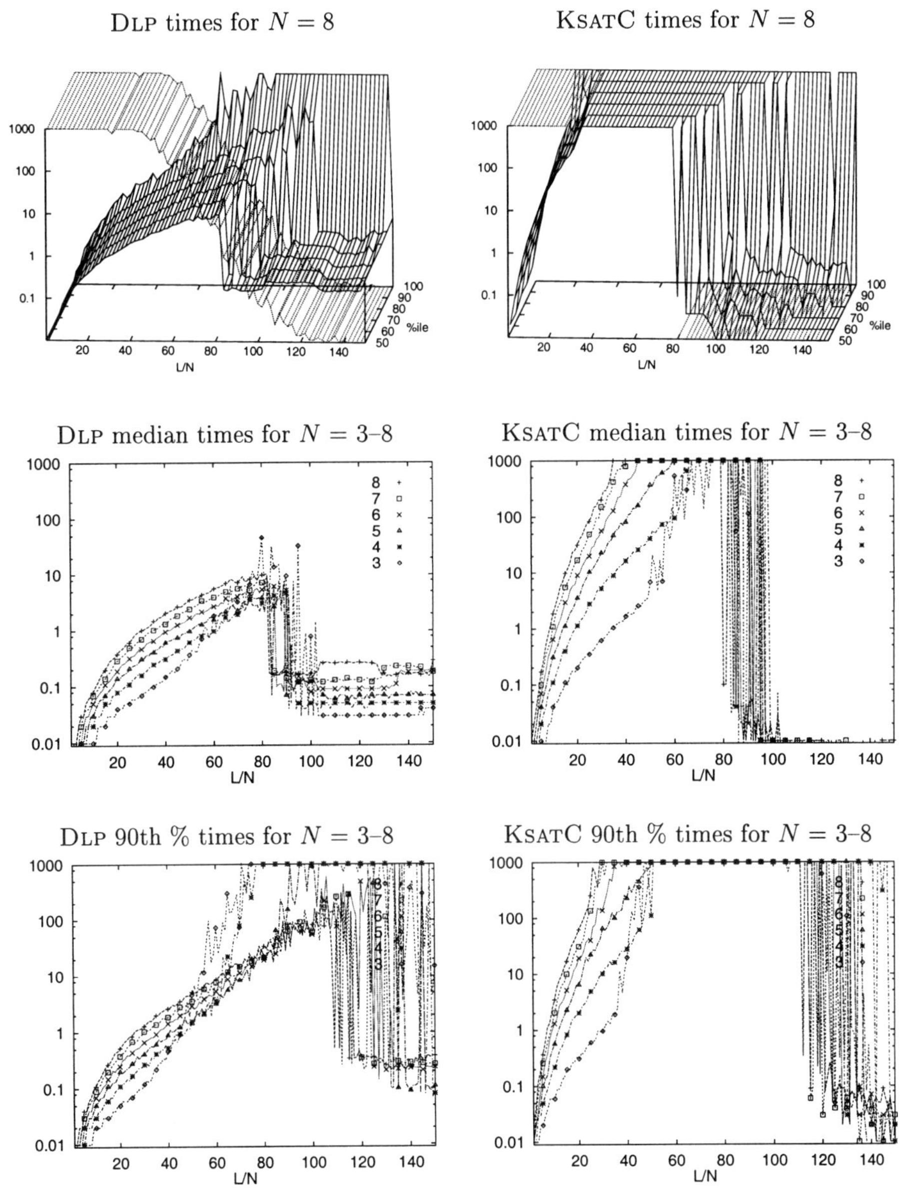

Figure 8. Results for test 6 ($d = 2$, $p = 0.4$, and $n_m = 0.5$)

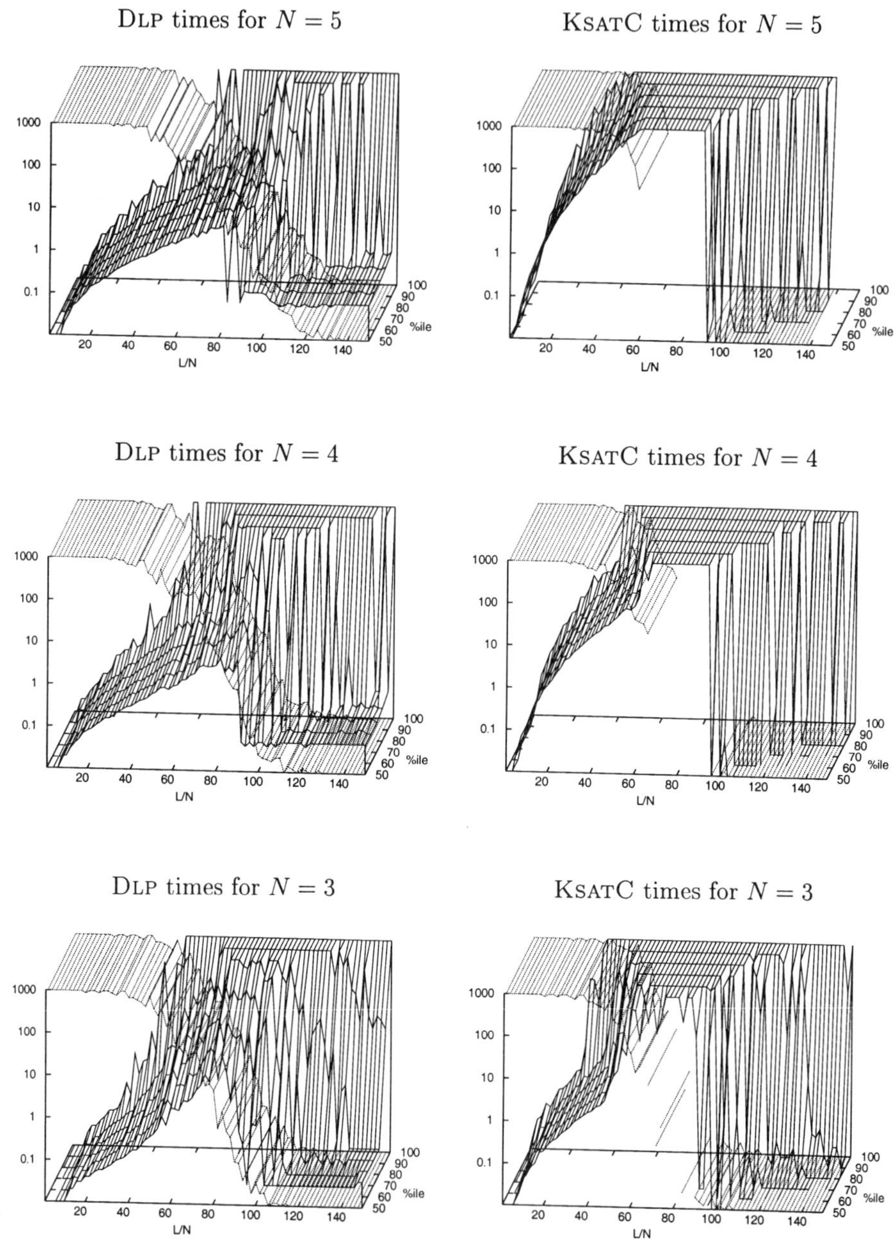

Figure 9. Detailed results for test 6 ($d = 2$, $p = 0.4$, and $n_m = 0.5$)

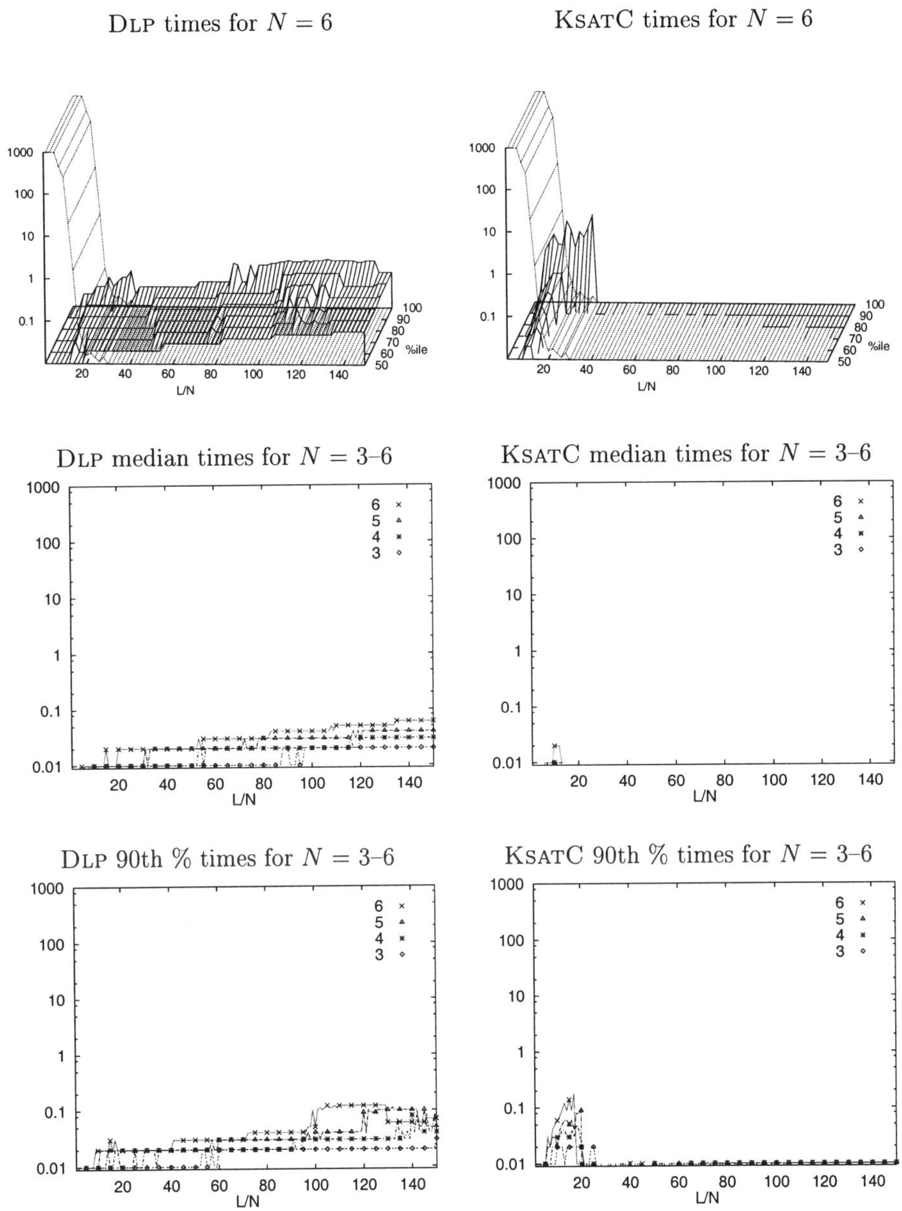

Figure 10. Results for test 7, part 1 ($d = 100$, $p = 0.75$, and $n_m = 0.5$)

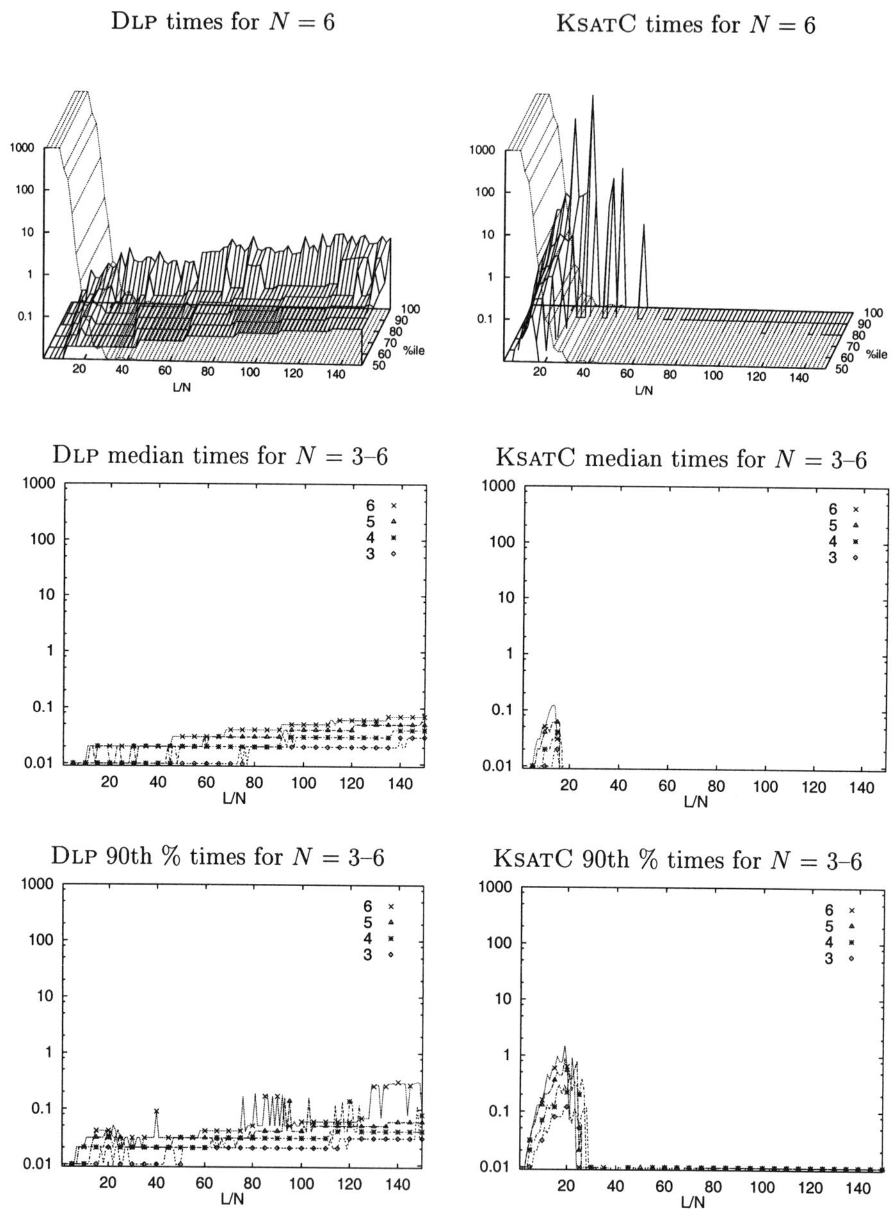

Figure 11. Results for test 7, part 2 ($d = 100$, $p = 0.7$, and $n_m = 0.5$)

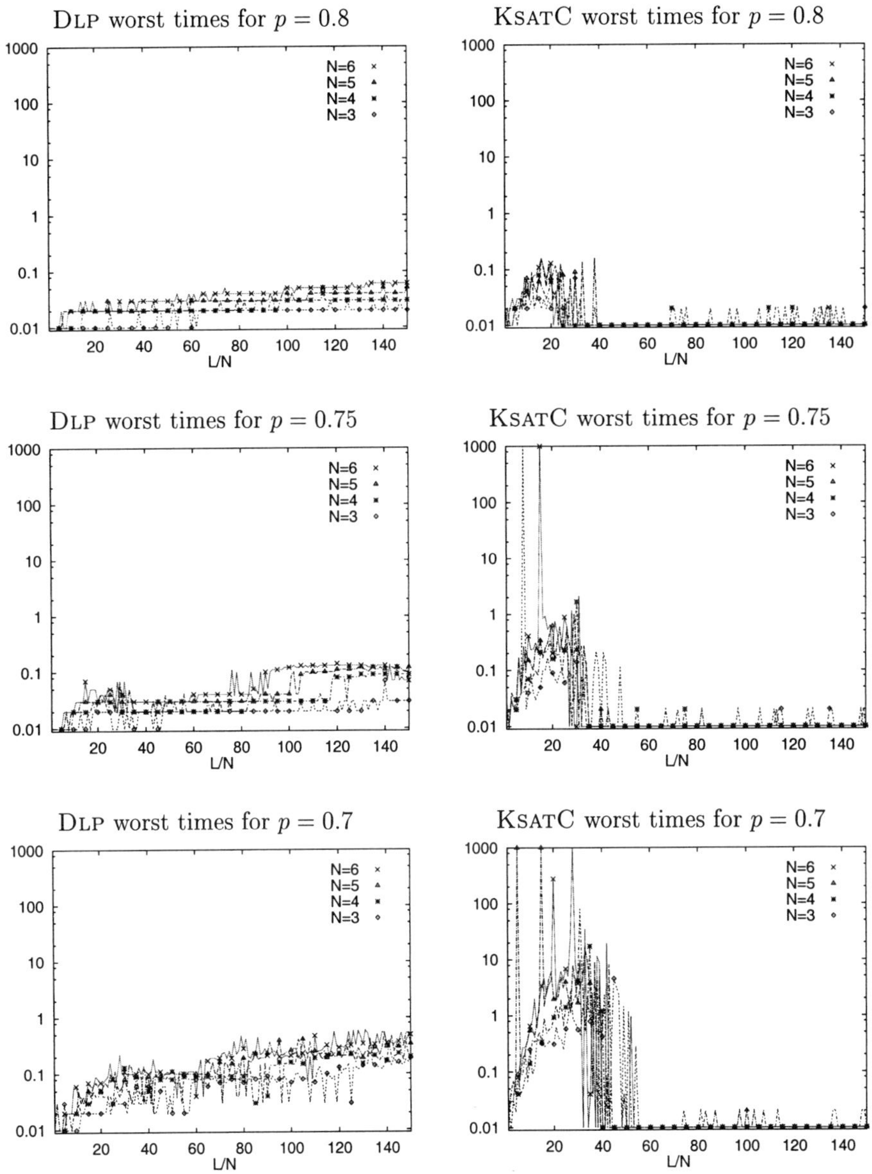

Figure 12. Worst-case for test 7 ($d = 100$; $p = 0.8, 0.75, 0.7$; $n_m = 0.5$)

References

1. Aiello, L. C., J. Doyle, and S. C. Shapiro (eds.): 1996, 'Principles of Knowledge Representation and Reasoning: Proceedings of the Fifth International Conference (KR'96)'. Morgan Kaufmann Publishers, San Francisco, CA.
2. Baader, F.: 1991, 'Augmenting Concept Languages by Transitive Closure of Roles: An Alternative to Terminological Cycles'. in [40], pp. 446–451.
3. Baader, F. and P. Hanschke: 1991, 'A Scheme for Integrating Concrete Domains into Concept Languages'. in [40], pp. 452–457.
4. Baader, F. and B. Hollunder: 1991, 'A Terminological Knowledge Representation System with Complete Inference Algorithms'. In: *Processing declarative knowledge: International workshop PDK'91*. Berlin, pp. 67–86.
5. Baader, F. and U. Sattler: 1996, 'Number Restrictions on Complex Roles in Description Logics'. in [1], pp. 328–339.
6. Baker, A. B.: 1995, 'Intelligent Backtracking on Constraint Satisfaction Problems: Experimental and Theoretical Results'. Ph.D. thesis, University of Oregon.
7. Balsiger, P. and A. Heuerding: 1998, 'Comparison of Theorem Provers for Modal Logics — Introduction and Summary'. in [12], pp. 25–26.
8. Buchheit, M., F. M. Donini, and A. Schaerf: 1993, 'Decidable Reasoning in Terminological Knowledge Representation Systems'. *Journal of Artificial Intelligence Research* **1**, 109–138.
9. Buro, M. and H. Buning: 1992, 'Report on a SAT competition'. Technical Report 110, University of Paderborn, Germany.
10. Cohn, A. G., L. Schubert, and S. C. Shapiro (eds.): 1998, 'Principles of Knowledge Representation and Reasoning: Proceedings of the Sixth International Conference (KR'98)'. Morgan Kaufmann Publishers, San Francisco, CA.
11. Davis, M., G. Logemann, and D. Loveland: 1962, 'A machine program for theorem proving'. *Communications of the ACM* **5**, 394–397.
12. de Swart, H. (ed.): 1998, 'Automated Reasoning with Analytic Tableaux and Related Methods: International Conference Tableaux'98', No. 1397 in Lecture Notes in Artificial Intelligence. Springer-Verlag.
13. Donini, F., G. D. Giacomo, and F. Massacci: 1996, 'EXPTIME Tableaux for $\mathcal{ALC}$'. In: L. Padgham, E. Franconi, M. Gehrke, D. L. McGuinness, and P. F. Patel-Schneider (eds.): *Collected Papers from the International Description Logics Workshop (DL'96)*. pp. 107–110.
14. Franco, J. and M. Paull: 1983, 'Probabilistic analysis of the Davis-Putnam procedure for solving the satisfiability problem'. *Discrete Applied Mathematics* **5**, 77–87.
15. Franconi, E., G. D. Giacomo, R. M. MacGregor, W. Nutt, C. A. Welty, and F. Sebastiani (eds.): 1998, 'Collected Papers from the International Description Logics Workshop (DL'98)'.
16. Freeman, J. W.: 1995, 'Improvements to propositional satisfiability search algorithms'. Ph.D. thesis, Department of Computer and Information Science, University of Pennsylvania, Philadelphia, PA, USA.
17. Freeman, J. W.: 1996, 'Hard random 3-SAT problems and the Davis-Putnam procedure'. *Artificial Intelligence* **81**, 183–198.
18. Gent, I. P. and T. Walsh: 1999, 'Beyond NP: the QSAT phase transition'. In: *Proceedings of AAAI'99*. Orlando, Florida.
19. Giacomo, G. D. and F. Massacci: 1996, 'Tableaux and algorithms for propositional dynamic logic with converse'. in [37], pp. 613–628.
20. Ginsberg, M. L.: 1993, 'Dynamic Backtracking'. *Journal of Artificial Intelligence Research* **1**, 25–46.
21. Giunchiglia, E., F. Giunchiglia, R. Sebastiani, and A. Tacchella: 1998, 'More evaluation of decision procedures for modal logics'. in [10], pp. 626–635.
22. Giunchiglia, F. and R. Sebastiani: 1996a, 'Building decision procedures for modal logics from propositional decision procedures—the case study of modal K'. in [37], pp. 583–597.
23. Giunchiglia, F. and R. Sebastiani: 1996b, 'A SAT-based decision procedure for $\mathcal{ALC}$'. in [1], pp. 304–314.
24. Haarslev, V., R. Möller, and A.-Y. Turhan: 1998, 'Implementing an $\mathcal{ALCRP}(\mathcal{D})$ ABox Reasoner - Progress Report'. in [15], pp. 82–86.
25. Heuerding, A. and S. Schwendimann: 1996, 'A benchmark method for the propositional modal logics K, KT, and S4'. Technical report IAM-96-015, University of Bern, Switzerland.

26. Hollunder, B. and W. Nutt: 1990, 'Subsumption Algorithms for Concept Languages'. Research Report RR-90-04, Deutsches Forschungszentrum für Künstliche Intelligenz GmbH (DFKI).
27. Horrocks, I.: 1997, 'Optimising Tableaux Decision Procedures for Description Logics'. Ph.D. thesis, University of Manchester.
28. Horrocks, I.: 1998, 'Using an Expressive Description Logic: FaCT or Fiction?'. in [10], pp. 636–647.
29. Horrocks, I. and P. F. Patel-Schneider: 1998a, 'Comparing Subsumption Optimizations'. in [15], pp. 90–94.
30. Horrocks, I. and P. F. Patel-Schneider: 1998b, 'FaCT and DLP'. in [12], pp. 27–30.
31. Horrocks, I. and P. F. Patel-Schneider: 1998c, 'Optimising Propositional Modal Satisfiability for Description Logic Subsumption'. In: *International Conference AISC'98.*
32. Horrocks, I. and P. F. Patel-Schneider: to appear, 'Optimising Description Logic Subsumption'. *Journal of Logic and Computation.*
33. Horrocks, I. and U. Sattler: to appear, 'A Description Logic with Transitive and Inverse Roles and Role Hierarchies'. *Journal of Logic and Computation.*
34. Hustadt, U. and R. A. Schmidt: 1997a, 'On evaluating decision procedures for modal logic'. Technical Report MPI-I-97-2-003, Max-Planck-Institut Für Informatik, Im Stadtwald, D 66123 Saarbrücken, Germany.
35. Hustadt, U. and R. A. Schmidt: 1997b, 'On evaluating decision procedures for modal logic'. In: *Proceedings of the 15th International Joint Conference on Artificial Intelligence (IJCAI-97)*, Vol. 1. pp. 202–207.
36. Jeroslow, R. and J. Wang: 1990, 'Solving propositional satisfiability problems'. *Annals of Mathematics and Artificial Intelligence* **1**, 167–187.
37. McRobbie, M. and J. Slaney (eds.): 1996, 'Proceedings of the Thirteenth International Conference on Automated Deduction (CADE-13)', No. 1104 in Lecture Notes in Artificial Intelligence. Springer-Verlag.
38. Oppacher, F. and E. Suen: 1988, 'HARP: A Tableau-Based Theorem Prover'. *Journal of Automated Reasoning* **4**, 69–100.
39. Patel-Schneider, P. F.: 1998, 'DLP System Description'. in [15], pp. 87–89.
40. Proceedings of IJCAI-91: 1991, 'Proceedings of the 12th International Joint Conference on Artificial Intelligence, (IJCAI-91)'.
41. Sattler, U.: 1996, 'A concept language extended with different kinds of transitive roles'. In: G. Görz and S. Hölldobler (eds.): *20. Deutsche Jahrestagung für Künstliche Intelligenz.* pp. 333–345.
42. Selman, B., D. G. Mitchell, and H. J. Levesque: 1996, 'Generating hard satisfiability problems'. *Artificial Intelligence* **81**, 17–29.
43. Vellino, A.: 1989, 'The Complexity of Automated Reasoning'. Ph.D. thesis, University of Toronto.
44. Weidenbach, C., B. Gaede, and G. Rock: 1996, 'SPASS & FLOTTER version 0.42.'. in [37], pp. 141–145.

SAT2000
I. Gent et al. (Eds.)
IOS Press, 2000

Using Resolution for Testing Modal Satisfiability and Building Models

Ullrich Hustadt † and Renate A. Schmidt §
Centre for Agent Research and Development, Department of Computing and Mathematics, Manchester Metropolitan University, Chester Street, Manchester M1 5GD, United Kingdom

Abstract. This paper presents a translation-based resolution decision procedure for the multi-modal logic $K_{(m)}(\cap, \cup, \smile)$ defined over families of relations closed under intersection, union and converse. The relations may satisfy certain additional frame properties. Different from previous resolution decision procedures which are based on ordering refinements our procedure is based on a selection refinement, the derivations of which correspond to derivations of tableaux or sequent proof systems. This procedure has the advantage that it can be used both as a satisfiability checker and a model builder. We show that tableaux and sequent-style proof systems can be polynomially simulated with our procedure. Furthermore, the finite model property follows for a number of extended modal logics.

Keywords: modal logic, automated theorem proving, resolution decision procedures, tableaux proof systems, satisfiability testing, model generation, simulation, relative proof complexity, relative search space complexity.

1. Introduction

Recently a number of results concerning resolution decision procedures for subclasses of first-order logic have been obtained. The considered subclasses are expressive enough to encompass a variety of non-classical logics, in particular, various extended modal logics as well as description logics. De Nivelle [11] describes a resolution decision procedure for the guarded fragment using a non-liftable ordering refinement. The guarded fragment is a generalisation of the restricted quantifier fragment corresponding to basic modal logic and allows for the embedding of a variety of extended modal logics [1]. Modal logics can also be embedded into the class $\overline{\text{DK}}$ (the dual of Maslov's class K) [25], and its subclasses One-Free [14] and the class of DL-clauses [26]. Again, ordering refinements of resolution provide decision procedures for these classes. A non-standard translation into path logics combined with resolution and arbitrary refinements provide decision procedures for the satisfiability of the modal logics *K*, *KD*, *KT*, *KD4*, *S4* and *S5* [40]. This approach was adopted in the experiments of [23, 27]. Experiments using the standard translation and a combination of a first-order theorem prover augmented with a finite-model finder are described in [37].

The motivation for this work has been our interest in different refinements for translation-based theorem proving for modal logics. Different refinements result in better performance for different problem sets. Experimental evidence for this is that for some problem sets good performance can be achieved with SPASS using ordered resolution while not so good performance with tableaux proof systems, and for some problem sets the situation is reversed, cf. [22, 24, 27]. However, by competitive testing alone it is near impossible to identify the major factors having a positive or negative influence on the performance of a theorem prover [20]. As long as the theorem provers

† `u.hustadt@doc.mmu.ac.uk`
§ `r.a.schmidt@doc.mmu.ac.uk`

which are being compared follow different search strategies this difference is likely to have a dominating effect on the overall performance. This has two consequences. One, we can say little about the other factors influencing the performance, for example, fundamental differences between the underlying proof systems or sophisticated redundancy elimination techniques used by the theorem prover. Two, while it is easy to find benchmark problems illustrating the superiority of one theorem prover it is just as easy to find benchmark problems showing the opposite. Therefore, it is always advisable to complement empirical investigations with theoretical study so that some insight about the different approaches is gained.

To this end we study a selection refinement of resolution, called $R^{\mathcal{MOD}}$, which adopts a very different approach to ordered refinements. It provides a decision procedure for satisfiability in the multi-modal logic $K_{(m)}(\cap, \cup, \smile)$ with modalities defined over intersection, union and converse of relations, and any normal modal logic below it, as well as a number of extensions with additional frame properties. We show that on the basis of this proof system we can polynomially simulate tableaux proof systems for the familiar lattice of standard normal modal logics below *S5*. Moreover, for the logics *K*, *KD*, *KT*, *KB*, *KDB* and *KTB*, there is a polynomial reduction of the search space of a tableaux procedure to that of our procedure for any modal formula. We focus on Massacci's single-step prefixed tableaux systems [31], but this choice is arbitrary. The technique described in this paper can also be applied for obtaining simulation results of modal tableaux systems with implicit or explicit accessibility relation and analytic modal KE tableaux [32], or even sequent proof systems.

As a side-effect the procedure described in this paper provides a solution to the problem of backward translation of resolution proofs. In general, the modal form is lost during transformation to clausal form and subsequent deduction. By using a different translation method, for example, translation methods based on the functional translation where accessibility is encoded in terms of paths [2, 19, 36], this problem can be reduced and eliminated for certain logics [9, 12]. There is another well-known technique, called structural transformation or renaming, which enables the preservation of the structure of the original formula in the clausal form. This technique is used in connection with most resolution decision procedures, but the problem is that the connection to the original formula is generally lost after a few inference steps. This makes it difficult to convert resolution proofs into more user friendly tableaux style or natural deduction style proofs. The resolution procedure described in this paper does not have this drawback. It has the property that it is always possible to translate inferred information back to modal logic. An immediate consequence of this property and the termination result is the finite model property. More important, and of practical value, is the direct utilisation of the resolution procedure for automatically generating models for satisfiable input formulae.

The structure of the paper is as follows. We begin with some preliminary definitions in the next section. Section 3 defines the syntax and semantics of the multi-modal logic $K_{(m)}(\cap, \cup, \smile)$ and extensions with first-order frame properties or axiom schemas. The resolution framework which we adopt is described in Section 4. Section 5 recalls the definition of structural transformation. The main parts are Sections 6, 7, 9 and 10. Section 6 defines the selection-based resolution procedure $R^{\mathcal{MOD}}$ and proves termination results for a certain class of extensions of logics in-between K and $K_{(m)}(\cap, \cup, \smile)$. $R^{\mathcal{MOD}}$ immediately gives a procedure for effectively finding models for satisfiable input formulae. This is shown in Section 7. In Section 8 we recall the definition of single-step prefixed tableaux calculi, for which simulation results are presented in Section 9. In Section 10 we describe an implementation of $R^{\mathcal{MOD}}$ and some initial experiments which illustrate differences to ordered resolution. The final section is the Conclusion.

2. Some basic definitions

The polarity of (occurrences of) modal or first-order subformulae is defined as usual: Any occurrence of a proper subformula of an equivalence has *zero polarity.* For occurrences of subformulae not below a '$\leftrightarrow$' symbol, an occurrence of a subformula has *positive polarity* if it is one inside the scope of an even number of (explicit or implicit) negations, and it has *negative polarity* if it is one inside the scope of an odd number of negations.

First-order variables are denoted by x, y and z, terms by s and t, atoms by $A, A_1, A_2, \ldots$, and clauses by C and D. For sets of clauses we use the symbols $N, N_1, N_2, \ldots$. A literal is an atom or the negation of an atom. The former is said to be a *positive literal* and the latter a *negative literal.* As usual *clauses* are assumed to be multisets of literals, and will be denoted by $P(x) \vee P(x) \vee \neg R(x, y)$, for example. The components in the variable partition of a clause are called *split components*, that is, split components do not share variables. Two formulae or clauses are said to be *variants* of each other if one is equal to the other modulo variable renaming.

3. The modal logic $K_{(m)}(\cap, \cup, \smile)$

We have not come across any mention of the logic $K_{(m)}(\cap, \cup, \smile)$ in the literature of modal logic, but it is closely related to a number of known logics. It can be viewed as an extension of the multi-modal version of the basic tense logic K_t with intersection and union of relations. Unlike Boolean modal logic [16] we admit converse relations but not complementation of relations. In the field of knowledge representation, description logics closely related to $K_{(m)}(\cap, \cup, \smile)$ and moderate extensions with inclusion axioms are prominent (see for example [13]).

$K_{(m)}(\cap, \cup, \smile)$ is the multi-modal logic defined over families of binary relations closed under intersection, union and converse. Formally, the language is defined over countably many propositional variables $p, p_1, p_2, \ldots$, and countably many relational variables $r, r_1, r_2, \ldots$. A *propositional atom* is a propositional variable, $\top$ or $\bot$. A *modal formula* is either a propositional atom or a formula of the form $\neg\varphi$, $\varphi \wedge \psi$, $\varphi \vee \psi$, $\langle\alpha\rangle\varphi$ and $[\alpha]\varphi$, where φ is a modal formula and α is a relational formula. A *relational formula* is a relational variable or has one of the following forms:

$$\alpha \wedge \beta \text{ (conjunction)}, \ \alpha \vee \beta \text{ (disjunction), and } \alpha^{\smile} \text{ (converse)},$$

where α and β are relational formulae. Other connectives are defined to be abbreviations, for example, $\varphi \rightarrow \psi = \neg\varphi \vee \psi$. A modal formula is in *negation normal form* iff for every subformula of the form $\neg\varphi$, φ is a propositional variable.

The semantics of $K_{(m)}(\cap, \cup, \smile)$ is defined in terms of relational structures or frames. A frame is a tuple (W, R) of a non-empty set W (of worlds) and a mapping R from relational formulae to binary relations over W satisfying:

$$\begin{aligned} R(\alpha \wedge \beta) &= R(\alpha) \cap R(\beta) \\ R(\alpha \vee \beta) &= R(\alpha) \cup R(\beta) \\ R(\alpha^{\smile}) &= R(\alpha)^{\smile}. \end{aligned}$$

The defining class of frames of a modal logic determines, and is determined by, a corresponding class of models. A model (an interpretation) is given by a triple $\mathcal{M} = (W, R, \iota)$, where (W, R) is a frame and ι is a mapping from modal formulae to subsets of W satisfying:

$$\iota(\bot) = \emptyset \qquad \iota(\top) = W$$

Seriality, for $D = \langle r \rangle \top$:	$R(x, f(x))$
Reflexivity, for $T = [r]p \to p$:	$R(x, x)$
Symmetry, for $B = p \to [r]\langle r \rangle p$:	$\neg R(x, y) \vee R(y, x)$
Inclusion, for $\langle r_1 \rangle p \to \langle r_2 \rangle p$:	$\neg R_1(x, y) \vee R_2(x, y)$
For $(\langle r_1 \rangle p \wedge \langle r_2{}^{\smile} \rangle p) \to \langle r_3 \rangle p$:	$\neg R_1(x, y) \vee \neg R_2(y, x) \vee R_3(x, y)$

Figure 1. Some correspondence properties

$$\iota(\varphi \wedge \psi) = \iota(\varphi) \cap \iota(\psi)$$

$$\vdots \quad \text{(as expected for the other propositional connectives)}$$

$$\iota(\langle \alpha \rangle \varphi) = \{x \mid \exists y \in W\ (x, y) \in R(\alpha) \wedge y \in \iota(\varphi)\}$$

$$\iota([\alpha]\varphi) = \{x \mid \forall y \in W\ (x, y) \in R(\alpha) \to y \in \iota(\varphi)\}.$$

A modal formulae is satisfiable if an $\mathcal{M}$ exists such that for some x in W, $x \in \iota(\varphi)$.

By $L\Delta$ we denote the extension of a logic L characterised by the class of frames satisfying the conjunction of relational (frame) properties in Δ. By $L\Sigma$ we denote the extension of L closed under the additional axiom schemas in Σ. Examples of first-order frame properties (in Skolemised clausal form) and the corresponding axiom schemas are given in Figure 1.

Our results will apply to certain classes of logics $L\Delta$ with the L being logics in-between K and $K_{(m)}(\cap, \cup, \smile)$. Formally, by a logic in-between K and $K_{(m)}(\cap, \cup, \smile)$ we mean a logic $K_{(m)}(\star_1, \ldots, \star_k)$ where $m \geq 1$, $1 \leq k \leq 3$ and the $\star_i$ are distinct operations from $\{\cap, \cup, {}^{\smile}\}$.

For testing the satisfiability of a modal formula we utilise the following translation mappings.

$$\begin{aligned}
\pi(\top, x) &= \top \\
\pi(\bot, x) &= \bot \\
\pi(p_i, x) &= P_i(x) \\
\pi(\neg\varphi, x) &= \neg\pi(\varphi, x) \\
\pi(\varphi \star \psi, x) &= \pi(\varphi, x) \star \pi(\psi, x) \quad \text{for } \star \in \{\wedge, \vee, \to, \leftrightarrow\} \\
\pi(\langle \alpha \rangle \varphi, x) &= \exists y\ (\tau(\alpha, x, y) \wedge \pi(\varphi, y)) \\
\pi([\alpha]\varphi, x) &= \forall y\ (\tau(\alpha, x, y) \to \pi(\varphi, y))
\end{aligned}$$

Relational formulae are translated according to:

$$\begin{aligned}
\tau(r_j, x, y) &= R_j(x, y) \\
\tau(\alpha^{\smile}, x, y) &= \tau(\alpha, y, x) \\
\tau(\alpha \star \beta, x, y) &= \tau(\alpha, x, y) \star \tau(\beta, x, y) \quad \text{for } \star \in \{\wedge, \vee\}
\end{aligned}$$

In the translation each propositional or relational variable (p_i or r_j) is uniquely associated with a unary or binary predicate variable, denoted by the corresponding capital letter (P_i or R_j).

By definition, Π maps any modal formula φ to $\pi(\varphi, \underline{a})$, where $\underline{a}$ denotes a constant.

THEOREM 3.1. *Let Δ be a finite (possibly empty) set of first-order frame properties, and let L be a logic in-between K and $K_{(m)}(\cap, \cup, \smile)$. For any modal formula φ, φ is satisfiable in $L\Delta$ iff $\Delta \wedge \Pi(\varphi)$ is first-order satisfiable.*

Proof. It not difficult to define a first-order interpretation from a modal interpretation, and vice versa.

It will be helpful to keep in mind the following list of equivalences which may be employed as rewrite rules (from left to right), thereby simplifying formulae and possibly transforming them into negation normal form.

$$\begin{array}{rlrl} \neg\langle\alpha\rangle\psi & \leftrightarrow [\alpha]\neg\psi & \neg[\alpha]\psi & \leftrightarrow \langle\alpha\rangle\neg\psi \\ \langle\alpha\rangle(\psi \vee \phi) & \leftrightarrow \langle\alpha\rangle\psi \vee \langle\alpha\rangle\phi & [\alpha](\psi \wedge \phi) & \leftrightarrow [\alpha]\psi \wedge [\alpha]\phi \\ \langle\alpha \vee \beta\rangle\psi & \leftrightarrow \langle\alpha\rangle\psi \vee \langle\beta\rangle\psi & [\alpha \vee \beta]\psi & \leftrightarrow [\alpha]\psi \wedge [\beta]\psi \\ \alpha^{\smile\smile} & \leftrightarrow \alpha & (\alpha \star \beta)^{\smile} & \leftrightarrow \alpha^{\smile} \star \beta^{\smile} \quad \text{for } \star \in \{\wedge, \vee\} \end{array}$$

4. First-order resolution

We briefly describe the general ordered resolution calculus R (with selection and simplification) of Bachmair and Ganzinger [5, 6, 7, 8].

In the calculus inference rules are parameterised by an admissible ordering $\succ$ on literals and a selection function S. Essentially, an admissible ordering is a total (well-founded) strict ordering on the ground level such that for literals: $\ldots \succ \neg A_n \succ A_n \succ \ldots \succ \neg A_1 \succ A_1$. This is extended to the non-ground level in a canonical manner. For the exact definition the interested reader may refer to [5, 6, 7, 8]. A *selection* function assigns to each clause a possibly empty set of occurrences of negative literals. If C is a clause, then the literal occurrences in $S(C)$ are *selected.* No restrictions are imposed on the selection function.

The calculus consists of general *expansion rules* of the form:

$$\frac{N}{N_1 \mid \cdots \mid N_n}$$

Each represents a finite derivation of alternatives $N_1, \ldots, N_n$ from N. The following rules describe how derivations can be expanded at the leaves.

Deduce: $$\frac{N}{N \cup \{\textsc{Norm}(C)\}}$$

if C is either a resolvent or a factor of clauses in N, $\textsc{Norm}(C)$ is a clause which is logically equivalent to C and $C \succeq \textsc{Norm}(C)$.

Delete: $$\frac{N \cup \{C\}}{N}$$

if C is a tautology or N contains a clause which is a variant of C.

Split: $$\frac{N \cup \{C \vee D\}}{N \cup \{C\} \mid N \cup \{D\}}$$

if C and D are variable-disjoint.

Resolvents and factors are derived by the following rules.

Resolution: $$\frac{C \vee A_1 \quad \neg A_2 \vee D}{(C \vee D)\sigma}$$

where (i) σ is the most general unifier of A_1 and A_2, (ii) no literal is selected in C, and $A_1\sigma$ is strictly $\succ$-maximal with respect to $C\sigma$, and (iii) $\neg A_2$ is either selected, or $\neg A_2\sigma$ is maximal with respect to $D\sigma$ and no literal is selected in D.

The left premise is called the *positive premise* and the right premise is called the *negative premise.* We implicitly assume that the premises have no common variables.

Factoring:
$$\frac{C \vee A_1 \vee A_2}{(C \vee A_1)\sigma}$$

where (i) σ is the most general unifier of A_1 and A_2, and (ii) no literal is selected in C and $A_1\sigma$ is $\succ$-maximal with respect to $C\sigma$.

The calculus is refutationally complete and compatible with a general notion of *redundancy* for clauses and inferences, with which additional don't-care non-deterministic simplification and deletion rules can be sanctioned [5, 6, 7, 8]. Essentially, a ground clause is redundant in a set N with respect to the ordering $\succ$ if it follows from smaller instances of clauses in N, and a non-ground clause is redundant in N if all its ground instances are redundant in N. For example, any tautologous clause is redundant, and C is redundant with respect to $N \cup \text{NORM}(C)$. By definition, a set of clauses is *saturated up to redundancy* (with respect to ordered inference) if the conclusion of every inference from non-redundant premises in N is either contained in N, or else is redundant in N.

THEOREM 4.1. ([5, 6, 7, 8]). *Let N be a set of clauses. Then, N is unsatisfiable iff the R-saturation (up to redundancy) of N contains the empty clause.*

Commonly, in resolution decision procedures the normalisation function in the "Deduce" is required to be the condensation mapping. The *condensation* $\text{COND}(C)$ of a clause C is a minimal subclause of C which is a factor of C. However, for the purposes of obtaining the decidability and simulation results below no normalisation is required.

5. Structural transformation

Structural transformation, also known as renaming or transformation to definitional form, is a standard technique for transforming formulae into a more suitable normal form, and is used in many areas, including automated deduction [4, 38, 41], modal logic [33, 34] and description logics [3]. In this paper its primary purpose is to keep a tight link between the structure of modal formulae and their translated clausal form.

Let $\text{Pos}(\varphi)$ be the set of positions of a first-order formula φ. If λ is a position in φ, then $\varphi|_\lambda$ denotes the subformula of φ at position λ and $\varphi[\lambda \leftarrow \psi]$ is the result of replacing φ at position λ by ψ.

We associate with each element λ of $\Lambda \subseteq \text{Pos}(\varphi)$ a predicate symbol Q_λ and a literal $Q_\lambda(x_1, \dots, x_n)$, where $x_1, \dots, x_n$ are the free variables of $\varphi|_\lambda$, the symbol Q_λ does not occur in φ and two symbols Q_λ and $Q_{\lambda'}$ are equal only if $\varphi|_\lambda$ and $\varphi|_{\lambda'}$ are variant formulae. Let

$$\text{Def}^+_\lambda(\varphi) = \forall x_1 \dots x_n \, (Q_\lambda(x_1, \dots, x_n) \rightarrow \varphi|_\lambda) \quad \text{and}$$
$$\text{Def}^-_\lambda(\varphi) = \forall x_1 \dots x_n \, (\varphi|_\lambda \rightarrow Q_\lambda(x_1, \dots, x_n)).$$

The *definition* of Q_λ is the formula

$$\text{Def}_\lambda(\varphi) = \begin{cases} \text{Def}^+_\lambda(\varphi) & \text{if } \varphi|_\lambda \text{ has positive polarity} \\ \text{Def}^-_\lambda(\varphi) & \text{if } \varphi|_\lambda \text{ has negative polarity} \\ \text{Def}^+_\lambda(\varphi) \wedge \text{Def}^-_\lambda(\varphi) & \text{otherwise.} \end{cases}$$

The corresponding clauses will be called *definitional clauses.* Now, define $\mathrm{Def}_\Lambda(\varphi)$ inductively by:

$$\mathrm{Def}_\emptyset(\varphi) = \varphi \quad \text{and}$$
$$\mathrm{Def}_{\Lambda\cup\{\lambda\}}(\varphi) = \mathrm{Def}_\Lambda(\varphi[\lambda \leftarrow Q_\lambda(x_1,\ldots,x_n)]) \wedge \mathrm{Def}_\lambda(\varphi),$$

where λ is maximal in $\Lambda \cup \{\lambda\}$ with respect to the prefix ordering on positions. A *definitional form* of φ is $\mathrm{Def}_\Lambda(\varphi)$, where Λ is a subset of all positions of subformulae (usually, non-atomic or non-literal subformulae).

THEOREM 5.1. *Let φ be a first-order formula.* $\mathrm{Def}_\Lambda(\varphi)$ *can be computed in polynomial time and φ is satisfiable iff* $\mathrm{Def}_\Lambda(\varphi)$ *is satisfiable, for any* $\Lambda \subseteq \mathrm{Pos}(\varphi)$.

Consequently (by Theorems 5.1 and 3.1):

COROLLARY 5.2. *Let Δ be a finite (possibly empty) set of first-order frame properties, and let L be a logic in-between K and $K_{(m)}(\cap, \cup, \smile)$. For any given modal formula φ,* $\mathrm{Def}_\Lambda(\Pi(\varphi))$ *can be computed in polynomial time and φ is satisfiable in $L\Delta$ iff $\Delta \wedge$* $\mathrm{Def}_\Lambda(\Pi(\varphi))$ *is satisfiable, for any* $\Lambda \subseteq \mathrm{Pos}(\Pi(\varphi))$.

6. A structure preserving resolution decision procedure

In this section we define a selection-based resolution decision procedure which retains the modal structure of formulae.

As only negative literals can be selected and we aim not to destroy the connection to the original modal formulae, we transform modal formulae into negation normal form first. This is achieved by eliminating $\rightarrow$ and $\leftrightarrow$ in the usual way, moving negation symbols inward as far as possible, and deleting double negations along the way. So henceforth we will assume that the given modal formula is already in negation normal form.[1]

Let $\varphi' = \Pi(\varphi)$ be the translation of any $K_{(m)}(\cap, \cup, \smile)$-formula φ. To ensure a one-to-one correspondence between clauses of the clausal form of φ' and subformulae of φ we require a particular form of structural transformation. Let Ξ denote the mapping Def_Λ where Λ is the subset of positions in φ' which correspond to non-atomic subformulae in φ. For reasons explained below Ξ introduces the same symbol for variant subformulae with the same polarity. Because by assumption φ is in negation normal form, all occurrences of non-atomic subformulae of φ' with one free variable have positive polarity. This means $\mathrm{Def}_\lambda(\varphi') = \mathrm{Def}^+_\lambda(\varphi')$ for the positions λ associated with these occurrences. But subformulae corresponding to relational formulae, that is, subformulae with two free variables, can occur both positively and negatively. Here, Ξ introduces one symbol for all variant occurrences of subformulae corresponding to non-atomic relational subformulae with positive polarity and a different symbol for all variant occurrences with negative polarity.

For example, Ξ will introduce for the subformula ψ corresponding to $\langle r_j\rangle p_i$ the definition $\forall x\, (Q_\psi(x) \rightarrow \exists y\, (R_j(x,y) \wedge P_i(y)))$. For $\psi = [\alpha]\langle\alpha\rangle p_i$ with $\alpha = r_{j_1} \wedge r_{j_2}$ and $\phi = \langle\alpha\rangle p_i$ it will introduce the definitions:

$$\forall x\, (Q_\psi(x) \rightarrow \forall y\, (Q^n_\alpha(x,y) \rightarrow Q_\phi(y)))$$

[1] An extra transformation, which is described in section 5 of [26], is necessary if we do not want to make this assumption.

1. $Q_\varphi(\underline{a})$
2. $\neg Q_\varphi(x)^+ \lor Q_\Box(x)$
3. $\neg Q_\varphi(x)^+ \lor Q_\neg(x)$
4. $\neg Q_\Box(x)^+ \lor \neg R(x,y) \lor Q_\lor(y)$
5. $\neg Q_\lor(x)^+ \lor P(x) \lor Q_\Diamond(x)$
6. $\neg Q_\Diamond(x)^+ \lor R(x, f(x))$
7. $\neg Q_\Diamond(x)^+ \lor P(f(x))$
8. $\neg Q_\neg(x)^+ \lor \neg P(x)$

Figure 2. The clausal form of $\Xi\Pi(\varphi)$ for $\varphi = \Box(p \lor \Diamond p) \land \neg p$.

$$\forall x\ (Q_\phi(x) \to \exists y\ (Q^p_\alpha(x,y) \land P_i(y)))$$
$$\forall xy\ (Q^p_\alpha(x,y) \to (R_{j1}(x,y) \land R_{j2}(x,y)))$$
$$\forall xy\ ((R_{j1}(x,y) \land R_{j2}(x,y)) \to Q^n_\alpha(x,y)).$$

Figure 2 gives the clausal form of a small example which will also be used for illustration later.

From a computational perspective, the renaming of formulae associated with $\alpha^\smile$ and also negative literals is not necessary. In this case the decidability results of this section remain true. The sole purpose of these renamings is the reconstruction of the corresponding modal formulae from derived clauses (in Section 7), and the simulation of tableaux proof systems (in Section 9).

Note how the exact correspondence between introduced symbols and subformulae is made explicit in our notation: We denote introduced predicate symbols by Q_ψ and Q_α, if Q_ψ represents an occurrence of a modal subformula ψ and Q_α represents an occurrence of a relational subformula α. We also find it convenient to use the notation

$$\begin{array}{ll} \mathcal{P}(s) & \text{for some literal in } \{P_i(s), Q_\psi(s)\}_{i,\psi}, \text{ and} \\ \mathcal{R}(s,t) & \text{for some literal in } \{R_j(s,t), R_j(t,s), Q_\alpha(s,t), Q_\alpha(t,s)\}_{j,\alpha}. \end{array}$$

Two occurrences of $\mathcal{P}(s)$, or $\mathcal{R}(s,t)$, need not be identical. For example, $\neg Q_\psi(x) \lor \mathcal{P}(x) \lor \mathcal{P}(x)$ can represent $\neg Q_\psi(x) \lor P_i(x) \lor Q_\chi(x)$. Also, $\neg Q_\psi(x) \lor \neg\mathcal{R}(x,y) \lor \mathcal{P}(y)$ can represent $\neg Q_\psi(x) \lor \neg R_j(y,x) \lor Q_\chi(y)$ or $\neg Q_\psi(x) \lor \neg Q_\alpha(x,y) \lor Q_\chi(y)$.

The inference calculus, denoted by $R^{\mathcal{MOD}}$, is given by a minimal calculus of resolution and factoring with selection by a function $S_{\mathcal{MOD}}$ (to be defined next) plus splitting, and NORM being the identity function. We assume all derivations in $R^{\mathcal{MOD}}$ are generated by strategies in which no application of the "Deduce" expansion rule with identical premises and identical consequence may occur twice on the same path in any derivation. In addition, "Delete", "Split", and "Deduce" are applied in this order, except that "Split" is not applied to clauses which contain a selected literal. An ordering refinement is optional.

We define a dependency relation $\succ_d$ on the predicate symbols by $S_1 \succ_d S_2$, if there is a definition $\psi \to \phi$ in $\Xi\Pi(\varphi)$ such that S_1 occurs in ψ and S_2 occurs in ϕ. Let $\succ_D$ be any ordering on the predicate symbols in $\Xi\Pi(\varphi)$ which is compatible with the transitive closure of $\succ_d$, that is, $\succ_d^+ \subseteq \succ_D$. Such an ordering can always be found. For this, it was important to introduce different predicate symbols for positive and negative subformulae associated with relational subformulae.

$Q_{\varphi}(\underline{a})$	$P_i(\underline{a})$ (when $\varphi = p_i$)
$\neg Q_{\psi}(x)^+ \vee \mathcal{P}(x)$	$\neg Q_{\psi}(x)^+ \vee \neg P_i(x)$
$\neg Q_{\psi}(x)^+ \vee \mathcal{P}(x) \vee \mathcal{P}(x)$	$\neg Q_{\psi}(x)^+ \vee \neg\mathcal{R}(x,y)\ [\vee\ \mathcal{P}(y)]$
$\neg Q_{\psi}(x)^+ \vee \mathcal{P}(f(x))$	$\neg Q_{\psi}(x)^+ \vee \mathcal{R}(x, f(x))$
$\neg Q_{\alpha}(x,y)^+ \vee \mathcal{R}(x,y)$	$\neg Q_{\alpha}(x,y)^+ \vee \mathcal{R}(x,y) \vee \mathcal{R}(x,y)$
$Q_{\alpha}(x,y) \vee \neg\mathcal{R}(x,y)^+$	$Q_{\alpha}(x,y) \vee \neg\mathcal{R}(x,y) \vee \neg\mathcal{R}(x,y)^+$

Figure 3. Schematic clausal forms for $\Xi\Pi(\varphi)$.

Now, for any clause C which contains an occurrence of a negative literal, the function $S_{\mathcal{MOD}}$ selects a literal $\neg A$ iff either

1. the predicate symbol of A is $\succ_D$-maximal in C, or
2. $\neg A$ is a binary literal and C does not contain a literal which would have been selected according to condition 1.

In the sample clause set of Figure 2 selected literals are indicated by $^+$. These are the literals which may be resolved upon, as well as any literals[2] of clauses without selected literals.

LEMMA 6.1. *Let φ be any modal formula. The clausal form of $\Xi\Pi(\varphi)$ is defined by a subset of instances of the schemas of Figure 3. (Again, selected literals are indicated by $^+$.)*

We now consider what happens during deduction with the clausal form of $\Xi\Pi(\varphi)$. Our goal is to show the existence of a term depth bound for all inferred clauses, as well as the existence of a bound on the number of variables occurring in any inferred clause. It then follows that $R^{\mathcal{MOD}}$ is a decision procedure [29].

As all non-unit clauses contain a selected literal no factoring steps are possible and all definitional clauses can only be used as negative premises of resolution steps. We note that the selected literals contain all the variables of any clause except for those in the form

$$(*) \qquad \neg Q_{\psi}(x)^+ \vee \neg\mathcal{R}(x,y) \vee \mathcal{P}(y).$$

With the exception of

$$\neg Q_{\psi}(x)^+ \vee \mathcal{P}(f(x)) \quad \text{and} \quad \neg Q_{\psi}(x)^+ \vee \mathcal{R}(x, f(x))$$

no variables occur as arguments of compound terms.

To begin with the only candidates for positive premises are unit ground clauses. Inference with these produce either ground clauses consisting of unary literals only, which can be split into ground unit clauses, clauses of the form $\mathcal{R}(s, f(s))$, or

$$(**) \qquad \neg\mathcal{R}(s,y)^+\ [\vee\ \mathcal{P}(y)],$$

for s a ground term. Since $\neg\mathcal{R}(s,y)$ is a binary literal and it is the only negative literal in $(**)$, it is selected either by condition 1 or condition 2 above. Now, inferences

[2] ... any strictly maximal literals ... , in case an ordering restriction is assumed.

on (**) with ground binary unit clauses produce ground clauses only. Inferences with the definitional clauses associated with relational subformulae produce ground clauses, which can be split into units of the form $(\neg)\mathcal{R}(s, f(s))$.

Thus, assuming φ is any modal formula and N is the clausal form of $\Xi\Pi(\varphi)$, we have:

LEMMA 6.2. *Any derivation by $R^{\mathcal{MOD}}$ from N contains only (i) ground clauses of the form $(\neg)\mathcal{P}(s)$ and $(\neg)\mathcal{R}(s, f(s))$, (ii) clauses satisfying the schematic definition of Figure 3, and (iii) clauses of the form (**).*

LEMMA 6.3. *All clauses occurring in an $R^{\mathcal{MOD}}$-derivation from N contain at most two variables.*

It remains to exhibit a term depth bound. Resolvents may contain terms of larger depth than both their parent clauses. However $R^{\mathcal{MOD}}$ has the property that derived clauses are always strictly smaller than their parent clauses with respect to a well-founded ordering which is based on the ordering $\succ_D$. This implies the number of conclusions is finitely bounded, and consequently, there is an upper bound on the depth of terms. Formally:

LEMMA 6.4. *There is a finite bound on the maximal term depth of clauses derived by $R^{\mathcal{MOD}}$ from N.*

Proof. Define $\succ_d$ as above with the additional requirement that if Q_ψ is the symbol introduced for a diamond formula ψ, and Q_ϕ is the symbol introduced for a box formula ϕ, and ψ and ϕ occur at the same modal depth in φ, then $Q_\psi \succ_d Q_\phi$. Let $\succ'_D$ be any ordering on predicate symbols compatible with $\succ_d^+$. Now, with every clause C which can occur as a positive premise or as a conclusion in a derivation we associate a complexity measure c_C. We let $c_C = (Q, Q)$, if $C = (\neg)Q(s)$. If $C = (\neg)R(s,t)$ then $c_C = (Q, R)$, where Q is the predicate symbol associated with the leading function symbol of the maximal term in $\{s, t\}$. By definition, a predicate symbol Q is *associated with a function symbol* f, written Q_f, if there is a clause $\neg Q(x) \vee \mathcal{R}(x, f(x))$ in N. For example, the measure of a clause $(\neg)\mathcal{R}(s, f(s))$ is (Q_f, R). For clauses of the form (**), let $c_C = (Q_\psi, Q_\phi)$ where $\neg Q_\psi(x) \vee \neg\mathcal{R}(x, y) \vee Q_\phi(y)$ is the negative premise of C and $\psi = [\alpha]\phi$. Complexity measures c_C are compared by the lexicographic combination $\succ_c = (\succ'_D, \succ'_D)$. Now, it is routine to verify that any inference step from a positive premise C by resolution or factoring will result in a clause D such that $c_C \succ_c c_D$.[3] Termination and the existence of a term depth bound follows.

Consequently (by Lemmas 6.1 to 6.4 and Theorem 4.1):

THEOREM 6.5. *Let φ be any modal formula and let N be the clausal form of $\Xi\Pi(\varphi)$. Then,*

1. *any $R^{\mathcal{MOD}}$-derivation from N (with or without redundancy elimination) terminates, and*

2. *φ is unsatisfiable in $K_{(m)}(\cap, \cup, \smile)$ iff the $R^{\mathcal{MOD}}$-saturation (up to redundancy) of N contains the empty clause.*

Strictly, splitting is optional for this result to hold, but it is essential for the subsequent sections.

[3] Notice that the ordering $\succ_c$ is merely used to show termination, not to restrict inferences.

Procedures based on $R^{\mathcal{MOD}}$ can be used to decide also extensions of $K_{(m)}$ below $K_{(m)}(\cap, \cup, \smile)$ in which the R_j satisfy additional frame properties. It goes beyond the scope of this paper to investigate which extensions $K_{(m)}(\cap, \cup, \smile)\Delta$ can be decided with $R^{\mathcal{MOD}}$. However it is not difficult to verify the following result, which proves that inference with the properties of Figure 1 does not lead to unbounded computation.

In the following theorem, the notation $\mathcal{R}(s,t)$ represents either an atom $R_j(s,t)$ or an atom $R_j(t,s)$ for some j.

THEOREM 6.6. *Theorem 6.5 is true for any extension $L\Delta$ of a logic L in-between K and $K_{(m)}(\cap, \cup, \smile)$, for which the $R^{\mathcal{MOD}}$-saturation (up to redundancy) of Δ is a conjunction of universal closures of relational properties:*

1. $R_j(x,x)$,
2. $\mathcal{R}(\underline{b}, \underline{c})$, *where $\underline{b}$ and $\underline{c}$ denote any constants,*
3. $\mathcal{R}(x, f(x))$, *or*
4. *any clause built from literals of the forms $\mathcal{R}(x,y)$, $\mathcal{R}(x,x)$, $\mathcal{R}(y,y)$, or their negations, containing at least one negative literal $\neg\mathcal{R}(x,y)$.*

Proof. Consider inferences between Δ clauses and clauses of N containing only binary predicate symbols. The latter contain at least one selected negative literal. Thus, no inferences are possible between theory clauses satisfying condition 4 and clauses in N. Resolving clauses $Q^n_\alpha(x,y) \vee \neg\mathcal{R}(x,y)^+$ $[\vee \neg\mathcal{R}'(x,y)]$ and $\mathcal{R}(\underline{b}, \underline{c})$ produce ground clauses of the same form. Non-ground conclusions are produced by resolving $\mathcal{R}(x, f(x))$, or $\mathcal{R}(x,x)$, with $Q^n_\alpha(x,y) \vee \neg\mathcal{R}(x,y)^+$ $[\vee \neg\mathcal{R}'(x,y)]$. The outcome are clauses of the form: $Q^n_\alpha(x, f(x))$, $Q^n_\alpha(x,x)$,

$$(') \qquad Q^n_\alpha(x, f(x)) \vee \neg\mathcal{R}'(x, f(x))^+ \quad \text{and} \quad Q^n_\alpha(x,x) \vee \neg\mathcal{R}'(x,x)^+.$$

The superscript of Q^n_α makes explicit that it is a name linked with a negative occurrence of the formula α. Recall, that we have introduced different predicate symbols for positive and negative occurrences of the same relational formula. No inference will be possible between $Q^n_\alpha(x, f(x))$, or $Q^n_\alpha(x,x)$, and clauses satisfying condition 4. Inferences between clauses $(')$ and theory clauses are only possible if $\mathcal{R}'$ is a non-introduced primitive symbol R_j. Such inferences produce $Q^n_\alpha(x, f(x))$, $Q^n_\alpha(x,x)$ or $Q^n_\alpha(\underline{b}, \underline{b})$.

('') The saturation Δ' of Δ and the subset of clauses in N which contain only binary predicate symbols is bounded.

This is immediate since inferred clauses contain at most two variables and there is no increase of the term depth.

We now establish that, except for $(**)$, conclusions of further inferences are ground. Resolution with positive premises from Δ' and clauses of the form $(**)$ produces ground conclusions. Inferences with clauses $(')$ and clauses not in Δ' are with ground clauses, and produce ground clauses. The remaining inferences are as in Lemma 6.2. It follows that split ground conclusions have the form

$$(\neg)P(s), \quad (\neg)\mathcal{R}(s, f(s)), \quad (\neg)\mathcal{R}(s,s) \quad \text{or} \quad \mathcal{R}(\underline{b}, \underline{c}).$$

Termination of any derivation from $N \cup \Delta$ is now shown as follows. Let $\mathtt{T}$ be a new symbol which does not occur in either N or Δ. Let this symbol be the largest symbol with respect to $\succ_d$. In addition, let

$$\Gamma(T) = \{(\neg)R(s,t) \mid s,t \in T \text{ and } R \text{ is a binary predicate symbol}\}.$$

9. $R(x,x)$
10. $Q_{\Box}(\underline{a})$ [1, 2]
11. $Q_{\neg}(\underline{a})$ [1, 3]
12. $\neg R(\underline{a},y)^{+} \vee Q_{\vee}(y)$ [4, 10]
13. $Q_{\vee}(\underline{a})$ [9, 12]
14. $P(\underline{a}) \vee Q_{\Diamond}(\underline{a})$ [5, 13]
15. $\neg P(\underline{a})$ [11, 8]

16.1.1. $P(\underline{a})$ [14, split]
16.1.2. $\emptyset$ [15, 16.1.1]

16.2.1. $Q_{\Diamond}(\underline{a})$ [14, split]
16.2.2. $R(\underline{a}, f(\underline{a}))$ [6, 16.2.1]
16.2.3. $P(f(\underline{a}))$ [7, 16.2.1]
16.2.4. $Q_{\vee}(f(\underline{a}))$ [12, 16.2.2]
16.2.5. $P(f(\underline{a})) \vee Q_{\Diamond}(f(\underline{a}))$ [5, 16.2.4]

16.2.5.1.1. $P(f(\underline{a}))$ [16.2.5, split]
16.2.5.1.2. $Q_{\Diamond}(f(\underline{a}))$ [16.2.5, split]

Figure 4. Derivation for $\varphi = \Box(p \vee \Diamond p) \wedge \neg p$.

Let N_C denote the set of clauses derived prior to C, and C itself. Now, define a measure (a subset of) clauses in a derivation by:

- $c_C = (Q, Q, \emptyset)$, if $C = (\neg)Q(s)$,
- $c_C = (Q_\psi, Q_\phi, \emptyset)$, if C has the form (**), $\neg Q_\psi(x) \vee \neg\mathcal{R}(x,y) \vee Q_\phi(y)$ is the negative premise of C, and $\psi = [\alpha]\phi$, and
- $c_C = (Q, Q, \Gamma(\{s,t\}) \setminus N_C)$, if $C = (\neg)R(s,t)$ and Q is the predicate symbol associated with the the leading function symbol of the maximal term in $\{s,t\}$, whenever such a symbol exists, and T otherwise. Here, maximality is with respect to the proper subterm ordering.

Let $\succ'_D$ be the ordering specified in the proof of Lemma 6.4. The ordering on the complexity measures c_C of positive premises and conclusions is defined to be the lexicographic combination of $\succ'_D$, $\succ'_D$, and the proper superset relationship. This ordering is well-founded. Now we need to verify that split ground conclusions are strictly smaller than their positive premises. As this is tedious, we omit the details. Termination follows.

A characteristic of the clausal class associated with the procedure $R^{\mathcal{MOD}}$ is that (at any point after exhaustive splitting) positive information is given by ground unit clauses, and that additionally, inferred clauses contain at most one variable. For being able to systematically construct a model in the tableaux manner, it is crucial, in particular, that any unary unit clause is ground, for otherwise, the conclusion of an inference with a clause (*) or (**) associated with a box formula would contain more than one variable. This is the reason for having excluded relational negation and the universal modality from consideration. In these cases also non-ground unary unit clauses would have been produced.

Finally, let us consider the example from Figure 2 and give a sample derivation, see Figure 4. We assume R is reflexive, for otherwise not many inference steps are possible. Notice how the correspondence to modal subformulae is retained during inference in $R^{\mathcal{MOD}}$. For example, 16.1.1 and 16.2.1 say that p and $\Diamond p$ are true in the initial world

$\underline{a}$, 16.2.2, 16.2.3 and 16.2.4 say that p and $p \vee \Diamond p$ are true in a successor world of $\underline{a}$. The correspondence is elaborated on in the next section. Evidently, a similar derivation would have been obtained with a tableaux procedure, which will be formally established in Section 9.

7. Automatic model generation

Any clause set N_∞ saturated up to redundancy which does not include the empty clause provides a characterisation of models for the input set N. On the basis of the model construction of the completeness proof it is possible to effectively build a model from N_∞ for N. However, this model will in general be infinite. We now consider how finite models can be generated by using our selection-based procedure.

By a *model* of a clause set we mean a set I of ground atoms. The presence of an atom A in I means A is true in I, and the absence of A means $\neg A$ is true in I. In general, a clause C is true in I iff for all ground substitutions σ there is a literal L in $C\sigma$ which is true in I. Falsehood is defined dually.

LEMMA 7.1. *Let φ be a $K_{(m)}(\cap, \cup, \smile)$-formula. Let N be the clausal form of $\Xi\Pi(\varphi)$, and let N_∞ denote the $R^{\mathcal{MOD}}$-saturated (up to redundancy) clause set derivable from N. Let I be the set of positive ground unit clauses in N_∞. If N_∞ does not contain the empty clause then I is a model of N_∞ and N.*

Proof. As was noted before, during the derivation only ground unit clauses and clauses of the form $\neg\mathcal{R}(s, y) \vee \mathcal{P}(y)$ (with s ground) are generated. To prove that I is a model of N_∞ we have to show that any ground instance of a clause C in N_∞ is true in I. This obviously holds for any of the positive ground unit clauses in N_∞. Next, consider a negative ground unit clause $\neg A$ in N_∞. Then, N_∞ does not contain the positive ground unit clause A (and $A \notin I$), since otherwise the empty clause would also be in N_∞. So, $\neg A$ is true in I. Let $C\sigma = \neg A\sigma \vee D\sigma$ be any ground instance of a clause C in N_∞ with selected literal $\neg A$. If $A\sigma$ is not in I, then $C\sigma$ is true. Otherwise, $A\sigma$ is an element of I and hence of N_∞. This implies we have derived $D\sigma$ at one stage of the derivation. Consequently, one of the split components of $D\sigma$ is in N_∞. The split components of a ground clause are unit ground clauses, for which we have already shown that they are true in I. It follows that $C\sigma$ is true in I. Hence I is a model of N_∞, and also N, by completeness of the procedure (Theorem 4.1).

Now it is an easy matter to construct a modal model $\mathcal{M} = (W, R, \iota)$ for φ from I. Essentially, the set of worlds is defined by the set of ground terms occurring in I. The valuation mapping for relational formulae is determined by the set of R_i and Q_α literals in I. More precisely, if $R_i(s,t)$ (resp. $Q_\alpha(s,t)$) is in I then $(s,t) \in R(r_i)$ (resp. $(s,t) \in R(\alpha)$), which can be extended to a homomorphism for complex relational formulae. Similarly, the valuation mapping for modal formulae is defined: for any unary literal $P_i(s)$ (resp. $Q_\psi(s)$) in I, $s \in \iota(p_i)$ (resp. $s \in \iota(\psi)$), that is, p_i (resp. ψ) is true in the world s. Again, this is homomorphically extended in the expected way.

This proves:

THEOREM 7.2. *For any modal formula satisfiable in $K_{(m)}(\cap, \cup, \smile)$ a finite modal model can be effectively constructed on the basis of $R^{\mathcal{MOD}}$.*

On the side we remark that the satisfiability of some complex formulae is already explicit in I and N_∞. For example, if $Q_\psi(f(g(s)))$ is in $I \subseteq N_\infty$ then ψ is true in the world $f(g(s))$, $\langle\beta_g\rangle\psi$ is true in $g(s)$, and $\langle\beta_f\rangle\langle\beta_g\rangle\psi$ is true in s, where β_f and β_g are the relational formulae associated with f and g. Clauses in $N_\infty \setminus I$ give information about the satisfiability of box formulae. For example, if $\neg Q_\alpha(f(s), y) \vee Q_\psi(y)$ is contained in N_∞ then this implies $[\alpha]\psi$ is true in $f(s)$, and $\langle\beta_f\rangle[\alpha]\psi$ is true in s.

The previous result can be strengthened to the following.

THEOREM 7.3. *For any modal formula which is satisfiable in any logic $L\Delta$ as defined in Theorem 6.6 a finite modal model can be effectively constructed on the basis of R^{MOD}.*

Proof. Construct a modal model $\mathcal{M}$ from the set of positive ground unit clauses in N_∞, as described above, and consistently complete $\mathcal{M}$ in accordance with the background theory Δ. Because Δ contains no clauses requiring the creation of new worlds this is always possible. For example, if $\Delta = \{R_i(x, f(x))\}$ then add $(s, s) \in R(r_i)$ for each dead end world s.

COROLLARY 7.4. *Let L be any logic in-between K and $K_{(m)}(\cap, \cup, \smile)$, and let Δ be defined as in Theorem 6.6. Then, $L\Delta$ has the finite model property.*

8. Tableaux systems for $K\Sigma$

We consider the single-step prefixed tableaux of Massacci [31] (with minor corrections by [18]) for the lattice of normal uni-modal logics defined over the axiom schemas K, D, T, B, 4 and 5.

The basic entities are formulae labelled with prefixes. A labelled (prefixed) formula has the form $\sigma : \varphi$, where σ is a sequence of positive integers and φ is a modal formula. We think of σ as representing a world in which φ is true.

Tableaux proofs have a tree structure. Assuming that we are interested whether a given formula φ is satisfiable, the root node contains the formula, $1 : \varphi$. Successor nodes are constructed by the application of expansion rules. The classical expansion rules for formulae in negation normal form are:

$$(\bot)\ \frac{\sigma : \psi,\ \sigma : \neg\psi}{\sigma : \bot} \qquad (\wedge)\ \frac{\sigma : \psi \wedge \phi}{\sigma : \psi,\ \sigma : \phi} \qquad (\vee)\ \frac{\sigma : \psi \vee \phi}{\sigma : \psi \mid \sigma : \phi}$$

The modal expansion rules include the diamond rule

$$(\Diamond)\ \frac{\sigma : \Diamond\psi}{\sigma.n : \psi}\ \text{with } \sigma.n \text{ new to the current branch}$$

and for the logics we consider the following box rules:

$$(\Box)\ \frac{\sigma : \Box\psi}{\sigma.n : \psi} \qquad (D)\ \frac{\sigma : \Box\psi}{\sigma : \Diamond\psi} \qquad (T)\ \frac{\sigma : \Box\psi}{\sigma : \psi}$$

$$(B)\ \frac{\sigma.n : \Box\psi}{\sigma : \psi} \qquad (4)\ \frac{\sigma : \Box\psi}{\sigma.n : \Box\psi} \qquad (4^r)\ \frac{\sigma.n : \Box\psi}{\sigma : \Box\psi}$$

$$(4^d)\ \frac{\sigma.n : \Box\psi}{\sigma.n.m : \Box\psi} \qquad (5)\ \frac{1.n : \Box\psi}{1 : \Box\Box\psi}$$

The prefixes occurring in the conclusions of the box rules are required to be present in the current branch.

For K:	$(\Diamond), (\Box)$
For KD:	$(\Diamond), (\Box), (D)$
For KT:	$(\Diamond), (\Box), (T)$
For KB:	$(\Diamond), (\Box), (B)$
For $K4$:	$(\Diamond), (\Box), (4)$
For $K5$:	$(\Diamond), (\Box), (4^r), (4^d), (5)$
For KDB:	$(\Diamond), (\Box), (D), (B)$
For $KD4$:	$(\Diamond), (\Box), (D), (4)$
For $KD5$:	$(\Diamond), (\Box), (D), (4^r), (4^d), (5)$
For KTB:	$(\Diamond), (\Box), (T), (B)$
For $S4$:	$(\Diamond), (\Box), (T), (4)$
For $KB4$:	$(\Diamond), (\Box), (B), (4), (4^r)$
For $K45$:	$(\Diamond), (\Box), (4), (4^r), (4^d)$
For $KD45$:	$(\Diamond), (\Box), (D), (4), (4^r), (4^d)$
For $S5$:	$(\Diamond), (\Box), (T), (4), (4^r)$

Figure 5. Modal tableaux rules

The tableaux calculi of the standard logics below $S5$ are given by the classical rules plus the modal rules of Figure 5.[4]

THEOREM 8.1. ([31, 18]). *A formula φ is satisfiable in a logic $K\Sigma$ iff a tableaux containing a branch X can be constructed by the tableaux calculus for $K\Sigma$ such that X does not contain the falsum and no more rules can be applied.*

9. Simulation of tableaux for $K\Sigma$

In this section we prove that inference in the tableaux calculi described in the previous section can be polynomially simulated by the selection-based decision procedure of Section 6. More specifically, we consider the relative proof and search space complexity of the two systems.

In general, when concerned with the relative proof complexity of two systems $\mathcal{A}$ and $\mathcal{B}$ the task is to determine whether one proof system is able to polynomially simulate the other proof system. This is to say, there is a function g, computable in polynomial time, mapping proofs in $\mathcal{B}$ for any given formula φ to proofs in $\mathcal{A}$ for φ. Then, $\mathcal{A}$ *polynomially simulates* (*p-simulates*) the system $\mathcal{B}$ [10]. More generally, a system $\mathcal{A}$ *p-simulates derivations* (not only proofs) of a system $\mathcal{B}$ iff there is a function g, computable in polynomial time, such that for any formula φ, g maps derivations from φ in $\mathcal{B}$ to derivations from φ in $\mathcal{A}$. Clearly, if a system p-simulates derivations in another system, then it also p-simulates the other system. For determining the relative size of the search space we must determine the potential number of inference steps performed until a proof is found [39]. For this purpose we introduce the notion of p-simulation of search. A system $\mathcal{A}$ *p-simulates search* of a system $\mathcal{B}$ iff there is a polynomial function g such that for any formula φ, g maps derivations from φ in $\mathcal{A}$ to derivations from φ in $\mathcal{B}$. Then, $\mathcal{A}$ does not perform any inference steps for which no corresponding inference steps exist in $\mathcal{B}$.

[4] Remember $KT = KDT$, $S4 = KT4$, $KB4 = KB5$, $S5 = KTB4 = KDB4 = KT5$.

In our simulation the first-order background theories for the different axiom schemas are determined by the following clauses:[5]

$$
\begin{aligned}
T_K &= \emptyset & T_{KD4} &= T_{KD} \cup T_{K4}\\
T_{KD} &= \{R(x, f(x))\} & T_{KD5} &= T_{KD} \cup T_{K5}\\
T_{KT} &= \{R(x, x)\} & T_{KTB} &= T_{KT} \cup T_{KB}\\
T_{KB} &= \{\neg R(x, y)^+ \vee R(y, x)\} & T_{S4} &= T_{KT} \cup T_{K4}\\
T_{K4} &= \{\neg R(x, y)^+ \vee \neg R(y, z) \vee R(x, z)\} & T_{KB4} &= T_{KB} \cup T_{K4}\\
T_{K5} &= \{\neg R(x, y) \vee \neg R(x, z) \vee R(y, z), & &\\
&\quad\ \neg R(x, y) \vee R(y, y)\} & T_{K45} &= T_{K4} \cup T_{K5}\\
T_{KDB} &= T_{KD} \cup T_{KB} & T_{S5} &= T_{S4} \cup T_{KB}
\end{aligned}
$$

The previous selection function $S_{\mathcal{MOD}}$ needs to be restricted somewhat, as we do not want to select certain negative binary literals which are generated by inference steps with theory clauses. Here, we define $S_{\mathcal{TAB}}$ to be the selection function which selects

1. a unary literal $\neg A$ in a clause C, if the predicate symbol of A is $\succ_D$-maximal in C,
2. a binary literal, if it is of the form $\neg \mathcal{R}(s, y)$ and no ground term distinct from s occurs in the clause, and
3. the indicated literals in the symmetry clause and the transitivity clause.

The restriction of condition 2, that no ground term distinct from s occurs in the clause, is needed for the simulation of the rules (4) and (4^r), see below.

A subset of the rules of the general resolution calculus R, and also $R^{\mathcal{MOD}}$, are required for the simulation. Let $R^{\mathcal{TAB}}$ be the resolution calculus consisting of the rules "Split" and "Deduce" parameterised by the selection function $S_{\mathcal{TAB}}$, no ordering, and $\text{Norm}(C) = C$.[6] The rules are applied in this order and it is assumed that no derivation step is performed twice on one clause (or any of its variants).

The exact correspondence between the inference steps of the single-step prefixed tableaux procedure and our resolution procedure is not hard to see. In more detail, as was noted before, each non-atomic subformula or modal literal ψ of the given modal formula is uniquely associated with a predicate symbol Q_ψ in the clausal form, and each atomic subformula (p_i or r_j) is uniquely mapped to a predicate symbol by the translation mapping. Furthermore, every prefix σ can be uniquely associated with ground term t_σ.

- The clause associated with $1 : \varphi$ is the ground unit clause $Q_\varphi(\underline{a})$ and $t_1 = \underline{a}$.
- A derivation of falsum by the ($\perp$) rule corresponds to the derivation of the empty clause from $Q_\psi(t_\sigma)$, $Q_{\neg\psi}(t_\sigma)$ and $\neg Q_{\neg\psi}(x)^+ \vee \neg Q_\psi(x)$, the definition of $\neg\psi$.
- An application of the ($\wedge$) rule corresponds to two resolution steps with a ground clause $Q_{\psi\wedge\phi}(t_\sigma)$ and clauses $\neg Q_{\psi\wedge\phi}(x)^+ \vee Q_\psi(x)$ and $\neg Q_{\psi\wedge\phi}(x)^+ \vee Q_\phi(x)$, producing resolvents $Q_\psi(t_\sigma)$ and $Q_\phi(t_\sigma)$.
- An application of the ($\vee$) rule corresponds to one resolution step between clauses $Q_{\psi\vee\phi}(t_\sigma)$ and $\neg Q_{\psi\vee\phi}(x)^+ \vee Q_\psi(x) \vee Q_\phi(x)$. The conclusion is $Q_\psi(t_\sigma) \vee Q_\phi(t_\sigma)$, to which we can apply the splitting rule. The two newly created branches contain $Q_\psi(t_\sigma)$ and $Q_\phi(t_\sigma)$, respectively.

[5] Note that we do not select any literal in the theory clauses for 5.

[6] It turns out, we do not even need factoring. This is because all positive premises are ground and subject to the application of the splitting rule.

- For the simulation of the ($\Diamond$) rule assume $Q_{\Diamond\psi}(t_\sigma)$ is present in the clauses set. Then an application of the ($\Diamond$) rule corresponds to resolving $Q_{\Diamond\psi}(t_\sigma)$ with $\neg Q_{\Diamond\psi}(x)^+ \vee R(x, f(x))$, and $\neg Q_{\Diamond\psi}(x)^+ \vee Q_\psi(f(x))$. This will add $R(t_\sigma, f(t_\sigma))$ and $Q_\psi(f(t_\sigma))$ to the clause set. The term $f(t_\sigma)$ corresponds to the new prefix $\sigma.n$, that is, $t_{\sigma.n} = f(t_\sigma)$.

  Observe that if the set already contains $Q_\psi(t_{\sigma.n})$ no inference step is necessary. Similarly, for all other rules: Whenever the conclusion of an inference is already present in the clause set then the inference is redundant.

For the box rules we will assume that the current set of clauses includes a clause $\neg R(s, y)^+ \vee Q_\psi(y)$ of the appropriate form (s is either t_σ or $t_{\sigma.n}$). If it does not, then it can be derived from the given clause $Q_{\Box\psi}(s)$ and the definitional clause $\neg Q_{\Box\psi}(x)^+ \vee \neg R(x, y) \vee Q_\psi(y)$.

- For the ($\Box$) rule: Resolving $\neg R(t_\sigma, y)^+ \vee Q_\psi(y)$ with $R(t_\sigma, t_{\sigma.n})$ gives $Q_\psi(t_{\sigma.n})$.

- For the (D) rule: A resolution step with $\neg R(t_\sigma, y)^+ \vee Q_\psi(y)$ and the seriality clause $R(x, f(x))$ generates $Q_\psi(f(t_\sigma))$ ($= Q_\psi(t_{\sigma.n})$ for some n already present in the branch).

- For the (T) rule: A resolution step between $\neg R(t_\sigma, y)^+ \vee Q_\psi(y)$ and the reflexivity clause $R(x, x)$ generates $Q_\psi(t_\sigma)$.

- For the (B) rule: Resolve the given clause $R(t_\sigma, t_{\sigma.n})$ with the symmetry clause, which gives $R(t_{\sigma.n}, t_\sigma)$. With $\neg R(t_{\sigma.n}, y)^+ \vee Q_\psi(y)$ we can derive $Q_\psi(t_\sigma)$.

- For the (4) rule: A resolution step between $R(t_\sigma, t_{\sigma.n})$ and the transitivity clause gives $\neg R(t_{\sigma.n}, z) \vee R(t_\sigma, z)$. This resolves with $\neg R(t_\sigma, y)^+ \vee Q_\psi(y)$ so that we get $\neg R(t_{\sigma.n}, z) \vee Q_\psi(z)$.[7]

- For the (4^r) rule, we distinguish two cases:

  a. 5 is a theorem. Inference with $R(t_\sigma, t_{\sigma.n})$ and Euclideanness results in $\neg R(t_\sigma, z) \vee R(t_{\sigma.n}, z)$, which gives $\neg R(t_\sigma, y)^+ \vee Q_\psi(y)$ when resolved with $\neg R(t_{\sigma.n}, y)^+ \vee Q_\psi(y)$.

  b. B and 4 are theorems. Resolving $R(t_\sigma, t_{\sigma.n})$ with symmetry produces $R(t_{\sigma.n}, t_\sigma)$, and with transitivity we derive $\neg R(t_\sigma, z) \vee \neg R(t_{\sigma.n}, z)$. Resolving with $\neg R(t_{\sigma.n}, y)^+ \vee Q_\psi(y)$ produces the clause $\neg R(t_\sigma, z)^+ \vee Q_\psi(z)$.

- For the (4^d) rule: We can assume 5 is a theorem and $\neg R(t_{\sigma.n}, y)^+ \vee Q_\psi(y)$ is available. Resolving this twice with Euclideanness gives

  $$\neg R(x, t_{\sigma.n})^+ \vee \neg R(x, y) \vee \neg R(y, z) \vee Q_\psi(z).$$

  Now, we resolve with $\neg R(x, y) \vee R(y, y)$, producing $\neg R(x, t_{\sigma.n})^+ \vee \neg R(t_{\sigma.n}, y)^+ \vee \neg R(y, z) \vee Q_\psi(z)$. Inference with the given clauses $R(t_\sigma, t_{\sigma.n})$ and $R(t_{\sigma.n}, t_{\sigma.n.m})$ produces $\neg R(t_{\sigma.n.m}, z)^+ \vee Q_\psi(z)$, as required.

- For the (5) rule: Two resolution steps upon $R(t_1, t_{1.n})$, Euclideanness and $\neg R(t_{1.n}, y)^+ \vee Q_\psi(y)$ generates $\neg R(t_1, z)^+ \vee Q_\psi(z)$.

[7] It is here, for example, where we do not want to have the first literal in $\neg R(t_{\sigma.n}, z) \vee R(t_\sigma, z)$ selected.

All these inference steps strictly adhere to the restrictions enforced by the selection function S_{TAB}. It turns out that each application of a tableaux rule can be simulated by at most six inference steps in R^{TAB}.

The above proves that every tableaux derivation (or proof) can be polynomially mapped to a resolution derivation (or proof). That is:

THEOREM 9.1. *For $K\Sigma$ with $\Sigma \subseteq \{D, T, B, 4, 5\}$, derivations in the single-step prefixed tableaux calculi can be p-simulated by the selection-based resolution procedure R^{TAB}.*

COROLLARY 9.2. *The single-step prefixed tableaux calculi for $K\Sigma$ with $\Sigma \subseteq \{D, T, B, 4, 5\}$ can be p-simulated by a selection-based resolution procedure.*

By Theorem 6.6 termination is certain for both procedures.

COROLLARY 9.3. *Procedures based on R^{TAB}, and the single-step prefixed tableaux calculi provide decision procedures for $K\Sigma$ with $\Sigma \subseteq \{D, T, B\}$.*

Now, we may ask whether the tableaux procedure also p-simulates search in R^{TAB}. The answer is yes, for $K\Sigma$ with $\Sigma \subseteq \{D, T, B\}$, and modulo the addition of a factoring rule. The tableaux rules constitute in effect macro inference steps in the resolution calculus. As previously mentioned factoring is not essential for completeness with respect to the concerned clausal class. We can therefore conclude:

THEOREM 9.4. *R^{TAB} p-simulates search in single step prefix tableaux for $K\Sigma$ with $\Sigma \subseteq \{D, T, B\}$.*

In effect, by Theorem 9.1 and 9.4, there is a bisimulation relationship between the two methods. It follows that, the soundness and completeness of the tableaux procedure is a consequence of the soundness and completeness of R^{TAB} (Theorem 4.1).

COROLLARY 9.5. *The single-step prefix tableaux calculi for $K\Sigma$ with $\Sigma \subseteq \{D, T, B\}$ are sound and complete.*

Moreover:

COROLLARY 9.6. *Derivations based on the single-step prefixed tableaux calculi for $K\Sigma$ with $\Sigma \subseteq \{D, T, B\}$ can be simulated by a resolution procedure with the same time and space complexity.*

The above results generalise in the expected way to independent joins of countably many $K\Sigma$, where $\Sigma \subseteq \{D, T, B, 4, 5\}$.

10. Implementation and experiments

So as to obtain a first impression of the behaviour of an implementation of the selection-based resolution calculus we modified the theorem prover SPASS. SPASS is a resolution theorem prover for first-order logic with equality developed by Weidenbach et al. [43]. SPASS contains, amongst others, the inference rules of the general ordered resolution calculus R described in Section 4. Thus, to realise the calculi R^{MOD} and R^{TAB} we have extended SPASS (Version 0.95) with an implementation of the selection functions $S_{\mathcal{MOD}}$ and $S_{\mathcal{TAB}}$.

For the later discussion of the experimental results we need some basic understanding of the proof search strategy, heuristics and optimisations implemented in SPASS, which we briefly describe now.

The inference loop in SPASS is controlled by two sets of clauses: The set of worked-off clauses and the set of usable clauses. At the beginning all input clauses are usable. The theorem prover starts by choosing, according to some heuristic, a clause from the usable clause set and moving it to the worked-off clause set. Then all inference rules are applied to the chosen clause and clauses from the worked-off clause set. The derived clauses are subjected to the reduction rules, for example, subsumption deletion and clause reduction, and non-redundant clauses are added to the usable clause set. If the empty clause is derived or the set of usable clauses is empty, the theorem prover stops, having derived a contradiction or a satisfiable clause set. Otherwise, the next clause is chosen from the usable clause set, moved to the worked-off clause set, and the loop is repeated. The heuristic used by SPASS for choosing clauses is based on the number of symbols in a clause and its depth in the search space.

Among the inference rules, splitting has priority. If splitting is applicable to a clause, a heuristic is used to determine which subclauses are generated and in which order they are considered. The heuristic used by SPASS will simply branch on the first (in the order literals are stored internally) positive literal of the chosen clause.

While the heuristics implemented in SPASS work reasonably well for first-order problems, they provide little guidance on the randomly generated modal formulae we used in the comparison detailed below. Therefore, we have replaced these by new heuristics. If the set of usable clauses contains either a unit clause or a clause containing selected literals, then one of these is chosen. Otherwise, a clause is chosen which is shortest and which contains the literal L for which the function $JW(L)$ is maximal. $JW(L)$ is defined to be the sum of 2^{-n_i} over all clauses C_i containing L, where n_i is the number of literals in C_i.

For the clause sets under consideration, all non-ground clauses contain a selected literal and will therefore be chosen before any non-unit ground clause. Furthermore, all non-ground clauses are indecomposable. If the set of usable clauses contains no clauses with selected literals, then it consists of ground clauses only. On such clause sets the heuristic described above is identical to the Jeroslow-Wang heuristic for propositional problems [28]. Splitting is only applicable if the chosen clause is ground. Thus, the chosen clause contains a literal L for which the function $JW(L)$ is maximal and the splitting heuristic branches on this particular literal.

SPASS provides a variety of reduction rules. We will concentrate on subsumption deletion and unit propagation, which is an instance of clause reduction. A clause C *subsumes* a clause D if there exists a substitution σ such that $C\sigma$ is a subclause of D. For example, the clause $P_1(\underline{a}) \vee \neg P_2(\underline{a})$ subsumes $P_1(\underline{a}) \vee \neg P_2(\underline{a}) \vee P_3(\underline{a})$. A clause C *reduces* a clause D to D' if D' is a (condensed) resolvent of C and D, and D' is a subclause of D. For example, the clause $P_1(\underline{a}) \vee \neg P_2(\underline{a})$ reduces $P_1(\underline{a}) \vee P_2(\underline{a})$ to $P_1(\underline{a})$. In Figure 4, subsumption deletion would have avoided the second splitting (because clause 16.2.3 subsumes clause 16.2.5), and unit propagation (of 15 into 14) followed by subsumption deletion would have avoided also the first splitting of the derivation.

Subsumption deletion and unit propagation correspond to familiar inference rules and notions in the context of tableaux calculi. A (prefixed) disjunction Φ is *fulfilled* on a branch if there is a (prefixed) proper subdisjunction Φ' of Φ on the branch. A tableau is *regular* if the $(\vee)$ rule is not applied to a (prefixed) disjunction which is fulfilled on a branch. Thus, if $\sigma : \varphi$ and $\sigma : \varphi \vee \psi$ occur on a branch, the $(\vee)$ rule will not be applied to the second formula, since this application would produce an irregular tableaux. If $\sigma : \varphi$ and $\sigma : \neg\varphi \vee \psi$ are present on a branch, we can apply the $(\vee)$ rule to the second formula which results in a branch containing $\sigma : \neg\varphi$ and a branch containing $\sigma : \psi$. Obviously, the first branch can be closed with the $(\bot)$ rule. Considering proof length only, both subsumption deletion (regularity) and unit propagation do not improve the computational behaviour of the procedure. The shortest proof for a formula contains no application of subsumption deletion and any application of unit propagation can be simulated by applications of the $(\vee)$ and $(\bot)$ rules, as just explained.

SPASS was augmented with the translation mapping defined in Section 3, as well as the structural transformation defined in Section 6. The implementation differs from the definitions in that during the structural transformation only non-literal subformula occurrences are renamed, and for any pair of unary predicate symbols Q_ψ and Q_ϕ such that ψ is the negation normal form of $\neg\phi$, the first-order formula $\forall x\, (\neg Q_\psi(x) \vee \neg Q_\phi(x))$ is added. With the latter extension contradictions are found earlier which improves the performance. This corresponds to normalisation optimisations and techniques for early detection of contradictions in tableaux provers [21].

In the following, the modified version of SPASS using selection will be called TAB-SPASS. It remains a sound and complete theorem prover for first-order logic with equality.

The ordered resolution procedure with which we compare TABSPASS is a realisation in SPASS of the ordering refinement described in [26]. The ordering is a liftable ordering determined by the multiset extension of the strict subterm ordering on ground arguments. It is realised in SPASS by specifying a suitable precedence on the vocabulary for the built in extended Knuth Bendix ordering.

The experiments were performed on randomly generated formulae analysed in [23, 24]. The generated formulae are in modal conjunctive normal form determined by five parameters: N, the number of propositional variables, M, the number of modalities, K, the number of disjuncts, L, the number of conjuncts, D, the modal degree, and P, the probability of being a propositional variable. The graphs in Figures 6 and 7 are for the parameter settings

$$\text{PS0 } (N{=}5,\ M{=}1,\ K{=}3,\ D{=}2,\ P{=}0.5) \text{ and}$$
$$\text{PS1 } (N{=}4,\ M{=}1,\ K{=}3,\ D{=}1,\ P{=}0.0).$$

PS0 was generated using the original generator of [17]. PS1 was generated in accordance with the guidelines of [24]. The parameter L (the number of conjuncts) ranges from N to $40N$. For each value of the ratio L/N a set of 100 random modal formulae of degree D is generated. For small L the generated formulae are most likely satisfiable and for larger L the generated formulae are most likely unsatisfiable. The tests were performed under Sun Solaris 2.6 on a cluster of PCs equipped with 300 MHz Pentium II processors and 256 MB main memory. Each figure includes three percentile graphs of TABSPASS with and without reductions, and SPASS employing the ordering refinement with reductions. Each figure also includes a graph displaying the median CPU time plots.

It is important to note that formulae generated using the parameter settings PS0 and PS1 have particular properties which have to be carefully taken into account in an analysis of the experimental results [24]. However, they are well-suited to illustrate some basic differences between various decision procedures for modal logic.

As is evident in Figures 6 and 7, enabling the reduction rules in TABSPASS greatly enhances its performance. Of particular interest here are ratios L/N greater than 18 for PS0 and greater than 17 for PS1 for which more than half of the formulae are unsatisfiable. As mentioned above, theoretical considerations would lead us to expect

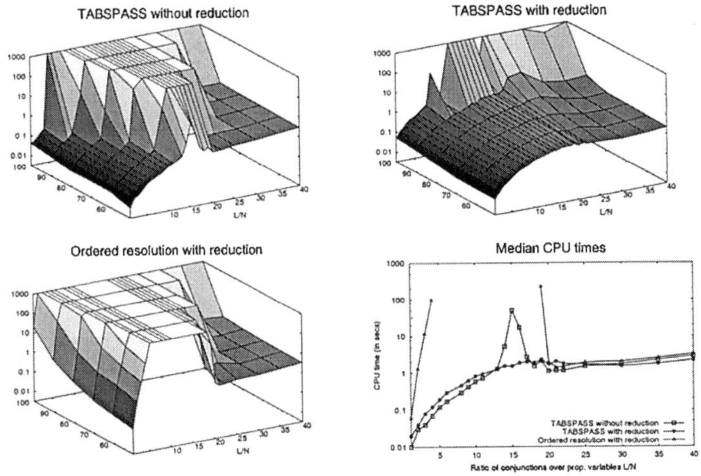

Figure 6. Graphs for PS0 (N=5, M=1, K=3, D=2, P=0.5)

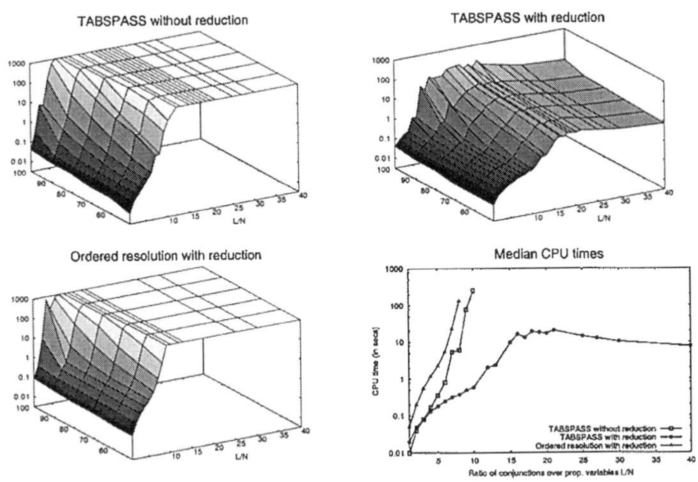

Figure 7. Graphs for PS1 (N=4, M=1, K=3, D=1, P=0.0)

little difference in the performance of TABSPASS with and without reductions on these formulae. However, for PS1 there is a visible improvement for the reduction rules.

Consider a clause set containing a unit clause $Q_\varphi(t)$ and ground clauses $\bigcup_j\{\neg Q_\varphi(t) \vee C_j\}$. If $Q_\varphi(t)$ is the chosen clause in the inference loop and the reduction rules are enabled, then TABSPASS will replace each ground clause $\neg Q_\varphi(t) \vee C_j$ by C_j. To achieve the same effect if the reduction rules are disabled, we need to chose the clauses $\neg Q_\varphi(t) \vee C_j$ one after the other, apply the splitting rule in such a way that we obtain a branch contain $\neg Q_\varphi(t)$ and one containing C_j, and close the first branch by a resolution inference step. However, the choice of clauses and the application of splitting is determined by the heuristics described above. For PS0, it happens that due to the particular probability with which literals occur in clause sets, the heuristics will actually achieve the desired effect. For PS1 this is not the case.

To understand why TABSPASS with reduction performs better than ordered resolution with reduction on PS0 and PS1 we take a closer look at the way ordered resolution deals with the clause sets under consideration. Due to the structural transformation performed, these clause sets contain a considerable number of clauses of the form

$$(\dagger) \qquad \neg Q_{\Diamond\varphi}(x) \vee R(x, f(x))_* \quad \text{and}$$
$$(\dagger\dagger) \qquad \neg Q_{\Box\psi}(x) \vee \neg R(x, y)_* \vee Q_\psi(y).$$

The maximal literals are marked by a $_*$. Recall, that in the framework presented in Section 6, $\neg Q_{\Diamond\varphi}(x)$ and $\neg Q_{\Box\psi}(x)$ are selected literals, which prevents any inference steps between such clauses. Here, however, whenever a clause of the form (†) is chosen, resolvents with *all* clauses of form (††) will be computed. Consequences of these inference steps have the form $\neg Q_{\Diamond\varphi}(x) \vee \neg Q_{\Box\psi}(x) \vee Q_\psi(f(x))_*$. Further inference steps can lead to clauses of the form $\neg Q_{\Diamond\varphi}(x) \vee \neg Q_{\Box\psi}(x) \vee (\neg)P_i(f(x))_*$. Maximal literals with a predicate symbol associated with a propositional variable potentially lead to very many inference steps.

Recall, that the satisfiability of a clause set is established only after all possible inference steps have been performed. Proof search as described above leads to a large number of derived clauses before this is the case. Thus, on all but the smallest problem this approach will not terminate within the given time limit. Even on unsatisfiable problems, the fact that we always have to compute *all* consequences with the chosen clause and the fact that the heuristics of SPASS provide very little guidance for the proof search, results in unsatisfactory performance.

The only exceptions are the clause sets obtained from the random modal formulae for the ratios L/N greater than 19 for PS0. Most of these formulae contain propositional subproblems which are unsatisfiable. The unsatisfiability of these formulae is easily detected by the procedure based on ordered resolution without any inference steps between clauses of the form (†) and (††).

It should be stressed that these experimental results are only preliminary and do not allow any strong conclusions to be drawn for or against either selection-based approaches or ordered resolution approaches. In many cases ordered resolution is easier to use, and it would be interesting to investigate whether a different organisation of the proof search could improve the performance of the ordered resolution procedure for unsatisfiable formulae. A notable difference between the ordered resolution procedure and the selection-based resolution procedure is that for transitive modal logics the former can be extended to a terminating resolution procedure which does not require a loop detection mechanism [15].

11. Conclusion

We have described a new resolution decision procedure for certain extended modal logics. Due to careful transformation to clausal form and the implementation of a tableaux-style refinement, the procedure provides also a tool for automatically building models, and additionally, proofs can be easily translated back into (tableaux proofs of) the original source logic. Logical and model-theoretic implications are decidability and the finite model property. These results are not all new, for example, Theorems 6.5 and 6.6 and Corollary 7.4 follow also from results for more expressive logics, for example [16, 35]. However, the significance of the results is that the method of obtaining them is new. Moreover, we believe the methods described here have the potential to be used for obtaining new results for less well-studied logics. For instance, one could imagine that by studying selection-based resolution refinements a tableaux proof system could be obtained for the guarded fragment.[8]

An important contribution of this paper is on the issue of relative efficiency of proof. We have focused on a particular tableaux proof system and showed how this system can be simulated with polynomial overhead in the context of resolution. As already mentioned, we expect similar results can also be obtained for other forms of tableaux proof systems or sequent calculi. The results provide new insight into the relative proof and search complexity of tableaux and resolution proof systems, similar to corresponding results for propositional logic [42]. With respect to the runtime behaviour, the difference between modal tableaux systems and selection-based resolution procedures is at most a polynomial factor. Naturally, good implementations incorporate various optimisations. A standard optimisation, in both resolution and tableaux procedures, is the utilisation of unit propagation and subsumption deletion for minimising the number of applications of the splitting rule, thereby reducing the size of the search space. It follows from our results that optimisation techniques can be readily transferred between the corresponding tableaux and resolution proof systems.

The resolution decision procedure described in this paper offers just one of many possible refinements. Other resolution refinements utilised in the literature, mentioned in the Introduction and the previous section, are implemented by ordering restrictions. Yet another alternative is hyperresolution, which is closely related to a selection-based procedure based on maximal selection [6, 8]. Consequently, the results of this paper also hold for hyperresolution. The main reason for using the Bachmair-Ganzinger framework is that it allows for all the various refinements to be presented uniformly in a common formalism.

As there is much room for further refinement, this paper may be regarded as a starting point for further in depth analysis, including an extended theoretical and empirical comparison of selection-based refinements and ordering refinements. Going on from there, a goal of further work is to establish guidelines for good search strategies for different classes of modal problems.

Acknowledgements

We thank the anonymous reviewers for their helpful comments. Also, we are grateful for the permission to perform the experiments on the PC cluster of the Max-Planck-Institut für Informatik in Saarbrücken, Germany. The work of the first author was supported by EPSRC Grant GR/K57282.

References

1. Andréka, H., J. van Benthem, and I. Németi: 1995, 'Back and Forth Between Modal Logic and Classical Logic'. *Bulletin of the IGPL* **3**(5), 685–720.
2. Auffray, Y. and P. Enjalbert: 1992, 'Modal Theorem Proving: An Equational Viewpoint'. *Journal of Logic and Computation* **2**(3), 247–297.
3. Baader, F., B. Hollunder, B. Nebel, H.-J. Profitlich, and E. Franconi: 1992, 'An Empirical Analysis of Optimization Techniques for Terminological Representation Systems, or: Making KRIS get a move on'. In: B. Nebel, C. Rich, and W. Swartout (eds.): *Proceedings of the Third International Conference on Principles of Knowledge Representation and Reasoning (KR'92)*. Morgan Kaufmann, pp. 270–281.

[8] It so happens that during the final revision of this paper we became aware of a tableaux system for a fragment of the guarded fragment, proposed in [30]. This system can be p-simulated (and generalised) by the method described in this paper.

4. Baaz, M., C. Fermüller, and A. Leitsch: 1994, 'A Non-Elementary Speed-Up in Proof Length by Structural Clause Form Transformation'. In: *Proceedings of the Ninth Annual IEEE Symposium on Logic in Computer Science (LICS'94)*. IEEE Computer Society Press, pp. 213–219.
5. Bachmair, L. and H. Ganzinger: 1994, 'Rewrite-Based Equational Theorem Proving with Selection and Simplification'. *Journal of Logic and Computation* 4(3), 217–247.
6. Bachmair, L. and H. Ganzinger: 1997, 'A Theory of Resolution'. Research Report MPI-I-97-2-005, Max-Planck-Institut für Informatik, Saarbrücken, Germany.
7. Bachmair, L. and H. Ganzinger: 1998, 'Equational Reasoning in Saturation-Based Theorem Proving'. In: *Automated Deduction—A Basis for Applications. Volume I.* Kluwer, Chapt. 11, pp. 353–397.
8. Bachmair, L. and H. Ganzinger: 2000, 'Resolution Theorem Proving'. To appear in J. A. Robinson and A. Voronkov (eds.): *Handbook of Automated Reasoning*, Elsevier.
9. Caferra, R. and S. Demri: 1993, 'Cooperation Between Direct Method and Translation Method in Non Classical Logics: Some Results in Propositional S5'. In: R. Bajcsy (ed.): *Proceedings of the Thirteenth International Joint Conference on Artificial Intelligence (IJCAI'93)*. Morgan Kaufmann, pp. 74–79.
10. Cook, S. A. and R. A. Reckhow: 1979, 'The Relative Efficiency of Propositional Proof Systems'. *Journal of Symbolic Logic* **44**(1), 36–50.
11. de Nivelle, H.: 1998, 'A Resolution Decision Procedure for the Guarded Fragment'. In: C. Kirchner and H. Kirchner (eds.): *Automated Deduction: CADE-15*, Vol. 1421 of *Lecture Notes in Artificial Intelligence.* Springer, pp. 191–204.
12. Demri, S.: 1995, 'A Hierarchy of Backward Translations: Applications to Modal Logics'. In: M. de Glas and Z. Pawlak (eds.): *Proceedings of the Second World Conference on the Fundamentals of Artificial Intelligence (WOCFAI 95)*. Paris: Angkor, pp. 121–132.
13. Donini, F. M., M. Lenzerini, D. Nardi, and A. Schaerf: 1996, 'Reasoning in Description Logics'. In: G. Brewka (ed.): *Principles in Knowledge Representation*, Studies in Logic, Language and Information. Stanford: CSLI Publications, pp. 191–236.
14. Fermüller, C., A. Leitsch, T. Tammet, and N. Zamov: 1993, *Resolution Method for the Decision Problem*, Vol. 679 of *Lecture Notes in Computer Science.* Springer.
15. Ganzinger, H., U. Hustadt, C. Meyer, and R. A. Schmidt: 1999, 'A Resolution-Based Decision Procedure for Extensions of K4'. To appear in *Advances in Modal Logic, Volume 2*, Stanford: CSLI Publications.
16. Gargov, G. and S. Passy: 1990, 'A Note on Boolean Modal Logic'. In: P. P. Petkov (ed.): *Mathematical Logic: Proceedings of the 1988 Heyting Summerschool.* New York: Plenum Press, pp. 299–309.
17. Giunchiglia, F. and R. Sebastiani: 1996, 'Building Decision Procedures for Modal Logics From Propositional Decision Procedures: The Case Study of Modal K'. In: M. A. McRobbie and J. K. Slaney (eds.): *Automated Deduction: CADE-13*, Vol. 1104 of *Lecture Notes in Artificial Intelligence.* Springer, pp. 583–597.
18. Goré, R.: 1995, 'Tableau Methods for Modal and Temporal Logics'. Technical Report TR-ARP-15-95, Australian National University, Canberra. To appear in M. D'Agostino, D. Gabbay, R. Hähnle and J. Posegga (eds.): *Handbook of Tableau Methods*, Kluwer.
19. Herzig, A.: 1989, 'Raisonnement automatique en logique modale et algorithmes d'unification.'. Ph.D. thesis, Univ. Paul-Sabatier, Toulouse.
20. Hooker, J. N.: 1996, 'Testing heuristics: We have it all wrong'. *Journal of Heuristics* **1**, 33–42.
21. Horrocks, I.: 1998, 'Using an Expressive Description Logic: FaCT or Fiction?'. In: A. Cohn, L. Schubert, and S. Shapiro (eds.): *Proceedings of the Sixth International Conference on Principles of Knowledge Representation and Reasoning (KR-98).* Morgan Kaufmann, pp. 636–647.
22. Horrocks, I. and P. F. Patel-Schneider: 1998, 'FaCT and DLP'. In: H. de Swart (ed.): *Automated Reasoning with Analytic Tableaux and Related Methods: TABLEAUX'98*, Vol. 1397 of *Lecture Notes in Computer Science.* Springer, pp. 27–30.
23. Hustadt, U. and R. A. Schmidt: 1997, 'On Evaluating Decision Procedures for Modal Logics'. In: M. Pollack (ed.): *Proceedings of the Fifteenth International Joint Conference on Artificial Intelligence (IJCAI'97).* Morgan Kaufmann, pp. 202–207.
24. Hustadt, U. and R. A. Schmidt: 1999a, 'An Empirical Analysis of Modal Theorem Provers'. *Journal of Applied Non-Classical Logics* **9**(4).
25. Hustadt, U. and R. A. Schmidt: 1999b, 'Maslov's Class K Revisited'. In: H. Ganzinger (ed.): *Automated Deduction—CADE-16*, Vol. 1632 of *Lecture Notes in Artificial Intelligence.* Springer, pp. 172–186.

26. Hustadt, U. and R. A. Schmidt: 2000, 'Issues of Decidability for Description Logics in the Framework of Resolution'. In: R. Caferra and G. Salzer (eds.): *Automated Deduction in Classical and Non-Classical Logics*, Vol. 1761 of *Lecture Notes in Artificial Intelligence*. pp. 192–206.
27. Hustadt, U., R. A. Schmidt, and C. Weidenbach: 1998, 'Optimised Functional Translation and Resolution'. In: H. de Swart (ed.): *Automated Reasoning with Analytic Tableaux and Related Methods: TABLEAUX'98*, Vol. 1397 of *Lecture Notes in Computer Science*. Springer, pp. 36–37.
28. Jeroslow, R. and J. Wang: 1990, 'Solving Propositional Satisfiability Problems'. *Annals of Mathematics and Artificial Intelligence* **1**, 167–187.
29. Joyner Jr., W. H.: 1976, 'Resolution Strategies as Decision Procedures'. *Journal of the ACM* **23**(3), 398–417.
30. Lutz, C., U. Sattler, and S. Tobies: 1999, 'A Suggestion of an n-ary Description Logic'. In: P. Lambrix, A. Borgida, M. Lenzerini, R. Möller, and P. Patel-Schneider (eds.): *Proc. of Intern. Workshop on Description Logics'99*. Linköping University, pp. 81–85.
31. Massacci, F.: 1994, 'Strongly Analytic Tableaux for Normal Modal Logics'. In: *Automated Deduction: CADE-12*, Vol. 814 of *Lecture Notes in Artificial Intelligence*. Springer, pp. 723–737.
32. Massacci, F.: 1998, 'Simplification: A General Constraint Propagation Technique for Propositional and Modal Tableaux'. In: H. de Swart (ed.): *Automated Reasoning with Analytic Tableaux and Related Methods: TABLEAUX'98*, Vol. 1397 of *Lecture Notes in Artificial Intelligence*. Springer, pp. 217–231.
33. Mints, G.: 1986, 'A Resolution Method for Non-Classical Logics'. *Semiotika and Informatika* **25**, 120–135.
34. Mints, G.: 1989, 'Resolution Calculi for Modal Logics'. *American Mathematical Society Translations* **143**, 1–14.
35. Mortimer, M.: 1975, 'On Languages with two Variables'. *Zeitschrift für mathematische Logik und Grundlagen der Mathematik* **21**, 135–140.
36. Ohlbach, H. J. and R. A. Schmidt: 1997, 'Functional Translation and Second-Order Frame Properties of Modal Logics'. *Journal of Logic and Computation* **7**(5), 581–603.
37. Paramasivam, M. and D. A. Plaisted: 1998, 'Automated Deduction Techniques for Classification in Description Logic Systems'. *Journal of Automated Reasoning* **20**(3), 337–364.
38. Plaisted, D. A. and S. Greenbaum: 1986, 'A Structure-Preserving Clause Form Translation'. *Journal of Symbolic Computation* **2**, 293–304.
39. Plaisted, D. A. and Y. Zhu: 1997, *The Efficiency of Theorem Proving Strategies*. Vieweg.
40. Schmidt, R. A.: 1999, 'Decidability by Resolution for Propositional Modal Logics'. *Journal of Automated Reasoning* **22**(4), 379–396.
41. Tseitin, G. S.: 1970, 'On the complexity of derivations in propositional calculus'. In: A. O. Slisenko (ed.): *Studies in Constructive Mathematics and Mathematical Logic, Part II*. New York: Consultants Bureau:, pp. 115–125.
42. Urquhart, A.: 1995, 'The Complexity of Propositional Proofs'. *Bulletin of Symbolic Logic* **1**(4), 425–467.
43. Weidenbach, C. et al.: 1999, 'System Description: SPASS Version 1.0.0'. In: H. Ganzinger (ed.): *Automated Deduction—CADE-16*, Vol. 1632 of *Lecture Notes in Artificial Intelligence*. pp. 378–382.

SAT2000
I. Gent et al. (Eds.)
IOS Press, 2000

An Algorithm to Evaluate Quantified Boolean Formulae and its Experimental Evaluation †

Marco Cadoli, Marco Schaerf§ and Andrea Giovanardi, Massimo Giovanardi||
Dipartimento di Informatica e Sistemistica, Università di Roma "La Sapienza", Via Salaria 113, I-00198 Roma, Italy

Abstract. The high computational complexity of advanced reasoning tasks such as reasoning about knowledge and planning calls for efficient and reliable algorithms for reasoning problems harder than NP. In this paper we propose Evaluate, an algorithm for evaluating *Quantified Boolean Formulae* (QBFs). Algorithms for evaluation of QBFs are suitable for the experimental analysis on problems that belong to a wide range of complexity classes, a property not easily found in other formalisms. Evaluate is a generalization of the Davis-Putnam procedure for SAT, and is guaranteed to work in polynomial space. Before presenting the algorithm, we discuss several abstract properties of QBFs that we singled out to make it more efficient. We also discuss various options that were investigated about heuristics and data structures, and report the main results of the experimental analysis. In particular Evaluate is orders of magnitude more efficient than a nested backtracking procedure which resorts to a Davis-Putnam algorithm for handling the innermost set of quantifiers. Moreover experiments show that randomly generated QBFs exhibit regular patterns such as phase transition and easy-hard-easy distribution.

1. Introduction

Interest in algorithms for the SAT problem has been constant in the AI community. SAT is obviously relevant to AI, and, being the prototypical NP-complete problem, challenges our ability to reason effectively in the presence of large knowledge bases. Usage of algorithms for SAT for reasoning tasks different from classical propositional reasoning has been recently emphasized in the literature. For example, real-world problems such as many forms of constraint-based planning can be encoded in SAT (see [18] for more details), and theorem provers for modal logic can use SAT solvers as black boxes [13].

The optimization of algorithms for SAT is not enough for the goals of Knowledge Representation: theoretical analysis showed that advanced forms of reasoning such as belief revision, non-monotonic reasoning, reasoning about knowledge, and STRIPS-like planning, have computational complexity higher that the complexity of SAT, see, for example, [8, 3, 9] that show Σ_2^p- and PSPACE-complete reasoning problems. This calls for efficient and reliable algorithms for reasoning problems harder than NP.

In this paper we propose Evaluate, an algorithm for evaluating a *Quantified Boolean Formula* (QBF). Intuitively, QBFs extend propositional logic in a way similar to the extension from first- to second-order logic: in QBFs propositional variables can be

† Parts of this work appeared in a preliminary form in [4, 5]

§ cadoli@dis.uniroma1.it, schaerf@dis.uniroma1.it
|| giovanardi@dis.uniroma1.it, mgiovana@dis.uniroma1.it

quantified over, either existentially or universally. As an example,

$$\forall x_1 \exists x_2 \ (x_1 \vee x_2) \wedge (\neg x_1 \vee \neg x_2)$$

means "for each truth assignment to x_1 there exists a truth assignment to x_2 such that $(x_1 \vee x_2) \wedge (\neg x_1 \vee \neg x_2)$ is true". The above QBF is indeed true: if $x_1 =$ true then x_2 can be assigned to false; if $x_1 =$ false then x_2 can be assigned to true; in both cases $(x_1 \vee x_2) \wedge (\neg x_1 \vee \neg x_2)$ is true. The *evaluation problem* for a QBF is to decide whether a given QBF is true or not.

QBFs are both harder to cope with, and much more expressive, than pure propositional logic. In fact, many advanced forms of reasoning such as reasoning about knowledge using modal logics, temporal and description logics, can be formulated as evaluation of a QBF.

Evaluation of QBFs is similar to SAT also because it is the prototypical problem complete for an important complexity class, that is, PSPACE. Moreover, syntactically restricted QBFs offer complete problems for other complexity classes relevant to knowledge representation such as Σ_2^p and Σ_3^p. Therefore, algorithms for evaluation of QBFs are very suitable for the experimental analysis on problems that belong to a wide range of complexity classes, a property not easily found in other formalisms. While several other PSPACE-complete reasoning problems have been analyzed from an experimental point of view [12, 13], we believe that the structure of QBFs makes their analysis of special interest. As an example, generating Σ_3^p-complete instances for the problem of satisfiability of a modal formula of system K is difficult, because fixing the modal depth to any integer makes the problem NP-complete [14].

An algorithm for evaluation of QBFs appears in [19], and is based on resolution. Very recently, another algorithm appeared in [20]. A linear-time algorithm for a restricted form of QBFs appeared in [1]. Evaluate is a generalization of the Davis-Putnam procedure for SAT, and is guaranteed to work in polynomial space. Implementations of the Davis-Putnam procedure are still among the most efficient complete algorithms for SAT. Like the Davis-Putnam procedure, Evaluate (first shown in [5]) exploits the idea of performing unit propagation as much as possible, and resorts to branching when all other simplifying rules fail. Of course, the different nature of evaluation of QBF and SAT forced us to use specific rules in the design of Evaluate, for example, variables bound by the external quantifier must be dealt with before others. In particular, some of the rules that we will present in Section 3 do not affect soundness and/or completeness (see Table I), but rather improve the overall efficiency of the algorithm. As an example of such a rule, Lemma 2.1 states that if a QBF F has a non-tautologous clause in which all literals are universally quantified, then F is false.

We implemented the algorithm in C++ and performed an extensive analysis of its performances for the evaluation of randomly generated QBFs. The analysis, part of which has been reported in [4], is the first of its kind. In particular, experiments show that Evaluate is orders of magnitude more efficient than the simplest algorithm for evaluation, that is, a nested backtracking procedure which resorts to the Davis-Putnam procedure for handling the innermost set of quantifiers. Moreover, we were able to find patterns for *shift of crossover point* (the point at which half of the instances evaluate to true), *phase transition* (sharp differences in the complexity of evaluation between instances close to the crossover point from instances far from it), and *easy-hard-easy* distribution. Some of the result generalize those shown in [22] for SAT, while others do not. Moreover, the richer structure of QBFs raises the possibility of analyzing experimental behavior for parameters that do not have any counterpart in the propositional case (for example, number of quantifier alternations in a QBF). To this end we show an interesting set of experiments on PSPACE-complete instances.

Evaluate and the programs for the generation of random instances are available at www.dis.uniroma1.it/~cadoli/projects/QBF

The structure of this paper is the following. In Section 2 we quickly recall the basic notions about QBFs, and then prove several properties of such formulae that are useful for the design of the algorithm. The Evaluate algorithm is shown in Section 3, while the basic choices about its implementation, that is, the heuristics adopted, the data structures used, and the resulting complexity of the basic operations, are discussed in Section 4. The experimental analysis is shown in Section 5, where performance of the algorithm is analyzed in detail, and regular patterns of the randomly generated formulae are highlighted. Related work is discussed in Section 6, while possible extensions of the research are reported in Section 7.

2. Quantified Boolean Formulae: definition and properties

In the first subsection we recall syntax and semantics of QBFs, and in the second one we introduce some new results that will be used to design an efficient algorithm for evaluation of such formulae.

2.1. Syntax and semantics

A QBF has the form

$$Q_1x_1 \cdots Q_nx_n \quad E(x_1, \ldots, x_n)$$

where E is a propositional formula involving the propositional variables $x_1, \ldots, x_n$ and every Q_i ($1 \leq i \leq n$) is either an existential quantifier $\exists$ or a universal one $\forall$. The expression $\exists x_i \phi$ means that "there exists a truth assignment to x_i such that ϕ is true". Analogously, $\forall x_i \phi$ is an abbreviation for "for each truth assignment to x_i, ϕ is true". Inverting quantifiers in a QBF may change its truth value. As an example, inverting quantifiers in $\forall x_1 \exists x_2 \quad (x_1 \vee x_2) \wedge (\neg x_1 \vee \neg x_2)$ (which is true, see Section 1) yields $\exists x_2 \forall x_1 \quad (x_1 \vee x_2) \wedge (\neg x_1 \vee \neg x_2)$, which is indeed false.

Given a generic QBF, we can group in the same set all consecutive variables having the same quantifier. In such a format, each quantifier is applied to a set of variables rather than to a single propositional variable. Moreover, the sequence of quantifiers alternates: a group of existential quantifiers follows a group of universal quantifiers and vice-versa.

A *kQBF*, where k is a constant integer, is a QBF in which the quantifiers are applied to k disjoint sets of variables and the sequence of quantifiers alternates; sometimes we will add a subscript denoting the type of the most external quantifier in the formula. For example, if X_1, X_2, and X_3 are mutually disjoint sets of propositional variables, then the formula $\exists X_1 \forall X_2 \exists X_3 \quad E(X_1, X_2, X_3)$ is a 3QBF$_\exists$. SAT coincides with the evaluation problem for 1QBF$_\exists$. From the standpoint of computational complexity, evaluating a QBF is inherently more difficult than deciding satisfiability of a propositional formula. The evaluation problem for a QBF is PSPACE-complete, and plays the role of prototypical problem for such a class, while the problem of evaluating a kQBF$_\exists$ is Σ_k^p-complete, whereas the problem of evaluating a kQBF$_\forall$ is Π_k^p-complete, Σ_k^p and Π_k^p being the classes at the k-th level of the Polynomial Hierarchy [23]. We remind that $\text{NP} \subseteq \Sigma_2^p \subseteq \cdots \subseteq \Sigma_k^p \subseteq \cdots \subseteq \text{PSPACE}$ and that most researchers in computational complexity believe these containments to be strict. There is also a structural difference in the nature of the solutions for SAT and QBF problems. In fact, like for all problems in NP, the solution to a SAT problem (that is, a satisfying model) can be represented in space at most linear in the size of the input, while the proof that a QBF is solvable might require a tree of size exponential in the size of the input formula. This difference makes the application of local-search based algorithms very problematic for QBF, since the current solution cannot be represented compactly.

In the rest of this paper we refer to QBFs in *Conjunctive Normal Form* (CNF), that is, QBFs of the form $Q_1 x_1 \cdots Q_n x_n E(x_1, \ldots, x_n)$ in which the Boolean formula E is a conjunction of *clauses*, each one being a disjunction of *literals* —a negated or non-negated variable. In this case E is called *matrix* of the formula. A QBF is said to be in *hCNF* if every clause contains exactly h literals. A clause is *tautological* if it contains both a literal and its negation. Since QBFs are extensions of the propositional calculus, many semantical properties of the propositional calculus carry over to the QBFs. In fact, many simplification rules that are valid in the propositional calculus can also be applied to the matrix of a QBF. In the sequel we will take use the following properties:

$$\begin{aligned}
\mathsf{true} \lor \gamma &\mapsto \mathsf{true} \\
\mathsf{false} \lor \gamma &\mapsto \gamma \\
\mathsf{true} \land \delta &\mapsto \delta \\
\mathsf{false} \land \delta &\mapsto \mathsf{false}
\end{aligned}$$

where γ is a clause, δ is a conjunction of clauses and $\mapsto$ denotes the rewriting. In the following we implicitly assume that all these simplifications are performed whenever we assign a truth value to a literal, that is, when we substitute a literal with true or false.

Considering QBF in CNF is not a restriction, since the problem of evaluating such formulae is still PSPACE-complete. With respect to kQBFs, the evaluation problem of kQBFs in 3CNF is complete for the same complexity class of the general case if the most internal quantifier is an existential [24]. As a consequence, in the following we will consider kQBFs of the form

$$Q_1 X_1 \cdots \exists X_k \;\; E(X_1, \ldots, X_k) \tag{1}$$

in which $E(X_1, \ldots, X_n)$ is in CNF, the most internal quantifier is existential and the sequence of quantifiers alternates. Fixing the type of the most internal quantifier makes the use of subscripts in, for example, $k\text{QBF}_\exists$ useless. As an example, a 2QBF has the form $\forall X_1 \exists X_2 \; E(X_1, X_2)$, while a 3QBF has the form $\exists X_1 \forall X_2 \exists X_3 \; E(X_1, X_2, X_3)$.

2.2. Rules for simplification and evaluation

It is easy to design a dumb algorithm for evaluating a QBF: just apply the semantics and do nested backtracking, always selecting a variable from the outermost set X_1; when the QBF is reduced to a 1QBF, apply any algorithm for SAT. In the following we show some properties of QBFs that can make the algorithm more efficient, because they make it possible to simplify the literals even if they are not bound by the most external quantifier. First of all, we define a partition of the variables occurring in a QBF.

DEFINITION 2.1. (Sets Σ and Π). *Given a kQBF of the form $Q_1 X_1 \cdots \exists X_k \;\; E(X_1, \ldots, X_k)$, we define the sets Σ and Π as follows:*

$$\begin{aligned}
\Sigma &= X_k \cup X_{k-2} \cup \cdots \\
\Pi &= X_{k-1} \cup X_{k-3} \cup \cdots
\end{aligned}$$

that is, Σ is the union of all the sets of existentially quantified variables, while Π collects all the universally quantified variables.

We also say that a literal belongs to either Σ or Π if the corresponding variable does.

EXAMPLE 2.1. *Let F be the QBF, where $W = \{w_1, w_2\}$, $Z = \{z_1\}$, $X = \{x_1, x_2\}$ and $Y = \{y_1, y_2\}$:*

$$\forall W \exists Z \forall X \exists Y \ [(x_1 \vee \neg y_1 \vee z_1) \wedge (y_1) \wedge (w_1 \vee \neg w_2 \vee \neg z_1) \wedge (\neg x_2) \wedge (y_2 \vee \neg w_1 \vee \neg x_1) \wedge (\neg y_2 \vee z_1)]$$

Then $\Pi = W \cup X = \{w_1, w_2, x_1, x_2\}$, while $\Sigma = Z \cup Y = \{z_1, y_1, y_2\}$.

Now, we partition the set of clauses of the matrix.

DEFINITION 2.2. (Sets H, G, and L). *Given a kQBF of the form $Q_1X_1 \cdots \exists X_k \ \ E(X_1, \ldots, X_k)$, we partition its matrix $E(X_1, \ldots, X_k)$ into three sub-matrices:*

1. *$H(\Sigma)$, containing the clauses in which only variables of Σ occur;*
2. *$G(\Pi)$, containing the clauses in which only variables of Π occur;*
3. *$L(\Sigma, \Pi)$, containing the remaining clauses.*

Therefore, any such kQBF can be rewritten as:

$$Q_1X_1 \cdots \exists X_k \ \ [H(\Sigma) \wedge G(\Pi) \wedge L(\Sigma, \Pi)]$$

EXAMPLE 2.2. *Referring to Example 2.1:*

$$\begin{aligned} H(\Sigma) &\equiv (y_1) \wedge (\neg y_2 \vee z_1) \\ G(\Pi) &\equiv (\neg x_2) \\ L(\Sigma, \Pi) &\equiv (x_1 \vee \neg y_1 \vee z_1) \wedge (w_1 \vee \neg w_2 \vee \neg z_1) \wedge (y_2 \vee \neg w_1 \vee \neg x_1) \end{aligned}$$

The partition allows us to obtain a first simple sufficient condition for a QBF to be false.

LEMMA 2.1. (Trivial falsity on Π). *A QBF F of the form $Q_1X_1 \cdots \exists X_k \ \ [H(\Sigma) \wedge G(\Pi) \wedge L(\Sigma, \Pi)]$ is false if $G'(\Pi) \neq \emptyset$, where $G'(\Pi)$ is obtained from $G(\Pi)$ by deleting all tautological clauses.*

Proof. Let us assume that $G'(\Pi)$ is non-empty. Then there exists at least one non-tautological clause $C = l_1 \vee \cdots \vee l_m$, where $l_1, \ldots, l_m$ are literals. The truth assignment $l_i = \mathsf{false}$ for $i = 1, \ldots, m$ makes G false. Since all variables corresponding to the literals $l_1, \ldots, l_m$ are universally quantified, F is false. □

Notice that the formula in Example 2.1 is trivially false since $G'(\Pi)$ is non-empty $(\neg x_2)$. The simple check required in Lemma 2.1 can be accomplished in time linear in the size of the matrix. As a consequence, in all the interesting cases we always have that $G(\Pi) = \emptyset$. In the following we assume that this is the case. Thus, the generic form of a QBF becomes:

$$Q_1X_1 \cdots \exists X_k \ \ [H(\Sigma) \wedge L(\Sigma, \Pi)]$$

Based on such generic form, we now show two sufficient conditions for immediate evaluation of a QBF.

LEMMA 2.2. (Trivial falsity on Σ). *A QBF F of the form $Q_1X_1 \cdots \exists X_k \quad [H(\Sigma) \wedge L(\Sigma, \Pi)]$ is false if $H(\Sigma)$ is unsatisfiable.*

Proof. If $H(\Sigma)$ is unsatisfiable, there are no truth assignments to the existentially quantified variables that can make the matrix true. Therefore, F is false. □

A corollary of Lemma 2.2 is that, if a unit clause occurs in $H(\Sigma)$, then it is useless to try to falsify it. In other words, the unit propagation rule of the Davis-Putnam algorithm is also applicable to QBFs *when applied to variables in* Σ. On the contrary, unit propagation is ruled out for variables in Π by Lemma 2.1. In fact, if there exists a unit clause whose only variable belongs to Π then the QBF is false. Next example shows an application of the above lemma.

EXAMPLE 2.3. *Let F be the following QBF, where $X = \{x_1, x_2\}$ and $Y = \{y_1, y_2, y_3\}$:*

$$F = \forall X \exists Y \; [y_2 \wedge (\neg y_1 \vee y_2 \vee y_3) \wedge (\neg y_2 \vee y_1) \wedge (x_1 \vee x_2 \vee y_3) \wedge (\neg y_1 \vee x_1 \vee \neg x_2)]$$

F is false: in fact, $H(Y) \equiv y_2 \wedge (\neg y_1 \vee y_2 \vee y_3) \wedge (\neg y_2 \vee y_1)$ must be satisfiable (Lemma 2.2), and therefore, $y_2 =$ true. By unit propagation $y_1 =$ true and F can be simplified as

$$\forall X \exists Y [(x_1 \vee x_2 \vee y_3) \wedge (x_1 \vee \neg x_2)]$$

Now there exists a clause $(x_1 \vee \neg x_2)$ with all variables in Π. Thus, by Lemma 2.1, F is false.

LEMMA 2.3. (Trivial truth). *A QBF F of the form $Q_1X_1 \cdots \exists X_k \quad [H(\Sigma) \wedge L(\Sigma, \Pi)]$ is true if $H(\Sigma) \wedge L'(\Sigma)$ is satisfiable, where $L'(\Sigma)$ is obtained from $L(\Sigma, \Pi)$ by deleting all variables in Π.*

Proof. Since all clauses in $L'(\Sigma)$ are obtained from those in $L(\Sigma, \Pi)$ by deleting some of the literals, all models of $L'(\Sigma)$ are also models of $L(\Sigma, \Pi)$. Let us assume $H(\Sigma) \wedge L'(\Sigma)$ is satisfiable, and M is one of its models. M makes $H(\Sigma) \wedge L(\Sigma, \Pi)$ true for any truth assignment to the variables in Π. Therefore, F is true. □

Next example shows an application of the above lemma.

EXAMPLE 2.4. *The following QBF, where $W = \{w_1\}$, $Z = \{z_1, z_2, z_3\}$, $X = \{x_1, x_2\}$ and $Y = \{y_1, y_2\}$:*

$$\forall W \exists Z \forall X \exists Y \; [(\neg w_1 \vee x_2 \vee y_1) \wedge (\neg x_1 \vee y_2 \vee z_3) \wedge (\neg x_2 \vee w_1 \vee \neg z_1) \wedge (x_1 \vee z_2 \vee y_1) \wedge (\neg z_2 \vee \neg y_2 \vee y_1)]$$

is trivially true. In fact, $H(\Sigma) \wedge L'(\Sigma) \equiv y_1 \wedge (y_2 \vee z_3) \wedge (\neg z_1) \wedge (z_2 \vee y_1) \wedge (\neg z_2 \vee \neg y_2 \vee y_1)$ is satisfiable since the assignment $y_1 =$ true, $y_2 =$ true, $z_1 =$ false satisfies it.

Lemmata 2.2 and 2.3 present sufficient conditions which are not necessary. For example, the QBF $\forall X \exists Y \; [(x_1 \vee y_1) \wedge (\neg x_1 \vee \neg y_1)]$ is true while $L'(\Sigma) \equiv y_1 \wedge \neg y_1$ is unsatisfiable. Notice that verifying the conditions of the above lemmata requires to perform a satisfiability test (therefore, unless P = NP, it cannot be performed in polynomial time). Nevertheless, our experimental analysis has shown that there are several cases in which application of the lemmata, in particular of Lemma 2.3, makes the algorithm Evaluate more efficient (see Section 5.2).

There are other conditions that can help us to simplify QBFs. Following the terminology used for the Davis-Putnam procedure, we call a literal l *monotone* if its complementary literal does not appear in the matrix E of the QBF. Monotone literals are important because (like in the Davis-Putnam procedure) we can immediately assign them a value without any need for branching. The truth value we need to assign them is a function of the set (either Σ or Π) to which they belong, as shown by the next two lemmata. We remind that whenever a literal is replaced with true or false, the set of simplifications presented in the Section 2.2 are applied.

LEMMA 2.4. (Monotone literals in Σ). *Given a QBF F of the form $Q_1X_1 \cdots \exists X_k \;\; E(X_1, \ldots, X_k)$ and a monotone literal $l \in \Sigma$, then F is true if and only if $F' = Q_1X_1 \cdots \exists X_k \;\; E'(X_1, \ldots, X_k)$ is true, where $E'(X_1, \ldots, X_k)$ is obtained from $E(X_1, \ldots, X_k)$ by replacing l with* true.

Proof. Let x be the variable corresponding to l. Proof is by induction on the index i of the set of variables to which x belongs.

$i = 1$: In this case x belongs to the most external group, that is, $x \in X_1$. Since $l \in \Sigma$, X_1 is existentially quantified. Let $E''(X_1, \ldots, X_k)$ be obtained from $E(X_1, \ldots, X_k)$ by replacing l with false, and let F'' be $\exists X_1 \cdots \exists X_k \;\; E''(X_1, \ldots, X_k)$. Clearly F is true if and only if either F' or F'' is true. Since l is monotone, by substituting l with true all clauses containing l will be simplified, while when we substitute l with false this same set of clauses is only shortened by deleting the literal l. As a consequence, E' contains a subset of the clauses of E''. Therefore if F'' is true then F' is true. Since there is no way for F'' to be true and F' being false, it follows that F is true if and only if F' is true.

$i = h + 1$: In this case $x \in X_{h+1}$. Let n be the cardinality of X_1. We denote with $E_1(X_2, \ldots, X_k), \ldots, E_{2^n}(X_2, \ldots, X_k)$ the matrices obtained from E applying all 2^n possible substitutions of truth values for the variables of X_1.

We assume $Q_1 = \forall$. Then F is true if and only if all the following QBFs are true.

$$\exists X_2 \cdots \exists X_{h+1} \cdots \exists X_k \;\; E_j(X_2, \ldots, X_k), \;\; (1 \leq j \leq 2^n) \qquad (2)$$

In each of these QBFs, the set X_{h+1} is at the h-th level, hence, by inductive hypothesis, each QBFs of the set (2) is true if and only if the corresponding QBF in the following set is true.

$$\exists X_2 \cdots \exists X_{h+1} \cdots \exists X_k \;\; E'_j(X_2, \ldots, X_k), \;\; (1 \leq j \leq 2^n) \qquad (3)$$

where for each j $(1 \leq j \leq 2^n)$, E'_j is obtained from E_j by replacing l with true. Clearly each QBFs of the set (3) is true if and only if $\forall X_1 \cdots \exists X_k \;\; E'(X_1, \ldots, X_k)$ is true, that is, F' is true. As already pointed out in the base case, F is true if and only if F' is true, hence the thesis follows.

If $Q_1 = \exists$, then the proof goes in a similar way, except that now *at least one* QBF in sets (2) and (3) must be true. □

LEMMA 2.5. (Monotone literals in Π). *Given a QBF F of the form $Q_1X_1 \cdots \exists X_k \;\; E(X_1, \ldots, X_k)$ and a monotone literal $l \in \Pi$, then F is true if and only if $F' = Q_1X_1 \cdots \exists X_k \;\; E'(X_1, \ldots, X_k)$ is true, where $E'(X_1, \ldots, X_k)$ is obtained from $E(X_1, \ldots, X_k)$ by replacing l with* false.

Proof. Let x be the variable corresponding to l. Like in the proof of Lemma 2.4, we prove the statement by induction on the index i of the set of variables to which x belongs.

$i = 1$: In this case x belongs to the most external group, that is, $x \in X_1$. Since $l \in \Pi$, X_1 is universally quantified. Let $E''(X_1, \ldots, X_k)$ be obtained from $E(X_1, \ldots, X_k)$ by replacing l with true, and let F'' be $\exists X_1 \cdots \exists X_k \; E''(X_1, \ldots, X_k)$. Clearly F is true if and only if both F' and F'' are true. Since l is monotone, E'' contains a subset of the clauses of E'. Therefore if F' is true then F'' is true. Hence, F is true iff F' is true.

$i = h + 1$: In this case the proof can be obtained with the same technique used in the corresponding case of Lemma 2.4. □

Summing up, the effect of the last two lemmata can be described as follows: if we have a monotone literal l and this literal belongs to Σ (that is, it is existentially quantified) then all the clauses that contain l are deleted. If l is a monotone literal and it belongs to Π (that is, it is universally quantified) then all occurrences of l can be deleted.

The following example shows the application of Lemmata 2.4 and 2.5.

EXAMPLE 2.5. *Let F be the following 2QBF, where $X = \{x_1, x_2\}$ and $Y = \{y_1, y_2, y_3\}$:*

$$\forall X \exists Y \; ((x_1 \vee x_2 \vee \neg y_1) \wedge (x_1 \vee \neg y_2 \vee \neg y_3) \wedge (\neg y_1 \vee y_2 \vee y_3) \wedge (\neg x_2 \vee \neg y_2 \vee y_3)).$$

The literal $x_1 \in \Pi$ is monotone in F, hence by Lemma 2.5 F is true if and only if the formula F' is true, where F' is

$$\forall X \exists Y \; ((x_2 \vee \neg y_1) \wedge (\neg y_2 \vee \neg y_3) \wedge (\neg y_1 \vee y_2 \vee y_3) \wedge (\neg x_2 \vee \neg y_2 \vee y_3)),$$

that is, x_1 is assigned to true. *Now, $\neg y_1 \in \Sigma$ is monotone in F'. Therefore we define F'' as*

$$\forall X \exists Y \; ((\neg y_2 \vee \neg y_3) \wedge (\neg x_2 \vee \neg y_2 \vee y_3)),$$

that is, $\neg y_1$ is assigned to true. *By Lemma 2.4, F'' is true if and only if F' is true. Now, $\neg x_2 \in \Pi$ is monotone in F''. We define F''' as*

$$\forall X \exists Y \; ((\neg y_2 \vee \neg y_3) \wedge (\neg y_2 \vee y_3)),$$

that is, assign $\neg x_2$ to false. *Now, $\neg y_2 \in \Sigma$ is monotone in F''', and can be assigned to* true. *The resulting QBF has an empty matrix, hence it is true, and the original QBF F is also true.*

The conditions of Lemmata 2.4 and 2.5 can be checked in polynomial time.

Next lemma generalizes the idea of unit propagation to literals in Σ occurring in clauses in which some literals of Π occur. Its conditions can be checked in polynomial time. In the following, when we assign a truth value to a literal, we implicitly assign the opposite truth value to the complementary one.

LEMMA 2.6. (Forced assignment for Σ).
Let F be a QBF of the form $Q_1 X_1 \cdots \exists X_k \;\; E(X_1, \ldots, X_k)$ and C a clause in E such that:

1.there exists a literal $l \in X_i \subseteq \Sigma$ in C, and

2. all other literals of C belong to the set $X_{i+1} \cup X_{i+3} \cup \cdots \cup X_{k-1} \subseteq \Pi$.

Then the formula F is true if and only if the formula $F' = Q_1 X_1 \cdots \exists X_k\, E'(X_1, \ldots, X_k)$ is true, where $E'(X_1, \ldots, X_k)$ is obtained from $E(X_1 \ldots, X_k)$ by substituting all occurrences of l with true.

Proof. Let C be $l \vee l_1 \vee \cdots \vee l_s$.

- If l is monotone, then the thesis follows from Lemma 2.4.
- If all literals $l_1, \ldots, l_s$ are monotone, then by Lemma 2.5 they can be assigned to false, preserving the truth value of the formula. As a consequence, C is simplified to l, and F is true iff l is assigned to true.
- The last case is that some literals of C, including l, are non-monotone. Let C' be the disjunction of such literals. By assumption, l must be assigned a truth value before the other literals in C'. If l is assigned false, then C' is simplified to a clause with all literals in Π, hence F is false by Lemma 2.1. Therefore F is true iff l is assigned to true. □

Note that the conditions of Lemma 2.6 require the literal l to belong to the most external set of quantified variables of the clause C. As an example, the lemma does not apply in $\forall y \exists x\ (y \vee x) \wedge (\neg y \vee \neg x)$.

Gent and Walsh ([10]) point out the possibility of having the following lemma, by showing that, for some generation models, there is a high probability of having a pair of clauses that satisfy it.

LEMMA 2.7. (Pairwise falsity). *A QBF F of the form $Q_1 X_1 \cdots \exists X_k\ E(X_1, \ldots, X_k)$ is false if E contains two clauses:*

$$C_1 = P_1 \vee x \vee Q_1 \quad (4)$$
$$C_2 = P_2 \vee \neg x \vee Q_2 \quad (5)$$

such that the following conditions hold:

- $\exists i\ 1 \leq i \leq k$ *s.t.*
  - $x \in X_i \subseteq \Sigma$
  - $W = X_{i+1} \cup X_{i+3} \cup \cdots \cup X_{k-1} \subseteq \Pi$
  - $Y = X_{i-1} \cup X_{i-3} \cup \cdots \subseteq \Pi$;
- *P_1 and P_2 are clauses that only contain literals from the set Y, while Q_1 and Q_2 are clauses that only contain literals from the set W;*
- *at least one of the following conditions is true*

  1. $P_1 = \emptyset$, or $P_2 = \emptyset$;

  2. $P_1 \neq \emptyset$, $P_2 \neq \emptyset$, and for each literal l in P_1, $\neg l$ is not in P_2.

Proof. Cases 1 and 2 are considered separately.

1. Let's assume that $P_1 = \emptyset$. If $Q_1 \neq \emptyset$, then conditions of Lemma 2.6 apply, and x can be assigned to **true**. Clause C_2 simplifies to a clause in which all literals belong to Π, hence by Lemma 2.1 F is false. If $Q_1 = \emptyset$, then C_1 is a unit clause; by Lemma 2.2 x must be assigned to **true**, and C_2 simplifies to a clause in which all literals belong to Π, hence F is false.

   By symmetry, the lemma can be proven if $P_2 = \emptyset$.

2. Variables in Y are assigned before the others. We consider the variable assignment that makes both P_1 and P_2 false (such an assignment exists because for each literal l in P_1, $\neg l$ is not in P_2). For proving the lemma, it is sufficient to show that the formula is false for such assignment. C_1 and C_2 simplify, respectively, to $C_1' = x \vee Q_1$ and $C_2' = \neg x \vee Q_2$.

   If $Q_1 \neq \emptyset$ and $Q_2 \neq \emptyset$, for both C_1' and C_2' Lemma 2.6 applies. Considering C_1', x is assigned to **true**, and C_2' simplifies to a clause in which all literals belong to Π, hence F is false.

   If $Q_1 = \emptyset$, then C_1' is a unit clause; by Lemma 2.6 x must be assigned to **true**, and C_2' simplifies to a clause in which all literals belong to Π, hence F is false. In a similar way, the lemma can be proven if $Q_2 = \emptyset$. □

The following example shows the application of Lemma 2.7.

EXAMPLE 2.6. *Let F be the following 4QBF:*

$$\forall t_1, t_2, t_3 \exists x_1, x_2 \forall s_1, s_2 \exists z_1, z_2 \quad (t_1 \vee t_2 \vee \neg x_1 \vee s_1) \wedge (x_2 \vee t_2 \vee z_1)$$
$$(t_1 \vee t_3 \vee x_1 \vee s_2) \wedge \wedge (z_2 \vee t_3 \vee \neg x_1)$$

Referring to notation of Lemma 2.7, the first and the third clauses form a pair C_1, C_2, where $Y = \{t_1, t_2, t_3\}$, $W = \{s_1, s_2\}$, $P_1 = t_1 \vee t_2$, $P_2 = t_1 \vee t_3$. In particular, condition 2 applies, hence F is false.

Table I summarizes the rules for evaluation and simplification of a QBF obtained so far, with their complexity and their nature.

3. The Algorithm

In this section we design the Evaluate algorithm for the evaluation of a QBF of the form (1). This algorithm uses all the lemmata presented in the previous section in order to reduce the search space. The algorithm Evaluate is shown in Figure 3 in pseudo-C. In order to decide the truth of a QBF, Evaluate uses two recursive procedures Σ_Evaluate and Π_Evaluate, where Σ_Evaluate is a procedure that works on a QBF in which the most external quantifier is existential (that is, a Σ-formula). Dually, Π_Evaluate works on Π-formulae, that is, formulae in which the most external quantifier is universal. We assume that the matrix of both Σ- and Π-formulae is in CNF.

The main procedure Evaluate takes as input a QBF F and returns its truth value. It performs two simple actions: first, all tautological clauses in F (if any) are removed[1]. Then, Evaluate invokes either Σ_Evaluate or Π_Evaluate according to whether F is a Σ-formula or a Π-formula.

[1] Notice that the elimination of tautological clauses can be performed once and for all, because, none of the successive manipulations that the algorithm makes on the input formula can create a tautological clause.

Table I. Summary of rules for evaluation of a QBF

NAME	COMPLEXITY	EFFECT ON QBF	CONDITION
Trivial falsity on Π 2.1	P	evaluates to false	sufficient
Trivial falsity on Σ 2.2	NP-complete	evaluates to false	sufficient
Trivial truth 2.3	NP-complete	evaluates to true	sufficient
Monotone literals in Σ 2.4	P	is simplified	necessary and sufficient
Monotone literals in Π 2.5	P	is simplified	necessary and sufficient
Forced assignment for Σ 2.6	P	is simplified	necessary and sufficient
Pairwise falsity 2.7	P	evaluates to false	sufficient

Algorithm Evaluate
Input: a kQBF CNF formula F of the form $Q_1X_1 \cdots \exists X_k \;\; E(X_1, \ldots, X_k)$
Output: true if F is true, false otherwise.

```
boolean Evaluate (QBF F)
  { while (F contains a tautological clause C)
            remove C from F;
    if (F is a Π-formula) return Π_Evaluate(F);
    else return Σ_Evaluate(F);
  }
```

Figure 1. The Evaluate algorithm

Figure 3 shows the procedure Π_Evaluate. The procedure takes in input a Π-formula and returns its truth value by applying the following steps:

Base of recursion. First of all, Π_Evaluate checks whether the input formula F is formed by all existentially quantified variables; in this case, F is indeed a 1QBF and then, for evaluating it, it is sufficient to invoke a procedure for SAT (see line (1)), that, in our implementation, is the Davis-Putnam algorithm. Successively, Π_Evaluate verifies whether F is trivially true by using Lemma 2.3. To this end, it computes the 1QBF G, obtained by removing from F all the universally quantified variables (see line (2)), and checks its satisfiability. If G is satisfiable, the input formula F is true, and then Π_Evaluate can stop and return true (see line (3)).

Iteration and forced assignments. If F is not trivially true, the algorithm proceeds iteratively: during the generic iteration, the formula F is simplified by means of truth values assignments to one or more of its variables. The assignments made by

Procedure Π_Evaluate
Input: a Π-formula of the form: $F = \forall X_1 \exists X_2 \cdots \forall X_{k-1} \exists X_k \;\; E(X_1, \ldots, X_k)$
Output: true if F is true, false otherwise.

```
boolean Π_Evaluate (QBF F)
(1) { /* recursions++; */
      if (all the variables in F are existentially quantified)
        return SAT(F);
(2)   remove from F all the universally quantified
      variables, thus obtaining the formula G;
(3)   if (SAT(G)) return true;
(4)   while (there are uninstantiated variables in X1)
(5)       { if (E is an empty set of clauses)
(6)               return true;
(7)         if (E contains an empty clause)
(8)               return false;
(9)         if (there is a clause made of all universally quantified variables in E)
(10)              return false;
(11)        if (there is a unit clause c formed by a literal l ∈ Σ in E)
(12)           { assign true to l;    /* tries++; */
(13)             simplify F with l = true;
               }
(14)        else if (there is a monotone literal l ∈ Σ in E)
(15)           { assign true to l;    /* tries++; */
(16)             simplify F with l = true;
               }
(17)        else if (there is a monotone literal l ∈ Π in E)
(18)           { assign false to l;    /* tries++; */
(19)             simplify F with l = false;
               }
(20)        else if (there is a clause C including a literal l ∈ Xh ⊆ Σ in E
                   and all other literals of C are in Xh+1 ∪ ··· ∪ Xk-1 ⊆ Π)
(21)              { assign true to l;    /* tries++; */
(22)                simplify F with l = true;
                  }
(23)        else if (there are two clauses C1, C2 satisfying condition 2 of Lemma 2.7)
(24)               return false;
(25)        else { choose a literal l ∈ X1;
(26)               QBF OldF = F;
(27)               assign false to l;    /* tries++; */
(28)               simplify F with l = false;
(29)               if (Π_Evaluate(F) == false)    return false;
(30)               else { F = OldF;
(31)                      assign true to l;    /* tries++; */
(32)                      simplify F with l = true;
(33)                      return Π_Evaluate(F);
                        }
                 }
          } /* while */
(34)      return Σ_Evaluate(F);
    }
```

Figure 2. The Π_Evaluate procedure

Π_Evaluate can be of two kinds: *forced* and *unforced.* A *forced assignment* to a variable x in F causes F to be simplified in an other QBF G such that F is true *if and only if* G is true. Thus, forced assignments are very important, since they simplify the evaluation process without making backtracking necessary.

Unforced assignments are performed on variables that belong to X_1, that is, the most external set of variables in the input formula F (see the input of Π_Evaluate). Unforced assignment generally require the use of backtracking, as we will see later.

The formula F can be simplified when one of the following cases is verified:

1. Simplifications made on F cause all the variables in X_1 to be instantiated (see line (4)); in this case X_1 is empty, and F is indeed a Σ-Formula. For evaluating F, Π_Evaluate invokes the Σ_Evaluate procedure (see line (34)).

2. Simplifications made on F cause the matrix E to be empty (see line (5)); this means that all clauses in E have been satisfied, and so F is true. As a consequence, the algorithm returns true (see line (6)).

3. Simplifications made on F cause the matrix E to contain an empty clause (see line (7)); in this case F is trivially false and the algorithm returns false (see line (8)).

4. Simplifications made on F cause the matrix E to contain a clause formed by all universally quantified variables (see line (9)). By Lemma 2.1 the formula F is false. So, the algorithm returns false (see line (10)).

If none of the above cases is verified, Π_Evaluate checks whether it is possible to perform forced assignments on variables in F. Using Lemmata 2.3-2.6 and unit propagation (using Lemma 2.2), we have characterized four different situations where forced assignments can be performed (see lines (11-22)). We note that Lemma 2.2 is not fully exploited, but is used only for justifying unit propagation of Σ-variables. Finally, Lemma 2.7 is applied (lines (23-24)). Note that only condition 2 of the lemma is tested: Lemma 2.6 has just been applied (lines (20-22)), and if condition 1 applies, then the correct answer false is returned at the next iteration (lines (9-10)), because Lemma 2.1 applies (see proof of Lemma 2.6). In general, the sequence of application of the lemmata has been decided with the criterion of using first the more effective and less computationally expensive.

Branch. If no forced assignments can be performed, Π_Evaluate simplifies the input formula by means of an unforced assignment made on a literal l in X_1 (see lines (25-33)). Since there is no way for excluding neither the value true nor the value false for l, the evaluation of F is split in the evaluation of the two subformulae obtained assigning respectively false and true to l. Since l corresponds to a universally quantified variable, F is true if and only if both these subformulae are true. The instantiation of l is indeed a branch in the evaluation process of F; for this reason, we call l the *branch literal.* Several heuristics for choosing the branch literal have been tested, and they are described in Section 4.1.

After having chosen the branch literal (see line (25)), the data structure representing F is saved for future backtracking (see line (26)). Successively, Π_Evaluate is recursively invoked on the formula obtained assigning false to the branch literal l (see lines (27-29)). If the result of the recursive call of Π_Evaluate is false, the procedure can stop and return false (see line (29)). Otherwise, Π_Evaluate backtracks and restores the data structure representing F (see line (30)). The formula F is then simplified assigning true to the branch literal (see line (31) and (32)). Lastly, the procedure returns the result obtained applying recursively Π_Evaluate on F (see line (33)).

The statement `tries++` (commented, because it has no impact on the soundness of the algorithm) is reported in lines in which a truth assignment to a variable is made. The number of tries is a parameter that estimates the cost of a run of the algorithm, and will be explained in more details in Section 5. This same comment also applies to the statement `recursions++`.

The procedure Σ_Evaluate is very similar to Π_Evaluate, and so is omitted. Σ_Evaluate differs from Π_Evaluate only in case of branch: now X_1 is a set of existentially quantified variables. While in Π_Evaluate a logical "and" between the two recursive calls is performed, in Σ_Evaluate is necessary to perform a logical "or" between them.

4. Implementation issues

In this section we show the main decisions about heuristics and data structures for the implementation of Evaluate.

4.1. *Heuristics*

Apart from the choice of the branching literal when dealing with kQBFs with $k > 1$, we were also faced with the choice of an appropriate heuristics for the underlying SAT problems. More precisely (see lines (1) and (3) of Π_Evaluate), our algorithm solves instances of the satisfiability problem. In this case we used a pure Davis-Putnam procedure[2], and adopt a specific heuristics for the choice of the branch literal.

Concerning heuristics, the main decisions we made are:

- heuristics for the choice of the branching literal in Evaluate (see line (25) of Π_Evaluate) and in the SAT solver are possibly distinct;
- as for the SAT solver, we considered only two well-known heuristics (Lexicographic and NonHornFirst);
- as for Evaluate, we considered two kinds of heuristics:
  - depending on the type (universally or existentially quantified) of the branching literal (we called them *type-sensitive*);
  - non depending on such a type (*type-insensitive*).

In the literature there are no heuristics specifically designed for QBF evaluation, although we can of course take inspiration from the large body of work on SAT, which does not take into account type. Our first choice was to use the Lexicographic heuristics also for the selection of the branching literal in Evaluate. We also tried a simplification of Lexicographic, which we called BinaryFirst, which just tries to simplify binary clauses and to obtain many unit clauses. We made this choice because the simplification rules reported in Section 2 are very effective for short clauses, as shown in Section 5.3. Finally, we modified BinaryFirst (obtaining BinaryFirst2) by adding a criterion based on the type of the literal, which tries to reduce the instance to a 1QBF evaluation as soon as possible.

The heuristics we implemented are described below.

[2] In the case of the call to SAT in line (3) we are implementing a sufficient condition (see Lemma 2.3). Therefore we could, without compromising soundness of Evaluate, either check satisfiability only when polynomiality is guaranteed, for example, when the matrix is Horn, or use an incomplete algorithm such as GSAT [21]. While the former idea did not give positive results, impact on performance of the latter one has still to be evaluated.

Table II. Various heuristics used

IMPLEMENTATION	HEURISTICS FOR SAT	HEURISTICS FOR kQBF ($k > 1$)
1	NonHornFirst	BinaryFirst2
2	NonHornFirst	BinaryFirst
3	NonHornFirst	Lexicographic
4	Lexicographic	BinaryFirst

- Fixed order: the literals are always chosen in the same order.
- Lexicographic: this is an heuristics for SAT which is described in [2], and its basic idea is to select a literal occurring as often as possible in the shortest clauses of the formula; moreover the number of occurrences of the complementary literal is also accounted for, by using appropriate weights. When used for SAT problems, this is the best heuristics, among those we used.
- NonHornFirst: this is an heuristics for SAT based on ideas described in [7], and tries to maximize the number of Horn/Dual-Horn clauses in the matrix after simplification.
- BinaryFirst: A simplification of the criterion of the lexicographic heuristics, restricting the attention only to binary clauses, *and ignoring the number of occurrences of the complementary literal.* This heuristics works as follows:
  1. compute the set W of literals which occur more often in binary clauses;
  2. if $|W| > 1$, then $W :=$ literals that occur more frequently in the matrix;
  3. if $|W| > 1$, then $W :=$ literals whose variable occurs more frequently in the matrix;
  4. if $|W| > 1$, then make a random choice.
- BinaryFirst2: this heuristics (unlike the previous ones) does not ignore the distinction between Σ and Π variables. In particular, if the literal to be selected belongs to Π, W is refined by selecting literals which occur more often in clauses with no other universally quantified variables: in this way, at least one resulting clause is "purely existential", and the resulting problem should intuitively be easier to solve (especially in the 2QBF case).

As for experimental results, in general, the heuristics for SAT did not prove to be very important for the efficiency of the algorithm (see discussion in Section 5.2), because a kQBF is typically solved before it is simplified to a 1QBF. The heuristics for $k > 1$ had more impact, but did not change drastically performance of the algorithm. We tried several combinations of the heuristics, which are reported in Table II[3]. The results we obtained are still not definitive, and are summarized in the following.

[3] Results in [4] have been obtained with implementation 1.

Comparing implementations 1 and 2: the refinement of BinaryFirst2 makes performance worse, both in terms of number of recursions and in terms of execution time (implementation 2 is 30% to 80% more efficient than implementation 1, for 2/3QBF-5CNF instances).

This shows that designing an heuristics sensitive to the type of the literal (Σ or Π) is a difficult task.

Comparing implementations 2 and 3: Lexicographic, which is better than BinaryFirst for SAT, is worse for evaluation of QBF. In the latter case (implementation 3), the number of recursions is 10% to 60% higher, for 2/3/4/5QBF-4/5/6/7CNF (we tried very long clauses because, as long as SAT is concerned, Lexicographic is better for such instances).

This shows that a good heuristics for SAT is not necessarily as good for QBF evaluation.

Comparing implementations 2 and 4: we tried to take "the best of both worlds", by choosing the best heuristics for the two cases (in our implementation, the Davis-Putnam procedure with Lexicographic is about three times faster than using NonHornFirst). Actually, the number of recursions decreased, but only for a small amount (typically 2-3%, as in the 2QBF-5CNF case). In fact, as shown in Section 5.2, the Davis-Putnam procedure is not called very often. This modest improvement is paid in terms of time, because implementing the Lexicographic heuristics needs a special data structure: in general time is 5-10% higher.

4.2. Data structures

As for the choice of the data structures, we had the following goals:

- verify conditions for applicability of Lemmata 2.1 and 2.4-2.7 efficiently (obviously checking conditions for applicability of Lemmata 2.2 and 2.3 needs exponential time);
- implement the effect of Lemmata 2.4-2.6, that is, unit propagation, efficiently (the effect of the other lemmata is an evaluation, not a simplification of the formula);
- select the branching literal, according to the various heuristics presented in Subsection 4.1, efficiently.

To this end, we chose a redundant representation. In particular, for representing a kQBF of the kind (1), with m clauses, h literals (maximum) per clause, and n variables (maximum) for each set $X_1, \ldots, X_k$, we have the following structures:

representation of E: an array M such that, for each i ($1 \leq i \leq m$), $M[i] = \langle \gamma_i^\Pi, \gamma_i^\Sigma, |\gamma_i^\Pi|, |\gamma_i^\Sigma| \rangle$, where:

- γ_i^Π is the set of literals of the i-th clause which belong to Π;
- γ_i^Σ is the set of literals of the i-th clause which belong to Σ;

representation of $X_1, \ldots, X_k$:

Table III. Complexity of various procedures

RULE	VERIFICATION	EFFECT
Lemma 2.1	$O(m)$	$O(1)$
Lemma 2.4	$O(k \cdot n)$	$O(h \cdot m^2 + k \cdot n)$
Lemma 2.5	$O(k \cdot n)$	$O(h \cdot m^2 + k \cdot n)$
Lemma 2.6	$O(h \cdot m)$	$O(h \cdot m^2 + k \cdot n)$
Lemma 2.7	$O(h \cdot m^2)$	$O(1)$

HEURISTICS	SELECTION
Lexicographic	$O(h \cdot n)$
NonHornFirst	$O(m \cdot n)$
BinaryFirst	$O(m \cdot n)$
BinaryFirst2	$O(m \cdot n)$

- an array S such that, for each i $(1 \leq i \leq k)$, $S[i] = X_i$;
- an array P such that, for each i $(1 \leq i \leq k \cdot n)$, $P[i] = \langle o_i^+, o_i^-, |o_i^+|, |o_i^-| \rangle$, where $id(\gamma)$ is an identifier for clause γ, and:
  - $o_i^+ = \{id(\gamma) \mid i \text{ occurs positively in clause } \gamma\}$;
  - $o_i^- = \{id(\gamma) \mid i \text{ occurs negatively in clause } \gamma\}$.

During evaluation, the size of the formula decreases because variables are assigned a value, and clauses disappear when they are satisfied. When an assignment is made (see lines (26) and (30)) arrays are automatically resized by using auxiliary data structures. Moreover, an $h \times (k \cdot n)$ matrix L is needed for the Lexicographic heuristics, where $L[i][j]$ is the number of positive and negative occurrences of variable j in clauses of length i.

The implementation of the main operations has, in the worst case, the cost reported in Table III.

We remind that the effect of Lemmata 2.4, 2.5, and 2.6 is the unit propagation of a certain literal l. Let i be the variable corresponding to l; it is necessary to update, for each variable j of each clause γ such that $id(\gamma) \in P[i].o_i^+ \cup P[i].o_i^-$, the corresponding entry $P[j]$. This accounts for the $h \cdot m^2$ term in the cost function. Actually, the term m^2 is a very coarse estimate of the number of clauses involved: since E contains at most $h \cdot m$ occurrences of variables, and the number of distinct variables is at most $k \cdot n$, a variable occurs on average[4] in $\frac{h \cdot m}{k \cdot n}$ clauses. Therefore, $|o_i^+| + |o_i^-|$ is about $\frac{h \cdot m}{k \cdot n}$, and the cost of unit propagation is $O(h \cdot \frac{h^2 \cdot m^2}{k^2 \cdot n^2} + k \cdot n)$. We note that, in all the experiments of Section 5, m is linear in n.

We do not claim that the chosen data structures are the most effective, and believe there is room for improvement. All the code has been implemented in C++, using O-O methodologies for obtaining a high level of modularization and reusability.

[4] This is true in the randomly generated formulae considered in Section 5.

5. Experimental results

In this section we present the most important experimental results obtained applying our evaluation algorithm on randomly generated QBF instances. First of all we show the various models of generations used (Subsection 5.1), then analyze costs and benefits of various rules shown in Section 2.2 (Subsection 5.2). Finally (Subsection 5.3), we highlight some regular patterns exhibited by the formulae.

5.1. Models of generation

In our earliest tests (see [4]) we have mainly generated kQBF instances according to the *Fixed Clause Length* (FCL) model (see, for example, [22]).

The FCL model for QBFs has the following parameters:

- the number k of distinct sets of propositional variables in formula $Q_1X_1 \cdots \exists X_k \;\; E(X_1, \dots, X_k)$,
- the cardinalities $|X_1|, \dots, |X_k|$,
- the number m of clauses in E,
- the number h of literals per clause.

In this model each formula is generated so that every clause contains h literals. If V is the set $X_1 \cup X_2 \cup \cdots \cup X_k$, then a clause is produced by randomly choosing h distinct variables in V and negating each one with probability 0.5. The FCL model for QBF directly extends the FCL model for SAT.

In our tests we ensured that all the m clauses were different from one another and that none of them included both a literal and its complement. Moreover, to avoid generating trivially false kQBF instances (see Lemma 2.1), we disallowed a clause to contain only universally quantified variables.

Gent and Walsh ([10]) noted that with the FCL model the probability of generating instances containing two clauses like (4) and (5) (see statement of Lemma 2.7) increases very quickly when m increases. Such instances are therefore false, and we decided to investigate also another model (which we called FCL2) in which one of the clauses is removed and replaced. FCL2 is similar to two models (named A and B) investigated in [10], the difference being that the selection criterion of FCL2 is more precise: for example, in model A a clause with less than two existential variables (which does not necessarily make the formula false) is disallowed. With FCL2 we made a lot of new tests on the same kind of formulae experimented with FCL, and also on deeper instances of QBF (for example 30QBF-5CNF, not reported in this paper).

We also considered the *Constant Density* (CD) model (see for example, [22]) which has the same parameters of the FCL model, except for h, which represents in this case the average number of literals per clause in the formula. In this model, in fact, the m clauses of the formula have different lengths, each one being produced including a variable $v \in V$ with a fixed probability P and negating it with probability 0.5. Since it can be proved that, with this method, the average number of literals per clause is $h = P \cdot |V|$, we could easily determine the value of the probability P for having clauses with a certain average length. Lastly, in the CD model, we discarded both empty and unit clauses, since their presence makes the evaluation process much easier.

For all the considered parameters settings we ran 500 experiments; for each one we recorded several data like: the truth value of the randomly generated QBF, the CPU time for evaluation, the number of *recursions*, and the number of *tries*. Recursions and tries are two parameters that should give an idea of the size of the portion of search space actually explored by the algorithm. In particular, the number of tries is incremented at each unit propagation, which may happen either in the Davis-Putnam procedure implementing SAT(), or in Σ_Evaluate, or Π_Evaluate, while the number of recursions is incremented at each call of SAT(), Σ_Evaluate, or Π_Evaluate (see Figure 3).

Clearly, there is some dependency between numbers of tries and recursions, but for each call to, for example, Π_Evaluate there might be zero, one, or many unit propagations (anyway, if there are zero unit propagations, then the sub-formula can be immediately evaluated by means of one of the lemmata shown in Section 2.2). Tries are more adequate for small instances, for example, 30 variables, because there are few recursions. Anyway for larger instances, numbers of tries and recursions always gave the same qualitative results.

Such data were successively processed to obtain the mean and the median values. Moreover, we split these results considering separately data for the true and false instances. We performed our tests on a SparcStation Ultra2, equipped with a 200MHz processor and 80 MB of RAM.

In the following we primarily give results in terms of number of tries as opposed to CPU time, for several reasons. CPU times can be estimated with an accuracy of one millisecond, and such a precision is not enough for classes of formulae like 2QBF-3CNF, which can be evaluated very efficiently. Moreover, using tries is much easier to separate costs, as an example, for knowing how much effort is spent at each different level when evaluating a kQBF with $k > 1$. Finally, number of tries highlights in a more evident way the easy-hard-easy pattern, as shown by Figure 3. This situation is rather typical: for few clauses (those on the left side) there is a good correspondence between the two parameters; for larger instances CPU time is affected by costs that depend on our implementation (as shown by Table III, costs depend on the number of clauses m).

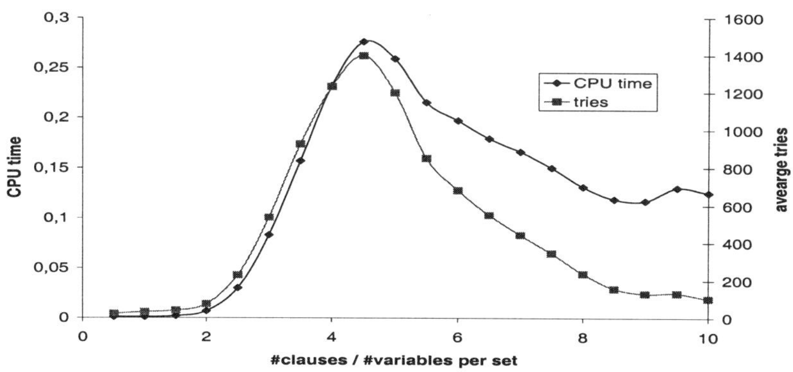

Figure 3. Number of tries versus CPU time in Evaluate (2QBF-5CNF, 20 vars per set, FCL2 model)

All the experiments reported here have been run using the implementation 2 (see Table II), which turned out to be the best in our comparison tests.

5.2. *Impact of the rules on performance*

The first aim of our analysis is to evaluate the impact on the efficiency of the algorithm of Lemmata 2.1-2.7 (performances of the various heuristics has been analyzed in Section 4.1). The results are shown in Figures 4, 5, and 6.

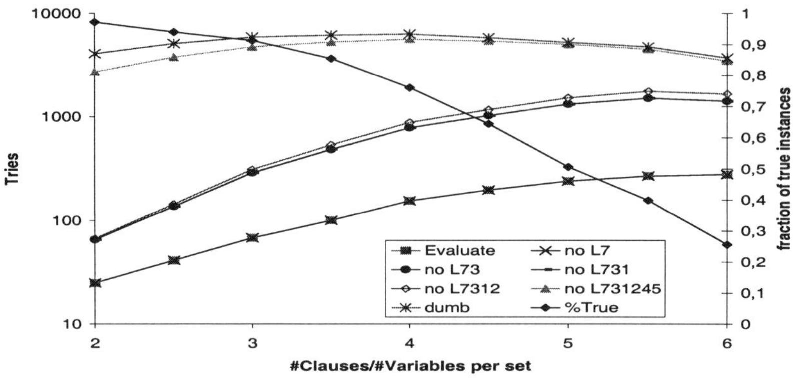

Figure 4. Performance of Evaluate disabling lemmata progressively (2QBF-5CNF, 10 vars per set, FCL2 model)

Figure 4 refers to 2QBF-5CNF instances of the kind $\forall X_1 \exists X_2\ E(X_1, X_2)$, generated according to the FCL2 model. The two sets of variables X_1 and X_2 have the same cardinality, that is, 10, and we varied the #clauses/#variables per set ratio (represented in the x-axis) from 2 to 6, with a step of 0.5. The y-axis represents, in logarithmic scale, the average number of tries and the fraction of true instances. In particular, the figure shows seven curves for the number of tries (plus one for the fraction of true instances), which refer, respectively, to the performance of Evaluate and of various versions of the algorithm in which one or more lemmata are disabled (for example, "no L731" means that Lemmata 2.7, 2.3, and 2.1 are disabled); "dumb" means that all lemmata are disabled and the branching literal is chosen always in the same order, that is, no heuristics is applied.

The figure shows that disabling Lemma 2.7 has almost no impact (we remind that clauses are filtered according to the FCL2 model), while performance decreases significantly if Lemma 2.3 is also disabled. Elimination of Lemmata 2.1 and 2.2 has little impact, while removing also Lemmata 2.4 and 2.5 (they are removed together, because of their similarity) increases number of tries of about one order of magnitude, especially for true instances. The impact of the heuristics if all lemmata are disabled (Lemma 2.6 does not apply for 2QBF) is shown by comparing curves "noL732145" and "dumb": the heuristics is helpful for true instances, but it gives almost no improvement for false ones. The overall gain of Evaluate with respect to the dumb version is about two orders of magnitude for high percentages of true instances, and about one for low percentages. Data about CPU time are very similar.

Figure 5 refers to the same setting, with the exception that lemmata are disabled separately. Lemma 2.6 is not considered because it does not apply for 2QBFs. Results confirm that the most effective rule is the one of Lemma 2.3, and that also Lemmata

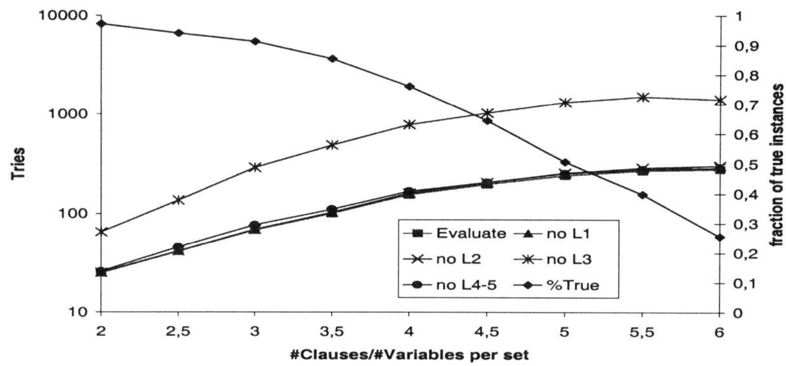

Figure 5. Performance of Evaluate disabling lemmata separately (2QBF-5CNF, 10 vars per set, FCL2 model)

2.4 and 2.5 have a significant impact. As for Lemmata 2.1 and 2.2 they are not invoked frequently.

As for 4QBFs, the situation is similar, but Lemmata 2.4 and 2.5 are now more effective than Lemma 2.3. As for 3QBF, Lemma 2.3 does not appear to be useful (see below for an explanation), and actually disabling it makes number of tries lower, when false instances are considered (see Figure 6). For these formulae, Lemma 2.6 is useful, and increases the performance.

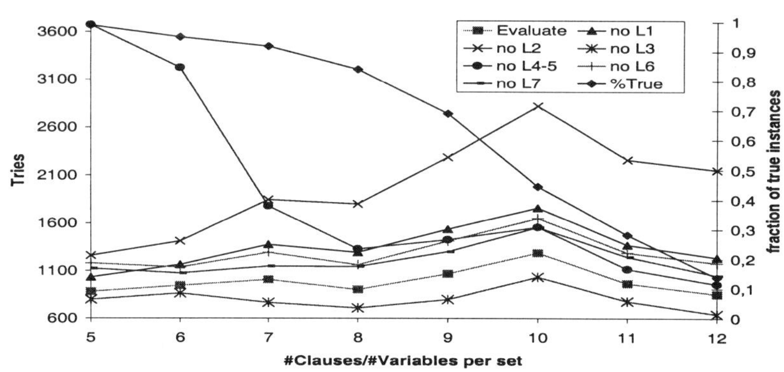

Figure 6. Performance of Evaluate disabling lemmata separately (3QBF-5CNF, 10 vars per set, false instances, FCL2 model)

Summing up, the Evaluate algorithm is much more efficient than a dumb algorithm which adopts the simple strategy of backtracking for higher levels and resorts to the

Davis-Putnam procedure when the outer variables are eliminated and the problem is reduced to an instance of SAT: for 3QBF the gain is about 2.5 orders of magnitude, and for 4QBF we had to interrupt experiments for lack of resources.

The rules of Section 2 have various merits in the performance of the algorithm: some of them have always a positive impact, some of them appears to be of little impact, and one seems to be negative (at least in some cases). In particular, it seems that all lemmata that simplify the QBF, that is, 2.4, 2.5, and 2.6, are useful: in fact they are invoked several times for each instance. As an example, Lemma 2.4 is applied 5 to 15 times for each instance of 2QBF-5CNF with 10 variables per set, and Lemma 2.6 is applied up to 16 times for 3QBF-5CNF instances with 10 variables per set. Moreover, their application does not seem to degrade CPU time (this is intuitive, because their verification and application is a polynomial task).

The situation for the lemmata that evaluate the QBF, that is, Lemmata 2.1, 2.3, and 2.7, is different:

- Lemma 2.1 is applied very rarely in kQBF for k even, while it is applied frequently if k is odd: as an example, it is applied 30 times on average for 3QBF-5CNF instances with 10 variables per set. Intuitively, this lemma is therefore useful for proving that a sub-formula obtained after simplification is false. Its cost is quite low, and its impact on CPU time is always positive.

- As for Lemma 2.3, a consideration is in order. Applying the lemma means that an expensive call to the Davis-Putnam procedure is made. Moreover, this call might be useless, if the instance evaluates to false. As a consequence, in cases such as 3QBF, where false instances are harder, it is better not to apply it. A possible solution is to use an incomplete method such as GSAT.

- Lemma 2.7 is applied rarely in the FCL2 model, while it is very useful for the FCL model. As an example, the number of tries without the lemma increases of about 15% for 3QBF-5CNF instances.

As for the number of calls to SAT() made by Π_ and Σ_Evaluate, it seems that the condition in the "if" statement of line (1) is rarely true, because the value of a QBF can typically be settled before all external quantifiers are eliminated. As an example, for 2QBF-5CNF with 10 variables per set, 2 or 3 calls maximum per instance are done. Considering deeper instances does not change the situation: for 5QBF-5CNF with 10 variables per set, about 20 calls to SAT() in line (1) are done; this must be compared with the analogous figures for Lemmata 2.4 and 2.5, which are applied more than 200 times each; as for lemmata which settle the value of a QBF, that is, Lemmata 2.1, 2.3, and 2.7, for such formulae they are applied about 30, 10, and 5 times, respectively.

5.3. Phase transition and easy-hard-easy patterns

Another goal of our analysis is to understand whether certain computational phenomena observed in the experimental analysis of several polynomial and NP-complete problems also arise in the context of QBF evaluation. Among these phenomena, the most important ones are *phase transition* and *easy-hard-easy* patterns. A phase transition is an abrupt change of a global value due to a small local change. In the SAT problem it has been observed that there exists a crucial parameter, the #clauses/#variables ratio, whose small changes can cause a large change in the probability that a formula is satisfiable. This phenomenon only occurs when the value of the parameter is close to the *crossover point*, that is, the point where the probability of a formula being satisfiable is 50%. In SAT, it has also been observed that the phase transition is related to the computational resources needed to solve the problem. In fact, instances that are far away from the phase transition appear to be computationally simple (on average), while instances close to the phase transition are computationally very demanding. This pattern is known as easy-hard-easy.

One more goal of our experimental analysis is to find out whether we can confirm theoretical results about the complexity of evaluating QBFs, in particular, by choosing and comparing PSPACE-complete, Σ_k^p-complete, and NP-complete instances of the QBF evaluation problem.

The rest of this subsection shows results of the experimental analysis. We primarily report tests on the FCL2 model, but also mention the other two models introduced in Subsection 5.1. For making it easier to understand the results, we now briefly summarize them.

- Our first experiment concerned 2QBF-3CNF (such instances are interesting because they are already Π_2^p-complete). Experiment showed that such instances are actually easier to evaluate than 1QBF-3CNF, that is an NP-complete problem.

- In the quest for harder instances, we considered deeper nesting (3QBF-3CNF), and longer clauses (2QBF-4CNF), but obtained the same qualitative results.

- Clauses even longer (2QBF-5CNF) eventually proved to be more difficult than the corresponding NP-complete problem (1QBF-5CNF).

  At this point we could investigate more aspects, such as unbalancing existential and universal variables.

- Finally, we experimented with the FCL and CD models. The former differs from FCL2 only as far as short clauses are concerned (as an example in 2QBF-3CNF), while in the latter we were able to confirm the results known from SAT, that is, it is easier.

5.3.1. *FCL2 model*

5.3.1.1. *2QBF-3CNF results.* Formulae of the kind $\forall X_1 \exists X_2\ E(X_1,\ X_2)$ were generated choosing the same cardinality for the two different sets of variables (that is, $|X_1| = |X_2|$). The tests were executed varying the number of variables *per set* from 100 to 500, with a step of 100 variables. Note that, as an example, a 2QBF with 500 variables per set contains 1,000 variables. For every number of variables per set, we varied the #clauses/#variables per set ratio from 0.05 to 1, with a step of 0.05.

Figure 7 (top) reports the fraction of true 2QBF-3CNF instances as a function of the #clauses/#variables per set ratio, for 100, 200, 300, 400, and 500 variables per set, respectively. The curves show that phase transition occurs. Moreover, as in the 1QBF case, the phase transition becomes steeper and steeper as the number of variables is increased; in the meanwhile, the crossover point moves to the left. The curves in Figure 7 (top) do not intersect, whereas in the 1QBF case they do (see, for example, [6]).

Figure 7 (bottom) shows the median number of tries needed, as a function of the #clauses/#variables per set ratio. The curves follow an easy-hard-easy pattern: the number of tries initially increases as the ratio is increased, reaches a peak (sharper for higher number of variables), and successively settles on almost constant values. We also noticed a correlation between the hardness of evaluating 2QBF-3CNF instances and the crossover point.

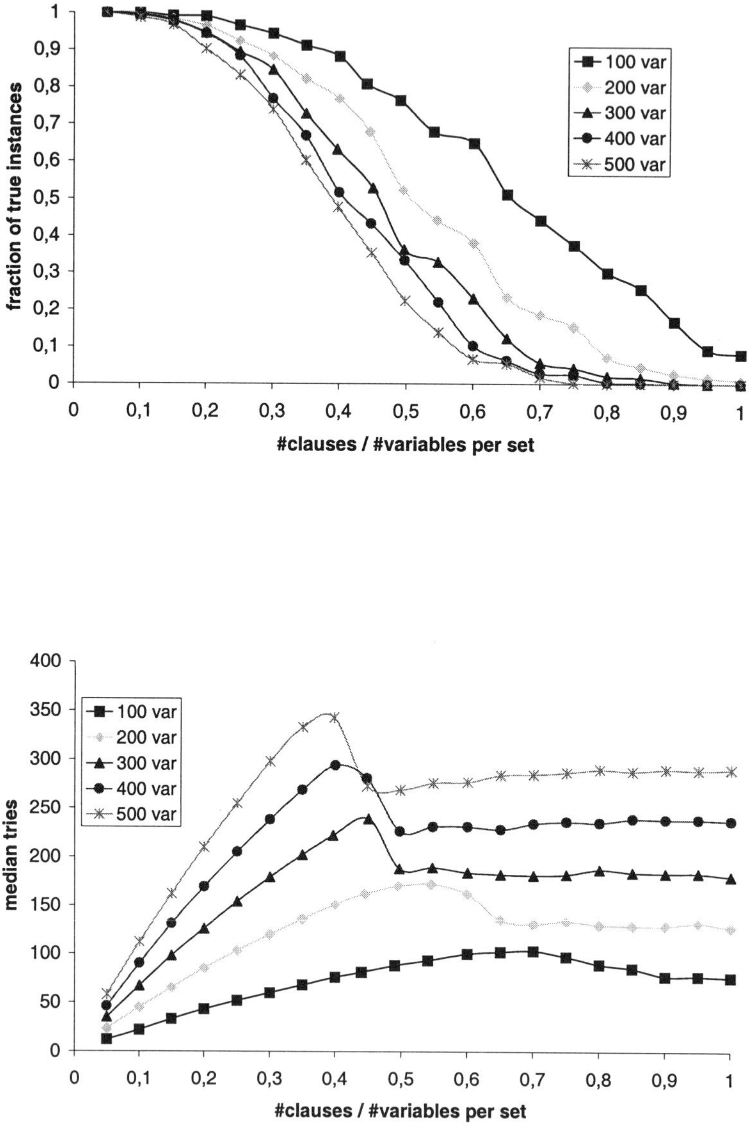

Figure 7. Fraction of true instances (top) and number of tries (bottom) for 2QBF-3CNF

The Evaluate algorithm performed the evaluation of this kind of formulae quite easily, as Figure 7 (bottom) displays. For example, in the most difficult test cases, Evaluate needed on average 350 tries for evaluating a 2QBF-3CNF with 500 variables per set —that is, it was necessary to instantiate only one variable out of three. As for the CPU time, a 2QBF-3CNF with 500 variables per set and 200 clauses was evaluated in about 0.07 seconds close to the peak of tries. For comparison, Evaluate with Lexicographic heuristics, needs about 3,950 tries, 296 recursions, and 1.14 seconds on average for 1QBFs with 100 variables and 430 clauses, that is, close to the crossover point. Intuitively, 2QBF-3CNF are easier than 1QBF-3CNF because short clauses can be simplified very often using our rules.

We noticed that true instances are harder to evaluate than false ones, and this was confirmed in all sets of experiments for k even (see Figure 9-bottom). Intuitively, this holds because when k is even the outermost quantifiers are universal, and all truth assignments must be considered for proving that a QBF is true. On top of that, constraints are apparently unable to cut branches early. This also gives a partial explanation for the easy-hard-easy pattern (see also Subsection 5.3.1.3). On the other hand, when k is odd, we found false instances to be harder to evaluate. In the case of $k = 1$, that is of SAT, this is well-known from the literature.

5.3.1.2. *2QBF-4CNF and 3QBF-3CNF results.* The results we obtained for 3QBF-3CNF are very similar to the 2QBF-3CNF ones. In particular, we could verify in both cases the existence of phase transition, which becomes steeper and steeper as the number of variables is increased. Moreover, there is an easy-hard-easy pattern, with the peak of tries close to the crossover point, and the computational effort for evaluating instances is quite modest: for 500 variables per set, the average number of recursions was about 2, while the number of tries is about twice the number of tries for 2QBF-3CNF (the peak of tries is about 620, see Figure 8-bottom). As for 2QBF-4CNF, the main difference is that the easy-hard-easy pattern is much less marked for this formulae (this behavior is similar to the one obtained using FCL model; see Subsection 5.3.2).

An interesting phenomenon we observed is that, considering the same number of variables per set, the phase transitions for 2QBF-3CNF are steeper than the 2QBF-4CNF and 3QBF-3CNF ones. This phenomenon is shown in Figure 8 (top) for formulae with 500 variables per set: the slope of the phase transitions progressively decreases considering 2QBF-3CNF, 2QBF-4CNF, and 3QBF-3CNF. In particular, the crossover points for 2QBF-4CNF, 2QBF-3CNF, and 3QBF-3CNF are respectively at about 0.4, 0.5, and 0.85 #clauses per #variables per set. The relation between 2QBF-3CNF and 2QBF-4CNF can be intuitively explained as follows: considering the same number of clauses, 4CNF formulae are less constrained than 3CNF ones, hence more likely to be true. As for the relation between 2QBF-3CNF and 3QBF-3CNF, considering the same number of clauses per set of variables, intuitively the most external quantifier (existential) of the 3QBFs makes them more likely to be true.

Figure 8 (bottom) shows the average number of tries needed for evaluating formulae with 500 variables per set, in the 2QBF-3CNF, 2QBF-4CNF, and 3QBF-3CNF cases. As it can be seen, 2QBF-4CNF are harder than 2QBF-3CNF. This can be intuitively explained as follows: for k even true instances are harder; 4CNF formulae are less constrained than 3CNF ones, hence more likely to be true, as shown by Figure 8 (top). For few clauses, 3QBF-3CNF are the easiest, then (when the #clauses/#variables per set ratio is ≥ 0.7) they become the hardest. Intuitively, for k odd false instances are harder; such instances are initially few, then, as shown by Figure 8 (top), they increase, and make the formula hard to evaluate.

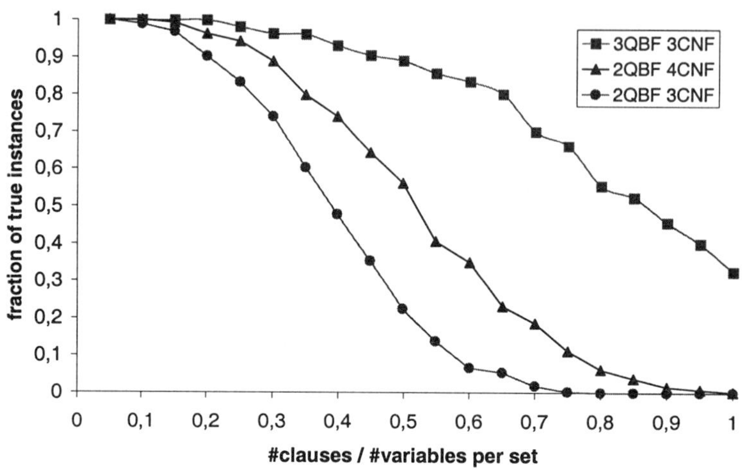

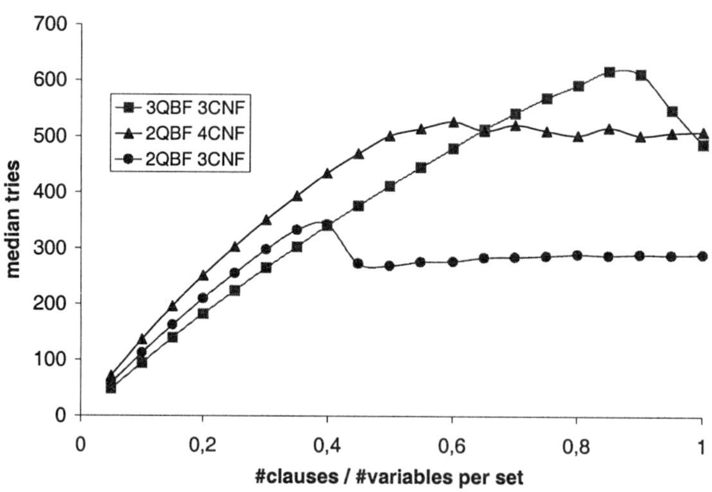

Figure 8. Fraction of true instances (top) and number of tries (bottom) for 2QBF-3CNF, 2QBF-4CNF, 3QBF-3CNF (500 vars per set)

5.3.1.3. *2QBF-5CNF results.* The hardness of evaluating 2QBFs increases sharply considering 5CNF rather than 4CNF. As a matter of fact, for 2QBF-5CNF we could not consider a wide range for the number of variables per set, as we did, instead, for the type of formulae previously seen. As an example, the evaluation process of 2QBF-5CNF instances with 50 variables per set needed, on average, about 17,200 tries (with a peak of about 46,200) and about 3 seconds (with a peak of about 8 seconds for all the instances and of about 43 seconds for the true ones); since we ran, as usual, 500 different tests, this means that the collection of the data for 2QBF-5CNF with 50 variables per set required several hours.

In our experiments, we considered primarily 10 and 20 variables per set; we also ran some experiments with formulae with up to 100 variables per set, always obtaining the same qualitative results. For 10 variables per set we varied the #clauses/#variables per set ratio from 0.5 to 15, incrementing by 0.25; for 20 variables per set we varied the #clauses/#variables per set ratio from 0.5 to 10, incrementing by 0.5. Figure 9 (top) shows the results we obtained for 10 variables per set (the results for 20 variables are quite similar). For convenience, three different curves are drawn: the percentage of true instances, the average number of tries, and the average number of recursions, all as a function of the #clauses/#variables per set ratio. As usual there is phase transition, and an easy-hard-easy pattern for the number of tries and for the number of recursions. The peak of the tries curve is located in correspondence to a #clauses/#variables per set ratio of 6 and a percentage of true instance of about 20% –thus not in the crossover point. The value of the crossover point, instead, is about 5.1, much higher than the previous ones.

The number of tries needed for evaluating this kind of formulae is remarkably higher with respect to the formulae considered before: as an example, Evaluate needed on average less than 500 tries for evaluating 2QBF-4CNF with 500 variables per set, whereas it needed about 280 tries, in the peak point, for evaluating 2QBF-5CNF with only 10 variables per set (the peak of tries for 50 variables per set reaches 46,200, as said before). Apparently, going from 4 to 5 literals per clause causes a drastic reduction of forced assignments in the Evaluate algorithm.

In Figure 9 (bottom) the number of tries needed for evaluating 2QBF-5CNF with 10 variables per set is split considering the false and true instances separately. It can be seen that the hardness of the true instances increases as the #clauses/#variables ratio is increased, whereas the difficulty of the false instances remains modest for every value of the ratio.

We believe that the easy-hard-easy pattern for the number of tries in 2QBF-5CNF is mostly due to the true instances: for a #clauses/#variables per set ratio of about 6, they are already so hard and still so many to influence the average values of tries. Instead, the absence of an easy-hard-easy pattern for the number of tries in 2QBF-4CNF, and the limited pattern for 2QBF-3CNF, could be due to the fact that their phase transitions are sharper than the 2QBF-5CNF ones: increasing the number of clauses, the true instances become rare, and cannot influence significantly the average number of tries.

5.3.1.4. *Unbalancing existential and universal variables.* All the previous results have been obtained for 2QBFs in which the cardinality of two sets of variables is the same. An interesting question is the following one: how do these results change if we modify the proportion between the number of universally-quantified variables (that is, variables in Π, see Definition 2.1) and the existentially-quantified ones (that is, variables in Σ)? For example, what happens if we consider formulae where the number of variables in Π is twice as much the number of variables in Σ, and vice-versa?

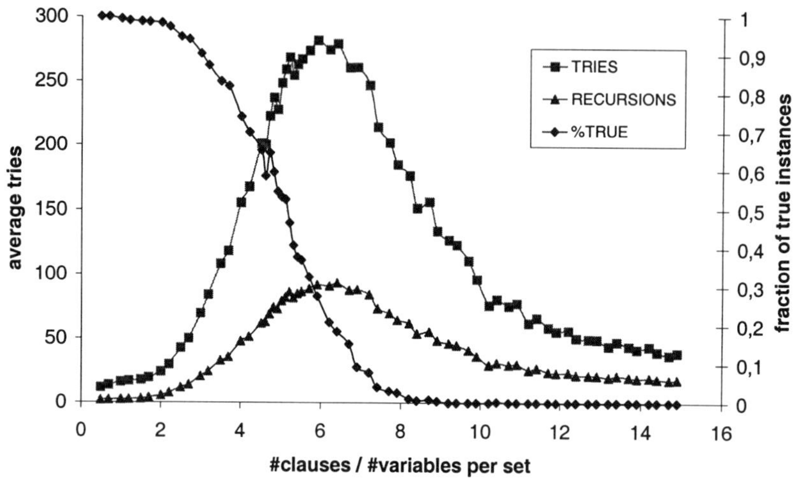

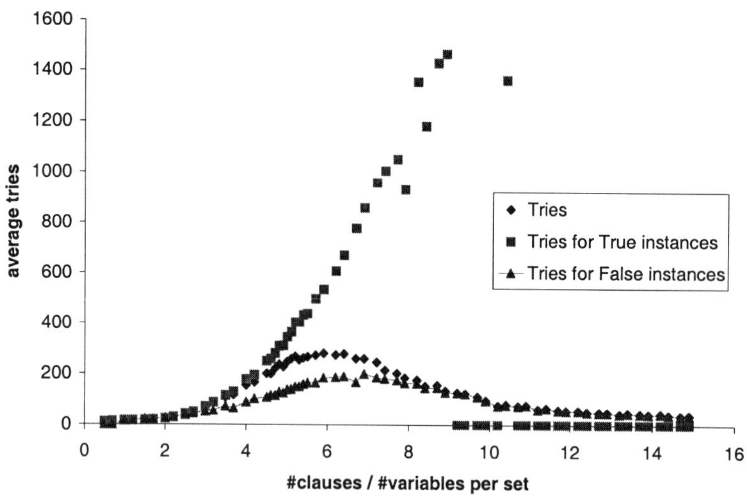

Figure 9. Results for 2QBF-5CNF (10 vars per set)

In order to understand whether the proportion between the number of universally-quantified variables and the existentially-quantified ones has an impact on our results, we ran two different groups of tests; in the first group, we considered 2QBF-5CNF with 14 variables in Π and 7 variables in Σ. We call this kind of formulae 2QBF-5CNF 14-7 vars. We also considered 2QBF-5CNF 7-14 vars. Since both kinds of formulae contain a total number of 21 variables, the corresponding results can be compared with the 2QBF-5CNF 10 variables per set ones.

Figure 10 (top and bottom) shows the fraction of true instances and the average number of tries we obtained respectively for 2QBF-5CNF 14-7 vars and 2QBF-5CNF 7-14 vars. In both figures, the x-axis represents the ratio between the number of clauses and the *average number of variables per set*—a value that in this case is $(14+7)/2 = 10.5$.

Comparing Figures 9 (top) and 10 (top), we can notice that evaluating 2QBF-5CNF 14-7 vars formulae is much easier than evaluating formulae with 10 variables for each set: though in both cases we can observe an easy-hard-easy pattern, in the former case the highest number of tries needed is 90, whereas in the latter case is over 280. We believe that such a drastic reduction in the number of tries can be explained as follows: an increase of the number of variables in Π with respect to the number of variables in Σ causes a reduction of the number of true instances; in fact, the phase transition is steeper for 14-7 vars than in 10 variables per set. Since the true instances are harder for k even (see Figure 9 (bottom)), their decrease causes a reduction of the average number of tries.

Figure 10 (bottom) shows an opposite phenomenon for formulae of the type 2QBF-5CNF 7-14 vars: they are harder than those with 10 variables per set. In fact, in the former case the number of tries in the peak point is about 850, whereas in the latter case is 280. This fact can be explained in the same way as before: increasing the number of variables in Σ and decreasing the number of variables in Π causes an increase of the number of true instances; this, in turn, causes an increase of the average number of tries, together with a decrease in the slope of the phase transition. Clearly this is true as long as the formula remains a 2QBF: if there are no universal variables, the formula is actually a 1QBF, and true instances are actually easier to evaluate.

As mentioned in Subsection 5.3.1.1, balanced 2QBF-3CNF are easier to evaluate than 1QBF-3CNF. This remains true for unbalanced 2QBF-3CNF, even if more variables in Σ make the evaluation more difficult. As an example, evaluation of 2QBF-3CNF 70-140 vars needs 136 tries at the peak, which is slightly worse than 2QBF-3CNF 105-105 vars, i.e., 103 tries, but much better than 1QBF-3CNF 100 vars, i.e., 3,950 tries.

5.3.2. *FCL model*

With this model the main results, compared to the FCL2 model, are the following (more details can be found in [4]):

- There is no easy-hard-easy pattern for the 2QBF-3CNF and the 3QBF-3CNF case.

  Figure 11 (FCL model) is the analogous of Figure 7 (FCL2 model), and shows that the curves do not follow an easy-hard-easy pattern: the number of tries initially increases as the ratio is increased, and successively settles on almost constant values.

  Moreover, we did not notice any correlation between the hardness of evaluating 2QBF-3CNF instances and the crossover point, which is located more on the left (for example, at 0,15 #clause/#variables per set ratio for 500 variables). Gent and Walsh ([10]) explained this phenomenon, which depends on the high probability

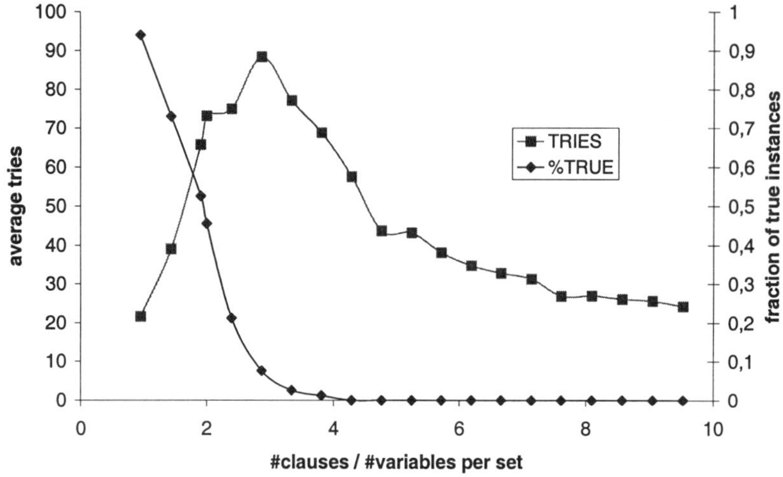

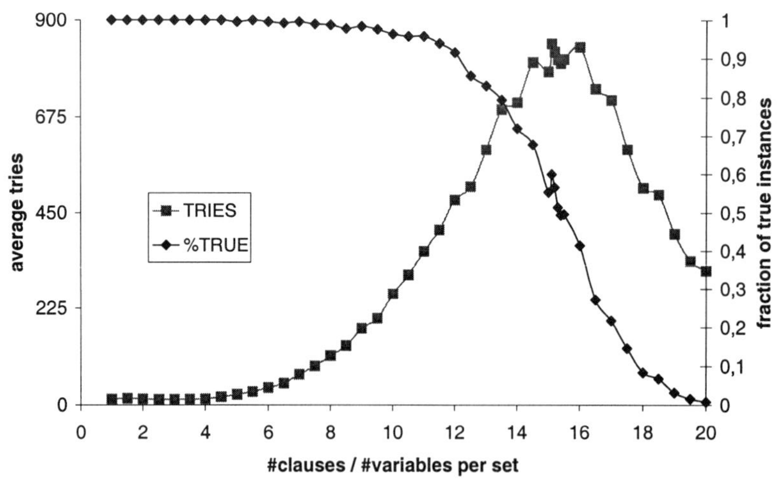

Figure 10. Results for 2QBF-5CNF 14-7 vars (top) and 7-14 vars (bottom)

of generating instances containing two clauses like (4) and (5) (see statement of Lemma 2.7). In Subection 5.3.1.1 we have confirmed their results, showing that the easy-hard-easy pattern occurs for the FCL2 model.

Instances are now moderately easier (from 350 to 250 tries in the worst case for 500 variables).

– The situation for all the other instances is qualitatively similar to the FCL2 one: they exhibit an easy-hard-easy pattern even for FCL. The only differences are:

  - the crossover point moves, obviously, towards the left;
  - instances are on average easier: as an example 2QBF-4CNF are twice harder in the FCL2 model.

5.3.3. *CD model*

When this model is applied to 1QBF, instances can be easily evaluated (see [22]). With the aim of verifying if this is also the case for kQBF with $k > 1$, we ran the **Evaluate** algorithm on 2QBF randomly generated instances with 10 variables per set and an average of 6 literals per clause; the tests were executed varying the number of clauses from 10 to 200, with a step of 1.

Figure 12 reports the fraction of true instances and the number of tries as a function of the #clauses/#variables per set ratio. The curve of the number of tries shows an easy-hard-easy pattern, with the peak point at 31% of the true instances. Comparing 2QBF-6CNF results for the FCL2 and CD models, we can notice a remarkable difference between the number of tries in the peak points: 940 tries for 2QBF-6CNF in the FCL2 model and 51 tries for 2QBF-6CNF in the CD model. Thus, these results seem to confirm that, also for kQBF with $k > 1$, the instances generated with the FCL model are, on an average, much harder than the instances generated by means of the CD model. Apparently, in the latter model, short clauses allow simplifications in the evaluation process that are predominant with respect to complications due to long clauses.

6. Related work

The first work that, to the best of our knowledge, defines an algorithm for QBFs is the paper by Kleine Büning, Karpinski, and Flögel ([19]), where they present a resolution-based algorithm. In particular, the authors define a variant of resolution called Q-resolution that is shown to be sound and complete for QBFs.

While the proposed algorithm is very interesting and it has led to an implementation, in this paper we took a rather different approach, by defining an algorithm based on the Davis-Putnam procedure.

We now compare our approach with that used by other authors who address reasoning problems harder than NP, in order to understand whether the techniques used by the various researchers are similar or if there are differences.

In the last years there has been a proliferation of systems to decide the satisfiability of modal formulae and concept descriptions, as an example, the work of Giunchiglia and Sebastiani ([13, 12]). Their algorithms are, in their terms, SAT-based, since they define algorithms that try to reduce, whenever possible, the problem to an instance of SAT, and use the satisfiability test as a sufficient or necessary condition. While this approach seems to work fine for the problems considered by Giunchiglia and Sebastiani, our experimental analysis shows that most of the instances of QBFs are evaluated with

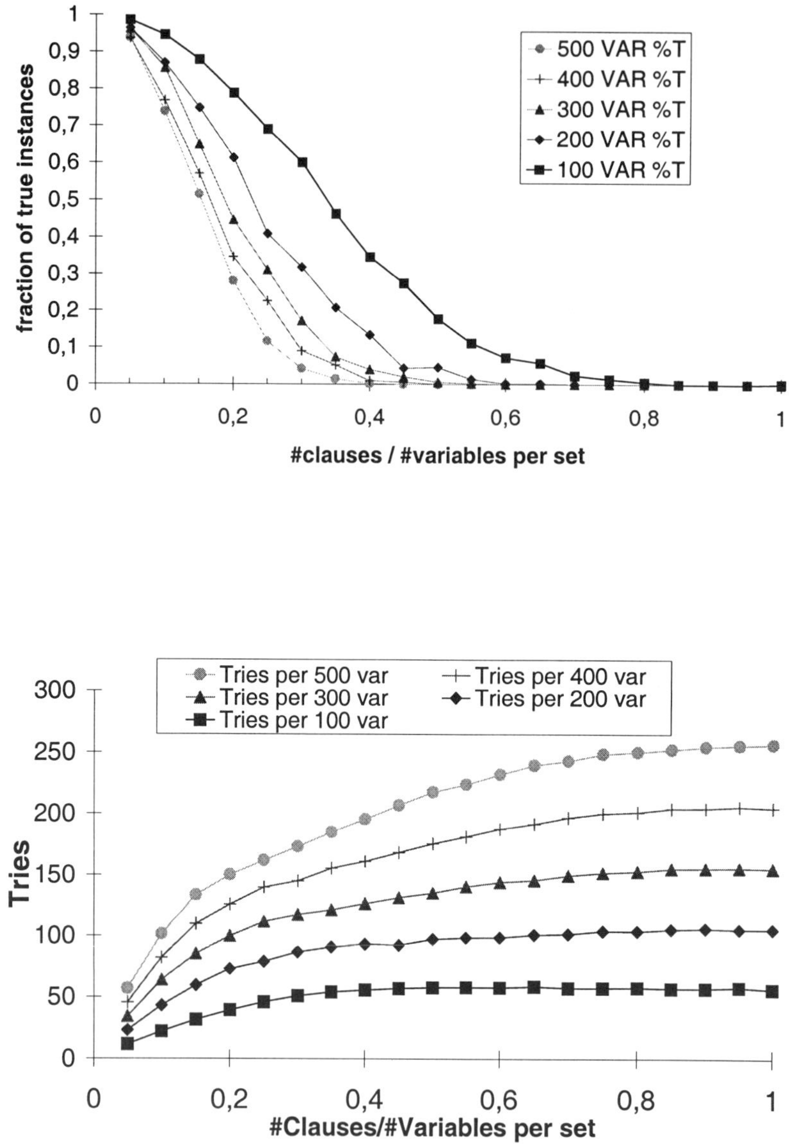

Figure 11. Fraction of true instances (top) and number of tries (bottom) for 2QBF-3CNF

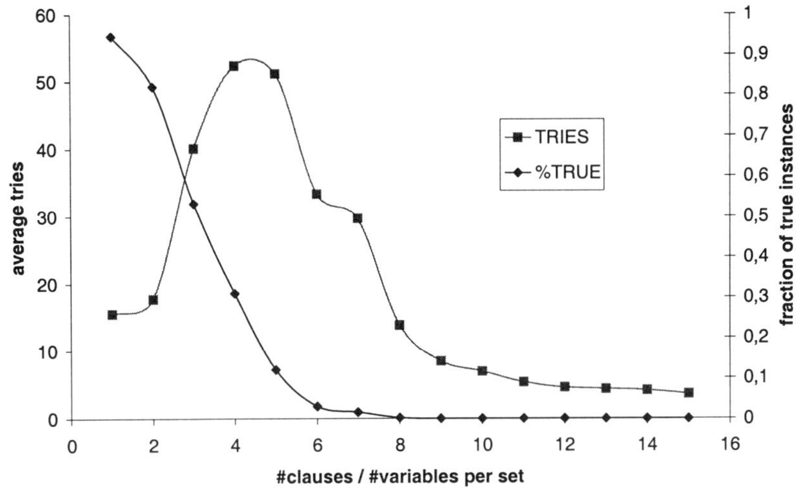

Figure 12. Results for 2QBF-Average 6CNF (10 vars per set)

a limited number of calls to the satisfiability solver. As pointed out in Section 4, when discussing the heuristics, and in Section 5, when analyzing the experiments, trying to reduce a QBF into an instance of SAT does not seem to be the most promising approach in our case.

Other algorithms and implemented systems have been developed, among the others, by Horrocks ([15]). In his work he shows that satisfiability in very expressive terminological logics, whose complexity is even higher than PSPACE, can be checked in a reasonable amount of time by using specialized heuristics. While his approach appears very promising, it is difficult to directly compare our results since there is no clear counterpart of the kQBFs in his terminological logics.

More interestingly, the set of techniques used by the algorithms is rather complementary. Following the classification of optimizations listed in [16], both algorithms use the techniques of *lexical normalization*, *Boolean constraint propagation* and *heuristic guided search*, but we do not use techniques such as *dependency directed backtracking* or *caching*. On the other hand, we have devised a set of necessary or sufficient conditions that can greatly reduce the search space. We are currently exploring how their techniques can be integrated in our framework.

The interesting discussion arisen with the two papers [17, 11] emphasizes the necessity of carefully tuning the generation model and the preprocessing steps. In fact, the choice of the parameters of the generation model and the selection of which preprocessing steps are accomplished influences which algorithm will perform better in the given experiments.

We conclude this section noting that QBFs, and in particular kQBFs, have an experimental advantage over other kinds of logical formulae. As an example, it appears to be difficult to generate in a random fashion modal formulae which are Σ_k^p-complete, because fixing the modal depth to any integer makes the problem NP-complete, as shown by Halpern ([14]).

7. Conclusions and Future Work

In this paper we have presented Evaluate, an algorithm to evaluate quantified Boolean formulae. With this algorithm we were able to consider large instances of problems that belong to some of the complexity classes captured by QBFs, in particular, various levels of the Polynomial Hierarchy, discovering in this way some properties exhibited by randomly generated formulae. We do not claim Evaluate is the best conceivable algorithm, but it is reasonably efficient.

The main results we obtained are listed in the following.

- Concerning efficiency, Evaluate is much more efficient than a dumb algorithm, because of the application of the rules of Section 2.2 and, partially, the heuristics. The various rules have different merits on the performance, but their impact is generally positive, with the exception of Lemma 2.3, which seems to have a negative impact on the performances when we analyze false instances of 3QBFs.

  According to our experiments, the satisfiability test, implemented by the Davis-Putnam procedure, is not invoked frequently, because the value of the QBF is typically settled during evaluation of external sets of variables. Therefore, it seems more important to strive for the optimization of those phases of the evaluation process. Moreover, very smart implementations of Davis-Putnam do not seem to be necessary, and actually could make the data structure too complex.

- Concerning the heuristics for the choice of the branching literal, good heuristics for SAT, for example, Lexicographic, can be used safely only at the purely propositional level, that is, 1QBF, but their performance is not guaranteed for kQBF when $k > 1$.

  We found it difficult to find type-sensitive, that is, Σ or Π, heuristics. Intuitively, such heuristics should be very helpful (actually Evaluate has several rules sensitive to the type of a literal), and are the subject of current research.

- As for the regularity of randomly generated formulae, we analyzed three different generation models, obtaining the following results.

  - Phase transition phenomena exist in all the investigated cases of QBF.
  - With FCL2 model, which has more true instances than FCL, the easy-hard-easy pattern has been observed for all classes of generated formulae.

    With FCL model, an easy-hard-easy pattern has not been observed for short clauses, that is in 2QBF-3/4CNF.
  - Instances generated with the FCL2 model are (on average) more difficult than those generated with the FCL model. FCL2 corrects a flaw in the generation model FCL that appears when the length of the clauses is small (≤ 4). Therefore, it is the only adequate model for instances composed of short clauses. When we deal with instances containing longer clauses, FCL and FCL2 exhibit the same qualitative results.

- 2QBFs are harder than 1QBFs only if long clauses (i.e., ≥ 5) are considered. Actually, the hardness of evaluating 2QBFs increases sharply considering 5CNF rather than 4CNF.
- As in the 1QBF case, instances generated according to the CD model are, on average, much easier than those generated by means of the FCL model.
- In all the considered cases, for kQBF with k odd the true instances are easier, whereas for k even the false ones are easier.
- Unbalancing the number of existentially-quantified and universally-quantified variables has remarkable effects on the difficulty of 2QBF instances. If existentially quantified variables are increased, the instances become much harder. An opposite phenomenon occurs when universally quantified variables are increased. Notice that this phenomenon has been so far only observed for 2QBF instances.
- Considering instances with deep nesting (kQBF-5CNF, $1 \leq k \leq 10$, experiments not reported here), we could prove that difficulty of evaluation increases with nesting, and that instances with k odd are more difficult.
- We could confirm such results considering instances in which the number of variables is equal to the number of alternations (experiments not reported here).

Summing up, we singled out some cases which appear in practice to require more computational resources, hence made a first step in the development of algorithms which are efficient in the average case. Development of the algorithm has also been one step for our long-term goal to characterize the computational complexity, from an experimental point of view, of the most widely accepted Knowledge Representation formalisms.

While QBFs are of great theoretical interest, their usage as a Knowledge Representation formalism has been limited so far. Nevertheless, we claim that our algorithm can be of practical use in the mechanization of many reasoning tasks. In fact, the reasoning services of many Knowledge Representation formalisms are easily (and often efficiently) translatable into computing the truth value of a QBF.

Since the upper bound of the computational complexity of problems in the Polynomial Hierarchy is, sometimes, established via a reduction to QBFs, such reductions can also be used to translate instances of the problem into checking truthness of a QBF.

In order to substantiate this claim, we are currently experimenting on the usage of our algorithm to solve decision problems that are not in NP, such as satisfiability of modal formulae and entailment in circumscription.

For the future, our aim is also to perform tests on kQBF classes that are not taken into consideration in this paper. Another interesting question concerns the function binding number of clauses and number of variables at the crossover point, using the FCL2 model. Further optimizations of the algorithm include using incomplete algorithms for SAT when performing the test required by Lemma 2.3, and using new techniques, for example, caching and dependency directed backtracking.

Acknowledgements

The authors are grateful to Paolo Liberatore and Fabio Massacci for interesting comments on the experiments. They also appreciate the very useful comments of the anonymous reviewers, which helped to improve the reading of the paper. This work has been supported by ASI (Italian Space Agency), MURST (Italian Ministry for University and Scientific and Technological Research) and CNR (Italian Research Council).

References

1. B. Aspvall, M. F. Plass, and R. E. Tarjan. A linear time algorithm for testing the truth of certain quantified boolean formulas. *Information Processing Letters*, 8:121–123, 1979.
2. M. Buro and H. Kleine Büning. Report on a SAT competition. *EATCS Bulletin*, 49:143–151, 1993.
3. M. Cadoli and M. Schaerf. A survey of complexity results for non-monotonic logics. *Journal of Logic Programming*, 17:127–160, 1993.
4. Marco Cadoli, Andrea Giovanardi, and Marco Schaerf. Experimental analysis of the computational cost of evaluating quantified boolean formulae. In *Proceedings of the Fifth Conference of the Italian Association for Artificial Intelligence (AI*IA'97). Springer LNAI 1321.*, number 1321 in Lecture Notes in Artificial Intelligence, pages 207–218. Springer-Verlag, 1997.
5. Marco Cadoli, Andrea Giovanardi, and Marco Schaerf. An algorithm to evaluate quantified boolean formulae. In *Proceedings of the Fifteenth National Conference on Artificial Intelligence (AAAI'98)*, pages 262–267, 1998.
6. J. Crawford and L. Auton. Experimental results on the crossover point in random 3-SAT. *Artificial Intelligence*, 81:31–57, 1996.
7. J. M. Crawford and L. D. Auton. Experimental results on the crossover point in satisfiability problems. In *Proceedings of the Eleventh National Conference on Artificial Intelligence (AAAI'93)*, pages 21–27, 1993.
8. T. Eiter and G. Gottlob. On the complexity of propositional knowledge base revision, updates and counterfactuals. *Artificial Intelligence*, 57:227–270, 1992.
9. T. Eiter and G. Gottlob. The complexity of logic-based abduction. *Journal of the ACM*, 42(1):3–42, 1995.
10. I. P. Gent and T. Walsh. Beyond np: the qsat phase transition. In *Proceedings of the Sixteenth National Conference on Artificial Intelligence (AAAI'99)*, 1999. Also available as APES report, APES-05-1998 from http://apes.cs.strath.ac.uk/reports/apes-05-1998.ps.gz.
11. E. Giunchiglia, F. Giunchiglia, R. Sebastiani, and A. Tacchella. More evaluation of decision procedures for modal logics. In *Proceedings of the Sixth International Conference on Principles of Knowledge Representation and Reasoning (KR'98)*, pages 626–635, 1998.
12. F. Giunchiglia and R. Sebastiani. Building decision procedures for modal logics from propositional decision procedures - the case study of modal K. In *Proceedings of the Thirteenth International Conference on Automated Deduction (CADE'96)*, pages 583–597. Lecture Notes on Artificial Intelligence, 1996.
13. F. Giunchiglia and R. Sebastiani. A SAT-based decision procedure for $\mathcal{ALC}$. In *Proceedings of the Fifth International Conference on the Principles of Knowledge Representation and Reasoning (KR'96)*, pages 304–314, 1996.
14. Joseph Y. Halpern. The effect of bounding the number of primitive propositions and the depth of nesting on the complexity of modal logic. *Artificial Intelligence*, 75(2):361–372, 1995.
15. Ian Horrocks. Using an expressive description logic: FaCT or fiction? In *Proceedings of the Sixth International Conference on Principles of Knowledge Representation and Reasoning (KR'98)*, pages 636–647, 1998.
16. Ian Horrocks and Peter F. Patel Schneider. Optimising propositional modal satisfiability for description logic subsumption. In *Proceedings of AISC-98*, 1998.
17. U. Hustadt and R. A. Schmidt. On evaluating decision procedures for modal logic. In *Proceedings of the Fifteenth International Joint Conference on Artificial Intelligence (IJCAI'97)*, pages 202–207, 1997.
18. H. A. Kautz and B. Selman. Pushing the envelope: planning, propositional logic, and stochastic search. In *Proceedings of the Thirteenth National Conference on Artificial Intelligence (AAAI'96)*, pages 1194–1201, 1996.
19. H. Kleine Büning, M. Karpinski, and A. Flögel. Resolution for quantified boolean formulas. *Information and Computation*, 117:12–18, 1995.
20. J. Rintanen. Improvements to the evaluation of quantified boolean formulae. In *Proceedings of the Sixteenth International Joint Conference on Artificial Intelligence (IJCAI'99)*, pages 1192–1197, July-August 1999.

21. B. Selman, H. Levesque, and D. Mitchell. A new method for solving hard satisfiability problems. In *Proceedings of the Tenth National Conference on Artificial Intelligence (AAAI'92)*, pages 440–446, 1992.
22. B. Selman, D. Mitchell, and H. Levesque. Generating hard satisfiability problems. *Artificial Intelligence*, 81:17–29, 1996.
23. L. J. Stockmeyer. The polynomial-time hierarchy. *Theoretical Computer Science*, 3:1–22, 1976.
24. L. J. Stockmeyer and A. R. Meyer. Word problems requiring exponential time. In *Proceedings of the Fifth ACM Symposium on Theory of Computing (STOC'73)*, pages 1–9, 1973.

SAT2000
I. Gent et al. (Eds.)
IOS Press, 2000

Stochastic Boolean Satisfiability

Michael L. Littman[†] [‡]
Stephen M. Majercik[¶] [||]
Department of Computer Science, Duke University, Durham, NC 27708-0129, USA

Toniann Pitassi[††] [‡‡]
Department of Computer Science, The University of Arizona, Tucson, AZ 85721-0077, USA

Abstract. Satisfiability problems and probabilistic models are core topics of artificial intelligence and computer science. This paper looks at the rich intersection between these two areas, opening the door for the use of satisfiability approaches in probabilistic domains. The paper examines a generic stochastic satisfiability problem, SSAT, which can function for probabilistic domains as SAT does for deterministic domains. It shows the connection between SSAT and well studied problems in belief network inference and planning under uncertainty, and defines algorithms, both systematic and stochastic, for solving SSAT instances. These algorithms are validated on random SSAT formulae generated under the fixed-clause model. In spite of the large complexity gap between SSAT (PSPACE) and SAT (NP), the paper suggests that much of what we have learned about SAT transfers to the probabilistic domain.

1. Introduction

There has been a recent focus in artificial intelligence (AI) on solving problems exhibiting various forms of uncertainty. In parallel, there is a great deal of work in AI and computer science on solving deterministic problems using techniques for testing Boolean satisfiability. Some recent work has looked at combinations of these ideas, viewing planning under uncertainty as stochastic Boolean satisfiability [34]. This paper extends these ideas, and provides a general approach for combining reasoning about uncertainty and satisfiability.

The remainder of this section reviews deterministic satisfiability, introduces the stochastic satisfiability (SSAT) framework, describes the relationship between special cases of SSAT and planning and reasoning under uncertainty, and discusses the family of random SSAT instances. Section 2 describes three algorithms for SSAT, one based on the Davis-Putnam-Logemann-Loveland (DPLL) algorithm for SAT, a variation based on a "universal" search algorithm for SAT, and one that combines stochastic sampling and local search. Section 4 presents empirical results and puts them into perspective.

1.1. Deterministic Satisfiability

In the deterministic satisfiability problem, or SAT, we are given a Boolean formula and wish to determine whether there is some assignment to the variables in the formula that results in the formula evaluating to `True`. This problem is connected to problems

† `mlittman@cs.duke.edu`
¶ `majercik@cs.duke.edu`
†† `toni@cs.arizona.edu`
‡ Research supported in part by NSF CAREER grant IRI-9702576.
|| Research supported by a NASA Graduate Student Research Program Fellowship.
‡‡ Research supported by NSF grant CCR-9457782 and US-Israel BSF Grant 95-00238.

Table I. Summary of notation used for Boolean formulae. Some notation is introduced in later sections.

$0 < n$	number of Boolean variables
$0 < k$	number of literals per clause
$0 < m \leq \sum_{i=1}^{k} \binom{2n}{i}$	number of clauses
$b \in \{0,1\}$	Boolean value
$\mathbf{x} = \langle x_1, x_2, \ldots, x_n \rangle$	Boolean variables, $x_i \in \{0,1\}$
$\phi(\mathbf{x})$	Boolean formula in CNF
$\phi\lceil_{x_i=b}$	restriction (variable assignment) of ϕ (renumbers variables)
α	assignment to $\mathbf{x}$
$Q(x_i) \in \{\exists, \forall, \text{Я}\}$	quantifier for variable x_i (existential, universal, or randomized)
$\mathcal{F}_m^{k,n}$	fixed-clause distribution
$3 \leq s \leq 2^{n+1} - 1$	size of smallest DPLL tree
$0 \leq w$	size of an assignment sample
$0 \leq \theta \leq 1$	stochastic satisfaction threshold
$0 \leq t \leq n$	satisfaction threshold, where 2^t is the number of assignments needed for a positive instance
$0 \leq c \leq n$	number of choice variables in E-MAJSAT

throughout computer science, from circuit design and complexity theory to AI. The last several years has seen tremendous progress in our ability to solve SAT problems. In part due to the success of solving satisfiability problems, researchers are finding efficient ways of modeling diverse problems within the satisfiability framework, such as planning [27].

A formal definition of the SAT decision problem follows. Let $\mathbf{x} = \langle x_1, x_2, \ldots, x_n \rangle$ be a collection of n Boolean (0/1) variables, and $\phi(\mathbf{x})$ be a k-CNF Boolean formula on these variables with m clauses. For example, $(x_1 \vee \overline{x_2} \vee x_4)(x_2 \vee x_3 \vee x_4)(\overline{x_1} \vee \overline{x_2} \vee \overline{x_3})$ is a formula with $k = 3$ literals per clause, $n = 4$ variables and $m = 3$ clauses. An assignment α to the Boolean variables $\mathbf{x}$ is *satisfying* if it makes the formula `True` ($\phi(\alpha) = 1$) and unsatisfying if it makes the formula `False` ($\phi(\alpha) = 0$). The decision problem SAT asks, given a Boolean formula $\phi(\mathbf{x})$ in k-CNF, does it have a satisfying assignment? Or, symbolically, we want to know whether $\exists x_1, \ldots, \exists x_n (\phi(\mathbf{x}) = 1)$. Table I summarizes notation.

1.2. Stochastic Satisfiability

[38] ([38]) explored an extension of SAT in which a randomized quantifier is introduced. The stochastic SAT (SSAT) problem is to evaluate a Boolean formula containing both existential and randomized quantifiers. For example:

$$\exists x_1, \text{Я} y_2, \exists x_3, \ldots, \exists x_{n-1}, \text{Я} y_n (E[\phi(\mathbf{x})] \geq \theta).$$

In words, this formula asks whether there is a value for x_1 such that *for random* values of y_2 (choose 0 or 1 with equal probability), there exists a value of x_3, such that... the *expected* value of the Boolean formula $\phi(\mathbf{x})$ meets or exceeds a threshold $0 \leq \theta \leq 1$. This particular example of stochastic satisfiability consists of alternating between making a choice of value for an x variable (perhaps based on values of lower-numbered variables) and a chance selection of a value for a y variable. For this reason, Papadimitriou referred to SSAT as a "game against nature." An instance of SSAT is *positive* if the threshold is met or exceeded. This paper also considers a generalization of Papadimitriou's class, Extended SSAT, that allows universal, existential and randomized quantifiers, and a more constrained version, Alternating SSAT, in which existential and randomized quantifiers strictly alternate.

1.2.1. *Semantics of Extended* SSAT *and Decision Trees*
An Extended SSAT formula is defined by a triple (ϕ, θ, Q) where ϕ is a CNF formula with underlying ordered variables $x_1, \ldots, x_n$, $0 \leq \theta \leq 1$ is a threshold, and Q is a mapping from variables to quantifiers (existential $\exists$, universal $\forall$, and randomized Ⴏ). Define $\phi' = \phi\lceil_{x_i=b}$, where ϕ' is the $(n-1)$-variable CNF formula obtained from assigning the single variable x_i the Boolean value b in the n-variable CNF formula ϕ and simplifying the result (including any necessary variable renumbering). Variables are numbered so that x_1 corresponds to the outermost (leftmost) quantifier and x_n to the innermost.

The value of ϕ (under quantifier order Q), $val(\phi, Q)$, is defined by induction on the number of quantifiers as follows. Let x_1 be the variable associated with the outermost quantifier:

(1) if ϕ contains an empty clause, then $val(\phi, Q) = 0$;

(2) if ϕ contains no clauses then $val(\phi, Q) = 1$;

(3) if $Q(x_1) = \exists$, then $val(\phi, Q) = \max(val(\phi\lceil_{x_1=0}, Q), val(\phi\lceil_{x_1=1}, Q))$;

(4) if $Q(x_1) = \forall$, then $val(\phi, Q) = \min(val(\phi\lceil_{x_1=0}, Q), val(\phi\lceil_{x_1=1}, Q))$;

(5) if $Q(x_1) =$ Ⴏ, then $val(\phi, Q) = (val(\phi\lceil_{x_1=0}, Q) + val(\phi\lceil_{x_1=1}, Q))/2$.

For example, the formula

$$Ⴏx, \exists y, Ⴏz(E[(x \vee y)(y \vee \overline{z})(\overline{x} \vee \overline{y})] \geq 1/2).$$

has value 3/4. Now, given ϕ, Q, and a threshold θ, (ϕ, θ, Q) is `True` if and only if $val(\phi, Q) \geq \theta$.

Note that this coincides with the usual definition of the quantified Boolean formula problem (QBF), where all of the quantifiers are $\forall$ or $\exists$. The usual definition of truth for ϕ on an instance of QBF is as follows. If ϕ contains an empty clause, then ϕ is `False`; if ϕ contains no clauses, then ϕ is `True`; otherwise, if $\phi = \exists x_1 \phi'$, then ϕ is `True` if and only if $\phi'\lceil_{x_1=0}$ is `True` or $\phi'\lceil_{x_1=1}$ is `True`, and finally if $\phi = \forall x_1 \phi'$, then ϕ is `True` if and only if both $\phi'\lceil_{x_1=0}$ and $\phi'\lceil_{x_1=1}$ are `True`. Using the definition of value, ϕ is `True` if and only if $val(\phi, Q) > 0$. The base case, when ϕ contains an empty clause or no clauses clearly coincide. If $\phi = \exists x_1 \phi'$, then ϕ is `True` if and only if $\phi'\lceil_{x_1=0}$ is `True` or $\phi'\lceil_{x_1=1}$ is `True`, which is the case if and only if $\max(val(\phi'\lceil_{x_1=0}, Q), val(\phi'\lceil_{x_1=1}, Q)) > 0$, as desired. The definitions similarly coincide when $\phi = \forall x_1 \phi'$.

It will be useful to visualize the above inductive procedure as a decision tree. A *decision tree* T over variables $x_1, \ldots, x_n$ is a binary decision tree where each internal node in the tree is labeled with a variable x_i, and the two outgoing edges are labeled with the two different settings of x_i: $x_i = 0$ and $x_i = 1$. Each leaf of the tree is labeled with either 0 or 1. Note that any total truth assignment α to the underlying variables is consistent with exactly one path of T. A decision tree T over $x_1, \ldots, x_n$ represents a CNF formula $\phi(x_1, \ldots, x_n)$ if for every truth assignment α, the value of the leaf node on the path consistent with α is equal to $\phi(\alpha)$. A decision tree T for ϕ is *complete* if it is a full binary tree of height n; notice that a given ϕ will have many decision trees that can represent it; some may be very small while others (such as the complete

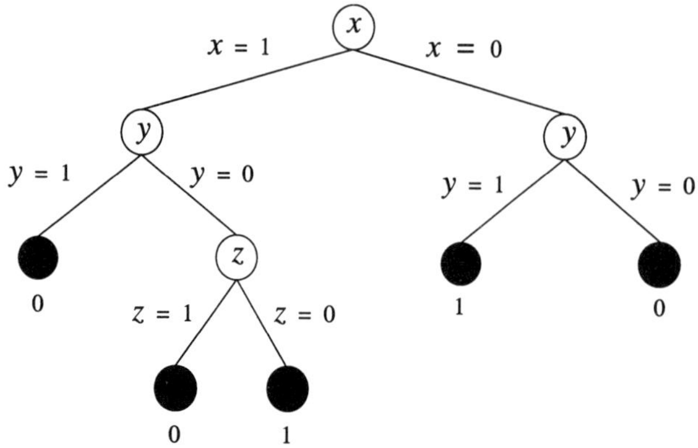

Figure 1. A decision tree for the formula $(x \vee y)(y \vee \overline{z})(\overline{x} \vee \overline{y})$ encodes which assignments are satisfying and which are not.

tree) can have exponential size in n. Figure 1 gives an example of a decision tree for $(x \vee y)(y \vee \overline{z})(\overline{x} \vee \overline{y})$.

A *canonical* decision tree for an Extended SSAT instance (ϕ, θ, Q) is a decision tree T where the ordering of the variables in T is consistent with the quantifier order.

Given a canonical tree T for an Extended SSAT formula ϕ, the value of ϕ, $val(\phi, Q)$, can be computed from T by labeling the intermediate nodes of T in a bottom-up fashion: Inductively, if v is unlabeled, and has children v', v'' with labels $L(v')$, $L(v'')$ respectively, then: (i) if $Q(v) = \exists$, then $L(v) = \max(L(v'), L(v''))$; (ii) if $Q(v) = \forall$, then $L(v) = \min(L(v'), L(v''))$; and (iii) if $Q(v) = \reflectbox{R}$, then $L(v) = (L(v') + L(v''))/2$. The value of ϕ is the value of the root, and ϕ is a positive instance if and only if that value is greater than or equal to θ.

Note that, while not explored in detail in this paper, the definition of the randomized quantifier $\reflectbox{R}$ can be extended to allow arbitrary rational probability distributions over the set $\{0, 1\}$ instead of the uniform distribution considered in this paper. The resulting generalization does not change any of the complexity results described in the next section, and is key to making a connection between SSAT, planning under uncertainty, and belief network inference.

1.3. *Satisfiability and Uncertainty*

As AI techniques are used more and more to attack real-world problems, many researchers have embraced probability theory as a way of representing the pervasive uncertainty they find. Two specific examples of this trend are the increasing use of Markov decision process models in planning and learning, and belief networks in reasoning and knowledge representation; however, the influence of probabilistic models in AI is felt quite broadly.

Whereas many basic deterministic problems are complete for the well-known complexity class NP, and are therefore formally equivalent to SAT, many planning and reasoning problems in probabilistic models lie in other complexity classes, such as #P or PP [43, 32]. This means that, with respect to the current state of complexity theory, these problems cannot be polynomially reduced to SAT. However, many standard uncertain reasoning problems can be reduced to special cases of SSAT, as described next. The probabilistic problems discussed are complete for NP, PP, NP^{PP}, and PSPACE.

The NP-complete problem SAT is the SSAT problem obtained by using only existential quantifiers and setting $\theta = 1$. The problem of finding the most probable explanation

(MPE) in a belief network [15] is (polynomially) equivalent to SAT. A related problem from planning under uncertainty is determining whether there is some choice of actions such that the probability of the most likely trajectory through state space to the goal exceeds a given probability threshold.

The class PP, or probabilistic polynomial time, can be defined in several ways. For the purposes of this paper, it is useful to define it by one of its complete problems, MAJSAT. In its standard formulation, MAJSAT asks whether, given a Boolean formula $\phi(\mathbf{x})$ in CNF, at least half of its assignments are satisfying. Thus, MAJSAT is concerned, not just with the existence of a satisfying assignment, but the *number* of satisfying assignments.

The MAJSAT problem connects satisfiability to probability in the sense that, if we imagine that all assignments are equally likely, MAJSAT asks whether the probability of a satisfying assignment is at least 1/2. Thus, MAJSAT can be expressed as an instance of SSAT:

$$\text{ᴚ}x_1, \ldots, \text{ᴚ}x_n(E[\phi(\mathbf{x})] \geq 1/2)$$

(or θ, more generally; [38] ([38]) refers to this as "Threshold SAT", but this paper uses simply "MAJSAT" for this generalization). Thus, MAJSAT is obtained from SSAT by using only randomized quantifiers.

As with many decision problems, MAJSAT is polynomially equivalent to the problem of actually computing the probability of a satisfying assignment, since binary search on θ can be used to find the exact value of θ for which the probability is at least as big, but no bigger than, θ. Thus, the class PP can be viewed as the decision-problem version of #P, which actually *counts* the number of satisfying assignments.

The problem of belief network inference—given a belief network, values for its evidence nodes, and the value for a query node, what is the probability that the query node takes on the given value given the evidence?—is #P-complete [43]. In addition, any belief network (with rational conditional probability tables) can be represented as a Boolean formula. Thus, belief network inference is equivalent to MAJSAT. A PP-complete planning problem is plan evaluation in a probabilistic domain [32].

The complexity class NP^{PP} is formed by combining NP and PP. It is the class of problems that can be solved by guessing a solution (NP) and then performing a PP calculation for verification. A satisfiability problem that is complete for this class is E-MAJSAT ("exists" MAJSAT) [32], which combines elements of SAT and MAJSAT. An E-MAJSAT instance is defined by a CNF Boolean formula $\phi(\mathbf{x})$ on n Boolean variables, a threshold value θ, and a number $0 \leq c \leq n$. The variables $x_{c+1}, \ldots, x_n$ are the "chance" variables, and the decision problem is to report whether there is an assignment to the "choice" variables $x_1, \ldots, x_c$ so that the probability that they combine with the chance variables to constitute a satisfying assignment of $\phi(\mathbf{x})$ is at least θ. Thus, E-MAJSAT is also an SSAT problem:

$$\exists x_1, \ldots, \exists x_c, \text{ᴚ}x_{c+1}, \ldots, \text{ᴚ}x_n(E[\phi(\mathbf{x})] \geq \theta).$$

Note that, if $c = n$, E-MAJSAT is simply SAT (for $\theta = 1$). If $c = 0$, E-MAJSAT is exactly MAJSAT. In terms of complexity classes, $\text{NP} \subseteq \text{PP} \subseteq \text{NP}^{\text{PP}}$; E-MAJSAT is at least as hard as MAJSAT, which is at least as hard as SAT. In some sense, then, the peak complexity for E-MAJSAT is achieved with intermediate values of c.

Other problems have been shown to be NP^{PP}-complete, such as finding optimal size-bounded plans in uncertain domains [32] and generating "explanations" in belief networks [42]. In addition, the belief network problems of calculating a maximum a posteriori (MAP) hypothesis or a maximum expected utility (MEU) solution [15] are also complete for NP^{PP}. In these problems, the choice variables correspond to the plan or explanation and the chance variables to the uncertainty.

Table II. Different arrangements of quantifiers result in SSAT problems complete for different complexity classes and correspond to basic problems in uncertain reasoning and planning.

class	satisfiability problem Boolean formula	belief network problem planning problem
NP	SAT $\exists x_1, \ldots, \exists x_n (E[\phi(\mathbf{x})] \geq \theta)$	most probable explanation best trajectory
PP	MAJSAT $\text{Ɐ} x_1, \ldots, \text{Ɐ} x_n (E[\phi(\mathbf{x})] \geq \theta)$	belief updating (inference) plan evaluation
$\mathrm{NP}^{\mathrm{PP}}$	E-MAJSAT $\exists x_1, \ldots, \exists x_c, \text{Ɐ} x_{c+1}, \ldots, \text{Ɐ} x_n (E[\phi(\mathbf{x})] \geq \theta)$	maximum a posteriori hypothesis best polynomial-size plan
PSPACE	Alternating SSAT $\exists x_1, \text{Ɐ} x_2, \ldots, \exists x_{n-1}, \text{Ɐ} x_n (E[\phi(\mathbf{x})] \geq \theta)$	influence diagrams best polynomial-horizon plan

The class PSPACE consists of the problems solvable using a polynomial amount of space. All the previously mentioned classes (NP, PP, $\mathrm{NP}^{\mathrm{PP}}$) can be solved in polynomial space by enumerating all assignments and combining the results in the appropriate way. The stochastic SAT problem SSAT and the deterministic QBF are satisfiability problems that are PSPACE-complete. As mentioned earlier, each existential quantifier in an SSAT problem can be viewed as a simple type of maximization operator; the problem then becomes one of maximizing the probability that $\phi(\mathbf{x})$ is satisfied, given that some of the variables are under the control of "nature." This is closely related to solving a finite-horizon partially observable Markov decision process (POMDP), which is also PSPACE-complete [39]. The problem remains PSPACE-complete when the domain is specified compactly via probabilistic STRIPS operators or an equivalent representation [37], even if the domain is "fully observable" [31]. The connection between SSAT and these planning problems has been exploited to create a competitive planning algorithm [35]. Influence diagrams [46] are a belief-network-like representation for the same type of problem.

Table II summarizes the relations between the complexity classes, stochastic satisfiability problems, belief network problems, and planning problems discussed.

1.3.1. *Approximability of* SSAT

For applications in planning and decision making, the underlying problem is often the related optimization problem associated with SSAT: Given an instance (ϕ, θ, Q) output $val(\phi)$. Moreover, an efficient algorithm that will return a close approximation to the actual value is nearly as good as an exact solution. Below is a brief review of what is known about the approximability of SSAT.

Let *Opt* be an optimization problem; that is, $Opt(x)$ is a real-valued function with domain $D \subseteq \{0,1\}^*$ (bit strings). Let A be an algorithm that approximates $Opt(x)$: on input $x \in \{0,1\}^*$, the algorithm produces an output $A(x)$. Let ϵ be a function from integers (input string lengths) to real numbers between 0 and 1. We say that algorithm A *approximates* *Opt* to within ratio $0 < \epsilon(\cdot) < 1$ if for all $x \in D$, $\epsilon(|x|) \leq A(x)/Opt(x) \leq 1/(\epsilon(|x|))$. In other words, for all inputs x, $A(x)$ and $Opt(x)$ differ by a factor of at most $\epsilon(|x|)$, where $|x|$ is the length of the input string x. If such an A exists for *Opt*, then *Opt* can be *approximated* to within ratio $\epsilon(\cdot)$. [12] ([12]) observed that there exists a constant $c > 0$ such that approximating SSAT to within ratio 2^{-n^c} is

PSPACE-hard. Thus, the general problem, with unbounded alternations of quantifiers, is very hard to approximate. However, what about special cases of SSAT, such as SSAT with i alternations of quantifiers where i is a small constant, independent of n? The argument of [12] ([12]) breaks down, and it is open whether or not the problem remains as hard to approximate as the general version.

[33] ([33]) found that approximating solutions to Markov decision processes to within ratio δ is also intractable.

1.4. Random Formulae

To empirically evaluate algorithms for satisfiability and stochastic satisfiability, it is useful to have a good testbed of hard formulae. This is a nontrivial problem: specific hand-coded instances of SAT are known to be satisfiable or not, and usually for a clear (easily computable) reason. What is sought is a natural distribution over SAT instances that is hard on average. This has led many researchers to study randomly generated formulae (although this distribution is not known to be average-case hard). The usual fixed-clause random k-CNF model is used in this paper, which is defined in terms of three integer parameters n, k and m; a formula is generated by selecting m clauses of size k independently. A clause is generated by randomly selecting one of n variables k times, rejecting duplicate selections, and randomly negating it with probability 1/2. This distribution is denoted $\mathcal{F}_m^{k,n}$. In the experiments described in Section 3, a program called `makewff`, available from AT&T Labs – Research, was used to generate random formulae from this distribution.

The random k-CNF model has been widely studied for several good reasons. First, it is an intrinsically natural model, analogous to the random graph model, that sheds light on fundamental structural properties of the satisfiability problem. As with SAT, it is possible to gain insight into the mathematical structure of SSAT by looking at the behavior of randomly generated formulae. Second, using an appropriate choice of parameters, randomly chosen formulae are empirically difficult for satisfiability algorithms, and are a commonly used benchmark [22]. The next section briefly reviews some analytical results concerning random SAT and MAJSAT instances.

1.4.1. *Random* SAT

An interesting property of random k-CNF formulae is that when m is small relative to n, almost all formulae are satisfiable, and most algorithms find it easy to show this satisfiability. When m is large relative to n, almost all formulae are unsatisfiable and unsatisfiability is relatively easy to show. For intermediate values of m (around $4.2n$ for $k = 3$), approximately half of the formulae are satisfiable and it is very difficult to show satisfiability. Thus, with respect to m, random SAT instances exhibit an "easy-hardest-hard" pattern. This pattern is consistent for various values of n but becomes more pronounced with larger n. In addition, the hard region is very large for large n.

A key conjecture about the random k-CNF SAT formula model is that there exists a constant α_k such that a random k-CNF formula from $\mathcal{F}_m^{k,n}$ is almost certainly satisfiable for $m/n < \alpha_k$ (as n gets large), and almost certainly unsatisfiable if $m/n > \alpha_k$. As mentioned above, empirical evidence [44] suggests that this 0–1 threshold value for $k = 3$ occurs at around 4.2, and a recent theoretical result by [17] ([17]) shows that for each n, there is a sharp 0–1 threshold $\alpha_k(n)$ that possibly varies with n. It is known that $\alpha_2 = 1$ [9, 21], and that for $k = 3$, $3.003 \leq \alpha_k(n) \leq 4.601$ [18, 29].

An interesting feature of the threshold is that the dual problems of bounding the threshold value from above and below appear to be asymmetric. At slightly below the 0–1 threshold, there are simple linear-time algorithms for finding a satisfying assignment, but at slightly above the 0–1 threshold, there are no known algorithms that quickly produce proofs of unsatisfiability. Moreover, it has been proven that no Resolution-based method (including the DPLL procedure that forms the basis of several algorithms in this paper) will succeed in sub-exponential time on a broad range of randomly generated formulae [9, 4, 3]. In particular, [3] ([3]) show that for $k = 3$ and $m \geq n^2/\log n$, almost certainly a random formula has a polynomial-size decision tree, but for $m < n^{6/5}$, almost certainly a random formula requires a superpolynomial-size decision tree. This suggests that DPLL will perform very badly (asymptotically in n) even for ranges of m way above the 0–1 threshold (up to $n^{6/5}$), and that the easy-hardest-hard pattern observed empirically may actually be misleading—for large enough n, the expected pattern is more like easy-hardest-...-hardest-easy. This points out that when analyzing algorithms for random instances of SAT it is important to know whether the algorithm is applied above, below, or at the threshold.

1.4.2. *Random* MAJSAT

A random MAJSAT instance is defined in terms of four integer parameters, k, n, m, and t. A random MAJSAT formula with these parameters is obtained by selecting a k-CNF formula uniformly and at random from the distribution $\mathcal{F}_m^{k,n}$. The instance is positive if and only if the probability of a satisfying assignment is at least $\theta = 1/2^{n-t}$, that is, there are at least 2^t satisfying assignments.

Let $f(k, n, m, t)$ be the probability that a random k-CNF formula on n variables with m clauses has at least 2^t satisfying truth assignments. Given m and a function $t(n)$ of n, what can be said about the limit of f as n gets large? Surprisingly, in spite of a number of articles concerning the counting of satisfying assignments, there are very few analytical results known about this function f, and its 0–1 threshold behavior is far from determined. Some simple results are summarized next.

The expected number of satisfying assignments for a random 3-CNF formula from $\mathcal{F}_m^{3,n}$ is $2^n(7/8)^m = (2(7/8)^{m/n})^n$. For $m \geq (\log_{8/7} 2)n$ (about $5.19n$), $2(7/8)^{m/n} < 1$, and, thus, by Markov's inequality, with probability $1 - o(1)$, a random formula with parameters $(3, n, m, t = 0)$ is unsatisfiable for m in this range. What happens to this calculation for larger values of t? We want to calculate for what values of m does $(2(7/8)^{m/n})^n 2^{-t}$ go to zero as n goes to infinity. This will happen whenever $2(7/8)^{m/n} < 2^{t/n}$. Solving for m, whenever

$$m \geq (\log_{8/7} 2)(n - t) \approx 5.19(n - t), \tag{1}$$

a random 3-CNF formula with m clauses and n variables almost certainly has fewer than 2^t satisfying assignments. As expected, as t increases, fewer random clauses are needed to generate an instance that is not positive. Empirical estimates of the 0–1 threshold in Section 3.1 confirm the form of Equation 1.

While the above calculation gives an upper bound on m as a function of t and n, this upper bound is likely larger than the actual number. In several papers [26, 29], it has been demonstrated that most formulae will have a much smaller number of satisfying assignments than the expected number of satisfying assignments, because for those formulae that are satisfiable, they actually have many satisfying assignments (thus skewing the average). In particular, [26] ([26]) show that if a random k-CNF formula is satisfiable, then with exponentially high probability (probability at least $1 - 2^{-\epsilon n}$) it has an exponential number of satisfying truth assignments. Let Z be the number of variables that are not mentioned at all when m clauses are chosen randomly. For $k = 3$, the expectation of Z, $E[Z]$, is $n(1 - 1/n)^{3m}$, which is approximately $ne^{-3m/n}$. [26] ([26]) show amazingly tight tail bounds on this quantity. In fact, the weakest of their results shows that the probability of being more than a constant factor away from the expectation is exponentially small in n. This implies that if ϕ is a random formula where m is below the 0–1 threshold, then ϕ almost certainly will be satisfiable and, by the above result, almost certainly will have at least $2^{ne^{-3m/n}}$ satisfying assignments, since each of the variables that are not mentioned at all can be set in any possible way. Thus, almost certainly, whenever m is less than the 0–1 threshold, a random MAJSAT instance with parameters $(3, m, n, t)$ is positive whenever $t \leq ne^{-3m/n}$.

The above argument states that while the expected number of satisfying assignments is $(2(7/8)^{m/n})^n$, almost certainly the number of satisfying assignments will be substantially below the expected value. The beautifully simple argument of [29] ([29]) demonstrates that this is not the only source of wastefulness in these calculations. (See the thesis of [1] ([1]) for more details.)

What can be said of a lower bound on m as a function of t? Here again, very little seems to be known. Assume that almost certainly, there are l disjoint clauses, $C_1, C_2, \ldots, C_l$ in a random MAJSAT formula with parameters k, m, n, t.

Let $k = 3$. There are 2^{3l} total assignments for the l disjoint clauses. There are 7 ways to make each clause `True` for 3-CNF formulae. Since the clauses are disjoint, there are 7^l ways to make all the clauses true, so the exact number of assignments that make one or more clauses `False` is $2^{3l} - 7^l$, which is between $2^{3(l-1)}$ and 2^{3l}. This gives a lower bound on m as a function of t, the number of satisfying assignments, since l can be chosen as a function of m and n such that almost certainly a 3-CNF random formula with m clauses over n variables contains at least l variable-disjoint clauses.

The above gives very coarse upper and lower bounds on the value of m for which a random MAJSAT formula is `False`/`True` almost certainly as a function of t. Do we know that $f(k, m, n, t)$ actually exhibits a sharp 0–1 threshold behavior? As mentioned earlier, [17] ([17]) has proven that random SAT has a sharp 0–1 threshold, although the 0–1 threshold value α_k may be a function of n. The ideas in his proof are general enough that they extend to MAJSAT. In other words, from [17] ([17]), it follows that there exists a function $\alpha_k(n)$ such that for any $\epsilon > 0$, there exists $t > 1$ such that a random MAJSAT instance with parameters (k, m, n, t), where $m = (\alpha_k(n) - \epsilon)n$, is positive with high probability, while a random formula with parameters (k, m, n, t), where $m = (\alpha_k(n) + \epsilon)n$, is not a positive instance with high probability, and moreover has zero satisfying truth assignments with high probability. Therefore, although this line of argument doesn't lead to a prediction of where the 0–1 threshold is, or even whether it is a linear function of n, it does imply that it exists.

For random instances of more general SSAT problems, there are more parameters, since the validity of the formula is highly dependent on the exact sequence of quantifiers. To date, there are no theoretical results concerning the threshold behavior of random instances of general SSAT.

2. Algorithms for Stochastic Satisfiability

The SSAT problem is PSPACE complete, and therefore would seem to require a different set of algorithmic approaches from those developed for the NP-complete SAT. In fact, this section shows that the fundamental algorithmic ideas developed in the SAT community provide an excellent starting point for SSAT algorithms—the gap between NP and PSPACE may not be as large as it seems.

This section describes three algorithms for SSAT. Section 2.1 develops a DPLL-based algorithm. It shows that the basic structure of the SAT DPLL algorithm is applicable to Extended SSAT.

Section 2.2 describes another algorithm that is similar to the DPLL-based algorithm, but that has a guarantee of being efficient with respect to other decision-tree-based algorithms. This type of algorithm can be viewed as a "universal" search algorithm for DPLL-based procedures. The algorithm is guaranteed to solve the Extended SSAT instance in time that is efficient in the size of the smallest decision tree. As discussed in Section 4, although the theoretical performance of the universal algorithm is superior in the worst case, it does not perform as well on random formulae as the DPLL algorithm.

The algorithms in Section 2.1 and Section 2.2 are both sound and complete algorithms: given an arbitrary Extended SSAT instance (ϕ, θ, Q), both of these algorithms are guaranteed to return the correct answer, although the running time can be exponential. As with SAT, incomplete or approximate algorithms can often solve large problems more quickly than complete algorithms like DPLL. For SAT, randomized local search procedures like WALKSAT have been shown to be successful for large problem instances. Similarly, MAJSAT instances are very naturally approximated using random sampling. Section 2.3 describes a new SSAT algorithm that combines local search with random sampling to compute approximate answers to SSAT problems (existential and randomized quantifiers only).

2.1. A Davis-Putnam-Logemann-Loveland Algorithm

The Davis-Putnam-Logemann-Loveland (DPLL) algorithm for Boolean satisfiability [14] works by enumerating partial assignments and monitoring for opportunities to simplify the formula. These simplifications, or pruning rules, make it possible to solve problems whose entire set of assignments could not be fully enumerated.

DPLL is designed to solve SAT problems, and, thus, only needs to deal with existential quantifiers. The algorithm described in this section can be viewed as an extension of the DPLL algorithm to Extended SSAT by providing pruning rules for universal and randomized quantifiers. [8] ([8]) provide a set of pruning rules for universal quantifiers (for solving QBF problems); the purification and unit propagation pruning rules described here are introduced and justified there. [6] ([6]) describe a similar adaptation to DPLL for counting satisfying assignments.

The evalssat algorithm in Figure 2 takes formula ϕ and low and high thresholds θ_l and θ_h. It returns a value less than θ_l if and only if the value of the Extended SSAT formula is less than θ_l, a value greater than θ_h if and only if the value of the Extended SSAT formula is greater than θ_h, and otherwise the exact value of the Extended SSAT formula. Thus, it can be used to solve the Extended SSAT decision problem by setting $\theta_l = \theta_h = \theta$. It can also be used to compute the exact value of the formula by setting $\theta_l = 0$ and $\theta_h = 1$. The algorithm's basic structure is to compute the value of the Extended SSAT formula from its definition (Section 1.2.1); this takes place in the section of the pseudocode labeled "*Splitting*", which enumerates all assignments, applying operators recursively from left to right. However, it is made more complex (and efficient) by a set of pruning rules, described next.

2.1.1. *Unit Resolution*

When a Boolean formula ϕ is evaluated that contains a variable x_i that appears alone in a clause in ϕ with *sign* b (0 if $\overline{x_i}$ is in the clause, 1 if x_i is in the clause), the normal left-to-right evaluation of quantifiers can be interrupted to deal with this variable. This is called *unit resolution*, by analogy with DPLL.

If the quantifier associated with x_i is existential, x_i can be eliminated from the formula by assigning it value b and recursing. As in DPLL, this is because assigning $x_i = 1 - b$ is guaranteed to make ϕ `False`, so $x_i = b$ can be no worse. Similarly, if

```
evalssat(φ, Q, θ_l, θ_h) := {
  if φ is the empty set, return 1
  if φ contains an empty clause, return 0
  /* Unit Resolution */
  if x_i is a unit variable with sign b and Q(x_i) = ∃,
    return evalssat(φ⌈_{x_i=b}, Q, θ_l, θ_h)
  if x_i is a unit variable and Q(x_i) = ∀,
    return 0
  if x_i is a unit variable with sign b and Q(x_i) = ꓤ,
    return evalssat(φ⌈_{x_i=b}, Q, 2θ_l, 2θ_h)/2
  /* Purification */
  if x_i is a pure variable with sign b and Q(x_i) = ∃,
    return evalssat(φ⌈_{x_i=b}, Q, θ_l, θ_h)
  if x_i is a pure variable with sign b and Q(x_i) = ∀,
    return evalssat(φ⌈_{x_i=1-b}, Q, θ_l, θ_h)
  /* Splitting */
  if Q(x_1) = ∃, {
    v_0 = evalssat(φ⌈_{x_1=0}, Q, θ_l, θ_h)
    if v_0 ≥ θ_h, return v_0
    v_1 = evalssat(φ⌈_{x_1=1}, Q, max(θ_l, v_0), θ_h)
    return max(v_0, v_1)
  }
  if Q(x_1) = ∀, {
    v_0 = evalssat(φ⌈_{x_1=0}, Q, θ_l, θ_h)
    if v_0 < θ_l, return v_0
    v_1 = evalssat(φ⌈_{x_1=1}, Q, θ_l, min(v_0, θ_h))
    return min(v_0, v_1)
  }
  if Q(x_1) = ꓤ, {
    v_0 = evalssat(φ⌈_{x_1=0}, Q, 2θ_l − 1, 2θ_h)
    if (v_0 + 1)/2 < θ_l, return v_0/2
    if v_0/2 ≥ θ_h, return v_0/2
    v_1 = evalssat(φ⌈_{x_1=1}, Q, 2θ_l − v_0, 2θ_h − v_0)
    return (v_0 + v_1)/2
  }
}
```

Figure 2. The evalssat algorithm generalizes the DPLL algorithm for satisfiability to solve Extended SSAT problems.

the quantifier associated with x_i is randomized, it is the case that one branch of the computation will return a zero, so x_i can be eliminated from the formula by assigning it value b and continuing recursively. The resulting value is divided by two (or multiplied by the probability associated with the randomized quantifier, more generally), since it represents the value of only one branch.

On the other hand, if the quantifier associated with x_i is universal, it is immediate that the entire formula is `False` since it will not be the case that all values of x_i make the formula `True`. The algorithm can return a zero in this case. This is stronger than the pruning possible for either existential or randomized variables.

2.1.2. *Purification and Thresholding*

The *purification* pruning rules apply when there is a variable x_i that appears only with one sign b in ϕ. If $Q(x_i) = \exists$, the algorithm assigns $x_i = b$ and recurses. This is valid because any clause satisfied by an assignment with $x_i = 1 - b$ will also be satisfied by assigning $x_i = b$. By similar reasoning, if $Q(x_i) = \forall$, the algorithm recurses after assigning $x_i = 1-b$. Interestingly, purification pruning does not appear possible for randomized variables. Both assignments to a randomized variable give *some* contribution to the value of the Extended SSAT formula, and must be considered independently.

Another useful class of pruning rules concerns the *threshold* parameters θ_l and θ_h. While some care must be taken to pass meaningful thresholds when applying unit resolution, threshold pruning mainly comes into play when variables are split to try to prevent recursively computing both assignments to x_1, the outermost quantified variable.

If $Q(x_1) = \exists$, after the first recursive call computing v_0 (the value of the current formula with x_1 set to `False`), it is possible that θ_h has already been exceeded. In this case, the algorithm can simply return v_0, without ever computing v_1 (the value of the current formula with x_1 set to `True`). In particular, it is possible that $v_1 > v_0$, but all that is significant is whether the larger of the two exceeds θ_h. If v_0 exceeds θ_l but falls short of θ_h, this can be used to increase the lower threshold for the recursive computation of v_1; since the algorithm must take the larger of v_0 and v_1, the precise value of v_1 is not needed if it less than v_0.

The complement of this argument provides a threshold pruning rule for universal quantifiers.

Threshold pruning is not as strong for randomized variables, although it can be done. There are two types of threshold pruning that apply. First, if assigning 0 to x_1 is sufficient to meet the threshold θ_h, then the algorithm need not recurse on assigning the variable to 1: if $v_0/2 \geq \theta_h$, return $v_0/2$.

If the first value v_0 is so low that, even if $v_1 = 1$, $(v_0 + v_1)/2 < \theta_l$, then again the algorithm need not compute v_1. If both tests fail, the algorithm needs to compute v_1, but can adjust the thresholds accordingly.

All of these pruning rules are incorporated into the algorithm given in Figure 2. Appendix A gives a correctness proof for the algorithm.

2.1.3. *Complexity of* evalssat

Not surprisingly, the worst-case running time of evalssat is exponential in the size of the formula. The reason is that on even simple instances, often the underlying decision tree is always large, and in addition, pruning does not help. A particular example of this is applying evalssat to unsatisfiable SAT formulae that are known to require exponential size Resolution proofs. Since the algorithm (in this special case) produces a Resolution refutation, the Resolution lower bounds for specific formulae (such as the propositional pigeonhole principle) imply exponential time lower bounds on the running time of evalssat on these examples.

It is also interesting to understand the average-case running time of evalssat and its performance on more general formulae, such as instances of MAJSAT or Alternating SSAT. This question can be partially answered in the context of random formulae, yielding results on the complexity of the DPLL algorithm assuming no pruning rules, that is, assuming that the algorithm needs to generate the entire decision tree before terminating. This is interesting, since for many hard formulae the entire decision tree must be generated in order to determine truth or falsity of the formula, and, thus, lower bounds on the decision-tree size yield lower bounds on the running time of the algorithm. The following theorem follows from the results of [3] ([3]).

THEOREM 1. *Let ϕ be a 3-CNF formula chosen uniformly at random from $\mathcal{F}_m^{k,n}$. For all n sufficiently large, for all m, $n \leq m \leq n^{5/4}$, with high probability any decision tree for ϕ requires exponential size in n.*

This theorem shows that for random formulae in a large range, the decision-tree complexity of the underlying 3-CNF formula will be huge, and therefore the running time of any decision-tree-based algorithm without pruning will be exponential. To make matters worse, the DPLL algorithm above searches for a decision tree in a very specific way; that is, it is not guaranteed to even search for the smallest tree. This leads to the following interesting question: Given a CNF formula ϕ, is it possible to efficiently produce a decision tree for ϕ that is close to an optimal one? An affirmative answer to this question suggests a more efficient algorithm for SAT, and moreover suggests that if one is using a decision-tree-based method, that an "optimal" algorithm within this class exists. The next section describes such an algorithm: it is guaranteed to find a close-to-optimal size tree efficiently.

2.2. *A Universal Search Algorithm for Extended* SSAT

As indicated earlier, it may be possible to determine whether a MAJSAT instance (ϕ, θ, Q) is positive without actually constructing the entire decision tree, via pruning. On the other hand, to determine the exact value of ϕ, the entire decision tree must be examined, and therefore a lower bound on the best possible running time of the algorithm described here will be a linear function of the size of the smallest decision tree for ϕ. Thus, it is useful to understand how hard it is to search for the smallest such decision tree.

Let (ϕ, θ, Q) be an instance of Extended SSAT. A *block* is a maximal set of variables that appear in the formula with the same quantifier and are adjacent in the quantifier ordering. Note that, within a block, quantifiers commute. In what follows, assume that (ϕ, θ, Q) has κ consecutive blocks of variables $X^1, \ldots, X^\kappa$.

If ϕ is an Extended SSAT formula, then ϕ can be determined to be `True` or `False` by examining a canonical decision tree for ϕ as described in Section 1.2.1. Given an Extended SSAT instance ϕ, the evalssat algorithm described in Section 2.1 can be generalized to search for a decision tree that is more general than a canonical decision tree (splits need not follow the precise quantifier ordering), but has the following properties: for every i, j $i < j$, every variable in the block X^i is split upon in the decision tree before every variable in the block X^j, with the possible exception of variables that appear in unit clauses or pure variables. A decision tree for ϕ with these properties will be called a *DPLL tree* for ϕ. The evaluation of a DPLL tree for ϕ is again obtained by evaluating each vertex, starting at the leaves, in the manner described in Section 1.2.1. To summarize, a decision tree ignores the quantifier ordering, a canonical tree follows it precisely, and the DPLL tree can consider variables in a block in any order.

It was shown implicitly by [10] ([10]) and more explicitly by [4] ([4]) and [5] ([5]) that there is a relatively efficient deterministic procedure for finding a small tree-like Resolution proof. Following the proof of their theorem, it can be shown that there is an efficient deterministic procedure for finding a small DPLL tree.

THEOREM 2. *There is a deterministic algorithm that takes as input an Extended* SSAT *formula ϕ with m clauses and n underlying variables and outputs a DPLL decision tree, T for ϕ. Moreover, the running time of the algorithm is at most $n^{O(\log s)}O(m)$, where s is the size of the smallest DPLL decision tree for ϕ.*

Proof: The proof follows [3] ([3]), with small modifications. As above, let (ϕ, θ, Q) be an instance of Extended SSAT with κ blocks of consecutive variables $X^1, \ldots, X^\kappa$. Assume that ϕ has a size s DPLL decision tree, and assume without loss of generality that the root node is labeled by the variable x. It follows that one of the two subtrees has size at most $s/2$. Therefore, the algorithm can search through all literals l occurring in the first block until it finds one, l^*, such that $\phi\lceil_{l^*=1}$ has a decision tree of size at most $s/2$. The tree T constructed for ϕ will, thus, have root labeled with l^* (not necessarily x, but not much worse, as indicated by the overall running time).

The main algorithm, **DPLLsearch**, takes as input a Boolean formula ϕ. If there is a literal l occurring in a unit clause, then the output of **DPLLsearch**(ϕ) consists of a DPLL tree for $\phi\lceil_{l=1}$ followed by a DPLL tree for $\phi\lceil_{l=0}$, and then these two trees are combined by adding a top node and splitting on l. Otherwise (if there is no unit clause), then for each of the literals l occurring in the current block (the leftmost block of variables that have not already been set), apply **DPLLsearch** to the formula $\phi\lceil_{l=1}$ to identify the literal l for which **DPLLsearch**($\phi\lceil_{l=1}$) terminates fastest.

These calls to **DPLLsearch** are executed in a sequence of parallel rounds so that in round i the ith step of each of the calls is performed. In other words, if $l_1, \ldots, l_p$ are the variables in the current block, then the algorithm will execute the p recursive calls, **DPLLsearch**($\phi\lceil_{l_i=1}$), $i = 1, \ldots, p$, in a dovetail fashion, executing each for one time step, and then each for two time steps, etc. The first time that one of the recursive calls terminates, say for literal l^*, **DPLLsearch**($\phi\lceil_{l^*=1}$) terminates, then we abort all other calls, except for the call corresponding to $\overline{l^*}$, which is run to completion.

The output of **DPLLsearch**(ϕ) consists of a DPLL tree for $\phi\lceil_{l^*=1}$ followed by a DPLL tree for $\phi\lceil_{l^*=0}$, and then these two trees are combined by adding a top node and splitting on l^*.

The analysis of the algorithm follows that of [3] ([3]). Let $T_1(n, s; m)$ denote the maximum running time of **DPLLsearch**(ϕ) over all formulae ϕ with at most n variables, m clauses and such that there exists a decision tree for ϕ of size at most s. Consider a decision tree of size at most s and let x be the splitting variable at the root. The left and right branches of the tree give decision trees for $\phi\lceil_{x=0}$ and $\phi\lceil_{x=1}$, and the smaller of these is of size at most $s/2$. Hence, at least one of the recursive calls terminates after at most $T_1(n-1, s/2; m)$ steps, and so the literal l^* is found after at most that number of rounds. The time for each round is at most Cn for some constant C. Once l^* is found, it takes at most $T_1(n-1, s; m)$ steps to complete the call to **DPLLsearch**($\phi\lceil_{l^*=0}$) (the smallest tree for $l^* = 0$ can be no larger than the smallest tree). Thus, for fixed m, the following recurrence relation is obtained: $T_1(n, s) \leq CnT_1(n-1, s/2) + T_1(n-1, s)$ whenever $n \geq 1$ and $s > 1$; $T_1(0, s) = 1$ and $T_1(n, 1) = \text{time}(O(m))$, which is the time to compute the value of a CNF formula with m clauses under a given truth assignment. It can be shown by induction that $T_1(n, s) \leq O(m)n^{O(\log s)}$. ∎

For SAT and MAJSAT formulae, any decision tree is a DPLL tree, but for more complicated Extended SSAT instances, the DPLL tree is more restricted since it must split on all the variables in the outermost block before splitting on any variables that appear later in the quantifier ordering (with the exception of unit resolution and purification). In particular, it might be that for a given formula ϕ, there is a small decision tree for ϕ but not a small DPLL tree for ϕ, because of the quantifier ordering. Unfortunately, the following theorem due to [47] ([47]) shows that an arbitrary decision tree cannot be used to evaluate an Extended SSAT formula efficiently.

THEOREM 3. ([47] ([47])). *Let* QBF(i) *denote the complexity class of deciding an Extended* SSAT *formula with only* $\exists$ *and* $\forall$ *quantifiers, and with* i *quantifier alternations (blocks). Let* QBF*-tree(i) be the following problem. The input is a pair* (ϕ, T)*, where* ϕ *is a* QBF(i) *formula and where* T *is a decision tree that captures the CNF part of the formula* ϕ *(ignoring quantifiers). Then,* QBF*-tree(i) is in* P *if and only if* QBF$(i-1) =$ P.

In other words, the above theorem tells us that it is impossible to determine in polynomial time the value of an Extended SSAT formula given an *arbitrary* polynomial-size decision tree for the CNF part of the formula, unless a surprising collapse of complexity classes occurs. Thus, the restriction to searching for DPLL trees, which respect quantifier order, is necessary, in a sense. Nonetheless, there are somewhat less restricted decision trees than DPLL trees that could be used to evaluate an Extended SSAT formula. For instance, variables can be skipped altogether and still the values of the internal nodes can be calculated, as long as the variables that are mentioned are consistent with the quantification ordering (again, with the exception of unit resolution). However, at this time, there is no method known to efficiently search for these more general types of trees.

2.3. *A Stochastic Sampling Algorithm*

Randomized local search algorithms, like WALKSAT [27], have been extremely successful in solving difficult satisfiability problems. WALKSAT initially makes a random assignment to the variables in the SAT formula. If this is not a satisfying assignment, it randomly selects an unsatisfied clause. If it can satisfy this clause by flipping a variable without unsatisfying any other clauses, it does so. If not, with probability 1/2, it randomly flips that variable that would unsatisfy the fewest clauses. This process continues until a satisfying assignment is found or until a specified maximum number of variables have been flipped. This entire process can also be repeated a specified number of times starting with a new random assignment. Clearly, WALKSAT is not complete; it may not find a satisfying assignment when one exists. Further, it cannot determine when no satisfying assignment exists. But, compared to existing systematic solvers, randomized local search algorithms can solve random satisfiability problems that are orders of magnitude larger [45].

The presence of randomly quantified variables in SSAT problems, however, makes it impossible to apply local search techniques directly to SSAT problems. A possible approach is suggested by an approximation technique for MAJSAT problems: stochastic sampling. In this approach, some number of assignments to the random variables are generated according to their probabilities, and then the probability that the formula is satisfiable is estimated from that sample. This section develops an approximation algorithm for SSAT problems that combines stochastic sampling to reduce the size of the problem (Section 2.3.2) and randomized local search to solve the reduced problem efficiently (Section 2.3.3).

2.3.1. *Policy Trees*

The starting point for the stochastic sampling algorithm for SSAT is the policy-tree representation. Figure 3 provides an example policy tree for the SSAT instance

$$\exists x_1, \exists x_2, \text{Я} y_1, \text{Я} y_2, \exists x_3, \exists x_4, \text{Я} y_3, \text{Я} y_4, E[(\overline{x_1} \vee x_3 \vee \overline{y_3})(\overline{x_2} \vee \overline{x_4} \vee y_2)(x_3 \vee y_1 \vee \overline{y_4})] \geq \theta.$$

Each existential variable can take on a different Boolean value as a function of the assignment to the randomized variables that appear to its left in the quantifier ordering. The *policy-tree* representation makes this evident by including a copy of the variable for each of these assignments. Existential variables, and their copies, can be called *decision*

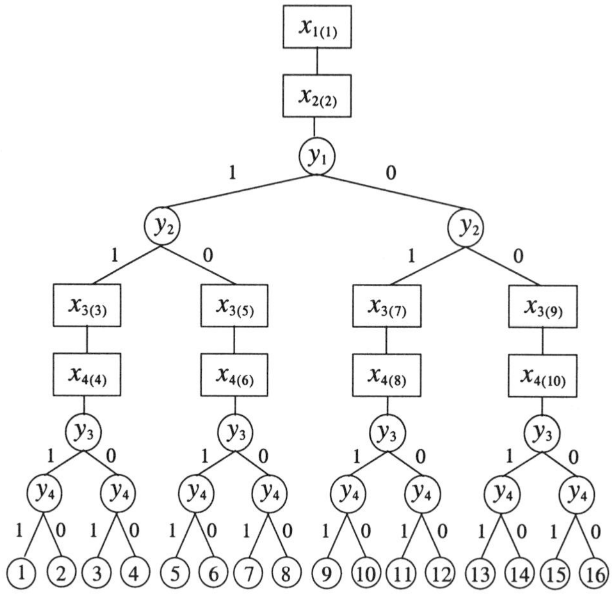

Original Formula: $(\bar{x}_1 \vee x_3 \vee \bar{y}_3)(\bar{x}_2 \vee \bar{x}_4 \vee y_2)(x_3 \vee y_1 \vee \bar{y}_4)$

Simplified Formulae at Leaves Given Random Variable Assignments

Leaf 1:	$(\bar{x}_1 \vee x_3)$	Leaf 9:	$(\bar{x}_1 \vee x_7)(x_7)$
Leaf 2:	$(\bar{x}_1 \vee x_3)$	Leaf 10:	$(\bar{x}_1 \vee x_7)$
Leaf 3:	Satisfied	Leaf 11:	(x_7)
Leaf 4:	Satisfied	Leaf 12:	Satisfied
Leaf 5:	$(\bar{x}_1 \vee x_5)(\bar{x}_2 \vee \bar{x}_6)$	Leaf 13:	$(\bar{x}_1 \vee x_9)(\bar{x}_2 \vee \bar{x}_{10})(x_9)$
Leaf 6:	$(\bar{x}_1 \vee x_5)(\bar{x}_2 \vee \bar{x}_6)$	Leaf 14:	$(\bar{x}_1 \vee x_9)(\bar{x}_2 \vee \bar{x}_{10})$
Leaf 7:	$(\bar{x}_2 \vee \bar{x}_6)$	Leaf 15:	$(\bar{x}_2 \vee \bar{x}_{10})(x_9)$
Leaf 8:	$(\bar{x}_2 \vee \bar{x}_6)$	Leaf 16:	$(\bar{x}_2 \vee \bar{x}_{10})$

Figure 3. A policy tree represents the set of contingent choices in an SSAT problem.

variables and are represented as rectangular *decision nodes* in the policy tree. If x_i is an existential variable such that r randomized variables are to its left, then there will be 2^r copies of x_i in the policy-tree representation. In the policy tree in Figure 3, for example, two randomized variables (y_1 and y_2) appear to the left of the existential variables x_3 and x_4 in the quantifier ordering, so there are four copies of x_3 and x_4. To emphasize that the value of each instance of a copied variable can be set independently, these variables are renumbered in the policy tree such that, given two decision nodes at the same level in the tree (and, therefore, containing the same variables), the variables in one decision node will be distinct from the variables in the other decision node. The renumbering of a variable appears in a parenthesized subscript next to the original number. Thus, $x_{3(7)}$ is the relevant copy of variable x_3 when y_1 is `False` and y_2 is `True`. Note that the existential variables in the simplified formulae in Figure 3 are subscripted only with the new numbers.

Each leaf of the policy tree represents a partial assignment consisting of an assignment to all randomized variables in the SSAT formula. The *probability of a leaf* is $1/2^R$ in a formula with R randomized variables (more generally, it is the product of the probabilities of the outcomes along the path from the root to the leaf). A *policy* is an assignment of Boolean values to the existential nodes in the policy tree (boxes in Figure 3). Given a policy, all the root-to-leaf paths in the policy tree represent complete assignments to the variables in the formula, each of which is either satisfying (value 1) or unsatisfying (value 0). The *value of a policy* is the weighted sum of the probabilities of the satisfied leaves. For example, the policy that assigns "0" to all existential nodes in the policy tree in Figure 3 has value 3/4 (leaves 9, 11, 13, and 15 are unsatisfied).

The *value of a policy tree* is the maximum over all policies of the policy values. The value of the policy tree in Figure 3 is 1 because the policy $x_{1(1)} = 0$, $x_{2(2)} = 0$, $x_{3(7)} = 1$, $x_{3(9)} = 1$ satisfies all leaves (unmentioned variables can take on either value). Note that a policy tree is simply an alternative representation of the DPLL tree for a formula (Section 2.2), and the value of a policy tree is exactly that of a DPLL tree for the formula. However, it is a convenient representation for organizing the sampling algorithm described next.

2.3.2. *Stochastic Sampling*

The value of a fixed policy with respect to an SSAT instance can be computed in time linear in the size of the policy tree. However, in a formula with R randomized variables, the size of the policy tree is roughly 2^R. An accurate estimate of the value of the policy can be obtained by constructing and evaluating a *partial policy tree*. Choose a set W of w assignments to the randomized variables proportional to their probability and independently of the policy. The sampled assignments select out a set of leaves from the full policy tree, with the probability of an assignment given by its frequency of selection in the random sample. The top of Figure 4 gives a partial policy tree derived from the sample in the bottom of the figure and the policy tree of Figure 3. The value of the policy is estimated as the proportion of the w sampled leaves that are satisfied by the policy. Let v be the true value of the policy and $\hat{v}$ be the estimate found via sampling.

LEMMA 4. *Let $\epsilon > 0$ be a target approximation error. The probability that $|v - \hat{v}| > \epsilon$ is less than $2e^{-2\epsilon^2 w}$.*

This is a direct application of a Chernoff bound.

Thus, to be sure with probability $1 - \delta$ of having an estimate no further than ϵ away from the true value, $w = O(\frac{1}{\epsilon^2}\log(\frac{1}{\delta}))$ samples are sufficient. Note that this number does not depend on n, m, k, or how the SSAT formula or the policy was created!

Lemma 4 directly gives an approximation algorithm for MAJSAT and can be extended to solve SSAT problems via systematic search, described next.

Given a sample W of size w of assignments to the randomized variables in an SSAT formula, it is straightforward to recursively compute the value of the policy with the largest approximate value. Figure 5 sketches this procedure; as before x_1 refers to the outermost quantified variable.

The running time of sampleevalssat is $w \cdot 2^E$, where E is the number of existential variables in the formula. The next theorem shows that, if the random sample W is large enough, sampleevalssat gives a good approximation to the true value of the given SSAT formula with high probability.

THEOREM 5. *Let (ϕ, Q, θ) be an instance of* SSAT *and W be a size w random sample of the assignments to the randomized variables in ϕ. Let P be the number of possible policies for the* SSAT *instance. Let $v = val(\phi, Q)$ be the true value of the* SSAT *formula*

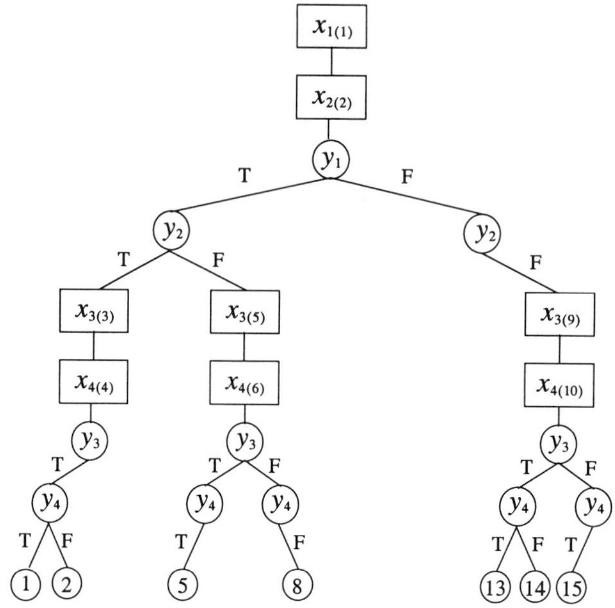

Original Formula: $(\bar{x}_1 \vee x_3 \vee \bar{y}_3)(\bar{x}_2 \vee \bar{x}_4 \vee y_2)(x_3 \vee y_1 \vee \bar{y}_4)$

Assignments Responsible for Leaves in Partial Decision Tree

Leaf 1:	$y_1 = 1$	$y_2 = 1$	$y_3 = 1$	$y_4 = 1$
Leaf 2:	$y_1 = 1$	$y_2 = 1$	$y_3 = 1$	$y_4 = 0$
Leaf 5:	$y_1 = 1$	$y_2 = 0$	$y_3 = 1$	$y_4 = 1$
Leaf 8:	$y_1 = 1$	$y_2 = 0$	$y_3 = 0$	$y_4 = 0$
Leaf 13:	$y_1 = 0$	$y_2 = 0$	$y_3 = 1$	$y_4 = 1$
Leaf 14:	$y_1 = 0$	$y_2 = 0$	$y_3 = 1$	$y_4 = 0$
Leaf 15:	$y_1 = 0$	$y_2 = 0$	$y_3 = 0$	$y_4 = 1$

Figure 4. Randomized local search can be applied to a partial policy tree, obtained by sampling, to provide an approximate answer for an SSAT instance. Boxes in the figure represent decision nodes and circles random nodes.

and $\hat{v}$ be the estimate found via sampleevalssat. *Let $\epsilon > 0$ be a target approximation error. The probability that $|v - \hat{v}| > \epsilon$ is less than $P2e^{-2\epsilon^2 w}$. Thus,*

$$w = O\left(\frac{1}{\epsilon^2}\log\left(\frac{1}{\delta}\right) + \frac{1}{\epsilon^2}\log(P)\right)$$

samples are sufficient to be sure with probability $1 - \delta$ of having an estimate no further than ϵ away from the true value.

Proof: Imagine that we use the sample W to approximately evaluate all P policies. By Lemma 4, the probability that any given estimate is off by more than ϵ is $2e^{-2\epsilon^2 w}$. Therefore, the probability that at least one estimate out of P is off by more than ϵ is less than $P2e^{-2\epsilon^2 w}$. If all P policies have approximate values within ϵ of their true values, then the maximum of the approximate values, that is, $\hat{v}$, cannot differ by more than ϵ from the maximum of the true values, that is, v. ∎

```
sampleevalssat(φ, Q, W) := {
  if φ is the empty set, return 1
  if φ contains an empty clause, return 0
  if Q(x_1) = ∃, return
      max(sampleevalssat(φ⌈_{x_1=0}, Q, W),
          sampleevalssat(φ⌈_{x_1=1}, Q, W))
  else if Q(x_1) = Я, {
    Let W_0 be the samples in W that assign x_1 = 0
    Let W_1 be the samples in W that assign x_1 = 1
    return |W_0|/|W| sampleevalssat(φ⌈_{x_1=0}, Q, W_0)+
           |W_1|/|W| sampleevalssat(φ⌈_{x_1=1}, Q, W_1)
  }
}
```

Figure 5. A stochastic sampling algorithm for SSAT problems chooses the best approximate value.

The *sample complexity* of the algorithm is the number of samples needed to insure an accurate estimate of the value of the formula with high probability. Note that for SAT, the number of policies is $P = 2^n$, MAJSAT, $P = 1$, and E-MAJSAT, $P = 2^c \leq 2^n$. Since the sample complexity for sampleevalssat is logarithmically dependent on P, these SSAT problems have polynomial sample complexity. However, for Alternating SSAT, $P = \Theta(2^{2^{n/2}})$, so Theorem 5 gives an exponential sample bound. Appendix B shows that this is a necessary feature of the algorithm by providing a family of SSAT instances that require an exponential sized sample for sampleevalssat to give accurate results with high probability.

2.3.3. *Randomized Local Search*

The basic approach described in the previous section is to randomly sample a set of assignments to be used to evaluate policies, then systematically search the space of policies to find one with the best approximate value. Although, for many problems, the number of samples required is not too large, the search for the best policy will be exponential in the number of existential variables in the formula.

Randomized local search can be used to substantially reduce the search time for a good policy, at the cost of finding one that is only locally optimal. As described in Section 2.3.2, stochastic sampling can be used to construct a partial policy tree and, given a policy, the partial policy tree can be evaluated (its value is the proportion of the sample corresponding to satisfied leaves). The goal is to search the space of policies to find one with high value.

The randevalssat algorithm in Figure 6 takes SSAT formula ϕ and returns an approximation of its value, along with the policy that approximately produces this value. The algorithm's local search component operates by first converting the partial policy tree to a two-level Boolean formula, called a *treeSAT* formula (function construct_treesat_formula in Figure 6). As illustrated in Figure 3, the effect of a policy on a leaf can be summarized by a Boolean formula, called a *path formula*, for that leaf. Each random sample can potentially produce a different path formula, and the union of all the path formulae produces the treeSAT formula. Thus, on one level the treeSAT formula is a collection of clauses, while on another level it is a collection of path formulae.

A satisfying assignment to the treeSAT formula corresponds to a setting of the decision variables that satisfies the original SSAT formula along all paths in the partial policy tree. In general, it will not be possible to find such a setting, so the challenge here is to find an assignment to the treeSAT formula that maximizes the number of path formulae that are satisfied. This can be accomplished by randomized local search. In the experiments in this paper, this is done by hillclimbing on an objective function that counts both clauses satisfied and path formulae satisfied. A satisfied path formula is weighted as heavily as the number of clauses in the original SSAT formula, so that satisfying all the clauses in a path formula contributes more to the treeSAT formula's value than satisfying the same number of clauses scattered over more than one path formula. The function eval_treesat_formula calculates the value of the treeSAT formula using this objective function.

The operation of randevalssat is similar to that of WALKSAT [27]. The main difference is in the objective function. WALKSAT searches for an assignment that maximizes the number of satisfied clauses. As described above, the two-level structure of the treeSAT formula requires randevalssat to use an objective function that counts both clauses satisfied and path formulae satisfied. (In fact, in the tests conducted, counting satisfied clauses did not seem to be as important as counting satisfied path formulae; randevalssat performed as well with an objective function that counted only satisfied path formulae. Larger problems might exhibit different behavior.)

Essentially, randevalssat randomly sets the values of the treeSAT variables, then hill-climbs on the objective function described above. On each iteration (up to a maximum of IterationLimit iterations), the algorithm randomly chooses an unsatisfied clause. If it is possible to improve the value of the objective function by flipping the truth value of a variable in that clause, it does so. Otherwise, it calculates which variable flip in that clause will lead to the least decrease in the value of the objective function, and accepts that flip with a probability of 0.5. The algorithm returns the treeSAT assignment that produced the highest value of the objective function over all iterations. If the algorithm fails to make progress on a prespecified number of consecutive iterations (FailureLimit) it restarts with a new random setting of the treeSAT variables. A prespecified number of restarts (RestartLimit) is allowed.

Empirical results with randevalssat are discussed in Section 3.4.

2.3.4. *Related Work*

Many other researchers have explored approximations for probability-based problems. [43] ([43]) studied the complexity of inference in belief networks. He showed that computing the probability of a query node (akin to evaluating a MAJSAT formula) is #P-complete. In addition, approximating the probability of a query node to within a multiplicative factor of its true value is just as hard as computing the exact value. In contrast, Lemma 4 shows that the complexity of getting within an *additive* factor for MAJSAT is polynomial.

[28] ([28]) show how approximately optimal actions can be chosen with high probability in infinite-horizon discounted Markov decision processes. Their strategy is to show that it is sufficient to consider the first H actions in the sequence, for an appropriate choice of H. The space of all H-step action sequences is then evaluated using random sampling. The sampleevalssat algorithm in Section 2.3.2 was directly inspired by this work.

2.3.5. *Summary*

In summary, the stochastic sampling algorithm randevalssat appears to be a promising approximation method for SSAT problems. Its primary strength is the use of sampling to convert the problem to a lower complexity problem and its use of randomized local search to solve that problem efficiently. A feature of this process is that it does not

```
randevalssat(φ, W) := {
  ρ := construct_treesat_formula(φ, W);
  currentpolicy := generate a random truth assignment for ρ;
  P := eval_treesat_formula(ρ); bestP := P;
  bestpolicy := currentpolicy;
  for (r = 1 to RestartLimit) {
    numfailures := 0;
    for (i = 1 to IterationLimit) {
      if (all clauses in ρ are satisfied)
        return(P, currentpolicy);
      randomly choose an unsatisfied clause c in ρ;
      bestflipvar := 0; bestnewP := 0;
      for (each literal l in c) {
        flip the truth assignment of the variable v corresponding to l;
        newP = eval_treesat_formula(ρ);
        if (newP > P) {
          numfailures = 0;
          P = newP;
          if (newP > bestP) {
            bestP = newP; bestpolicy = currentpolicy;
          }
          break out of literal loop and start next iteration;
        }
        else if (newP > bestnewP) {
          bestflipvar = v; bestnewP = newP;
        }
        restore the truth assignment of the variable v corresponding to l;
      } /* literal loop */
      with probability 0.5 {
        flip the truth assignment of variable bestflipvar;
        P = bestnewP;
      }
      numfailures := numfailures + 1;
      if (numfailures > FailureLimit){
        currentpolicy := generate a random truth assignment for ρ;
        P := eval_treesat_formula(ρ);
        break out of iteration loop and start next restart;
    } /* iteration loop */
  } /* restart loop */
  return(bestP, bestpolicy);
}
```

Figure 6. A randomized algorithm for SSAT problems uses hillclimbing on a SAT formula derived from a partial policy tree created by sampling.

necessarily completely discard the probabilities of the original problem (as would, say, a conversion that merely rounded off the probabilities of the random variables to 0 and 1 and set their truth values accordingly). It would, for example, be possible to modify the algorithm such that the probabilities of the random variables are used to direct the construction of the partial policy tree. A more substantial modification would be to iteratively build the partial policy tree by using the solution of the partial policy tree in a given iteration to construct a better partial policy tree (and solution) in the next iteration.

This algorithm has some weaknesses. First, unlike WALKSAT, randevalssat does not return an answer whose correctness is "easy" to certify; this is to be expected, given the complexity of SSAT problems. Second, there are SSAT problems for which the algorithm needs provably large samples (see Section B for an example of such a problem). Third, randevalssat is subject to the same pitfalls as other randomized local search algorithms; in particular, it may become stuck in local optima. Allowing the algorithm to restart after a period of no progress helps minimize, but does not erase, this problem. Finally, the memory requirements of the algorithm can be prohibitively large. This weakness can be partially overcome by more memory-efficient implementations, but problems that require a large number of samples to produce an accurate answer will inherently generate large treeSAT formulae.

3. Results

This section describes some empirical explorations of solving SSAT problems of various types using the algorithms presented in Section 2.

3.1. Varying Problem Type

Throughout the experiments in this section, the DPLL-based SSAT algorithm from Section 2.1 (variable to split next chosen by strict quantifier order) is used. A set of 1,000 formulae with $n = 20$ variables, $k = 3$ literals per clause, and 141 clauses were randomly generated using `makewff`. All thresholds were expressed as $\theta = 1/2^{n-t}$ for integer t in the range 0 to n; this defines t so that 2^t is the number of satisfying assignments required. Formulae with m clauses were created by using the first m clauses from each of the 1,000 formulae.

3.1.1. MAJSAT *vs.* SAT

The first experiment compares and contrasts MAJSAT with SAT. Figure 7 illustrates the average work required to solve random MAJSAT instances, varying the number of clauses and values of the threshold parameter t.

The line on the plot labeled $t = 0$ is the curve for SAT; this problem is asking whether the probability of satisfaction is at least $1/2^n$, which is reached as long as there is even a single satisfying assignment. The classic easy-hardest-hard pattern is visible. In fact, nearly all the threshold values produce the same basic shape.

Note that the peak difficulty over all thresholds occurs at $t = 16$; it is much higher than the peak difficulty for SAT and occurs at a much lower setting of the number of clauses m. High values of the threshold are difficult because the threshold pruning rules for randomized quantifiers rarely apply—it is almost always necessary to check both branches to determine whether the probability threshold can be met.

Note that when no pruning rules are used, MAJSAT and SAT are equally difficult for the DPLL algorithm; it must create the entire DPLL tree for both, and has the

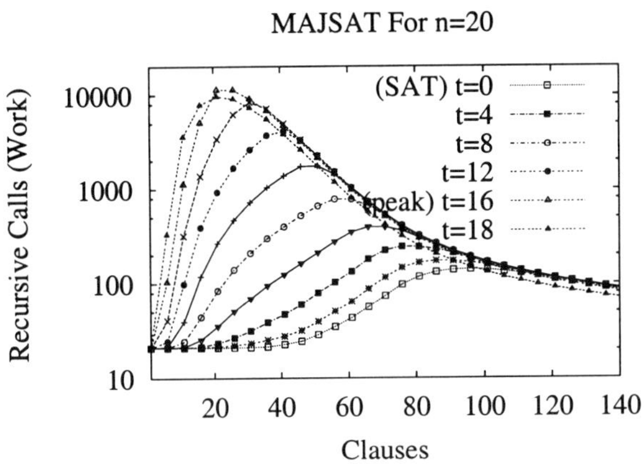

Figure 7. For random $n = 20$ variable formulae ($k = 3$ literals per clause), the difficulty of solving random MAJSAT instances via DPLL varies with both the number of clauses to variables and the satisfaction threshold t. The plot includes curves for thresholds $t = 0$ through $t = 18$ by 2s (not all curves are labeled). Peak difficulty occurs at $t = 16$ at roughly 20 clauses.

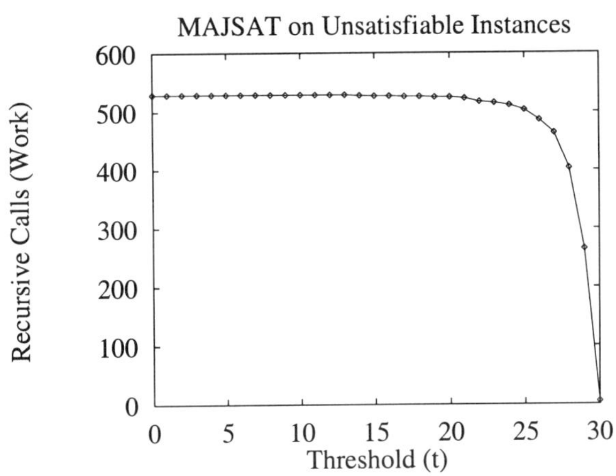

Figure 8. For random unsatisfiable $n = 30$ variable formulae ($m = 141$ clauses, $k = 3$ literals per clause), the difficulty of solving random MAJSAT instances via DPLL varies with the satisfaction threshold t. When the threshold is high, pruning becomes more effective, allowing instances to be solved more quickly.

freedom to split in any order. This implies that, for unsatisfiable formulae, MAJSAT is actually *easier* to decide than SAT, since threshold pruning is only possible in the case of MAJSAT. Figure 8 shows that the average difficulty for solving MAJSAT problems based on the 689 random $n = 30$ formulae that are unsatisfiable at $m = 141$ clauses does decrease with increasing satisfiability threshold.

3.1.2. E-MAJSAT

On average, MAJSAT instances were substantially more difficult to solve than SAT instances. That MAJSAT is more difficult to solve on average than SAT is not surprising, since it belongs to a higher complexity class. A more interesting pattern occurs in E-MAJSAT formulae. As mentioned in Section 1.3, the E-MAJSAT parameter c interpolates between MAJSAT ($c = 0$) and SAT ($c = n$). In terms of complexity theory,

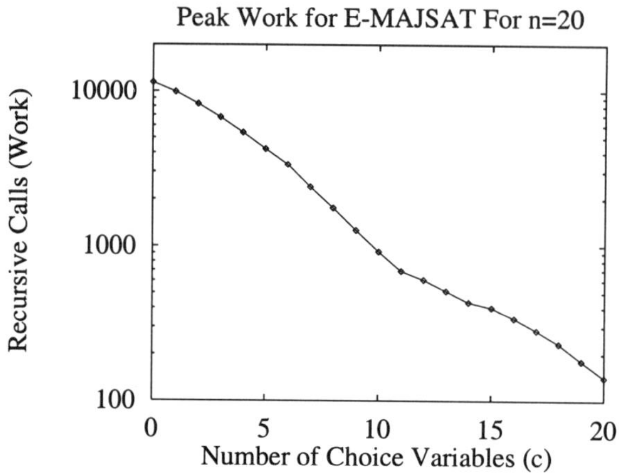

Figure 9. The difficulty of solving random E-MAJSAT instances via DPLL decreases with increasing number of choice variables c. The plot is for random formulae with $k = 3$ literals per clause.

however, intermediate values of c place E-MAJSAT in a more difficult complexity class than either endpoint. This suggests analyzing the peak difficulty of E-MAJSAT as a function of c.

The following experiment was carried out. For each value of c from 0 to $n = 20$, the formulae were solved for each clause size m from 1 to 141 by 5s and threshold parameter t from 0 to 19. Work was averaged separately for each combination of settings, and the value for t and m that resulted in the maximum average work was selected for each value of c. Figure 9 summarizes the results.

The results of these experiments are somewhat counterintuitive. Instead of the peak difficulty being obtained for $c = n/2$ as might be assumed from complexity theory, the difficulty is *logarithmically* related to the number of choice variables. It appears that the main effect is that each randomized quantifier that is changed to an existential quantifier results in a constant fraction of savings of work. This result calls for more careful study—perhaps by systematically varying the instance size.

3.1.3. SSAT *Subtypes*

Figure 10 plots the work vs. number of clauses for each of four types of SSAT problems described earlier. For each problem class, the most difficult (on average) setting of the threshold parameter observed was used. There are several things to note here. One is that all these randomized satisfiability problems exhibit the same easy-hardest-hard pattern described for SAT. However, the number of clauses corresponding to the peak work differs for each problem. Also, the higher the peak, the smaller the number of clauses at the peak.

Another observation is that the relative peak difficulty of different problems does not match what might be predicted by complexity theory. In particular, as $\mathrm{NP} \subseteq \mathrm{PP} \subseteq \mathrm{NP}^{\mathrm{PP}} \subseteq \mathrm{PSPACE}$, one might expect SAT < MAJSAT < E-MAJSAT < Alternating SSAT in terms of peak work (here, "<" is being used as shorthand for "requiring less work than"). In fact, the experiments come out with SAT < E-MAJSAT < Alternating SSAT < MAJSAT. That is, MAJSAT comes out as the hardest instead of the second easiest. This pattern can be observed with a wide range of values of n, with the MAJSAT instances getting harder much faster than the other problems with increasing n.

The facts that E-MAJSAT is easier for DPLL than MAJSAT and that SAT is easier than Alternating SSAT probably stem from the fact that randomized quantifiers are

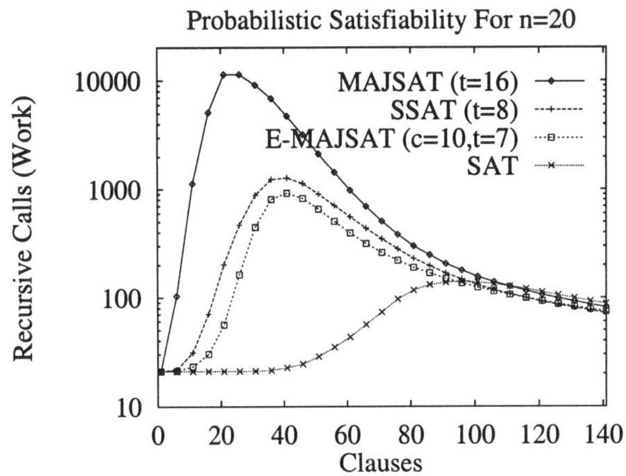

Figure 10. The peak difficulty of solving different SSAT instances via DPLL varies with the structure of the operators and the number of clauses. The plot is for random formulae with $k = 3$ literals per clause. MAJSAT problems appear to be the hardest, on average.

harder to prune than are existential quantifiers. Recall from the DPLL algorithm of Section 2.1 that existential quantifiers can be simplified by purification whereas randomized quantifiers cannot. In addition, the threshold pruning rules for randomized quantifiers are weaker and will apply less often. Thus, the presence of randomized quantifiers can make an SSAT problem more challenging. Supporting this observation is the fact that Alternating SSAT and E-MAJSAT ($c = n/2$) both consist of half existential and half randomized quantifiers, and have very similar curves in Figure 10.

A similar observation concerning problem difficulty and quantifier type was made by [20] ([20]); they argue that random QBF formulae are trivially easy because of the fact that a single clause consisting of all (or nearly all) universal variables can be solved with no backtracking at all. Thus, in spite of the fact that QBF is PSPACE-complete, QBF $<$ SAT for random CNF formulae. This effect was also observed by [7] ([7]), who found that increasing the number of universal quantifiers at the expense of existential quantifiers makes problems easier to solve.

Figure 11 shows a similar pattern when the number of literals per clause $k = 5$, although the curves for MAJSAT and Alternating SSAT have grown closer together.

3.1.4. *Threshold*

With SAT, the peak hardness of determining whether an instance is positive appears to correspond to the point at which about half of all random instances are positive; informal tests support the same conclusion for MAJSAT. Figure 12 examines the threshold, showing results for MAJSAT for $k = 3$, $n = 30$, varying the number of clauses m and threshold t. As the satisfaction threshold increases, few clauses are needed to prevent a random instance from being positive. There is a strong linear relationship between m and t visible in the graph that begs explanation; the observed relationship between n, m, and t at the threshold is $m \approx 4.2(n - t)$. This relation makes sense for $t = 0$, since it says that the 0–1 threshold for SAT occurs at $m \approx 4.2n$. It also makes sense for $t = n$, since only a single clause is needed to prevent there from being $2^t = 2^n$ satisfying assignments. Equation 1 gives a lower bound on this threshold with this form, but no upper bound of this type has been proven.

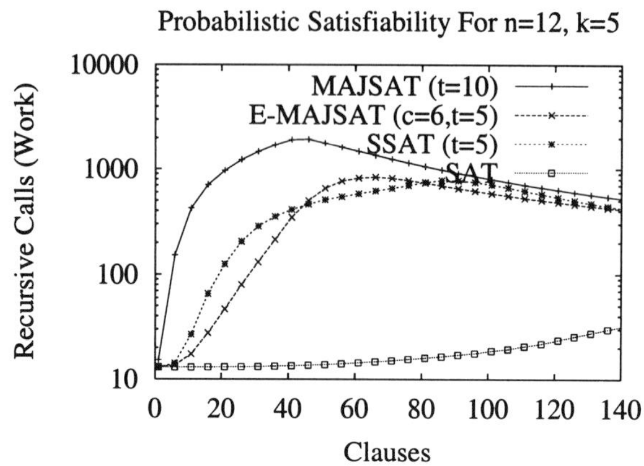

Figure 11. The peak difficulty of solving different SSAT instances via DPLL varies with the structure of the operators and the number of clauses. With more than $k = 3$ literals per clause, the difference in difficulty of the problem types lessens.

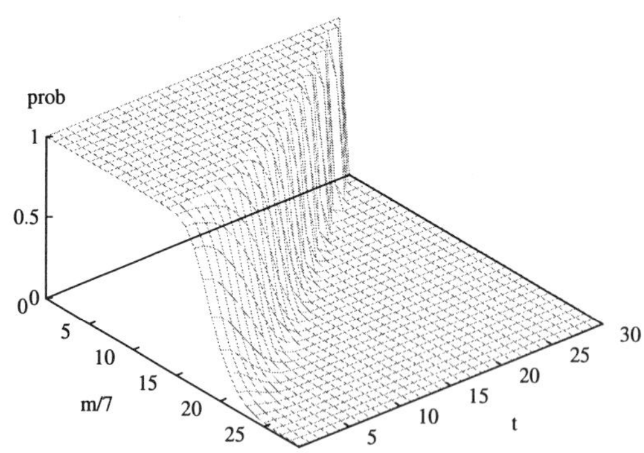

Figure 12. The probability that a random instance of MAJSAT ($n = 30$, $k = 3$) is positive varies with both the satisfaction threshold t and the number of clauses m. Peak difficulty for a fixed t occurs around the number of clauses m for which half of the instances are positive.

3.2. Varying Problem Size

To see how peak problem difficulty scales with n, the following experiment was carried out. For each of $n = 5, 10, 15, 20, 25, 30$, a thousand $k = 3$-CNF MAJSAT formulae were generated. For each n, the DPLL solver solved all 1,000 formulae for all values of t from 0 to n and all values of m from 1 to about $7n$ (at intervals of approximately $n/4$ clauses). This was used to identify the hardest settings of t and m. At this point, all values of m and t in the vicinity of the maximum were run to get a more accurate answer. Finally, a peak combination of values of m and t was identified for each n.

The results were quite clean (the lines are sufficiently straight that they are not shown). For all values of n, the peak work was achieved with $t \approx 0.80n$ and $m \approx 1.14n$. The peak work for these settings follows a clear exponential growth curve of 3.96×1.49^n. This is interesting, because, even with a difficult problem like MAJSAT, this simple version of DPLL achieves a running time that is asymptotically faster than that of full enumeration ($O(2^n)$).

3.3. *An Evaluation of Heuristics for* evalssat

In all but the most trivial SAT problems, the DPLL algorithm will exhaust opportunities to apply unit resolution and purification before a satisfying assignment has been discovered. When this occurs, the algorithm must select an unassigned variable x from the current simplified formula to split on, *i.e.* check for satisfying assignments both when x is assigned `True` and when x is assigned `False`. For peak performance, the order in which variables are selected is critical. For example, suppose a SAT problem is presented to DPLL with n variables and, for the sake of this example, that no pruning is done. Suppose further that if the variable x_a is set to `True` the formula becomes unsatisfiable. If x_a is the last variable the algorithm chooses to split on, it will potentially generate 2^{n-1} assignments, discovering as many times that setting x_a to `True` makes the formula unsatisfiable. If, however, it selects x_a as the first variable to split on, it will discover that setting that variable to `True` leads to unsatisfiability *before* generating and checking those 2^{n-1} assignments. Unit resolution, as described in Section 2.1.1, handles this extreme case; other ideas are needed to address this more generally.

Considerations such as this have prompted a great deal of research into efficient splitting heuristics for SAT [24, 2, 19, 23, 25, 30, 13, 16]. An appropriate splitting heuristic can reduce the running time of the DPLL algorithm by several orders of magnitude. But, do these splitting heuristics improve efficiency in SSAT problems?

Relative to its counterpart in SAT problems, splitting in SSAT is restricted to selection from among a specific class of variables: To ensure that the value of the formula is computed correctly, splitting heuristics for SSAT must choose a variable from the first (leftmost or outermost) block, as described in Section 1.2.1.

The reasoning behind this restriction is because adjacent quantifiers commute if they are of the same type, but not if they are of different types. Returning to the example from Section 1.2, consider the formula

$$\rotatebox[origin=c]{180}{R}x, \rotatebox[origin=c]{180}{R}z, \exists y, E[(x \vee y)(y \vee \overline{z})(\overline{x} \vee \overline{y})] \geq 3/5.$$

The value of the formula is 3/4, and this can be determined by splitting either on x or z first (both are in the first block). On the other hand, if y is used as the variable in the first split, the value is calculated incorrectly as 1/2.

A hypothesis is that splitting heuristics would have the greatest impact when there are large blocks of interchangeable variables (the extremes being SAT and MAJSAT, both of which consist of a single block of size n), and would not be as useful when there was a great deal of quantifier alternation (since, barring unit clauses and pure variables, DPLL must split on all variables in the first block before splitting on a variable from another block). In the case where blocks are single variables, the splitting heuristic can be expected to have no impact on performance.

To test this hypothesis, tests were conducted using six splitting heuristics (where, in all cases, it is understood that the choice is made from the outermost block of variables):

- RAND chooses a variable randomly,
- SATS_MOST finds the literal that satisfies the most clauses in the current formula and chooses that variable,
- 2S_JW (2-sided Jeroslow-Wang, described by [24] ([24])) chooses a variable whose literals appear in a large number of short clauses,

- POS_2S_JW (positive, 2-sided Jeroslow-Wang, described by [24] ([24])) is 2S_JW applied to the subset of variables that appear in at least one clause containing all positive literals,

- MOMS chooses the variable that has Maximum Occurrences in clauses of Minimum Size, and

- MAX_UNIT, a splitting heuristic used by [2] ([2]) in some of their work on satisfiability algorithms, is similar to heuristics used by the successful POSIT [16] and TABLEAU [13] solvers, preferring variables that will lead to a maximal number of unit resolutions.

With the exception of RAND, these heuristics try to select the variable that will most simplify the formula and establish its satisfiability (or lack thereof) most quickly. SATS_MOST attempts to do this by choosing the literal that will satisfy, and thus eliminate, the most clauses. The remaining heuristics try to choose a variable that maximizes the number of unit clauses likely to be produced. The baseline for comparison is the splitting rule in Figure 2, which splits on the next variable in the initially specified quantifier ordering.

To test the performance of these heuristics on problems with varying block sizes, eight sets of 100 random formulae were generated with the following characteristics:

24 variables, 24 clauses, 3 literals per clause
24 variables, 48 clauses, 3 literals per clause
24 variables, 72 clauses, 3 literals per clause
24 variables, 96 clauses, 3 literals per clause
32 variables, 32 clauses, 3 literals per clause
32 variables, 64 clauses, 3 literals per clause
32 variables, 96 clauses, 3 literals per clause
32 variables, 128 clauses, 3 literals per clause.

These sets were generated according to $\mathcal{F}_m^{k,n}$ (Section 1.4) using `makewff`. In order to ensure that the formulae generated contained exactly n variables, however, `makewff` was modified to repeatedly generate a formula with the desired characteristics until one was generated that contained all n variables. For each block size in a specified range of block sizes (1, 2, 3, 4, 6, 12, and 24 for problems with 24 variables and 1, 2, 4, 8, 16, and 32 for problems with 32 variables) two problem types were generated: a type E problem, which has an existentially quantified outermost block, and an R problem, which has a randomly quantified outermost block. The block sizes chosen were all those that generate an equal number of existential and randomized quantifiers, plus SAT and E-MAJSAT (block size 24 or 32). In this manner, each set of 100 24-variable problems generated 1400 instances, and each set of 100 32-variable problems generated 1200 instances.

The evalssat algorithm was implemented in C and each splitting heuristic was tested on all 10,400 problem instances generated as described above. These tests were conducted on a Sun Ultra-1 running SunOS-5.7 with 128 MB of RAM. Performance was measured by counting the change in the number of recursive calls to the central function in the algorithm. This function first tests for satisfaction of the formula; if the current partial assignment is insufficient to establish satisfaction or unsatisfaction, the function extends the partial assignment. In the most general case, the function selects an unassigned variable, first setting the variable to `True` and calling itself recursively, and then setting the variable to `False` and calling itself recursively. Whenever possible, as in the case of a variable in a unit clause, one of these recursive calls is eliminated. Measuring the number of calls to this function is equivalent to measuring the size of the DPLL tree generated by the algorithm and is thus a more direct measure of the efficiency of the heuristic than measuring, for example, CPU time. For perspective, however, the running time, measured in CPU seconds, for a non-MAJSAT 24-variable, 48-clause problem was typically less than a second. Running times for MAJSAT problems varied from 1 to 5 seconds. A connection between these two ways of measuring performance is provided by the fact that for the results reported below (problems with 24 variables, 48 clauses, 3 literals per clause) the algorithm performs approximately 20,000 recursive calls per cpu second.

Although the results of the tests (Figure 13) generally supported the hypothesis stated above, there are some peculiarities that warrant further study. (Note that the results for all eight sets of problems were similar; we show the results only for 24-variable, 48-clause problems.) On both type E and type R problems, four of the heuristics tested (POS_2S_JW, MAX_UNIT, SATS_MOST, and MOMS) provided some improvement in performance (reduction in the size of the DPLL tree generated). For type E problems, this improvement was positively correlated with block size (see Figure 13(b)). For type R problems the improvement was positively correlated with block size up to a block size of 12; all four of these heuristics show less improvement for a block size of 24 (MAJSAT problems, in which the formula cannot be simplified by purification) than they do for a block size of 12 (see Figure 13(a)). SATS_MOST and MOMS were particularly effective, reducing the number of recursive calls in DPLL by approximately half (over both problem types) for a block size of 12. RAND performed as expected on type R problems, neither improving nor degrading performance. 2S_JW, a heuristic which might have demonstrated improved performance, was similarly neutral. Neither of these two heuristics performed as expected on type E problems; both heuristics degraded performance, and this degradation was positively correlated with block size. The fact that 2S_JW performed no better than RAND agrees with results reported by [24] ([24]); on a set of hard, random SAT instances, they reported that the DPLL trees constructed using the 2S_JW heuristic were significantly larger than those constructed using a random heuristic.

For the heuristics that improved performance, the block size did not have to be very large to produce significant reductions in the size of the DPLL tree generated. For the four successful heuristics, tree size was reduced as soon as blocks were larger than a single variable and, in some cases, the reduction became significant even for relatively small block sizes. MAX_UNIT, SATS_MOST, and MOMS, for example, provided average reductions in tree size of approximately 23%, 28%, and 32%, respectively, for a block size of six.

The results suggest that a successful SAT heuristic is likely to be a successful heuristic in MAJSAT and SSAT problems, but block size is a limiting factor. In the case where blocks are single variables, the splitting heuristic has no impact on performance. It is important to note, however, that the tests were conducted on small, random problems. For problems with more structure, such as SSAT formulae that encode planning problems, these results may not hold. In addition, there may be other good splitting heuristics that take advantage of this structure. For example, [34] ([34]) report improved performance on such SSAT problems using a *time-ordered* splitting heuristic in which variables with a lower time index are chosen first. The success of SATS_MOST, which is computationally much simpler than MAX_UNIT or MOMS, was somewhat surprising and warrants further study. It is possible that performance disparities might appear in these three splitting heuristics as the problem size increases beyond that of the problems in these tests. Finally, it is possible that splitting heuristics unique to Extended SSAT

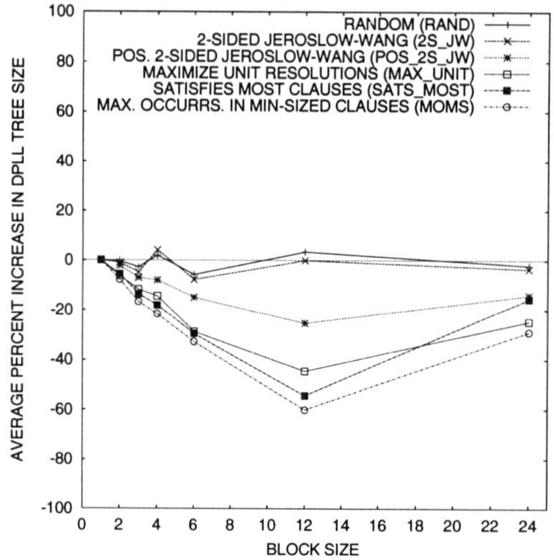

(a) first block R

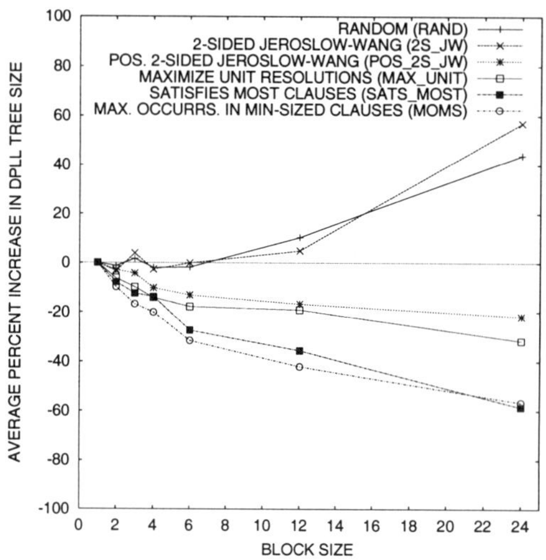

(b) first block E

Figure 13. The heuristics POS_2S_JW, MAX_UNIT, SATS_MOST, and MOMS reduce the size of the DPLL tree generated relative to splitting in strict quantifier order when the formula block size is greater than 1. For the most part, larger block sizes yield more improvement.

problems could be developed. Such heuristics might use the probabilities associated with the random variables to select variables in a way that provides potentially greater simplification of the problem.

3.4. *Experiments with the Stochastic Sampling Algorithms*

The performance of randevalssat for computing the value of SSAT instances was tested on 27 sets of 100 random formulae. The characteristics of these 27 sets were generated by taking the cross product of the following sets: $\{n = 8, 12, 16\}$, $\{m = n, 2n, 3n\}$, and $\{k = 3, 4, 5\}$. As was the case for the evaluation of heuristics in Section 3.3, these sets

were generated according to $\mathcal{F}_m^{k,n}$ (Section 1.4) using a modified version of `makewff` that guarantees a formula with exactly n variables. For each problem a SAT instance (all existential variables), a MAJSAT instance (all randomized variables), and all possible instances that contain an equal number of existential and randomized variables in alternating blocks of the same size were constructed. This generated 8 instances for each 8-variable problem (block sizes 1, 2, 4, and 8, each with an instance in which the initial block is existentially quantified and an instance in which the initial block is randomly quantified), 10 instances for each 12-variable problem (block sizes 1, 2, 3, 6, and 12 with instances differing by initial quantifier), and 10 instances for 16-variable problems (block sizes 1, 2, 4, 8, and 16 with instances differing by initial quantifier). Thus, each set of 100 8-variable problems generated 800 distinct problems, and all other sets generated 1000 distinct problems, for a total of 25,200 problems. For each of these problems, 10 different partial policy trees were created by sampling random variable assignments and constructing the tree paths specified by the samples. The number of assignments sampled w ranged from 5 to 4086 on an approximate logarithmic scale; the larger the number of samples, the greater the similarity of the partial tree to the full tree.

Both sampleevalssat and randevalssat were implemented in C. Each of the partial policy trees generated for the 25,200 problem instances described above was solved using randevalssat. For comparison, those problem instances with 12 variables, 24 clauses, and 3 literals per clause were also solved using sampleevalssat. For randevalssat, the number of restarts and the number of iterations were both specified as a multiple of the number of variables in the CNF formula constructed from the tree, so increasing the number of samples tended to increase the number of restarts and iterations. Performance was measured by comparing the estimate of (or, in the case of sampleevalssat, the exact calculation of) the value of the partial policy tree to the exact value of the full policy tree (and, hence, the formula). This difference is referred to below as the error in the value estimate. Note that since the running time is proportional to the number of restarts and iterations allowed, and since these limits are increased for larger problems, running time is not a very informative measure of performance. For perspective, however, running times, measured in CPU seconds, for 12-variable, 24-clause problems, with 4086 assignment samples, varied from 1 to 5 seconds.

Figure 14 shows results for the sampleevalssat algorithm on problems with 12 variables, 24 clauses, and 3 literals per clause; the graph shows mean squared error in the value estimate as a function of the number of sampled assignments for all problem types. Since the algorithm is performing perfect optimization on the partial tree, any error is due entirely to the incompleteness of the partial tree due to sampling. As expected, the mean and variance of the squared error approach zero as the number of assignment samples increases, and the partial tree constructed approaches the full policy tree.

Figure 15 shows the same graphs for the results of the randevalssat algorithm. (Note that the results for all 27 sets of problems were similar; we show the results only for the set of problems with 12 variables, 24 clauses, and 3 literal per clause.) Here, the mean and variance of the squared error decrease as the number of assignment samples increases. But, even in the limiting case, where the number of assignments sampled is sufficient to construct the full policy tree with high probability, randevalssat is not always capable of finding the optimal setting of the decision variables. (Note that in some cases, however, randevalssat can generate almost as accurate an answer as sampleevalssat in far less time. For one problem with 36 variables, 72 clauses, and 3 literals per clause, randevalssat was able to return an answer with squared error of approximately 10^{-4} in 442 cpu seconds, while sampleevalssat required over 4 times as long to compute an answer with squared error of approximately 10^{-5}.)

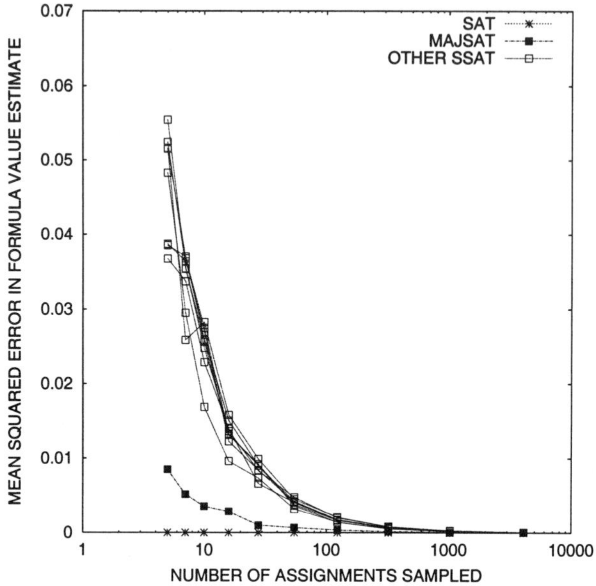

Figure 14. The partial policy tree produced by random sampling can be solved exactly using a DPLL-style approach. Approximation error decreases as sample size increases.

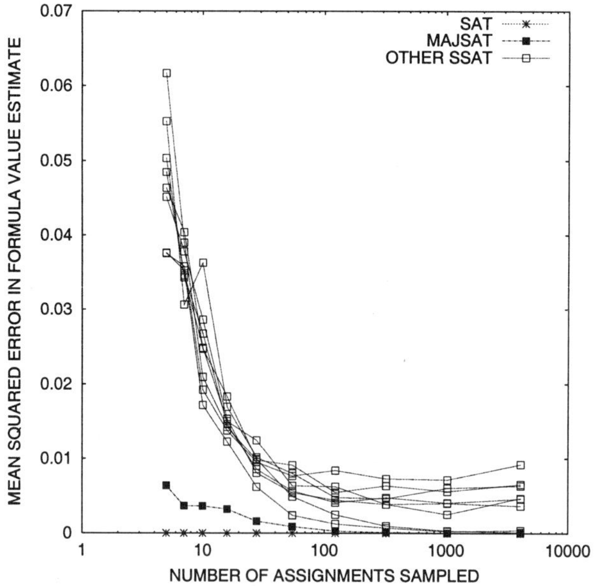

Figure 15. As the number of sampled assignments increases, the accuracy of the randomized local search algorithm increases. Because of local optima in the search space, increasing the number of sampled assignments does not drive the error to zero.

It should also be noted that the randevalssat algorithm can exhibit anomalous behavior as the number of assignment samples increases. A set of 100 random problems with 12 variables, 24 clauses, and 3 literals per clause was generated, but with a block size of 4 and an initial block of existential variables. This set was not included in the results reported above, since this quantifier ordering results in problem instances with an unequal number of existential and random variables. The mean squared error for this set of problems decreases to approximately 0.008 as the number of sampled assignments increases to 55. As the number of sampled assignments increases further, however, the mean squared error also increases, appearing to asymptote at approximately 0.016. Since this behavior does not appear when the same problem instances are solved using sampleevalssat, the anomaly appears to be due to the imperfect optimization technique employed by randevalssat becoming trapped in local optima. Initially, generating a policy tree with more branches allows the algorithm to return a more accurate estimate of the value of the formula. Beyond a certain point, however, this advantage seems to be outweighed by the increasing difficulty of the optimization problem; because more policy-tree nodes means more treeSAT variables, the algorithm is increasingly likely to become stuck in local maxima and so less likely to find the global maximum within the permitted number of restarts. Future work will examine striking the proper balance between sampling completeness and optimization difficulty.

Future work will also consider more sophisticated randomized local search procedures. For instance, the algorithm could be modified to select the decision node or the variable to flip in that decision node according to some set of criteria. Another variation would use the entire local search algorithm in Figure 6 as a subroutine in an algorithm that periodically restarts with a new set of samples. The approach could also be refined using simulated annealing.

4. Conclusion and Future Work

This paper described a stochastic satisfiability framework, relating it to existing problems in reasoning and planning under uncertainty. It described several algorithms, inspired by work in deterministic satisfiability: a DPLL-based algorithm, a "universal" search algorithm, and a stochastic sampling algorithm. The paper also explored the behavior of the algorithms on randomly generated satisfiability problems.

This paper takes a first stab at developing practical algorithms for SSAT, with particular emphasis on understanding which algorithms, intuitions and ideas developed for the satisfiability problem extend to more general satisfiability-type problems. In spite of the gap in computational complexity between the general form of stochastic satisfiability (SSAT, PSPACE-complete) and deterministic satisfiability (SAT, NP-complete), this work shows that many insights obtained from studying SAT carry over to the more general probabilistic setting. Many more questions remain unanswered; some directions for future work are sketched next.

A primary motivation for studying Extended SSAT problems is to gain a better understanding of algorithms for decision making under uncertainty. These problems are modeled by Extended SSAT in that existential quantifiers act like "maximizing" decisions, universal quantifiers act like a "minimizing" decisions, and randomized quantifiers act like an oblivious random influence. [11] ([11]) studied a simple stochastic game model with precisely these three types of nodes. There are two fundamental differences between simple stochastic games and stochastic satisfiability. Stochastic games have no predefined "horizon"; games can continue indefinitely. Extended SSAT problems, in contrast, model domains with a fixed number of decisions or events (one for each quantifier), at which point the "game" ends. On the other hand, Extended SSAT problems model very complex decisions, in that a value for an existential quantifier can be conditioned on all the preceding randomized quantifiers—possibly an exponential-sized set of conditions. This allows Extended SSAT problems to model compactly represented AI planning domains, an insight that has led to an implemented state-of-the-art planning algorithm [35]. Representing a planning problem via a simple stochastic game, however, leads to a state-space explosion, rendering it an inefficient formalism for complex domains. An important direction for future work involves combining the core propositional representation of Extended SSAT with the unbounded horizon of simple stochastic games.

The study of randomized satisfiability algorithms has helped spur the development of algorithms and applications of deterministic satisfiability. While this paper has proposed an initial stochastic sampling algorithm for SSAT, more experiments and more algorithmic insights are needed. One area in need of more research is how the approximation algorithm can be applied to solve planning problems. In particular, the algorithm returns a partial assignment strategy, or policy, that specifies how each existential variable should be set given the settings of the variables that precede it in the quantifier ordering, but this only happens for those situations represented by paths in the random sample. The algorithm implicitly assumes that performance on missing branches is the same as the average performance over all paths in the partial tree, but doesn't actually find a plan that achieves this performance. A topic for future work is extending the stochastic sampling algorithm to return successful plans, perhaps in an iterative approach that integrates planning and execution.

In addition, it is not clear how to apply the proposed algorithm to formulae with intermixed existential, randomized, *and* universal quantifiers. Such problems arise, for example, in applications in which two competitive agents interact with a stochastic environment, and a randomized algorithm for this broader class of SSAT problems would be useful.

The proposed universal search algorithm is a promising approach to solving Extended SSAT problems exactly and efficiently. Future work will be to implement and test the algorithm, comparing it to the splitting heuristics examined in Section 3.3. Although they are not well understood theoretically, the threshold pruning rules described in Section 2.1.2 could be helpful in a practical implementation of the universal search algorithm.

There has been a recent flurry of activity in analyzing common Davis-Putnam algorithms, and proving that these algorithms are guaranteed to solve any k-SAT instance in subexponential-time [36, 41, 40]. (For example, a very simple randomized DPLL-type algorithm solves 3-CNF SAT in worst-case time $2^{(2/3)n}$.) It would be interesting to show that these analyses carry over to the SSAT setting.

In addition to Resolution-based methods, there are several alternative methods for solving satisfiability instances. In particular, algebraic approaches based on discrete versions of the Grobner basis algorithm are looking promising for solving satisfiability problems [10]. Future work will examine to what extent these methods carry over to the SSAT domain.

A number of recent studies have shown that the satisfiability framework is useful for examining a variety of search problems. An exciting element of the present work is that it illustrates how the satisfiability approach applies outside of SAT's complexity class, greatly expanding the realm of problems that can be attacked.

Acknowledgements

Thanks to Pankaj Agarwal, Julien Basch, Ian Gent, Judy Goldsmith, Moises Goldszmidt, Henry Kautz, Don Loveland, Matt Peters, John Reif, Bart Selman, and Toby Walsh for feedback and suggestions. Avrim Blum suggested the use of sampling and Chernoff bounds, and Noam Shazeer provided the insight behind the counter example in Appendix B. We would also like to thank Steve Cook, Mike Molloy, and especially Dimitris Achlioptas for illuminating conversations on the 0–1 threshold properties of SAT and MAJSAT formulae.

Appendix

A. Correctness of evalssat

This section proves that the evalssat algorithm described in Section 2.1 produces the correct value of the given SSAT instance (ϕ, Q, θ).

LEMMA 6. *For all n, for all formulae ϕ with at most n variables, for all thresholds θ_l, θ_h, such that $\theta_l \leq \theta_h$, evalssat$(\phi, Q, \theta_l, \theta_h)$ returns a value v such that: (i) if $\theta_l \leq val(\phi, Q) \leq \theta_h$, then $val(\phi, Q) = v$; (ii) if $val(\phi, Q) \leq \theta_l$, then $v \leq \theta_l$; and (iii) if $val(\phi, Q) \geq \theta_h$, then $v \geq \theta_h$.*

Proof: The correctness of the algorithm will be proved by induction on the number of variables of the formula. If there are no variables, then ϕ either consists of no clauses (*i.e.*, it contains the empty set), or it contains an empty clause. If ϕ consists of no clauses, then ϕ evaluates to 1 by definition. Likewise, if ϕ contains an empty clause, this implies that $val(\phi, Q) = 0$, and thus the lemma holds in this case.

Now, assume that ϕ has $n > 0$ variables, and as usual, the variables are named $x_1, \ldots, x_n$ where x_1 is the outermost quantified variable. As above, the lemma holds if ϕ consists of no clauses or contains an empty clause. In all other cases, a single variable is removed. The first case is where a variable x_i is removed because it occurs in a singleton clause in ϕ with sign b, and $Q(x_i) = \exists$. In this case, $val(\phi, Q) = val(\phi\lceil_{x_i=b}, Q)$ because when x_i is set to $1-b$, ϕ evaluates to 0. Then, by the inductive hypothesis, the algorithm outputs a correct value on $\phi\lceil_{x_i=b}$. Similarly, if x_i is a unit variable in ϕ and $Q(x_i) = \forall$, then $val(\phi, Q) = 0$ and, thus, the algorithm outputs a correct value. Finally, if x_i is a unit variable and $Q(x_i) = \text{Я}$, then $val(\phi, Q) = (val(\phi\lceil_{x_i=b}, Q) + val(\phi\lceil_{x_i=1-b}, Q))/2 = val(\phi\lceil_{x_i=b}, Q)/2$. In this case, when calling evalssat recursively on $\phi\lceil_{x_i=b}$, the low and high bounds θ_l and θ_h must be shifted by a factor of two. That is, when $val(\phi, Q) = x$, $val(\phi\lceil_{x_i=b}, Q)$ is $2x$; thus if $\theta_l \leq x \leq \theta_h$, then by induction evalssat$(\phi\lceil_{x_i=b}, Q, 2\theta_l, 2\theta_h)$ will return the value $2x$ since $2\theta_l \leq 2x \leq 2\theta_h$. Similarly, the algorithm is correct for $x \leq \theta_l$ and $x \geq \theta_h$.

The second case is where x_i is a pure variable with sign b and $Q(x_i) = \forall$. In this case, $val(\phi, Q) = \min(val(\phi\lceil_{x_i=b}, Q), val(\phi\lceil_{x_i=1-b}, Q)) = val(\phi\lceil_{x_i=1-b}, Q)$, so by induction the algorithm is correct. Similarly, when x_i is a pure variable and $Q(x_i) = \exists$, then

$$val(\phi, Q) = \max(val(\phi\lceil_{x_i=b}, Q), val(\phi\lceil_{x_i=1-b}, Q)) = val(\phi\lceil_{x_i=b}, Q).$$

The third case is when x_1 is removed and $Q(x_1) = \exists$. Let $v_0 = $ evalssat$(\phi\lceil_{x_1=0}, Q, \theta_l, \theta_h)$. If $val(\phi\lceil_{x_1=0}, Q) \geq \theta_h$, then $v_0 \geq \theta_h$ by the induction hypothesis, so v_0 is a correct value. Otherwise, $v_0 < \theta_h$. Let $v_1 = $ evalssat$(\phi\lceil_{x_1=1}, Q, \max(\theta_l, v_0), \theta_h)$. There are several simple cases to check: If $val(\phi\lceil_{x_1=0}, Q) \geq \theta_l$, then v_0 will equal $val(\phi\lceil_{x_1=0}, Q)$ by the inductive hypothesis, so $\max(\theta_l, v_0) = v_0$, and thus it is easy to check that $\max(v_0, v_1)$ is a correct answer. Similarly, it can be checked that the answer returned is correct if $val(\phi\lceil_{x_1=0}, Q) < \theta_l$.

The fourth case, when x_1 is removed and $Q(x_1) = \forall$, is very similar to the above case.

The fifth and final case is when x_1 is removed and $Q(x_1) = ᖱ$. Let $v_0' = val(\theta\lceil_{x_1=0}, Q)$ and let $v_1' = val(\theta\lceil_{x_1=1}, Q)$. If $v_0' < 2\theta_l - 1$ then $(v_0' + v_1')/2 < (2\theta_l - 1 + 1)/2 = \theta_l$. If $v_0' > 2\theta_h$, then $(v_0' + v_1')/4 > (2\theta_h)/2 = \theta_h$. So, no detailed answer is needed if $v_0' < 2\theta_l - 1$ or $v_0' > 2\theta_h$. Thus, it suffices to calculate $v_0 = \mathsf{evalssat}(\theta\lceil_{x_1=0}, Q, 2\theta_l - 1, 2\theta_h)$. If $(v_0 + 1)/2 < \theta_l$, then $(v_0' + v_1')/2 < \theta_l$, so return $v_0/2$ (anything less than θ_l). If $v_0/2 \geq \theta_h$, then $(v_0' + v_1')/2 \geq v_0/2 \geq \theta_h$, so return $v_0/2$. Otherwise, calculate $v_1 = \mathsf{evalssat}(\theta\lceil_{x_1=1}, 2\theta_l - v_0, 2\theta_h - v_0)$. Now, if $v_1 < 2\theta_l - v_0$, then $(v_0' + v_1')/2 < \theta_l$, and if $v_1 > 2\theta_h - v_0$, then $(v_0' + v_1')/2 > \theta_h$. ■

B. A Difficult Instance for sampleevalssat

This section shows that sampleevalssat can require exponentially many samples to accurately approximate some SSAT problems. Consider the n-variable SSAT formula

$$ᖱ y_1, ᖱ y_2, \ldots, ᖱ y_{n-2}, \exists x_{n-1}, ᖱ y_n((x_{n-1} \vee \overline{y_n})(\overline{x_{n-1}} \vee y_n)).$$

The value of this formula is 1/2, since the formula is `True` if and only if $x_{n-1} = y_n$, which happens half of the time regardless of the value of x_{n-1}.

The number of policies for this SSAT formula is $P = 2^{2^{n-2}}$ since the setting for x_{n-1} can be conditioned on the preceding $n-2$ randomized variables.

Let W be a size w sample of the assignments to the randomized variables in the formula. The estimated value of the formula is

$$\sum_{\alpha \in W} \text{match}(\alpha, W, n)/\text{match}(\alpha, W, n-2),$$

where match(α, W, i) is the number of samples in W that match α in the setting of the first i variables. The justification for this expression is that the existential variable immediately above any given sampled leaf will be set to maximize the number of sampled leaves below it that are made `True`. That is, it will be set to match the majority of the assignments to y_n immediately below it. For example, if a decision node has only one leaf beneath, the value of that leaf will be 1.

For any sample, α, with probability at least $1 - w/2^{n-1}$,

$$\text{match}(\alpha, W, n) = \text{match}(\alpha, W, n-2)$$

because the second set is only larger than the first set if there is a sample that matches α in its assignment to $y_1, \ldots, y_{n-2}$ but differs in its assignment to y_n. Thus, the expected value of the sampleevalssat estimate $E[\hat{v}] \geq 1 - w/2^{n-1}$.

Let ϵ be a target approximation error and $1 - \delta$ be the desired probability of the estimate being within ϵ of the true value. This restricts $E[\hat{v}] \leq (1-\delta)(1/2+\epsilon) + (\delta)(1)$. Thus, $1 - w/2^{n-1} \leq E[\hat{v}] \leq (1-\delta)(1/2+\epsilon) + \delta$, or

$$w \geq 2^{n-2}(1 - \delta(1 - 2\epsilon) - 2\epsilon)).$$

This means that the number of samples needed to insure a good estimate from sampleevalssat is exponential in n.

References

1. Dimitris Achlioptas. *Threshold phenomena in random graph colouring and satisfiability.* PhD thesis, University of Toronto, 1999.
2. Robert J. Bayardo, Jr. and Robert C. Schrag. Using CSP look-back techniques to solve real-world SAT instances. In *Proceedings of the Fourteenth National Conference on Artificial Intelligence*, pages 203–208. AAAI Press/The MIT Press, 1997.
3. P. Beame, R. Karp, T. Pitassi, and M. Saks. On the complexity of unsatisfiability of random k-CNF formulas. In *Proceedings of the Thirtieth Annual ACM Symposium on Theory of Computing*, pages 561–571, 1998.
4. Paul Beame and Toniann Pitassi. Simplified and improved resolution lower bounds. In *37th Annual Symposium on Foundations of Computer Science*, pages 274–282. IEEE, 1996.
5. Eli Ben-Sasson and Avi Wigderson. Short proofs are narrow: Resolution made simple. To appear in STOC 1999, 1999.
6. Elazar Birnbaum and Eliezer L. Lozinskii. The good old Davis-Putnam procedure helps counting models. *Journal of Artificial Intelligence Research*, 10:457–477, 1999.
7. Marco Cadoli, Andrea Giovanardi, and Marco Schaerf. Experimental analysis of the computational cost of evaluating quantified Boolean formulae. In *Fifth Conference of the Italian Association for Artificial Intelligence (AI*IA '97)*, number 1321, pages 207–218. Springer-Verlag, 1997.
8. Marco Cadoli, Andrea Giovanardi, and Marco Schaerf. An algorithm to evaluate quantified Boolean formulae. In *Proceedings of the Fifteenth National Conference on Artificial Intelligence (AAAI-98)*, pages 262–267. The AAAI Press/The MIT Press, 1998.
9. V. Chvátal and B. Reed. Mick gets some (the odds are on his side). In *33nd Annual Symposium on Foundations of Computer Science*, pages 620–627, 1992.
10. M. Clegg, J. Edmonds, and R. Impagliazzo. Using the Gröbner basis algorithm to find proofs of unsatisfiability. In *Proceedings of the Twenty-Eighth Annual ACM Symposium on Theory of Computing*, pages 174–183, 1996.
11. Anne Condon. The complexity of stochastic games. *Information and Computation*, 96(2):203–224, February 1992.
12. Anne Condon, Joan Feigenbaum, Carsten Lund, and Peter Shor. Random debators and the hardness of approximating stochastic functions. *SIAM Journal on Computing*, 26(2):369–400, 1997.
13. J. M. Crawford and L. D. Auton. Experimental results in the crossover point in random 3SAT. *Artificial Intelligence*, 81(1-2):31—57, 1996.
14. M. Davis, G. Logemann, and D. Loveland. A machine program for theorem proving. *Communications of the ACM*, 5:394–397, 1962.
15. Rina Dechter. Bucket elimination: A unifying framework for probabilistic inference. In *Proceedings of the 12th Conference on Uncertainty in Artificial Intelligence (UAI-96)*, pages 211–219. Morgan Kaufmann Publishers, 1996.
16. J. W. Freeman. *Improvements to propositional satisfiability search algorithms.* PhD thesis, Department of Computer and Information Science, University of Pennsylvania, 1995.
17. E. Friedgut. Necessary and sufficient conditions for sharp thresholds of graph properties, and the k-SAT problem. Preprint, 1997.
18. A. Frieze and S. Suen. Analysis of two simple heuristics on a random instance of k-SAT. *Journal of Algorithms*, 20(2):312–355, 1996.
19. G. Gallo and G. Urbani. Algorithms for testing the satisfiability of propositional formulae. *Journal of Logic Programming*, 7:45–61, 1989.
20. Ian Gent and Toby Walsh. Beyond NP: the QSAT phase transition. Technical Report APES-05-1998, 1998.
21. A. Goerdt. A threshold for unsatisfiability. *Journal of Computer and System Sciences*, 53:469–486, 1996.
22. J. Gu, P. W. Purdom, J. Franco, and B. J. Wah. Algorithms for the satisfiability (SAT) problem: A survey. In *Satisfiability (SAT) Problem*, pages 19–151. DIMACS, American Mathematical Society, 1997.
23. F. Harche, J. N. Hooker, and G. Thompson. A computational study of satisfiability algorithms for propositional logic. *ORSA Journal on Computing*, 6:423—435, 1994.
24. J. N. Hooker and V. Vinay. Branching rules for satisfiability. Technical Report GSIA Working Paper 1994-09, Carnegie Mellon University, April 1994. Revised January 1995.

25. R. Jeroslow and J. Wang. Solving propositional satisfiability problems. *Annals of Mathematics and AI*, 1:167—187, 1990.
26. A. Kamath, R. Motwani, K. Palem, and P. Spirakis. Tail bounds for occupancy and the satisfiability threshold conjecture. *Random Structures and Algorithms*, 7(1):59–80, 1995.
27. Henry Kautz and Bart Selman. Pushing the envelope: Planning, propositional logic, and stochastic search. In *Proceedings of the Thirteenth National Conference on Artificial Intelligence*, pages 1194–1201. AAAI Press/The MIT Press, 1996.
28. Michael Kearns, Yishay Mansour, and Andrew Y. Ng. A sparse sampling algorithm for near-optimal planning large markov decision processes. Submitted, 1999.
29. L. M. Kirousis, E. Kranakis, D. Krizanc, and Y. C. Stamatiou. Approximating the unsatisfiability threshold of random formulas. *Random Structures and Algorithms*, 12(3):253–269, 1998.
30. Chu Min Li and Anbulagan. Heuristics based on unit propagation for satisfiability problems. In *Proceedings of the Fifteenth International Joint Conference on Artificial Intelligence*, pages 366—371, Nagoya, Aichi, Japan, 1997.
31. Michael L. Littman. Probabilistic propositional planning: Representations and complexity. In *Proceedings of the Fourteenth National Conference on Artificial Intelligence*, pages 748–754. AAAI Press/The MIT Press, 1997.
32. Michael L. Littman, Judy Goldsmith, and Martin Mundhenk. The computational complexity of probabilistic plan existence and evaluation. *Journal of Artificial Intelligence Research*, 9:1–36, 1998.
33. Christopher Lusena, Judy Goldsmith, and Martin Mundhenk. Nonapproximability results for Markov decision processes. Technical Report UK CS Dept TR 275-98, University of Kentucky, 1998.
34. Stephen M. Majercik and Michael L. Littman. MAXPLAN: A new approach to probabilistic planning. In Reid Simmons, Manuela Veloso, and Stephen Smith, editors, *Proceedings of the Fourth International Conference on Artificial Intelligence Planning*, pages 86–93. AAAI Press, 1998.
35. Stephen M. Majercik and Michael L. Littman. Contingent planning under uncertainty via probabilistic satisfiability. In *Proceedings of the Sixteenth National Conference on Artificial Intelligence*, pages 549–556. The AAAI Press, 1999.
36. B. Monien and E. Speckenmeyer. Solving satisfiability in less than 2^n steps. *Discrete Applied Mathematics*, 10:287–295, 1985.
37. Martin Mundhenk, Judy Goldsmith, Christopher Lusena, and Eric Allender. Encyclopaedia of complexity results for finite-horizon Markov decision process problems. Technical Report UK CS Dept TR 273-97, University of Kentucky, 1997.
38. C. H. Papadimitriou. Games against nature. *Journal of Computer Systems Science*, 31:288–301, 1985.
39. Christos H. Papadimitriou and John N. Tsitsiklis. The complexity of Markov decision processes. *Mathematics of Operations Research*, 12(3):441–450, August 1987.
40. R. Paturi, P. Pudlak, M.E. Saks, and F. Zane. An improved exponential time algorithm for k-SAT. 1998.
41. R. Paturi, P. Pudlak, and F. Zane. Satisfiability coding lemma. In *FOCS*, pages 566–574, 1997.
42. Mark Peot. Personal communication. 1998.
43. Dan Roth. On the hardness of approximate reasoning. *Artificial Intelligence*, 82(1–2):273–302, 1996.
44. B. Selman, D. Mitchell, and H. Levesque. Generating hard satisfiability problems. *Artificial Intelligence*, 81:17–29, 1996.
45. Bart Selman, Henry Kautz, and Bram Cohen. Local search strategies for satisfiability testing. In David S. Johnson and Michael A. Trick, editors, *Cliques, Coloring, and Satisfiability*, pages 521–531. American Mathematical Society, 1996. DIMACS Series in Discrete Mathematics and Theoretical Computer Science, v. 26.
46. R. D. Shachter. Evaluating influence diagrams. *Operations Research*, 34(6):871–882, 1986.
47. Chris Umans. Personal communication. 1999.

Author Index